2012 North America
Coins & Prices

A GUIDE TO U.S., CANADIAN AND MEXICAN COINS

21st EDITION

David C. Harper, Editor

Harry Miller & Thomas Michael, Market Analysts

The World's Best-Selling Coin Books

Published by

Krause Publications, a division of F+W Media, Inc.
700 East State Street • Iola, WI 54990-0001
715-445-2214 • 888-457-2873
www.krausebooks.com

To order books or other products call toll-free 1-800-258-0929
or visit us online at www.shopnumismaster.com

ISSN 1935-0562
ISBN-13: 978-1-4402-1725-8
ISBN-10: 1-4402-1725-4

Cover Design by Sandi Carpenter
Designed by Sandi Carpenter
Edited by George Cuhaj

Printed in the United States of America

Contents

Preface

Providing coin collectors with accurate, independently produced pricing information on collectible coins has become a trademark of Krause Publication's numismatic division in its 55 years of publishing. Visit our website at www.shopnumismaster.com for more information about us. We employ a full-time staff of market analysts who monitor auction results, trading on the Internet and trading at major shows.

This information is compiled by our analysts who determine what price most accurately reflects the trading that has occurred for each date and mintmark in each grade listed in *North American Coins & Prices*. By studying this information and referring back to it repeatedly, a collector can arm himself with the necessary knowledge to go out in the market and make wise purchasing decisions. It must be remembered that these prices are intended solely as a guide. They are neither offers to buy nor offers to sell. Because prices do fluctuate, those that appear in this book may be in some cases obsolete by the time of publication. By checking the more than 40 price charts in the U.S. section, you can get a feel as to how price swings have occurred since 1972.

U.S. coins are the most popularly collected issues in the world. This is attributable in part to the popularity of coin collecting in the United States, but collectors in many other countries also covet collectible U.S. coins. After collecting U.S. coins for a while, many collectors in the United States branch out into issues of Canada and Mexico. These coins also enjoy a popular following in their countries of origin.

Thus, *North American Coins & Prices* brings together pricing information on all three of these countries. But this book also takes the price-guide concept a step further by providing information on the nuts and bolts of collecting coins: acquiring coins, grading them, organizing them into a collection, storing them properly and much more. Novice collectors can gain the necessary knowledge to collect coins enjoyably; veterans can pick up some pointers to add to their knowledge.

"A Small Beginning"
The U.S. Mint grew from a modest start

By Robert R. Van Ryzin

It was a "small beginning" but a significant one. In July 1792, a site for the new U.S. Mint not yet having been secured, 1,500 silver half dismes were struck on a small screw press nestled in the cellar of a Philadelphia building owned by sawmaker John Harper. Though some have since categorized these early emissions of the fledgling U.S. Mint as patterns, it is clear that first President George Washington – who is said to have deposited the silver from which the coins were struck – considered this small batch of half dismes the first official U.S. coins.

It is true that this limited coinage, the first since passage of the act establishing the Mint on April 2, 1792, pales by comparison to modern U.S. Mint presses. Today's machines can churn out up to 750 coins a minute, striking as many as four coins at a time and boasting yearly mintages in the billions. But it is also true that these first small pieces – struck from silver and stamped with a plump Liberty on the obverse and a scrawny eagle in flight on the reverse – have tremendous historical importance.

For within what Washington would declare in his 1792 address to Congress as a "small beginning" were the seeds of a monetary system that has lasted more than 200 years and has become the study and admiration of many.

Before the U.S. Mint

Collectors today can trace much of the nation's development and learn of its struggles and growth through its coinage: from a cumbersome system first proposed by Robert Morris, a Revolutionary War financier and first superintendent of finance, to the refinements tendered by Thomas Jefferson and Alexander Hamilton, which firmly placed the nation on an easily understood decimal system of coinage.

At first there was little coinage in circulation, except for foreign coins that arrived through trade or in the purses of the first settlers. Despite a dire need for coinage in the Colonies, Great Britain considered it a royal right and granted franchises sparingly. Much of the Colonial economy, therefore, revolved around barter, with food staples, crops, and goods serving as currency. Indian wampum or bead money also was used, first in the fur trade and later as a form of money for Colonial use.

Copper pieces were produced around 1616 for the Sommer Islands (now Bermuda), but coinage within the American Colonies apparently didn't begin until 1652, when John Hull struck silver threepence, sixpence and shillings under authority of the General Court of Massachusetts. This coinage continued, with design changes (willow, oak and pine trees), through 1682. Most of the coins were dated 1652, apparently to avoid problems with England.

In 1658 Cecil Calvert, second Lord Baltimore, commissioned coins to be struck in England for use in Maryland. Other authorized and unauthorized coinages – including those of Mark Newby, John Holt, William Wood, and Dr. Samuel Higley – all became part of the landscape of circulating coins. In the 1780s this hodgepodge of coinage was augmented by influxes of counterfeit British halfpenny coins and various state coinages.

In terms of the latter, the Articles of Confederation had granted individual states the right to produce copper coins. Many states found this to be appealing, and merchants in the mid-1780s traded copper coins of Vermont, Connecticut, Massachusetts, New Jersey, and New York. Not all were legal issues; various entrepreneurs used this as an invitation to strike imitation state coppers and British halfpence. Mutilated and worn foreign coins also circulated in abundance. Included among these were coins of Portugal, Great Britain and France, with the large majority of the silver arriving from Spain.

The accounting system used by the states was derived from the British system of pounds, shillings and pence. Each state was allowed to set its own rates at which foreign gold and silver coins would trade in relation to the British pound.

In 1782 Robert Morris, newly named superintendent of finance, was appointed to head a committee to determine the values and weights of the gold and silver coins in circulation. Asked simply to draw up a table of values, Morris took the opportunity to propose the establishment of a federal mint. In his Jan. 15, 1782, report (largely prepared by his assistant, Gouverneur Morris), Morris noted that the exchange rates between the states were complicated.

He observed that a farmer in New Hampshire would be hard-pressed if asked to determine the value of a bushel of wheat in South Carolina. Morris recorded that an amount of wheat worth four shillings in his home state of New Hampshire would be worth 21 shillings and eightpence under the accounting system used in South Carolina.

Robert Morris devised a complicated plan for a national coinage based on a common denominator of 1,440.

Morris claimed these difficulties plagued not only farmers, but that "they are perplexing to most Men and troublesome to all." Morris further pressed for the adoption of an American coin to solve the problems of the need for small change and debased foreign coinages in circulation.

In essence, what he was advocating was a monometallic system based on silver. He said that gold and silver had fluctuated throughout history. Because these fluctuations resulted in the more valuable metal leaving the country, any nation that adopted a bimetallic coinage was doomed to have its gold or silver coins disappear from circulation.

Gouverneur Morris calculated the rate at which the Spanish dollar traded to the British pound in the various states. Leaving out South Carolina, because it threw off his calculations, Gouverneur Morris arrived at a common denominator of 1,440. Robert Morris, therefore, recommended a unit of value of 1/1,440, equivalent to a quarter grain of silver. He suggested the striking of a silver 100-unit coin, or cent; a silver 500-unit coin, or quint; a silver 1,000-unit coin, or mark; and two copper coins, one of eight units and the other of five units.

On Feb. 21, 1782, the Grand Committee of Congress approved the proposal and directed Morris to press forward and report with a plan to establish a mint. Morris had already done so. Apparently feeling confident that Congress would like his coinage ideas, Morris (as shown by his diary) began efforts at the physical establishment prior to his January 1782 report. He had already engaged Benjamin Dudley to acquire necessary equipment for the mint and hoped to have sample coins available to submit with his original report to Congress.

Things went awry, however.

By Dec. 12, 1782, 10 months after Congress had approved his plan, Morris still could not show any samples of his coins. He was forced, ironically, to suggest that Congress draw up a table of rates for foreign coins to be used until his report was ready. It was not until April 2, 1783, that Morris was able to note in his diary that the first of his pattern coins were being struck.

"I sent for Mr. Dudley who delivered me a piece of Silver Coin," he wrote, "being the first that has been struck as an American Coin."

He also recorded that he had urged Dudley to go ahead with production of the silver patterns.

It wasn't until April 23, 1783, that Morris was able to send his Nova Constellatio patterns to Congress and suggest that he was ready to report on establishing a mint. Apparently nothing came of Morris' efforts. Several committees looked into the matter, but nothing was accomplished. Dudley was eventually discharged as Morris' hopes dimmed.

Thomas Jefferson was the next to offer a major plan. Jefferson liked the idea of a decimal system of coinage, but disliked Morris' basic unit of value. As chairman of the Currency Committee, Jefferson reviewed Morris' plan and formulated his own ideas.

To test public reaction, Jefferson gave his "Notes on Coinage" to The Providence Gazette, and Country Journal, which published his plan in its July 24, 1784, issue. Jefferson disagreed with Morris' suggestion for a 1/1,440 unit of value and instead proposed a decimal coinage based on the dollar, with the lowest unit of account being the mil, or 1/1,000.

"The most easy ratio of multiplication and division is that by ten," Jefferson wrote. "Every one knows the facility of Decimal Arithmetic."

Jefferson argued that although Morris' unit would have eliminated the unwanted fraction that occurred when merchants converted British farthings to dollars, this was of little significance. After all, the original idea of establishing a mint was to get rid of foreign currencies.

Morris' unit, Jefferson said, was too cumbersome for use in normal business transactions. According to Jefferson, under Morris' plan a horse valued at 80 Spanish dollars would require a notation of six figures and would be shown as 115,200 units.

Jefferson' coinage plan suggested the striking of a dollar, or unit; half dollar, or five-tenths; a double tenth, or fifth of a dollar, equivalent to a pistereen; a tenth, equivalent to a Spanish bit; and a one-fifth copper coin, relating to the British farthing. He also wanted a gold coin of $10, corresponding to the British double guinea; and a copper one-hundredth coin, relating to the British halfpence.

In reference to his coinage denominations, Jefferson said, it was important that the coins "coincide in value with some of the known coins so nearly, that the people may by quick reference in the mind, estimate their value."

Thomas Jefferson proposed that the United States adopt a decimal system of coinage.

More than a year, however, passed without any further action on his plan or that proposed by Morris. In a letter to William Grayson, a member of the Continental Congress, Washington expressed concern for the establishment of a national coinage system, terming it "indispensably necessary." Washington also complained of the coinage in circulation: "A man must travel with a pair of scales in his pocket, or run the risk of receiving gold at one-fourth less than it counts."

A plan at last

On May 13, 1785, the 13-member Grand Committee, to whom Jefferson's plan had been submitted, filed its report, generally favoring Jefferson's coinage system. The committee did, however, make slight alterations, including the elimination of the gold $10 coin, the addition of a gold $5 coin, and the dropping of Jefferson's double tenth, which it replaced with a quarter dollar. The committee also added a coin equal to 1/200th of a dollar (half cent). On July 6, 1785, Congress unanimously approved the Grand Committee's plan. It failed, however, to set a standard weight for the silver dollar or to order plans drawn up for a mint.

These two factors led to new proposals.

On April 8, 1786, the Board of Treasury, which had been reinstated after Morris' resignation as superintendent of finance two years prior, tendered three distinct coinage proposals based on varying weights and bimetallic ratios for the silver dollar. The first of these three plans (the one passed by Congress on Aug. 8, 1786) required the silver dollar to contain 375.64 grains of pure silver. The board's proposal varied from earlier coinage plans in that it advocated a higher bimetallic ratio of 15.256-to-1 and differing charges to depositors for coining of gold and silver. It called for minting of gold $5 and $10 coins, and silver denominations of the dime, double dime, half dollar, and dollar. In copper were a cent and half cent. The proposal came during the peak of state coinages and influxes of debased coppers, which, as the board reported, were being "Imported into or manufactured in the Several States."

Concerned over the need to control state coinages and foreign coppers, the board suggested that, within nine months of passage of its proposal, the legal-tender status of all foreign coppers be repealed and that values be set at which the state coppers would circulate. The board obviously expected immediate action and ordered a supply of copper that was being stored in Boston to be brought to New York in the hope that it might soon be coined. Their hopes, however, rested on the positive and quick action of Congress, something that hadn't occurred with the other proposals and would not occur this time.

Opposition to the mint was beginning to surface. Several members of Congress expressed their belief that the supply of foreign gold and silver coins in circulation was sufficient to preclude any need for a mint. They also argued that the problem with debased coppers could be solved by contracting with private individuals to strike the nation's cents and half cents.

Several proposals were offered for a contract coinage. On April 21, 1787, the board accepted a proposal by James Jarvis to strike 300 tons of copper coin at the federal standard. Jarvis, however, delivered slightly less than 9,000 pounds of his contract. The contract was voided the following year for his failure to meet scheduled delivery times, but helped to delay further action on a mint. Concerted action on a coinage system and a mint would wait until the formation of the new government.

Alexander Hamilton, named in September 1789 to head the new Treasury, offered three different methods by which the new nation could achieve economic stability, including the funding of the national debt, establishment of the Bank of North America, and the founding of the U.S. Mint. On Jan. 21, 1791, Hamilton submitted to Congress a "Report on the Establishment of a Mint." It was compiled through his study of European economic theories and the earlier works of Morris and Jefferson, along with the 1786 report of the Board of Treasury.

Hamilton agreed with Jefferson that the dollar seemed to be best suited to serve as the basic unit, but believed it necessary to establish a proper weight and fineness for the new coin. To do so, Hamilton had several Spanish coins assayed to determine the fine weight of the Spanish dollar. He also watched the rate at which Spanish dollars traded for fine gold (24 3/4 grains per dollar) on the world market.

From his assays and observations he determined that the Spanish dollar contained 371 grains of silver. He then multiplied 24 3/4 by 15 (the gold value of silver times his suggested bimetallic ratio) and arrived at 371 1/4 as the proper fine silver weight for the new silver dollar.

In regard to his findings, Hamilton admitted that Morris had made similar assays and had arrived at a weight of 373 grains for the Spanish dollar. Hamilton attributed the discrepancy to the differing equipment used in making the assays. He failed, however, to observe that silver coins were traded in the world market at actual weight rather than the weight at time of issue. The Spanish dollar contained 376 grains of pure silver when new, 4 3/4 grains more than Hamilton's proposed silver dollar.

Hamilton also wanted a bimetallic ratio of 15-to-1, in contrast to the Board of Treasury's 15.6-to-1 ratio. Hamilton said his ratio was closer to Great Britain's, which would be important for trade, and Holland's, which would be important for repaying loans from that country.

His report suggested the striking of a gold $10; gold dollar; silver dollar; silver tenth, or disme; and copper one-hundredth and half-hundredth. Hamilton felt the last of these, the half cent, was necessary because it would enable merchants to lower their prices, which would help the poor.

Congress passed the act establishing the U.S. Mint in April 1792. It reinstated several coin denominations left out by Hamilton and dropped his gold dollar. In gold, the act authorized at $10 coin, or "eagle"; a $5 coin, or "half eagle"; and a $2.50 coin, or "quarter eagle." In silver were to be a dollar, half dollar, quarter dollar, disme, and half disme, and in copper a cent and half cent.

Though it established a sound system of U.S. coinage, the act failed to address the problem of foreign coins in circulation. It was amended in February 1793 to cancel their legal-tender status within three years of the Mint's opening.

Coinage begins

Coinage totals at the first mint were understandably low. Skilled coiners, assayers and others who could handle the mint's daily operations were in short supply in the United States. Also in want were adequate equipment and supplies of metal for coinage. Much of the former had to be built or imported. Much of the latter was also imported or salvaged from various domestic sources, including previously struck tokens and coins, and scrap metal.

Coinage began in earnest in 1793 with the striking of half cents and cents at the new mint located at Seventh Street between Market and Arch streets in Philadelphia. Silver coinage followed in 1794, with half dimes, half dollars and dollars. Gold coinage did not begin until 1795 with the minting of the first $5 and $10 coins. Silver dimes and quarters and gold $2.50 coins did not appear until 1796.

Production at the first U.S. mint, in Philadelphia, was minuscule by today's standards.

Under the bimetallic system of coinage by which gold and silver served as equal representations of the unit of value, much of the success and failure of the nation's coinage to enter and remain in circulation revolved around the supply and valuation of precious metals. One need only to gain a cursory knowledge of such movements to understand what role precious metals played in development of U.S. coinage. That role, to a large extent, determined why some coins today are rare and why some passed down from generation to generation are still plentiful and of lower value to collectors.

From the Mint's beginning, slight miscalculations in the proper weight for the silver dollar and a proper bimetallic ratio led gold and silver to disappear from circulation. The U.S. silver dollar traded at par with Spanish and Mexican dollars, but because the U.S. coin was lighter, it was doomed to export.

A depositor at the first mint could make a profit at the mint's expense by sending the coins to the West Indies. There they could be traded at par for the heavier Spanish or Mexican eight reales, which were then shipped back to the United States for recoinage. As a result, few early silver dollars entered domestic circulation; most failed to escape the melting pots.

Gold fared no better. Calculations of the bimetallic ratio by which silver traded for gold on the world market were also askew at first and were always subject to fluctuations. Gold coins either disappeared quickly after minting or never entered circulation, languishing in bank vaults. These problems led President Jefferson to halt coinage of the gold $10 and silver dollar.

The gold $10 reappeared in 1838 at a new, lower-weight standard. The silver dollar, not coined for circulation since 1803, returned in 1836 with a limited mintage. Full-scale coinage waited until 1840.

Nor was the coinage of copper an easy matter for the first mint. Severe shortages of the metal led the Mint to explore various avenues of obtaining sufficient supplies for striking cents and half cents.

Witness, for example, the half-cent issues of 1795 and 1797 struck over privately issued tokens of the New York firm of Talbot, Allum & Lee because of a shortage of copper for the federal issue. Rising copper prices and continued shortages forced the Mint to lower the cent's weight from 208 grains to 168 grains in 1795.

By that same year Congress had begun to investigate the Mint. Complaints about high costs and low production had been raised. Suggestions that a contract coinage might be more suitable for the new nation surfaced again, despite bad experiences with previous attempts.

The Mint survived this and another investigation, but the problems of fluctuating metal supplies continued to plague the nation. In 1798, because of the coinage shortage, the legal-tender status of foreign coins was restored. Several more extensions were given during the 1800s, ending with the withdrawal of legal-tender status for Spanish coins in 1857.

In the 1830s great influxes of silver from foreign mints raised the value of gold in relation to silver, which made it necessary for the Mint to lower the standard weight of all gold coins in 1834. It also led to the melting of great numbers of gold coins of the old specifications.

By the 1850s discovery of gold in California had again made silver the dearer metal. All silver quickly disappeared from circulation. Congress reacted in 1853 by lowering the weight of the silver half dime, dime, quarter, and half dollar, hoping to keep silver in circulation. A new gold coin of $20 value was introduced to absorb a great amount of the gold from Western mines.

Not long after, silver was discovered in Nevada. By the mid-1870s the various mines that made up what was known as the Comstock Lode (after its colorful early proprietor, Henry P. Comstock) had hit the mother lode. Large supplies of silver from the Comstock, combined with European demonetization, caused a severe drop in its value, which continued through the close of the 19th century.

It was believed that the introduction of a heavier, 420-grain silver dollar in 1873, known as the Trade dollar, would create a market for much of the Comstock silver, bolster its price, and at the same time wrest control from Great Britain of lucrative trade with the Orient. It didn't. Large numbers of Trade dollars eventually flooded back into the United States, where they were, ironically, accepted only at a discount to the lesser-weight Morgan dollars.

The latter had been introduced in 1878 as a panacea to the severe economic problems following the Civil War. Those who proudly carried the banner of free silver contended that by taking the rich output of the Comstock mines and turning it into silver dollars, a cheaper, more plentiful form of money would become available. In its wake, they believed, would be a much needed economic recovery.

The Free Silver Movement gained its greatest support during the late 19th century when William Jennings Bryan attempted to gain the White House on a plank largely based on restoration of the free and unlimited coinage of the standard 412.5-grain silver dollar. He failed. Silver failed. Shortly thereafter the United States officially adopted a gold standard.

Silver continued to be a primary coinage metal until 1964, when rising prices led the Mint to remove it from the dime and quarter. Mintage of the silver dollar had ended in 1935. The half dollar continued to be coined through 1970 with a 40-percent-silver composition. It, too, was then debased.

Gold coinage ended in 1933 and exists today only in commemorative issues and American Eagle bullion coins with fictive face values. A clad composition of copper and nickel is now the primary coinage metal. Even the cent is no longer all copper; a copper-coated zinc composition has been used since 1982.

Precious-metal supplies were also linked to the opening of additional mints, which served the parent facility in Philadelphia. The impact of gold discoveries in the 1820s in the southern Appalachian Mountains was directly tied to the construction of branch mints in Dahlonega, Ga., and Charlotte, N.C., in 1838. These new mints struck only gold coins. New Orleans also became the site of a branch mint in the same year as Dahlonega and Charlotte. It took in some of the outflow of gold from Southern mines, but also struck silver coins.

Discovery of gold in California in the late 1840s created a gold rush, and from it sprang a great western migration. Private issues of gold coinage, often of debased quality, were prevalent, and the cost of shipping the metal eastward for coinage at Philadelphia was high. A call for an official branch mint was soon heard and heeded in 1852 with the authorization of the San Francisco Mint, which began taking deposits in 1854.

The discovery of silver in the Comstock Lode led to yet another mint. Located only a short distance via Virginia & Truckee Railroad from the fabulous Comstock Lode, the Carson City mint began receiving bullion in early 1870.

Denver, also located in a mineral-rich region, became the site of an assay office in 1863 when the government purchased the Clark, Gruber & Co. private mint. It became a U.S. branch mint in 1906. In addition to the Denver and Philadelphia mints, San Francisco and a facility in West Point, N.Y., continue to serve as U.S. mints, but the others have left behind a rich legacy.

The collector taking a more extended journey into the history of U.S. coinage can find plenty of interesting tales – some as tall as the day is long and others factually based – all of which are part of the rich and ever-changing panoply of U.S. coinage history. There are stories of denominations that failed, great discoveries, great rarities, great collectors, and, for those with an artistic bent, a rich field of pattern coins to be explored and a wealth of much-heralded designs by famous sculptors such as Augustus Saint-Gaudens, Adolph Weinman, James Earle Fraser, and others.

For those who are drawn to the hobby by the allure of age-old relics of days gone by, or by coins handed down through the family, or even by dreams of great wealth, coin collecting has much to offer. The history of the U.S. Mint, with its small but ever so important beginning, is the starting point.

The Grading Factor
How to classify a coin's condition

By Arlyn G. Sieber

Grading is one of the most important factors in buying and selling coins as collectibles. Unfortunately, it's also one of the most controversial. Since the early days of coin collecting in the United States, buying through the mail has been a convenient way for collectors to acquire coins. As a result, there has always been a need in numismatics for a concise way to classify the amount of wear on a coin and its condition in general.

A look back

In September 1888, Dr. George Heath, a physician in Monroe, Mich., published a four-page pamphlet titled *The American Numismatist*. Publication of subsequent issues led to the founding of the American Numismatic Association, and *The Numismatist*, as it's known today, is the association's official journal. Heath's first issues were largely devoted to selling world coins from his collection. There were no formal grades listed with the coins and their prices, but the following statement by Heath indicates that condition was a consideration for early collectors:

"The coins are in above average condition," Heath wrote, "and so confident am I that they will give satisfaction, that I agree to refund the money in any unsatisfactory sales on the return of the coins."

As coin collecting became more popular and *The Numismatist* started accepting paid advertising from others, grading became more formal. The February 1892 issue listed seven "classes" for the condition of coins (from worst to best): mutilated, poor, fair, good, fine, uncirculated, and proof. Through the years, the hobby has struggled with developing a grading system that would be accepted by all and could apply to all coins. The hobby's growth was accompanied by a desire for more grades, or classifications, to more precisely define a coin's condition. The desire for more precision, however, was at odds with the basic concept of grading: to provide a concise method for classifying a coin's condition.

For example, even the conservatively few classifications of 1892 included fudge factors.

"To give flexibility to this classification," *The Numismatist* said, "such modification of fine, good and fair, as 'extremely,' 'very,' 'almost,' etc., are used to express slight variations from the general condition."

The debate over grading continued for decades in *The Numismatist*. A number of articles and letters prodded the ANA to write grading guidelines and endorse them as the association's official standards. Some submitted specific suggestions for terminology and accompanying standards for each grade. But grading remained a process of "instinct" gained through years of collecting or dealing experience.

A formal grading guide in book form finally appeared in 1958, but it was the work of two individuals rather than the ANA. *A Guide to the Grading of United States Coins* by Martin R. Brown and John W. Dunn was a breakthrough in the great grading debate. Now collectors had a reference that gave them specific guidelines for specific coins and could be studied and restudied at home.

The first editions of Brown and Dunn carried text only, no illustrations. For the fourth edition, in 1964, publication was assumed by Whitman Publishing Co. of Racine, Wis., and line drawings were added to illustrate the text.

The fourth edition listed six principal categories for circulated coins (from worst to best): good, very good, fine, very fine, extremely fine, and about uncirculated. But again, the desire for more precise categories were evidenced. In the book's introduction, Brown and Dunn wrote, "Dealers will sometimes advertise coins that are graded G-VG, VG-F, F-VF, VF-XF. Or the description may be ABT. G. or VG plus, etc. This means that the coin in question more than meets minimum standards for the lower grade but is not quite good enough for the higher grade."

When the fifth edition appeared, in 1969, the "New B & D Grading System" was introduced. The six principal categories for circulated coins were still intact, but variances within those categories were now designated by up to four letters: "A," "B," "C" or "D." For example, an EF-A coin was "almost about uncirculated." An EF-B was "normal extra fine" within the B & D standards. EF-C had a "normal extra fine" obverse, but the reverse was "obviously not as nice as obverse due to poor strike or excessive wear." EF-D had a "normal extra fine" reverse but a problem obverse.

But that wasn't the end. Brown and Dunn further listed 29 problem points that could appear on a coin – from No. 1 for an "edge bump" to No. 29 for "attempted re-engraving outside of the Mint." The number could be followed by the letter "O" or "R" to designate whether the problem appeared on the obverse or reverse and a Roman numeral corresponding to a clock face to designate where the problem appears on the obverse or reverse. For example, a coin described as "VG-B-9-O-

X" would grade "VG-B"; the "9" designated a "single rim nick"; the "O" indicated the nick was on the obverse; and the "X" indicated it appeared at the 10 o'clock position, or upper left, of the obverse.

The authors' goal was noble – to create the perfect grading system. They again, however, fell victim to the age-old grading-system problem: Precision comes at the expense of brevity. Dealer Kurt Krueger wrote in the January 1976 issue of *The Numismatist*, "Under the new B & D system, the numismatist must contend with a minimum of 43,152 different grading combinations! Accuracy is apparent, but simplicity has been lost." As a result, the "New B & D Grading System" never caught on in the marketplace.

The 1970s saw two important grading guides make their debut. The first was *Photograde* by James F. Ruddy. As the title implies, Ruddy uses photographs instead of line drawings to show how coins look in the various circulated grades. Simplicity is also a virtue of Ruddy's book. Only seven circulated grades are listed (about good, good, very good, fine, very fine, extremely fine, and about uncirculated), and the designations stop there.

In 1977 the longtime call for the ANA to issue grading standards was met with the release of *The Official A.N.A. Grading Standards for United States Coins*. Like Brown and Dunn, the first edition of the ANA grading guide used line drawings to illustrate coins in various states of wear. But instead of using adjectival descriptions, the ANA guide adopted a numerical system for designating grades.

The numerical designations were based on a system used by Dr. William H. Sheldon in his book *Early American Cents*, first published in 1949. He used a scale of 1 to 70 to designate the grades of large cents.

"On this scale," Sheldon wrote, "1 means that the coin is identifiable and not mutilated – no more than that. A 70-coin is one in flawless Mint State, exactly as it left the dies, with perfect mint color and without a blemish or nick." (Sheldon's scale also had its pragmatic side. At the time, a No. 2 large cent was worth about twice a No. 1 coin; a No. 4 was worth about twice a No. 2, and so on up the scale.)

With the first edition of its grading guide, the ANA adopted the 70-point scale for grading all U.S. coins. It designated 10 categories of circulated grades: AG-3, G-4, VG-8, F-12, VF-20, VF-30, EF-40, EF-45, AU-50, and AU-55. The third edition, released in 1987, replaced the line drawings with photographs, and another circulated grade was added: AU-58. A fourth edition was released in 1991.

Grading circulated U.S. coins

Dealers today generally use either the ANA guide or Photograde when grading circulated coins for their inventories. (Brown and Dunn is now out of print.) Many local coin shops sell both books. Advertisers in *Numismatic News*, *Coins* magazine, and *Coin Prices* must indicate which standards they are using in grading their coins. If the standards are not listed, they must conform to ANA standards.

Following are some general guidelines, accompanied by photos, for grading circulated U.S. coins. Grading even circulated pieces can be subjective, particularly when attempting to draw the fine line between, for example, AU-55 and AU-58. Two longtime collectors or dealers can disagree in such a case.

But by studying some combination of the following guidelines, the ANA guide, and *Photograde*, and by looking at a lot of coins at shops and shows, collectors can gain enough grading knowledge to buy circulated coins confidently from dealers and other collectors. The more you study, the more knowledge and confidence you will gain. When you decide which series of coins you want to collect, focus on the guidelines for that particular series. Read them, reread them, and then refer back to them again and again.

AU-50

AU-50 (about uncirculated): Just a slight trace of wear, result of brief exposure to circulation or light rubbing from mishandling, may be evident on elevated design

Indian cent

Lincoln cent

Buffalo nickel

Jefferson nickel

Mercury dime   *Standing Liberty quarter*

Washington quarter   *Walking Liberty half dollar*

Morgan dollar   *Barber coins*

areas. These imperfections may appear as scratches or dull spots, along with bag
marks or edge nicks. At least half of the original mint luster generally is still evident.

XF-40

Indian cent

Lincoln cent

Buffalo nickel

Jefferson nickel

Mercury dime

Standing Liberty quarter

Washington quarter

Walking Liberty half dollar

Morgan dollar

Barber coins

XF-40 (extremely fine): The coin must show only slight evidence of wear on the highest points of the design, particularly in the hair lines of the portrait on the obverse. The same may be said for the eagle's feathers and wreath leaves on the reverse of most U.S. coins. A trace of mint luster may still show in protected areas of the coin's surface.

VF-20

Indian cent

Lincoln cent

Buffalo nickel

Jefferson nickel

Mercury dime

Standing Liberty quarter

Washington quarter

Walking Liberty half dollar

Morgan dollar

Barber coins

VF-20 (very fine): The coin will show light wear at the fine points in the design, though they may remain sharp overall. Although the details may be slightly smoothed, all lettering and major features must remain sharp.

Indian cent: All letters in "Liberty" are complete but worn. Headdress shows considerable flatness, with flat spots on the tips of the feathers.

Lincoln cent: Hair, cheek, jaw, and bow-tie details will be worn but clearly separated, and wheat stalks on the reverse will be full with no weak spots.

Buffalo nickel: High spots on hair braid and cheek will be flat but show some detail, and a full horn will remain on the buffalo.

Jefferson nickel: Well over half of the major hair detail will remain, and the pillars on Monticello will remain well defined, with the triangular roof partially visible.

Mercury dime: Hair braid will show some detail, and three-quarters of the detail will remain in the feathers. The two diagonal bands on the fasces will show completely but will be worn smooth at the middle, with the vertical lines sharp.

Standing Liberty quarter: Rounded contour of Liberty's right leg will be flattened, as will the high point of the shield.

Washington quarter: There will be considerable wear on the hair curls, with feathers on the right and left of the eagle's breast showing clearly.

Walking Liberty half dollar: All lines of the skirt will show but will be worn on the high points. Over half the feathers on the eagle will show.

Morgan dollar: Two-thirds of the hair lines from the forehead to the ear must show. Ear should be well defined. Feathers on the eagle's breast may be worn smooth.

Barber coins: All seven letters of "Liberty" on the headband must stand out sharply. Head wreath will be well outlined from top to bottom.

F-12

Indian cent

Lincoln cent

Buffalo nickel

Jefferson nickel

Mercury dime

Standing Liberty quarter

Washington quarter

Walking Liberty half dollar

Morgan dollar

Barber coins

F-12 (fine): Coins show evidence of moderate to considerable but generally even wear on all high points, though all elements of the design and lettering remain bold. Where the word "Liberty" appears in a headband, it must be fully visible. On 20th century coins, the rim must be fully raised and sharp.

VG-8

Indian cent

Lincoln cent

Buffalo nickel

Jefferson nickel

Mercury dime

Standing Liberty quarter

Washington quarter

Walking Liberty half dollar

Morgan dollar

Barber coins

VG-8 (very good): The coin will show considerable wear, with most detail points worn nearly smooth. Where the word "Liberty" appears in a headband, at least three letters must show. On 20th century coins, the rim will start to merge with the lettering.

G-4

Indian cent

Lincoln cent

Buffalo nickel

Jefferson nickel

Mercury dime

Standing Liberty quarter

Washington quarter

Walking Liberty half dollar

Morgan dollar

Barber coins

G-4 (good): Only the basic design remains distinguishable in outline form, with all points of detail worn smooth. The word "Liberty" has disappeared, and the rims are almost merging with the lettering.

About good or fair: The coin will be identifiable by date and mint but otherwise badly worn, with only parts of the lettering showing. Such coins are of value only as fillers in a collection until a better example of the date and mintmark can be obtained. The only exceptions would be rare coins

Collectors have a variety of grading services from which to choose. This set of Arkansas half dollars that appeared in an Early American History Auctions sale used two of the services.

Grading uncirculated U.S. coins

The subjectivity of grading and the trend toward more classifications becomes more acute when venturing into uncirculated, or mint-state, coins. A minute difference between one or two grade points can mean a difference in value of hundreds or even thousands of dollars. In addition, the standards are more difficult to articulate in writing and illustrate through drawings or photographs. Thus, the possibilities for differences of opinion on one or two grade points increase in uncirculated coins.

Back in Dr. George Heath's day and continuing through the 1960s, a coin was either uncirculated or it wasn't. Little distinction was made between uncirculated coins of varying condition, largely because there was little if any difference in value. When *Numismatic News* introduced its value guide in 1962 (the forerunner of today's *Coin Market* section in the *News*), it listed only one grade of uncirculated for Morgan dollars.

But as collectible coins increased in value and buyers of uncirculated coins became more picky, distinctions within uncirculated grade started to surface. In 1975 *Numismatic News* still listed only one uncirculated grade in *Coin Market*, but added this note: "Uncirculated and proof specimens in especially choice condition will also command proportionately higher premiums than these listed."

The first edition of the ANA guide listed two grades of uncirculated, MS-60 and MS-65, in addition to the theoretical but non-existent MS-70 (a flawless coin). MS-60 was described as "typical uncirculated" and MS-65 as "choice uncirculated." *Numismatic News* adopted both designations for *Coin Market*. In 1981, when the second edition of the ANA grading guide was released, MS-67 and MS-63 were added. In 1985 *Numismatic News* started listing six grades of uncirculated for Morgan dollars: MS-60, MS-63, MS-65, MS-65+, and MS-63 prooflike.

Then in 1986, a new entity appeared that changed the nature of grading and trading uncirculated coins ever since. A group of dealers led by David Hall of Newport Beach, Calif., formed the Professional Coin Grading Service. For a fee, collectors could submit a coin through an authorized PCGS dealer and receive a professional opinion of its grade.

The concept was not new; the ANA had operated an authentication service since 1972 and a grading service since 1979. A collector or dealer could submit a coin directly to the service and receive a certificate giving the service's opinion on authenticity and grade. The grading service was the source of near constant debate among dealers and ANA officials. Dealers charged that ANA graders were too young and inexperienced, and that their grading was inconsistent.

Grading stability was a problem throughout the coin business in the early 1980s, not just with the ANA service. Standards among uncirculated grades would tighten during a bear market and loosen during a bull market. As a result, a coin graded MS-65 in a bull market may have commanded only MS-63 during a bear market.

PCGS created several innovations in the grading business in response to these problems:

1. Coins could be submitted through PCGS-authorized dealers only.

2. Each coin would be graded by at least three members of a panel of "top graders," all prominent dealers in the business. (Since then, however, PCGS does not allow its graders to also deal in coins.)

3. After grading, the coin would be encapsulated in an inert, hard-plastic holder with a serial number and the grade indicated on the holder.

4. PCGS-member dealers pledged to make a market in PCGS-graded coins and honor the grades assigned.

5. In one of the most far-reaching moves, PCGS said it would use all 11 increments of uncirculated on the 70-point numerical scale: MS-60, MS-61, MS-62, MS-63, MS-64, MS-65, MS-66, MS-67, MS-68, MS-69, and MS-70.

The evolution of more uncirculated grades had reached another milestone.

Purists bemoaned the entombment of classic coins in the plastic holders and denounced the 11 uncirculated grades as implausible. Nevertheless, PCGS was an immediate commercial success. The plastic holders were nicknamed "slabs," and dealers couldn't get coins through the system fast enough.

In subsequent years, a number of similar services have appeared. Among them, one of the original PCGS "top graders," John Albanese, left PCGS to found the Numismatic Guaranty Corp (NGC). The ANA grading service succumbed to "slab mania" and introduced its own encapsulated product.

There now are numerous other reputable private third-party grading services. PCGS and NGC are the oldest and remain the leaders. In 1990 the ANA sold its grading service to a private company. It operates under the ANACS acronym.

How should a collector approach the buying and grading of uncirculated coins? Collecting uncirculated coins worth thousands of dollars implies a higher level of numismatic expertise by the buyer. Those buyers without that level of expertise should cut their teeth on more inexpensive coins, just as today's experienced collectors did. Inexperienced collectors can start toward that level by studying the guidelines for mint-state coins in the ANA grading guide and looking at lots of coins at shows and shops.

Study the condition and eye appeal of a coin and compare it to other coins of the same series. Then compare prices. Do the more expensive coins look better? If so, why? Start to make your own judgments concerning relationships between condition and value.

According to numismatic legend, a collector walked up to a crusty old dealer at a show one time and asked the dealer to grade a coin the collector had with him. The dealer looked at the coin and said, "I grade it a hundred dollars." Such is the bottom line to coin grading.

Grading U.S. proof coins

Because proof coins are struck by a special process using polished blanks, they receive their own grading designation. A coin does not start out being a proof and then become mint state if it becomes worn. Once a proof coin, always a proof coin.

In the ANA system, proof grades use the same numbers as circulated and uncirculated grades, and the amount of wear on the coin corresponds to those grades. But the number is preceded by the word "proof." For example, Proof-65, Proof-55, Proof-45, and so on. In addition, the ANA says a proof coin with many marks, scratches or other defects should be called an "impaired proof."

Grading world coins

The state of grading non-U.S. issues is similar to U.S. coin grading before Brown and Dunn. There is no detailed, illustrated guide that covers the enormous scope and variety of world coins; collectors and dealers rely on their experience in the field and knowledge of the marketplace.

The *Standard Catalog of World Coins* gives the following guidelines for grading world coins, which apply to the Canadian and Mexican value listings in this book:

In grading world coins, there are two elements to look for: (1) overall wear and (2) loss of design details, such as strands of hair, feathers on eagles, designs on coats of arms, and so on. Grade each coin by the weaker of the two sides. Age, rarity or type of coin should not be considered in grading.

Grade by the amount of overall wear and loss of detail evident in the main design on each side. On coins with a moderately small design element that is prone to early wear, grade by that design alone.

In the marketplace, adjectival grades are still used for Mexican coins. The numerical system for Canadian coins is now commonplace:

Uncirculated, MS-60: No visible signs of wear or handling, even under a 30X microscope. Bag marks may be present.

Visit Our Website @ coinbuys.com

Almost uncirculated, AU-50: All detail will be visible. There will be wear on only the highest points of the coin. There will often be half or more of the original mint luster present.

Extremely fine, XF-40: About 95 percent of the original detail will be visible. Or, on a coin with a design that has no inner detail to wear down, there will be light wear over nearly the entire coin. If a small design is used as the grading area, about 90 percent of the original detail will be visible. This latter rule stems from the logic that a smaller amount of detail needs to be present because a small area is being used to grade the whole coin.

Very fine, VF-20: About 75 percent of the original detail will be visible. Or, on a coin with no inner detail, there will be moderate wear over the entire coin. Corners of letters and numbers may be weak. A small grading area will have about 60 percent of the original detail.

Fine, F-12: About 50 percent of the original detail will be visible. Or, on a coin with no inner detail, there will be fairly heavy wear over the entire coin. Sides of letters will be weak. A typically uncleaned coin will often appear dirty or dull. A small grading area will have just under 50 percent of the original detail.

Very good, VG-8: About 25 percent of the original detail will be visible. There will be heavy wear on the entire coin.

Good, G-4: Design will be clearly outlined but with substantial wear. Some of the larger detail may be visible. The rim may have a few weak spots of wear.

About good, AG-3: Typically only a silhouette of a large design will be visible. The rim will be worn down into the letters, if any.

Where to write for more information

American Numismatic Association: 818 N. Cascade Ave.,
     Colorado Springs, CO 80903-3279

Independent Coin Grading Co.: 7901 E. Belleview Ave., Suite 50,
     Englewood, CO 80111

Numismatic Guaranty Corp: P.O. Box 4776, Sarasota, FL 34230

NTC (Numistrust Corp.): 2500 N. Military Trail, Suite 210, Boca Raton, FL 33431

Professional Coin Grading Service: P.O. Box 9458, Newport Beach, CA 92658

Sovereign Entities Grading Service: 401 Chestnut St., Suite 103,
     Chattanooga, TN 37402-4924

Visit the Krause Publications website
www.numismaster.com

Get a Map
How to organize a collection

By David C. Harper

Do you have a jar full of old coins? Did a favorite relative give you a few silver dollars over the years? Or did you just come across something unusual that you set aside?

All three circumstances make good beginnings for collecting coins. It may surprise you, but this is how just about everybody starts in the hobby. It is a rare collector who decides to start down the hobby road without first having come into a few coins one way or another.

What these random groupings lack is organization. It is organization that makes a collection. But think about it another way: Organization is the map that tells you where you can go in coin collecting and how you can get there.

Have you ever been at a large fair or a huge office building and seen the maps that say "you are here?" Did you ever consider that, over time, thousands of other people have stood on the same spot? This is true in numismatics also. Figuratively, you are standing on the same spot on which the writers of this book stood at some point in their lives.

At a fair, the map helps you consider various ways of seeing all the sights. In coin collecting, too, there are different ways to organize a collection. The method you choose helps you see the hobby sights you want to see.

It should be something that suits you. Remember, do what you want to do. See what you want to see. But don't be afraid to make a mistake; there aren't any. Just as one can easily retrace steps at a fair, one can turn around and head in another direction in the coin-collecting hobby. Besides, when you start off for any given point, often you see something along the way that was unplanned but more interesting. That's numismatics.

There are two major ways to organize a collection: by type, and by date and mintmark. These approaches work in basically the same fashion for coins of the United States, Canada and Mexico. Naturally, there are differences. But to establish the concepts, let's focus first on U.S. coins.

United States

Let's take collecting by type first. Look at your jar of coins, or take the change out of your pocket. You find Abraham Lincoln and the Lincoln Memorial on most cents and four commemorative reverse designs in 2009. You find Thomas Jefferson and his home, Monticello, on most nickels, but special reverse designs were produced in 2004 and 2005 and a new obverse began in 2006. Franklin D. Roosevelt and a torch share the dime. George Washington and an eagle (or since 1999, designs honoring states and the District of Columbia and territories) appear on the quarter. John F. Kennedy and the presidential seal are featured on the half dollar. Sacagawea paired with an eagle or a woman planting and Presidents paired with the Statue of Liberty are on dollars.

Each design is called a "type." If you took one of each and put them in a holder, you would have a type set of recent coins.

With just these six denominations, you can study various metallic compositions. You can evaluate their states of preservation and assign a grade to each. You can learn about the artists who designed the coins, and you can learn of the times in which these designs were created.

As you might have guessed, many different coin types have been used in the United States over the years. You may remember seeing some of them circulating. These designs reflect the hopes and aspirations of people over time. Putting all of them together forms a wonderful numismatic mosaic of American history.

George Washington did not mandate that his image appear on the quarter. Quite the contrary. He would have been horrified. When he was president, he headed off those individuals in Congress who thought the leader of the country should have his image on its coins. Washington said it smacked of monarchy and would have none of it.

Almost a century and a half later, during the bicentennial of Washington's birth in 1932, a nation searching for its roots during troubled economic times decided that it needed his portrait on its coins as a reminder of his great accomplishments and as reassurance that this nation was the same place it had been in more prosperous days.

In its broadest definition, collecting coins by type requires that you obtain an example of every design that was struck by the U.S. Mint since it was founded in 1792. That's a tall order. You would be looking for denominations like the half cent, 2-cent piece, 3-cent piece, and 20-cent piece, which have not been produced in more than a century. You would be looking for gold coins ranging in face value from $1 to $50 and current bullion coins.

But even more important than odd-sounding denominations or high face values is the question of rarity. Some of the pieces in this multi-century type set are rare and expensive. That's why type collectors often divide the challenge into more digestible units.

Type collecting can be divided into 18th, 19th, 20th and 21st century units. The 21st century set is rapidly growing. Starting type collectors can focus on 20th century coin designs, which are easily obtainable. The fun and satisfaction of putting the 20th century set together then creates the momentum to continue backward in time.

In the process of putting a 20th century type set together, one is also learning how to grade, learning hobby jargon, and discovering how to obtain coins from dealers, the U.S. Mint, and other collectors. All of this knowledge is then refined as the collector increases the challenge to himself.

This book is designed to help. How many dollar types were struck in the 20th century? Turn to the U.S. price guide section and check it out. We see the Morgan dollar, Peace dollar, Eisenhower dollar, and Anthony dollar. Hobbyists could also add the Ike dollar with the Bicentennial design of 1976 and the silver American Eagle bullion coin struck since 1986. One can also find out their approximate retail prices from the listings.

The beauty of type collecting is that one can choose the most inexpensive example of each type. There is no need to select a 1903-O Morgan when the 1921 will do just as well. With the 20th century type set, hobbyists can dodge some truly big-league prices.

As a collector's hobby confidence grows, he can tailor goals to fit his desires. He can take the road less traveled if that is what suits him. Type sets can be divided by denomination. You can choose more than two centuries of one-cent coins. You can take just obsolete denominations or copper, silver or gold denominations.

You can even collect by size. Perhaps you would like to collect all coin types larger than 30 millimeters or all coins smaller than 20 millimeters. Many find this freedom of choice stimulating.

Type collecting has proven itself to be enduringly popular over the years. It provides a maximum amount of design variety while allowing collectors to set their own level of challenge.

The second popular method of collecting is by date and mintmark. What this means, quite simply, is that a collector picks a given type – Jefferson nickels, for example – and then goes after an example of every year, every mintmark, and every type of manufacture that was used with the Jefferson design.

Looking at this method of collecting brings up the subject of mintmarks. The "U.S. Mint" is about as specific as most non-collectors get in describing the government agency that provides everyday coins. Behind that label are the various production facilities that actually do the work.

In the more than two centuries of U.S. coinage, there have been eight such facilities. Four are still in operation. Those eight in alphabetical order are Carson City, Nev., which used a "CC" mintmark to identify its work; Charlotte, N.C.

A basic type set of
20th century dollar
coins would consist of
(from top) a Morgan
type, Peace type,
Eisenhower type and
Anthony type.

("C"); Dahlonega, Ga. ("D"); Denver (also uses a "D," but it opened long after the Dahlonega Mint closed, so there was never any confusion); New Orleans ("O"); Philadelphia (because it was the primary mint, it used no mintmark for much of its history, but currently uses a "P"); San Francisco ("S"); and West Point, N.Y. ("W").

A person contemplating the collecting of Jefferson nickels by date and mintmark will find that three mints produced them: San Francisco, Denver and Philadelphia. Because the first two are branch mints serving smaller populations, their output has tended over time to be smaller than that of Philadelphia. This fact, repeated in other series, has helped give mintmarks quite an allure to collectors. It provides one of the major attractions in collecting coins by date and mintmark.

The key date for Jeffersons is the 1950-D when using mintages as a guide. In that year, production was just 2.6 million pieces. Because collectors of the time

Jefferson nickels have been produced at the (from top) Philadephia, Denver and San Francisco Mints. Note the Denver and San Francisco mintmarks to the right of Monticello.

The wartime nickels of 1942-1945 marked the first time a "P" mintmark, for Philadelphia, was used.

were aware of the coin's low mintage, many examples were saved. As a result, prices are reasonable.

The Depression-era 1939-D comes in as the most valuable regular-issue Jefferson nickel despite a mintage of 3.5 million – almost 1 million more than the 1950-D. The reason: Fewer were saved for later generations of coin collectors.

Date and mintmark collecting teaches hobbyists to use mintage figures as a guide but to take them with a grain of salt. Rarity, after all, is determined by the number of surviving coins, not the number initially created.

The Jefferson series is a good one to collect by date and mintmark, because the mintmarks have moved around, grown in size, and expanded in number.

When the series was first introduced, the Jefferson nickel was produced at the three mints previously mentioned. In 1942, because of a diversion of certain metals to wartime use, the coin's alloy of 75 percent copper and 25 percent nickel was changed. The new alloy was 35 percent silver, 56 percent copper, and 9 percent manganese.

To denote the change, the mintmarks were moved and greatly enlarged. The pre-1942 mintmarks were small and located to the right of Monticello; the wartime mintmarks were enlarged and placed over the dome. What's more, for the first time in American history, the Philadelphia Mint used a mintmark ("P").

The war's end restored the alloy and mintmarks to their previous status. The "P" disappeared. This lasted until the 1960s, when a national coin shortage saw all mintmarks removed for three years (1965-1967) and then returned, but in a different location. Mintmarks were placed on the obverse, to the right of Jefferson's portrait near the date in 1968. In 1980 the "P" came back in a smaller form and is still used.

Another consideration arises with date and mintmark collecting: Should the hobbyist include proof coins in the set? This can be argued both ways. Suffice to say that anyone who has the desire to add proof coins to the set will have a larger one. It is not necessary nor is it discouraged.

Some of the first proof coins to carry mintmarks were Jefferson nickels. When proof coins were made in 1968 after lapsing from 1965 to 1967, production occurred at San Francisco instead of Philadelphia. The "S" mintmark was placed on the proof coins of that year, including the Jefferson nickel, to denote the change. Since that time, mintmarks used on proof examples of various denominations have included the "P," "D," "S," and "W."

In 1968 the mintmarks reappeared on U.S. coins and production of proof coins resumed, this time at the San Francisco Mint. On the nickels, the mintmark moved from the reverse to the obverse below the date.

For all of the mintmark history that is embodied in the Jefferson series, prices are reasonable. For a first attempt at collecting coins by date and mintmark, it provides excellent background for going on to the more expensive and difficult types. After all, if you are ever going to get used to the proper handling of a coin, it is far better to experiment on a low-cost coin than a high-value rarity.

As one progresses in date and mintmark collecting and type collecting, it is important to remember that all of the coins should be of similar states of preservation. Sets look slapdash if one coin is VG and another is MS-65 and still another is VF. Take a look at the prices of all the coins in the series before you get too far, figure out what you can afford, and then stick to that grade or range of grades.

Sure, there is a time-honored practice of filling a spot with any old example until a better one comes along. That is how we got the term "filler." But if you get a few placeholders, don't stop there. By assembling a set of uniform quality, you end up with a more aesthetically pleasing collection.

The date and mintmark method used to be the overwhelmingly dominant form of collecting. It still has many adherents. Give it a try if you think it sounds right for you.

Before we leave the discussion of collecting U.S. coins, it should be pointed out that the two major methods of organizing a collection are simply guidelines. They are not hard-and-fast rules that must be followed without questions. Collecting should be satisfying to the hobbyist. It should never be just one more item in the daily grind. Take the elements of these collecting approaches that you like or invent your own.

It should also be pointed out that U.S. coinage history does not start with 1792, nor do all of the coins struck since that time conform precisely to the two major organizational approaches. But these two areas are good places to start.

There are coins and tokens from the American Colonial period (1607-1776) that are just as fascinating and collectible as regular U.S. Mint issues. There are federal issues struck before the Mint was actually established. See the Colonial price-guide section in this book.

There are special coins called commemoratives, which have been struck by the U.S. Mint since 1892 to celebrate some aspect of American history or a contemporary event. They are not intended for circulation. There was a long interruption between 1954 and 1982, but currently annual commemoratives are being offered for sale directly to collectors by the Mint.

Collecting commemoratives has always been considered something separate from collecting regular U.S. coinage. It is, however, organized the same way. Commemoratives can be collected by date and mintmark or by type.

Current commemoratives can be purchased from the U.S. Mint. Check the U.S. Mint website at www.usmint.gov. Hobbyists who order from the U.S. Mint's website receive notices of product availability by e-mail. Hobbyists will get the various solicitations for not only commemoratives, but regular proof sets and mint sets and proof American Eagle bullion coins. Buying coins from the Mint can be considered a hobby pursuit in its own right. Some collectors let the Mint organize their holdings for them. They buy complete sets and put them away. They never buy anything from anywhere else.

Admittedly, this is a passive form of collecting, but there are individuals around the world who enjoy collecting at this level without ever really going any deeper. They like acquiring every new issue as it comes off the Mint's presses.

Once done, there is a certain knowledge that one has all the examples of the current year. Obviously, too, collectors by date and mintmark of the current types would have to buy the new coins each year, but, of course, they do not stop there.

Varieties and errors make up another area. Under this heading come the coins the Mint did not intend to make. There are all kinds of errors. Many of them are inexpensive. Check out the "U.S. Minting Varieties and Errors" section in the price guide. If you want to pursue it further, there are specialty books that deal with the topic in more detail.

Canada

Starting point for the national coinage of Canada is popularly fixed at 1858. In that year a large cent was first produced for use in Upper and Lower Canada (Ontario and Quebec). These prices were intended to supplant local copper coinage, which in turn had been attempts to give various regions a medium of exchange.

What was circulating in Canada at the time was a hodgepodge of world issues. The large cent predates a unified national government by nine years, but it is considered the beginning of national issues nevertheless.

There are many similarities between the United States and Canada and their respective monetary systems. Both continent-sized nations thought in terms of taming the frontier, new settlements, and growth. Both came to use the dollar as the unit of account because of the pervasiveness of the Spanish milled dollar in trade. For each, the dollar divides into 100 cents.

However, Canada had a far longer colonial history. Many of its residents resisted the tide that carried the United States to independence and worked to preserve their loyalties to the British crown. As a result, Canada was firmly a part of the British Empire. So even today with its constitution (the British North America Act transferred from Westminster to Ottawa in 1982), parliamentary democracy, and a national consciousness perhaps best symbolized by the maple leaf, Canada retains a loyalty to the crown in the person of Queen Elizabeth II of the United Kingdom. Canada is a member of the British Commonwealth of Nations.

Canadian coins
have depicted (from
top) Queen Victoria,
King Edward VII,
King George V,
King George VI and
Queen Elizabeth II.

The effect of this on coins is obvious. Current issues carry the queen's effigy. How Canada got its coins in the past was also influenced. The fledgling U.S. government set about creating its own mint as one of its earliest goals, despite that better-quality pieces could be purchased abroad at lower cost. Canada found that ties to mints located in England were logical and comfortable.

The Royal Canadian Mint was not established until 1908, when it was called the Ottawa branch of the British Royal Mint, and it was not given its present name until 1931. Both events are within living memory. Canadian coins, therefore, have a unique mixture of qualities. They are tantalizingly familiar to U.S. citizens yet distinctly different.

The coinage of a monarchy brings its own logic to the organization of a collection. Type collecting is delineated by the monarch. United Canada has had six. The first was Queen Victoria, whose image appeared on those large cents of 1858. Her reign began in 1837 and lasted until 1901.

She was followed by Edward VII, 1901-1910; George V, 1910-1936; Edward VIII, 1936; George VI, 1936-1952; and Queen Elizabeth II, 1952-present. All but Edward VIII had coins struck for circulation in Canada. The collectible monarchs, therefore, number five, but the longer reigns inspired changes of portraits over time to show the aging process at work. Legends also changed. When George VI ceased being emperor of India, Canada's coins were modified to recognize the change.

Like U.S. coins, sizes and alloys were altered to meet new demands placed on the coinage. However, the separateness of each nation might best be summed up this way: Though the United States abolished its large cent in 1857, Canada's was just getting under way in 1858. The United States put an end to the silver dollar in 1935, the very year Canada finally got its series going.

And Canada, the nickel-mining giant, used a small-sized silver five-cent coin until 1921, almost 50 years after the half dime was abolished in the United States. But whereas the Civil War was the major cause of the emergence of modern U.S. coinage as specified by the Coinage Act of 1873, World War I influenced the alterations that made Canada's coins what they are today.

It might be assumed that change in the monarch also signaled a change in the reverse designs of the various denominations. A check of the Canadian price guide section shows this is not necessarily the case. Current designs paired with Queen Elizabeth II basically date back to the beginning of her father's reign. The familiar maple-leaf cent, beaver 5-cent piece, schooner 10-cent, caribou 25-cent, and coat-of-arms 50-cent have been running for more than 50 years. Significant changes were made to the 50-cent coin in 1959, but the reverse design remains the coat of arms.

So where does that leave type collectors? It puts them in a situation similar to categorizing the various eagles on U.S. coins. They can be universalists and accept the broadest definitions of type, or they can narrow the bands to whatever degree suits them best.

By checking the price guide section, date and mintmark collectors will quickly note that their method of organization more or less turns into collecting by date. Though currently there are three mints in Canada – Hull, Quebec; Ottawa, Ontario; and Winnipeg, Manitoba – they don't use mintmarks. Historically, few mintmarks were employed.

Ottawa used a "C" on gold sovereigns of 1908-1919 and on some exported colonial issues. The private Heaton Mint in Birmingham, England, used an "H" on coins it supplied to Canada from 1871 to 1907.

But the coins supplied to Canada by the British Royal Mint and later by its Ottawa branch did not carry any identifying mark. Collectors who confine their activities to the more recent issues need never think about a mintmark.

It would be easy to slant a presentation on Canadian issues to stress similarities or differences to U.S. issues. One should remember that the monetary structures of each evolved independently, but each was always having an impact on the other.

Common events, such as World War II, had a similar impact. For example, the Canadian 5-cent coin changed in much the same way as the U.S. nickel. In Canada, nickel was removed and replaced first by a tombac (brass) alloy and then by chromium-plated steel. Peace brought with it a return to the prewar composition.

To see an example of differences between the United States and Canada, take the Canadian approach to the worldwide trend of removing silver from coinage. Canada made its move in 1968, three years after the United States. Instead of choosing a copper-nickel alloy as a substitute for silver, Canada looked to its own vast natural resources and employed pure nickel.

Canada also seems more comfortable with its coinage than the United States. Whereas the United States often feared confusion and counterfeiting from making the least little changes in its coins, Canada has long embraced coinage to communicate national events, celebrations and culture. Its silver-dollar series actually began as a celebration of George V's 25 years on the throne.

Succeeding years saw additional commemorative $1 designs interspersed with the regular Voyageur design. When the centennial of national confederation was observed in 1967, all of the denominations were altered for one year. The United States only reluctantly tried out the idea on three of its denominations for the nation's Bicentennial.

Ultimately, Canada began an annual commemorative dollar series in 1971. It issued coins for the 1976 Montreal Olympic Games and again in 1988 for the Calgary Olympic Games. Bullion coins were created to market its gold, silver and platinum output. A commemorative series of gold $100 coins was also undertaken. Canada, too, issues special proof, prooflike and specimen sets, similar to the United States.

Hobbyists who would like to be informed of new issues should write Royal Canadian Mint, P.O. Box 457, Station A, Ontario K1A 8V5, Canada. The mint also main-

Like the U.S. Mint, the Royal Canadian Mint offers sets of coins in a variety of finishes to the collector market.

tains special toll-free lines. In the United States, hobbyists may telephone the Royal Canadian Mint at 1-800-268-6468. In Canada, the number is 1-800-267-1871. You can get on the mailing list by using these numbers and you can buy currently available coins. (See Chapter 6 for Web information.)

When collecting Canada, another thing to remember is the importance varieties play in the nation's various series. Certainly, a type collector has no need to dwell on this information, but the date and mintmark collector may puzzle over the many extra identifying abbreviations in the price guide for certain coins. These varieties should not be confused with the U.S. variety-and-error category.

Here the varieties are not mistakes; they are deliberately created and issued variations of the standard design. We see Voyageur dollars on which the number of water lines changes. Other dollars count the number of beads.

These differences are minor. Though they were deliberately done to meet varying mint needs, they were not intended to be set apart in the public mind. The hobby, however, likes to look at things under a microscope.

Some varieties were indeed intended to be deliberately and noticeably different. An example of this occurs with 1947-dated issues. A maple leaf was placed on the 1947-dated cent through 50-cent issues. This indicated the coin was struck after George VI lost his title of emperor of India, as proclaimed in the Latin legend, but that the design had not yet been altered to reflect this. All of these varieties are considered integral parts of the Canadian series, and they are listed as such.

Do not construe any of this to mean there is no collecting of varieties and errors of the type common in the United States. There is. Collecting Royal Canadian Mint mistakes is just as active, just as interesting, and just as rewarding. After all, mint errors are universal. The methods of manufacture are the same. So the mistakes can be classified in the same manner.

Canada's numismatic listings also include items from various provinces issued before they were part of the confederation. The largest portion of this section is devoted to Newfoundland, because it retained a separate status far longer than the other provinces – until 1949, in fact.

Advice given to collectors of U.S. coins also applies to collectors of Canadian coins: Do what interests you. Do what you can afford. Create sets of uniform grade.

The rules of rarity transcend national boundaries. The only thing to keep in mind is the relative size of the collecting population. Because Canada has only a tenth of the U.S. population, it stands to reason that the number of collectors in that nation is but a fraction of the U.S. number. A mintage that seems to indicate scarcity for U.S. coin, therefore, could indicate something quite common in Canada. Don't forget that mintage is just a guide. The same factors that caused loss of available specimens or preserved unusually large quantities were at work in Canada, too.

Mexico

Coinage produced in Mexico dates to the establishment of a mint in Mexico City in 1536, more than 250 years before a federal mint was set up in the United States and more than 300 years before Canada circulated its own coins. The output of those extra centuries alone would make organizing a Mexican coin collection more challenging than a collection of U.S. or Canadian coins. But there are numerous other factors involved.

You say you like the kings and queens on Canada's coins? Mexico has kings, too – nearly 300 years' worth, plus a couple of emperors. You say the ideals of liberty embodied by the great men and women on U.S. coins is more your cup of tea? Mexico's coins also feature men and women committed to liberty.

In addition, Mexico is the crossroads of civilizations and empires. The great pyramid-building society of southern Mexico and Central America met its end at the hands of the Spanish conquistadors led initially by Hernando Cortez. The great Aztec empire was looted and overturned in 1519-1521 in the name of Spain.

The great natural resources of the area then supported successive Spanish kings in their grand dreams of dominating Europe. Through the doors of the Mexico City Mint and later facilities scattered about the country passed legendary quantities of silver. Even today the country ranks at the top of the list of silver producers.

But while Spain could dominate Mexico for a long time, the basic ideals of liberty and human dignity eventually motivated the people to throw off the foreign yoke. Unfortunately, victory was often neither complete nor wisely led. And in more recent years, the scourge of inflation had exacted a high toll on the currency itself. The numismatic consequences of a long history punctuated by periods of turmoil are an abundance of denominations, metals and types.

It is tempting for a would-be collector of Mexican coins to forget about anything that happened in the country prior to its monetary reform of 1905. By starting at that point, a hobbyist can happily overlook anything other than a decimal monetary system in which 100 centavos equal 1 peso. That system is as modern as any. The coins' striking quality is high. Legends are easy to read and understand, and the variety of issues is wide but not overwhelming.

There always is a certain logic to begin the collecting of any country with recent issues. The costs of learning are minimized, and as one becomes comfortable, a level of confidence can be built up sufficient to prompt diving further into the past.

*One thousand of
these equaled one
new peso as 1993 began.*

The issues of 1905 to date also more easily fit into the mold of type collecting and collecting by date and mintmark. To take type collecting, for example, let's look at the peso. In 1905 it was a silver-dollar-sized coin with a silver-dollar-sized quantity of bullion in it, 0.786 ounces. In 1918 it was reduced to 0.4663 ounces; in 1920, 0.3856 ounces; in 1947, 0.2250 ounces; 1950, 0.1285 ounces; 1957, 0.0514 ounces; and in 1970 silver was eliminated completely in favor of a copper-nickel alloy.

At almost every one of those steps, the design changed, too. After sinking to 3,300 to the U.S. dollar, monetary reform dropped three zeroes in 1993. The new peso, equal to 1,000 old ones, is now about 14 to the U.S. dollar.

By beginning with 1905, a date and mintmark collector misses out on issues of the various branch mints that were located around the country. Regular issues were all struck in Mexico City. Yearly output was reasonably regular for the various denominations, so date sets are extensive.

There have been rumblings since the early 1980s that Mexico would abandon the peso because of its greatly reduced value. The government, however, has been working hard to retain it since the monetary reform. So far it has succeeded.

One thing the government cannot do, however, is turn the clock back to a time when the fractional denominations of 1, 2, 5, 10, 20, 25, and 50 centavos were relatively high face values. However, it is stimulating to assemble sets because they offer a range of rarities. They are neither so expensive that it would prevent a collector from acquiring them at some point, but neither are they so common that you can walk into a shop, write a check, and come away with all of the 20th century sets complete. Check out the price guide section and see.

Gold in the post-1905 era is basically so much bullion. There are some scarcer pieces and some strikingly beautiful designs, such as the Centenario, a gold 50-peso coin containing 1.2 ounces of bullion. It was first struck in 1921 to mark 100 years of independence. Because Mexico actively restruck its gold coins, however, it is virtually impossible to tell an original issue from the newer version.

The result is a retail price structure based on metallic content. Gold, however, does not conjure up the images that silver does. Silver is the magic word for Mexico. That, of course, means the peso.

The modern Mexico City Mint also strikes commemoratives and collector sets from time to time. These are generally marketed to collectors through private firms,

Mexico also strikes commemorative coins for the collector market. They are available through private firms in the United States.

details of which are published in hobby newspapers like World Coin News. Mexico, like the United States and Canada, also issues gold and silver bullion coins.

These also are marketed through arrangements with private firms. Interestingly, Mexico's many gold-coin restrikes were the bullion coins of their day. They had the advantage of ready identification, and they were legally tradable according to gold-coin regulations that existed in the United States from 1933 through 1974.

It is appropriate that we conclude discussion of the modern period on the concept of bullion, because bullion is at the root of Mexico's numismatic history. That is a period to which we now turn.

When Cortez toppled the Aztec Empire, for a time the wealth returning to Spain was merely that taken by the victors from the vanquished. But the business of permanently administering a vast area in the name of the Spanish king, exploiting its natural resources, and funneling the proceeds to Spain quite soon involved the establishment of a mint in Mexico City. This was undertaken in 1536, just 15 years after the end of Aztec dominion.

At first, the authorized coins were low denominations: silver quarter, half, 1, 2, 3, and 4 reales, and copper 2 and 4 maravedis. To understand their face values and how they related to each other, let's take the common reference point of a silver dollar. The silver dollar is 8 reales, and you might recognize the nickname for the denomination of "piece of eight" from pirate lore. The eighth part, the silver real, was divided into 34 copper maravedis. That means the 8 reales was worth 272 copper maravedis.

The copper coinage was hated and soon abolished, not to reappear until 1814. The silver coins were fine as far as they went. When the mines of Mexico began producing undreamed of quantities of metal, however, it was the 8 reales that took center stage. This occurred after 1572. The piece of eight became the standard form for shipping silver back to Spain.

Mexico City's output was prodigious. Minting standards were crude. All denominations produced are called "cobs," because they are basically little more than irregular-looking lumps of metal on which bits and pieces of design can be seen. The only constant was weight, fineness, and the appearance of assayer's initials (which guaranteed the weight and fineness). Not showing those initials was cause for severe punishment.

Designs showed the arms of the monarch on one side, a cross on the other, appropriate legends, and an indication of denomination. The period of cob issues lasted until 1732. Rulers of the period start with Charles and Johanna, 1516-1556; Philip II, 1556-1598; Philip III, 1598-1621; Philip IV, 1621-1665; Charles II, 1665-1700; Philip V, 1700-1724 and 1724-1746; and Luis I, 1724.

Modern mint machinery began turning out coins in 1732. Quality was similar to today. The arms design was continued. It was not until 1772 that the monarch's portrait began appearing. The honor of this numismatic debut belongs to Charles III. Kings of this period are Ferdinand VI, 1746-1759; Charles III, 1760-1788; Charles IV, 1788-1808; and Ferdinand VII, 1808-1821. *The Standard Catalog of Mexican Coins* by Colin R. Bruce II and Dr. George W. Vogt is recommended to those who want to study this period in greater depth.

The revolutionary period begins in 1810, when a parish priest, Miguel Hidalgo y Costilla, issued the call for independence. The first attempts to achieve this were violently suppressed. Hidalgo was executed, but independence did come in 1821.

With revolt against central authority came a dispersal of the right to strike coins. Mexico City continued as the major facility, but other operations began. The list of these over the next century is lengthy. Mintmarks and assayer initials proliferated.

The old colonial coinage standard survived the period. The 8 reales and its parts carried on. A slight reduction in bullion content had been ordered by the king in 1760, but otherwise things continued as they were. Gold was coined during the colonial period beginning in 1679 based on an 8-escudo piece, which divided into eighths just like the 8 reales. Gold, however, was not as important as silver.

Mexico's first emperor came shortly after independence. He was a leader in the struggle that set Mexico free from Spain. Augustin de Iturbide, originally an officer in the service of Spain, was proclaimed emperor in 1822. He abdicated in 1823 and was executed in 1824.

The second emperor had a reign almost as short as the first. Maximilian I, emperor only because he had a French army to secure the throne, reigned from 1863 to 1867. He was shot by a firing squad when the French left.

He is remembered numismatically because he decided to decimalize the coinage. The centavo and peso were born. Soon afterward, the republic was re-established. Further monetary changes were minor thereafter until 1905.

Collectors focusing on Mexico can devote much time to the study of the quasi-official issues of rebels during the periods of instability. They can look at hacienda tokens, which were issued by large farms or ranches that employed hundreds or thousands of people. Or they can pick whichever period in Mexico's history that fascinates them most. Whatever collectors of Mexico eventually settle on, they will find it rewarding.

Where to write for more information:

World Coin News: 700 E. State St., Iola, WI 54990.

Caring For Coins
How to store and preserve your collection

By Alan Herbert

From the day you acquire your first collectible coin, you have to consider where and how to store your collection. Often a shoebox or a small cardboard or plastic box of some kind will be the principal storage point as you start to gather coins, even before they can be considered a collection. Sooner or later you will outgrow that first box and need to think seriously about what to do with your coins to protect and preserve them.

All too often security takes precedence over preservation. We're more worried that the kids will dip into the coins for candy or ice cream or that burglars will somehow learn about your "valuable" collection and pay a visit. It often isn't until years later when you suddenly notice that your once beautiful coins are now dingy and dull, with spots and fingerprints all over them, that preservation becomes a primary consideration.

Learning good storage habits should be one of the first things to do right along with acquiring those first coins. There are a multitude of storage products on the market that are intended for more or less specific situations, so learning which to use and how to use them is vital to the health of your collection. Most, if not all, of the products mentioned here should be available at your nearest coin shop or hobby store.

Safe storage methods

The common impulse is to use what's available around the house; never allow that impulse to control your collecting. Plastic wrap, aluminum foil, cardboard, stationery envelopes, and other common household products are not designed for coin storage and never should be used for your collection. The same goes for soaps and cleansers found around the home.

Two-by-two cardboard holders are a common form of short-term, inexpensive coin storage.

Many dealers sell coins in 2-by-2 plastic "flips," but these should not be used for long-term storage.

There are specific products that have been designed, tested and found safe to use for coins. These are the media your collection deserves. The slight added expense will pay a thousand dividends years from now when you sell you collection or pass it on to your heirs.

The most common storage media are 2-inch by 2-inch cardboard holders with Mylar windows, 2-by-2 plastic "flips," coin tubes, hard-plastic holders, coin boards, and coin albums.

The 2-by-2 cardboard holders are the cheapest and most commonly used storage method. They are usually folded and stapled around the coin. They are intended for short-term general storage. They are not airtight or watertight, and staples driven too close to the coin can ruin it.

The 2-by-2 plastic flips come in good and bad varieties. The old, usually soft flips are made of plastics that contain polyvinyl chloride, a chemical found in many plastics. Over time it breaks down into substances that put a green slime on your coins, which attacks the surface and ruins them.

The good flips are made of Mylar, but they are brittle and prone to splitting. So they should not be used to mail coins or when the coins are moved about frequently. Mylar flips, too, are for short-term general storage.

Often you will find coins in PVC holders when you buy them from a dealer. Remove them immediately and put them in some better storage medium.

Coin tubes are often used for bulk storage, but there is a proper technique to placing the coins in the tube.

Coin tubes come in clear and cloudy, or translucent, plastic. These are made of an inert plastic that will not harm your coins. Tubes are intended for bulk, medium- to long-term storage, with one caution: Use care when inserting the coins. Merely dropping one coin onto another in a tube can damage both coins. The best technique is to make a stack or pile of the coins, then slide the pile carefully into the tube while holding it at an angle.

Hard-plastic holders are the elite items for storing your collection. There are a number of varieties, some of which come in three parts that are screwed together. Some come in two pieces that fit together. Some of these are airtight and watertight. They are more expensive, but they deserve to be used for any really valuable coins in your collection.

Coins processed by the third-party grading services come in hard-plastic holders, most of which are at least semi-airtight. The hard-plastic holders used by the U.S. Mint for proof sets since 1968 are not airtight, so coins should be watched carefully for signs of problems. In recent years these holders have been improved, but you should check your proof sets periodically.

Any stored coins should be checked regularly, at least twice a year. Check coins for signs of spotting or discoloration. Check the storage media for any signs of deterioration, rust, mildew, or other problems.

The older mint sets and proof sets – issued from 1955 to 1964 – come in soft-plastic envelopes that are not intended for long-term storage. Coins in these envelopes should be put in better storage media for the long term. In recent years the Mint has switched to an inert, stiffer plastic for the mint sets. This plastic is safe.

A coin folder is frequently the first piece of equipment the beginning collector buys. It is simply a piece of cardboard with holes to hold the coins. The holder folds up for storage. It is intended for inexpensive circulated coins only.

Hard-plastic holders are the top of the line in coin storage.

Coin albums also provide attractive storage for inexpensive circulated coins.

They give no protection from contamination or fingerprints. Worn coins will often fall out of the holes, which leads some novice collectors to tape the coins in the album. This is another example of misuse of a household product; tape can permanently damage a coin's surface.

Pride of ownership and the desire to show off a collection are the moving forces behind the sale of thousands of coin albums. They should also be used for inexpensive circulated coins only, with a couple of exceptions.

Some albums are merely coin boards mounted between covers. Others have pages with sliding plastic strips on both sides of the page so both sides of the coin can be seen.

The open-face albums are subject to fingerprints and contamination. Sneezing on your coins can do as much damage as gouging them with a knife. The

Placing coins in folders can bring generations together.

slides will rub on your coins, damaging the high points of the design over time. These two types of albums should never be used for expensive uncirculated or proof coins, although they are fine for circulated coins that you want to display.

Fairly new on the market are albums designed for coins in inert, airtight holders. This allows you to display your coins and still keep them safe from handling and contact with the atmosphere.

One more storage medium that deserves mention is the clear-plastic notebook page that has pockets for 2-by-2 holders or flips. Here again there are good and bad. Most old pocket sheets contain PVC, so they cannot be used to hold coins in non-airtight holders because the gases will migrate into the holders and damage the coins. The newer Mylar pages are brittle but will not generate damaging gases or liquids.

When buying storage media, make sure the dealer guarantees that his products are safe for coins. Many of the old albums, flips and pocket pages are still around, especially at flea markets. If you are in doubt, don't buy.

There are also thin, two-piece, inert plastic holders that many collectors use to protect coins put in flips or 2-by-2 cardboard holders, especially to protect them from moving about against the holder and getting scratched. They are virtually airtight, so they do offer some protection.

Coins need to be protected from burglars. A box under the bed or in the closet offers no protection. If you must keep coins at home, a good, fireproof safe is a must. Otherwise, rent a safe-deposit box at a bank, but read the fine print on your box contract to make sure a coin collection is covered.

Most homeowner's insurance policies will not cover a coin collection or will cover only a fraction of its value. Special riders are expensive, but if you keep most of your coins at the bank, this will cut costs. For details, consult your insurance agent. The American Numismatic Association also offers collection insurance to its members.

Where to store coins is often a problem. The most common solution is to put them in the attic or basement. Those are the two worst places for your collection. Attics are notoriously hot. Heat can damage almost any storage media, and if there is the slightest hint of PVC, you've got trouble.

Basements are equally bad. They can flood, and humidity is high. Mildew can attack holders and other material stored with your coins.

So what's left? Ideally coins should be treated like a family member. They should be stored in some part of the house where temperature and humidity are relatively constant year round. If it's comfortable for you, it's probably much more comfortable for your coins than the basement or attic.

Protecting coins from humidity is always a good idea, even in areas where it is not a major health problem. For your coins, too much dampness can become a serious problem, often before you realize it. A good solution is to get several good-sized packets of silica gel and store them with your coins in your safe or a container of some kind that will isolate them from the general climate in the home.

To clean or not to clean

Before you store your coins, you should be aware that coins are like dishes: They should never be put away dirty. Ah, but you've probably already heard or read that you should never clean a coin. If you haven't, I'll say it now: Never clean a coin.

OK, so there are exceptions, but be careful of those exceptions and for good reason. Ignoring the exception can be excruciatingly and embarrassingly expensive.

Coins get dirty, just like anything else. The impulse is to shine them up – polish them to a brilliance that will dazzle the viewer. If you've already succumbed to the temptation to clean even a single coin, stand up, kick yourself, then sit back down and read on. The one exception is loose dirt, grease, oil, or something similar, and there are even exceptions to that rule.

Use a neutral solvent to dissolve the grease and oils that usually coat uncirculated coins as they come from the mint. Follow the instructions on the container exactly, and if the directions say to use the product outdoors, they mean it.

For circulated coins, lighter fluid will often dissolve the accumulated "gunk" that sticks to them, but I don't recommend it for uncirculated coins, especially copper alloy coins. Air dry the coins; don't rub or wipe them. Even the softest cloth or paper towel can pick up sharp-edged particles that will ruin a coin's surface. Proof coins are clean when they are packaged, so this should not be necessary and should be done only as a last resort if they have somehow picked up oil in handling.

Using dips, household cleansers, metal polish, and even soap can permanently damage a coin. Avoid acid-based cleaners at all costs. They work by eating away the coin's surface to remove the embedded dirt or discoloration. Cleaning a coin with any of these products will sharply reduce its collectible value. To put it simply, collectors do not want cleaned coins, so they are heavily discounted.

One of the reasons for this is that once a coin has been cleaned, it will discolor much more quickly, requiring fresh cleaning. Each time it is cleaned, the surface is further dulled, reducing the coin's appeal and reducing its value.

Obviously this advice applies especially to uncirculated and proof coins, but it applies to any coin that is or has the potential to become valuable. But if you clean it, its career ends right there.

There are products specifically designed for removing the green PVC slime from coins. They do not contain acid, so they are safe. They will stop but cannot reverse the damage that the PVC has already done to the coin. Read the label, and use exactly as directed.

I frequently am asked about ultrasonic cleaners. They fall under the same heading as the various cleaning products I've described. In other words, the apparatus should not be used for uncirculated, proof, or other valuable coins. If you do use one, do one coin at a time so there is no chance for the vibration to rub two coins together. Change or filter the cleaning solution frequently to keep abrasive particles from coming in contact with the vibrating coin.

Like anything else, cleaning can be carried to an extreme, so I'll give you one horror story and just such a mistake: Years ago I had a collector fly several hundred miles to bring his collection for me to sell for him. When he laid out the coins on the table, I was shocked to discover that the hundreds of coins had all been harshly cleaned.

When I questioned him he calmly recounted that he had decided that the coins needed cleaning, so he dumped them all into a rock tumbler and left it on for several hours. It ruined all his coins, reducing them to face value. With his passion for cleanliness he had destroyed several thousand dollars worth of collectible value, plus air fare, a rental car, and a motel bill.

The key to a long-term collection that might appreciate in value is to learn what not to do to your coins and what care they need to survive years of waiting in the wings. Learning to protect your coins with the best available storage methods and media is a key first step toward enjoying your collection for years to come.

A private firm, Numismatic Conservation Services, LLC, will clean coins that need it for a fee. The firm's Web site address is www.ncscoin.com.

Where to write for more information

American Numismatic Association: 818 N. Cascade Ave., Colorado Springs, CO 80903-3279. Web address is http://www.money.org.

New 5-Ounce Hits Market
Rarity or flash in the pan?

By David C. Harper

What do you call a coin that is twice the diameter of a Morgan silver dollar that says "Quarter Dollar" on it?

Give up?

The Mint calls it a silver bullion coin, that is, a coin of known design, weight and fineness that contains a standard amount of silver in it.

Confused? How can such a large coin be called a quarter?

Welcome to the wacky world of the U.S. Congress.

When that supreme legislative body of the United States decided that the state quarter program needed an encore in the form of the America the Beautiful series that honors national parks, forests, monuments and seashores, it didn't stop at that.

Language in the legislation also required the U.S. Mint to strike a much larger version of the circulating quarter in .999 fine silver. It is to have a diameter of 3 inches as compared to the Morgan dollar's 1.5 inches and it is to contain 5 troy ounces of silver, five times more than the popular 1-ounce U.S. American Eagle bullion coin that has been struck since 1986.

In addition to being large, the 5-ounce bullion coins are fairly thin and have lettered edges spelling out weight and fineness.

Five quarter designs were authorized for each year starting in 2010 and that also meant five corresponding 5-ounce silver coin designs.

The Mint had trouble striking such a large coin. It had to import a German Graebener coining press and specially install it at the Philadelphia Mint.

As every collector knows, trouble in striking a coin can mean scarcity and in this hobbyists were not disappointed.

The Mint was able to strike just 33,000 of each of the five 2010 designs. This number was viewed as low by would-be buyers and a feeding frenzy followed the announcement of their availability Dec. 6, 2010.

Initially, the Mint had intended simply to sell the coins in bulk to its 11 silver bullion coin Authorized Purchasers, which would in turn sell them in the usual manner to bullion coin buyers. Such was not to be. The Mint was forced to backtrack in just days.

On Dec. 10, 2010, the Mint told the APs that they could sell only one set per customer. The Mint also imposed strict price controls, fixing the price at between $900 and $1,000 a set, depending on the price of silver on the day the coins were bought from the Mint, a 10 percent mark-up and the inclusion of a reasonable shipping and handling charge.

This blind sided the APs. They were deluged with telephone calls in December 2010 by would-be buyers. But they didn't have individual packages for the coins, nor did they have the retail staffing to handle sales of one set at a time.

Delays resulted. Tempers flared. It took until March 2011 for the coins to reach the market in quantity. The result was that a few early recipients were able to sell their five-coin sets at online auctions for $2,500 to $5,000 each, depending on whether they were graded by third-party graders and how high the grades were.

America the Beautiful quarters

America the Beautiful quarters will be issued at the rate of five per year 2010-2021 in the order the sites gained congressional recognition.

STATES	SITE
Arkansas (2010)	Hot Springs National Park
Wyoming	Yellowstone National Park
California	Yosemite National Park
Arizona	Grand Canyon National Park
Oregon	Mount Hood National Park
Pennsylvania (2011)	Gettysburg National Park
Montana	Glacier National Park
Washington	Olympic National Park
Mississippi	Vicksburg National Military Park
Oklahoma	Chickasaw National Recreation Area
Puerto Rico (2012)	El Yunque National Forest
New Mexico	Chaco Culture National Historical Park
Maine	Acadia National Park
Hawaii	Hawaii Volcanoes National Park
Alaska	Denali National Park
New Hampshire (2013)	White Mountain National Forest
Ohio	Perry's Victory and Internat'l Peace Memorial
Nevada	Great Basin National Park
Maryland	Fort McHenry National Monument
South Dakota	Mount Rushmore National Memorial
Tennessee (2014)	Great Smokey Mountains Nat. Park
Virgina	Shenandoah National Park
Utah	Arches National Park
Colorado	Great Sand Dunes National Park
Florida	Everglades National Park

The buyers lucky enough to get early delivery made up to five times their investment in a matter of weeks. By March, any set was trading routinely in the $1,400-$1,700 range, while the top grades still brought higher prices.

Numismatic versions of the 2010 coins were to be struck as special uncirculated pieces and sold by the Mint directly to collectors.

The supply of these coins was only 27,000 per design and this even lower mintage number put the Mint in a greater bind. It delayed their sale until after the bullion versions of the 2010 coins were disposed of. It even announced the availability of the 2011 coins starting in late April 2011 before it offered the 2010 numismatic pieces.

When the 2011 coins became available, the Mint ensured a far higher supply (126,700 each as this book goes to press) and this in turn allowed the APs to sell the coins in bulk as is their usual practice.

The 2011 designs became available one at a time, starting with the Gettysburg design. With silver at $37 a troy ounce, the silver value alone of the five coins in the 2010 or 2011 set is $925.

Remember, the five designs are being released to circulation on the standard quarter size copper-nickel planchet. It is also selling silver versions of the standard quarter size in its silver proof sets.

Imagine that? Three coins called quarters that are really very different, and they will be issued every year to 2021.

America the Beautiful quarters

Here is the order of issue for the years 2015 to 2021. The final year of 2021 features just one quarter design.

STATES	SITE
Nebraska (2015)	Homestead National Monument
Louisiana	Kisatchie National Forest
North Carolina	Blue Ridge Parkway
Delaware	Bombay Hook Nat. Wildlife Refuge
New York	Saratoga National Historic Park
Illinois (2016)	Shawnee National Forest
Kentucky	Cumberland Gap Nat. Historic Park
West Virginia	Harpers Ferry Nat. Historic Park
North Dakota	Theodore Roosevelt National Park
South Carolina	Ft. Moultrie (Ft. Sumter) Nat. Monument
Iowa (2017)	Effigy Mounds National Monument
District of Columbia	Frederick Douglass Nat. Historic Site
Missouri	Ozark National Scenic Riverways
New Jersey	Ellis Island Nat. Monument (Statue of Liberty)
Indiana	George Rogers Clark Nat. Historical Park
Michigan (2018)	Pictured Rocks National Lakeshore
Wisconsin	Apostle Islands National Lakeshore
Minnesota	Voyageurs National Park
Georgia	Cumberland Island National Seashore
Rhode Island	Block Island Nat. Wildlife Refuge
Massachusetts (2019)	Lowell National Historical Park
N, Mariana Islands	American Memorial Park
Guam	War in the Pacific Nat. Historical Park
Texas	San Antonio Missions Nat. Historical Park
Idaho	Frank Church River of No Return Wilderness
American Samoa (2020)	National Park of American Samoa
Connecticut	Weir Farm National Historic Site
U.S. Virgin Islands	Salt River Bay Nat. Historical Park
Vermont	Marsh-Billings-Rockefeller Nat. Historical Park
Kansas	Tallgrass Prairie National Preserve
Alabama (2021)	Tuskegee Airmen Nat. Historic Site

What's Hot in 2012?
Many collectors feel rich(er)

Rising silver and gold markets made every collector look like an investment genius in early 2011 as long as they owned some coins made of the two precious metals. With silver now at roughly $37 a troy ounce, any old U.S. silver dime, quarter or half dollar struck before 1965 has seen its metallic value soar from roughly 13 times face value to 26 times face value in just over a year's time. With gold at $1,430 a troy ounce, gold coins' metallic values have jumped by nearly a quarter in the same time span. It didn't matter what collectors think of the coins. Only the view of bullion investors count. They have been bidding prices higher.

There is nothing wrong with feeling good about being a little richer, especially after the financial crash of 2008 and the high unemployment it caused.

These peak bullion prices are the culmination of a decade of increases that have seen silver rise from less than $5 a troy ounce and gold run higher from $256 an ounce since 2001. Making eight times their money in silver and something less than seven times their money in gold left some gold and silver owners wanting still more. As this edition of *North American Coins & Prices* was assembled, all that can be said for sure is that they might just get their wish – then again, they might not.

What's a sensible collector to do? As welcome as windfall bullion profits might be, it is confusing to see coins that were once valued for their relative scarcity now considered to be just so much precious metal.

In the 2001 edition of *North American Coins & Prices*, the 1937-S Washington quarter was priced at $3 in G-4 condition. That was almost triple the $1.20 price of the incredibly common 1964-D in XF-40. But why should it not trade for more than the 1964-D when it has a mintage of just 1,652,000 compared to 704 million? That price relationship is just one of thousands that have been swept away by the upwelling of silver values. The value of the two coins have been equalized at their melt value of $6.50. Will the old relationship ever come back? Will a G-4

Of the three 1986 Statue of Liberty coins, only the half dollar remains a disappointment to buyers today. Rising gold and silver prices have rewarded patient holders of the silver dollar and the $5 gold piece. The $5 alone is worth $346, double the issue price of the three-piece set.

1937-S quarter once again be worth 2.5 times an XF-40 1964-D? Probably, but there might be a long wait. When silver soared in 1979-1980, price relationships were swept away, but silver then fell rapidly after the $50 peak price. What might follow the current 10-year run of higher silver prices could be vastly different from what followed the two-year run that ended in early 1980. However, collectors will be active. They will be aware of low mintages, so the odds are that in future low-mintage coins will be priced at higher levels than common pieces.

If you believe that – and you probably should – then the thing to do now is to dig out your old price guides and see if you can buy coins like the 1937-S for bullion value. Better yet, take your stash of common date silver coins and see if you can trade them even up, or nearly so, for coins that once had premiums.

Alternatively, if you are one of hundreds of thousands of coin collectors who purchased modern commemoratives from the U.S. Mint only to see prices later fall well below issue price, now might be a good time to sell these or trade these for scarcer coins. Bullion has helped you make back your losses.

As an example, if you had purchased the proof 1986 Statue of Liberty three-coin set for $175 and then simply held onto it, at first you saw the gold $5 coin fall to $80, the silver dollar to under $10 and the clad half dollar to $3. But now, thanks to high bullion prices, you have a tidy profit. The $5 gold piece is worth almost $346. The silver dollar, thanks to its weight of .7734 ounces of silver, is worth almost $29. The clad half is still $3 if you want to go to the bother of selling it. But that means the set you paid $175 for and felt bad about is now worth $378. Grab the profit. Those coins will always be common when evaluated by mintages. Change them into other gold or silver coins that have low mintages, but today are trading only for their metallic value. By doing this, you will always have coins of high metallic value and you also will know that should bullion cool off, the scarcity factor from the low mintages might just power the value of your collection ahead for many years to come. That would be mighty smart collecting.

Glossary of Coin Terms

Adjustment marks: Marks made by use of a file to correct the weight of overweight coinage planchets prior to striking. Adjusting the weight of planchets was a common practice at the first U.S. Mint in Philadelphia and was often carried out by women hired to weigh planchets and do any necessary filing of the metal.

Altered coin: A coin that has been changed after it left the mint. Such changes are often to the date or mintmark of a common coin in an attempt to increase its value by passing to an unsuspecting buyer as a rare date or mint.

Alloy: A metal or mixture of metals added to the primary metal in the coinage composition, often as a means of facilitating hardness during striking. For example, most U.S. silver coins contain an alloy of 10 percent copper.

Anneal: To heat in order to soften. In the minting process planchets are annealed prior to striking.

Authentication: The act of determining whether a coin, medal, token or other related item is a genuine product of the issuing authority.

Bag marks: Scrapes and impairments to a coin's surface obtained after minting by contact with other coins. The term originates from the storage of coins in bags, but such marks can occur as coins leave the presses and enter hoppers. A larger coin is more susceptible to marks, which affect its grade and, therefore, its value.

Base metal: A metal with low intrinsic value.

Beading: A form of design around the edge of a coin. Beading once served a functional purpose of deterring clipping or shaving parts of the metal by those looking to make a profit and then return the debased coin to circulation.

Beading

Blank: Often used in reference to the coinage planchet or disc of metal from which the actual coin is struck. Planchets or blanks are punched out of a sheet of metal by what is known as a blanking press.

Business strike: A coin produced for circulation.

Cast copy: A copy of a coin or medal made by a casting process in which molds are used to produce the finished product. Casting imparts a different surface texture to the finished product than striking and often leaves traces of a seam where the molds came together.

Center dot: A raised dot at the center of a coin caused by use of a compass to aid the engraver in the circular positioning of die devices, such as stars, letters, and dates. Center dots are prevalent on early U.S. coinage.

Chop: A mark used by Oriental merchants as a means of guaranteeing the silver content of coins paid out. The merchants' chop, or stamped insignia, often obliterated the original design of the host coin. U.S. Trade dollars, struck from 1873 through 1878 and intended for use in trade with China, are sometimes found bearing multiple marks.

Chop

Clash marks: Marks impressed in the coinage dies when they come together without a planchet between them. Such marks will affect coins struck subsequently by causing portions of the obverse design to appear in raised form on the reverse, and vice versa.

Clipping: The practice of shaving or cutting small pieces of metal from a coin in circulation. Clipping was prevalent in Colonial times as a means of surreptitiously extracting precious metal from a coin before placing it back into circulation. The introduction of beading and a raised border helped to alleviate the problem.

Coin alignment: U.S. coins are normally struck with an alignment by which, when a coin is held by the top and bottom edge and rotated from side-to-side, the reverse will appear upside down.

Collar: A ring-shaped die between which the obverse and reverse coinage dies are held during striking. The collar contains the outward flow during striking and can be used to produce edge reeding.

Commemorative: A coin issued to honor a special event or person. United States commemorative coins have historically been produced for sale to collectors and not placed in circulation, though the 50-states quarters are circulating commemoratives.

Copy: A replica of an original issue. Copies often vary in quality and metallic composition from the original. Since passage of the Hobby Protection Act (Public Law 93-167) of Nov. 29, 1973, it has been illegal to produce or import copies of coins or other numismatic items that are not clearly and permanently marked with the word "Copy."

Counterfeit: A coin or medal or other numismatic item made fraudulently, either for entry into circulation or sale to collectors.

Denticles: The toothlike pattern found around a coin's obverse or reverse border.

Die: A cylindrical piece of metal containing an incuse image that imparts a raised image when stamped into a planchet.

Die crack: A crack that develops in a coinage die after extensive usage, or if the die is defective or is used to strike harder metals. Die cracks, which often run through border lettering, appear as raised lines on the finished coin.

Device: The principal design element.

Double eagle: Name adopted by the Act of March 3, 1849, for the gold coin valued at 20 units or $20.

Eagle: Name adopted by the Coinage Act of 1792 for a gold coin valued at 10 units or $10. Also a name used to refer to gold, silver, and platinum coins of the American Eagle bullion coinage program begun in 1986.

Edge: The cylindrical surface of a coin between the two sides. The edge can be plain, reeded, ornamented, or lettered.

Electrotype: A copy of a coin, medal, or token made by electroplating.

Exergue: The lower segment of a coin, below the main design, generally separated by a line and often containing the date, designer initials, and mintmark.

Face value: The nominal legal-tender value assigned to a given coin by the governing authority.

Fasces: A Roman symbol of authority consisting of a bound bundle of rods and an axe.

Field: The flat area of a coin's obverse or reverse, devoid of devices or inscriptions.

Galvano: A reproduction of a proposed design from an artist's original model produced in plaster or other substance and then electroplated with metal. The galvano is then used in a reducing lathe to make a die or hub.

Glory: A heraldic term for stars, rays or other devices placed as if in the sky or luminous.

Grading: The largely subjective practice of providing a numerical or adjectival ranking of the condition of a coin, token, or medal. The grade is often a major determinant of value.

Gresham's law: The name for the observation made by Sir Thomas Gresham, 16th century English financier, that when two coins with the same face value but different intrinsic values are in circulation at the same time, the one with the lesser intrinsic value will remain in circulation while the other is hoarded.

Half eagle: Name adopted by the Coinage Act of 1792 for a gold coin valued at five units or $5.

Hub: A piece of die steel showing the coinage devices in relief. The hub is used to produce a die that, in contrast, has the relief details incuse. The die is then used to produce the final coin, which looks much the same as the hub. Hubs may be reused to make new dies.

Legend: A coin's principal lettering, generally shown along its outer perimeter.

Rim

Field

Mintmark

Exergue

Obverse

Legend

Reverse

Lettered edge: Incuse or raised lettering on a coin's edge.

Matte proof: A proof coin on which the surface is granular or dull. On U.S. coins this type of surface was used on proofs of the early 20th century. The process has since been abandoned.

Magician's coin: A term sometimes used to describe a coin with two heads or two tails. Such a coin is considered impossible in normal production due to physical differences in obverse and reverse die mountings, though as of 2001 two have been certified as genuine by professional coin authenticators. The vast majority are products made outside the Mint as novelty pieces.

These Canadian Olympic commemoratives have lettered edges.

Medal: Made to commemorate an event or person. Medals differ from coins in that a medal is not legal tender and, in general, is not produced with the intent of circulating as money.

Medal alignment: Medals are generally struck with the coinage dies facing the same direction during striking. When held by the top and bottom edge and rotated from side-to-side, a piece struck in this manner will show both the obverse and reverse right side up.

Mintage: The total number of coins struck during a given time frame, generally one year.

Mintmark: A letter or other marking on a coin's surface to identify the mint at which the coin was struck.

Mule: The combination of two coinage dies not intended for use together.

A medal usually commemorates an event but has no monetary value. It can be issued by a private entity or a government.

Numismatics: The science, study or collecting of coins, tokens, medals, paper money, and related items.

Obverse: The front or "heads" side of a coin, medal, or token.

Overdate: Variety produced when one or more digits of the date are repunched over an old date on a die at the Mint, generally to save on dies or correct an error. Portions of the old date can still be seen under the new one.

Overmintmark: Variety created at the Mint when a different mintmark is punched over an already existing mintmark, generally done to make a coinage die already punched for one mint usable at another. Portions of the old mintmark can still be seen under the new one.

Overstrike: A coin, token or medal struck over another coin, token, or medal.

Pattern: A trial strike of a proposed coin design, issued by the Mint or authorized agent of a governing authority. Patterns can be in a variety of metals, thicknesses, and sizes.

Phrygian cap: A close-fitting, egg-shell-shaped hat placed on the head of a freed slave when Rome was in its ascendancy. Hung from a pole, it was a popular symbol of freedom during the French Revolution and in 18th century United States.

Planchet: A disc of metal or other material on which the image of the dies are impressed, resulting in a finished coin. Also sometimes called a blank.

Proof: A coin struck twice or more from specially polished dies and polished planchets. Modern proofs are prepared with a mirror finish. Early 20th century proofs were prepared with a matte surface.

Prooflike: A prooflike coin exhibits some of the characteristics of a proof despite having been struck by regular production processes. Many Morgan dollars are found with prooflike surfaces. The field will have a mirror background similar to that of a proof, and design details are frosted like some proofs.

Quarter eagle: Name adopted by the Coinage Act of 1792 for a gold coin valued at 2.5 units or $2.50.

Reeding: Serrated (toothlike) ornamentation applied to the coin's edge during striking.

Relief: The portion of a design raised above the surface of a coin, medal, or token.

Restrike: A coin, medal or token produced from original dies at a later date, often with the purpose of sale to collectors.

This U.S. Trade dollar has a reeded edge.

A token is issued by a private entity and can be redeemed for its face value in trade or service.

Reverse: The backside or "tails" side of a coin, medal or token, opposite from the principal figure of the design or obverse.

Rim: The raised area bordering the edge and surrounding the field.

Series: The complete group of coins of the same denomination and design and representing all issuing mints.

Token: A privately issued piece, generally in metal, with a represented value in trade or offer of service. Tokens are also produced for advertising purposes.

Type coin: A coin from a given series representing the basic design. A type coin is collected as an example of a particular design rather than for its date and mintmark.

Variety: Any coin noticeably different in dies from another of the same design, date and mint. Overdate and overmintmarks are examples of varieties.

Wire edge: Created when coinage metal flows between the coinage die and collar, producing a thin flange of coin metal at the outside edge or edges of a coin.

Introduction to Pricing

The following value guide is divided into six sections:
1. U.S. minting varieties and errors.
2. Colonial coins, issued prior to the establishment of the United States
3. U.S. issues of 1792.
4. U.S. issues of 1793-present.
5. Canadian coins.
6. Mexican coins.

Value listings

Values listed in the following price guide are average retail prices. These are the approximate prices collectors can expect to pay when purchasing coins from dealers. They are not offers to buy or sell. The pricing section should be considered a guide only; actual selling prices will vary.

The values were compiled by Krause Publications' independent staff of market analysts. They derived the values listed by monitoring auction results, business on electronic dealer trading networks, and business at major shows, and in consultation with a panel of dealers. For rare coins, when only a few specimens of a particular date and mintmark are known, a confirmed transaction may occur only once every several years. In those instances, the most recent auction result is listed.

Grading

Values are listed for coins in various states of preservation, or grades. Standards used in determining grades for U.S. coins are those set by the American Numismatic Association. See Chapter 2 for more on grading.

Dates and mintmarks

The dates listed are the individual dates that appear on each coin. The letter that follows the date is the mintmark and indicates where the coin was struck: "C" — Charlotte, N.C. (1838-1861); "CC" — Carson City, Nev. (1870-1893); "D" — Dahlonega, Ga. (1838-1861), and Denver (1906-present); "O" New Orleans (1838-1909); "P" — Philadelphia (1793-present); "S" San Francisco (1854-present); and "W" — West Point, N.Y. (1984-present). Coins without mintmarks were struck at Philadelphia.

A slash mark in a date indicates an overdate. This means a new date was engraved on a die over an old date. For example, if the date is listed as "1899/8," an 1898 die had a 9 engraved over the last 8 in the date. Portions of the old numeral are still visible on the coin.

A slash mark in a mintmark listing indicates an overmintmark (example: "1922-P/D"). The same process as above occurred, but this time a new mintmark was engraved over an old.

See the "U.S. Minting Varieties and Errors" section for more information on overdates and overmintmarks.

Price charts

Pricing data for the selected charts in the U.S. section were taken from the January issues of *Coin Prices* for the years indicated.

Mexican coin mintages

Quantities minted of each date are indicated when that information is available.

Precious-metal content

Throughout this book precious-metal content is indicated in troy ounces. One troy ounce equals 480 grains, or 31.103 grams.

Abbreviations

AGW. Actual gold weight.

APW. Actual platinum weight.

ASW. Actual silver weight.

BV. Bullion value. This indicates the coin's current value is based on the amount of its precious-metal content and the current price for that metal.

Est. Indicates the exact mintage is not known and the figure listed is an estimate.

G. Grams.

Inc. Abv. Indicates the mintage for the date and mintmark listed is included in the previous listing.

KM#. Indicates "Krause-Mishler number." This sequential cataloging numbering system originated with the *Standard Catalog of World Coins* and provides collectors with a means for identifying coins.

Leg. Legend.

Mkt value. Market value.

MM. Millimeters.

Obv. Obverse.

P/L. Indicates "prooflike," a type of finish used on some Canadian coins.

Rev. Reverse.

Spec. Indicates "specimen," a type of finish used on some Canadian coins.

U.S. Minting Varieties and Errors

Introduction

By Alan Herbert

The P.D.S. cataloging system used here to list minting varieties was originally compiled by Alan Herbert in 1971. PDS stands for the three main divisions of the minting process, "planchet," "die" and "striking." Two more divisions cover collectible modifications after the strike, as well as non-collectible alterations, counterfeits and damaged coins.

This listing includes 445 classes, each a distinct part of the minting process or from a specific non-mint change in the coin. Classes from like causes are grouped together. The PDS system applies to coins of the world, but is based on U.S. coinage with added classes for certain foreign minting practices.

Price ranges are based on a U.S. coin in MS-60 grade (uncirculated.) The ranges may be applied in general to foreign coins of similar size or value although collector values are not usually as high as for U.S. coins. Prices are only a guide as the ultimate price is determined by a willing buyer and seller.

To define minting varieties, "A coin which exhibits a variation of any kind from the normal, as a result of any portion of the minting process, whether at the planchet stage, as a result of a change or modification of the die, or during the striking process. It includes those classes considered to be intentional changes, as well as those caused by normal wear and tear on the dies or other minting equipment and classes deemed to be "errors."

The three causes are represented as follows:
1. (I) = Intentional Changes
2. (W) = Wear and Tear
3. (E) = Errors
Note: A class may show more than one cause and could be listed as (IWE).

Rarity level

The rarity ratings are based on the following scale:
1 - Very Common. Ranges from every coin struck down to 1,000,000.
2 - Common. From 1,000,000 down to 100,000.
3 - Scarce. From 100,000 down to 10,000.
4 - Very Scarce. From 10,000 down to 1,000.
5 - Rare. From 1,000 down to 100.
6 - Very Rare. From 100 down to 10.
7 - Extremely Rare. From 10 down to 1.

Unknown: If there is no confirmed report of a piece fitting a particular class, it is listed as Unknown. Reports of finds by readers would be appreciated in order to update future presentations.

An Unknown does not mean that your piece automatically is very valuable. Even a Rarity 7 piece, extremely rare, even unique, may have a very low collector value because of a lack of demand or interest in that particular class.

Classes, definitions and price ranges are based on material previously offered in Alan Herbert's book, The Official Price Guide to Minting Varieties and Errors and in Coin Prices Magazine.

Pricing information has also been provided by John A. Wexler and Ken Potter, with special pricing and technical advice from Del Romines.

Also recommended is the Cherrypicker's Guide to Rare Die Varieties by Bill Fivaz and J.T. Stanton. Check your favorite coin shop, numismatic library or book seller for availability of the latest edition.

For help with your coin questions, to report significant new finds and for authentication of your minting varieties, include a loose first class stamp and write to Alan Herbert, 700 E. State St., Iola, WI 54990-0001. Don't include any numismatic material until you have received specific mailing instructions from me.

Quick check index

If you have a coin and are not sure where to look for the possible variety:

If your coin shows doubling, first check V-B-I.
Then try II-A, II-B, II-C, II-I (4 & 5), III-J, III-L, or IV-C.
If part of the coin is missing, check III-B, III-C, or III-D.
If there is a raised line of coin metal, check II-D, II-G.
If there is a raised area of coin metal, check II-E, II-F, or III-F.
If the coin is out of round, and too thin, check III-G.
If coin appears to be the wrong metal, check III-A, III-E, III-F-3 and III-G.
If the die appears to have been damaged, check II-E, II-G. (Damage to the coin itself usually is not a minting variety.)
If the coin shows incomplete or missing design, check II-A, II-E, III-B-3, III-B-5 or III-D.
If only part of the planchet was struck, check III-M.
If something was struck into the coin, check III-J and III-K.
If something has happened to the edge of the coin, check II-D-6, II-E-10, III-I, III-M and III-O.
If your coin shows other than the normal design, check II-A or II-C.
If a layer of the coin metal is missing, or a clad layer is missing, check III-B and III-D.
If you have an unstruck blank, or planchet, check I-G.
If your coin may be a restrike, check IV-C.
If your coin has a counterstamp, countermark, additional engraving or apparent official modifications, check IV-B and V-A-8.

Do not depend on the naked eye to examine your coins. Use a magnifying lens whenever possible, as circulation damage, wear and alterations frequently can be mistaken for legitimate minting varieties.

Division I: planchet varieties

The first division of the PDS System includes those minting varieties that occur in the manufacture of the planchet upon which the coins will ultimately be struck and includes classes resulting from faulty metallurgy, mechanical damage, faulty processing, or equipment or human malfunction prior to the actual coin striking.

Planchet alloy mix (I-A)

This section includes those classes pertaining to mixing and processing the various metals which will be used to make a coin alloy.

I-A-1 Improper Alloy Mix (WE), Rarity Level: 3-4 . . . . Values: $5 to $10
I-A-2 Slag Inclusion Planchet (WE), Rarity Level: 5-6. . . . . Values: $25 up

Damaged and defective planchets (I-B)

To be a class in this section the blank, or planchet, must for some reason not meet the normal standards or must have been damaged in processing. The classes cover the areas of defects in the melting, rolling, punching and processing of the planchets up to the point where they are sent to the coin presses to be struck.

I-B-1 Defective Planchet (WE), Rarity Level: 6 . . . . .Values: $25 up
I-B-2 Mechanically Damaged Planchet (WE), Rarity Level: – . . . . Values: No Value
    (See values for the coin struck on a mechanically damaged planchet.)
I-B-3 Rolled Thin Planchet (WE), Rarity Level: 6 - *(Less rare on half cents of 1795, 1797 and*
    restrikes of 1831-52.). . . . . .Values: $10 up
I-B-4 Rolled Thick Planchet (WE), Rarity Level: 7 - *(Less rare in Colonial copper coins. Notable examples occur*
    on the restrike half cents of 1840-52.) . . . . .Values: $125 up
I-B-5 Tapered Planchet (WE), Rarity Level: 7 . . . . .Values: $25 up
I-B-6 Partially Unplated Planchet (WE), Rarity Level: 6. . . . . .Values: $15 up
I-B-7 Unplated Planchet (WE), Rarity Level: 6-7. . . . . .Values: $50 up
I-B-8 Bubbled Plating Planchet (WE), Rarity Level: 1 . . . . Values: No Value
I-B-9 Included Gas Bubble Planchet (WE), Rarity Level: 6-7. . . . . .Values: $50 up
I-B-10 Partially Unclad Planchet (WE), Rarity Level: 6 . . . . .Values: $20 up
I-B-11 Unclad Planchet (WE), Rarity Level: 6-7 . . . . .Values: $50 up
I-B-12 Undersize Planchet (WE), Rarity Level: 7. . . . . .Values: $250 up
I-B-13 Oversize Planchet (WE), Rarity Level: 7 . . . . .Values: $250 up
I-B-14 Improperly Prepared Proof Planchet (WE), Rarity Level: 7. . . . . .Values: $100 up
I-B-15 Improperly Annealed Planchet (WE), Rarity Level: - . . . . Values: No Value
I-B-16 Faulty Upset Edge Planchet (WE), Rarity Level: 5-6. . . . . .Values: $10 up
I-B-17 Rolled-In Metal Planchet (WE), Rarity Level: 6-7. . . . . .Values: $50 up
I-B-18 Weld Area Planchet (WE), Rarity Level: Unknown . . . . .Values: No Value Established
    (See values for the coins struck on weld area planchets.)
I-B-19 Strike Clip Planchet (WE), Rarity Level: 7 . . . . .Values: $150 up
I-B-20 Unpunched Center-Hole Planchet (WE), Rarity Level: 5-7. . . . . Values: $5 and up
I-B-21 Incompletely Punched Center-Hole Planchet (WE), Rarity Level: 6-7. . . . . .Values: $15 up
I-B-22 Uncentered Center-Hole Planchet (WE), Rarity Level: 6-7. . . . . Values: $10 up
I-B-23 Multiple Punched Center-Hole Planchet (WE), Rarity Level: 7. .Values: $35 up
I-B-24 Unintended Center-Hole Planchet (WE), Rarity Level: Unknown . . . . .Values: -
I-B-25 Wrong Size or Shape Center-Hole Planchet (IWE), Rarity Level: 5-7 . . . . .Values: $10 up

Clipped planchets (I-C)

Clipped blanks, or planchets, occur when the strip of coin metal fails to move forward between successive strokes of the gang punch to clear the previously punched holes, in the same manner as a cookie cutter overlapping a previously cut hole in the dough. The size of the clip is a function of the amount of overlap of the next punch.

The overlapping round punches produce a missing arc with curve matching the outside circumference of the blanking punch. Straight clips occur when the punch overlaps the beginning or end of a strip which has had the end sheared or sawed off. Ragged clips occur in the same manner when the ends of the strip have been left as they were rolled out.

The term "clip" as used here should not be confused with the practice of clipping or shaving small pieces of metal from a bullion coin after it is in circulation.

I-C-1 Disc Clip Planchet (WE), Rarity Level: 3-5 . . . . .Values: $5 up
I-C-2 Curved Clip Planchet - (To 5%) (WE), Rarity Level: 5-6 . . . . .Values: $5 up
I-C-3 Curved Clip Planchet - (6 to 10%) (WE), Rarity Level: 6. . . . . .Values: $10 up
I-C-4 Curved Clip Planchet - (11 to 25%) (WE), Rarity Level: 5-6. . . . . Values: $15 up
I-C-5 Curved Clip Planchet - (26 to 60%) (WE), Rarity Level: 6-7. . . . . Values: $25 up
I-C-6 Double Curved Clip Planchet (WE), Rarity Level: 6. . . . . .Values: $10 up
I-C-7 Triple Curved Clip Planchet (WE), Rarity Level: 5-6 . . . . .Values: $25 up
I-C-8 Multiple Curved Clip Planchet (WE), Rarity Level: 6-7 . . . . .Values: $35 up
I-C-9 Overlapping Curved Clipped Planchet (WE), Rarity Level: 6-7 . . . . .Values: $50 up
I-C-10 Incompletely Punched Curved Clip Planchet (WE), Rarity Level: 6 . . . . .Values: $35 up
I-C-11 Oval Curved Clip Planchet (WE), Rarity Level: 6-7 . . . . .Values: $50 up
I-C-12 Crescent Clip Planchet - (61% or more) (WE), Rarity Level: 7 .Values: $200 up
I-C-13 Straight Clip Planchet (WE), Rarity Level: 6. . . . . .Values: $30 up

I-C-14 Incompletely Sheared Straight Clip Planchet (WE), Rarity Level: 6 . . . . .Values: $50 up
I-C-15 Ragged Clip Planchet (WE), Rarity Level: 6-7 . . . . .Values: $35 up
I-C-16 Outside Corner Clip Planchet (E), Rarity Level: -. . . . . Values: No Value
I-C-17 Inside Corner Clip Planchet (E), Rarity Level: - . . . . Values: No Value
I-C-18 Irregularly Clipped Planchet (E) Rarity Level: - .Values: Value not established
I-C-19 Incompletely Punched Scalloped or Multi-Sided Planchet (E), Rarity Level: 7 . . . . .Values: $25 up

Laminated, split, or broken planchet (I-D)

For a variety of reasons the coin metal may split into thin layers (delaminate) and either split completely off the coin, or be retained. Common causes are included gas or alloy mix problems. Lamination cracks usually enter the surface of the planchet at a very shallow angle or are at right angles to the edge. The resulting layers differ from slag in that they appear as normal metal.

Lamination cracks and missing metal of any size below a split planchet are too common in the 35 percent silver 1942-1945 nickels to be collectible or have any significant value.

I-D-1 Small Lamination Crack Planchet (W), Rarity Level: 4-5 . . . . .Values: $1 up
I-D-2 Large Lamination Crack Planchet (W), Rarity Level: 3-4 . . . . .Values: $5 up
I-D-3 Split Planchet (W), Rarity Level: 5-6 . . . . .Values: $15 up
I-D-4 Hinged Split Planchet (W), Rarity Level: 6-7 . . . . .Values: $75 up
I-D-5 Clad Planchet With a Clad Layer Missing (W), Rarity Level: 5-6. . . . . .Values: $35 up
I-D-6 Clad Planchet With Both Clad Layers Missing (W), Rarity Level: 6-7 . . . . .Values: $75 up
I-D-7 Separated Clad Layer (W), Rarity Level: 5 . . . . .Values: $25 up
I-D-8 Broken Planchet (WE), Rarity Level: 3-4 . . . . .Values: $5 up

Wrong stock planchet (I-E)

The following classes cover those cases where the wrong coin metal stock was run through the blanking press, making blanks of the correct diameter, but of the wrong thickness, alloy or metal or a combination of the wrong thickness and the wrong metal.

I-E-1 Half Cent Stock Planchet (IE), Rarity Level: Unknown . . . . .Values: No Value Established
I-E-2 Cent Stock Planchet (IE), Rarity Level: Unknown . . . . .Values: No Value Established
I-E-3 Two Cent Stock Planchet (E), Rarity Level: Unknown. . . . . .Values: No Value Established
I-E-4 Three Cent Silver Stock Planchet (E), Rarity Level: Unknown. . . . . .Values: No Value Established
I-E-5 Three Cent Nickel Stock Planchet (E), Rarity Level: Unknown . . . . .Values: No Value Established
I-E-6 Half Dime Stock Planchet (E), Rarity Level: Unknown . . . . .Values: No Value Established
I-E-7 Dime Stock Planchet (E), Rarity Level: 7 . . . . .Values: $200 up
I-E-8 Twenty Cent Stock Planchet (E), Rarity Level: Unknown. . . . . .Values: No Value Established
I-E-9 Quarter Stock Planchet (E), Rarity Level: Unknown .Values: No Value Established
I-E-10 Half Dollar Stock Planchet (E), Rarity Level: Unknown. . . . . .Values: No Value Established
I-E-11 Dollar Stock Planchet (E), Rarity Level: 7. . . . . .Values: $300 up
I-E-12 Token or Medal Stock Planchet (E), Rarity Level: Unknown . . . . .Values: No Value Established
I-E-13 Wrong Thickness Spoiled Planchet (IWE), Rarity Level: Unknown. . . . . . . .Values: No Value Established
I-E-14 Correct Thickness Spoiled Planchet (IWE), Rarity Level: Unknown . . . . . . .Values: No Value Established
I-E-15 Cut Down Struck Token Planchet (IWE), Rarity Level: Unknown . . . . .Values: No Value Established
I-E-16 Experimental or Pattern Stock Planchet (IE), Rarity Level: Unknown . . . . . .Values: No Value Established
I-E-17 Proof Stock Planchet (IE), Rarity Level: Unknown .Values: No Value Established
I-E-18 Adjusted Specification Stock Planchet (IE), Rarity Level: 7. . . . . .Values: $25 up
I-E-19 Trial Strike Stock Planchet (IE), Rarity Level: Unknown . . . . .Values: No Value Established
I-E-20 U.S. Punched Foreign Stock Planchet (E), Rarity Level: 7 . . . . Values: $75 up
I-E-21 Foreign Punched Foreign Stock Planchet (E), Rarity Level: 7. .Values: $75 up
I-E-22 Non-Standard Coin Alloy Planchet (IE), Rarity Level: 7 . . . . .Values: Unknown

Extra metal on a blank, or planchet (I-F)

True extra metal is only added to the blank during the blanking operation. This occurs as metal is scraped off the sides of the blanks as they are driven down through the thimble, or lower die in the blanking press. The metal is eventually picked up by a blank passing through, welded to it by the heat of friction.

A second form of extra metal has been moved to this section, the sintered coating planchet, the metal deposited on the planchet in the form of dust during the annealing operation.

I-F-1 Extra Metal on a Type 1 Blank (W), Rarity Level: 7 . . . . Values: $50 up
I-F-2 Extra Metal on a Type 2 Planchet (W), Rarity Level: 6-7 . . . . Values: $75 up
I-F-3 Sintered Coating Planchet (W), Rarity Level: 7 . . . . Values: $75 up

Normal or abnormal planchets (I-G)

This section consists of the two principal forms – the blank as it comes from the blanking press – and in the form of a planchet after it has passed through the upsetting mill. It also includes a class for purchased planchets and one for planchets produced by the mint.

I-G-1 Type I Blank (IWE), Rarity Level: 3-5 . . . . Values: $2 up
I-G-2 Type II Planchet (IWE), Rarity Level: 3-4 . . . . Values: 50 up
I-G-3 Purchased Planchet (I), Rarity Level: 1 . . . . Values: No Value
I-G-4 Mint Made Planchet (I), Rarity Level: 1 . . . . Values: No Value
I-G-5 Adjustment-Marked Planchet (I), Rarity Level: Unknown . . . . Values: No Value
I-G-6 Hardness Test-Marked Planchet (I), Rarity Level: - . . . . Values: No Value Established
Note: There are no classes between I-G-6 and I-G-23
I-G-23 Proof Planchet (IE), Rarity Level: 6-7 . . . . Values: $1 up

Coin metal strip (I-H)

When the coin metal strip passes through the blanking press it goes directly to a chopper. This cuts the remaining web into small pieces to be sent back to the melting furnace. Pieces of the web or the chopped up web may escape into the hands of collectors.

I-H-1 Punched Coin Metal Strip (IWE), Rarity Level: 4-6 . . . . Values: $5 up,
depending on size, denomination and number of holes showing
I-H-2 Chopped Coin Metal Strip (IE), Rarity Level: 3-5 . . . . Values: $5 up

The die varieties

Division II

Die varieties may be unique to a given die, but will repeat for the full life of the die unless a further change occurs. Anything that happens to the die will affect the appearance of the struck coin. This includes all the steps of the die making:

- Cutting a die blank from a tool steel bar.
- Making the design.
- Transferring it to a model.
- Transferring it to the master die or hub.
- The hubbing process of making the die.
- Punching in the mintmark.
- Heat treating of the die.

The completed dies are also subject to damage in numerous forms, plus wear and tear during the striking process and repair work done with abrasives. All of these factors can affect how the struck coin looks.

Engraving varieties (II-A)

In all cases in this section where a master die, or master hub is affected by the class, the class will affect all the working hubs and all working dies descending from it.

Identification as being on a master die or hub depends on it being traced to two or more of the working hubs descended from the same master tools.

II-A-1 Overdate (IE), Rarity Level: 1-7 . . . . Values: $1 up
II-A-2 Doubled Date (IE), Rarity Level: 1-7 . . . . Values: $1 up
II-A-3 Small Date (IE), Rarity Level: 2-5 . . . . Values: $1 up
II-A-4 Large Date (IE), Rarity Level: 2-5 . . . . Values: $1 up
II-A-5 Small Over Large Date (IE), Rarity Level: 4-6 . . . . Values: $15 up
II-A-6 Large Over Small Date (IE), Rarity Level: 3-5 . . . . Values: $10 up
II-A-7 Blundered Date (E), Rarity Level: 6-7 . . . . Values: $50 up
II-A-8 Corrected Blundered Date (IE), Rarity Level: 3-5. . . . . Values: $5 up
II-A-9 Wrong Font Date Digit (IE), Rarity Level: 5-6 . . . . Values: Minimal
II-A-10 Worn, Broken or Damaged Punch (IWE), Rarity Level: 5-6. . . . . Values: $5 up
II-A-11 Expedient Punch (IWE), Rarity Level: 5-6 . . . . Values: $10 up
II-A-12 Blundered Digit (E), Rarity Level: 4-5 . . . . Values: $50 up
II-A-13 Corrected Blundered Digit (IE), Rarity Level: 3-6 . . . . Values: $10 up
II-A-14 Doubled Digit (IWE), Rarity Level: 2-6 . . . . Values: $2 up
II-A-15 Wrong Style or Font Letter or Digit (IE), Rarity Level: 3-5. . . . . Values: Minimal
II-A-16 One Style or Font Over Another (IE), Rarity Level: 4-6 . . . . Values: $10 up
II-A-17 Letter Over Digit (E), Rarity Level: 6-7 . . . . Values: $25 up
II-A-18 Digit Over Letter (E), Rarity Level: 6-7 . . . . Values: $25 up
II-A-19 Omitted Letter or Digit (IWE), Rarity Level: 4-6. . . . . Values: $5 up
II-A-20 Blundered Letter (E), Rarity Level: 6-7 . . . . Values: $50 up
II-A-21 Corrected Blundered Letter (IE), Rarity Level: 1-3. . . . . Values: $10 up
II-A-22 Doubled Letter (IWE), Rarity Level: 2-6. . . . . Values: $2 up
II-A-23 Blundered Design Element (IE), Rarity Level: 6-7 . . . . Values: $50 up
II-A-24 Corrected Blundered Design Element (IE), Rarity Level: 3-5 . . . . Values: $10 up
II-A-25 Large Over Small Design Element (IE), Rarity Level: 4-6 . . . . Values: $2 up
II-A-26 Omitted Design Element (IWE), Rarity Level: 5-7 . . . . Values: $10 up
II-A-27 Doubled Design Element (IWE), Rarity Level: 2-6. . . . . Values: $2 up
II-A-28 One Design Element Over Another (IE), Rarity Level: 3-6 . . . . Values: $5 up
II-A-29 Reducing Lathe Doubling (WE), Rarity Level: 6-7. . . . . Values: $50 up
II-A-30 Extra Design Element (IE), Rarity Level: 3-5 . . . . Values: $10 up
II-A-31 Modified Design (IWE), Rarity Level: 1-5 . . . . Values: No Value up
II-A-32 Normal Design (I), Rarity Level: 1. . . . . Values: No Extra Value
II-A-33 Design Mistake (IE), Rarity Level: 2-6. . . . . Values: $1 up
II-A-34 Defective Die Design (IWE), Rarity Level: 1. . . . . Values: No Value
II-A-35 Pattern (I), Rarity Level: 6-7 . . . . Values: $100 up
II-A-36 Trial Design (I), Rarity Level: 5-7 . . . . Values: $100 up
II-A-37 Omitted Designer's Initial (IWE), Rarity Level: 3-7 . . . . Values: $1 up
II-A-38 Layout Mark (IE), Rarity Level: 5-7 . . . . Values: Minimal
II-A-39 Abnormal Reeding (IWE), Rarity Level: 2-5. . . . . Values: $1 up
II-A-40 Modified Die or Hub (IWE), Rarity Level: 1-5 . . . . Values: No Value up
II-A-41 Numbered Die (I), Rarity Level: 3-5 . . . . Values: $5 up
II-A-42 Plugged Die (IW), Rarity Level: 5-6 . . . . Values: Minimal
II-A-43 Cancelled Die (IE), Rarity Level: 3-6. . . . . Values: No Value up
II-A-44 Hardness Test Marked Die (IE), Rarity Level: 7 . . . . Values: $100 up
II-A-45 Coin Simulation (IE), Rarity Level: 6-7 . . . . Values: $100 up, but may be illegal to own
II-A-46 Punching Mistake (IE), Rarity Level: 2-6. . . . . Values: $1 up
II-A-47 Small Over Large Design (IE), Rarity Level: 4-6 . . . . Values: $5 up
II-A-48 Doubled Punch (IE), Rarity Level: 5-7. . . . . Values: $5 up
II-A-49 Mint Display Sample (I) Rarity Level: 7. . . . . Values not established
II-A-50 Center Dot, Stud or Circle (IE) Rarity Level: 7, much more common on early cents. . Values not established

Hub doubling varieties (II-B)

Rotated hub doubling   *Hub break*

This section includes eight classes of hub doubling. Each class is from a different cause, described by the title of the class. At the latest count over 2,500 doubled dies have been reported in the U.S. coinage, the most famous being examples of the 1955, 1969-S and 1972 cent dies.

II-B-I Rotated Hub Doubling (WE), Rarity Level: 3-6 . . . . Values: $1 up
II-B-II Distorted Hub Doubling (WE), Rarity Level: 3-6 . . . . Values: $1 up
II-B-III Design Hub Doubling (IWE), Rarity Level: 3-6. . . . . Values: $1 up to five figure amounts
II-B-IV Offset Hub Doubling (WE), Rarity Level: 4-6 . . . . Values: $15 up
II-B-V Pivoted Hub Doubling (WE), Rarity Level: 3-6 . . . . Values: $10 up
II-B-VI Distended Hub Doubling (WE), Rarity Level: 2-5. . . . . Values: $1 up
II-B-VII Modified Hub Doubling (IWE), Rarity Level: 2-5 . . . . Values: $1 up
II-B-VIII Tilted Hub Doubling (WE), Rarity Level: 4-6 . . . . Values: $5 up

Mintmark varieties (II-C)

Double   *Triple*

Mintmarks are punched into U.S. coin dies by hand (Up to 1985 for proof coins, to 1990 for cents and nickels and 1991 for other denominations). Variations resulting from mistakes in the punching are listed in this section. Unless exceptionally mispunched, values are usually estimated at 150 percent of numismatic value. Slightly tilted or displaced mintmarks have no value.

II-C-1 Doubled Mintmark (IE), Rarity Level: 2-6 . . . . Values: 50 cents up
II-C-2 Separated Doubled Mintmark (IE), Rarity Level: 5-6. . . . . Values: $15 up
II-C-3 Over Mintmark (IE), Rarity Level: 3-6 . . . . Values: $2 up
II-C-4 Tripled Mintmark (IE), Rarity Level: 3-5 . . . . Values: 50 up
II-C-5 Quadrupled Mintmark (IE), Rarity Level: 4-6 . . . . Values: $1 up
II-C-6 Small Mintmark (IE), Rarity Level: 2-5 . . . . Values: No Extra Value up
II-C-7 Large Mintmark (IE), Rarity Level: 2-5 . . . . Values: No Extra Value up
II-C-8 Large Over Small Mintmark (IE), Rarity Level: 2-5 . . . . Values: $2 up
II-C-9 Small Over Large Mintmark (IE), Rarity Level: 3-6 . . . . Values: $5 up
II-C-10 Broken Mintmark Punch (W), Rarity Level: 5-6 . . . . Values: $5 up
II-C-11 Omitted Mintmark (IWE), Rarity Level: 4-7. . . . . Values: $125 up
II-C-12 Tilted Mintmark (IE), Rarity Level: 5-7 . . . . Values: $5 up
II-C-13 Blundered Mintmark (E), Rarity Level: 4-6 . . . . Values: $5 up

II-C-14 Corrected Horizontal Mintmark (IE), Rarity Level: 4-6 . . . . .Values: $5 up
II-C-15 Corrected Upside Down Mintmark (IE), Rarity Level: 4-6. . . . . .Values: $5 up
II-C-16 Displaced Mintmark (IE), Rarity Level: 4-6. . . . . .Values: $5 to $10
II-C-17 Modified Mintmark (IWE), Rarity Level: 1-4 . . . . Values: No Extra Value up
II-C-18 Normal Mintmark (I), Rarity Level: 1. . . . . .Values: No Extra Value
II-C-19 Doubled Mintmark Punch (I), Rarity Level: 6-7 . . . . Values: No Extra Value up
II-C-20 Upside Down Mintmark (E) Rarity Level 6-7. . . . . .Values: $5 up
II-C-21 Horizontal Mintmark (E) Rarity Level 6-7 . . . . .Values: $5 up
II-C-22 Wrong Mintmark (E) Rarity Level 6-7 . . . . Values $15 up
(Example has a D mintmark in the date, but was used at Philadelphia.)

Die, collar and hub cracks (II-D)

Die cracks

Cracks in the surface of the die allow coin metal to be forced into the crack during the strike, resulting in raised irregular lines of coin metal above the normal surface of the coin. These are one of the commonest forms of die damage and wear, making them easily collectible.

Collar cracks and hub cracks are added to this section because the causes and effects are similar or closely associated.

Die cracks, collar cracks and hub cracks are the result of wear and tear on the tools, with intentional use assumed for all classes.

II-D-1 Die Crack (W), Rarity Level: 1-3 . . . . .Values: 10 to $1, $25 up on a proof coin
with a rarity level of 6-7
II-D-2 Multiple Die Cracks (W), Rarity Level: 1-3 . . . . Values: 25 cents to $2
II-D-3 Head-To-Rim Die Crack (Lincoln Cent) (W), Rarity Level: 2-6 . . Values: 25 to $10 for multiple die cracks
II-D-4 Split Die (W), Rarity Level: 5-6. . . . . .Values: $10 up
II-D-5 Rim-To-Rim Die Crack (W), Rarity Level: 2-5. . . . . .Values: $1 up
II-D-6 Collar Crack (W), Rarity Level: 4-6. . . . . .Values: $10 up
II-D-7 Hub Crack (W), Rarity Level: 3-5 . . . . .Values: $1-$2

Small die break II-E-2

Clogged letter II-E-1

Major die break, date missing, II-E-5

Rim die break II-E-4

Die breaks (II-E)

Breaks in the surface of the die allow coin metal to squeeze into the resulting holes, causing raised irregular areas above the normal surface of the coin. Die chips and small die breaks are nearly as common as the die cracks, but major die breaks, which extend in from the edge of the coin, are quite rare on the larger coins.

If the broken piece of the die is retained, the resulting design will be above or below the level of the rest of the surface.

II-E-1 Die Chip (W), Rarity Level: 1-2. . . . . .Values: 10 to $1
II-E-2 Small Die Break (W), Rarity Level: 1-3 . . . . .Values: 10 to $2
II-E-3 Large Die Break (W), Rarity Level: 3-5 . . . . .Values: $1 to $50 and up
II-E-4 Rim Die Break (W), Rarity Level: 2-3. . . . . Values: 25 cents to $5
II-E-5 Major Die Break (WE), Rarity Level: 3-6 . . . . Values: $5 to $100 and up
II-E-6 Retained Broken Die (W), Rarity Level: 3-5. . . . . Values: $1 to $10 and up
II-E-7 Retained Broken Center of the Die (W), Rarity Level: 6-7 . . . . .Values: $100 up
II-E-8 Laminated Die (W), Rarity Level: 3-5 . . . . Values: 10 cents to $5
II-E-9 Chipped Chrome Plating (W), Rarity Level: 4-5 . . . . .Values: $10 to $25 on proofs
II-E-10 Collar Break (W), Rarity Level: 4-6 . . . . .Values: $5 to $25 and up
II-E-11 Broken Letter or Digit on an Edge Die (W), Rarity Level: 4-6. Values: Minimal.
II-E-12 "Bar" Die Break (W), Rarity Level: 3-5. . . . . .Values: 25 to $20
II-E-13 Hub Break (W), Rarity Level: 4-6. . . . . Values: 50 to $10 and up

"BIE" varieties (II-F)

A series of small die breaks or die chips in the letters of "LIBERTY" mostly on the wheat-reverse Lincoln cent are actively collected. The name results from the resemblance to an "I" between the "B" and "E" on many of the dies, but they are found between all of the letters in different cases. Well over 1,500 dies are known and cataloged. Numerous more recent examples are known.

II-F-1 ILI Die Variety (W), Rarity Level: 4-5. . . . . Values: 25 cents to $10
II-F-2 LII Die Variety (W), Rarity Level: 3-5. . . . . Values: 50 cents to $15
II-F-3 IIB Die Variety (W), Rarity Level: 3-5. . . . . Values: 50 cents to $15
II-F-4 BIE Die Variety (W), Rarity Level: 3-5 . . . . .Values: $1 to $20
II-F-5 EIR Die Variety (W), Rarity Level: 3-5 . . . . .Values: 50 to $15
II-F-6 RIT Die Variety (W), Rarity Level: 4-5 . . . . .Values: $2 to $25
II-F-7 TIY Die Variety (W), Rarity Level: 4-5 . . . . .Values: $5 to $30
II-F-8 TYI Die Variety (W), Rarity Level: 4-5 . . . . .Values: $2 to $25

Worn and damaged dies, collars and hubs (II-G)

Many dies are continued deliberately in service after they have been damaged, dented, clashed or show design transfer, since none of these classes actually affect anything but the appearance of the coin. The root cause is wear, but intent or mistakes may enter the picture.

II-G-1 Dented Die, Collar or Hub (IWE), Rarity Level: 3-5. . . . . .Values: 25 to $5
II-G-2 Damaged Die, Collar or Hub (IWE), Rarity Level: 3-5. . . . . .Values: 25 to $5
II-G-3 Worn Die, Collar or Hub (IWE), Rarity Level: 2-3 . . . . .Values: No Extra Value to Minimal Value
II-G-4 Pitted or Rusted Die, Collar or Hub (IWE), Rarity Level: 3-4. . . . . .Values: No Extra Value, marker only
II-G-5 Heavy Die Clash (IWE), Rarity Level: 4-5 . . . . Values: $1 to $10 and up
II-G-6 Heavy Collar Clash (IWE), Rarity Level: 3-4 . . . . Values: $1 to $5 and up
II-G-7 Heavy Design Transfer (IWE), Rarity Level: 3-4 . . . . Values: 10 cents to $1

Die progressions (II-H)

The progression section consists of three classes. These are useful as cataloging tools for many different die varieties, but especially the die cracks and die breaks which may enlarge, lengthen or increase in number.

II-H-1 Progression (W), Rarity Level: 3-5. . . . . .Values: $1 up

II-H-2 Die Substitution (IW), Rarity Level: 2-4 . . . . .Values: No Extra Value to Minimal Value
II-H-3 Die Repeat (I), Rarity Level: 2-4 . . . . .Values: No Extra Value to Minimal Value

Die scratches, polished and abraded dies (II-I)

This section consists of those classes having to do with the use of an abrasive in some form to intentionally polish proof dies, or repair the circulating die surface. Several classes that previously were referred to as "polished" now are listed as "abraded."

II-I-1 Die Scratch (IW), Rarity Level: 1-2. . . . . .Values: No Extra Value to 10 cents to 25 cents, as a marker
II-I-2 Polished (proof) Die (IW), Rarity Level: 1. . . . . .Values: No Extra Value
II-I-3 Abraded (Circulation) Die (IW), Rarity Level: 1-2. . . . . .Values: No Extra Value up to $10
II-I-4 Inside Abraded Die Doubling (IW), Rarity Level: 1-3 . . . . Values: No Extra Value to $1
II-I-5 Outside Abraded Die Doubling (IW), Rarity Level: 1-3. . . . . Values: No Extra Value to $1
II-I-6 Lathe Marks (IW), Rarity Level: 5-7 . . . . .Values: No Extra Value, marker only

Striking varieties
Division III

Once the dies are made and the planchets have been prepared, they are struck by a pair of dies and become a coin. In this division, we list the misstrikes resulting from human or mechanical malfunction in the striking process. These are one-of-a-kind varieties, but there may be many similar coins that fall in a given class.

Multiples and combinations of classes must be considered on a case by case basis. The first several sections match the planchet sections indicated in the title.

Struck on defective alloy mix planchets (III-A)

This section includes those classes of coins struck on planchets that were made from a defective alloy.

III-A-1 Struck on an Improper Alloy Mix Planchet (IE), Rarity Level: 2-3 . . . . Values: 10 cents to $2
III-A-2 Struck on a Planchet With Slag Inclusions(IE), Rarity Level: 5-6 . . . . .Values: $10 up

Struck on damaged, defective or abnormal planchet (III-B)

Struck on a defective planchet III-B-1   *Struck on a tapered planchet III-B-5*

Coins get struck on many strange objects. The more common, of course, are planchets that have been damaged in some way in the production process. In most of the classes in this section, intent is at least presumed, if not specifically listed as a cause.

III-B-1 Struck on a Defective Planchet (IWE), Rarity Level: 4-6. . . . . .Values: $5 to $10 and up
III-B-2 Struck on a Mechanically Damaged Planchet (IWE), Rarity Level: 5-6. . . . . . .Values: $10 to $20 and up
III-B-3 Struck on a Rolled Thin Planchet (IWE), Rarity Level: 5-6 . . . . Values: $2 to $5 and up
III-B-4 Struck on a Rolled Thick Planchet (IWE), Rarity Level: 5-6 . . . . .Values: $35 to $50 and up
III-B-5 Struck on a Tapered Planchet (WE), Rarity Level: 4-6 . . . . Values: $2 to $5 and up
III-B-6 Struck on a Partially Unplated Planchet (WE), Rarity Level: 5 . . . . .Values: $10 up
III-B-7 Struck on an Unplated Planchet (WE), Rarity Level: 6-7 . . . . Values: $100 up
III-B-8 Struck on a Bubbled Plating Planchet (IWE), Rarity Level: 1 . . . . Values: No Value
III-B-9 Struck on an Included Gas Bubble Planchet (WE), Rarity Level: 5-6 . . . . .Values: $5 up
III-B-10 Struck on a Partially Unclad Planchet (WE), Rarity Level: 5-6 . . . . .Values: $5 up

III-B-11 Struck on an Unclad Planchet (WE), Rarity Level: 4-5 . . . . Values: $5 and up
III-B-12 Struck on an Undersize Planchet (WE), Rarity Level: 4-6 . . . . .Values: Minimal
III-B-13 Struck on an Oversize Planchet (WE), Rarity Level: 6-7 . . . . Values: Minimal
III-B-14 Struck on an Improperly Prepared Proof Planchet (IWE), Rarity Level: 3-5 . . . . Values: $5 up
III-B-15 Struck on an Improperly Annealed Planchet (IWE), Rarity Level: 4-5 . . . . Values: $5 up
III-B-16 Struck on a Faulty Upset Edge Planchet (IWE), Rarity Level: 4-5 . . . . .Values: $1 to $2
III-B-17 Struck on a Rolled In Metal Planchet (WE), Rarity Level: 4-6. . . . . .Values: $2 up
III-B-18 Struck on a Weld Area Planchet (WE), Rarity Level: 6 . . . . .Values: $25 to $50
III-B-19 Struck on a Strike Clip Planchet (W), Rarity Level: 6-7 . . . . .Values: $25 up
III-B-20 Struck on an Unpunched Center Hole Planchet (WE), Rarity Level: 4-6. . . . . Values: $1 and up
III-B-21 Struck on an Incompletely Punched Center Hole Planchet (WE), Rarity Level: 6-7 . . . . . . Values: $5 up
III-B-22 Struck on an Uncentered Center Hole Planchet (WE), Rarity Level: 6-7. . . . . .Values: $10 up
III-B-23 Struck on a Multiple Punched Center Hole Planchet (WE), Rarity Level: 7. . . . . .Values: $25 up
III-B-24 Struck on an Unintended Center Hole Planchet (WE), Rarity Level: 6-7. . . . . Values: $25 and up
III-B-25 Struck on a Wrong Size or Shape Center Hole Planchet (WE), Rarity Level: 5-7 . . . . .Values: $5 up
III-B-26 Struck on Scrap Coin Metal (E), Rarity Level: 4-6 . . . . .Values: $10 up
III-B-27 Struck on Junk Non Coin Metal (E), Rarity Level: 4-6 . . . . .Values: $15 up
III-B-28 Struck on a False Planchet (E), Rarity Level: 3-5 . . . . .Values: $35 up
III-B-29 Struck on Bonded Planchets (E), Rarity Level: 6-7. . . . . .Values: $50 up

Struck on a clipped planchet (III-C)

Ragged edge clip III-C-15

Multiple clip III-C-8   *Incomplete curved clip III-C-10*

Coins struck on clipped blanks, or planchets, exhibit the same missing areas as they did before striking, modified by the metal flow from the strike which rounds the edges and tends to move metal into the missing areas. Values for blanks will run higher than planchets with similar clips.

III-C-1 Struck on a Disc Clip Planchet (WE), Rarity Level: 4-5 . . . . Values: $1 on regular coins,
$20 and up for clad coins
III-C-2 Struck on a Curved Clip Planchet - to 5% (WE), Rarity Level: 3-5 . . . . Values: 50 cents up
III-C-3 Struck on a Curved Clip Planchet - (6 to 10%) (WE), Rarity Level: 4-5. . . . . .Values: $1 up
III-C-4 Struck on a Curved Clip Planchet - (11 to 25%) (WE), Rarity Level: 4-5. . . . . .Values: $2 up
III-C-5 Struck on a Curved Clip Planchet - (26 to 60%) (WE), Rarity Level: 4-6 . . . . .Values: $10 up
III-C-6 Struck on a Double Curved Clip Planchet (WE), Rarity Level: 3-4. . . . . .Values: $2 up
III-C-7 Struck on a Triple Curved Clip Planchet (WE), Rarity Level: 4-5 . . . . .Values: $5 up
III-C-8 Struck on a Multiple Curved Clip Planchet (WE), Rarity Level: 4-6 . . . . .Values: $5 up
III-C-9 Struck on an Overlapping Curved Clipped Planchet (WE), Rarity Level: 5-6 . . . . .Values: $15 up
III-C-10 Struck on an Incomplete Curved Clip Planchet (WE), Rarity Level: 4-5. . . . . .Values: $10 up
III-C-11 Struck on an Oval Clip Planchet (WE), Rarity Level: 5-6 . . . . .Values: $20 up
III-C-12 Struck on a Crescent Clip Planchet - (61% or more) (WE), Rarity Level: 6-7 . . . . .Values: $100 up
III-C-13 Struck on a Straight Clip Planchet (E), Rarity Level: 4-6 . . . . .Values: $10 up

III-C-14 Struck on an Incomplete Straight Clip Planchet (WE), Rarity Level: 5-6 . . . . Values: $20 up
III-C-15 Struck on a Ragged Clip Planchet (E), Rarity Level: 4-6 . . . . Values: $15 up
III-C-16 Struck on an Outside Corner Clip Planchet (E), Rarity Level: 7 . . . . Values: $100 up
III-C-17 Struck on an Inside Corner Clip Planchet (E), Rarity Level: Unknown outside mint . . . . Values:
III-C-18 Struck on an Irregularly Clipped Planchet (E), Rarity Level: 6-7 . . . . Values: $20 up.
III-C-19 Struck on an Incompletely Punched Scalloped or Multi-Sided Planchet (E), Rarity Level: 7
. . . . Values: $20 up.

Struck on a laminated, split or broken planchet (III-D)

Lamination crack III-D-1   *Layer peeled off III-D-2*   *Split planchet III-D-3*

This section has to do with the splitting, cracking or breaking of a coin parallel to the faces of the coin, or at least very nearly parallel, or breaks at right angles to the faces of the coin.

Lamination cracks and missing metal of any size below a split planchet are too common in the 35-percent silver 1942-1945 nickels to be collectible or have any significant value.

III-D-1 Struck on a Small Lamination Crack Planchet (W), Rarity Level: 3-4. . . . . Values: 10 up
III-D-2 Struck on a Large Lamination Crack Planchet (W), Rarity Level: 3-6. . . . . Values: $1 up
III-D-3 Struck on a Split Planchet (W), Rarity Level: 4-6. . . . . Values: $5 up
III-D-4 Struck on a Hinged Split Planchet (W), Rarity Level: 5-6. . . . . Values: $35 up
III-D-5 Struck on a Planchet With a Clad Layer Missing (W), Rarity Level: 4-5. . . . . Values: $15 up
III-D-6 Struck on a Planchet With Both Clad Layers Missing (W), Rarity Level: 4-5 . . . . Values: $25 up
III-D-7 Struck on a Separated Clad Layer or Lamination (W), Rarity Level: 6-7. . . . . Values: $75 up
III-D-8 Struck on a Broken Planchet Before the Strike (W), Rarity Level: 3-5 . . . . Values: $10 up
III-D-9 Broken Coin During or After the Strike (W), Rarity Level: 4-6 . . . . Values: $20 up
III-D-10 Struck Coin Fragment Split or Broken During or After the Strike (W), Rarity Level: 3-5. . . Values: $5 up
III-D-11 Reedless Coin Broken During or After the Strike (W), Rarity Level: Unknown . . . . Values: -

Struck on wrong stock planchets (III-E)

Quarter on dime stock
III-E-7 (lower coin edge)

These classes cover those cases where the wrong stock was run through the blanking press, making planchets of the correct diameter, but of the wrong thickness, alloy or metal or a combination of incorrect thickness and metal.

III-E-1 Struck on a Half Cent-Stock Planchet (IE), Rarity Level: Unknown. . . . . Values: No Value Established
III-E-2 Struck on a Cent-Stock Planchet (IE), Rarity Level: Unknown . . . . Values: No Value Established
III-E-3 Struck on a Two-Cent-Stock Planchet (E), Rarity Level: Unknown . . . . Values: -
III-E-4 Struck on a Three-Cent-Silver Stock Planchet (E), Rarity Level: Unknown . . . . Values: -
III-E-5 Struck on a Three-Cent-Nickel Stock Planchet (E), Rarity Level: Unknown . . . . Values: -
III-E-6 Struck on a Half Dime-Stock Planchet (E), Rarity Level: Unknown. . . . . Values: -
III-E-7 Struck on a Dime-Stock Planchet (E), Rarity Level: 5-6 . . . . Values: $20 up
III-E-8 Struck on a Twenty-Cent-Stock Planchet (E), Rarity Level: Unknown. . . . . Values: -

III-E-9 Struck on a Quarter-Stock Planchet (E), Rarity Level: 6 . . . . .Values: $50 up
III-E-10 Struck on a Half Dollar-Stock Planchet (E), Rarity Level: 6-7 . . . . .Values: $100 up
III-E-11 Struck on a Dollar-Stock Planchet (E), Rarity Level: 6-7 . . . . .Values: $300 up
III-E-12 Struck on a Token/Medal-Stock Planchet (E), Rarity Level: 7 . . . . .Values: No Value Established
III-E-13 Struck on a Wrong Thickness Spoiled Planchet (IWE), Rarity Level: 7 . . . . .Values: $50 up
III-E-14 Struck on a Correct Thickness Spoiled Planchet (IWE), Rarity Level: Unknown. Values: No Value Established
III-E-15 Struck on a Cut Down Struck Token (IWE), Rarity Level: 6-7 . . . . .Values: $50 up
III-E-16 Struck on an Experimental or Pattern-Stock Planchet (IE), Rarity Level: 7 . . . . .Values: $50 up
III-E-17 Struck on a Proof-Stock Planchet (IE), Rarity Level: 7 . . . . .Values: $100 up
III-E-18 Struck on an Adjusted Specification-Stock Planchet (IE), Rarity Level: 3-7. Values: No Value to $5 and up
III-E-19 Struck on a Trial Strike-Stock Planchet (IE), Rarity Level: Unknown. . . . . . .Values: No Value Established
III-E-20 U.S. Coin Struck on a Foreign-Stock Planchet. (E), Rarity Level: 5 . . . . .Values: $35 up
III-E-21 Foreign Coin Struck on a Foreign-Stock Planchet (E), Rarity Level: 5-6 . . . . .Values: $25 up
III-E-22 Struck on a Non-Standard Coin Alloy (IE), Rarity Level: 4-7 . . . . .Values: $20 up

Extra metal (III-F)

*Extra metal on a
struck coin (III-F-2)*

Sintered coating III-F-3

The term "extra metal" for the purpose of this section includes both extra metal added to the blank during the blanking operation and metal powder added to the planchet during the annealing operation.

III-F-1 Struck on a Type 1 Blank With Extra Metal (W), Rarity Level: Unknown . . . . .Values: -
III-F-2 Struck on a Type 2 Planchet With Extra Metal (W), Rarity Level: 4-5 . . . . .Values: $10 up
III-F-3 Struck on a Sintered Coating Planchet (W), Rarity Level: 6-7 . . . . .Values: $35 up

Struck on normal or abnormal blanks, or planchets (III-G)

*Half on dime
planchet III-G-10*

*Cent on dime
planchet III-G-10*

*Half on quarter
planchet III-G-10*

This section includes coins struck on either a blank, as it comes from the blanking press, or as a planchet that has passed through the upsetting mill. Added to this section are those planchets that are normal until they are struck by the wrong dies. These differ from the wrong stock planchets because the wrong stock planchets are already a variety before they are struck.

III-G-1 Struck on a Type 1 Blank (IWE), Rarity Level: 4-6 . . . . .Values: $10 up
III-G-2 Struck on a Type 2 Planchet (I), Rarity Level: 1 . . . . .Values: No Extra Value
III-G-3 Struck on a Purchased Planchet (I), Rarity Level: 1 . . . . .Values: No Extra Value
III-G-4 Struck on a Mint-Made Planchet (I), Rarity Level: 1 . . . . .Values: No Extra Value
III-G-5 Struck on an Adjustment-Marked Planchet (I), Rarity Level: 4-7 . . . . Values: Minimal, and may
   reduce value of coin in some cases

III-G-6 Struck on a Hardness Test-Marked Planchet (I), Rarity Level: 6-7 . . . . .Values: $10 up

III-G-7 Wrong Planchet or Metal on a Half Cent Planchet (IE), Rarity Level: 5-7 . . . . .Values: $100 up

III-G-8 Wrong Planchet or Metal on a Cent Planchet (IE), Rarity Level: 3-6 . . . . .Values: $25 up

III-G-9 Wrong Planchet or Metal on a Nickel Planchet (E), Rarity Level: 4-6 . . . . .Values: $35 up

III-G-10 Wrong Planchet or Metal on a Dime Planchet (E), Rarity Level: 4-6 . . . . .Values: $50 up

III-G-11 Wrong Planchet or Metal on a Quarter Planchet (E), Rarity Level: 4-6 . . . . .Values: $100 up

III-G-12 Wrong Planchet or Metal on a Half Dollar Planchet (E), Rarity Level: 6-7 . . . . .Values: $500 up

III-G-13 Wrong Planchet or Metal on a Dollar Planchet (E), Rarity Level: 7 . . . . .Values: $500 up

III-G-14 Wrong Planchet or Metal on a Gold Planchet (E), Rarity Level: 7 . . . . .Values: $1000 up

III-G-15 Struck on a Wrong Series Planchet (IE), Rarity Level: 6-7 . . . . .Values: $1500 up

III-G-16 U.S. Coin Struck on a Foreign Planchet (E), Rarity Level: 5-7 .Values: $35 up

III-G-17 Foreign Coin Struck on a U.S. Planchet (E), Rarity Level: 6-7 . . . . .Values: $500 up

III-G-18 Foreign Coin Struck on a Wrong Foreign Planchet (E), Rarity Level: 6-7 . . . . .Values: $50 up

III-G-19 Struck on a Medal Planchet (E), Rarity Level: 6-7 . . . . .Values: $100 up

III-G-20 Medal Struck on a Coin Planchet (IE), Rarity Level: 3-5 . . . . .Values: $10 up

III-G-21 Struck on an Official Sample Planchet (IE), Rarity Level: Unknown . . . . . .Values: No Value Established

III-G-22 Struck Intentionally on a Wrong Planchet (I), Rarity Level: 6-7 . . Values: Mainly struck as Presentation Pieces, full numismatic value

III-G-23 Non-Proof Struck on a Proof Planchet (IE), Rarity Level: 6-7 . . . . .Values: $500 up

Struck on coin metal strip (III-H)

Pieces of the coin metal strip do manage at times to escape into the coin press.

III-H-1 (See I-H-1 Punched Coin Metal Strip), Rarity Level: Impossible . . . . .Values: -

III-H-2 Struck on Chopped Coin Metal Strip (E), Rarity Level: 6-7 . . . . .Values: $25 up

Die adjustment strikes (III-I)

As the dies are set up and adjusted in the coin press, variations in the strike occur until the dies are properly set. Test strikes are normally scrapped, but on occasion reach circulation.

III-I-1 Die Adjustment Strike (IE), Rarity Level: 5-6 . . . . .Values: $35 up

III-I-2 Edge Strike (E), Rarity Level: 5-6 . . . . Values: $10 to $20 and up

III-I-3 Weak Strike (W), Rarity Level: 1 . . . . .Values: No Extra Value

III-I-4 Strong Strike (IWE), Rarity Level: 1 . . . . .Values: No value except for the premium that might be paid for a well struck coin

III-I-5 Jam Strike (IE), Rarity Level: 7 . . . . .Values: $50 up

III-I-6 Trial Piece Strike (I), Rarity Level: 6-7 . . . . .Values: $100 up

III-I-7 Edge-Die Adjustment Strike (I), Rarity Level: 5-7 . . . . .Values: $5 up

III-I-8 Uniface Strike (I), Rarity Level 7 . . . . .Values: $50 up

Indented, brockage and counter-brockage strikes (III-J)

Indented strike
III-J-1

Counter-brockage strike
III-J-11

Capped die strike
III-J-15

Indented and uniface strikes involve an extra unstruck planchet between one of the dies and the planchet being struck. Brockage strikes involve a struck coin between one of the dies and the planchet and a counter-brockage requires a brockage coin between one of the dies and the planchet.

A cap, or capped die strike results when a coin sticks to the die and is squeezed around it in the shape of a bottle cap.

III-J-1 Indented Strike (W), Rarity Level: 3-6 . . . . .Values: $5 up

III-J-2 Uniface Strike (W), Rarity Level: 3-5 . . . . .Values: $15 up

III-J-3 Indented Strike By a Smaller Planchet (WE), Rarity Level: 5-7 . . . . .Values: $100 up
III-J-4 Indented Second Strike (W), Rarity Level: 3-5 . . . . Values: $10 up, about the same as a regular double strike of comparable size
III-J-5 Partial Brockage Strike (W), Rarity Level: 3-6. . . . . .Values: $15 up
III-J-6 Full Brockage Strike (W), Rarity Level: 3-6. . . . . .Values: $5 up
III-J-7 Brockage Strike of a Smaller Coin (WE), Rarity Level: 6-7 . . . . .Values: $200 up
III-J-8 Brockage Strike of a Struck Coin Fragment (WE), Rarity Level: 4-6 . . . . .Values: $5 up
III-J-9 Brockage Second Strike (WE), Rarity Level: 3-5. . . . . .Values: $5 up
III-J-10 Partial Counter-Brockage Strike (WE), Rarity Level: 3-5. . . . . .Values: $10 up
III-J-11 Full Counter-Brockage Strike (WE), Rarity Level: 5-7. . . . . .Values: $100 up
III-J-12 Counter-Brockage Second Strike (WE), Rarity Level: 4-6. . . . . .Values: $10 up
III-J-13 Full Brockage-Counter-Brockage Strike (WE), Rarity Level: 6-7. . . . . .Values: $150 up
III-J-14 Multiple Brockage or Counter-Brockage Strike (WE), Rarity Level: 5-7 . . . . .Values: $100 up
III-J-15 Capped Die Strike (WE), Rarity Level: 6-7 . . . . .Values: $500 up
III-J-16 Reversed Capped Die Strike (WE), Rarity Level: 7 . . . . .Values: $1,000 up

Struck through abnormal objects (III-K)

| Struck through cloth | Struck through a filled die | Struck through a |
| III-K-1 | III-K-4 | dropped filling III-K-5 |

This section covers most of the objects or materials that might come between the planchet and the die and be struck into the surface of the coin. Unless noted, the materials - even the soft ones - are driven into the surface of the coin.

III-K-1 Struck Through Cloth (IWE), Rarity Level: 3-6. . . . . .Values: $35 up
III-K-2 Struck Through Wire (IWE), Rarity Level: 3-6 . . . . .Values: $5 up
III-K-3 Struck Through Thread (IWE), Rarity Level: 3-6. . . . . .Values: $5 up
III-K-4 Struck Through Dirt-and-Grease-Filled Die (IWE), Rarity Level: 1-4
. . . . Values: 10 cents to 25 cents up, but no value on a worn or circulated coin
III-K-5 Struck Through a Dropped Filling (IWE), Rarity Level: 5-6 . . . . .Values: $10 up
III-K-6 Struck Through Wrong Metal Fragments (IWE), Rarity Level: 4-6 . . . . .Values: $1 up
III-K-7 Struck Through an Unstruck Planchet Fragment (IWE), Rarity Level: 3-5 . . . . .Values: $1 up
III-K-8 Struck Through a Rim Burr (IWE), Rarity Level: 3-5. . . . . Values: $1 to $2 and up
III-K-9 Struck Through plit-Off Reeding (IWE), Rarity Level: 5-6. . . . . .Values: $25 up
III-K-10 Struck Through a Feed Finger (IWE), Rarity Level: 5-7 . . . . Values: $25 to $50 and up
III-K-11 Struck Through Miscellaneous Objects (IWE), Rarity Level: 4-6 . . . . .Values: $1 up
III-K-12 Struck Through Progression (IWE), Rarity Level: 4-6 . . . . .Values: $1 up
Note: Some 1987 through 1994 quarters are found without mintmarks, classed as III-K-4, a Filled Die. Values depend on market conditions. Filled dies have value ONLY on current, uncirculated grade coins.

Double strikes (III-L)

Only coins that receive two or more strikes by the die pair fall in this section and are identified by the fact that both sides of the coin are affected. Unless some object interferes, an equal area of both sides of the coin will be equally doubled.

The exception is the second strike with a loose die, which will double only one side of a coin, but is a rare form usually occurring only on proofs. A similar effect is flat field doubling from die chatter.

III-L-1 Close Centered Double Strike (WE), Rarity Level: 4-6 . . . . .Values: $15 up
III-L-2 Rotated Second Strike Over a Centered First Strike (WE), Rarity Level: 4-6 . . . . .Values: $15 up

Off-center second strike over centered first strike III-L-3

Non-overlapping double strike III-L-8

Multiple strike III-L-16

Chain strike III-L-10

III-L-3 Off-Center Second Strike Over a Centered First Strike (WE), Rarity Level: 4-6 . . . . Values: $15 up
III-L-4 Off-Center Second Strike Over an Off-Center First Strike (WE), Rarity Level: 4-6 . . . . Values: $10 up
III-L-5 Off-Center Second Strike Over a Broadstrike (WE), Rarity Level: 5-6 . . . . Values: $20 up
III-L-6 Centered Second Strike Over an Off-Center First Strike (WE), Rarity Level: 5-6 . . . . Values: $50 up
III-L-7 Obverse Struck Over Reverse (WE), Rarity Level: 5-6 . . . . Values: $25 up
III-L-8 Nonoverlapping Double Strike (WE), Rarity Level: 5-6 . . . . Values: $20 up
III-L-9 Struck Over a Different Denomination or Series (WE), Rarity Level: 6 . . . . Values: $300 and up
III-L-10 Chain Strike (WE), Rarity Level: 6 . . . . . Values: $300 up for the pair of coins that were struck together
III-L-11 Second-Strike Doubling From a Loose Die (W), Rarity Level: 6-7 . . . . Values: $200 up
III-L-12 Second-Strike Doubling From a Loose Screw Press Die (W), Rarity Level: 5-6 . . . . . . Values: $100 up
III-L-13 Second Strike on an Edge Strike (WE), Rarity Level: 5-6 . . . . Values: $20 up
III-L-14 Folded Planchet Strike (WE), Rarity Level: 5-7 . . . . Values: $100 up
III-L-15 Triple Strike (WE), Rarity Level: 6-7 . . . . Values: $100 up
III-L-16 Multiple Strike (WE), Rarity Level: 6-7 . . . . Values: $200 up
III-L-17 U.S. Coin Struck Over a Struck Foreign Coin (WE), Rarity Level: 6-7 . . . . Values: $300 up
III-L-18 Foreign Coin Struck Over a Struck U.S. Coin (WE), Rarity Level: 6-7 . . . . Values: $400 up
III-L-19 Foreign Coin Struck Over a Struck Foreign Coin (WE), Rarity Level: 7 . . . . Values: $500 up
III-L-20 Double Strike on Scrap or Junk (E), Rarity Level: 6 . . . . Values: $50 up
III-L-21 Struck on a Struck Token or Medal (E), Rarity Level: 5-6 . . . . Values: $100 up
III-L-22 Double-Struck Edge Motto or Design (E), Rarity Level: 6-7 . . . . Values: $200 up
III-L-23 One Edge Motto or Design Struck Over Another (E), Rarity Level: 7 . . . . Values: $300 up
III-L-24 Flat Field Doubling (W), Rarity Level: 2-3 . . . . Values: $1 to $5
III-L-25 Territorial Struck over Struck U.S. Coin: (I) Rarity Level: 6-7 . . . . Values: $200 up
III-L-26 Pattern Struck over Struck U.S. Coin: (I) Rarity Level: 6-7 . . . . Values: $200 up
III-L-27 Pattern Struck over Struck Pattern:(I) Rarity Level 6-7 . . . . Values: $200 up
III-L-28 Pattern Struck Over Foreign Coin:(I) Rarity Level 6-7 . . . . Values - $200 up

Collar striking varieties (III-M)

The collar is often referred to as the "Third Die," and is involved in a number of forms of misstrikes. The collar normally rises around the planchet, preventing it from squeezing sideways between the dies and at the same time forming the reeding on reeded coins.

If the collar is out of position or tilted, a partial collar strike results; if completely missing, it causes a broadstrike; if the planchet is not entirely between the dies, an off-center strike.

Flanged partial collar III-M-1

Struck off center
10 to 30 percent III-M-7

Struck off center
31 to 70 percent III-M-8

Struck off center
71 percent or more
III-M-9

III-M-1 Flanged Partial Collar Strike (WE), Rarity Level: 5-6. . . . . Values: $20 up
III-M-2 Reversed Flanged Partial Collar Strike (WE), Rarity Level: 6-7 . . . . Values: $35 up
III-M-3 Tilted Partial Collar Strike (WE), Rarity Level: 5-6 . . . . Values: $20 up
III-M-4 Centered Broadstrike (WE), Rarity Level: 5-6 . . . . Values: $5 up
III-M-5 Uncentered Broadstrike (WE), Rarity Level: 5 . . . . Values: $3 up
III-M-6 Reversed Broadstrike (WE), Rarity Level: 6 . . . . Values: $10 up
III-M-7 Struck Off-Center 10-30% (W), Rarity Level: 3-6 . . . . Values: $3 up
III-M-8 Struck Off-Center 31-70% (W), Rarity Level: 4-6 . . . . Values: $5 up
III-M-9 Struck Off-Center 71% or More (W), Rarity Level: 3-5 . . . . Values: $2 up
III-M-10 Rotated Multi-sided Planchet Strike (W), Rarity Level: 5-6 . . . . Values: $10 up
III-M-11 Wire Edge Strike (IWE), Rarity Level: 1-2 . . . . Values: No Extra Value
III-M-12 Struck With the Collar Too High (WE), Rarity Level: 6-7 . . . . Values: $20 up
III-M-13 Off-Center Slide Strike (W), Rarity Level: 3-6 . . . . Values: $4 up

Misaligned and rotated (die) strike varieties (III-N)

Misaligned die III-N-1

Normal rotation   *90 degrees*   *180 degrees*

One (rarely both) of the dies may be Offset Misaligned, off to one side, or may be tilted (Vertically Misaligned). One die may either have been installed so that it is turned in relation to the other die, or may turn in the holder, or the shank may break allowing the die face to rotate in relation to the opposing die.

Vertical misaligned dies are rarely found, and, like rotated dies, find only limited collector interest. Ninety- and 180-degree rotations are the most popular. Rotations of 14 degrees or less have no value. The 1989-D Congress dollar is found with a nearly 180-degree rotated reverse, currently retailing for around $2,000. Only about 30 have been reported to date.

III-N-1 Offset Die Misalignment Strike (WE), Rarity Level: 3-5 . . . . .Values: $2 up
III-N-2 Vertical Die Misalignment Strike (WE), Rarity Level: 4-6. . . . . .Values: $1 up
III-N-3 Rotated Die Strike - 15 to 45 Degrees (IWE), Rarity Level: 4-6 .Values: $2 up
III-N-4 Rotated Die Strike - 46 to 135 Degrees (IWE), Rarity Level: 5-6 . . . . .Values: $10 up
III-N-5 Rotated Die Strike - 136 to 180 Degrees (IWE), Rarity Level: 5-6 . . . . .Values: $25 up

Lettered and design edge strike varieties (III-O)

Overlapping edge letters III-O-1

Early U.S. coins and a number of foreign coins have either lettered edges or designs on the edge of the coin. Malfunctions of the application of the motto or design to the edge fall in this section.

III-O-1 Overlapping Edge Motto or Design (WE), Rarity Level: 3-4 . . . . Values: $5 to $10 and up
III-O-2 Wrong Edge Motto or Design (WE), Rarity Level: 5-6-7 . . . . .Values: $50 up
III-O-3 Missing Edge Motto, Design or Security Edge (IWE), Rarity Level: 5-6-7 . . . . .Values: $50 up
III-O-4 Jammed Edge Die Strike (W), Rarity Level: 6. . . . . .Values: $10 up
III-O-5 Misplaced Segment of an Edge Die (E), Rarity Level: 4-7 . . . . .Values: $25 up
III-O-6 Reeded Edge Struck Over a Lettered Edge (IE), Rarity Level: 3-6 . . . . Values: No Extra Value up

Defective strikes and mismatched dies (III-P)

The final section of the Striking Division covers coins that are not properly struck for reasons other than those in previous classes, such as coins struck with mismatched (muled) dies. The mismatched die varieties must be taken on a case by case basis, while the other classes presently have little collector demand or premium.

III-P-1 Defective Strike (WE), Rarity Level: 1. . . . . .Values: No Extra Value
III-P-2 Mismatched Die Strike (E), Rarity Level: 4-7 . . . . .Values: $25 up
III-P-3 Single-Strike Proof (WE), Rarity Level: 4-5 . . . . .Values: Minimal
III-P-4 Single Die-Proof Strike (IE), Rarity Level: 5-6 . . . . .Values: $100 up
III-P-5 Reversed Die Strike (I), Rarity Level: 4-5 . . . . .Values: No Extra Value to Minimal

Official Mint modifications

Division IV

Several mint-produced varieties occur after the coin has been struck, resulting in the addition of the fourth division to my PDS System. Since most of these coins are either unique or are special varieties, each one must be taken on a case by case basis. All classes listed here are by definition intentional.

I have not listed values as the coins falling in these classes, which are sold through regular numismatic channels, are cataloged with the regular issues or are covered in specialized catalogs in their particular area.

Matte proofs (IV-A)

Matte proofs IV-A-1

Matte proofs as a section include several of the forms of proof coins that have the striking characteristics of a mirror proof but have been treated AFTER striking to give them a grainy, non-reflective surface.

IV-A-1 Matte Proof (I), Rarity Level: 3-5 . . . . .Values: Normal Numismatic Value
IV-A-2 Matte Proof on One Side (I), Rarity Level: 7 .Values: Normal Numismatic Value
IV-A-3 Sandblast Proof (I), Rarity Level: 4-6 . . . . .Values: Normal Numismatic Value

Additional engraving (IV-B)

Counterstamp IV-B-3

This section includes any added markings that are placed on the struck coin and struck coins that later were cut into pieces for various purposes. The warning is repeated: Anything done to a coin after the strike is extremely difficult t o authenticate and is much easier to fake than a die struck coin.

IV-B-1 Counterstamp and Countermark (I), Rarity Level: 3-6 . . . . .Values: Normal Numismatic Value
IV-B-2 Perforated and Cut Coins (I), Rarity Level: 4-6 . . . . .Values: Normal Numismatic Value

Restrikes (IV-C)

Restrike with new dies IV-C-7

Restrikes cover a complicated mixture of official use of dies from a variety of sources. Whether or not some were officially sanctioned is always a problem for the collector.

IV-C-1) Restrike on the Same Denomination Planchet (I), Rarity Level: 4-6. . .Values: Normal Numismatic Value

IV-C-2 Restrike on a Different Denomination or Series Planchet (I), Rarity Level: 4-6
. . . . .Values: Normal Numismatic Value

IV-C-3 Restrike on a Foreign Coin (I), Rarity Level: 6-7 . . . . .Values: Normal Numismatic Value

IV-C-4 Restrike on a Token or Medal (I), Rarity Level: 5-6 . . . . .Values: Normal Numismatic Value

IV-C-5 Restruck With the Original Dies (I), Rarity Level: 4-6 . . . . .Values: Normal Numismatic Value

IV-C-6 Restruck With Mismatched Dies (I), Rarity Level: 4-6 . . . . .Values: Normal Numismatic Value

IV-C-7 Copy Strike With New Dies (I), Rarity Level: 3-5 . . . . .Values: Normal Numismatic Value

IV-C-8 Fantasy Strike (I), Rarity Level: 4-6 . . . . .Values: Normal Numismatic Value

After strike modifications

Division V

This division includes both modifications that have value to collectors – and those that don't. I needed a couple of divisions to cover other things that happen to coins to aid in cataloging them. This avoids the false conclusion that an unlisted coin is quite rare, when the exact opposite is more likely to be the case.

Collectible modifications after strike (V-A)

Mint modification V-A-8

This section includes those classes having to do with deliberate modifications of the coin done with a specific purpose or intent that makes them of some value to collectors. Quite often these pieces were made specifically to sell to collectors, or at least to the public, under the guise of being collectible.

V-A-1 Screw Thaler, Rarity Level: 5-6 . . . . Values: Normal Numismatic Value
V-A-2 Love Token, Rarity Level: 3-6 . . . . .Values: $10 up
V-A-3 Satirical or Primitive Engraving, Rarity Level: 6-7 . . . . Values: $5 up
V-A-4 Elongated Coin, Rarity Level: 2-7 . . . . Values: 50 cents to $1 and up
V-A-5 Coin Jewelry, Rarity Level: 2-5 . . . . .Values: $1 up
V-A-6 Novelty Coin, Rarity Level: 1-3 . . . . .Values: No Value up to $5 to $10
V-A-7 Toning, Rarity Level: 3-6 . . . . Values: No value up, depending on coloration. Easily faked
V-A-8 Mint Modification, Rarity Level: 4-7 . . . . Values: $5 up. Easily faked
V-A-9 Mint Packaging Mistake, Rarity Level: 5-7 . . . . Values: Nominal $1. Very easily faked

Alterations and damage after the strike (V-B)

Machine doubling damage V-B-1

This section includes those changes in a coin that have no collector value. In most cases, their effect on the coin is to reduce or entirely eliminate any collector value - and in the case of counterfeits they are actually illegal to even own.

V -B-1 Machine Doubling Damage: *NOTE: Machine doubling damage is defined as: "Damage to a coin after the strike, due to die bounce or chatter or die displacement, showing on the struck coin as scrapes on the sides of the design elements, with portions of the coin metal in the relief elements either displaced sideways or downward, depending on the direction of movement of the loose die."* Machine doubling damage, or MDD, is by far the most common form of doubling found on almost any coin in the world.
Rarity Level: 0 . . . . Values: Reduces the coin's value
V-B-2 Accidental or Deliberate Damage, Rarity Level: 0 . . . . Values: Reduces the coin's value
V-B-3 Test Cut or Mark, Rarity Level: 0 . . . . Values: Reduces value of coin to face or bullion value
V-B-4 Alteration, Rarity Level: 0 . . . . .Values: Reduces value to face or bullion value
V-B-5 Whizzing, Rarity Level: 0 . . . . . . Values: Reduces value sharply and may reduce it to face or bullion value
V-B-6 Counterfeit, Copy, Facsimile, Forgery or Fake, Rarity Level: 0 . . Values: No Value and may be illegal to own
V-B-7 Planchet Deterioration. Very common on copper-plated zinc cents. Rarity level: 0 . . . . .Values: No Value

Pricing Section

COLONIAL COINAGE

MARYLAND

Lord Baltimore

PENNY (DENARIUM)

KM# 1 • Copper • Obv. Legend: CAECILIVS Dns TERRAE MARIAE

Date	AG	Good	VG	Fine	VF	XF
(1659) 5 known	—	—	—	—	—	—100,000

Note: Stack's Auction 5-04, proof realized $241,500

4 PENCE (GROAT)

KM# 2 • Silver • Obv: Large bust **Obv. Legend:** CAECILIVS Dns TERRAE MARIAE **Rev:** Large shield

Date	AG	Good	VG	Fine	VF	XF
(1659)	1,250	1,850	3,500	6,250	13,500	20,000

KM# 3 • Silver • Obv: Small bust **Obv. Legend:** CAECILIVS Dns TERRAE MARIAE **Rev:** Small shield

Date	AG	Good	VG	Fine	VF	XF
(1659) unique	—	—	—	—	—	—

Note: Norweb $26,400

6 PENCE

KM# 4 • Silver • Obv: Small bust **Obv. Legend:** CAECILIVS Dns TERRAE MARIAE **Note:** Known in two other rare small-bust varieties and two rare large-bust varieties.

Date	AG	Good	VG	Fine	VF	XF
(1659)	850	1,400	2,400	4,900	9,000	15,000

SHILLING

KM# 6 • Silver • Obv. Legend: CAECILIVS Dns TERRAE MARIAE **Note:** Varieties exist; one is very rare.

Date	AG	Good	VG	Fine	VF	XF
(1659)	1,100	1,800	3,000	5,750	13,500	20,000

MASSACHUSETTS

New England

3 PENCE

KM# 1 • Silver • Obv: NE **Rev:** III

Date	AG	Good	VG	Fine	VF
(1652) Unique	—	—	—	—	—

Note: Massachusetts Historical Society specimen

6 PENCE

KM# 2 • Silver • Obv: NE **Rev:** VI

Date	Good	VG	Fine	VF
(1652) 8 known	25,000	50,000	90,000	175,000

Note: Garrett $75,000

SHILLING

KM# 3 • Silver • Obv: NE **Rev:** XII

Date	Good	VG	Fine	VF	XF
(1652)	35,000	65,000	100,000	200,000	—

Oak Tree

2 PENCE

KM# 7 • **Silver** • **Note:** Small 2 and large 2 varieites exist

Date	Good	VG	Fine	VF	XF	Unc
1662	500	900	2,000	3,850	6,500	15,000

3 PENCE

KM# 8 • **Silver** • **Note:** Two types of legends.

Date	AG	Good	VG	Fine	VF	XF
1652	350	600	1,000	2,500	5,500	9,000

6 PENCE

KM# 9 • **Silver** • **Note:** Three types of legends.

Date	AG	Good	VG	Fine	VF	XF	Unc
1652	400	900	1,100	2,700	6,400	9,500	25,000

SHILLING

KM# 10 • **Silver** • **Note:** Two types of legends.

Date	AG	Good	VG	Fine	VF	XF	Unc
1652	350	650	1,100	2,600	5,400	8,800	25,000

Pine Tree

3 PENCE

KM# 11 • **Silver** • **Obv:** Tree without berries

Date	AG	Good	VG	Fine	VF	XF	Unc
1652	250	500	700	1,650	3,000	5,600	17,500

KM# 12 • **Silver** • **Obv:** Tree with berries

Date	AG	Good	VG	Fine	VF	XF	Unc
1652	250	500	700	1,650	3,200	5,750	18,500

6 PENCE

KM# 13 • **Silver** • **Obv:** Tree without berries; "spiney tree"

Date	AG	Good	VG	Fine	VF	XF	Unc
1652	400	700	1,400	2,000	3,750	6,500	20,000

KM# 14 • **Silver** • **Obv:** Tree with berries

Date	AG	Good	VG	Fine	VF	XF	Unc
1652	300	500	800	1,750	3,500	6,250	18,000

SHILLING

KM# 15 • **Silver** • **Note:** Large planchet. Many varieties exist; some are very rare.

Date	AG	Good	VG	Fine	VF	XF	Unc
1652	350	600	950	2,000	4,350	7,500	20,000

KM# 16 • **Silver** • **Note:** Small planchet; large dies. All examples are thought to be contemporary fabrications.

Date	AG	Good	VG	Fine	VF	XF
1652	—	—	—	—	—	—

KM# 17 • Silver • Note: Small planchet; small dies. Many varieties exist; some are very rare.

Date	AG	Good	VG	Fine	VF	XF	Unc
1652	285	525	800	1,700	3,750	6,950	22,500

Willow Tree

3 PENCE

KM# 4 • Silver

Date	AG	Good	VG	Fine	VF	XF
1652 3 known	—	—	—	—	—	—

6 PENCE

KM# 5 • Silver

Date	AG	Good	VG	Fine	VF	XF
1652						
14 known	9,000	17,500	30,000	57,500	125,000	200,000

SHILLING

KM# 6 • Silver

Date	AG	Good	VG	Fine	VF	XF
1652	9,800	18,000	34,000	80,000	150,000	225,000

NEW JERSEY
St. Patrick or Mark Newby

FARTHING

KM# 1 • Copper • Obv. Legend: FLOREAT REX Rev. Legend: QUIESCAT PLEBS

Date	AG	Good	VG	Fine	VF	XF
(1682)	70.00	125	285	700	2,250	4,500

Note: One very rare variety is known with reverse legend: QUIESAT PLEBS

KM# 1a • Silver • Obv. Legend: FLOREAT REX Rev. Legend: QUIESCAT PLEBS

Date	AG	Good	VG	Fine	VF	XF
(1682)	800	1,500	2,200	4,500	8,000	12,500

HALFPENNY

KM# 2 • Copper • Obv. Legend: FLOREAT REX Rev. Legend: ECCE GREX

Date	AG	Good	VG	Fine	VF	XF	Unc
(1682)	180	365	850	1,650	4,000	10,500	—

EARLY AMERICAN TOKENS
American Plantations

1/24 REAL

KM# Tn5.1 • Tin • Obv. Legend: ET HIB REX

Date	AG	Good	VG	Fine	VF	XF	Unc
(1688)	125	200	300	450	750	2,000	—

KM# Tn5.3 • **Tin** • **Rev:** Horizontal 4

Date	AG	Good	VG	Fine	VF	XF	Unc
(1688)	275	400	900	1,500	2,700	5,000	—

KM# Tn5.4 • **Tin** • **Obv. Legend:** ET HIB REX

Date	AG	Good	VG	Fine	VF	XF	Unc
(1688)	—	250	450	750	1,400	2,650	9,000

KM# Tn6 • **Tin** • **Rev:** Arms of Scotland left, Ireland right

Date	AG	Good	VG	Fine	VF	XF	Unc
(1688)	450	750	1,250	2,000	3,000	6,500	—

KM# Tn5.2 • **Tin** • **Obv:** Rider's head left of "B" in legend **Note:** Restrikes made in 1828 from two obverse dies.

Date	AG	Good	VG	Fine	VF	XF	Unc
(1828)	75.00	110	175	275	500	1,000	—

Elephant

KM# Tn1.1 • 15.5500 g., **Copper** • **Note:** Thick planchet.

Date	AG	Good	VG	Fine	VF	XF	Unc
(1664)	125	200	300	500	1,000	1,750	3,850

KM# Tn1.2 • **Copper** • **Note:** Thin planchet.

Date	AG	Good	VG	Fine	VF	XF	Unc
(1664)	175	300	500	850	3,000	5,500	11,750

KM# Tn2 • **Copper** • **Rev:** Diagonals tie shield

Date	AG	Good	VG	Fine	VF	XF	Unc
(1664)	250	450	650	2,250	6,500	10,000	17,500

KM# Tn3 • **Copper** • **Rev:** Sword right side of shield

Date	VG	Fine	VF	XF	Unc
(1664) 3 known	—	—	12,500	—	—
Note: Norweb $1,320					

KM# Tn4 • **Copper** • **Rev. Legend:** LON DON

Date	AG	Good	VG	Fine	VF	XF	Unc
(1684)	340	650	1,000	2,250	4,000	7,000	17,500

KM# Tn7 • **Copper** • **Rev. Legend:** NEW ENGLAND

Date	VG	Fine	VF	XF
(1694) 2 known	50,000	75,000	95,000	140,000
Note: Norweb $25,300				

KM# Tn8.1 • **Copper** • **Rev. Legend:** CAROLINA (PROPRIETORS)

Date	VG	Fine	VF	XF	Unc
(1694) 5 known	4,750	6,500	14,000	22,500	—
Note: Norweb $35,200					

KM# Tn8.2 • **Copper** • **Rev. Legend:** CAROLINA (PROPRIETORS, O over E)

Date	AG	Good	VG	Fine	VF	XF
1694	1,300	2,500	4,000	6,000	12,000	17,500
Note: Norweb $17,600						

Gloucester

KM# Tn15 • **Copper** • **Obv. Legend:** GLOVCESTER COVRTHOVSE VIRGINIA **Rev. Legend:** RIGHAVLT DAWSON.ANNO.DOM.1714.

Date	Good	VG	Fine	VF	XF	Unc
(1714) 2 known	—	—	—	—	—	—
Note: Garrett $36,000						

Hibernia-Voce Populi

FARTHING

KM# Tn21.1 • **Copper** • **Note:** Large letters

Date	AG	Good	VG	Fine	VF	XF	Unc
1760	125	200	325	600	1,600	3,000	8,500

KM# Tn21.2 • **Copper** • **Note:** Small letters

Date	AG	Good	VG	Fine	VF	XF	Unc
1760	—	650	1,250	2,750	7,500	13,500	—
Note: Norweb $5,940.							

HALFPENNY

KM# Tn22 • Copper •

Date	AG	Good	VG	Fine	VF	XF	Unc
1700 Extremely rare	—	—	—	—	—	—	—

Note: Date is in error; ex-Roper $575. Norweb $577.50. Stack's Americana, VF, $2,900.

Date	AG	Good	VG	Fine	VF	XF	Unc
1760	40.00	70.00	135	175	365	675	2,500
1760	50.00	80.00	135	195	425	775	3,500

Note: legend VOOE POPULI

Date	AG	Good	VG	Fine	VF	XF	Unc
1760 P below bust	65.00	100.00	185	350	700	1,750	8,000
1760 P in front of bust	55.00	90.00	170	325	600	1,400	6,500

Higley or Granby

KM# Tn16 • Copper • Obv. Legend: CONNECTICVT **Rev. Legend:** THE VALVE OF THREE PENCE

Date	AG	Good	VG	Fine	VF
1737	—	10,000	18,000	40,000	80,000

Note: Garrett $16,000

KM# Tn17 • Copper • Obv. Legend: THE VALVE OF THREE PENCE **Rev. Legend:** I AM GOOD COPPER

Date	AG	Good	VG	Fine	VF
1737 2 known	—	11,000	20,000	40,000	85,000

Note: ex-Norweb $6,875

KM# Tn18.1 • Copper • Obv. Legend: VALUE ME AS YOU PLEASE **Rev. Legend:** I AM GOOD COPPER

Date	AG	Good	VG	Fine	VF	XF
1737	6,500	10,000	18,000	40,000	80,000	—

KM# Tn18.2 • Copper • Obv. Legend: VALVE.ME.AS.YOU.PLEASE. **Rev. Legend:** I AM GOOD COPPER.

Date	VG	Fine	VF	XF
1737 2 known	—	—	—	275,000

KM# Tn19 • Copper • Rev: Broad axe

Date	AG	Good	VG	Fine	VF
(1737)	—	10,000	18,000	35,000	125,000

Note: Garrett $45,000

Date	AG	Good	VG	Fine	VF
1739 5 known	—	—	—	—	—

Note: Eliasberg $12,650. Oechsner $9,900. Steinberg (holed) $4,400.

KM# Tn20 • Copper • Obv. Legend: THE WHEELE GOES ROUND **Rev:** J CUT MY WAY THROUGH

Date	AG	Good	VG	Fine	VF
(1737) unique	—	—	—	150,000	—

Note: Roper $60,500

New Yorke

KM# Tn9 • Brass • Obv. Legend:
NEW.YORK.IN.AMERICA

Date	AG	Good	VG	Fine	VF	XF
1700	1,800	3,500	5,500	13,000	22,500	35,000

KM# Tn9a • White Metal • Obv. Legend:
NEW.YORK.IN.AMERICA

Date	Good	VG	Fine	VF	XF
1700 4 known	—	6,000	15,000	28,000	50,000

Pitt

FARTHING

KM# Tn23 • Copper

Date	AG	Good	VG	Fine	VF	XF
1766	—	—	—	7,500	22,000	35,000

HALFPENNY

KM# Tn24 • Copper

Date	AG	Good	VG	Fine	VF	XF	Unc
1766	140	250	400	700	1,500	2,750	7,500

KM# Tn24a • Silver Plated Copper •

Date	VG	Fine	VF	XF	Unc
1766	—	—	2,250	5,000	12,000

ROYAL PATENT COINAGE
Hibernia

FARTHING

KM# 20 • Copper   Note: Pattern.

Date	AG	Good	VG	Fine	VF	XF	Unc
1722	135	235	375	500	1,000	2,600	7,750

KM# 24 • Copper • Obv: 1722 obverse Obv. Legend: …D:G:REX.

Date	AG	Good	VG	Fine	VF	XF
1723	20.00	40.00	60.00	90.00	150	350

KM# 25 • Copper • Obv. Legend: DEI • GRATIA • REX •

Date	AG	Good	VG	Fine	VF	XF	Unc
1723	25.00	45.00	60.00	180	300	550	950
1724	—	90.00	125	225	600	1,350	3,500

KM# 25a • Silver •

Date	Good	VG	Fine	VF	XF	Unc
1723	—	1,600	2,250	4,000	5,500	10,000

HALFPENNY

KM# 21 • Copper • Obv: Bust right Obv. Legend:
GEORGIUS • DEI • GRATIA • REX • **Rev:** Harp left,
head left **Rev. Legend:** • HIBERNIA • 1722 •

Date	AG	Good	VG	Fine	VF	XF	Unc
1722	50.00	90.00	110	160	325	700	1,750

KM# 22 • Copper • Obv: Bust right **Obv. Legend:** GEORGIVS D: G: REX **Rev:** Harp left, head right **Rev. Legend:** • HIBERNIÆ • **Note:** "Rocks Reverse" pattern.

Date	AG	Good	VG	Fine	VF	XF	Unc
1722	—	—	—	2,750	3,850	8,500	

KM# 23.1 • Copper • Rev: Harp right

Date	AG	Good	VG	Fine	VF	XF	Unc
1722	35.00	60.00	80.00	120	285	600	1,400
1723	20.00	35.00	45.00	75.00	190	280	800
1723/22	35.00	60.00	80.00	150	375	750	1,750
1724	25.00	50.00	90.00	160	360	825	2,000

KM# 23.2 • Copper • Obv: DEII error in legend

Date	AG	Good	VG	Fine	VF	XF	Unc
1722	75.00	125	160	325	750	1,400	2,750

KM# 26 • Copper • Rev: Large head **Note:** Rare. Generally mint state only. Probably a pattern.

Date	AG	Good	VG	Fine	VF	XF	Unc
1723	—	—	—	—	—	—	—

KM# 27 • Copper • Rev: Continuous legend over head

Date	AG	Good	VG	Fine	VF	XF	Unc
1724	45.00	80.00	150	300	900	1,500	3,500

Rosa Americana

HALFPENNY

KM# 1 • Copper • Obv. Legend: D • G • REX •

Date	AG	Good	VG	Fine	VF	XF	Unc
1722	20.00	50.00	140	250	525	1,050	4,000

KM# 2 • Copper • Obv: Uncrowned rose **Obv. Legend:** ... • DEI • GRATIA • REX • **Note:** Several varieties exist.

Date	AG	Good	VG	Fine	VF	XF	Unc
1722	50.00	90.00	135	250	450	950	3,500
1723	385	700	850	1,750	3,600	—	—

KM# 3 • Copper • Rev. Legend: VTILE DVLCI

Date	AG	Good	VG	Fine	VF	XF	Unc
1722	250	450	850	2,200	3,800	7,500	—

KM# 9 • Copper • Rev: Crowned rose

Date	AG	Good	VG	Fine	VF	XF	Unc
1723	45.00	85.00	110	165	425	1,000	4,500

PENNY

KM# 4 • Copper • Rev. Legend: UTILE DULCI **Note:** Several varieties exist.

Date	AG	Good	VG	Fine	VF	XF	Unc
1722	60.00	100.00	135	240	450	950	3,750

KM# 5 • Copper • Note: Several varieties exist. Also known in two rare pattern types with long hair ribbons, one with V's for U's on the obverse.

Date	AG	Good	VG	Fine	VF	XF	Unc
1722	18.00	35.00	150	275	750	1,350	5,600

KM# 10 • Copper • Note: Several varieties exist.

Date	AG	Good	VG	Fine	VF	XF	Unc
1723	40.00	75.00	110	175	425	900	3,600

KM# 12 • Copper • Note: Pattern.

Date	AG	Good	VG	Fine	VF	XF	Unc
1724 2 known	—	—	—	—	—	—	—

KM# 13 • Copper • Rev. Legend: ROSA: SINE: SPINA •

Date	Good	VG	Fine	VF	XF	Unc
(1724) 5 known	—	—	—	—	—	—

Note: Norweb $2,035

KM# 14 • Copper • Obv: George II **Note:** Pattern.

Date	Good	VG	Fine	VF	XF	Unc
1727 2 known	—	—	—	—	—	—

2 PENCE

KM# 6 • Copper • Rev: Motto with scroll

Date	AG	Good	VG	Fine	VF	XF	Unc
(1722)	80.00	150	200	425	700	1,200	6,250

KM# 7 • Copper • Rev: Motto without scroll

Date	AG	Good	VG	Fine	VF	XF	Unc
(1722) 3 known	—	—	—	—	—	—	—

KM# 8.1 • Copper • Obv. Legend: ...REX • **Rev:** Dated

Date	AG	Good	VG	Fine	VF	XF	Unc
1722	70.00	125	175	275	750	1,500	5,500

KM# 8.2 • Copper • Obv. Legend: ...REX

Date	AG	Good	VG	Fine	VF	XF	Unc
1722	70.00	125	175	275	775	1,600	6,000

KM# 11 • Copper • Obv: No stop after REX **Rev:** Stop after 1723 **Note:** Several varieties exist.

Date	AG	Good	VG	Fine	VF	XF	Unc
1723	65.00	120	160	285	550	1,200	3,500

KM# 15 • Copper • Note: Pattern. Two varieties exist; both extremely rare.

Date	AG	Good	VG	Fine	VF	XF	Unc
1724	—	—	—	—	—	—	—

Note: Stack's 5-05 choice AU realized $25,300. Ex-Garrett $5,775. Stack's Americana, XF, $10,925

KM# 16 • **Copper** • **Obv:** Bust left **Rev:** Crowned rose **Note:** Pattern.

Date	Good	VG	Fine	VF	XF	Unc
1733	4 known	—	—	—	—	—

Note: Norweb $19,800

Virginia Halfpenny

KM# Tn25.1 • **Copper** • **Rev:** Small 7s in date. **Note:** Struck on Irish halfpenny planchets.

Date	Good	VG	Fine	VF	XF	Unc	Proof
1773	—	—	—	—	—	—	22,000

KM# Tn25.2 • **Copper** • **Obv. Legend:** GEORGIVS •... **Rev:** Varieties with 7 or 8 strings in harp

Date	AG	Good	VG	Fine	VF	XF	Unc
1773	30.00	50.00	70.00	110	235	425	1,000

KM# Tn25.3 • **Copper** • **Obv. Legend:** GEORGIVS... **Rev:** Varieties with 6, 7 or 8 strings in harp

Date	AG	Good	VG	Fine	VF	XF	Unc
1773	35.00	60.00	75.00	135	275	500	1,250

KM# Tn25.4 • **Copper** • **Obv. Legend:** GEORGIVS... **Rev:** 8 harp strings, dot on cross

Date	AG	Good	VG	Fine	VF	XF	Unc
1773	—	—	—	—	—	—	—

Note: ex-Steinberg $2,600

KM# Tn26 • **Silver** • **Note:** So-called "shilling" silver proofs.

Date	Good	VG	Fine	VF	XF	Unc
1774	6 known	—	—	—	—	—

Note: Garrett $23,000

REVOLUTIONARY COINAGE
Continental "Dollar"

KM# EA1 • **Pewter** • **Obv. Legend:** CURRENCY.

Date	AG	Good	VG	Fine	VF	XF	Unc
1776	—	7,500	9,350	12,000	21,000	32,500	70,000

KM# EA2 • **Pewter** • **Obv. Legend:** CURRENCY, EG FECIT.

Date	AG	Good	VG	Fine	VF	XF	Unc
1776	—	8,000	10,500	13,500	25,000	36,000	75,000

KM# EA2a • **Silver** • **Obv. Legend:** CURRENCY, EG FECIT.

Date	Good	VG	Fine	VF	XF
1776	2 known	—	300,000	450,000	—

KM# EA3 • **Pewter** • **Obv. Legend:** CURRENCEY

Date	Good	VG	Fine	VF	XF
1776	extremely rare	—	—	—	—100,000

KM# EA4 • **Pewter** • **Obv. Legend:** CURRENCY. **Rev:** Floral cross.

Date	Good	VG	Fine	VF	XF
1776	3 recorded	—	—	—	400,000

Note: Norweb $50,600. Johnson $25,300

KM# EA5 • Pewter • Obv. Legend: CURENCY.

Date	Good	VG	Fine	VF	XF	Unc
1776	7,500	9,500	12,000	22,500	33,000	65,000

KM# EA5a • Brass • Obv. Legend: CURENCY.
Note: Two varieties exist.

Date	Good	VG	Fine	VF	XF	Unc
1776	22,500	28,500	36,000	70,000	110,000	—

KM# EA5b • Silver • Obv. Legend: CURENCY.

Date	Good	VG	Fine	VF
1776 unique	—	—	300,000	450,000

Note: Romano $99,000

STATE COINAGE
CONNECTICUT

KM# 1 • Copper • Obv: Bust facing right.

Date	AG	Good	VG	Fine	VF	XF	Unc
1785	35.00	55.00	90.00	200	650	1,750	—

KM# 2 • Copper • Obv: "African head."

Date	AG	Good	VG	Fine	VF	XF	Unc
1785	55.00	85.00	150	600	1,500	3,800	—

KM# 3.1 • Copper • Obv: Mailed bust facing left.

Date	AG	Good	VG	Fine	VF	XF
1785	125	220	375	750	1,800	3,850
1786	30.00	50.00	90.00	175	475	1,200
1787	30.00	50.00	85.00	160	450	1,350
1788	30.00	50.00	80.00	160	435	1,100

KM# 3.3 • Copper • Obv: Perfect date. **Rev. Legend:** IN DE ET.

Date	AG	Good	VG	Fine	VF	XF	Unc
1787	50.00	80.00	125	350	750	1,500	—

KM# 3.4 • Copper • Obv. Legend: CONNLC.

Date	AG	Good	VG	Fine	VF	XF	Unc
1788	44.00	60.00	120	240	650	1,850	—

KM# 4 • Copper • Obv: Small mailed bust facing left. **Rev. Legend:** ETLIB INDE.

Date	AG	Good	VG	Fine	VF	XF	Unc
1786	45.00	75.00	150	350	900	2,100	—

KM# 5 • Copper • Obv: Small mailed bust facing right. **Rev. Legend:** INDE ET LIB.

Date	AG	Good	VG	Fine	VF	XF	Unc
1786	60.00	100.00	175	450	2,000	4,250	—

KM# 6 • Copper • Obv: Large mailed bust facing right.

Date	AG	Good	VG	Fine	VF	XF	Unc
1786	55.00	90.00	160	400	1,750	3,750	—

KM# 7 • Copper • Obv: "Hercules head."

Date	AG	Good	VG	Fine	VF	XF	Unc
1786	60.00	110	220	600	2,500	5,800	—

KM# 8.1 • Copper • Obv: Draped bust.

Date	AG	Good	VG	Fine	VF	XF	Unc
1786	50.00	90.00	175	475	1,150	2,750	—

KM# 8.2 • Copper • Obv: Draped bust. **Note:** Many varieties.

Date	AG	Good	VG	Fine	VF	XF	Unc
1787	28.00	42.00	70.00	115	325	750	—

KM# 8.3 • Copper • Obv. Legend: AUCIORI.

Date	AG	Good	VG	Fine	VF	XF	Unc
1787	30.00	55.00	90.00	175	450	1,000	—

KM# 8.4 • Copper • Obv. Legend: AUCTOPI.

Date	AG	Good	VG	Fine	VF	XF	Unc
1787	35.00	65.00	110	200	650	1,650	—

KM# 8.5 • Copper • Obv. Legend: AUCTOBI.

Date	AG	Good	VG	Fine	VF	XF	Unc
1787	35.00	65.00	110	200	625	1,550	—

KM# 8.6 • Copper • Obv. Legend: CONNFC.

Date	AG	Good	VG	Fine	VF	XF	Unc
1787	32.00	60.00	90.00	160	475	1,000	—

KM# 8.7 • Copper • Obv. Legend: CONNLC.

Date	AG	Good	VG	Fine	VF	XF	Unc
1787	50.00	75.00	150	300	650	1,850	—

KM# 8.8 • Copper • Rev. Legend: FNDE.

Date	AG	Good	VG	Fine	VF	XF	Unc
1787	35.00	55.00	80.00	160	475	1,400	—

KM# 8.9 • Copper • Rev. Legend: ETLIR.

Date	AG	Good	VG	Fine	VF	XF	Unc
1787	32.00	50.00	75.00	150	440	1,175	—

KM# 8.10 • Copper • Rev. Legend: ETIIB.

Date	AG	Good	VG	Fine	VF	XF	Unc
1787	35.00	50.00	75.00	150	450	1,200	—

KM# 9 • Copper • Obv: Small head. **Rev. Legend:** ETLIB INDE.

Date	AG	Good	VG	Fine	VF	XF	Unc
1787	65.00	110	180	375	1,500	3,750	—

KM# 10 • Copper • Obv: Small head. **Rev. Legend:** INDE ET LIB.

Date	AG	Good	VG	Fine	VF	XF	Unc
1787	75.00	135	200	450	2,000	4,000	—

KM# 11 • Copper • Obv: Medium bust. **Note:** Two reverse legend types exist.

Date	AG	Good	VG	Fine	VF	XF	Unc
1787	60.00	90.00	150	350	1,500	3,000	—

KM# 12 • Copper • Obv: "Muttonhead" variety. **Note:** Extremely rare with legend INDE ET LIB.

Date	AG	Good	VG	Fine	VF	XF	Unc
1787	60.00	90.00	175	500	2,200	4,500	—

KM# 13 • Copper • Obv: "Laughing head"

Date	AG	Good	VG	Fine	VF	XF	Unc
1787	35.00	60.00	120	240	650	1,800	—

KM# 14 • Copper • Obv: "Horned head"

Date	AG	Good	VG	Fine	VF	XF	Unc
1787	30.00	50.00	80.00	165	450	1,200	—

KM# 15 • Copper • Rev. Legend: IND ET LIB

Date	AG	Good	VG	Fine	VF	XF	Unc
1787/8	50.00	85.00	170	450	1,500	4,000	—
1787/1887	85.00	150	225	600	1,750	4,500	—

KM# 16 • Copper • Obv. Legend: CONNECT.
Rev. Legend: INDE ET LIB. **Note:** Two additional scarce reverse legend types exist.

Date	AG	Good	VG	Fine	VF	XF	Unc
1787	35.00	50.00	120	240	550	1,500	—

KM# 22.1 • Copper • Obv: Draped bust facing left. **Rev. Legend:** INDE ET LIB.

Date	AG	Good	VG	Fine	VF	XF	Unc
1788	45.00	70.00	125	285	675	1,650	—

KM# 22.2 • Copper • Rev. Legend: INDLET LIB.

Date	AG	Good	VG	Fine	VF	XF	Unc
1788	55.00	80.00	175	375	800	1,750	—

KM# 22.3 • Copper • Obv. Legend: CONNEC.
Rev. Legend: INDE ET LIB.

Date	AG	Good	VG	Fine	VF	XF	Unc
1788	58.00	85.00	190	400	875	1,850	—

KM# 22.4 • Copper • Obv. Legend: CONNEC.
Rev. Legend: INDL ET LIB.

Date	AG	Good	VG	Fine	VF	XF	Unc
1788	58.00	85.00	190	400	875	1,850	—

KM# 20 • Copper • Obv: Mailed bust facing right.

Date	AG	Good	VG	Fine	VF	XF	Unc
1788	28.00	40.00	85.00	180	550	1,450	—

KM# 21 • Copper • Obv: Small mailed bust facing right.

Date	AG	Good	VG	Fine	VF	XF	Unc
1788	850	1,500	2,950	4,150	9,500	18,500	—

MASSACHUSETTS

HALFPENNY

KM# 17 • Copper •

Date	AG	Good	VG	Fine	VF	XF
1776 unique	—	—	—	200,000	—	—

Note: Garrett $40,000

PENNY

KM# 18 • Copper

Date	AG	Good	VG	Fine	VF	XF	Unc
1776 unique	—	—	—	—	—	—	—

HALF CENT

KM# 19 • **Copper** • **Note:** Varieties exist; some are rare.

Date	AG	Good	VG	Fine	VF	XF	Unc
1787	60.00	90.00	140	210	550	1,000	3,250
1788	70.00	110	175	260	585	1,100	3,500

CENT

KM# 20.1 • **Copper** • **Rev:** Arrows in right talon

Date	Good	VG	Fine	VF	XF	Unc
1787 7 known	9,000	22,500	45,000	—	—	350,000

Note: Ex-Bushnell-Brand $8,800. Garrett $5,500

KM# 20.2 • **Copper** • **Rev:** Arrows in left talon

Date	AG	Good	VG	Fine	VF	XF	Unc
1787	60.00	90.00	165	240	650	1,250	6,800

KM# 20.3 • **Copper** • **Rev:** "Horned eagle" die break

Date	AG	Good	VG	Fine	VF	XF	Unc
1787	70.00	110	190	275	775	1,500	7,750

KM# 20.4 • **Copper** • **Rev:** Without period after Massachusetts

Date	AG	Good	VG	Fine	VF	XF	Unc
1788	70.00	105	190	260	675	1,600	6,250

KM# 20.5 • **Copper** • **Rev:** Period after Massachusetts, normal S's

Date	AG	Good	VG	Fine	VF	XF	Unc
1788	60.00	90.00	170	235	600	1,375	5,750

KM# 20.6 • **Copper** • **Rev:** Period after Massachusetts, S's like 8's

Date	AG	Good	VG	Fine	VF	XF	Unc
1788	50.00	75.00	135	200	575	1,250	5,400

NEW HAMPSHIRE

KM# 1 • **Copper**

Date	Good	VG	Fine	VF	XF
1776 extremely rare	—	75,000	—	—	—

Note: Garrett $13,000

NEW JERSEY

KM# 8 • Copper • Obv: Date below draw bar.

Date	Good	VG	Fine	VF
1786 extremely rare	—	—	48,000	110,000

Note: Garrett $52,000

KM# 9 • Copper • Obv: Large horse head, date below plow, no coulter on plow.

Date	AG	Good	VG	Fine	VF	XF	Unc
1786	450	750	1,450	2,350	7,500	20,000	—

KM# 10 • Copper • Rev: Narrow shield, straight beam.

Date	AG	Good	VG	Fine	VF	XF	Unc
1786	38.00	60.00	140	210	550	1,350	—

KM# 11.1 • Copper • Rev: Wide shield, curved beam. **Note:** Varieties exist.

Date	AG	Good	VG	Fine	VF	XF	Unc
1786	45.00	75.00	150	225	600	2,000	—

KM# 11.2 • Copper • Obv: Bridle variety (die break). **Note:** Reverse varieties exist.

Date	AG	Good	VG	Fine	VF	XF	Unc
1786	45.00	70.00	145	235	650	2,400	—

KM# 12.1 • Copper • Rev: Plain shield. **Note:** Small planchet. Varieties exist.

Date	AG	Good	VG	Fine	VF	XF	Unc
1787	35.00	55.00	110	200	500	1,050	—

KM# 12.2 • Copper • Rev: Shield heavily outlined. **Note:** Small planchet.

Date	AG	Good	VG	Fine	VF	XF	Unc
1787	38.00	60.00	120	215	550	1,150	—

KM# 13 • Copper • Obv: "Serpent head."

Date	AG	Good	VG	Fine	VF	XF	Unc
1787	55.00	85.00	200	375	1,500	3,750	—

KM# 14 • Copper • Rev: Plain shield. **Note:** Large planchet. Varieties exist.

Date	AG	Good	VG	Fine	VF	XF	Unc
1787	45.00	60.00	135	240	750	1,650	—

KM# 15 • Copper • Rev. Legend: PLURIBS.

Date	AG	Good	VG	Fine	VF	XF	Unc
1787	85.00	150	275	450	1,000	2,800	—

KM# 16 • Copper • Obv: Horse's head facing right. Note: Varieties exist.

Date	AG	Good	VG	Fine	VF	XF	Unc
1788	42.00	60.00	115	190	700	1,275	—

KM# 17 • Copper • Rev: Fox before legend. Note: Varieties exist.

Date	AG	Good	VG	Fine	VF	XF	Unc
1788	75.00	135	285	550	1,750	4,400	—

KM# 18 • Copper • Obv: Horse's head facing left. Note: Varieties exist.

Date	AG	Good	VG	Fine	VF	XF	Unc
1788	235	400	850	1,500	4,800	13,000	—

NEW YORK
Nova Eboracs

KM# 1 • Copper • Obv: Bust right Obv. Legend: NON VI VIRTUTE VICI. Rev. Legend: NEO-EBORACENSIS

Date	AG	Good	VG	Fine	VF	XF
1786	3,250	5,000	7,500	15,000	35,000	—

KM# 2 • Copper • Obv: Eagle on globe facing

right. Obv. Legend: EXCELSIOR Rev. Legend: E. PLURIBUS UNUM

Date	AG	Good	VG	Fine	VF	XF
1787	1,400	2,250	3,850	7,000	17,500	32,500

KM# 3 • Copper • Obv: Eagle on globe facing left. Obv. Legend: EXCELSIOR Rev. Legend: E. PLURIBUS UNUM

Date	AG	Good	VG	Fine	VF	XF
1787	1,250	2,000	3,500	6,500	16,500	32,000

KM# 4 • Copper • Obv. Legend: EXCELSIOR Rev: Large eagle, arrows in right talon. Rev. Legend: E. PLURIBUS UNUM

Date	AG	Good	VG	Fine	VF	XF
1787	—	4,500	9,000	16,500	35,000	55,000

Note: Norweb $18,700

KM# 5 • Copper • Obv: George Clinton. Rev. Legend: EXCELSIOR

Date	AG	Good	VG	Fine	VF	XF
1787	4,500	7,500	14,500	26,000	48,500	125,000

KM# 6 • Copper • Obv: Indian. Obv. Legend: LIBERNATUS LIBERTATEM DEFENDO Rev: New York arms. Rev. Legend: EXCELSIOR

Date	AG	Good	VG	Fine	VF	XF
1787	4,500	7,000	10,000	17,500	40,000	90,000

KM# 7 • **Copper** • **Obv:** Indian. **Obv. Legend:** LIBERNATUS LIBERTATEM DEFENDO **Rev:** Eagle on globe. **Rev. Legend:** NEO EBORACUS EXCELSIOR

Date	AG	Good	VG	Fine	VF	XF
1787	6,000	11,000	15,000	27,500	55,000	120,000

KM# 8 • **Copper** • **Obv:** Indian. **Rev:** George III.

Date		AG	Good	VG	Fine	VF	XF
1787	3 Known	—	—	60,000	—	—	—

KM# 12 • **Copper** • **Obv:** Large head, two quatrefoils left. **Obv. Legend:** NOVA EBORAC. **Rev:** Figure seated left **Rev. Legend:** VIRT.ET.LIB.

Date	AG	Good	VG	Fine	VF	XF	Unc
1787	350	600	1,250	2,250	7,500	15,000	—

Machin's Mill

KM# 13 • **Copper** • **Note:** Crude, lightweight imitations of the British Halfpenny were struck at Machin's Mill in large quantities bearing the obverse legends: GEORGIVS II REX, GEORGIVS III REX, and GEORGIUS III REX, with the BRITANNIA reverse. There are many different mulings. Plain crosses in the shield of Britannia are noticeable on high grade pieces, unlike common British made imitations, which usually have outlined crosses in the shield. Some Machin's Mill varieties are very rare.

Date	AG	Good	VG	Fine	VF	XF
(1747-1788)	40.00	70.00	120	250	750	2,200

Note: Prices are for most common within date ranges. Examples are dated: 1747, 1771, 1772, 1774, 1775, 1776, 1777, 1778, 1784, 1785, 1786, 1787 and 1788. Other dates may exist

KM# 9 • **Copper** • **Obv:** Bust right **Obv. Legend:** NOVA EBORAC. **Rev:** Figure seated right. **Rev. Legend:** VIRT.ET.LIB.

Date	AG	Good	VG	Fine	VF	XF	Unc
1787	75.00	115	220	360	1,150	2,700	—

KM# 10 • **Copper** • **Obv:** Bust right **Obv. Legend:** NOVA EBORAC **Rev:** Figure seated left. **Rev. Legend:** VIRT.ET.LIB.

Date	AG	Good	VG	Fine	VF	XF	Unc
1787	60.00	100	200	325	825	1,750	—

VERMONT

KM# 1 • **Copper** • **Rev. Legend:** IMMUNE COLUMBIA

Date	AG	Good	VG	Fine	VF	XF	Unc
(1785)	3,750	5,500	9,000	12,750	32,000	—	—

KM# 11 • **Copper** • **Obv:** Small head, star above. **Obv. Legend:** NOVA EBORAC. **Rev:** Figure seated left **Rev. Legend:** VIRT.ET.LIB.

Date	AG	Good	VG	Fine	VF	XF	Unc
1787	2,450	3,500	5,200	7,500	20,000	55,000	—

KM# 2 • Copper • Obv: Sun rising over field with plow **Obv. Legend:** VERMONTIS. RES. PUBLICA. **Rev:** Eye, with rays and stars **Rev. Legend:** QUARTA. DECIMA. STELLA.

Date	AG	Good	VG	Fine	VF	XF	Unc
1785	120	290	650	1,450	4,500	11,000	—

KM# 3 • Copper • Obv: Sun rising over field with plow **Obv. Legend:** VERMONTS. RES. PUBLICA. **Rev:** Eye, with rays and stars **Rev. Legend:** QUARTA. DECIMA. STELLA.

Date	AG	Good	VG	Fine	VF	XF	Unc
1785	150	275	600	1,250	3,100	7,500	—

KM# 4 • Copper • Obv: Sun rising over field with plow **Obv. Legend:** VERMONTENSIUM. RES. PUBLICA **Rev:** Eye, with pointed rays and stars **Rev. Legend:** QUARTA. DECIMA. STELLA.

Date	AG	Good	VG	Fine	VF	XF	Unc
1786	140	235	400	750	2,000	4,400	—

KM# 5 • Copper • Obv: "Baby head." **Obv. Legend:** AUCTORI: VERMON: **Rev:** Seated figure left **Rev. Legend:** ET:LIB: INDE

Date	AG	Good	VG	Fine	VF	XF	Unc
1786	200	350	650	1,750	4,800	12,500	—

KM# 6 • Copper • Obv: Bust facing left. **Obv. Legend:** VERMON: AUCTORI: **Rev:** Seated figure left **Rev. Legend:** INDE ETLIB

Date	Good	VG	Fine	VF	XF
1786	175	350	800	2,800	4,750
1787 extremely rare	—	4,500	11,000	27,500	44,000

KM# 7 • Copper • Obv: Bust facing right. **Obv. Legend:** VERMON. AUCTORI. **Rev:** Seated figure left **Rev. Legend:** INDE ETLIB **Note:** Varieties exist.

Date	AG	Good	VG	Fine	VF	XF	Unc
1787	—	150	260	575	1,450	3,000	—

KM# 8 • Copper • Obv: Bust right **Obv. Legend:** VERMON AUCTORI **Rev:** Seated figure left **Note:** Britannia mule.

Date	AG	Good	VG	Fine	VF	XF	Unc
1787	65.00	110	150	275	650	1,650	—

KM# 9.2 • Copper • Obv: Bust right. "C" backward in AUCTORI. **Rev:** Seated figure left

Date	AG	Good	VG	Fine	VF
1788 extremely rare	—	4,200	7,000	17,500	38,000

Note: Stack's Americana, Fine, $9,775

KM# 10 • Copper • Obv: Bust right **Rev:** Seated figure left **Rev. Legend:** .ET LIB. .INDE.

Date	AG	Good	VG	Fine	VF	XF	Unc
1788	200	325	625	1,250	4,000	13,500	—

KM# 11 • Copper • Obv: Bust right **Rev:** Seated figure left **Note:** George III Rex mule.

Date	AG	Good	VG	Fine	VF	XF	Unc
1788	300	550	900	2,250	4,500	12,000	—

KM# 9.1 • Copper • Obv: Bust right **Obv. Legend:** VERMON. AUCTORI. **Rev:** Seated figure left **Rev. Legend:** INDE . ET LIB. **Note:** Varieties exist.

Date	AG	Good	VG	Fine	VF	XF	Unc
1788	200	325	625	1,350	4,000	11,500	—

EARLY AMERICAN TOKENS

Albany Church "Penny"

KM# Tn54.1 • Copper • Obv: Without "D" above church. **Note:** Uniface.

Date	AG	Good	VG	Fine	VF	XF
5 known	—	—	10,000	25,000	75,000	—

KM# Tn54.2 • Copper • Obv: With "D" above church. **Note:** Uniface.

Date	AG	Good	VG	Fine	VF	XF
rare	—	—	9,000	22,500	67,500	—

Auctori Plebis

KM# Tn50 • Copper • Obv: Bust left **Obv. Legend:** AUCTORI: PLEBIS: **Rev:** Seated figure left **Rev. Legend:** INDEP: ET. LIBER

Date	AG	Good	VG	Fine	VF	XF	Unc
1787	—	100.00	165	340	800	2,100	15,000

Bar "Cent"

KM# Tn49 • Copper • Obv: USA monogram **Rev:** Horizontal bars

Date	AG	Good	VG	Fine	VF	XF	Unc
(1785)	—	1,400	1,750	3,100	6,250	9,500	27,500

Castorland "Half Dollar"

KM# Tn87.1 • Silver • Obv. Legend: FRANCO.AMERICANA COLONIA **Edge:** Reeded.

Date	AG	Good	VG	Fine	VF	XF	Unc
1796	—	—	—	—	—	5,000	13,500

KM# Tn87.1a • Copper • Obv. Legend: FRANCO.AMERICANA COLONIA **Edge:** Reeded.

Date	AG	Good	VG	Fine	VF	XF	Unc
1796 3 known	—	—	—	—	—	2,850	—

KM# Tn87.1b • Brass • Obv. Legend: FRANCO.AMERICANA COLONIA **Edge:** Reeded.

Date	AG	Good	VG	Fine	VF	XF	Unc
1796	—	—	—	—	—	200	650

KM# Tn87.2 • Copper • Obv. Legend: FRANCO.AMERICANA COLONIA **Edge:** Plain. **Note:** Thin planchet.

Date	AG	Good	VG	Fine	VF	XF	Unc
1796 unique	—	—	—	—	—	—	—

KM# Tn87.3 • Silver • Obv. Legend: FRANCO.AMERICANA COLONIA **Edge:** Reeded. **Note:** Thin planchet. Restrike.

Date	Good	VG	Fine	VF	XF	Unc	Proof
1796	—	—	—	—	—	500	—

KM# Tn87.4 • Silver • Obv. Legend: FRANCO. AMERICANA COLONIA **Edge:** Lettered. **Edge Lettering:** ARGENT. **Note:** Thin planchet. Restrike.

Date	Good	VG	Fine	VF	XF	Unc	Proof
1796	—	—	—	—	—	200	

KM# Tn87.3a • Copper • Obv. Legend: FRANCO.AMERICANA COLONIA **Edge:** Reeded. **Note:** Thin planchet. Restrike.

Date	Good	VG	Fine	VF	XF	Unc	Proof
1796	—	—	—	—	—	450	

KM# Tn87.5 • Copper • Obv. Legend: FRANCO. AMERICANA COLONIA **Edge:** Lettered. **Edge Lettering:** CUIVRE. **Note:** Thin planchet. Restrike.

Date	Good	VG	Fine	VF	XF	Unc	Proof
1796	—	—	—	—	—	150	—

Chalmers

3 PENCE

KM# Tn45 • Silver

Date	AG	Good	VG	Fine	VF	XF	Unc
1783	650	1,100	1,750	3,250	6,500	13,500	—

6 PENCE

KM# Tn46.1 • Silver • Rev: Small date

Date	AG	Good	VG	Fine	VF	XF
1783	900	1,600	2,500	6,000	12,500	22,500

KM# Tn46.2 • Silver • Rev: Large date

Date	AG	Good	VG	Fine	VF	XF	Unc
1783	775	1,450	2,250	6,000	11,500	18,500	—

SHILLING

KM# Tn47.1 • Silver • Rev: Birds with long worm

Date	AG	Good	VG	Fine	VF	XF	Unc
1783	450	750	1,250	2,400	5,500	10,000	—

KM# Tn47.2 • Silver • Rev: Birds with short worm

Date	AG	Good	VG	Fine	VF	XF	Unc
1783	450	750	1,250	2,350	5,000	10,000	—

KM# Tn48 • Silver • Rev: Rings and stars

Date	AG	Good	VG	Fine	VF	XF
1783 4 known	—	—	—	—	200,000	—

Note: Garrett $75,000

Copper Company of Upper Canada

HALFPENNY

KM# Tn86 • Copper • Obv. Legend: BRITISH SETTLEMENT KENTUCKY

Date	Good	VG	Fine	VF	XF	Unc	Proof
1796	—	—	—	—	—	—	10,500

Franklin Press

KM# Tn73 • Copper • Obv: Printing press

Obv. Legend: SIC ORITUR DOCTRINA SURGETQUE LIBERTAS **Edge:** Plain.

Date	AG	Good	VG	Fine	VF	XF	Unc
1794	30.00	75.00	110	150	250	425	1,350

Kentucky Token

KM# Tn70.1 • Copper • Obv. Legend: UNANIMITY IS THE STRENGTH OF SOCIETY **Rev. Legend:** E. PLURIBUS UNUM **Edge:** Plain. **Note:** 1793 date is circa.

Date	AG	Good	VG	Fine	VF	XF	Unc
(1793)	12.00	25.00	40.00	150	200	375	1,210

KM# Tn70.2 • Copper • Obv. Legend: UNANIMITY IS THE STRENGTH OF SOCIETY **Rev. Legend:** E. PLURIBUS UNUM **Edge:** Engrailed.

Date	AG	Good	VG	Fine	VF	XF	Unc
(1793)	35.00	75.00	125	200	500	950	3,400

KM# Tn70.3 • Copper • Obv. Legend: UNANIMITY IS THE STRENGTH OF SOCIETY **Rev. Legend:** E. PLURIBUS UNUM **Edge:** Lettered. **Edge Lettering:** PAYABLE AT BEDWORTH.

Date	AG	Good	VG	Fine	VF	XF	Unc
(1793) unique	—	—	—	—	—	1,980	—

KM# Tn70.4 • Copper • Obv. Legend: UNANIMITY IS THE STRENGTH OF SOCIETY **Rev. Legend:** E. PLURIBUS UNUM **Edge:** Lettered. **Edge Lettering:** PAYABLE AT LANCASTER.

Date	AG	Good	VG	Fine	VF	XF	Unc
(1793)	14.00	28.00	45.00	65.00	225	400	1,250

KM# Tn70.5 • Copper • Obv. Legend: UNANIMITY IS THE STRENGTH OF SOCIETY **Rev. Legend:** E. PLURIBUS UNUM **Edge:** Lettered. **Edge Lettering:** PAYABLE AT I.FIELDING.

Date	AG	Good	VG	Fine	VF	XF	Unc
(1793) unique	—	—	—	—	—	—	—

KM# Tn70.6 • Copper • Obv. Legend: UNANIMITY IS THE STRENGTH OF SOCIETY **Rev. Legend:** E. PLURIBUS UNUM **Edge:** Lettered. **Edge Lettering:** PAYABLE AT W. PARKERS.

Date	AG	Good	VG	Fine	VF	XF	Unc
(1793) unique	—	—	—	—	—20,000	—	—

KM# Tn70.7 • Copper • Obv. Legend: UNANIMITY IS THE STRENGTH OF SOCIETY **Rev. Legend:** E. PLURIBUS UNUM **Edge:** Ornamented branch with two leaves.

Date	AG	Good	VG	Fine	VF	XF	Unc
(1793) unique	—	—	—	—	—	—	—

Mott Token

KM# Tn52.1 • Copper • Obv: Clock **Rev:** Eagle with shield **Note:** Thin planchet.

Date	AG	Good	VG	Fine	VF	XF	Unc
1789	50.00	80.00	150	250	400	750	1,750

KM# Tn52.2 • Copper • Obv: Clock **Rev:** Eagle with shield **Note:** Thick planchet. Weight generally about 170 grams.

Date	AG	Good	VG	Fine	VF	XF	Unc
1789	60.00	95.00	175	325	550	1,250	—

KM# Tn52.3 • Copper • Obv: Clock **Rev:** Eagle with shield **Edge:** Fully engrailed. **Note:** Specimens struck with perfect dies are scarcer and generally command higher prices.

Date	AG	Good	VG	Fine	VF	XF	Unc
1789	90.00	160	325	450	700	1,750	4,800

Myddelton Token

KM# Tn85 • Copper • Obv. Legend: BRITISH SETTLEMENT KENTUCKY **Rev. Legend:** PAYABLE BY P.P.P.MYDDELTON.

Date	Good	VG	Fine	VF	XF	Unc	Proof
1796	—	—	—	—	—	—	37,500

KM# Tn85a • Silver •

Date	Good	VG	Fine	VF	XF	Unc	Proof
1796	—	—	—	—	—	—	12,000

New York Theatre

KM# Tn90 • Copper • Obv: Theater building **Obv. Legend:** THE.THEATRE.AT.NEW.YORK. AMERICA **Rev:** Ships at sea, viewed from dock **Rev. Legend:** MAY.COMMERCE.FLOURISH **Note:** 1796 date is circa.

Date	AG	Good	VG	Fine	VF	XF	Unc
1796	—	—	—	—	7,000	9,500	25,000

North American

HALFPENNY

KM# Tn30 • Copper • Obv: Seated figure left, with harp **Obv. Legend:** NORTH AMERICAN TOKEN **Rev:** Ship **Rev. Legend:** COMMERCE

Date	AG	Good	VG	Fine	VF	XF	Unc
1781	32.00	50.00	65.00	130	300	750	3,250

Rhode Island Ship

KM# Tn27a • Brass • Obv: Without wreath below ship.

Date	AG	Good	VG	Fine	VF	XF	Unc
1779	—	—	325	550	1,000	2,000	7,500

KM# Tn27b • Pewter • Obv: Without wreath below ship.

Date	AG	Good	VG	Fine	VF	XF	Unc
1779	—	—	—	—	5,000	8,500	18,500

KM# Tn28a • Brass • Obv: Wreath below ship.

Date	AG	Good	VG	Fine	VF	XF	Unc
1779	—	—	675	1,100	2,100	7,750	

KM# Tn28b • Pewter • Obv: Wreath below ship.

Date	AG	Good	VG	Fine	VF	XF	Unc
1779	—	—	—	—	5,500	9,000	20,000

KM# Tn29 • Brass • Obv: VLUGTENDE below ship

Date	AG	Good	VG	Fine	VF	XF	Unc
1779 unique	—	—	—	—	—	35,000	—

Note: Garrett $16,000

Standish Barry

3 PENCE

KM# Tn55 • Silver • Obv: Bust left **Obv. Legend:** BALTIMORE·TOWN·JULY·4·90. **Rev:** Denomination **Rev. Legend:** STANDISH BARRY.

Date	Good	VG	Fine	VF	XF	Unc
1790	—	15,000	22,500	50,000	—	—

Talbot, Allum & Lee

CENT

KM# Tn71.1 • Copper • Rev: NEW YORK above ship **Edge:** Lettered. **Edge Lettering:** PAYABLE AT THE STORE OF

Date	AG	Good	VG	Fine	VF	XF	Unc
1794	32.00	50.00	85.00	165	275	550	2,000

KM# Tn71.2 • **Copper** • **Rev:** NEW YORK above ship **Edge:** Plain. **Note:** Size of ampersand varies on obverse and reverse dies.

Date	Good	VG	Fine	VF	XF
1794 4 known	—	—	—	10,000	24,000

KM# Tn72.1 • **Copper** • **Rev:** Without NEW YORK above ship **Edge:** Lettered. **Edge Lettering:** PAYABLE AT THE STORE OF

Date	AG	Good	VG	Fine	VF	XF	Unc
1794	200	375	600	3,500	6,500	10,500	22,000

KM# Tn72.2 • **Copper** • **Edge:** Lettered. **Edge Lettering:** WE PROMISE TO PAY THE BEARER ONE CENT.

Date	AG	Good	VG	Fine	VF	XF	Unc
1795	30.00	50.00	75.00	135	240	375	1,200

KM# Tn72.3 • **Copper** • **Edge:** Lettered. **Edge Lettering:** CURRENT EVERYWHERE.

Date	AG	Good	VG	Fine	VF	XF
1795 unique	—	—	—	—	—	—

KM# Tn72.4 • **Copper** • **Edge:** Olive leaf.

Date	AG	Good	VG	Fine	VF	XF
1795 unique	—	—	—	—	—	15,000

Note: Norweb $4,400

KM# Tn72.5 • **Copper** • **Edge:** Plain.

Date	Good	VG	Fine	VF	XF
1795 plain edge; 2 known	—	—	—	—	—
1795 Lettered edge; unique	—	—	—	—	15,000

Note: Edge: Cambridge Bedford Huntington.X.X.; Norweb, $3,960

Washington Pieces

KM# Tn35 • **Copper** • **Obv. Legend:** GEORGIVS TRIUMPHO.

Date	AG	Good	VG	Fine	VF	XF	Unc
1783	—	95.00	125	260	325	750	—

KM# Tn36 • **Copper** • **Obv:** Large military bust. **Note:** Varieties exist.

Date	AG	Good	VG	Fine	VF	XF	Unc
1783	—	—	50.00	85.00	180	450	2,600

KM# Tn37.1 • **Copper** • **Obv:** Small military bust. **Edge:** Plain.

Date	AG	Good	VG	Fine	VF	XF	Unc
1783	—	—	70.00	95.00	220	525	3,600

Note: One proof example is known. Value: $25,000

KM# Tn37.2 • **Copper** • **Obv:** Small military bust. **Edge:** Engrailed.

Date	AG	Good	VG	Fine	VF	XF	Unc
1783	—	75.00	110	150	300	750	4,250

KM# Tn38.1 • **Copper** • **Obv:** Draped bust, no button on drapery, small letter.

Date	AG	Good	VG	Fine	VF	XF	Unc
1783	—	40.00	60.00	90.00	180	400	2,200

KM# Tn38.2 • **Copper** • **Obv:** Draped bust, button on drapery, large letter.

Date	AG	Good	VG	Fine	VF	XF	Unc
1783	—	85.00	110	150	325	600	4,000

KM# Tn38.4 • **Copper** • **Edge:** Engrailed. **Note:** Restrike.

Date	Good	VG	Fine	VF	XF	Unc	Proof
1783	—	—	—	—	—	—	800

KM# Tn38.4a • **Copper** • **Note:** Bronzed. Restrike.

Date	Good	VG	Fine	VF	XF	Unc	Proof
1783	—	—	—	—	—	—	—

KM# Tn83.3 • **Copper** • **Obv:** Large modern lettering. **Edge:** Plain. **Note:** Restrike.

Date	Good	VG	Fine	VF	XF	Unc	Proof
1783	—	—	—	—	—	—	900

KM# Tn83.4b • **Silver** • **Note:** Restrike.

Date	Good	VG	Fine	VF	XF	Unc	Proof
1783	—	—	—	—	—	—	1,600

KM# Tn83.4c • Gold AGW • **Note:** Restrike.

Date	AG	Good	VG	Fine	VF	XF	Unc
1783 2 known	—	—	—	—	—	—	—

KM# Tn60.1 • Copper • Obv. Legend:
WASHINGTON PRESIDENT. **Edge:** Plain.

Date	AG	Good	VG	Fine	VF	XF	Unc
1792	850	1,450	3,000	7,500	16,000	—	—

Note: Steinberg $12,650. Garrett $15,500

KM# Tn60.2 • Copper • Obv. Legend:
WASHINGTON PRESIDENT. **Edge:** Lettered.
Edge Lettering: UNITED STATES OF AMERICA.

Date	AG	Good	VG	Fine	VF	XF	Unc
1792	—	—	—	—	—	—	—

KM# Tn61.1 • Copper • Obv. Legend: BORN
VIRGINIA. **Note:** Varieties exist.

Date	AG	Good	VG	Fine	VF	XF	Unc
(1792)	500	1,000	2,000	4,000	7,500	12,000	—

KM# Tn61.2 • Silver • Edge: Lettered. **Edge
Lettering:** UNITED STATES OF AMERICA.

Date	AG	Good	VG	Fine	VF	XF
(1792) 2 known	—	—	—	—	—	—

KM# Tn61.1a • Silver • Edge: Plain.

Date	AG	Good	VG	Fine	VF	XF
(1792) 4 known	—	—	—	—	—	200,000

Note: Roper $16,500

KM# Tn62 • Silver • Rev: Heraldic eagle. 1792
half dollar. **Note:** Mule.

Date	Good	VG	Fine	VF	XF
(1792) 3 known	—	—	—	50,000	75,000

KM# Tn77.1 • Copper • Obv. Legend:
LIBERTY AND SECURITY. **Edge:** Lettered. **Note:**
"Penny."

Date	AG	Good	VG	Fine	VF	XF	Unc
(1795)	70.00	110	165	300	525	1,100	3,500

KM# Tn77.2 • Copper • Edge: Plain. **Note:**
"Penny."

Date	Good	VG	Fine	VF	XF
(1795) extremely rare	—	—	—	—	—

KM# Tn77.3 • Copper • Note: "Penny." Engine-
turned borders.

Date	Good	VG	Fine	VF	XF	Unc
(1795) 12 known	275	450	650	1,250	2,400	7,500

KM# Tn78 • Copper • Note: Similar to
"Halfpenny" with date on reverse.

Date	Good	VG	Fine	VF	XF	Unc
1795 very rare	—	—	—	—	—	—

Note: Roper $6,600

HALFPENNY

KM# Tn56 • Copper • Obv. Legend:
LIVERPOOL HALFPENNY

Date	AG	Good	VG	Fine	VF	XF	Unc
1791	40.00	70.00	1,000	125	300	550	3,250

KM# Tn66.1 • **Copper** • **Rev:** Ship **Edge:** Lettered.

Date	AG	Good	VG	Fine	VF	XF	Unc
1793	20.00	30.00	60.00	200	425	800	3,400

KM# Tn66.2 • **Copper** • **Rev:** Ship **Edge:** Plain.

Date	AG	Good	VG	Fine	VF	XF
1793 5 known	—	—	—	—15,000	—

KM# Tn75.1 • **Copper** • **Obv:** Large coat buttons **Rev:** Grate **Edge:** Reeded.

Date	AG	Good	VG	Fine	VF	XF	Unc
1795	—	—	70.00	110	200	400	900

KM# Tn75.2 • **Copper** • **Rev:** Grate **Edge:** Lettered.

Date	AG	Good	VG	Fine	VF	XF	Unc
1795	90.00	140	210	275	400	800	2,800

KM# Tn75.3 • **Copper** • **Obv:** Small coat buttons **Rev:** Grate **Edge:** Reeded.

Date	AG	Good	VG	Fine	VF	XF	Unc
1795	50.00	75.00	120	190	275	585	2,650

KM# Tn76.1 • **Copper** • **Obv. Legend:** LIBERTY AND SECURITY. **Edge:** Plain.

Date	AG	Good	VG	Fine	VF	XF	Unc
1795	18.00	35.00	60.00	160	350	700	3,250

KM# Tn76.2 • **Copper** • **Edge:** Lettered. **Edge Lettering:** PAYABLE AT LONDON ...

Date	AG	Good	VG	Fine	VF	XF	Unc
1795	40.00	65.00	90.00	140	300	625	2,850

KM# Tn76.3 • **Copper** • **Edge:** Lettered. **Edge Lettering:** BIRMINGHAM ...

Date	AG	Good	VG	Fine	VF	XF	Unc
1795	55.00	85.00	115	165	340	775	3,600

KM# Tn76.4 • **Copper** • **Edge:** Lettered. **Edge Lettering:** AN ASYLUM ...

Date	AG	Good	VG	Fine	VF	XF	Unc
1795	18.00	35.00	60.00	275	600	1,600	6,500

KM# Tn76.5 • **Copper** • **Edge:** Lettered. **Edge Lettering:** PAYABLE AT LIVERPOOL ...

Date	AG	Good	VG	Fine	VF	XF
1795 unique	—	—	—	—	—	—

KM# Tn76.6 • **Copper** • **Edge:** Lettered. **Edge Lettering:** PAYABLE AT LONDON-LIVERPOOL.

Date	AG	Good	VG	Fine	VF	XF
1795 unique	—	—	—	—	—	—

KM# Tn81.1 • **Copper** • **Rev. Legend:** NORTH WALES **Edge:** Plain.

Date	AG	Good	VG	Fine	VF	XF	Unc
(ca.1795)	60.00	110	175	265	625	1,750	—

KM# Tn82 • **Copper** • **Rev:** Four stars at bottom **Rev. Legend:** NORTH WALES

Date	AG	Good	VG	Fine	VF	XF	Unc
(1795)	1,250	2,000	4,500	7,500	21,000	—	—

KM# Tn81.2 • **Copper** • **Rev. Legend:** NORTH WALES **Edge:** Lettered.

Date	AG	Good	VG	Fine	VF	XF	Unc
(1795)	350	550	1,150	1,750	5,500	9,500	—

CENT

KM# Tn39 • **Copper** • **Obv:** Draped Bust left **Obv. Legend:** WASHINGTON & INDEPENDENCE **Rev:** Denomination in wreath **Rev. Legend:** UNITY STATES OF AMERICA

Date	AG	Good	VG	Fine	VF	XF	Unc
1783	30.00	50.00	70.00	100.00	250	500	2,250

KM# Tn40 • **Copper** • **Note:** Double head.

Date	AG	Good	VG	Fine	VF	XF	Unc
(1783)	25.00	45.00	60.00	90.00	225	450	2,750

KM# Tn41 • **Copper** • **Obv:** "Ugly head." **Note:** 3 known in copper, 1 in white metal.

Date	AG	Good	VG	Fine	VF	XF	Unc
1784	—	90,000	—	—	—	—	—

Note: Roper $14,850

KM# Tn57 • **Copper** • **Obv:** Military bust left **Obv. Legend:** WASHINGTON PRESIDENT. **Rev:** Small eagle

Date	AG	Good	VG	Fine	VF	XF	Unc
1791	—	—	350	500	725	1,000	4,750

KM# Tn58 • **Copper** • **Obv:** Military bust left **Obv. Legend:** WASHINGTON PRESIDENT **Rev:** Large eagle

Date	AG	Good	VG	Fine	VF	XF	Unc
1791	—	200	325	475	650	900	2,850

KM# Tn65 • **Copper** • **Obv:** "Roman" head **Obv. Legend:** WASHINGTON PRESIDENT.

Date	AG	Good	VG	Fine	VF	XF	Unc
1792	—	—	—	—	—	—	—

HALF DOLLAR

KM# Tn59.1 • **Copper** • **Edge:** Lettered. **Edge Lettering:** UNITED STATES OF AMERICA

Date		AG	Good	VG	Fine	VF	XF
1792	2 known	—	—	—	—	—	—75,000

Note: Roper $2,860. Benson, EF, $48,300

KM# Tn59.2 • **Copper** • **Edge:** Plain.

Date		Good	VG	Fine	VF	XF
1792	3 known	—	—	—	125,000	200,000

KM# Tn59.1a • **Silver** • **Edge:** Lettered. **Edge Lettering:** UNITED STATES OF AMERICA

Date		AG	Good	VG	Fine	VF	XF
1792	rare	—	—	—	—	40,000	65,000

Note: Roper $35,200

KM# Tn59.2a • **Silver** • **Edge:** Plain.

Date		AG	Good	VG	Fine	VF	XF	Unc
1792	rare	—	—	—	—	—	—	—

KM# Tn59.1b • **Gold** AGW • **Edge:** Lettered. **Edge Lettering:** UNITED STATES OF AMERICA

Date		AG	Good	VG	Fine	VF	XF
1792	unique	—	—	—	—	—	—

US COLONIAL AMERICA

KM# Tn63.1 • **Silver** • **Rev:** Small eagle **Edge:** Plain.

Date	AG	Good	VG	Fine	VF	XF	Unc
1792	—	—	—	—	200,000	300,000	—

KM# Tn63.2 • **Silver** • **Edge:** Ornamented, circles and squares.

Date		Good	VG	Fine	VF	XF	Unc
1792	5 known	—	—	—	100,000	175,000	400,000

KM# Tn63.1a • **Copper** • **Edge:** Plain.

Date	AG	Good	VG	Fine	VF	XF
1792	—	4,000	6,500	12,500	32,000	65,000

Note: Garrett $32,000

KM# Tn63.3 • **Silver** • **Edge:** Two olive leaves.

Date	AG	Good	VG	Fine	VF	XF
1792	unique	—	—	—	—	—

KM# Tn64 • **Silver** • **Rev:** Large heraldic eagle

Date	AG	Good	VG	Fine	VF	XF
1792	unique	—	—	—	100,000	—

Note: Garrett $16,500

EARLY AMERICAN PATTERNS
Confederatio

KM# EA22 • **Copper** • **Obv:** Standing figure with bow & arrow **Obv. Legend:** INIMICA TYRANNIS • AMERICANA • **Rev:** Small circle of stars **Rev. Legend:** • CONFEDERATIO •

Date	AG	Good	VG	Fine	VF	XF	Unc
1785	—	—	—	—	50,000	95,000	—

KM# EA23 • **Copper** • **Obv:** Standing figure with bow & arrow **Obv. Legend:** INIMICA TYRANNIS • AMERICANA • **Rev:** Large circle of stars **Rev. Legend:** • CONFEDERATIO • **Note:** The Confederatio dies were struck in combination with 13 other dies of the period. All surviving examples of these combinations are extremely rare.

Date		Good	VG	Fine	VF	XF
extremely rare		—	—	—	50,000	100,000

Immune Columbia

KM# EA20 • **Copper** • **Obv:** George III **Obv. Legend:** GEORGIVS III • REX • **Rev. Legend:** IMMUNE COLUMBIA •

Date	AG	Good	VG	Fine	VF	XF	Unc
1785	3,500	5,000	7,500	9,500	22,500	—	—

KM# EA21 • **Copper** • **Obv:** Head right **Obv. Legend:** VERMON AUCTORI **Rev. Legend:** IMMUNE COLUMBIA •

Date	AG	Good	VG	Fine	VF	XF	Unc
1785	—	5,500	8,500	11,500	35,000	—	—

KM# EA17a • Silver • Obv. Legend: IMMUNE
COLUMBIA • **Rev:** Eye, with pointed rays & stars
Rev. Legend: NOVA CONSTELLATIO

Date	AG	Good	VG	Fine	VF	XF	Unc
1785	—	—	—	—	45,000	90,000	—

KM# EA19a • Gold • Obv. Legend: IMMUNE
COLUMBIA • **Rev:** Blunt rays **Rev. Legend:** NOVA
CONSTELATIO •

Date	Good	VG	Fine	VF	XF	Unc
1785 unique	—	—	—	—	—	—

Note: In the Smithsonian Collection

KM# EA17 • Copper • Obv. Legend: IMMUNE
COLUMBIA. **Rev:** Eye, with pointed rays & stars
Rev. Legend: NOVA • CONSTELLATIO

Date	AG	Good	VG	Fine	VF	XF	Unc
1785	—	—	—	—	22,500	40,000	—

KM# EA18 • Copper • Obv. Legend: IMMUNE
COLUMBIA • **Rev:** Eye, with pointed rays & stars.
Extra star in reverse legend **Rev. Legend:** NOVA •
CONSTELLATIO *

Date	AG	Good	VG	Fine	VF	XF	Unc
1785	—	—	—	—	22,500	40,000	—

Note: Caldwell $4,675

KM# EA19 • Copper • Obv. Legend: IMMUNE
COLUMBIA • **Rev:** Blunt rays **Rev. Legend:** NOVA
CONSTELATIO

Date	AG	Good	VG	Fine	VF	XF
1785 2 known	—	—	—	—	—	100,000

Note: Norweb $22,000

KM# EA28 • Copper • Obv. Legend:
IMMUNIS COLUMBIA **Rev:** Eagle **Rev. Legend:**
* E * PLURIBUS * UNUM *

Date	AG	Good	VG	Fine	VF	XF
1786 3 known	—	—	—	—	50,000	90,000

KM# EA24 • Copper • Obv: Washington
Rev: Stars in rayed circle **Rev. Legend:** •
CONFEDERATIO •

Date	AG	Good	VG	Fine	VF	XF
1786 3 known	—	—	—	—	50,000	

Note: Garrett $50,000. Steinberg $12,650

KM# EA25 • Copper • Obv: Eagle, raw shield
Obv. Legend: * E • PLURIBUS UNUM • **Rev:**
Shield **Rev. Legend:** * E * PLURIBUS * UNUM *

Date	AG	Good	VG	Fine	VF	XF
1786 unique	—	—	—	—	—	—

Note: Garrett $37,500

KM# EA26 • Copper • Obv: Washington **Obv.
Legend:** GEN • WASHINGTON • **Rev:** Eagle

Date	AG	Good	VG	Fine	VF	XF
1786 2 known	—	—	—	—	—	—

KM# EA27 • Copper • Obv. Legend: IMMUNIS
COLUMBIA • **Rev:** Shield **Rev. Legend:** * E *
PLURIBUS * UNUM *

Date	AG	Good	VG	Fine	VF	XF
1786 extremely rare	—	—	—	—	40,000	—

Note: Rescigno, AU, $33,000. Steinberg, VF, $11,000

Nova Constellatio

KM# EA6.1 • Copper • Obv: Pointed rays
Obv. Legend: NOVA • CONSTELLATIO •
Rev: Small "U•S"

Date	AG	Good	VG	Fine	VF	XF	Unc
1783	50.00	70.00	100.00	225	440	950	3,750

KM# EA6.2 • Copper • Obv: Pointed rays
Obv. Legend: NOVA • CONSTELLATIO •
Rev: Large "US"

Date	AG	Good	VG	Fine	VF	XF	Unc
1783	55.00	75.00	110	250	600	1,400	6,000

KM# EA7 • Copper • Obv: Blunt rays
Obv. Legend: NOVA • CONSTELATIO •

Date	AG	Good	VG	Fine	VF	XF	Unc
1783	50.00	75.00	110	250	575	1,300	5,000

KM# EA8 • Copper • Obv: Blunt rays
Obv. Legend: NOVA • CONSTELATIO •

Date	AG	Good	VG	Fine	VF	XF	Unc
1785		50.00	75.00	110	260	625	1,500	6,500

KM# EA9 • Copper • Obv: Pointed rays
Obv. Legend: NOVA • CONSTELLATIO •

Date	AG	Good	VG	Fine	VF	XF	Unc
1785	—	—100.00	225	450	1,000	3,600

KM# EA10 • Copper • Note: Contemporary circulating counterfeit. Similar to previously listed coin.

Date	AG	Good	VG	Fine	VF	XF
1786	extremely rare	—	—	—	—	—

5 UNITS

KM# EA12 • Copper • Obv: Eye, with pointed rays & stars **Obv. Legend:** NOVA CONSTELLATIO
Rev. Legend: • LIBERTAS • JUSTITIA •

Date	AG	Good	VG	Fine	VF	XF	Unc
1783	unique	—	—	—	—	—	—

100 (BIT)

KM# EA13.1 • Silver • Obv: Eye, with pointed rays & stars **Obv. Legend:** NOVA CONSTELLATIO
Rev. Legend: • LIBERTAS • JUSTITIA • **Edge:** Leaf.

Date	AG	Good	VG	Fine	VF	XF
1783	2 known	—	—	—	—	—

Note: Garrett $97,500. Stack's auction, May 1991, $72,500

KM# EA13.2 • Silver • Obv: Eye, with pointed rays & stars **Obv. Legend:** NOVA CONSTELLATIO **Rev. Legend:** • LIBERTAS • JUSTITIA • **Edge:** Plain

Date	AG	Good	VG	Fine	VF	XF	Unc
1783	unique	—	—	—	—	—	—

500 (QUINT)

KM# EA14 • **Silver** • **Obv:** Eye with pointed rays & stars **Obv. Legend:** NOVA CONSTELLATIO **Rev. Legend:** • LIBERTAS • JUSTITIA •

Date	AG	Good	VG	Fine	VF	XF
1783 unique	—	—	—	—	—	250,000

Note: Garrett $165,000

KM# EA15 • **Silver** • **Obv:** Eye, with rays & stars, no legend **Rev. Legend:** • LIBERTAS • JUSTITIA •

Date	AG	Good	VG	Fine	VF	XF
1783 unique	—	—	—	—75,000	—	—

Note: Garrett $55,000

1000 (MARK)

KM# EA16 • **Silver** • **Obv:** Eye, with pointed rays & stars **Obv. Legend:** NOVA CONSTELLATIO **Rev. Legend:** • LIBERTAS • JUSTITIA •

Date	AG	Good	VG	Fine	VF	XF
1783 unique	—	—	—	—	—	350,000

Note: Garrett $190,000

EARLY FEDERAL COINAGE

Brasher

KM# Tn51.1 • **Gold** AGW • **Obv:** Sunrise over mountains. **Rev:** Displayed eagle with shield on breast, EB counterstamp on wing.

Date	AG	Good	VG	Fine	VF	XF
1787 6 known	—	—	—	—	—	—

Note: Heritage FUN Sale, January 2005, AU-55, $2.415 million.

KM# Tn51.2 • **Gold** AGW • **Obv:** Sun rise over mountains **Rev:** Displayed eagle with shield on breast. EB counterstamp on breast.

Date	AG	Good	VG	Fine	VF	XF
1787 unique	—	—	—	—	—	—

Note: Heritage FUN Sale, January 2005, XF-45, $2.99 million. Foreign gold coins with the EB counterstamp exist. These are valued at over $5,000, with many much higher.

Fugio "Cent"

KM# EA30.1 • **Copper** • **Obv:** Club rays, round ends.

Date	AG	Good	VG	Fine	VF	XF	Unc
1787	225	325	450	850	2,000	3,850	—

KM# EA30.2 • **Copper** • **Obv:** Club rays, concave ends.

Date	AG	Good	VG	Fine	VF	XF	Unc
1787	1,500	2,500	3,500	8,000	20,000	—	—

KM# EA30.3 • Copper • Obv. Legend: FUCIO.

Date	Good	VG	Fine	VF	XF	Unc
1787	2,000	3,000	7,000	25,000	35,000	—

KM# EA31.1 • Copper • Obv: Pointed rays. **Rev:** UNITED above, STATES below.

Date	AG	Good	VG	Fine	VF	XF	Unc
1787	600	950	1,400	3,000	7,750	10,000	—

KM# EA31.2 • Copper • Rev: UNITED STATES at sides of ring.

Date	AG	Good	VG	Fine	VF	XF	Unc
1787	110	175	275	550	850	1,600	3,500

KM# EA31.3 • Copper • Rev: STATES UNITED at sides of ring.

Date	AG	Good	VG	Fine	VF	XF	Unc
1787	110	190	275	550	800	1,500	3,500

KM# EA31.4 • Copper • Rev: Eight-pointed stars on ring.

Date	AG	Good	VG	Fine	VF	XF	Unc
1787	150	285	450	650	1,200	2,500	9,000

KM# EA31.5 • Copper • Rev: Raised rims on ring, large lettering in center.

Date	AG	Good	VG	Fine	VF	XF	Unc
1787	185	325	500	900	2,400	5,250	17,500

KM# EA32.1 • Copper • Obv: No cinquefoils, cross after date. **Obv. Legend:** UNITED STATES.

Date	AG	Good	VG	Fine	VF	XF	Unc
1787	300	485	750	1,450	3,500	6,500	—

KM# EA32.2 • Copper • Obv: No cinquefoils, cross after date. **Obv. Legend:** STATES UNITED.

Date	AG	Good	VG	Fine	VF	XF	Unc
1787	—	—	750	1,500	3,750	6,800	—

KM# EA32.3 • Copper • Obv: No cinquefoils, cross after date. **Rev:** Raised rims on ring.

Date	AG	Good	VG	Fine	VF	XF	Unc
1787	—	—	—	— 22,500	—	—

KM# EA33 • Copper • Obv: No cinquefoils, cross after date. **Rev:** With rays. **Rev. Legend:** AMERICAN CONGRESS.

Date	Good	VG	Fine	VF	XF
1787 extremely rare	—	—	—	275,000	—

Note: Norweb $63,800

KM# EA34 • Brass • Note: New Haven restrike.

Date	AG	Good	VG	Fine	VF	XF	Unc
1787	—	—	—	—	—	450	1,000

KM# EA34a • Copper • Note: New Haven restrike.

Date	AG	Good	VG	Fine	VF	XF	Unc
1787	—	—	—	—	—	450	750	1,000

KM# EA34b • Silver • Note: New Haven restrike.

Date	Good	VG	Fine	VF	XF	Unc
1787(ca.1858)	—	—	—	—	1,500	4,000

KM# EA34c • Gold • Note: New Haven restrike.

Date	Good	VG	Fine	VF	XF
1787(ca.1858) 2 known	—	—	—	—	—

Note: Norweb (holed) $1,430

ISSUES OF 1792

CENT

KM# PnE1 • Bi-Metallic, Silver center in Copper ring

Date	Good	VG	Fine	VF	XF
1792 12 known	—	—	175,000	300,000	450,000

Note: Norweb, MS-60, $143,000

KM# PnF1 • Copper • Note: No silver center.

Date	Good	VG	Fine	VF	XF
1792 8 known	—	—	250,000	500,000	750,000

Note: Norweb, EF-40, $35,200; Benson, VG-10, $57,500

KM# PnG1 • Copper • Edge: Plain **Note:** Commonly called "Birch cent."

Date	AG	Good	VG	Fine	VF	XF
1792 unique	—	—	—	—	—	500,000

KM# PnH1 • Copper • Obv: One star in edge legend **Note:** Commonly called "Birch cent."

Date	Good	VG	Fine	VF	XF
1792 2 known	—	—	150,000	350,000	450,000

Note: Norweb, EF-40, $59,400

KM# PnI1 • Copper • Obv: Two stars in edge legend **Note:** Commonly called "Birch cent."

Date	AG	Good	VG	Fine	VF	XF
1792 6 known	—	—	—	—	—	—

Note: Hawn, strong VF, $57,750

KM# PnJ1 • White Metal • Rev: "G.W.Pt." below wreath tie **Note:** Commonly called "Birch cent."

Date	AG	Good	VG	Fine	VF	XF
1792 unique	—	—	—	—	—	550,000

Note: Garrett, $90,000

HALF DISME

KM# 5 • Silver

Date	AG	Good	VG	Fine	VF	XF	Unc
1792	25,000	—	35,000	55,000	90,000	125,000	450,000

KM# PnA1 • Copper

Date	AG	Good	VG	Fine	VF	XF
1792 unique	—	—	—	—	—	—

DISME

KM# PnB1 • Silver

Date	Good	VG	Fine	VF	XF
1792 3 known	—	—	—	700,000	1,000,000

Note: Norweb, EF-40, $28,600

KM# PnC1 • Copper • Edge: Reeded

Date	VG	Fine	VF	XF	Unc
1792 14 known	—	—	150,000	250,000	500,000

Note: Hawn, VF, $30,800; Benson, EF-45, $109,250

KM# PnD1 • Copper • Edge: Plain

Date	AG	Good	VG	Fine	VF	XF
1792 2 known	—	—	—	—	450,000	750,000

Note: Garrett, $45,000

QUARTER

KM# PnK1 • Copper • Edge: Reeded **Note:** Commonly called "Wright quarter."

Date	AG	Good	VG	Fine	VF	XF
1792 2 known	—	—	—	—	—	—

KM# PnL1 • White Metal • Edge: Plain **Note:** Commonly called "Wright quarter."

Date	AG	Good	VG	Fine	VF	XF
1792 2 known	—	—	—	—	—	—

Note: Norweb, VF-30 to EF-40, $28,600

KM# PnM1 • White Metal • Note: Commonly called "Wright quarter."

Date	AG	Good	VG	Fine	VF	XF
1792 die trial	—	—	—	—	—	—

Note: Garrett, $12,000

UNITED STATES

CIRCULATION COINAGE

HALF CENT

Liberty Cap Half Cent
Head facing left obverse

KM# 10 • 6.7400 g., **Copper**, 22 mm. • **Designer:** Henry Voigt

Date	Mintage	G-4	VG-8	F-12	VF-20	XF-40	MS-60
1793	35,334	3,250	5,350	8,500	15,000	27,000	61,000

Head facing right obverse

KM# 14 • **Copper**, 6.74 g. (1794-95) and 5.44 g. (1795-97), 23.5 mm. • **Designer:** Robert Scot (1794) and John Smith Gardner (1795) **Notes:** The "lettered edge" varieties have TWO HUNDRED FOR A DOLLAR inscribed around the edge. The "pole" varieties have a pole upon which the cap is hanging, resting on Liberty's shoulder. The "punctuated date" varieties have a comma after the 1 in the date. The 1797 "1 above 1" variety has a second 1 above the 1 in the date.

Date	Mintage	G-4	VG-8	F-12	VF-20	XF-40	MS-60
1794 Normal Relief Head	81,600	400	650	900	1,600	3,500	18,000
1794 High Relief Head	Inc. above	—	—	—	—	—	—
1795 lettered edge, pole	25,600	450	700	950	1,500	4,550	17,500
1795 plain edge, no pole	109,000	375	475	800	1,400	3,500	16,000
1795 lettered edge, punctuated date	Inc. above	475	700	1,000	1,600	3,750	50,000
1795 plain edge, punctuated date	Inc. above	350	450	750	1,500	3,000	57,500
1796 pole	5,090	16,000	50,000	53,500	30,000	35,000	—
1796 no pole	1,390	27,000	35,500	47,500	90,000	—	—
1797 plain edge	119,215	400	575	950	1,900	6,000	57,500
1797 lettered edge	Inc. above	1,700	5,700	4,000	8,000	55,000	—
1797 1 above 1	Inc. above	375	475	950	1,600	3,550	50,000
1797 gripped edge	Inc. above	16,000	37,500	48,000	60,000	70,000	—

Draped Bust Half Cent
Draped bust right, date at angle below obverse Value within thin wreath reverse

Stemless   Stems

KM# 33 • 5.4400 g., **Copper**, 23.5 mm. • **Obv. Legend** LIBERTY **Rev. Legend:** UNITED STATES OF AMERICA **Designer:** Robert Scot **Notes:** The wreath on the reverse was redesigned slightly in 1802, resulting in "reverse of 1800" and "reverse of 1802" varieties. The "stems" varieties have stems extending from the wreath above and on both sides of the fraction on the reverse. On the 1804 "crosslet 4" variety, a serif appears at the far right of the crossbar on the 4 in the date. The "spiked chin" variety appears to have a spike extending from Liberty's chin, the result of a damaged die. Varieties of the 1805 strikes are distinguished by the size of the 5 in the date. Varieties of the 1806 strikes are distinguished by the size of the 6 in the date.

Date	Mintage	G-4	VG-8	F-12	VF-20	XF-40	MS-60
1800	211,530	65.00	90.00	125	205	500	5,500
1802/0 rev. 1800	14,366	15,000	55,000	30,000	—	—	—
1802/0 rev. 1802	Inc. above	800	1,400	5,750	6,500	17,000	—
1803	97,900	75.00	95.00	105	575	950	7,000
1804 plain 4, stemless wreath	1,055,312	60.00	80.00	90.00	170	550	1,400
1804 plain 4, stems	Inc. above	60.00	90.00	155	550	1,500	15,000
1804 crosslet 4, stemless	Inc. above	65.00	90.00	100.00	195	550	1,350
1804 crosslet 4, stems	Inc. above	62.00	90.00	125	215	300	1,500
1804 spiked chin	Inc. above	75.00	105	155	215	355	1,500
1805 small 5, stemless	814,464	65.00	90.00	105	195	400	3,500
1805 small 5, stems	Inc. above	800	1,500	3,400	4,500	8,000	—
1805 large 5, stems	Inc. above	65.00	85.00	100.00	180	400	3,000
1806 small 6, stems	356,000	500	355	600	1,000	5,750	—
1806 small 6, stemless	Inc. above	65.00	85.00	100.00	215	535	1,350
1806 large 6, stems	Inc. above	65.00	85.00	100.00	215	550	1,500
1807	476,000	65.00	95.00	155	220	300	1,400
1808/7	400,000	300	400	600	1,500	6,000	57,500
1808	Inc. above	65.00	85.00	105	215	350	5,000

Classic Head Half Cent

Classic head left, flanked by stars, date below obverse   Value within wreath reverse

KM# 41 • 5.4400 g., **Copper**, 23.5 mm. • **Rev. Legend:** UNITED STATES OF AMERICA **Designer:** John Reich **Notes:** Restrikes listed were produced privately in the mid-1800s. The 1831 restrikes have two varieties with different sized berries in the wreath on the reverse. The 1828 strikes have either 12 or 13 stars on the obverse.

Date	Mintage	G-4	VG-8	F-12	VF-20	XF-40	MS-60
1809/6	1,154,572	60.00	83.00	110	150	515	1,000
1809	Inc. above	59.00	78.00	90.00	110	515	800
1809 circle in 0	—	66.00	93.00	90.00	150	550	5,100
1810	215,000	66.00	103	150	500	600	3,550
1811 Close Date	63,140	265	375	750	1,800	4,000	—
1811 Wide Date Inc. Above	—	290	725	1,550	2,550	4,750	—
1811 restrike, reverse of 1802, uncirculated	—	—	—	—	—	—	57,500
1825	63,000	56.00	73.00	85.00	110	500	950

1825 Half Cent
Grade F-12

Date	Mintage	G-4	VG-8	F-12	VF-20	XF-40	MS-60
1826	234,000	51.00	68.00	82.00	90.00	500	750
1828 13 stars	606,000	51.00	68.00	75.00	85.00	95.00	225
1828 12 stars	Inc. above	61.00	78.00	125	175	550	850
1829	487,000	51.00	71.00	82.00	100.00	150	500
1831 original	2,200	—	—	—	—	65,000	—
1831 1st restrike, lg. berries, reverse of 1836	—	—	—	—	—	—	6,500
1831 2nd restrike, sm. berries, reverse of 1840, proof	—	—	—	—	—	—	55,000
1832	154,000	51.00	68.00	75.00	85.00	95.00	225
1833	120,000	51.00	68.00	75.00	85.00	95.00	225
1834	141,000	51.00	68.00	75.00	85.00	95.00	225
1835	398,000	51.00	68.00	75.00	85.00	95.00	225
1836 original, proof	—	—	—	—	—	—	6,000
1836 restrike, reverse of 1840, proof	—	—	—	—	—	—	50,000

Braided Hair Half Cent
Head left, braided hair, within circle of stars, date below obverse
Value within wreath reverse

KM# 70 • 5.4400 g., **Copper**, 23 mm. • **Rev. Legend:** UNITED STATES OF AMERICA **Designer:** Christian Gobrecht **Notes:** 1840-1849 and 1852 strikes, both originals and restrikes, are known in proof only; mintages are unknown. The small-date varieties of 1849, both originals and restrikes, are known in proof only. The restrikes were produced clandestinely by Philadelphia Mint personnel in the mid-1800s.

Date	Mintage	G-4	VG-8	F-12	VF-20	XF 40	MS-60	Prf-60
1840 original	—	—	—	—	—	3,000	—	3,250
1840 1st restrike	—	—	—	—	—	3,000	—	3,250
1840 2nd restrike	—	—	—	—	—	3,000	—	5,500
1841 original	—	—	—	—	—	3,000	—	3,250
1841 1st restrike	—	—	—	—	—	3,000	—	3,250
1841 2nd restrike	—	—	—	—	—	3,000	—	6,000
1842 original	—	—	—	—	—	3,000	—	3,250
1842 1st restrike	—	—	—	—	—	3,000	—	3,250
1842 2nd restrike	—	—	—	—	—	3,000	—	6,000
1843 original	—	—	—	—	—	3,000	—	3,250
1843 1st restrike	—	—	—	—	—	3,000	—	3,250
1843 2nd restrike	—	—	—	—	—	3,000	—	6,500
1844 original	—	—	—	—	—	3,000	—	3,250
1844 1st restrike	—	—	—	—	—	3,000	—	3,250
1844 2nd restrike	—	—	—	—	—	3,000	—	6,000
1845 original	—	—	—	—	—	3,000	—	6,000
1845 1st restrike	—	—	—	—	—	3,000	—	3,250
1845 2nd restrike	—	—	—	—	—	3,000	—	6,000
1846 original	—	—	—	—	—	3,000	—	3,250
1846 1st restrike	—	—	—	—	—	3,000	—	3,250
1846 2nd restrike	—	—	—	—	—	3,000	—	6,000
1847 original	—	—	—	—	—	3,000	—	3,250
1847 1st restrike	—	—	—	—	—	5,500	—	3,250
1847 2nd restrike	—	—	—	—	—	3,000	—	6,000
1848 original	—	—	—	—	—	3,000	—	6,000
1848 1st restrike	—	—	—	—	—	3,000	—	3,250
1848 2nd restrike	—	—	—	—	—	3,000	—	6,000
1849 original, small date	—	—	—	—	—	3,000	—	3,250
1849 1st restrike small date	—	—	—	—	—	3,000	—	3,250
1849 large date	39,864	58.00	75.00	82.00	92.00	110	300	—
1850	39,812	58.00	75.00	82.00	92.00	110	340	—
1851	147,672	54.00	70.00	77.00	84.00	96.00	195	—
1852 original	—	15,000	55,000	30,000	35,000	40,000	—	90,000
1852 1st restrike	—	1,000	1,500	1,850	2,600	3,000	—	5,000
1852 2nd restrike	—	1,000	1,500	1,850	2,600	3,000	—	7,000
1853	129,694	54.00	70.00	77.00	84.00	96.00	195	—
1854	55,358	54.00	70.00	77.00	84.00	96.00	195	—
1855	56,500	54.00	70.00	77.00	84.00	96.00	195	3,250
1856	40,430	54.00	70.00	77.00	84.00	96.00	195	3,250
1857	35,180	59.00	77.00	87.00	102	126	270	3,250

CENT

Flowing Hair Cent
Chain reverse

KM# 11 • 13.4800 g., **Copper**, 26-27 mm. • **Designer:** Henry Voigt

Date	Mintage	G-4	VG-8	F-12	VF-20	XF-40	MS-60
1793 "AMERI"	36,103	8,950	13,750	25,500	45,500	86,000	245,000
1793 "AMERICA"	Inc. above	6,950	10,500	17,750	36,500	61,500	140,000
1793 periods after "LIBERTY"	Inc. above	7,850	11,250	18,850	38,500	63,500	147,000

Flowing Hair Cent
Wreath reverse

KM# 12 • 13.4800 g., **Copper**, 26-28 mm. • **Designer:** Henry Voigt

Date	Mintage	G-4	VG-8	F-12	VF-20	XF-40	MS-60
1793 vine and bars edge	63,353	1,950	2,950	4,750	7,500	12,500	30,000
1793 lettered edge	Inc. above	2,100	3,250	5,200	8,000	14,000	—
1793 strawberry leaf; 4 known	—	350,000	450,000	875,000	—	—	—

Liberty Cap Cent

KM# 13 • **Copper**, 13.48 g. (1793-95) and 10.89 g. (1795-96), 29 mm. • **Designer:** Joseph Wright (1793-1795) and John Smith Gardner (1795-1796) **Notes:** The heavier pieces were struck on a thicker planchet. The Liberty design on the obverse was revised slightly in 1794, but the 1793 design was used on some 1794 strikes. A 1795 "lettered edge" variety has ONE HUNDRED FOR A DOLLAR and a leaf inscribed on the edge.

Date	Mintage	G-4	VG-8	F-12	VF-20	XF-40	MS-60
1793 cap	11,056	3,500	6,500	11,500	36,500	67,500	—
1794 head '93	918,521	1,350	2,600	4,000	8,450	20,000	—
1794 head '94	Inc. above	465	555	825	1,600	3,750	9,000
1794 head '95	Inc. above	455	520	770	1,545	3,350	—
1794 starred rev.	Inc. above	10,500	23,500	44,500	115,000	275,000	—
1795 plain edge	501,500	390	455	675	1,450	3,750	12,500
1795 reeded edge	Inc. above	350,000	700,000	—	—	—	—
1795 Jefferson head	Inc. above	24,500	49,500	95,000	150,000	—	—
1795 Jefferson head lettered edge	Inc. above	75,000	95,000	155,000	250,000	—	—

Liberty Cap Cent

KM# 13a • 10.8900 g., **Copper**, 29 mm. • **Designer:** Joseph Wright (1793-1795) and John Smith Gardner (1795-1796)

Date	Mintage	G-4	VG-8	F-12	VF-20	XF-40	MS-60
1795 lettered edge, "One Cent" high in wreath	37,000	410	480	725	1,850	4,750	15,000
1796	109,825	390	455	875	4,000	9,500	21,000

Draped Bust Cent
Draped bust right, date at angle below obverse
Value within wreath reverse

Stemless   Stems

KM# 22 • 10.9800 g., **Copper**, 29 mm. • **Obv. Legend** LIBERTY **Rev. Legend:** UNITED STATES OF AMERICA **Designer:** Robert Scot **Notes:** The 1801 "3 errors" variety has the fraction on the reverse reading "1/000," has only one stem extending from the wreath above and on both sides of the fraction on the reverse, and UNITED in UNITED STATES OF AMERICA appears as "linited."

Date	Mintage	G-4	VG-8	F-12	VF-20	XF-40	MS-60
1796 Rev. of 1794	363,375	300	450	900	2,800	6,850	—
1796 Rev. of 1796	Inc. above	260	375	700	3,250	9,500	—
1796 Rev. of 1797	Inc. above	240	350	650	1,500	3,250	—
1796 Liberty error	Inc. above	300	750	1,500	5,500	13,500	—
1797 reverse of 1796 plain edge	897,510	165	300	600	3,450	5,500	—
1797 reverse of 1796 gripped edge	Inc. above	185	375	550	1,350	4,750	—
1797	Inc. above	135	225	450	1,250	2,600	3,300
1797 stemless	Inc. above	300	495	600	910	3,200	—
1798/7	1,841,745	200	300	375	1,200	3,900	—
1798 reverse of 1796	Inc. above	—	—	—	—	—	—
1798 1st hair style	Inc. above	90.00	130	200	350	1,300	3,100
1798 2nd hair style	Inc. above	—	—	—	—	—	—
1799	42,540	2,750	4,650	10,000	24,500	58,500	—
1799/98	Inc. above	2,600	4,300	9,200	21,000	46,000	—
1800	2,822,175	70.00	130	285	650	1,750	—
1800/798	Inc. above	—	—	—	—	—	—
1800/79	Inc. above	—	—	—	—	—	—
1801	1,362,837	60.00	85.00	195	375	850	—
1801 3 errors	Inc. above	225	500	925	1,750	5,500	—
1801 1/000	Inc. above	—	—	—	—	—	—
1801 100/000	Inc. above	—	—	—	—	—	—
1802	3,435,100	60.00	85.00	185	360	780	2,250
1802 stemless	Inc. above	68.00	95.00	200	350	—	—
1802 fraction 1/000	Inc. above	—	—	—	—	—	—
1803 small date, small fraction	2,471,353	60.00	85.00	185	350	750	2,250
1803 small date, large fraction	Inc. above	60.00	85.00	185	360	800	—
1803 large date, small fraction	Inc. above	4,600	6,950	14,500	26,500	75,000	—
1803 large date, large fraction	Inc. above	—	—	—	—	—	—
1804	96,500	1,650	2,650	4,000	8,950	15,500	—
1804 Restrike of 1860	—	—	—	650	750	800	1,000
1805	941,116	60.00	90.00	160	300	875	2,450
1806	348,000	70.00	100.00	150	375	1,100	4,700
1807 small fraction	727,221	60.00	85.00	185	350	750	2,250
1807 large fraction	Inc. above	60.00	85.00	185	350	750	—

Date	Mintage	G-4	VG-8	F-12	VF-20	XF-40	MS-60
1807/6 large 7/6	Inc. above	60.00	85.00	185	350	750	—
1807/6 small 7/6	Inc. above	1,900	4,250	9,500	24,500	49,500	—
1807 Comet Variety	Inc. above	95.00	125	250	575	2,000	—

Classic Head Cent
Classic head left, flanked by stars, date below obverse
Value within wreath reverse

KM# 39 • 10.8900 g., **Copper**, 29 mm. • **Rev. Legend:** UNITED STATES OF AMERICA **Designer:** John Reich

Date	Mintage	G-4	VG-8	F-12	VF-20	XF-40	MS-60
1808	1,109,000	85.00	150	250	575	1,450	3,600
1809	222,867	135	250	450	1,050	2,650	6,300
1810/09	1,458,500	—	—	—	—	—	—
1810	Inc. above	75.00	95.00	210	550	1,100	3,850
1811/10	218,025	130	200	440	1,200	2,200	—
1811	Inc. above	110	175	400	1,000	1,500	7,000
1812 small date	1,075,500	54.00	88.00	215	550	975	2,800
1812 large date	—	—	—	—	—	—	—
1813	418,000	60.00	175	400	800	1,200	—
1814 Plain 4	357,830	54.00	93.00	225	530	975	2,800
1814 Crosslet 4	Inc. above	54.00	88.00	215	550	975	—

Coronet Cent
Coronet head left, within circle of stars, date below obverse
Value within wreath reverse

KM# 45 • 10.8900 g., **Copper**, 28-29 mm. • **Rev. Legend:** UNITED STATES OF AMERICA **Designer:** John Reich

Date	Mintage	G-4	VG-8	F-12	VF-20	XF-40	MS-60
1816	2,820,982	31.00	37.00	60.00	115	200	420
1817 13 obverse stars	3,948,400	29.00	33.00	40.00	72.00	120	500
1817 15 obverse stars	Inc. above	35.00	44.00	70.00	163	550	1,600
1818	3,167,000	29.00	33.00	40.00	72.00	120	270
1819 Large date, 9/8	2,671,000	31.00	36.00	46.00	84.00	140	285
1819 Large date	Inc. above	29.00	33.00	40.00	72.00	120	—
1819 Small date	Inc. above	30.00	35.00	43.00	76.00	130	—
1820	4,407,550	29.00	33.00	40.00	72.00	120	300
1821	389,000	40.00	75.00	250	400	1,500	6,000
1822	2,072,339	31.00	35.00	45.00	100.00	195	750
1823 Included in 1824 mintage	1,824	90.00	200	310	690	2,750	—
1823/22 Included in 1824 mintage	—	80.00	110	300	675	2,450	—
1823 Restrike	—	600	750	850	1,000	1,200	2,000
1824	1,262,000	31.00	35.00	38.00	160	350	950
1824/22	Inc. above	40.00	49.00	90.00	375	1,000	9,850
1825	1,461,100	30.00	35.00	50.00	110	300	960
1826	1,517,425	30.00	35.00	40.00	84.00	175	750
1826/25	Inc. above	40.00	55.00	95.00	250	850	2,000
1827	2,357,732	29.00	33.00	40.00	91.00	125	750
1828	2,260,624	29.00	33.00	40.00	81.00	150	450
1829 Large letters	1,414,500	29.00	33.00	40.00	91.00	130	475
1829 Medium letters	Inc. above	—	—	—	—	—	—
1830 Large letters	1,711,500	25.00	29.00	36.00	68.00	120	400
1830 Medium letters	Inc. above	—	—	—	—	—	—
1831 Large letters	3,359,260	25.00	29.00	36.00	68.00	115	315
1831 Medium letters	—	29.00	34.00	41.00	74.00	130	—
1832 Large letters	2,362,000	25.00	29.00	36.00	68.00	120	380
1832 Medium letters	—	27.00	32.00	39.00	72.00	125	—
1833	2,739,000	25.00	29.00	36.00	68.00	113	300
1834 Large 8, stars and letters	1,855,100	75.00	120	145	250	625	375
1834 Large 8 & stars, medium letters	Inc. above	190	275	600	1,100	3,250	62,000
1834 Large 8, small stars, medium letters	Inc. above	25.00	29.00	36.00	68.00	125	—
1834 Small 8 & stars	Inc. above	25.00	29.00	36.00	68.00	125	—
1835 Large 8 & stars	3,878,400	25.00	29.00	36.00	68.00	105	300
1835 Small 8 & stars	—	—	—	—	—	—	—
1835 Head '36	—	—	—	—	—	—	—
1836	2,111,000	25.00	29.00	36.00	68.00	105	350
1837 Plain hair cords, medium letters	5,558,300	25.00	29.00	36.00	68.00	105	300
1837 Plain hair cords, small letters	Inc. above	—	—	—	—	—	—
1837 Head '38	Inc. above	—	—	—	—	—	—
1838	6,370,200	25.00	29.00	36.00	68.00	105	300
1839 Head '38, beaded hair cords	3,128,661	29.00	33.00	40.00	72.00	110	350
1839/36 Plain hair cords	Inc. above	300	600	1,250	2,450	4,900	—
1839 Silly head	Inc. above	35.00	40.00	50.00	88.00	145	—
1839 Booby head	Inc. above	34.00	38.00	47.00	83.00	133	—

Braided Hair Cent
Head left, braided hair, within circle of stars, date below obverse
Value within wreath reverse

KM# 67 • 10.8900 g., **Copper**, 27.5 mm. • **Rev. Legend:** UNITED STATES OF AMERICA **Designer:** Christian Gobrecht **Notes:** 1840 and 1842 strikes are known with both small and large dates, with little difference in value. A slightly larger Liberty head and larger reverse lettering were used beginning in 1843.

Date	Mintage	G-4	VG-8	F-12	VF-20	XF-40	MS-60
1839	3,128,661	29.00	33.00	38.00	46.00	85.00	—
1840 Large date	2,462,700	25.00	28.00	31.00	36.00	69.00	475
1840 Small date	Inc. above	30.00	35.00	40.00	49.00	90.00	—
1840 Small date over large 18	Inc. above	40.00	50.00	75.00	125	210	—
1841	1,597,367	25.00	28.00	31.00	39.00	79.00	440
1842 Small date	2,383,390	25.00	28.00	31.00	36.00	69.00	425
1842 Large date	Inc. above	28.00	32.00	40.00	54.00	100.00	—
1843	2,425,342	25.00	28.00	31.00	36.00	69.00	445
1843 obverse 1842 with reverse of 1844	Inc. above	27.00	30.00	33.00	38.00	79.00	400
1844	2,398,752	25.00	28.00	31.00	36.00	69.00	300
1844/81	Inc. above	40.00	50.00	60.00	100.00	225	700
1845	3,894,804	25.00	28.00	31.00	36.00	69.00	250
1846	4,120,800	23.00	26.00	29.00	34.00	69.00	250
1847	6,183,669	23.00	26.00	29.00	34.00	69.00	250
1847/7	Inc. above	32.00	50.00	90.00	150	385	1,350
1848	6,415,799	25.00	28.00	31.00	36.00	61.00	250
1849	4,178,500	25.00	28.00	31.00	36.00	61.00	325
1850	4,426,844	25.00	28.00	31.00	36.00	61.00	250
1851	9,889,707	23.00	26.00	29.00	34.00	59.00	165
1851/81	Inc. above	36.00	45.00	55.00	85.00	175	700
1852	5,063,094	23.00	26.00	29.00	34.00	59.00	165
1853	6,641,131	23.00	26.00	29.00	34.00	59.00	165
1854	4,236,156	23.00	26.00	29.00	34.00	59.00	165
1855 Upright 5's	Inc. above	23.00	26.00	29.00	34.00	59.00	165
1855 Slanted 5's	1,574,829	43.00	56.00	66.00	71.00	95.00	200
1855 Slanted 5's Knob on Ear	Inc. above	29.00	34.00	41.00	52.00	99.00	—
1856 Slanted 5	2,690,463	23.00	26.00	29.00	34.00	59.00	165
1856 Upright 5	Inc. above	30.00	40.00	50.00	55.00	80.00	—
1857 Large date	333,456	125	150	175	235	310	600
1857 Small date	Inc. above	85.00	110	140	190	265	—

Flying Eagle Cent
Flying eagle above date obverse
Value within wreath reverse

Large letters AM touch at bottom

Small letters Space between AM

KM# 85 • 4.6700 g., **Copper-Nickel**, 19 mm. • **Obv. Legend** UNITED STATES OF AMERICA **Designer:** James B. Longacre **Notes:** On the large-letter variety of 1858, the "A" and "M" in AMERICA are connected at their bases; on the small-letter variety, the two letters are separated.

Date	Mintage	G-4	VG-8	F-12	VF-20	XF-40	AU-50	MS-60	MS-65	Prf-65
1856	Est. 2,500	6,250	7,250	9,000	10,750	12,850	13,500	16,500	65,000	28,500
1857	17,450,000	27.50	39.00	40.00	47.00	125	165	320	3,500	29,000
1858/7	Inc. below	65.00	92.50	175	380	760	1,500	3,300	60,000	—
1858 large letters	24,600,000	27.50	41.00	43.50	56.00	150	220	340	3,850	24,500
1858 small letters	Inc. above	26.00	39.00	42.00	47.00	135	175	320	3,650	30,000

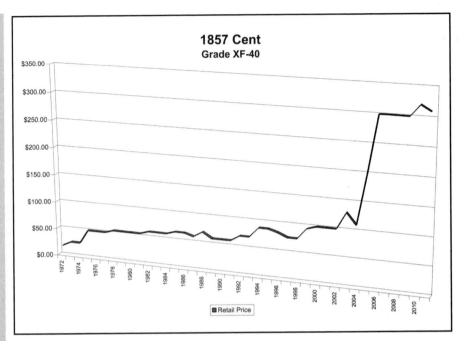

1857 Cent
Grade XF-40

Indian Head Cent
Indian head with headdress left above date obverse
Value within wreath reverse

KM# 87 • 4.6700 g., **Copper-Nickel**, 19 mm. • **Obv. Legend** UNITED STATES OF AMERICA
Designer: James B. Longacre

Date	Mintage	G-4	VG-8	F-12	VF-20	XF-40	AU-50	MS-60	MS-65	Prf-65
1859	36,400,000	13.00	16.00	22.50	48.00	100.00	175	230	3,650	5,200

Indian Head Cent
Indian head with headdress left above date obverse
Value within wreath, shield above reverse

KM# 90 • 4.6700 g., **Copper-Nickel**, 19 mm. • **Obv. Legend** UNITED STATES OF AMERICA **Designer:**
James B. Longacre

Date	Mintage	G-4	VG-8	F-12	VF-20	XF-40	AU-50	MS-60	MS-65	Prf-65
1860 Rounded Bust	20,566,000	11.00	15.00	22.00	46.00	68.00	110	190	965	3,600
1860	1,000	—	—	—	—	—	—	—	—	—
1860 Pointed Bust	Inc. above	20.00	30.00	42.00	60.00	100.00	160	300	6,000	—
1861	10,100,000	20.00	30.00	42.00	58.00	95.00	160	180	975	7,250
1862	28,075,000	11.00	11.50	12.50	15.00	28.00	60.00	80.00	1,050	2,350
1863	49,840,000	7.50	9.25	11.00	12.50	25.00	58.00	75.00	1,050	3,100
1864	13,740,000	16.50	28.50	35.00	72.00	125	175	220	1,350	3,200

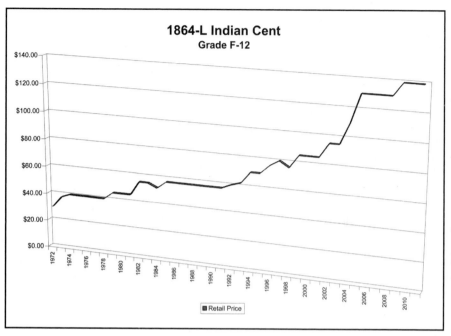

1864-L Indian Cent
Grade F-12

Retail Price

Indian Head Cent
Indian head with headdress left above date obverse
Value within wreath, shield above reverse

   1864 "L"

KM# 90a • 3.1100 g., **Bronze**, 19 mm. • **Obv. Legend** UNITED STATES OF AMERICA **Designer:** James B. Longacre **Notes:** The 1864 "L" variety has the designer's initial in Liberty's hair to the right of her neck.

Date	Mintage	G-4	VG-8	F-12	VF-20	XF-40	AU-50	MS-60	MS-65	Prf-65
1864	39,233,714	8.00	20.00	25.00	45.00	70.00	80.00	110	335	10,500
1864 L pointed bust	Inc. above	52.50	72.50	139	185	275	325	410	1,700	200,000
1865 plain 5	35,429,286	7.00	11.00	20.00	25.00	45.00	60.00	90.00	485	6,750
1865 fancy 5	Inc. above	6.00	10.50	18.50	23.00	40.00	55.00	85.00	465	—
1866	9,826,500	46.00	66.00	80.00	115	195	240	280	1,350	4,500
1867	9,821,000	52.00	72.00	110	120	195	240	285	1,350	6,100
1867/1867	Inc. above	60.00	85.00	130	190	275	385	565	1,950	—
1868	10,266,500	37.50	50.00	77.00	120	180	245	265	985	5,750
1869/9	6,420,000	145	280	495	660	825	1,000	1,250	2,350	—
1869	Inc. above	90.00	125	230	335	450	560	625	1,750	3,100
1870	5,275,000	62.00	118	225	285	410	510	600	1,400	2,650
1871	3,929,500	88.00	125	280	310	420	510	610	2,400	2,500
1872	4,042,000	90.00	180	390	425	625	750	840	3,850	4,250
1873 closed 3	11,676,500	30.00	52.00	95.00	135	235	300	400	2,850	2,950
1873 open 3	Inc. above	20.00	34.00	65.00	82.00	175	215	250	1,300	—
1873 Double Liberty die 1	Inc. above	275	450	950	1,500	2,400	4,250	7,500	—	—
1873 Double Liberty die 2	Inc. above	—	—	450	900	1,650	2,800	4,500	—	—
1874	14,187,500	15.00	22.50	46.00	65.00	112	150	225	700	2,850
1875	13,528,000	16.00	29.00	56.00	72.00	120	165	215	800	8,500
1876	7,944,000	27.00	38.50	74.00	130	230	295	335	975	2,600
1877	852,500	985	1,190	1,600	2,050	2,650	3,000	3,450	13,000	12,500
1878	5,799,850	26.00	35.00	68.00	135	245	290	350	875	1,375
1879	16,231,200	7.00	10.00	16.50	33.00	75.00	90.00	100.00	365	1,250
1880	38,964,955	3.50	5.50	6.50	11.00	28.00	48.00	66.00	360	1,250
1881	39,211,575	3.50	4.25	6.50	8.00	22.00	30.00	43.00	325	1,250
1882	38,581,100	3.50	4.25	5.00	10.00	22.00	30.00	40.00	325	1,450
1883	45,589,109	3.00	4.00	4.50	7.50	17.50	30.00	42.00	325	1,600

Date	Mintage	G-4	VG-8	F-12	VF-20	XF-40	AU-50	MS-60	MS-65	Prf-65
1884	23,261,742	3.50	4.50	7.00	12.50	29.00	40.00	60.00	460	1,250
1885	11,765,384	6.75	8.00	12.00	27.00	62.00	82.00	105	725	1,500
1886 Type 1 obverse	17,654,290	3.75	6.60	19.80	56.00	148	170	190	1,250	2,650
1886 Type 2 obverse	Inc. above	7.00	10.00	35.00	90.00	200	250	325	2,500	7,500
1887	45,226,483	2.50	3.00	4.00	7.00	19.00	28.00	50.00	400	6,200
1888	37,494,414	2.75	3.25	5.00	8.00	21.00	28.00	48.00	900	5,400
1889	48,869,361	2.25	2.75	3.50	6.00	12.00	26.00	40.00	400	1,900
1890	57,182,854	2.10	2.50	3.00	5.50	10.00	23.00	37.50	400	1,800
1891	47,072,350	2.25	2.75	3.25	5.50	13.00	23.00	37.00	400	2,150
1892	37,649,832	2.40	3.25	4.40	6.00	18.50	25.00	35.00	400	1,325
1893	46,642,195	2.10	2.75	3.25	5.50	10.00	22.00	30.00	340	1,250
1894	16,752,132	5.00	6.00	13.00	20.00	50.00	65.00	85.00	375	1,350
1894/94	Inc. above	24.00	34.00	80.00	150	275	440	800	8,000	—
1895	38,343,636	2.10	2.40	3.50	4.50	11.00	22.00	32.00	200	1,275
1896	39,057,293	1.95	2.50	3.25	4.75	13.00	26.00	34.00	225	1,900
1897	50,466,330	1.95	2.40	2.75	4.00	10.00	22.00	30.00	195	1,600
1898	49,823,079	1.95	2.40	2.75	4.00	10.00	22.00	30.00	195	1,275
1899	53,600,031	1.95	2.20	2.60	4.00	10.00	22.00	30.00	165	1,275
1900	66,833,764	1.95	2.20	2.50	4.00	12.00	23.00	30.00	175	1,275
1901	79,611,143	1.85	2.20	2.50	4.00	11.00	22.00	29.00	165	1,275
1902	87,376,722	1.85	2.20	2.50	4.00	10.00	22.00	28.00	165	1,325
1903	85,094,493	1.85	2.20	2.50	4.00	10.00	21.00	28.00	165	1,275
1904	61,328,015	1.75	2.20	2.50	4.00	10.00	21.00	28.00	165	1,275
1905	80,719,163	1.75	2.20	2.50	3.50	9.00	20.00	28.00	165	1,350
1906	96,022,255	1.75	2.20	2.50	3.50	9.00	21.00	28.00	165	1,275
1907	108,138,618	1.75	2.20	2.50	3.50	8.50	20.00	28.00	165	1,950
1908	32,327,987	1.75	2.30	2.50	3.50	9.00	20.00	28.00	165	1,275
1908S	1,115,000	77.00	82.00	105	122	166	195	285	2,650	—
1909S	309,000	590	655	720	825	900	950	1,000	2,250	—
1909	14,370,645	14.00	14.80	15.50	15.90	18.50	30.00	38.00	155	1,275

Lincoln Cent
Wheat Ears reverse

KM# 132 • 3.1100 g., **Bronze**, 19 mm. • **Designer:** Victor D. Brenner **Notes:** The 1909 "VDB" varieties have the designer's initials inscribed at the 6 o'clock position on the reverse. The initials were removed until 1918, when they were restored on the obverse • MS60 prices are for brown coins and MS65 prices are for coins that are at least 90% original red.

Date	Mintage	G-4	VG-8	F-12	VF-20	XF-40	AU-50	MS-60	MS-65	Prf-65
1909 VDB	27,995,000	12.50	13.00	13.25	13.50	14.00	16.00	25.00	195	12,500
1909 VDB Doubled Die Obverse	Inc. above	—	—	55.00	75.00	100.00	120	150	4,650	—
1909S VDB	484,000	750	940	1,120	1,365	1,475	1,600	1,825	6,600	—
1909	72,702,618	3.65	3.85	4.35	4.75	5.50	12.00	14.50	85.00	950
1909S	1,825,000	115	120	142	185	245	265	350	1,275	—
1909S/S S over horizontal S	Inc. above	115	120	135	180	255	280	350	1,600	—
1910	146,801,218	.50	.60	.75	1.00	4.25	10.00	17.50	250	800
1910S	6,045,000	16.50	20.00	21.00	27.50	47.50	72.00	98.00	825	—
1911	101,177,787	.60	.80	2.00	2.50	6.75	11.00	18.50	350	765
1911D	12,672,000	4.75	5.85	9.50	22.50	50.00	70.00	88.00	1,450	—
1911S	4,026,000	49.00	53.00	55.00	60.00	75.00	105	175	2,850	—
1912	68,153,060	1.60	1.85	2.35	5.50	13.50	26.00	32.00	520	975
1912D	10,411,000	6.50	9.75	11.00	26.00	69.00	105	160	2,350	—
1912S	4,431,000	24.00	26.00	29.00	42.00	78.00	115	175	4,150	—
1913	76,532,352	.90	1.10	1.65	3.25	18.50	28.00	34.00	385	750
1913D	15,804,000	2.75	3.25	3.60	10.50	49.00	61.50	90.00	2,650	—
1913S	6,101,000	13.50	16.50	20.00	32.00	57.00	105	190	6,350	—
1914	75,238,432	.60	.95	2.10	6.00	18.00	40.00	52.00	415	775
1914D	1,193,000	205	235	395	450	945	1,475	2,000	24,500	—
1914S	4,137,000	25.00	27.50	31.00	39.00	88.00	175	300	9,350	—
1915	29,092,120	1.65	2.90	4.00	18.00	60.00	68.00	82.00	1,300	775
1915D	22,050,000	1.75	2.85	4.50	6.85	24.00	44.00	70.00	1,250	—
1915S	4,833,000	21.00	24.50	28.00	32.00	72.00	94.00	185	4,650	—
1916	131,833,677	.45	.60	1.10	2.40	8.50	14.50	18.50	385	2,450
1916D	35,956,000	1.35	2.00	3.25	6.50	17.50	38.00	72.00	3,150	—
1916S	22,510,000	1.85	3.25	4.40	9.50	27.50	48.00	102	7,450	—
1917	196,429,785	.35	.40	.55	1.85	4.75	13.00	16.00	475	—
1917 Doubled Die Obverse	Inc. above	90.00	110	175	350	900	1,750	2,500	27,500	—
1917D	55,120,000	1.15	1.60	2.85	5.00	36.50	44.00	70.00	2,900	—

CENT

1914-D Cent
Grade F-12

Date	Mintage	G-4	VG-8	F-12	VF-20	XF-40	AU-50	MS-60	MS-65	Prf-65
1917S	32,620,000	.65	1.00	1.50	2.50	11.50	25.00	63.00	6,500	—
1918	288,104,634	.35	.40	.50	1.00	4.25	9.50	13.00	375	—
1918D	47,830,000	1.20	1.45	2.65	5.50	15.50	34.00	75.00	3,500	—
1918S	34,680,000	.40	1.00	1.65	3.65	11.00	31.00	66.00	7,950	—
1919	392,021,000	.30	.40	.50	.80	1.60	5.25	8.00	115	—
1919D	57,154,000	1.10	1.35	1.85	4.85	12.75	35.00	57.50	2,650	—
1919S	139,760,000	.40	.60	1.80	2.65	5.75	17.50	42.00	3,950	—
1920	310,165,000	.30	.35	.75	1.25	2.80	7.50	15.00	235	—
1920D	49,280,000	1.15	1.65	2.90	6.85	18.50	37.00	68.50	2,650	—
1920S	46,220,000	.75	.80	1.50	2.75	13.00	34.50	100.00	8,250	—
1921	39,157,000	.60	.80	1.15	1.50	10.50	21.00	41.50	365	—
1921S	15,274,000	1.65	2.10	3.50	6.25	34.50	68.00	100.00	6,150	—
1922D	7,160,000	20.00	21.00	23.00	25.00	37.50	75.00	100.00	2,350	—
1922D Weak Rev	Inc. above	18.00	18.50	19.50	21.00	34.00	65.00	90.00	1,850	—
1922D Weak D	Inc. above	30.00	44.00	60.00	100.00	185	285	550	—	—
1922 No D Die 2 Strong Rev	Inc. above	700	760	975	1,375	2,300	4,500	10,500	160,000	—
1922 No D Die 3 Weak Rev	Inc. above	300	400	650	885	1,650	3,350	8,500	—	—
1923	74,723,000	.50	.70	.95	1.25	5.75	10.50	13.50	435	—
1923S	8,700,000	4.00	5.25	7.00	10.00	38.00	88.00	185	14,850	—
1924	75,178,000	.35	.45	.60	1.00	5.25	11.00	17.50	385	—
1924D	2,520,000	36.00	44.00	49.00	60.00	118	170	255	12,500	—
1924S	11,696,000	1.45	1.65	2.75	5.35	32.50	68.00	105	10,000	—
1925	139,949,000	.30	.35	.50	.70	2.75	6.50	9.00	100.00	—
1925D	22,580,000	1.25	1.65	3.10	5.85	15.50	30.00	60.00	4,650	—
1925S	26,380,000	.95	1.25	1.85	2.75	11.50	31.00	83.00	9,850	—
1926	157,088,000	.25	.35	.50	.60	1.65	5.25	7.00	62.00	—
1926D	28,020,000	1.50	1.70	3.40	5.25	15.50	34.00	80.00	3,950	—
1926S	4,550,000	9.00	10.00	11.50	16.00	35.00	70.00	135	110,000	—
1927	144,440,000	.20	.25	.35	.60	1.60	5.25	7.00	92.00	—
1927D	27,170,000	1.35	1.70	2.25	3.35	7.50	25.00	58.50	2,100	—
1927S	14,276,000	1.50	1.85	2.65	5.25	14.50	40.00	62.50	6,350	—
1928	134,116,000	.20	.25	.35	.60	1.25	4.00	7.50	84.00	—
1928D	31,170,000	1.10	1.40	2.15	3.65	6.75	19.00	34.00	985	—
1928S Small S	17,266,000	1.20	1.65	2.60	4.00	9.50	31.00	71.50	5,450	—
1928S Large S	Inc. above	2.00	2.85	4.25	7.50	16.50	55.00	135	6,850	—
1929	185,262,000	.20	.25	.35	.55	2.75	5.25	6.25	85.00	—
1929D	41,730,000	.60	1.10	1.40	2.75	5.85	13.50	24.00	590	—
1929S	50,148,000	.70	1.15	1.85	2.80	7.00	14.75	19.00	525	—
1930	157,415,000	.20	.25	.35	.60	1.25	2.75	3.75	31.50	—
1930D	40,100,000	.30	.40	.55	.90	2.00	5.50	9.75	92.00	—
1930S	24,286,000	.30	.40	.58	.80	1.50	6.50	9.50	47.50	—
1931	19,396,000	.65	.75	1.10	2.00	4.00	9.50	18.50	130	—
1931D	4,480,000	4.85	5.85	6.50	7.50	12.75	33.50	48.50	925	—
1931S	866,000	112	118	120	125	138	145	160	685	—
1932	9,062,000	1.50	1.95	2.85	3.50	6.75	13.00	17.50	82.00	—

Date	Mintage	G-4	VG-8	F-12	VF-20	XF-40	AU-50	MS-60	MS-65	Prf-65
1932D	10,500,000	1.40	1.90	2.50	2.85	4.15	11.00	18.50	110	—
1933	14,360,000	1.40	1.80	2.65	2.85	6.50	11.50	15.50	82.00	—
1933D	6,200,000	3.50	4.25	5.65	7.50	13.50	19.00	23.00	100.00	—
1934	219,080,000	.20	.25	.40	.60	1.25	4.00	8.00	35.00	—
1934D	28,446,000	.35	.50	.80	1.50	3.00	9.00	20.00	60.00	—
1935	245,338,000	.20	.30	.40	.55	.90	1.50	3.50	40.00	—
1935D	47,000,000	.15	.20	.30	.40	.95	2.50	4.50	40.00	—
1935S	38,702,000	.25	.35	.60	1.75	3.00	5.00	12.00	95.00	—
1936 (Proof in Satin Finish)	309,637,569	.20	.30	.40	.55	.85	1.40	2.00	15.00	1,000
1936 Brilliant Proof	Inc. above	—	—	—	—	—	—	—	—	1,100
1936D	40,620,000	.20	.30	.40	.55	.90	1.50	3.50	18.00	—
1936S	29,130,000	.20	.30	.45	.60	1.50	1.75	3.00	26.00	—
1937	309,179,320	.20	.30	.40	.55	.85	1.40	1.60	16.00	180
1937D	50,430,000	.20	.30	.40	.60	.80	1.00	2.20	20.00	—
1937S	34,500,000	.20	.30	.40	.55	.90	1.25	2.40	22.50	—
1938	156,696,734	.20	.30	.40	.55	.85	1.20	3.00	25.00	125
1938D	20,010,000	.20	.30	.45	.60	1.00	1.50	3.50	27.00	—
1938S	15,180,000	.30	.40	.50	.70	1.00	2.00	2.80	30.00	—
1939	316,479,520	.20	.30	.40	.55	.75	.90	1.00	20.00	85.00
1939D	15,160,000	.35	.45	.50	.60	.85	1.90	2.50	22.00	—
1939S	52,070,000	.30	.40	.50	.60	.80	1.10	2.00	18.00	—
1940	586,825,872	.10	.20	.30	.40	.50	.75	1.00	15.00	65.00
1940D	81,390,000	.20	.30	.40	.55	.75	.90	1.20	13.00	—
1940S	112,940,000	.20	.30	.40	.55	.90	1.25	1.40	14.00	—
1941	887,039,100	.10	.20	.30	.40	.50	.70	.85	16.00	80.00
1941 Doubled Die Obv	Inc. above	35.00	50.00	70.00	80.00	95.00	135	200	2,800	—
1941D	128,700,000	.20	.30	.40	.55	.75	1.25	2.25	15.00	—
1941S	92,360,000	.20	.30	.40	.55	.75	1.75	2.75	23.00	—
1942	657,828,600	.10	.20	.30	.40	.50	.70	.85	16.00	85.00
1942D	206,698,000	.20	.25	.30	.35	.40	.50	.65	18.00	—
1942S	85,590,000	.25	.35	.45	.85	1.25	2.50	4.50	26.00	—

Lincoln Cent
Wheat Ears reverse

KM# 132a • 2.7000 g., Zinc Coated Steel, 19 mm. • Designer: Victor D. Brenner

Date	Mintage	G-4	VG-8	F-12	VF-20	XF-40	AU-50	MS-60	MS-65	Prf-65
1943	684,628,670	.25	.30	.35	.45	.60	.85	1.25	18.00	—
1943D	217,660,000	.35	.40	.45	.50	.70	1.00	1.25	20.00	—
1943D/D RPM	Inc. above	30.00	38.00	50.00	65.00	90.00	125	200	1,400	—
1943S	191,550,000	.40	.45	.50	.65	.90	1.40	3.00	28.00	—

Lincoln Cent
Wheat Ears reverse

KM# A132 • 3.1100 g., Brass, 19 mm. •
Designer: Victor D. Brenner **Notes:** KM#132
design and composition resumed • MS60 prices are
for brown coins and MS65 prices are for coins that
are at least 90% original red.

Date	Mintage	XF-40	MS-65	Prf-65
1944	1,435,400,000	.40	8.00	—
1944D	430,578,000	.50	12.50	—
1944D/S Type 1	Inc. above	235	3,750	—
1944D/S Type 2	Inc. above	175	1,600	—
1944S	282,760,000	.40	11.00	—
1945	1,040,515,000	.40	13.50	—
1945D	226,268,000	.40	12.50	—
1945S	181,770,000	.40	8.50	—
1946	991,655,000	.30	9.00	—
1946D	315,690,000	.30	10.00	—
1946S	198,100,000	.30	12.00	—
1946S/D	—	70.00	600	—
1947	190,555,000	.45	10.00	—
1947D	194,750,000	.40	9.00	—
1947S	99,000,000	.35	12.00	—
1948	317,570,000	.40	10.00	—
1948D	172,637,000	.40	6.50	—

Date	Mintage	XF-40	MS-65	Prf-65
1948S	81,735,000	.40	8.00	—
1949	217,775,000	.40	12.50	—
1949D	153,132,000	.40	15.00	—
1949S	64,290,000	.50	10.00	—
1950	272,686,386	.40	13.50	65.00
1950D	334,950,000	.35	7.50	—
1950S	118,505,000	.40	9.00	—
1951	295,633,500	.40	14.00	70.00
1951D	625,355,000	.30	8.50	—
1951S	136,010,000	.40	10.00	—
1952	186,856,980	.40	16.00	42.00
1952D	746,130,000	.30	8.50	—
1952S	137,800,004	.60	12.00	—
1953	256,883,800	.30	15.00	30.00
1953D	700,515,000	.30	9.50	—
1953S	181,835,000	.40	10.00	—
1954	71,873,350	.25	14.00	17.00
1954D	251,552,500	.25	10.00	—
1954S	96,190,000	.25	12.00	—
1955	330,958,000	.25	15.00	16.00
1955 Doubled Die	Inc. above	2,350	38,500	—

Note: The 1955 "doubled die" has distinct doubling of the date and lettering on the obverse.

Date	Mintage	XF-40	MS-65	Prf-65
1955D	563,257,500	.20	12.00	—
1955S	44,610,000	.35	12.00	—
1956	421,414,384	.20	16.00	10.00
1956D	1,098,201,100	.20	8.00	—
1957	283,787,952	.20	9.00	6.00
1957D	1,051,342,000	.20	8.00	—
1958	253,400,652	.20	9.00	6.50
1958D	800,953,300	.20	8.00	—

Lincoln Cent
Lincoln Memorial reverse

Large date   Small date   Large date   Small date

KM# 201 • 3.1100 g., **Brass**, 19 mm. • **Rev. Designer:** Frank Gasparro **Notes:** MS60 prices are for brown coins and MS65 prices are for coins that are at least 90% original red. The dates were modified in 1960, 1970 and 1982, resulting in large-date and small-date varieties for those years. The 1972 "doubled die" shows doubling of IN GOD WE TRUST. The 1979-S and 1981-S Type II proofs have a clearer mint mark than the Type I proofs of those years. Some 1982 cents have the predominantly copper composition; others have the predominantly zinc composition. They can be distinguished by weight.

Date	Mintage	XF-40	MS-65	Prf-65
1959	610,864,291	—	18.00	10.00
1959D	1,279,760,000	—	16.00	—
1960 small date, low 9	588,096,602	2.10	12.00	18.00
1960 large date, high 9	Inc. above	—	10.00	10.00
1960D small date, low 9	1,580,884,000	—	10.00	—
1960D large date, high 9	Inc. above	—	11.00	—
1960D/D small over large date	Inc. above	—	—	—
1961	756,373,244	—	6.50	9.00
1961D	1,753,266,700	—	15.00	—
1962	609,263,019	—	8.00	8.00
1962D	1,793,148,400	—	14.00	—
1963	757,185,645	—	10.00	8.00
1963D	1,774,020,400	—	12.00	—
1964	2,652,525,762	—	6.50	8.00
1964D	3,799,071,500	—	7.00	—
1965	1,497,224,900	—	10.00	—
1965 SMS	Inc. above	—	7.50	—
1966	2,188,147,783	—	10.00	—
1966 SMS	Inc. above	—	8.00	—
1967	3,048,667,100	—	10.00	—
1967 SMS	Inc. above	—	8.00	—
1968	1,707,880,970	—	12.00	—
1968D	2,886,269,600	—	12.00	—
1968S	261,311,510	—	8.00	1.00
1969	1,136,910,000	—	6.50	—
1969D	4,002,832,200	—	10.00	—
1969S	547,309,631	—	8.00	1.10
1969S Doubled Die Obverse	Inc. above	—	—	—
1970	1,898,315,000	—	8.00	—
1970D	2,891,438,900	—	6.00	—
1970S	693,192,814	—	—	—
1970S small date, level 7	Inc. above	—	75.00	60.00
1970S large date, low 7	Inc. above	—	16.00	—
1970S Doubled Die Obverse	Inc. above	—	—	—
1971	1,919,490,000	—	25.00	—
1971D	2,911,045,600	—	5.50	—
1971S	528,354,192	—	6.00	1.20
1971S Doubled Die Obverse	Inc. above	—	—	—
1972	2,933,255,000	—	6.00	—
1972 Doubled Die Obverse	Inc. above	285	800	—
1972D	2,665,071,400	—	10.00	—
1972S	380,200,104	—	30.00	1.15
1973	3,728,245,000	—	8.00	—

Date	Mintage	XF-40	MS-65	Prf-65
1973D	3,549,576,588	—	11.00	—
1973S	319,937,634	—	8.00	0.80
1974	4,232,140,523	—	12.00	—
1974D	4,235,098,000	—	12.00	—
1974S	412,039,228	—	10.00	0.75
1975	5,451,476,142	—	8.00	—
1975D	4,505,245,300	—	13.50	—
1975S	2,845,450	—	—	5.50
1976	4,674,292,426	—	18.00	—
1976D	4,221,592,455	—	20.00	—
1976S	4,149,730	—	—	5.00
1977	4,469,930,000	—	.25	—
1977D	4,149,062,300	—	.25	—
1977S	3,251,152	—	—	3.00
1978	5,558,605,000	—	.25	—
1978D	4,280,233,400	—	.25	—
1978S	3,127,781	—	—	3.50
1979	6,018,515,000	—	.25	—
1979D	4,139,357,254	—	.25	—
1979S type I, proof	3,677,175	—	—	4.00
1979S type II, proof	Inc. above	—	—	4.25
1980	7,414,705,000	—	.25	—
1980D	5,140,098,660	—	.25	—
1980S	3,554,806	—	—	2.25
1981	7,491,750,000	—	.25	—
1981D	5,373,235,677	—	.25	—
1981S type I, proof	4,063,083	—	—	3.50
1981S type II, proof	Inc. above	—	—	60.00
1982 large date	10,712,525,000	—	.25	—
1982 small date	Inc. above	—	.25	—
1982D large date	6,012,979,368	—	.25	—
1982S	3,857,479	—	—	3.00

Lincoln Cent
Lincoln Memorial reverse

KM# 201a • 2.5000 g., **Copper Plated Zinc**, 19 mm. • **Notes:** MS60 prices are for brown coins and MS65 prices are for coins that are at least 90% original red.

Date	Mintage	XF-40	MS-65	Prf-65
1982 large date	—	—	.50	—
1982 small date	—	—	2.00	—
1982D large date	—	—	.30	—
1982D small date	—	—	.25	—

Lincoln Cent
Lincoln Memorial reverse

KM# 201b • Copper Plated Zinc, 19 mm. •
Notes: MS60 prices are for brown coins and MS65 prices are for coins that are at least 90% original red.

Date	Mintage	XF-40	MS-65	Prf-65
1982S	3,857,479	—	—	3.00
1983	7,752,355,000	—	.25	—
1983 Doubled Die	Inc. above	—	400	—
1983D	6,467,199,428	—	.50	—
1983S	3,279,126	—	—	4.00
1984	8,151,079,000	—	.25	. —
1984 Doubled Die	Inc. above	—	275	—
1984D	5,569,238,906	—	.75	—
1984S	3,065,110	—	—	4.50
1985	5,648,489,887	—	.25	—
1985D	5,287,399,926	—	.25	—
1985S	3,362,821	—	—	6.00
1986	4,491,395,493	—	1.50	—
1986D	4,442,866,698	—	1.25	—
1986S	3,010,497	—	—	7.50
1987	4,682,466,931	—	.25	—
1987D	4,879,389,514	—	.25	—
1987S	4,227,728	—	—	5.00
1988	6,092,810,000	—	.25	—
1988D	5,253,740,443	—	.25	—
1988S	3,262,948	—	—	4.00
1989	7,261,535,000	—	.25	—
1989D	5,345,467,111	—	.25	—
1989S	3,220,194	—	—	6.00
1990	6,851,765,000	—	.25	—
1990D	4,922,894,533	—	.25	—
1990S	3,299,559	—	—	5.00
1990 no S, Proof only	Inc. above	—	—	2,750
1991	5,165,940,000	—	.25	—
1991D	4,158,442,076	—	.25	—
1991S	2,867,787	—	—	5.00
1992	4,648,905,000	—	.25	—
1992D	4,448,673,300	—	.25	—
1992D Close AM, Proof Reverse Die	Inc. above	—	—	—
1992S	4,176,560	—	—	5.00
1993	5,684,705,000	—	.25	—
1993D	6,426,650,571	—	.25	—
1993S	3,394,792	—	—	7.00
1994	6,500,850,000	—	.25	—
1994D	7,131,765,000	—	.25	—
1994S	3,269,923	—	—	4.00
1995	6,411,440,000	—	.25	—
1995 Doubled Die Obverse	Inc. above	20.00	50.00	—
1995D	7,128,560,000	—	.25	—
1995S	2,707,481	—	—	9.50
1996	6,612,465,000	—	.25	—
1996D	6,510,795,000	—	.25	—
1996S	2,915,212	—	—	6.50
1997	4,622,800,000	—	.25	—
1997D	4,576,555,000	—	.25	—
1997S	2,796,678	—	—	11.50
1998	5,032,155,000	—	.25	—
1998 Wide AM, reverse from proof die	Inc. above	—	—	—
1998D	5,255,353,500	—	.25	—
1998S	2,957,286	—	—	9.50
1999	5,237,600,000	—	.25	—

Date	Mintage	XF-40	MS-65	Prf-65
1999 Wide AM, reverse from proof die	Inc. above	—	—	—
1999D	6,360,065,000	—	.25	—
1999S	3,362,462	—	—	5.00
2000	5,503,200,000	—	.25	—
2000 Wide AM, reverse from proof die	Inc. above	—	—	—
2000D	8,774,220,000	—	.25	—
2000S	4,063,361	—	—	4.00
2001	4,959,600,000	—	.25	—
2001D	5,374,990,000	—	.25	—
2001S	3,099,096	—	—	4.00
2002	3,260,800,000	—	.25	—
2002D	4,028,055,000	—	.25	—
2002S	3,157,739	—	—	4.00
2003	3,300,000,000	—	.25	—
2003D	3,548,000,000	—	.25	—
2003S	3,116,590	—	—	4.00
2004	3,379,600,000	—	.25	—
2004D	3,456,400,000	—	.25	—
2004S	2,992,069	—	—	4.00
2005	3,935,600,000	—	.25	—
2005D	3,764,450,000	—	.25	—
2005S	3,273,000	—	—	4.00
2006	4,290,000,000	—	.25	—
2006D	3,944,000,000	—	.25	—
2006S	2,923,105	—	—	4.00
2007	—	—	1.50	—
2007D	—	—	1.50	—
2007S	—	—	—	4.00
2008	—	—	1.50	—
2008D	—	—	1.50	—
2008S	—	—	—	4.00

Lincoln Bicentennial
Bust right obverse   Log cabin reverse

KM# 441 • 2.5000 g., Copper Plated Zinc, 19 mm. • **Rev. Designer:** Richard Masters and James Licaretz

Date	Mintage	XF-40	MS-65	Prf-65
2009P	284,400,000	—	1.50	—
2009D	350,400,000	—	1.50	—

KM# 441a • 3.3100 g., Brass • Rev. Designer: Richard Masters and James Licaretz

Date	Mintage	XF-40	MS-65	Prf-65
2009S	—	—	—	4.00

Lincoln seated on log reverse

KM# 442 • 2.5000 g., Copper Plated Zinc, 19 mm. • **Rev. Designer:** Charles Vickers

Date	Mintage	XF-40	MS-65	Prf-65
2009P	376,000,000	—	1.50	—
2009D	363,600,000	—	1.50	—

KM# 442a • 3.1100 g., Brass, 19 mm. • **Rev. Designer:** Charles Vickers

Date	Mintage	XF-40	MS-65	Prf-65
2009S	—	—	—	4.00

CENT

Lincoln standing before Illinois Statehouse reverse

KM# 443 • 2.5000 g., **Copper Plated Zinc**, 19 mm. • **Rev. Designer:** Joel Ishowitz and Don Everhart

Date	Mintage	XF-40	MS-65	Prf-65
2009P	316,000,000	—	1.50	—
2009D	336,000,000	—	1.50	—

KM# 443a • 3.1100 g., **Brass**, 19 mm. • **Rev. Designer:** Joel Iskowitz and Don Everhart

Date	Mintage	XF-40	MS-65	Prf-65
2009S	—	—	—	4.00

Capitol Building reverse

KM# 444 • 2.5000 g., **Copper Plated Zinc** • **Rev. Designer:** Susan Gamble and Joseph Menna

Date	Mintage	XF-40	MS-65	Prf-65
2009P	129,600,000	—	1.50	—
2009D	198,000,000	—	1.50	—

KM# 444a • 3.1100 g., **Brass**, 19 mm. • **Rev. Designer:** Susan Ganmble and Joseph Menna

Date	Mintage	XF-40	MS-65	Prf-65
2009S	—	—	—	4.00

Lincoln bust right obverse   Shield reverse

KM# 468 • 2.5000 g., **Copper Plated Zinc**, 19 mm. • **Obv. Designer:** Victor D. Brenner **Rev. Designer:** Lyndall Bass and Joseph Menna

Date	Mintage	XF-40	MS-65	Prf-65
2010P	—	—	1.50	—
2010D	—	—	1.50	—
2010S	—	—	—	4.00
2011P	—	—	1.50	—
2011D	—	—	1.50	—
2011S	—	—	—	4.00

2 CENTS

Shield in front of crossed arrows, banner above, date below
Value within wheat wreath reverse

Small motto   Large motto

KM# 94 • 6.2200 g., **Copper-Tin-Zinc**, 23 mm. • **Rev. Legend:** UNITED STATES OF AMERICA **Designer:** James B. Longacre **Notes:** The motto IN GOD WE TRUST was modified in 1864, resulting in small-motto and large-motto varieties for that year.

Date	Mintage	G-4	VG-8	F-12	VF-20	XF-40	AU-50	MS-60	MS-65	Prf-65
1864 small motto	19,847,500	140	210	285	425	650	725	1,125	7,500	75,000
1864 large motto	Inc. above	16.50	18.50	20.00	27.50	42.50	70.00	84.00	1,650	3,950
1865 fancy 5	13,640,000	16.50	18.50	20.00	27.50	42.50	70.00	84.00	1,650	850
1865 plain 5	Inc. above	16.50	18.50	21.00	29.00	45.00	75.00	90.00	1,750	2,950
1866	3,177,000	17.00	20.00	21.50	29.00	46.00	75.00	94.00	2,550	2,850
1867	2,938,750	18.00	21.00	36.00	46.00	60.00	96.00	125	2,900	2,900
1867 double die obverse	Inc. above	—	65.00	135	200	275	440	575	12,500	—
1868	2,803,750	18.00	22.00	37.50	47.50	65.00	105	135	2,900	2,850
1869	1,546,000	20.00	23.00	40.00	50.00	79.00	125	165	2,400	2,850
1869 repunched 18	Inc. above	35.00	45.00	75.00	150	325	550	—	—	—
1869/8 die crack	Inc. above	150	185	375	435	650	900	—	—	—
1870	861,250	31.00	42.00	60.00	82.00	135	190	295	8,250	2,850
1871	721,250	43.00	49.00	70.00	110	155	215	285	3,850	2,850
1872	65,000	325	395	550	740	925	1,050	1,500	8,850	2,950
1873 closed 3 proof only	Est. 600	1,250	1,375	1,500	1,625	1,750	2,000	—	—	4,250
1873 open 3 proof only	Est. 500	1,275	1,400	1,575	1,700	1,875	2,150	—	—	5,500

SILVER 3 CENTS

Silver 3 Cents - Type 1
Shield within star, no outlines in star obverse
Roman numeral in designed C, within circle of stars reverse

KM# 75 • 0.8000 g., 0.7500 **Silver**, 0.0193 oz. ASW, 14 mm. • **Obv. Legend** UNITED STATES OF AMERICA **Designer:** James B. Longacre

Date	Mintage	G-4	VG-8	F-12	VF-20	XF-40	AU-50	MS-60	MS-65	Prf-65
1851	5,447,400	32.00	48.50	51.00	58.50	68.00	145	180	825	—
1851O	720,000	38.50	58.50	61.00	95.00	160	275	500	3,100	—
1852	18,663,500	32.00	48.50	51.00	58.50	68.00	145	180	825	—
1853	11,400,000	32.00	48.50	51.00	58.50	68.00	145	180	825	—

1851-O Silver Three-Cent Piece
Grade XF-40

■ Retail Price

Silver 3 Cents - Type 2
Shield within star, three outlines in star obverse
Roman numeral in designed C, within circle of stars reverse

KM# 80 • 0.7500 g., 0.9000 **Silver**, 0.0217 oz. ASW, 14 mm. • **Obv. Legend** UNITED STATES OF AMERICA **Designer:** James B. Longacre

Date	Mintage	G-4	VG-8	F-12	VF-20	XF-40	AU-50	MS-60	MS-65	Prf-65
1854	671,000	32.00	48.50	51.00	59.50	112	205	340	2,700	33,500
1855	139,000	44.00	57.50	75.00	125	200	325	520	7,400	15,000
1856	1,458,000	34.00	50.50	54.00	67.00	119.5	205	260	3,250	15,500
1857	1,042,000	34.00	50.50	54.00	67.00	112	223	285	2,375	13,500
1858	1,604,000	33.00	49.50	52.00	62.00	122	205	230	2,350	6,400

Silver 3 Cents - Type 3
Shield within star, two outlines in star obverse
Roman numeral in designed C, within circle of stars reverse

KM# 88 • 0.7500 g., 0.9000 **Silver**, 0.0217 oz. ASW, 14 mm. • **Obv. Legend** UNITED STATES OF AMERICA **Designer:** James B. Longacre

Date	Mintage	G-4	VG-8	F-12	VF-20	XF-40	AU-50	MS-60	MS-65	Prf-65
1859	365,000	333	50.00	52.00	61.00	87.00	160	185	975	2,150
1860	287,000	33.00	50.00	52.00	61.00	83.00	160	185	1,050	4,000
1861	498,000	33.00	50.00	52.00	61.00	83.00	160	185	1,050	1,800
1862	343,550	39.00	52.00	54.00	63.00	88.00	180	225	935	1,400
1862/1	Inc. above	36.00	54.00	58.00	68.00	94.00	177	210	865	—
1863	21,460	375	420	450	485	520	725	825	2,250	1,350
1863/62 proof only; Rare	Inc. above	—	—	—	—	—	—	—	—	5,400
1864	12,470	375	420	450	485	520	725	850	1,675	1,350
1865	8,500	475	525	550	620	665	700	875	1,650	1,350
1866	22,725	375	420	450	485	520	675	775	1,950	1,325
1867	4,625	475	525	575	625	675	725	850	2,750	1,300
1868	4,100	475	535	585	640	690	750	875	5,750	1,400
1869	5,100	475	535	585	640	690	750	875	2,450	1,400
1869/68 proof only; Rare	Inc. above	—	—	—	—	—	—	—	—	—
1870	4,000	450	460	525	600	665	750	950	5,650	1,350
1871	4,360	440	450	535	625	670	710	835	1,800	1,450
1872	1,950	465	485	550	645	690	750	875	5,500	1,350
1873 proof only	600	—	—	—	—	950	1,050	—	—	2,950

NICKEL 3 CENTS

Coronet head left, date below obverse
Roman numeral value within wreath reverse

KM# 95 • 1.9400 g., **Copper-Nickel**, 17.9 mm. • **Obv. Legend** UNITED STATES OF AMERICA
Designer: James B. Longacre

Date	Mintage	G-4	VG-8	F-12	VF-20	XF-40	AU-50	MS-60	MS-65	Prf-65
1865	11,382,000	15.50	16.50	17.50	22.50	37.50	60.00	100.00	650	6,500
1866	4,801,000	15.50	16.50	17.50	22.50	37.50	60.00	100.00	650	1,725
1867	3,915,000	15.50	16.50	17.50	22.50	37.50	60.00	100.00	770	1,575
1868	3,252,000	15.50	16.50	17.50	22.50	37.50	60.00	100.00	650	1,450
1869	1,604,000	16.50	17.50	19.50	25.50	40.50	61.00	120	795	1,050
1870	1,335,000	17.50	18.50	20.50	26.50	41.50	62.00	135	795	2,250
1871	604,000	17.50	19.00	22.50	27.50	42.50	64.00	155	800	1,200
1872	862,000	19.00	22.50	24.50	28.50	43.50	68.00	175	1,075	910
1873	1,173,000	16.50	18.50	22.50	25.50	40.50	62.00	145	1,375	1,125
1874	790,000	17.50	20.50	22.50	27.50	42.50	66.00	160	1,050	950
1875	228,000	19.00	22.50	27.50	30.50	45.50	80.00	190	850	1,500
1876	162,000	20.50	23.50	26.50	34.50	49.50	95.00	225	1,550	1,025
1877 proof	Est. 900	1,100	1,150	1,175	1,250	1,300	1,350	—	—	3,750
1878 proof	2,350	615	645	720	770	795	830	—	—	1,200
1879	41,200	65.00	75.00	96.00	110	115	180	320	850	690
1880	24,955	100.00	115	130	165	185	235	375	800	700
1881	1,080,575	15.50	16.50	19.00	23.50	39.50	60.00	100.00	670	680
1882	25,300	130	150	180	225	300	325	425	1,100	700
1883	10,609	200	225	260	305	375	425	480	4,850	690
1884	5,642	400	445	550	600	645	730	800	6,250	700
1885	4,790	470	520	645	700	745	775	900	2,300	720
1886 proof	4,290	320	330	345	385	385	420	—	—	715
1887/6 proof	7,961	350	390	415	450	460	515	—	—	940
1887	Inc. above	305	355	395	440	455	500	540	1,350	1,125
1888	41,083	54.00	63.00	70.00	80.00	100.00	170	315	725	690
1889	21,561	90.00	115	140	180	220	255	320	800	690

HALF DIME

Flowing Hair Half Dime

KM# 15 • 1.3500 g., 0.8920 **Silver**, 0.0387 oz. ASW, 16.5 mm. • **Designer:** Robert Scot

Date	Mintage	G-4	VG-8	F-12	VF-20	XF-40	MS-60
1794	86,416	1,325	1,625	2,150	3,125	7,325	19,850
1795	Inc. above	1,050	1,350	1,875	2,850	5,750	13,850

Draped Bust Half Dime
Draped bust right obverse   Small eagle reverse

KM# 23 • 1.3500 g., 0.8920 **Silver**, 0.0387 oz. ASW, 16.5 mm. • **Designer:** Robert Scot

Date	Mintage	G-4	VG-8	F-12	VF-20	XF-40	MS-60
1796	10,230	1,435	1,550	3,000	4,700	8,700	19,550
1796 LIKERTY	Inc. above	1,485	1,600	3,050	4,750	8,750	19,600
Note: In 1796 the word LIBERTY was spelled LIKERTY on a die.							
1796/5	Inc. above	1,555	1,700	3,150	4,850	8,850	19,700
1797 13 stars	44,527	2,100	2,650	4,100	5,800	9,800	32,750
1797 15 stars	Inc. above	1,385	1,500	2,950	4,650	8,650	19,500
1797 16 stars	Inc. above	1,535	1,750	3,200	4,900	8,900	19,750

Draped Bust Half Dime
Draped bust right, flanked by stars, date at angle below   Heraldic eagle reverse

KM# 34 • 1.3500 g., 0.8920 **Silver**, 0.0387 oz. ASW, 16.5 mm. • **Obv. Legend** LIBERTY **Rev. Legend:** UNITED STATES OF AMERICA **Designer:** Robert Scot

Date	Mintage	G-4	VG-8	F-12	VF-20	XF-40	MS-60
1800	24,000	1,000	1,250	1,875	2,350	6,750	13,850
1800 LIBEKTY	Inc. above	1,000	1,250	1,875	2,350	7,250	15,400
1801	33,910	1,225	1,500	2,125	2,600	7,000	18,100
1802	3,060	44,500	65,000	95,000	135,000	300,000	—
1803 Large 8	37,850	1,100	1,375	2,000	2,475	6,875	13,975
1803 Small 8	Inc. above	1,325	1,625	2,250	2,725	7,125	16,200
1805	15,600	1,225	1,525	2,350	2,825	10,150	31,350

1802 Half Dime
Grade F-12

Retail Price

Liberty Cap Half Dime
Classic head left, flanked by stars, date below
Eagle with arrows in talons, banner above reverse

KM# 47 • 1.3500 g., 0.8920 **Silver**, 0.0387 oz. ASW, 15.5 mm. • **Rev. Legend:** UNITED STATES OF AMERICA **Designer:** William Kneass

Date	Mintage	G-4	VG-8	F-12	VF-20	XF-40	AU-50	MS-60	MS-65
1829	1,230,000	55.00	60.00	72.00	125	185	275	365	3,300
1830	1,240,000	47.50	52.50	62.00	95.00	155	215	350	3,150
1831	1,242,700	47.50	52.50	62.00	95.00	155	215	350	3,150
1832	965,000	47.50	52.50	62.00	95.00	155	215	350	3,150
1833	1,370,000	47.50	52.50	62.00	95.00	155	215	350	3,150
1834	1,480,000	47.50	52.50	62.00	95.00	155	215	350	3,150
1835 large date and 5C.	2,760,000	47.50	60.00	74.00	110	170	235	350	3,150
1835 large date, small 5C.	Inc. above	47.50	52.50	62.00	95.00	155	215	410	4,350
1835 small date, large 5C.	Inc. above	47.50	52.50	62.00	95.00	155	215	375	4,050
1835 small date and 5C.	Inc. above	47.50	52.50	62.00	95.00	155	215	350	3,150
1836 large 5C.	1,900,000	47.50	52.50	62.00	95.00	155	215	350	3,150
1836 small 5C.	Inc. above	49.50	52.50	66.00	105	167	227	362	3,650
1837 large 5C.	2,276,000	47.50	52.50	70.00	113	170	235	395	4,350
1837 small 5C.	Inc. above	54.50	62.50	77.00	125	235	465	950	11,000

Seated Liberty Half Dime
Seated Liberty, no stars around border, date below
Value within wreath reverse

KM# 60 • 1.3400 g., 0.9000 **Silver**, 0.0388 oz. ASW, 15.5 mm. • **Rev. Legend:** UNITED STATES OF AMERICA **Designer:** Christian Gobrecht **Notes:** A design modification in 1837 resulted in small-date and large-date varieties for that year.

Date	Mintage	G-4	VG-8	F-12	VF-20	XF-40	AU-50	MS-60	MS-65
1837 small date	Inc. above	35.00	46.50	75.00	135	220	485	770	4,450
1837 large date	Inc. above	39.00	49.50	82.00	150	235	435	640	3,650
1838O	70,000	110	130	250	475	975	1,450	2,500	29,500

Seated Liberty Half Dime
Seated Liberty, stars around top 1/2 of border, date below
Value within wreath reverse

KM# 62.1 • 1.3400 g., 0.9000 **Silver**, 0.0388 oz. ASW, 15.5 mm. • **Rev. Legend:** UNITED STATES OF AMERICA **Designer:** Christian Gobrecht **Notes:** The two varieties of 1838 are distinguished by the size of the stars on the obverse. The 1839-O with reverse of 1838-O was struck from rusted reverse dies. The result is a bumpy surface on this variety's reverse.

Date	Mintage	G-4	VG-8	F-12	VF-20	XF-40	AU-50	MS-60	MS-65
1838 large stars	2,255,000	21.50	25.50	29.00	36.00	88.00	173	280	2,475
1838 small stars	Inc. above	25.50	31.50	46.00	115	189	274	610	3,950
1839	1,069,150	22.50	26.50	30.00	37.00	93.00	178	280	2,400
1839O	1,034,039	26.50	30.50	34.00	41.00	88.00	173	730	6,850
1839O reverse 1838O	Inc. above	500	700	1,200	1,750	3,000	—	—	—
1840	1,344,085	23.50	27.50	31.00	38.00	80.00	165	270	2,275
1840O	935,000	28.50	32.50	38.00	48.00	138	343	1,250	—

Seated Liberty Half Dime
Seated Liberty, stars around top 1/2 of border, date below

KM# 62.2 • 1.3400 g., 0.9000 **Silver**, 0.0388 oz. ASW, 15.5 mm. • **Rev. Legend:** UNITED STATES OF AMERICA **Designer:** Christian Gobrecht **Notes:** In 1840 drapery was added to Liberty's left elbow. Varieties for the 1848 Philadelphia strikes are distinguished by the size of the numerals in the date.

Date	Mintage	G-4	VG-8	F-12	VF-20	XF-40	AU-50	MS-60	MS-65
1840	Inc. above	20.00	18.00	75.00	135	210	350	490	3,850
1840O	Inc. above	51.00	60.00	115	225	650	1,350	6,500	—
1841	1,150,000	17.00	21.50	23.50	31.00	58.00	125	180	1,325
1841O	815,000	20.00	24.50	30.00	50.00	125	300	650	6,750
1842	815,000	16.00	21.50	23.50	28.00	55.00	125	175	1,850
1842O	350,000	38.00	45.00	75.00	225	550	1,050	2,250	16,500
1843	1,165,000	16.00	21.50	23.50	28.00	55.00	120	175	1,365
1844	430,000	19.00	24.50	26.50	34.00	58.00	125	180	1,250
1844O	220,000	80.00	110	210	600	1,300	2,650	5,400	27,500
1845	1,564,000	16.00	21.50	23.50	35.00	58.00	120	175	1,250
1845/1845	Inc. above	19.00	24.50	26.50	38.00	85.00	130	190	1,300
1846	27,000	410	550	850	1,250	2,475	3,600	11,500	—
1847	1,274,000	16.00	21.50	23.50	28.00	55.00	125	175	1,250
1848 medium date	668,000	19.00	24.50	26.50	34.00	65.00	135	215	3,150
1848 large date	Inc. above	22.50	28.00	48.00	65.00	145	275	635	4,250
1848O	600,000	20.00	25.50	33.00	62.00	135	265	450	2,450
1849/8	1,309,000	28.50	35.00	47.50	67.50	140	250	785	2,950
1849/6	Inc. above	24.00	26.00	30.00	56.50	110	200	425	2,900
1849	Inc. above	19.00	18.50	27.50	52.50	65.00	135	190	1,925
1849O	140,000	29.00	40.00	95.00	225	540	1,100	2,350	—
1850	955,000	19.00	24.50	26.50	34.00	60.00	125	190	1,400
1850O	690,000	20.00	24.50	35.00	65.00	125	280	685	4,450
1851	781,000	16.00	21.50	23.50	28.00	57.00	120	175	1,450
1851O	860,000	19.00	24.50	26.50	41.50	110	220	500	4,350
1852	1,000,500	16.00	21.50	23.50	28.00	57.00	120	175	1,250
1852O	260,000	25.00	44.50	79.00	135	275	475	885	11,500
1853	135,000	40.00	60.00	90.00	175	300	525	850	2,850
1853O	160,000	285	325	450	850	1,800	3,500	6,450	27,500

1846 Half Dime
Grade XF-40

Retail Price

Seated Liberty Half Dime
Seated Liberty, stars around top 1/2 of border, arrows at date obverse
Value within wreath reverse

KM# 76 • 1.2400 g., 0.9000 **Silver**, 0.0359 oz. ASW • **Rev. Legend:** UNITED STATES OF AMERICA
Designer: Christian Gobrecht

Date	Mintage	G-4	VG-8	F-12	VF-20	XF-40	AU-50	MS-60	MS-65	Prf-65
1853	13,210,020	16.00	19.00	22.50	28.00	58.00	135	200	2,100	—
1853O	2,200,000	19.00	27.00	30.50	36.00	66.00	143	315	3,950	—
1854	5,740,000	16.00	19.00	24.50	30.00	60.00	137	210	2,100	15,000
1854O	1,560,000	17.00	20.00	32.50	38.00	88.00	165	240	4,250	—
1855	1,750,000	17.00	20.00	24.50	30.00	60.00	137	205	2,500	15,000
1855O	600,000	21.00	25.00	38.50	54.00	140	220	545	4,950	—

Seated Liberty Half Dime
Seated Liberty, stars around top 1/2 of border, date below
Value within wreath reverse

KM# A62.2 • 1.2400 g., 0.9000 **Silver**, 0.0359 oz. ASW • **Rev. Legend:** UNITED STATES OF AMERICA
Designer: Christian Gobrecht **Notes:** On the 1858/inverted date variety, the date was engraved into the die upside down and then re-engraved right side up. Another 1858 variety has the date doubled.

Date	Mintage	G-4	VG-8	F-12	VF-20	XF-40	AU-50	MS-60	MS-65	Prf-65
1856	4,880,000	16.00	21.00	23.00	27.00	52.50	115	175	1,400	15,000
1856O	1,100,000	17.00	22.00	26.00	28.00	97.50	260	470	2,350	—
1857	7,280,000	16.00	21.00	23.00	27.00	52.50	115	175	1,250	5,600
1857O	1,380,000	17.00	22.00	24.00	28.00	62.50	185	320	1,950	—
1858	3,500,000	16.00	21.00	23.00	27.00	52.50	115	175	1,350	5,500
1858 inverted date	Inc. above	30.00	43.50	62.50	100.00	225	300	675	3,950	—
1858 double date	Inc. above	45.00	60.00	90.00	175	285	425	800	—	—

HALF DIME

Date	Mintage	G-4	VG-8	F-12	VF-20	XF-40	AU-50	MS-60	MS-65	Prf-65
1858O	1,660,000	17.00	22.00	24.00	28.00	71.50	137	245	1,850	—
1859	340,000	18.00	23.00	25.00	29.00	54.50	117	225	1,550	4,000
1859O	560,000	19.00	24.00	26.00	42.00	128.5	200	285	2,050	—

Seated Liberty Half Dime
Seated Liberty, date below
Value within wreath reverse

KM# 91 • 1.2400 g., 0.9000 **Silver**, 0.0359 oz. ASW • **Obv. Legend** UNITED STATES OF AMERICA
Designer: Christian Gobrecht

Date	Mintage	G-4	VG-8	F-12	VF-20	XF-40	AU-50	MS-60	MS-65	Prf-65
1860	799,000	16.00	20.00	23.00	26.00	47.00	77.00	145	1,025	1,550
1860O	1,060,000	16.00	20.00	23.00	29.00	49.00	79.00	170	1,375	—
1861	3,361,000	16.00	20.00	22.00	25.00	45.00	75.00	145	1,025	1,600
1861/0	Inc. above	25.00	32.50	59.00	125	260	435	560	3,650	—
1862	1,492,550	20.00	25.00	34.00	44.00	64.00	94.00	154	1,025	1,550
1863	18,460	200	250	300	400	485	550	800	1,575	1,550
1863S	100,000	35.00	45.00	70.00	95.00	165	300	750	3,450	—
1864	48,470	375	475	575	750	950	1,100	1,375	2,350	1,600
1864S	90,000	60.00	75.00	115	175	250	450	785	3,750	—
1865	13,500	375	475	575	750	950	1,100	1,350	1,950	1,550
1865S	120,000	29.00	40.00	60.00	85.00	145	375	975	5,450	—
1866	10,725	350	475	550	700	875	1,000	1,225	2,575	1,550
1866S	120,000	29.00	40.00	60.00	85.00	145	285	485	5,000	—
1867	8,625	550	650	775	900	1,100	1,200	1,375	2,350	1,550
1867S	120,000	29.00	40.00	60.00	85.00	150	325	850	3,850	—
1868	89,200	60.00	90.00	190	225	300	425	625	2,400	1,550
1868S	280,000	20.00	25.00	35.00	42.00	59.00	125	325	3,250	—
1869	208,600	20.00	25.00	35.00	42.00	59.00	135	200	1,375	1,560
1869S	230,000	18.00	24.00	30.00	35.00	55.00	125	310	4,150	—
1870	536,600	18.00	24.00	30.00	35.00	55.00	125	185	975	1,550
1870S unique	—	—	—	—	—	—	—	—	—	—
Note: 1870S, Superior Galleries, July 1986, brilliant uncirculated, $253,000.										
1871	1,873,960	16.00	20.00	22.00	25.00	45.00	75.00	135	975	1,550
1871S	161,000	25.00	30.00	45.00	60.00	90.00	175	320	2,425	—
1872	2,947,950	16.00	20.00	22.00	25.00	45.00	75.00	135	975	1,550
1872S mint mark in wreath	837,000	16.00	20.00	22.00	25.00	45.00	75.00	135	975	—
1872S mint mark below wreath	Inc. above	17.00	21.00	24.00	27.00	47.00	80.00	135	975	—
1873	712,600	16.00	20.00	22.00	25.00	45.00	75.00	135	1,375	1,550
1873S	324,000	20.00	25.00	30.00	42.00	62.00	90.00	150	975	—

5 CENTS

Shield Nickel
Draped garland above shield, date below
Value within center of rays between stars reverse

KM# 96 • 5.0000 g., **Copper-Nickel**, 20.5 mm. • **Obv. Legend** IN GOD WE TRUST **Rev. Legend:**
UNITED STATES OF AMERICA **Designer:** James B. Longacre

Date	Mintage	G-4	VG-8	F-12	VF-20	XF-40	AU-50	MS-60	MS-65	Prf-65
1866	14,742,500	27.50	38.50	50.00	75.00	155	235	260	2,700	3,850
1867	2,019,000	37.50	50.00	67.50	100.00	200	295	350	4,150	75,000

Draped garland above shield, date below
Value within circle of stars reverse

KM# 97 • 5.0000 g., **Copper-Nickel** • **Obv. Legend** IN GOD WE TRUST **Rev. Legend:** UNITED STATES OF AMERICA

Date	Mintage	G-4	VG-8	F-12	VF-20	XF-40	AU-50	MS-60	MS-65	Prf-65
1867	28,890,500	18.00	21.00	28.00	37.50	60.00	120	160	900	3,450
1868	28,817,000	18.00	21.00	28.00	37.50	60.00	120	160	975	1,500
1869	16,395,000	18.00	21.00	28.00	37.50	60.00	120	160	775	1,000
1870	4,806,000	27.00	34.00	52.00	65.00	90.00	145	200	1,700	1,250
1871	561,000	70.00	90.00	125	170	265	325	375	2,100	1,100
1872	6,036,000	35.00	42.00	70.00	80.00	115	150	235	1,350	820
1873 Open 3	4,550,000	28.00	36.00	52.00	65.00	80.00	135	200	2,400	840
1873 Closed 3	Inc. above	34.00	42.00	65.00	90.00	150	220	350	3,250	—
1874	3,538,000	29.00	39.00	70.00	82.00	105	140	225	1,500	1,000
1875	2,097,000	40.00	55.00	80.00	110	145	190	250	2,000	1,650
1876	2,530,000	38.00	50.00	74.00	100.00	135	175	230	1,900	900
1877 proof	Est. 900	1,500	1,650	1,750	2,000	2,150	2,300	—	—	4,300
1878 proof	2,350	800	875	900	1,100	1,300	1,450	—	—	2,150
1879	29,100	415	520	625	675	750	825	970	2,000	840
1879/8	Inc. above	—	—	—	—	—	—	—	—	850
1880	19,995	560	620	775	950	1,300	1,750	3,450	47,500	700
1881	72,375	270	340	445	500	600	730	800	1,900	660
1882	11,476,600	18.00	20.00	27.00	36.00	58.00	115	150	750	660
1883	1,456,919	18.00	21.00	32.00	37.50	60.00	118	160	750	660
1883/2	Inc. above	210	285	425	650	850	1,000	1,400	4,000	—

Liberty Nickel
Liberty head left, within circle of stars, date below
Roman numeral value within wreath, without CENTS below reverse

KM# 111 • 5.0000 g., **Copper-Nickel**, 21.2 mm. • **Rev. Legend:** UNITED STATES OF AMERICA
Designer: Charles E. Barber

Date	Mintage	G-4	VG-8	F-12	VF-20	XF-40	AU-50	MS-60	MS-65	Prf-65
1883	5,479,519	7.00	7.75	8.50	8.75	9.25	12.00	25.50	215	1,075

Liberty head left, within circle of stars, date below
Roman numeral value within wreath, CENTS below reverse

KM# 112 • 5.0000 g., **Copper-Nickel**, 21.2 mm. • **Rev. Legend:** UNITED STATES OF AMERICA

Date	Mintage	G-4	VG-8	F-12	VF-20	XF-40	AU-50	MS-60	MS-65	Prf-65
1883	16,032,983	19.00	29.50	39.50	55.00	85.00	120	160	625	610
1884	11,273,942	22.50	33.50	39.50	59.00	92.00	135	190	1,675	610
1885	1,476,490	585	635	875	1,050	1,350	1,650	1,950	8,650	3,150
1886	3,330,290	285	335	400	500	685	850	1,950	7,250	1,950
1887	15,263,652	16.00	25.00	31.00	44.00	78.00	115	150	1,025	585
1888	10,720,483	28.00	44.00	68.00	130	185	250	295	1,500	585
1889	15,881,361	14.50	19.50	30.00	52.50	77.00	125	155	850	585
1890	16,259,272	10.50	20.50	26.00	39.50	68.50	115	165	1,365	585
1891	16,834,350	5.75	11.00	22.00	37.50	60.00	120	160	1,050	585
1892	11,699,642	6.50	11.00	22.50	39.00	65.00	120	165	1,300	585
1893	13,370,195	5.50	11.00	24.00	37.50	60.00	120	155	1,050	585
1894	5,413,132	16.50	31.00	98.00	165	230	295	350	1,500	585
1895	9,979,884	5.75	7.50	24.00	45.00	66.00	120	145	2,200	585
1896	8,842,920	9.00	21.00	41.50	68.50	98.00	150	205	1,950	585
1897	20,428,735	3.25	4.50	12.50	27.50	46.00	69.50	95.00	925	585
1898	12,532,087	2.15	4.25	11.00	23.50	40.00	68.50	130	1,025	585
1899	26,029,031	1.80	3.00	8.50	19.50	34.00	62.50	89.00	560	585
1900	27,255,995	1.60	2.50	8.50	19.00	34.00	69.50	84.00	650	585
1901	26,480,213	1.60	2.50	7.00	14.50	34.00	65.00	100.00	550	585
1902	31,480,579	1.60	2.50	4.00	15.00	32.00	65.00	102	550	585
1903	28,006,725	1.80	2.50	4.75	14.50	32.00	60.00	77.00	500	585
1904	21,404,984	1.60	2.40	4.75	11.50	30.00	65.00	96.00	500	585
1905	29,827,276	1.60	2.40	4.00	12.00	30.00	65.00	96.00	550	585
1906	38,613,725	1.80	2.40	4.00	11.50	30.00	65.00	96.00	650	585
1907	39,214,800	1.50	2.20	4.00	12.00	30.00	65.00	96.00	1,000	585
1908	22,686,177	1.80	2.20	4.00	12.00	30.00	68.00	104	1,100	585
1909	11,590,526	2.50	2.80	4.35	13.00	33.00	80.00	112	1,075	585
1910	30,169,353	1.50	1.85	4.00	10.00	30.00	52.00	62.00	550	585
1911	39,559,372	1.50	1.85	4.00	10.00	30.00	52.00	62.00	500	585
1912	26,236,714	1.50	1.85	4.00	10.00	30.00	52.00	62.00	570	585
1912D	8,474,000	2.75	3.60	11.50	38.00	70.00	170	280	2,200	—
1912S	238,000	165	190	220	480	810	1,300	1,475	5,900	—
1913 5 known	—	—	—	—	—	—	—	—	—	—

Note: 1913, Heritage Sale, January 2010, Proof-64 (Olsen), $3,737,500. Private treaty, 2007, (Eliasburg) Proof-66 $5 million.

Buffalo Nickel
American Bison standing on a mound reverse

KM# 133 • 5.0000 g., **Copper-Nickel**, 21.2 mm. • **Designer:** James Earle Fraser

Date	Mintage	G-4	VG-8	F-12	VF-20	XF-40	AU-50	MS-60	MS-65	Prf-65
1913	30,993,520	8.00	14.50	15.00	16.00	19.00	25.00	32.50	190	3,150
1913D	5,337,000	16.00	19.50	21.00	25.00	35.00	57.00	62.50	310	—
1913S	2,105,000	43.00	47.00	50.00	60.00	75.00	100.00	125	690	—

American Bison standing on a line reverse

1937D 3-legged   1918/17D

KM# 134 • 5.0000 g., **Copper-Nickel**, 21.2 mm. • **Designer:** James Earle Fraser **Notes:** In 1913 the reverse design was modified so the ground under the buffalo was represented as a line rather than a mound. On the 1937D 3-legged variety, the buffalo's right front leg is missing, the result of a damaged die.

Date	Mintage	G-4	VG-8	F-12	VF-20	XF-40	AU-50	MS-60	MS-65	Prf-65
1913	29,858,700	8.00	12.00	13.00	14.00	19.00	25.00	34.00	355	2,500
1913D	4,156,000	125	155	180	190	265	240	285	1,450	—
1913S	1,209,000	350	400	420	430	575	675	885	3,850	—
1914	20,665,738	18.00	21.00	22.00	23.00	27.50	37.50	47.00	420	2,250
1914/3	Inc. above	150	300	425	525	700	1,050	2,850	30,000	—
1914D	3,912,000	90.00	132	165	200	335	390	475	1,600	—
1914/3D	Inc. above	115	225	335	450	625	900	3,500	—	—
1914S	3,470,000	26.00	37.50	45.00	62.50	90.00	145	165	22,350	—
1914/3S	Inc. above	250	500	750	1,000	1,450	2,260	4,300	—	—
1915	20,987,270	6.25	7.00	7.75	11.00	21.50	38.50	50.00	325	2,100
1915D	7,569,500	21.50	31.00	41.50	66.00	115	150	235	2,250	—
1915S	1,505,000	47.00	74.00	105	185	326	490	625	3,150	—
1916	63,498,066	5.50	6.40	7.00	8.00	13.50	24.00	43.50	315	3,250
1916 2 Feathers	Inc. above	35.00	—	45.00	—	—	—	—	150	—
1916/16	Inc. above	1,800	3,650	7,150	10,850	16,500	34,500	49,500	375,000	—
1916D	13,333,000	15.00	26.50	29.00	38.50	82.50	110	165	2,250	—
1916S	11,860,000	11.00	13.50	26.00	35.00	75.00	125	185	2,300	—
1917	51,424,029	7.50	8.00	8.75	10.00	16.00	32.50	59.00	535	—
1917 2 Feathers	Inc. above	40.00	—	50.00	—	—	—	—	165	—
1917D	9,910,800	26.00	31.00	55.00	80.00	135	255	345	3,250	—
1917S	4,193,000	23.00	42.00	80.00	110	180	285	395	4,850	—
1917S 2 Feathers	Inc. above	50.00	—	95.00	—	—	—	—	315	—
1918	32,086,314	5.25	6.75	8.00	15.00	31.00	48.50	105	1,550	—
1918/17D	8,362,314	1,000	1,475	2,600	4,950	7,950	10,750	36,500	350,000	—
1918D	Inc. above	22.50	39.00	66.00	135	226	330	430	4,650	—
1918 2 Feathers	Inc. above	50.00	—	95.00	—	—	—	—	315	—
1918S	4,882,000	14.00	27.50	55.00	100.00	175	300	495	25,500	—
1919	60,868,000	2.60	3.50	3.90	7.00	16.00	32.00	58.00	535	—
1919D	8,006,000	15.50	31.00	66.00	115	235	335	570	6,850	—
1919S	7,521,000	8.00	26.00	50.00	110	225	360	540	24,000	—
1920	63,093,000	1.50	2.75	3.25	8.00	16.00	30.00	59.00	700	—
1920D	9,418,000	8.50	19.00	35.00	125	275	340	575	6,850	—
1920S	9,689,000	4.50	12.75	30.00	100.00	260	300	525	25,500	—
1921	10,663,000	4.00	6.25	8.50	25.00	53.50	73.00	125	800	—
1921S	1,557,000	64.00	100.00	180	400	825	1,150	1,575	7,350	—
1923	35,715,000	1.70	3.25	4.25	7.00	14.00	37.50	59.00	575	—
1923S	6,142,000	8.00	11.00	27.00	125	275	335	625	11,500	—
1924	21,620,000	1.25	2.40	4.50	10.00	19.00	41.00	73.50	850	—
1924D	5,258,000	8.00	12.00	30.00	90.00	215	315	375	4,950	—
1924S	1,437,000	16.50	32.00	96.00	455	1,100	1,700	2,300	12,850	—
1925	35,565,100	2.50	3.00	3.75	8.50	16.50	32.00	42.00	490	—
1925D	4,450,000	10.00	26.00	38.00	80.00	160	240	375	5,650	—
1925S	6,256,000	4.50	9.00	17.50	77.50	170	250	425	28,500	—
1926	44,693,000	1.50	2.00	2.80	5.40	11.50	26.00	31.50	235	—

5 CENTS

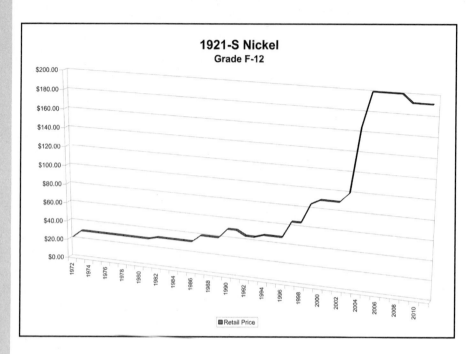

1921-S Nickel
Grade F-12

Date	Mintage	G-4	VG-8	F-12	VF-20	XF-40	AU-50	MS-60	MS-65	Prf-65
1926D	5,638,000	10.00	17.50	28.50	100.00	170	295	335	5,850	—
1926S	970,000	20.00	42.00	100.00	345	850	2,450	4,950	125,000	—
1927	37,981,000	1.40	1.75	2.50	4.50	12.50	26.00	35.00	290	—
1927D	5,730,000	3.00	6.00	7.00	27.50	75.00	115	155	7,950	—
1927S	3,430,000	2.00	3.00	6.00	31.00	80.00	160	490	18,500	—
1928	23,411,000	1.40	1.75	2.50	4.50	12.50	25.00	32.50	310	—
1928D	6,436,000	1.90	2.50	3.75	16.00	40.00	46.50	53.00	685	—
1928S	6,936,000	1.75	2.35	3.00	12.00	27.50	105	225	4,750	—
1929	36,446,000	1.40	1.75	2.50	4.50	13.00	21.00	35.00	325	—
1929D	8,370,000	1.50	1.85	3.00	6.75	32.50	42.50	60.00	1,850	—
1929S	7,754,000	1.50	1.85	2.25	4.00	12.50	25.00	49.50	485	—
1930	22,849,000	1.40	1.75	2.50	4.50	12.00	21.00	32.50	235	—
1930S	5,435,000	1.50	2.00	3.00	4.50	16.00	37.50	65.00	480	—
1931S	1,200,000	15.00	16.00	17.00	19.00	31.00	46.00	59.00	300	—
1934	20,213,003	1.40	1.75	2.50	4.50	11.00	19.00	47.50	355	—
1934D	7,480,000	2.00	3.00	4.75	9.60	22.00	50.00	79.50	800	—
1935	58,264,000	1.25	1.60	2.25	3.00	4.00	11.00	20.00	145	—
1935 Double Die Rev.	Inc. above	50.00	75.00	125	250	675	1,800	4,000	75,000	—
1935D	12,092,000	1.60	2.50	3.00	9.00	26.00	48.00	72.00	415	—
1935S	10,300,000	1.35	1.75	2.50	3.50	4.50	17.50	48.50	250	—
1936	119,001,420	1.25	1.60	2.25	3.00	4.00	6.75	14.50	105	1,650
1936 Brilliant	Inc. above	—	—	—	—	—	—	—	—	2,450
1936D	24,814,000	1.35	1.75	2.75	4.00	5.35	11.50	33.50	118	—
1936D 3-1/2 leg	Inc. above	750	1,250	2,000	3,500	6,000	10,500	17,500	—	—
1936D/S	Inc. above	1.35	—	10.00	16.00	25.00	—	—	—	—
1936S	14,930,000	1.35	1.75	2.50	3.50	4.50	11.00	33.50	115	—
1937	79,485,769	1.25	1.60	2.25	3.00	4.00	6.75	14.50	69.00	2,100
1937D	17,826,000	1.35	1.75	2.50	3.50	4.50	9.00	29.00	73.00	—
1937D 3-legged	Inc. above	535	660	725	775	965	1,225	2,375	37,000	—
1937S	5,635,000	1.35	1.75	2.50	3.50	4.50	10.00	27.50	72.00	—
1938D	7,020,000	3.50	3.75	3.90	4.00	4.50	8.00	26.00	66.00	—
1938D/D	Inc. above	4.00	4.50	6.00	8.00	10.00	17.00	32.00	125	—
1938D/S	Inc. above	4.50	6.75	9.00	12.50	19.00	32.50	50.00	185	—

Jefferson Nickel
Monticello, mintmark to right side reverse

KM# 192 • 5.0000 g., **Copper-Nickel**, 21.2 mm. • **Designer:** Felix Schlag **Notes:** Some 1939 strikes have doubling of the word MONTICELLO on the reverse.

Date	Mintage	VG-8	F-12	VF-20	XF-40	MS-60	MS-65	-65FS	Prf-65
1938	19,515,365	.50	.75	1.00	2.25	7.50	18.00	125	130
1938D	5,376,000	1.00	1.25	1.50	2.00	4.00	15.00	95.00	—
1938S	4,105,000	1.75	2.00	2.50	3.00	5.25	12.00	165	—
1939 T I, wavy steps, Rev. of 1939	120,627,535	—	—	—	—	—	—	300	70.00
1939 T II, even steps, Rev. of 1940	Inc. above	—	.20	.25	.30	1.75	3.50	50.00	130
1939 doubled MONTICELLO T II	Inc. above	40.00	60.00	90.00	165	300	1,250	2,000	—
1939D T IT I, wavy steps, Rev. of 1939	3,514,000	—	—	10.00	17.50	75.00	160	275	—
1939D T IIT II, even steps, Rev. of 1940	Inc. above	4.00	5.00	8.00	14.00	55.00	105	400	—
1939S T IT I, wavy steps, Rev. of 1939	6,630,000	.45	.60	1.50	4.00	17.00	45.00	250	—
1939S T IIT II, even steps, Rev. of 1940	Inc. above	—	—	—	5.00	24.00	250	275	—
1940	176,499,158	—	—	—	.25	1.00	12.00	60.00	135
1940D	43,540,000	—	.20	.30	.40	1.50	2.75	25.00	—
1940S	39,690,000	.25	.40	.50	1.25	4.50	20.00	55.00	—
1941	203,283,720	—	—	—	.20	.75	20.00	55.00	130
1941D	53,432,000	—	.20	.30	.50	2.25	7.50	25.00	—
1941S	43,445,000	.25	.40	.50	1.35	5.00	14.00	60.00	—
1942	49,818,600	—	—	—	.40	5.00	22.00	75.00	115
1942D	13,938,000	1.00	1.75	3.00	5.00	38.00	65.00	85.00	—
1942D D over horizontal D	Inc. above	35.00	60.00	100.00	165	750	10,000	25,000	—

Note: Fully Struck Full Step nickels command higher prices. Bright, Fully Struck coins command even higher prices. 1938 thru 1989 - 5 Full Steps. 1990 to date - 6 Full Steps. Without bag marks or nicks on steps.

Monticello, mint mark above reverse

1943/2P

KM# 192a • 0.3500 **Copper-Silver-Manganese**, 21.2 mm. • **Designer:** Felix Schlag **Notes:** War-time composition nickels have the mint mark above MONTICELLO on the reverse.

Date	Mintage	VG-8	F-12	VF-20	XF-40	MS-60	MS-65	-65FS	Prf-65
1942P	57,900,600	1.60	1.70	1.90	2.00	9.00	20.00	70.00	150
1942S	32,900,000	1.60	1.70	1.90	2.50	11.00	30.00	125	—
1943P	271,165,000	1.60	1.70	1.90	2.00	5.00	20.00	35.00	—
1943P	—	—	—	32.00	54.00	135	650	1,100	—
1943/2P	Inc. above	35.00	50.00	75.00	110	250	650	1,000	—
1943D	15,294,000	1.90	2.00	2.20	2.10	4.00	20.00	30.00	—
1943S	104,060,000	1.60	1.70	1.90	2.00	6.75	18.50	55.00	—
1944P	119,150,000	1.60	1.70	1.90	2.00	14.00	28.00	75.00	—
1944D	32,309,000	1.70	1.80	2.00	2.30	12.00	22.50	38.00	—
1944S	21,640,000	1.70	1.80	3.00	2.10	9.50	20.00	185	—
1945P	119,408,100	1.60	1.70	1.90	2.00	6.00	26.00	120	—
1945D	37,158,000	1.70	1.80	2.10	2.20	5.50	20.00	40.00	—
1945S	58,939,000	1.60	1.70	1.90	2.00	5.00	20.00	250	—

Note: Fully Struck Full Step nickels command higher prices. Bright, Fully Struck coins command even higher prices. 1938 thru 1989 - 5 Full Steps. 1990 to date - 6 Full Steps. Without bag marks or nicks on steps.

Pre-war design resumed reverse

KM# A192 • 5.0000 g., **Copper-Nickel**, 21.2 mm. • **Designer:** Felix Schlag **Edge Desc:** Plain

Date	Mintage	XF-40	MS-65	Prf-65	Date	Mintage	XF-40	MS-65	Prf-65
1946	161,116,000	.25	20.00	—	1970D	515,485,380	—	.50	—
1946D	45,292,200	.35	16.00	—	1970S	241,464,814	—	8.00	3.00
1946S	13,560,000	.40	17.00	—	1971	106,884,000	—	2.00	—
1947	95,000,000	.25	18.00	—	1971D	316,144,800	—	.50	—
1947D	37,822,000	.30	15.00	—	1971S	3,220,733	—	—	2.00
1947S	24,720,000	.25	15.00	—	1972	202,036,000	—	.50	—
1948	89,348,000	.25	16.00	—	1972D	351,694,600	—	.50	—
1948D	44,734,000	.35	14.00	—	1972S	3,260,996	—	—	2.00
1948S	11,300,000	.50	14.00	—	1973	384,396,000	—	.50	—
1949	60,652,000	.30	18.00	—	1973D	261,405,000	—	.50	—
1949D	36,498,000	.40	12.00	—	1973S	2,760,339	—	—	1.75
1949D/S	Inc. above	65.00	400	—	1974	601,752,000	—	.50	—
1949S	9,716,000	.90	10.00	—	1974D	277,373,000	—	.50	—
1950	9,847,386	.75	12.00	75.00	1974S	2,612,568	—	—	2.00
1950D	2,630,030	10.00	20.00	—	1975	181,772,000	—	.75	—
1951	28,609,500	.50	18.00	70.00	1975D	401,875,300	—	.50	—
1951D	20,460,000	.50	14.00	—	1975S	2,845,450	—	—	2.25
1951S	7,776,000	1.10	18.50	—	1976	367,124,000	—	.75	—
1952	64,069,980	.25	17.00	42.00	1976D	563,964,147	—	.60	—
1952D	30,638,000	.45	18.00	—	1976S	4,149,730	—	—	3.00
1952S	20,572,000	.25	18.00	—	1977	585,376,000	—	.40	—
1953	46,772,800	.25	9.00	45.00	1977D	297,313,460	—	.55	—
1953D	59,878,600	.25	16.00	—	1977S	3,251,152	—	—	1.75
1953S	19,210,900	.25	20.00	—	1978	391,308,000	—	.40	—
1954	47,917,350	—	9.00	20.00	1978D	313,092,780	—	.40	—
1954D	117,136,560	—	10.00	—	1978S	3,127,781	—	—	1.75
1954S	29,384,000	.20	16.00	—	1979	463,188,000	—	.40	—
1954S/D	Inc. above	20.00	250	—	1979D	325,867,672	—	.40	—
1955	8,266,200	.45	6.50	13.50	1979S type I, proof	3,677,175	—	—	1.50
1955D	74,464,100	—	16.00	—	1979S type II, proof	Inc. above	—	—	1.75
1955D/S	Inc. above	25.00	225	—	1980P	593,004,000	—	6.00	—
1956	35,885,384	—	16.00	3.00	1980D	502,323,448	—	.40	—
1956D	67,222,940	—	16.00	—	1980S	3,554,806	—	—	1.50
1957	39,655,952	—	12.00	2.50	1981P	657,504,000	—	.40	—
1957D	136,828,900	—	12.00	—	1981D	364,801,843	—	.40	—
1958	17,963,652	.20	28.00	8.00	1981S type I, proof	4,063,083	—	—	2.00
1958D	168,249,120	—	13.00	—	1981S type II, proof	Inc. above	—	—	2.50

Note: Fully Struck Full Step nickels command higher prices. Bright, Fully Struck coins command even higher prices. 1938 thru 1989 - 5 Full Steps. 1990 to date - 6 Full Steps. Without bag marks or nicks on steps.

Date	Mintage	XF-40	MS-65	Prf-65	Date	Mintage	XF-40	MS-65	Prf-65
					1982P	292,355,000	—	12.50	—
					1982D	373,726,544	—	3.50	—
1959	28,397,291	—	8.00	1.40	1982S	3,857,479	—	—	3.50
1959D	160,738,240	—	5.50	—	1983P	561,615,000	—	4.00	—
1960	57,107,602	—	6.00	1.25	1983D	536,726,276	—	2.50	—
1960D	192,582,180	—	20.00	—	1983S	3,279,126	—	—	4.00
1961	76,668,244	—	6.00	1.00	1984P	746,769,000	—	3.00	—
1961D	229,342,760	—	20.00	—	1984D	517,675,146	—	.85	—
1962	100,602,019	—	5.00	1.00	1984S	3,065,110	—	—	5.00
1962D	280,195,720	—	75.00	—	1985P	647,114,962	—	.75	—
1963	178,851,645	—	.55	1.00	1985D	459,747,446	—	.75	—
1963D	276,829,460	—	.55	—	1985S	3,362,821	—	—	4.00
1964	1,028,622,762	—	.55	1.00	1986P	536,883,483	—	1.00	—
1964D	1,787,297,160	—	.50	—	1986D	361,819,140	—	2.00	—
1965	136,131,380	—	.50	—	1986S	3,010,497	—	—	7.00
1966	156,208,283	—	.50	—	1987P	371,499,481	—	.75	—
1967	107,325,800	—	.50	—	1987D	410,590,604	—	.75	—
1968 none minted	—	—	—	—	1987S	4,227,728	—	—	3.50
1968D	91,227,880	—	4.50	—	1988P	771,360,000	—	.75	—
1968S	103,437,510	—	.50	0.75	1988D	663,771,652	—	.75	—
1969 none minted	—	—	—	—	1988S	3,262,948	—	—	6.50
1969D	202,807,500	—	.50	—	1989P	898,812,000	—	.75	—
1969S	123,099,631	—	.50	2.00	1989D	570,842,474	—	.75	—
1970 none minted	—	—	—	—	1989S	3,220,194	—	—	5.50
					1990P	661,636,000	—	.75	—
					1990D	663,938,503	—	.75	—

Date	Mintage	XF-40	MS-65	Prf-65
1990S	3,299,559	—	—	5.50
1991P	614,104,000	—	.75	—
1991D	436,496,678	—	.75	—
1991S	2,867,787	—	—	5.00
1992P	399,552,000	—	2.00	—
1992D	450,565,113	—	.75	—
1992S	4,176,560	—	—	4.00
1993P	412,076,000	—	.75	—
1993D	406,084,135	—	.75	—
1993S	3,394,792	—	—	4.50
1994P	722,160,000	—	.75	—
1994P matte proof	167,703	—	—	70.00
1994D	715,762,110	—	.75	—
1994S	3,269,923	—	—	4.00
1995P	774,156,000	—	.75	—
1995D	888,112,000	—	.85	—
1995S	2,707,481	—	—	4.00
1996P	829,332,000	—	.75	—
1996D	817,736,000	—	.75	—
1996S	2,915,212	—	—	4.00
1997P	470,972,000	—	.75	—
1997P matte proof	25,000	—	—	200
1997D	466,640,000	—	2.00	—
1997S	1,975,000	—	—	5.00
1998P	688,272,000	—	.80	—
1998D	635,360,000	—	.80	—
1998S	2,957,286	—	—	4.50
1999P	1,212,000,000	—	.80	—
1999D	1,066,720,000	—	.80	—
1999S	3,362,462	—	—	3.50
2000P	846,240,000	—	.80	—
2000D	1,509,520,000	—	.80	—
2000S	4,063,361	—	—	2.00
2001P	675,704,000	—	.50	—
2001D	627,680,000	—	.50	—
2001S	3,099,096	—	—	4.00
2002P	539,280,000	—	.50	—
2002D	691,200,000	—	.50	—
2002S	3,157,739	—	—	2.00
2003P	441,840,000	—	.50	—
2003D	383,040,000	—	.50	—
2003S	3,116,590	—	—	2.00

Jefferson - Westward Expansion - Lewis & Clark Bicentennial

Jefferson era peace medal design: two clasped hands, pipe and hatchet reverse

KM# 360 • 5.0000 g., **Copper-Nickel**, 21.2 mm. • **Obv. Designer:** Felix Schlag **Rev. Designer:** Norman E. Nemeth

Date	Mintage	MS-65	Prf-65
2004P	361,440,000	1.50	—
2004D	372,000,000	1.50	—
2004S	—	—	10.00

Jefferson - Westward Expansion - Lewis & Clark Bicentennial

Lewis and Clark's Keelboat reverse

KM# 361 • 5.0000 g., **Copper-Nickel**, 21.2 mm. • **Obv. Designer:** Felix Schlag **Rev. Designer:** Al Maletsky

Date	Mintage	MS-65	Prf-65
2004P	366,720,000	1.50	—
2004D	344,880,000	1.50	—
2004S	—	—	10.00

Thomas Jefferson large profile right obverse   American Bison right reverse

KM# 368 • 5.0000 g., **Copper-Nickel**, 21.2 mm. • **Obv. Designer:** Joe Fitzgerald and Don Everhart II **Rev. Designer:** Jamie Franki and Norman E. Nemeth

Date	Mintage	MS-65	Prf-65
2005P	448,320,000	1.50	—
2005D	487,680,000	1.50	—
2005S	—	—	6.50

Jefferson, large profile obverse Pacific coastline reverse

KM# 369 • 5.0000 g., **Copper-Nickel**, 21.2 mm. • **Obv. Designer:** Joe Fitzgerald and Don Everhart **Rev. Designer:** Joe Fitzgerald and Donna Weaver

Date	Mintage	MS-65	Prf-65
2005P	394,080,000	1.25	—
2005D	411,120,000	1.25	—
2005S	—	—	5.50

5 CENTS

Jefferson head facing obverse
Monticello, enhanced design reverse

KM# 381 • 5.0000 g., **Copper-Nickel**, 21.2 mm. •
Obv. Designer: Jamie N. Franki and Donna
Weaver **Rev. Designer:** Felix Schlag and John
Mercanti

Date	Mintage	MS-65	Prf-65
2006P	693,120,000	2.50	—
2006P Satin finish	—	4.00	—
2006D	809,280,000	2.50	—
2006D Satin finish	—	4.00	—
2006S	—	—	5.00
2007P	—	2.50	—

Date	Mintage	MS-65	Prf-65
2007P Satin finish	—	4.00	—
2007D	—	2.50	—
2007D Satin finish	—	4.00	—
2007S	—	—	4.00
2008P	—	2.50	—
2008P Satin finish	—	4.00	—
2008D	—	2.50	—
2008D Satin finish	—	4.00	—
2008S	—	—	4.00
2009P	—	2.50	—
2009P Satin finish	—	4.00	—
2009D	—	2.50	—
2009D Satin finish	—	4.00	—
2009S	—	—	3.00
2010P	—	2.50	—
2010P Satin finish	—	4.00	—
2010D	—	2.50	—
2010D Satin finish	—	4.00	—
2010S	—	—	3.00
2011P	—	2.50	—
2011D	—	2.50	—
2011S	—	—	3.00

DIME

Draped Bust Dime
Draped bust right   Small eagle reverse

KM# 24 • 2.7000 g., 0.8920 **Silver**, 0.0774 oz. ASW, 19 mm. • **Designer:** Robert Scot

Date	Mintage	G-4	VG-8	F-12	VF-20	XF-40	MS-60
1796	22,135	2,850	3,465	5,350	7,350	12,350	24,500
1797 13 stars	25,261	3,000	3,615	5,600	7,750	13,150	25,100
1797 16 stars	Inc. above	2,850	3,490	5,425	7,500	12,650	25,100

Draped bust right   Heraldic eagle reverse

KM# 31 • 2.7000 g., 0.8920 **Silver**, 0.0774 oz. ASW, 19 mm. • **Obv. Legend** LIBERTY **Rev. Legend:**
UNITED STATES OF AMERICA **Designer:** Robert Scot **Notes:** The 1805 strikes have either 4 or 5 berries
on the olive branch held by the eagle.

Date	Mintage	G-4	VG-8	F-12	VF-20	XF-40	MS-60
1798 large 8	27,550	725	1,250	1,550	1,850	3,375	8,850
1798 small 8	Inc. above	975	1,450	1,750	2,150	4,350	53,500
1798/97 13 stars	Inc. above	2,150	3,850	5,650	8,850	14,750	59,000
1798/97 16 stars	Inc. above	775	1,125	1,800	2,650	4,350	10,500
Note: The 1798 overdates have either 13 or 16 stars under the clouds on the reverse; Varieties of the regular 1798 strikes are distinguished by the size of the 8 in the date							
1800	21,760	700	1,075	1,400	2,550	4,100	34,500
1801	34,640	750	1,150	1,650	2,750	7,250	47,500
1802	10,975	1,750	2,650	3,500	4,750	11,000	36,500
1803	33,040	675	1,150	1,900	2,750	5,900	49,500
1804 13 stars	8,265	2,650	4,450	10,500	19,000	41,500	—
1804 14 stars	Inc. above	4,850	6,500	12,500	24,500	46,500	—
1805 5 berries	Inc. above	625	1,000	1,400	1,950	3,450	9,100
1805 4 berries	120,780	575	900	1,200	1,500	2,700	6,850
1807	165,000	575	900	1,200	1,500	2,700	6,850

5 CENTS

1809 Dime
Grade F-12

Retail Price

Liberty Cap Dime
Draped bust left, flanked by stars, date below
Eagle with arrows in talons, banner above, value below reverse

KM# 42 • 2.7000 g., 0.8920 **Silver**, 0.0774 oz. ASW, 18.8 mm. • **Rev. Legend:** UNITED STATES OF AMERICA **Designer:** John Reich **Notes:** The 1820 varieties are distinguished by the size of the 0 in the date. The 1823 overdates have either large E's or small E's in UNITED STATES OF AMERICA on the reverse.

Date	Mintage	G-4	VG-8	F-12	VF-20	XF-40	AU-50	MS-60	MS-65
1809	51,065	140	220	450	700	1,500	2,850	4,500	24,500
1811/9	65,180	110	175	275	650	1,350	2,000	4,000	33,500
1814 small date	421,500	60.00	80.00	145	300	650	1,250	2,000	19,500
1814 large date	Inc. above	43.00	52.00	75.00	135	435	670	1,175	15,000
1814 STATESOF	Inc. above	70.00	88.00	160	335	750	1,400	2,350	24,500
1820 large O	942,587	42.00	50.00	71.00	122	430	665	1,160	12,750
1820 small O	Inc. above	43.00	52.00	75.00	137	450	750	1,425	15,250
1820 STATESOF	Inc. above	43.00	52.00	75.00	135	435	670	1,175	14,500
1821 large date	1,186,512	42.00	50.00	71.00	122	430	665	1,160	12,750
1821 small date	Inc. above	43.00	52.00	75.00	137	450	750	1,425	17,000
1822	100,000	1,000	1,850	3,250	4,500	6,250	7,850	13,500	70,000
1823/22 large E's	440,000	42.00	50.00	71.00	130	450	685	1,210	14,850
1823/22 small E's	Inc. above	42.00	50.00	71.00	130	450	685	1,210	13,600
1824/22	—	50.00	80.00	145	300	650	1,250	2,000	19,500
1825	510,000	39.00	46.00	65.00	112	410	625	1,100	12,850
1827	1,215,000	39.00	46.00	65.00	112	410	625	1,100	12,500
1827/7	Inc. above	250	—	—	750	1,100	1,500	—	—
1828 large date	125,000	70.00	110	175	375	750	1,250	2,850	6,850

Liberty Cap Dime
Draped bust left, flanked by stars, date below
Eagle with arrows in talons, banner above, value below reverse

KM# 48 • Silver, 18.5 mm. • **Rev. Legend:** UNITED STATES OF AMERICA **Designer:** John Reich
Notes: The three varieties of 1829 strikes and two varieties of 1830 strikes are distinguished by the size of "10C." on the reverse. On the 1833 "high 3" variety, the last 3 in the date is higher thatn the first 3. The two varieties of the 1834 strikes are distinguished by the size of the 4 in the date.

Date	Mintage	G-4	VG-8	F-12	VF-20	XF-40	AU-50	MS-60	MS-65
1828 small date	Inc. above	40.00	48.00	80.00	155	425	625	1,250	12,500
1829 very large 10C.	770,000	60.00	75.00	120	235	550	800	1,500	—
1829 large 10C.	Inc. above	54.00	65.00	110	200	400	600	1,150	9,250
1829 medium 10C.	Inc. above	36.00	42.00	54.00	85.00	255	375	775	6,850
1829 small 10C.	Inc. above	36.00	42.00	56.00	90.00	270	395	795	7,050
1829 curl base 2	Inc. above	7,750	10,500	16,500	27,500	38,500	44,000	—	—
1830 large 10C.	510,000	36.00	42.00	56.00	85.00	255	375	775	6,850
1830 small 10C.	Inc. above	36.00	42.00	54.00	90.00	270	400	825	8,850
1830/29	Inc. above	52.00	75.00	120	220	430	750	1,500	—
1831	771,350	36.00	42.00	54.00	85.00	255	375	775	6,850
1832	522,500	36.00	42.00	54.00	85.00	255	375	775	6,850
1833	485,000	36.00	42.00	54.00	85.00	260	390	790	6,850
1833 last 3 high	Inc. above	36.00	42.00	54.00	85.00	260	390	820	9,350
1834 small 4	635,000	36.00	42.00	54.00	85.00	255	375	775	7,000
1834 large 4	Inc. above	36.00	42.00	54.00	85.00	255	375	775	6,850
1835	1,410,000	36.00	42.00	54.00	85.00	255	375	775	6,850
1836	1,190,000	36.00	42.00	54.00	85.00	255	375	775	6,850
1837	1,042,000	36.00	42.00	56.00	90.00	270	395	795	7,000

Seated Liberty Dime
Seated Liberty, date below
Value within wreath reverse

KM# 61 • 2.6700 g., 0.9000 Silver, 0.0773 oz. ASW, 17.9 mm. • **Rev. Legend:** UNITED STATES OF AMERICA **Designer:** Christian Gobrecht

Date	Mintage	G-4	VG-8	F-12	VF-20	XF-40	AU-50	MS-60	MS-65
1837 flat top	Inc. above	40.00	50.00	85.00	290	550	750	1,100	6,500
1837 curly top	Inc. above	40.00	50.00	85.00	290	550	750	1,100	6,500
1838O	406,034	40.00	60.00	110	375	725	1,250	3,500	21,000

Seated Liberty, stars around top 1/2 of border, date below
Value within wreath reverse

No drapery at elbow

KM# 63.1 • 2.6700 g., 0.9000 Silver, 0.0773 oz. ASW, 17.9 mm. • **Obv. Designer:** Christian Gobrecht
Rev. Legend: UNITED STATES OF AMERICA **Notes:** The 1839-O with reverse of 1838-O variety was struck from rusted dies, it has a bumpy reverse surface.

Date	Mintage	G-4	VG-8	F-12	VF-20	XF-40	AU-50	MS-60	MS-65
1838 small stars	1,992,500	25.00	30.00	50.00	80.00	165	350	600	—
1838 large stars	Inc. above	17.50	20.00	30.00	37.50	110	215	280	8,500
1838 partial drapery	Inc. above	35.00	50.00	85.00	150	225	350	550	—
1839	1,053,115	16.00	18.50	25.00	35.00	105	195	280	3,000
1839O	1,323,000	18.50	22.50	35.00	60.00	150	365	1,250	6,000

Date	Mintage	G-4	VG-8	F-12	VF-20	XF-40	AU-50	MS-60	MS-65
1839O reverse 1838O	Inc. above	165	225	375	550	1,150	—	—	—
1840	1,358,580	16.00	18.50	25.00	35.00	105	195	300	4,000
1840O	1,175,000	18.50	22.50	40.00	70.00	165	365	975	6,500

Seated Liberty, stars around top 1/2 of border, date below
Value within wreath reverse

Drapery at elbow

KM# 63.2 • 2.6700 g., 0.9000 **Silver**, 0.0773 oz. ASW, 17.9 mm. • **Rev. Legend:** UNITED STATES OF AMERICA **Designer:** Christian Gobrecht **Notes:** Drapery added to Liberty's left elbow

Date	Mintage	G-4	VG-8	F-12	VF-20	XF-40	AU-50	MS-60	MS-65
1840	Inc. above	35.00	50.00	95.00	185	350	1,250	—	—
1841	1,622,500	16.00	18.50	21.50	27.50	50.00	175	260	2,700
1841O	2,007,500	18.50	22.50	28.50	45.00	75.00	250	1,500	5,000
1841O large O	Inc. above	600	900	1,200	2,500	—	—	—	—
1842	1,887,500	15.00	17.50	21.50	26.00	45.00	175	260	2,700
1842O	2,020,000	18.50	23.50	30.00	75.00	225	1,350	2,900	—
1843	1,370,000	15.00	17.50	21.50	26.00	45.00	175	260	3,000
1843/1843	Inc. above	16.00	18.50	22.50	30.00	75.00	200	295	—
1843O	150,000	50.00	80.00	135	325	1,100	2,250	—	—
1844	72,500	275	350	550	800	1,450	2,200	3,000	—
1845	1,755,000	16.00	18.50	21.50	27.50	45.00	120	260	2,600
1845/1845	Inc. above	17.00	20.00	35.00	55.00	100.00	175	—	—
1845O	230,000	25.00	35.00	95.00	250	750	1,750	—	—
1846	31,300	250	350	500	950	1,750	2,750	5,500	—
1847	245,000	19.00	25.00	40.00	85.00	150	350	950	9,000
1848	451,500	18.50	21.50	25.00	50.00	95.00	250	750	7,000
1849	839,000	17.50	19.50	23.50	33.50	60.00	140	500	4,000
1849O	300,000	21.50	30.00	50.00	135	275	750	2,200	—
1850	1,931,500	17.50	19.50	23.50	32.50	55.00	120	260	5,900
1850O	510,000	21.50	25.00	40.00	90.00	175	475	1,250	—
1851	1,026,500	17.50	20.00	22.50	30.00	60.00	120	325	5,000
1851O	400,000	21.50	25.00	40.00	90.00	175	500	1,850	—
1852	1,535,500	15.00	16.00	18.50	23.50	50.00	120	290	2,550
1852O	430,000	22.50	30.00	45.00	125	235	550	1,800	—
1853	95,000	95.00	125	200	295	425	575	800	—

Seated Liberty, stars around top 1/2 of border, arrows at date
Value within wreath reverse

KM# 77 • 2.4900 g., 0.9000 **Silver**, 0.0720 oz. ASW • **Rev. Legend:** UNITED STATES OF AMERICA **Designer:** Christian Gobrecht

Date	Mintage	G-4	VG-8	F-12	VF-20	XF-40	AU-50	MS-60	MS-65	Prf-65
1853	12,078,010	8.00	9.00	10.00	14.00	45.00	125	330	2,500	31,500
1853O	1,100,000	11.00	14.00	20.00	45.00	145	400	900	—	—
1854	4,470,000	8.75	9.25	10.00	15.00	45.00	125	330	2,500	31,500
1854O	1,770,000	10.00	11.00	14.00	25.00	75.00	175	600	—	—
1855	2,075,000	8.75	9.25	14.00	20.00	55.00	150	350	3,800	31,500

Seated Liberty, stars around top 1/2 of border, date below
Value within wreath reverse

KM# A63.2 • 2.4900 g., 0.9000 **Silver**, 0.0720 oz. ASW • **Rev. Legend:** UNITED STATES OF AMERICA **Designer:** Christian Gobrecht

Date	Mintage	G-4	VG-8	F-12	VF-20	XF-40	AU-50	MS-60	MS-65	Prf-65
1856 small date	5,780,000	14.00	15.00	18.00	22.00	37.50	115	250	7,050	38,000
1856 large date	Inc. above	16.00	18.50	19.50	25.00	65.00	175	475	—	—
1856O	1,180,000	16.00	18.50	19.50	35.00	85.00	215	625	5,250	—
1856S	70,000	160	225	375	550	1,200	1,750	—	—	—
1857	5,580,000	14.00	15.50	16.50	22.50	37.50	110	260	2,600	3,400
1857O	1,540,000	14.00	16.00	18.50	27.50	70.00	200	375	2,600	—
1858	1,540,000	14.00	15.50	16.50	22.50	55.00	145	260	2,600	3,400
1858O	290,000	19.00	25.00	40.00	85.00	165	280	800	5,000	—
1858S	60,000	150	200	325	475	1,000	1,500	—	—	—
1859	430,000	16.00	20.00	25.00	45.00	70.00	140	350	—	3,400
1859O	480,000	16.00	20.00	25.00	45.00	80.00	225	550	—	—
1859S	60,000	160	225	375	550	1,350	3,000	—	—	—
1860S	140,000	40.00	55.00	75.00	145	325	800	—	—	—

UNITED STATES OF AMERICA replaced stars
Value within wreath reverse

KM# 92 • 2.4900 g., 0.9000 **Silver**, 0.0720 oz. ASW • **Obv. Legend** UNITED STATES OF AMERICA **Obv. Designer:** Christian Gobrecht **Notes:** The 1873 "closed-3" and "open-3" varieties are distinguished by the amount of space between the upper left and lower left serifs of the 3 in the date.

Date	Mintage	G-4	VG-8	F-12	VF-20	XF-40	AU-50	MS-60	MS-65	Prf-65
1860	607,000	15.00	22.00	29.00	31.00	55.00	125	275	1,350	1,400
1860O	40,000	450	600	1,000	1,950	3,500	5,500	8,500	—	—
1861	1,884,000	15.00	17.00	20.00	23.00	34.00	85.00	150	1,250	1,400
1861S	172,500	55.00	90.00	165	275	400	900	1,400	—	—
1862	847,550	16.00	17.50	19.50	25.00	45.00	77.50	105	1,250	1,400
1862S	180,750	45.00	65.00	95.00	185	375	775	1,000	—	—
1863	14,460	425	500	650	900	950	1,100	1,300	—	1,400
1863S	157,500	40.00	55.00	80.00	145	275	650	1,200	—	—
1864	11,470	425	500	650	750	900	1,000	1,200	—	1,400
1864S	230,000	35.00	45.00	75.00	110	225	425	1,200	—	—
1865	10,500	475	575	700	875	1,000	1,200	1,350	—	1,400
1865S	175,000	45.00	55.00	85.00	145	325	850	—	—	—
1866	8,725	500	600	775	950	1,100	1,200	1,800	—	1,750
1866S	135,000	50.00	65.00	100.00	150	325	700	1,900	—	—

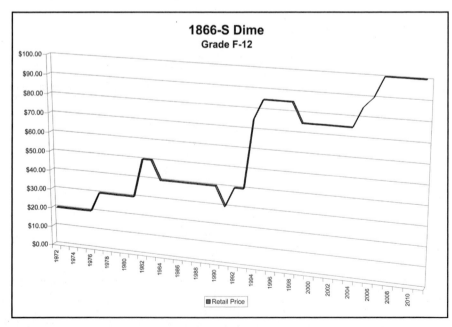

Date	Mintage	G-4	VG-8	F-12	VF-20	XF-40	AU-50	MS-60	MS-65	Prf-65
1867	6,625	600	700	950	1,100	1,450	1,600	1,800	—	1,750
1867S	140,000	50.00	60.00	90.00	150	325	700	1,200	—	—
1868	464,000	18.00	22.00	29.00	39.00	85.00	175	300	—	1,400
1868S	260,000	30.00	35.00	50.00	85.00	165	300	600	—	—
1869	256,600	25.00	35.00	45.00	80.00	135	250	600	—	1,400
1869S	450,000	25.00	30.00	40.00	55.00	85.00	175	400	—	—
1870	471,000	18.00	22.00	30.00	40.00	50.00	80.00	150	—	1,400
1870S	50,000	300	375	500	650	850	1,200	2,000	—	—
1871	907,710	16.00	20.00	25.00	33.00	55.00	175	300	—	1,400
1871CC	20,100	2,500	3,500	4,500	6,500	10,000	—	—	—	—
1871S	320,000	35.00	55.00	75.00	130	195	350	900	—	—
1872	2,396,450	12.00	15.00	17.00	20.00	31.00	95.00	175	—	1,400
1872CC	35,480	950	1,250	1,850	3,000	6,500	—	—	—	—
1872S	190,000	40.00	65.00	85.00	150	250	450	1,100	—	—
1873 closed 3	1,568,600	12.50	15.00	18.00	22.00	50.00	100.00	200	—	1,400
1873 open 3	Inc. above	28.00	35.00	50.00	75.00	125	250	650	—	—
1873CC	12,400	—	—	—	—	—	—	—	—	—

Note: 1873-CC, Heritage Sale, April 1999, MS-64, $632,500.

Seated Liberty, arrows at date
Value within wreath reverse

KM# 105 • 2.5000 g., 0.9000 **Silver**, 0.0723 oz. ASW • **Obv. Legend** UNITED STATES OF AMERICA
Designer: Christian Gobrecht

Date	Mintage	G-4	VG-8	F-12	VF-20	XF-40	AU-50	MS-60	MS-65	Prf-65
1873	2,378,500	15.00	18.50	25.00	55.00	150	350	500	4,500	4,500
1873CC	18,791	2,350	3,250	4,250	6,500	10,000	—	—	—	—
1873S	455,000	20.00	30.00	40.00	70.00	190	400	1,500	—	—
1874	2,940,700	13.50	17.50	22.50	50.00	150	315	500	4,500	4,500
1874CC	10,817	5,000	6,500	8,000	12,500	25,000	—	—	—	—
1874S	240,000	60.00	75.00	100.00	160	250	450	1,500	—	—

Seated Liberty, date below
Value within wreath reverse

KM# A92 • 2.5000 g., 0.9000 **Silver**, 0.0723 oz. ASW • **Obv. Legend** UNITED STATES OF AMERICA
Designer: Christian Gobrecht **Notes:** On the 1876-CC doubled-obverse variety, doubling appears in the words OF AMERICA in the legend.

Date	Mintage	G-4	VG-8	F-12	VF-20	XF-40	AU-50	MS-60	MS-65	Prf-65
1875	10,350,700	14.00	16.00	17.50	20.00	30.00	75.00	125	2,250	4,600
1875CC mint mark in wreath	4,645,000	15.00	19.00	22.50	35.00	47.50	90.00	190	2,700	—
1875CC mint mark under wreath	Inc. above	15.00	19.00	27.50	45.00	75.00	165	235	3,000	—
1875S mint mark in wreath	9,070,000	20.00	25.00	30.00	43.00	65.00	125	225	3,100	—
1875S mint mark under wreath	Inc. above	12.50	15.50	17.50	20.00	27.50	72.50	125	1,100	—
1876 Type 1 rev	11,461,150	14.00	16.00	17.50	20.00	30.00	75.00	125	1,100	1,200
1876 Type 2 rev	Inc. above	20.00	25.00	30.00	40.00	60.00	120	200	—	—
1876CC Type 1 rev	8,270,000	20.00	25.00	30.00	40.00	65.00	125	225	—	—
1876CC Type 2 rev	Inc. above	25.00	35.00	48.00	65.00	90.00	175	300	—	—
1876CC doubled die obverse	Inc. above	20.00	26.00	44.00	100.00	185	340	600	—	—
1876S Type 1 rev	10,420,000	14.00	16.00	17.50	20.00	30.00	75.00	125	1,750	—
1876S Type 2 rev	Inc. above	18.00	20.00	24.00	30.00	40.00	90.00	150	—	—
1877 Type 1 rev	7,310,510	14.00	16.00	17.50	20.00	30.00	75.00	125	1,100	1,200
1877 Type 2 rev	Inc. above	18.00	20.00	24.00	30.00	40.00	90.00	150	—	—
1877CC Type 1 rev	7,700,000	25.00	35.00	48.00	65.00	90.00	175	300	1,100	—
1877CC Type 2 rev	Inc. above	20.00	25.00	30.00	40.00	65.00	125	225	—	—
1877S Type 1 rev	2,340,000	—	—	—	—	—	—	—	—	—
1877S Type 2 rev	Inc. above	14.00	18.00	20.00	30.00	50.00	105	225	—	—
1878 Type 1 rev	1,678,800	28.00	35.00	50.00	65.00	100.00	175	—	—	—
1878 Type 2 rev	Inc. above	14.00	16.00	20.00	30.00	36.00	72.50	125	1,500	1,200
1878CC Type 1 rev	200,000	100.00	135	175	285	450	700	—	—	—
1878CC Type 2 rev	Inc. above	65.00	90.00	125	225	370	500	900	3,500	—

Date	Mintage	G-4	VG-8	F-12	VF-20	XF-40	AU-50	MS-60	MS-65	Prf-65
1879	15,100	275	310	375	425	500	575	675	1,750	1,500
1880	37,335	250	275	315	350	400	450	550	1,750	1,500
1881	24,975	265	300	350	400	475	550	650	2,500	1,600
1882	3,911,100	14.00	16.00	17.50	20.00	30.00	75.00	125	1,100	1,200
1883	7,675,712	14.00	16.00	17.50	20.00	30.00	75.00	125	1,100	1,200
1884	3,366,380	14.00	16.00	17.50	20.00	30.00	75.00	125	1,100	1,200
1884S	564,969	30.00	35.00	45.00	55.00	125	280	650	—	—
1885	2,533,427	14.00	16.00	17.50	20.00	30.00	75.00	125	1,100	1,200
1885S	43,690	450	650	950	1,750	2,400	3,600	5,000	—	—
1886	6,377,570	12.50	15.00	17.00	20.00	27.50	72.50	125	1,100	1,200
1886S	206,524	50.00	70.00	80.00	125	175	280	600	—	—
1887	11,283,939	14.00	16.00	17.50	20.00	30.00	75.00	125	1,100	1,200
1887S	4,454,450	12.50	15.00	17.00	20.00	38.00	80.00	125	1,100	—
1888	5,496,487	14.00	16.00	17.50	20.00	30.00	75.00	125	1,100	1,200
1888S	1,720,000	12.50	15.00	17.00	25.00	40.00	95.00	200	—	—
1889	7,380,711	14.00	16.00	17.50	20.00	30.00	75.00	125	1,100	1,200
1889S	972,678	14.00	18.00	25.00	45.00	70.00	150	475	4,500	—
1890	9,911,541	14.00	16.00	17.50	20.00	30.00	75.00	125	1,100	1,200
1890S	1,423,076	14.00	15.00	22.50	50.00	85.00	155	400	4,900	—
1891	15,310,600	14.00	16.00	17.50	20.00	30.00	75.00	125	1,100	1,200
1891O	4,540,000	12.50	15.00	17.00	20.00	27.50	72.50	175	1,750	—
1891O /horizontal O	Inc. above	65.00	95.00	125	175	225	400	—	—	—
1891S	3,196,116	13.50	15.00	17.50	20.00	30.00	75.00	225	1,650	—
1891S/S	Inc. above	25.00	30.00	40.00	85.00	135	250	—	—	—

Barber Dime
Laureate head right, date at angle below
Value within wreath reverse

KM# 113 • 2.5000 g., 0.9000 **Silver**, 0.0723 oz. ASW, 17.9 mm. • **Obv. Legend** UNITED STATES OF AMERICA **Designer:** Charles E. Barber

Date	Mintage	G-4	VG-8	F-12	VF-20	XF-40	AU-50	MS-60	MS-65	Prf-65
1892	12,121,245	6.75	7.50	16.00	25.00	27.50	63.00	105	710	1,485
1892O	3,841,700	11.00	15.00	32.50	56.00	75.00	96.00	135	1,275	—
1892S	990,710	66.00	115	210	245	285	340	425	3,500	—
1893/2	3,340,792	135	155	175	225	300	325	450	4,850	—
1893	Inc. above	8.25	12.50	20.00	30.00	46.00	80.00	165	1,000	1,485
1893O	1,760,000	31.00	45.00	135	168	190	250	315	2,950	—
1893S	2,491,401	14.00	25.00	39.00	50.00	85.00	155	360	3,750	—
1894	1,330,972	25.00	45.00	122	165	190	235	310	1,150	1,485
1894O	720,000	70.00	105	215	280	425	650	1,550	15,500	—
1894S	24	—	—	—	—	—	—	—	1,900,000	—
Note: 1894S, Eliasberg Sale, May 1996, Prf-64, $451,000.										
1895	690,880	85.00	180	355	480	565	650	750	2,650	1,485
1895O	440,000	385	575	900	1,285	2,500	3,650	6,000	19,500	—
1895S	1,120,000	43.50	60.00	135	190	240	320	500	7,500	—
1896	2,000,762	11.50	23.00	56.00	82.00	100.00	120	145	1,450	1,485
1896O	610,000	80.00	155	305	375	465	700	975	9,500	—
1896S	575,056	85.00	160	310	335	385	525	770	4,650	—
1897	10,869,264	3.50	3.75	8.00	15.00	31.50	73.00	125	710	1,485
1897O	666,000	69.50	115	290	385	480	600	975	4,450	—
1897S	1,342,844	21.00	45.00	98.00	125	185	265	435	3,950	—
1898	16,320,735	3.50	3.75	7.50	15.00	28.00	68.00	125	710	1,485
1898O	2,130,000	13.50	27.50	88.00	145	200	285	450	3,850	—
1898S	1,702,507	8.50	15.00	33.00	48.00	78.00	160	370	3,750	—
1899	19,580,846	3.50	3.75	7.50	12.00	26.00	68.00	110	710	1,485
1899O	2,650,000	10.00	19.50	72.00	110	150	230	415	4,450	—
1899S	1,867,493	9.00	16.00	34.00	37.00	46.00	105	300	4,350	—
1900	17,600,912	4.00	5.00	7.00	11.00	26.00	63.00	105	740	1,485
1900O	2,010,000	19.50	38.50	115	165	225	355	595	5,750	—
1900S	5,168,270	5.00	6.25	12.50	19.50	31.50	75.00	155	1,850	—
1901	18,860,478	4.00	5.00	6.50	10.00	27.50	63.00	105	755	1,485
1901O	5,620,000	4.00	5.50	16.00	27.50	67.50	175	450	4,350	—
1901S	593,022	80.00	150	360	475	520	675	985	5,350	—
1902	21,380,777	4.00	5.00	6.25	8.00	23.00	63.00	105	755	1,485
1902O	4,500,000	4.00	5.50	15.00	32.50	62.50	145	350	4,500	—
1902S	2,070,000	8.00	21.00	58.00	90.00	135	195	375	3,950	—
1903	19,500,755	4.00	5.00	6.25	8.00	25.00	63.00	105	1,100	1,485
1903O	8,180,000	4.00	5.50	13.50	23.50	50.00	110	250	4,850	—
1903S	613,300	84.00	130	350	490	750	840	1,100	3,150	—

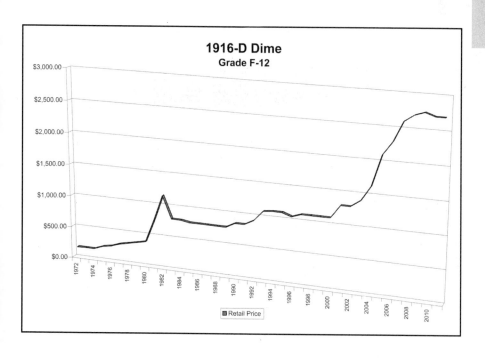

DIME

DIME

Date	Mintage	G-4	VG-8	F-12	VF-20	XF-40	AU-50	MS-60	MS-65	Prf-65
1904	14,601,027	4.00	5.00	7.00	9.75	25.00	63.00	110	1,850	1,485
1904S	800,000	45.00	75.00	165	245	335	465	725	4,500	—
1905	14,552,350	4.25	5.25	6.75	9.75	25.00	63.00	105	735	1,485
1905O	3,400,000	4.25	14.50	36.50	57.50	92.00	155	285	1,650	—
1905O micro O	Inc. above	35.00	50.00	75.00	140	235	375	1,750	12,500	—
1905S	6,855,199	3.50	5.00	9.00	18.50	43.50	96.00	210	775	—
1906	19,958,406	3.25	4.50	4.50	7.25	22.00	58.00	100.00	735	1,485
1906D	4,060,000	3.75	4.85	7.00	15.00	35.00	78.00	175	1,650	—
1906O	2,610,000	5.50	13.00	50.00	78.00	100.00	135	195	1,150	—
1906S	3,136,640	4.25	6.25	12.50	22.50	44.00	110	240	1,350	—
1907	22,220,575	3.25	3.50	4.25	7.25	22.00	58.00	100.00	700	1,485
1907D	4,080,000	3.75	5.00	8.75	17.50	43.50	115	275	3,950	—
1907O	5,058,000	4.25	6.75	33.50	50.00	62.50	110	210	1,350	—
1907S	3,178,470	4.25	5.50	16.00	27.50	67.50	150	410	2,450	—
1908	10,600,545	3.25	3.50	4.25	7.25	22.00	58.00	100.00	700	1,485
1908D	7,490,000	3.25	3.50	5.75	9.75	29.00	63.00	125	990	—
1908O	1,789,000	5.25	11.00	44.50	64.00	92.00	150	290	1,350	—
1908S	3,220,000	4.50	6.25	11.50	22.00	46.00	175	310	2,350	—
1909	10,240,650	3.25	3.50	4.25	7.25	22.00	58.00	100.00	700	1,485
1909D	954,000	7.25	18.50	60.00	100.00	135	225	485	3,150	—
1909O	2,287,000	4.00	7.25	12.50	22.00	50.00	92.50	185	1,650	—
1909S	1,000,000	8.75	19.50	88.00	130	182	315	525	3,150	—
1910	11,520,551	3.25	3.50	4.00	9.75	22.00	58.00	100.00	700	1,485
1910D	3,490,000	3.50	4.00	8.50	19.00	47.50	100.00	210	1,650	—
1910S	1,240,000	5.25	9.00	50.00	74.00	110	195	425	2,450	—
1911	18,870,543	3.25	3.50	4.00	7.00	22.00	58.00	100.00	700	1,485
1911D	11,209,000	3.25	3.50	4.00	7.00	22.00	58.00	100.00	700	—
1911S	3,520,000	4.00	4.75	8.50	18.50	39.50	105	195	1,050	—
1912	19,350,700	3.25	3.50	4.00	7.00	22.00	58.00	100.00	700	1,485
1912D	11,760,000	3.25	3.50	4.00	7.00	22.00	58.00	100.00	700	—
1912S	3,420,000	3.50	4.50	5.60	12.50	34.00	92.50	155	775	—
1913	19,760,622	3.25	3.50	4.00	7.00	22.00	58.00	100.00	700	1,485
1913S	510,000	35.00	50.00	120	190	240	325	480	1,375	—
1914	17,360,655	3.25	3.50	4.00	7.00	22.00	58.00	100.00	700	1,485
1914D	11,908,000	3.25	3.50	4.00	7.00	22.00	58.00	100.00	700	—
1914S	2,100,000	3.50	4.50	8.00	17.50	39.50	78.00	150	1,250	—
1915	5,620,450	3.25	3.50	4.00	7.00	22.00	58.00	100.00	700	1,485
1915S	960,000	7.50	11.50	34.50	49.50	66.50	135	250	1,550	—
1916	18,490,000	3.25	3.50	4.00	8.00	22.00	58.00	100.00	700	—
1916S	5,820,000	3.50	4.50	5.00	8.50	25.50	63.00	105	795	—

Mercury Dime

Mint mark   1942/41

Full split bands

KM# 140 • 2.5000 g., 0.9000 Silver, 0.0723 oz. ASW, 17.8 mm. • **Designer:** Adolph A. Weinman **Notes:** All specimens listed as -65FSB are for fully struck MS-65 coins with fully split and rounded horizontal bands on the fasces.

Date	Mintage	G-4	VG-8	F-12	VF-20	XF-40	MS-60	MS-65	Prf-65	-65FSB
1916	22,180,080	3.50	4.75	6.00	7.00	12.00	30.00	110	—	165
1916D	264,000	1,000	1,650	2,700	3,850	6,200	13,750	26,500	—	48,500
1916S	10,450,000	4.00	5.00	9.25	15.00	25.00	46.00	210	—	800
1917	55,230,000	3.40	3.80	4.10	5.50	8.00	28.00	155	—	375
1917D	9,402,000	4.30	6.00	12.50	26.00	52.50	120	1,100	—	5,650
1917S	27,330,000	3.50	4.00	3.50	7.50	15.00	64.00	470	—	1,265
1918	26,680,000	4.00	5.30	5.75	12.00	34.00	70.00	420	—	1,325
1918D	22,674,800	3.00	3.25	6.50	13.00	32.00	105	600	—	27,500
1918S	19,300,000	2.90	3.00	3.85	11.00	24.00	96.00	660	—	7,450

Date	Mintage	G-4	VG-8	F-12	VF-20	XF-40	MS-60	MS-65	Prf-65	-65FSB
1919	35,740,000	2.90	3.00	3.25	5.50	12.00	37.00	315	—	685
1919D	9,939,000	3.50	6.00	13.50	31.00	46.00	180	2,100	—	38,500
1919S	8,850,000	2.90	3.25	10.50	20.00	42.00	180	1,250	—	14,350
1920	59,030,000	3.00	3.00	3.20	4.00	8.50	28.00	235	—	540
1920D	19,171,000	2.90	2.90	4.75	9.00	24.00	110	750	—	4,750
1920S	13,820,000	2.90	2.90	7.00	9.00	21.00	110	1,300	—	8,250
1921	1,230,000	60.00	72.00	115	260	525	1,175	3,100	—	4,350
1921D	1,080,000	78.00	120	200	380	660	1,325	3,250	—	5,200
1923	50,130,000	2.90	3.00	3.00	3.50	7.00	28.00	115	—	340
1923S	6,440,000	2.90	3.00	8.25	19.00	75.00	160	1,150	—	7,450
1924	24,010,000	3.20	3.50	4.30	4.50	13.50	42.00	175	—	500
1924D	6,810,000	3.00	4.25	9.00	23.50	63.00	175	1,050	—	1,365
1924S	7,120,000	2.90	3.60	4.25	12.00	59.00	170	1,100	—	16,750
1925	25,610,000	3.20	3.50	4.00	4.00	11.00	28.00	210	—	990
1925D	5,117,000	3.90	4.40	12.75	46.50	135	350	1,750	—	3,500
1925S	5,850,000	2.90	3.20	7.75	18.50	85.00	185	1,400	—	4,650
1926	32,160,000	2.90	3.00	3.00	3.50	5.75	25.00	240	—	525
1926D	6,828,000	3.00	4.00	5.00	12.00	32.00	125	550	—	2,500
1926S	1,520,000	11.75	13.50	29.00	67.50	275	900	3,000	—	6,750
1927	28,080,000	2.90	3.00	3.00	3.50	6.00	26.00	138	—	350
1927D	4,812,000	2.90	5.00	7.75	25.50	88.00	175	1,285	—	8,500
1927S	4,770,000	3.00	3.75	5.50	11.00	30.00	285	1,400	—	7,600
1928	19,480,000	2.90	3.00	3.00	3.50	4.75	27.50	120	—	345
1928D	4,161,000	3.70	4.00	11.50	25.50	62.50	175	875	—	2,750
1928S Large S	7,400,000	3.20	3.25	5.00	12.00	40.00	225	750	—	6,500
1928S Small S	Inc. above	2.90	2.90	3.25	6.50	19.00	125	425	—	2,000
1929	25,970,000	2.90	3.00	3.00	3.50	4.50	21.00	60.00	—	175
1929D	5,034,000	2.90	3.00	3.75	8.00	15.00	27.00	75.00	—	225
1929S	4,730,000	3.00	3.20	3.10	5.00	7.50	32.50	90.00	—	560
1929S Doubled Die Obv	Inc. above	5.00	9.00	16.00	25.00	40.00	90.00	275	—	1,150
1930	6,770,000	2.90	3.00	3.00	3.50	7.00	26.00	120	—	575
1930S	1,843,000	2.90	3.50	4.80	6.50	19.00	82.00	200	—	685
1931	3,150,000	2.90	3.00	3.30	4.70	12.50	33.00	135	—	800
1931D	1,260,000	8.50	10.00	15.00	19.50	48.00	100.00	285	—	375
1931 Doubled Die Obv & Rev	Inc. above	—	—	—	50.00	70.00	135	485	—	650
1931S	1,800,000	4.00	5.00	5.50	11.00	23.50	96.00	275	—	2,500
1931S Doubled Die Obv	Inc. above	7.50	10.00	13.00	25.00	35.00	140	425	—	3,850
1934	24,080,000	2.80	2.80	2.90	2.90	6.50	29.00	42.00	—	130
1934D	6,772,000	3.50	3.70	3.30	7.50	14.00	50.00	78.00	—	320
1935	58,830,000	2.80	2.80	2.90	2.90	4.25	10.00	30.00	—	68.00
1935D	10,477,000	3.20	3.20	3.30	6.50	13.00	37.00	84.00	—	500
1935S	15,840,000	3.20	3.20	3.30	3.30	5.50	24.00	37.00	—	360
1936	87,504,130	2.80	2.80	2.90	2.90	3.50	9.00	26.50	1,950	84.00
1936 Doubled Die Obv	Inc. above	—	—	8.00	15.00	25.00	50.00	165	—	—
1936D	16,132,000	3.20	3.20	3.30	4.30	8.50	28.00	53.00	—	290
1936S	9,210,000	—	3.20	3.30	3.50	6.00	20.00	33.00	—	88.00
1937	56,865,756	2.80	2.80	2.90	2.90	3.75	8.00	24.00	800	52.00
1937 Doubled Die Obv	Inc. above	—	—	—	6.00	9.00	20.00	60.00	—	175
1937D	14,146,000	3.20	3.20	3.30	3.50	6.00	22.00	43.00	—	105
1937S	9,740,000	3.20	3.20	3.30	3.50	5.50	22.00	36.00	—	190
1937S Doubled Die Obv	Inc. above	—	—	—	5.00	8.00	28.00	80.00	—	275
1938	22,198,728	2.80	2.80	2.90	2.90	3.75	13.00	25.00	480	80.00
1938D	5,537,000	3.20	3.20	3.30	5.00	6.00	18.00	34.00	—	62.00
1938S	8,090,000	3.20	3.20	3.30	3.50	5.00	21.00	37.00	—	160
1939	67,749,321	2.80	2.80	2.90	2.90	3.30	9.00	25.00	425	170
1939 Doubled Die Obv	Inc. above	—	—	—	4.00	6.00	14.00	35.00	—	450
1939D	24,394,000	2.90	3.00	3.10	3.20	3.50	7.50	26.00	—	49.00
1939S	10,540,000	3.30	3.30	3.40	3.60	6.75	25.00	50.00	—	765
1940	65,361,827	2.80	2.80	2.90	2.90	3.30	6.00	30.00	325	48.00
1940D	21,198,000	2.90	3.00	3.10	3.20	4.70	8.00	32.00	—	48.00
1940S	21,560,000	2.90	3.00	3.10	3.20	4.70	8.50	32.00	—	95.00
1941	175,106,557	2.80	2.80	2.90	2.90	3.30	6.00	30.00	325	46.00
1941 Doubled Die Obv	Inc. above	—	—	—	10.00	16.00	55.00	140	—	295
1941D	45,634,000	2.90	3.00	3.10	3.20	3.70	8.00	23.00	—	46.00
1941D Doubled Die Obv	Inc. above	—	—	—	9.00	14.00	30.00	90.00	—	250
1941S Small S	43,090,000	2.90	3.00	3.10	3.20	3.70	7.00	30.00	—	46.00
1941S Large S	Inc. above	3.00	4.00	8.00	15.00	25.00	110	250	—	425
1941S Doubled Die Rev	Inc. above	3.00	3.50	3.75	4.00	5.00	18.00	50.00	—	85.00
1942	205,432,329	2.80	2.80	2.90	2.90	3.30	6.00	24.00	325	46.00
1942/41	Inc. above	525	545	610	640	750	2,250	12,500	—	35,000
1942D	60,740,000	2.90	3.00	3.10	3.20	3.70	8.00	27.50	—	46.00
1942/41D	Inc. above	475	540	600	650	825	2,650	7,000	—	26,500
1942S	49,300,000	2.90	3.00	3.10	3.20	3.70	9.50	24.00	—	145
1943	191,710,000	2.80	2.80	2.90	2.90	3.30	6.00	31.00	—	50.00
1943D	71,949,000	2.90	3.00	3.10	3.20	3.70	7.75	30.00	—	47.00
1943S	60,400,000	2.90	3.00	3.10	3.20	3.70	9.00	26.50	—	66.00
1944	231,410,000	2.80	2.80	2.90	2.90	3.30	6.00	23.00	—	75.00
1944D	62,224,000	2.90	3.00	3.10	3.20	3.70	7.50	23.00	—	46.00
1944S	49,490,000	2.90	3.00	3.10	3.20	3.70	7.50	30.00	—	50.00

DIME

Date	Mintage	G-4	VG-8	F-12	VF-20	XF-40	MS-60	MS-65	Prf-65	-65FSB
1945	159,130,000	2.80	2.80	2.90	2.90	3.30	6.00	23.00	—	9,750
1945D	40,245,000	2.90	3.00	3.10	3.20	3.70	6.50	24.00	—	4,650
1945S	41,920,000	2.90	3.00	3.10	3.20	3.70	7.00	24.00	—	105
1945S micro S	Inc. above	3.30	4.00	6.00	9.00	13.00	28.00	115	—	685

Roosevelt Dime

Mint mark 1946-64

KM# 195 • 2.5000 g., 0.9000 **Silver**, 0.0723 oz. ASW, 17.9 mm. • **Designer:** John R. Sinnock

Date	Mintage	G-4	VG-8	F-12	VF-20	XF-40	AU-50	MS-60	MS-65	Prf-65
1946	225,250,000	—	—	—	—	2.80	3.10	3.20	14.00	—
1946D	61,043,500	—	—	—	—	2.80	3.30	3.20	15.00	—
1946S	27,900,000	—	—	—	—	2.80	3.30	3.20	17.00	—
1947	121,520,000	—	—	—	—	2.80	3.00	3.50	15.00	—
1947D	46,835,000	—	—	—	—	2.80	3.00	4.50	17.00	—
1947S	34,840,000	—	—	—	—	2.80	3.00	3.50	16.00	—
1948	74,950,000	—	—	—	—	2.80	3.00	3.30	15.00	—
1948D	52,841,000	—	—	—	—	2.80	3.00	5.00	17.00	—
1948S	35,520,000	—	—	—	—	2.80	3.00	4.50	14.00	—
1949	30,940,000	—	—	2.80	2.80	3.00	8.00	16.00	45.00	—
1949D	26,034,000	—	—	2.80	2.80	2.80	5.00	9.00	22.00	—
1949S	13,510,000	—	—	2.80	3.50	8.00	15.00	35.00	65.00	—
1950	50,181,500	—	—	—	2.80	2.80	3.50	7.00	25.00	55.00
1950D	46,803,000	—	—	—	—	—	3.00	3.50	12.00	—
1950S	20,440,000	—	—	2.80	2.80	3.75	9.00	23.00	60.00	—
1951	102,937,602	—	—	—	—	—	3.20	3.20	10.00	60.00
1951D	56,529,000	—	—	—	—	—	3.10	3.20	8.00	—
1951S	31,630,000	—	—	—	2.80	2.80	4.00	10.00	26.00	—
1952	99,122,073	—	—	—	—	—	3.00	3.20	9.00	35.00
1952D	122,100,000	—	—	—	—	—	3.00	3.20	10.00	—
1952S	44,419,500	—	—	—	2.80	3.20	3.50	5.50	15.00	—
1953	53,618,920	—	—	—	—	—	3.00	3.20	8.00	42.00
1953D	136,433,000	—	—	—	—	—	3.00	3.60	8.00	—
1953S	39,180,000	—	—	—	—	—	3.40	5.50	15.00	—
1954	114,243,503	—	—	—	—	—	3.00	3.20	7.00	18.00
1954D	106,397,000	—	—	—	—	—	3.00	3.20	7.00	—
1954S	22,860,000	—	—	—	—	—	3.00	3.30	10.00	—
1955	12,828,381	—	—	—	2.80	2.80	3.00	3.20	8.50	17.00
1955D	13,959,000	—	—	—	2.80	2.80	3.00	3.20	8.50	—
1955S	18,510,000	—	—	—	2.80	2.80	3.00	3.20	8.00	—
1956	109,309,384	—	—	—	—	—	3.00	3.20	9.00	8.00
1956D	108,015,100	—	—	—	—	—	3.00	3.30	10.00	—
1957	161,407,952	—	—	—	—	—	3.00	3.20	8.00	5.00
1957D	113,354,330	—	—	—	—	—	3.00	3.20	8.00	—
1958	32,785,652	—	—	—	—	—	3.00	3.20	8.50	6.00
1958D	136,564,600	—	—	—	—	—	3.00	3.20	9.00	—
1959	86,929,291	—	—	—	—	—	3.00	3.20	8.00	4.50
1959D	164,919,790	—	—	—	—	—	3.00	3.20	8.00	—
1960	72,081,602	—	—	—	—	—	3.00	3.20	7.50	4.50
1960D	200,160,400	—	—	—	—	—	3.00	3.20	7.50	—
1961	96,758,244	—	—	—	—	—	3.00	3.20	6.50	4.00
1961D	209,146,550	—	—	—	—	—	3.00	3.20	6.50	—
1962	75,668,019	—	—	—	—	—	3.00	3.20	7.00	4.00
1962D	334,948,380	—	—	—	—	—	3.00	3.20	7.00	—
1963	126,725,645	—	—	—	—	—	3.00	3.20	6.50	3.75
1963D	421,476,530	—	—	—	—	—	3.00	3.20	6.50	—
1964	933,310,762	—	—	—	—	—	3.00	3.20	6.00	3.75
1964D	1,357,517,180	—	—	—	—	—	3.00	3.20	6.00	—

Roosevelt Dime

Mint mark 1968- present   1982 No mint mark

KM# 195a • 2.2680 g., **Copper-Nickel Clad Copper**, 17.91 mm. • **Designer:** John R. Sinnock **Notes:** The 1979-S and 1981-S Type II proofs have clearer mint marks than the Type I proofs of those years. On the 1982 no-mint-mark variety, the mint mark was inadvertently left off.

Date	Mintage	MS-65	Prf-65	Date	Mintage	MS-65	Prf-65
1965	1,652,140,570	1.00	—	1987P	762,709,481	1.00	—
1966	1,382,734,540	1.00	—	1987D	653,203,402	1.00	—
1967	2,244,007,320	1.50	—	1987S	4,227,728	—	1.00
1968	424,470,000	1.00	—	1988P	1,030,550,000	1.00	—
1968D	480,748,280	1.00	—	1988D	962,385,488	1.00	—
1968S	3,041,506	—	1.00	1988S	3,262,948	—	3.00
1969	145,790,000	3.00	—	1989P	1,298,400,000	1.00	—
1969D	563,323,870	1.00	—	1989D	896,535,597	1.00	—
1969S	2,934,631	—	0.80	1989S	3,220,194	—	4.00
1970	345,570,000	1.00	—	1990P	1,034,340,000	1.00	—
1970S No S	—	—	1,300	1990D	839,995,824	1.00	—
1970D	754,942,100	1.00	—	1990S	3,299,559	—	2.00
1970S	2,632,810	—	1.00	1991P	927,220,000	1.00	—
1971	162,690,000	2.00	—	1991D	601,241,114	1.00	—
1971D	377,914,240	1.00	—	1991S	2,867,787	—	3.00
1971S	3,220,733	—	1.00	1992P	593,500,000	1.00	—
1972	431,540,000	1.00	—	1992D	616,273,932	1.00	—
1972D	330,290,000	1.00	—	1992S	2,858,981	—	4.00
1972S	3,260,996	—	1.00	1993P	766,180,000	1.00	—
1973	315,670,000	1.00	—	1993D	750,110,166	1.50	—
1973D	455,032,426	1.00	—	1993S	2,633,439	—	7.00
1973S	2,760,339	—	1.00	1994P	1,189,000,000	1.00	—
1974	470,248,000	1.00	—	1994D	1,303,268,110	1.00	—
1974D	571,083,000	1.00	—	1994S	2,484,594	—	5.00
1974S	2,612,568	—	1.00	1995P	1,125,500,000	1.50	—
1975	585,673,900	1.00	—	1995D	1,274,890,000	2.00	—
1975D	313,705,300	1.00	—	1995S	2,010,384	—	20.00
1975S	2,845,450	—	2.00	1996P	1,421,163,000	1.00	—
1976	568,760,000	1.50	—	1996D	1,400,300,000	1.00	—
1976D	695,222,774	1.00	—	1996W	1,457,949	25.00	—
1976S	4,149,730	—	1.00	1996S	2,085,191	—	2.50
1977	796,930,000	1.00	—	1997P	991,640,000	2.00	—
1977D	376,607,228	1.00	—	1997D	979,810,000	1.00	—
1977S	3,251,152	—	2.00	1997S	1,975,000	—	11.00
1978	663,980,000	1.00	—	1998P	1,163,000,000	1.00	—
1978D	282,847,540	1.00	—	1998D	1,172,250,000	1.25	—
1978S	3,127,781	—	1.00	1998S	2,078,494	—	4.00
1979	315,440,000	1.00	—	1999P	2,164,000,000	1.00	—
1979D	390,921,184	1.00	—	1999D	1,397,750,000	1.00	—
1979 type I	—	—	1.00	1999S	2,557,897	—	4.00
1979S type I	3,677,175	—	1.00	2000P	1,842,500,000	1.00	—
1979S type II	Inc. above	—	2.00	2000D	1,818,700,000	1.00	—
1980P	735,170,000	1.00	—	2000S	3,097,440	—	1.00
1980D	719,354,321	.70	—	2001P	1,369,590,000	1.00	—
1980S	3,554,806	—	1.00	2001D	1,412,800,000	1.00	—
1981P	676,650,000	1.00	—	2001S	2,249,496	—	1.00
1981D	712,284,143	1.00	—	2002P	1,187,500,000	1.00	—
1981S type I	—	—	1.00	2002D	1,379,500,000	1.00	—
1981S type II	—	—	2.00	2002S	2,268,913	—	2.00
1982P	519,475,000	8.50	—	2003P	1,085,500,000	1.00	—
1982 no mint mark	Inc. above	300	—	2003D	986,500,000	1.00	—
1982D	542,713,584	3.00	—	2003S	2,076,165	—	2.00
1982S	3,857,479	—	2.00	2004P	1,328,000,000	1.00	—
1983P	647,025,000	7.00	—	2004D	1,159,500,000	1.00	—
1983D	730,129,224	2.50	—	2004S	1,804,396	—	4.75
1983S	3,279,126	—	2.00	2005P	1,412,000,000	1.00	—
1984P	856,669,000	1.00	—	2005D	1,423,500,000	1.00	—
1984D	704,803,976	2.00	—	2005S	—	—	2.25
1984S	3,065,110	—	2.00	2006P	1,381,000,000	1.00	—
1985P	705,200,962	1.00	—	2006D	1,447,000,000	1.00	—
1985D	587,979,970	1.00	—	2006S	—	—	2.25
1985S	3,362,821	—	1.00	2007P	—	1.00	—
1986P	682,649,693	2.00	—	2007D	—	1.00	—
1986D	473,326,970	2.00	—	2007S	—	—	2.25
1986S	3,010,497	—	2.75	2008P	—	1.00	—

DIME

Date	Mintage	MS-65	Prf-65
2008D	—	1.00	—
2008S	—	—	2.25
2009P	—	1.00	—
2009D	—	1.00	—
2009S	—	—	2.25
2010P	—	1.00	—
2010D	—	1.00	—
2010S	—	—	2.25
2011P	—	1.00	—
2011D	—	1.00	—
2011S	—	—	2.25

KM# 195b • 2.5000 g., 0.9000 **Silver**, 0.0723 oz. ASW, 17.9 mm. • **Designer:** John R. Sinnock

Date	Mintage	Prf-65
1992S	1,317,579	5.00
1993S	761,353	9.00
1994S	785,329	9.00

Date	Mintage	Prf-65
1995S	838,953	25.00
1996S	830,021	9.00
1997S	821,678	25.00
1998S	878,792	9.00
1999S	804,565	6.50
2000S	965,921	4.00
2001S	849,600	5.00
2002S	888,826	5.00
2003S	1,090,425	4.00
2004S	—	4.50
2005S	—	3.50
2006S	—	3.50
2007S	—	3.50
2008S	—	3.50
2009S	—	3.50
2010S	—	3.50
2011S	—	3.50

20 CENTS

Seated Liberty within circle of stars, date below
Eagle with arrows in talons, value below reverse

KM# 109 • 5.0000 g., 0.9000 **Silver**, 0.1447 oz. ASW, 22 mm. • **Rev. Legend:** UNITED STATES OF AMERICA **Designer:** William Barber

Date	Mintage	G-4	VG-8	F-12	VF-20	XF-40	AU-50	MS-60	MS-65	Prf-65
1875	39,700	165	210	270	325	415	550	835	5,500	9,500
1875S Clear S	Inc. above	110	120	135	200	235	350	600	5,500	—
1875S	1,155,000	100.00	110	120	175	210	320	500	4,900	—
Note: 1875-S exists as a branch mint proof										
1875S over horizontal S	Inc. above	100.00	110	120	175	210	320	500	4,900	—
Note: Also known as filled S										
1875S as $	Inc. above	—	120	130	150	225	260	375	1,300	—
1875CC	133,290	335	385	475	600	775	1,150	1,650	10,000	—
1876	15,900	185	225	285	350	410	535	800	5,600	9,400
1876CC	10,000	20,000	25,000	30,000	35,000	50,000	60,000	—	—	175,000
Note: 1876CC, Eliasberg Sale, April 1997, MS-65, $148,500. Heritage 1999 ANA, MS-63, $86,500.										
1877 proof only	510	—	—	2,700	2,900	3,300	3,500	—	—	10,000
1878 proof only	600	—	—	2,000	2,300	2,400	2,800	—	—	9,500

1876 20-Cent
Grade F-12

QUARTER

Draped Bust Quarter
Draped bust right
Small eagle reverse

KM# 25 • 6.7400 g., 0.8920 **Silver**, 0.1933 oz. ASW, 27.5 mm. • **Designer:** Robert Scot

Date	Mintage	G-4	VG-8	F-12	VF-20	XF-40	AU-50	MS-60	MS-65
1796	6,146	11,000	16,500	30,000	39,500	42,500	68,000	82,500	235,000

Draped bust right, flanked by stars, date at angle below
Heraldic eagle reverse

KM# 36 • 6.7400 g., 0.8920 **Silver**, 0.1933 oz. ASW, 27.5 mm. • **Obv. Legend** LIBERTY **Rev. Legend:** UNITED STATES OF AMERICA **Designer:** Robert Scot

Date	Mintage	G-4	VG-8	F-12	VF-20	XF-40	AU-50	MS-60	MS-65
1804	6,738	5,500	6,750	9,000	14,500	46,500	54,500	88,500	335,000
1805	121,394	230	285	520	960	2,500	4,450	6,600	62,000
1806/5	206,124	250	375	650	1,400	2,850	5,000	7,150	72,000
1806	Inc. above	220	275	500	900	2,350	4,250	6,300	56,000
1807	220,643	220	275	500	925	2,350	4,250	6,300	58,000

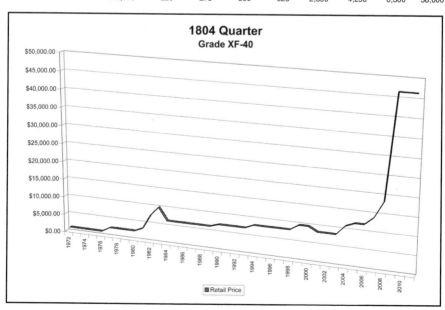

1804 Quarter
Grade XF-40

Liberty Cap Quarter
Draped bust left, flanked by stars, date below
Eagle with arrows in talons, banner above, value below reverse

KM# 44 • 6.7400 g., 0.8920 **Silver**, 0.1933 oz. ASW, 27 mm. • **Rev. Legend:** UNITED STATES OF AMERICA **Designer:** John Reich **Notes:** Varieties of the 1819 strikes are distinguished by the size of the 9 in the date. Varieties of the 1820 strikes are distinguished by the size of the 0 in the date. One 1822 variety and one 1828 variety have "25" engraved over "50" in the denomination. The 1827 restrikes were produced privately using dies sold as scrap by the U.S. Mint.

Date	Mintage	G-4	VG-8	F-12	VF-20	XF-40	AU-50	MS-60	MS-65
1815	89,235	100.00	135	200	425	1,375	1,750	3,250	30,000
1818/15	361,174	100.00	130	190	450	1,350	1,850	3,200	28,500
1818	Inc. above	95.00	125	180	410	1,200	1,600	2,850	19,500
1819 small 9	144,000	95.00	125	180	410	1,225	1,659	2,900	23,500
1819 large 9	Inc. above	95.00	130	185	435	1,300	1,750	3,100	25,000
1820 small 0	127,444	95.00	125	180	420	1,300	1,700	3,100	34,500
1820 large 0	Inc. above	95.00	125	180	415	1,225	1,600	2,900	32,500
1821	216,851	100.00	130	185	420	1,275	1,650	2,875	20,000
1822	64,080	110	135	200	440	1,225	2,750	4,200	—
1822 25/50C.	Inc. above	1,650	3,350	4,350	6,800	12,500	20,000	33,000	125,000
1823/22	17,800	30,000	35,000	48,500	58,500	68,000	100,000	175,000	—
Note: 1823/22, Superior, Aug. 1990, Proof, $62,500.									
1824/2	—	275	425	600	1,650	4,200	7,000	14,500	—
1825/22	168,000	125	175	260	500	1,550	2,100	3,000	
1825/23	Inc. above	115	150	235	450	1,400	1,850	3,400	25,000
1825/24	Inc. above	100.00	135	210	420	1,325	1,700	3,150	22,000
1827 original curl base 2	4,000	—	—	—	70,000	75,000	80,000	—	—
Note: Eliasberg, April 1997, VF-20, $39,600.									
1827 restrike, square base 2	Inc. above	—	—	—	—	—	—	—	—
Note: 1827 restrike, Eliasberg, April 1997, Prf-65, $77,000.									
1828	102,000	90.00	120	180	400	1,100	1,650	3,000	26,000
1828 25/50C.	Inc. above	165	320	550	1,250	2,650	4,250	9,500	—

Draped bust left, flanked by stars, date below
Eagle with arrows in talons, value below reverse

KM# 55 • 0.8920 **Silver**, 24.3 mm. • **Rev. Legend:** UNITED STATES OF AMERICA **Designer:** William Kneass **Notes:** Varieties of the 1831 strikes are distinguished by the size of the lettering on the reverse.

Date	Mintage	G-4	VG-8	F-12	VF-20	XF-40	AU-50	MS-60	MS-65
1831 small letter rev.	398,000	70.00	95.00	115	160	400	850	1,175	19,500
1831 large letter rev.	Inc. above	70.00	90.00	110	150	385	775	1,100	17,000
1832	320,000	70.00	90.00	110	150	385	775	1,075	22,750
1833	156,000	75.00	100.00	115	170	420	855	1,400	20,500
1834	286,000	70.00	90.00	110	150	385	775	1,100	17,000
1834 0 over O	Inc. above	—	—	—	—	—	—	—	—
1835	1,952,000	70.00	90.00	110	150	385	775	1,100	23,750
1836	472,000	70.00	90.00	110	150	385	775	1,100	18,850
1837	252,400	70.00	90.00	110	150	385	775	1,100	17,000
1838	832,000	70.00	90.00	110	150	385	775	1,100	19,500

QUARTER

Seated Liberty Quarter
Seated Liberty, stars around top 1/2 of border, date below
Eagle with arrows in talons, value below reverse

KM# 64.1 • 6.6800 g., 0.9000 **Silver**, 0.1933 oz. ASW, 24.3 mm. • **Rev. Legend:** UNITED STATES OF AMERICA **Designer:** Christian Gobrecht

Date	Mintage	G-4	VG-8	F-12	VF-20	XF-40	AU-50	MS-60	MS-65
1838	Inc. above	36.00	44.00	55.00	95.00	365	510	1,250	36,500
1839	491,146	35.00	42.00	53.00	90.00	365	510	1,250	36,500
1840O	425,200	46.00	54.00	75.00	135	425	575	1,850	48,500

Drapery added to Liberty's left elbow, stars around top 1/2 of border
Eagle with arrows in talons, value below reverse

KM# 64.2 • 6.6800 g., 0.9000 **Silver**, 0.1933 oz. ASW, 24.3 mm. • **Rev. Legend:** UNITED STATES OF AMERICA **Designer:** Christian Gobrecht

Date	Mintage	G-4	VG-8	F-12	VF-20	XF-40	AU-50	MS-60	MS-65
1840	188,127	31.00	36.50	60.00	110	200	300	1,100	33,000
1840O	Inc. above	34.00	39.00	70.00	115	250	450	1,000	—
1841	120,000	65.00	90.00	125	170	275	385	750	11,000
1841O	452,000	21.50	27.50	50.00	85.00	165	350	700	10,000
1842 small date	88,000	—	—	—	—	—	—	—	—
Note: 1842 small date, Eliasberg, April 1997, Prf-63, $66,000.									
1842 large date	Inc. above	100.00	125	190	275	375	850	1,850	—
1842O small date	769,000	425	650	1,200	1,950	4,000	—	—	—
1842O large date	Inc. above	31.00	44.50	55.00	70.00	135	300	900	—
1843	645,600	28.00	31.50	34.00	44.00	75.00	175	400	6,750
1843O	968,000	31.00	44.50	55.00	125	250	750	2,000	11,000
1844	421,200	28.00	31.50	34.00	44.00	80.00	160	450	5,500
1844O	740,000	31.00	44.50	40.00	75.00	140	280	1,000	6,000
1845	922,000	28.00	31.50	34.00	44.00	70.00	150	465	5,000
1846	510,000	30.00	33.50	36.00	46.00	85.00	175	475	6,000
1847	734,000	28.00	31.50	34.00	11.00	70.00	150	450	5,000
1847O	368,000	36.00	45.00	70.00	135	300	750	1,900	—
1848	146,000	38.00	60.00	110	185	225	375	1,000	10,000
1849	340,000	30.00	33.50	45.00	65.00	125	275	750	9,000
1849O	—	550	750	1,150	1,850	3,250	5,750	—	—
1850	190,800	40.00	50.00	80.00	125	175	275	800	—
1850O	412,000	31.00	44.50	60.00	110	175	450	1,300	—
1851	160,000	60.00	75.00	125	225	285	400	850	8,500
1851O	88,000	185	275	425	700	1,250	2,250	4,000	—
1852	177,060	50.00	60.00	100.00	185	225	350	500	4,800
1852O	96,000	195	275	475	800	1,350	3,500	8,000	—
1853 recut date	44,200	450	650	900	1,100	1,350	1,800	2,600	9,000

Seated Liberty, arrows at date
Rays around eagle reverse

KM# 78 • 6.2200 g., 0.9000 **Silver**, 0.1800 oz. ASW, 24.3 mm. • **Rev. Legend:** UNITED STATES OF AMERICA **Designer:** Christian Gobrecht

Date	Mintage	G-4	VG-8	F-12	VF-20	XF-40	AU-50	MS-60	MS-65	Prf-65
1853	15,210,020	27.50	31.00	34.00	44.00	135	265	900	17,000	100,000
1853/4	Inc. above	40.00	70.00	110	200	400	950	1,950	45,000	—
1853O	1,332,000	29.50	45.00	54.00	85.00	300	1,100	2,750	—	—

Seated Liberty, arrows at date
Eagle with arrows in talons, value below reverse

KM# 81 • 6.6800 g., 0.9000 **Silver**, 0.1933 oz. ASW, 24.3 mm. • **Rev. Legend:** UNITED STATES OF AMERICA **Designer:** Christian Gobrecht

Date	Mintage	G-4	VG-8	F-12	VF-20	XF-40	AU-50	MS-60	MS-65	Prf-65
1854	12,380,000	27.50	31.00	33.00	42.00	70.00	210	460	8,900	17,500
1854O	1,484,000	29.50	33.00	35.00	60.00	125	300	1,750	—	—
1854O huge O	Inc. above	800	1,350	2,850	4,750	7,500	12,500	17,000	—	—
1855	2,857,000	27.50	31.00	33.00	42.00	70.00	210	460	8,900	18,500
1855O	176,000	50.00	75.00	110	240	475	950	2,750	—	—
1855S	396,400	40.00	60.00	80.00	225	500	1,250	2,000	—	—

Seated Liberty, date below
Eagle with arrows in talons, value below reverse

KM# A64.2 • 6.2200 g., 0.9000 **Silver**, 0.1800 oz. ASW, 24.3 mm. • **Rev. Legend:** UNITED STATES OF AMERICA **Designer:** Christian Gobrecht

Date	Mintage	G-4	VG-8	F-12	VF-20	XF-40	AU-50	MS-60	MS-65	Prf-65
1856	7,264,000	28.00	31.50	34.00	44.00	75.00	170	280	4,250	15,000
1856O	968,000	30.00	33.50	40.00	60.00	110	250	1,000	8,500	—
1856S	286,000	45.00	65.00	110	250	450	900	2,200	—	—
1856S/S	Inc. above	150	275	500	1,250	2,000	—	—	—	—
1857	9,644,000	28.00	31.50	34.00	44.00	75.00	170	280	4,000	9,500
1857O	1,180,000	30.00	33.50	36.00	46.00	80.00	275	975	—	—
1857S	82,000	125	175	275	450	700	950	2,750	—	—
1858	7,368,000	28.00	31.50	34.00	44.00	75.00	170	280	4,000	6,500
1858O	520,000	32.00	35.50	45.00	70.00	135	360	1,350	—	—
1858S	121,000	70.00	110	175	300	750	1,250	—	—	—
1859	1,344,000	30.00	33.50	36.00	46.00	75.00	175	375	6,000	7,000
1859O	260,000	32.00	30.00	50.00	80.00	150	400	1,000	15,000	—
1859S	80,000	125	150	250	500	1,500	2,500	—	—	—
1860	805,400	32.00	35.50	38.00	48.00	60.00	160	500	—	5,250
1860O	388,000	32.00	30.00	40.00	55.00	100.00	275	1,200	—	—
1860S	56,000	200	350	600	975	4,000	6,000	—	—	—
1861	4,854,600	30.00	19.00	27.00	32.00	55.00	150	290	4,200	5,500

1856-S Quarter
Grade F-12

Date	Mintage	G-4	VG-8	F-12	VF-20	XF-40	AU-50	MS-60	MS-65	Prf-65
1861S	96,000	90.00	145	235	400	1,250	2,750	—	—	—
1862	932,550	32.00	22.00	33.00	40.00	65.00	165	300	4,350	5,350
1862S	67,000	80.00	125	200	325	700	1,600	2,750	—	—
1863	192,060	45.00	57.00	75.00	140	220	360	650	4,850	5,650
1864	94,070	90.00	120	160	245	345	400	650	5,000	5,500
1864S	20,000	400	600	900	1,350	2,350	3,750	7,000	—	—
1865	59,300	85.00	115	150	235	325	375	875	9,500	5,500
1865S	41,000	125	175	250	425	750	1,250	2,350	11,500	—
1866 unique	—	—	—	—	—	—	—	—	—	—

Seated Liberty, date below
IN GOD WE TRUST above eagle reverse

KM# 98 • 6.2200 g., 0.9000 **Silver**, 0.1800 oz. ASW, 24.3 mm. • **Rev. Legend:** UNITED STATES OF AMERICA **Designer:** Christian Gobrecht **Notes:** The 1873 closed-3 and open-3 varieties are distinguished by the amount of space between the upper left and lower left serifs in the 3.

Date	Mintage	G-4	VG-8	F-12	VF-20	XF-40	AU-50	MS-60	MS-65	Prf-65
1866	17,525	375	600	750	1,000	1,200	1,500	2,250	7,500	3,000
1866S	28,000	250	375	675	1,050	1,450	2,000	3,000	—	—
1867	20,625	260	325	500	675	850	975	1,200	—	2,450
1867S	48,000	200	385	600	900	1,350	1,700	—	—	—
1868	30,000	150	250	325	400	500	650	900	7,000	3,450
1868S	96,000	95.00	110	195	300	625	1,350	2,000	—	—
1869	16,600	350	450	600	800	900	1,000	1,275	—	2,500
1869S	76,000	100.00	135	225	375	700	1,400	2,400	16,000	—
1870	87,400	55.00	80.00	145	245	295	425	850	6,000	2,750
1870CC	8,340	8,500	10,000	14,500	24,500	42,500	55,000	—	—	—
1871	119,160	30.00	65.00	75.00	150	195	350	650	6,000	2,500
1871CC	10,890	3,500	4,500	7,500	12,500	18,000	—	—	—	—
1871S	30,900	300	500	700	950	1,200	1,850	3,000	10,000	—
1872	182,950	30.00	40.00	80.00	110	155	300	600	6,500	2,500
1872CC	22,850	1,100	1,500	2,250	3,750	6,500	7,500	14,000	—	—
1872S	83,000	850	1,250	1,750	2,400	3,500	4,500	7,500	—	—

Date	Mintage	G-4	VG-8	F-12	VF-20	XF-40	AU-50	MS-60	MS-65	Prf-65
1873 closed 3	212,600	225	350	475	800	1,200	1,800	2,800	—	2,600
1873 open 3	Inc. above	32.00	42.50	80.00	120	175	250	450	5,000	—
1873CC 6 known	4,000	—	75,000	—	—	100,000	135,000	200,000	—	—

Note: 1873CC, Heritage, April 1999, MS-62, $106,375.

Seated Liberty, arrows at date
"In God We Trust" above eagle reverse

KM# 106 • 6.2500 g., 0.9000 **Silver**, 0.1808 oz. ASW, 24.3 mm. • **Rev. Legend:** UNITED STATES OF AMERICA **Designer:** Christian Gobrecht

Date	Mintage	G-4	VG-8	F-12	VF-20	XF-40	AU-50	MS-60	MS-65	Prf-65
1873	1,271,700	28.00	32.00	37.50	60.00	190	390	725	3,900	8,000
1873CC	12,462	3,500	4,500	8,000	11,000	17,000	—	—	—	—
1873S	156,000	35.00	39.00	49.50	140	275	550	1,200	8,000	—
1874	471,900	28.00	32.00	37.50	60.00	190	390	725	3,650	6,750
1874S	392,000	33.00	37.00	47.50	110	240	425	900	4,500	—

Seated Liberty, date below
"In God We Trust" above eagle reverse

KM# A98 • 6.2500 g., 0.9000 **Silver**, 0.1808 oz. ASW, 24.3 mm. • **Rev. Legend:** UNITED STATES OF AMERICA **Designer:** Christian Gobrecht **Notes:** The 1876-CC fine-reeding variety has a more finely reeded edge.

Date	Mintage	G-4	VG-8	F-12	VF-20	XF-40	AU-50	MS-60	MS-65	Prf-65
1875	4,293,500	27.50	31.50	33.50	40.00	62.50	140	245	1,600	2,300
1875CC	140,000	75.00	110	225	350	550	850	1,600	15,000	—
1875S	680,000	25.00	36.00	67.00	110	175	275	575	3,200	—
1876	17,817,150	27.50	31.50	33.50	40.00	62.50	140	245	1,600	2,250
1876CC	4,944,000	50.00	68.00	80.00	100.00	135	235	450	2,600	—
1876CC fine reeding	Inc. above	30.00	40.00	50.00	65.00	90.00	150	325	3,600	—
1876S	8,596,000	27.50	31.50	33.50	40.00	62.50	140	245	2,000	—
1877	10,911,710	27.50	31.50	33.50	40.00	62.50	140	245	1,600	2,250
1877CC	4,192,000	50.00	68.00	80.00	100.00	135	235	450	2,600	—
1877S	8,996,000	27.50	31.50	33.50	40.00	62.50	140	245	1,600	—
1877S over horizontal S	Inc. above	45.00	60.00	95.00	175	250	375	650	—	—
1878	2,260,800	27.50	31.50	33.50	40.00	62.50	150	265	2,750	2,300
1878CC	996,000	55.00	75.00	90.00	125	150	265	550	3,650	—
1878S	140,000	165	200	300	400	650	875	1,450	—	—
1879	14,700	190	235	285	325	400	485	575	1,700	2,250
1880	14,955	190	235	285	325	400	485	575	1,600	2,250
1881	12,975	200	250	300	350	425	500	600	1,650	2,200
1882	16,300	200	250	300	350	425	500	600	1,850	2,200
1883	15,439	210	265	315	365	435	525	625	2,450	2,200
1884	8,875	375	450	550	650	750	750	850	1,900	2,200
1885	14,530	210	265	315	365	435	525	625	2,600	2,200
1886	5,886	500	600	700	800	900	1,000	1,250	2,600	2,400
1887	10,710	300	350	450	550	650	750	850	2,350	2,200
1888	10,833	275	325	425	500	600	700	800	2,000	2,350
1888S	1,216,000	27.50	31.50	33.50	40.00	62.50	150	265	2,450	—
1889	12,711	250	300	375	425	500	575	675	1,750	2,350
1890	80,590	65.00	85.00	100.00	125	200	300	425	—	2,350
1891	3,920,600	27.50	31.50	33.50	40.00	62.50	140	245	1,750	2,350
1891O	68,000	150	225	325	550	950	1,250	3,000	14,500	—
1891S	2,216,000	28.50	32.50	35.50	45.00	62.50	150	265	2,400	—

Barber Quarter
Laureate head right, flanked by stars, date below
Heraldic eagle reverse

KM# 114 • 6.2500 g., 0.9000 **Silver**, 0.1808 oz. ASW, 24.3 mm. • **Obv. Legend** IN GOD WE TRUST **Rev. Legend:** UNITED STATES OF AMERICA **Designer:** Charles E. Barber

Date	Mintage	G-4	VG-8	F-12	VF-20	XF-40	AU-50	MS-60	MS-65	Prf-65
1892	8,237,245	10.00	14.50	35.00	65.00	100.00	150	285	—	2,450
1892 Type 2 Rev	Inc. above	7.50	8.50	26.00	46.00	75.00	115	220	1,550	2,450
1892O	2,640,000	22.00	30.00	55.00	90.00	155	235	400	—	—
1892O Type 2 Rev	Inc. above	15.00	21.50	43.50	63.50	100.00	150	290	1,875	—
1892S	964,079	50.00	75.00	135	200	300	465	650	—	—
1892S Type 2 Rev	Inc. above	35.00	57.50	95.00	145	195	300	450	4,650	—
1893	5,484,838	6.50	9.00	27.50	41.50	70.00	115	220	1,650	2,450
1893O	3,396,000	13.50	22.00	44.00	75.00	165	285	390	—	—
1893O MM far right	Inc. above	9.00	15.00	31.00	57.50	115	170	265	2,100	—
1893S	1,454,535	26.00	47.50	82.00	158	255	390	635	—	—
1893S MM far right	Inc. above	21.00	38.00	67.50	125	195	310	450	7,950	—
1894	3,432,972	7.10	9.50	34.00	50.00	93.50	140	235	1,550	2,450
1894O	2,852,000	12.50	24.00	50.00	95.00	165	285	415	—	—
1894O MM far right	Inc. above	10.00	18.50	43.00	80.00	142	220	325	2,650	—
1894S	2,648,821	11.00	17.00	50.00	100.00	180	265	410	—	—
1894S MM far right	Inc. above	8.30	13.50	38.00	68.50	128	195	295	2,750	—
1895	4,440,880	7.00	10.50	31.50	41.50	78.00	130	235	1,850	2,450
1895O	2,816,000	17.50	27.50	60.00	92.00	175	290	525	—	—
1895O MM far right	Inc. above	12.50	19.50	46.00	75.00	145	225	390	2,850	—
1895S	1,764,681	28.00	40.00	85.00	165	235	375	560	—	—
1895S MM far right	Inc. above	22.00	30.00	68.50	120	175	290	425	4,450	—
1896	3,874,762	7.10	7.00	25.00	41.50	80.00	130	225	1,550	2,450
1896O	1,484,000	32.00	53.50	122	250	435	725	815	9,850	—
1896S	188,039	900	1,650	2,350	3,350	4,650	6,250	9,750	56,000	—
1897	8,140,731	7.10	6.30	21.50	33.50	72.00	115	220	1,550	2,450
1897O	1,414,800	19.50	40.00	130	255	400	625	900	3,950	—
1897S	542,229	75.00	115	235	290	440	665	900	7,000	—

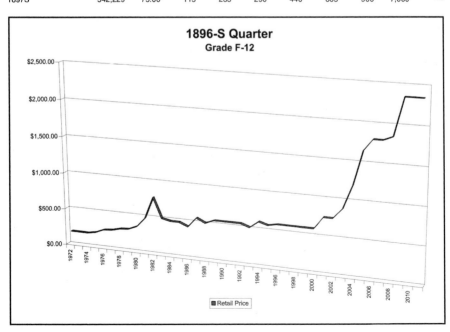

1896-S Quarter
Grade F-12

QUARTER

Date	Mintage	G-4	VG-8	F-12	VF-20	XF-40	AU-50	MS-60	MS-65	Prf-65
1898	11,100,735	7.10	6.30	22.50	35.00	75.00	115	210	1,550	2,450
1898O	1,868,000	16.00	28.50	75.00	160	300	430	665	10,000	—
1898S	1,020,592	12.50	19.00	50.00	70.00	100.00	210	385	6,950	—
1899	12,624,846	7.10	7.50	22.50	35.00	75.00	115	220	1,550	2,450
1899O	2,644,000	14.00	21.00	38.50	72.00	145	290	415	3,750	—
1899S	708,000	18.00	28.50	70.00	92.50	145	275	410	3,650	—
1900	10,016,912	7.10	8.00	23.50	36.00	71.50	130	220	1,550	2,450
1900O	3,416,000	16.00	29.00	69.50	118	170	320	575	3,750	—
1900S	1,858,585	8.00	15.00	38.00	55.00	80.00	135	375	4,950	—
1901	8,892,813	11.00	13.00	25.00	41.50	80.00	135	215	1,850	2,450
1901O	1,612,000	42.50	60.00	145	275	455	665	885	5,850	—
1901S	72,664	6,250	14,000	17,500	25,500	30,000	35,000	40,000	82,500	—
1902	12,197,744	7.10	8.50	19.50	32.50	65.00	120	220	1,275	2,450
1902O	4,748,000	8.50	16.00	52.50	89.00	150	245	485	5,000	—
1902S	1,524,612	14.50	22.00	55.00	95.00	170	260	525	3,750	—
1903	9,670,064	7.10	8.50	19.50	32.50	62.00	112	220	2,600	2,450
1903O	3,500,000	8.00	13.50	41.50	65.00	125	260	435	6,250	—
1903S	1,036,000	15.50	26.00	46.00	88.00	145	285	435	2,900	—
1904	9,588,813	8.00	9.80	20.00	34.50	69.00	120	230	1,375	2,450
1904O	2,456,000	11.50	21.50	62.50	120	225	460	850	3,250	—
1905	4,968,250	13.50	15.00	27.50	39.50	72.00	120	220	1,650	2,450
1905O	1,230,000	18.50	33.50	82.50	170	265	365	500	6,600	—
1905S	1,884,000	12.80	15.00	43.50	66.00	110	220	335	3,650	—
1906	3,656,435	7.10	8.50	18.50	32.50	65.00	112	215	1,275	2,450
1906D	3,280,000	7.10	8.50	25.00	42.50	69.00	155	230	2,250	—
1906O	2,056,000	7.10	13.50	41.50	60.00	110	200	290	1,575	—
1907	7,192,575	7.10	8.00	16.50	32.50	62.00	112	215	1,275	2,450
1907D	2,484,000	7.10	9.00	29.00	52.50	78.00	175	250	2,750	—
1907O	4,560,000	7.10	13.50	19.00	38.50	66.00	135	215	2,600	—
1907S	1,360,000	10.00	18.50	47.50	75.00	135	275	465	4,250	—
1908	4,232,545	7.10	7.50	18.50	33.50	66.00	112	215	1,275	2,450
1908D	5,788,000	7.10	7.50	17.50	35.00	66.00	116	250	1,750	—
1908O	6,244,000	7.10	8.50	17.50	38.50	72.00	120	215	1,275	—
1908S	784,000	18.50	40.00	90.00	165	295	500	775	4,950	—
1909	9,268,650	7.10	7.50	17.50	33.50	66.00	108	215	1,275	2,450
1909D	5,114,000	7.10	8.00	22.00	41.50	88.00	160	215	2,350	—
1909O	712,000	19.50	45.00	95.00	200	375	600	800	8,500	—
1909S	1,348,000	8.00	13.50	37.50	57.50	96.00	200	300	2,500	—
1910	2,244,551	7.80	10.00	30.00	46.00	80.00	140	215	1,275	2,450
1910D	1,500,000	8.00	11.00	47.50	75.00	130	260	375	2,250	—
1911	3,720,543	7.10	8.50	19.50	33.50	72.50	125	225	1,275	2,450
1911D	933,600	9.00	19.50	95.00	215	330	500	700	6,250	—
1911S	988,000	7.10	13.00	51.50	90.00	180	300	400	1,600	—
1912	4,400,700	7.10	8.00	17.50	33.50	70.00	108	215	1,275	2,485
1912S	708,000	9.00	13.00	46.00	84.00	130	230	390	2,750	—

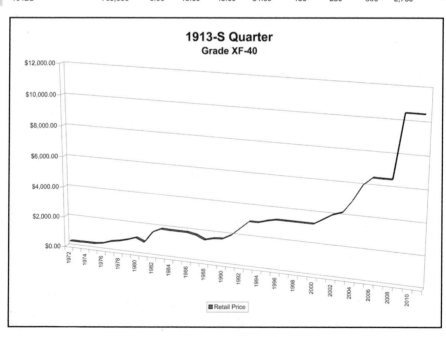

1913-S Quarter
Grade XF-40

Date	Mintage	G-4	VG-8	F-12	VF-20	XF-40	AU-50	MS-60	MS-65	Prf-65
1913	484,613	16.00	26.00	75.00	190	390	535	960	5,000	2,485
1913D	1,450,800	12.50	14.50	38.50	58.50	94.00	185	275	1,400	—
1913S	40,000	1,850	2,500	5,000	7,750	10,500	12,850	15,000	37,500	—
1914	6,244,610	7.10	7.50	17.00	28.00	55.00	108	215	1,275	2,550
1914D	3,046,000	7.10	7.50	17.00	28.00	55.00	108	215	1,275	—
1914S	264,000	82.00	120	235	425	620	775	1,000	3,450	—
1915	3,480,450	7.10	7.50	17.00	28.00	55.00	108	215	1,275	2,485
1915D	3,694,000	7.10	7.50	17.00	28.00	55.00	108	215	1,275	—
1915S	704,000	9.00	13.00	35.00	57.50	110	220	285	1,375	—
1916	1,788,000	7.10	7.50	17.00	28.00	55.00	108	215	1,275	—
1916D	6,540,800	7.10	7.50	17.00	28.00	55.00	108	215	1,275	—
1916D/D	Inc. above	10.00	14.00	24.00	45.00	95.00	150	400	—	—

Standing Liberty Quarter
Right breast exposed; Type 1 obverse

Right breast exposed

KM# 141 • 6.2500 g., 0.9000 **Silver**, 0.1808 oz. ASW, 24.3 mm. • **Designer:** Hermon A. MacNeil

Date	Mintage	G-4	VG-8	F-12	VF-20	XF-40	AU-50	MS-60	MS-65	-65FH
1916	52,000	2,850	5,650	6,900	9,000	10,000	12,000	14,500	26,500	37,500
1917	8,792,000	—	50.00	66.50	89.00	118	170	205	685	1,500
1917D	1,509,200	28.00	67.50	98.00	130	200	255	310	900	2,550
1917S	1,952,000	30.00	75.00	110	155	220	280	340	1,150	4,100

Right breast covered; Type 2 obverse
Three stars below eagle reverse

Mint mark   Right breast covered

KM# 145 • 6.2500 g., 0.9000 **Silver**, 0.1808 oz. ASW, 24.3 mm. • **Designer:** Hermon A. MacNeil

Date	Mintage	G-4	VG-8	F-12	VF-20	XF-40	AU-50	MS-60	MS-65	-65FH
1917	13,880,000	25.00	35.00	52.00	72.00	96.50	145	200	610	900
1917D	6,224,400	40.00	45.00	88.00	120	160	210	265	1,550	3,350
1917S	5,522,000	40.00	45.00	63.00	75.00	108	155	215	1,100	3,650
1918	14,240,000	17.00	21.00	29.00	35.00	46.00	80.00	135	560	1,750
1918D	7,380,000	26.00	36.00	66.00	78.00	122	195	250	1,485	4,850
1918S	11,072,000	17.00	21.00	32.00	35.00	48.00	95.00	185	1,250	13,500
1918/17S	Inc. above	1,550	2,250	3,850	5,200	7,500	13,500	17,850	110,000	320,000
1919	11,324,000	33.00	44.00	55.00	74.00	80.00	118	175	600	1,650
1919D	1,944,000	85.00	110	195	345	565	695	825	2,950	28,500
1919S	1,836,000	80.00	105	185	285	510	585	750	4,200	30,000
1920	27,860,000	15.00	18.00	25.00	37.00	51.00	90.00	165	600	2,100
1920D	3,586,400	48.00	65.00	88.00	120	160	215	325	2,250	7,200
1920S	6,380,000	19.00	25.00	30.00	37.00	57.00	110	235	2,650	24,000
1921	1,916,000	165	210	450	635	825	1,125	1,625	3,850	5,500
1923	9,716,000	15.00	18.00	35.00	37.00	55.00	95.00	155	620	4,000
1923S	1,360,000	300	425	675	1,000	1,500	2,000	2,600	5,500	7,500
1924	10,920,000	15.00	18.00	25.00	34.00	45.00	90.00	170	585	1,650
1924D	3,112,000	56.00	68.00	108	135	185	220	300	610	5,750
1924S	2,860,000	27.00	32.00	43.00	57.00	105	220	315	1,850	6,500
1925	12,280,000	6.10	6.90	8.10	16.50	44.00	90.00	150	575	950
1926	11,316,000	6.10	6.50	7.40	12.80	28.00	58.00	135	535	2,250
1926D	1,716,000	6.50	10.00	20.00	40.00	75.00	118	170	485	22,500
1926S	2,700,000	6.40	6.80	11.00	30.00	110	225	325	2,175	28,000
1927	11,912,000	6.10	6.50	7.40	10.50	40.00	83.00	92.00	485	1,300
1927D	976,400	14.00	19.00	32.00	70.00	140	210	250	600	2,650
1927S	396,000	35.00	48.00	110	285	1,000	2,650	4,750	12,000	165,000
1928	6,336,000	6.10	6.50	7.40	11.50	28.00	58.00	92.00	485	2,150
1928D	1,627,600	6.60	7.00	7.50	20.00	42.50	90.00	135	485	5,650
1928S Large S	2,644,000	7.60	8.40	10.30	25.00	65.00	115	200	—	—

Date	Mintage	G-4	VG-8	F-12	VF-20	XF-40	AU-50	MS-60	MS-65	-65FH
1928S Small S	Inc. above	6.40	6.80	8.00	16.50	38.00	75.00	125	525	900
1929	11,140,000	6.10	6.50	7.40	11.50	28.00	58.00	92.00	485	900
1929D	1,358,000	6.60	7.00	6.75	16.00	38.50	79.00	135	485	5,850
1929S	1,764,000	6.40	6.80	6.50	15.00	34.00	75.00	120	485	875
1930	5,632,000	6.10	6.50	7.40	10.50	28.00	58.00	92.00	485	875
1930S	1,556,000	6.40	6.80	7.40	10.50	34.00	70.00	115	485	925

Washington Quarter

Mint mark 1932-64

KM# 164 • 6.2500 g., 0.9000 **Silver**, 0.1808 oz. ASW, 24.3 mm. • **Designer:** John Flanagan

Date	Mintage	G-4	VG-8	F-12	VF-20	XF-40	AU-50	MS-60	MS-65	Prf-65
1932	5,404,000	7.40	7.50	7.60	7.70	9.50	14.50	25.00	310	—
1932D	436,800	115	125	140	180	290	440	1,150	13,000	—
1932S	408,000	125	140	150	165	225	260	465	4,000	—
1934 Medium Motto	31,912,052	7.40	8.00	8.30	8.70	10.00	10.50	26.00	110	—
1934 Heavy Motto	Inc. above	7.20	7.30	9.00	12.50	18.00	30.00	50.00	265	—
1934 Light motto	Inc. above	7.80	8.60	10.00	12.00	15.00	26.00	45.00	350	—
1934 Doubled Die Obverse	Inc. above	75.00	100.00	165	200	320	450	850	4,250	—
1934D Medium Motto	3,527,200	7.20	7.30	11.50	17.50	28.00	85.00	235	1,050	—
1934D Heavy Motto	Inc. above	7.40	7.50	12.50	20.00	34.00	100.00	265	1,350	—
1935	32,484,000	7.20	7.40	737	8.20	9.70	10.00	20.00	115	—
1935D	5,780,000	7.90	8.20	8.90	15.50	33.50	125	245	635	—
1935S	5,660,000	7.40	7.60	8.60	9.70	15.50	36.50	95.00	310	—
1936	41,303,837	7.20	7.40	7.70	8.20	9.70	9.50	26.00	108	1,550
1936D	5,374,000	7.90	8.20	10.50	26.00	52.00	255	600	1,000	—
1936S	3,828,000	7.60	7.90	8.60	9.10	14.50	48.50	108	345	—
1937 Double Die Obverse	Inc. above	75.00	100.00	235	340	450	850	1,850	11,500	—
1937	19,701,542	7.20	7.40	7.70	9.60	10.00	16.50	22.00	92.00	475
1937D	7,189,600	7.40	7.60	8.60	9.00	16.50	38.00	6,750	150	—
1937S	1,652,000	7.90	8.20	9.00	22.00	34.00	95.00	160	400	—
1938	9,480,045	7.40	7.60	8.60	9.00	18.00	49.00	90.00	215	350
1938S	2,832,000	7.90	8.10	8.30	9.75	22.50	55.00	108	215	—
1939	33,548,795	7.20	7.40	7.70	8.20	9.30	7.00	15.50	50.00	250
1939D	7,092,000	7.40	7.60	8.20	9.70	12.00	19.50	42.00	128	—

1932-D Quarter
Grade F-12

Date	Mintage	G-4	VG-8	F-12	VF-20	XF-40	AU-50	MS-60	MS-65	Prf-65
1939S	2,628,000	7.90	8.20	8.70	12.00	24.00	60.00	105	260	—
1940	35,715,246	7.20	7.40	7.70	8.20	9.20	7.50	17.50	53.50	160
1940D	2,797,600	7.40	7.60	7.70	12.50	26.00	65.00	130	300	—
1940S	8,244,000	7.40	7.60	7.70	7.80	9.00	16.50	28.50	54.00	—
1941	79,047,287	—	—	—	—	7.40	7.60	9.50	36.00	175
1941 Double Die Obv.	Inc. above	—	—	—	20.00	40.00	50.00	65.00	120	—
1941D	16,714,800	—	—	—	7.90	9.00	15.00	33.00	66.00	—
1941S	16,080,000	—	—	—	8.10	8.20	12.50	30.00	65.00	—
1941 Lg S	Inc. above	—	8.20	12.00	20.00	30.00	50.00	100.00	350	—
1942	102,117,123	—	—	—	—	7.30	7.50	9.00	29.00	135
1942D	17,487,200	—	—	—	7.90	9.10	11.00	18.00	38.00	—
1942D Double Die Obv.	Inc. above	—	115	250	440	650	1,350	2,150	5,000	—
1942D Double Die Rev.	Inc. above	—	22.00	40.00	60.00	75.00	150	350	1,850	—
1942S	19,384,000	—	—	—	8.00	11.00	22.50	72.00	140	—
1943	99,700,000	—	—	—	—	7.30	7.50	9.00	39.00	—
1943 Double Die Obv.	Inc. above	—	12.00	20.00	35.00	50.00	90.00	175	450	—
1943D	16,095,600	—	—	—	8.10	9.20	16.50	29.00	50.00	—
1943S	21,700,000	—	—	7.80	8.20	8.60	14.50	27.00	51.50	—
1943S Double Die Obv.	Inc. above	30.00	60.00	80.00	110	150	265	400	1,200	—
1943 Trumpet tail S	Inc. above	10.00	15.00	25.00	40.00	60.00	100.00	175	675	—
1944	104,956,000	—	—	—	—	7.30	7.50	8.10	29.00	—
1944D	14,600,800	—	—	—	7.80	7.90	11.00	19.00	38.50	—
1944S	12,560,000	—	—	—	7.80	7.90	9.50	14.50	31.00	—
1945	74,372,000	—	—	—	—	7.30	7.50	8.10	37.50	—
1945D	12,341,600	—	—	—	7.90	7.50	11.00	18.00	40.00	—
1945S	17,004,001	—	—	—	7.70	7.80	8.00	8.50	32.00	—
1946	53,436,000	—	—	—	—	7.30	7.50	8.10	38.00	—
1946D	9,072,800	—	—	—	7.80	8.40	8.60	9.75	40.00	—
1946S	4,204,000	—	—	—	7.80	8.40	8.60	9.30	35.00	—
1947	22,556,000	—	—	—	—	8.40	8.60	11.50	40.00	—
1947D	15,338,400	—	—	—	7.80	8.30	8.50	11.00	40.00	—
1947S	5,532,000	—	—	—	7.80	8.30	8.50	9.25	29.00	—
1948	35,196,000	—	—	—	7.80	8.30	8.50	8.30	30.00	—
1948D	16,766,800	—	—	—	7.80	8.40	8.80	13.00	53.00	—
1948S	15,960,000	—	—	—	7.80	8.30	8.50	9.10	41.00	—
1949	9,312,000	—	—	—	7.90	6.50	15.00	36.00	62.00	—
1949D	10,068,400	—	—	—	7.70	8.40	9.50	16.50	48.00	—
1950	24,971,512	—	—	—	—	7.90	10.00	10.00	40.00	65.00
1950D	21,075,600	—	—	—	—	7.40	7.60	8.30	32.00	—
1950D/S	Inc. above	30.00	37.00	45.00	75.00	140	225	350	5,000	—
1950S	10,284,004	—	—	—	—	8.00	7.50	15.00	32.00	—
1950S/D	Inc. above	32.00	44.00	65.00	125	180	285	400	1,250	—
1950S/S	Inc. above	4.00	5.00	7.00	10.00	14.00	18.00	35.00	135	—
1951	43,505,602	—	—	—	—	7.30	7.50	8.00	32.00	60.00
1951D	35,354,800	—	—	—	—	7.50	8.10	7.00	26.00	—
1951S	9,048,000	—	—	7.10	8.00	7.50	11.00	24.00	54.00	—
1952	38,862,073	—	—	—	—	7.30	8.20	11.50	36.00	46.00
1952D	49,795,200	—	—	—	—	7.30	7.50	9.10	32.00	—
1952S	13,707,800	—	—	—	7.90	8.00	12.50	20.00	52.00	—
1953	18,664,920	—	—	—	—	7.90	8.80	10.00	42.00	44.00
1953D	56,112,400	—	—	—	—	7.30	7.50	8.60	22.00	—
1953S	14,016,000	—	—	—	—	7.30	7.50	8.90	28.00	—
1954	54,645,503	—	—	—	—	7.30	7.50	8.10	24.00	18.00
1954D	42,305,500	—	—	—	—	7.30	7.50	8.10	24.00	—
1954S	11,834,722	—	—	—	—	7.30	7.50	8.60	23.00	—
1955	18,558,381	—	—	—	—	7.30	7.50	8.10	23.00	22.00
1955D	3,182,400	—	—	—	—	8.00	8.40	9.10	22.00	—
1956	44,813,384	—	—	—	—	7.30	7.50	8.10	26.00	15.00
1956 Double Bar 5	Inc. above	—	8.00	8.10	8.20	8.30	9.00	20.00	125	—
1956 Type B rev, proof rev die	Inc. above	—	—	8.00	12.00	18.00	25.00	35.00	275	—
1956D	32,334,500	—	—	—	—	7.30	7.50	8.10	15.00	—
1957	47,779,952	—	—	—	—	7.30	7.50	8.10	12.00	12.00
1957 Type B rev, proof rev die	Inc. above	—	—	—	7.50	10.00	20.00	40.00	125	—
1957D	77,924,160	—	—	—	—	7.30	7.50	8.10	12.00	—
1958	7,235,652	—	—	—	—	7.30	7.50	8.10	12.00	12.00
1958 Type B rev, proof rev die	Inc. above	—	—	—	7.50	10.00	16.00	24.00	90.00	—
1958D	78,124,900	—	—	—	—	7.30	7.50	8.10	12.00	—
1959	25,533,291	—	—	—	—	7.30	7.50	8.10	12.00	12.00
1959 Type B rev, proof rev die	Inc. above	—	—	—	8.20	8.30	12.00	18.00	65.00	—
1959D	62,054,232	—	—	—	—	7.30	7.50	8.10	22.00	—
1960	30,855,602	—	—	—	—	7.30	7.50	8.10	12.00	12.00
1960 Type B rev, proof rev die	Inc. above	—	—	—	7.50	10.00	16.00	24.00	90.00	—
1960D	63,000,324	—	—	—	—	7.30	7.50	8.10	12.00	—
1961	40,064,244	—	—	—	—	7.30	7.50	8.10	15.00	12.00
1961 Type B rev, proof rev die	Inc. above	—	—	—	8.20	10.00	14.00	20.00	200	—
1961D	83,656,928	—	—	—	—	7.30	7.50	8.10	20.00	—
1962	39,374,019	—	—	—	—	7.30	7.50	8.10	15.00	12.00
1962 Type B rev, proof rev die	Inc. above	—	—	—	8.00	12.00	15.00	30.00	175	—.
1962D	127,554,756	—	—	—	—	7.30	7.50	8.10	22.00	—

QUARTER

Date	Mintage	G-4	VG-8	F-12	VF-20	XF-40	AU-50	MS-60	MS-65	Prf-65
1963	77,391,645	—	—	—	—	7.30	7.50	8.10	12.00	12.00
1963 Type B rev, proof rev die	Inc. above	—	—	—	8.20	8.30	8.00	15.00	50.00	—
1963D	135,288,184	—	—	—	—	7.30	7.50	8.10	15.00	—
1964	564,341,347	—	—	—	—	7.30	7.50	8.10	12.00	12.00
1964 Type B rev, proof rev die	Inc. above	—	—	—	8.20	10.00	14.00	25.00	75.00	—
1964 SMS	Inc. above	—	—	—	—	—	250	750	1,400	—
1964D	704,135,528	—	—	—	—	7.30	7.50	8.10	12.00	—
1964D Type C rev, clad rev die	Inc. above	—	—	—	40.00	55.00	75.00	125	450	—

KM# 164a • 5.6700 g., Copper-Nickel Clad Copper, 24.3 mm. • Designer: John Flanagan

Date	Mintage	MS-65	Prf-65	Date	Mintage	MS-65	Prf-65
1965	1,819,717,540	12.00	—	1971	109,284,000	15.00	—
1965 SMS	2,300,000	9.00	—	1971D	258,634,428	6.50	—
1966	821,101,500	7.50	—	1971S	3,220,733	—	2.00
1966 SMS	2,261,583	9.00	—	1972	215,048,000	7.50	—
1967	1,524,031,848	12.00	—	1972D	311,067,732	10.00	—
1967 SMS	1,863,344	9.00	—	1972S	3,260,996	—	2.00
1968	220,731,500	15.00	—	1973	346,924,000	10.00	—
1968D	101,534,000	8.00	—	1973D	232,977,400	12.50	—
1968S	3,041,506	—	2.00	1973S	2,760,339	—	1.75
1969	176,212,000	14.00	—	1974	801,456,000	8.00	—
1969D	114,372,000	10.00	—	1974D	353,160,300	15.00	—
1969S	2,934,631	—	2.25	1974S	2,612,568	—	2.10
1970	136,420,000	12.00	—	1975 none minted	—	—	—
1970D	417,341,364	9.50	—	1975D none minted	—	—	—
1970S	2,632,810	—	2.00	1975S none minted	—	—	—

Bicentennial design, drummer boy reverse

Mint mark
1968-present

KM# 204 • 5.6700 g., Copper-Nickel Clad Copper, 24.3 mm. • Rev. Designer: Jack L. Ahr

Date	Mintage	G-4	VG-8	F-12	VF-20	XF-40	MS-60	MS-65	Prf-65
1976	809,784,016	—	—	—	—	—	.50	8.00	—
1976D	860,118,839	—	—	—	—	—	.50	10.00	—
1976S	4,149,730	—	—	—	—	—	—	—	3.25

Bicentennial design, drummer boy reverse

KM# 204a • 5.7500 g., Silver Clad, 24.3 mm. • Rev. Designer: Jack L. Ahr

Date	Mintage	G-4	VG-8	F-12	VF-20	XF-40	MS-60	MS-65	Prf-65
1976S	4,908,319	—	—	—	—	—	1.50	6.00	—
1976S	3,998,621	—	—	—	—	—	—	—	4.50

Regular design resumed reverse

KM# A164a • 5.6700 g., Copper-Nickel Clad Copper, 24.3 mm. • Edge Desc: Reeded Notes: KM#164 design and composition resumed. The 1979-S and 1981 Type II proofs have clearer mint marks than the Type I proofs for those years.

Date	Mintage	MS-65	Prf-65
1977	468,556,000	10.00	—
1977D	256,524,978	8.00	—
1977S	3,251,152	—	2.75
1978	521,452,000	9.00	—
1978D	287,373,152	11.00	—
1978S	3,127,781	—	2.75

Date	Mintage	MS-65	Prf-65
1979	515,708,000	10.00	—
1979D	489,789,780	9.00	—
1979S T-I	3,677,175	—	2.50
1979S T-II	Inc. above	—	4.00
1980P	635,832,000	8.00	—
1980D	518,327,487	8.50	—
1980S	3,554,806	—	2.75
1981P	601,716,000	8.00	—
1981D	575,722,833	6.50	—
1981S T-I	4,063,083	—	2.75
1981S T-II	Inc. above	—	7.50
1982P	500,931,000	28.00	—
1982D	480,042,788	15.00	—
1982S	3,857,479	—	2.75
1983P	673,535,000	45.00	—
1983D	617,806,446	30.00	—
1983S	3,279,126	—	3.00
1984P	676,545,000	16.00	—
1984D	546,483,064	12.50	—
1984S	3,065,110	—	3.00
1985P	775,818,962	15.00	—
1985D	519,962,888	10.00	—
1985S	3,362,821	5.00	3.00
1986P	551,199,333	12.00	—

Date	Mintage	MS-65	Prf-65
1986D	504,298,660	15.00	—
1986S	3,010,497	—	3.00
1987P	582,499,481	10.50	—
1987D	655,594,696	10.00	—
1987S	4,227,728	—	3.00
1988P	562,052,000	16.00	—
1988D	596,810,688	14.00	—
1988S	3,262,948	—	3.00
1989P	512,868,000	18.00	—
1989D	896,535,597	7.50	—
1989S	3,220,194	—	3.00
1990P	613,792,000	17.00	—
1990D	927,638,181	7.00	—
1990S	3,299,559	—	4.50
1991P	570,968,000	15.00	—
1991D	630,966,693	12.00	—
1991S	2,867,787	—	3.00
1992P	384,764,000	20.00	—
1992D	389,777,107	27.50	—
1992S	2,858,981	—	3.00
1993P	639,276,000	11.00	—
1993D	645,476,128	14.00	—
1993S	2,633,439	—	3.00
1994P	825,600,000	18.00	—

Date	Mintage	MS-65	Prf-65
1994D	880,034,110	8.00	—
1994S	2,484,594	—	3.00
1995P	1,004,336,000	22.00	—
1995D	1,103,216,000	20.00	—
1995S	2,117,496	—	9.00
1996P	925,040,000	15.00	—
1996D	906,868,000	14.00	—
1996S	1,750,244	—	4.50
1997P	595,740,000	12.50	—
1997D	599,680,000	16.00	—
1997S	2,055,000	—	9.00
1998P	896,268,000	13.50	—
1998D	821,000,000	13.50	—
1998S	2,086,507	—	9.00

KM# A164b • 6.2000 g., 0.9000 **Silver**, 0.1794 oz. ASW, 24.3 mm. •

Date	Mintage	Prf-65
1992S	1,317,579	5.00
1993S	761,353	6.50
1994S	785,329	8.50
1995S	838,953	10.00
1996S	775,021	9.50
1997S	741,678	10.00
1998S	878,792	8.50

50 State Quarters

Connecticut

KM# 297 • 5.6700 g., **Copper-Nickel Clad Copper**

Date	Mintage	MS-63	MS-65	Prf-65
1999P	688,744,000	1.00	10.00	—
1999D	657,480,000	1.00	9.00	—
1999S	3,713,359	—	—	12.00

KM# 297a • 6.2500 g., 0.9000 **Silver**, 0.1808 oz. ASW

Date	Mintage	MS-63	MS-65	Prf-65
1999S	804,565	—	—	65.00

Georgia

KM# 296 • 5.6700 g., **Copper-Nickel Clad Copper**

Date	Mintage	MS-63	MS-65	Prf-65
1999P	451,188,000	1.20	14.00	—
1999D	488,744,000	1.20	14.00	—
1999S	3,713,359	—	—	12.00

KM# 296a • 6.2500 g., 0.9000 **Silver**, 0.1808 oz. ASW

Date	Mintage	MS-63	MS-65	Prf-65
1999S	804,565	—	—	65.00

Delaware

KM# 293 • 5.6700 g., **Copper-Nickel Clad Copper**, 24.3 mm.

Date	Mintage	MS-63	MS-65	Prf-65
1999P	373,400,000	1.00	8.00	—
1999D	401,424,000	1.25	20.00	—
1999S	3,713,359	—	—	12.00

KM# 293a • 6.2500 g., 0.9000 **Silver**, 0.1808 oz. ASW

Date	Mintage	MS-63	MS-65	Prf-65
1999S	804,565	—	—	65.00

New Jersey

KM# 295 • 5.6700 g., **Copper-Nickel Clad Copper**

Date	Mintage	MS-63	MS-65	Prf-65
1999P	363,200,000	1.00	10.00	—
1999D	299,028,000	1.00	9.00	—
1999S	3,713,359	—	—	12.00

KM# 295a • 6.2500 g., 0.9000 **Silver**, 0.1808 oz. ASW

Date	Mintage	MS-63	MS-65	Prf-65
1999S	804,565	—	—	65.00

Pennsylvania

KM# 294 • 5.6700 g., **Copper-Nickel Clad Copper,** 24.3 mm.

Date	Mintage	MS-63	MS-65	Prf-65
1999P	349,000,000	1.00	15.00	—
1999D	358,332,000	1.00	20.00	—
1999S	3,713,359	—	—	12.00

KM# 294a • 6.2500 g., 0.9000 **Silver,** 0.1808 oz. ASW

Date	Mintage	MS-63	MS-65	Prf-65
1999S	804,565	—	—	65.00

Maryland

KM# 306 • 5.6700 g., **Copper-Nickel Clad Copper**

Date	Mintage	MS-63	MS-65	Prf-65
2000P	678,200,000	1.00	11.00	—
2000D	556,526,000	1.00	11.00	—
2000S	4,078,747	—	—	3.50

KM# 306a • 6.2500 g., 0.9000 **Silver,** 0.1808 oz. ASW

Date	Mintage	MS-63	MS-65	Prf-65
2000S	965,921	—	—	5.50

Massachusetts

KM# 305 • 5.6700 g., **Copper-Nickel Clad Copper**

Date	Mintage	MS-63	MS-65	Prf-65
2000P	629,800,000	1.00	7.00	—
2000D	535,184,000	1.00	8.00	—
2000S	4,078,747	—	—	3.50

KM# 305a • 6.2500 g., 0.9000 **Silver,** 0.1808 oz. ASW

Date	Mintage	MS-63	MS-65	Prf-65
2000S	965,921	—	—	5.50

New Hampshire

KM# 308 • 5.6700 g., **Copper-Nickel Clad Copper**

Date	Mintage	MS-63	MS-65	Prf-65
2000P	673,040,000	1.00	8.00	—
2000D	495,976,000	1.00	9.00	—
2000S	4,078,747	—	—	3.50

KM# 308a • 6.2500 g., 0.9000 **Silver,** 0.1808 oz. ASW

Date	Mintage	MS-63	MS-65	Prf-65
2000S	965,921	—	—	5.50

South Carolina

KM# 307 • 5.6700 g., **Copper-Nickel Clad Copper**

Date	Mintage	MS-63	MS-65	Prf-65
2000P	742,756,000	1.40	6.00	—
2000D	566,208,000	1.40	9.00	—
2000S	4,078,747	—	—	3.50

KM# 307a • 6.2500 g., 0.9000 **Silver,** 0.1808 oz. ASW

Date	Mintage	MS-63	MS-65	Prf-65
2000S	965,921	—	—	5.50

Virginia

KM# 309 • 5.6700 g., **Copper-Nickel Clad Copper**

Date	Mintage	MS-63	MS-65	Prf-65
2000P	943,000,000	1.00	6.50	—
2000D	651,616,000	1.00	6.50	—
2000S	4,078,747	—	—	3.35

KM# 309a • 6.2500 g., 0.9000 **Silver,** 0.1808 oz. ASW

Date	Mintage	MS-63	MS-65	Prf-65
2000S	965,921	—	—	5.50

QUARTER

Kentucky

KM# 322 • 5.6700 g., **Copper-Nickel Clad Copper**

Date	Mintage	MS-63	MS-65	Prf-65
2001P	353,000,000	1.20	6.50	—
2001D	370,564,000	1.00	7.00	—
2001S	3,094,140	—	—	11.00

KM# 322a • 6.2500 g., 0.9000 **Silver,** 0.1808 oz. ASW

Date	Mintage	MS-63	MS-65	Prf-65
2001S	889,697	—	—	21.00

New York

KM# 318 • 5.6700 g., **Copper-Nickel Clad Copper**

Date	Mintage	MS-63	MS-65	Prf-65
2001P	655,400,000	1.00	5.50	—
2001D	619,640,000	1.00	5.50	—
2001S	3,094,140	—	—	11.00

KM# 318a • 6.2500 g., 0.9000 **Silver,** 0.1808 oz. ASW

Date	Mintage	MS-63	MS-65	Prf-65
2001S	889,697	—	—	24.00

North Carolina

KM# 319 • 5.6700 g., **Copper-Nickel Clad Copper**

Date	Mintage	MS-63	MS-65	Prf-65
2001P	627,600,000	1.00	5.50	—
2001D	427,876,000	1.00	6.50	—
2001S	3,094,140	—	—	11.00

KM# 319a • 6.2500 g., 0.9000 **Silver,** 0.1808 oz. ASW

Date	Mintage	MS-63	MS-65	Prf-65
2001S	889,697	—	—	22.00

Rhode Island

KM# 320 • 5.6700 g., **Copper-Nickel Clad Copper**

Date	Mintage	MS-63	MS-65	Prf-65
2001P	423,000,000	1.00	5.50	—
2001D	447,100,000	1.00	6.00	—
2001S	3,094,140	—	—	11.00

KM# 320a • 6.2500 g., 0.9000 **Silver,** 0.1808 oz. ASW

Date	Mintage	MS-63	MS-65	Prf-65
2001S	889,697	—	—	19.00

Vermont

KM# 321 • 5.6700 g., **Copper-Nickel Clad Copper**

Date	Mintage	MS-63	MS-65	Prf-65
2001P	423,400,000	1.20	6.50	—
2001D	459,404,000	1.00	6.50	—
2001S	3,094,140	—	—	11.00

KM# 321a • 6.2500 g., 0.9000 **Silver,** 0.1808 oz. ASW

Date	Mintage	MS-63	MS-65	Prf-65
2001S	889,697	—	—	19.00

Indiana

KM# 334 • 5.6700 g., **Copper-Nickel Clad Copper**

Date	Mintage	MS-63	MS-65	Prf-65
2002P	362,600,000	1.00	5.00	—
2002D	327,200,000	1.00	5.00	—
2002S	3,084,245	—	—	4.00

KM# 334a • 6.2500 g., 0.9000 **Silver,** 0.1808 oz. ASW •

Date	Mintage	MS-63	MS-65	Prf-65
2002S	892,229	—	—	9.00

Louisiana

KM# 333 • 5.6700 g., **Copper-Nickel Clad Copper**

Date	Mintage	MS-63	MS-65	Prf-65
2002P	362,000,000	1.00	5.50	—
2002D	402,204,000	1.00	6.00	—
2002S	3,084,245	—	—	4.00

KM# 333a • 6.2500 g., 0.9000 **Silver,** 0.1808 oz. ASW

Date	Mintage	MS-63	MS-65	Prf-65
2002S	892,229	—	—	9.00

Tennessee

KM# 331 • 5.6700 g., **Copper-Nickel Clad Copper**

Date	Mintage	MS-63	MS-65	Prf-65
2002P	361,600,000	1.40	6.50	—
2002D	286,468,000	1.40	7.00	—
2002S	3,084,245	—	—	4.00

KM# 331a • 6.2500 g., 0.9000 **Silver,** 0.1808 oz. ASW

Date	Mintage	MS-63	MS-65	Prf-65
2002S	892,229	—	—	9.00

Mississippi

KM# 335 • 5.6700 g., **Copper-Nickel Clad Copper**

Date	Mintage	MS-63	MS-65	Prf-65
2002P	290,000,000	1.00	5.00	—
2002D	289,600,000	1.00	5.00	—
2002S	3,084,245	—	—	4.00

KM# 335a • 6.2500 g., 0.9000 **Silver,** 0.1808 oz. ASW

Date	Mintage	MS-63	MS-65	Prf-65
2002S	892,229	—	—	9.00

Alabama

KM# 344 • 5.6700 g., **Copper-Nickel Clad Copper**

Date	Mintage	MS-63	MS-65	Prf-65
2003P	225,000,000	1.00	5.00	—
2003D	232,400,000	1.00	5.00	—
2003S	3,408,516	—	—	3.50

KM# 344a • 6.2500 g., 0.9000 **Silver,** 0.1808 oz. ASW

Date	Mintage	MS-63	MS-65	Prf-65
2003S	1,257,555	—	—	5.25

Ohio

KM# 332 • 5.6700 g., **Copper-Nickel Clad Copper**

Date	Mintage	MS-63	MS-65	Prf-65
2002P	217,200,000	1.00	5.50	—
2002D	414,832,000	1.00	5.50	—
2002S	3,084,245	—	—	4.00

KM# 332a • 6.2500 g., 0.9000 **Silver,** 0.1808 oz. ASW

Date	Mintage	MS-63	MS-65	Prf-65
2002S	892,229	—	—	9.00

Arkansas

KM# 347 • 5.6700 g., **Copper-Nickel Clad Copper**

Date	Mintage	MS-63	MS-65	Prf-65
2003P	228,000,000	1.00	5.00	—
2003D	229,800,000	1.00	5.00	—
2003S	3,408,516	—	—	3.50

KM# 347a • 6.2500 g., 0.9000 **Silver,** 0.1808 oz. ASW

Date	Mintage	MS-63	MS-65	Prf-65
2003S	1,257,555	—	—	5.25

QUARTER

Illinois

KM# 343 • 5.6700 g., **Copper-Nickel Clad Copper**

Date	Mintage	MS-63	MS-65	Prf-65
2003P	225,800,000	1.10	5.00	—
2003D	237,400,000	1.10	5.00	—
2003S	3,408,516	—	—	3.50

KM# 343a • 6.2500 g., 0.9000 **Silver**, 0.1808 oz. ASW

Date	Mintage	MS-63	MS-65	Prf-65
2003S	1,257,555	—	—	5.25

Maine

KM# 345 • 5.6700 g., **Copper-Nickel Clad Copper**

Date	Mintage	MS-63	MS-65	Prf-65
2003P	217,400,000	1.00	5.00	—
2003D	213,400,000	1.00	5.00	—
2003S	3,408,516	—	—	3.50

KM# 345a • 6.2500 g., 0.9000 **Silver**, 0.1808 oz. ASW

Date	Mintage	MS-63	MS-65	Prf-65
2003S	1,257,555	—	—	5.25

Missouri

KM# 346 • **Copper-Nickel Clad Copper**

Date	Mintage	MS-63	MS-65	Prf-65
2003P	225,000,000	1.00	5.00	—
2003D	228,200,000	1.00	5.00	—
2003S	3,408,516	—	—	3.50

KM# 346a • 6.2500 g., 0.9000 **Silver**, 0.1808 oz. ASW

Date	Mintage	MS-63	MS-65	Prf-65
2003S	1,257,555	—	—	5.25

Florida

KM# 356 • 5.6700 g., **Copper-Nickel Clad Copper**

Date	Mintage	MS-63	MS-65	Prf-65
2004P	240,200,000	.75	5.00	—
2004D	241,600,000	.75	5.00	—
2004S	2,740,684	—	—	5.00

KM# 356a • 6.2500 g., 0.9000 **Silver**, 0.1808 oz. ASW

Date	Mintage	MS-63	MS-65	Prf-65
2004S	1,775,370	—	—	6.00

Iowa

KM# 358 • 5.6700 g., **Copper-Nickel Clad Copper**

Date	Mintage	MS-63	MS-65	Prf-65
2004P	213,800,000	.75	5.00	—
2004D	251,800,000	.75	5.00	—
2004S	2,740,684	—	—	5.00

KM# 358a • 6.2500 g., 0.9000 **Silver**, 0.1808 oz. ASW

Date	Mintage	MS-63	MS-65	Prf-65
2004S	—	—	—	6.00

Michigan

KM# 355 • 5.6700 g., **Copper-Nickel Clad Copper**

Date	Mintage	MS-63	MS-65	Prf-65
2004P	233,800,000	.75	5.00	—
2004D	225,800,000	.75	5.00	—
2004S	2,740,684	—	—	5.00

KM# 355a • 6.2500 g., 0.9000 **Silver**, 0.1808 oz. ASW

Date	Mintage	MS-63	MS-65	Prf-65
2004S	1,775,370	—	—	6.00

QUARTER

Texas

KM# 357 • 5.6700 g., Copper-Nickel Clad Copper

Date	Mintage	MS-63	MS-65	Prf-65
2004P	278,800,000	.75	5.00	—
2004D	263,000,000	.75	5.00	—
2004S	2,740,684	—	—	5.00

KM# 357a • 6.2500 g., 0.9000 Silver, 0.1808 oz. ASW

Date	Mintage	MS-63	MS-65	Prf-65
2004S	1,775,370	—	—	6.00

Wisconsin

KM# 359 • 5.6700 g., Copper-Nickel Clad Copper

Date	Mintage	MS-63	MS-65	Prf-65
2004P	226,400,000	1.00	5.00	—
2004D	226,800,000	1.00	5.00	—
2004D Extra Leaf Low	Est. 9,000	300	600	—
2004D Extra Leaf High	Est. 3,000	400	900	—
2004S	—	—	—	5.00

KM# 359a • 6.2500 g., 0.9000 Silver, 0.1808 oz. ASW

Date	Mintage	MS-63	MS-65	Prf-65
2004S	1,775,370	—	—	6.00

California

KM# 370 • 5.6700 g., Copper-Nickel Clad Copper

Date	Mintage	MS-63	MS-65	Prf-65
2005P	257,200,000	.75	5.00	—
2005P Satin Finish	Inc. above	3.50	4.50	—
2005D	263,200,000	.75	5.00	—
2005D Satin Finish	Inc. above	3.50	4.50	—
2005S	3,262,960	—	—	3.00

KM# 370a • 6.2500 g., 0.9000 Silver, 0.1808 oz. ASW

Date	Mintage	MS-63	MS-65	Prf-65
2005S	1,679,600	—	—	5.50

Kansas

KM# 373 • 5.6700 g , Copper-Nickel Clad Copper

Date	Mintage	MS-63	MS-65	Prf-65
2005P	263,400,000	.75	5.00	—
2005P Satin Finish	Inc. above	3.50	4.50	—
2005D	300,000,000	.75	5.00	—
2005D Satin Finish	Inc. above	3.50	4.50	—
2005S	3,262,960	—	—	3.00

KM# 373a • 6.2500 g., 0.9000 Silver, 0.1808 oz. ASW

Date	Mintage	MS-63	MS-65	Prf-65
2005S	1,679,600	—	—	5.50

Minnesota

KM# 371 • 5.6700 g., Copper-Nickel Clad Copper

Date	Mintage	MS-63	MS-65	Prf-65
2005P	226,400,000	.75	5.00	—
2005P Satin Finish	Inc. above	3.50	4.50	—
2005D	226,800,000	.75	5.00	—
2005D Satin Finish	Inc. above	3.50	4.50	—
2005S	3,262,960	—	—	3.00

KM# 371a • 6.2500 g., 0.9000 Silver, 0.1808 oz. ASW

Date	Mintage	MS-63	MS-65	Prf-65
2005S	1,679,600	—	—	5.50

Oregon

KM# 372 • 5.6700 g., Copper-Nickel Clad Copper

Date	Mintage	MS-63	MS-65	Prf-65
2005P	316,200,000	.75	5.00	—
2005P Satin Finish	Inc. above	3.50	4.50	—
2005D	404,000,000	.75	5.00	—
2005D Satin Finish	Inc. above	3.50	4.50	—
2005S	3,262,960	—	—	3.00

KM# 372a • 6.2500 g., 0.9000 Silver, 0.1808 oz. ASW

Date	Mintage	MS-63	MS-65	Prf-65
2005S	1,679,600	—	—	5.50

West Virginia

KM# 374 • 5.6700 g., **Copper-Nickel Clad Copper**

Date	Mintage	MS-63	MS-65	Prf-65
2005P	365,400,000	.75	5.00	—
2005P Satin Finish	Inc. above	3.50	4.50	—
2005D	356,200,000	.75	5.00	—
2005D Satin Finish	Inc. above	3.50	4.50	—
2005S	3,262,960	—	—	3.00

KM# 374a • 6.2500 g., 0.9000 **Silver**, 0.1808 oz. ASW

Date	Mintage	MS-63	MS-65	Prf-65
2005S	1,679,600	—	—	5.50

Colorado

KM# 384 • 5.7100 g., **Copper-Nickel Clad Copper**, 24.2 mm.

Date	Mintage	MS-63	MS-65	Prf-65
2006P	274,800,000	.75	5.00	—
2006P Satin Finish	Inc. above	3.00	4.50	—
2006D	294,200,000	.75	5.00	—
2006D Satin Finish	Inc. above	3.00	4.50	—
2006S	2,862,078	—	—	5.00

KM# 384a • 6.2500 g., 0.9000 **Silver**, 0.1808 oz. ASW

Date	Mintage	MS-63	MS-65	Prf-65
2006S	1,571,839	—	—	5.75

Nebraska

KM# 383 • 5.6700 g., **Copper-Nickel Clad Copper**

Date	Mintage	MS-63	MS-65	Prf-65
2006P	318,000,000	.75	5.00	—
2006P Satin Finish	Inc. above	3.00	4.50	—
2006D	273,000,000	.75	5.00	—
2006D Satin Finish	Inc. above	3.00	4.50	—
2006S	2,862,078	—	—	5.00

KM# 383a • 6.2500 g., 0.9000 **Silver**, 0.1808 oz. ASW

Date	Mintage	MS-63	MS-65	Prf-65
2006S	1,571,839	—	—	5.75

Nevada

KM# 382 • 5.6700 g., **Copper-Nickel Clad Copper**

Date	Mintage	MS-63	MS-65	Prf-65
2006P	277,000,000	.75	5.00	—
2006P Satin Finish	Inc. above	3.00	4.50	—
2006D	312,800,000	.75	5.00	—
2006D Satin Finish	Inc. above	3.00	4.50	—
2006S	2,862,078	—	—	5.00

KM# 382a • 6.2500 g., 0.9000 **Silver**, 0.1808 oz. ASW

Date	Mintage	MS-63	MS-65	Prf-65
2006S	1,571,839	—	—	5.75

North Dakota

KM# 385 • 5.7200 g., **Copper-Nickel Clad Copper**, 24.2 mm.

Date	Mintage	MS-63	MS-65	Prf-65
2006P	305,800,000	.75	5.00	—
2006P Satin Finish	Inc. above	3.00	4.50	—
2006D	359,000,000	.75	5.00	—
2006D Satin Finish	Inc. above	3.00	4.50	—
2006S	2,862,078	—	—	5.00

KM# 385a • 6.2500 g., 0.9000 **Silver**, 0.1808 oz. ASW

Date	Mintage	MS-63	MS-65	Prf-65
2006S	1,571,839	—	—	5.75

South Dakota

KM# 386 • 5.6500 g., **Copper-Nickel Clad Copper**, 24.3 mm.

Date	Mintage	MS-63	MS-65	Prf-65
2006P	245,000,000	.75	5.00	—
2006P Satin Finish	Inc. above	3.00	4.50	—
2006D	265,800,000	.75	5.00	—
2006D Satin Finish	Inc. above	3.00	4.50	—
2006S	2,862,078	—	—	5.00

KM# 386a • 6.2500 g., 0.9000 **Silver**, 0.1808 oz. ASW

Date	Mintage	MS-63	MS-65	Prf-65
2006S	1,571,839	—	—	5.75

QUARTER

Idaho

KM# 398 • 5.6700 g., Copper-Nickel Clad Copper

Date	Mintage	MS-63	MS-65	Prf-65
2007P	294,600,000	.75	8.00	—
2007P Satin finish	—	3.00	4.50	—
2007D	286,800,000	.75	8.00	—
2007D Satin finish	—	3.00	4.50	—
2007S	2,374,778	—	—	4.00

KM# 398a • 6.2500 g., 0.9000 Silver, 0.1808 oz. ASW

Date	Mintage	MS-63	MS-65	Prf-65
2007S	1,299,878	—	—	6.50

Washington

KM# 397 • 5.6700 g., Copper-Nickel Clad Copper

Date	Mintage	MS-63	MS-65	Prf-65
2007P	265,200,000	.75	8.00	—
2007P Satin Finish	—	3.00	4.50	—
2007D	280,000,000	.75	8.00	—
2007D Satin Finish	—	3.00	4.50	—
2007S	2,374,778	—	—	4.00

KM# 397a • 6.2500 g., 0.9000 Silver, 0.1808 oz. ASW

Date	Mintage	MS-63	MS-65	Prf-65
2007S	1,299,878	—	—	6.50

Montana

KM# 396 • 5.6700 g., Copper-Nickel Clad Copper

Date	Mintage	MS-63	MS-65	Prf-65
2007P	257,000,000	.75	8.00	—
2007D	256,240,000	.75	5.00	—
2007S	2,374,778	—	—	4.00

KM# 396a • 6.2500 g., 0.9000 Silver, 0.1808 oz. ASW

Date	Mintage	MS-63	MS-65	Prf-65
2007S	1,299,878	—	—	6.50

Wyoming

KM# 399 • 5.6700 g., Copper-Nickel Clad Copper

Date	Mintage	MS-63	MS-65	Prf-65
2007P	243,600,000	.75	5.00	—
2007P Satin finish	—	3.00	4.50	—
2007D	320,800,000	.75	5.00	—
2007 Satin finish	—	3.00	4.50	—
2007S	2,374,778	—	—	4.00

KM# 399a • 6.2500 g., 0.9000 Silver, 0.1808 oz. ASW

Date	Mintage	MS-63	MS-65	Prf-65
2007S	1,299,878	—	—	6.50

Utah

KM# 400 • Copper-Nickel Clad Copper

Date	Mintage	MS-63	MS-65	Prf-65
2007P	255,000,000	.75	5.00	—
2007P Satin finish	—	3.00	4.50	—
2007D	253,200,000	.75	5.00	—
2007CC Satin finish	—	3.00	4.50	—
2007S	2,374,778	—	—	4.00

KM# 400a • 6.2500 g., 0.9000 Silver, 0.1808 oz. ASW

Date	Mintage	MS-63	MS-65	Prf-65
2007S	1,299,878	—	—	6.50

Alaska

KM# 424 • 5.6700 g., Copper-Nickel Clad Copper

Date	Mintage	MS-63	MS-65	Prf-65
2008P	251,800,000	.75	5.00	—
2008P Satin finish	—	3.00	4.50	—
2008D	254,000,000	.75	5.00	—
2008D Satin finish	—	3.00	4.50	—
2008S	2,100,000	—	—	4.00

KM# 424a • 6.2500 g., 0.9000 Silver, 0.1808 oz. ASW

Date	Mintage	MS-63	MS-65	Prf-65
2008S	1,200,000	—	—	6.50

Arizona

KM# 423 • 5.6700 g., **Copper-Nickel Clad Copper**

Date	Mintage	MS-63	MS-65	Prf-65
2008D Satin finish	—	3.00	4.50	—
2008P Satin finish	—	3.00	4.50	—
2008P	244,600,000	.75	5.00	—
2008D	265,000,000	.75	5.00	—
2008S	2,100,000	—	—	4.00

KM# 423a • 6.2500 g., 0.9000 **Silver,**
0.1808 oz. ASW

Date	Mintage	MS-63	MS-65	Prf-65
2008S	1,200,000	—	—	6.50

Hawaii

KM# 425 • 5.6700 g., **Copper-Nickel Clad Copper**

Date	Mintage	MS-63	MS-65	Prf-65
2008P	254,000,000	.75	5.00	—
2008P Satin finish	—	3.00	4.50	—
2008D	263,600,000	.75	5.00	—
2008D Satin finish	—	3.00	4.50	—
2008S	2,100,000	—	—	4.00

KM# 425a • 6.2500 g., 0.9000 **Silver,**
0.1808 oz. ASW

Date	Mintage	MS-63	MS-65	Prf-65
2008S	1,200,000	—	—	6.50

New Mexico

KM# 422 • 5.6700 g., **Copper-Nickel Clad Copper**

Date	Mintage	MS-63	MS-65	Prf-65
2008P	244,200,000	.75	5.00	—
2008P Satin finish	—	3.00	4.50	—
2008D	244,400,000	.75	5.00	—
2008D Satin finish	—	3.00	4.50	—
2008S	2,100,000	—	—	4.00

KM# 422a • 6.2500 g., 0.9000 **Silver,**
0.1808 oz. ASW

Date	Mintage	MS-63	MS-65	Prf-65
2008S	1,200,000	—	—	6.50

Oklahoma

KM# 421 • 5.6700 g., **Copper-Nickel Clad Copper**

Date	Mintage	MS-63	MS-65	Prf-65
2008P	222,000,000	.75	5.00	—
2008P Satin finish	—	3.00	4.50	—
2008D	194,600,000	.75	5.00	—
2008D Satin finish	—	3.00	4.50	—
2008S	2,100,000	—	—	4.00

KM# 421a • 6.2500 g., 0.9000 **Silver,**
0.1808 oz. ASW

Date	Mintage	MS-63	MS-65	Prf-65
2008S	1,200,000	—	—	6.50

DC and Territories

American Samoa

KM# 448 • 5.6700 g., **Copper-Nickel Clad Copper,**
24 mm. • **Rev. Designer:** Charles Vickers

Date	Mintage	MS-63	MS-65	Prf-65
2009P	42,600,000	.75	8.00	—
2009D	39,600,000	.75	8.00	—
2009S	—	—	—	4.00

KM# 448a • 6.2500 g., 0.9000 **Silver,**
0.1808 oz. ASW, 24 mm.

Date	Mintage	MS-63	MS-65	Prf-65
2009S	—	—	—	6.50

District of Columbia

KM# 445 • 5.6700 g., **Copper-Nickel Clad Copper,**
24 mm. • **Rev. Designer:** Don Everhart

Date	Mintage	MS-63	MS-65	Prf-65
2009P	83,600,000	.75	8.00	—
2009D	88,800,000	.75	8.00	—
2009S	—	—	—	4.00

KM# 445a • 6.2500 g., 0.9000 **Silver,**
0.1808 oz. ASW, 24 mm.

Date	Mintage	MS-63	MS-65	Prf-65
2009S	—	—	—	6.50

QUARTER

Guam

KM# 447 • 5.6700 g., **Copper-Nickel Clad Copper,** 24 mm. • **Rev. Designer:** James Licaretz

Date	Mintage	MS-63	MS-65	Prf-65
2009P	45,000,000	.75	8.00	—
2009D	42,600,000	.75	8.00	—
2009S	—	—	—	4.00

KM# 447a • 6.2500 g., 0.9000 **Silver,** 0.1808 oz. ASW, 24 mm.

Date	Mintage	MS-63	MS-65	Prf-65
2009S	—	—	—	6.50

Puerto Rico

KM# 446 • 5.6700 g., **Copper-Nickel Clad Copper,** 24 mm. • **Rev. Designer:** Joseph Menna

Date	Mintage	MS-63	MS-65	Prf-65
2009P	53,200,000	.75	8.00	—
2009D	86,000,000	.75	8.00	—
2009S	—	—	—	4.00

KM# 446a • 6.2500 g., 0.9000 **Silver,** 0.1808 oz. ASW, 24 mm.

Date	Mintage	MS-63	MS-65	Prf-65
2009S	—	—	—	6.50

Northern Mariana Islands

KM# 466 • 5.6700 g., **Copper-Nickel Clad Copper** • **Rev. Designer:** Pheve Hemphill

Date	Mintage	MS-63	MS-65	Prf-65
2009P	35,200,000	.75	8.00	—
2009D	37,600,000	.75	8.00	—
2009S	—	—	—	4.00

KM# 466a • 6.2500 g., 0.9000 **Silver,** 0.1808 oz. ASW

Date	Mintage	MS-63	MS-65	Prf-65
2009S	—	—	—	6.50

US Virgin Islands

KM# 449 • 5.6700 g., **Copper-Nickel Clad Copper,** 24 mm. • **Rev. Designer:** Joseph Menna

Date	Mintage	MS-63	MS-65	Prf-65
2009P	41,000,000	.75	8.00	—
2009D	41,000,000	.75	8.00	—
2009S	—	—	—	4.00

KM# 449a • 6.2500 g., 0.9000 **Silver,** 0.1808 oz. ASW, 24 mm.

Date	Mintage	MS-63	MS-65	Prf-65
2009S	—	—	—	6.50

America the Beautiful

Grand Canyon National Park

KM# 472 • 5.6700 g., **Copper-Nickel Clad Copper,** 24.3 mm.

Date	Mintage	MS-63	MS-65	Prf-65
2010P	—	.75	8.00	—
2010D	—	.75	8.00	—
2010S	—	—	—	4.00

KM# 472a • 6.2500 g., 0.9000 **Silver,** 0.1808 oz. ASW

Date	Mintage	MS-63	MS-65	Prf-65
2010	—	—	—	6.50

Hot Springs, Ark.

KM# 469 • 5.6700 g., **Copper-Nickel Clad Copper,** 24.3 mm.

Date	Mintage	MS-63	MS-65	Prf-65
2010P	—	.75	8.00	—
2010D	—	.75	8.00	—
2010S	—	—	—	4.00

KM# 469a • 6.2500 g., 0.9000 **Silver,** 0.1808 oz. ASW

Date	Mintage	MS-63	MS-65	Prf-65
2010S	—	—	—	6.50

Mount Hood National Park

KM# 473 • 5.6700 g., **Copper-Nickel Clad Copper**

Date	Mintage	MS-63	MS-65	Prf-65
2010P	—	.75	8.00	—
2010D	—	.75	8.00	—
2010S	—	—	—	4.00

KM# 473a • 6.2500 g., 0.9000 **Silver**, 0.1808 oz. ASW

Date	Mintage	MS-63	MS-65	Prf-65
2010	—	—	—	6.50

Yellowstone National Park

KM# 470 • 5.6700 g., **Copper-Nickel Clad Copper**
• **Edge Desc:** 24.3

Date	Mintage	MS-63	MS-65	Prf-65
2010P	—	.75	8.00	—
2010D	—	.75	8.00	—
2010S	—	—	—	4.00

KM# 470a • 6.2500 g., 0.9000 **Silver**, 0.1808 oz. ASW

Date	Mintage	MS-63	MS-65	Prf-65
2010	—	—	—	6.50

Yosemite National Park

KM# 471 • 5.6700 g., **Copper-Nickel Clad Copper**, 24.3 mm.

Date	Mintage	MS-63	MS-65	Prf-65
2010P	—	.75	8.00	—
2010D	—	.75	8.00	—
2010S	—	—	—	4.00

KM# 471a • 6.2500 g., 0.9000 **Silver**, 0.1808 oz. ASW

Date	Mintage	MS-63	MS-65	Prf-65
2010	—	—	—	6.50

Chickasaw National Recreation Area

KM# 498a • 6.2500 g., 0.9000 **Silver**, 0.1808 oz. ASW

Date	Mintage	MS-63	MS-65	Prf-65
2011S	—	—	—	6.50

KM# 498 • 5.6700 g., **Copper-Nickel Clad Copper**, 24 mm.

Date	Mintage	MS-63	MS-65	Prf-65
2011P	—	.75	8.00	—
2011D	—	.75	8.00	—
2011S	—	—	—	4.00

Gettysburg National Military Park

KM# 494a • 6.2500 g., 0.9000 **Silver**, 0.1808 oz. ASW

Date	Mintage	MS-63	MS-65	Prf-65
2011S	—	—	—	6.50

KM# 494 • 5.6700 g., **Copper-Nickel Clad Copper**, 24 mm.

Date	Mintage	MS-63	MS-65	Prf-65
2011P	—	.75	8.00	—
2011D	—	.75	8.00	—
2011S	—	—	—	4.00

Glacier National Park

KM# 495a • 6.2500 g., 0.9000 **Silver**, 0.1808 oz. ASW

Date	Mintage	MS-63	MS-65	Prf-65
2011S	—	—	—	6.50

KM# 495 • 5.6700 g., **Copper-Nickel Clad Copper**, 24 mm.

Date	Mintage	MS-63	MS-65	Prf-65
2011P	—	.75	8.00	—
2011D	—	.75	8.00	—
2011S	—	—	—	4.00

QUARTER

Olympic National Park

KM# 496a • 6.2500 g., 0.9000 Silver, 0.1808 oz. ASW

Date	Mintage	MS-63	MS-65	Prf-65
2011S	—	—	—	6.50

KM# 496 • 5.6700 g., Copper-Nickel Clad Copper, 24 mm.

Date	Mintage	MS-63	MS-65	Prf-65
2011P	—	.75	8.00	—
2011D	—	.75	8.00	—
2011S	—	—	—	4.00

Vicksburg National Military Park

KM# 497a • 6.2500 g., 0.9000 Silver, 0.1808 oz. ASW

Date	Mintage	MS-63	MS-65	Prf-65
2011S	—	—	—	6.50

KM# 497 • 5.6700 g., Copper-Nickel Clad Copper, 24 mm.

Date	Mintage	MS-63	MS-65	Prf-65
2011P	—	.75	8.00	—
2011D	—	.75	8.00	—
2011S	—	—	—	4.00

HALF DOLLAR

Flowing Hair Half Dollar

KM# 16 • 13.4800 g., 0.8920 Silver, 0.3866 oz. ASW, 32.5 mm. • Designer: Robert Scot Notes: The 1795 "recut date" variety had the date cut into the dies twice, so both sets of numbers are visible on the coin. The 1795 "3 leaves" variety has three leaves under each of the eagle's wings on the reverse.

Date	Mintage	G-4	VG-8	F-12	VF-20	XF-40	MS-60
1794	23,464	2,850	5,750	8,850	19,500	37,500	225,000
1795	299,680	1,025	1,450	2,850	4,850	13,850	46,500
1795 recut date	Inc. above	1,040	1,470	2,895	5,200	14,250	46,500
1795 3 leaves	Inc. above	2,600	3,150	5,350	8,350	17,500	59,500

Draped Bust Half Dollar
Draped bust right   Small eagle reverse

KM# 26 • 13.4800 g., 0.8920 Silver, 0.3866 oz. ASW, 32.5 mm. • Designer: Robert Scot

Date	Mintage	G-4	VG-8	F-12	VF-20	XF-40	MS-60
1796 15 obverse stars	3,918	36,500	46,000	62,000	73,500	118,000	300,000
1796 16 obverse stars	Inc. above	39,500	50,000	67,000	79,500	128,000	320,000
1797	Inc. above	36,700	46,300	62,500	74,300	121,000	310,000

QUARTER

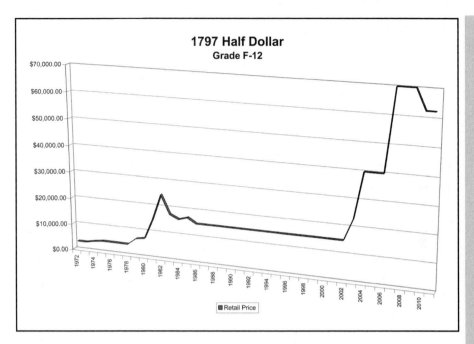

1797 Half Dollar
Grade F-12

Retail Price

Draped Bust Half Dollar
Draped bust right, flanked by stars, date at angle below obverse
Heraldic eagle reverse

KM# 35 • 13.4800 g., 0.8920 **Silver**, 0.3866 oz. ASW, 32.5 mm. • **Obv. Legend** LIBERTY **Rev. Legend:** UNITED STATES OF AMERICA **Designer:** Robert Scot **Notes:** The two varieties of the 1803 strikes are distinguished by the size of the 3 in the date. The several varieties of the 1806 strikes are distinguished by the style of 6 in the date, size of the stars on the obverse, and whether the stem of the olive branch held by the reverse eagle extends through the claw.

Date	Mintage	G-4	VG-8	F-12	VF-20	XF-40	MS-60
1801	30,289	850	1,250	2,550	4,250	10,500	50,000
1802	29,890	900	1,350	2,750	4,500	11,000	52,000
1803 small 3	188,234	255	325	425	825	2,325	17,250
1803 large 3	Inc. above	195	235	295	715	1,925	14,750
1805	211,722	195	235	295	685	1,865	10,750
1805/4	Inc. above	270	385	570	1,515	3,325	30,000
1806 knobbed 6, large stars	839,576	195	235	295	665	1,825	—
1806 knobbed 6, small stars	Inc. above	195	235	295	680	2,025	13,500
1806 knobbed 6, stem not through claw	Inc. above	20,000	35,000	42,000	57,500	95,000	—
1806 pointed-top 6, stem not through claw	Inc. above	195	235	295	665	1,825	15,250
1806 pointed-top 6, stem through claw	Inc. above	195	235	295	665	1,825	9,750
1806/5	Inc. above	215	270	355	775	2,050	10,075
1806 /inverted 6	Inc. above	255	355	845	1,615	4,375	28,500
1807	301,076	195	235	295	665	1,825	9,750

HALF DOLLAR

Capped Bust
Draped bust left, flanked by stars, date at angle below
"50 C." below eagle reverse

KM# 37 • 13.4800 g., 0.8920 **Silver**, 0.3866 oz. ASW, 32.5 mm. • **Rev. Legend:** UNITED STATES OF
AMERICA **Designer:** John Reich **Notes:** There are three varieties of the 1807 strikes. Two are distinguished
by the size of the stars on the obverse. The third was struck from a reverse die that had a 5 cut over a 2 in the
"50C" denomination. Two varieties of the 1811 are distinguished by the size of the 8 in the date. A third has a
period between the 8 and second 1 in the date. One variety of the 1817 has a period between the 1 and 7 in
the date. Two varieties of the 1820 are distinguished by the size of the date. On the 1823 varieties, the
"broken 3" appears to be almost separated in the middle of the 3 in the date; the "patched 3" has the error
repaired; the "ugly 3" has portions of its detail missing. The 1827 "curled-2" and "square-2" varieties are
distinguished by the numeral's base -- either curled or square. Among the 1828 varieties, "knobbed 2" and "no
knob" refers to whether the upper left serif of the digit is rounded. The 1830 varieties are distinguished by the
size of the 0 in the date. The four 1834 varieties are distinguished by the sizes of the stars, date and letters in
the inscriptions. The 1836 "50/00" variety was struck from a reverse die that has "50" recut over "00" in the
denomination.

Date	Mintage	G-4	VG-8	F-12	VF-20	XF-40	AU-50	MS-60	MS-65
1807 small stars	750,500	125	175	350	750	1,900	6,500	9,850	54,000
1807 large stars	Inc. above	115	165	300	660	1,750	5,650	8,900	—
1807 50/20 C.	Inc. above	85.00	125	195	450	1,500	3,150	6,500	30,000
1807 bearded goddess	—	450	775	1,500	3,350	6,850	22,500	—	—
1808	1,368,600	67.00	84.00	93.00	145	350	550	1,800	20,000
1808/7	Inc. above	90.00	110	135	240	440	1,850	5,400	32,500
1809 XXXX edge	Inc. above	80.00	105	135	185	550	950	4,450	—
1809 IIIIIII edge	Inc. above	85.00	110	140	210	450	850	4,000	—
1809 Normal edge	1,405,810	65.00	82.00	90.00	140	375	750	1,500	14,000
1810	1,276,276	64.00	81.00	87.00	135	265	650	1,950	19,500
1811 small 8	1,203,644	70.00	80.00	84.00	125	350	800	2,350	28,500
1811 large 8	Inc. above	80.00	107	115	175	425	1,000	2,400	28,500
1811 dated 18.11	Inc. above	78.00	100.00	110	165	650	1,250	3,500	28,500
1812	1,628,059	64.00	81.00	84.00	110	254	405	1,350	14,800
1812/1 small 8	Inc. above	80.00	97.00	115	200	500	1,350	2,500	—
1812/1 large 8	Inc. above	1,650	2,450	4,500	6,750	12,000	21,000	—	—
1812 Single leaf below wing	Inc. above	750	950	1,250	2,400	4,000	6,800	12,500	—
1813	1,241,903	64.00	81.00	84.00	110	184	445	1,400	14,000
1813 50/UNI reverse	1,241,903	74.00	101	120	175	650	1,350	3,650	27,500
1814	1,039,075	64.00	81.00	84.00	120	285	650	1,650	12,800
1814/3	Inc. above	100.00	165	245	300	850	1,650	3,250	—
1814 E/A in States	Inc. above	85.00	110	150	225	385	950	3,950	—
1814 Single leaf below wing	Inc. above	75.00	97.00	120	190	575	1,350	2,250	—
1815/2	47,150	1,100	1,550	2,250	3,650	5,500	7,950	14,500	85,000
1817	1,215,567	67.00	84.00	87.00	115	195	415	1,300	13,000
1817/3	Inc. above	115	175	280	525	1,150	2,350	4,850	—
1817/4	—	60,000	80,000	150,000	200,000	240,000	—	—	—
1817 dated 181.7	Inc. above	100.00	87.00	90.00	100.00	575	1,350	3,950	27,500
1817 Single leaf below wing	Inc. above	75.00	98.00	120	205	550	2,100	2,750	—
1818	1,960,322	64.00	81.00	84.00	115	225	405	1,350	12,600
1818/7 Large 8	Inc. above	100.00	115	145	190	325	950	1,850	17,500
1818/7 Small 8	Inc. above	98.00	110	130	150	250	850	1,650	16,500
1819	2,208,000	64.00	81.00	84.00	115	175	395	1,350	15,000
1819/8 small 9	Inc. above	75.00	92.00	105	180	290	650	1,900	13,000
1819/8 large 9	Inc. above	85.00	105	150	275	385	850	2,000	27,000
1820 Curl Base 2, small date	751,122	70.00	85.00	92.00	120	285	950	2,250	13,000
1820 Square Base 2 with knob, large date	Inc. above	72.00	90.00	100.00	135	400	800	2,400	14,500
1820 Square Base 2 without know, large date	Inc. above	72.00	90.00	100.00	150	475	1,100	2,500	26,500
1820 E's without Serifs	Inc. above	260	450	900	2,150	3,500	5,500	—	—
1820/19 Square Base 2	Inc. above	110	130	165	240	775	1,650	3,250	25,000
1820/19 Curled Base 2	Inc. above	95.00	115	140	200	650	1,450	2,900	24,500
1821	1,305,797	58.00	76.00	85.00	97.00	185	575	1,350	12,600
1822	1,559,573	58.00	76.00	85.00	97.00	180	450	1,250	12,300
1822/1	Inc. above	83.00	100.00	125	275	385	800	1,900	—

Date	Mintage	G-4	VG-8	F-12	VF-20	XF-40	AU-50	MS-60	MS-65
1823	1,694,200	58.00	76.00	85.00	97.00	175	425	1,150	12,500
1823 broken 3	Inc. above	68.00	88.00	100.00	135	500	1,500	3,200	—
1823 patched 3	Inc. above	73.00	94.00	115	155	550	950	2,000	16,500
1823 ugly 3	Inc. above	78.00	99.00	125	180	750	1,750	4,200	—
1824	3,504,954	58.00	76.00	85.00	97.00	175	360	1,075	11,500
1824/21	Inc. above	63.00	82.00	95.00	122	275	650	2,000	17,000
1824/4	Inc. above	61.00	80.00	87.00	110	225	500	1,350	—
1824 1824/various dates	Inc. above	60.00	79.00	87.00	100.00	300	875	2,000	16,500
1825	2,943,166	58.00	76.00	85.00	97.00	175	350	1,050	11,500
1826	4,004,180	58.00	76.00	85.00	97.00	175	350	1,050	11,500
1827 curled 2	5,493,400	61.00	81.00	95.00	130	185	450	1,400	14,000
1827 square 2	Inc. above	58.00	76.00	85.00	97.00	175	350	1,050	11,500
1827/6	Inc. above	85.00	95.00	120	155	265	650	1,450	13,000
1828 curled-base 2, no knob	3,075,200	58.00	76.00	85.00	97.00	175	350	1,150	12,500
1828 curled-base 2, knobbed 2	Inc. above	78.00	99.00	125	180	245	460	1,300	—
1828 small 8s, square-base 2, large letters	Inc. above	60.00	80.00	95.00	120	175	350	1,050	14,000
1828 small 8s, square-base 2, small letters	Inc. above	58.00	76.00	85.00	102	250	750	1,900	
1828 large 8s, square-base 2	Inc. above	58.00	76.00	85.00	97.00	175	350	1,050	12,500
1829	3,712,156	55.00	72.00	75.00	85.00	159	315	1,000	11,500
1829 Large letters	Inc. above	59.00	79.00	85.00	100.00	180	420	1,250	14,000
1829/7	Inc. above	78.00	99.00	125	170	200	475	1,250	14,000
1830 Small O rev	4,764,800	55.00	72.00	75.00	85.00	159	315	1,000	11,500
1830 Large O	Inc. above	60.00	78.00	84.00	105	189	550	2,000	14,500
1830 Large letter rev	Inc. above	1,500	2,250	3,000	3,750	4,800	9,800	—	—
1831	5,873,660	55.00	72.00	75.00	85.00	159	315	1,000	11,500
1832 small letters	4,797,000	55.00	72.00	75.00	85.00	159	315	1,000	11,500
1832 large letters	Inc. above	58.00	75.00	81.00	95.00	175	375	1,350	14,000
1833	5,206,000	55.00	72.00	75.00	85.00	159	325	1,000	11,750
1834 small date, large stars, small letters	6,412,004	55.00	74.00	77.00	87.00	163	325	1,025	11,750
1834 small date, small stars, small letters	Inc. above	55.00	74.00	77.00	87.00	163	325	1,025	11,750
1834 large date, small letters	Inc. above	55.00	74.00	77.00	87.00	163	325	1,025	11,750
1834 large date, large letters	Inc. above	55.00	72.00	75.00	85.00	159	315	1,000	11,500
1835	5,352,006	55.00	72.00	75.00	85.00	159	315	1,000	11,500
1836	6,545,000	55.00	72.00	75.00	85.00	159	315	1,000	11,500
1836	Inc. above	80.00	95.00	120	265	450	1,000	2,500	—
1836 50/00	Inc. above	93.00	112	125	165	300	800	1,750	19,500

Bust Half Dollar

Draped bust left, flanked by stars, date at angle below
"50 Cents" below eagle reverse

KM# 58 • 13.3600 g., 0.9000 **Silver**, 0.3866 oz. ASW, 30 mm. • **Rev. Legend:** UNITED STATES OF AMERICA **Designer:** Christian Gobrecht **Edge Desc:** Reeded.

Date	Mintage	G-4	VG-8	F-12	VF-20	XF-40	AU-50	MS-60	MS-65
1836	1,200	850	1,075	1,600	2,000	3,350	4,400	8,850	66,500
1837	3,629,820	58.00	73.00	80.00	115	200	345	1,100	24,500

Draped bust left, flanked by stars, date below
HALF DOL. below eagle reverse

KM# 65 • 13.3600 g., 0.9000 **Silver**, 0.3866 oz. ASW, 30 mm. • **Rev. Legend:** UNITED STATES OF AMERICA **Designer:** Christian Gobrecht

Date	Mintage	G-4	VG-8	F-12	VF-20	XF-40	AU-50	MS-60	MS-65
1838	3,546,000	58.00	70.00	82.00	120	205	360	1,125	21,500
1838O proof only	Est. 20	—	—	—	—	250,000	300,000	—	—
1839	1,392,976	60.00	76.00	92.00	130	245	410	1,350	39,500
1839O	178,976	240	325	425	650	1,350	2,350	4,500	46,500

Seated Liberty Half Dollar
Seated Liberty, date below obverse
"Half Dol." below eagle reverse

KM# 68 • 13.3600 g., 0.9000 **Silver**, 0.3866 oz. ASW, 30.6 mm. • **Rev. Legend:** UNITED STATES OF AMERICA **Designer:** Christian Gobrecht

Date	Mintage	G-4	VG-8	F-12	VF-20	XF-40	AU-50	MS-60	MS-65
1839 no drapery from elbow	Inc. above	40.00	80.00	160	335	900	1,850	6,250	200,000
1839 drapery	Inc. above	32.00	41.00	58.00	86.00	165	265	1,000	25,000
1840 small letters	1,435,008	35.00	41.00	59.00	84.00	150	325	600	7,500
1840 reverse 1838	Inc. above	150	200	275	350	650	1,350	3,400	30,000
1840O	855,100	32.00	48.00	58.00	90.00	140	275	450	—
1841	310,000	50.00	65.00	100.00	150	235	325	1,200	6,850
1841O	401,000	32.00	44.00	58.00	82.00	180	230	600	7,000
1842 small date	2,012,764	32.00	55.00	75.00	120	175	325	1,300	13,500
1842 medium date	Inc. above	30.00	41.00	51.00	64.00	115	220	750	8,800
1842O small date	957,000	650	850	1,400	2,450	4,650	7,750	16,500	—
1842O medium date	Inc. above	35.00	42.00	55.00	90.00	185	500	1,250	10,500
1843	3,844,000	30.00	39.00	51.00	65.00	110	225	500	4,500
1843O	2,268,000	30.00	41.00	51.00	65.00	120	240	550	—
1844	1,766,000	30.00	41.00	51.00	65.00	110	210	440	4,500
1844O	2,005,000	30.00	41.00	51.00	70.00	110	225	550	—
1844/1844O	Inc. above	500	775	1,000	1,300	2,500	5,750	10,000	—
1845	589,000	35.00	44.00	65.00	125	210	325	850	12,000
1845O	2,094,000	30.00	41.00	51.00	70.00	135	240	550	9,400
1845O no drapery	Inc. above	35.00	44.00	58.00	115	185	375	750	—
1846 medium date	2,210,000	30.00	41.00	51.00	70.00	110	200	500	9,000
1846 tall date	Inc. above	35.00	47.00	70.00	85.00	145	250	650	12,000
1846 /horizontal 6	Inc. above	175	250	325	450	625	1,000	2,500	—
1846O medium date	2,304,000	35.00	41.00	58.00	65.00	110	225	550	12,000
1846O tall date	Inc. above	165	285	365	620	1,050	2,000	6,650	—
1847/1846	1,156,000	2,000	2,750	3,750	5,250	7,700	12,500	21,000	—
1847	Inc. above	30.00	45.00	54.00	67.00	105	250	480	9,000
1847O	2,584,000	30.00	41.00	51.00	65.00	120	275	640	7,000
1848	580,000	45.00	65.00	95.00	185	265	485	1,000	9,000
1848O	3,180,000	30.00	41.00	51.00	70.00	110	285	750	9,000
1849	1,252,000	35.00	45.00	58.00	67.00	108	365	1,250	15,000
1849O	2,310,000	30.00	41.00	51.00	70.00	110	250	650	9,000
1850	227,000	275	325	400	550	675	1,000	1,500	—

Date	Mintage	G-4	VG-8	F-12	VF-20	XF-40	AU-50	MS-60	MS-65
1850O	2,456,000	32.00	41.00	56.00	80.00	135	275	650	9,000
1851	200,750	335	450	550	850	950	1,200	2,250	—
1851O	402,000	35.00	55.00	59.00	120	185	300	700	9,000
1852	77,130	425	500	700	925	1,100	1,350	1,700	—
1852O	144,000	70.00	125	200	350	600	1,250	3,850	26,000
1853O mintage unrecorded	—	—	250,000	—	—	450,000	—	—	—

Note: 1853O, Eliasberg Sale, 1997, VG-8, $154,000.

Seated Liberty, arrows at date
Rays around eagle reverse

KM# 79 • 12.4400 g., 0.9000 **Silver**, 0.3599 oz. ASW • **Rev. Legend:** UNITED STATES OF AMERICA
Designer: Christian Gobrecht

Date	Mintage	G-4	VG-8	F-12	VF-20	XF-40	AU-50	MS-60	MS-65	Prf-65
1853	3,532,708	31.00	36.50	50.00	88.00	245	575	1,400	24,500	175,000
1853O	1,328,000	36.00	41.50	55.00	115	275	695	2,250	29,500	—

Seated Liberty, arrows at date
HALF DOL. below eagle reverse

KM# 82 • 12.4400 g., 0.9000 **Silver**, 0.3599 oz. ASW • **Rev. Legend:** UNITED STATES OF AMERICA
Designer: Christian Gobrecht

Date	Mintage	G-4	VG-8	F-12	VF-20	XF-40	AU-50	MS-60	MS-65	Prf-65
1854	2,982,000	28.00	38.00	47.00	60.00	100.00	270	675	8,000	37,500
1854O	5,240,000	28.00	38.00	47.00	60.00	100.00	270	600	8,000	—
1855	759,500	30.00	40.00	49.00	63.00	120	325	700	9,000	39,500
1855/4	Inc. above	65.00	84.00	160	250	375	600	2,000	17,500	37,000
1855O	3,688,000	28.00	38.00	47.00	60.00	100.00	270	650	8,000	—
1855S	129,950	350	475	800	1,500	3,150	6,850	19,500	—	—

1855-S Half Dollar
Grade XF-40

Seated Liberty, date below
HALF DOL. below eagle reverse

KM# A68 • 12.4400 g., 0.9000 **Silver**, 0.3599 oz. ASW • **Rev. Legend:** UNITED STATES OF AMERICA
Designer: Christian Gobrecht

Date	Mintage	G-4	VG-8	F-12	VF-20	XF-40	AU-50	MS-60	MS-65	Prf-65
1856O	2,658,000	28.00	38.00	52.00	60.00	100.00	190	385	12,500	—
1856	938,000	30.00	39.00	50.00	72.00	105	215	425	6,500	12,500
1856S	211,000	85.00	120	160	260	500	1,250	3,500	19,000	—
1857	1,988,000	30.00	38.00	50.00	60.00	100.00	190	385	5,150	12,500
1857O	818,000	33.00	40.00	52.00	85.00	135	275	885	12,500	—
1857S	158,000	100.00	120	145	285	575	975	3,500	19,000	—
1858	4,226,000	30.00	39.00	50.00	72.00	105	215	385	6,500	12,500
1858O	7,294,000	30.00	39.00	50.00	72.00	105	215	385	12,500	—
1858S	476,000	38.00	48.00	62.00	110	215	400	950	12,500	—
1859	748,000	30.00	41.00	51.00	70.00	120	200	650	6,600	5,500
1859O	2,834,000	30.00	39.00	50.00	72.00	105	215	450	6,500	—
1859S	566,000	38.00	44.00	59.00	100.00	215	375	750	12,500	—
1860	303,700	38.00	42.00	51.00	100.00	150	350	1,000	6,500	5,500
1860O	1,290,000	30.00	39.00	50.00	72.00	110	230	450	5,150	—
1860S	472,000	35.00	44.00	55.00	80.00	135	245	850	12,500	—
1861	2,888,400	30.00	39.00	50.00	72.00	105	190	440	5,150	5,500
1861O	2,532,633	35.00	44.00	55.00	80.00	125	235	450	5,150	—
1861S	939,500	35.00	44.00	57.00	85.00	150	195	975	9,500	—
1862	253,550	38.00	51.00	57.00	120	200	295	750	5,150	5,500
1862S	1,352,000	30.00	39.00	50.00	72.00	105	195	460	9,000	—
1863	503,660	35.00	48.00	57.00	85.00	135	250	750	5,150	5,500
1863S	916,000	33.00	45.00	52.00	70.00	120	195	460	9,000	—
1864	379,570	30.00	48.00	57.00	120	195	250	750	5,150	5,500
1864S	658,000	33.00	45.00	51.00	70.00	125	215	675	9,000	—

Date	Mintage	G-4	VG-8	F-12	VF-20	XF-40	AU-50	MS-60	MS-65	Prf-65
1865	511,900	28.00	47.00	55.00	90.00	150	275	750	5,150	5,500
1865S	675,000	35.00	45.00	52.00	70.00	150	235	500	9,000	—
1866 proof, unique	—	—	—	—	—	—	—	—	—	—
1866S	60,000	460	575	850	1,250	2,550	3,350	5,400	68,000	—

Seated Liberty, date below
IN GOD WE TRUST above eagle reverse

KM# 99 • 12.4400 g., 0.9000 **Silver**, 0.3599 oz. ASW • **Rev. Legend:** UNITED STATES OF AMERICA
Designer: Christian Gobrecht

Date	Mintage	G-4	VG-8	F-12	VF-20	XF-40	AU-50	MS-60	MS-65	Prf-65
1866	745,625	35.00	45.00	53.00	80.00	120	225	350	4,800	3,750
1866S	994,000	33.00	43.00	51.00	70.00	110	275	650	5,000	—
1867	449,925	38.00	48.00	59.00	110	165	250	350	4,800	3,750
1867S	1,196,000	32.00	42.00	51.00	70.00	110	250	350	7,000	—
1868	418,200	48.00	55.00	95.00	185	225	300	525	7,100	3,750
1868S	1,160,000	32.00	42.00	51.00	70.00	110	250	350	7,000	—
1869	795,900	35.00	45.00	49.00	70.00	110	190	385	4,600	3,750
1869S	656,000	35.00	47.00	51.00	70.00	120	265	600	7,000	—
1870	634,900	35.00	45.00	50.00	80.00	125	250	475	7,000	3,750
1870CC	54,617	900	1,500	1,900	3,900	12,500	30,000	100,000	—	—
1870S	1,004,000	31.00	43.00	53.00	85.00	150	275	575	7,000	—
1871	1,204,560	32.00	42.00	52.00	75.00	120	165	350	7,000	3,750
1871CC	153,950	225	325	600	1,200	1,950	10,000	15,000	—	—
1871S	2,178,000	30.00	41.00	49.00	70.00	110	215	400	7,000	—
1872	881,550	32.00	40.00	49.00	75.00	120	195	430	2,850	3,750
1872CC	272,000	85.00	125	275	400	1,500	4,000	8,000	50,000	—
1872S	580,000	31.00	47.00	67.00	135	225	375	975	7,000	—
1873 closed 3	801,800	35.00	46.00	64.00	98.00	135	250	545	4,500	3,750
1873 open 3	Inc. above	2,650	3,400	4,350	5,500	7,900	13,500	30,000	—	—
1873CC	122,500	225	320	425	950	1,900	6,500	12,000	80,000	—
1873S no arrows	5,000	—	—	—	—	—	—	—	—	—

Note: 1873S no arrows, no specimens known to survive.

Seated Liberty, arrows at date
IN GOD WE TRUST above eagle reverse

KM# 107 • 12.5000 g., 0.9000 **Silver**, 0.3617 oz. ASW • **Rev. Legend:** UNITED STATES OF AMERICA
Designer: Christian Gobrecht

Date	Mintage	G-4	VG-8	F-12	VF-20	XF-40	AU-50	MS-60	MS-65	Prf-65
1873	1,815,700	32.00	49.00	60.00	90.00	230	400	850	17,500	9,000
1873CC	214,560	150	275	375	850	2,000	2,400	5,700	42,000	—
1873S	233,000	55.00	78.00	130	245	425	675	2,200	40,000	—
1874	2,360,300	33.00	42.00	60.00	84.00	215	400	900	15,500	9,000
1874CC	59,000	400	575	1,000	1,750	3,600	5,600	10,500	—	—
1874S	394,000	43.00	65.00	85.00	185	365	685	1,850	20,000	—

HALF DOLLAR

Seated Liberty, date below obverse
IN GOD WE TRUST above eagle reverse

HALF DOLLAR

KM# A99 • 12.5000 g., 0.9000 **Silver**, 0.3617 oz. ASW • **Rev. Legend:** UNITED STATES OF AMERICA
Designer: Christian Gobrecht

Date	Mintage	G-4	VG-8	F-12	VF-20	XF-40	AU-50	MS-60	MS-65	Prf-65
1875	6,027,500	34.00	38.00	47.00	56.00	88.00	180	420	3,500	3,375
1875CC	1,008,000	50.00	56.00	75.00	125	200	325	650	8,350	—
1875S	3,200,000	34.00	38.00	47.00	63.00	100.00	165	360	2,700	—
1876	8,419,150	32.00	38.00	47.00	56.00	88.00	165	360	5,300	3,775
1876S	4,528,000	32.00	38.00	47.00	56.00	88.00	165	360	2,700	—
1876CC	1,956,000	50.00	60.00	75.00	100.00	180	275	560	4,200	—
1877	8,304,510	32.00	38.00	47.00	56.00	88.00	165	360	2,700	3,825
1877CC	1,420,000	50.00	56.00	75.00	115	180	275	630	3,250	—
1877S	5,356,000	32.00	38.00	47.00	56.00	88.00	165	360	2,700	—
1878	1,378,400	34.00	46.00	67.00	80.00	120	165	425	3,650	3,900
1878CC	62,000	385	525	1,000	1,500	3,150	4,850	7,000	43,500	—
1878S	12,000	27,500	37,500	45,000	47,500	52,000	60,000	70,000	175,000	—
1879	5,900	275	310	360	400	465	575	700	3,650	3,150
1880	9,755	260	280	315	355	410	535	700	3,750	3,150
1881	10,975	270	300	335	385	455	565	700	4,000	3,150
1882	5,500	340	365	385	450	525	600	750	3,850	3,150
1883	9,039	325	340	365	435	500	575	775	3,950	3,150
1884	5,275	385	375	415	500	560	635	800	3,850	3,150
1885	6,130	390	425	475	550	625	700	825	3,850	3,150
1886	5,886	400	500	600	700	775	875	1,000	3,900	3,150
1887	5,710	500	525	650	775	875	950	1,100	3,900	3,150
1888	12,833	280	300	365	400	485	550	800	3,900	3,150
1889	12,711	275	315	350	400	485	550	800	3,900	3,150
1890	12,590	275	310	365	415	500	550	800	3,850	3,150
1891	200,600	55.00	75.00	94.00	122	155	240	480	3,850	3,150

1878-S Half Dollar
Grade F-12

Barber Half Dollar

Laureate head right, flanked by stars, date below   **Heraldic eagle reverse**

Mint mark

KM# 116 • 12.5000 g., 0.9000 **Silver**, 0.3617 oz. ASW, 30.6 mm. • **Obv. Legend** IN GOD WE TRUST
Rev. Legend: UNITED STATES OF AMERICA **Designer:** Charles E. Barber

Date	Mintage	G-4	VG-8	F-12	VF-20	XF-40	AU-50	MS-60	MS-65	Prf-65
1892	935,245	28.50	40.00	65.00	120	195	345	475	2,945	4,650
1892O	390,000	310	420	515	575	630	690	850	4,350	—
1892O micro O	Inc. above	2,000	3,750	4,500	7,000	10,000	17,500	24,000	64,000	—
1892S	1,029,028	250	330	425	530	600	700	940	4,850	—
1893	1,826,792	20.00	36.00	75.00	135	205	335	520	3,125	4,650
1893O	1,389,000	36.00	65.00	130	220	360	435	625	9,650	—
1893S	740,000	165	225	300	500	595	725	1,275	25,000	—
1894	1,148,972	32.50	50.00	115	200	280	355	500	3,850	4,650
1894O	2,138,000	22.00	34.00	90.00	170	290	365	525	6,250	—
1894S	4,048,690	18.00	28.00	67.00	125	230	345	490	9,850	—
1895	1,835,218	18.00	25.00	72.00	150	225	345	595	3,900	4,650
1895O	1,766,000	23.00	43.00	110	195	285	385	620	6,950	—
1895S	1,108,086	30.00	54.00	130	235	310	410	580	8,250	—
1896	950,762	21.50	28.00	88.00	160	265	355	565	5,450	4,650
1896O	924,000	42.00	56.00	185	290	475	775	1,750	14,750	—
1896S	1,140,948	115	145	210	350	495	750	1,450	10,500	—
1897	2,480,731	15.20	18.00	47.50	100.00	180	345	485	2,945	4,650
1897O	632,000	170	230	485	835	1,100	1,350	1,800	9,500	—
1897S	933,900	155	225	385	535	840	1,050	1,500	7,350	—
1898	2,956,735	15.20	18.00	38.50	94.00	180	335	485	2,975	4,650
1898O	874,000	37.50	75.00	225	355	525	625	1,250	9,450	—
1898S	2,358,550	27.50	53.00	87.50	175	340	440	950	10,250	—
1899	5,538,846	15.70	18.00	39.50	98.00	180	365	475	2,945	4,650
1899O	1,724,000	26.00	38.00	80.00	170	300	400	675	8,150	—
1899S	1,686,411	23.00	43.00	88.00	135	205	355	660	6,900	—
1900	4,762,912	15.70	18.00	36.50	90.00	180	335	475	3,075	4,650
1900O	2,744,000	17.50	23.00	62.00	165	285	335	860	15,500	—
1900S	2,560,322	15.00	19.00	46.50	98.00	200	335	640	10,000	—
1901	4,268,813	15.70	18.00	38.50	94.00	180	335	510	4,250	4,650
1901O	1,124,000	16.50	27.00	80.00	205	350	475	1,350	14,850	—
1901S	847,044	34.00	55.00	160	355	610	1,050	1,850	19,500	—
1902	4,922,777	14.20	16.00	32.50	86.00	180	335	475	3,925	4,650
1902O	2,526,000	13.50	17.00	52.50	105	225	355	725	11,500	—
1902S	1,460,670	16.00	19.00	62.50	150	260	420	750	7,750	—
1903	2,278,755	15.70	18.00	47.50	100.00	200	335	500	9,250	4,650
1903O	2,100,000	15.20	17.00	53.00	115	210	335	665	9,500	—
1903S	1,920,772	15.00	18.00	55.00	125	220	380	610	5,750	—
1904	2,992,670	14.20	16.00	33.00	85.00	180	345	475	6,450	4,650
1904O	1,117,600	20.00	30.00	80.00	220	385	590	1,100	12,500	—
1904S	553,038	38.50	75.00	260	555	1,075	1,775	9,000	41,500	—
1905	662,727	22.50	33.00	95.00	180	270	370	565	7,500	4,650
1905O	505,000	30.00	45.00	125	235	340	440	760	4,850	—
1905S	2,494,000	15.50	18.00	50.00	125	230	350	615	9,750	—
1906	2,638,675	14.20	16.00	32.00	83.00	180	335	465	3,800	4,650
1906D	4,028,000	14.20	16.00	33.00	89.00	180	335	465	4,500	—
1906O	2,446,000	14.20	16.00	44.00	98.00	190	350	600	6,350	—
1906S	1,740,154	15.70	17.00	57.50	110	215	380	590	5,950	—
1907	2,598,575	14.20	16.00	30.00	83.00	180	335	465	2,925	4,650
1907D	3,856,000	14.20	16.00	30.00	75.00	180	335	465	2,925	—
1907O	3,946,000	14.20	16.00	32.00	89.00	180	335	575	3,025	—
1907S	1,250,000	18.50	20.00	80.00	165	315	650	1,275	12,500	—
1908	1,354,545	14.20	16.00	30.00	80.00	180	335	465	4,350	4,650
1908D	3,280,000	14.20	16.00	30.00	80.00	180	335	485	4,250	—
1908O	5,360,000	14.20	16.00	30.00	89.00	180	345	540	2,925	—
1908S	1,644,828	18.50	25.00	72.00	160	285	435	850	6,350	—
1909	2,368,650	15.20	18.00	32.00	83.00	180	335	465	2,925	4,650
1909O	925,400	18.50	24.00	56.00	140	300	510	775	4,850	—
1909S	1,764,000	14.50	16.00	37.00	100.00	180	335	600	4,450	—
1910	418,551	20.00	29.00	90.00	170	330	445	610	3,900	4,650

Date	Mintage	G-4	VG-8	F-12	VF-20	XF-40	AU-50	MS-60	MS-65	Prf-65
1910S	1,948,000	17.70	18.00	36.00	100.00	180	355	625	6,650	—
1911	1,406,543	14.20	16.00	30.00	83.00	180	335	465	2,925	4,650
1911D	695,080	15.20	18.00	40.00	91.00	180	345	565	3,025	—
1911S	1,272,000	15.70	18.00	42.00	98.00	180	345	580	5,950	—
1912	1,550,700	14.20	16.00	30.00	83.00	180	335	465	3,425	4,650
1912D	2,300,800	14.20	16.00	30.00	81.00	180	335	465	2,925	—
1912S	1,370,000	17.50	20.00	41.50	100.00	180	335	535	5,850	—
1913	188,627	77.00	88.00	235	420	600	875	1,150	5,250	4,800
1913D	534,000	17.00	20.00	44.00	100.00	200	335	485	5,450	—
1913S	604,000	20.00	25.00	53.50	110	225	385	725	4,650	—
1914	124,610	155	175	325	550	775	1,025	1,400	11,500	5,000
1914S	992,000	17.50	19.00	41.00	98.00	190	355	575	4,950	—
1915	138,450	112	168	285	380	575	920	1,350	6,650	5,000
1915D	1,170,400	14.20	16.00	30.00	75.00	180	335	465	2,925	—
1915S	1,604,000	18.00	20.00	41.50	94.00	195	350	480	2,925	—

1923-S Half Dollar
Grade XF-40

Retail Price

Walking Liberty Half Dollar
Liberty walking left wearing U.S. flag gown, sunrise at left
Eagle advancing left reverse

Obverse mint mark
1916-1917

Reverse mint mark
1917-1947

KM# 142 • 12.5000 g., 0.9000 **Silver**, 0.3617 oz. ASW, 30.6 mm. • **Designer:** Adolph A. Weinman **Notes:** The mint mark appears on the obverse below the word "Trust" on 1916 and some 1917 issues. Starting with some 1917 issues and continuing through the remainder of the series, the mint mark was changed to the reverse, at about the 8 o'clock position near the rim.

Date	Mintage	G-4	VG-8	F-12	VF-20	XF-40	AU-50	MS-60	MS-65	Prf-65
1916	608,000	47.00	55.00	95.00	170	240	275	345	1,950	—
1916D	1,014,400	48.50	55.00	80.00	135	220	255	360	2,500	—
1916S	508,000	108	135	280	440	600	720	1,050	6,250	—
1917	12,292,000	14.20	14.50	15.20	19.50	42.00	72.00	130	1,050	—
1917D obv. mint mark	765,400	23.50	33.00	80.00	155	235	335	625	7,900	—
1917S obv. mint mark	952,000	27.00	44.00	135	365	700	1,200	2,300	22,500	—
1917D rev. mint mark	1,940,000	14.20	14.50	45.00	135	275	555	940	18,500	—
1917S rev. mint mark	5,554,000	14.20	14.50	16.50	32.00	65.00	155	330	13,850	—
1918	6,634,000	14.20	14.50	15.50	64.00	150	265	565	3,800	—
1918D	3,853,040	14.20	14.50	35.00	90.00	225	500	1,300	24,500	—
1918S	10,282,000	14.20	14.50	16.00	34.00	60.00	190	485	17,750	—
1919	962,000	26.00	32.50	78.50	265	535	885	1,325	7,750	—
1919D	1,165,000	25.00	38.50	95.00	320	765	1,750	5,950	130,000	—
1919S	1,552,000	17.50	28.50	72.00	310	825	1,750	3,300	20,000	—
1920	6,372,000	14.20	14.50	15.50	42.00	75.00	155	330	5,250	—
1920D	1,551,000	14.20	14.50	65.00	240	460	920	1,485	17,500	—
1920S	4,624,000	14.20	14.50	19.00	78.00	235	510	850	14,500	—
1921	246,000	165	210	350	750	1,575	2,650	4,500	19,500	—
1921D	208,000	310	370	550	950	2,200	3,150	5,650	29,500	—
1921S	548,000	45.00	65.00	210	750	4,850	7,950	12,950	130,000	—
1923S	2,178,000	14.20	14.50	27.50	110	295	650	1,375	16,500	—
1927S	2,392,000	14.50	14.80	16.50	46.00	165	425	990	9,750	—
1928S Large S	1,940,000	14.50	17.50	28.00	110	325	600	1,650	—	—
1928S Small S	Inc. above	14.20	14.50	18.50	66.00	195	450	985	10,750	—
1929D	1,001,200	14.20	14.50	17.50	32.00	98.00	195	390	3,350	—
1929S	1,902,000	14.20	14.50	15.50	28.50	115	220	400	3,750	—
1933S	1,786,000	14.20	14.50	17.60	20.00	58.00	240	590	4,500	—
1934	6,964,000	14.00	14.50	15.20	15.80	17.60	25.00	85.00	565	—
1934D	2,361,400	14.20	14.90	18.90	17.50	36.00	88.00	150	1,625	—
1934S	3,652,000	14.00	14.70	15.80	18.00	30.00	100.00	385	4,800	—
1935	9,162,000	14.00	14.50	15.20	15.80	17.76	21.50	45.00	365	—
1935D	3,003,800	14.00	14.70	15.80	16.20	33.00	66.00	140	2,450	—
1935S	3,854,000	14.00	14.70	15.60	13.50	32.00	95.00	285	2,850	—
1936	12,617,901	14.00	14.50	15.20	15.80	17.76	21.00	37.50	265	6,600
1936D	4,252,400	14.00	14.70	15.60	16.00	20.00	52.00	78.00	665	—
1936S	3,884,000	14.00	14.70	15.60	16.00	21.50	58.00	132	1,000	—
1937	9,527,728	14.00	14.50	15.20	15.80	17.76	22.00	38.00	285	1,700
1937D	1,676,000	14.00	14.70	17.20	17.60	33.50	105	220	965	—
1937S	2,090,000	14.00	14.70	15.80	17.20	25.50	62.00	168	785	—
1938	4,118,152	14.00	14.70	15.60	16.20	19.21	38.00	66.00	460	1,275
1938D	491,600	70.00	75.00	100.00	125	185	250	475	1,750	—
1939	6,820,808	14.00	14.30	15.00	15.80	17.76	22.00	41.00	210	1,150
1939D	4,267,800	14.00	14.50	15.20	16.80	18.51	26.00	45.00	225	—
1939S	2,552,000	14.00	14.70	15.60	16.00	25.00	76.00	145	375	—
1940	9,167,279	14.00	14.30	15.00	15.40	16.80	17.60	31.00	185	1,000
1940S	4,550,000	14.00	14.50	15.20	15.80	17.76	21.00	50.00	315	—
1941	24,207,412	14.00	14.30	15.00	15.36	16.10	17.60	30.00	155	850
1941D	11,248,400	14.00	14.50	15.20	15.80	16.20	18.00	37.50	180	—
1941S	8,098,000	14.00	14.50	15.20	15.80	19.60	27.50	70.00	925	—
1942	47,839,120	14.00	14.30	15.00	15.36	15.80	17.60	30.00	130	850
1942D	10,973,800	14.00	14.50	15.20	15.80	16.20	19.00	37.00	315	—
1942S	12,708,000	14.00	14.50	15.20	15.80	16.20	18.60	37.00	475	—
1943	53,190,000	14.00	14.30	15.00	15.36	16.10	17.60	30.00	140	—
1943D	11,346,000	14.00	14.50	15.20	15.80	16.20	25.00	42.00	240	—
1943D Double Die Obverse	—	14.20	15.00	17.00	19.00	22.00	30.00	55.00	450	—
1943S	13,450,000	14.00	14.50	15.20	15.80	16.20	18.50	42.00	290	—
1944	28,206,000	14.00	14.30	15.00	15.36	16.10	17.60	30.00	170	—
1944D	9,769,000	14.00	14.50	15.20	15.80	16.20	20.00	37.00	165	—
1944S	8,904,000	14.00	14.50	15.20	15.80	16.20	18.00	36.00	500	—
1945	31,502,000	14.00	14.30	15.00	15.36	16.10	17.60	30.00	130	—
1945D	9,966,800	14.00	14.50	15.20	15.80	16.20	19.00	36.00	130	—
1945S	10,156,000	14.00	14.50	15.20	15.80	16.20	17.50	36.00	135	—
1946 Double Die Reverse	Inc. above	16.00	24.00	35.00	50.00	85.00	175	325	2,750	—
1946	12,118,000	14.00	14.30	15.00	15.36	16.10	17.60	30.00	155	—
1946D	2,151,000	14.00	14.70	15.20	15.80	16.20	25.50	38.50	47.50	125	—
1946S	3,724,000	14.00	14.50	15.20	15.80	16.90	19.00	43.50	175	—
1947	4,094,000	14.00	14.30	15.00	15.80	16.20	22.00	50.00	220	—
1947D	3,900,600	14.00	14.70	15.20	15.80	16.20	31.50	52.50	145	—

HALF DOLLAR

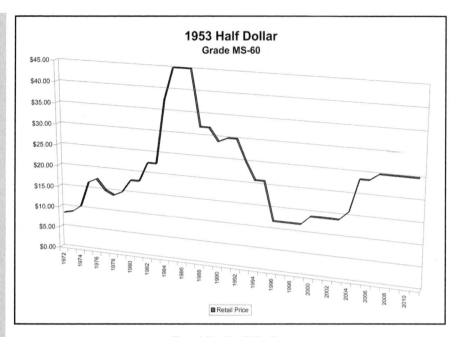

1953 Half Dollar
Grade MS-60

☐ Retail Price

Franklin Half Dollar
Franklin bust right obverse
Liberty Bell, small eagle at right reverse

Mint mark

KM# 199 • 12.5000 g., 0.9000 **Silver**, 0.3617 oz. ASW, 30.6 mm. • **Designer:** John R. Sinnock

Date	Mintage	G-4	VG-8	F-12	VF-20	XF-40	AU-50	MS-60	MS-65	-65FBL	-65CAM
1948	3,006,814	—	13.80	13.90	14.50	15.10	15.30	17.00	75.00	190	—
1948D	4,028,600	—	13.80	13.90	14.50	14.60	15.00	16.00	125	260	—
1949	5,614,000	—	—	—	—	15.60	14.00	38.50	120	250	—
1949D	4,120,600	—	—	—	14.30	16.60	25.00	43.50	900	1,750	—
1949S	3,744,000	—	—	—	14.50	16.50	30.00	62.50	160	700	—
1950	7,793,509	—	—	—	—	13.90	13.00	26.00	110	285	2,000
1950D	8,031,600	—	—	—	—	14.90	15.10	22.00	425	900	—
1951	16,859,602	—	—	—	—	13.60	16.60	17.60	75.00	340	1,450
1951D	9,475,200	—	—	—	—	17.90	17.50	26.00	170	540	—
1951S	13,696,000	—	—	—	13.90	14.60	15.00	23.50	125	750	—
1952	21,274,073	—	—	—	—	13.80	16.60	17.00	70.00	210	775
1952D	25,395,600	—	—	—	—	13.80	16.60	17.00	130	450	—
1952S	5,526,000	—	—	13.90	16.50	16.00	32.00	52.00	140	1,500	—
1953	2,796,920	—	—	13.90	14.00	14.40	16.00	25.00	140	1,000	475
1953D	20,900,400	—	—	—	—	13.60	13.80	14.10	150	400	—
1953S	4,148,000	—	—	—	13.90	14.60	18.50	25.00	65.00	16,000	—
1954	13,421,503	—	—	—	—	13.60	14.60	14.80	75.00	225	175
1954D	25,445,580	—	—	—	—	13.60	14.60	14.80	110	235	—
1954S	4,993,400	—	—	—	—	14.00	14.60	15.10	42.00	440	—
1955	2,876,381	—	15.50	16.00	17.50	18.00	18.50	20.00	70.00	140	120
1955 Bugs Bunny	Inc. above	—	20.00	22.00	23.00	25.00	26.00	28.00	120	750	—
1956 Type 1 rev.	4,701,384	—	13.50	13.60	13.70	14.00	14.80	15.40	55.00	125	300
1956 Type 2 rev.	Inc. above	—	—	—	—	—	—	—	—	—	40.00
1957 Type 1 rev.	6,361,952	—	—	—	—	13.60	14.80	15.70	63.00	95.00	55.00
1957 Type 2 rev.	Inc. above	—	—	—	—	—	—	—	—	—	—

Date	Mintage	G-4	VG-8	F-12	VF-20	XF-40	AU-50	MS-60	MS-65	-65FBL	-65CAM
1957D	19,966,850	—	—	—	—	13.60	14.80	15.50	60.00	100.00	—
1958 Type 1 rev.	4,917,652	—	—	—	—	13.60	14.80	15.50	55.00	110	60.00
1958 Type 2 rev.	Inc. above	—	—	—	—	14.30	20.00	26.00	—	—	—
1958D	23,962,412	—	—	—	—	13.60	14.80	15.50	55.00	80.00	—
1959 Type 1 rev.	7,349,291	—	—	—	—	13.60	14.80	15.50	110	250	75.00
1959 Type 2 rev.	Inc. above	—	—	—	—	14.10	16.00	30.00	115	—	—
1959D	13,053,750	—	—	—	—	13.60	14.80	15.50	125	215	—
1960 Type 1 rev.	7,715,602	—	—	—	—	13.60	14.80	15.50	110	340	45.00
1960 Type 2 rev.	Inc. above	—	—	—	—	—	—	—	—	—	—
1960D	18,215,812	—	—	—	—	13.60	14.80	15.50	400	1,350	—
1961 Type 1 rev.	11,318,244	—	—	—	—	13.60	14.80	15.50	125	1,300	40.00
1961 Type 2 rev.	Inc. above	—	—	—	—	25.00	—	—	—	—	—
1961 Double die rev.	Inc. above	—	—	—	—	—	—	—	—	—	3,500
1961D	20,276,442	—	—	—	—	13.60	14.80	15.50	155	875	—
1962 Type 1 rev.	12,932,019	—	—	—	—	13.60	14.80	15.50	145	1,850	35.00
1962 Type 2 rev.	Inc. above	—	—	—	—	—	—	—	—	—	—
1962D	35,473,281	—	—	—	—	13.60	14.80	15.50	175	800	—
1963 Type 1 rev.	25,239,645	—	—	—	—	13.60	14.80	15.50	55.00	1,200	35.00
1963 Type 2 rev.	Inc. above	—	—	—	—	—	—	—	—	—	—
1963D	67,069,292	—	—	—	—	13.60	14.80	15.50	75.00	165	—

Kennedy Half Dollar

Mint mark 1964

KM# 202 • 12.5000 g., 0.9000 **Silver**, 0.3617 oz. ASW, 30.6 mm. • **Obv. Designer:** Gilroy Roberts
Rev. Designer: Frank Gasparro **Edge Desc:** Reeded

Date	Mintage	XF-40	MS-60	MS-65	Prf-65
1964	277,254,766	13.20	13.40	20.00	14.50
1964 Accented Hair	Inc. above	—	—	—	40.00
1964D	156,205,446	13.30	13.60	24.00	—

Mint mark 1968 - present

KM# 202a • 11.5000 g., 0.4000 **Silver**, 0.1479 oz. ASW, 30.6 mm. • **Obv. Designer:** Gilroy Roberts
Rev. Designer: Frank Gasparro **Edge Desc:** Reeded

Date	Mintage	MS-60	MS-65	Prf-65
1965	65,879,366	6.20	18.00	—
1965 SMS	2,360,000	—	15.00	—
1966	108,984,932	6.20	14.00	—
1966 SMS	2,261,583	—	17.00	—
1967	295,046,978	6.20	22.00	—
1967 SMS	1,863,344	—	18.00	—
1968D	246,951,930	6.20	18.00	—
1968S	3,041,506	—	—	7.00
1969D	129,881,800	6.20	20.00	—
1969S	2,934,631	—	—	7.00
1970D	2,150,000	13.00	50.00	—
1970S	2,632,810	—	—	20.00

KM# 202b • 11.3400 g., **Copper-Nickel Clad Copper**, 30.6 mm. • **Obv. Designer:** Gilroy Roberts
Rev. Designer: Frank Gasparro

Date	Mintage	XF-40	MS-60	MS-65	Prf-65
1971	155,640,000	—	1.00	15.00	—
1971D	302,097,424	—	1.00	15.00	—

Date	Mintage	XF-40	MS-60	MS-65	Prf-65
1971S	3,244,183	—	—	—	8.00
1972	153,180,000	—	1.00	20.00	—
1972D	141,890,000	—	1.00	14.00	—
1972S	3,267,667	—	—	—	7.00
1973	64,964,000	—	1.00	14.00	—
1973D	83,171,400	—	—	12.00	—
1973S	2,769,624	—	—	—	7.00
1974	201,596,000	—	1.00	18.00	—
1974D	79,066,300	—	1.00	20.00	—
1974D DDO	Inc. above	24.00	32.00	165	—
1974S	2,617,350	—	—	—	6.00
1975 none minted	—	—	—	—	—
1975D none minted	—	—	—	—	—
1975S none minted	—	—	—	—	—

Bicentennial design, Independence Hall reverse

KM# 205 • 11.2000 g., **Copper-Nickel**, 30.6 mm.
• **Rev. Designer:** Seth Huntington

Date	Mintage	MS-60	MS-65	Prf-65
1976	234,308,000	1.00	22.00	—
1976D	287,565,248	1.00	9.00	—
1976S	7,059,099	—	—	5.00

KM# 205a • 11.5000 g., 0.4000 **Silver**, 0.1479 oz.
ASW, 30.6 mm. • **Rev. Designer:** Seth
Huntington

Date	Mintage	MS-60	MS-65	Prf-65
1976S	4,908,319	—	12.00	6.00
1976S	3,998,621	—	—	6.00

Regular design resumed reverse

KM# A202b • 11.1000 g., **Copper-Nickel Clad
Copper**, 30.4 mm. • **Edge Desc:** Reeded **Notes:**
KM#202b design and composition resumed. The
1979-S and 1981-S Type II proofs have clearer
mint marks than the Type I proofs of those years.

Date	Mintage	MS-65	Prf-65
1977	43,598,000	18.00	—
1977D	31,449,106	20.00	—
1977S	3,251,152	—	4.50
1978	14,350,000	12.00	—
1978D	13,765,799	10.00	—
1978S	3,127,788	—	6.00
1979	68,312,000	11.00	—
1979D	15,815,422	9.00	—
1979S Type I	3,677,175	—	6.00
1979S Type II	Inc. above	—	20.00
1980P	44,134,000	9.00	—

Date	Mintage	MS-65	Prf-65
1980D	33,456,449	6.50	—
1980S	3,547,030	—	6.00
1981P	29,544,000	8.00	—
1981D	27,839,533	8.50	—
1981S Type I	4,063,083	—	5.00
1981S Type II	Inc. above	—	17.50
1982P	10,819,000	10.00	—
1982P no initials FG	Inc. above	40.00	—
1982D	13,140,102	9.00	—
1982S	38,957,479	—	6.50
1983P	34,139,000	20.00	—
1983D	32,472,244	10.00	—
1983S	3,279,126	—	6.50
1984P	26,029,000	13.00	—
1984D	26,262,158	18.00	—
1984S	3,065,110	—	7.00
1985P	18,706,962	10.00	—
1985D	19,814,034	12.00	—
1985S	3,962,138	—	6.00
1986P	13,107,633	25.00	—
1986D	15,336,145	17.00	—
1986S	2,411,180	—	8.00
1987P	2,890,758	14.00	—
1987D	2,890,758	10.00	—
1987S	4,407,728	—	6.50
1988P	13,626,000	16.00	—
1988D	12,000,096	12.00	—
1988S	3,262,948	—	6.00
1989P	24,542,000	18.00	—
1989D	23,000,216	14.00	—
1989S	3,220,194	—	8.00
1990P	22,780,000	18.00	—
1990D	20,096,242	15.00	—
1990S	3,299,559	—	7.00
1991P	14,874,000	15.00	—
1991D	15,054,678	16.00	—
1991S	2,867,787	—	13.00
1992P	17,628,000	12.00	—
1992D	17,000,106	8.00	—
1992S	2,858,981	—	8.00
1993P	15,510,000	15.00	—
1993D	15,000,006	14.00	—
1993S	2,633,439	—	14.00
1994P	23,718,000	8.00	—
1994D	23,828,110	8.00	—
1994S	2,484,594	—	11.00
1995P	26,496,000	9.00	—
1995D	26,288,000	8.00	—
1995S	2,010,384	—	35.00
1996P	24,442,000	10.00	—
1996D	24,744,000	8.00	—
1996S	2,085,191	—	16.00
1997P	20,882,000	14.00	—
1997D	19,876,000	10.00	—
1997S	1,975,000	—	34.00
1998P	15,646,000	12.50	—
1998D	15,064,000	12.50	—
1998S	2,078,494	—	22.00
1999P	8,900,000	9.00	—
1999D	10,682,000	9.00	—
1999S	2,557,897	—	18.00
2000P	22,600,000	9.00	—

Date	Mintage	MS-65	Prf-65
2000D	19,466,000	7.00	—
2000S	3,082,944	—	8.00
2001P	21,200,000	9.00	—
2001D	19,504,000	9.00	—
2001S	2,235,000	—	8.00
2002P	3,100,000	10.00	—
2002D	2,500,000	10.00	—
2002S	2,268,913	—	8.00
2003P	2,500,000	14.00	—
2003D	2,500,000	14.00	—
2003S	2,076,165	—	6.00
2004P	2,900,000	7.00	—
2004D	2,900,000	7.00	—
2004S	1,789,488	—	13.00
2005P	3,800,000	9.00	—
2005P Satin finish	1,160,000	8.00	—
2005D	3,500,000	9.00	—
2005D Satin finish	1,160,000	10.00	—
2005S	2,275,000	—	7.00
2006P	2,400,000	12.00	—
2006P Satin finish	847,361	12.00	—
2006D	2,000,000	20.00	—
2006D Satin finish	847,361	14.00	—
2006S	1,934,965	—	10.00
2007P	—	7.00	—
2007P Satin finish	—	8.00	—
2007D	—	7.00	—
2007D Satin finish	—	8.00	—
2007S	—	—	10.00
2008P	—	7.00	—
2008P Satin finish	—	8.50	—
2008D	—	7.00	—
2008D Satin finish	—	8.50	—
2008S	—	—	12.00
2009P	—	7.00	—
2009P Satin finish	—	8.50	—
2009D	—	7.00	—
2009D Satin finish	—	8.50	—
2009S	—	—	6.00
2010P	—	7.00	—
2010P Satin finish	—	8.50	—
2010D	—	7.00	—
2010D Satin finish	—	8.50	—
2010S	—	—	6.00
2011P	—	7.00	—
2011D	—	7.00	—
2011S	—	—	6.00

KM# A202c • 12.5000 g., 0.9000 **Silver**, 0.3617 oz. ASW, 30.6 mm. • **Designer:** Gilroy Roberts

Date	Mintage	Prf-65
1992S	1,317,579	14.50
1993S	761,353	32.00
1994S	785,329	36.00
1995S	838,953	92.00
1996S	830,021	40.00
1997S	821,678	75.00
1998S	878,792	25.00
1998S Matte Proof	62,350	250
1999S	804,565	40.00
2000S	965,921	14.50
2001S	849,600	20.00
2002S	888,816	14.50
2003S	1,040,425	14.50
2004S	1,175,935	14.50
2005S	1,069,679	14.50
2006S	988,140	14.50
2007S	1,384,797	14.50
2008S	620,684	14.50
2009S	—	20.00
2010S	—	20.00

DOLLAR

Flowing Hair Dollar

KM# 17 • 26.9600 g., 0.8920 **Silver**, 0.7731 oz. ASW, 39-40 mm. • **Designer:** Robert Scot **Notes:** The two 1795 varieties have either two or three leaves under each of the eagle's wings on the reverse.

Date	Mintage	F-12	VF-20	XF-40	AU-50	MS-60	MS-63
1794	1,758	120,000	170,000	245,000	365,000	575,000	950,000
1795 2 leaves	203,033	4,450	7,800	16,150	25,500	80,500	196,500
1795 3 leaves	Inc. above	4,200	7,250	14,500	22,500	69,500	182,500
1795 Silver plug	Inc. above	9,850	13,950	28,500	48,500	115,000	235,000

1794 Silver Dollar
Grade XF-40

Draped Bust Dollar
Small eagle reverse

KM# 18 • 26.9600 g., 0.8920 **Silver**, 0.7731 oz. ASW, 39-40 mm. • **Designer:** Robert Scot

Date	Mintage	F-12	VF-20	XF-40	AU-50	MS-60	MS-63
1795 Off-center bust	Inc. above	3,850	5,850	12,500	17,000	52,000	126,000
1795 Centered bust	—	3,900	5,950	12,700	17,250	52,500	126,000
1796 small date, small letters	72,920	4,100	6,300	13,750	18,500	70,000	—
1796 small date, large letters	Inc. above	3,875	6,400	13,700	19,400	—	—
1796 large date, small letters	Inc. above	4,250	6,750	14,350	19,200	57,000	136,000
1797 9 stars left, 7 stars right, small letters	7,776	5,200	9,000	18,850	36,500	—	—
1797 9 stars left, 7 stars right, large letters	Inc. above	4,250	6,850	13,950	20,300	55,500	—
1797 10 stars left, 6 stars right	Inc. above	4,050	6,350	13,600	18,500	53,500	125,000
1798 13 stars	327,536	4,150	6,300	13,750	21,000	85,000	—
1798 15 stars	Inc. above	4,700	7,450	16,150	25,500	95,000	—

Draped bust right, flanked by stars, date below obverse
Heraldic eagle reverse

KM# 32 • 26.9600 g., 0.8920 **Silver**, 0.7731 oz. ASW, 39-40 mm. • **Obv. Legend** LIBERTY **Rev. Legend:**
UNITED STATES OF AMERICA **Designer:** Robert Scot **Notes:** The 1798 "knob 9" variety has a serif on the
lower left of the 9 in the date. The 1798 varieties are distinguished by the number of arrows held by the eagle
on the reverse and the number of berries on the olive branch. On the 1798 "high-8" variety, the 8 in the date is
higher than the other numberals. The 1799 varieties are distinguished by the number and positioning of the
stars on the obverse and by the size of the berries in the olive branch on the reverse. On the 1700 "irregular
date" variety, the first 9 in the date is smaller than the other numerals. Some varieties of the 1800 strikes had
letters in the legend cut twice into the dies; as between the numerals in the date are wider than other varieties
and the 8 is lower than the other numerals. The 1800 "small berries" variety refers to the size of the berries in
the olive branch on the reverse. The 1800 "12 arrows" and "10 arrows" varieties refer to the number of arrows
held by the eagle. The 1800 "Americai" variety appears to have the faint outline of an "I" after "America" in the
reverse legend. The "close" and "wide" varieties of the 1802 refer to the amount of space between the
numberals in the date. The 1800 large-3 and small-3 varieties are distinguished by the size of the 3 in the date.

Date	Mintage	F-12	VF-20	XF-40	AU-50	MS-60	MS-63
1798 knob 9, 4 stripes	423,515	1,785	2,735	5,550	9,850	21,750	95,000
1798 knob 9, 10 arrows	Inc. above	1,785	2,735	5,550	9,850	21,750	87,000
1798 knob 9, 5 stripes	Inc. above	—	—	—	—	—	124,500
1798 pointed 9, 4 berries	Inc. above	1,785	2,735	5,550	9,850	21,750	43,500
1798 5 berries, 12 arrows	Inc. above	1,785	2,735	5,550	9,850	21,750	43,500
1798 high 8	Inc. above	1,785	2,735	5,550	9,850	21,750	43,500
1798 13 arrows	Inc. above	1,785	2,735	5,550	9,850	21,750	45,000
1799/98 13-star reverse	Inc. above	2,000	2,950	4,300	8,600	23,500	45,000
1799/98 15-star reverse	Inc. above	1,875	2,850	4,000	8,300	24,500	47,500
1799 irregular date, 13-star reverse	Inc. above	1,825	3,000	3,900	8,200	23,500	45,000
1799 irregular date, 15-star reverse	Inc. above	1,825	3,200	5,550	9,850	21,500	42,500
1799 perfect date, 7- and 6-star obverse, no berries	Inc. above	1,750	2,700	3,850	8,150	18,500	42,500
1799 perfect date, 7- and 6-star obverse, small berries	Inc. above	1,750	2,700	3,850	8,150	18,500	42,500
1799 perfect date, 7- and 6-star obverse, medium large berries	Inc. above	1,750	2,700	3,850	8,150	18,500	42,500
1799 perfect date, 7- and 6-star obverse, extra large berries	Inc. above	1,750	2,700	3,850	8,150	18,500	51,500
1799 8 stars left, 5 stars right on obverse	Inc. above	1,825	2,800	3,900	8,200	24,000	45,000
1800 "R" in "Liberty" double cut	220,920	1,825	2,775	5,550	9,850	21,500	45,000
1800 first "T" in "States" double cut	Inc. above	1,800	2,750	5,550	9,850	21,500	45,000
1800 both letters double cut	Inc. above	1,800	2,750	5,550	9,850	21,500	45,000
1800 "T" in "United" double cut	Inc. above	1,800	2,750	5,550	9,850	21,500	45,000
1800 very wide date, low 8	Inc. above	1,800	2,750	5,550	9,850	21,500	—
1800 small berries	Inc. above	1,850	2,800	3,900	8,200	22,000	48,500
1800 dot date	Inc. above	2,000	3,000	4,300	8,600	21,500	45,000
1800 12 arrows	Inc. above	1,825	3,200	5,550	9,850	31,000	—
1800 10 arrows	Inc. above	1,825	3,200	5,550	9,850	—	—
1800 "Americai"	Inc. above	2,000	3,300	4,300	8,600	21,500	49,000
1801	54,454	2,050	3,200	4,000	8,300	25,000	—
1801 proof restrike	—	—	—	—	—	—	—
1802/1 close	Inc. above	2,000	3,300	4,300	8,600	20,500	—
1802/1 wide	Inc. above	2,000	3,300	4,300	8,600	20,500	—
1802 close, perfect date	Inc. above	1,850	2,800	3,900	8,200	20,500	—
1802 wide, perfect date	Inc. above	1,825	2,775	3,950	8,250	21,500	—
1802 proof restrike, mintage unrecorded	—	—	—	—	—	—	—
1803 large 3	85,634	1,875	3,000	4,000	8,300	20,500	47,500
1803 small 3	Inc. above	2,000	3,300	4,300	8,600	21,500	48,500
1803 proof restrike, mintage unrecorded	—	—	—	—	—	—	—
1804 15 known	—	—	—	—	— 3,000,000	—	—

Note: 1804, Childs Sale, Aug. 1999, Prf-68, $4,140,000.

Gobrecht Dollar
"C Gobrecht F." in base   Eagle flying left amid stars reverse

KM# 59.1 • 26.7300 g., 0.9000 **Silver**, 0.7734 oz. ASW, 38.1 mm. • **Obv. Designer:** Christian Gobrecht
Rev. Legend: UNITED STATES OF AMERICA **Edge Desc:** Plain.

Date	Mintage	VF-20	XF-40	AU-50	Prf-60
1836	1,000	11,500	14,850	—	25,500

"C. Gobrecht F." in base   Eagle flying in plain field reverse

KM# 59.2 • 26.7300 g., 0.9000 **Silver**, 0.7734 oz. ASW, 38.1 mm. • **Obv. Designer:** Christian Gobrecht.
Edge Desc: Plain.

Date	Mintage	VF-20	XF-40	AU-50	Prf-60
1836 Restrike	—	—	—	—	24,000

"C. Gobrecht F." in base

KM# 59a.1 • 26.7300 g., 0.9000 **Silver**, 0.7734 oz. ASW, 38.1 mm. • **Obv. Legend** Eagle flying left amid
stars. **Edge Desc:** Plain.

Date	Mintage	VF-20	XF-40	AU-50	Prf-60
1836	600	—	—	—	—

"C. Gobrecht F." in base obverse   Eagle flying left amid stars reverse

KM# 59a.2 • 26.7300 g., 0.9000 **Silver**, 0.7734 oz. ASW, 38.1 mm. • **Edge Desc:** Reeded.

Date	Mintage	VF-20	XF-40	AU-50	Prf-60
1836 Restrike	—	—	—	—	—

Designer's name omitted in base   Eagle in plain field reverse

KM# 59a.3 • 26.7300 g., 0.9000 **Silver**, 0.7734 oz. ASW, 38.1 mm. • **Edge Desc:** Reeded.

Date	Mintage	VF-20	XF-40	AU-50	Prf-60
1839	300	—	—	—	38,000

Designer's name omitted in base obverse   Eagle in plain field reverse

KM# 59a.4 • 26.7300 g., 0.9000 **Silver**, 0.7734 oz. ASW, 38.1 mm.

Date	Mintage	VF-20	XF-40	AU-50	Prf-60
1839 Restrike	—	—	—	—	36,500

Note: All other combinations are restrikes of the late 1850's.

Seated Liberty Dollar
Seated Liberty, date below
No motto above eagle reverse

KM# 71 • 26.7300 g., 0.9000 **Silver**, 0.7734 oz. ASW, 38.1 mm. • **Rev. Legend:** UNITED STATES OF AMERICA **Designer:** Christian Gobrecht

Date	Mintage	G-4	VG-8	F-12	VF-20	XF-40	AU-50	MS-60	MS-63	MS-65	Prf-65
1840	61,005	290	320	340	420	680	1,075	4,000	21,500	—	—
1841	173,000	265	295	315	395	610	1,000	2,950	5,500	100,000	—
1842	184,618	265	295	315	395	630	925	2,650	4,700	—	—
1843	165,100	265	295	315	395	465	925	2,750	9,000	—	—
1844	20,000	280	313	360	455	785	1,250	6,450	15,000	100,000	—
1845	24,500	300	335	385	455	900	1,750	10,500	26,500	—	75,000
1846	110,600	275	313	345	490	650	1,100	2,750	5,200	98,000	125,000
1846O	59,000	285	330	370	480	775	1,325	3,250	20,000	—	—
1847	140,750	265	295	315	395	465	900	2,950	7,500	100,000	—
1848	15,000	325	385	515	795	1,250	1,700	4,100	12,500	100,000	—
1849	62,600	275	305	350	420	600	1,000	3,200	7,950	100,000	155,000
1850	7,500	465	545	380	845	1,750	2,650	7,850	15,000	—	80,000
1850O	40,000	335	400	515	750	1,550	3,950	12,850	34,500	—	—
1851	1,300	4,000	4,850	5,750	7,750	18,000	27,000	43,500	68,500	150,000	225,000
1851 Restrike	—	—	—	—	—	—	—	—	—	—	90,000
1852	1,100	3,500	4,150	5,200	7,000	15,000	26,000	38,500	60,000	150,000	200,000
1852 Restrike	—	—	—	—	—	—	—	—	—	—	70,000
1853	46,110	335	400	550	660	1,100	1,425	4,000	7,950	100,000	90,000
1853 Restrike	—	—	—	—	—	—	—	—	—	—	—
1854	33,140	1,100	1,450	2,000	2,850	4,500	5,750	8,500	13,500	100,000	80,000
1855	26,000	900	1,150	1,500	2,150	3,750	4,950	8,850	31,500	—	55,000
1856	63,500	400	450	650	775	1,650	2,850	4,350	11,500	—	39,500
1857	94,000	345	525	675	800	1,500	1,850	3,650	9,000	95,000	39,500
1858 proof only	Est. 800	3,200	3,600	4,000	4,800	7,250	8,850	—	—	—	42,500
Note: Later restrike.											
1859	256,500	285	335	400	515	655	1,000	2,850	5,850	95,000	17,500
1859O	360,000	265	295	315	395	465	800	2,250	4,150	56,000	—
1859S	20,000	330	390	515	750	1,550	3,500	15,000	36,500	—	—
1860	218,930	275	310	380	510	660	900	2,550	5,500	90,000	15,700
1860O	515,000	265	295	315	395	465	800	2,250	3,850	56,000	—
1861	78,500	600	750	900	985	1,750	1,975	2,950	5,650	90,000	15,700
1862	12,090	440	600	850	945	1,450	1,650	3,250	5,750	90,000	15,700
1863	27,660	375	525	575	660	985	1,400	3,250	6,000	90,000	18,000
1864	31,170	350	410	500	565	920	1,375	3,350	6,400	90,000	15,700
1865	47,000	300	350	420	585	1,050	1,750	3,250	6,250	90,000	15,700
1866 2 known without motto	—										

Seated Liberty, date below
IN GOD WE TRUST above eagle reverse

KM# 100 • 26.7300 g., 0.9000 **Silver**, 0.7734 oz. ASW, 38.1 mm. • **Rev. Legend:** UNITED STATES OF AMERICA **Designer:** Christian Gobrecht **Notes:** In 1866 the motto IN GOD WE TRUST was added to the reverse above the eagle.

Date	Mintage	G-4	VG-8	F-12	VF-20	XF-40	AU-50	MS-60	MS-63	MS-65	Prf-65
1866	49,625	320	350	440	590	795	1,250	2,400	5,000	85,000	16,000
1867	47,525	315	345	405	565	670	895	2,435	5,050	85,000	16,000
1868	162,700	325	355	395	535	650	920	3,500	7,350	85,000	16,000
1869	424,300	290	320	370	490	640	985	2,400	5,000	85,000	16,000
1870	416,000	280	320	350	430	595	970	2,300	4,950	67,500	16,000
1870CC	12,462	475	600	825	1,375	3,650	8,250	27,500	44,500	—	—
1870S 12-15 known	—	150,000	235,000	350,000	600,000	850,000	1,350,000	1,850,000	2,500,000	—	—

Note: 1870S, Eliasberg Sale, April 1997, EF-45 to AU-50, $264,000.

Date	Mintage	G-4	VG-8	F-12	VF-20	XF-40	AU-50	MS-60	MS-63	MS-65	Prf-65
1871	1,074,760	270	300	330	410	545	970	2,300	4,950	67,500	16,000
1871CC	1,376	2,000	2,850	4,750	7,450	14,500	25,000	68,500	175,000	—	—
1872	1,106,450	270	300	330	410	495	820	2,300	4,850	67,500	16,000
1872CC	3,150	900	1,400	2,850	4,300	4,850	13,500	28,500	120,000	385,000	—
1872S	9,000	310	365	550	700	2,000	4,500	11,000	26,000	—	—
1873	293,600	275	310	340	420	510	840	2,350	4,900	67,500	16,000
1873CC	2,300	6,250	7,250	11,500	19,000	31,500	43,500	125,000	225,000	625,000	—
1873S none known	700	—	—	—	—	—	—	—	—	—	—

Trade Dollar
Seated Liberty, IN GOD WE TRUST in base above date
TRADE DOLLAR below eagle reverse

KM# 108 • 27.2200 g., 0.9000 **Silver**, 0.7876 oz. ASW, 38.1 mm. • **Rev. Legend:** UNITED STATES OF AMERICA. **Designer:** William Barber

Date	Mintage	G-4	VG-8	F-12	VF-20	XF-40	AU-50	MS-60	MS-65	Prf-65
1873	397,500	108	155	165	190	250	360	1,050	12,500	11,000
1873CC	124,500	230	275	330	450	700	1,475	8,850	122,000	—
1873S	703,000	115	135	155	210	265	385	1,450	15,500	—
1874	987,800	118	130	150	185	250	365	1,150	13,850	10,800
1874CC	1,373,200	235	265	310	375	600	775	3,250	26,500	—
1874S	2,549,000	108	155	160	175	235	285	975	11,000	—
1875	218,900	160	185	375	460	590	850	2,450	13,000	10,700
1875CC	1,573,700	200	255	285	335	510	675	2,150	40,000	—
1875S	4,487,000	98.00	145	150	165	225	275	960	13,750	—
1875S/CC	Inc. above	220	285	375	560	925	1,450	4,650	65,000	—
1876	456,150	108	155	160	175	235	285	950	7,500	10,500
1876CC	509,000	235	265	300	365	525	720	6,000	78,500	—
1876CC	Inc. above	—	—	375	650	1,250	2,000	8,500	—	—

1875 Trade Dollar
Grade F-12

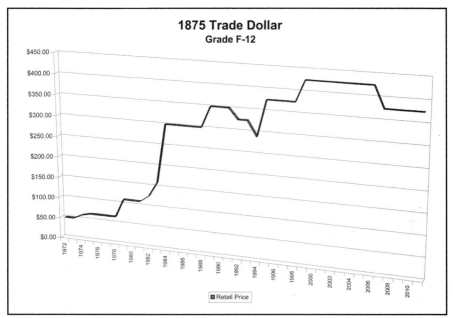

Legend: ■ Retail Price

Date	Mintage	G-4	VG-8	F-12	VF-20	XF-40	AU-50	MS-60	MS-65	Prf-65
1876S	5,227,000	98.00	145	150	165	225	275	940	13,750	—
1877	3,039,710	108	155	160	175	235	285	950	16,000	10,500
1877CC	534,000	235	275	320	410	700	800	2,450	60,000	—
1877S	9,519,000	98.00	145	150	165	225	275	940	13,750	—
1878 proof only	900	—	—	—	1,200	1,300	1,500	—	—	13,500
1878CC	97,000	425	525	710	1,050	2,400	4,200	12,000	112,000	—
1878S	4,162,000	98.00	145	150	165	225	275	940	13,750	—
1879 proof only	1,541	—	—	—	1,175	1,275	1,400	—	—	10,500
1880 proof only	1,987	—	—	—	1,150	1,250	1,350	—	—	10,500
1881 proof only	960	—	—	—	1,200	1,300	1,400	—	—	10,500
1882 proof only	1,097	—	—	—	1,175	1,275	1,375	—	—	10,500
1883 proof only	979	—	—	—	1,200	1,300	1,400	—	—	10,500
1884 proof only	10	—	—	—	—	—	100,000	—	—	—

Note: 1884, Eliasberg Sale, April 1997, Prf-66, $396,000.

1885 proof only	5	—	—	—	—	—	—	—	—	200,000

Note: 1885, Eliasberg Sale, April 1997, Prf-65, $907,500.

Morgan Dollar
Laureate head left, date below flanked by stars
Eagle within 1/2 wreath reverse

| 8 Tail feathers | 7 Tail feathers | 7/8 Tail feathers |

KM# 110 • 26.7300 g., 0.9000 **Silver**, 0.7734 oz. ASW, 38.1 mm. • **Obv. Legend** E.PLURIBUS.UNUM **Rev. Legend:** UNITED STATES OF AMERICA **Designer:** George T. Morgan **Notes:** "65DMPL" values are for coins grading MS-65 deep-mirror prooflike. The 1878 "8 tail feathers" and "7 tail feathers" varieties are distinguished by the number of feathers in the eagle's tail. On the "reverse of 1878" varieties, the top of the top feather in the arrows held by the eagle is straight across and the eagle's breast is concave. On the "reverse of 1879 varieties," the top feather in the arrows held by the eagle is slanted and the eagle's breast is convex. The 1890-CC "tail-bar" variety has a bar extending from the arrow feathers to the wreath on the reverse, the result of a die gouge. The Pittman Act of 1918 authorized the melting of 270 Million pieces of various dates. They were not indivudually recorded.

Date	Mintage	VG-8	F-12	VF-20	XF-40	AU-50	MS-60	MS-63	MS-64	MS-65	65DMPL	Prf-65
1878 8 tail feathers	750,000	41.30	42.30	42.70	46.00	74.00	127	205	385	1,500	23,500	8,350
1878 7 over 8 tail feathers	9,759,550	39.30	40.30	41.70	41.50	75.00	140	260	465	2,385	17,000	—
1878 7 tail feathers, reverse of 1878	Inc. above	39.30	40.30	40.70	42.70	45.00	61.00	102	225	1,215	11,650	11,500
1878 7 tail feathers, reverse of 1879	Inc. above	39.30	40.30	40.70	44.70	49.00	80.00	178	485	2,650	24,500	185,000
1878CC	2,212,000	88.00	96.00	100.00	125	150	225	315	495	1,800	10,800	—
1878S	9,744,000	41.30	42.30	42.70	45.70	47.50	63.00	84.00	120	275	10,500	—
1879	14,807,100	39.30	40.30	40.70	41.70	45.00	51.50	66.00	138	895	17,250	7,550
1879CC	756,000	150	170	260	735	1,850	3,850	6,350	9,350	29,850	49,000	—
1879CC capped CC	Inc. above	145	165	270	700	1,700	3,750	6,100	9,650	46,500	63,500	—
1879O	2,887,000	39.30	40.30	40.70	41.70	50.50	76.00	185	510	3,750	28,500	—
1879S reverse of 1878	9,110,000	39.30	40.30	40.70	42.70	48.50	125	445	1,450	6,500	24,000	—
1879S reverse of 1879	9,110,000	39.30	40.30	40.70	41.70	45.00	54.50	67.00	68.00	245	1,300	—
1880	12,601,335	39.30	40.30	40.70	41.90	45.50	51.50	82.00	135	790	6,350	7,350
1880CC reverse of 1878	591,000	175	210	245	300	355	575	660	1,080	2,375	21,500	—
1880CC 80/79 reverse of 1878	Inc. above	190	230	270	335	410	640	850	1,700	4,000	—	—
1880CC 8/7 reverse of 1878	Inc. above	170	200	235	290	360	600	700	1,300	2,950	—	—
1880CC reverse of 1879	Inc. above	170	200	240	285	345	510	565	675	1,175	9,850	—
1880CC 8/7 high 7 reverse of 1879	Inc. above	175	205	245	290	355	525	620	775	1,800	—	—

1889-O Silver Dollar
Grade F-12

$35.00
$30.00
$25.00
$20.00
$15.00
$10.00
$5.00
$0.00

1972 1974 1976 1978 1980 1982 1984 1986 1988 1990 1992 1994 1996 1998 2000 2002 2004 2006 2008 2010

■ Retail Price

Date	Mintage	VG-8	F-12	VF-20	XF-40	AU-50	MS-60	MS-63	MS-64	MS-65	65DMPL	Prf-65
1880CC 8/7 low 7 reverse of 1879	Inc. above	175	205	245	290	355	525	620	775	1,800	—	—
1880O	5,305,000	39.60	40.30	40.70	42.70	45.50	66.00	420	2,200	28,500	70,000	—
1880S	8,900,000	39.30	40.30	40.70	41.70	45.00	51.50	75.00	115	245	725	—
1880S 8/7 crossbar	—	43.30	45.30	47.70	45.00	75.00	90.00	265	335	450	—	—
1881	9,163,975	39.30	40.30	40.70	41.70	43.00	56.00	69.00	140	625	21,750	7,650
1881CC	296,000	375	385	410	425	460	540	520	550	915	3,050	—
1881O	5,708,000	39.30	40.30	40.70	41.70	43.00	51.50	67.00	195	1,375	35,000	—
1881S	12,760,000	39.30	40.30	40.70	41.70	45.00	51.50	75.00	115	245	850	—
1882	11,101,100	39.30	40.30	40.70	41.70	43.00	53.00	82.00	76.00	550	6,800	7,350
1882CC	1,133,000	92.00	96.00	110	130	155	192	225	260	475	1,950	—
1882O	6,090,000	39.60	40.30	40.70	42.70	45.00	55.50	52.00	100.00	1,175	4,950	—
1882O/S	Inc. above	30.00	40.00	48.00	72.00	120	245	900	2,550	61,500	65,000	—
1882S	9,250,000	39.30	40.30	40.70	41.70	45.00	50.50	79.50	120	247	4,000	—
1883	12,291,039	39.30	40.30	40.70	41.70	43.00	53.50	79.00	132	195	1,650	7,500
1883CC	1,204,000	92.00	96.00	110	125	148	185	210	255	505	1,450	—
1883O	8,725,000	39.30	40.30	40.70	41.70	43.00	48.50	75.00	115	170	1,400	—
1883S	6,250,000	39.30	41.30	44.20	46.70	145	635	2,550	5,500	46,500	94,500	—
1884	14,070,875	39.30	40.30	40.70	41.70	43.00	51.50	78.00	125.5	330	4,350	7,350
1884CC	1,136,000	125	135	140	145	160	185	210	255	470	1,450	—
1884O	9,730,000	39.30	40.30	40.70	41.70	43.00	49.50	75.00	115	277	1,000	—
1884S	3,200,000	39.30	40.80	42.70	43.00	310	6,250	35,500	110,000	235,000	220,000	—
1885	17,787,767	39.30	40.30	40.70	41.70	43.00	48.50	78.00	115	259	845	7,350
1885CC	228,000	550	565	580	585	595	615	645	685	1,075	2,400	—
1885O	9,185,000	39.30	40.30	40.70	41.70	43.00	48.50	75.00	115	245	1,000	—
1885S	1,497,000	41.40	43.90	45.70	64.00	125	220	340	700	2,000	42,500	—
1886	19,963,886	39.30	40.30	40.70	41.70	43.00	48.50	75.00	115	245	1,275	7,350
1886O	10,710,000	39.30	40.30	41.20	49.70	78.00	685	3,550	10,500	190,000	300,000	—
1886S	750,000	47.50	62.50	85.00	90.00	165	300	510	810	3,350	30,000	—
1887	20,290,710	39.30	40.30	40.70	41.70	43.00	48.50	75.00	115	245	1,200	7,350
1887/6	Inc. above	42.80	43.80	45.20	55.00	165	425	585	875	2,300	44,750	—
1887O	11,550,000	39.30	40.30	42.70	44.70	46.00	52.00	110	360	2,300	12,000	—
1887/6O	—	42.80	43.80	45.20	65.00	190	450	2,050	5,850	29,500	—	—
1887S	1,771,000	39.80	40.80	44.20	48.70	51.50	115	250	700	2,750	29,500	—
1888	19,183,833	39.30	40.30	40.70	41.70	43.00	51.50	75.00	115	178	3,000	7,500
1888O	12,150,000	39.30	40.30	40.70	43.70	45.50	51.50	79.00	74.00	615	2,850	—
1888O Hot Lips	Inc. above	55.00	125	250	600	3,000	—	—	—	—	—	—
1888S	657,000	115	190	210	225	235	300	465	915	3,050	16,500	—
1889	21,726,811	39.30	40.30	40.70	41.70	43.00	50.50	75.00	118	340	4,050	7,350
1889CC	350,000	610	935	1,265	2,700	5,500	23,000	43,500	66,000	320,000	—	—
1889O	11,875,000	39.60	40.30	42.70	43.70	45.00	140	375	825	7,000	14,500	—
1889S	700,000	51.00	60.00	65.00	82.00	125	195	365	610	2,000	38,500	—
1890	16,802,590	39.30	40.30	40.70	41.70	43.00	51.50	75.00	145	2,850	19,750	7,350
1890CC	2,309,041	85.00	96.00	105	140	235	450	775	1,400	4,975	15,500	—
1890CC tail bar	Inc. above	155	175	225	400	700	1,450	3,600	5,500	—	—	—
1890O	10,701,000	39.80	40.80	42.70	43.70	45.00	70.00	98.00	275	2,150	10,000	—
1890S	8,230,373	39.60	40.60	41.20	43.70	45.00	60.00	105	280	1,125	10,500	—
1891	8,694,206	39.80	41.30	41.70	43.70	45.00	55.00	165	775	9,000	27,500	7,350
1891CC	1,618,000	85.00	96.00	105	135	215	365	680	1,100	4,150	34,500	—
1891CC Spitting Eagle	Inc. above	105	115	135	185	260	425	900	1,600	6,000	—	—
1891O	7,954,529	39.80	40.70	41.20	43.70	45.50	135	345	700	8,850	37,500	—
1891S	5,296,000	39.80	40.80	41.70	43.70	50.50	56.00	135	280	1,475	21,500	—
1892	1,037,245	42.80	44.30	46.70	50.20	75.00	145	400	960	4,850	20,500	7,500
1892CC	1,352,000	190	210	290	485	725	1,485	1,760	2,450	8,550	39,500	—
1892O	2,744,000	42.80	44.30	46.70	47.70	67.50	150	360	950	7,750	52,500	—
1892S	1,200,000	39.80	40.80	136	315	1,750	35,500	66,500	122,000	205,000	225,000	—
1893	378,792	245	250	260	300	400	700	1,045	2,300	7,000	66,000	7,500
1893CC	677,000	245	315	665	1,475	2,100	3,500	5,100	9,250	70,000	90,000	—
1893O	300,000	205	250	380	620	850	2,250	6,350	16,750	210,000	215,000	—
1893S	100,000	3,300	4,100	5,250	8,250	21,000	90,000	205,000	350,000	715,000	735,000	—
1894	110,972	1,425	1,485	1,550	1,650	1,825	3,500	5,500	10,600	49,000	78,000	7,500
1894O	1,723,000	55.00	57.00	59.00	96.00	310	580	3,450	11,750	63,500	61,500	—
1894S	1,260,000	62.00	65.00	110	150	510	725	1,075	1,825	5,650	26,000	—
1895 proof only	12,880	21,500	29,500	36,500	38,000	40,000	—	—	—	—	—	75,000
1895O	450,000	315	350	480	585	1,225	15,500	57,500	85,000	165,000	—	—
1895S	400,000	495	625	935	1,275	1,950	3,850	6,650	7,750	27,500	42,500	—
1896	9,967,762	39.30	40.30	40.70	41.70	43.00	48.50	75.00	115	185	1,450	7,350
1896O	4,900,000	39.80	41.30	41.70	49.20	155	1,450	71,500	46,000	180,000	180,000	—
1896S	5,000,000	42.80	43.80	60.00	235	895	1,775	3,450	4,850	19,500	110,000	—
1897	2,822,731	39.30	40.30	40.70	41.70	43.00	51.50	76.00	122	345	3,950	7,350
1897O	4,004,000	39.80	41.30	42.70	57.70	110	735	4,850	15,900	70,000	72,500	—
1897S	5,825,000	39.80	41.30	41.70	43.70	48.50	58.00	127	155	575	3,250	—
1898	5,884,735	39.30	40.30	40.70	42.20	43.00	51.50	76.00	118	240	1,440	7,350
1898O	4,440,000	39.30	40.30	40.70	42.20	43.00	52.00	76.00	116	250	1,000	—
1898S	4,102,000	41.30	42.80	43.20	55.00	105	260	465	625	2,300	18,000	—
1899	330,846	170	185	215	220	248	295	310	380	950	2,850	7,350
1899O	12,290,000	39.30	40.30	40.70	41.70	43.00	51.50	75.00	122	287	1,550	—

DOLLAR

DOLLAR

Date	Mintage	VG-8	F-12	VF-20	XF-40	AU-50	MS-60	MS-63	MS-64	MS-65	65DMPL	Prf-65
1899S	2,562,000	41.80	42.80	43.70	62.50	125	320	485	775	2,075	26,000	—
1900	8,880,938	39.30	40.30	40.70	41.70	43.00	51.50	75.00	122	195	42,500	7,350
1900O	12,590,000	39.30	40.30	40.70	41.70	43.00	51.50	75.00	122	180	6,250	—
1900O/CC	Inc. above	39.00	47.50	62.50	100.00	190	285	740	965	1,975	19,000	—
1900S	3,540,000	41.30	45.80	46.20	49.20	85.00	310	400	615	1,575	38,500	—
1901	6,962,813	39.00	40.00	57.50	110	350	2,350	17,250	55,000	375,000	—	7,850
1901 doubled die reverse	Inc. above	275	450	900	2,000	3,850	—	—	—	—	—	—
1901O	13,320,000	41.30	42.30	42.70	43.70	46.00	51.50	75.00	118	185	10,000	—
1901S	2,284,000	41.30	42.80	43.70	48.00	220	470	750	1,050	3,400	24,500	—
1902	7,994,777	41.30	42.30	42.70	43.70	45.00	46.50	135	145	465	19,500	7,350
1902O	8,636,000	39.30	40.30	40.70	41.70	43.00	50.50	75.00	116	259	16,000	—
1902S	1,530,000	93.50	102	160	220	315	425	630	950	2,800	15,000	—
1903	4,652,755	48.00	50.00	52.00	58.00	60.00	75.00	85.00	105	285	36,850	7,350
1903O	4,450,000	325	350	375	395	400	412	455	495	685	5,950	—
1903S	1,241,000	95.00	130	215	425	1,750	3,950	6,500	7,150	11,750	40,000	—
1903S Micro S	Inc. above	135	225	450	1,150	3,000	—	—	—	—	—	—
1904	2,788,650	41.30	42.30	42.70	43.70	45.00	78.00	255	575	3,100	86,500	7,350
1904O	3,720,000	39.80	41.80	42.20	43.70	45.00	53.00	76.00	115	263	1,175	—
1904S	2,304,000	39.80	47.50	87.00	230	570	1,225	3,800	5,000	10,500	19,000	—
1921	44,690,000	37.80	38.30	39.10	40.00	41.30	50.90	69.00	88.00	185	11,500	—
1921D	20,345,000	38.20	38.70	39.50	40.40	41.70	52.00	83.00	145	375	10,000	—
1921S	21,695,000	38.20	38.70	39.50	40.40	41.70	51.50	82.00	137.5	1,350	31,000	—

Peace Dollar
Liberty Head left obverse
Eagle facing right perched on rock reverse

Mint mark

KM# 150 • 26.7300 g., 0.9000 **Silver**, 0.7734 oz. ASW, 38.1 mm. • **Designer:** Anthony DeFrancisci

Date	Mintage	G-4	VG-8	F-12	VF-20	XF-40	AU-50	MS-60	MS-63	MS-64	MS-65
1921	1,006,473	95.00	120	130	136	146	160	260	440	700	1,980
1922	51,737,000	37.90	38.90	39.80	40.30	42.10	44.00	46.50	70.00	99.00	225
1922D	15,063,000	37.90	39.10	40.10	40.50	42.40	44.90	47.50	53.00	105	550
1922S	17,475,000	37.90	39.10	40.10	40.50	42.40	44.90	49.00	69.00	245	2,700
1923	30,800,000	37.90	38.90	39.80	40.30	42.10	44.00	46.50	70.00	99.00	220
1923D	6,811,000	37.90	39.10	40.10	40.50	42.40	48.00	48.50	140	330	1,250
1923S	19,020,000	37.90	39.10	40.10	40.50	42.40	44.90	47.40	74.00	360	8,500
1924	11,811,000	37.90	38.90	40.10	40.30	42.10	44.00	48.50	70.00	99.00	243
1924S	1,728,000	39.90	41.90	44.80	46.30	44.00	66.50	190	530	1,375	10,000
1925	10,198,000	37.90	38.90	39.00	40.30	42.10	44.00	48.50	70.00	99.00	232
1925S	1,610,000	38.80	39.80	40.70	44.30	42.10	46.00	77.00	210	965	25,000
1926	1,939,000	38.80	39.80	40.90	41.60	42.10	44.00	47.40	72.00	112	475
1926D	2,348,700	38.80	39.80	40.70	41.40	42.10	44.00	66.00	190	310	910
1926S	6,980,000	38.50	39.50	40.40	40.90	42.70	47.00	51.50	98.00	235	990
1927	848,000	39.90	41.90	44.80	46.30	48.10	50.00	70.00	185	535	3,350
1927D	1,268,900	38.50	39.90	40.80	43.30	46.10	80.00	170	350	865	5,450
1927S	866,000	38.50	39.90	40.80	43.30	46.10	80.00	170	440	1,225	10,850
1928	360,649	345	385	390	395	400	415	495	875	1,100	4,650
1928S Large S	1,632,000	39.00	42.00	46.00	50.00	56.00	90.00	220	800	2,100	29,500
1928S Small S	Inc. above	38.50	39.90	40.80	41.30	44.10	66.00	170	495	885	24,850
1934	954,057	39.40	40.90	42.80	44.30	46.10	48.00	120	215	400	735
1934D Large D	1,569,500	41.40	44.10	46.50	48.00	49.80	65.00	165	600	925	3,000
1934D Small D	Inc. above	40.70	41.80	43.50	44.00	45.80	46.00	155	385	585	1,800
1934S	1,011,000	32.00	38.00	53.00	80.00	172	475	1,800	3,200	4,850	7,750
1935	1,576,000	40.70	41.80	43.50	44.40	46.10	48.00	65.00	105	205	765
1935S 3 Rays	1,964,000	40.70	41.80	43.50	44.30	47.60	92.00	245	350	550	1,125
1935S 4 Rays	—	41.10	43.60	43.80	46.10	50.10	105	275	440	625	1,350

Eisenhower Dollar

Bicentennial design, moon behind Liberty Bell reverse

Type I	Type II
Squared "T"	Slant-top "T"

KM# 203 • 22.8000 g., **Copper-Nickel Clad Copper**, 38 mm. • **Designer:** Frank Gasparro

Date	Mintage	Proof	MS-63	Prf-65
1971	47,799,000	—	10.00	—
1971D	68,587,424	—	8.00	—
1972 Low Relief	75,890,000	—	18.00	—
1972 High Relief	Inc. above	—	175	—
1972 Modified High Relief	Inc. above	—	35.00	—
1972D	92,548,511	—	9.00	—
1973	2,000,056	—	12.00	—
1973D	2,000,000	—	12.00	—
1973S	—(2,769,624)	—	—	12.00
1974	27,366,000	—	15.00	—
1974D	35,466,000	—	7.50	—
1974S	—(2,617,350)	—	—	11.00

KM# 203a • 24.5900 g., 0.4000 **Silver**, 0.3162 oz. ASW, 38.1 mm. • **Designer:** Frank Gasparro

Date	Mintage	Proof	MS-63	Prf-65
1971S	6,868,530	—	15.80	11.00
1971S	—(4,265,234)	—	—	—
1971S Peg Leg "R" Variety	Inc. above	—	—	17.00
1971S Partial Peg Leg "R" Variety	Inc. above	—	—	18.00
1972S	2,193,056	—	15.80	—
1972S	—(1,811,631)	—	—	9.00
1973S	1,833,140	—	15.80	—
1973S	—(1,005,617)	—	—	45.00
1974S	1,720,000	—	15.80	—
1974S	—(1,306,579)	—	—	11.00

KM# 206 • 22.6800 g., **Copper-Nickel Clad Copper**, 38.1 mm. • **Rev. Designer:** Dennis R. Williams **Notes:** In 1976 the lettering on the reverse was changed to thinner letters, resulting in the Type II variety for that year. The Type I variety was minted 1975 and dated 1976.

Date	Mintage	Proof	MS-63	Prf-65
1976 type I	117,337,000	—	12.00	—
1976 type II	Inc. above	—	8.00	—
1976D type I	103,228,274	—	7.50	—
1976D type II	Inc. above	—	6.00	—
1976S type I	—(2,909,369)	—	—	10.00
1976S type II	—(4,149,730)	—	—	9.00

KM# 206a • 24.5900 g., 0.4000 **Silver**, 0.3162 oz. ASW • **Rev. Designer:** Dennis R. Williams

Date	Mintage	Proof	MS-63	Prf-65
1976S	—(3,998,621)	—	—	—
1976S	4,908,319	—	15.80	14.00

Regular design resumed reverse

KM# A203 • **Copper-Nickel Clad Copper**, 38.1 mm

Date	Mintage	Proof	MS-63	Prf-65
1977	12,596,000	—	5.00	—
1977D	32,983,006	—	4.00	—
1977S	—(3,251,152)	—	—	9.00
1978	25,702,000	—	4.00	—
1978D	33,012,890	—	4.75	—
1978S	—(3,127,788)	—	—	9.00

DOLLAR

Susan B. Anthony Dollar

Susan B. Anthony bust right obverse
Eagle landing on moon, symbolic of
Apollo manned moon landing reverse

KM# 207 • 8.1000 g., **Copper-Nickel Clad Copper**, 26.5 mm. • **Designer:** Frank Gasparro **Edge Desc:** Reeded **Notes:** The 1979-S and 1981-S Type II coins have a clearer mint mark than the Type I varieties for those years.

Date	Mintage	MS-63	Prf-65
1979P Near date	360,222,000	70.00	—
1979P	Inc. above	2.50	—
1979D	288,015,744	3.00	—
1979S Proof, Type I	3,677,175	—	8.00
1979S Proof, Type II	Inc. above	—	110
1979S	109,576,000	3.00	—
1980P	27,610,000	3.00	—
1980D	41,628,708	3.00	—
1980S	20,422,000	3.50	—
1980S Proof	3,547,030	—	8.00
1981P	3,000,000	7.50	—
1981D	3,250,000	7.50	—
1981S	3,492,000	7.50	—
1981S Proof, Type I	4,063,083	—	8.00
1981S Proof, Type II	Inc. above	—	230
1999P	29,592,000	4.00	—
1999P Proof	Est. 750,000	—	25.00
1999D	11,776,000	4.00	—

Sacagawea Dollar

Sacagawea bust right, with
baby on back obverse
Eagle in flight left reverse

KM# 310 • 8.0700 g., **Copper-Zinc-Manganese-Nickel Clad Copper**, 26.5 mm. •

Date	Mintage	MS-63	Prf-65
2000P	767,140,000	2.00	—
2000D	518,916,000	2.00	—
2000S	4,048,000	—	10.00
2001P	62,468,000	2.00	—
2001D	70,939,500	2.00	—
2001S	3,190,000	—	100.00
2002P	3,865,610	2.00	—
2002D	3,732,000	2.00	—
2002S	3,210,000	—	28.50
2003P	3,080,000	3.00	—
2003D	3,080,000	3.00	—
2003S	3,300,000	—	20.00
2004P	2,660,000	2.50	—

Date	Mintage	MS-63	Prf-65
2004D	2,660,000	2.50	—
2004S	2,965,000	—	22.50
2005P	2,520,000	2.50	—
2005D	2,520,000	2.50	—
2005S	3,273,000	—	22.50
2006P	4,900,000	2.50	—
2006D	2,800,000	5.00	—
2006S	3,028,828	—	22.50
2007P	3,640,000	2.50	—
2007D	3,920,000	2.50	—
2007S	2,563,563	—	22.50
2008P	9,800,000	2.50	—
2008D	14,840,000	2.50	—
2008S	—	—	22.50

Native American Dollar - Planting crops reverse

Sacagawea bust right with
baby on back obverse
Native American female planting corn,
beans and squash reverse

KM# 467 • 8.0700 g., **Copper-Zinc-Manganese-Nickel Clad Copper**, 26.5 mm. •

Date	Mintage	MS-63	Prf-65
2009P	37,380,000	—	—
2009D	33,880,000	—	—
2009S	—	—	22.50

Native American Dollar - Hiawatha belt reverse

Sacagawea bust right with
baby on back obverse
Hiawatha belt and bundle of
five arrows reverse

KM# 474 • 8.0700 g., **Copper-Zinc-Manganese-Nickel Clad Copper**, 26.5 mm. •

Date	Mintage	MS-63	Prf-65
2010P	—	—	—
2010D	—	—	—
2010S	—	—	22.50

Native American Dollar - Peace Pipe reverse

Sacagawea bust right with baby on back obverse   Hands passing peace pipe reverse

KM# 503 • 8.0700 g., **Copper-Zinc-Manganese-Nickel Clad Copper**, 26.5 mm. •

Date	Mintage	MS-63	Prf-65
2011P	—	—	—
2011D	—	—	—
2011S	—	—	8.00

Presidential Dollars

George Washington

KM# 401 • 8.0700 g., **Copper-Zinc-Manganese-Nickel Clad Copper**, 26.5 mm. • **Edge Lettering:** IN GOD WE TRUST date, mint mark E PLURIBUS UNUM **Notes:** Date and mint mark incuse on edge.

Date	Mintage	MS-63	MS-65	Prf-65
2007P	176,680,000	2.00	5.00	—
(2007) Plain edge error	Inc. above	75.00	—	—
2007D	163,680,000	2.00	5.00	—
2007S	3,883,103	—	—	8.00

John Adams

KM# 402 • 8.0700 g., **Copper-Zinc-Manganese-Nickel Clad Copper**, 26.5 mm. • **Edge Lettering:** IN GOD WE TRUST date, mint mark E PLURIBUS UNUM **Notes:** Date and mint mark incuse on edge.

Date	Mintage	MS-63	MS-65	Prf-65
2007P	112,420,000	2.00	5.00	—
2007P Double edge lettering	Inc. above	250	—	—
2007D	112,140,000	2.00	5.00	—
2007S	3,877,409	—	—	8.00

James Madison

KM# 404 • 8.0700 g., **Copper-Zinc-Manganese-Nickel Clad Copper**, 26.5 mm. • **Edge Lettering:** IN GOD WE TRUST date, mint mark E PLURIBUS UNUM **Notes:** Date and mint mark incuse on edge.

Date	Mintage	MS-63	MS-65	Prf-65
2007P	84,560,000	2.00	5.00	—
2007D	87,780,000	2.00	5.00	—
2007S	3,876,829	—	—	8.00

Thomas Jefferson

KM# 403 • 8.0700 g., **Copper-Zinc-Manganese-Nickel Clad Copper**, 26.5 mm. • **Edge Lettering:** IN GOD WE TRUST date, mint mark E PLURIBUS UNUM **Notes:** Date and mint mark incuse on edge.

Date	Mintage	MS-63	MS-65	Prf-65
2007P	100,800,000	2.00	5.00	—
2007D	102,810,000	2.00	5.00	—
2007S	3,877,573	—	—	8.00

DOLLAR

Andrew Jackson

KM# 428 • 8.0700 g., **Copper-Zinc-Manganese-Nickel Clad Copper**, 26.5 mm. • **Edge Lettering:** IN GOD WE TRUST date, mint mark E PLURIBUS UNUM **Notes:** Date and mint mark incuse on edge.

Date	Mintage	MS-63	MS-65	Prf-65
2008P	61,180,000	2.00	5.00	—
2008D	61,070,000	2.00	5.00	—
2008S	3,000,000	—	—	8.00

Martin van Buren

KM# 429 • 8.0700 g., **Copper-Zinc-Manganese-Nickel Clad Copper**, 26.5 mm. • **Edge Lettering:** IN GOD WE TRUST date, mint mark E PLURIBUS UNUM **Notes:** Date and mint mark incuse on edge.

Date	Mintage	MS-63	MS-65	Prf-65
2008P	51,520,000	2.00	5.00	—
2008D	50,960,000	2.00	5.00	—
2008S	3,000,000	—	—	8.00

James Monroe

KM# 426 • 8.0700 g., **Copper-Zinc-Manganese-Nickel Clad Copper**, Date and mint mark incuse on edge., 26.5 mm. • **Edge Lettering:** IN GOD WE TRUST date, mint mark E PLURIBUS UNUM

Date	Mintage	MS-63	MS-65	Prf-65
2008P	64,260,000	2.00	5.00	—
2008D	60,230,000	2.00	5.00	—
2008S	3,000,000	—	—	8.00

James K. Polk

KM# 452 • 8.0700 g., **Copper-Zinc-Manganese-Nickel Clad Copper**, 26.5 mm. • **Edge Lettering:** E PLURIBUS UNUM, date, mint mark **Notes:** Date and mint mark on edge

Date	Mintage	MS-63	MS-65	Prf-65
2009P	46,620,000	2.00	5.00	—
2009D	41,720,000	2.00	5.00	—
2009S	—	—	—	8.00

John Quincy Adams

KM# 427 • 8.0700 g., **Copper-Zinc-Manganese-Nickel Clad Copper**, 26.5 mm. • **Edge Lettering:** IN GOD WE TRUST date, mint mark E PLURIBUS UNUM **Notes:** Date and mint mark incuse on edge.

Date	Mintage	MS-63	MS-65	Prf-65
2008P	57,540,000	2.00	5.00	—
2008D	57,720,000	2.00	5.00	—
2008S	3,000,000	—	—	8.00

John Tyler

KM# 451 • 8.0700 g., **Copper-Zinc-Manganese-Nickel Clad Copper**, 26.5 mm. • **Edge Lettering:** E PLURIBUS UNUM, date, mint mark **Notes:** Date and mint mark on edge.

Date	Mintage	MS-63	MS-65	Prf-65
2009P	43,540,000	2.00	5.00	—
2009D	43,540,000	2.00	5.00	—
2009S	—	—	—	8.00

William Henry Harrison

KM# 450 • 8.0700 g., **Copper-Zinc-Manganese-Nickel Clad Copper**, 26.5 mm. • **Edge Lettering:** E PLURIBUS UNUM, date, mint mark **Notes:** Date and mint mark on edge

Date	Mintage	MS-63	MS-65	Prf-65
2009P	43,260,000	2.00	5.00	—
2009D	55,160,000	2.00	5.00	—
2009S	—	—	—	8.00

Zachary Taylor

KM# 453 • 8.0700 g., **Copper-Zinc-Manganese-Nickel Clad Copper**, 26.5 mm. • **Edge Lettering:** E PLURIBUS UNUM, date, mint mark **Notes:** Date and mint mark on edge.

Date	Mintage	MS-63	MS-65	Prf-65
2009P	41,580,000	2.00	5.00	—
2009D	36,680,000	2.00	5.00	—
2009S	—	—	—	8.00

Abraham Lincoln

KM# 478 • 8.0700 g., **Copper-Zinc-Manganese-Nickel Clad Copper**, 26.5 mm. • **Edge Lettering:** E PLURIBUS UNUM, date, mint mark **Notes:** Date and mint mark on edge.

Date	Mintage	MS-63	MS-65	Prf-65
2010P	—	2.00	5.00	—
2010D	—	2.00	5.00	—
2010S	—	—	—	8.00

Franklin Pierce

KM# 476 • 8.0700 g., **Copper-Zinc-Manganese-Nickel Clad Copper**, 26.5 mm. • **Edge Lettering:** E PLURIBUS UNUM, date, mint mark **Notes:** Date and mint mark on edge.

Date	Mintage	MS-63	MS-65	Prf-65
2010P	—	2.00	5.00	—
2010D	—	2.00	5.00	—
2010S	—	—	—	8.00

James Buchanan

KM# 477 • 8.0700 g., **Copper-Zinc-Manganese-Nickel Clad Copper**, 26.5 mm. • **Edge Lettering:** E PLURIBUS UNUM, date, mint mark **Notes:** Date and mint mark on edge.

Date	Mintage	MS-63	MS-65	Prf-65
2010P	—	2.00	5.00	—
2010D	—	2.00	5.00	—
2010S	—	—	—	8.00

Millard Filmore

KM# 475 • 8.0700 g., **Copper-Zinc-Manganese-Nickel Clad Copper**, 26.5 mm. • **Edge Lettering:** E PLURIBUS UNUM, date, mint mark **Notes:** Date and mint mark on edge.

Date	Mintage	MS-63	MS-65	Prf-65
2010P	—	2.00	5.00	—
2010D	—	2.00	5.00	—
2010S	—	—	—	8.00

Andrew Johnson

KM# 499 • 8.0700 g., **Copper-Zinc-Manganese-Nickel Clad Copper**, 26.5 mm. • **Edge Lettering:** E PLURIBUS UNUM, date, mint mark **Notes:** Date and mint mark on edge.

Date	Mintage	MS-63	MS-65	Prf-65
2011P	—	2.00	5.00	—
2011D	—	2.00	5.00	—
2011S	—	—	—	8.00

Rutherford B. Hayes

KM# 501 • 8.0700 g., **Copper-Zinc-Manganese-Nickel Clad Copper**, 26.5 mm. • **Edge Lettering:** E PLURIBUS UNUM, date, mint mark **Notes:** Date and mint mark on edge.

Date	Mintage	MS-63	MS-65	Prf-65
2011P	—	2.00	5.00	—
2011D	—	2.00	5.00	—
2011S	—	—	—	8.00

James Garfield

KM# 502 • 8.0700 g., **Copper-Zinc-Manganese-Nickel Clad Copper**, 26.5 mm. • **Edge Lettering:** E PLURIBUS UNUM, date, mint mark **Notes:** Date and mint mark on edge.

Date	Mintage	MS-63	MS-65	Prf-65
2011P	—	2.00	5.00	—
2011D	—	2.00	5.00	—
2011S	—	—	—	8.00

Ulysses S. Grant

KM# 500 • 8.0700 g., **Copper-Zinc-Manganese-Nickel Clad Copper**, 26.5 mm. • **Edge Lettering:** E PLURIBUS UNUM, date, mint mark **Notes:** Date and mint mark on edge.

Date	Mintage	MS-63	MS-65	Prf-65
2011P	—	2.00	5.00	—
2011D	—	2.00	5.00	—
2011S	—	—	—	8.00

GOLD

Liberty Head - Type 1
Liberty head left within circle of stars obverse   Value, date within 3/4 wreath reverse

KM# 73 • 1.6720 g., 0.9000 **Gold**, 0.0484 oz. AGW, 13 mm. • **Rev. Legend:** UNITED STATES OF AMERICA **Designer:** James B. Longacre **Notes:** On the "closed wreath" varieties of 1849, the wreath on the reverse extends closer to the numeral 1.

Date	Mintage	F-12	VF-20	XF-40	AU-50	MS-60
1849 open wreath	688,567	175	225	265	300	650
1849 small head, no L	—	—	—	—	—	—
1849 closed wreath	Inc. above	175	210	245	270	335
1849C closed wreath	11,634	800	950	1,450	2,400	8,850
1849C open wreath	Inc. above	135,000	240,000	320,000	475,000	600,000
1849D open wreath	21,588	1,050	1,300	1,875	2,600	6,000
1849O open wreath	215,000	195	235	310	390	800
1850	481,953	175	210	245	270	335
1850C	6,966	900	1,150	1,600	2,350	9,000
1850D	8,382	1,050	1,250	1,725	2,950	12,500
1850O	14,000	200	275	390	775	3,300
1851	3,317,671	175	210	245	270	335
1851C	41,267	840	1,150	1,500	1,700	3,150
1851D	9,882	1,000	1,250	1,675	2,500	5,650
1851O	290,000	160	195	240	265	775

Date	Mintage	F-12	VF-20	XF-40	AU-50	MS-60
1852	2,045,351	175	210	245	270	335
1852C	9,434	845	1,040	1,400	1,700	5,100
1852D	6,360	1,025	1,250	1,675	2,300	10,000
1852O	140,000	130	175	260	385	1,400
1853	4,076,051	175	210	245	270	335
1853C	11,515	900	1,100	1,400	2,000	5,600
1853D	6,583	1,040	1,250	1,700	2,650	9,700
1853O	290,000	135	160	235	270	665
1854	736,709	175	210	245	270	335
1854D	2,935	1,050	1,400	2,350	6,000	13,000
1854S	14,632	260	360	525	775	2,450

Indian Head - Type 2
Indian head with headdress left obverse
Value, date within wreath reverse

KM# 83 • 1.6720 g., 0.9000 **Gold**, 0.0484 oz. AGW, 15 mm. • **Obv. Legend** UNITED STATES OF AMERICA **Designer:** James B. Longacre

Date	Mintage	F-12	VF-20	XF-40	AU-50	MS-60
1854	902,736	250	280	410	535	1,680
1855	758,269	250	280	410	535	1,680
1855C	9,803	975	1,450	3,750	11,500	33,000
1855D	1,811	3,250	4,750	9,800	22,000	48,000
1855O	55,000	345	440	600	1,500	7,800
1856S	24,600	525	820	1,325	2,500	8,650

Indian Head - Type 3
Indian head with headdress left obverse
Value, date within wreath reverse

KM# 86 • 1.6720 g., 0.9000 **Gold**, 0.0484 oz. AGW, 15 mm. • **Obv. Legend** UNITED STATES OF AMERICA **Designer:** James B. Longacre **Notes:** The 1856 varieties are distinguished by whether the 5 in the date is slanted or upright. The 1873 varieties are distinguished by the amount of space between the upper left and lower left serifs in the 3.

Date	Mintage	F-12	VF-20	XF-40	AU-50	MS-60	Prf-65
1856 upright 5	1,762,936	225	260	310	335	510	—
1856 slanted 5	Inc. above	220	250	285	300	360	55,000
1856D	1,460	2,350	3,650	5,800	8,000	32,000	—
1857	774,789	210	245	285	300	360	32,000
1857C	13,280	900	1,150	1,750	3,750	13,250	—
1857D	3,533	1,000	1,300	2,300	4,400	11,000	—
1857S	10,000	260	520	650	1,300	6,200	—
1858	117,995	210	245	285	300	360	28,500
1858D	3,477	1,025	1,250	1,600	2,850	10,000	—
1858S	10,000	300	400	575	1,450	5,350	—
1859	168,244	210	245	285	300	360	17,000
1859C	5,235	885	1,050	1,700	4,250	9,850	—
1859D	4,952	1,050	1,500	2,100	3,250	10,500	—
1859S	15,000	210	265	525	1,250	5,500	—
1860	36,668	210	245	285	300	360	16,500
1860D	1,566	2,150	2,500	4,200	7,000	19,500	—
1860S	13,000	300	380	500	750	2,900	—
1861	527,499	210	245	285	300	360	14,850
1861D mintage unrecorded	—	4,950	7,000	11,000	21,000	41,500	—
1862	1,361,390	210	245	285	300	360	15,000
1863	6,250	370	500	925	2,100	3,900	18,000
1864	5,950	290	370	475	825	1,050	18,000
1865	3,725	290	370	590	750	1,600	18,000
1866	7,130	300	385	470	685	1,025	18,000
1867	5,250	325	420	525	675	1,160	17,500
1868	10,525	265	290	415	500	1,025	19,000
1869	5,925	315	460	530	725	1,150	17,000

DOLLAR

Date	Mintage	F-12	VF-20	XF-40	AU-50	MS-60	Prf-65
1870	6,335	255	290	410	500	875	16,000
1870S	3,000	300	475	785	1,250	2,650	—
1871	3,930	260	290	390	480	750	18,000
1872	3,530	260	295	400	480	975	18,500
1873 closed 3	125,125	325	425	825	950	1,650	—
1873 open 3	Inc. above	210	245	285	300	360	—
1874	198,820	210	245	285	300	360	30,000
1875	420	1,650	2,350	4,650	5,200	10,000	32,500
1876	3,245	240	300	360	475	725	16,750
1877	3,920	210	210	340	460	725	18,000
1878	3,020	195	250	365	480	675	15,500
1879	3,030	210	225	285	330	525	14,000
1880	1,636	235	180	300	300	475	14,000
1881	7,707	235	270	300	300	460	11,500
1882	5,125	245	275	300	300	460	10,500
1883	11,007	235	265	300	300	460	11,000
1884	6,236	235	265	—	300	460	10,000
1885	12,261	235	265	300	300	460	10,000
1886	6,016	235	265	300	300	460	10,000
1887	8,543	235	265	300	300	460	10,000
1888	16,580	235	265	300	300	460	10,000
1889	30,729	235	265	300	300	390	10,000

$2.50 (QUARTER EAGLE)

GOLD
Liberty Cap

Liberty cap on head, right, flanked by stars obverse
Heraldic eagle reverse

KM# 27 • 4.3700 g., 0.9160 **Gold**, 0.1287 oz. AGW, 20 mm. • **Obv. Legend** LIBERTY **Rev. Legend:** UNITED STATES OF AMERICA **Designer:** Robert Scot **Notes:** The 1796 "no stars" variety does not have stars on the obverse. The 1804 varieties are distinguished by the number of stars on the obverse.

Date	Mintage	F-12	VF-20	XF-40	MS-60
1796 no stars	963	55,000	71,500	100,000	245,000
1796 stars	432	26,500	32,500	65,000	185,000
1797	427	20,000	25,000	45,000	125,000
1798 close date	1,094	6,250	8,650	16,500	60,000
1798 wide date	Inc. above	5,250	7,650	15,500	57,500
1802/1	3,035	4,250	6,650	14,500	34,500
1804 13-star reverse	3,327	45,000	65,000	125,000	—
1804 14-star reverse	Inc. above	4,550	7,150	15,500	46,500
1805	1,781	4,250	6,650	14,500	37,000
1806/4	1,616	4,250	6,650	15,000	38,000
1806/5	Inc. above	6,250	8,650	21,500	95,000
1807	6,812	4,250	6,650	14,500	34,500

Turban Head
Turban on head left flanked by stars
Banner above eagle reverse

KM# 40 • 4.3700 g., 0.9160 **Gold**, 0.1287 oz. AGW, 20 mm. • **Rev. Legend:** UNITED STATES OF AMERICA **Designer:** John Reich

Date	Mintage	F-12	VF-20	XF-40	MS-60
1808	2,710	26,500	36,500	54,500	175,000

Turban on head left within circle of stars
Banner above eagle reverse

KM# 46 • 4.3700 g., 0.9160 **Gold**, 0.1287 oz. AGW, 18.5 mm. • **Rev. Legend:** UNITED STATES OF AMERICA **Designer:** John Reich

Date	Mintage	F-12	VF-20	XF-40	MS-60
1821	6,448	5,950	7,150	10,350	30,000
1824/21	2,600	5,950	7,150	10,250	29,500
1825	4,434	5,950	7,150	10,250	27,500
1826/25	760	6,450	7,900	11,000	100,000
1827	2,800	6,050	7,350	10,750	29,500

Turban on head left within circle of stars
Banner above eagle reverse

KM# 49 • 4.3700 g., 0.9160 **Gold**, 0.1287 oz. AGW, 18.2 mm. • **Rev. Legend:** UNITED STATES OF AMERICA **Designer:** John Reich

Date	Mintage	F-12	VF-20	XF-40	MS-60
1829	3,403	5,400	6,250	7,950	18,500
1830	4,540	5,400	6,250	7,950	18,500
1831	4,520	5,400	6,250	7,950	19,000
1832	4,400	5,400	6,250	7,950	18,500
1833	4,160	5,400	6,250	7,950	19,000
1834	4,000	8,900	11,750	15,450	48,500

Classic Head
Classic head left within circle of stars
No motto above eagle reverse

KM# 56 • 4.1800 g., 0.8990 **Gold**, 0.1208 oz. AGW, 18.2 mm. • **Rev. Legend:** UNITED STATES OF AMERICA **Designer:** William Kneass

Date	Mintage	VF-20	XF-40	AU-50	MS-60	MS-65
1834	112,234	475	675	965	3,300	27,000
1835	131,402	475	675	950	3,200	32,000
1836	547,986	475	675	940	3,100	29,000
1837	45,080	500	800	1,500	4,000	35,000
1838	47,030	500	625	1,100	3,200	30,000
1838C	7,880	1,700	3,000	8,000	27,000	55,000
1839	27,021	500	900	1,900	5,500	—
1839C	18,140	1,500	2,650	4,500	26,500	—
1839/8	Inc. above	—	—	—	—	—
1839D	13,674	1,750	3,450	8,000	24,000	—
1839O	17,781	700	1,100	2,500	7,250	—

Coronet Head
Coronet head left within circle of stars
No motto above eagle reverse

1848 "Cal." reverse

KM# 72 • 4.1800 g., 0.9000 **Gold**, 0.1209 oz. AGW, 18 mm. • **Rev. Legend:** UNITED STATES OF AMERICA **Designer:** Christian Gobrecht

Date	Mintage	F-12	VF-20	XF-40	AU-50	MS-60	Prf-65
1840	18,859	160	190	900	2,950	6,000	—
1840C	12,822	975	1,400	1,600	6,000	13,000	—
1840D	3,532	2,000	3,200	8,700	15,500	35,000	—
1840O	33,580	250	400	825	2,100	11,000	—
1841	—	—	48,000	85,000	96,000	—	—
1841C	10,281	750	1,500	2,000	3,500	18,500	—
1841D	4,164	950	2,100	4,750	11,000	25,000	—
1842	2,823	500	900	2,600	6,500	20,000	140,000
1842C	6,729	700	1,700	3,500	8,000	27,000	—
1842D	4,643	900	2,100	4,000	11,750	38,000	—
1842O	19,800	240	370	1,200	2,500	14,000	—
1843	100,546	160	180	450	915	3,000	140,000
1843C small date, Crosslet 4	26,064	1,500	2,400	5,500	9,000	29,000	—
1843C large date, Plain 4	Inc. above	800	1,600	2,200	3,500	8,800	—
1843D small date, Crosslet 4	36,209	920	1,800	2,350	3,250	10,500	—
1843O small date, Crosslet 4	288,002	165	190	250	350	1,700	—
1843O large date, Plain 4	76,000	210	260	465	1,600	8,000	—
1844	6,784	225	365	850	2,000	7,500	140,000
1844C	11,622	700	1,600	2,600	7,000	20,000	—
1844D	17,332	785	1,650	2,200	3,200	7,800	—
1845	91,051	190	250	350	600	1,275	140,000
1845D	19,460	950	1,900	2,600	3,900	15,000	—
1845O	4,000	550	1,050	2,300	9,000	20,000	—
1846	21,598	200	275	500	950	6,000	140,000
1846C	4,808	725	1,575	3,500	8,950	18,750	—
1846D	19,303	800	1,400	2,000	3,000	12,000	—
1846O	66,000	170	280	400	1,150	6,500	—
1847	29,814	140	220	360	825	3,800	—
1847C	23,226	900	1,800	2,300	3,500	7,250	—
1847D	15,784	800	1,650	2,250	3,250	10,500	—
1847O	124,000	160	240	400	1,000	4,000	—
1848	7,497	315	500	850	2,400	7,000	125,000
1848 "CAL."	1,389	8,000	15,000	26,000	36,000	50,000	—
1848C	16,788	800	1,600	2,100	3,800	13,750	—
1848D	13,771	1,000	2,000	2,500	4,500	12,000	—
1849	23,294	180	275	475	1,000	2,600	—
1849C	10,220	800	1,475	2,150	5,150	23,500	—
1849D	10,945	950	2,000	2,500	4,500	18,000	—
1850	252,923	265	310	360	385	1,100	—
1850C	9,148	800	1,500	2,000	3,600	13,500	—
1850D	12,148	950	1,700	2,350	3,450	1,600	—
1850O	84,000	300	345	485	1,300	4,500	—
1851	1,372,748	265	300	330	345	495	—
1851C	14,923	900	1,650	2,250	3,450	9,850	—
1851D	11,264	1,000	1,800	2,500	3,850	12,000	—
1851O	148,000	300	335	370	900	4,450	—
1852	1,159,681	265	300	330	345	495	—
1852C	9,772	975	1,500	2,050	4,250	16,500	—
1852D	4,078	1,100	1,650	2,950	7,000	17,500	—
1852O	140,000	300	335	365	1,000	5,000	—
1853	1,404,668	265	300	330	345	495	—
1853D	3,178	1,250	1,975	3,450	4,850	18,000	—
1854	596,258	265	300	330	345	495	—
1854C	7,295	1,100	1,450	2,450	4,750	13,500	—
1854D	1,760	2,100	3,350	6,950	11,500	27,500	—
1854O	153,000	300	335	365	420	1,600	—
1854S	246	95,000	175,000	300,000	—	—	—
1855	235,480	270	305	335	350	495	—
1855C	3,677	1,050	1,675	3,250	6,350	19,500	—
1855D	1,123	2,100	3,350	7,500	16,500	50,000	—
1856	384,240	270	305	335	350	515	75,000
1856C	7,913	985	1,600	2,500	4,000	14,500	—
1856D	874	3,850	6,500	12,850	30,000	72,500	—

Date	Mintage	F-12	VF-20	XF-40	AU-50	MS-60	Prf-65
1856O	21,100	300	345	750	1,350	7,500	—
1856S	71,120	300	335	425	950	4,350	—
1857	214,130	270	305	335	350	515	75,000
1857D	2,364	1,025	1,650	2,775	3,700	13,200	—
1857O	34,000	300	335	425	1,050	4,450	—
1857S	69,200	300	335	365	875	5,350	—
1858	47,377	275	310	340	395	1,250	59,000
1858C	9,056	965	1,500	2,100	3,350	9,250	—
1859	39,444	275	310	350	425	1,250	61,000
1859D	2,244	1,150	1,850	3,100	3,950	18,500	—
1859S	15,200	310	365	950	2,350	5,000	—
1860	22,675	275	310	340	450	1,150	58,000
1860C	7,469	985	1,475	2,175	3,100	20,000	—
1860S	35,600	310	365	625	1,150	3,850	—
1861	1,283,878	270	305	335	350	850	31,500
1861S	24,000	320	400	900	3,250	7,250	—
1862	98,543	310	340	600	1,950	5,150	32,500
1862/1	Inc. above	650	875	1,850	3,450	7,500	—
1862S	8,000	650	875	2,050	4,200	17,500	—
1863	30	—	—	—	—	—	95,000
1863S	10,800	465	475	1,475	3,150	13,500	—
1864	2,874	3,750	5,450	11,500	22,500	47,500	27,000
1865	1,545	2,950	4,750	7,750	18,000	37,500	30,000
1865S	23,376	320	335	595	1,450	4,400	—
1866	3,110	775	1,250	3,150	5,750	11,500	25,000
1866S	38,960	365	400	625	1,500	5,950	—
1867	3,250	350	395	850	1,150	4,750	27,000
1867S	28,000	300	335	575	1,600	4,100	—
1868	3,625	300	335	395	640	1,625	27,000
1868S	34,000	270	305	365	1,050	3,850	—
1869	4,345	300	335	435	685	2,750	24,500
1869S	29,500	300	365	445	800	4,000	—
1870	4,555	290	375	550	900	4,150	33,500
1870S	16,000	270	345	465	1,000	4,900	—
1871	5,350	295	360	385	850	3,100	36,500
1871S	22,000	270	345	415	550	2,350	—
1872	3,030	305	450	800	1,250	4,650	33,500
1872S	18,000	275	340	485	1,150	4,350	—
1873 closed 3	178,025	270	330	375	395	435	42,500
1873 open 3	Inc. above	270	325	355	375	405	—
1873S	27,000	280	345	395	900	2,800	—
1874	3,940	285	345	425	850	2,250	42,500
1875	420	1,950	3,500	5,500	11,000	24,000	70,000
1875S	11,600	270	330	375	850	3,950	—
1876	4,221	285	345	675	1,250	3,350	27,500
1876S	5,000	285	345	625	1,150	2,850	—
1877	1,652	310	395	875	1,250	3,250	35,000
1877S	35,400	265	325	355	415	750	—
1878	286,260	265	320	345	370	410	35,000
1878S	178,000	265	320	345	375	415	—
1879	88,990	270	325	355	385	435	26,000
1879S	43,500	270	340	365	765	2,500	—
1880	2,996	275	345	385	750	1,400	26,000
1881	691	950	2,150	3,150	5,250	9,850	26,500
1882	4,067	270	330	375	550	1,050	23,500
1883	2,002	280	395	750	1,350	3,350	23,500
1884	2,023	275	375	440	750	1,600	23,500
1885	887	400	750	1,850	2,650	4,850	22,500
1886	4,088	275	340	375	650	1,150	23,500
1887	6,282	275	340	365	500	850	17,500
1888	16,098	270	335	365	450	520	18,000
1889	17,648	270	335	365	450	535	20,500
1890	8,813	275	340	365	500	600	18,500
1891	11,040	—	—	—	—	—	17,500
1891 DDR	Inc. above	275	335	365	475	585	—
1892	2,545	275	330	365	500	950	15,500
1893	30,106	270	330	355	375	400	15,500
1894	4,122	275	330	365	440	800	18,000
1895	6,199	265	325	355	400	525	16,750
1896	19,202	265	325	350	370	400	16,750
1897	29,904	270	325	350	370	400	16,750
1898	24,165	265	325	345	365	385	15,000
1899	27,350	265	325	345	365	385	15,000
1900	67,205	265	325	345	365	385	15,000
1901	91,322	265	325	345	365	385	15,000
1902	133,733	265	320	345	365	385	15,000
1903	201,257	265	320	345	365	385	15,000
1904	160,960	265	320	345	365	385	15,000
1905	217,944	265	320	345	365	385	15,000

Date	Mintage	F-12	VF-20	XF-40	AU-50	MS-60	Prf-65
1906	176,490	265	320	345	365	385	15,000
1907	336,448	265	320	345	365	385	15,000

Indian Head

KM# 128 • 4.1800 g., 0.9000 **Gold**, 0.1209 oz. AGW, 18 mm. • **Designer:** Bela Lyon Pratt

Date	Mintage	VF-20	XF-40	AU-50	MS-60	MS-63	MS-65	Prf-65
1908	565,057	285	325	340	380	1,250	4,150	25,000
1909	441,899	285	325	340	390	1,650	6,540	53,000
1910	492,682	285	325	340	380	1,550	7,500	35,000
1911	704,191	285	325	340	380	1,265	8,500	25,000
1911D D strong D	55,680	2,750	3,850	4,750	8,750	20,500	77,500	—
1911 1D weak D	Inc. above	1,150	1,950	2,850	4,950	—	—	—
1912	616,197	285	325	345	405	1,750	11,850	25,000
1913	722,165	285	325	340	380	1,190	7,500	25,000
1914	240,117	290	340	365	565	4,950	34,500	30,000
1914D	448,000	285	325	350	395	1,500	36,500	—
1915	606,100	285	325	335	380	1,225	6,500	32,500
1925D	578,000	285	325	335	370	975	3,550	—
1926	446,000	285	325	335	370	975	3,550	—
1927	388,000	285	325	335	370	975	3,550	—
1928	416,000	285	325	335	370	975	3,550	—
1929	532,000	290	335	350	400	1,065	7,000	—

1911-D $2.50 Gold
Grade MS-60

$3

GOLD

Indian head with headdress, left   Value, date within wreath reverse

KM# 84 • 5.0150 g., 0.9000 **Gold**, 0.1451 oz. AGW, 20.5 mm. • **Obv. Legend** UNITED STATES OF AMERICA **Designer:** James B. Longacre **Notes:** The 1873 "closed-3" and "open-3" varieties are distinguished by the amount of space between the upper left and lower left serifs of the 3 in the date.

Date	Mintage	VF-20	XF-40	AU-50	MS-60	MS-65	Prf-65
1854	138,618	850	1,100	2,000	3,400	18,000	125,000
1854D	1,120	8,300	15,000	29,000	65,000	—	—
1854O	24,000	1,000	2,000	4,000	20,000	—	—
1855	50,555	900	1,100	2,000	3,300	32,000	120,000
1855S	6,600	1,025	2,150	5,700	25,000	—	—
1856	26,010	880	1,100	2,150	3,500	27,000	—
1856S	34,500	900	1,500	2,350	10,000	—	—
1857	20,891	900	1,100	2,100	3,500	—	62,500
1857S	14,000	950	2,200	5,500	18,000	—	—
1858	2,133	950	1,800	3,000	9,000	—	62,500
1859	15,638	900	1,800	1,800	3,000	—	60,000
1860	7,155	900	1,600	2,000	3,600	21,000	46,000
1860S	7,000	950	2,000	7,000	17,000	—	—
1861	6,072	925	1,500	2,200	3,600	27,000	46,000
1862	5,785	925	1,850	2,200	3,600	28,000	46,500
1863	5,039	900	1,450	2,200	3,600	20,000	43,000
1864	2,680	950	1,500	2,300	3,600	29,000	42,000
1865	1,165	1,350	2,500	6,000	10,000	39,000	40,000
1866	4,030	970	1,100	2,000	3,600	27,500	42,000
1867	2,650	950	1,100	2,400	4,000	28,000	41,500
1868	4,875	740	1,100	2,100	3,000	22,000	42,000
1869	2,525	1,150	2,200	2,600	4,000	—	46,000
1870	3,535	1,000	1,500	2,400	5,000	—	47,000
1870S unique	—	—	—	—	—	—	—
Note: H. W. Bass Collection. AU50, cleaned. Est. value, $1,250,000.							
1871	1,330	1,000	1,500	2,000	4,000	27,500	47,000
1872	2,030	900	1,800	2,250	3,600	—	33,000
1873 open 3, proof only	25	3,300	5,000	8,700	—	—	—
1873 closed 3, mintage unknown	—	4,000	6,000	10,000	—	—	42,000
1874	41,820	800	1,300	1,900	3,000	16,000	42,000
1875 proof only	20	20,000	28,000	47,500	—	—	175,000
1876	45	6,000	10,000	16,500	—	—	60,000
1877	1,488	1,200	2,900	5,200	12,000	60,000	43,500
1878	82,324	800	1,300	1,900	3,000	16,000	43,000
1879	3,030	850	1,300	2,000	2,650	19,000	32,000
1880	1,036	850	1,700	3,000	4,000	20,000	29,500
1881	554	1,400	2,750	5,500	8,000	24,000	25,000
1882	1,576	925	1,400	2,000	3,500	22,000	25,000
1883	989	1,000	1,600	3,500	3,600	24,000	25,000
1884	1,106	1,250	1,700	2,200	3,600	24,000	24,000
1885	910	1,300	1,800	2,850	3,900	24,000	25,000
1886	1,142	1,250	1,800	3,000	4,000	20,000	24,000
1887	6,160	900	1,300	2,000	3,000	18,000	21,000
1888	5,291	950	1,500	2,000	3,300	20,000	23,000
1889	2,429	925	1,300	1,700	3,100	18,000	22,000

$2.50

$5 (HALF EAGLE)

GOLD

Liberty Cap

Liberty Cap on head, right, flanked by stars obverse
Small eagle reverse

KM# 19 • 8.7500 g., 0.9160 **Gold**, 0.2577 oz. AGW •

Date	Mintage	F-12	VF-20	XF-40	MS-60
1795	8,707	19,500	25,000	31,000	79,500
1796/95	6,196	20,500	25,350	32,750	84,500
1797 15 obverse stars	Inc. above	23,000	27,500	42,250	—
1797 16 obverse stars	Inc. above	21,000	25,850	41,000	210,000
1798	—	112,000	185,000	350,000	—

Liberty cap on head, right, flanked by stars
Large Heraldic eagle reverse

KM# 28 • 8.7500 g., 0.9160 **Gold**, 0.2577 oz. AGW, 25 mm. • **Obv. Legend** LIBERTY **Rev. Legend:** UNITED STATES OF AMERICA **Designer:** Robert Scot

Date	Mintage	F-12	VF-20	XF-40	MS-60
1795	Inc. above	10,000	16,500	22,500	85,000
1797/95	3,609	10,850	17,500	24,000	155,000
1797 15 star obv.; Unique	—	—	—	—	—
Note: Smithsonian collection					
1797 16 star obv.; Unique	—	—	—	—	—
Note: Smithsonian collection					
1798 small 8	24,867	4,850	6,650	10,100	—
1798 large 8, 13-star reverse	Inc. above	4,050	5,050	8,350	33,500
1798 large 8, 14-star reverse	Inc. above	5,050	6,650	10,950	—
1799 small reverse stars	7,451	3,850	4,900	11,100	21,500
1799 large reverse stars	Inc. above	3,950	4,750	14,200	31,700
1800	37,628	3,850	4,650	7,100	15,850
1802/1	53,176	3,850	4,650	7,100	15,850
1803/2	33,506	3,850	4,650	7,100	15,850
1804 small 8	30,475	3,850	4,650	7,100	15,850
1804 small 8 over large 8	Inc. above	3,950	4,850	7,600	17,850
1805	33,183	3,850	4,650	7,100	15,850
1806 pointed 6	64,093	3,850	4,650	7,100	17,750
1806 round 6	Inc. above	3,850	4,650	7,100	15,850
1807	32,488	3,850	4,650	7,100	15,850

Turban Head
Capped draped bust, left, flanked by stars
Heraldic eagle reverse

KM# 38 • 8.7500 g., 0.9160 **Gold**, 0.2577 oz. AGW, 25 mm. • **Rev. Legend:** UNITED STATES OF AMERICA **Designer:** John Reich

Date	Mintage	F-12	VF-20	XF-40	MS-60
1807	51,605	3,100	3,850	5,100	13,850
1808	55,578	3,600	4,500	5,950	18,850
1808/7	Inc. above	3,100	3,850	5,100	13,850
1809/8	33,875	3,100	3,850	5,100	13,850
1810 small date, small 5	100,287	17,500	32,500	48,500	125,000
1810 small date, large 5	Inc. above	3,100	3,850	5,100	16,250
1810 large date, small 5	Inc. above	17,500	37,500	60,000	135,000
1810 large date, large 5	Inc. above	3,100	3,850	5,100	13,850
1811 small 5	99,581	3,100	3,850	5,100	13,850
1811 tall 5	Inc. above	3,100	3,850	5,100	13,850
1812	58,087	3,100	3,850	5,100	13,850

Capped head, left, within circle of stars
Heraldic eagle reverse

KM# 43 • 8.7500 g., 0.9160 **Gold**, 0.2577 oz. AGW, 25 mm. • **Rev. Legend:** UNITED STATES OF AMERICA **Designer:** John Reich

Date	Mintage	F-12	VF-20	XF-40	MS-60
1813	95,428	3,100	3,850	5,500	13,250
1814/13	15,454	5,000	6,250	8,250	19,000
1815	635	32,500	50,000	200,000	250,000
Note: 1815, private sale, Jan. 1994, MS-61, $150,000.					
1818	48,588	5,000	6,450	13,500	20,000
1818 5D over 50 Inc. Above	—	5,500	6,450	10,500	23,500
1819	51,723	8,800	16,500	50,000	64,000
1819 5D over 50 Inc. Above	—	5,500	11,000	35,000	64,000
1820 curved-base 2, small letters	263,806	5,250	6,600	12,850	22,500
1820 curved-base 2, large letters	Inc. above	5,100	6,400	12,000	20,000
1820 square-base 2	Inc. above	5,000	6,250	11,500	19,000
1821	34,641	12,000	22,000	43,000	115,000
1822 3 known	—	500,000	900,000	1,250,000	1,000,000
Note: 1822, private sale, 1993, VF-30, $1,000,000.					
1823	14,485	5,500	6,250	11,500	19,000
1824	17,340	5,500	10,500	32,000	38,000
1825/21	29,060	5,750	9,500	25,000	39,500
1825/24	Inc. above	—	—	550,000	750,000
Note: 1825/4, Bowers & Merena, March 1989, XF, $148,500.					
1826	18,069	5,500	7,800	16,500	30,000
1827	24,913	6,000	10,000	23,500	34,500
1828/7	28,029	15,000	28,500	66,000	125,000
Note: 1828/7, Bowers & Merena, June 1989, XF, $20,900.					
1828	Inc. above	6,000	13,000	30,000	60,000
1829 large planchet	57,442	15,000	28,500	65,000	125,000
Note: 1829 large planchet, Superior, July 1985, MS-65, $104,500.					
1829 small planchet	Inc. above	37,500	54,000	86,500	140,000
Note: 1829 small planchet, private sale, 1992 (XF-45), $89,000.					
1830 small "5D."	126,351	16,500	27,500	44,650	70,000
1830 large "5D."	Inc. above	16,500	27,500	44,650	70,000

Date	Mintage	F-12	VF-20	XF-40	MS-60
1831	140,594	16,500	27,500	44,650	70,000
1832 curved-base 2, 12 stars	157,487	50,000	80,000	175,000	
1832 square-base 2, 13 stars	Inc. above	16,500	27,500	44,650	70,000
1833 small date	193,630	17,500	29,500	54,650	90,000
1833 large date	Inc. above	16,500	27,500	44,650	70,000
1834 plain 4	50,141	16,500	27,500	44,650	70,000
1834 crosslet 4	Inc. above	17,500	29,500	54,650	80,000

Classic Head
Classic head, left, within circle of stars
No motto above eagle reverse

KM# 57 • 8.3600 g., 0.8990 **Gold**, 0.2416 oz. AGW, 22.5 mm. • **Rev. Legend:** UNITED STATES OF AMERICA **Designer:** William Kneass

Date	Mintage	VF-20	XF-40	AU-50	MS-60	MS-65
1834 plain 4	658,028	550	790	1,400	3,000	48,000
1834 crosslet 4	Inc. above	1,650	2,900	6,000	20,000	—
1835	371,534	550	790	1,450	3,150	—
1836	553,147	550	790	1,450	2,950	70,000
1837	207,121	550	790	1,650	3,500	75,000
1838	286,588	550	890	1,450	3,700	58,000
1838C	17,179	2,550	5,500	13,000	42,500	—
1838D	20,583	2,100	4,650	9,750	31,000	—

Coronet Head
Coronet head, left, within circle of stars
No motto above eagle reverse

KM# 69 • 8.3590 g., 0.9000 **Gold**, 0.2419 oz. AGW, 21.6 mm. • **Rev. Legend:** UNITED STATES OF AMERICA **Designer:** Christian Gobrecht **Notes:** Varieties for 1843 are distinguished by the size of the numerals in the date. One 1848 variety has "Cal." incsribed on the reverse, indicating it was made from California gold. The 1873 "closed-3" and "open-3" varieties are distinguished by the amount of space between the upper left and lower left serifs in the 3 in the date.

Date	Mintage	F-12	VF-20	XF-40	MS-60	Prf-65
1839	118,143	250	275	480	4,000	—
1839/8 curved date	Inc. above	275	325	700	2,250	—
1839C	17,205	1,250	2,300	2,900	24,000	—
1839D	18,939	1,125	2,200	3,200	22,000	—
1840	137,382	432	462	360	3,700	—
1840C	18,992	1,200	2,200	3,000	26,000	—
1840D	22,896	1,200	2,200	3,000	16,000	—
1840O	40,120	442	365	875	11,000	—
1841	15,833	442	400	875	5,500	—
1841C	21,467	1,200	1,850	2,400	20,000	—
1841D	30,495	1,400	1,800	2,350	15,000	—
1841O 2 known	50	—	—	—	—	—
1842 small letters	27,578	200	345	1,100	—	—
1842 large letters	Inc. above	350	750	2,000	11,000	—
1842C small date	28,184	4,500	10,000	23,000	110,000	—
1842C large date	Inc. above	900	1,800	2,200	18,000	—
1842D small date	59,608	1,000	2,000	2,300	15,000	—
1842D large date	Inc. above	1,400	2,350	6,500	48,000	—
1842O	16,400	550	1,000	3,400	22,000	—
1843	611,205	432	462	491	1,850	—
1843C	44,201	1,250	1,850	2,500	14,000	—
1843D	98,452	1,250	1,950	2,600	13,000	—

Date	Mintage	F-12	VF-20	XF-40	MS-60	Prf-65
1843O small letters	19,075	300	660	1,700	26,000	—
1843O large letters	82,000	442	496	1,175	12,000	—
1844	340,330	432	462	491	2,000	—
1844C	23,631	1,300	1,900	3,000	24,000	—
1844D	88,982	1,500	1,950	2,400	12,000	—
1844O	364,600	329	349	375	4,700	—
1845	417,099	432	462	260	2,000	—
1845D	90,629	1,300	1,900	2,400	12,500	—
1845O	41,000	466	415	800	9,900	—
1846	395,942	432	462	330	2,400	—
1846C	12,995	1,350	1,900	3,000	24,000	—
1846D	80,294	1,250	1,800	2,400	13,000	—
1846O	58,000	329	375	1,000	11,500	—
1847	915,981	432	462	491	2,200	—
1847C	84,151	1,350	1,800	2,400	13,000	—
1847D	64,405	1,400	2,000	2,000	10,000	—
1847O	12,000	550	2,200	6,750	28,000	—
1848	260,775	432	462	275	1,500	—
1848C	64,472	1,400	1,900	2,250	19,250	—
1848D	47,465	1,450	2,000	2,350	14,500	—
1849	133,070	432	462	280	2,800	—
1849C	64,823	1,500	1,900	2,400	14,000	—
1849D	39,036	1,550	2,000	2,600	16,500	—
1850	64,491	432	300	625	4,250	—
1850C	63,591	1,350	1,850	2,300	14,000	—
1850D	43,984	1,450	1,950	2,500	33,000	—
1851	377,505	432	462	250	2,800	—
1851C	49,176	1,300	1,900	2,350	17,500	—
1851D	62,710	1,400	1,950	2,400	15,000	—
1851O	41,000	280	590	1,500	13,000	—
1852	573,901	432	462	260	1,400	—
1852C	72,574	1,350	1,900	2,450	7,750	—
1852D	91,584	1,450	2,000	2,450	13,000	—
1853	305,770	432	462	250	1,400	—
1853C	65,571	1,500	1,950	2,350	8,500	—
1853D	89,678	1,550	2,000	2,500	11,000	—
1854	160,675	432	462	260	2,000	—
1854C	39,283	1,400	1,900	2,300	14,000	—
1854D	56,413	1,400	1,875	2,200	11,500	—
1854O	46,000	325	300	525	8,250	—
1854S	268	—	—	—	—	—
Note: 1854S, Bowers & Merena, Oct. 1982, AU-55, $170,000.						
1855	117,098	432	462	250	1,800	—
1855C	39,788	1,400	1,900	2,300	16,000	—
1855D	22,432	1,500	1,950	2,400	19,000	—

$5

1852-C $5 Gold
Grade MS-60

Date	Mintage	F-12	VF-20	XF-40	MS-60	Prf-65
1855O	11,100	315	675	2,100	20,000	—
1855S	61,000	462	390	1,000	15,500	—
1856	197,990	432	462	491	2,850	—
1856C	28,457	1,450	1,875	2,400	20,000	—
1856D	19,786	1,475	1,950	2,600	15,000	—
1856O	10,000	370	650	1,600	14,000	—
1856S	105,100	305	300	700	6,750	—
1857	98,188	432	462	260	1,600	123,500
1857C	31,360	1,400	1,900	2,500	9,500	—
1857D	17,046	1,500	2,000	2,650	14,500	—
1857O	13,000	340	640	1,400	15,000	—
1857S	87,000	442	300	700	11,000	—
1858	15,136	442	240	550	3,850	190,000
1858C	38,856	1,400	1,900	2,350	11,000	—
1858D	15,362	1,500	2,000	2,450	12,500	—
1858S	18,600	400	825	2,350	31,000	—
1859	16,814	442	325	625	7,000	—
1859C	31,847	1,400	1,900	2,450	16,000	—
1859D	10,366	1,600	2,150	2,600	16,000	—
1859S	13,220	615	1,800	4,150	30,000	—
1860	19,825	200	280	575	3,650	100,000
1860C	14,813	1,500	2,100	3,000	15,000	—
1860D	14,635	1,500	1,900	2,600	15,000	—
1860S	21,200	500	1,100	2,100	27,000	—
1861	688,150	432	462	491	1,850	100,000
1861C	6,879	1,500	2,400	3,900	25,000	—
1861D	1,597	3,000	4,700	7,000	50,000	—
1861S	18,000	500	1,100	4,500	36,500	—
1862	4,465	400	800	1,850	20,000	96,000
1862S	9,500	1,500	3,000	6,000	62,000	—
1863	2,472	450	1,200	3,750	27,500	90,000
1863S	17,000	600	1,450	4,100	35,500	—
1864	4,220	350	650	1,850	15,000	72,000
1864S	3,888	2,300	4,750	16,000	55,000	—
1865	1,295	500	1,450	4,100	20,000	82,500
1865S	27,612	475	1,400	2,400	20,000	—
1866S	9,000	750	1,750	4,000	40,000	—

Coronet head, left, within circle of stars
IN GOD WE TRUST above eagle reverse

KM# 101 • 8.3590 g., 0.9000 **Gold**, 0.2419 oz. AGW, 21.6 mm. • **Rev. Legend:** UNITED STATES OF AMERICA **Designer:** Christian Gobrecht

Date	Mintage	VF-20	XF-40	AU-50	MS-60	MS-63	MS-65	Prf-65
1866	6,730	750	1,650	3,500	16,500	—	—	70,000
1866S	34,920	900	2,600	8,800	25,000	—	—	—
1867	6,920	500	1,500	3,300	11,500	—	—	70,000
1867S	29,000	1,400	2,900	8,000	34,500	—	—	—
1868	5,725	650	1,000	3,500	11,500	—	—	70,000
1868S	52,000	476	1,550	4,000	20,000	—	—	—
1869	1,785	925	2,400	3,500	17,500	34,000	—	65,000
1869S	31,000	500	1,750	4,000	26,000	—	—	—
1870	4,035	800	2,000	2,850	18,000	—	—	75,000
1870CC	7,675	5,250	15,000	30,000	110,000	137,500	200,000	—
1870S	17,000	950	2,600	8,250	29,000	—	—	—
1871	3,230	900	1,700	3,300	12,500	—	—	70,000
1871CC	20,770	1,250	3,000	12,000	60,000	—	—	—
1871S	25,000	500	950	2,950	13,000	—	—	—
1872	1,690	850	1,925	3,000	15,000	18,000	—	60,000
1872CC	16,980	1,250	5,000	20,000	60,000	—	—	—
1872S	36,400	527	800	3,400	13,500	—	—	—
1873 closed 3	49,305	462	477	489	1,200	6,500	24,000	70,000
1873 open 3	63,200	457	468	476	850	3,650	—	—
1873CC	7,416	2,600	12,500	27,500	60,000	—	—	—
1873S	31,000	525	1,400	3,250	21,000	—	—	—
1874	3,508	660	1,675	2,500	13,000	26,000	—	66,000
1874CC	21,198	850	1,700	9,500	36,000	—	—	—
1874S	16,000	640	2,100	4,800	22,500	—	—	—
1875	220	34,000	45,000	60,000	190,000	—	—	185,000

Date	Mintage	VF-20	XF-40	AU-50	MS-60	MS-63	MS-65	Prf-65
1875CC	11,828	1,400	4,500	11,500	52,000	—	—	—
1875S	9,000	715	2,250	5,000	16,500	32,500	—	—
1876	1,477	1,100	2,500	4,125	11,000	14,500	55,000	60,000
1876CC	6,887	1,450	5,000	14,000	46,500	82,500	165,000	—
1876S	4,000	2,000	3,600	9,500	30,000	—	—	—
1877	1,152	900	2,750	4,000	13,750	29,000	—	75,000
1877CC	8,680	1,000	3,300	11,000	52,500	—	—	—
1877S	26,700	489	650	1,400	9,200	—	—	—
1878	131,740	459	471	513	550	2,000	—	50,000
1878CC	9,054	3,100	7,200	20,000	60,000	—	—	—
1878S	144,700	457	466	3,000	675	4,250	—	—
1879	301,950	457	466	474	520	2,000	12,000	55,000
1879CC	17,281	1,000	1,500	3,150	22,000	—	—	—
1879S	426,200	459	471	513	950	3,300	—	—
1880	3,166,436	452	461	469	500	840	7,500	54,000
1880CC	51,017	625	815	1,375	9,900	—	—	—
1880S	1,348,900	452	461	469	490	800	5,750	—
1881	5,708,802	452	461	469	500	775	4,800	54,000
1881/80	Inc. above	330	600	750	1,500	4,500	—	—
1881CC	13,886	650	1,500	7,000	22,500	60,000	—	—
1881S	969,000	452	461	469	500	775	7,150	—
1882	2,514,568	452	461	469	500	800	6,150	54,000
1882CC	82,817	625	625	900	7,500	40,000	—	—
1882S	969,000	452	461	469	510	800	4,500	—
1883	233,461	469	478	486	530	1,200	—	40,000
1883CC	12,958	629	1,100	3,200	18,000	—	—	—
1883S	83,200	469	478	490	1,000	2,950	—	—
1884	191,078	469	478	489	650	2,250	—	35,000
1884CC	16,402	625	975	3,000	17,000	—	—	—
1884S	177,000	469	478	486	490	2,000	—	—
1885	601,506	452	461	469	505	825	4,800	35,000
1885S	1,211,500	452	461	469	510	790	4,000	—
1886	388,432	452	461	469	510	1,125	5,600	44,000
1886S	3,268,000	452	461	469	510	815	4,500	—
1887	87	—	14,500	20,000	—	—	—	120,000
1887S	1,912,000	452	461	469	510	800	4,800	—
1888	18,296	467	476	497	550	1,500	—	29,000
1888S	293,900	457	466	547	1,200	4,000	—	—
1889	7,565	566	575	557	1,150	2,400	—	30,000
1890	4,328	489	498	550	2,200	6,500	—	27,000
1890CC	53,800	566	575	615	1,600	7,500	55,000	—
1891	61,413	459	471	513	640	2,000	5,400	29,000
1891CC	208,000	551	565	800	1,350	3,500	28,500	—
1892	753,572	452	461	469	530	1,350	7,000	30,000
1892CC	82,968	566	585	750	1,500	6,500	33,500	—
1892O	10,000	515	1,000	1,375	3,300	15,000	—	—
1892S	298,400	452	461	477	525	2,850	—	—
1893	1,528,197	452	461	469	510	1,150	3,900	34,000
1893CC	60,000	586	625	825	1,550	6,650	—	—
1893O	110,000	467	572	585	950	5,950	—	—
1893S	224,000	452	461	474	510	1,150	9,000	—
1894	957,955	452	461	469	500	1,015	2,600	35,000
1894O	16,600	469	478	570	1,300	5,500	—	—
1894S	55,900	479	478	575	2,900	10,000	—	—
1895	1,345,936	452	461	469	495	1,015	4,500	29,000
1895S	112,000	457	478	486	3,150	6,500	26,000	—
1896	59,063	452	461	474	510	1,615	4,500	30,000
1896S	155,400	459	471	513	1,150	6,000	24,500	—
1897	867,883	452	461	469	495	1,015	4,500	35,000
1897S	354,000	452	461	474	865	5,150	—	—
1898	633,495	452	461	469	500	1,015	6,000	30,000
1898S	1,397,400	452	461	469	495	1,420	—	—
1899	1,710,729	452	461	469	495	1,000	3,600	30,000
1899S	1,545,000	452	461	469	495	1,370	9,600	—
1900	1,405,730	452	461	469	495	1,000	3,600	30,000
1900S	329,000	452	461	474	500	1,370	14,000	—
1901	616,040	452	461	469	495	1,000	3,650	27,000
1901S	3,648,000	452	461	469	495	1,000	3,600	—
1902	172,562	452	461	469	495	1,000	4,400	27,000
1902S	939,000	452	461	469	495	1,000	3,600	—
1903	227,024	452	461	469	500	1,015	4,000	27,000
1903S	1,855,000	452	461	469	495	1,000	3,600	—
1904	392,136	452	461	469	495	1,000	3,600	27,000
1904S	97,000	459	471	513	885	4,000	9,600	—
1905	302,308	452	461	469	500	1,015	4,000	27,000
1905S	880,700	452	461	469	495	3,350	9,600	—
1906	348,820	452	461	469	495	1,000	3,600	26,000
1906D	320,000	452	461	469	495	1,015	3,200	—
1906S	598,000	452	461	469	500	1,300	4,400	—

Date	Mintage	VF-20	XF-40	AU-50	MS-60	MS-63	MS-65	Prf-65
1907	626,192	452	461	469	495	1,000	3,400	23,000
1907D	888,000	452	461	469	495	1,000	3,400	—
1908	421,874	452	461	461	510	1,015	3,400	—

Indian Head

KM# 129 • 8.3590 g., 0.9000 **Gold**, 0.2419 oz. AGW, 21.6 mm. • **Designer:** Bela Lyon Pratt

Date	Mintage	VF-20	XF-40	AU-50	MS-60	MS-63	MS-65	Prf-65
1908	578,012	468.39	482	485	530	2,200	14,650	25,500
1908D	148,000	468.39	482	485	530	2,200	36,500	—
1908S	82,000	543.39	557	580	1,275	6,000	15,400	—
1909	627,138	468.39	482	485	510	2,200	14,650	36,000
1909D	3,423,560	468.39	482	485	510	1,650	14,650	—
1909O	34,200	2,150	3,350	7,250	27,500	64,500	475,000	—
1909S	297,200	498.39	522	545	1,350	11,000	45,000	—
1910	604,250	468.39	482	485	510	2,250	14,650	37,000
1910D	193,600	468.39	482	485	530	4,150	39,500	—
1910S	770,200	508.39	537	555	975	65,000	44,000	—
1911	915,139	468.39	482	485	510	1,650	14,650	28,500
1911D	72,500	575	700	1,100	4,650	38,500	255,000	—
1911S	1,416,000	478.39	517	540	600	5,850	41,500	—
1912	790,144	468.39	482	485	510	1,650	14,650	28,500
1912S	392,000	513.39	547	630	1,675	13,500	105,000	—
1913	916,099	468.39	482	485	510	2,200	15,400	28,000
1913S	408,000	508.39	542	670	1,450	11,500	125,000	—
1914	247,125	468.39	482	485	530	2,350	15,650	28,500
1914D	247,000	468.39	482	485	530	2,250	14,650	—
1914S	263,000	513.39	537	580	1,375	12,850	105,000	—
1915	588,075	468.39	482	485	510	2,250	14,650	39,000
1915S	164,000	523.39	557	665	1,950	17,000	110,000	—
1916S	240,000	493.39	517	565	710	5,750	28,500	—
1929	662,000	7,500	10,750	11,800	14,500	31,000	50,000	—

$10 (EAGLE)

GOLD

Liberty Cap

Small eagle reverse

KM# 21 • 17.5000 g., 0.9160 **Gold**, 0.5154 oz. AGW, 33 mm. • **Designer:** Robert Scot

Date	Mintage	F-12	VF-20	XF-40	MS-60
1795 13 leaves	5,583	28,500	33,850	48,500	122,500
1795 9 leaves	Inc. above	30,000	45,000	73,500	250,000
1796	4,146	27,500	36,000	50,000	135,000
1797 small eagle	3,615	31,500	40,000	55,000	200,000

Liberty Cap
Liberty cap on head, right, flanked by stars obverse
Heraldic eagle reverse

KM# 30 • 17.5000 g., 0.9160 **Gold**, 0.5154 oz. AGW, 33 mm. • **Obv. Legend** LIBERTY **Rev. Legend:**
UNITED STATES OF AMERICA **Designer:** Robert Scot

Date	Mintage	F-12	VF-20	XF-40	MS-60
1797 large eagle	10,940	9,800	12,850	21,400	58,500
1798/97CC 9 stars left, 4 right	900	13,500	19,000	34,500	127,500
1798/97 7 stars left, 6 right	842	28,500	38,500	87,500	235,000
1799 large star obv	37,449	9,350	10,750	18,200	37,500
1799 small star obv	Inc. above	9,350	10,750	18,200	37,500
1800	5,999	9,500	10,750	18,350	39,500
1801	44,344	9,250	10,900	17,400	37,500
1803 extra star	15,017	9,600	11,850	19,550	67,500
1803 large stars rev	Inc. above	9,250	11,400	17,800	37,500
1804 crosslet 4	3,757	16,500	22,750	31,500	92,500
1804 plain 4	—	—	—	—	400,000

Coronet Head
Old-style head, left, within circle of stars
No motto above eagle reverse

KM# 66.1 • 16.7180 g., 0.9000 **Gold**, 0.4837 oz. AGW, 27 mm. • **Rev. Legend:** UNITED STATES OF
AMERICA **Designer:** Christian Gobrecht

Date	Mintage	F-12	VF-20	XF-40	MS-60	Prf-65
1838	7,200	1,750	2,650	6,850	43,500	1,500,000
1839/8 Type of 1838	25,801	1,100	1,450	5,850	28,500	1,500,000
1839 large letters	Inc. above	800	1,150	2,150	32,000	—

New-style head, left, within circle of stars
No motto above eagle reverse

KM# 66.2 • 16.7180 g., 0.9000 **Gold**, 0.4837 oz. AGW, 27 mm. • **Rev. Legend:** UNITED STATES OF
AMERICA **Designer:** Christian Gobrecht

Date	Mintage	F-12	VF-20	XF-40	MS-60	Prf-65
1839 small letters	12,447	975	1,550	6,850	75,000	—
1840	47,338	884	949	1,223	11,500	—

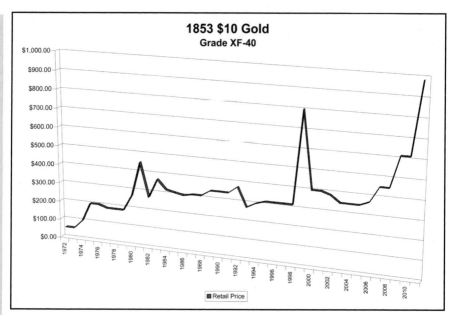

1853 $10 Gold
Grade XF-40

Date	Mintage	F-12	VF-20	XF-40	MS-60	Prf-65
1841	63,131	864	939	1,123	9,000	—
1841O	2,500	1,750	3,450	6,950	—	—
1842 small date	81,507	864	939	1,048	15,000	—
1842 large date	Inc. above	864	939	1,038	9,500	—
1842O	27,400	864	949	1,353	22,500	—
1843	75,462	864	939	1,153	16,750	—
1843O	175,162	864	949	1,108	12,000	—
1844	6,361	800	1,350	3,200	16,750	—
1844O	118,700	864	949	1,293	15,000	—
1845	26,153	899	1,109	1,233	17,500	—
1845O	47,500	884	949	875	16,500	—
1845O repunched	Inc. above	959	1,309	3,850	—	—
1846	20,095	909	1,179	1,250	—	—
1846O	81,780	864	949	1,150	—	—
1846/5	Inc. above	959	1,309	1,135	—	—
1847	862,258	864	939	983	3,450	—
1847O	571,500	864	939	983	6,500	—
1848	145,484	864	939	1,048	5,000	—
1848O	38,850	939	1,129	1,850	17,750	—
1849	653,618	864	939	983	3,400	—
1849O	23,900	939	1,129	2,450	27,500	—
1850 large date	291,451	864	939	983	4,500	—
1850 small date	Inc. above	939	1,129	1,150	8,500	—
1850O	57,500	884	964	1,275	19,500	—
1851	176,328	864	939	983	5,150	—
1851O	263,000	864	949	1,038	6,650	—
1852	263,106	864	939	983	5,250	—
1852O	18,000	939	1,109	1,650	27,500	—
1853	201,253	884	949	983	3,600	—
1853/2	Inc. above	884	964	1,318	14,950	—
1853O	51,000	864	964	1,048	14,500	—
1854	54,250	864	939	1,008	6,250	—
1854O small date	52,500	884	964	1,288	11,000	—
1854O large date	Inc. above	939	1,104	925	9,450	—
1854S	123,826	864	939	1,008	10,500	—
1855	121,701	864	939	983	4,750	—
1855O	18,000	884	964	2,100	28,000	—
1856	60,490	864	939	983	4,250	—
1856O	14,500	939	1,264	2,150	18,500	—
1856S	68,000	864	939	1,058	9,000	—
1857	16,606	884	964	1,050	13,500	—
1857O	5,500	1,039	1,800	3,650	—	—
1857S	26,000	884	949	1,050	11,500	—
1858	2,521	3,000	5,200	8,250	35,000	—
1858O	20,000	864	939	1,308	10,000	—
1858S	11,800	900	1,600	3,950	—	—

Date	Mintage	F-12	VF-20	XF-40	MS-60	Prf-65
1859	16,093	884	964	1,168	10,500	—
1859O	2,300	2,000	4,250	10,500	—	—
1859S	7,000	1,450	2,600	5,250	—	—
1860	15,105	909	1,004	1,218	8,450	175,000
1860O	11,100	929	1,104	1,850	13,750	—
1860S	5,000	1,400	2,950	6,400	—	—
1861	113,233	864	939	983	6,250	170,000
1861S	15,500	690	1,600	3,750	—	—
1862	10,995	939	1,094	1,200	—	170,000
1862S	12,500	700	2,000	3,450	—	—
1863	1,248	2,400	4,000	10,000	52,500	165,000
1863S	10,000	700	1,600	3,750	29,500	—
1864	3,580	775	1,800	4,950	18,000	165,000
1864S	2,500	2,600	5,100	17,500	—	—
1865	4,005	900	1,950	4,850	34,500	165,000
1865S	16,700	1,700	4,850	12,500	—	—
1865S over inverted 186	Inc. above	1,300	3,450	8,750	50,000	—
1866S	8,500	1,000	2,650	5,950	—	—

New-style head, left, within circle of stars
IN GOD WE TRUST above eagle reverse

KM# 102 • 16.7180 g., 0.9000 **Gold**, 0.4837 oz. AGW, 27 mm. • **Rev. Legend:** UNITED STATES OF AMERICA **Designer:** Christian Gobrecht

Date	Mintage	VF-20	XF-40	AU-50	MS-60	MS-63	MS-65	Prf-65
1866	3,780	850	2,450	5,000	—	—	—	120,000
1866S	11,500	1,550	3,850	8,000	—	—	—	—
1867	3,140	1,500	2,600	5,000	33,000	—	—	—
1867S	9,000	2,350	6,650	9,850	—	—	—	—
1868	10,655	945	1,200	2,250	19,000	—	—	110,000
1868S	13,500	1,350	2,400	3,900	—	—	—	—
1869	1,855	1,550	3,000	5,650	36,000	—	—	—
1869S	6,430	1,500	2,700	6,250	25,000	—	—	—
1870	4,025	985	1,650	3,950	—	—	—	—
1870CC	5,908	13,000	30,000	52,500	—	—	—	—
1870S	8,000	1,150	2,850	7,400	33,500	—	—	—
1871	1,820	1,500	3,000	5,000	20,000	—	—	110,000
1871CC	8,085	2,600	6,400	22,500	65,000	—	—	—
1871S	16,500	1,300	2,200	6,000	30,000	—	—	—
1872	1,650	2,400	5,500	8,700	15,000	34,000	—	90,000
1872CC	4,600	2,850	9,850	24,500	—	—	—	—
1872S	17,300	850	1,175	1,900	—	—	—	—
1873 closed 3	825	4,500	9,750	17,500	55,000	—	—	—
1873CC	4,543	6,000	13,500	32,000	—	—	—	—
1873S	12,000	1,150	2,850	5,200	27,500	—	—	—
1874	53,160	871	898	910	2,200	7,250	42,500	120,000
1874CC	16,767	1,150	3,650	12,000	52,500	75,000	—	—
1874S	10,000	1,275	3,400	7,250	—	—	—	—
1875	120	40,000	67,500	80,000	—	—	—	—
Note: 1875, Akers, Aug. 1990, Proof, $115,000.								
1875CC	7,715	4,250	9,850	25,000	71,500	—	—	—
1876	732	3,000	8,500	18,500	—	—	—	—
1876CC	4,696	3,600	7,750	21,500	—	—	—	—
1876S	5,000	1,300	2,950	7,500	—	—	—	—
1877	817	3,350	6,350	9,850	37,500	—	—	—
1877CC	3,332	2,400	6,750	15,000	—	—	—	—
1877S	17,000	873	1,250	2,450	33,500	—	—	—
1878	73,800	861	898	910	975	6,750	29,000	—
1878CC	3,244	3,850	10,000	19,000	—	—	—	—
1878S	26,100	873	925	2,150	16,500	29,500	—	—
1879	384,770	864	898	910	1,029	5,000	15,750	83,000
1879/78	Inc. above	871	910	1,195	1,250	2,850	—	—
1879CC	1,762	6,650	12,500	26,000	—	—	—	—
1879O	1,500	2,150	5,450	10,250	—	—	—	—
1879S	224,000	864	898	910	1,150	6,500	49,500	—
1880	1,644,876	846	860	872	884	3,650	—	—

Date	Mintage	VF-20	XF-40	AU-50	MS-60	MS-63	MS-65	Prf-65
1880CC	11,190	900	1,000	1,950	15,500	—	—	—
1880O	9,200	966	1,450	1,850	20,000	—	—	—
1880S	506,250	846	860	872	904	4,850	25,000	—
1881	3,877,260	846	860	872	884	3,650	16,500	63,000
1881CC	24,015	992	1,200	1,800	6,850	36,500	—	—
1881O	8,350	848	865	1,500	6,950	—	—	—
1881S	970,000	846	860	872	894	3,650	—	—
1882	2,324,480	846	860	872	884	3,650	19,500	63,000
1882CC	6,764	985	1,750	3,250	—	—	—	—
1882O	10,820	874	1,047	1,250	6,350	18,500	—	—
1882S	132,000	874	898	910	966	3,650	—	—
1883	208,740	846	860	872	894	3,100	—	63,000
1883CC	12,000	1,046	1,250	2,600	22,500	—	—	—
1883O	800	3,000	7,950	10,500	—	—	—	—
1883S	38,000	874	898	910	1,275	10,500	23,500	—
1884	76,905	874	898	910	1,064	5,100	15,000	53,000
1884CC	9,925	1,066	1,450	2,350	12,850	55,000	—	—
1884S	124,250	846	860	872	979	6,500	—	—
1885	253,527	846	860	872	884	4,850	—	53,000
1885S	228,000	846	860	872	884	4,400	—	—
1886	236,160	846	860	872	884	5,100	—	53,000
1886S	826,000	846	860	872	894	1,500	—	—
1887	53,680	874	898	910	979	6,150	—	53,000
1887S	817,000	846	860	872	894	2,950	—	—
1888	132,996	874	898	910	1,124	6,600	—	—
1888O	21,335	874	898	910	1,064	5,750	—	—
1888S	648,700	846	860	872	884	2,700	—	—
1889	4,485	904	1,087	1,200	2,700	—	—	53,000
1889S	425,400	846	860	872	894	1,500	18,500	—
1890	58,043	884	918	930	942	5,500	16,000	46,000
1890CC	17,500	986	1,080	1,200	3,850	18,500	—	—
1891	91,868	904	938	950	962	4,500	—	48,000
1891CC	103,732	986	1,040	1,125	1,300	7,150	—	—
1892	797,552	846	860	872	884	3,650	9,100	48,000
1892CC	40,000	986	1,040	1,165	3,800	22,500	—	—
1892O	28,688	904	918	930	942	11,000	—	—
1892S	115,500	874	922	934	946	4,500	—	—
1893	1,840,895	846	860	872	884	2,025	16,500	46,000
1893CC	14,000	986	1,080	1,800	8,500	—	—	—
1893O	17,000	874	898	952	1,164	5,450	—	—
1893S	141,350	874	898	910	930	4,950	19,500	—
1894	2,470,778	846	860	872	884	3,775	—	46,000
1894O	107,500	874	898	905.5	1,000	6,350	—	—
1894S	25,000	874	922	1,100	3,950	—	—	—
1895	567,826	846	860	872	884	3,650	17,500	43,500
1895O	98,000	874	898	922	1,034	8,000	—	—
1895S	49,000	874	910	980	2,400	9,500	—	—
1896	76,348	846	860	872	894	2,550	30,000	43,500
1896S	123,750	874	893	932	2,500	12,000	28,500	—
1897	1,000,159	846	860	872	884	3,775	10,000	—
1897O	42,500	874	898	910	800	5,850	27,500	—
1897S	234,750	874	893	905	870	5,750	22,500	—
1898	812,197	846	860	872	884	3,775	9,000	43,500
1898S	473,600	874	893	905	954	5,100	18,500	—
1899	1,262,305	846	860	872	884	3,650	6,500	43,500
1899O	37,047	874	898	912	1,064	8,450	—	—
1899S	841,000	846	860	872	894	3,650	12,850	—
1900	293,960	846	860	872	894	3,650	9,500	43,500
1900S	81,000	874	898	910	950	6,750	—	—
1901	1,718,825	846	860	872	884	3,650	12,850	43,500
1901O	72,041	874	898	910	1,004	3,750	12,500	—
1901S	2,812,750	846	860	872	884	3,650	6,250	—
1902	82,513	846	860	872	894	2,800	11,750	43,500
1902S	469,500	846	860	872	884	3,650	6,250	—
1903	125,926	846	860	872	894	2,450	13,500	43,500
1903O	112,771	874	898	910	994	3,250	18,000	—
1903S	538,000	846	860	872	894	3,675	5,350	—
1904	162,038	846	860	872	894	2,000	9,500	46,000
1904O	108,950	874	898	910	994	3,700	16,500	—
1905	201,078	846	860	872	884	1,450	8,500	43,500
1905S	369,250	874	893	937	1,200	5,600	22,500	—
1906	165,497	846	860	872	894	2,450	10,000	43,500
1906D	981,000	846	860	872	884	3,650	7,000	—
1906O	86,895	874	898	910	1,034	4,900	14,500	—
1906S	457,000	874	893	910	1,044	5,000	15,500	—
1907	1,203,973	846	860	872	884	3,650	12,850	43,500
1907D	1,030,000	846	860	872	894	2,250	—	—
1907S	210,500	874	893	932	1,084	5,450	17,000	—

Indian Head
No motto next to eagle reverse

KM# 125 • 16.7180 g., 0.9000 **Gold**, 0.4837 oz. AGW, 27 mm. • **Designer:** Augustus Saint-Gaudens
Notes: 1907 varieties are distinguished by whether the edge is rolled or wired, and whether the legend E PLURIBUS UNUM has periods between each word.

Date	Mintage	VF-20	XF-40	AU-50	MS-60	MS-63	MS-65
1907 wire edge, periods before and after legend	500	11,000	16,850	19,500	26,500	43,500	83,500
1907 same, without stars on edge, unique	—	—	—	—	—	—	—
1907 rolled edge, periods	42	26,000	38,500	49,000	66,500	98,500	250,000
1907 without periods	239,406	855	865	890	965	3,400	10,000
1908 without motto	33,500	840	850	875	950	4,650	14,500
1908D without motto	210,000	840	850	875	990	6,350	37,500

IN GOD WE TRUST left of eagle reverse

KM# 130 • 16.7180 g., 0.9000 **Gold**, 0.4837 oz. AGW, 27 mm. • **Designer:** Augustus Saint-Gaudens

Date	Mintage	VF-20	XF-40	AU-50	MS-60	MS-63	MS-65	Prf-65
1908	341,486	835	845	870	920	2,750	10,400	52,500
1908D	836,500	840	865	890	940	6,750	29,000	—
1908S	59,850	850	900	925	2,950	8,650	25,500	—
1909	184,863	835	845	870	900	3,550	16,500	54,500
1909D	121,540	840	850	875	965	6,100	34,500	—
1909S	292,350	840	850	875	965	6,350	17,500	—
1910	318,704	835	845	870	890	1,660	11,000	54,500
1910D	2,356,640	830	840	870	890	1,560	8,400	—
1910S	811,000	840	850	875	950	8,850	51,000	—
1911	505,595	830	840	865	905	1,650	9,250	52,500
1911D	30,100	900	975	1,450	5,850	25,000	122,500	—
1911S	51,000	870	880	915	1,050	9,000	17,000	—
1912	405,083	835	845	870	890	1,635	11,000	52,500
1912S	300,000	840	850	875	965	7,250	38,500	—
1913	442,071	835	845	870	890	1,700	11,500	52,500
1913S	66,000	885	895	975	4,000	28,500	100,000	—
1914	151,050	835	845	870	900	2,250	11,500	52,500
1914D	343,500	835	845	870	890	2,650	15,500	—
1914S	208,000	845	855	880	1,035	7,750	32,500	—
1915	351,075	835	845	870	890	2,000	12,750	55,000
1915S	59,000	885	910	1,050	3,150	15,250	58,500	—
1916S	138,500	870	880	905	955	6,350	20,000	—
1920S	126,500	9,800	16,500	20,000	36,500	86,000	245,000	—
1926	1,014,000	830	840	865	885	1,360	7,450	—
1932	4,463,000	830	840	865	885	1,360	7,500	—
1933	312,500	110,000	135,000	145,000	165,000	230,000	575,000	—

$10

$20 (DOUBLE EAGLE)

GOLD

Liberty Head
Coronet head, left, within circle of stars
TWENTY D. below eagle, no motto above eagle reverse

KM# 74.1 • 33.4360 g., 0.9000 **Gold**, 0.9675 oz. AGW, 34 mm. • **Rev. Legend:** UNITED STATES OF AMERICA **Designer:** James B. Longacre

Date	Mintage	VF-20	XF-40	AU-50	MS-60	MS-63	MS-65	Prf-65
1849 unique, in Smithsonian collection	1	—	—	—	—	—	—	—
1850	1,170,261	1,830	1,920	3,000	8,500	43,500	175,000	—
1850O	141,000	1,790	3,500	9,800	45,000	—	—	—
1851	2,087,155	1,870	2,050	2,325	3,850	13,500	—	—
1851O	315,000	1,945	2,750	4,250	23,000	58,500	—	—
1852	2,053,026	1,870	2,050	2,225	3,950	17,500	—	—
1852O	190,000	1,900	2,650	3,800	22,500	—	—	—
1853	1,261,326	1,870	2,050	2,050	5,000	27,500	—	—
1853/2	Inc. above	1,950	2,250	6,850	33,500	—	—	—
1853O	71,000	1,960	3,650	4,850	32,500	65,000	—	—
1854	757,899	1,870	2,050	2,350	9,250	26,500	—	—
1854	Inc. above	2,110	2,350	6,000	—	—	—	—
1854O	3,250	95,000	225,000	365,000	—	—	—	—
1854S	141,468	1,950	2,040	3,000	6,000	15,500	52,500	—

Date	Mintage	VF-20	XF-40	AU-50	MS-60	MS-63	MS-65	Prf-65
1855	364,666	1,870	2,050	2,250	8,850	66,500	—	—
1855O	8,000	3,650	19,500	24,500	110,000	—	—	—
1855S	879,675	1,850	2,050	2,325	7,200	19,500	—	—
1856	329,878	1,870	2,050	2,125	8,400	24,500	—	—
1856O	2,250	97,500	165,000	300,000	525,000	750,000	—	—
1856S	1,189,750	1,850	2,050	2,150	5,900	15,000	30,000	—
1857	439,375	1,870	2,050	2,250	3,400	26,500	—	—
1857O	30,000	1,925	2,950	6,400	31,000	115,000	—	—
1857S	970,500	1,850	2,050	2,250	4,500	7,250	12,850	—
1858	211,714	1,925	2,040	2,150	5,500	34,500	—	—
1858O	35,250	1,950	3,850	7,500	42,000	—	—	—
1858S	846,710	1,850	2,070	2,440	8,500	—	—	—
1859	43,597	1,925	2,450	4,400	28,000	—	—	280,000
1859O	9,100	6,400	16,500	44,000	110,000	—	—	—
1859S	636,445	1,850	2,050	2,400	5,000	35,000	—	—
1860	577,670	1,850	2,050	2,250	3,950	18,000	63,500	—
1860O	6,600	3,650	14,500	24,000	100,000	—	—	—
1860S	544,950	1,870	2,340	2,440	7,350	18,500	48,000	—
1861	2,976,453	1,850	2,050	2,200	3,950	12,850	41,500	275,000
1861O	17,741	5,650	17,500	24,000	88,000	—	—	—
1861S	768,000	1,870	2,150	2,250	10,500	31,500	—	—

Liberty
Coronet head, left, within circle of stars
Paquet design, TWENTY D. below eagle reverse

KM# 93 • 33.4360 g., 0.9000 **Gold**, 0.9675 oz. AGW • **Rev. Legend:** UNITED STATES OF AMERICA
Notes: In 1861 the reverse was redesigned by Anthony C. Paquet, but it was withdrawn soon after its release. The letters in the inscriptions on the Paquet-reverse variety are taller than on the regular reverse.

Date	Mintage	VF-20	XF-40	AU-50	MS-60	MS-63	MS-65	Prf-65
1861 2 Known	—	—	—	—	—	—	—	—

Note: 1861 Paquet reverse, Bowers & Merena, Nov. 1988, MS-67, $660,000.

Date	Mintage	VF-20	XF-40	AU-50	MS-60	MS-63	MS-65	Prf-65
1861S	—	19,500	54,000	92,500	275,000	—	—	—

Note: Included in mintage of 1861S, KM#74.1

Longacre design resumed reverse

KM# A74.1 • 33.4360 g., 0.9000 **Gold**, 0.9675 oz. AGW •

Date	Mintage	VF-20	XF-40	AU-50	MS-60	MS-63	MS-65	Prf-65
1862	92,133	1,850	3,500	6,000	17,500	36,500	—	250,000
1862S	854,173	1,835	1,925	2,100	12,400	36,000	—	—
1863	142,790	1,850	2,650	3,950	19,500	39,500	—	250,000
1863S	966,570	1,835	2,005	2,105	7,350	28,500	—	—
1864	204,285	1,850	1,940	2,450	14,500	40,000	—	250,000
1864S	793,660	1,835	1,985	2,085	8,600	32,000	—	—
1865	351,200	1,850	2,005	2,190	6,200	26,000	—	250,000
1865S	1,042,500	1,835	2,005	2,100	4,200	9,000	19,500	—
1866S	Inc. below	2,750	11,500	37,500	—	—	—	—

$20

Coronet head, left, within circle of stars
TWENTY D. below eagle. IN GOD WE TRUST above eagle reverse

KM# 74.2 • 33.4360 g., 0.9000 **Gold**, 0.9675 oz. AGW, 34 mm. • **Rev. Legend:** UNITED STATES OF AMERICA **Designer:** James B. Longacre

Date	Mintage	VF-20	XF-40	AU-50	MS-60	MS-63	MS-65	Prf-65
1866	698,775	1,833	2,003	2,063	6,950	28,500	—	200,000
1866S	842,250	1,833	2,013	2,100	15,500	—	—	—
1867	251,065	1,833	2,023	2,063	3,250	30,000	—	200,000
1867S	920,750	1,833	2,013	2,100	15,000	—	—	—
1868	98,600	1,873	2,113	2,250	11,500	50,000	—	200,000
1868S	837,500	1,833	1,983	2,150	10,000	—	—	—
1869	175,155	1,843	1,973	2,100	6,800	22,750	—	210,000
1869S	686,750	1,833	2,003	2,100	7,000	45,000	—	—
1870	155,185	1,853	2,003	2,300	9,250	50,000	—	215,000
1870CC	3,789	200,000	275,000	400,000	—	—	—	—
1870S	982,000	1,833	1,958	2,018	5,450	34,000	—	—
1871	80,150	1,843	1,958	2,100	4,500	24,500	—	—
1871CC	17,387	9,500	19,500	45,000	97,500	300,000	650,000	—
1871S	928,000	1,833	1,973	2,058	4,750	22,000	—	—
1872	251,880	1,833	2,003	2,088	3,750	24,500	—	—
1872CC	26,900	2,550	5,450	8,950	38,500	—	—	—
1872S	780,000	1,833	2,003	2,063	3,250	23,500	—	—
1873 closed 3	Est. 208,925	1,833	2,063	2,123	3,350	—	—	200,000
1873 open 3	Est. 1,500,900	1,833	2,003	2,073	2,477	12,000	85,000	—
1873CC	22,410	2,900	4,750	11,750	37,500	115,000	—	—
1873S closed 3	1,040,600	1,833	1,973	2,066	2,150	20,000	—	—
1873S open 3	Inc. above	1,833	2,003	2,063	5,900	29,500	—	—
1874	366,800	1,833	2,003	2,063	2,467	19,500	—	—
1874CC	115,085	2,100	2,450	3,400	11,500	—	—	—
1874S	1,214,000	1,833	1,973	2,066	2,359	24,000	—	—
1875	295,740	1,833	2,003	2,063	2,389	13,500	—	—
1875CC	111,151	1,950	2,250	2,650	4,850	26,500	—	—
1875S	1,230,000	1,833	1,973	2,066	2,498	16,850	—	—
1876	583,905	1,833	1,993	2,066	2,350	13,500	78,500	—
1876CC	138,441	1,960	2,300	2,700	7,750	—	—	—
1876S	1,597,000	1,833	1,973	2,066	2,477	12,400	90,000	—

Coronet head, left, within circle of stars
TWENTY DOLLARS below eagle reverse

KM# 74.3 • 33.4360 g., 0.9000 **Gold**, 0.9675 oz. AGW • **Rev. Legend:** UNITED STATES OF AMERICA

Date	Mintage	VF-20	XF-40	AU-50	MS-60	MS-63	MS-65	Prf-65
1877	397,670	1,648	1,793	1,843	1,941	11,500	—	—
1877CC	42,565	1,803	2,150	3,650	19,500	—	—	—
1877S	1,735,000	1,638	1,693	1,773	1,911	15,500	—	—
1878	543,645	1,658	1,793	1,853	2,031	12,500	—	—
1878CC	13,180	2,450	3,950	7,250	30,000	—	—	—

Date	Mintage	VF-20	XF-40	AU-50	MS-60	MS-63	MS-65	Prf-65
1878S	1,739,000	1,638	1,668	1,698	1,911	20,500	—	—
1879	207,630	1,718	1,793	1,803	1,911	16,500	—	—
1879CC	10,708	3,000	4,850	8,850	34,000	77,500	—	—
1879O	2,325	12,500	21,500	27,500	88,500	127,500	—	—
1879S	1,223,800	1,638	1,668	1,698	2,150	30,000	—	—
1880	51,456	1,748	1,823	1,878	3,150	25,000	—	110,000
1880S	836,000	1,638	1,668	1,708	2,050	17,500	—	—
1881	2,260	12,500	21,000	34,500	79,000	—	—	110,000
1881S	727,000	1,638	1,668	1,708	2,011	20,000	—	—
1882	630	13,500	39,500	88,000	130,000	225,000	—	130,000
1882CC	39,140	1,788	2,000	2,600	8,850	65,000	—	—
1882S	1,125,000	1,638	1,668	1,688	1,981	18,500	—	—
1883 proof only	92	—	—	27,500	—	—	—	195,000
1883CC	59,962	1,788	2,000	2,600	7,850	30,000	—	—
1883S	1,189,000	1,638	1,668	1,698	1,911	8,500	—	—
1884 proof only	71	—	—	35,000	—	—	—	225,000
1884CC	81,139	1,788	2,000	2,600	5,000	25,000	—	—
1884S	916,000	1,638	1,668	1,698	1,851	6,150	46,500	—
1885	828	8,450	13,850	18,500	60,000	100,000	—	115,000
1885CC	9,450	2,500	3,850	6,450	19,500	48,500	—	—
1885S	683,500	1,638	1,668	1,708	1,851	5,700	29,500	—
1886	1,106	10,500	18,500	37,500	70,000	140,000	—	105,000
1887	121	—	—	26,500	—	—	—	142,500
1887S	283,000	1,638	1,668	1,698	1,911	15,000	36,500	—
1888	226,266	1,638	1,668	1,718	1,961	7,900	36,500	93,500
1888S	859,600	1,638	1,668	1,698	1,851	4,650	—	—
1889	44,111	1,798	1,923	2,043	2,301	13,500	36,500	105,000
1889CC	30,945	1,788	2,150	3,000	7,950	25,500	—	—
1889S	774,700	1,638	1,668	1,698	1,861	5,400	—	—
1890	75,995	1,638	1,693	1,773	1,911	10,000	—	100,000
1890CC	91,209	1,788	2,000	2,450	4,850	32,500	—	—
1890S	802,750	1,638	1,668	1,698	1,851	6,350	30,000	—
1891	1,442	8,500	15,000	22,500	75,000	125,000	—	108,000
1891CC	5,000	4,950	9,000	11,000	24,500	71,500	—	—
1891S	1,288,125	1,638	1,668	1,698	1,851	3,000	—	—
1892	4,523	2,000	3,650	6,250	13,500	35,000	—	90,000
1892CC	27,265	1,788	2,100	2,850	7,500	36,500	—	—
1892S	930,150	1,638	1,668	1,753	1,841	2,950	24,500	—
1893	344,339	1,638	1,688	1,763	1,881	2,100	—	95,000
1893CC	18,402	1,885	2,100	2,850	7,000	29,500	—	—
1893S	996,175	1,598	1,623	1,648	1,686	2,850	28,500	—
1894	1,368,990	1,598	1,623	1,648	1,686	1,800	26,500	85,000
1894S	1,048,550	1,598	1,623	1,648	1,686	2,450	27,500	—
1895	1,114,656	1,598	1,623	1,648	1,686	1,650	17,500	82,500
1895S	1,143,500	1,598	1,623	1,648	1,686	2,200	15,500	—
1896	792,663	1,598	1,623	1,648	1,686	1,850	19,500	200,000
1896S	1,403,925	1,598	1,623	1,648	1,686	1,975	23,500	—
1897	1,383,261	1,598	1,623	1,648	1,686	2,350	18,500	200,000
1897S	1,470,250	1,598	1,623	1,648	1,686	1,450	21,500	—
1898	170,470	1,603	1,653	1,748	1,986	4,500	—	200,000
1898S	2,575,175	1,603	1,623	1,648	1,686	1,650	7,950	—
1899	1,669,384	1,598	1,623	1,648	1,686	1,625	12,500	200,000
1899S	2,010,300	1,598	1,623	1,648	1,686	1,750	21,500	—
1900	1,874,584	1,598	1,623	1,648	1,686	2,285	5,700	200,000
1900S	2,459,500	1,598	1,623	1,648	1,686	2,100	23,000	—
1901	111,526	1,598	1,623	1,648	1,686	2,285	5,850	200,000
1901S	1,596,000	1,598	1,623	1,648	1,686	3,850	21,500	—
1902	31,254	1,598	1,818	1,908	2,096	11,750	37,500	200,000
1902S	1,753,625	1,598	1,623	1,648	1,686	2,900	23,500	—
1903	287,428	1,598	1,623	1,648	1,686	2,285	5,500	200,000
1903S	954,000	1,598	1,623	1,648	1,686	2,315	13,500	—
1904	6,256,797	1,598	1,623	1,648	1,686	2,250	4,200	200,000
1904S	5,134,175	1,598	1,623	1,648	1,686	2,250	5,400	—
1905	59,011	1,603	1,643	1,683	1,986	14,500	—	200,000
1905S	1,813,000	1,598	1,623	1,648	1,686	3,250	20,500	—
1906	69,690	1,603	1,628	1,703	1,866	6,850	26,500	200,000
1906D	620,250	1,598	1,623	1,648	1,686	3,450	22,500	—
1906S	2,065,750	1,598	1,623	1,648	1,686	2,350	19,500	—
1907	1,451,864	1,598	1,623	1,648	1,686	2,250	8,200	200,000
1907D	842,250	1,598	1,623	1,648	1,686	2,650	7,350	—
1907S	2,165,800	1,598	1,623	1,648	1,686	2,650	27,000	—

$20

$20

Saint-Gaudens
Roman numerals in date obverse
No motto below eagle reverse

KM# 126 • 33.4360 g., 0.9000 **Gold**, 0.9675 oz. AGW, 34 mm. • **Designer:** Augustus Saint-Gaudens
Edge Desc: Plain.

Date	Mintage	VF-20	XF-40	AU-50	MS-60	MS-63	MS-65
MCMVII (1907) high relief, unique, AU-55, $150,000	—	—	—	—	—	—	—
MCMVII (1907) high relief, wire rim	11,250	7,650	8,750	10,350	14,000	24,500	45,000
MCMVII (1907) high relief, flat rim	Inc. above	7,900	9,250	11,350	15,250	26,000	46,500

Arabic numerals in date obverse   No motto below eagle reverse

KM# 127 • 33.4360 g., 0.9000 **Gold**, 0.9675 oz. AGW, 34 mm. • **Designer:** Augustus Saint-Gaudens
Edge Desc: Lettered; large letters.

Date	Mintage	VF-20	XF-40	AU-50	MS-60	MS-63	MS-65	Prf-65
1907 large letters on edge, unique	—	—	—	—	—	—	—	—
1907 small letters on edge	361,667	1,638	1,659	1,690	1,740	2,060	4,600	—
1908	4,271,551	1,628	1,649	1,670	1,700	1,850	2,525	—
1908D	663,750	1,638	1,659	1,680	1,725	1,960	11,800	—

Roman numerals in date obverse
No motto below eagle reverse

KM# Pn1874 • 33.4360 g., 0.9000 **Gold**, 0.9675 oz. AGW, 34 mm. • **Designer:** Augustus Saint-Gaudens
Edge Desc: Plain. **Notes:** The "Roman numerals" varieties for 1907 use Roman numerals for the date instead of Arabic numerals. The lettered-edge varieties have "E Pluribus Unum" on the edge, with stars between the words.

Date	Mintage	VF-20	XF-40	AU-50	MS-60	MS-63	MS-65	Prf-65
1907 extremely high relief, unique	—	—	—	—	—	—	—	—
1907 extremely high relief, lettered edge	—	—	—	—	—	—	—	—

Note: 1907 extremely high relief, lettered edge, Prf-68, private sale, 1990, $1,500,000.

IN GOD WE TRUST below eagle reverse

KM# 131 • 33.4360 g., 0.9000 **Gold**, 0.9675 oz. AGW, 34 mm. • **Designer:** Augustus Saint-Gaudens

Date	Mintage	VF-20	XF-40	AU-50	MS-60	MS-63	MS-65	Prf-65
1908	156,359	1,633	1,654	1,680	1,750	2,300	28,000	76,500
1908 Roman finish; Prf64 Rare	—	—	—	—	—	—	—	—
Note: Rare								
1908D	349,500	1,638	1,659	1,690	1,740	1,980	7,000	—
1908S	22,000	2,450	3,150	4,850	10,650	24,500	52,500	—
1909/8	161,282	1,638	1,659	1,730	1,850	6,250	52,000	—
1909	Inc. above	1,648	1,679	1,700	1,800	3,150	46,000	92,500
1909D	52,500	1,678	1,699	1,825	3,100	8,950	57,500	—
1909S	2,774,925	1,638	1,659	1,690	1,720	1,935	7,000	—
1910	482,167	1,633	1,654	1,680	1,750	1,950	9,000	84,500
1910D	429,000	1,633	1,654	1,680	1,725	1,920	3,450	—
1910S	2,128,250	1,638	1,659	1,695	1,730	1,985	11,350	—
1911	197,350	1,638	1,659	1,700	1,740	2,900	23,500	76,500
1911D	846,500	1,633	1,654	1,680	1,725	1,920	2,950	—
1911S	775,750	1,633	1,654	1,680	1,730	1,920	6,850	—
1912	149,824	1,638	1,659	1,695	1,765	2,050	31,000	76,500
1913	168,838	1,638	1,659	1,695	1,770	3,250	53,500	82,500
1913D	393,500	1,633	1,654	1,680	1,725	2,000	7,850	—
1913S	34,000	1,688	1,709	1,730	2,000	4,350	36,500	—
1914	95,320	1,648	1,669	1,730	1,275	3,900	25,000	81,500
1914D	453,000	1,633	1,654	1,680	1,725	1,930	3,450	—
1914S	1,498,000	1,633	1,654	1,680	1,725	1,920	3,150	—
1915	152,050	1,638	1,659	1,690	1,730	2,650	28,000	125,000
1915S	567,500	1,633	1,654	1,680	1,725	1,920	3,000	—
1916S	796,000	1,638	1,659	1,690	1,765	1,950	3,250	—
1920	228,250	1,628	1,649	1,670	1,725	2,450	118,000	—
1920S	558,000	14,500	18,500	28,500	53,000	105,000	355,000	—
1921	528,500	35,000	43,500	56,500	125,000	300,000	975,000	—
1922	1,375,500	1,628	1,649	1,670	1,700	1,870	6,850	—
1922S	2,658,000	1,748	1,150	1,300	2,450	5,650	63,500	—
1923	566,000	1,628	1,649	1,670	1,700	1,870	8,000	—
1923D	1,702,250	1,638	1,659	1,680	1,710	1,870	2,635	—
1924	4,323,500	1,628	1,649	1,670	1,700	1,850	2,525	—
1924D	3,049,500	1,851	1,872	2,100	3,950	11,200	115,000	—
1924S	2,927,500	1,665	1,750	2,200	3,800	12,250	180,000	—
1925	2,831,750	1,628	1,649	1,670	1,700	1,850	2,525	—
1925D	2,938,500	1,803	2,100	2,375	4,450	11,500	148,000	—
1925S	3,776,500	1,900	2,850	4,850	9,850	23,500	210,000	—
1926	816,750	1,628	1,649	1,670	1,700	1,850	2,525	—
1926D	481,000	10,000	15,500	19,350	27,500	35,000	235,000	—
1926S	2,041,500	1,831	1,550	1,725	3,050	5,650	37,500	—
1927	2,946,750	1,628	1,649	1,670	1,700	1,850	2,525	—
1927D	180,000	155,000	200,000	245,000	325,000	1,500,000	1,950,000	—
1927S	3,107,000	6,850	8,850	13,250	26,750	54,000	160,000	—
1928	8,816,000	1,628	1,649	1,670	1,700	1,850	2,525	—
1929	1,779,750	10,000	13,500	15,500	19,300	38,500	112,000	—
1930S	74,000	35,000	41,000	49,500	72,500	105,000	235,000	—
1931	2,938,250	10,500	13,500	20,500	31,500	63,500	120,000	—
1931D	106,500	8,850	11,500	21,500	42,500	83,500	140,000	—
1932	1,101,750	12,500	14,500	17,850	26,500	73,500	110,000	—
1933	445,500	—	—	—	—	—	9,000,000	—

Note: Sotheby/Stack's Sale, July 2002. Thirteen known, only one currently available.

MINT SETS

Mint, or uncirculated, sets contain one uncirculated coin of each denomination from each mint produced for circulation that year. Values listed here are only for those sets sold by the U.S. Mint. Sets were not offered in years not listed. In years when the Mint did not offer the sets, some private companies compiled and marketed uncirculated sets. Mint sets from 1947 through 1958 contained two examples of each coin mounted in cardboard holders, which caused the coins to tarnish. Beginning in 1959, the sets have been packaged in sealed Pliofilm packets and include only one specimen of each coin struck for that year (both P & D mints). Listings for 1965, 1966 and 1967 are for "special mint sets," which were of higher quality than regular mint sets and were prooflike. They were packaged in plastic cases. The 1970 large-date and small-date varieties are distinguished by the size of the date on the coin. The 1976 three-piece set contains the quarter, half dollar and dollar with the Bicentennial design. The 1971 and 1972 sets do not include a dollar coin; the 1979 set does not include an S-mint-marked dollar. Mint sets issued prior to 1959 were double sets (containing two of each coin) packaged in cardboard with a paper overlay. Original sets will always be toned and can bring large premiums if nicely preserved with good color.

Date	Sets Sold	Issue Price	Value	Date	Sets Sold	Issue Price	Value
1947 Est. 5,000	—	4.87	1,350	1979 Type I	2,526,000	8.00	4.50
1948 Est. 6,000	—	4.92	750	1980	2,815,066	9.00	6.50
1949 Est. 5,200	—	5.45	935	1981 Type I	2,908,145	11.00	9.75
1950 None issued	—	—	—	1982 & 1983 None			
1951	8,654	6.75	900	issued	—	—	—
1952	11,499	6.14	825	1984	1,832,857	7.00	3.65
1953	15,538	6.14	565	1985	1,710,571	7.00	4.25
1954	25,599	6.19	265	1986	1,153,536	7.00	8.75
1955 flat pack	49,656	3.57	168	1987	2,890,758	7.00	5.00
1956	45,475	3.34	165	1988	1,646,204	7.00	5.25
1957	32,324	24.50	275	1989	1,987,915	7.00	4.00
1958	50,314	4.43	150	1990	1,809,184	7.00	3.75
1959	187,000	2.40	60.00	1991	1,352,101	7.00	5.50
1960 large date	260,485	2.40	60.00	1992	1,500,143	7.00	5.25
1961	223,704	2.40	60.00	1993	1,297,094	8.00	6.15
1962	385,285	2.40	60.00	1994	1,234,813	8.00	5.00
1963	606,612	2.40	60.00	1995	1,038,787	8.00	7.50
1964	1,008,108	2.40	60.00	1996	1,457,949	8.00	15.00
1965 Special Mint Set	2,360,000	4.00	7.50	1997	950,473	8.00	11.00
1966 Special Mint Set	2,261,583	4.00	7.50	1998	1,187,325	8.00	4.50
1967 Special Mint Set	1,863,344	4.00	9.75	1999 9 piece	1,421,625	14.95	10.00
1968	2,105,128	2.50	7.50	2000	1,490,160	14.95	11.00
1969	1,817,392	2.50	7.50	2001	1,066,900	14.95	19.50
1970 large date	2,038,134	2.50	13.50	2002	1,139,388	14.95	21.00
1970 small date	Inc. above	2.50	70.00	2003	1,002,555	14.95	16.75
1971	2,193,396	3.50	2.95	2004	844,484	16.95	22.50
1972	2,750,000	3.50	2.95	2005	—	16.95	9.75
1973	1,767,691	6.00	13.50	2006	—	16.95	13.75
1974	1,975,981	6.75	7.25	2007	—	—	21.00
1975	1,921,488	6.00	6.00	2008	—	—	50.00
1976 3 coins	4,908,319	9.00	25.00	2009 18 pieces clad	—	—	34.50
1976	1,892,513	6.00	6.75	2010 28 piece clad coin			
1977	2,006,869	7.00	7.50	set	—	—	—
1978	2,162,609	7.00	5.65				

PROOF SETS

Proof coins are produced through a special process involving specially selected, highly polished planchets and dies. They usually receive two strikings from the coin press at increased pressure. The result is a coin with mirrorlike surfaces and, in recent years, a cameo effect on its raised design surfaces. Proof sets have been sold off and on by the U.S. Mint since 1858. Listings here are for sets from what is commonly called the modern era, since 1936. Values for earlier proofs are included in regular date listings. Sets were not offered in years not listed. Since 1968, proof coins have been produced at the San Francisco Mint; before that they were produced at the Philadelphia Mint. In 1942 the five-cent coin was struck in two compositions. Some proof sets for that year contain only one type (five-coin set); others contain both types. Two types of packaging were used in 1955 -- a box and a flat, plastic holder. The 1960 large-date and small-date sets are distinguished by the size of the date on the cent. Some 1968 sets are missing the mint mark on the dime, the result of an error in the preparation of an obverse die. The 1970 large-date and small-date sets are distinguished by the size of the date on the cent. Some 1970 sets are missing the mint mark on the dime, the result of an error in the preparation of an obverse die. Some 1971 sets are missing the mint mark on the five-cent piece, the result of an error in the preparation of an obverse die. The 1976 three-piece set contains the quarter, half dollar and dollar with the Bicentennial designs. The 1979 and 1981 Type II sets have clearer mint marks than the Type I sets for those years. Some 1983 sets are missing the mint mark on the dime, the result of an error in the preparation of an obverse die. Prestige sets contain the five regular-issue coins plus a commemorative silver dollar from that year. Sets issued prior to 1956 came in transparent envelopes stapled together in a small square box. In mid 1955 sets were changed to a flat clear cellophane envelope. In 1968 sets were changed to a clear hard plastic case as they still are currently issued.

Date	Sets Sold	Issue Price	Value
1795 (2006) XPn1-XPn3	—	—	—
1836 (2006) XPn4, 10-11	—	—	—
1863 (2006) XPn12-14	—	—	—
1871 (2006) XPn15-17	—	—	—
1879 (2006) XPn18-20	—	—	—
1879 (2006) XPn21-23	—	—	—
1936	3,837	1.89	7,500
1937	5,542	1.89	4,350
1938	8,045	1.89	1,900
1939	8,795	—	1,800
1940	11,246	—	1,385
1941	15,287	—	1,450
1942 6 coins	21,120	1.89	1,475
1942 5 coins	Inc. above	1.89	1,250
1950	51,386	2.10	690
1951	57,500	2.10	625
1952	81,980	2.10	270
1953	128,800	2.10	235
1954	233,300	2.10	100.00
1955 box	378,200	2.10	100.00
1955 flat pack	Inc. above	2.10	145
1956	669,384	2.10	40.00
1957	1,247,952	2.10	32.00
1958	875,652	2.10	33.00
1959	1,149,291	2.10	32.00
1960 large date	1,691,602	2.10	32.00
1960 small date	Inc. above	2.10	37.50
1961	3,028,244	2.10	32.00
1962	3,218,019	2.10	32.00
1963	3,075,645	2.10	32.00
1964	3,950,762	2.10	32.00
1965 Special Mint Set	—	—	—
1966 Special Mint Set	—	—	—
1967 Special mint set	—	—	—
1968S	3,041,509	5.00	7.75
1968S no mint mark dime	Inc. above	5.00	16,500
1969S	2,934,631	5.00	7.75
1970S large date	2,632,810	5.00	8.25
1970S small date	Inc. above	5.00	100.00
1970S no mint mark dime	Inc. above	5.00	1,050
1971S	3,224,138	5.00	5.00
1971S no mint mark nickel Est. 1,655	1,655	5.00	1,475
1972S	3,267,667	5.00	5.50
1973S	2,769,624	7.00	6.60
1974S	2,617,350	7.00	8.25
1975S no mint mark dime	Inc. above	7.00	45,500
1975S	2,909,369	7.00	11.00
1976S 3 coins	3,998,621	13.00	26.50
1976S	4,149,730	7.00	7.50
1977S	3,251,152	9.00	6.35
1978S	3,127,788	9.00	7.75
1979S Type I	3,677,175	9.00	5.65
1979S Type II	Inc. above	9.00	92.00
1980S	3,547,030	10.00	5.00
1981S Type I	4,063,083	11.00	6.15
1981S Type II	Inc. above	11.00	335
1982S	3,857,479	11.00	3.75
1983S	3,138,765	11.00	4.25
1983S Prestige Set	140,361	59.00	63.00
1983S no mint mark dime	Inc. above	11.00	755
1984S	2,748,430	11.00	4.85
1984S Prestige Set	316,680	59.00	39.50
1985S	3,362,821	11.00	3.85
1986S	2,411,180	11.00	4.50
1986S Prestige Set	599,317	48.50	41.00
1987S	3,972,233	11.00	3.75
1987S Prestige Set	435,495	45.00	39.50
1988S	3,031,287	11.00	4.95
1988S Prestige Set	231,661	45.00	39.50
1989S	3,009,107	11.00	5.50
1989S Prestige Set	211,087	45.00	46.50
1990S	2,793,433	11.00	4.50
1990S no S 1¢	3,555	11.00	5,750
1990S Prestige Set	506,126	45.00	41.00
1990S Prestige Set, no S 1¢	Inc. above	45.00	5,000
1991S	2,610,833	11.00	7.50
1991S Prestige Set	256,954	59.00	48.50
1992S	2,675,618	12.00	4.25
1992S Prestige Set	183,285	59.00	46.50
1992S Silver	1,009,585	21.00	30.00
1992S Silver premier	308,055	37.00	30.00
1993S	2,337,819	12.50	6.50
1993S Prestige Set	224,045	57.00	57.50
1993S Silver	570,213	21.00	30.00
1993S Silver premier	191,140	37.00	30.00
1994S	2,308,701	13.00	7.25
1994S Prestige Set	175,893	57.00	45.00
1994S Silver	636,009	21.00	30.00
1994S Silver premier	149,320	37.50	30.00
1995S	2,010,384	12.50	17.75
1995S Prestige Set	107,112	57.00	117
1995S Silver	549,878	21.00	72.00
1995S Silver premier	130,107	37.50	85.00
1996S	2,085,191	16.00	10.50
1996S Prestige Set	55,000	57.00	320
1996S Silver	623,655	21.00	32.50
1996S Silver premier	151,366	37.50	32.50
1997S	1,975,000	12.50	17.00
1997S Prestige Set	80,000	57.00	100.00
1997S Silver	605,473	21.00	53.50
1997S Silver premier	136,205	37.50	61.50
1998S	2,078,494	12.50	10.00
1998S Silver	638,134	21.00	30.00
1998S Silver premier	240,658	37.50	30.00
1999S 9 piece	2,557,899	19.95	16.50

Date	Sets Sold	Issue Price	Value	Date	Sets Sold	Issue Price	Value
1999S 5 quarter set	1,169,958	13.95	13.75	2006S 5 quarter set	—	15.95	8.00
1999S Silver	804,565	31.95	160	2006S Silver 10 piece	—	37.95	66.00
2000S 10 piece	3,097,442	19.95	6.25	2006S Silver 5 quarter set	—	23.95	44.00
2000S 5 quarter set	995,803	13.95	3.50	2007S Presidental $ set	—	—	10.50
2000S Silver	965,421	31.95	63.50	2007S American Legacy	—	—	175
2001S 10 piece	2,249,498	19.95	26.00	2007S 5 quarter set	—	13.95	9.00
2001S 5 quarter set	774,800	13.95	18.00	2007S Silver 5 quarter set	—	22.95	44.00
2001S Silver	849,600	31.95	72.50	2007S 14 piece clad	—	—	26.00
2002S 10 piece	2,319,766	19.95	9.90	2007S Silver 14 piece	—	—	66.00
2002S 5 quarter set	764,419	13.95	8.50	2008 14 pieces clad	—	—	59.00
2002S Silver	892,229	31.95	66.00	2008S American Legacy	—	—	158
2003 X#207, 208, 209.2	—	44.00	28.75	2008S Silver 14 piece	734,045	—	80.00
2003S 10 piece	2,175,684	16.75	8.50	2008S Presidental $ set	—	—	17.50
2003S 5 quarter set	1,225,507	13.95	5.00	2008S 5 quarter set	—	22.95	33.50
2003S Silver	1,142,858	31.95	64.00	2008S Silver 5 quarter set	—	—	43.50
2004S 11 piece	1,804,396	22.95	11.75	2009S 6 quarter set	—	—	11.00
2004S 5 quarter set	987,960	23.95	6.75	2009S Silver 6 quarter set	—	—	53.00
2004S Silver 11 piece	1,187,673	37.95	65.00	2009S 18 coin clad set	1,477,967	—	31.50
2004S Silver 5 quarter set	594,137	—	43.50	2009S Silver 18 coin set	694,406	—	67.50
2005S Silver 5 quarter set	—	23.95	44.00	2009S Presidental $ set	627,925	—	8.00
2005S American Legacy	—	—	98.00	2009S Lincoln Chronicle	—	—	169
2005S American Legacy	—	—	76.00	2009S Lincoln 4 piece	—	—	18.50
2005S 11 piece	—	22.95	5.75	2010S 14 coin clad set	—	—	—
2005S 5 quarter set	—	15.95	5.00	2010S 14 coin silver set	—	—	—
2005S Silver 11 piece	—	37.95	66.00	2010S Presidental $ set	—	—	—
2006S American Legacy	—	—	76.00	2010S 5 clad quarter set	—	—	—
2006S 10 piece clad	—	22.95	13.00	2010S 5 silver quarter set	—	—	—

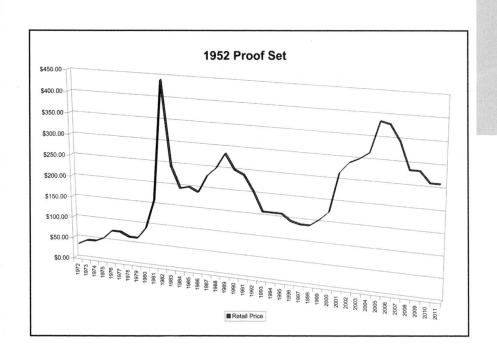

1952 Proof Set

■ Retail Price

PROOF SETS

UNCIRCULATED ROLLS

Listings are for rolls containing uncirculated coins. Large date and small date varieties for 1960 and 1970 apply to the one cent coins.

Date	Cents	Nickels	Dimes	Quarters	Halves	Date	Cents	Nickels	Dimes	Quarters	Halves
1934	585	3,500	2,350	1,650	2,350	1959	2.50	5.00	140	280	280
1934D	2,650	4,350	2,950	9,000	—	1959D	2.10	5.25	140	280	280
1934S	—	—	—	—	—	1960 large					
1935	885	1,700	1,450	1,725	1,250	date	1.60	4.40	140	280	280
1935D	750	3,150	2,950	8,850	4,000	1960 small					
1935S	2,500	1,725	1,950	4,650	6,500	date	220	—	—	—	—
1936	285	1,450	885	1,300	1,750	1960D large					
1936D	400	1,450	1,700	—	2,750	date	1.60	5.00	140	280	280
1936S	885	1,800	1,675	6,250	3,500	1960D small					
1937	250	1,100	710	1,250	1,150	date	2.85	—	—	—	—
1937D	250	1,200	1,550	3,450	5,000	1961	1.60	4.25	140	280	280
1937S	335	1,285	1,650	4,850	3,450	1961D	1.90	4.50	140	280	280
1938	665	535	1,100	3,100	1,850	1962	1.65	5.25	140	280	280
1938D	710	485	1,000	—	—	1962D	1.65	5.50	140	280	280
1938S	440	355	1,350	3,250	—	1963	1.50	4.25	140	280	280
1938D Buffalo	—	1,065	—	—	—	1963D	1.65	4.75	140	280	280
1939	180	160	630	1,040	1,250	1964	1.50	3.50	140	280	280
1939D	535	3,850	610	1,875	1,975	1964D	1.60	3.50	140	280	280
1939S	265	2,750	1,900	3,200	2,350	1965	2.25	8.75	8.00	25.00	120
1940	225	145	535	1,850	975	1966	3.75	6.00	10.00	53.00	120
1940D	265	120	780	5,350	—	1967	4.50	9.75	8.50	25.00	120
1940S	300	265	675	1,275	1,200	1968	1.75	—	8.50	25.00	—
1941	170	215	430	475	750	1968D	1.70	6.00	9.50	33.00	120
1941D	335	330	710	2,750	1,200	1968S	1.90	6.25	—	—	—
1941S	360	295	535	2,450	3,000	1969	7.75	—	44.00	100.00	—
1942	140	315	465	450	690	1969D	2.00	6.25	21.50	82.00	120
1942P	—	600	—	—	—	1969S	3.75	6.75	—	—	—
1942D	140	2,550	740	1,060	1,350	1970	2.10	—	8.00	26.00	—
1942S	585	525	1,050	5,350	1,475	1970D	2.10	4.00	7.75	16.00	235
1943	60.00	275	470	365	725	1970S	3.00	4.50	—	—	—
1943D	170	210	610	2,000	1,775	1970S small					
1943S	310	325	650	2,100	1,365	date	2,650	—	—	—	—
1944	30.00	720	460	280	715	1971	17.00	26.50	16.00	50.00	26.00
1944D	38.00	680	635	725	1,250	1971D	3.00	7.50	9.50	19.50	15.50
1944S	120	565	660	950	1,300	1971S	4.00	—	—	—	—
1945	125	375	410	325	730	1972	2.00	6.50	11.00	23.00	32.00
1945D	110	315	500	1,000	1,000	1972D	6.00	5.75	10.00	21.50	23.00
1945S	80.00	270	525	575	950	1972S	4.75	—	—	—	—
1946	39.00	80.00	140	365	1,025	1973	1.75	6.25	10.50	22.00	25.50
1946D	36.50	75.00	140	380	900	1973D	1.75	6.25	9.00	23.00	18.00
1946S	185	50.00	140	275	900	1973S	3.00	—	—	—	—
1947	220	58.00	215	735	1,000	1974	1.75	4.50	7.50	18.50	15.00
1947D	46.50	72.00	275	385	1,000	1974D	1.75	5.75	7.75	17.50	21.00
1947S	39.00	72.00	210	415	—	1974S	3.50	—	—	—	—
1948	72.50	55.00	188	270	450	1975	3.75	12.50	8.75	—	—
1948D	175	155	325	645	425	1975D	1.75	5.25	15.50	—	—
1948S	165	80.00	255	475	—	1976	1.75	13.50	21.00	17.50	18.00
1949	180	330	1,200	2,350	1,300	1976D	2.50	11.00	18.00	17.50	15.50
1949D	125	215	550	1,285	1,475	1977	1.75	6.25	9.75	16.50	21.50
1949S	140	138	2,350	—	2,250	1977D	2.85	5.75	8.50	17.50	24.00
1950	115	120	525	395	750	1978	3.00	4.50	7.25	16.00	32.00
1950D	42.00	385	200	440	875	1978D	10.00	5.00	8.00	16.50	46.50
1950S	78.00	—	1,550	850	—	1979	1.75	4.75	8.75	17.00	22.50
1951	165	230	140	435	390	1979D	3.00	5.75	8.00	22.50	22.50
1951D	26.50	285	140	325	800	1980	1.75	4.25	8.00	16.50	20.50
1951S	60.00	265	690	1,350	750	1980D	2.50	4.50	7.50	16.50	20.50
1952	165	145	140	535	385	1981	1.75	4.25	7.50	16.50	16.50
1952D	26.50	260	140	300	230	1981D	1.85	4.25	8.00	16.50	19.00
1952S	300	42.00	290	1,000	1,585	1982 Small					
1953	42.00	24.50	140	635	490	date	25.00	325	270	250	98.00
1953D	22.50	17.00	140	280	280	1982D Large					
1953S	35.00	39.00	140	280	850	date	4.00	54.00	66.00	165	80.00
1954	39.00	57.50	140	280	280	1982 Large					
1954D	22.50	24.00	140	280	280	date	2.50	—	—	—	—
1954S	22.50	39.50	140	280	400	1982 Copper					
1955	24.50	19.00	140	280	300	plated Zinc	8.00	—	—	—	—
1955D	19.00	7.00	170	280	—	1982 Small					
1955S	27.50	—	140	—	—	date, copper					
1956	10.50	7.50	140	280	280	plated zinc	3.00	—	—	—	—
1956D	12.50	9.25	140	280	—	1982D Large					
1957	10.00	12.50	140	280	280	date, copper					
1957D	9.50	4.75	140	280	280	plated zinc	35.00	—	—	—	—
1958	10.50	6.50	140	280	280	1982D Small					
1958D	9.75	5.50	140	280	280	date, copper					
						plated zinc	2.50	—	—	—	—
						1983	7.50	90.00	235	945	80.00

Date	Cents	Nickels	Dimes	Quarters	Halves
1983D	17.50	39.00	39.00	410	120
1984	5.50	22.00	8.50	17.00	26.00
1984D	14.50	6.50	21.00	29.00	37.00
1985	4.25	10.00	9.75	31.00	76.00
1985D	9.75	8.00	9.25	22.00	44.00
1986	20.00	8.75	25.00	85.00	75.00
1986D	31.50	24.50	22.50	210	90.00
1987	6.50	6.00	7.75	15.50	52.00
1987D	13.50	4.50	8.75	15.50	52.00
1988	6.25	5.50	9.75	39.00	75.00
1988D	12.50	9.00	9.25	22.50	45.00
1989	3.25	5.50	12.00	19.50	42.00
1989D	3.50	8.75	12.50	17.00	25.00
1990	4.00	11.50	14.50	20.00	39.00
1990D	5.85	13.75	10.00	25.00	52.00
1991	2.60	12.00	10.00	29.00	37.50
1991D	11.50	12.00	11.00	31.00	33.00
1992	3.00	46.00	8.00	42.00	21.00
1992D	5.00	9.00	8.00	27.50	50.00
1993	3.25	13.50	9.50	39.00	64.00
1993D	7.50	17.50	13.00	36.00	17.00
1994	2.00	7.75	12.00	42.00	15.00
1994D	2.00	8.00	12.00	47.50	20.00
1995	1.85	10.50	16.50	45.00	17.00
1995D	2.00	20.00	19.50	53.00	40.00
1996	2.25	8.75	11.00	19.00	17.00
1996D	2.85	8.25	11.50	27.50	19.00
1997	2.75	14.50	29.00	22.50	20.00
1997D	3.35	60.00	11.00	39.00	16.50
1998	2.00	13.75	9.75	17.00	20.00
1998D	1.85	14.00	12.00	18.00	16.50
1999P	2.35	5.50	8.50	—	20.00
1999D	2.25	6.25	8.50	—	19.00
2000P	2.50	6.25	7.75	—	15.00
2000D	1.75	4.75	7.00	—	17.00
2001P	3.75	4.75	7.75	—	16.50
2001D	2.00	6.50	7.25	—	16.00
2002P	2.00	4.00	7.25	—	20.00
2002D	3.25	4.10	7.25	—	20.00
2003P	3.35	7.50	7.00	—	22.50
2003D	2.00	3.50	7.00	—	19.50
2004P Peace Medal Nickel	1.75	6.75	7.00	—	30.00
2004D Peace Medal Nickel	2.50	7.00	7.00	—	30.00

Date	Cents	Nickels	Dimes	Quarters	Halves
2004P Keelboat Nickel	—	4.00	—	—	—
2004D Keelboat Nickel	—	3.50	—	—	—
2005P Bison Nickel	1.75	3.25	7.00	—	21.00
2005D Bison Nickel	2.75	3.25	7.00	—	21.00
2005P Ocean in view Nickel	—	3.25	—	—	—
2005D Ocean in view Nickel	—	3.25	—	—	—
2006P	2.75	3.25	8.50	—	29.00
2006D	1.75	3.25	8.50	—	29.00
2007P	1.75	3.50	8.00	—	21.00
2007D	1.75	3.50	7.75	—	21.00
2008P	1.75	3.75	8.00	—	24.50
2008D	1.75	3.75	7.50	—	25.50
2009P Log Cabin	2.00	23.00	13.50	—	18.50
2009D Log Cabin	2.15	13.50	13.50	—	18.50
2009P Log Splitter	1.75	—	—	—	—
2009D Log Splitter	1.75	—	—	—	—
2009P Professional	—	1.75	—	—	—
2009D Professional	1.75	—	—	—	—
2009P President	2.00	—	—	—	—
2009D President	2.00	—	—	—	—
2009 DC	18.00	15.50	—	—	—
2009 Puerto Rico	15.00	15.50	—	—	—
2009 Guam	15.00	16.50	—	—	—
2009 American Samoa	15.00	15.00	—	—	—
2009 Virgin Islands	15.00	15.00	—	—	—
2009 Marianna Islands	15.00	15.00	—	—	—

50 STATE QUARTERS UNCIRCULATED ROLLS

Listings are for rolls containing uncirculated coins.

State	Philadelphia	Denver	State	Philadelphia	Denver
1999 Delaware	15.00	15.50	2004 Michigan	13.75	14.50
1999 Pennsylvania	16.00	16.50	2004 Florida	13.75	14.50
1999 New Jersey	16.00	15.50	2004 Texas	14.00	15.00
1999 Georgia	28.00	30.00	2004 Iowa	14.00	14.50
1999 Connecticut	26.00	27.00	2004 Wisconsin	15.50	16.50
2000 Massachusetts	14.00	15.00	2005 California	21.00	22.50
2000 Maryland	14.00	15.50	2005 Minnesota	17.50	17.50
2000 South Carolina	15.50	15.50	2005 Oregon	13.75	13.75
2000 New Hampshire	13.50	14.50	2005 Kansas	13.75	14.50
2000 Virginia	14.50	14.50	2005 West Virginia	13.50	13.75
2001 New York	14.00	14.00	2006 Nevada	13.75	13.75
2001 North Carolina	14.50	15.00	2006 Nebraska	13.75	14.00
2001 Rhode Island	14.00	15.50	2006 Colorado	13.75	14.00
2001 Vermont	14.50	14.50	2006 North Dakota	13.75	14.50
2001 Kentucky	16.50	18.50	2006 South Dakota	13.75	13.75
2002 Mississippi	16.50	16.50	2007 Montana	14.00	17.00
2002 Tennessee	30.00	39.50	2007 Washington	18.00	18.75
2002 Ohio	21.50	21.50	2007 Idaho	15.50	15.50
2002 Louisiana	14.00	14.00	2007 Wyoming	14.75	15.00
2002 Indiana	14.50	15.50	2007 Utah	15.00	14.50
2003 Illinois	39.00	45.00	2008 Oklahoma	13.75	13.75
2003 Alabama	17.00	18.50	2008 New Mexico	14.00	15.50
2003 Maine	14.50	15.50	2008 Arizona	15.50	13.75
2003 Missouri	14.50	14.75	2008 Alaska	13.50	13.75
2003 Arkansas	14.50	15.50	2008 Hawaii	13.50	13.50

COMMEMORATIVE COINAGE
1892-1954

All commemorative half dollars of 1892-1954 have the following specifications: diameter — 30.6 millimeters; weight — 12.5000 grams; composition — 0.9000 silver, 0.3617 ounces actual silver weight. Values for PDS sets contain one example each from the Philadelphia, Denver and San Francisco mints. Type coin prices are the most inexpensive single coin available from the date and mint mark combinations listed.

QUARTER

KM# 115 COLUMBIAN EXPOSITION
Weight: 6.2500 g. **Composition:** 0.9000 Silver, 0.1808 oz. ASW **Diameter:** 24.3mm. **Obv:** Queen Isabella bust left **Rev:** Female kneeling with distaff adn spindle

Date	Mintage	AU-50	MS-60	MS-63	MS-64	MS-65
1893	24,214	450	525	650	950	2,750

HALF DOLLAR

KM# 117 COLUMBIAN EXPOSITION
Obv: Christopher Columbus bust right
Obv. Designer: Charles E. Barber **Rev:** Santa Maria sailing left, two globes below **Rev. Designer:** George T. Morgan

Date	Mintage	AU-50	MS-60	MS-63	MS-64	MS-65
1892	950,000	18.50	28.00	80.00	135	525
1893	1,550,405	17.00	28.00	75.00	145	465

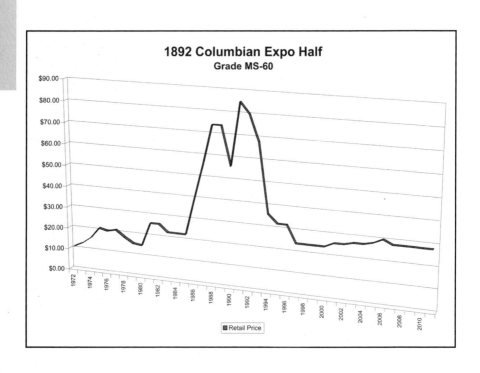

1892 Columbian Expo Half
Grade MS-60

Retail Price

KM# 135 PANAMA-PACIFIC EXPOSITION
Obv: Columbia standing, sunset in background
Rev: Eagle standing on shield **Designer:**
Charles E. Barber

Date	Mintage	AU-50	MS-60	MS-63	MS-64	MS-65
1915S	27,134	465	535	825	1,250	2,650

KM# 143 ILLINOIS CENTENNIAL-LINCOLN
Obv: Abraham Lincon bust right **Obv. Designer:**
George T. Morgan **Rev:** Eagle standing left **Rev.**
Designer: John R. Sinnock

Date	Mintage	AU-50	MS-60	MS-63	MS-64	MS-65
1918	100,058	135	150	165	200	565

KM# 146 MAINE CENTENNIAL
Obv: Arms of the State of Maine **Rev:** Legend
within wreath **Designer:** Anthony de Francisci

Date	Mintage	AU-50	MS-60	MS-63	MS-64	MS-65
1920	50,028	130	165	185	250	500

KM# 147.1 PILGRIM TERCENTENARY
Obv: William bradford half-length left **Rev:**
Mayflower sailing left **Designer:** Cyrus E. Dallin

Date	Mintage	AU-50	MS-60	MS-63	MS-64	MS-65
1920	152,112	80.00	100.00	110	120	375

KM# 147.2 PILGRIM TERCENTENARY
Obv: William Bradford half-length left, 1921 added
at left **Rev:** Mayflower sailing left **Designer:** Cyrus
E. Dallin

Date	Mintage	AU-50	MS-60	MS-63	MS-64	MS-65
1921	20,053	170	200	220	235	515

2x2

KM# 148.1 ALABAMA CENTENNIAL
Obv: William W. Bibb and T.E. Kilby conjoint busts
left. "2x2" at right above stars **Rev:** Ealge left on
shield **Designer:** Laura G. Fraser **Notes:** "Fake
2x2" counterstamps exist.

Date	Mintage	AU-50	MS-60	MS-63	MS-64	MS-65
1921	6,006	315	330	525	675	1,600

KM# 148.2 ALABAMA CENTENNIAL
Obv: William W. Bibb and T.E. Kilby conjoint busts
left **Obv. Designer:** Laura G. Fraser **Rev:** Eagle
standing left on shield

Date	Mintage	AU-50	MS-60	MS-63	MS-64	MS-65
1921	59,038	190	215	525	685	1,800

COMMEMORATIVES

KM# 149.1 MISSOURI CENTENNIAL
Obv: Frontiersman in coonskin cap left
Rev: Frontiersman and Native American standing
left **Designer:** Robert Aitken

Date	Mintage	AU-50	MS-60	MS-63	MS-64	MS-65
1921	15,428	400	600	885	1,275	3,650

2x4

KM# 149.2 MISSOURI CENTENNIAL
Obv: Frontiersman in coonskin cap left, 2(star)4 in
field at left **Rev:** Frontiersman and Native American
standing left **Designer:** Robert Aitken **Notes:** "Fake
"2*4" counterstamps exist.

Date	Mintage	AU-50	MS-60	MS-63	MS-64	MS-65
1921	5,000	620	720	1,050	1,500	3,450

KM# 151.1 GRANT MEMORIAL
Obv: Grant bust right **Rev:** Birthplace in Point
Pleasant, Ohio **Designer:** Laura G. Fraser

Date	Mintage	AU-50	MS-60	MS-63	MS-64	MS-65
1922	67,405	120	125	155	250	700

KM# 151.2 GRANT MEMORIAL
Obv: Grant bust left, star above the word GRANT
Rev: Birthplace in Point Pleasant, Ohio
Designer: Laura G. Fraser **Notes:** "Fake star"
counterstamps exist.

Date	Mintage	AU-50	MS-60	MS-63	MS-64	MS-65
1922	4,256	925	1,275	1,750	3,450	7,850

KM# 153 MONROE DOCTRINE CENTENNIAL
Obv: James Monroe and John Quincy Adams
conjoint busts left **Rev:** Western Hemisphere
portraied by two female figures **Designer:** Chester
Beach

Date	Mintage	AU-50	MS-60	MS-63	MS-64	MS-65
1923S	274,077	56.00	72.50	125	250	1,950

KM# 154 HUGUENOT-WALLOON
TERCENTENARY Obv: Huguenot leader
Gaspard de Coligny and William I of Orange
conjoint busts right **Rev:** Nieuw Nederland sailing
left **Designer:** George T. Morgan

Date	Mintage	AU-50	MS-60	MS-63	MS-64	MS-65
1924	142,080	135	145	150	215	385

COMMEMORATIVES

KM# 155 CALIFORNIA DIAMOND JUBILEE
Obv: Fourty-Niner kneeling panning for gold
Rev: Grizzly bear walking left **Designer:** Jo Mora

Date	Mintage	AU-50	MS-60	MS-63	MS-64	MS-65
1925S	86,594	195	225	270	485	900

KM# 157 STONE MOUNTAIN MEMORIAL
Obv: Generals Robert E. Lee and Thomas "Stonewall" Jackson mounted left. **Rev:** Eagle on rock at right **Designer:** Gutzon Borglum

Date	Mintage	AU-50	MS-60	MS-63	MS-64	MS-65
1925	1,314,709	62.00	67.50	80.00	190	315

KM# 156 LEXINGTON-CONCORD SESQUICENTENNIAL
Obv: Concord's Minute Man statue **Rev:** Old Belfry at Lexington **Designer:** Chester Beach

Date	Mintage	AU-50	MS-60	MS-63	MS-64	MS-65
1925	162,013	95.00	105	110	145	615

KM# 158 FORT VANCOUVER CENTENNIAL
Obv: John McLoughlin bust left **Rev:** Frontiersmen standing with musket, Ft. Vancouver in background **Designer:** Laura G. Fraser

Date	Mintage	AU-50	MS-60	MS-63	MS-64	MS-65
1925	14,994	320	360	420	475	1,250

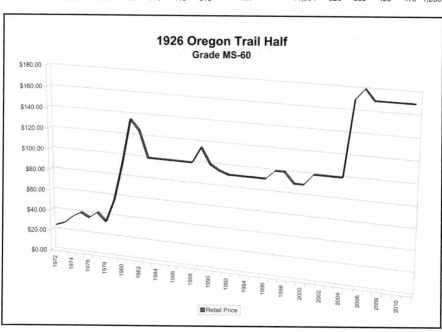

1926 Oregon Trail Half
Grade MS-60

■ Retail Price

KM# 159 OREGON TRAIL MEMORIAL
Obv: Native American standing in full headdress and holding bow, US Map in background **Rev:** Conestoga wagon pulled by oxen left towards sunset **Designer:** James E. and Laura G. Fraser

Date	Mintage	AU-50	MS-60	MS-63	MS-64	MS-65
1926	47,955	135	165	175	195	315
1926S	83,055	135	165	180	195	320
1928	6,028	220	245	275	285	375
1933D	5,008	365	380	385	390	465
1934D	7,006	195	205	215	220	365
1936	10,006	165	190	205	220	340
1936S	5,006	175	190	210	235	350
1937D	12,008	175	200	210	225	325
1938	6,006	155	170	205	210	335
1938D	6,005	155	170	205	220	335
1938S	6,006	155	170	205	215	335
1939	3,004	510	585	600	620	675
1939D	3,004	510	585	610	620	675
1939S	3,005	510	585	590	600	665

KM# 160 U.S. SESQUICENTENNIAL
Obv: George Washington and Calvin Coolidge conjoint busts right **Rev:** Liberty Bell **Designer:** John R. Sinnock

Date	Mintage	AU-50	MS-60	MS-63	MS-64	MS-65
1926	141,120	85.00	110	118	465	4,800

KM# 162 VERMONT SESQUICENTENNIAL
Obv: Ira Allen bust right **Obv. Designer:** Charles Keck **Rev:** Catamount advancing left

Date	Mintage	AU-50	MS-60	MS-63	MS-64	MS-65
1927	28,142	250	275	290	335	880

KM# 163 HAWAIIAN SESQUICENTENNIAL
Obv: Captain James Cook bust left **Rev:** Native Hawaiian standing over view of Diamond Head **Designer:** Juliette May Fraser and Chester Beach **Notes:** Counterfeits exist.

Date	Mintage	AU-50	MS-60	MS-63	MS-64	MS-65
1928	10,008	1,785	2,650	3,350	3,775	6,200

KM# 168 ARKANSAS CENTENNIAL
Obv: Liberty and Indian Chief's conjoint heads left **Rev:** Eagle with outstreatched wings and Flag of Arkansas in background **Designer:** Edward E. Burr

Date	Mintage	AU-50	MS-60	MS-63	MS-64	MS-65
1935	13,012	90.00	100.00	110	120	215
1935D	5,505	105	110	120	130	250
1935S	5,506	105	110	120	130	250
1936	9,660	90.00	100.00	110	120	225
1936D	9,660	105	110	120	130	255
1936S	9,662	105	110	120	130	255
1937	5,505	105	115	120	135	275
1937D	5,505	105	115	120	130	265
1937S	5,506	105	115	120	135	290
1938	3,156	155	180	190	200	590
1938D	3,155	160	180	190	200	580
1938S	3,156	160	180	190	200	640
1939	2,104	320	375	380	400	940
1939D	2,104	320	375	380	400	910
1939S	2,105	320	375	380	400	925

KM# 165.2 DANIEL BOONE BICENTENNIAL
Obv: Daniel Boone bust left **Rev:** Daniel Boone and Native American standing, "1934" added above the word "PIONEER." **Designer:** Augustus Lukeman

Date	Mintage	AU-50	MS-60	MS-63	MS-64	MS-65
1935	10,008	125	135	140	145	260
1935D	2,003	360	390	425	450	835
1935S	2,004	360	390	425	450	815
1936	12,012	120	125	135	140	250
1936D	5,005	130	135	145	155	295
1936S	5,006	130	135	145	155	285
1937	9,810	135	135	138	145	260
1937D	2,506	320	375	385	400	515
1937S	2,506	320	375	385	400	540
1938	2,100	340	380	390	400	535
1938D	2,100	340	380	390	410	525
1938S	2,100	340	380	390	400	565

KM# 167 TEXAS CENTENNIAL
Obv: Eagle standing left, large star in background
Rev: Winged Victory kneeling beside Alamo Mission, small busts of Sam Houston and Stephen Austin at sides **Designer:** Pompeo Coppini

Date	Mintage	AU-50	MS-60	MS-63	MS-64	MS-65
1934	61,463	135	140	150	165	300
1935	9,994	140	145	155	160	300
1935D	10,007	140	145	155	160	300
1935S	10,008	140	145	155	160	300
1936	8,911	140	145	155	160	310
1936D	9,039	140	145	155	160	310
1936S	9,055	140	145	155	160	325
1937	6,571	140	145	155	160	310
1937D	6,605	140	145	155	160	300
1937S	6,637	140	145	155	160	300
1938	3,780	235	250	260	305	425
1938D	3,775	240	255	265	305	415
1938S	3,814	235	250	260	305	415

KM# 165.1 DANIEL BOONE BICENTENNIAL
Obv: Daniel Boone bust left **Rev:** Daniel Boone and Native American standing **Designer:** Augustus Lukeman

Date	Mintage	AU-50	MS-60	MS-63	MS-64	MS-65
1934	10,007	120	125	135	140	250
1935	10,010	120	125	135	140	250
1935D	5,005	130	135	145	155	295
1935S	5,005	130	135	145	155	285

KM# 166 MARYLAND TERCENTENARY
Obv: Lord Baltimore, Cecil Calvert bust right **Rev:** Maryland state arms **Designer:** Hans Schuler

Date	Mintage	AU-50	MS-60	MS-63	MS-64	MS-65
1934	25,015	150	175	185	200	375

KM# 171 SAN DIEGO-PACIFIC INTERNATIONAL EXPOSITION
Obv: Seated female with bear at her side
Rev: State of California exposition building
Designer: Robert Aitken

Date	Mintage	AU-50	MS-60	MS-63	MS-64	MS-65
1935S	70,132	95.00	98.00	105	110	240
1936D	30,092	100.00	120	125	135	275

KM# 169 CONNECTICUT TERCENTENARY
Obv: Eagle standing left **Rev:** Charter oak tree
Designer: Henry Kreiss

Date	Mintage	AU-50	MS-60	MS-63	MS-64	MS-65
1935	25,018	240	265	275	325	500

KM# 170 HUDSON, N.Y., SESQUICENTENNIAL
Obv: Hudson's ship, the Half Moon sailing right
Rev: Seal of the City of Hudson **Designer:** Chester Beach

Date	Mintage	AU-50	MS-60	MS-63	MS-64	MS-65
1935	10,008	750	875	1,050	1,550	2,100

KM# 172 OLD SPANISH TRAIL
Obv: Long-horn cow's head facing **Rev:** The 1535

route of Cabeza de Vaca's expedition and a yucca tree **Designer:** L.W. Hoffecker **Notes:** Counterfeits exist.

Date	Mintage	AU-50	MS-60	MS-63	MS-64	MS-65
1935	10,008	1,250	1,375	1,650	1,750	2,000

KM# 173 ALBANY, N.Y., CHARTER ANNIVERSARY

Obv: Beaver knawing on maple branch **Rev:** Standing figures of Thomas Dongan, Peter Schyuyler and Robert Livingston **Designer:** Gertrude K. Lathrop

Date	Mintage	AU-50	MS-60	MS-63	MS-64	MS-65
1936	17,671	300	310	330	350	440

KM# 174 SAN FRANCISCO-OAKLAND BAY BRIDGE

Obv: Grizzly bear facing **Rev:** Oakland Bay Bridge **Designer:** Jacques Schnier

Date	Mintage	AU-50	MS-60	MS-63	MS-64	MS-65
1936	71,424	155	160	165	185	365

KM# 175 BRIDGEPORT, CONN., CENTENNIAL

Obv: P.T. Barnum bust left **Rev:** Eagle standing right **Designer:** Henry Kreiss

Date	Mintage	AU-50	MS-60	MS-63	MS-64	MS-65
1936	25,015	130	140	150	175	320

KM# 176 CINCINNATI MUSIC CENTER

Obv: Stephen Foster bust right **Rev:** Kneeling female with lyre **Designer:** Constance Ortmayer

Date	Mintage	AU-50	MS-60	MS-63	MS-64	MS-65
1936	5,005	295	310	335	410	725
1936D	5,005	295	310	335	410	750
1936S	5,006	295	310	335	410	750

KM# 177 CLEVELAND-GREAT LAKES EXPOSITION

Obv: Moses Cleaveland bust left **Rev:** Dividers and map of the Great Lakes **Designer:** Brenda Putnam

Date	Mintage	AU-50	MS-60	MS-63	MS-64	MS-65
1936	50,030	110	115	120	160	215

KM# 178 COLUMBIA, S.C., SESQUICENTENNIAL

Obv: Figure of Justice between capitols of 1786 and 1936 **Rev:** Palmetto tree **Designer:** A. Wolfe Davidson

Date	Mintage	AU-50	MS-60	MS-63	MS-64	MS-65
1936	9,007	250	265	270	275	310
1936D	8,009	260	270	280	285	340
1936S	8,007	260	270	280	285	340

KM# 179 DELAWARE TERCENTENARY

Obv: Old Swedes Church in Wilmington **Rev:** Kalmar Nyckel sailing left **Designer:** Carl L. Schmitz

Date	Mintage	AU-50	MS-60	MS-63	MS-64	MS-65
1936	20,993	255	265	275	290	465

KM# 180 ELGIN, ILL., CENTENNIAL
Obv: Pioneer head left **Rev:** Statue group
Designer: Trygve Rovelstad

Date	Mintage	AU-50	MS-60	MS-63	MS-64	MS-65
1936	20,015	195	205	215	225	355

KM# 181 BATTLE OF GETTYSBURG 75TH ANNIVERSARY
Obv: Union and Confederate veteran conjoint busts right **Rev:** Double blased fasces seperating two shields **Designer:** Frank Vittor

Date	Mintage	AU-50	MS-60	MS-63	MS-64	MS-65
1936	26,928	435	460	485	565	925

KM# 182 LONG ISLAND TERCENTENARY
Obv: Dutch settler and Native American conjoint head right **Rev:** Dutch sailing vessel **Designer:** Howard K. Weinman

Date	Mintage	AU-50	MS-60	MS-63	MS-64	MS-65
1936	81,826	85.00	92.00	98.00	105	325

KM# 183 LYNCHBURG, VA., SESQUICENTENNIAL
Obv: Sen. Carter Glass bust left **Rev:** Liberty standing, old Lynchburg courthouse at right **Designer:** Charles Keck

Date	Mintage	AU-50	MS-60	MS-63	MS-64	MS-65
1936	20,013	220	230	265	275	365

KM# 184 NORFOLK, VA., BICENTENNIAL
Obv: Seal of the City of Norfolk **Rev:** Royal Mace of Norfolk **Designer:** William M. and Marjorie E. Simpson

Date	Mintage	AU-50	MS-60	MS-63	MS-64	MS-65
1936	16,936	425	435	445	460	575

KM# 185 RHODE ISLAND TERCENTENARY
Obv: Roger Williams in canoe hailing Native American **Rev:** Shield with anchor **Designer:** Arthur G. Carey and John H. Benson

Date	Mintage	AU-50	MS-60	MS-63	MS-64	MS-65
1936	20,013	98.00	105	110	120	290
1936D	15,010	100.00	110	120	125	305
1936S	15,011	100.00	110	120	130	320

KM# 186 ROANOKE ISLAND, N.C.
Obv: Sir Walter Raleigh bust left **Rev:** Ellinor Dare holding baby Virginia, two small ships flanking **Designer:** William M. Simpson

Date	Mintage	AU-50	MS-60	MS-63	MS-64	MS-65
1937	29,030	220	225	235	245	315

KM# 187 ARKANSAS CENTENNIAL
Obv: Eagle with wings outstreatched, Arkansas flag in backgorund **Obv. Designer:** Henry Kreiss
Rev: Sen. Joseph T. Robinson bust right
Rev. Designer: Edward E. Burr

Date	Mintage	AU-50	MS-60	MS-63	MS-64	MS-65
1936	25,265	140	175	210	220	385

KM# 188 WISCONSIN TERRITORIAL
CENTENNIAL Obv: Badger from the Territorial seal **Rev:** Pick axe and mound of lead ore **Designer:** David Parsons

Date	Mintage	AU-50	MS-60	MS-63	MS-64	MS-65
1936	25,015	215	240	255	265	365

KM# 189 YORK COUNTY, MAINE,
TERCENTENARY Obv: Stockade **Rev:** York County seal **Designer:** Walter H. Rich

Date	Mintage	AU-50	MS-60	MS-63	MS-64	MS-65
1936	25,015	210	215	225	235	340

KM# 190 BATTLE OF ANTIETAM 75TH
ANNIVERSARY Obv: Generals Robert E. Lee and George McClellan conjoint busts left **Rev:** Burnside Bridge **Designer:** William M. Simpson

Date	Mintage	AU-50	MS-60	MS-63	MS-64	MS-65
1937	18,028	695	735	750	775	950

KM# 191 NEW ROCHELLE, N.Y.
Obv: John Pell and a calf **Rev:** Fleur-de-lis from the seal of the city **Designer:** Gertrude K. Lathrop

Date	Mintage	AU-50	MS-60	MS-63	MS-64	MS-65
1938	15,266	375	385	425	440	600

KM# 198 BOOKER T. WASHINGTON
Obv: Booker T. Washington bust right **Rev:** Cabin and NYU's Hall of Fame **Designer:** Isaac S. Hathaway **Notes:** Actual mintages are higher, but unsold issues were melted to produce Washington Carver issues.

Date	Mintage	AU-50	MS-60	MS-63	MS-64	MS-65
1946	1,000,546	14.00	18.00	21.00	23.00	64.00
1946D	200,113	16.50	20.00	32.00	37.00	72.00
1946S	500,729	15.00	18.50	23.00	27.00	66.00
1947	100,017	30.00	36.00	56.00	65.00	80.00
1947D	100,017	32.00	38.00	62.00	70.00	100.00
1947S	100,017	32.00	38.00	59.00	65.00	76.00
1948	8,005	46.00	64.00	77.00	80.00	84.00
1948D	8,005	46.00	62.00	77.00	80.00	84.00
1948S	8,005	46.00	65.00	78.00	82.00	88.00
1949	6,004	67.00	82.00	85.00	96.00	115
1949D	6,004	67.00	82.00	85.00	96.00	115
1949S	6,004	67.00	82.00	85.00	102	105
1950	6,004	46.00	68.00	78.00	82.00	90.00
1950D	6,004	46.00	68.00	75.00	82.00	88.00
1950S	512,091	18.00	20.00	24.00	26.00	65.00
1951	51,082	17.00	22.00	24.00	26.00	65.00
1951D	7,004	47.00	68.00	80.00	85.00	90.00
1951S	7,004	47.00	68.00	80.00	84.00	88.00

KM# 197 IOWA STATEHOOD CENTENNIAL
Obv: First Capitol building at Iowa City **Rev:** Iowa state seal **Designer:** Adam Pietz

Date	Mintage	AU-50	MS-60	MS-63	MS-64	MS-65
1946	100,057	100.00	105	108	112	160

KM# 200 BOOKER T. WASHINGTON AND
GEORGE WASHINGTON CARVER
Obv: Booker T. Washington and George Washington Carver conjoint busts right **Rev:** Map of the United States **Designer:** Isaac S. Hathaway

Date	Mintage	AU-50	MS-60	MS-63	MS-64	MS-65
1951	110,018	18.00	20.00	25.00	44.00	290
1951D	10,004	42.00	50.00	80.00	82.00	140
1951S	10,004	42.00	50.00	80.00	86.00	90.00
1952	2,006,292	17.00	18.00	24.00	42.00	83.00
1952D	8,006	40.00	50.00	80.00	85.00	190
1952S	8,006	40.00	50.00	80.00	84.00	185
1953	8,003	40.00	50.00	80.00	85.00	260
1953D	8,003	40.00	50.00	80.00	85.00	175
1953S	108,020	17.00	18.00	24.00	42.00	120
1954	12,006	39.00	48.00	70.00	75.00	200
1954D	12,006	39.00	48.00	70.00	80.00	83.00
1954S	122,024	17.00	18.00	24.00	42.00	83.00

DOLLAR

KM# 118 LA FAYETTE
Weight: 26.7300 g. **Composition:** 0.9000 Silver, 0.7734 oz. ASW **Diameter:** 38.1mm. **Obv:** George Washington and Marquis de La Fayette conjoint busts right **Rev:** La Fayette on horseback left **Designer:** Charles E. Barber

Date	Mintage	AU-50	MS-60	MS-63	MS-64	MS-65
1900	36,026	550	950	1,875	3,250	11,500

KM# 119 LOUISIANA PURCHASE EXPOSITION - JEFFERSON
Weight: 1.6720 g. **Composition:** 0.9000 Gold, 0.0484 oz. AGW **Diameter:** 15mm. **Obv:** Jefferson bust left **Rev:** Legend and laurel branch **Designer:** Charles E. Barber

Date	Mintage	AU-50	MS-60	MS-63	MS-64	MS-65
1903	17,500	600	660	925	1,450	2,150

KM# 120 LOUISIANA PURCHASE EXPOSITION - MCKINLEY
Weight: 1.6720 g. **Composition:** 0.9000 Gold, 0.0484 oz. AGW **Diameter:** 15mm. **Obv:** William McKinley bust left **Obv. Designer:** Charles E. Barber **Rev:** Legend and laurel branch

Date	Mintage	AU-50	MS-60	MS-63	MS-64	MS-65
1903	17,500	590	650	800	1,400	2,100

KM# 121 LEWIS AND CLARK EXPOSITION
Weight: 1.6720 g. **Composition:** 0.9000 Gold, 0.0484 oz. AGW **Diameter:** 15mm. **Obv:** Lewis bust left **Obv. Designer:** Charles E. Barber **Rev:** Clark bust left

Date	Mintage	AU-50	MS-60	MS-63	MS-64	MS-65
1904	10,025	950	1,100	1,850	3,650	7,900
1905	10,041	975	1,450	2,250	3,950	15,000

KM# 136 PANAMA-PACIFIC EXPOSITION
Weight: 1.6720 g. **Composition:** 0.9000 Gold, 0.0484 oz. AGW **Diameter:** 15mm. **Obv:** Canal laborer bust left **Obv. Designer:** Charles Keck **Rev:** Value within two dolphins

Date	Mintage	AU-50	MS-60	MS-63	MS-64	MS-65
1915S	15,000	565	625	775	1,100	1,700

KM# 144 MCKINLEY MEMORIAL
Weight: 1.6720 g. **Composition:** 0.9000 Gold, 0.0484 oz. AGW **Diameter:** 15mm. **Obv:** William McKinley head left **Obv. Designer:** Charles E. Barber **Rev:** Memorial building at Niles, Ohio **Rev. Designer:** George T. Morgan

Date	Mintage	AU-50	MS-60	MS-63	MS-64	MS-65
1916	9,977	520	600	685	1,000	1,750
1917	10,000	575	700	900	1,475	2,250

KM# 152.1 GRANT MEMORIAL
Weight: 1.6720 g. **Composition:** 0.9000 Gold, 0.0484 oz. AGW **Diameter:** 15mm. **Obv:** U.S. Grant bust right **Obv. Designer:** Laura G. Fraser **Rev:** Birthplace **Notes:** Without an incuse "star" above the word GRANT on the obverse.

Date	Mintage	AU-50	MS-60	MS-63	MS-64	MS-65
1922	5,000	1,875	1,900	2,350	3,650	4,900

Star

KM# 152.2 GRANT MEMORIAL
Weight: 1.6720 g. **Composition:** 0.9000 Gold, 0.0484 oz. AGW **Diameter:** 15mm. **Obv:** U.S. Grant bust right **Obv. Designer:** Laura G. Fraser **Rev:** Birthplace **Notes:** Variety with an incuse "star" above the word GRANT on the obverse.

Date	Mintage	AU-50	MS-60	MS-63	MS-64	MS-65
1922	5,016	1,650	1,775	2,100	2,150	3,100

$2.50 (QUARTER EAGLE)

KM# 137 PANAMA-PACIFIC EXPOSITION
Weight: 4.1800 g. **Composition:** 0.9000 Gold,
0.1209 oz. AGW **Diameter:** 18mm. **Obv:** Columbia
holding cadueus while seated on a hippocamp
Obv. Designer: Charles E. Barber **Rev:** Eagle
standing left **Rev. Designer:** George T. Morgan

Date	Mintage	AU-50	MS-60	MS-63	MS-64	MS-65
1915S	6,749	1,550	1,950	4,100	5,650	6,750

KM# 161 U.S. SESQUICENTENNIAL
Weight: 4.1800 g. **Composition:** 0.9000 Gold,
0.1209 oz. AGW **Diameter:** 18mm. **Obv:** Liberty
standing holding torch and scroll **Obv. Designer:**
John R. Sinnock **Rev:** Independence Hall

Date	Mintage	AU-50	MS-60	MS-63	MS-64	MS-65
1926	46,019	425	500	800	1,375	3,450

$50

Obv: Minerva bust helmeted left **Obv. Designer:**
Robert Aitken **Rev:** Owl pearched on California pin
branch

Date	Mintage	AU-50	MS-60	MS-63	MS-64	MS-65
1915S	483	46,500	57,500	90,000	105,000	160,000

KM# 139 PANAMA-PACIFIC EXPOSITION
OCTAGONAL Weight: 83.5900 g. **Composition:**
0.9000 Gold, 2.4186 oz. AGW **Diameter:** 44mm.
Obv: Minerva bust helmeted left **Obv. Designer:**
Robert Aitken **Rev:** Owl pearched on California
pine branch

Date	Mintage	AU-50	MS-60	MS-63	MS-64	MS-65
1915S	645	50,000	52,500	84,500	98,000	146,000

KM# 138 PANAMA-PACIFIC EXPOSITION
ROUND Weight: 83.5900 g. **Composition:**
0.9000 Gold, 2.4186 oz. AGW **Diameter:** 44mm.

COMMEMORATIVE COINAGE 1882-PRESENT

All commemorative silver dollar coins of 1982-present have the following specifications: diameter — 38.1 millimeters; weight — 26.7300 grams; composition — 0.9000 silver, 0.7736 ounces actual silver weight. All commemorative $5 coins of 1982-present have the following specificiations: diameter — 21.6 millimeters; weight — 8.3590 grams; composition: 0.9000 gold, 0.242 ounces actual gold weight.

Note: In 1982, after a hiatus of nearly 20 years, coinage of commemorative half dollars resumed. Those designated with a 'W' were struck at the West Point Mint. Some issues were struck in copper-nickel. Those struck in silver have the same size, weight and composition as the prior commemorative half-dollar series.

HALF DOLLAR

KM# 208 GEORGE WASHINGTON, 250TH BIRTH ANNIVERSARY
Weight: 12.5000 g. Composition: 0.9000 Silver, 0.3617 oz. ASW Diameter: 30.6mm. Obv: George Washington on horseback facing Obv. Designer: Elizabeth Jones Rev: Mount Vernon

Date	UNC Mintage	Proof Mintage	MS-65	Prf-65
1982D	2,210,458	—	14.90	—
1982S	—	4,894,044	—	14.90

KM# 212 STATUE OF LIBERTY CENTENNIAL
Weight: 11.3400 g. Composition: Copper-Nickel Clad Copper Obv: State of Liberty and sunrise Obv. Designer: Edgar Z. Steever Rev: Emigrant family looking toward mainland Rev. Designer: Sherl Joseph Winter

Date	UNC Mintage	Proof Mintage	MS-65	Prf-65
1986D	928,008	—	3.75	—
1986S	—	6,925,627	—	3.75

KM# 224 CONGRESS BICENTENNIAL
Weight: 11.3400 g. Composition: Copper-Nickel Clad Copper Obv: Statue of Freedom head Obv. Designer: Patricia L. Verani Rev: Capitol building Rev. Designer: William Woodward and Edgar Z. Steever

Date	UNC Mintage	Proof Mintage	MS-65	Prf-65
1989D	163,753	—	7.50	—
1989S	762,198	—	—	7.50

KM# 228 MOUNT RUSHMORE 50TH ANNIVERSARY
Weight: 11.3400 g. Composition: Copper-Nickel Clad Copper Obv. Designer: Marcel Jovine Rev: Mount Rushmore portraits Rev. Designer: T. James Ferrell

Date	UNC Mintage	Proof Mintage	MS-65	Prf-65
1991D	172,754	—	18.50	—
1991S	753,257	—	—	16.00

KM# 233 1992 OLYMPICS
Weight: 11.3400 g. Composition: Copper-Nickel Clad Copper Obv: Torch and laurel Obv.

Designer: William Cousins **Rev:** Female gymnast and large flag **Rev. Designer:** Steven M. Bieda

Date	UNC Mintage	Proof Mintage	MS-65	Prf-65
1992P	161,607	—	8.50	—
1992S	—	519,645	—	9.00

KM# 237 COLUMBUS VOYAGE - 500TH ANNIVERSARY   Weight: 11.3400 g.
Composition: Copper-Nickel Clad Copper **Obv:** Columbus standing on shore **Rev:** Nina, Pinta and Santa Maria sailing right **Designer:** T. James Ferrell

Date	UNC Mintage	Proof Mintage	MS-65	Prf-65
1992D	135,702	—	11.50	—
1992S	—	390,154	—	9.50

KM# 240 JAMES MADISON - BILL OF RIGHTS
Weight: 12.5000 g. **Composition:** 0.9000 Silver, 0.3617 oz. ASW **Obv:** James Madison writing, Montpelier in background **Obv. Designer:** T. James Ferrell **Rev:** Statue of Liberty torch **Rev. Designer:** Dean McMullen

Date	UNC Mintage	Proof Mintage	MS-65	Prf-65
1993W	193,346	—	16.50	—
1993S	586,315	—	—	15.00

KM# 243 WORLD WAR II 50TH ANNIVERSARY
Weight: 11.3400 g. **Composition:** Copper-Nickel Clad Copper **Obv:** Three portraits, plane above, large V in backgound **Obv. Designer:** George Klauba **Rev:** Pacific island battle scene **Rev. Designer:** William J. Leftwich

Date	UNC Mintage	Proof Mintage	MS-65	Prf-65
(1993)P	197,072	—	17.50	—
(1993)P	317,396	—	—	17.50

KM# 246 1994 WORLD CUP SOCCER
Weight: 11.3400 g. **Composition:** Copper-Nickel Clad Copper **Obv:** Soccer player with ball **Obv. Designer:** Richard T. LaRoche **Rev:** World Cup 94 logo **Rev. Designer:** Dean McMullen

Date	UNC Mintage	Proof Mintage	MS-65	Prf-65
1994D	168,208	—	8.25	—
1994P	—	609,354	—	8.00

KM# 254 CIVIL WAR BATTLEFIELD PRESERVATION   Weight: 11.3400 g.
Composition: Copper-Nickel Clad Copper **Obv:** Drummer and fenceline **Obv. Designer:** Don Troiani **Rev:** Canon overlooking battlefield **Rev. Designer:** T. James Ferrell

Date	UNC Mintage	Proof Mintage	MS-65	Prf-65
1995S	119,510	—	36.50	—
1995S	330,099	—	—	33.50

KM# 257 1996 ATLANTA OLYMPICS - BASKETBALL   Weight: 11.3400 g.
Composition: Copper-Nickel Clad Copper **Obv:** Three players, one jumping for a shot **Rev:** Hemisphere and Atlanta Olympics logo

Date	UNC Mintage	Proof Mintage	MS-65	Prf-65
1995S	—	169,655	—	16.50
1995S	171,001	—	18.00	—

KM# 262 1996 ATLANTA OLYMPICS - BASEBALL Weight: 11.3400 g. Composition:
Copper-Nickel Clad Copper Obv: Baseball batter at plate, catcher and umpire Obv. Designer: Edgar Z. Steever Rev: Hemisphere and Atlanta Olympics logo

Date	UNC Mintage	Proof Mintage	MS-65	Prf-65
1995S	164,605	—	19.50	—
1995S	—	118,087	—	18.00

KM# 271 1996 ATLANTA OLYMPICS - SOCCER
Weight: 11.3400 g. Composition: Copper-Nickel Clad Copper Obv: Two female soccer players Rev: Atlanta Olympics logo

Date	UNC Mintage	Proof Mintage	MS-65	Prf-65
1996S	52,836	—	135	—
1996S	—	122,412	—	88.00

KM# 267 1996 ATLANTA OLYMPICS - SWIMMING Weight: 11.3400 g. Composition:
Copper-Nickel Clad Copper Obv: Swimmer right in butterfly stroke Rev: Atlanta Olympics logo

Date	UNC Mintage	Proof Mintage	MS-65	Prf-65
1996S	49,533	—	140	—
1996S	—	114,315	—	33.50

KM# 323 U. S. CAPITOL VISITOR CENTER
Weight: 11.3400 g. Composition: Copper-Nickel Clad Copper Obv: Capitol sillouete, 1800 structure in detail Obv. Designer: Dean McMullen Rev: Legend within circle of stars Rev. Designer: Alex Shagin and Marcel Jovine

Date	UNC Mintage	Proof Mintage	MS-65	Prf-65
2001P	99,157	—	14.50	—
2001P	—	77,962	—	15.50

KM# 348 FIRST FLIGHT CENTENNIAL
Weight: 11.3400 g. Composition: Copper-Nickel Clad Copper Obv: Wright Monument at Kitty Hawk Obv. Designer: John Mercanti Rev: Wright Flyer in flight Rev. Designer: Donna Weaver

Date	UNC Mintage	Proof Mintage	MS-65	Prf-65
2003P	57,726	—	15.00	—
2003P	109,710	—	—	16.00

KM# 438 AMERICAN BALD EAGLE
Weight: 11.3400 g. Composition: Copper-Nickel Clad Copper Diameter: 30.6mm. Obv: Two eaglets in nest with egg Rev: Eagle Challenger facing right, American Flag in background

Date	UNC Mintage	Proof Mintage	MS-65	Prf-65
2008S	120,000	—	12.00	—
2008S	175,000	—	—	14.50

KM# 506 U.S. ARMY Composition: Copper-Nickel Obv: Army contributions during peacetime, surveying, building a flood wall and space exploration Obv. Designer: Donna Weaver and Charles L. Vickers Rev: Continental soldier with musket Rev. Designer: Thomas Cleveland and Joseph Menna

Date	UNC Mintage	Proof Mintage	MS-65	Prf-65
2011	—	—	—	—

COMMEMORATIVES

DOLLAR

KM# 209 1984 LOS ANGELES OLYMPICS -
DISCUS **Obv:** Trippled discus thrower and five star logo **Obv. Designer:** Elizabeth Jones **Rev:** Eagle bust left

Date	UNC Mintage	Proof Mintage	MS-65	Prf-65
1983P	294,543	—	33.20	—
1983D	174,014	—	33.70	—
1983S	174,014	—	33.20	—
1983S	—	1,577,025	—	33.20

KM# 210 1984 LOS ANGELES OLYMPICS -
STADIUM STATUES **Obv:** Statues at exterior of Los Angeles Memorial Coliseum **Obv. Designer:** Robert Graham **Rev:** Eagle standing on rock

Date	UNC Mintage	Proof Mintage	MS-65	Prf-65
1984P	217,954	—	33.20	—
1984D	116,675	—	33.70	—
1984S	116,675	—	33.70	—
1984S	—	1,801,210	—	33.20

KM# 214 STATUE OF LIBERTY CENTENNIAL
Obv: Statue of Liberty and Ellis Island great hall **Obv. Designer:** John Mercanti **Rev:** Statue of Liberty torch **Rev. Designer:** John Mercanti and Matthew Peloso

Date	UNC Mintage	Proof Mintage	MS-65	Prf-65
1986P	723,635	—	33.20	—
1986S	—	6,414,638	—	33.20

KM# 220 CONSTITUTION BICENTENNIAL
Obv: Feather pen and document **Obv. Designer:** Patricia L. Verani **Rev:** Group of people

Date	UNC Mintage	Proof Mintage	MS-65	Prf-65
1987P	451,629	—	33.20	—
1987S	—	2,747,116	—	33.20

KM# 222 1988 OLYMPICS
Obv: Olympic torch and Statue of Liberty torch within laurel wreath **Obv. Designer:** Patricia L. Verani **Rev:** Olympic rights within olive wreath **Rev. Designer:** Sherl Joseph Winter

Date	UNC Mintage	Proof Mintage	MS-65	Prf-65
1988D	191,368	—	33.20	—
1988S	—	1,359,366	—	33.20

KM# 225 CONGRESS BICENTENNIAL
Obv: Statue of Freedom in clouds and sunburst
Rev: Mace from the House of Represenatives
Designer: William Woodward and Chester Y. Martin

Date	UNC Mintage	Proof Mintage	MS-65	Prf-65
1989D	135,203	—	33.20	—
1989S	—	762,198	—	33.20

KM# 229 MOUNT RUSHMORE 50TH
ANNIVERSARY Obv: Mount Rushmore portraits,
wreath below **Obv. Designer:** Marika Somogyi
Rev: Great seal in rays, United States map in
background **Rev. Designer:** Frank Gasparro

Date	UNC Mintage	Proof Mintage	MS-65	Prf-65
1991P	133,139	—	33.20	—
1991S	—	738,419	—	33.20

KM# 227 EISENHOWER CENTENNIAL
Obv: Two Eisenhower profiles, as general, left, as
President, right **Obv. Designer:** John Mercanti
Rev: Eisenhower home at Gettysburg
Rev. Designer: Marcel Jovine and John Mercanti

Date	UNC Mintage	Proof Mintage	MS-65	Prf-65
1990W	241,669	—	33.70	—
1990P	1,144,461	—	—	33.70

KM# 231 KOREAN WAR - 38TH ANNIVERSARY
Obv: Solder advancing right up a hill; planes
above, ships below **Obv. Designer:** John Mercanti
Rev: Map of Korean pensiluar, eagle's head
Rev. Designer: T. James Ferrell

Date	UNC Mintage	Proof Mintage	MS-65	Prf-65
1991D	213,049	—	33.70	—
1991P	—	618,488	—	22.00

KM# 232 USO 50TH ANNIVERSARY
Obv: USO banner **Obv. Designer:** Robert Lamb
Rev: Eagle pearched right atop globe
Rev. Designer: John Mercanti

Date	UNC Mintage	Proof Mintage	MS-65	Prf-65
1991D	124,958	—	33.20	—
1991S	—	321,275	—	34.20

KM# 236 WHITE HOUSE BICENTENNIAL
Obv: White House's north portico **Obv. Designer:**
Edgar Z. Steever **Rev:** John Hoban bust left, main
entrance doorway **Rev. Designer:** Chester Y.
Martin

Date	UNC Mintage	Proof Mintage	MS-65	Prf-65
1992D	123,803	—	33.20	—
1992W	—	375,851	—	33.20

KM# 234 1992 OLYMPICS - BASEBALL
Obv: Baseball pitcher, Nolan Ryan as depicted on
card **Obv. Designer:** John R. Deecken and Chester
Y. Martin **Rev:** Shield flanked by stylized wreath,
olympic rings above **Rev. Designer:** Marcel Jovine

Date	UNC Mintage	Proof Mintage	MS-65	Prf-65
1992D	187,552	—	33.20	—
1992S	—	504,505	—	33.20

KM# 238 COLUMBUS DISCOVERY - 500TH
ANNIVERSARY
Obv: Columbus standing with
banner, three ships in background **Obv. Designer:**
John Mercanti **Rev:** Half view of Santa Maria on
left, Space Shuttle Discovery on right
Rev. Designer: Thomas D. Rogers, Sr.

Date	UNC Mintage	Proof Mintage	MS-65	Prf-65
1992D	106,949	—	33.20	—
1992P	—	385,241	—	33.20

KM# 247 1994 WORLD CUP SOCCER
Obv: Two players with ball **Obv. Designer:** Dean McMullen and T. James Ferrell **Rev:** World Cup 94 logo **Rev. Designer:** Dean McMullen

Date	UNC Mintage	Proof Mintage	MS-65	Prf-65
1994D	81,698	—	33.20	—
1994S	—	576,978	—	33.20

KM# 241 JAMES MADISON - BILL OF RIGHTS
Obv: James Madison bust right, at left **Obv. Designer:** William Krawczewicz and Thomas D. Rogers, Sr. **Rev:** Montpelier home **Rev. Designer:** Dean McMullen and Thomas D. Rogers, Sr.

Date	UNC Mintage	Proof Mintage	MS-65	Prf-65
1993D	98,383	—	33.20	—
1993S	—	534,001	—	34.20

KM# 244 WORLD WAR II 50TH ANNIVERSARY
Obv: Soldier on Normandy beach **Rev:** Insignia of the Supreme Headquarters of the AEF above Eisenhower quote **Designer:** Thomas D. Rogers, Sr.

Date	UNC Mintage	Proof Mintage	MS-65	Prf-65
1993D	94,708	—	33.20	—
1993W	342,041	—	—	37.50

KM# 249 THOMAS JEFFERSON 250TH BIRTH ANNIVERSARY **Obv:** Jefferson's head left
Rev: Monticello home **Designer:** T. James Ferrell

Date	UNC Mintage	Proof Mintage	MS-65	Prf-65
1993P	266,927	—	33.20	—
1993S	—	332,891	—	33.70

COMMEMORATIVES

KM# 250 VIETNAM VETERANS MEMORIAL
Obv: Outstretched hand touching names on the Wall, Washington Monument in background **Obv. Designer:** John Mercanti **Rev:** Service Medals **Rev. Designer:** Thomas D. Rogers, Sr.

Date	UNC Mintage	Proof Mintage	MS-65	Prf-65
1994W	57,317	—	70.00	—
1994P	—	226,262	—	58.00

KM# 252 WOMEN IN MILITARY SERVICE MEMORIAL
Obv: Five uniformed women left **Obv. Designer:** T. James Ferrell **Rev:** Memorial at Arlington National Cemetery **Rev. Designer:** Thomas D. Rogers, Sr.

Date	UNC Mintage	Proof Mintage	MS-65	Prf-65
1994W	53,054	—	34.00	—
1994P	—	213,201	—	33.20

KM# 251 NATIONAL PRISONER OF WAR MUSEUM
Obv: Eagle in flight left within circle of barbed wire **Obv. Designer:** Thomas Nielson and Alfred Maletsky **Rev:** National Prisioner of War Museum **Rev. Designer:** Edgar Z. Steever

Date	UNC Mintage	Proof Mintage	MS-65	Prf-65
1994W	54,790	—	75.00	—
1994P	—	220,100	—	36.00

KM# 253 U.S. CAPITOL BICENTENNIAL
Obv: Capitol dome, Statue fo Freedom surrounded by stars **Rev:** Eagle on shield, flags flanking

Date	UNC Mintage	Proof Mintage	MS-65	Prf-65
1994D	68,352	—	34.20	—
1994S	—	279,416	—	33.20

KM# 255 CIVIL WAR
Obv: Soldier giving water to wounded soldier
Obv. Designer: Don Troiani and Edgar Z. Steever
Rev: Chamberlain quote and battlefield monument
Rev. Designer: John Mercanti

Date	UNC Mintage	Proof Mintage	MS-65	Prf-65
1995P	45,866	—	69.00	—
1995S	—	437,114	—	66.00

KM# 260 1996 ATLANTA OLYMPICS - GYMNASTICS
Obv: Two gymnasts, female on floor exercise and male on rings **Rev:** Two clasped hands, Atlanta Olympic logo above

Date	UNC Mintage	Proof Mintage	MS-65	Prf-65
1995D	42,497	—	57.50	—
1995P	—	182,676	—	41.00

KM# 259 1996 ATLANTA PARALYMPICS - BLIND RUNNER
Obv: Blind runner **Rev:** Two clasped hands, Atlanta Olympic logo above

Date	UNC Mintage	Proof Mintage	MS-65	Prf-65
1995D	28,649	—	72.00	—
1995P	—	138,337	—	51.00

KM# 263 1996 ATLANTA OLYMPICS - CYCLING
Obv: Three cyclists approaching **Obv. Designer:** John Mercanti **Rev:** Two clasped hands, Atlanta Olympic logo above

Date	UNC Mintage	Proof Mintage	MS-65	Prf-65
1995D	19,662	—	135	—
1995P	—	118,795	—	45.00

COMMEMORATIVES

COMMEMORATIVES

KM# 264 1996 ATLANTA OLYMPICS - TRACK AND FIELD
Obv: Two runners on a track, one crossing finish line **Obv. Designer:** John Mercanti **Rev:** Two clasped hands, Atlanta Olympic logo above

Date	UNC Mintage	Proof Mintage	MS-65	Prf-65
1995D	24,796	—	88.00	—
1995P	—	136,935	—	41.00

KM# 268 1996 ATLANTA PARALYMPICS - WHEELCHAIR RACER
Obv: Wheelchair racer approaching with uplifted arms **Rev:** Atlanta Olympics logo **Rev. Designer:** Thomas D. Rogers, Sr.

Date	UNC Mintage	Proof Mintage	MS-65	Prf-65
1996D	14,497	—	310	—
1996P	—	84,280	—	73.00

KM# 266 SPECIAL OLYMPICS WORLD GAMES
Obv: Eunice Schriver head left; founder of the Special Olympics **Obv. Designer:** Jamie Wyeth and T. James Ferrell **Rev:** Special Olympics Logo on an award medal, rose, quote from Schriver **Rev. Designer:** Thomas D. Rogers, Sr.

Date	UNC Mintage	Proof Mintage	MS-65	Prf-65
1995W	89,301	—	33.20	—
1995P	—	351,764	—	33.20

KM# 269 1996 ATLANTA OLYMPICS - TENNIS
Obv: Female tennis player **Rev:** Atlanta Olympics logo **Rev. Designer:** Thomas D. Rogers, Sr.

Date	UNC Mintage	Proof Mintage	MS-65	Prf-65
1996D	15,983	—	260	—
1996P	—	92,016	—	83.00

KM# A272 1996 ATLANTA OLYMPICS - HIGH JUMP
Obv: High jumper **Rev. Designer:** Thomas D. Rogers, Sr.

Date	UNC Mintage	Proof Mintage	MS-65	Prf-65
1996D	15,697	—	315	—
1996P	—	124,502	—	48.00

KM# 275 NATIONAL COMMUNITY SERVICE
Obv: Female standing with lamp and shield **Obv. Designer:** Thomas D. Rogers, Sr. **Rev:** Legend within wreath **Rev. Designer:** William C. Cousins

Date	UNC Mintage	Proof Mintage	MS-65	Prf-65
1996S	23,500	—	200	—
1996S	—	101,543	—	60.00

KM# 272 1996 ATLANTA OLYMPICS - ROWING
Obv: Four man crew rowing left **Rev:** Atlanta Olympic logo **Rev. Designer:** Thomas D. Rogers, Sr.

Date	UNC Mintage	Proof Mintage	MS-65	Prf-65
1996D	16,258	—	290	—
1996P	—	151,890	—	63.00

KM# 276 SMITHSONIAN INSTITUTION 150TH ANNIVERSARY
Obv: Original Smithsonian building, the "Castle" designed by James Renwick **Obv. Designer:** Thomas D. Rogers, Sr. **Rev:** Female seated with torch and scroll on globe **Rev. Designer:** John Mercanti

Date	UNC Mintage	Proof Mintage	MS-65	Prf-65
1996D	31,230	—	120	—
1996P	—	129,152	—	45.00

KM# 278 U.S. BOTANIC GARDENS 175TH ANNIVERSARY **Obv:** National Botanic Gardens Conservatory building **Rev:** Rose **Designer:** Edgar Z. Steever

Date	UNC Mintage	Proof Mintage	MS-65	Prf-65
1997P	57,272	—	38.50	—
1997P	—	264,528	—	36.50

KM# 281 NATIONAL LAW ENFORCEMENT OFFICERS MEMORIAL **Obv:** Male and female officer admiring name on monument **Rev:** Rose on a plain shield **Designer:** Alfred Maletsky

Date	UNC Mintage	Proof Mintage	MS-65	Prf-65
1997P	—	110,428	—	82.00
1997P	28,575	—	145	—

KM# 279 JACKIE ROBINSON **Obv:** Jackie Robinson sliding into base **Obv. Designer:** Alfred Maletsky **Rev:** Anniversary logo **Rev. Designer:** T. James Ferrell

Date	UNC Mintage	Proof Mintage	MS-65	Prf-65
1997S	30,007	—	83.00	—
1997S	—	110,495	—	100.00

KM# 287 ROBERT F. KENNEDY **Obv:** Kennedy bust facing **Obv. Designer:** Thomas D. Rogers, Sr. **Rev:** Eagle on sheild, Senate Seal **Rev. Designer:** James M. Peed and Thomas D. Rogers, Sr.

Date	UNC Mintage	Proof Mintage	MS-65	Prf-65
1998S	106,422	—	36.00	—
1998S	—	99,020	—	45.00

KM# 299 YELLOWSTONE
Obv: Old Faithful gyser erupting **Obv. Designer:** Edgar Z. Steever **Rev:** Bison and vista as on National Parks shield **Rev. Designer:** William C. Cousins

Date	UNC Mintage	Proof Mintage	MS-65	Prf-65
1999P	23,614	—	48.50	—
1999P	—	128,646	—	41.50

KM# 288 BLACK REVOLUTIONARY WAR PATRIOTS **Obv:** Crispus Attucks bust right **Obv. Designer:** John Mercanti **Rev:** Family standing **Rev. Designer:** Ed Dwight

Date	UNC Mintage	Proof Mintage	MS-65	Prf-65
1998S	37,210	—	145	—
1998S	—	75,070	—	89.00

KM# 298 DOLLEY MADISON
Obv: Madison bust right, at left **Rev:** Montpelier home **Designer:** Tiffany & Co.

Date	UNC Mintage	Proof Mintage	MS-65	Prf-65
1999P	89,104	—	41.00	—
1999P	224,403	—	—	33.20

KM# 311 LIBRARY OF CONGRESS BICENTENNIAL **Obv:** Open and closed book, torch in background **Obv. Designer:** Thomas D. Rogers, Sr. **Rev:** Skylight dome above the main reading room **Rev. Designer:** John Mercanti

Date	UNC Mintage	Proof Mintage	MS-65	Prf-65
2000P	52,771	—	37.50	—
2000P	—	196,900	—	33.20

COMMEMORATIVES

COMMEMORATIVES

KM# 313 LEIF ERICSON
Obv: Ericson bust helmeted right **Obv. Designer:**
John Mercanti **Rev:** Viking ship sailing left
Rev. Designer: T. James Ferrell

Date	UNC Mintage	Proof Mintage	MS-65	Prf-65
2000P	28,150	—	82.50	—
2000 Iceland	15,947	—	—	29.20
2000P	58,612	—	—	62.50

KM# 325 NATIVE AMERICAN - BISON
Obv: Native American bust right **Rev:** Bison
standing left **Designer:** James E. Fraser

Date	UNC Mintage	Proof Mintage	MS-65	Prf-65
2001D	197,131	—	159	—
2001P	272,869	—	—	169

KM# 324 CAPITOL VISITOR CENTER
Obv: Original and current Capital facades **Obv.
Designer:** Marika Somogyi **Rev:** Eagle with sheild
and ribbon **Rev. Designer:** John Mercanti

Date	UNC Mintage	Proof Mintage	MS-65	Prf-65
2001P	66,636	—	33.20	—
2001P	143,793	—	—	33.20

KM# 336 2002 WINTER OLYMPICS - SALT LAKE CITY
Obv: Salt Lake City Olympic logo **Obv. Designer:**
John Mercanti **Rev:** Stylized skyline with mountains
in background **Rev. Designer:** Donna Weaver

Date	UNC Mintage	Proof Mintage	MS-65	Prf-65
2002P	35,388	—	33.20	—
2002P	142,873	—	—	36.50

KM# 338 U.S. MILITARY ACADEMY AT WEST POINT -BICENTENNIAL
Obv: Cadet Review flagbearers, Academy buildings in background **Obv. Designer:** T. James Ferrell **Rev:** Academy emblems - Corinthian helmet and sword **Rev. Designer:** John Mercanti

Date	UNC Mintage	Proof Mintage	MS-65	Prf-65
2002W	103,201	—	33.20	—
2002W	—	288,293	—	33.20

KM# 362 THOMAS A. EDISON - ELECTRIC LIGHT 125TH ANNIVERSARY
Obv: Edison half-length figure facing holding light bulb **Obv. Designer:** Donna Weaver **Rev:** Light bulb and rays **Rev. Designer:** John Mercanti

Date	UNC Mintage	Proof Mintage	MS-65	Prf-65
2004P	68,031	—	33.20	—
2004P	—	213,409	—	33.20

KM# 349 FIRST FLIGHT CENTENNIAL
Obv: Orville and Wilbur Wright busts left **Obv. Designer:** T. James Ferrell **Rev:** Wright Flyer over dunes **Rev. Designer:** Norman E. Nemeth

Date	UNC Mintage	Proof Mintage	MS-65	Prf-65
2003P	53,761	—	33.20	—
2003P	—	193,086	—	33.20

KM# 363 LEWIS AND CLARK CORPS OF DISCOVERY BICENTENNIAL
Obv: Lewis and Clark standing **Rev:** Jefferson era clasped hands peace medal

Date	UNC Mintage	Proof Mintage	MS-65	Prf-65
2004P	90,323	—	33.20	—
2004P	—	288,492	—	33.20

KM# 375 JOHN MARSHALL, 250TH BIRTH ANNIVERSARY Obv: Marshall bust left
Obv. Designer: John Mercanti Rev: Marshall era Supreme Court Chamber Rev. Designer: Donna Weaver

Date	UNC Mintage	Proof Mintage	MS-65	Prf-65
2005P	48,953	—	33.20	—
2005P	—	141,993	—	34.20

KM# 387 BENJAMIN FRANKLIN, 300TH BIRTH ANNIVERSARY Obv: Youthful Franklin flying kite
Obv. Designer: Norman E. Nemeth
Rev: Revolutionary era "JOIN, or DIE" snake cartoon illustration

Date	UNC Mintage	Proof Mintage	MS-65	Prf-65
2006P	58,000	—	33.20	—
2006P	—	142,000	—	42.50

KM# 376 U.S. MARINE CORPS, 230TH ANNIVERSARY Obv: Flag Raising at Mt. Suribachi on Iwo Jima Rev: Marine Corps emblem

Date	UNC Mintage	Proof Mintage	MS-65	Prf-65
2005P	130,000	—	38.00	—
2005P	—	370,000	—	46.50

KM# 388 BENJAMIN FRANKLIN, 300TH BIRTH ANNIVERSARY Obv: Bust 3/4 right, signature in oval below Rev: Continental Dollar of 1776 in center

Date	UNC Mintage	Proof Mintage	MS-65	Prf-65
2006P	58,000	—	33.20	—
2006P	—	142,000	—	43.50

KM# 394 SAN FRANCISCO MINT MUSEUM
Obv: 3/4 view of building **Obv. Designer:** Sherl J. Winter **Rev:** Reverse of 1880s Morgan silver dollar

Date	UNC Mintage	Proof Mintage	MS-65	Prf-65
2006S	65,609	—	33.20	—
2006S	—	255,700	—	33.20

KM# 418 CENTRAL HIGH SCHOOL
DESEGREGATION Obv: Children's feet walking left with adult feet in military boots **Rev:** Little Rock's Central High School **Rev. Designer:** Don Everhart II

Date	UNC Mintage	Proof Mintage	MS-65	Prf-65
2007P	66,093	—	50.00	—
2007P	—	124,618	—	50.00

KM# 405 JAMESTOWN - 400TH ANNIVERSARY
Obv: Two settlers and Native American
Obv. Designer: Donna Weaver **Rev:** Three ships
Rev. Designer: Don Everhart II

Date	UNC Mintage	Proof Mintage	MS-65	Prf-65
2007P	79,801	—	33.20	—
2007P	—	258,802	—	33.20

KM# 439 AMERICAN BALD EAGLE
Obv: Eagle with flight, mountain in background at right **Rev:** Great Seal of the United States

Date	UNC Mintage	Proof Mintage	MS-65	Prf-65
2008P	110,073	—	391	—
2008P	—	243,558	—	396

KM# 454 LINCOLN BICENTENNIAL
Obv: 3/4 portrait facing right **Obv. Designer:** Justin Kunz and Don Everhart II **Rev:** Part of Gettysburg Address within wreath **Rev. Designer:** Phebe Hemphill

Date	UNC Mintage	Proof Mintage	MS-65	Prf-65
2009P	125,000	—	55.00	—
2009P	—	375,000	—	63.50

KM# 455 LOUIS BRAILLE BIRTH
BICENTENNIAL   Obv: Louis Braille bust facing
Obv. Designer: Joel Iskowitz and Phebe Hemphill
Rev: School child reading book in Braille, BRL in
Braille code above **Rev. Designer:** Susan Gamble
and Joseph Menna

Date	UNC Mintage	Proof Mintage	MS-65	Prf-65
2009P	82,639	—	32.50	—
2009P	—	135,235	—	42.50

KM# 480 BOY SCOUTS OF AMERICA, 100TH
ANNIVERSARY   Obv: Cub Scout, Boy Scout and
Venturer saluting **Obv. Designer:** Donna Weaver
Rev: Boy Scouts of America logo **Rev. Designer:**
Jim Licaretz

Date	UNC Mintage	Proof Mintage	MS-65	Prf-65
2010P	—	—	35.00	—
2010P	—	—	—	45.00

KM# 504 MEDAL OF HONOR
Obv: Medal of Honor designs for Army, Navy adn Air
Force awards **Obv. Designer:** James Licaretz
Rev: Army infantry doldier carrying another to safety
Rev. Designer: Richard Masters and Phebe Hemphill

Date	UNC Mintage	Proof Mintage	MS-65	Prf-65
2011	—	—	—	—

KM# 507 U.S. ARMY
Obv: Male and femlae soldier heads looking
outward **Obv. Designer:** Richard Masters and
Michael Gaudioso **Rev:** Seven core values of the
Army, Eagle from the great seal **Rev. Designer:**
Susan Gamble and Don Everhart, II

Date	UNC Mintage	Proof Mintage	MS-65	Prf-65
2011	—	—	—	—

$5 (HALF EAGLE)

KM# 479 AMERICAN VETERANS DISABLED
FOR LIFE   Obv: Soldier's feet, crutches **Rev:**
Legend within wreath

Date	UNC Mintage	Proof Mintage	MS-65	Prf-65
2010W	77,859	—	41.00	—
2010W	—	189,881	—	42.50

KM# 215 STATUE OF LIBERTY CENTENNIAL
Obv: Statue of Liberty head right **Rev:** Eagle in
flight left **Designer:** Elizabeth Jones

Date	UNC Mintage	Proof Mintage	MS-65	Prf-65
1986W	95,248	—	376	—
1986W	—	404,013	—	376

KM# 221 CONSTITUTION BICENTENNIAL

Obv: Eagle left with quill pen in talon **Rev:** Upright quill pen **Designer:** Marcel Jovine

Date	UNC Mintage	Proof Mintage	MS-65	Prf-65
1987W	214,225	—	376	—
1987W	—	651,659	—	376

KM# 235 1992 OLYMPICS

Obv: Sprinter, U.S. Flag in background **Obv. Designer:** James C. Sharpe and T. James Ferrell **Rev:** Heraldic eagle, olympic rings above **Rev. Designer:** James M. Peed

Date	UNC Mintage	Proof Mintage	MS-65	Prf-65
1992W	27,732	—	395	—
1992W	—	77,313	—	396

KM# 223 1988 OLYMPICS

Obv: Nike head wearing olive wreath **Obv. Designer:** Elizabeth Jones **Rev:** Stylized olympic couldron **Rev. Designer:** Marcel Jovine

Date	UNC Mintage	Proof Mintage	MS-65	Prf-65
1988W	62,913	—	376	—
1988W	—	281,456	—	376

KM# 239 COLUMBUS QUINCENTENARY

Obv: Columbus' profile left, at right, map of Western Hemisphere at left **Obv. Designer:** T. James Ferrell **Rev:** Arms of Spain, and parchment map **Rev. Designer:** Thomas D. Rogers, Sr.

Date	UNC Mintage	Proof Mintage	MS-65	Prf-65
1992W	24,329	—	395	—
1992W	—	79,730	—	376

KM# 226 CONGRESS BICENTENNIAL

Obv: Capitol dome **Obv. Designer:** John Mercanti **Rev:** Eagle atop of the canopy from the Old Senate Chamber

Date	UNC Mintage	Proof Mintage	MS-65	Prf-65
1989W	46,899	—	376	—
1989W	—	164,690	—	376

KM# 242 JAMES MADISON - BILL OF RIGHTS

Obv: Madison at left holding document **Obv. Designer:** Scott R. Blazek **Rev:** Eagle above legend, torch and laurel at sides **Rev. Designer:** Joseph D. Peña

Date	UNC Mintage	Proof Mintage	MS-65	Prf-65
1993W	22,266	—	410	—
1993W	—	78,651	—	376

KM# 230 MOUNT RUSHMORE 50TH ANNIVERSARY

Obv: Eagle in flight towards Mount Rushmore **Obv. Designer:** John Mercanti **Rev:** Legend at center **Rev. Designer:** Robert Lamb and William C. Cousins

Date	UNC Mintage	Proof Mintage	MS-65	Prf-65
1991W	31,959	—	395	—
1991W	—	111,991	—	376

KM# 245 WORLD WAR II 50TH ANNIVERSARY

Obv: Soldier with expression of victory **Obv. Designer:** Charles J. Madsen **Rev:** Morse code dot-dot-dot-dash for V, large in background; V for Victory **Rev. Designer:** Edward S. Fisher

Date	UNC Mintage	Proof Mintage	MS-65	Prf-65
1993W	23,089	—	440	—
1993W	—	65,461	—	376

KM# 248 1994 WORLD CUP SOCCER
Obv: World Cup trophy **Obv. Designer:** William J. Krawczewicz **Rev:** World Cup 94 logo **Rev. Designer:** Dean McMullen

Date	UNC Mintage	Proof Mintage	MS-65	Prf-65
1994W	22,464	—	391	—
1994W	—	89,619	—	396

KM# 256 CIVIL WAR
Obv: Bugler on horseback right **Obv. Designer:** Don Troiani **Rev:** Eagle on shield **Rev. Designer:** Alfred Maletsky

Date	UNC Mintage	Proof Mintage	MS-65	Prf-65
1995W	12,735	—	750	—
1995W	—	55,246	—	410

KM# 261 1996 OLYMPICS - TORCH RUNNER
Obv: Torch runner, Atlanta skyline and logo in background **Rev:** Eagle advancing right

Date	UNC Mintage	Proof Mintage	MS-65	Prf-65
1995W	14,675	—	750	—
1995W	—	57,442	—	400

KM# 265 1996 OLYMPICS - STADIUM
Obv: Atlanta Stadium and logo **Rev:** Eagle advancing right

Date	UNC Mintage	Proof Mintage	MS-65	Prf-65
1995W	10,579	—	1,200	—
1995W	—	43,124	—	396

KM# 270 1996 OLYMPICS - CAULDRON
Obv: Torch bearer lighting cauldron **Rev:** Atlanta Olympics logo flanked by laurel

Date	UNC Mintage	Proof Mintage	MS-65	Prf-65
1996W	9,210	—	1,500	—
1996W	—	38,555	—	410

KM# 274 1996 OLYMPICS - FLAG BEARER
Obv: Flag bearer advancing **Rev:** Atlanta Olympic logo flanked by laurel

Date	UNC Mintage	Proof Mintage	MS-65	Prf-65
1996W	9,174	—	900	—
1996W	—	32,886	—	450

KM# 277 SMITHSONIAN INSTITUTION 150TH ANNIVERSARY
Obv: Smithson bust left **Obv. Designer:** Alfred Maletsky **Rev:** Sunburst museum logo **Rev. Designer:** T. James Ferrell

Date	UNC Mintage	Proof Mintage	MS-65	Prf-65
1996W	9,068	—	800	—
1996W	—	29,474	—	400

KM# 280 JACKIE ROBINSON
Obv: Robinson head right **Obv. Designer:** William C. Cousins **Rev:** Legend on baseball **Rev. Designer:** James M. Peed

Date	UNC Mintage	Proof Mintage	MS-65	Prf-65
1997W	5,202	—	3,000	—
1997W	—	24,072	—	560

KM# 282 FRANKLIN DELANO ROOSEVELT
Obv: Roosevelt bust right **Obv. Designer:** T. James Ferrell **Rev:** Eagle shield **Rev. Designer:** James M. Peed and Thomas D. Rogers, Sr.

Date	UNC Mintage	Proof Mintage	MS-65	Prf-65
1997W	11,894	—	900	—
1997W	—	29,474	—	385

KM# 300 GEORGE WASHINGTON DEATH BICENTENNIAL
Obv: Washington's head right **Rev:** Eagle with wings outstretched **Designer:** Laura G. Fraser

Date	UNC Mintage	Proof Mintage	MS-65	Prf-65
1999W	22,511	—	390	—
1999W	—	41,693	—	381

KM# 326 CAPITOL VISITOR CENTER
Obv: Column at right **Rev:** First Capital building **Designer:** Elizabeth Jones

Date	UNC Mintage	Proof Mintage	MS-65	Prf-65
2001W	6,761	—	1,750	—
2001W	—	27,652	—	381

KM# 337 2002 WINTER OLYMPICS
Obv: Salt Lake City Olympics logo **Rev:** Stylized cauldron **Designer:** Donna Weaver

Date	UNC Mintage	Proof Mintage	MS-65	Prf-65
2002W	10,585	—	410	—
2002W	—	32,877	—	391

KM# 395 SAN FRANCISCO MINT MUSEUM
Obv: Front entrance façade **Rev:** Eagle as on 1860's $5. Gold

Date	UNC Mintage	Proof Mintage	MS-65	Prf-65
2006S	16,230	—	376	—
2006S	—	41,517	—	376

KM# 406 JAMESTOWN - 400TH ANNIVERSARY
Obv: Settler and Native American **Rev:** Jamestown Memorial Church ruins

Date	UNC Mintage	Proof Mintage	MS-65	Prf-65
2007W	18,843	—	376	—
2007W	—	47,050	—	376

KM# 440 AMERICAN BALD EAGLE
Obv: Two eagles on branch **Rev:** Eagle with shield

Date	UNC Mintage	Proof Mintage	MS-65	Prf-65
2008W	13,467	—	384	—
2008W	—	59,269	—	384

KM# 505 MEDAL OF HONOR Obv: 1861 Medal of Honor design for the Navy **Obv. Designer:** Joseph Menna **Rev:** Minerva standing with shield and Union flag, field artillery canon flanking **Rev. Designer:** Joel Iskowitz and Michael Gaudioso

Date	UNC Mintage	Proof Mintage	MS-65	Prf-65
2011	—	—	—	—

KM# 508 U.S. ARMY Obv: Five Soldiers of different eras **Obv. Designer:** Joel Iskowitz and Phebe Hemphill **Rev:** Elements from the Army's emblem **Rev. Designer:** Joseph Menna

Date	UNC Mintage	Proof Mintage	MS-65	Prf-65
2011	—	—	—	—

$10 (EAGLE)

Date	UNC Mintage	Proof Mintage	MS-65	Prf-65
2000W	6,683	—	3,750	—
2000W	—	27,167	—	975

KM# 211 1984 OLYMPICS
Weight: 16.7180 g. **Composition:** 0.9000 Gold, 0.4837 oz. AGW **Diameter:** 27mm. **Obv:** Male and female runner with torch **Obv. Designer:** James M. Peed and John Mercanti **Rev:** Heraldic eagle **Rev. Designer:** John Mercanti

Date	UNC Mintage	Proof Mintage	MS-65	Prf-65
1984W	75,886	—	758	—
1984P	—	33,309	—	755
1984D	—	34,533	—	755
1984S	—	48,551	—	755
1984W	—	381,085	—	755

KM# 350 FIRST FLIGHT CENTENNIAL
Weight: 16.7180 g. **Composition:** 0.9000 Gold, 0.4837 oz. AGW **Obv:** Orvile and Wilbur Wright busts facing **Rev:** Wright flyer and eagle **Designer:** Donna Weaver

Date	UNC Mintage	Proof Mintage	MS-65	Prf-65
2003P	10,129	—	900	—
2003P	—	21,846	—	755

$20 (DOUBLE EAGLE)

KM# 312 LIBRARY OF CONGRESS
Weight: 16.2590 g. **Composition:** Bi-Metallic **Obv:** Torch and partial facade **Obv. Designer:** John Mercanti **Rev:** Stylized eagle within laurel wreath **Rev. Designer:** Thomas D. Rogers, Sr.

KM# 464   Composition: 0.9990 Gold AGW **Diameter:** 27mm. **Obv:** Ultra high relief Liberty holding torch, walking forward **Rev:** Eagle in flight left, sunrise in background **Designer:** Augustus Saint-Gaudens

Date	UNC Mintage	Proof Mintage	MS-65	Prf-65
2009	—	115,178	—	2,200

MODERN COMMEMORATIVE COIN SETS

Olympic, 13-1984

Date	Price
1983 collectors 3 coin set: 1983 PDS uncirculated dollars; KM209.	100.00
1983 & 1984 3 coin set: 1983 and one 1984 uncirculated dollar and 1984W uncirculated gold $10; KM209, 210, 211.	684
1983S & 1984S 3 coin set: proof 1983 and 1984 dollar and 1984W gold $10; KM209, 210, 211.	812
1983 & 1984 6 coin set in a cherrywood box: 1983S and 1984S uncirculated and proof dollars, 1984W uncirculated and proof gold $10; KM209, 210, 211.	1,636
1983S & 1984S 2 coin set: proof dollars.	66.00
1984 collectors 3 coin set: 1984 PDS uncirculated dollars; KM210.	101
Bald Eagle proof half dollar, dollar and $5 gold, KM438, KM439, KM440	440

Statue of Liberty

Date	Price
1986 2 coin set: uncirculated silver dollar and clad half dollar; KM212, 214.	37.00
1986 2 coin set: proof silver dollar and clad half dollar; KM212, 214.	37.00
1986 3 coin set: uncirculated silver dollar, clad half dollar and gold $5; KM212, 214, 215.	413
1986 3 coin set: proof silver dollar, clad half dollar and gold $5; KM212, 214, 215.	413
1986 6 coin set: 1 each of the proof and uncirculated issues; KM212, 214, 215.	825
Bald Eagle proof half dollar, dollar and $5 gold, KM438, KM439, KM440	440

Constitution

Date	Price
1987 2 coin set: uncirculated silver dollar and gold $5; KM220, 221.	409
1987 2 coin set: proof silver dollar and gold $5; KM220, 221.	409
1987 4 coin set: silver dollar and $5 gold proof and uncirculated issues; KM220, 221.	820
Bald Eagle proof half dollar, dollar and $5 gold, KM438, KM439, KM440	440

Olympic, 1988

Date	Price
1988 2 coin set: uncirculated silver dollar and gold $5; KM222, 223.	409
1988 2 coin set: proof silver dollar and gold $5; KM222, 223.	409
1988 4 coin set: silver dollar and $5 gold proof and uncirculated issues; KM222, 223.	820
Bald Eagle proof half dollar, dollar and $5 gold, KM438, KM439, KM440	440

Congress

Date	Price
1989 2 coin set: uncirculated silver dollar and clad half dollar; KM224, 225.	41.00
1989 2 coin set: proof silver dollar and clad half dollar; KM224, 225.	41.00
1989 3 coin set: uncirculated silver dollar, clad half and gold $5; KM224, 225, 226.	416
1989 3 coin set: proof silver dollar, clad half and gold $5; KM224, 225, 226.	416
1989 6 coin set: 1 each of the proof and uncirculated issues; KM224, 225, 226.	835
Bald Eagle proof half dollar, dollar and $5 gold, KM438, KM439, KM440	440

Mt. Rushmore

Date	Price
1991 2 coin set: uncirculated half dollar and silver dollar; KM228, 229.	52.00
1991 2 coin set: proof half dollar and silver dollar; KM228, 229.	50.00
1991 3 coin set: uncirculated half dollar, silver dollar and gold $5; KM228, 229, 230.	447
1991 3 coin set: proof half dollar, silver dollar and gold $5; KM228, 229, 230.	426
1991 6 coin set: 1 each of proof and uncirculated issues; KM228, 229, 230.	875
Bald Eagle proof half dollar, dollar and $5 gold, KM438, KM439, KM440	440

Olympic, 1992

Date	Price
1992 2 coin set: uncirculated half dollar and silver dollar; KM233, 234.	42.00
1992 2 coin set: proof half dollar and silver dollar; KM233, 234.	42.00
1992 3 coin set: uncirculated half dollar, silver dollar and gold $5; KM233, 234, 235.	437
1992 3 coin set: proof half dollar, silver dollar and gold $5; KM233, 234, 235.	438
1992 6 coin set: 1 each of proof and uncirculated issues; KM233, 234, 235.	875
Bald Eagle proof half dollar, dollar and $5 gold, KM438, KM439, KM440	440

Columbus Quincentenary

Date	Price
1992 2 coin set: uncirculated half dollar and silver dollar; KM237, 238.	45.00
1992 2 coin set: proof half dollar and silver dollar; KM237, 238.	43.00
1992 3 coin set: uncirculated half dollar, silver dollar and gold $5; KM237, 238, 239.	440
1992 3 coin set: proof half dollar, silver dollar and gold $5; KM237, 238, 239.	418
1992 6 coin set: 1 each of proof and uncirculated issues; KM237, 238, 239.	860
Bald Eagle proof half dollar, dollar and $5 gold, KM438, KM439, KM440	440

Jefferson

Date	Price
1993 Jefferson: dollar, 1994 matte proof nickel and $2 note; KM249, 192.	48.50
Bald Eagle proof half dollar, dollar and $5 gold, KM438, KM439, KM440	440

Madison / Bill of Rights

Date	Price
1993 2 coin set: uncirculated half dollar and silver dollar; KM240, 241.	50.00
1993 2 coin set: proof half dollar and silver dollar; KM240, 241.	49.00
1993 3 coin set: uncirculated half dollar, silver dollar and gold $5; KM240, 241, 242.	460
1993 3 coin set: proof half dollar, silver dollar and gold $5; KM240, 241, 242.	425
1993 6 coin set: 1 each of proof and uncirculated issues; KM240, 241, 242.	885
Bald Eagle proof half dollar, dollar and $5 gold, KM438, KM439, KM440	440

World War II

Date	Price
1993 2 coin set: uncirculated half dollar and silver dollar; KM243, 244.	51.00
1993 2 coin set: proof half dollar and silver dollar; KM243, 244.	55.00
1993 3 coin set: uncirculated half dollar, silver dollar and gold $5; KM243, 244, 245.	491
1993 3 coin set: proof half dollar, silver dollar and gold $5; KM243, 244, 245.	431
1993 6 coin set: 1 each of proof and uncirculated issues; KM243, 244, 245.	925
Bald Eagle proof half dollar, dollar and $5 gold, KM438, KM439, KM440	440

World Cup

Date	Price
1994 2 coin set: uncirculated half dollar and silver dollar; KM246, 247.	42.00
1994 2 coin set: proof half dollar and silver dollar; KM246, 247.	41.00
1994 3 coin set: uncirculated half dollar, silver dollar and gold $5; KM246, 247, 248.	433
1994 3 coin set: proof half dollar, silver dollar and gold $5; KM246, 247, 248.	437
1994 6 coin set: 1 each of proof and uncirculated issues; KM246, 247, 248.	876
Bald Eagle proof half dollar, dollar and $5 gold, KM438, KM439, KM440	440

U.S. Veterans

Date	Price
1994 3 coin set: uncirculated POW, Vietnam, Women dollars; KM250, 251, 252.	179
1994 3 coin set: proof POW, Vietnam, Women dollars; KM250, 251, 252.	127
Bald Eagle proof half dollar, dollar and $5 gold, KM438, KM439, KM440	440

Olympic, 1995-96

Date	Price
1995 4 coin set: uncirculated basketball half, $1 gymnast & blind runner, $5 torch runner; KM257, 259, 260, 261.	898
1995 4 coin set: proof basketball half, $1 gymnast & blind runner, $5 torch runner; KM257, 259, 260, 261.	500
1995P 2 coin set: proof $1 gymnast & blind runner; KM259, 260.	92.00
1995P 2 coin set: proof $1 track & field, cycling; KM263, 264.	86.00
1995-96 4 coin set: proof halves, basketball, baseball, swimming, soccer; KM257, 262, 267, 271.	110
1995 & 96 8 coins in cherry wood case: proof silver dollars: blind runner, gymnast, cycling, track & field, wheelchair, tennis, rowing, high jump; KM259, 260, 263, 264, 268, 269, 272, 272A.	445
1995 & 96 16 coins in cherry wood case: proof silver dollars: blind runner, gymnast, cycling, track & field, wheelchair, tennis, rowing, high jump; KM259, 260, 263, 264, 268, 269, 272, 272A.	1,970
1995 & 96 16 coins in cherry wood case: proof half dollars: basketball, baseball, swimming, soccer, KM257, 262, 267, 271. Proof silver dollars: blind runner, gymnast, cycling, track & field, wheelchair, tennis, rowing, high jump, KM259, 260, 263, 264, 268, 269, 272, 272A. Proof $5 gold: torch runner, stadium, cauldron, flag bearer, KM 261, 265, 270, 274.	2,200
1995 & 96 32 coins in cherry wood case: bu & proof half dollars: basketball, baseball, swimming, soccer, KM257, 262, 267, 271. BU & proof silver dollars: blind runner, gymnast, cycling, track & field, wheelchair, tennis, rowing, high jump, KM259, 260, 263, 264, 268, 269, 272, 272A. BU & proof $5 gold: torch runner, stadium, cauldron, flag bearer, KM261, 265, 270, 274.	8,425
1996P 2 coin set: proof $1 wheelchair & tennis; KM268, 269.	156
1996P 2 coin set: proof $1 rowing & high jump; KM272, 272A.	111
Bald Eagle proof half dollar, dollar and $5 gold, KM438, KM439, KM440	440

Civil War

Date	Price
1995 2 coin set: uncirculated half and dollar; KM254, 255.	90.00
1995 2 coin set: proof half and dollar; KM254, 255.	92.00
1995 3 coin set: uncirculated half, dollar and gold $5; KM254, 255, 256.	840
1995 3 coin set: proof half, dollar and gold $5; KM254, 255, 256.	502
1995 6 coin set: 1 each of proof and uncirculated issues; KM254, 255, 256.	1,342
Bald Eagle proof half dollar, dollar and $5 gold, KM438, KM439, KM440	440

Smithsonian

Date	Price
1996 2 coin set: proof dollar and $5 gold; KM276, 277.	445
1996 4 coin set: proof and B.U. ; KM276, 277.	1,365
Bald Eagle proof half dollar, dollar and $5 gold, KM438, KM439, KM440	440

Jackie Robinson

Date	Price
1997 2 coin set: proof dollar & $5 gold; KM279, 280.	660
1997 4 coin set: proof & BU; KM279, 280.	3,750
1997 legacy set.	950
Bald Eagle proof half dollar, dollar and $5 gold, KM438, KM439, KM440	440

Botanic Garden

Date	Price
1997 2 coin set: dollar, Jefferson nickel and $1 note; KM278, 192.	172
Bald Eagle proof half dollar, dollar and $5 gold, KM438, KM439, KM440	440

Franklin Delano Roosevelt

Date	Price
1997W 2 coin set: uncirculated and proof; KM282.	1,285
Bald Eagle proof half dollar, dollar and $5 gold, KM438, KM439, KM440	440

Kennedy

Date	Price
1998 2 coin set: proof; KM287.	80.00
1998 2 coin collectors set: Robert Kennedy dollar and John Kennedy half dollar; KM287, 202b. Matte finished.	210
Bald Eagle proof half dollar, dollar and $5 gold, KM438, KM439, KM440	440

Black Patriots

Date	Price
1998S 2 coin set: uncirculated and proof; KM288.	220
Bald Eagle proof half dollar, dollar and $5 gold, KM438, KM439, KM440	440

George Washington

Date	Price
1999 2 coin set: proof and uncirculated gold $5; KM300.	775
Bald Eagle proof half dollar, dollar and $5 gold, KM438, KM439, KM440	440

Dolley Madison

Date	Price
1999 2 coin set: proof and uncirculated silver dollars; KM298.	80.00
Bald Eagle proof half dollar, dollar and $5 gold, KM438, KM439, KM440	440

Yellowstone National Park

Date	Price
1999 2 coin set: proof and uncirculated silver dollars; KM299.	74.00
Bald Eagle proof half dollar, dollar and $5 gold, KM438, KM439, KM440	440

Millennium Coin & Currency

Date	Price
2000 2 coin set: uncirculated Sacagewea $1, silver Eagle & $1 note.	67.50
Bald Eagle proof half dollar, dollar and $5 gold, KM438, KM439, KM440	440

Leif Ericson

Date	Price
2000 2 coin set: proof and uncirculated silver dollars; KM313.	92.00
Bald Eagle proof half dollar, dollar and $5 gold, KM438, KM439, KM440	440

American Buffalo

Date	Price
2001 2 coin set: 90% silver unc. & proof $1.; KM325.	328
2001 coin & currency set 90% unc. dollar & replicas of 1899 $5 silver cert.; KM325.	174
Bald Eagle proof half dollar, dollar and $5 gold, KM438, KM439, KM440	440

Capitol Visitor Center

Date	Price
2001 3 coin set: proof half, silver dollar, gold $5; KM323, 324, 326.	429
Bald Eagle proof half dollar, dollar and $5 gold, KM438, KM439, KM440	440

Winter Olympics - Salt Lake City

Date	Price
2002 2 coin set: proof 90% silver dollar KM336 & $5.00 Gold KM337.	410
2002 4 coin set: 90% silver unc. & proof $1, KM336 & unc. & proof gold $5, KM337.	820
Bald Eagle proof half dollar, dollar and $5 gold, KM438, KM439, KM440	440

First Flight Centennial

Date	Price
2003 3 coin set: proof gold ten dollar KM350, proof silver dollar KM349 & proof clad half dollar KM348.	805
Bald Eagle proof half dollar, dollar and $5 gold, KM438, KM439, KM440	440

Lewis and Clark Bicentennial

Date	Price
2004 Coin and pouch set.	75.00
2004 coin and currency set: Uncirculated silver dollar, two 2005 nickels, replica 1901 $10 Bison note, silver plated peace medal, three stamps & two booklets.	42.00
2004 Westward Journey Nickel series coin and medal set: Proof Sacagawea dollar, two 2005 proof nickels and silver plated peace medal.	35.00
Bald Eagle proof half dollar, dollar and $5 gold, KM438, KM439, KM440	440

Thomas Alva Edison

Date	Price
2004 Uncirculated silver dollar and light bulb.	60.00
Bald Eagle proof half dollar, dollar and $5 gold, KM438, KM439, KM440	440

U.S. Marine Corps.

Date	Price
2005 Uncirculated silver dollar and stamp set.	53.00
2005 American Legacy: Proof Marine Corps dollar, Proof John Marshall dollar and 10 piece proof set.	180
Bald Eagle proof half dollar, dollar and $5 gold, KM438, KM439, KM440	440

Chief Justice John Marshall

Date	Price
2005 Coin and Chronicles set: Uncirculated silver dollar, booklet and BEP intaglio portrait.	53.00
Bald Eagle proof half dollar, dollar and $5 gold, KM438, KM439, KM440	440

Benjamin Franklin Tercentennary

Date	Price
2006 Coin and Chronicles set: Uncirculated "Scientist" silver dollar, four stamps, Poor Richards Almanac and intaglio print.	41.00
Bald Eagle proof half dollar, dollar and $5 gold, KM438, KM439, KM440	440

BULLION COINS

AMERICAN EAGLE SILVER BULLION

SILVER DOLLAR

Date	Mintage	Unc	Prf.
1991	7,191,066	45.80	—
1991S	511,924	—	62.00
1992	5,540,068	45.80	—
1992S	498,543	—	64.00
1993	6,763,762	45.80	—
1993P	405,913	—	80.00
1994	4,227,319	46.80	—
1994P	372,168	—	98.00
1995	4,672,051	48.30	—
1995P	407,822	—	75.00
1995W 10th Anniversary	30,102	—	2,950
1996	3,603,386	48.00	—
1996P	498,293	—	85.00
1997	4,295,004	45.80	—
1997P	440,315	—	132
1998	4,847,547	46.80	—
1998P	450,728	—	44.00
1999	7,408,640	46.80	—
1999P	549,330	—	47.00
2000P	600,743	—	62.00
2000	9,239,132	45.80	—
2001	9,001,711	43.10	—
2001W	746,398	—	62.00
2002	10,539,026	43.10	—
2002W	647,342	—	62.00
2003	8,495,008	43.10	—
2003W	747,831	—	62.00
2004	8,882,754	43.10	—
2004W	801,602	—	62.00
2005	8,891,025	43.10	—
2005W	816,663	—	62.00
2006	10,676,522	45.30	—
2006W	1,093,600	—	62.00
2006P Reverse Proof	—	—	195
2006W Burnished Unc.	468,000	75.00	—
2006 20th Aniv. 3 pc. set	—	—	345
2007	9,028,036	43.30	—
2007W	821,759	—	62.00
2007W Burnished Unc.	690,891	49.10	—
2008	20,583,000	43.10	—
2008W Reverse of '07	—	450	—
2008	—	—	79.00
2008W Burnished Unc.	—	36.50	—
2009	—	43.10	—
2010	—	43.10	—
2010	—	—	62.00

KM# 273 • 31.1050 g., 0.9993 **Silver**, 0.9993 oz., 40.6mm. • **Obv. Desc:** Liberty walking left **Rev. Desc:** Eagle with shield **Obv. Designer:** Adolph A. Weinman **Rev. Designer:** John Mercanti

Date	Mintage	Unc	Prf.
1986	5,393,005	46.60	—
1986S	1,446,778	—	62.00
1987	11,442,335	45.80	—
1987S	904,732	—	62.00
1988	5,004,646	45.80	—
1988S	557,370	—	64.00
1989	5,203,327	43.10	—
1989S	617,694	—	64.00
1990	5,840,110	46.80	—
1990S	695,510	—	62.00

AMERICA THE BEAUTIFUL SILVER BULLION

SILVER QUARTER

KM# 489 • 155.5500 g., 0.9990 **Silver**, 4.9958 oz. • **Subject:** Hot Springs, Ark. **Rev. Desc:** Park Headquarters and fountain **Rev. Designer:** Don Everhart II and Joseph Menna

Date	Mintage	Unc	Prf.
2010	—	—	—

KM# 490 • 155.5500 g., 0.9990 **Silver**, 4.9958 oz. • **Subject:** Yellowstone National Park **Rev. Desc:** Old Faithful geyser and bison **Rev. Designer:** Don Everhart II

Date	Mintage	Unc	Prf.
2010	—	—	—

KM# 491 • 155.5500 g., 0.9990 **Silver**, 4.9958 oz. • **Subject:** Yosemite National Park **Rev. Desc:** El Capitan, largest monolith of granite in the world **Rev. Designer:** Joseph Menna and Phebe Hemphill

Date	Mintage	Unc	Prf.
2010	—	—	—

KM# 492 • 155.5500 g., 0.9990 **Silver**, 4.9958 oz. • **Subject:** Grand Canyon National Park **Rev. Desc:** Grabarues abive the Nankoweap Delta in Marble Canyon near the Colorado River **Rev. Designer:** Phebe Hemphill

Date	Mintage	Unc	Prf.
2010	—	—	—

KM# 493 • 155.5500 g., 0.9990 **Silver**, 4.9958 oz.
• **Subject:** Mount Hood National Park **Rev. Desc:**
Mt. Hood with Lost Lake in teh foreground **Rev.**
Designer: Phebe Hemphill

Date	Mintage	Unc	Prf.
2010	—	—	—

KM# 513 • 155.5500 g., 0.9990 **Silver**, 4.9958 oz.
• **Subject:** Gettysburg National Military Park **Rev.**
Desc: 72nd Pennsylvania Infantry Monumnet on
the battle line of the Union Army at Cemetery Ridge
Rev. Designer: Joel Iskowitz and Phebe Hemphill

Date	Mintage	Unc	Prf.
2011	—	—	—

KM# 514 • 155.5500 g., 0.9990 **Silver**, 4.9958 oz.
• **Subject:** Glacier National Park **Rev. Desc:**
Northeast slope of Mount Reynolds **Rev. Designer:**
Barbara Fox and Charles L. Vickers

Date	Mintage	Unc	Prf.
2011	—	—	—

KM# 515 • 155.5500 g., 0.9990 **Silver**, 4.9958 oz.
• **Subject:** Olympic National Park **Rev. Desc:**
Roosevelt elk on a gravel river bar along the Hoh
River, Mount Olympus in the background **Rev.**
Designer: Susan Gambel and Michael Gaudioso

Date	Mintage	Unc	Prf.
2011	—	—	—

KM# 516 • 155.5500 g., 0.9990 **Silver**, 4.9958 oz.
• **Subject:** Vicksburg National Military Park **Rev.**
Desc: U.S.S. Cairo on the Yazoo River **Rev.**
Designer: Thomas Cleveland and Joseph menna

Date	Mintage	Unc	Prf.
2011	—	—	—

KM# 517 • 155.5500 g., 0.9990 **Silver**, 4.9958 oz.
• **Subject:** Chickasaw National Recreation Area
Rev. Desc: Limestone Lincoln Bridge **Rev.**
Designer: Donna Weaver and James Licaretz

Date	Mintage	Unc	Prf.
2011	—	—	—

AMERICAN EAGLE GOLD BULLION

GOLD $5

KM# 216 • 3.3930 g., 0.9167 **Gold**, 0.1000 oz.,
16.5mm. • **Obv. Designer:** Augustus Saint-
Gaudens **Rev. Designer:** Miley Busiek

Date	Mintage	Unc	Prf.
MCMLXXXVI (1986)	912,609	184	—
MCMLXXXVII (1987)	580,266	184	—
MCMLXXXVIII (1988)	159,500	205	—
MCMLXXXVIII (1988)P	143,881	—	186
MCMLXXXIX (1989)	264,790	208	—
MCMLXXXIX (1989)P	84,647	—	194
MCMXC (1990)	210,210	205	—
MCMXC (1990)P	99,349	—	194
MCMXCI (1991)	165,200	205	—
MCMXCI (1991)P	70,334	—	189
1992	209,300	199	—
1992P	64,874	—	189
1993	210,709	176	—
1993P	45,960	—	189
1994	206,380	176	—
1994W	62,849	—	189
1995	223,025	174	—
1995W	62,667	—	189
1996	401,964	174	—
1996W	57,047	—	189
1997	528,515	174	—

Date	Mintage	Unc	Prf.
1997W	34,977	—	189
1998	1,344,520	174	—
1998W	39,395	—	189
1999	2,750,338	174	—
1999W	48,428	—	165
1999W Unfinished Proof die	—	615	—

> **Note:** The 1999 W issues are standard matte finished gold that were struck with unfinished proof dies.

Date	Mintage	Unc	Prf.
2000	569,153	184	—
2000W	49,971	—	189
2001	269,147	174	—
2001W	37,530	—	189
2002	230,027	174	—
2002W	40,864	—	189
2003	245,029	174	—
2003W	40,027	—	189
2004	250,016	174	—
2004W	35,131	—	189
2005	300,043	174	—
2005W	49,265	—	189
2006	285,006	174	—
2006W	47,277	—	189
2006W Burnished Unc.	20,643	175	—
2007	190,010	174	—
2007W	58,553	—	204
2007W Burnished Unc.	22,501	175	—
2008	305,000	184	—
2008W	—	—	204
2008W Burnished Unc.	12,657	245	—
2009	27,000	145	—
2010	—	—	—
2010W	—	—	189

GOLD $10

KM# 217 • 8.4830 g., 0.9167 **Gold**, 0.2500 oz.,
22mm. • **Obv. Designer:** Augustus Saint-
Gaudens **Rev. Designer:** Miley Busiek

Date	Mintage	Unc	Prf.
MCMLXXXVI (1986)	726,031	432	—
MCMLXXXVII (1987)	269,255	432	—
MCMLXXXVIII (1988)	49,000	432	—
MCMLXXXVIII (1988)P	98,028	—	516
MCMLXXXIX (1989)	81,789	432	—
MCMLXXXIX (1989)P	54,170	—	516

Date	Mintage	Unc	Prf.
MCMXC (1990)	41,000	432	—
MCMXC (1990)P	62,674	—	516
MCMXCI (1991)	36,100	432	—
MCMXCI (1991)P	50,839	—	516
1992	59,546	417	—
1992P	46,269	—	516
1993	71,864	417	—
1993P	33,775	—	516
1994	72,650	417	—
1994W	47,172	—	516
1995	83,752	417	—
1995W	47,526	—	516
1996	60,318	417	—
1996W	38,219	—	516
1997	108,805	417	—
1997W	29,805	—	516
1998	309,829	417	—
1998W	29,503	—	516
1999	564,232	417	—
1999W	34,417	—	516
1999W Unfinished Proof die	—	1,100	—

Note: The 1999 W issues are standard matte finished gold that were struck with unfinished proof dies.

Date	Mintage	Unc	Prf.
2000	128,964	417	—

Date	Mintage	Unc	Prf.
2000W	36,036	—	516
2001	71,280	417	—
2001W	25,613	—	516
2002	62,027	417	—
2002W	29,242	—	516
2003	74,029	417	—
2003W	30,292	—	516
2004	72,014	417	—
2004W	28,839	—	516
2005	72,015	417	—
2005W	37,207	—	516
2006	60,004	417	—
2006W	36,127	—	516
2006W Burnished Unc.	15,188	785	—
2007	34,004	417	—
2007W	46,189	—	456
2007W Burnished Unc.	12,786	785	—
2008	—	417	—
2008W	28,000	—	456
2008W Burnished Unc.	8,883	1,285	—
2009	27,500	417	—
2010	—	—	—
2010W	—	—	516

GOLD $25

KM# 218 • 16.9660 g., 0.9167 **Gold**, 0.5000 oz., 27mm. • **Obv. Designer:** Augustus Saint-Gaudens **Rev. Designer:** Miley Busiek

Date	Mintage	Unc	Prf.
MCMLXXXVI (1986)	599,566	843	—
MCMLXXXVII (1987)	131,255	806	—
MCMLXXXVII (1987)P	143,398	—	933
MCMLXXXVIII (1988)	45,000	1,125	—
MCMLXXXVIII (1988)P	76,528	—	933
MCMLXXXIX (1989)	44,829	1,100	—
MCMLXXXIX (1989)P	44,798	—	933
MCMXC (1990)	31,000	1,500	—
MCMXC (1990)P	51,636	—	933
MCMXCI (1991)	24,100	2,250	—
MCMXCI (1991)P	53,125	—	933
1992	54,404	935	—
1992P	40,976	—	933
1993	73,324	806	—
1993P	31,130	—	933
1994	62,400	806	—
1994W	44,584	—	933

Date	Mintage	Unc	Prf.
1995	53,474	935	—
1995W	45,388	—	933
1996	39,287	975	—
1996W	35,058	—	933
1997	79,605	840	—
1997W	26,344	—	933
1998	169,029	806	—
1998W	25,374	—	933
1999	263,013	806	—
1999W	30,427	—	933
2000	79,287	806	—
2000W	32,028	—	933
2001	48,047	900	—
2001W	23,240	—	933
2002	70,027	806	—
2002W	26,646	—	933
2003	79,029	806	—
2003W	28,270	—	933
2004	98,040	806	—
2004W	27,330	—	933
2005	80,023	806	—
2005W	34,311	—	933
2006	66,004	809	—
2006W	34,322	—	933
2006W Burnished Unc.	15,164	1,600	—
2007	47,002	840	—
2007W	44,025	—	933
2007W Burnished Unc.	11,458	1,600	—
2008	61,000	809	—
2008W	27,800	—	933
2008W Burnished Unc.	15,683	1,100	—
2009	55,000	809	—
2010	—	—	—
2010W	—	—	933

GOLD $50

Date	Mintage	Unc	Prf.
1993	480,192	1,540	—
1993W	34,369	—	1,745
1994	221,663	1,540	—
1994W	46,674	—	1,745
1995	200,636	1,540	—
1995W	46,368	—	1,745
1995W 10th Anniversary	—	—	—
1996	189,148	1,540	—
1996W	36,153	—	1,745
1997	664,508	1,540	—
1997W	28,034	—	1,745
1998	1,468,530	1,540	—
1998W	25,886	—	1,755
1999	1,505,026	1,540	—
1999W	31,427	—	1,745
1999W Die error	—	1,800	—

Note: The 1999 W issues are standard matte finished gold that were struck with unfinished proof dies.

Date	Mintage	Unc	Prf.
2000	433,319	1,540	—
2000W	33,007	—	1,745
2001	143,605	1,540	—
2001W	24,555	—	1,745
2002	222,029	1,540	—
2002W	27,499	—	1,745
2003	416,032	1,540	—
2003W	28,344	—	1,745
2004	417,149	1,540	—
2004W	28,215	—	1,745
2005	356,555	1,540	—
2005W	35,246	—	1,745
2006	237,510	1,540	—
2006W	47,000	—	1,745
2006W Reverse Proof	10,000	—	2,200
2006W Burnished Unc.	45,912	1,575	—
2007	140,016	1,554	—
2007W	51,810	—	1,745
2007W Burnished Unc.	18,609	1,575	—
2008W	710,000	1,540	—
2008W Proof	29,000	—	1,745
2008W Burnished Unc.	11,908	—	1,885
2008W Reverse of '07	—	—	—
2009	122,000	1,540	—
2010	—	1,540	—
2010W	—	—	1,745

KM# 219 • 33.9310 g., 0.9167 **Gold**, 100000 oz., 32.7mm. • **Obv. Designer:** Augustus Saint-Gaudens **Rev. Designer:** Miley Busiek

Date	Mintage	Unc	Prf.
MCMLXXXVI (1986)	1,362,650	1,540	—
MCMLXXXVI (1986)W	446,290	—	—
MCMLXXXVII (1987)	1,045,500	1,540	—
MCMLXXXVII (1987)W	147,498	—	1,795
MCMLXXXVIII (1988)	465,000	1,540	—
MCMLXXXVIII (1988)W	87,133	—	1,795
MCMLXXXIX (1989)	415,790	1,540	—
MCMLXXXIX (1989)W	54,570	—	1,795
MCMXC (1990)	373,219	1,540	—
MCMXC (1990)W	62,401	—	1,795
MCMXCI (1991)	243,100	1,540	—
MCMXCI (1991)W	50,411	—	1,795
1992	275,000	1,540	—
1992W	44,826	—	1,745

AMERICAN EAGLE PLATINUM BULLION

PLATINUM $10

KM# 283 • 3.1100 g., 0.9995 **Platinum**, 0.0999 oz., 17mm. • **Rev. Desc:** Eagle flying right over sunrise **Obv. Designer:** John Mercanti **Rev. Designer:** Thomas D. Rogers Sr

Date	Mintage	Unc	Prf.
1997	70,250	205	—
1997W	36,996	—	258
1998	39,525	205	—
1999	55,955	205	—
2000	34,027	205	—
2001	52,017	205	—
2002	23,005	205	—
2003	22,007	205	—
2004	15,010	205	—

Date	Mintage	Unc	Prf.
2005	14,013	205	—
2006	11,001	205	—
2006W Burnished Unc.	—	425	—
2007	13,003	280	—
2007W Burnished Unc.	—	205	—
2008	17,000	205	—
2008 Burnished Unc.	—	210	—
2009	—	—	—

KM# 289 • 3.1100 g., 0.9995 **Platinum**, 0.0999 oz. • **Rev. Desc:** Eagle in flight over New England costal lighthouse **Obv. Designer:** John Mercanti

Date	Mintage	Unc	Prf.
1998W	19,847	—	258

KM# 301 • 3.1100 g., 0.9995 **Platinum**, 0.0999 oz.
• **Rev. Desc:** Eagle in flight over Southeastern
Wetlands **Obv. Designer:** John Mercanti

Date	Mintage	Unc	Prf.
1999W	19,133	—	253

KM# 314 • 3.1100 g., 0.9995 **Platinum**, 0.0999
oz. • **Rev. Desc:** Eagle in flight over Heartland
Obv. Designer: John Mercanti

Date	Mintage	Unc	Prf.
2000W	15,651	—	253

KM# 327 • 3.1100 g., 0.9995 **Platinum**, 0.0999
oz., 17mm. • **Rev. Desc:** Eagle in flight over
Southwestern cactus desert **Obv. Designer:** John
Mercanti

Date	Mintage	Unc	Prf.
2001W	12,174	—	253

KM# 339 • 3.1100 g., 0.9995 **Platinum**, 0.0999
oz., 17mm. • **Rev. Desc:** Eagle fishing in
America's Northwest **Obv. Designer:** John
Mercanti

Date	Mintage	Unc	Prf.
2002W	12,365	—	253

KM# 351 • 3.1100 g., 0.9995 **Platinum**, 0.0999
oz., 17mm. • **Rev. Desc:** Eagle pearched on a
Rocky Mountain Pine branch against a flag
backdrop **Obv. Designer:** John Mercanti **Rev.
Designer:** Al Maletsky

Date	Mintage	Unc	Prf.
2003W	9,534	—	258

KM# 364 • 3.1100 g., 0.9995 **Platinum**, 0.0999
oz., 17mm. • **Rev. Desc:** Chester French, 1907.
The sculpture is outside the N.Y. Customs House,
now part of the Smithsonian's Museum of the
American Indian **Obv. Designer:** John Mercanti

Date	Mintage	Unc	Prf.
2004W	7,161	—	535

KM# 377 • 3.1100 g., 0.9995 **Platinum**, 0.0999
oz., 17mm. • **Rev. Desc:** Eagle with cornucopiae
Obv. Designer: John Mercanti **Rev. Designer:**
Donna Weaver

Date	Mintage	Unc	Prf.
2005W	8,104	—	265

KM# 389 • 3.1100 g., 0.9995 **Platinum**, 0.0999
oz., 17mm. • **Subject:** Legislative **Rev. Desc:**
Liberty seated writing between two columns **Obv.
Designer:** John Mercanti

Date	Mintage	Unc	Prf.
2006W	10,205	—	253

KM# 414 • 3.1100 g., 0.9995 **Platinum**, 0.0999
oz., 17mm. • **Subject:** Executive **Obv. Designer:**
John Mercanti

Date	Mintage	Unc	Prf.
2007W	8,176	—	253

KM# 434 • 3.1100 g., 0.9995 **Platinum**, 0.0999
oz., 17mm. • **Obv. Designer:** John Mercanti

Date	Mintage	Unc	Prf.
2008W	8,176	—	585

KM# 460 • 3.1100 g., 0.9995 **Platinum**, 0.0999
oz., 17mm. • **Subject:** Judicial **Obv. Designer:**
John Mercanti

Date	Mintage	Unc	Prf.
2009W	5,600	—	—

PLATINUM $25

KM# 284 • 7.7857 g., 0.9995 **Platinum**, 0.2502 oz., 22mm. • **Rev. Desc:** Eagle in flight over sunrise **Obv. Designer:** John Mercanti **Rev. Designer:** Thomas D. Rogers Sr

Date	Mintage	Unc	Prf.
1997	27,100	498	—
1997W	18,628	—	520
1998	38,887	498	—
1999	39,734	498	—
2000	20,054	498	—
2001	21,815	498	—
2002	27,405	498	—
2003	25,207	498	—
2004	18,010	498	—
2005	12,013	498	—
2006	12,001	498	—
2006W Burnished Unc.	—	585	—
2007	8,402	516	—
2007W Burnished Unc.	—	498	—
2008	22,800	498	—
2008 Burnished Unc.	—	498	—
2009	—	—	—

KM# 290 • 7.7857 g., 0.9995 **Platinum**, 0.2502 oz. • **Rev. Desc:** Eagle in flight over New England costal lighthouse **Obv. Designer:** John Mercanti

Date	Mintage	Unc	Prf.
1998W	14,873	—	520

KM# 302 • 7.7857 g., 0.9995 **Platinum**, 0.2502 oz. • **Rev. Desc:** Eagle in flight over Southeastern Wetlands **Obv. Designer:** John Mercanti

Date	Mintage	Unc	Prf.
1999W	13,507	—	520

KM# 315 • 7.7857 g., 0.9995 **Platinum**, 0.2502 oz. • **Rev. Desc:** Eagle in flight over Heartland **Obv. Designer:** John Mercanti

Date	Mintage	Unc	Prf.
2000W	11,995	—	520

KM# 328 • 7.7857 g., 0.9995 **Platinum**, 0.2502 oz., 22mm. • **Rev. Desc:** Eagle in flight over Southwestern cactus desert **Obv. Designer:** John Mercanti

Date	Mintage	Unc	Prf.
2001W	8,847	—	520

KM# 340 • 7.7857 g., 0.9995 **Platinum**, 0.2502 oz., 22mm. • **Rev. Desc:** Eagle fishing in America's Northwest **Obv. Designer:** John Mercanti

Date	Mintage	Unc	Prf.
2002W	9,282	—	520

KM# 352 • 7.7857 g., 0.9995 **Platinum**, 0.2502 oz., 22mm. • **Rev. Desc:** Eagle pearched on a Rocky Mountain Pine branch against a flag backdrop. **Obv. Designer:** John Mercanti **Rev. Designer:** Al Maletsky

Date	Mintage	Unc	Prf.
2003W	7,044	—	520

KM# 365 • 7.7857 g., 0.9995 **Platinum**, 0.2502 oz., 22mm. • **Rev. Desc:** Chester French, 1907. The sculpture is outside the N.Y. Customs House, now part of the Smithsonian's Museum of the American Indian **Obv. Designer:** John Mercanti

Date	Mintage	Unc	Prf.
2004W	5,193	—	1,075

KM# 378 • 7.7857 g., 0.9995 **Platinum**, 0.2502 oz., 22mm. • **Rev. Desc:** Eagle with cornucopiae **Obv. Designer:** John Mercanti **Rev. Designer:** Donna Weaver

Date	Mintage	Unc	Prf.
2005W	6,592	—	595

KM# 390 • 7.7857 g., 0.9995 **Platinum**, 0.2502 oz., 22mm. • **Subject:** Legislative **Rev. Desc:** Liberty seated writing between two columns **Obv. Designer:** John Mercanti

Date	Mintage	Unc	Prf.
2006W	7,813	—	445

KM# 415 • 7.7857 g., 0.9995 **Platinum**, 0.2502 oz., 22mm. • **Subject:** Executive **Obv. Designer:** John Mercanti

Date	Mintage	Unc	Prf.
2007W	6,017	—	440

KM# 435 • 7.7857 g., 0.9995 **Platinum**, 0.2502 oz., 22mm. • **Obv. Designer:** John Mercanti

Date	Mintage	Unc	Prf.
2008W	6,017	—	985

KM# 461 • 7.7857 g., 0.9995 **Platinum**, 0.2502 oz., 22mm. • **Subject:** Judicial **Obv. Designer:** John Mercanti

Date	Mintage	Unc	Prf.
2009W	3,800	—	—

PLATINUM $50

KM# 285 • 15.5520 g., 0.9995 **Platinum**, 0.4997 oz., 27mm. • **Rev. Desc:** Eagle flying right over sunrise **Obv. Designer:** John Mercanti **Rev. Designer:** Thomas D. Rogers Sr

Date	Mintage	Unc	Prf.
1997	20,500	997	—
1997W	15,432	—	1,049
1998	32,419	997	—
1999	32,309	997	—
2000	18,892	997	—
2001	12,815	997	—
2002	24,005	997	—
2003	17,409	997	—
2004	13,236	997	—
2005	9,013	997	—
2006	9,602	997	—
2006W Burnished Unc.	—	1,139	—
2007	7,001	1,032	—
2007W Burnished Unc.	—	997	—
2008	14,000	997	—
2008W Burnished Unc.	—	1,200	—
2009	—	—	—

KM# 291 • 15.5520 g., 0.9995 **Platinum**, 0.4997 oz. • **Rev. Desc:** Eagle in flight over New England costal lighthouse **Obv. Designer:** John Mercanti

Date	Mintage	Unc	Prf.
1998W	13,836	—	1,049

KM# 303 • 15.5520 g., 0.9995 **Platinum**, 0.4997 oz. • **Rev. Desc:** Eagle in flight over Southeastern Wetlands **Obv. Designer:** John Mercanti

Date	Mintage	Unc	Prf.
1999W	11,103	—	1,040

KM# 316 • 15.5520 g., 0.9995 **Platinum**, 0.4997 oz. • **Rev. Desc:** Eagle in flight over Heartland **Obv. Designer:** John Mercanti

Date	Mintage	Unc	Prf.
2000W	11,049	—	1,040

KM# 329 • 15.5520 g., 0.9995 **Platinum**, 0.4997 oz., 27mm. • **Rev. Desc:** Eagle in flight over Southwestern cactus desert **Obv. Designer:** John Mercanti

Date	Mintage	Unc	Prf.
2001W	8,254	—	1,040

KM# 341 • 15.5520 g., 0.9995 **Platinum**, 0.4997 oz., 27mm. • **Rev. Desc:** Eagle fishing in America's Northwest **Obv. Designer:** John Mercanti

Date	Mintage	Unc	Prf.
2002W	8,772	—	1,040

KM# 353 • 15.5520 g., 0.9995 **Platinum**, 0.4997 oz., 27mm. • **Rev. Desc:** Eagle pearched on a Rocky Mountain Pine branch against a flag backdrop. **Obv. Designer:** John Mercanti **Rev. Designer:** Al Maletsky

Date	Mintage	Unc	Prf.
2003W	7,131	—	1,040

KM# 366 • 15.5520 g., 0.9995 **Platinum**, 0.4997 oz., 27mm. • **Rev. Desc:** Chester French, 1907. The sculpture is outside the N.Y. Customs House, now part of the Smithsonian's Museum of the American Indian **Obv. Designer:** John Mercanti

Date	Mintage	Unc	Prf.
2004W	5,063	—	1,750

KM# 379 • 15.5520 g., 0.9995 **Platinum**, 0.4997 oz., 27mm. • **Rev. Desc:** Eagle with cornucopiae **Obv. Designer:** John Mercanti **Rev. Designer:** Donna Weaver

Date	Mintage	Unc	Prf.
2005W	5,942	—	1,175

KM# 391 • 15.5520 g., 0.9995 **Platinum**, 0.4997 oz., 27mm. • **Subject:** Legislative **Rev. Desc:** Liberty seated writing between two columns **Obv. Designer:** John Mercanti

Date	Mintage	Unc	Prf.
2006W	7,649	—	1,040

KM# 416 • 15.5520 g., 0.9995 **Platinum**, 0.4997 oz., 27mm. • **Subject:** Executive **Obv. Designer:** John Mercanti

Date	Mintage	Unc	Prf.
2007W	22,873	—	1,040
2007W Reverse Proof	16,937	—	1,040

KM# 436 • 15.5520 g., 0.9995 **Platinum**, 0.4997 oz., 27mm. • **Obv. Designer:** John Mercanti

Date	Mintage	Unc	Prf.
2008W	22,873	—	1,600

KM# 462 • 15.5520 g., 0.9995 **Platinum**, 0.4997 oz., 27mm. • **Subject:** Judicial **Obv. Designer:** John Mercanti

Date	Mintage	Unc	Prf.
2009	3,600	—	—

PLATINUM $100

KM# 286 • 31.1050 g., 0.9995 **Platinum**, 0.9995 oz., 33mm. • **Rev. Desc:** Eagle in flight over sun rise **Obv. Designer:** John Mercanti **Rev. Designer:** Thomas D. Rogers Sr

Date	Mintage	Unc	Prf.
1997	56,000	1,994	—
1997W	15,885	—	2,098
1998	133,002	1,994	—
1999	56,707	1,994	—
2000	10,003	1,994	—
2001	14,070	1,994	—
2002	11,502	1,994	—
2003	8,007	1,994	—
2004	7,009	1,994	—
2005	6,310	1,994	—
2006	6,000	1,994	—
2006W Burnished Unc.	—	2,154	—
2007	7,202	2,047	—
2007W Burnished Unc.	—	1,994	—
2008	21,800	1,994	—
2008W Burnished Unc.	—	2,154	—
2009	—	—	—

KM# 317 • 31.1050 g., 0.9995 **Platinum**, 0.9995 oz. • **Rev. Desc:** Eagle in flight over Heartland **Obv. Designer:** John Mercanti

Date	Mintage	Unc	Prf.
2000W	12,453	—	2,079

KM# 330 • 31.1050 g., 0.9995 **Platinum**, 0.9995 oz., 33mm. • **Rev. Desc:** Eagle in flight over Southwestern cactus desert **Obv. Designer:** John Mercanti

Date	Mintage	Unc	Prf.
2001W	8,969	—	2,079

KM# 292 • 31.1050 g., 0.9995 **Platinum**, 0.9995 oz. • **Rev. Desc:** Eagle in flight over New England costal lighthouse **Obv. Designer:** John Mercanti

Date	Mintage	Unc	Prf.
1998W	14,912	—	2,079

KM# 342 • 31.1050 g., 0.9995 **Platinum**, 0.9995 oz., 33mm. • **Rev. Desc:** Eagle fishing in America's Northwest **Obv. Designer:** John Mercanti

Date	Mintage	Unc	Prf.
2002W	9,834	—	2,079

KM# 304 • 31.1050 g., 0.9995 **Platinum**, 0.9995 oz. • **Rev. Desc:** Eagle in flight over Southeastern Wetlands **Obv. Designer:** John Mercanti

Date	Mintage	Unc	Prf.
1999W	12,363	—	2,079

KM# 354 • 31.1050 g., 0.9995 **Platinum**, 0.9995

oz., 33mm. • **Rev. Desc:** Eagle pearched on a
Rocky Mountain Pine branch against a flag
backdrop **Obv. Designer:** John Mercanti **Rev.
Designer:** Al Maletsky

Date	Mintage	Unc	Prf.
2003W	8,246	—	2,098

KM# 367 • 31.1050 g., 0.9995 **Platinum**, 0.9995
oz., 33mm. • **Rev. Desc:** Inspired by the sculpture
"America" by Daniel Chester French, 1907. The
sculpture is outside the N.Y. Customs House, now
part of the Smithsonian's Museum of the American
Indian **Obv. Designer:** John Mercanti **Rev.
Designer:** Donna Weaver

Date	Mintage	Unc	Prf.
2004W	6,007	—	2,406

KM# 380 • 31.1050 g., 0.9995 **Platinum**, 0.9995
oz., 33mm. • **Rev. Desc:** Eagle with cornucopiae
Obv. Designer: John Mercanti **Rev. Designer:**
Donna Weaver

Date	Mintage	Unc	Prf.
2005W	6,602	—	2,400

KM# 392 • 31.1050 g., 0.9995 **Platinum**, 0.9995
oz., 33mm. • **Subject:** Legislaive **Rev. Desc:**
Liberty seated writing between two columns **Obv.
Designer:** John Mercanti

Date	Mintage	Unc	Prf.
2006W	9,152	—	2,079

KM# 417 • 31.1050 g., 0.9995 **Platinum**, 0.9995
oz., 33mm. • **Subject:** Executive Branch
Rev. Desc: Eagle holding shield **Obv. Designer:**
John Mercanti

Date	Mintage	Unc	Prf.
2007W	8,363	—	2,079

KM# 437 • 31.1050 g., 0.9995 **Platinum**, 0.9995
oz., 33mm. • **Rev. Desc:** Female holding scales
of Justice, eagle in background **Obv. Designer:**
John Mercanti

Date	Mintage	Unc	Prf.
2008W	8,363	—	2,825

KM# 463 • 31.1020 g., 0.9995 **Platinum**, 0.9994
oz., 33mm. • **Subject:** A more perfect Union **Rev.
Desc:** Four portraits **Obv. Designer:** John Mercanti

Date	Mintage	Unc	Prf.
2009W Proof	4,900	—	2,600

KM# 488 • 31.1050 g., 0.9990 **Platinum**, 0.9990
oz. • **Obv. Designer:** John Mercanti

Date	Mintage	Unc	Prf.
2010W	—	—	2,200

BISON BULLION COINAGE

GOLD $5

KM# 411 • 3.1100 g., 0.9999 **Gold**, 0.1000 oz. •
Obv. Desc: Indian Head right **Rev. Desc:** Bison

Date	Mintage	Unc	Prf.
2008W	19,300	—	575
2008W	19,000	550	—
2009W	—	550	—
2009W	—	—	575

GOLD $10

KM# 412 • 7.7857 g., 0.9999 **Gold**, 0.2503 oz. •
Obv. Desc: Indian Head right **Rev. Desc:** Bison

Date	Mintage	Unc	Prf.
2008W	13,900	—	1,500
2008W	10,500	1,425	—
2009W	—	1,425	—
2009W	—	—	1,500

GOLD $25

KM# 413 • 15.5520 g., 0.9990 **Gold**, 0.4995 oz. •
Obv. Desc: Indian Head right **Rev. Desc:** Bison

Date	Mintage	Unc	Prf.
2008W	12,500	—	1,600
2008W	17,000	1,300	—
2009W	—	1,300	—
2009W	—	—	1,600

GOLD $50

KM# 393 • 31.1050 g., 0.9999 **Gold**, 0.9999 oz.,
32mm. • **Obv. Desc:** Indian head right **Rev.
Desc:** Bison standing left on mound **Designer:**
James E. Fraser

Date	Mintage	Unc	Prf.
2006W	246,267	—	1,584
2006W	337,012	1,540	—
2007W	136,503	1,540	—
2007W	58,998	—	1,594
2008W	189,500	1,540	—
2008W	19,500	—	3,300
2008W Moy Family Chop	—	3,500	—
2009W	—	1,540	—
2009W	—	—	1,584
2010W	—	—	1,634

FIRST SPOUSE GOLD COINAGE

GOLD $10

Date	Mintage	Unc	Prf.
2007W	20,000	791	—
2007W	20,000	—	791

KM# 409 • 15.5520 g., 0.9999 **Gold**, 0.4999 oz. •
Subject: Jefferson - Bust coinage design **Obv.
Desc:** Bust design from coinage **Rev. Desc:**
Jefferson's tombstone **Obv. Designer:** Robert Scot
and Phebe Hemphill **Rev. Designer:** Charles Vickers

Date	Mintage	Unc	Prf.
2007W	20,000	791	—
2007W	20,000	—	791

KM# 407 • 15.5520 g., 0.9999 **Gold**, 0.4999 oz. •
Subject: Martha Washington **Obv. Desc:** Bust 3/4
facing **Rev. Desc:** Martha Washington seated
sewing **Obv. Designer:** Joseph Menna **Rev.
Designer:** Susan Gamble and Don Everhart

Date	Mintage	Unc	Prf.
2007W	20,000	791	—
2007W	20,000	—	791

KM# 408 • 15.5520 g., 0.9999 **Gold**, 0.4999 oz. •
Subject: Abigail Adams **Obv. Desc:** Bust 3/4
facing **Rev. Desc:** Abigail Adams seated at desk
writing to John during the Revolutionary War **Obv.
Designer:** Joseph Menna **Rev. Designer:** Thomas
Cleveland and Phebe Hemphill

KM# 410 • 15.5520 g., 0.9999 **Gold**, 0.4999 oz. •
Subject: Dolley Madison **Obv. Desc:** Bust 3/4
facing **Rev. Desc:** Dolley standing before painting
of Washington, which she saved from the White

House **Obv. Designer:** Don Everhart **Rev.**
Designer: Joel Iskowitz and Don Everhart

Date	Mintage	Unc	Prf.
2007W	12,500	791	—
2007W	18,300	—	791

KM# 430 • 15.5520 g., 0.9990 **Gold**, 0.4995 oz. •
Subject: Elizabeth Monroe **Obv. Desc:** Bust 3/4
facing right **Rev. Desc:** Elizabeth standing before
mirror **Obv. Designer:** Joel Iskowitz and Don
Everhart **Rev. Designer:** Donna Weaver and
Charles Vickers

Date	Mintage	Unc	Prf.
2008W	4,500	—	—
2008W	7,900	—	—

KM# 431 • 15.5520 g., 0.9990 **Gold**, 0.4995 oz. •
Subject: Lousia Adams **Obv. Desc:** Bust 3/4 facing
right **Rev. Desc:** Lousia and son Charles before
entrance **Obv. Designer:** Susan Gamble and Phebe
Hemphill **Rev. Designer:** Joseph Menna

Date	Mintage	Unc	Prf.
2008W	4,200	—	—
2008W	7,400	—	—

KM# 432 • 15.5520 g., 0.9990 **Gold**, 0.4995 oz. •
Subject: Jackson's Liberty **Obv. Desc:** Capped
and draped bust left **Rev. Desc:** Andrew Jackson
on horseback right **Obv. Designer:** John Reich
Rev. Designer: Justin Kunz and Don Everhart

Date	Mintage	Unc	Prf.
2008W	4,800	—	—
2008W	7,800	—	—

KM# 433 • 15.5520 g., 0.9990 **Gold**, 0.4995 oz. •
Subject: van Buren's Liberty **Obv. Desc:** Seated
Liberty with shiled **Rev. Desc:** Youthful van Buren
seated under tree, family tavern in distance **Obv.**

Designer: Christian Gobrecht **Rev. Designer:**
Thomas Cleveland and James Licaretz

Date	Mintage	Unc	Prf.
2008W	15,000	—	—
2008W	Inc. above	—	—

KM# 456 • 15.5520 g., 0.9990 **Gold**, 0.4995 oz. •
Subject: Anna Harrison **Obv. Desc:** Bust 3/4 left
Rev. Desc: Anna reading to her three children **Obv.**
Designer: Donna Weaver and Joseph Menna **Rev.**
Designer: Thomas Cleveland and Charles Vickers

Date	Mintage	Unc	Prf.
2009W	15,000	—	—
2009W	Inc. above	—	—

KM# 457 • 15.5520 g., 0.9990 **Gold**, 0.4995 oz. •
Subject: Lettia Tyler **Obv. Desc:** Bust facing
Rev. Desc: Letitia and two children playing outside
of Cedar Grove Plantation **Obv. Designer:** Phebe
Hemphill **Rev. Designer:** Susan Gamble and Norm
Nemeth

Date	Mintage	Unc	Prf.
2009W	15,000	—	—
2009W	Inc. above	—	—

KM# 458 • 15.5520 g., 0.9990 **Gold**, 0.4995 oz. •
Subject: Julia Tyler **Obv. Desc:** Bust facing
Rev. Desc: Julia and John Tyler dancing
Designer: Joel Iskowitz and Don Everhart

Date	Mintage	Unc	Prf.
2009W	15,000	—	—
2009W	Inc. above	—	—

KM# 459 • 15.5520 g., 0.9990 **Gold**, 0.4995 oz. •
Subject: Sarah Polk **Obv. Desc:** Bust 3/4 right
Rev. Desc: Sarah seated at desk as personal
secretary to James Polk **Designer:** Phebe Hemphill

Date	Mintage	Unc	Prf.
2009W	3,501	—	—
2009W	5,157	—	—

KM# 465 • 15.5520 g., 0.9990 **Gold**, 0.4995 oz. • **Subject:** Margaret Taylor **Obv. Desc:** Bust 3/4 left **Rev. Desc:** Margaret Taylor nurses wounded soldier during the Seminole War **Obv. Designer:** Phebe Hemphill and Charles Vickers **Rev. Designer:** Mary Beth Zeitz and James Licaretz

Date	Mintage	Unc	Prf.
2009W	3,430	—	—
2009W	4,787	—	—

KM# 481 • 15.5200 g., 0.9990 **Gold**, 0.4985 oz. • **Subject:** Abigail Filmore **Rev. Desc:** Abigail Filmore placing books on library shelf **Obv. Designer:** Phebe Hemphill **Rev. Designer:** Susan Gamble and Joseph Menna

Date	Mintage	Unc	Prf.
2010W	15,000	—	—
2010W	Inc. above	—	—

KM# 482 • 15.5200 g., 0.9990 **Gold**, 0.4985 oz. • **Subject:** Jane Pierce **Rev. Desc:** Jane Pierce seated on porch **Obv. Designer:** Donna Weaver and Don Everhart **Rev. Designer:** Donna Weaver and Charles Vickers

Date	Mintage	Unc	Prf.
2010W	15,000	—	—
2010W	Inc. above	—	—

KM# 483 • 15.5200 g., 0.9990 **Gold**, 0.4985 oz. • **Subject:** Buchanan's Liberty **Rev. Desc:** Buchanan as clerk **Obv. Designer:** Christian Gobrecht **Rev. Designer:** Joseph Menna

Date	Mintage	Unc	Prf.
2010W	15,000	—	—
2010W	Inc. above	—	—

KM# 484 • 15.5200 g., 0.9990 **Gold**, 0.4985 oz. • **Subject:** Mary Todd Lincoln **Rev. Desc:** Mary Lincoln visiting soldiers at hospital **Obv. Designer:** Phebe Hemphill **Rev. Designer:** Joel Iskowitz and Pheve Hemphill

Date	Mintage	Unc	Prf.
2010	15,000	—	—
2010	Inc. above	—	—

KM# 509 • 15.5500 g., 0.9990 **Gold**, 0.4994 oz. • **Subject:** Eliza Johnson **Obv. Desc:** Bust of Eliza Johnson

Date	Mintage	Unc	Prf.
2011W	15,000	—	—
2011W	Inc. above	—	—

KM# 510 • 15.5520 g., 0.9990 **Gold**, 0.4995 oz. • **Subject:** Julia Grant **Obv. Desc:** Bust of Julia Grant

Date	Mintage	Unc	Prf.
2011W	15,000	—	—
2011W	Inc. above	—	—

KM# 511 • 15.5520 g., 0.9990 **Gold**, 0.4995 oz. • **Subject:** Lucy Hayes **Obv. Desc:** Bust of Lucy Hayes

Date	Mintage	Unc	Prf.
2011W	15,000	—	—
2011W	Inc. above	—	—

KM# 512 • 15.5520 g., 0.9990 **Gold**, 0.4995 oz. • **Subject:** Lucretia Garfield **Obv. Desc:** Bust of Lucretia Garfield

Date	Mintage	Unc	Prf.
2011W	15,000	768	—
2011W	Inc. above	—	781

CANADA

CONFEDERATION

CIRCULATION COINAGE

CENT

KM# 1 4.5400 g. Bronze **Obv:** Laureate head left **Obv. Legend:** VICTORIA DEI GRATIA REGINA. CANADA **Rev:** Denomination and date within beaded circle, chain of leaves surrounds **Rev. Legend:** ONE CENT **Edge:** plain

Date	Mintage	VG-8	F-12	VF-20	XF-40	MS-60	MS-63	Proof
1858	421,000	75.00	100.00	125	200	500	2,000	—
1859 Narrow 9	9,579,000	2.25	3.00	5.00	7.00	45.00	250	—
1859/8 Wide 9	Inc. above	30.00	45.00	60.00	125	350	1,800	—
1859 Double punched narrow 9 type I	Inc. above	200	250	350	550	1,300	5,000	—
1859 Double punched narrow 9 type II	Inc. above	55.00	75.00	125	175	550	3,000	—

KM# 7 5.6700 g. Bronze 25.5 mm. **Obv:** Crowned head left within beaded circle **Obv. Legend:** VICTORIA DEI GRATIA REGINA. CANADA **Obv. Designer:** Leonard C. Wyon **Rev:** Denomination and date within beaded circle, chain of leaves surrounds **Edge:** Plain

Date	Mintage	VG-8	F-12	VF-20	XF-40	MS-60	MS-63	Proof
1876H	4,000,000	3.00	4.00	6.00	9.00	45.00	250	—
1881H	2,000,000	4.00	5.00	11.00	18.00	75.00	300	—
1882H	4,000,000	3.00	3.50	4.00	7.50	40.00	250	—
1884	2,500,000	3.00	4.00	6.50	11.00	60.00	300	—
1886	1,500,000	4.00	7.00	13.00	20.00	95.00	450	—
1887	1,500,000	3.50	5.00	8.00	14.00	70.00	225	—
1888	4,000,000	3.00	4.00	5.00	v7.50	40.00	175	—
1890H	1,000,000	8.00	12.00	19.00	30.00	125	450	—
1891 Large date	1,452,000	8.00	11.00	17.00	35.00	150	450	—
1891 S.D.L.L.	Inc. above	65.00	125	200	300	1,000	4,000	—
1891 S.D.S.L.	Inc. above	60.00	95.00	125	200	450	1,750	—
1892	1,200,000	5.50	8.00	12.00	15.00	60.00	225	—
1893	2,000,000	3.00	4.00	5.00	9.50	45.00	200	—
1894	1,000,000	11.00	15.00	20.00	40.00	125	300	—
1895	1,200,000	5.00	9.50	13.00	16.00	60.00	225	—
1896	2,000,000	3.00	5.00	6.50	7.50	40.00	150	—
1897	1,500,000	3.00	5.00	6.50	9.00	45.00	200	—
1898H	1,000,000	9.00	13.00	17.00	35.00	100.00	300	—
1899	2,400,000	3.00	3.50	5.00	7.00	45.00	150	—
1900	1,000,000	9.00	13.50	20.00	30.00	125	500	—
1900H	2,600,000	3.00	3.50	5.00	7.50	30.00	95.00	—
1901	4,100,000	3.00	4.00	6.00	11.00	45.50	110	—

KM# 8 5.6700 g. Bronze 25.5 mm. **Obv:** Kings bust right within beaded circle **Obv. Designer:** G. W. DeSaulles **Rev:** Denomination above date within circle, chain of leaves surrounds **Edge:** Plain

Date	Mintage	VG-8	F-12	VF-20	XF-40	MS-60	MS-63	Proof
1902	3,000,000	2.25	3.00	5.00	8.00	32.50	100.00	—
1903	4,000,000	2.25	3.00	4.00	8.00	39.00	105	—
1904	2,500,000	2.50	5.00	7.00	10.00	45.50	110	—
1905	2,000,000	5.00	8.00	10.00	16.00	60.00	195	—
1906	4,100,000	2.25	3.00	4.00	8.00	45.50	230	—
1907	2,400,000	2.50	5.00	6.00	12.00	45.50	260	—
1907H	800,000	16.00	30.00	39.00	65.00	230	725	—
1908	2,401,506	4.00	5.00	7.00	10.00	39.00	115	195
1909	3,973,339	2.25	3.00	4.00	8.00	39.00	130	—
1910	5,146,487	2.25	3.00	4.00	7.00	33.75	90.00	—

KM# 15 5.6700 g. Bronze 25.5 mm. **Obv:** King's bust left **Obv. Designer:** E. B. MacKennal **Rev:** Denomination above date within beaded circle, chain of leaves surrounds **Edge:** Plain

Date	Mintage	VG-8	F-12	VF-20	XF-40	MS-60	MS-63	Proof
1911	4,663,486	0.80	1.50	2.25	3.50	25.00	75.00	250

KM# 21 5.6700 g. Bronze 25.5 mm. **Obv:** King's bust left **Obv. Designer:** E. B. MacKennal **Rev:** Denomination above date within beaded circle, chain of leaves surrounds **Edge:** Plain

Date	Mintage	VG-8	F-12	VF-20	XF-40	MS-60	MS-63	Proof
1912	5,107,642	0.90	1.75	2.75	4.00	30.00	95.00	—
1913	5,735,405	0.90	1.75	2.75	5.00	27.50	95.00	—
1914	3,405,958	1.25	1.75	3.00	5.00	42.00	150	—
1915	4,932,134	0.90	2.50	4.00	5.00	36.00	120	—
1916	11,022,367	0.60	0.80	1.50	4.00	19.00	60.00	—
1917	11,899,254	0.60	0.80	1.00	2.75	16.00	55.00	—
1918	12,970,798	0.60	0.80	1.00	2.75	14.00	55.00	—
1919	11,279,634	0.60	0.80	1.00	2.75	14.00	55.00	—
1920	6,762,247	0.70	0.90	1.25	2.75	25.00	120	—

Dot below date

KM# 28 3.2400 g. Bronze 19.10 mm. **Obv:** King's bust left **Obv. Designer:** E. B. MacKennal **Rev:** Denomination above date, leaves flank **Rev. Designer:** Fred Lewis **Edge:** Plain

Date	Mintage	VG-8	F-12	VF-20	XF-40	MS-60	MS-63	Proof
1920	15,483,923	0.20	0.45	0.95	1.75	15.00	50.00	—
1921	7,601,627	0.45	0.75	1.75	5.00	35.00	200	—
1922	1,243,635	13.00	16.00	21.00	40.00	200	1,200	—
1923	1,019,002	29.00	35.00	40.00	50.00	300	2,000	—
1924	1,593,195	5.00	6.50	8.50	15.00	125	850	—
1925	1,000,622	18.00	21.00	27.00	40.00	200	1,300	—
1926	2,143,372	3.50	4.50	7.00	11.00	100.00	650	—
1927	3,553,928	1.25	1.75	3.50	6.00	40.00	225	—
1928	9,144,860	0.15	0.30	0.65	1.50	20.00	90.00	—
1929	12,159,840	0.15	0.30	0.65	1.50	20.00	80.00	—
1930	2,538,613	2.00	2.50	4.50	8.50	50.00	225	—
1931	3,842,776	0.65	1.00	2.50	5.50	40.00	200	—
1932	21,316,190	0.15	0.20	0.50	1.50	14.00	45.00	—
1933	12,079,310	0.15	0.30	0.50	1.50	15.00	55.00	—
1934	7,042,358	0.20	0.30	0.75	1.50	14.00	45.00	—
1935	7,526,400	0.20	0.30	0.75	1.50	14.00	45.00	—
1936	8,768,769	0.15	0.30	0.75	1.50	14.00	45.00	—
1936 dot below date; Rare	678,823	—	—	—	—	—	250,000	—

Note: Only one possible business strike is known to exist. No other examples (or possible business strikes) have ever surfaced.

1936 dot below date, specimen, 3 known	—	—	—	—	—	—	—	—

Note: At the David Akers auction of the John Jay Pittman collection (Part 1, 10-97), a gem specimen realized $121,000. At the David Akers auction of the John Jay Pittman collection (Part 3, 10-99), a near choice specimen realized $115,000.

Maple leaf

KM# 32 3.2400 g. Bronze 19.10 mm. **Obv:** Head left **Obv. Designer:** T. H. Paget **Rev:** Maple leaf divides date and denomination **Rev. Designer:** George E. Kruger-Gray **Edge:** Plain

Date	Mintage	VG-8	F-12	VF-20	XF-40	MS-60	MS-63	Proof
1937	10,040,231	0.35	0.45	0.70	0.95	2.50	9.00	—
1938	18,365,608	0.15	0.20	0.30	0.75	2.50	13.00	—
1939	21,600,319	0.10	0.20	0.30	0.70	1.75	6.00	—
1940	85,740,532	0.10	0.15	0.25	0.50	2.25	6.00	—
1941	56,336,011	0.10	0.15	0.25	0.50	8.00	60.00	—
1942	76,113,708	0.10	0.15	0.25	0.50	8.00	60.00	—
1943	89,111,969	0.10	0.15	0.25	0.45	3.50	25.00	—
1944	44,131,216	0.10	0.15	0.30	0.60	12.00	75.00	—
1945	77,268,591	0.10	0.15	0.20	0.35	2.50	22.00	—
1946	56,662,071	0.10	0.15	0.20	0.35	2.50	9.00	—
1947	31,093,901	0.10	0.15	0.20	0.35	2.50	7.50	—
1947 maple leaf	47,855,448	0.10	0.15	0.20	0.35	2.50	8.50	—

KM# 41 3.2400 g. Bronze 19.10 mm. **Obv:** Modified legend **Obv. Designer:** T. H. Paget **Rev. Designer:** George E. Kruger-Gray **Edge:** Plain

Date	Mintage	VG-8	F-12	VF-20	XF-40	MS-60	MS-63	Proof
1948	25,767,779	—	0.15	0.25	0.70	4.00	30.00	—
1949	33,128,933	—	0.10	0.15	0.35	2.50	9.00	—
1950	60,444,992	—	0.10	0.15	0.25	1.75	9.00	—
1951	80,430,379	—	0.10	0.15	0.20	1.75	13.00	—
1952	67,631,736	—	0.10	0.15	0.20	1.25	7.00	—

No strap   With strap

KM# 49 3.2400 g. Bronze 19.10 mm. **Obv:** Laureate bust right **Obv. Designer:** Mary Gillick **Rev:** Maple leaf divides date and denomination **Rev. Designer:** George E. Kruger-Gray

Date	Mintage	VG-8	F-12	VF-20	XF-40	MS-60	MS-63	Proof
1953	67,806,016	0.10	0.10	0.10	0.25	0.65	1.50	—
Note: Without strap								
1953	Inc. above	0.50	1.00	1.50	2.50	12.00	55.00	—
Note: With strap								
1954	22,181,760	0.10	0.10	0.10	0.40	1.75	6.00	—
Note: With strap								
1954 Prooflike only	Inc. above	—	—	—	—	450	600	—
Note: Without strap								
1955	56,403,193	—	0.10	0.10	0.15	0.50	2.50	—
Note: With strap								

Date	Mintage	VG-8	F-12	VF-20	XF-40	MS-60	MS-63	Proof
1955	Inc. above	85.00	125	150	250	600	1,800	—
Note: Without strap								
1956	78,658,535	—	—	—	0.15	0.30	1.75	—
1957	100,601,792	—	—	—	0.10	0.10	1.00	—
1958	59,385,679	—	—	—	0.10	0.10	1.00	—
1959	83,615,343	—	—	—	0.10	0.10	0.50	—
1960	75,772,775	—	—	—	0.10	0.10	0.50	—
1961	139,598,404	—	—	—	—	0.10	0.50	—
1962	227,244,069	—	—	—	—	0.10	0.30	—
1963	279,076,334	—	—	—	—	0.10	0.30	—
1964	484,655,322	—	—	—	—	0.10	0.30	—

KM# 59.1 3.2400 g. Bronze 19.10 mm. **Obv:** Queens bust right **Obv. Designer:** Arnold Machin **Rev:** Maple leaf divides date and denomination **Rev. Designer:** George E. Kruger-Gray **Edge:** Plain

Date	Mintage	VG-8	F-12	VF-20	XF-40	MS-60	MS-63	Proof
1965	304,441,082	—	—	—	0.40	1.00	4.00	—
Note: Small beads, pointed 5								
1965	Inc. above	—	—	—	—	0.10	0.35	—
Note: Small beads, blunt 5								
1965	Inc. above	1.75	3.00	4.50	7.50	18.00	40.00	—
Note: Large beads, pointed 5								
1965	Inc. above	—	—	—	—	0.10	0.35	—
Note: Large beads, blunt 5								
1966	184,151,087	—	—	—	—	0.10	0.35	—
1968	329,695,772	—	—	—	—	0.10	0.35	—
1969	335,240,929	—	—	—	—	0.10	0.35	—
1970	311,145,010	—	—	—	—	0.10	0.35	—
1971	298,228,936	—	—	—	—	0.10	0.35	—
1972	451,304,591	—	—	—	—	0.10	0.35	—
1973	457,059,852	—	—	—	—	0.10	0.30	—
1974	692,058,489	—	—	—	—	0.10	0.35	—
1975	642,318,000	—	—	—	—	0.10	0.35	—
1976	701,122,890	—	—	—	—	0.10	0.35	—
1977	453,762,670	—	—	—	—	0.10	0.35	—

KM# 65 3.2400 g. Bronze 19.10 mm. **Subject:** Confederation Centennial **Obv:** Queen's bust right **Obv. Designer:** Arnold Machin **Rev:** Dove with wings spread, denomination above, two dates below **Rev. Designer:** Alex Coville

Date	Mintage	VG-8	F-12	VF-20	XF-40	MS-60	MS-63	Proof
1967	345,140,645	—	—	—	—	0.10	0.30	1.00

KM# 59.2 3.2400 g. Bronze 19.10 mm. **Obv:** Queen's bust right **Obv. Designer:** Arnold Machin **Rev:** Maple leaves **Rev. Designer:** George E. Kruger-Gray **Edge:** Plain **Note:** Thin planchet.

Date	Mintage	VG-8	F-12	VF-20	XF-40	MS-60	MS-63	Proof
1978	911,170,647	—	—	—	—	0.10	0.30	—
1979	754,394,064	—	—	—	—	0.10	0.30	—

KM# 127 2.8000 g. Bronze 19.10 mm. **Obv:** Queen's bust right **Obv. Designer:** Arnold Machin **Rev. Designer:** George E. Kruger-Gray **Edge:** Plain **Note:** Reduced weight.

Date	Mintage	VG-8	F-12	VF-20	XF-40	MS-60	MS-63	Proof
1980	912,052,318	—	—	—	—	0.10	0.30	—
1981	1,209,468,500	—	—	—	—	0.10	0.30	—
1981 Proof	199,000	—	—	—	—	—	—	1.50

KM# 132 2.5000 g. Bronze 19.10 mm. **Obv:** Queen's bust right **Obv. Designer:** Arnold Machin **Rev:** Maple leaf divides date and denomination **Rev. Designer:** George E. Kruger-Gray **Edge:** Plain **Note:** Reduced weight.

Date	Mintage	VG-8	F-12	VF-20	XF-40	MS-60	MS-63	Proof
1982	911,001,000	—	—	—	—	0.10	0.30	—
1982 Proof	180,908	—	—	—	—	—	—	1.50
1983	975,510,000	—	—	—	—	0.10	0.30	—
1983 Proof	168,000	—	—	—	—	—	—	1.50
1984	838,225,000	—	—	—	—	0.10	0.30	—
1984 Proof	161,602	—	—	—	—	—	—	1.50
1985	771,772,500	0.95	1.75	2.50	3.50	10.00	19.00	—
Note: Pointed 5								
1985	Inc. above	—	—	—	—	0.10	0.30	—
Note: Blunt 5								
1985 Proof	157,037	—	—	—	—	—	—	1.50
Note: Blunt 5								
1986	740,335,000	—	—	—	—	0.10	0.30	—
1986 Proof	175,745	—	—	—	—	—	—	1.50
1987	774,549,000	—	—	—	—	0.10	0.30	—
1987 Proof	179,004	—	—	—	—	—	—	1.50
1988	482,676,752	—	—	—	—	0.10	0.30	—
1988 Proof	175,259	—	—	—	—	—	—	1.50
1989	1,077,347,200	—	—	—	—	0.10	0.30	—
1989 Proof	170,928	—	—	—	—	—	—	1.50

KM# 181 2.5000 g. Bronze 19.10 mm. **Obv:** Crowned Queen's head right **Obv. Designer:** Dora dePedery-Hunt **Rev:** Maple leaf divides date and denomination **Rev. Designer:** George E. Kruger-Gray **Edge:** Plain

Date	Mintage	MS-63	Proof
1990	218,035,000	0.30	—
1990 Proof	140,649	—	2.50
1991	831,001,000	0.30	—
1991 Proof	131,888	—	3.50
1993	752,034,000	0.30	—
1993 Proof	145,065	—	2.00
1994	639,516,000	0.30	—
1994 Proof	146,424	—	2.50
1995	624,983,000	0.30	—
1995 Proof	—	—	2.50
1996	445,746,000	0.30	—
1996 Proof	—	—	2.50

KM# 204 Bronze 19.10 mm. **Subject:** Confederation 125 **Obv:** Crowned Queen's head right **Obv. Designer:** Dora dePedery-Hunt **Rev:** Maple leaf divides date and denomination **Rev. Designer:** George E. Kruger-Gray

Date	Mintage	MS-63	Proof
1992	673,512,000	0.30	—
1992 Proof	147,061	—	2.50

KM# 289 2.2500 g. Copper Plated Steel 19.05 mm. **Obv:** Crowned head right **Obv. Designer:** Dora dePédery-Hunt **Rev:** Maple twig design **Rev. Designer:** George E. Kruger-Gray **Edge:** Round and plain

Date	Mintage	MS-63	Proof
1997	549,868,000	0.30	—
1997 Proof	—	—	2.75
1998	999,578,000	0.30	—
1998 Proof	—	—	3.00
1998W	—	1.75	—
1999P	—	6.00	—
1999	1,089,625,000	0.30	—
1999W	—	—	—
1999 Proof	—	—	4.00
2000	771,908,206	0.30	—
2000 Proof	—	—	4.00
2000W	—	1.75	—
2001	919,358,000	0.30	—
2001P Proof	—	—	5.00
2003	92,219,775	0.30	—
2003P Proof	—	—	5.00
2003P	235,936,799	1.50	—

KM# 289a Bronze 19.10 mm.

Date	Mintage	MS-63	Proof
1998	—	0.75	—
Note: In Specimen sets only			

KM# 309 5.6700 g. 0.9250 Copper Plated Silver 0.1686 oz. **Subject:** 90th Anniversary Royal Canadian Mint - 1908-1998 **Obv. Designer:** Dora dePedery-Hunt **Rev. Designer:** G. W. DeSaulles

Date	Mintage	MS-63	Proof
1998	25,000	16.00	—
Note: Antique finish			
1998 Proof	—	—	—

KM# 332 5.6700 g. 0.9250 Silver 0.1686 oz. ASW **Subject:** 90th Anniversary Royal Canadian Mint - 1908-1998 **Obv:** Crowned Queen's head right, with "Canada" added to head **Obv. Designer:** Dora dePedery-Hunt **Rev:** Denomination above dates withn beaded circle, chain of leaves surrounds **Rev. Designer:** G. W. DeSaulles

Date	Mintage	MS-63	P/L	Proof
2000 Proof	25,000	—	—	16.00

Note: Mirror finish

KM# 445 2.2500 g. Copper Plated Steel 19.1 mm. **Subject:** Elizabeth II Golden Jubilee **Obv:** Crowned head right, Jubilee commemorative dates 1952-2002 **Obv. Designer:** Dora dePedery-Hunt **Rev:** Denomination above maple leaves **Rev. Designer:** George E. Kruger-Gray **Edge:** Plain

Date	Mintage	MS-63	Proof
2002	716,366,000	0.75	—
2002P	114,212,000	1.00	—
2002P Proof	32,642	—	5.00

KM# 445a 0.9250 Silver **Subject:** Elizabeth II Golden Jubilee **Obv:** Crowned head right, Jubilee commemorative dates 1952-2002 **Obv. Designer:** Dora dePédery-Hunt **Rev:** Denomination above maple leaves **Rev. Designer:** George E. Kruger-Gray

Date	Mintage	MS-63	Proof
2002	21,537	—	3.00

KM# 490 2.2500 g. Copper Plated Zinc 19.05 mm. **Obv:** New effigy of Queen Elizabeth II right **Obv. Designer:** Susanna Blunt **Rev:** Two maple leaves **Edge:** Plain

Date	Mintage	MS-63	Proof
2003	56,877,144	0.25	—
2004	653,317,000	0.25	—
2004 Proof	—	—	2.50
2005	759,658,000	0.25	—
2005 Proof	—	—	2.50
2006	886,275,000	0.25	—
2006 Proof	—	—	2.50

KM# 490a 2.2500 g. Copper Plated Steel 19.05 mm. **Obv:** Bust right **Obv. Designer:** Susanna Blunt **Rev:** Two maple leaves **Rev. Designer:** G. E. Kruger-Gray

Date	Mintage	MS-63	Proof
2003P	591,257,000	0.25	—
2003 WP	Inc. above	0.25	—
2004P	134,906,000	0.25	—
2005P	30,525,000	0.25	—
2006P	137,733,000	0.25	—
2006(ml)	Inc. above	0.25	—
2007(ml)	938,270,000	0.25	—
2007(ml) Proof	—	—	2.50
2008(ml)	787,625,000	0.25	—
2008(ml) Proof	—	—	2.50
2009(ml)	455,680,000	0.25	—
2009(ml) Proof	—	—	2.50
2010(ml)	—	0.25	—
2010(ml) Proof	—	—	2.50
2011(ml)	—	0.25	—
2011(ml) Proof	—	—	2.50

KM# 468 2.5000 g. Copper **Subject:** 50th Anniversary of the Coronation of Elizabeth II **Obv:** 1953 Effigy of the Queen, Jubilee commemorative dates 1952-2002 **Obv. Designer:** Mary Gillick

Date	Mintage	MS-63	Proof
2002 Proof	—	—	2.50

KM# 490b 2.2500 g. Copper Plated Zinc **Obv:** Head right **Rev:** Maple leaf, selectively gold plated **Note:** Bound into Annual Report.

Date	Mintage	MS-63	Proof
2003 Proof	7,746	—	35.00

KM# 1023 Copper 19.1 mm. **Obv:** George V bust left **Rev:** Value within wreath, dual dates below

Date	Mintage	MS-63	Proof
2010 Proof	—	—	10.00

3 CENTS

KM# 410 3.1100 g. 0.9250 Silver Gilt 0.0925 oz. ASW 21.3 mm. **Subject:** 1st Canadian Postage Stamp **Obv:** Crowned head right **Obv. Designer:** Dora dePédery-Hunt **Rev:** Partial stamp design **Rev. Designer:** Sandford Fleming **Edge:** Plain

Date	Mintage	MS-63	Proof
2001 Proof	59,573	—	12.50

5 CENTS

Oval O's

Round O's

KM# 2 1.1620 g. 0.9250 Silver 0.0346 oz. ASW **Obv:** Head left **Obv. Legend:** VICTORIA DEI GRATIA REGINA. CANADA **Rev:** Denomination and date within wreath, crown above

Date	Mintage	VG-8	F-12	VF-20	XF-40	MS-60	MS-63	Proof
1858 Small date	1,500,000	19.00	30.00	45.00	80.00	250	550	—
1858 Large date over small date	Inc. above	150	225	350	550	1,500	3,500	—
1870	2,800,000	15.00	24.00	40.00	75.00	250	850	—
Note: Flat rim								
1870	Inc. above	15.00	24.00	40.00	75.00	250	600	—
Note: Wire rim								
1871	1,400,000	15.00	24.00	40.00	75.00	300	800	—
1872H	2,000,000	13.00	20.00	35.00	80.00	350	1,250	—
1874H Plain 4	800,000	22.00	45.00	90.00	150	450	1,000	—
1874H Crosslet 4	Inc. above	18.00	40.00	75.00	150	500	1,100	—
1875H Large date	1,000,000	300	500	800	1,400	5,000	15,000	—
1875H Small date	Inc. above	150	225	500	700	2,100	6,000	—
1880H	3,000,000	6.00	12.00	27.00	65.00	300	800	—
1881H	1,500,000	9.00	15.00	30.00	70.00	300	800	—
1882H	1,000,000	12.00	18.00	28.00	80.00	300	800	—
1883H	600,000	23.00	40.00	85.00	200	900	3,000	—
1884	200,000	125	200	350	750	3,500	9,000	—
1885 Small 5	1,000,000	16.00	24.00	50.00	125	750	2,900	—
1885 Large 5	Inc. above	15.00	27.00	55.00	150	850	3,000	—
1885 Large 5 over small 5	Inc. above	65.00	125	200	500	4,000	—	—
1886 Small 6	1,700,000	9.00	15.00	30.00	60.00	400	1,300	—
1886 Large 6	Inc. above	11.00	18.00	40.00	70.00	425	1,500	—
1887	500,000	30.00	60.00	75.00	175	500	1,000	—
1888	1,000,000	6.00	9.00	18.00	50.00	175	450	—
1889	1,200,000	24.00	40.00	90.00	175	600	1,600	—
1890H	1,000,000	6.00	12.00	22.00	50.00	200	450	—
1891	1,800,000	6.00	9.00	15.00	30.00	150	400	—
1892	860,000	6.00	10.00	20.00	50.00	250	700	—
1893	1,700,000	6.00	9.00	14.00	30.00	175	500	—
1894	500,000	19.00	30.00	75.00	125	450	1,400	—
1896	1,500,000	6.00	9.00	14.00	35.00	175	450	—
1897	1,319,283	4.50	6.50	20.00	45.00	150	450	—
1898	580,717	12.00	20.00	40.00	90.00	350	950	—
1899	3,000,000	4.50	6.50	12.00	25.00	125	350	—
1900 Oval 0's	1,800,000	4.50	6.50	12.00	25.00	125	400	—
1900 Round 0's	Inc. above	21.00	40.00	60.00	150	450	1,000	—
1901	2,000,000	6.00	8.00	16.00	45.50	195	525	—

KM# 9 3.3200 g. 0.9250 Silver 0.0987 oz. ASW 20.1 mm. **Obv. Designer:** G. W. DeSaulles **Rev. Designer:** Leonard C. Wyon

Date	Mintage	VG-8	F-12	VF-20	XF-40	MS-60	MS-63	Proof
1902	2,120,000	3.00	4.00	5.00	9.00	45.50	70.00	—
1902	2,200,000	3.00	4.00	7.00	14.00	45.50	80.00	—
Note: Large broad H								
1902	Inc. above	10.00	17.00	31.25	50.00	130	230	—
Note: Small narrow H								

KM# 13 1.1500 g. 0.9250 Silver 0.0342 oz. ASW 15.5 mm. **Obv:** King's bust right **Rev:** Denomination and date within wreath, crown at top

Date	Mintage	VG-8	F-12	VF-20	XF-40	MS-60	MS-63	Proof
1903 22 leaves	1,000,000	5.00	9.00	22.50	45.50	195	450	—
1903H 21 leaves	2,640,000	2.25	4.00	9.00	20.00	130	400	—
1904	2,400,000	4.00	6.00	9.00	30.00	230	650	—
1905	2,600,000	2.25	4.00	12.00	20.00	130	295	—
1906	3,100,000	3.00	4.00	8.00	17.00	110	295	—
1907	5,200,000	3.00	4.00	5.00	13.00	70.00	195	—
1908	1,220,524	8.00	13.00	30.00	45.50	130	230	—
1909 Round leaves	1,983,725	4.00	8.00	13.00	39.00	230	650	—
1909 Pointed leaves	Inc. above	16.00	22.50	45.50	125	725	1,700	—
1910 Pointed leaves	3,850,325	3.00	4.00	7.00	14.00	65.00	125	—
1910 Round leaves	Inc. above	20.00	22.50	39.00	110	525	1,700	—

KM# 16 1.1620 g. 0.9250 Silver 0.0346 oz. ASW   **Obv:** King's bust left **Obv. Designer:** E. B. MacKennal
Rev: Denomination and date within wreath, crown above **Rev. Designer:** Leonard C. Wyon

Date	Mintage	VG-8	F-12	VF-20	XF-40	MS-60	MS-63	Proof
1911	3,692,350	2.50	4.00	8.00	12.00	80.00	130	—

KM# 22 1.1300 g. 0.9250 Silver 0.0336 oz. ASW 15.5 mm.   **Obv:** King's bust left **Obv. Designer:** E. B.
MacKennal **Rev:** Denomination and date within wreath, crown above **Rev. Designer:** Leonard C. Wyon

Date	Mintage	VG-8	F-12	VF-20	XF-40	MS-60	MS-63	Proof
1912	5,863,170	2.50	4.00	7.00	12.00	65.00	195	—
1913	5,488,048	2.50	4.00	6.00	10.00	33.75	65.00	—
1914	4,202,179	2.50	4.00	7.00	12.00	65.00	165	—
1915	1,172,258	14.00	20.00	33.75	65.00	425	775	—
1916	2,481,675	4.00	10.00	17.00	27.50	130	325	—
1917	5,521,373	2.25	3.00	4.00	9.00	39.00	105	—
1918	6,052,298	2.25	3.00	4.00	8.00	39.00	85.00	—
1919	7,835,400	2.25	3.00	4.00	8.00	39.00	85.00	—

KM# 22a 1.1664 g. 0.8000 Silver 0.0300 oz. ASW 15.48 mm.   **Obv. Designer:** E. B. MacKennal **Rev.
Designer:** Leonard C. Wyon

Date	Mintage	VG-8	F-12	VF-20	XF-40	MS-60	MS-63	Proof
1920	10,649,851	1.75	2.50	3.00	6.50	26.00	50.00	—
1921	2,582,495	3,000	4,000	5,500	7,000	12,000	21,000	—

Note: Approximately 460 known; balance remelted. Stack's A.G. Carter Jr. Sale (12-89) choice BU, finest known, realized $57,200

Near 6   Far 6

KM# 29 4.6000 g. Nickel 21.2 mm.   **Obv:** King's bust left **Obv. Designer:** E. B. MacKennal **Rev:** Maple
leaves divide denomination and date **Rev. Designer:** W. H. J. Blakemore

Date	Mintage	VG-8	F-12	VF-20	XF-40	MS-60	MS-63	Proof
1922	4,794,119	0.30	0.95	1.75	7.00	45.00	95.00	—
1923	2,502,279	0.40	1.25	5.50	16.00	100.00	300	—
1924	3,105,839	0.30	1.00	4.00	10.00	85.00	225	—
1925	201,921	55.00	70.00	100.00	225	1,200	4,000	—
1926 Near 6	938,162	3.00	7.00	16.00	60.00	400	1,300	—
1926 Far 6	Inc. above	100.00	150	300	600	1,500	4,500	—
1927	5,285,627	0.30	0.65	3.00	14.50	60.00	150	—
1928	4,577,712	0.30	0.65	3.00	14.50	55.00	100.00	—
1929	5,611,911	0.30	0.65	3.00	14.50	60.00	150	—
1930	3,704,673	0.30	1.25	3.00	15.00	90.00	225	—
1931	5,100,830	0.30	1.25	3.50	18.00	175	500	—
1932	3,198,566	0.30	1.00	3.50	16.00	150	400	—
1933	2,597,867	0.40	1.50	6.00	18.00	175	650	—
1934	3,827,304	0.30	1.00	3.00	16.00	150	400	—
1935	3,900,000	0.30	1.00	3.00	11.00	95.00	250	—
1936	4,400,450	0.30	0.65	1.75	9.00	50.00	125	—

KM# 33 4.5000 g. Nickel 21.2 mm. **Obv:** Head left **Obv. Designer:** T. H. Paget **Rev:** Beaver on rock divides denomination and date **Rev. Designer:** George E. Kruger-Gray

Date	Mintage	VG-8	F-12	VF-20	XF-40	MS-60	MS-63	Proof
1937 Dot	4,593,263	0.20	0.30	1.25	2.50	9.00	22.00	—
1938	3,898,974	0.30	0.90	2.00	7.00	75.00	150	—
1939	5,661,123	0.20	0.35	1.25	3.00	45.00	80.00	—
1940	13,920,197	0.20	0.30	0.75	2.25	18.00	55.00	—
1941	8,681,785	0.20	0.30	0.75	2.25	23.00	70.00	—
1942 Round	6,847,544	0.20	0.30	0.75	1.75	18.00	35.00	—

KM# 39 Tombac 21.2 mm. **Obv:** Head left **Obv. Designer:** T. H. Paget **Rev:** Beaver on rock divides denomination and date **Rev. Designer:** George E. Kruger-Gray **Shape:** 12-sided

Date	Mintage	VG-8	F-12	VF-20	XF-40	MS-60	MS-63	Proof
1942	3,396,234	0.40	0.65	1.25	1.75	3.00	14.00	—

KM# 40 Tombac 21.2 mm. **Subject:** Victory **Obv:** Head left **Obv. Designer:** T. H. Paget **Rev:** Torch on "V" divides date **Rev. Designer:** Thomas Shingles

Date	Mintage	VG-8	F-12	VF-20	XF-40	MS-60	MS-63	Proof
1943	24,760,256	0.20	0.30	0.40	0.80	3.00	9.00	—
1944	8,000	—	—	—	—	—	—	—

Note: 1 known

KM# 40a 4.4000 g. Chrome Plated Steel 21.2 mm. **Obv:** Head left **Rev:** Torch on "V" divides date

Date	Mintage	VG-8	F-12	VF-20	XF-40	MS-60	MS-63	Proof
1944	11,532,784	0.10	0.20	0.50	0.90	2.00	6.50	—
1945	18,893,216	0.10	0.20	0.40	0.80	2.00	6.50	—

Dot   Maple leaf

KM# 39a 4.5000 g. Nickel 21.2 mm. **Obv:** Head left **Obv. Designer:** T. H. Paget **Rev:** Beaver on rock divides denomination and date **Rev. Designer:** George E. Kruger-Gray

Date	Mintage	VG-8	F-12	VF-20	XF-40	MS-60	MS-63	Proof
1946	6,952,684	0.10	0.25	0.50	2.00	14.00	35.00	—
1947	7,603,724	0.20	0.25	0.50	1.25	10.00	25.00	—

5 CENTS

Date	Mintage	VG-8	F-12	VF-20	XF-40	MS-60	MS-63	Proof
1947 Dot	Inc. above	17.00	20.00	27.00	60.00	175	300	—
1947 Maple leaf	9,595,124	0.20	0.30	0.45	1.25	10.00	25.00	—

KM# 42 4.5400 g. Nickel 21.2 mm. **Obv:** Head left, modified legend **Obv. Designer:** T. H. Paget **Rev:** Beaver on rock divides date and denomination **Rev. Designer:** George E. Kruger-Gray

Date	Mintage	VG-8	F-12	VF-20	XF-40	MS-60	MS-63	Proof
1948	1,810,789	0.40	0.50	1.00	3.00	18.00	35.00	—
1949	13,037,090	0.15	0.25	0.45	0.75	6.00	12.00	—
1950	11,970,521	0.15	0.25	0.45	0.75	6.00	12.00	—

KM# 42a Chromium And Nickel Plated Steel 21.2 mm. **Obv:** Head left **Obv. Designer:** T. H. Paget **Rev:** Beaver on rock divides date and denomination **Rev. Designer:** George E. Kruger-Gray

Date	Mintage	VG-8	F-12	VF-20	XF-40	MS-60	MS-63	Proof
1951	4,313,410	0.10	0.20	0.50	0.80	3.50	11.00	—
Note: Low relief; Second "A" in GRATIA points between denticles								
1951	Inc. above	350	550	700	1,000	1,900	3,500	—
Note: High relief; Second "A" in GRATIA points to a denticle								
1952	10,891,148	0.10	0.20	0.45	0.80	3.00	7.50	—

KM# 48 4.5500 g. Nickel 21.2 mm. **Subject:** Nickel Bicentennial **Obv:** Head left **Obv. Designer:** T. H. Paget **Rev:** Buildings with center tower divide dates and denomination **Rev. Designer:** Stephen Trenka **Shape:** 12-sided

Date	Mintage	VG-8	F-12	VF-20	XF-40	MS-60	MS-63	Proof
1951	9,028,507	0.15	0.25	0.30	0.45	1.75	5.50	—

KM# 50 Chromium And Nickel Plated Steel 21.2 mm. **Obv:** Laureate queen's bust, right **Obv. Designer:** Mary Gillick **Rev:** Beaver on rock divides date and denomination **Rev. Designer:** George E. Kruger-Gray **Shape:** 12-sided

Date	Mintage	VG-8	F-12	VF-20	XF-40	MS-60	MS-63	Proof
1953	Inc. above	150	225	300	500	1,100	3,500	—
Note: With strap, far leaf								
1953	16,635,552	0.10	0.20	0.40	0.90	3.00	7.00	—
Note: Without strap								
1953	Inc. above	300	450	700	900	1,300	3,500	—
Note: Without strap, near leaf								
1953	Inc. above	0.10	0.20	0.40	0.90	3.50	7.00	—
Note: With strap								
1954	6,998,662	0.10	0.25	0.50	1.00	4.00	8.00	—

KM# 50a 4.5900 g. Nickel 21.2 mm. **Obv:** Laureate queen's bust right **Obv. Designer:** Mary Gillick **Rev:** Beaver on rock divides date and denomination **Rev. Designer:** George E. Kruger-Gray

Date	Mintage	VG-8	F-12	VF-20	XF-40	MS-60	MS-63	Proof
1955	5,355,028	0.15	0.20	0.40	0.75	3.50	4.50	—
1956	9,399,854	—	0.20	0.30	0.45	2.25	5.00	—
1957	7,387,703	—	—	0.25	0.30	1.25	3.00	—
1958	7,607,521	—	—	0.25	0.30	1.25	3.00	—
1959	11,552,523	—	—	—	0.20	0.45	1.50	—
1960	37,157,433	—	—	—	0.20	0.45	1.50	—
1961	47,889,051	—	—	—	—	0.30	0.80	—
1962	46,307,305	—	—	—	—	0.30	0.80	—

KM# 57 Nickel 21.2 mm. **Obv:** Laureate queen's bust right **Obv. Designer:** Mary Gillick **Rev:** Beaver on rock divides date and denomination **Rev. Designer:** George E. Kruger-Gray **Shape:** Round

Date	Mintage	VG-8	F-12	VF-20	XF-40	MS-60	MS-63	Proof
1963	43,970,320	—	—	—	—	0.20	0.50	—
1964	78,075,068	—	—	—	—	0.20	0.50	—
1964	—	14.00	16.00	18.00	21.00	35.00	100.00	—

Note: Extra water line

KM# 60.1 4.5400 g. Nickel 21.2 mm. **Obv:** Queen's bust right **Obv. Designer:** Arnold Machin **Rev:** Beaver on rock divides date and denomination **Rev. Designer:** George E. Kruger-Gray

Date	Mintage	MS-63	Proof
1965	84,876,018	0.50	—
1966	27,976,648	0.50	—
1968	101,930,379	0.50	—
1969	27,830,229	0.50	—
1970	5,726,010	1.00	—
1971	27,312,609	0.50	—
1972	62,417,387	0.50	—
1973	53,507,435	0.50	—
1974	94,704,645	0.50	—
1975	138,882,000	0.50	—
1976	55,140,213	0.50	—
1977	89,120,791	0.50	—
1978	137,079,273	0.50	—

KM# 66 Nickel 21.2 mm. **Subject:** Confederation Centennial **Obv:** Queen's bust right **Obv. Designer:** Arnold Machin **Rev:** Snowshoe rabbit bounding left divides dates and denomination **Rev. Designer:** Alex Coville

Date	Mintage	MS-63	Proof
1967	36,876,574	0.50	1.00

KM# 60.2 Nickel 21.2 mm. **Obv:** Queen's bust right **Obv. Designer:** Arnold Machin **Rev:** Beaver on rock divides date and denomination **Rev. Designer:** George E. Kruger-Gray

Date	Mintage	MS-63	Proof
1979	186,295,825	0.30	—
1980	134,878,000	0.30	—
1981	99,107,900	0.30	—
1981 Proof	199,000	—	1.50

KM# 60.2a 4.6000 g. Copper-Nickel 21.2 mm. **Obv:** Queen's bust right **Obv. Designer:** Arnold Machin **Rev:** Beaver on rock divides date and denomination **Rev. Designer:** George E. Kruger-Gray

Date	Mintage	MS-63	Proof
1982	64,924,400	0.30	—
1982 Proof	180,908	—	1.50
1983	72,596,000	0.30	—
1983 Proof	168,000	—	1.50
1984	84,088,000	0.30	—
1984 Proof	161,602	—	1.50

Date	Mintage	MS-63	Proof
1985	126,618,000	0.30	—
1985 Proof	157,037	—	1.50
1986	156,104,000	0.30	—
1986 Proof	175,745	—	1.50
1987	106,299,000	0.30	—
1987 Proof	179,004	—	1.50
1988	75,025,000	0.30	—
1988 Proof	175,259	—	1.50
1989	141,570,538	0.30	—
1989 Proof	170,928	—	1.50

KM# 182 4.6000 g. Copper-Nickel 19.55 mm. **Obv:** Crowned head right **Obv. Designer:** Dora dePedery-Hunt **Rev:** Beaver on rock divides dates and denomination **Rev. Designer:** George E. Kruger-Gray **Edge:** Plain

Date	Mintage	MS-63	Proof
1990	42,537,000	0.30	—
1990 Proof	140,649	—	2.50
1991	10,931,000	0.55	—
1991 Proof	131,888	—	7.00
1993	86,877,000	0.30	—
1993 Proof	143,065	—	2.50
1994	99,352,000	0.30	—
1994 Proof	146,424	—	3.00
1995	78,528,000	0.30	—
1995 Proof	50,000	—	2.50
1996 Far 6	36,686,000	2.25	—
1996 Near 6	Inc. above	2.25	—
1996 Proof	—	—	6.00
1997	27,354,000	0.30	—
1997 Proof	—	—	5.00
1998	156,873,000	0.30	—
1998W	—	1.50	—
1998 Proof	—	—	5.00
1999	124,861,000	0.30	—
1999W	—	—	—
1999 Proof	—	—	5.00
2000	108,514,000	0.30	—
2000W	—	1.50	—
2000 Proof	—	—	5.00
2001	30,035,000	12.50	—
2001P Proof	—	—	10.00
2003	—	0.30	—

KM# 205 4.6000 g. Copper-Nickel 21.2 mm.
Subject: Confederation 125 **Obv:** Crowned head
right **Obv. Designer:** Dora dePedery-Hunt **Rev:**
Beaver on rock divides date and denomination **Rev.
Designer:** George E. Kruger-Gray

Date	Mintage	MS-63	Proof
1992 Proof	147,061	—	4.00
1992	53,732,000	0.30	—

KM# 182b 3.9000 g. Nickel Plated Steel
21.2 mm. **Obv:** Crowned head right **Obv.
Designer:** Dora dePedery-Hunt **Rev:** Beaver on
rock divides date and denomination **Rev. Designer:**
George E. Kruger-Gray **Edge:** Plain

Date	Mintage	MS-63	Proof
1999 P	Est. 20,000	15.00	—
2000 P	Est. 2,300,000	3.50	—
2001 P	136,650,000	0.35	—
2003 P	32,986,921	0.35	—

KM# 182a 5.3500 g. 0.9250 Silver 0.1591 oz. ASW
21.2 mm. **Obv:** Crowned head right **Obv.
Designer:** Dora dePedery-Hunt **Rev:** Beaver on
rock divides date and denomination **Rev. Designer:**
George E. Kruger-Gray

Date	Mintage	MS-63	Proof
1996 Proof	—	—	5.00
1997 Proof	—	—	5.00
1998 Proof	—	—	5.00
1998O Proof	—	—	5.00
1999 Proof	—	—	5.00
2000 Proof	—	—	5.00
2001 Proof	—	—	5.00
2003 Proof	—	—	5.00

KM# 310 1.1670 g. 0.9250 Silver 0.0347 oz.
ASW **Subject:** 90th Anniversary Royal Canadian
Mint **Obv:** Crowned head right **Obv. Designer:** Dora
dePedery-Hunt **Rev:** Denomination and date within
wreath, crown above **Rev. Designer:** W. H. J.
Blackmore

Date	Mintage	MS-63	Proof
1998 Proof	25,000	—	12.00
1998	25,000	12.00	—

KM# 400 0.9250 Silver 21.2 mm. **Subject:** First
French-Canadian Regiment **Obv:** Crowned head
right **Obv. Designer:** Dora dePedery-Hunt **Rev:**
Regimental drums, sash and baton, denomination
above, date at right **Rev. Designer:** R. C. M. Staff
Edge: Plain

Date	Mintage	MS-63	Proof
2000 Proof	—	—	9.00

KM# 413 5.3500 g. 0.9250 Silver 0.1591 oz. ASW
21.2 mm. **Subject:** Royal Military College **Obv:**
Crowned head right **Rev:** Marching cadets and arch
Rev. Designer: Gerald T. Locklin **Edge:** Plain

Date	Mintage	MS-63	Proof
2001 Proof	25,834	—	7.00

KM# 446 3.9000 g. Nickel Plated Steel
21.2 mm. **Subject:** Elizabeth II Golden Jubilee
Obv: Crowned head right, Jubilee commemorative
dates 1952-2002 **Obv. Designer:** Dora dePedery-
Hunt **Rev. Designer:** George E. Kruger-Gray **Note:**
Magnetic.

Date	Mintage	MS-63	Proof
2002P Proof	32,642	—	10.00
2002P	135,960,000	0.45	—

KM# 446a 5.3500 g. 0.9250 Silver 0.1591 oz. ASW
21.2 mm. **Subject:** Elizabeth II Golden Jubilee
Obv: Queen, Jubilee commemorative dates 1952-
2002

Date	Mintage	MS-63	Proof
2002 Proof	21,573	—	11.50

KM# 453 5.3500 g. 0.9250 Silver 0.1591 oz. ASW
21.2 mm. **Subject:** Vimy Ridge - WWI **Obv:**
Crowned head right **Rev:** Vimy Ridge Memorial,
allegorical figure and dates 1917-2002 **Rev.
Designer:** S. A. Allward

Date	Mintage	MS-63	Proof
2002 Proof	22,646	—	11.50

KM# 491 3.9000 g. Nickel Plated Steel
21.2 mm. **Obv:** Bare head right **Obv. Designer:**
Susanna Blunt **Rev:** Beaver divides date and
denomination **Rev. Designer:** George E. Kruger-
Gray **Note:** Magnetic.

Date	Mintage	MS-63	Proof
2003P	61,392,180	0.45	—
2004P	132,097,000	0.45	—

Date	Mintage	MS-63	Proof
2004P Proof	—	—	2.50
2005P	89,664,000	0.45	—
2005P Proof	—	—	2.50
2006P	139,308,000	0.50	—
2006P Proof	—	—	2.50
2006(ml)	184,874,000	0.45	—
2006(ml) Proof	—	—	2.50
2007(ml)	221,472,000	0.45	—
2007(ml) Proof	—	—	2.50
2008(ml)	278,530,000	0.45	—
2008(ml) Proof	—	—	2.50
2009(ml)	266,488,000	0.45	—
2009(ml) Proof	—	—	2.50
2010(ml)	—	0.45	—
2010(ml) Proof	—	—	2.50
2011(ml)	—	0.45	—
2011(ml) Proof	—	—	2.50

KM# 469 5.3500 g. 0.9250 Silver 0.1591 oz. ASW 21.2 mm. **Subject:** 50th Anniversary of the Coronation of Elizabeth II **Obv:** Crowned head right, Jubilee commemorative dates 1953-2003 **Obv. Designer:** Mary Gillick

Date	Mintage	MS-63	Proof
2003 Proof	21,573	—	11.50

KM# 491a 5.3500 g. 0.9250 Silver 0.1591 oz. ASW 21.1 mm. **Obv:** Crowned head right **Obv. Designer:** Susanna Blunt **Rev:** Beaver divides date and denomination **Edge:** Plain

Date	Mintage	MS-63	Proof
2004 Proof	—	—	3.50

KM# 506 5.3500 g. 0.9250 Silver 0.1591 oz. ASW 21.3 mm. **Obv:** Bare head right **Rev:** "Victory " design of the KM-40 reverse **Edge:** Plain **Shape:** 12-sided

Date	Mintage	MS-63	Proof
2004 Proof	20,019	—	15.00

KM# 627 3.9000 g. Nickel 21.18 mm. **Subject:** 60th Anniversary, Victory in Europe 1945-2005 **Obv:** Head right **Rev:** Large V **Edge:** Plain

Date	Mintage	MS-63	Proof
2005P	59,269,192	4.50	—

KM# 758 5.3000 g. 0.9250 Silver 0.1576 oz. ASW **Obv:** George VI head left **Rev:** Torch and large V

Date	Mintage	MS-63	Proof
2005 Proof	42,792	—	35.00

KM# 758a 5.3000 g. 0.9250 Silver 0.1576 oz. ASW **Obv:** George VI head left **Rev:** Torch and large V **Note:** Bound into Annual Report.

Date	Mintage	MS-63	Proof
2005 Proof	6,065	—	40.00

KM# 491b 4.6000 g. Copper-Nickel **Obv:** Bust right **Rev:** Beaver

Date	Mintage	MS-63	Proof
2006	43,008,000	5.00	—

KM# 1024 Nickel 21.2 mm. **Obv:** George V bust left **Rev:** Denomination and 1935-2010 anniversary dates, two maple leaves below

Date	Mintage	MS-63	Proof
2010 Proof	—	—	15.00

10 CENTS

KM# 3 2.3240 g. 0.9250 Silver 0.0691 oz. ASW 18.03 mm. **Obv:** Head left **Obv. Legend:** VICTORIA DEI GRATIA REGINA. CANADA **Rev:** Denomination and date within wreath, crown above **Edge:** Reeded

Date	Mintage	VG-8	F-12	VF-20	XF-40	MS-60	MS-63	Proof
1858/5	900	1,400	2,100	4,000	12,000	—	—	
1858	1,250,000	20.00	35.00	65.00	125	350	850	—
1870 Narrow 0	1,600,000	18.00	40.00	75.00	125	400	1,300	—
1870 Wide 0	Inc. above	35.00	65.00	125	225	600	2,100	—
1871	800,000	29.00	50.00	125	200	600	2,500	—
1871H	1,870,000	35.00	60.00	125	225	600	2,100	—
1872H	1,000,000	150	225	400	600	1,750	4,000	—
1874H	600,000	14.00	24.00	50.00	125	350	1,100	—
1875H	1,000,000	400	800	1,200	2,000	7,000	16,000	—
1880H	1,500,000	18.00	30.00	65.00	125	350	1,200	—
1881H	950,000	21.00	35.00	70.00	150	400	1,300	—
1882H	1,000,000	21.00	35.00	70.00	150	450	1,500	—
1883H	300,000	65.00	125	250	500	1,300	3,000	—
1884	150,000	300	500	950	1,700	6,000	20,000	—
1885	400,000	65.00	125	250	500	1,700	7,000	—

Date	Mintage	VG-8	F-12	VF-20	XF-40	MS-60	MS-63	Proof
1886 Small 6	800,000	30.00	65.00	125	300	1,500	4,000	—
1886 Large 6	Inc. above	40.00	80.00	150	350	1,500	4,000	—
1887	350,000	65.00	125	225	450	1,700	4,000	—
1888	500,000	16.00	27.00	55.00	125	350	1,100	—
1889	600,000	750	1,200	2,000	4,000	13,000	35,000	—
1890H	450,000	21.00	45.00	90.00	200	500	1,100	—
1891 21 leaves	800,000	21.00	45.00	90.00	200	500	1,300	—
1891 22 leaves	Inc. above	21.00	45.00	90.00	200	500	1,200	—
1892/1	520,000	250	400	700	1,400	4,000	—	—
1892	Inc. above	20.00	35.00	75.00	150	450	1,200	—
1893 Flat-top 3	500,000	45.00	80.00	150	300	1,000	2,300	—
1893 Round-top 3	Inc. above	850	1,400	2,700	5,000	13,000	35,000	—
1894	500,000	45.00	80.00	150	250	750	1,800	—
1896	650,000	14.00	24.00	45.00	90.00	300	750	—
1898	720,000	14.00	24.00	45.00	90.00	300	750	—
1899 Small 9's	1,200,000	12.00	22.00	40.00	75.00	225	600	—
1899 Large 9's	Inc. above	24.00	45.00	85.00	150	500	1,200	—
1900	1,100,000	8.50	18.00	40.00	85.00	225	650	—
1901	1,200,000	11.00	22.50	50.00	110	295	850	—

KM# 10 2.3240 g. 0.9250 Silver 0.0691 oz. ASW 18.03 mm.   **Obv:** Crowned bust right **Obv. Designer:** G. W. DeSaulles **Rev:** Denomination and date within wreath, crown above **Rev. Designer:** Leonard C. Wyon **Edge:** Reeded

Date	Mintage	VG-8	F-12	VF-20	XF-40	MS-60	MS-63	Proof
1902	720,000	9.00	18.00	33.00	90.00	350	1,200	—
1902H	1,100,000	4.00	9.00	20.00	44.00	125	275	—
1903	500,000	15.00	33.00	85.00	220	1,100	2,300	—
1903H	1,320,000	8.00	18.00	33.00	70.00	275	600	—
1904	1,000,000	12.00	27.50	49.50	110	350	775	—
1905	1,000,000	7.00	27.50	60.00	125	525	1,200	—
1906	1,700,000	7.00	13.00	33.00	65.00	300	825	—
1907	2,620,000	5.00	12.00	25.00	45.00	225	475	—
1908	776,666	9.00	27.50	60.00	105	225	450	—
1909	1,697,200	7.00	20.00	44.00	105	425	1,100	—
Note: "Victorian" leaves, similar to 1902-08 coins								
1909	Inc. above	11.00	30.00	60.00	140	550	1,450	—
Note: Broad leaves, similar to 1910-12 coins								
1910	4,468,331	4.00	9.00	20.00	38.50	140	325	—

KM# 17 2.3240 g. 0.9250 Silver 0.0691 oz. ASW 23.5 mm.   **Obv:** Crowned bust left **Obv. Designer:** E. B. MacKennal **Rev:** Denomination and date within wreath, crown above **Rev. Designer:** Leonard C. Wyon **Edge:** Reeded

Date	Mintage	VG-8	F-12	VF-20	XF-40	MS-60	MS-63	Proof
1911	2,737,584	5.00	12.00	20.00	44.00	110	260	—

Small leaves

Large leaves

KM# 23 2.3240 g. 0.9250 Silver 0.0691 oz. ASW 17.8 mm.   **Obv:** Crowned bust left **Obv. Designer:** E. B. MacKennal **Rev:** Denomination and date within wreath, crown above **Rev. Designer:** Leonard C. Wyon **Edge:** Reeded

Date	Mintage	VG-8	F-12	VF-20	XF-40	MS-60	MS-63	Proof
1912	3,235,557	2.75	6.00	14.00	45.00	265	750	—
1913	3,613,937	2.35	3.00	13.00	34.50	190	500	—
Note: Small leaves								
1913	Inc. above	145	265	525	1,350	9,000	30,000	—
Note: Large leaves								

Date	Mintage	VG-8	F-12	VF-20	XF-40	MS-60	MS-63	Proof
1914	2,549,811	2.50	4.00	13.00	37.50	190	575	—
1915	688,057	9.00	22.50	45.00	150	500	975	—
1916	4,218,114	2.35	3.00	6.00	25.00	115	350	—
1917	5,011,988	BV	2.50	5.00	15.00	75.00	145	—
1918	5,133,602	BV	2.50	5.00	14.00	70.00	120	—
1919	7,877,722	BV	2.50	5.00	14.00	70.00	120	—

KM# 23a 2.3320 g. 0.8000 Silver 0.0600 oz. ASW 17.9 mm. **Obv:** Crowned bust left **Obv. Designer:** E. B. MacKennal **Rev:** Denomination and date within wreath, crown above **Edge:** Reeded

Date	Mintage	VG-8	F-12	VF-20	XF-40	MS-60	MS-63	Proof
1920	6,305,345	BV	2.25	3.50	12.00	75.00	140	—
1921	2,469,562	BV	2.75	6.00	20.00	80.00	250	—
1928	2,458,602	BV	2.50	4.00	12.00	55.00	140	—
1929	3,253,888	BV	2.75	3.50	12.00	55.00	110	—
1930	1,831,043	BV	3.00	4.50	14.00	60.00	140	—
1931	2,067,421	BV	2.50	4.00	12.00	55.00	110	—
1932	1,154,317	BV	3.00	9.00	23.00	90.00	250	—
1933	672,368	2.75	5.00	12.00	35.00	175	375	—
1934	409,067	4.00	7.00	22.00	60.00	250	550	—
1935	384,056	4.00	7.00	19.00	60.00	250	550	—
1936	2,460,871	BV	2.25	3.00	9.00	45.00	90.00	—
1936	—	—	—	—	—	—	—	—

Note: Dot on reverse. Specimen, 4 known; David Akers sale of John Jay Pittman collection, Part 1, 10-97, a gem specimen realized $120,000

Maple leaf

KM# 34 2.3328 g. 0.8000 Silver 0.0600 oz. ASW 18.03 mm. **Obv:** Head left **Obv. Designer:** T. H. Paget **Rev:** Bluenose sailing left, date at right, denomination below **Rev. Designer:** Emanuel Hahn **Edge:** Reeded

Date	Mintage	VG-8	F-12	VF-20	XF-40	MS-60	MS-63	Proof
1937	2,500,095	—	BV	2.50	4.00	12.00	18.00	—
1938	4,197,323	BV	2.25	4.00	7.00	40.00	90.00	—
1939	5,501,748	BV	2.00	3.00	6.00	45.00	90.00	—
1940	16,526,470	—	BV	2.00	4.00	15.00	30.00	—
1941	8,716,386	BV	2.00	3.00	7.00	35.00	90.00	—
1942	10,214,011	—	BV	2.00	5.00	30.00	50.00	—
1943	21,143,229	—	BV	2.00	5.00	18.00	35.00	—
1944	9,383,582	—	BV	2.00	5.00	25.00	45.00	—
1945	10,979,570	—	BV	2.00	5.00	18.00	27.00	—
1946	6,300,066	—	BV	2.50	5.00	30.00	50.00	—
1947	4,431,926	BV	2.00	3.00	7.00	30.00	50.00	—
1947	9,638,793	—	BV	2.00	4.00	10.00	15.00	—

Note: Maple leaf

KM# 43 2.3328 g. 0.8000 Silver 0.0600 oz. ASW 18.03 mm. **Obv:** Head left, modified legend **Obv. Designer:** T. H. Paget **Rev:** Bluenose sailing left, date at right, denomination below **Rev. Designer:** Emanuel Hahn

Date	Mintage	VG-8	F-12	VF-20	XF-40	MS-60	MS-63	Proof
1948	422,741	2.00	3.50	7.50	13.00	45.00	70.00	—
1949	11,336,172	—	—	BV	2.50	9.00	14.00	—
1950	17,823,075	—	—	BV	2.00	8.00	12.00	—
1951	15,079,265	—	—	BV	2.00	6.00	11.00	—
1951	—	—	3.50	5.00	8.00	35.00	60.00	—

Note: Doubled die

Date	Mintage	VG-8	F-12	VF-20	XF-40	MS-60	MS-63	Proof
1952	10,474,455	—	—	BV	2.00	5.00	9.00	—

KM# 51 2.3100 g. 0.8000 Silver 0.0594 oz. ASW 18 mm. **Obv:** Laureate bust right **Obv. Designer:** Mary Gllick **Rev:** Bluenose sailing left, date at right, denomination below **Rev. Designer:** Emanuel Hahn

Date	Mintage	VG-8	F-12	VF-20	XF-40	MS-60	MS-63	Proof
1953	17,706,395	—	—	BV	2.00	3.00	6.00	—
Note: Without straps								
1953	Inc. above	—	—	BV	2.00	5.00	9.00	—
Note: With straps								
1954	4,493,150	—	BV	2.00	2.75	10.00	17.00	—
1955	12,237,294	—	—	BV	2.00	4.50	7.00	—
1956	16,732,844	—	—	—	BV	3.00	6.00	—
1956	Inc. above	—	2.75	3.50	5.00	13.00	22.00	—
Note: Dot below date								
1957	16,110,229	—	—	—	BV	2.25	4.00	—
1958	10,621,236	—	—	—	BV	2.25	4.00	—
1959	19,691,433	—	—	—	BV	2.00	3.00	—
1960	45,446,835	—	—	—	BV	2.00	2.75	—
1961	26,850,859	—	—	—	BV	2.00	2.75	—
1962	41,864,335	—	—	—	—	BV	2.00	—
1963	41,916,208	—	—	—	—	BV	2.00	—
1964	49,518,549	—	—	—	—	BV	2.00	—

KM# 61 2.3328 g. 0.8000 Silver 0.0600 oz. ASW 18.03 mm. **Obv:** Young bust right **Obv. Designer:** Arnold Machin **Rev:** Bluenose sailing left, date at right, denomination below

Date	Mintage	VG-8	F-12	VF-20	XF-40	MS-60	MS-63	Proof
1965	56,965,392	—	—	—	—	BV	2.00	—
1966	34,567,898	—	—	—	—	BV	2.00	—

KM# 67 2.3328 g. 0.8000 Silver 0.0600 oz. ASW 18.03 mm. **Subject:** Confederation Centennial **Obv:** Bust right **Rev:** Atlantic mackeral left, denomination above, dates below **Rev. Designer:** Alex Colville

Date	Mintage	VG-8	F-12	VF-20	XF-40	MS-60	MS-63	Proof
ND(1967)	62,998,215	—	—	—	—	BV	2.00	2.50

KM# 67a 2.3328 g. 0.5000 Silver 0.0375 oz. ASW 18.03 mm. **Subject:** Confederation Centennial **Obv:** Young bust right **Rev:** Fish left, denomination above dates below

Date	Mintage	VG-8	F-12	VF-20	XF-40	MS-60	MS-63	Proof
ND(1967)	Inc. above	—	—	—	—	BV	1.75	—

Ottawa

KM# 72 2.3328 g. 0.5000 Silver 0.0375 oz. ASW 18.03 mm. **Obv:** Bust right **Obv. Designer:** Arnold Machin **Rev:** Bluenose sailing left, date at right, denomination below **Rev. Designer:** Emanuel Hahn **Note:** Ottawa Mint reeding has pointed deep areas in the edge reeding.

Date	Mintage	VG-8	F-12	VF-20	XF-40	MS-60	MS-63	Proof
1968	70,460,000	—	—	—	—	BV	1.75	—

Ottawa

KM# 72a Nickel 18.03 mm. **Obv:** Young bust right **Obv. Designer:** Arnold Machin **Rev:** Bluenose sailing left, date at right, denomination below **Rev. Designer:** Emanuel Hahn **Note:** Ottawa Mint reeding has pointed deep areas in the edge reeding.

Date	Mintage	VG-8	F-12	VF-20	XF-40	MS-60	MS-63	Proof
1968	87,412,930	—	—	—	0.10	0.15	0.35	—

Philadelphia

KM# 73 2.3300 g. Nickel 18.03 mm. **Obv:** Young bust right **Obv. Designer:** Arnold Machin **Rev:** Bluenose sailing left, date at right, denomination below **Rev. Designer:** Emanuel Hahn **Note:** Philadelphia Mint reeding has flat deep areas in the edge reeding.

Date	Mintage	VG-8	F-12	VF-20	XF-40	MS-60	MS-63	Proof
1968	85,170,000	—	—	—	0.10	0.15	0.35	—
1969	—	—	7,500	9,000	12,000	20,000	—	—

Note: Large date, large ship, 10-20 known

KM# 77.1 2.0700 g. Nickel 18.03 mm. **Obv:** Young bust right **Obv. Designer:** Arnold Machin **Rev:** Redesigned smaller Bluenose sailing left, date at right, denomination below **Rev. Designer:** Emanuel Hahn **Edge:** Reeded

Date	Mintage	MS-63	Proof
1969	55,833,929	0.50	—
1970	5,249,296	1.00	—
1971	41,016,968	0.50	—
1972	60,169,387	0.50	—
1973	167,715,435	0.50	—
1974	201,566,565	0.50	—
1975	207,680,000	0.50	—
1976	95,018,533	0.50	—
1977	128,452,206	0.50	—
1978	170,366,431	0.50	—

KM# 77.2 2.0700 g. Nickel 18.03 mm. **Obv:** Smaller young bust right **Obv. Designer:** Arnold Machin **Rev:** Redesigned smaller Bluenose sailing left, denomination below, date at right **Rev. Designer:** Emanuel Hahn **Edge:** Reeded

Date	Mintage	MS-63	Proof
1979	237,321,321	0.35	—
1980	170,111,533	0.35	—
1981	123,912,900	0.35	—
1981 Proof	199,000	—	1.50
1982	93,475,000	0.35	—
1982 Proof	180,908	—	1.50
1983	111,065,000	0.35	—
1983 Proof	168,000	—	1.50
1984	121,690,000	0.35	—
1984 Proof	161,602	—	1.50
1985	143,025,000	0.35	—
1985 Proof	157,037	—	1.50
1986	168,620,000	0.35	—
1986 Proof	175,745	—	1.50
1987	147,309,000	0.35	—
1987 Proof	179,004	—	1.50
1988	162,998,558	0.35	—
1988 Proof	175,259	—	1.50
1989	199,104,414	0.35	—
1989 Proof	170,528	—	1.50

KM# 183 2.1400 g. Nickel 18.03 mm. **Obv:** Crowned head right **Obv. Designer:** Dora dePedery-Hunt **Rev:** Bluenose sailing left, date at right, denomination below **Rev. Designer:** Emanuel Hahn **Edge:** Reeded

Date	Mintage	MS-63	Proof
1990	65,023,000	0.35	—
1990 Proof	140,649	—	2.50
1991	50,397,000	0.45	—
1991 Proof	131,888	—	4.00
1993	135,569,000	0.35	—
1993 Proof	143,065	—	2.00
1994	145,800,000	0.35	—
1994 Proof	146,424	—	2.50
1995	123,875,000	0.35	—
1995 Proof	50,000	—	2.50
1996	51,814,000	0.35	—
1996 Proof	—	—	2.50
1997	43,126,000	0.35	—
1997 Proof	—	—	2.50
1998	203,514,000	0.35	—
1998W	—	1.50	—
1998 Proof	—	—	2.50
1999	258,462,000	0.35	—
1999 Proof	—	—	2.50
2000	159,125,000	0.35	—
2000 Proof	—	—	2.50
2000W	—	1.50	—

KM# 206 Nickel 18.03 mm. **Subject:** Confederation 125 **Obv:** Crowned head right **Rev:** Bluenose sailing left, date at right, denomination below

Date	Mintage	MS-63	Proof
ND(1992)	174,476,000	0.35	—
ND(1992) Proof	147,061	—	3.00

KM# 183a 2.4000 g. 0.9250 Silver 0.0714 oz. ASW 18.03 mm. **Obv:** Crowned head right **Rev:** Bluenose sailing left, date at right, denomination below

Date	Mintage	MS-63	Proof
1996 Proof	—	—	5.50
1997 Proof	—	—	5.50

10 CENTS

Date	Mintage	MS-63	Proof
1998 Proof	—	—	4.00
1998O Proof	—	—	4.00
1999 Proof	—	—	5.00
2000 Proof	—	—	5.00
2001 Proof	—	—	5.00
2002 Proof	—	—	7.50
2003 Proof	—	—	7.50

KM# 299 2.4000 g. 0.9250 Silver 0.0714 oz. ASW 18.03 mm. **Subject:** John Cabot **Obv:** Crowned head right **Rev:** Ship with full sails divides dates, denomination below **Rev. Designer:** Donald H. Curley

Date	Mintage	MS-63	Proof
1997 Proof	49,848	—	17.50

KM# 311 2.3200 g. 0.9250 Silver 0.0690 oz. ASW 18.03 mm. **Subject:** 90th Anniversary Royal Canadian Mint **Obv:** Crowned head right **Rev:** Denomination and date within wreath, crown above

Date	Mintage	MS-63	Proof
1998 Matte	25,000	—	10.00
1998 Proof	25,000	—	10.00

KM# 183b 1.7700 g. Nickel Plated Steel 18.03 mm. **Obv:** Crowned head right **Obv. Designer:** Dora dePedery-Hunt **Rev:** Bluenose sailing left, date at right, denomination below **Rev. Designer:** Emanuel Hahn **Edge:** Reeded

Date	Mintage	MS-63	Proof
1999 P	Est. 20,000	15.00	—
2000 P	Est. 200	1,000	—
2001 P	266,000,000	0.45	—
2003 P	162,398,000	0.20	—

KM# 409 2.4000 g. 0.9250 Silver 0.0714 oz. ASW 18.03 mm. **Subject:** First Canadian Credit Union **Obv:** Crowned head right **Rev:** Alphonse Desjardins' house (founder of the first credit union in Canada), dates at right, denomination below **Edge:** Reeded

Date	Mintage	MS-63	Proof
2000 Proof	66,336	—	8.00

KM# 412a 2.4000 g. 0.9250 Silver 0.0714 oz. ASW 18 mm. **Subject:** Year of the Volunteer **Obv:** Crowned head right **Rev:** Three portraits left above banner, radiant sun below **Edge:** Reeded

Date	Mintage	MS-63	Proof
2001P Proof	40,634	—	9.00

KM# 412 1.7700 g. Nickel Plated Steel 18 mm. **Subject:** Year of the Volunteer **Obv:** Crowned head right **Rev:** Three portraits left and radiant sun **Edge:** Reeded

Date	Mintage	MS-63	Proof
2001P	224,714,000	4.50	—

KM# 447 1.7700 g. Nickel Plated Steel 18 mm. **Subject:** Elizabeth II Golden Jubilee **Obv:** Crowned head right, Jubilee commemorative dates 1952-2002

Date	Mintage	MS-63	Proof
2002P	252,563,000	1.00	—
2002 Proof	32,642	—	2.50

KM# 447a 2.3200 g. 0.9250 Silver 0.0690 oz. ASW 18 mm. **Subject:** Elizabeth II Golden Jubilee **Obv:** Crowned head right, Jubilee commemorative dates 1952-2002

Date	Mintage	MS-63	Proof
2002 Proof	21,537	—	12.50

KM# 492 1.7700 g. Nickel Plated Steel 18 mm. **Obv:** Head right **Obv. Designer:** Susanna Blunt **Rev:** Bluenose sailing left

Date	Mintage	MS-63	Proof
2003P	—	1.25	—
2004P	211,924,000	0.60	—
2004P Proof	—	—	2.50
2005P	212,175,000	0.60	—
2005P Proof	—	—	2.50
2006P	312,122,000	0.60	—
2006P Proof	—	—	2.50
2007(ml) Straight 7	304,110,000	0.60	—
2007(ml) Curved 7	Inc. above	0.60	—
2007(ml) Proof	—	—	2.50
2008(ml)	467,495,000	0.60	—
2008(ml) Proof	—	—	2.50
2009(ml)	370,700,000	0.60	—
2009(ml) Proof	—	—	2.50
2010(ml)	—	0.60	—
2010(ml) Proof	—	—	2.50
2011(ml)	—	0.60	—
2011(ml) Proof	—	—	2.50

KM# 470 2.3200 g. 0.9250 Silver 0.0690 oz. ASW **Subject:** 50th Anniversary of the Coronation of Elizabeth II **Obv:** Head right **Rev:** Bluenose sailing left

Date	Mintage	MS-63	Proof
2003 Proof	21,537	—	12.00

KM# 492a 2.4000 g. 0.9250 Silver 0.0714 oz. ASW 18 mm. **Obv:** Bare head right **Obv. Designer:** Susanna Blunt **Rev:** Sailboat **Edge:** Reeded

Date	Mintage	MS-63	Proof
2004 Proof	—	—	5.00

KM# 524 2.4000 g. 0.9250 Silver 0.0714 oz. ASW 18 mm. **Subject:** Golf, Championship of Canada, Centennial. **Obv:** Head right

Date	Mintage	MS-63	Proof
2004	39,486	12.50	—

KM# 1025 Silver 18.03 mm. **Obv:** George V bust left **Rev:** Value within wreath, dual dates below

Date	Mintage	MS-63	Proof
2010 Proof	—	—	20.00

20 CENTS

KM# 4 4.6480 g. 0.9250 Silver 0.1382 oz. ASW **Obv:** Head left **Obv. Legend:** VICTORIA DEI GRATIA REGINA. CANADA **Rev:** Denomination and date within wreath, crown above

Date	Mintage	VG-8	F-12	VF-20	XF-40	MS-60	MS-63	Proof
1858	750,000	60.00	100.00	125	225	900	2,500	—

25 CENTS

KM# 5 5.8100 g. 0.9250 Silver 0.1728 oz. ASW 23.88 mm. **Obv:** Crowned head left **Obv. Legend:** VICTORIA DEI GRATIA REGINA. CANADA **Obv. Designer:** Leonard C. Wyon **Rev:** Denomination and date within wreath, crown above

Date	Mintage	VG-8	F-12	VF-20	XF-40	MS-60	MS-63	Proof
1870	900,000	22.00	45.00	85.00	200	750	2,000	—
1871	400,000	27.00	50.00	125	250	1,000	2,400	—
1871H	748,000	35.00	60.00	150	300	1,100	2,100	—
1872H	2,240,000	13.00	25.00	45.00	125	550	1,800	—
1872H	Inc. above	—	—	—	—	2,500	6,000	—
Note: Inverted "A" for "V" in Victoria								
1874H	1,600,000	13.00	25.00	45.00	125	450	1,400	—
1875H	1,000,000	400	700	1,700	3,000	20,000	35,000	—
1880H Narrow 0	400,000	60.00	125	300	600	1,700	3,500	—
1880H Wide 0	Inc. above	150	350	600	1,400	4,500	8,000	—
1880H Narrow/wide 0	Inc. above	100.00	225	400	950	2,800	—	—
1881H	820,000	30.00	55.00	125	300	1,300	4,000	—
1882H	600,000	30.00	65.00	125	300	1,200	3,000	—
1883H	960,000	20.00	40.00	85.00	200	600	1,700	—
1885	192,000	150	300	5,500	1,100	4,000	10,000	—
1886/3	540,000	90.00	200	400	750	2,400	4,500	—
1886	Inc. above	45.00	90.00	200	450	1,700	4,500	—
1887	100,000	150	300	550	1,200	7,500	12,500	—
1888	400,000	26.00	40.00	90.00	200	750	2,200	—
1889	66,324	175	350	650	1,400	4,500	13,000	—
1890H	200,000	30.00	60.00	150	300	1,000	2,300	—
1891	120,000	125	225	400	750	1,800	3,500	—
1892	510,000	20.00	40.00	85.00	200	750	2,300	—
1893	100,000	150	300	550	1,000	2,000	3,000	—
1894	220,000	30.00	65.00	150	300	850	2,000	—
1899	415,580	12.00	25.00	60.00	150	600	1,500	—
1900	1,320,000	11.00	20.00	50.00	125	550	1,200	—
1901	640,000	18.00	33.00	75.00	225	825	1,800	—

KM# 11 5.8100 g. 0.9250 Silver 0.1728 oz. ASW 23.4 mm. **Obv:** Crowned bust right **Obv. Designer:** G. W.
DeSaulles **Rev:** Denomination and date within wreath, crown above

Date	Mintage	VG-8	F-12	VF-20	XF-40	MS-60	MS-63	Proof
1902	464,000	14.00	37.50	85.00	245	1,050	2,650	—
1902H	800,000	9.00	22.50	65.00	140	350	700	—
1903	846,150	20.00	40.50	105	280	1,100	2,650	—
1904	400,000	27.50	75.00	210	500	2,250	7,000	—
1905	800,000	20.00	42.00	140	425	1,950	6,400	—
1906 Large crown	1,237,843	11.00	30.00	75.00	325	1,050	2,400	—
1906 Small crown, Rare	Inc. above	3,500	5,500	8,400	19,000	25,000	35,000	—
1907	2,088,000	9.00	22.50	75.00	175	600	1,700	—
1908	495,016	20.00	49.00	135	280	550	1,050	—
1909	1,335,929	17.00	36.50	100.00	245	850	2,400	—

KM# 11a 5.8319 g. 0.9250 Silver 0.1734 oz. ASW   **Obv:** Crowned bust right **Rev:** Denomination and date
within wreath, crown above

Date	Mintage	VG-8	F-12	VF-20	XF-40	MS-60	MS-63	Proof
1910	3,577,569	8.00	22.50	55.00	120	425	850	—

KM# 18 5.8319 g. 0.9250 Silver 0.1734 oz. ASW   **Obv:** Crowned bust left **Obv. Legend:** GEORGIVS V REX
ET IND IMP **Obv. Designer:** E. B. MacKennal **Rev:** Denomination and date within wreath, crown above

Date	Mintage	VG-8	F-12	VF-20	XF-40	MS-60	MS-63	Proof
1911	1,721,341	10.00	30.00	55.00	135	400	725	—

KM# 24 5.8319 g. 0.9250 Silver 0.1734 oz. ASW 23.5 mm. **Obv:** Crowned bust left **Obv. Legend:**
GEORGIVS V DEI GRA REX ET IND IMP **Obv. Designer:** E. B. MacKennal **Rev:** Denomination and date
within wreath, crown above

Date	Mintage	VG-8	F-12	VF-20	XF-40	MS-60	MS-63	Proof
	2,544,199	9.00	15.00	34.00	70.00	450	1,550	—
1913	2,213,595	6.00	14.00	30.00	65.00	400	1,250	—
1914	1,215,397	9.00	17.00	39.00	80.00	650	2,100	—
1915	242,382	27.50	75.00	255	550	2,850	8,500	—
1916	1,462,566	5.00	13.00	30.50	50.00	295	900	—
1917	3,365,644	5.00	10.00	20.00	39.00	165	295	—
1918	4,175,649	5.00	9.00	20.00	33.75	125	230	—
1919	5,852,262	5.00	9.00	16.00	32.50	125	230	—

Dot below wreath

KM# 24a 5.8319 g. 0.8000 Silver 0.1500 oz. ASW **Obv:** Crowned bust left **Obv. Designer:** E. B. MacKennal
Rev: Denomination and date within wreath, crown below

Date	Mintage	VG-8	F-12	VF-20	XF-40	MS-60	MS-63	Proof
1920	1,975,278	5.00	9.00	18.00	39.00	195	525	—
1921	597,337	17.00	36.00	120	295	1,450	3,500	—
1927	468,096	40.50	75.00	150	295	975	2,100	—
1928	2,114,178	5.00	9.00	20.00	45.50	165	425	—
1929	2,690,562	5.00	9.00	20.00	45.50	165	425	—
1930	968,748	5.00	9.00	27.50	50.00	260	650	—
1931	537,815	5.00	10.00	30.00	65.00	260	650	—
1932	537,994	5.00	10.00	37.50	65.00	260	650	—
1933	421,282	5.00	10.00	42.00	85.00	230	450	—
1934	384,350	5.00	12.00	45.00	90.00	295	650	—
1935	537,772	5.00	10.00	33.00	65.00	195	450	—
1936	972,094	5.00	8.00	18.00	27.50	125	230	—
1936 Dot below wreath	153,322	39.00	100.00	225	400	1,050	2,350	—

Note: David Akers John Jay Pittman sale Part Three, 10-99, nearly Choice Unc. realized $6,900; considered a possible specimen example

Maple leaf after date

KM# 35 5.8320 g. 0.8000 Silver 0.1500 oz. ASW 23.5 mm. **Obv:** Head left **Obv. Designer:** T. H. Paget
Rev: Caribou left, denomination above, date at right **Rev. Designer:** Emanuel Hahn

Date	Mintage	VG-8	F-12	VF-20	XF-40	MS-60	MS-63	Proof
1937	2,690,176	—	BV	6.00	9.00	20.00	45.00	—
1938	3,149,245	—	BV	8.00	15.00	85.00	165	—
1939	3,532,495	—	BV	8.00	11.00	65.00	130	—
1940	9,583,650	—	—	BV	5.00	20.00	35.00	—
1941	6,654,672	—	—	BV	5.00	20.00	39.00	—
1942	6,935,871	—	—	BV	5.00	22.50	60.00	—
1943	13,559,575	—	—	BV	5.00	20.00	39.00	—
1944	7,216,237	—	—	BV	5.00	33.75	65.00	—
1945	5,296,495	—	—	BV	5.00	20.00	60.00	—
1946	2,210,810	—	BV	6.00	12.00	60.00	100.00	—
1947	1,524,554	—	BV	6.00	12.00	65.00	125	—
1947 Dot after 7	Inc. above	50.00	70.00	95.00	225	350	700	—
1947 Maple leaf after 7	4,393,938	—	—	BV	5.00	20.00	35.00	—

KM# 44 5.8319 g. 0.8000 Silver 0.1500 oz. ASW 23.5 mm. **Obv:** Head left, modified legend **Obv. Designer:**
T. H. Paget **Rev:** Caribou left, denomination above, date at right **Rev. Designer:** Emanuel Hahn

Date	Mintage	VG-8	F-12	VF-20	XF-40	MS-60	MS-63	Proof
1948	2,564,424	—	BV	5.00	20.00	85.00	115	—
1949	7,988,830	—	—	BV	5.00	15.00	30.00	—
1950	9,673,335	—	—	BV	5.00	12.00	22.50	—
1951	8,290,719	—	—	BV	5.00	11.00	18.00	—
1952	8,859,642	—	—	BV	5.00	9.00	17.00	—

25 CENTS

KM# 52 5.8319 g. 0.8000 Silver 0.1500 oz. ASW 23.8 mm.   **Obv:** Laureate bust right **Obv. Designer:** Mary Gillick **Rev:** Caribou left, denomination above, date at right **Rev. Designer:** Emanuel Hahn

Date	Mintage	VG-8	F-12	VF-20	XF-40	MS-60	MS-63	Proof
1953 Without strap	10,546,769	—	—	—	BV	8.00	15.00	—
1953 With strap	Inc. above	—	—	BV	5.00	10.00	27.50	—
1954	2,318,891	—	BV	5.00	11.00	37.50	60.00	—
1955	9,552,505	—	—	BV	5.00	9.00	22.50	—
1956	11,269,353	—	—	—	BV	5.00	8.00	—
1957	12,770,190	—	—	—	BV	5.00	6.00	—
1958	9,336,910	—	—	—	BV	5.00	6.00	—
1959	13,503,461	—	—	—	—	BV	5.50	—
1960	22,835,327	—	—	—	—	BV	5.50	—
1961	18,164,368	—	—	—	—	BV	5.50	—
1962	29,559,266	—	—	—	—	BV	5.50	—
1963	21,180,652	—	—	—	—	BV	5.00	—
1964	36,479,343	—	—	—	—	BV	5.00	—

KM# 62 5.8319 g. 0.8000 Silver 0.1500 oz. ASW 23.8 mm.   **Obv:** Young bust right **Obv. Designer:** Arnold Machin **Rev:** Caribou left, denomination above, date at right **Rev. Designer:** Emanuel Hahn

Date	Mintage	VG-8	F-12	VF-20	XF-40	MS-60	MS-63	Proof
1965	44,708,869	—	—	—	—	BV	5.00	—
1966	25,626,315	—	—	—	—	BV	5.00	—

KM# 68 5.8319 g. 0.8000 Silver 0.1500 oz. ASW 23.8 mm.   **Subject:** Confederation Centennial **Obv:** Young bust right **Rev:** Lynx striding left divides dates and denomination **Rev. Designer:** Alex Colville

Date	Mintage	VG-8	F-12	VF-20	XF-40	MS-60	MS-63	Proof
1967	48,855,500	—	—	—	—	BV	5.00	—

KM# 68a 5.8319 g. 0.5000 Silver 0.0937 oz. ASW 23.8 mm.   **Subject:** Confederation Centennial **Obv:** Young bust right **Rev:** Lynx striding left divides dates and denomination

Date	Mintage	VG-8	F-12	VF-20	XF-40	MS-60	MS-63	Proof
ND(1967)	Inc. above	—	—	—	BV	3.25	4.50	—

Date	Mintage	MS-63	Proof
1987 Proof	179,004	—	2.00
1988	80,368,473	0.95	—
1988 Proof	175,259	—	2.00
1989	119,796,307	0.75	—
1989 Proof	170,928	—	2.00

KM# 62a 5.8319 g. 0.5000 Silver 0.0937 oz. ASW 23.8 mm. **Obv:** Young bust right **Obv. Designer:** Machin **Rev:** Caribou left, denomination above, date at right

Date	Mintage	MS-63	Proof
1968	71,464,000	4.50	—

KM# 62b 5.0600 g. Nickel 23.8 mm. **Obv:** Young bust right **Obv. Designer:** Machin **Rev:** Caribou left, denomination above, date at right

Date	Mintage	MS-63	Proof
1968	88,686,931	0.75	—
1969	133,037,929	0.75	—
1970	10,302,010	2.00	—
1971	48,170,428	0.75	—
1972	43,743,387	0.75	—
1974	192,360,598	0.75	—
1975	141,148,000	0.75	—
1976	86,898,261	0.75	—
1977	99,634,555	0.75	—
1978	176,475,408	0.75	—

KM# 81.1 Nickel 23.8 mm. **Subject:** Royal Candian Mounted Police Centennial **Obv:** Young bust right **Rev:** Mountie divides dates, denomination above **Rev. Designer:** Paul Cedarberg **Note:** 120 beads.

Date	Mintage	MS-63	Proof
1973	134,958,587	0.90	—

KM# 81.2 Nickel 23.8 mm. **Subject:** RCMP Centennial **Obv:** Young bust right **Rev:** Mountie divides dates, denomination above **Note:** Large bust, 132 beads.

Date	Mintage	MS-63	Proof
1973	Inc. above	800	—

KM# 74 5.0700 g. Nickel 23.88 mm. **Obv:** Small young bust right **Obv. Designer:** Machin **Rev. Designer:** Emanuel Hahn

Date	Mintage	MS-63	Proof
1979	131,042,905	0.75	—
1980	76,178,000	0.75	—
1981	131,580,272	0.75	—
1981 Proof	199,000	—	2.00
1982	171,926,000	0.75	—
1982 Proof	180,908	—	2.00
1983	13,162,000	1.50	—
1983 Proof	168,000	—	3.00
1984	121,668,000	0.75	—
1984 Proof	161,602	—	2.00
1985	158,734,000	0.75	—
1985 Proof	157,037	—	2.00
1986	132,220,000	0.75	—
1986 Proof	175,745	—	2.00
1987	53,408,000	1.25	—

KM# 184 5.0700 g. Nickel 23.88 mm. **Obv:** Crowned head right **Obv. Designer:** Dora dePedery-Hunt **Rev:** Caribou left, denomination above, date at right **Rev. Designer:** Emanuel Hahn

Date	Mintage	MS-63	Proof
1990	31,258,000	0.90	—
1990 Proof	140,649	—	2.50
1991	459,000	12.00	—
1991 Proof	131,888	—	20.00
1993	73,758,000	0.70	—
1993 Proof	143,065	—	2.00
1994	77,670,000	0.70	—
1994 Proof	146,424	—	3.00
1995	89,210,000	0.70	—
1995 Proof	50,000	—	3.00
1996	28,106,000	0.70	—
1996 Proof	—	—	6.00
1997	—	0.70	—
1997 Proof	—	—	6.00
1998W	—	5.00	—
1999	258,888,000	0.75	—
1999 Proof	—	—	6.00
2000	434,087,000	0.75	—
2000 Proof	—	—	6.00
2000W	—	5.00	—
2001	8,415,000	5.00	—
2001 Proof	—	—	7.50

KM# 203 5.0000 g. Nickel 23.9 mm. **Series:** 125th Anniversary of Confederation **Subject:** New Brunswick **Obv:** Crowned head right **Rev:** Covered bridge in Newton, denomination below **Rev. Designer:** Ronald Lambert

Date	Mintage	MS-63	Proof
1992	12,174,000	0.70	—

KM# 203a 5.8319 g. 0.9250 Silver 0.1734 oz. ASW 23.8 mm. **Series:** 125th Anniversary of Confederation **Subject:** New Brunswick **Obv:** Crowned head right **Rev:** Covered bridge in Newton, denomination below

Date	Mintage	MS-63	Proof
1992 Proof	149,579	—	8.50

25 CENTS

KM# 207 Nickel 23.8 mm.   **Subject:** Confederation 125 **Obv:** Crowned head right **Obv. Designer:** Dora dePedery-Hunt **Rev:** Caribou left, denomination above, date at right **Rev. Designer:** Emanuel Hahn

Date	Mintage	MS-63	Proof
1992	442,986	12.50	—
1992 Proof	147,061	—	20.00

KM# 212 Nickel 23.8 mm.   **Series:** 125th Anniversary of Confederation **Subject:** Northwest Territories **Obv:** Crowned head right **Rev. Designer:** Beth McEachen

Date	Mintage	MS-63	Proof
1992	12,582,000	0.70	—

KM#212a 5.8319 g. 0.9250 Silver 0.1734 oz. ASW 23.8 mm.   **Series:** 125th Anniversary of Confederation **Subject:** Northwest Territories **Obv:** Crowned head right

Date	Mintage	MS-63	Proof
1992 Proof	149,579	—	8.50

KM# 213 Nickel 23.8 mm.   **Series:** 125th Anniversary of Confederation **Subject:** Newfoundland **Rev:** Fisherman rowing a dory, denomination below **Rev. Designer:** Christopher Newhook

Date	Mintage	MS-63	Proof
1992	11,405,000	0.70	—

KM#213a 5.8319 g. 0.9250 Silver 0.1734 oz. ASW 23.8 mm.   **Series:** 125th Anniversary of Confederation **Subject:** Newfoundland **Rev:** Fisherman rowing a dory, denomination below

Date	Mintage	MS-63	Proof
1992 Proof	149,579	—	8.50

KM# 214 Nickel 23.8 mm.   **Series:** 125th Anniversary of Confederation **Subject:** Manitoba **Obv:** Crowned head right **Rev. Designer:** Muriel Hope

Date	Mintage	MS-63	Proof
1992	11,349,000	0.70	—

KM#214a 5.8319 g. 0.9250 Silver 0.1734 oz. ASW 23.8 mm.   **Series:** 125th Anniversary of Confederation **Subject:** Manitoba **Obv:** Crowned head right

Date	Mintage	MS-63	Proof
1992 Proof	149,579	—	8.50

KM# 220 Nickel 23.8 mm.   **Series:** 125th Anniversary of Confederation **Subject:** Yukon **Obv:** Crowned head right **Rev. Designer:** Libby Dulac

Date	Mintage	MS-63	Proof
1992	10,388,000	0.70	—

KM#220a 5.8319 g. 0.9250 Silver 0.1734 oz. ASW 23.8 mm.   **Series:** 125th Anniversary of Confederation **Subject:** Yukon **Obv:** Crowned head right

Date	Mintage	MS-63	Proof
1992 Proof	149,579	—	8.50

KM# 221 Nickel 23.8 mm.   **Series:** 125th Anniversary of Confederation **Subject:** Alberta **Obv:** Crowned head right **Rev:** Rock formations in the badlands near Drumhelter, denomination below **Rev. Designer:** Mel Heath

Date	Mintage	MS-63	Proof
1992	12,133,000	0.70	—

KM#221a 5.8319 g. 0.9250 Silver 0.1734 oz. ASW 23.8 mm.   **Series:** 125th Anniversary of Confederation **Subject:** Alberta **Obv:** Crowned head right **Rev:** Rock formations in the badlands near Drumhelter, denomination below **Rev. Designer:** Mel Heath

Date	Mintage	MS-63	Proof
1992 Proof	—	—	5.50

KM# 222 Nickel 23.8 mm.   **Series:** 125th Anniversary of Confederation **Subject:** Prince Edward Island **Obv:** Crowned head right **Rev. Designer:** Nigel Roe

Date	Mintage	MS-63	Proof
1992	13,001,000	0.70	—

KM#222a 5.8319 g. 0.9250 Silver 0.1734 oz. ASW 23.8 mm.   **Series:** 125th Anniversary of Confederation **Subject:** Prince Edward Island **Obv:** Crowned head right **Rev. Designer:** Nigel Roe

Date	Mintage	MS-63	Proof
1992 Proof	149,579	—	8.50

KM# 223 Nickel 23.8 mm.   **Series:** 125th Anniversary of Confederation **Subject:** Ontario **Obv:** Crowned head right **Rev:** Jack pine, denomination below **Rev. Designer:** Greg Salmela

Date	Mintage	MS-63	Proof
1992	14,263,000	0.70	—

KM#223a 5.8319 g. 0.9250 Silver 0.1734 oz. ASW 23.8 mm.   **Series:** 125th Anniversary of Confederation **Subject:** Ontario **Obv:** Crowned head right **Rev:** Jack pine, denomination below **Rev. Designer:** Greg Salmela

Date	Mintage	MS-63	Proof
1992 Proof	149,579	—	8.50

25 CENTS

KM# 231 5.0300 g. Nickel 23.8 mm. **Series:** 125th Anniversary of Confederation **Subject:** Nova Scotia **Obv:** Crowned head right **Rev:** Lighthouse, denomination below **Rev. Designer:** Bruce Wood

Date	Mintage	MS-63	Proof
1992	13,600,000	0.70	—

KM#231a 5.8319 g. 0.9250 Silver 0.1734 oz. ASW 23.8 mm. **Series:** 125th Anniversary of Confederation **Subject:** Nova Scotia **Obv:** Crowned head right **Rev:** Lighthouse, denomination below **Rev. Designer:** Bruce Wood

Date	Mintage	MS-63	Proof
1992 Proof	149,579	—	8.50

KM# 232 Nickel 23.8 mm. **Series:** 125th Anniversary of Confederation **Subject:** British Columbia **Obv:** Crowned head right, dates below **Rev:** Large rock, whales, denomination below **Rev. Designer:** Carla Herrera Egan

Date	Mintage	MS-63	Proof
1992	14,001,000	0.70	—

KM#232a 5.8319 g. 0.9250 Silver 0.1734 oz. ASW 23.8 mm. **Series:** 125th Anniversary of Confederation **Subject:** British Columbia **Obv:** Crowned head right, dates below **Rev:** Large rock, whales, denomination below **Rev. Designer:** Carla Herrera Egan

Date	Mintage	MS-63	Proof
1992 Proof	149,579	—	8.50

KM# 233 Nickel 23.8 mm. **Series:** 125th Anniversary of Confederation **Subject:** Saskatchewan **Obv:** Crowned head right **Rev:** Buildings behind wall, grain stalks on right, denomination below **Rev. Designer:** Brian Cobb

Date	Mintage	MS-63	Proof
1992	14,165,000	0.70	—

KM#233a 5.8319 g. 0.9250 Silver 0.1734 oz. ASW 23.8 mm. **Series:** 125th Anniversary of Confederation **Subject:** Saskatchewan **Obv:** Crowned head right **Rev:** Buildings behind wall, grain stalks on right, denomination below **Rev. Designer:** Brian Cobb

Date	Mintage	MS-63	Proof
1992 Proof	149,579	—	8.50

KM# 234 Nickel 23.8 mm. **Series:** 125th Anniversary of Confederation **Subject:** Quebec **Obv:** Crowned head right **Rev:** Boats on water, large rocks in background, denomination below **Rev. Designer:** Romualdas Bukauskas

Date	Mintage	MS-63	Proof
1992	13,607,000	0.70	—

KM#234a 5.8319 g. 0.9250 Silver 0.1734 oz. ASW 23.8 mm. **Series:** 125th Anniversary of Confederation **Subject:** Quebec **Obv:** Crowned head right **Rev:** Boats on water, large rocks in background, denomination below **Rev. Designer:** Romualdas Bukauskas

Date	Mintage	MS-63	Proof
1992 Proof	149,579	—	8.50

KM#184a 5.9000 g. 0.9250 Silver 0.1755 oz. ASW 23.88 mm. **Obv:** Crowned head right **Rev:** Caribou left, denomination above, date at right

Date	Mintage	MS-63	Proof
1996 Proof	—	—	9.50
1997 Proof	—	—	9.50
1998 Proof	—	—	8.50
1998O Proof	—	—	8.50
1999 Proof	—	—	8.50
2001 Proof	—	—	9.50
2003 Proof	—	—	9.50

KM# 312 23.8 mm. **Subject:** 90th Anniversary Royal Canadian Mint **Obv:** Crowned head right **Rev:** Denomination and date within wreath, crown above

Date	Mintage	MS-63	Proof
1998 Matte	25,000	—	15.00
1998 Proof	—	—	15.00

KM# 184b 4.4000 g. Nickel Plated Steel 23.88 mm. **Obv:** Crowned head right **Rev:** Caribou left, denomination above, date at right

Date	Mintage	MS-63	Proof
1999 P	Est. 20,000	20.00	—
2000 P	—	5,500	—
Note: 3-5 known			
2001 P	55,773,000	0.95	—
2001 P Proof	—	—	5.00
2002 P	156,105,000	2.50	—
2002 P Proof	—	—	5.00
2003 P	87,647,000	2.50	—
2003 P Proof	—	—	5.00

KM# 342 5.0700 g. Nickel 23.8 mm. **Series:** Millennium **Subject:** January - A Country Unfolds **Obv:** Crowned head right **Rev:** Totem pole, portraits **Rev. Designer:** P. Ka-Kin Poon

Date	Mintage	MS-63	Proof
1999	12,181,200	0.65	—

KM#342a 5.8319 g. 0.9250 Silver 0.1734 oz. ASW 23.8 mm. **Series:** Millennium **Subject:** January **Obv:** Crowned head right **Rev:** Totem pole, portraits **Rev. Designer:** P. Ka-kin Poon

Date	Mintage	MS-63	Proof
1999 Proof	113,645	—	9.50

KM# 345 5.0700 g. Nickel 23.8 mm. **Series:** Millennium **Subject:** April - Our Northern Heritage **Obv:** Crowned head right **Rev:** Owl, polar bear **Rev. Designer:** Ken Ojnak Ashevac

Date	Mintage	MS-63	Proof
1999	15,446,000	0.65	—

KM#345a 5.8319 g. 0.9250 Silver 0.1734 oz. ASW 23.8 mm. **Series:** Millennium **Subject:** April **Obv:** Crowned head right **Rev:** Owl, polar bear **Rev. Designer:** Ken Ojnak Ashevac

Date	Mintage	MS-63	Proof
1999 Proof	113,645	—	9.50

KM# 343 5.0900 g. Nickel 23.8 mm. **Series:** Millennium **Subject:** February - Etched in Stone **Obv:** Crowned head right **Rev:** Native petroglyphs **Rev. Designer:** L. Springer

Date	Mintage	MS-63	Proof
1999	14,469,250	0.65	—

KM#343a 5.8319 g. 0.9250 Silver 0.1734 oz. ASW 23.8 mm. **Series:** Millennium **Subject:** February **Obv:** Crowned head right **Rev:** Native petroglyphs **Rev. Designer:** L. Springer

Date	Mintage	MS-63	Proof
1999 Proof	113,645	—	9.50

KM# 346 5.0700 g. Nickel 23.8 mm. **Series:** Millennium **Subject:** May - The Voyageures **Obv:** Crowned head right **Rev:** Voyageurs in canoe **Rev. Designer:** S. Mineok

Date	Mintage	MS-63	Proof
1999	15,566,100	0.65	—

KM#346a 5.8319 g. 0.9250 Silver 0.1734 oz. ASW 23.8 mm. **Series:** Millennium **Subject:** May **Obv:** Crowned head right **Rev:** Voyageurs in canoe **Rev. Designer:** S. Mineok

Date	Mintage	MS-63	Proof
1999 Proof	113,645	—	9.50

KM# 344 5.0700 g. Nickel 23.8 mm. **Series:** Millennium **Subject:** March - The Log Drive **Obv:** Crowned head right **Rev:** Lumberjack **Rev. Designer:** M. Lavoie

Date	Mintage	MS-63	Proof
1999	15,033,500	0.65	—

KM#344a 5.8319 g. 0.9250 Silver 0.1734 oz. ASW 23.8 mm. **Series:** Millennium **Subject:** March **Obv:** Crowned head right **Rev:** Lumberjack **Rev. Designer:** M. Lavoie

Date	Mintage	MS-63	Proof
1999 Proof	113,645	—	9.50

KM# 347 5.0300 g. Nickel 23.8 mm. **Series:** Millennium **Subject:** June - From Coast to Coast **Obv:** Crowned head right **Rev:** 19th-century locomotive **Rev. Designer:** G. Ho **Edge:** Reeded

Date	Mintage	MS-63	Proof
1999	20,432,750	0.65	—

KM#347a 5.8319 g. 0.9250 Silver 0.1734 oz. ASW 23.8 mm. **Series:** Millennium **Subject:** June **Obv:** Crowned head right **Rev:** 19th-century locomotive **Rev. Designer:** G. Ho **Edge:** Reeded

Date	Mintage	MS-63	Proof
1999 Proof	113,645	—	9.50

KM# 348 5.0700 g. Nickel 23.8 mm. **Series:** Millennium **Subject:** July - A Nation of People **Obv:** Crowned head right **Rev:** 6 stylized portraits **Rev. Designer:** M. H. Sarkany

Date	Mintage	MS-63	Proof
1999	17,321,000	0.65	—

KM#348a 5.8319 g. 0.9250 Silver 0.1734 oz. ASW 23.8 mm. **Series:** Millennium **Subject:** July **Obv:** Crowned head right **Rev:** 6 stylized portraits **Designer:** M.H. Sarkany

Date	Mintage	MS-63	Proof
1999 Proof	113,645	—	9.50

KM# 351 5.0700 g. Nickel 23.8 mm. **Series:** Millennium **Subject:** October - Tribute to the First Nations **Obv:** Crowned head right **Rev:** Aboriginal artwork **Rev. Designer:** J. E. Read

Date	Mintage	MS-63	Proof
1999	32,136,650	0.65	—

KM#351a 5.8319 g. 0.9250 Silver 0.1734 oz. ASW 23.8 mm. **Series:** Millennium **Subject:** October **Obv:** Crowned head right **Rev:** Aboriginal artwork **Rev. Designer:** J.E. Read

Date	Mintage	MS-63	Proof
1999 Proof	113,645	—	9.50

KM# 349 5.0700 g. Nickel 23.8 mm. **Series:** Millennium **Subject:** August - The Pioneer Spirit **Obv:** Crowned head right **Rev:** Hay harvesting **Rev. Designer:** A. Botelho

Date	Mintage	MS-63	Proof
1999	18,153,700	0.65	—

KM#349a 5.8319 g. 0.9250 Silver 0.1734 oz. ASW 23.8 mm. **Series:** Millennium **Subject:** August **Obv:** Crowned head right **Rev:** Hay harvesting **Rev. Designer:** A. Botelho

Date	Mintage	MS-63	Proof
1999 Proof	113,645	—	9.50

KM# 352 5.0700 g. Nickel 23.8 mm. **Series:** Millennium **Subject:** November - The Airplane Opens the North **Obv:** Crowned head right **Rev:** Bush plane with landing skis **Rev. Designer:** B. R. Brown

Date	Mintage	MS-63	Proof
1999	27,162,800	0.65	—

KM#352a 5.8319 g. 0.9250 Silver 0.1734 oz. ASW 23.8 mm. **Series:** Millennium **Subject:** November **Obv:** Crowned head right **Rev:** Bush plane with landing skis **Rev. Designer:** B.R. Brown

Date	Mintage	MS-63	Proof
1999 Proof	113,645	—	9.50

KM# 350 5.0700 g. Nickel 23.8 mm. **Series:** Millennium **Subject:** September - Canada Through a Child's Eye **Obv:** Crowned head right **Rev:** Childlike artwork **Rev. Designer:** Claudia Bertrand

Date	Mintage	MS-63	Proof
1999	31,539,350	0.65	—

KM#350a 5.8319 g. 0.9250 Silver 0.1734 oz. ASW 23.8 mm. **Series:** Millennium **Subject:** September **Obv:** Crowned head right **Rev:** Childlike artwork **Rev. Designer:** Claudia Bertrand

Date	Mintage	MS-63	Proof
1999 Proof	113,645	—	9.50

KM# 353 5.0700 g. Nickel 23.8 mm. **Series:** Millennium **Subject:** December - This is Canada **Obv:** Crowned head right **Rev:** Eclectic geometric design **Rev. Designer:** J. L. P. Provencher

Date	Mintage	MS-63	Proof
1999	43,339,200	0.70	—

KM#353a 5.1000 g. 0.9250 Silver 0.1517 oz. ASW 23.8 mm. **Series:** Millennium **Subject:** December **Obv:** Crowned head right **Rev:** Eclectic geometric design **Rev. Designer:** J.L.P. Provencher

Date	Mintage	MS-63	Proof
1999 Proof	113,645	—	9.50

KM# 373 Nickel 23.8 mm. **Subject:** Health **Obv:** Crowned head right, denomination below **Rev:** Ribbon and caduceus, date above **Rev. Designer:** Anny Wassef

Date	Mintage	MS-63	Proof
2000	35,470,900	0.65	—

KM# 373a 0.9250 Silver 23.8 mm. **Subject:** Health **Obv:** Crowned head right, denomination below **Rev:** Ribbon and caduceus, date above **Rev. Designer:** Anny Wassef

Date	Mintage	MS-63	Proof
2000 Proof	76,956	—	9.50

KM# 374 5.1000 g. Nickel 23.85 mm. **Subject:** Freedom **Obv:** Crowned head right, denomination below **Rev:** 2 children on maple leaf and rising sun, date above **Rev. Designer:** Kathy Vinish

Date	Mintage	MS-63	Proof
2000	35,188,900	0.65	—

KM# 374a 0.9250 Silver 23.8 mm. **Subject:** Freedom **Obv:** Crowned head right, denomination below **Rev:** 2 children on maple leaf and rising sun, date above **Rev. Designer:** Kathy Vinish

Date	Mintage	MS-63	Proof
2000 Proof	76,956	—	9.00

KM#375 Nickel 23.8 mm. **Subject:** Family **Obv:** Crowned head right, denomination below **Rev:** Wreath of native carvings, date above **Rev. Designer:** Wade Stephen Baker

Date	Mintage	MS-63	Proof
2000	35,107,700	0.65	—

KM# 375a 0.9250 Silver 23.8 mm. **Subject:** Family **Obv:** Crowned head right, denomination below **Rev:** Wreath of native carvings, date above **Rev. Designer:** Wade Stephen Baker

Date	Mintage	MS-63	Proof
2000 Proof	76,956	—	9.00

KM# 376 5.0800 g. Nickel 23.8 mm. **Subject:** Community **Obv:** Crowned head right, denomination below **Rev:** Map on globe, symbols surround, date above **Rev. Designer:** Michelle Thibodeau

Date	Mintage	MS-63	Proof
2000	35,155,400	0.65	—

KM# 376a 0.9250 Silver 23.8 mm. **Subject:** Community **Obv:** Crowned head right, denomination below **Rev:** Map on globe, symbols surround, date above **Rev. Designer:** Michelle Thibodeau

Date	Mintage	MS-63	Proof
2000 Proof	76,956	—	9.00

KM# 377 Nickel 23.8 mm. **Subject:** Harmony **Obv:** Crowned **Rev:** Maple leaf, date above **Rev. Designer:** Haver Demirer

Date	Mintage	MS-63	Proof
2000	35,184,200	0.65	—

KM# 377a 0.9250 Silver 23.8 mm. **Subject:** Harmony **Obv:** Crowned head right, denomination below **Rev:** Maple leaf **Rev. Designer:** Haver Demirer

Date	Mintage	MS-63	Proof
2000 Proof	76,956	—	9.00

KM# 378 Nickel 23.8 mm. **Subject:** Wisdom **Obv:** Crowned head right, denomination below **Rev:** Man with young child, date above **Rev. Designer:** Cezar Serbanescu

Date	Mintage	MS-63	Proof
2000	35,123,950	0.65	—

KM# 378a 0.9250 Silver 23.8 mm. **Subject:** Wisdom **Obv:** Crowned head right, denomination below **Rev:** Man with young child **Rev. Designer:** Cezar Serbanescu

Date	Mintage	MS-63	Proof
2000 Proof	76,956	—	9.00

KM# 379 Nickel 23.8 mm. **Subject:** Creativity **Obv:** Crowned head right, denomination below **Rev:** Canoe full of children, date above **Rev. Designer:** Kong Tat Hui

Date	Mintage	MS-63	Proof
2000	35,316,770	0.65	—

KM# 379a 0.9250 Silver 23.8 mm. **Subject:** Creativity **Obv:** Crowned head right, denomination below **Rev:** Canoe full of children **Rev. Designer:** Kong Tat Hui

Date	Mintage	MS-63	Proof
2000 Proof	76,956	—	9.00

KM# 380 Nickel 23.8 mm. **Subject:** Ingenuity **Obv:** Crowned head right, denomination below **Rev:** Crescent-shaped city views, date above **Rev. Designer:** John Jaciw

Date	Mintage	MS-63	Proof
2000	36,078,360	0.65	—

KM# 380a 0.9250 Silver 23.8 mm. **Subject:** Ingenuity **Obv:** Crowned head right, denomination below **Rev:** Crescent-shaped city views **Rev. Designer:** John Jaciw

Date	Mintage	MS-63	Proof
2000 Proof	76,956	—	9.00

KM# 381 Nickel 23.8 mm. **Subject:** Achievement **Obv:** Crowned head right, denomination below **Rev:** Rocket above jagged design, date above **Rev. Designer:** Daryl Dorosz

Date	Mintage	MS-63	Proof
2000	35,312,750	0.65	—

KM# 381a 0.9250 Silver 23.8 mm. **Subject:** Achievement **Obv:** Crowned head right, denomination below **Rev:** Rocket above jagged design **Rev. Designer:** Daryl Dorosz

Date	Mintage	MS-63	Proof
2000 Proof	76,956	—	9.00

KM# 382 Nickel 23.8 mm. **Subject:** Natural legacy **Obv:** Crowned head right, denomination below **Rev:** Environmental elements, date above **Rev. Designer:** Randy Trantau

Date	Mintage	MS-63	Proof
2000	36,236,900	0.65	—

KM# 382a 0.9250 Silver 23.8 mm. **Subject:** Natural legacy **Obv:** Crowned head right, denomination below **Rev:** Environmental elements **Rev. Designer:** Randy Trantau

Date	Mintage	MS-63	Proof
2000 Proof	76,956	—	9.00

KM# 383 Nickel 23.8 mm. **Subject:** Celebration **Obv:** Crowned head right, denomination below **Rev:** Fireworks, children behind flag, date above **Rev. Designer:** Laura Paxton

Date	Mintage	MS-63	Proof
2000	35,144,100	0.65	—

KM# 383a 0.9250 Silver 23.8 mm. **Subject:** Celebration **Obv:** Crowned head right, denomination below **Rev:** Fireworks, children behind flag **Rev. Designer:** Laura Paxton

Date	Mintage	MS-63	Proof
2000 Proof	76,956	—	9.00

KM# 384.1 Nickel 23.8 mm. **Subject:** Pride **Obv:** Crowned head right, denomination below **Rev:** Large ribbon 2 in red with 3 small red maple leaves on large maple leaf, date above **Rev. Designer:** Donald F. Warkentin **Edge:** Reeded **Note:** Colorized version.

Date	Mintage	MS-63	Proof
2000	49,399	6.50	—

KM# 384.2 Nickel 23.8 mm. **Subject:** Pride **Obv:** Crowned head right, denomination below **Rev:** Large ribbon 2 with three small maple leaves on large maple leaf, date above **Rev. Designer:** Donald F. Warkentin

Date	Mintage	MS-63	Proof
2000	50,666,800	0.65	—

KM# 384.2a 0.9250 Silver 23.8 mm. **Subject:** Pride **Obv:** Crowned head right, denomination below **Rev:** Ribbon 2 with 3 small maple leaves on large maple leaf **Rev. Designer:** Donald F. Warkentin

Date	Mintage	MS-63	Proof
2000 Proof	76,956	—	9.00

KM# 419 4.4000 g. Nickel Plated Steel
23.9 mm.   **Subject:** Canada Day **Obv:** Crowned
head right **Rev:** Maple leaf at center, children
holding hands below **Rev. Designer:** Silke Ware
Edge: Reeded

Date	Mintage	MS-63	Proof
2001	96,352	7.00	—

KM# 448 4.4000 g. Nickel Plated Steel
23.9 mm.   **Subject:** Elizabeth II Golden Jubilee
Obv: Crowned head right **Rev:** Caribou left

Date	Mintage	MS-63	Proof
2002P	152,485,000	2.00	—
2002P Proof	32,642	—	6.00

KM# 448a 5.9000 g. 0.9250 Silver 0.1755 oz. ASW
23.9 mm.   **Subject:** Elizabeth II Golden Jubilee
Obv: Crowned head right, Jubilee commemorative
dates 1952-2002

Date	Mintage	MS-63	Proof
2002 Proof	100,000	—	12.50

KM# 451 4.4000 g. Nickel Plated Steel
23.9 mm.   **Rev:** Small human figures supporting
large maple leaf

Date	Mintage	MS-63	Proof
2002P	30,627,000	5.00	—

KM# 451a 4.4000 g. Nickel Plated Steel
23.9 mm.   **Subject:** Canada Day **Obv:** Crowned
head right **Rev:** Human figures supporting large red
maple leaf **Edge:** Reeded

Date	Mintage	MS-63	Proof
2002P	49,903	6.00	—

KM# 471 5.9000 g. 0.9250 Silver 0.1755 oz. ASW
23.9 mm.   **Subject:** 50th Anniversary of the
Coronation of Elizabeth II **Obv:** 1953 Effigy of the
Queen, Jubilee commemorative dates 1952-2002
Obv. Designer: Mary Gillick

Date	Mintage	MS-63	Proof
2002 Proof	21,537	—	12.50

KM# 493 4.4000 g. Nickel Plated Steel
23.9 mm.   **Obv:** Bare head right **Obv. Designer:**

Susanna Blunt **Rev:** Caribou left, denomination
above, date at right

Date	Mintage	MS-63	Proof
2003P	66,861,633	2.00	—
2003P W	—	—	—
2004P	177,466,000	2.50	—
2004P Proof	—	—	5.00
2005P	206,346,000	2.50	—
2005P Proof	—	—	5.00
2006P	423,189,000	2.50	—
2006P Proof	—	—	5.00
2007(ml)	386,763,000	2.50	—
2007(ml) Proof	—	—	5.00
2008(ml)	387,222,000	2.50	—
2008(ml) Proof	—	—	5.00
2009(ml)	266,766,000	2.50	—
2009(ml) Proof	—	—	5.00
2010(ml)	—	2.50	—
2010(ml) Proof	—	—	5.00
2011(ml)	—	2.50	—
2011(ml) Proof	—	—	5.00

KM# 474 4.4000 g. 0.9250 Silver 0.1308 oz. ASW
23.9 mm.   **Subject:** Canada Day **Obv:** Queen's
head right **Rev:** Polar bear and red colored maple
leaves

Date	Mintage	MS-63	Proof
2003 Proof	—	—	12.00

KM# 493a 5.9000 g. 0.9250 Silver 0.1755 oz. ASW
23.9 mm.   **Obv:** Bare head right **Obv. Designer:**
Suanne Blunt **Rev:** Caribou **Edge:** Reeded

Date	Mintage	MS-63	Proof
2004 Proof	—	—	6.50

KM# 510 4.4000 g. Nickel Plated Steel
23.9 mm.   **Obv:** Bare head right **Rev:** Red poppy
in center of maple leaf **Edge:** Reeded

Date	Mintage	MS-63	Proof
2004	28,500,000	5.00	—

KM# 510a 5.9000 g. 0.9250 Silver 0.1755 oz. ASW
23.9 mm.   **Obv:** Bare head right **Rev:** Poppy at
center of maple leaf, selectively gold plated
Edge: Reeded **Note:** Housed in Annual Report.

Date	Mintage	MS-63	Proof
2004 Proof	12,677	—	20.00

KM# 525 4.4000 g. Nickel Plated Steel
23.9 mm.   **Obv:** Bare head right **Rev:** Maple leaf,
colorized

Date	Mintage	MS-63	Proof
2004	16,028	8.00	—

KM# 628 4.4000 g. Nickel Plated Steel
23.9 mm. **Subject:** First Settlement, Ile Ste Croix
1604-2004 **Obv:** Bare head right **Rev:** Sailing ship
Bonne-Renommee

Date	Mintage	MS-63	Proof
2004P	15,400,000	5.00	—

KM# 698 4.4000 g. Nickel Plated Steel
Rev: Santa, colorized

Date	Mintage	MS-63	Proof
2004	62,777	5.00	—

KM# 699 4.4000 g. Nickel Plated Steel
23.9 mm. **Series:** Canada Day **Rev:** Moose head,
humorous

Date	Mintage	MS-63	Proof
2004	44,752	5.00	—

KM# 529 4.4000 g. Nickel Plated Steel
23.9 mm. **Subject:** WWII, 60th Anniversary
Obv: Head right **Rev:** Three soldiers and flag

Date	Mintage	MS-63	Proof
2005	3,500	20.00	—

KM# 530 4.4000 g. Nickel Plated Steel
23.9 mm. **Subject:** Alberta **Obv:** Head right

Date	Mintage	MS-63	Proof
2005P	20,640,000	7.00	—

KM# 531 4.4000 g. Nickel Plated Steel
23.9 mm. **Subject:** Canada Day **Obv:** Head right
Rev: Beaver, colorized

Date	Mintage	MS-63	Proof
2005P	58,370	8.50	—

KM# 532 4.4000 g. Nickel Plated Steel
23.9 mm. **Subject:** Saskatchewan **Obv:** Head
right

Date	Mintage	MS-63	Proof
2005P	19,290,000	7.00	—

KM# 533 4.4000 g. Nickel Plated Steel
23.9 mm. **Obv:** Head right **Rev:** Stuffed bear in
Christmas stocking, colorized

Date	Mintage	MS-63	Proof
2005P	72,831	10.00	—

KM# 535 4.4000 g. Nickel Plated Steel
23.9 mm. **Subject:** Year of the Veteran **Obv:**

Head right **Rev:** Conjoined busts of young and
veteran left **Edge:** Reeded

Date	Mintage	MS-63	Proof
2005P	29,390,000	7.00	—

KM# 576 4.4000 g. Nickel Plated Steel
23.9 mm. **Subject:** Quebec Winter Carnival
Obv: Head right **Rev:** Snowman, colorized

Date	Mintage	MS-63	Proof
2006	8,200	10.00	—

KM# 534 4.4000 g. Nickel Plated Steel
23.9 mm. **Subject:** Toronto Maple Leafs
Obv: Head right **Rev:** Colorized team logo

Date	Mintage	MS-63	Proof
2006P		12.50	—

KM# 575 4.4000 g. Nickel Plated Steel
23.9 mm. **Subject:** Montreal Canadiens
Obv: Head right **Rev:** Colorized logo

Date	Mintage	MS-63	Proof
2006P		12.50	—

KM# 629 4.4000 g. Nickel Plated Steel
23.9 mm. **Obv:** Head right **Rev:** Medal of Bravery
Edge: Reeded

Date	Mintage	MS-63	Proof
2006(ml)	20,040,000	2.50	—

KM# 632 12.6100 g. Nickel Plated Steel 35 mm.
Subject: Queen Elizabeth II 80th Birthday
Rev: Crown, colorized

Date	Mintage	MS-63	Proof
2006 Specimen	24,977	—	25.00

KM# 633 4.4300 g. Nickel Plated Steel
23.9 mm. **Subject:** Canada Day **Obv:** Crowned
head right **Rev:** Boy marching with flag, colorized

Date	Mintage	MS-63	Proof
2006P	29,760	6.00	—

KM# 634 4.4300 g. Nickel Plated Steel **Subject:** Breast Cancer **Rev:** Four ribbons, all
colorized **Note:** Sold housed in a bookmark.

Date	Mintage	MS-63	Proof
2006P	40,911	10.00	—

KM# 636 4.4000 g. Nickel Plated Steel   **Obv:**
Head right **Obv. Designer:** Susana Blunt **Rev:**
Medal of Bravery design (maple leaf within wreath)

Date	Mintage	MS-63	Proof
2006	20,045,111	7.00	—

KM# 637 4.4300 g. Nickel Plated Steel   **Subject:**
Wedding **Rev:** Colorized bouquet of flowers

Date	Mintage	MS-63	Proof
2007(ml)	10,318	5.00	—

KM# 642 4.4300 g. Nickel Plated Steel   **Subject:**
Ottawa Senators **Obv:** Head right **Rev:** Logo

Date	Mintage	MS-63	Proof
2006P	—	12.50	—

KM# 644 4.4300 g. Nickel Plated Steel   **Subject:**
Calgary Flames **Obv:** Head right **Rev:** Logo

Date	Mintage	MS-63	Proof
2007(ml)	832	12.50	—

KM# 645 4.4300 g. Nickel Plated Steel   **Subject:**
Edmonton Oilers **Obv:** Head right **Rev:** Logo

Date	Mintage	MS-63	Proof
2007(ml)	2,213	12.50	—

KM# 647 4.4300 g. Nickel Plated Steel   **Subject:**
Santa and Rudolph **Rev:** Colorized Santa in sled
lead by Rudolph

Date	Mintage	MS-63	Proof
2006P	99,258	5.00	—

KM# 682 4.4300 g. Nickel Plated Steel   **Subject:**
Curling **Obv:** Head right

Date	Mintage	MS-63	Proof
2007	22,400,000	7.50	—
2008 Mule	—	—	—

KM# 683 4.4300 g. Nickel Plated Steel   **Subject:**
Ice Hockey **Obv:** Head right

Date	Mintage	MS-63	Proof
2007	22,400,000	7.50	—
2008 Mule	—	—	—

KM# 684 4.4300 g. Nickel Plated Steel
23.8 mm.   **Subject:** Paraolympic Winter Games
Obv: Head right **Rev:** Wheelchair curling

Date	Mintage	MS-63	Proof
2007	22,400,000	7.50	—
2008 Mule	—	—	—

KM# 685 4.4300 g. Nickel Plated Steel   **Subject:**
Biathlon **Obv:** Head right

Date	Mintage	MS-63	Proof
2007	22,400,000	7.50	—
2008 Mule	—	—	—

KM# 638 4.4300 g. Nickel Plated Steel   **Subject:**
Birthday **Rev:** Colorized baloons

Date	Mintage	MS-63	Proof
2007(ml)	24,531	5.00	—

KM# 639 4.4300 g. Nickel Plated Steel   **Subject:**
Baby birth **Rev:** Colorized baby rattle **Edge:** Reeded

Date	Mintage	MS-63	Proof
2007(ml)	29,964	5.00	—

KM# 640 4.4300 g. Nickel Plated Steel   **Subject:**
Oh Canada **Obv:** Head right **Rev:** Maple leaf,
colorized

Date	Mintage	MS-63	Proof
2006(ml)	23,582	8.50	—

KM# 641 4.4300 g. Nickel Plated Steel   **Subject:**
Congratulations **Obv:** Head right **Rev:** Fireworks,
colorized

Date	Mintage	MS-63	Proof
2006(ml)	8,910	8.00	—

KM# 643 4.4300 g. Nickel Plated Steel   **Subject:**
Vancouver Canucks **Obv:** Head right **Rev:** Logo

Date	Mintage	MS-63	Proof
2007(ml)	1,264	12.50	—

KM# 686 4.4300 g. Nickel Plated Steel
23.8 mm.   **Subject:** Alpine Skiing **Obv:** Head right

Date	Mintage	MS-63	Proof
2007	22,400,000	7.50	—
2008 Mule	—	—	—

KM# 701 4.4300 g. Nickel Plated Steel **Subject:** Birthday **Rev:** Party hat, multicolor

Date	Mintage	MS-63	Proof
2007	—	8.00	—

KM# 702 4.4300 g. Nickel Plated Steel **Subject:** Congratulations **Rev:** Trophy, multicolor

Date	Mintage	MS-63	Proof
2007	—	8.00	—

KM# 703 4.4300 g. Nickel Plated Steel **Subject:** Wedding **Rev:** Cake, multicolor

Date	Mintage	MS-63	Proof
2007	—	8.00	—

KM# 704 4.4300 g. Nickel Plated Steel **Subject:** Canada Day **Rev:** Mountie, colorized

Date	Mintage	MS-63	Proof
2007(ml)	27,743	8.00	—

KM# 705 4.4300 g. Nickel Plated Steel **Subject:** Christmas **Rev:** Multicolor tree

Date	Mintage	MS-63	Proof
2007	—	8.00	—

KM# 706 12.6100 g. Nickel Plated Steel 35.0 mm. **Subject:** Red-breasted Nuthatch **Obv:** Head right **Obv. Legend:** ELIZABETH II - D • G • REGINA **Obv. Designer:** Susanna Blunt **Rev:** Nuthatch perched on pine branch multicolor **Rev. Legend:** CANADA **Rev. Designer:** Arnold Nogy **Edge:** Plain

Date	Mintage	MS-63	Proof
2007(ml) Specimen	10,581	25.00	—

KM# 707 12.6100 g. Nickel Plated Steel 35 mm. **Obv:** Elizabeth II **Rev:** Multicolor ruby-throated hummingbird and flower **Edge:** Plain

Date	Mintage	MS-63	Proof
2007 Specimen	16,256	—	25.00

KM# 708 5.9000 g. 0.9250 Silver 0.1755 oz. ASW **Subject:** Queen's 60th Wedding Anniversary **Rev:** Royal carriage

Date	Mintage	MS-63	Proof
2007 Specimen	16,264	—	24.00

KM# 713 4.4000 g. Nickel Plated Steel **Rev:** Toronto Maple Leaf logo, colorized

Date	Mintage	MS-63	Proof
2007(ml)	3,527	5.00	—

KM# 714 4.4000 g. Nickel Plated Steel **Rev:** Ottawa Senators logo, colorized

Date	Mintage	MS-63	Proof
2007(ml)	1,634	5.00	—

KM# 723 4.4000 g. Nickel Plated Steel **Rev:** Montreal Canadiens logo, colorized

Date	Mintage	MS-63	Proof
2007(ml)	2,952	5.00	—

KM# 1039 4.4300 g. Nickel Plated Steel 23.9 mm. **Subject:** Canada Day **Rev:** Colorized moose head

Date	Mintage	MS-63	Proof
2008	—	12.50	—

KM# 760 4.4300 g. Nickel Plated Steel **Subject:**
Baby **Rev:** Multicolor blue teddy bear

Date	Mintage	MS-63	Proof
2008	—	8.00	—

KM# 761 4.4300 g. Nickel Plated Steel **Subject:**
Birthday **Rev:** Multicolor party hat

Date	Mintage	MS-63	Proof
2008	—	8.00	—

KM# 762 4.4300 g. Nickel Plated Steel **Subject:**
Congratulations **Rev:** Multicolor trophy

Date	Mintage	MS-63	Proof
2008	—	8.00	—

KM# 763 4.4300 g. Nickel Plated Steel **Subject:**
Wedding **Rev:** Multicolor wedding cake

Date	Mintage	MS-63	Proof
2008	—	8.00	—

KM# 764 4.4300 g. Nickel Plated Steel **Subject:**
Santa Claus **Rev:** Multicolor Santa

Date	Mintage	MS-63	Proof
2008	—	8.00	—

KM# 765 4.4300 g. Nickel Plated Steel
23.9 mm.   **Subject:** Vancouver Olympics **Rev:**
Freestyle skiing

Date	Mintage	MS-63	Proof
2008	—	2.00	—

KM# 766 4.4300 g. Nickel Plated Steel
23.8 mm.   **Subject:** Vancouver Olympics **Rev:**
Figure skating

Date	Mintage	MS-63	Proof
2008	—	2.00	—

KM# 768 4.4300 g. Nickel Plated Steel
23.9 mm.   **Subject:** Vancouver Olympics **Rev:**
Snow boarding

Date	Mintage	MS-63	Proof
2008	—	2.00	—

KM# 769 4.4300 g. Nickel Plated Steel **Subject:**
Vancouver Olympics **Rev:** Olympic mascott - Miga

Date	Mintage	MS-63	Proof
2008	—	3.00	—

KM# 770 4.4300 g. Nickel Plated Steel **Subject:**
Vancouver Olympics **Rev:** Olympic mascott -
Quatchi

Date	Mintage	MS-63	Proof
2008	—	3.00	—

KM# 771 4.4300 g. Nickel Plated Steel **Subject:**
Vancouver Olympics **Rev:** Olympic mascott - Sumi

Date	Mintage	MS-63	Proof
2008	—	3.00	—

KM# 772 4.4300 g. Nickel Plated Steel **Subject:**
Oh Canada **Rev:** Multicolor red flag

Date	Mintage	MS-63	Proof
2008	—	8.00	—

KM# 773 12.6100 g. Nickel Plated Steel 35 mm.
Obv: Bust right **Obv. Designer:** Susanna Blunt
Rev: Downy woodpecker in tree, multicolor **Rev.
Designer:** Arnold Nogy **Edge:** Plain **Note:** Prev.
KM#717.

Date	Mintage	MS-63	Proof
2008(ml)	25,000	24.00	—

KM# 774 12.6100 g. Nickel Plated Steel 35 mm.
Obv: Bust right **Obv. Designer:** Susanna Blunt
Rev: Northern cardinal perched on branch -
multicolor **Rev. Designer:** Arnold Nogy **Edge:** Plain
Note: Prev. KM#718.

Date	Mintage	MS-63	Proof
2008(ml)	25,000	25.00	—

25 CENTS

KM# 775 4.4300 g. Nickel Plated Steel
23.8 mm. **Subject:** End of WWI, 90th Anniversary
Rev: Multicolor poppy

Date	Mintage	MS-63	Proof
2008	—	8.00	—

KM# 776 12.6100 g. Nickel Plated Steel 35 mm.
Subject: Anne of Green Gables **Rev:** Image of young girl, multicolor **Rev. Designer:** Ben Stahl

Date	Mintage	MS-63	Proof
2008	25,000	20.00	—

KM# 841 4.4300 g. Nickel Plated Steel **Subject:** Vancouver Olympics **Rev:** Bobsleigh **Shape:** 23.8

Date	Mintage	MS-63	Proof
2008	—	3.00	—

KM# 1041 4.4300 g. Nickel Plated Steel
Subject: WWI **Rev:** Three military men standing over tomb

Date	Mintage	MS-63	Proof
2008(ml)	—	12.50	—

KM# 840 4.4300 g. Nickel Plated Steel
23.8 mm. **Subject:** Valcouver 2010 Olympics
Rev: Cross-country skiing

Date	Mintage	MS-63	Proof
2009	—	3.00	—

KM# 842 4.4300 g. Nickel Plated Steel
23.9 mm. **Subject:** Edmonton Olympics **Rev:** Speed skating

Date	Mintage	MS-63	Proof
2009	—	3.00	—

KM# 885 4.4000 g. Nickel Plated Steel 35 mm.
Subject: Canada Day **Rev:** Animals in boat with flag **Rev. Legend:** Canada 25 cents

Date	Mintage	MS-63	Proof
2009	—	5.00	—

KM# 886 12.6100 g. Nickel Plated Steel 35 mm.
Subject: Notre-Dame-Du-Saguenay **Obv:** Bust right **Obv. Legend:** Elizabeth II DG Regina **Obv. Designer:** Susanna Blunt **Rev:** Color photo of fjord and statue **Rev. Legend:** Canada 25 cents

Date	Mintage	MS-63	Proof
2009 Specimen	—	—	25.00

KM# 915 4.4300 g. Nickel Plated Steel
23.9 mm. **Subject:** Surprise Birthday **Obv:** Bust
right **Obv. Designer:** Susanna Blunt **Rev:** Colorized

Date	Mintage	MS-63	Proof
2009	—	12.50	—

KM# 916 4.4300 g. Nickel Plated Steel
23.9 mm. **Subject:** Share the Excitement **Obv:**
Bust right **Obv. Designer:** Susanna Blunt **Rev:**
Colorized

Date	Mintage	MS-63	Proof
2009	—	12.50	—

KM# 917 4.4300 g. Nickel Plated Steel
23.9 mm. **Subject:** Share the Love **Obv:** Bust
right **Obv. Designer:** Susanna Blunt **Rev:** Two
doves, coolored

Date	Mintage	MS-63	Proof
2009	—	12.50	—

KM# 918 4.4300 g. Nickel Plated Steel
23.9 mm. **Subject:** Thank You **Obv:** Bust right
Obv. Designer: Susanna Blunt **Rev:** Colorized

Date	Mintage	MS-63	Proof
2009	—	12.50	—

KM# 933 4.4000 g. Nickel Plated Steel
23.9 mm. **Rev:** Santa Claus, multicolor

Date	Mintage	MS-63	Proof
2009 In sets only	—	16.50	—

KM# 934 4.4000 g. Nickel Plated Steel
23.9 mm. **Rev:** Multicolor teddy bear, crescent
moon

Date	Mintage	MS-63	Proof
2009	—	16.50	—

KM# 935 4.4000 g. Nickel Plated Steel
23.9 mm. **Subject:** Oh Canada **Rev:** Maple
leaves, yellow color

Date	Mintage	MS-63	Proof
2009 In sets only	—	16.50	—

KM# 952 4.4000 g. Nickel Plated Steel
23.9 mm. **Rev:** Sledge hockey

Date	Mintage	MS-63	Proof
2009	—	3.00	—

KM# 1063 Nickel Plated Steel **Subject:** Men's
Hockey **Rev:** Hockey player and maple leaf outline

Date	Mintage	MS-63	Proof
2009	—	2.50	—

KM# 1063a Nickel Plated Steel **Subject:** Men's
Hockey **Rev:** Hockey player and maple leaf outline
in red

Date	Mintage	MS-63	Proof
2009	—	7.50	—

KM# 1064 Nickel Plated Steel **Subject:**
Women's Hockey **Rev:** Hockey player and maple
leaf outline

Date	Mintage	MS-63	Proof
2009	—	2.50	—

KM# 1064a Nickel Plated Steel **Subject:**
Women's Hockey **Rev:** Hockey player and male leaf
outline in red

Date	Mintage	MS-63	Proof
2009	—	7.50	—

KM# 1065 Nickel Plated Steel **Subject:** Klassen - Female hockey player **Rev:** Skater and maple leaf outline

Date	Mintage	MS-63	Proof
2009	—	2.50	—

KM# 1065a Nickel Plated Steel **Subject:** Klassen - female skater **Rev:** Skater and maple leaf outline in red

Date	Mintage	MS-63	Proof
2009	—	7.50	—

KM# 880 4.4000 g. Nickel Plated Steel 23.88 mm. **Subject:** Miga Mascot Vancouver Olympics **Rev:** Mica Mascot - color **Rev. Legend:** Vancouver 2010 25 cents

Date	Mintage	MS-63	Proof
2010	—	3.00	—

KM# 881 4.4000 g. Nickel Plated Steel 23.88 mm. **Subject:** Quatchi Mascot - Vancouver Olympics **Obv:** Bust right **Rev:** Quatchi Mascot color **Rev. Legend:** Vancouver 2010 25 cents

Date	Mintage	MS-63	Proof
2010	—	3.00	—

KM# 882 4.4000 g. Nickel Plated Steel 23.88 mm. **Subject:** Sumi Mascot **Rev:** Sumi Mascot color **Rev. Legend:** Vancouver 2010 25 cents

Date	Mintage	MS-63	Proof
2010	—	3.00	—

KM# 953 4.4000 g. Nickel Plated Steel 23.9 mm. **Rev:** Ice hockey

Date	Mintage	MS-63	Proof
2010	—	3.00	—

KM# 953a 4.4000 g. Nickel Plated Steel 23.9 mm. **Rev:** Ice Hockey - red enamel

Date	Mintage	MS-63	Proof
2010	—	8.00	—

KM# 954 4.4000 g. Nickel Plated Steel 23.9 mm. **Rev:** Curling

Date	Mintage	MS-63	Proof
2010	—	3.00	—

KM# 954a 4.4000 g. Nickel Plated Steel 23.9 mm. **Rev:** Curling red enamel

Date	Mintage	MS-63	Proof
2010	—	8.00	—

KM# 955 4.4000 g. Nickel Plated Steel 23.9 mm. **Rev:** Wheelchair curling

Date	Mintage	MS-63	Proof
2010	—	3.00	—

KM# 955a 4.4000 g. Nickel Plated Steel 23.9 mm. **Rev:** Wheelchair curling - red enamel

Date	Mintage	MS-63	Proof
2010	—	8.00	—

KM# 956 4.4000 g. Nickel Plated Steel 23.9 mm. **Rev:** Biathlon

Date	Mintage	MS-63	Proof
2010	—	3.00	—

KM# 956a 4.4000 g. Nickel Plated Steel 23.9 mm. **Rev:** Biathlon - red enamel

Date	Mintage	MS-63	Proof
2010	—	8.00	—

KM# 957 4.4000 g. Nickel Plated Steel 23.9 mm. **Rev:** Alpine skiing

Date	Mintage	MS-63	Proof
2010	—	3.00	—

KM# 957a 4.4000 g. Nickel Plated Steel 23.9 mm. **Rev:** Alpine skiing - red enamel

Date	Mintage	MS-63	Proof
2010	—	8.00	—

KM# 958 4.4000 g. Nickel Plated Steel 23.9 mm. **Rev:** Snowboarding

Date	Mintage	MS-63	Proof
2010	—	3.00	—

KM# 958a 4.4000 g. Nickel Plated Steel 23.9 mm. **Rev:** Snowboarding - red enamel

Date	Mintage	MS-63	Proof
2010	—	8.00	—

KM# 959 23.9000 g. Nickel Plated Steel 23.9 mm. **Rev:** Free-style skiing

Date	Mintage	MS-63	Proof
2010	—	3.00	—

KM# 959a 4.4000 g. Nickel Plated Steel 23.9 mm. **Rev:** Free-style skiing - red enamel

Date	Mintage	MS-63	Proof
2010	—	8.00	—

KM# 960 4.4000 g. Nickel Plated Steel 23.9 mm. **Rev:** Alpine skiing

Date	Mintage	MS-63	Proof
2010	—	3.00	—

KM# 960a 4.4000 g. Nickel Plated Steel 23.9 mm. **Rev:** Alpine skiing - red enamel

Date	Mintage	MS-63	Proof
2010	—	8.00	—

KM# 988 4.4000 g. Multi-Ply Plated Steel 23.88 mm. **Rev:** Blue baby carriage

Date	Mintage	MS-63	Proof
2010	—	10.00	—

KM# 989 4.4000 g. Nickel Plated Steel 23.9 mm. **Rev:** Purple gift box

Date	Mintage	MS-63	Proof
2010	—	10.00	—

KM# 991 4.4000 g. Nickel Plated Steel 23.9 mm. **Rev:** Three maple leaves

Date	Mintage	MS-63	Proof
2010	—	12.50	—

KM# 992 4.4000 g. Nickel Plated Steel
23.9 mm.   **Rev:** Three zinnias

Date	Mintage	MS-63	Proof
2010	—	12.50	—

KM# 993 23.9000 g. Nickel Plated Steel
23.9 mm.   **Rev:** Pink hearts and roses

Date	Mintage	MS-63	Proof
2010	—	10.00	—

KM# 994 12.6100 g. Nickel Plated Steel 35 mm.
Rev: Goldfinch, multicolor **Rev. Designer:** Arnold
Nogy

Date	Mintage	MS-63	Proof
2010 Proof	Est. 14,000	—	25.00

KM# 1001 12.6100 g. Nickel Plated Steel
35 mm.   **Subject:** Blue Jay **Rev:** Multicolor blue
jay on yellow maple leaves

Date	Mintage	MS-63	Proof
2010 Specimen	—	—	25.00

KM# 1006 0.5000 g. 0.9990 Gold 0.0161 oz. AGW
11 mm.   **Rev:** Caribou head left

Date	Mintage	MS-63	Proof
2010 Proof	15,000	—	80.00

KM# 1021 Nickel Plated Steel 23.9 mm.   **Rev:**
Santa Claus in color

Date	Mintage	MS-63	Proof
2010	—	15.00	—

KM# 1026 Silver 23.8 mm.   **Obv:** George V bust
left **Rev:** Value within wreath, dual dates below

Date	Mintage	MS-63	Proof
2010 Proof	—	—	25.00

KM# 1028 4.4000 g. Nickel Plated Steel
23.9 mm.   **Rev:** Soldier standing, two red poppies,
large maple leaf behind

Date	Mintage	MS-63	Proof
2010	—	15.00	—

KM# 1079 12.6100 g. Nickel Plated Steel
35 mm. **Rev:** Barn Swallow in color **Rev.**
Designer: Arnold Nagy

Date	Mintage	MS-63	Proof
2011	14,000	—	25.00

KM# 1080 4.4300 g. Nickel Plated Steel
23.88 mm. **Subject:** Oh Canada! **Rev:** Maple leaf
and circular legend

Date	Mintage	MS-63	Proof
2011	—	2.50	—

KM# 1081 4.4300 g. Nickel Plated Steel
23.88 mm. **Subject:** Wedding **Rev:** Two rings

Date	Mintage	MS-63	Proof
2011	—	2.50	—

KM# 1082 4.4300 g. Nickel Plated Steel
23.88 mm. **Subject:** Birthday **Rev:** Year in four
baloons

Date	Mintage	MS-63	Proof
2011	—	2.50	—

KM# 1083 4.4300 g. Nickel Plated Steel
23.88 mm. **Subject:** New Baby! **Rev:** Baby's feet

Date	Mintage	MS-63	Proof
2011	—	2.50	—

KM# 1084 4.4300 g. Nickel Plated Steel
23.88 mm. **Rev:** Tooth Fairy

Date	Mintage	MS-63	Proof
2011	—	2.50	—

50 CENTS

KM# 6 11.6200 g. 0.9250 Silver 0.3456 oz. ASW 29.7 mm. **Obv:** VICTORIA DEI GRATIA REGINA. CANADA
Obv. Designer: Leonard C. Wyon **Rev:** Denomination and date within wreath, crown above **Edge:** Reeded

Date	Mintage	VG-8	F-12	VF-20	XF-40	MS-60	MS-63	Proof
1870	450,000	900	1,400	2,400	5,000	25,000	40,000	—
1870 LCW	Inc. above	45.00	75.00	175	400	3,500	10,000	—
1871	200,000	75.00	150	350	650	7,000	15,000	—
1871H	45,000	150	225	450	1,100	8,500	22,000	—
1872H	80,000	55.00	95.00	200	450	4,000	10,500	—
1872H Inverted A for V in Victoria	Inc. above	500	700	1,900	5,000	25,000	—	—
1881H	150,000	60.00	125	225	550	5,500	16,000	—
1888	60,000	225	400	750	1,400	9,500	22,000	—
1890H	20,000	1,200	1,900	3,500	6,000	30,000	65,000	—
1892	151,000	70.00	125	350	650	9,000	21,000	—
1894	29,036	500	900	1,500	2,500	14,000	35,000	—
1898	100,000	75.00	150	350	750	9,000	26,000	—
1899	50,000	200	350	700	1,600	14,000	35,000	—
1900	118,000	60.00	100.00	200	500	5,000	10,500	—
1901	80,000	75.00	175	275	650	7,000	17,500	—

Victorian leaves

KM# 12 11.6200 g. 0.9250 Silver 0.3456 oz. ASW 29.7 mm. **Obv:** Crowned bust right **Obv. Designer:** G.
W. DeSaulles **Rev:** Denomination and date within wreath, crown above **Edge:** Reeded

Date	Mintage	VG-8	F-12	VF-20	XF-40	MS-60	MS-63	Proof
1902	120,000	22.50	55.00	150	375	1,950	5,300	—
1903H	140,000	33.00	70.00	265	675	2,250	6,000	—
1904	60,000	225	300	800	1,500	4,950	14,500	—
1905	40,000	225	450	900	2,100	9,000	22,500	—
1906	350,000	18.00	55.00	145	375	1,950	5,300	—
1907	300,000	18.00	55.00	145	375	2,100	6,000	—
1908	128,119	31.50	100.00	265	600	1,500	3,000	—
1909	302,118	25.00	90.00	265	750	3,600	12,000	—
1910 Victoria leaves	649,521	33.00	70.00	265	600	2,400	9,000	—

Edwardian leaves

KM# 12a 11.6200 g. 0.9250 Silver 0.3456 oz. ASW 29.7 mm. **Obv:** Crowned bust right **Obv. Designer:** G. W. DeSaulles **Rev:** Denomination and date within wreath **Edge:** Reeded

Date	Mintage	VG-8	F-12	VF-20	XF-40	MS-60	MS-63	Proof
1910 Edwardian leaves	Inc. above	14.00	37.75	110	325	1,550	4,200	—

KM# 19 11.6200 g. 0.9250 Silver 0.3456 oz. ASW 29.7 mm. **Obv:** Crowned bust left **Obv. Designer:** E. B. MacKennal **Rev:** Denomination and date within wreath, crown above **Edge:** Reeded

Date	Mintage	VG-8	F-12	VF-20	XF-40	MS-60	MS-63	Proof
1911	209,972	25.00	100.00	350	775	1,950	4,200	—

KM# 25 11.6200 g. 0.9250 Silver 0.3456 oz. ASW 29.7 mm. **Obv:** Crowned bust left, modified legend **Obv. Designer:** E. B. MacKennal **Rev:** Denomination and date within wreath, crown above **Edge:** Reeded

Date	Mintage	VG-8	F-12	VF-20	XF-40	MS-60	MS-63	Proof
1912	285,867	14.00	37.50	160	350	1,650	4,350	—
1913	265,889	14.00	37.50	240	475	2,100	7,500	—
1914	160,128	32.50	90.00	350	875	4,200	12,000	—
1916	459,070	11.00	22.50	75.00	280	975	3,150	—
1917	752,213	10.00	18.00	55.00	160	750	1,650	—
1918	754,989	10.00	16.00	42.00	145	600	1,500	—
1919	1,113,429	10.00	16.00	42.00	145	600	1,800	—

KM# 25a 11.6638 g. 0.8000 Silver 0.3000 oz. ASW 29.7 mm. **Obv:** Crowned bust left **Obv. Designer:** E. B. MacKennal **Rev:** Denomination and date within wreath, crown below **Edge:** Reeded

Date	Mintage	VG-8	F-12	VF-20	XF-40	MS-60	MS-63	Proof
1920	584,691	10.00	20.00	60.00	215	850	2,700	—
1921	—	33,000	36,000	47,500	59,500	85,000	135,000	—
Note: 75 to 100 known; David Akers John Jay Pittman sale, Part Three, 10-99, Gem Unc. realized $63,250								
1929	228,328	10.00	20.00	60.00	170	850	1,650	—
1931	57,581	17.00	42.50	135	375	1,350	2,700	—

Date	Mintage	VG-8	F-12	VF-20	XF-40	MS-60	MS-63	Proof
1932	19,213	225	300	675	1,350	6,800	13,000	—
1934	39,539	22.50	45.00	170	375	1,100	1,950	—
1936	38,550	22.50	45.00	170	300	850	1,500	—

KM# 36 11.6638 g. 0.8000 Silver 0.3000 oz. ASW 29.7 mm. **Obv:** Head left **Obv. Designer:** T. H. Paget **Rev:** Crowned arms with supporters, denomination above, date below **Rev. Designer:** George E. Kruger-Gray **Edge:** Reeded

Date	Mintage	VG-8	F-12	VF-20	XF-40	MS-60	MS-63	Proof
1937	192,016	BV	10.00	11.00	15.00	45.00	100.00	—
1938	192,018	BV	10.00	15.00	37.50	145	475	—
1939	287,976	BV	10.00	12.00	25.00	90.00	300	—
1940	1,996,566	—	—	BV	10.00	40.50	70.00	—
1941	1,714,874	—	—	BV	10.00	40.50	70.00	—
1942	1,974,164	—	—	BV	10.00	40.50	70.00	—
1943	3,109,583	—	—	BV	10.00	40.50	70.00	—
1944	2,460,205	—	—	BV	10.00	40.50	70.00	—
1945	1,959,528	—	—	BV	10.00	45.00	110	—
1946	950,235	—	BV	10.00	12.00	90.00	210	—
1946 hoof in 6	Inc. above	22.50	42.00	70.00	225	1,650	3,500	—
1947 straight 7	424,885	—	10.00	12.00	18.00	100.00	210	—
1947 curved 7	Inc. above	—	10.00	14.00	33.00	150	350	—
1947 maple leaf, straight 7	38,433	20.00	32.50	65.00	100.00	240	350	—
1947 maple leaf, curved 7	Inc. above	1,500	1,950	2,550	3,300	6,000	9,000	—

KM# 45 11.6638 g. 0.8000 Silver 0.3000 oz. ASW 29.7 mm. **Obv:** Head left, modified legend **Obv. Designer:** T. H. Paget **Rev:** Crowned arms with supporters, denomination above, date below **Rev. Designer:** George E. Kruger-Gray **Edge:** Reeded

Date	Mintage	VG-8	F-12	VF-20	XF-40	MS-60	MS-63	Proof
1948	37,784	90.00	130	150	225	375	525	—
1949	858,991	—	—	BV	11.00	55.00	225	—
1949 hoof over 9	Inc. above	15.00	27.50	55.00	90.00	525	1,150	—
1950 no lines in 0	2,384,179	10.00	15.00	17.00	55.00	190	350	—
1950 lines in 0	Inc. above	—	—	BV	10.00	14.00	45.00	—
1951	2,421,730	—	—	—	BV	14.00	39.00	—
1952	2,596,465	—	—	—	BV	11.00	27.50	—

KM# 53 11.6638 g. 0.8000 Silver 0.3000 oz. ASW 29.7 mm. **Obv:** Laureate bust right **Obv. Designer:** Mary Gillick **Rev:** Crowned arms with supporters, denomination above, date below **Edge:** Reeded

50 CENTS

Date	Mintage	VG-8	F-12	VF-20	XF-40	MS-60	MS-63	Proof
1953	1,630,429	—	—	—	BV	11.00	22.50	—
Note: small date								
1953	Inc. above	—	—	BV	10.00	28.00	55.00	—
Note: large date, straps								
1953	Inc. above	—	10.00	11.00	20.00	115	225	—
Note: large date without straps								
1954	506,305	—	BV	10.00	11.00	25.00	50.00	—
1955	753,511	—	—	BV	10.00	20.00	40.00	—
1956	1,379,499	—	—	—	BV	11.00	20.00	—
1957	2,171,689	—	—	—	BV	10.00	15.00	—
1958	2,957,266	—	—	—	BV	10.00	13.00	—

KM# 56 11.6638 g. 0.8000 Silver 0.3000 oz. ASW 30 mm. **Obv:** Luareate bust right **Obv. Designer:** Mary Gillick **Rev:** Crown divides date above arms with supporters, denomination at right **Rev. Designer:** Thomas Shingles **Edge:** Reeded

Date	Mintage	VG-8	F-12	VF-20	XF-40	MS-60	MS-63	Proof
1959	3,095,535	—	—	—	—	BV	11.00	—
Note: horizontal shading								
1960	3,488,897	—	—	—	—	BV	11.00	—
1961	3,584,417	—	—	—	—	BV	11.00	—
1962	5,208,030	—	—	—	—	BV	11.00	—
1963	8,348,871	—	—	—	—	BV	11.00	—
1964	9,377,676	—	—	—	—	BV	11.00	—

KM# 63 11.6638 g. 0.8000 Silver 0.3000 oz. ASW 29.7 mm. **Obv:** Young bust right **Obv. Designer:** Arnold Machin **Rev:** Crown divides date above arms with supporters, denomination at right **Rev. Designer:** Thomas Shingles **Edge:** Reeded

Date	Mintage	VG-8	F-12	VF-20	XF-40	MS-60	MS-63	Proof
1965	12,629,974	—	—	—	—	BV	11.00	—
1966	7,920,496	—	—	—	—	BV	11.00	—

KM# 69 11.6638 g. 0.8000 Silver 0.3000 oz. ASW 29.7 mm. **Subject:** Confederation Centennial **Obv:** Young bust right **Rev:** Seated wolf howling divides denomination at top, dates at bottom **Rev. Designer:** Alex Colville **Edge:** Reeded

Date	Mintage	VG-8	F-12	VF-20	XF-40	MS-60	MS-63	Proof
1967	4,211,392	—	—	—	—	BV	11.00	14.00

KM# 75.1 8.1000 g. Nickel 27.1 mm. **Obv:** Young bust right **Obv. Designer:** Arnold Machin **Rev:** Crown divides date above arms with supporters, denomination at right **Rev. Designer:** Thomas Shingles **Edge:** Reeded

Date	Mintage	VG-8	F-12	VF-20	XF-40	MS-60	MS-63	Proof
1968	3,966,932	—	—	—	0.50	0.65	1.00	—
1969	7,113,929	—	—	—	0.50	0.65	1.00	—
1970	2,429,526	—	—	—	0.50	0.65	1.00	—
1971	2,166,444	—	—	—	0.50	0.65	1.00	—
1972	2,515,632	—	—	—	0.50	0.65	1.00	—
1973	2,546,096	—	—	—	0.50	0.65	1.00	—
1974	3,436,650	—	—	—	0.50	0.65	1.00	—
1975	3,710,000	—	—	—	0.50	0.65	1.00	—
1976	2,940,719	—	—	—	0.50	0.65	1.00	—

KM# 75.2 8.1000 g. Nickel 27.1 mm. **Obv:** Small young bust right **Obv. Designer:** Arnold Machin **Rev:** Crown divides date above arms with supporters, denomination at right **Rev. Designer:** Thomas Shingles **Edge:** Reeded

Date	Mintage	VG-8	F-12	VF-20	XF-40	MS-60	MS-63	Proof
1977	709,839	—	—	0.50	0.75	1.25	2.00	—

KM# 75.3 8.1000 g. Nickel 27.1 mm. **Obv:** Young bust right **Obv. Designer:** Arnold Machin **Rev:** Crown divides date above arms with supporters, denomination at right, redesigned arms **Rev. Designer:** Thomas Shingles **Edge:** Reeded

Date	Mintage	VG-8	F-12	VF-20	XF-40	MS-60	MS-63	Proof
1978	3,341,892	—	—	—	0.50	0.65	1.00	—
Note: square jewels								
1978	Inc. above	—	—	1.00	2.50	4.50	6.00	—
Note: round jewels								
1979	3,425,000	—	—	—	0.50	0.65	1.00	—
1980	1,574,000	—	—	—	0.50	0.65	1.00	—
1981	2,690,272	—	—	—	0.50	0.65	1.00	—
1981 Proof	199,000	—	—	—	—	—	—	3.00
1982	2,236,674	—	—	—	30.00	65.00	95.00	—
Note: small beads								
1982 Proof	180,908	—	—	—	—	—	—	3.00
Note: small beads								
1982	Inc. above	—	—	—	0.50	0.65	1.00	—
Note: large beads								
1983	1,177,000	—	—	—	0.50	0.65	1.00	—
1983 Proof	168,000	—	—	—	—	—	—	3.00
1984	1,502,989	—	—	—	0.50	0.65	1.00	—
1984 Proof	161,602	—	—	—	—	—	—	3.00
1985	2,188,374	—	—	—	0.50	0.65	1.00	—
1985 Proof	157,037	—	—	—	—	—	—	3.00
1986	781,400	—	—	—	0.50	0.80	1.00	—
1986 Proof	175,745	—	—	—	—	—	—	3.00
1987	373,000	—	—	—	0.50	0.80	1.00	—
1987 Proof	179,004	—	—	—	—	—	—	3.50
1988	220,000	—	—	—	0.50	0.80	1.00	—
1988 Proof	175,259	—	—	—	—	—	—	3.00
1989	266,419	—	—	—	0.50	0.80	1.00	—
1989 Proof	170,928	—	—	—	—	—	—	3.00

KM# 185 8.2000 g. Nickel 27.1 mm.   **Obv:** Crowned head right **Obv. Designer:** Dora dePedery-Hunt **Rev:** Crown divides date above arms with supporters, denomination at right **Rev. Designer:** Thomas Shingles

Date	Mintage	VG-8	F-12	VF-20	XF-40	MS-60	MS-63	Proof
1990	207,000	—	—	—	0.50	0.80	1.00	—
1990 Proof	140,649	—	—	—	—	—	—	5.00
1991	490,000	—	—	—	0.50	0.85	1.00	—
1991 Proof	131,888	—	—	—	—	—	—	7.00
1993	393,000	—	—	—	0.50	0.85	1.00	—
1993 Proof	143,065	—	—	—	—	—	—	3.00
1994	987,000	—	—	—	0.50	0.75	1.00	—
1994 Proof	146,424	—	—	—	—	—	—	4.00
1995	626,000	—	—	—	0.50	0.75	1.00	—
1995 Proof	50,000	—	—	—	—	—	—	4.00
1996 Proof	—	—	—	—	—	—	—	4.00
1996	458,000	—	—	—	0.50	0.65	1.00	—

KM# 208 Nickel 27 mm.   **Subject:** Confederation 125 **Obv:** Crowned head right **Obv. Designer:** Dora dePedery-Hunt **Rev:** Crown divides date above arms with supporters, denomination at right **Rev. Designer:** Thomas Shingles

Date	Mintage	MS-63	Proof
1992	445,000	1.00	—
1992 Proof	147,061	—	5.00

KM# 262 11.6638 g. 0.9250 Silver 0.3469 oz. ASW   **Obv:** Crowned head right **Rev:** Whooping crane left, denomination and date at right **Rev. Designer:** Stan Witten

Date	Mintage	MS-63	Proof
1995 Proof	—	—	24.00

KM# 263 11.6638 g. 0.9250 Silver 0.3469 oz. ASW   **Obv:** Crowned head right **Rev:** Gray Jays, denomination and date at right **Rev. Designer:** Sheldon Beveridge

Date	Mintage	MS-63	Proof
1995 Proof	—	—	24.00

KM# 261 11.6638 g. 0.9250 Silver 0.3469 oz. ASW   **Obv:** Crowned head right **Rev:** Atlantic Puffin, denomination and date at right **Rev. Designer:** Sheldon Beveridge

Date	Mintage	MS-63	Proof
1995 Proof	—	—	24.00

KM# 264 11.6638 g. 0.9250 Silver 0.3469 oz.
ASW   **Obv:** Crowned head right **Rev:** White-tailed
ptarmigans, date and denomination at right **Rev.**
Designer: Cosme Saffioti

Date	Mintage	MS-63	Proof
1995 Proof	—	—	22.00

KM# 286 11.6638 g. 0.9250 Silver 0.3469 oz. ASW
27 mm.   **Obv:** Crowned head right **Rev:** Bear cubs
standing, date and denomination at right **Rev.**
Designer: Sheldon Beveridge

Date	Mintage	MS-63	Proof
1996 Proof	—	—	20.00

KM# 185a 11.6380 g. 0.9250 Silver 0.3461 oz.
ASW   **Obv:** Crowned head right **Obv. Designer:**
Dora dePedery-Hunt **Rev:** Crown divides date
above arms with supporters, denomination at right
Rev. Designer: Thomas Shingles

Date	Mintage	MS-63	Proof
1996 Proof	—	—	12.00

KM# 290 8.1000 g. Nickel 27.1 mm.   **Obv:**
Crowned head right **Obv. Designer:** Dora
dePedery-Hunt **Rev:** Redesigned arms **Rev.**
Designer: Cathy Bursey-Sabourin **Edge:** Reeded

Date	Mintage	MS-63	Proof
1997	387,000	1.00	—
1997 Proof	—	—	5.00
1998	308,000	1.00	—
1998 Proof	—	—	—
1998W	—	2.00	—
1999	496,000	1.00	—
1999 Proof	—	—	5.00
2000	559,000	1.00	—
2000 Proof	—	—	5.00
2000W	—	1.50	—
2001P	—	1.50	—
2001P Proof	—	—	5.00
2003P	—	1.50	—
2003P Proof	—	—	5.00

KM# 283 11.6638 g. 0.9250 Silver 0.3469 oz. ASW
27 mm.   **Obv:** Crowned head right **Rev:** Moose
calf left, denomination and date at right **Rev.**
Designer: Ago Aarand

Date	Mintage	MS-63	Proof
1996 Proof	—	—	20.00

KM# 284 11.6638 g. 0.9250 Silver 0.3469 oz. ASW
27 mm.   **Obv:** Crowned head right **Rev:** Wood
ducklings, date and denomination at right **Rev.**
Designer: Sheldon Beveridge

Date	Mintage	MS-63	Proof
1996 Proof	—	—	20.00

KM# 292 11.6638 g. 0.9250 Silver 0.3469 oz. ASW
27 mm.   **Obv:** Crowned head right **Rev:** Duck
Toling Retriever, date and denomination at right
Rev. Designer: Stan Witten

Date	Mintage	MS-63	Proof
1997 Proof	—	—	17.00

KM# 285 11.6638 g. 0.9250 Silver 0.3469 oz. ASW
27 mm.   **Obv:** Crowned head right **Rev:** Cougar
kittens, date and denomination at right **Rev.**
Designer: Stan Witten

Date	Mintage	MS-63	Proof
1996 Proof	—	—	20.00

KM# 293 11.6638 g. 0.9250 Silver 0.3469 oz.
ASW   **Obv:** Crowned head right **Rev:** Labrador

leaping left, date and denomination at right **Rev.**
Designer: Sheldon Beveridge

Date	Mintage	MS-63	Proof
1997 Proof	—	—	17.00

KM# 294 11.6638 g. 0.9250 Silver 0.3469 oz.
ASW **Obv:** Crowned head right **Rev:**
Newfoundland right, date and denomination at right
Rev. Designer: William Woodruff

Date	Mintage	MS-63	Proof
1997 Proof	—	—	17.00

KM# 295 11.6638 g. 0.9250 Silver 0.3469 oz. ASW
27 mm. **Obv:** Crowned head right **Rev:** Eskimo
dog leaping forward, date and denomination at right
Rev. Designer: Cosme Saffioti

Date	Mintage	MS-63	Proof
1997 Proof	—	—	17.00

KM# 290a 11.6380 g. 0.9250 Silver 0.3461 oz.
ASW 27.13 mm. **Obv:** Crowned head right **Obv.**
Designer: Dora dePedery-Hunt **Rev:** Redesigned
arms **Rev. Designer:** Cathy Bursey-Sabourin
Edge: Reeded

Date	Mintage	MS-63	Proof
1997 Proof	—	—	12.00
1998 Proof	—	—	12.00
1999 Proof	—	—	12.00
2000 Proof	—	—	12.00
2001 Proof	—	—	12.00
2003 Proof	—	—	12.00

KM# 313 11.6638 g. 0.9250 Silver 0.3469 oz.
ASW **Subject:** 90th Anniversary Royal Canadian
Mint **Obv:** Crowned head right **Rev:** Denomination
and date within wreath, crown above **Rev.**
Designer: W. H. J. Blakemore

Date	Mintage	MS-63	Proof
1998 Matte	25,000	—	15.00
1998 Proof	25,000	—	15.00

KM# 318 11.6638 g. 0.9250 Silver 0.3469 oz.
ASW **Obv:** Crowned head right **Rev:** Killer
Whales, date and denomination at right **Rev.**
Designer: William Woodruff

Date	Mintage	MS-63	Proof
1998 Proof	—	—	17.00

KM#319 11.6638 g. 0.9250 Silver 0.3469 oz. ASW
27 mm. **Obv:** Crowned head right **Rev:**
Humpback whale, date and denomination at right
Rev. Designer: Sheldon Beveridge

Date	Mintage	MS-63	Proof
1998 Proof	—	—	17.00

KM# 320 11.6638 g. 0.9250 Silver 0.3469 oz.
ASW **Obv:** Crowned head right **Rev:** Beluga
whales, date and denomination at right **Rev.**
Designer: Cosme Saffioti

Date	Mintage	MS-63	Proof
1998 Proof	—	—	17.00

KM#321 11.6638 g. 0.9250 Silver 0.3469 oz. ASW
27 mm. **Obv:** Crowned head right **Rev:** Blue
whale, date and denomination at right **Rev.**
Designer: Stan Witten

Date	Mintage	MS-63	Proof
1998 Proof	—	—	17.00

50 CENTS

KM# 327 11.6638 g. 0.9250 Silver 0.3469 oz. ASW **Subject:** 110 Years Canadian Soccer **Obv:** Crowned head right **Rev:** Soccer players, dates above, denomination at right **Rev. Designer:** Stan Witten

Date	Mintage	MS-63	Proof
1998 Proof	—	—	12.00

KM# 314 11.6638 g. 0.9250 Silver 0.3469 oz. ASW **Subject:** 110 Years Canadian Speed and Figure Skating **Obv:** Crowned head right **Rev:** Speed skaters, dates below, denomination above **Rev. Designer:** Sheldon Beveridge

Date	Mintage	MS-63	Proof
1998 Proof	—	—	12.00

KM# 315 11.6638 g. 0.9250 Silver 0.3469 oz. ASW **Subject:** 100 Years Canadian Ski Racing **Obv:** Crowned head right **Rev:** Skiers, dates below, denomination upper left **Rev. Designer:** Ago Aarand

Date	Mintage	MS-63	Proof
1998 Proof	—	—	12.00

KM# 328 11.6638 g. 0.9250 Silver 0.3469 oz. ASW **Subject:** 20 Years Canadian Auto Racing **Obv:** Crowned head right **Rev:** Race car divides date and denomination **Rev. Designer:** Cosme Saffioti

Date	Mintage	MS-63	Proof
1998 Proof	—	—	12.00

KM# 290b 6.9000 g. Nickel Plated Steel 27.13 mm. **Obv:** Crowned head right **Obv. Designer:** Dora dePedery-Hunt **Rev:** Redesigned arms **Rev. Designer:** Cathy Bursey-Sabourin **Edge:** Reeded

Date	Mintage	MS-63	Proof
1999 P	Est. 20,000	15.00	—
2000 P	Est. 50	3,500	—
Note: Available only in RCM presentation coin clocks			
2001 P	389,000	1.50	—
2003 P	—	5.00	—

KM# 335 11.6638 g. 0.9250 Silver 0.3469 oz. ASW **Series:** Canadian Cats **Obv:** Crowned head right **Rev:** Cymric cat, date below, denomination at bottom **Rev. Designer:** Susan Taylor

Date	Mintage	MS-63	Proof
1999 Proof	—	—	35.00

KM# 336 11.6638 g. 0.9250 Silver 0.3469 oz. ASW **Series:** Canadian Cats **Obv:** Crowned head right **Rev:** Tonkinese cat, date below, denomination at bottom **Rev. Designer:** Susan Taylor

Date	Mintage	MS-63	Proof
1999 Proof	—	—	35.00

KM# 337 11.6638 g. 0.9250 Silver 0.3469 oz. ASW **Series:** Canadian Cats **Obv:** Crowned head right **Rev:** Cougar, date and denomination below **Rev. Designer:** Susan Taylor

Date	Mintage	MS-63	Proof
1999 Proof	—	—	35.00

50 CENTS

KM# 338 11.6638 g. 0.9250 Silver 0.3469 oz.
ASW   **Series:** Canadian Cats **Obv:** Crowned head
right **Rev:** Lynx, date and denomination below **Rev.**
Designer: Susan Taylor

Date	Mintage	MS-63	Proof
1999 Proof	—	—	35.00

KM# 333 11.6638 g. 0.9250 Silver 0.3469 oz.
ASW   **Subject:** 1904 Canadian Open **Obv:**
Crowned head right **Rev:** Golfers, date at right,
denomination below **Rev. Designer:** William
Woodruff

Date	Mintage	MS-63	Proof
1999 Proof	—	—	15.00

KM# 334 11.6638 g. 0.9250 Silver 0.3469 oz.
ASW   **Subject:** First U.S.-Canadian Yacht Race
Obv: Crowned head right **Rev:** Yachts, dates at left,
denomination below **Rev. Designer:** Stan Witten

Date	Mintage	MS-63	Proof
1999 Proof	—	—	12.00

KM# 371 9.3600 g. 0.9250 Silver 0.2783 oz. ASW
27.1 mm.   **Subject:** Basketball **Obv:** Crowned
head right **Rev:** Basketball players **Rev. Designer:**
Sheldon Beveridge **Edge:** Reeded

Date	Mintage	MS-63	Proof
1999 Proof	—	—	10.00

KM# 372 9.3600 g. 0.9250 Silver 0.2783 oz. ASW
27.1 mm.   **Obv:** Crowned head right **Rev:** Football
players **Rev. Designer:** Cosme Saffioti **Edge:**
Reeded

Date	Mintage	MS-63	Proof
1999 Proof	—	—	11.00

KM# 389 9.3500 g. 0.9250 Silver 0.2781 oz.
ASW   **Obv:** Crowned head right **Rev:** Great
horned owl, facing, date and denomination at right
Rev. Designer: Susan Taylor

Date	Mintage	MS-63	Proof
2000 Proof	—	—	20.00

KM# 390 9.3500 g. 0.9250 Silver 0.2781 oz.
ASW   **Obv:** Crowned head right **Rev:** Red-tailed
hawk, dates and denomination at right

Date	Mintage	MS-63	Proof
2000 Proof	—	—	20.00

KM# 391 9.3500 g. 0.9250 Silver 0.2781 oz.
ASW   **Obv:** Crowned head right **Rev:** Osprey,
dates and denomination at right **Rev. Designer:**
Susan Taylor

Date	Mintage	MS-63	Proof
2000 Proof	—	—	20.00

KM# 392 9.3500 g. 0.9250 Silver 0.2781 oz.
ASW   **Obv:** Crowned head right **Rev:** Bald eagle,
dates and denomination at right **Rev. Designer:**
William Woodruff

Date	Mintage	MS-63	Proof
2000 Proof	—	—	20.00

KM# 393 0.9250 Silver **Subject:** Steeplechase **Obv:** Crowned head right **Rev:** Steeplechase, dates and denomination below **Rev. Designer:** Susan Taylor

Date	Mintage	MS-63	Proof
2000 Proof	—	—	12.00

KM# 394 0.9250 Silver **Subject:** Bowling **Obv:** Crowned head right **Rev. Designer:** William Woodruff

Date	Mintage	MS-63	Proof
2000 Proof	—	—	12.00

KM# 385 0.9250 Silver **Subject:** Ice Hockey **Obv:** Crowned head right **Rev:** 4 hockey players **Rev. Designer:** Stanley Witten

Date	Mintage	MS-63	Proof
2000 Proof	—	—	12.00

KM# 386 0.9250 Silver **Subject:** Curling **Obv:** Crowned head right **Rev:** Motion study of curlers, dates and denomination below **Rev. Designer:** Cosme Saffioti

Date	Mintage	MS-63	Proof
2000 Proof	—	—	12.00

KM# 420 9.3000 g. 0.9250 Silver 0.2766 oz. ASW 27.13 mm. **Series:** Festivals - Quebec **Obv:** Crowned head right **Rev:** Snowman and Chateau Frontenac **Rev. Designer:** Sylvie Daigneault **Edge:** Reeded

Date	Mintage	MS-63	Proof
2001 Proof	58,123	—	8.50

KM# 421 9.3000 g. 0.9250 Silver 0.2766 oz. ASW 27.13 mm. **Series:** Festivals - Nunavut **Obv:** Crowned head right **Rev:** Dancer, dog sled and snowmobiles **Rev. Designer:** John Mardon **Edge:** Reeded

Date	Mintage	MS-63	Proof
2001 Proof	58,123	—	8.50

KM# 422 9.3000 g. 0.9250 Silver 0.2766 oz. ASW 27.13 mm. **Series:** Festivals - Newfoundland **Obv:** Crowned head right **Rev:** Sailor and musical people **Rev. Designer:** David Craig **Edge:** Reeded

Date	Mintage	MS-63	Proof
2001 Proof	58,123	—	8.50

KM# 423 9.3000 g. 0.9250 Silver 0.2766 oz. ASW 27.13 mm. **Series:** Festivals - Prince Edward Island **Obv:** Crowned head right **Rev:** Family, juggler and building **Rev. Designer:** Brenda Whiteway **Edge:** Reeded

Date	Mintage	MS-63	Proof
2001 Proof	58,123	—	8.50

KM# 424 9.3000 g. 0.9250 Silver 0.2766 oz. ASW 27.13 mm. **Series:** Folklore - The Sled **Obv:** Crowned head right **Rev:** Family scene **Rev. Designer:** Valentina Hotz-Entin **Edge:** Reeded

Date	Mintage	MS-63	Proof
2001 Proof	28,979	—	9.00

KM# 425 9.3000 g. 0.9250 Silver 0.2766 oz. ASW 27.13 mm.   **Series:** Folklore - The Maiden's Cave **Obv:** Crowned head right **Rev:** Woman shouting **Rev. Designer:** Peter Kiss **Edge:** Reeded

Date	Mintage	MS-63	Proof
2001 Proof	28,979	—	9.00

KM# 426 9.3000 g. 0.9250 Silver 0.2766 oz. ASW 27.13 mm.   **Series:** Folklore - The Small Jumpers **Obv:** Crowned head right **Rev:** Jumping children on seashore **Rev. Designer:** Miynki Tanobe **Edge:** Reeded

Date	Mintage	MS-63	Proof
2001 Proof	28,979	—	9.00

KM# 509 6.9000 g. Nickel Plated Steel 27.13 mm.   **Obv:** Crowned head right **Rev:** National arms **Edge:** Reeded

Date	Mintage	MS-63	Proof
2001 P	—	1.50	—

KM# 444 6.9000 g. Nickel Plated Steel 27.13 mm.   **Subject:** Queen's Golden Jubilee **Obv:** Coronation crowned head right and monogram **Rev:** Canadian arms **Rev. Designer:** Bursey Sabourin **Edge:** Reeded

Date	Mintage	MS-63	Proof
2002P	14,440,000	2.50	—

KM# 444a 9.3000 g. 0.9250 Silver 0.2766 oz. ASW 27.13 mm.   **Subject:** Elizabeth II Golden Jubilee **Obv:** Crowned head right, Jubilee commemorative dates 1952-2002

Date	Mintage	MS-63	Proof
2002 Proof	100,000	—	17.50

KM# 444b 9.3000 g. 0.9250 Silver Gilt 0.2766 oz. ASW 27.13 mm.   **Subject:** Queen's Golden Jubilee **Obv:** Crowned head right and monogram **Rev:** Canadian arms **Edge:** Reeded **Note:** Special 24 karat gold-plated issue of KM#444.

Date	Mintage	MS-63	Proof
2002 Proof	32,642	—	35.00

KM# 454 9.3000 g. 0.9250 Silver 0.2766 oz. ASW 27.13 mm.   **Subject:** Nova Scotia Annapolis Valley Apple Blossom Festival **Obv:** Crowned head right **Rev. Designer:** Bonnie Ross

Date	Mintage	MS-63	Proof
2002 Proof	59,998	—	8.50

KM# 455 9.3000 g. 0.9250 Silver 0.2766 oz. ASW 27.13 mm.   **Subject:** Stratford Festival **Obv:** Crowned head right **Rev:** Couple with building in background **Rev. Designer:** Laurie McGaw

Date	Mintage	MS-63	Proof
2002 Proof	59,998	—	8.50

KM# 456 9.3000 g. 0.9250 Silver 0.2766 oz. ASW 27.13 mm.   **Subject:** Folklorama **Obv:** Crowned head right **Rev. Designer:** William Woodruff

Date	Mintage	MS-63	Proof
2002 Proof	59,998	—	8.50

KM# 457 9.3000 g. 0.9250 Silver 0.2766 oz. ASW 27.13 mm.   **Subject:** Calgary Stampede **Obv:** Crowned head right **Rev. Designer:** Stan Witten

Date	Mintage	MS-63	Proof
2002 Proof	59,998	—	8.50

KM# 458 9.3000 g. 0.9250 Silver 0.2766 oz. ASW 27.13 mm.   **Subject:** Squamish Days Logger Sports **Obv:** Crowned head right **Rev. Designer:** Jose Osio

Date	Mintage	MS-63	Proof
2002 Proof	59,998	—	8.50

KM# 459 9.3000 g. 0.9250 Silver 0.2766 oz. ASW 27.13 mm.   **Series:** Folklore and Legends **Obv:** Crowned head right **Rev:** The Shoemaker in Heaven **Rev. Designer:** Francine Gravel

Date	Mintage	MS-63	Proof
2002 Proof	19,267	—	9.50

KM# 460 9.3000 g. 0.9250 Silver 0.2766 oz. ASW 27.13 mm.   **Series:** Folklore and Legends **Subject:** The Ghost Ship **Obv:** Crowned head right **Rev. Designer:** Colette Boivin

Date	Mintage	MS-63	Proof
2002 Proof	19,267	—	9.50

KM# 461 9.3000 g. 0.9250 Silver 0.2766 oz. ASW 27.13 mm.   **Series:** Folklore and Legends **Subject:** The Pig That Wouldn't Get Over the Stile **Obv:** Crowned head right **Rev. Designer:** Laura Jolicoeur

Date	Mintage	MS-63	Proof
2002 Proof	19,267	—	9.50

KM# 494 6.9000 g. Nickel Plated Steel 27.13 mm. **Obv:** Crowned head right **Obv. Designer:** Susanna Blunt **Rev:** Reeded **Rev. Designer:** Cathy Bursey-Sabourin

Date	Mintage	MS-63	Proof
2003P W	—	5.00	—
2003P W Proof	—	—	7.50
2004P	—	5.00	—
2004P Proof	—	—	7.50
2005P	200,000	1.50	—
2005P Proof	—	—	5.00
2006P	98,000	1.50	—
2006P Proof	—	—	5.00
2007(ml)	250,000	1.50	—
2007(ml) Proof	—	—	5.00
2008(ml)	211,000	1.50	—
2008(ml) Proof	—	—	5.00
2009(ml)	150,000	1.50	—
2009(ml) Proof	—	—	5.00
2010(ml)	—	1.50	—
2010(ml) Proof	—	—	5.00
2011(ml)	—	1.50	—
2011(ml) Proof	—	—	5.00

KM# 472 11.6200 g. 0.9250 Silver 0.3456 oz. ASW 27.13 mm. **Subject:** 50th Anniversary of the Coronation of Elizabeth II **Obv:** Crowned head right, Jubilee commemorative dates 1952-2002 **Obv. Designer:** Mary Gillick

Date	Mintage	MS-63	Proof
2003 Proof	30,000	—	15.00

KM# 475 9.3000 g. 0.9250 Silver 0.2766 oz. ASW 27.13 mm. **Obv:** Crowned head right **Obv. Designer:** Dora dePédery-Hunt **Rev:** Golden daffodil **Rev. Designer:** Christie Paquet, Stan Witten

Date	Mintage	MS-63	Proof
2003 Proof	36,293	—	25.00

KM# 476 9.3000 g. 0.9250 Silver 0.2766 oz. ASW 27.13 mm. **Subject:** Yukon International Storytelling Festival **Obv:** Crowned head right **Obv. Designer:** Dora dePédery-Hunt **Rev. Designer:** Ken Anderson, Jose Oslo

Date	Mintage	MS-63	Proof
2003 Proof	—	—	11.00

KM# 477 9.3000 g. 0.9250 Silver 0.2766 oz. ASW 27.13 mm. **Subject:** Festival Acadien de Caraquet **Obv:** Crowned head right **Obv. Designer:** Dora dePédery-Hunt **Rev:** Sailboat and couple **Rev. Designer:** Susan Taylor, Hudson Design Group

Date	Mintage	MS-63	Proof
2003 Proof	—	—	11.00

KM# 478 9.3000 g. 0.9250 Silver 0.2766 oz. ASW 27.13 mm. **Subject:** Back to Batoche **Obv:** Crowned head right **Obv. Designer:** Dora dePédery-Hunt **Rev. Designer:** David Hannan, Stan Witten

Date	Mintage	MS-63	Proof
2003 Proof	—	—	11.00

KM# 479 9.3000 g. 0.9250 Silver 0.2766 oz. ASW 27.13 mm. **Subject:** Great Northern Arts Festival **Obv:** Crowned head right **Obv. Designer:** Dora dePédery-Hunt **Rev. Designer:** Dawn Oman, Susan Taylor

Date	Mintage	MS-63	Proof
2003 Proof	—	—	11.00

KM# 494a 9.3000 g. 0.9250 Silver 0.2766 oz. ASW 27.13 mm. **Obv:** Crowned head right **Obv. Designer:** Susanna Blunt **Rev:** Canadian coat of arms **Edge:** Reeded

Date	Mintage	MS-63	Proof
2004 Proof	—	—	7.50

KM# 526 1.2700 g. 0.9999 Gold 0.0408 oz. AGW 14 mm. **Subject:** Moose **Obv:** Head right **Rev:** Moose head facing right

Date	Mintage	MS-63	Proof
2004 Proof	—	—	85.00

KM# 606 9.3000 g. 0.9250 Silver 0.2766 oz. ASW 27.13 mm. **Obv:** Head right **Obv. Designer:** Susanna Blunt **Rev:** Clouded Sulphur Butterfly, hologram **Rev. Designer:** Susan Taylor

Date	Mintage	MS-63	Proof
2004 Proof	15,281	—	30.00

KM# 712 9.3000 g. 0.9250 Silver 0.2766 oz. ASW 27.13 mm. **Rev:** Hologram of Tiger Swallowtail butterfly

Date	Mintage	MS-63	Proof
2004 Proof	20,462	—	30.00

KM# 536 9.3000 g. 0.9250 Silver 0.2766 oz. ASW 27.13 mm. **Subject:** Golden rose **Obv:** Head right **Obv. Designer:** Susanna Blunt **Rev. Designer:** Christie Paquet

Date	Mintage	MS-63	Proof
2005 Proof	17,418	—	19.00

KM# 537 9.3000 g. 0.9250 Silver 0.2766 oz. ASW 27.13 mm. **Obv:** Head right **Obv. Designer:** Susanna Blunt **Rev:** Great Spangled Fritillary butterfly, hologram **Rev. Designer:** Jianping Yan

Date	Mintage	MS-63	Proof
2005 Proof	20,000	—	35.00

KM# 538 9.3000 g. 0.9250 Silver 0.2766 oz. ASW 27.13 mm. **Subject:** Toronto Maple Leafs **Obv:** Head right **Obv. Designer:** Susanna Blunt **Rev:** Darryl Sittler

Date	Mintage	MS-63	Proof
2005 Specimen	25,000	—	16.00

KM# 539 9.3000 g. 0.9250 Silver 0.2766 oz. ASW 27.13 mm. **Subject:** Toronto Maple Leafs **Obv:** Head right **Obv. Designer:** Susanna Blunt **Rev:** Dave Keon

Date	Mintage	MS-63	Proof
2005 Specimen	25,000	—	16.00

KM# 540 9.3000 g. 0.9250 Silver 0.2766 oz. ASW 27.13 mm. **Subject:** Toronto Maple Leafs **Obv:** Head right **Obv. Designer:** Susanna Blunt **Rev:** Jonny Bover

Date	Mintage	MS-63	Proof
2005 Specimen	25,000	—	16.00

KM# 541 9.3000 g. 0.9250 Silver 0.2766 oz. ASW 27.13 mm. **Subject:** Toronto Maple Leafs **Obv:** Head right **Obv. Designer:** Susanna Blunt **Rev:** Tim Horton

Date	Mintage	MS-63	Proof
2005 Specimen	25,000	—	16.00

KM# 542 1.2700 g. 0.9999 Gold 0.0408 oz. AGW **Subject:** Voyageurs **Obv:** Head right

Date	Mintage	MS-63	Proof
2005 Proof	—	—	65.00

KM# 543 9.3000 g. 0.9250 Silver 0.2766 oz. ASW **Subject:** WWII - Battle of Britain **Obv:** Head right **Rev:** Fighter plane in sky

Date	Mintage	MS-63	Proof
2005 Specimen	20,000	—	22.50

KM# 544 9.3000 g. 0.9250 Silver 0.2766 oz. ASW 27.13 mm. **Subject:** WWII - Battle of Scheldt **Obv:** Head right **Obv. Designer:** Susanna Blunt **Rev:** Four soldiers walking down road **Rev. Designer:** Peter Mossman

Date	Mintage	MS-63	Proof
2005 Specimen	20,000	—	19.00

KM# 545 9.3000 g. 0.9250 Silver 0.2766 oz. ASW 27.13 mm. **Subject:** WWII - Battle of the Atlantic **Obv:** Head right **Obv. Designer:** Susanna Blunt **Rev:** Merchant ship sinking **Rev. Designer:** Peter Mossman

Date	Mintage	MS-63	Proof
2005 Specimen	20,000	—	19.00

KM# 546 9.3000 g. 0.9250 Silver 0.2766 oz. ASW 27.13 mm. **Subject:** WWII - Conquest of Sicily **Obv:** Head right **Obv. Designer:** Susanna Blunt **Rev:** Tank among town ruins **Rev. Designer:** Peter Mossman

Date	Mintage	MS-63	Proof
2005 Specimen	20,000	—	19.00

KM# 547 9.3000 g. 0.9250 Silver 0.2766 oz. ASW 27.13 mm. **Subject:** WWII - Liberation of the Netherlands **Obv:** Head right **Obv. Designer:** Susanna Blunt **Rev:** Soldiers in parade, one holding flag **Rev. Designer:** Peter Mossman

Date	Mintage	MS-63	Proof
2005 Specimen	20,000	—	19.00

KM# 548 9.3000 g. 0.9250 Silver 0.2766 oz. ASW 27.13 mm. **Subject:** WWII - Raid of Dieppe **Obv:** Head right **Obv. Designer:** Susanna Blunt **Rev:** Three soldiers exiting landing craft **Rev. Designer:** Peter Mossman

Date	Mintage	MS-63	Proof
2005 Specimen	20,000	—	19.00

KM# 577 9.3000 g. 0.9250 Silver 0.2766 oz. ASW 27.13 mm. **Subject:** Montreal Canadiens **Obv:** Head right **Obv. Designer:** Susanna Blunt **Rev:** Guy LaFleur

Date	Mintage	MS-63	Proof
2005 Specimen	25,000	—	17.50

KM# 578 9.3000 g. 0.9250 Silver 0.2766 oz. ASW 27.13 mm. **Subject:** Montreal Canadiens **Obv:** Head right **Obv. Designer:** Susanna Blunt **Rev:** Jaque Plante

Date	Mintage	MS-63	Proof
2005 Specimen	25,000	—	17.50

KM# 579 9.3000 g. 0.9250 Silver 0.2766 oz. ASW 27.13 mm. **Subject:** Montreal Canadiens **Obv:** Head right **Obv. Designer:** Susanna Blunt **Rev:** Jean Beliveau

Date	Mintage	MS-63	Proof
2005 Specimen	25,000	—	17.50

KM# 580 9.3000 g. 0.9250 Silver 0.2766 oz. ASW 27.13 mm. **Subject:** Montreal Canadiens **Obv:** Head right **Obv. Designer:** Susanna Blunt **Rev:** Maurice Richard

Date	Mintage	MS-63	Proof
2005 Specimen	25,000	—	17.50

KM# 599 9.3000 g. 0.9250 Silver 0.2766 oz. ASW 27.13 mm. **Obv:** Head right **Obv. Designer:** Susanna Blunt **Rev:** Monarch butterfly, colorized **Rev. Designer:** Susan Taylor

Date	Mintage	MS-63	Proof
2005 Proof	20,000		35.00

KM# 925a 1.2700 g. 0.9990 Gold 0.0408 oz. AGW 13.92 mm. **Rev:** Voyagers with northern lights above **Rev. Designer:** Emanuel Hahn

Date	Mintage	MS-63	Proof
2005 Proof	Est. 25,000	—	100

KM# 648 9.3000 g. 0.9250 Silver 0.2766 oz. ASW **Subject:** Golden Daisy **Obv:** Head right

Date	Mintage	MS-63	Proof
2006	18,190	22.00	

KM# 649 9.3000 g. 0.9250 Silver 0.2766 oz. ASW **Subject:** Short-tailed swallowtail **Obv:** Head right **Rev:** Colorized butterfly

Date	Mintage	MS-63	Proof
2006	20,000	25.00	—

KM# 650 9.3000 g. 0.9250 Silver 0.2766 oz. ASW **Obv:** Head right **Rev:** Silvery blue hologram

Date	Mintage	MS-63	Proof
2006	16,000	25.00	—

KM# 651 9.3000 g. 0.9250 Silver 0.2766 oz. ASW **Subject:** Cowboy **Obv:** Head right

Date	Mintage	MS-63	Proof
2006	—	17.50	—

KM# 716 9.3000 g. 0.9250 Silver 0.2766 oz. ASW **Rev:** Multicolor holiday ornaments

Date	Mintage	MS-63	Proof
2006	16,989	17.50	—

KM# 717 1.2400 g. 0.9990 Gold 0.0398 oz. AGW 13.9 mm. **Rev:** Wolf

Date	Mintage	MS-63	Proof
2006 Proof	—	—	100

KM# 926 1.2400 g. 0.9990 Gold 0.0398 oz. AGW 13.9 mm. **Rev:** Cowboy and bronco rider

Date	Mintage	MS-63	Proof
2006 Proof	—	—	100

KM# 715 9.3000 g. 0.9250 Silver 0.2766 oz. ASW 27.12 mm. **Rev:** Forget-me-not flower

Date	Mintage	MS-63	Proof
2007 Proof	22,882	—	29.00

KM# 927 1.2400 g. 0.9990 Gold 0.0398 oz. AGW 13.9 mm. **Subject:** Gold Louis

Date	Mintage	MS-63	Proof
2007 Proof	—	—	100

KM# 777 1.2400 g. 0.9990 Gold 0.0398 oz. AGW 13.9 mm. **Subject:** DeHavilland beaver

Date	Mintage	MS-63	Proof
2008 Proof	20,000	—	100

KM# 778 20.0000 g. 0.9250 Silver 0.5948 oz. ASW 34.06 mm. **Subject:** Milk delivery **Obv:** Bust right **Rev:** Cow head and milk can **Shape:** Triangle

Date	Mintage	MS-63	Proof
2008 Proof	25,000	—	35.00

KM# 779 9.3000 g. 0.9250 Silver 0.2766 oz. ASW **Rev:** Multicolor snowman

Date	Mintage	MS-63	Proof
2008	—	17.50	—

KM# 780 9.3000 g. 0.9250 Silver 0.2766 oz. ASW **Subject:** Ottawa Mint Centennial 1908-2008

Date	Mintage	MS-63	Proof
2008	—	20.00	—

KM# 845 9.3000 g. 0.9250 Silver 0.2766 oz. ASW 27.13 mm. **Rev:** Calgary Flames lenticular design, old and new logos

Date	Mintage	MS-63	Proof
2009	—	15.00	—

KM# 846 9.3000 g. 0.9250 Silver 0.2766 oz. ASW 27.13 mm. **Rev:** Edmonton Oiler's lenticular design, old and new logos

Date	Mintage	MS-63	Proof
2009	—	15.00	—

KM# 847 9.3000 g. 0.9250 Silver 0.2766 oz. ASW 27.13 mm. **Rev:** Montreal Canadiens lenticular design, old and new logos

Date	Mintage	MS-63	Proof
2009	—	15.00	—

KM# 848 9.3000 g. 0.9250 Silver 0.2766 oz. ASW 27.13 mm. **Rev:** Ottawa Senators lenticular design, old and new logos

Date	Mintage	MS-63	Proof
2009	—	15.00	—

KM# 849 9.3000 g. 0.9250 Silver 0.2766 oz. ASW 27.13 mm. **Rev:** Toronto Maple Leafs lenticular design, old and new logos

Date	Mintage	MS-63	Proof
2009	—	15.00	—

KM# 850 9.3000 g. 0.9250 Silver 0.2766 oz. ASW 27.13 mm. **Rev:** Vancouver Canucks lenticular design, old and new logos

Date	Mintage	MS-63	Proof
2009	—	15.00	—

KM# 857 6.9000 g. Nickel Plated Steel 35 mm. **Rev:** Calgary Flames lenticular old and new logos

Date	Mintage	MS-63	Proof
2009	—	25.00	—

KM# 858 6.9000 g. Nickel Plated Steel 35 mm. **Rev:** Edmonton Oilers lenticular old and new logos

Date	Mintage	MS-63	Proof
2009	—	25.00	—

KM# 859 35.0000 g. Nickel Plated Steel 35 mm. **Rev:** Montreal Canadians lenticular old and new logo

Date	Mintage	MS-63	Proof
2009	—	25.00	—

KM# 860 6.9000 g. Nickel Plated Steel 35 mm. **Rev:** Ottawa Senators lenticular old and new logos

Date	Mintage	MS-63	Proof
2009	—	25.00	—

KM# 861 6.9000 g. Nickel Plated Steel 35 mm. **Rev:** Toronto Maple Leafs lenticular old and new logos

Date	Mintage	MS-63	Proof
2009	—	25.00	—

KM# 862 6.9000 g. Nickel Plated Steel 35 mm. **Rev:** Vancouver Canucks lenticular old and new logos

Date	Mintage	MS-63	Proof
2009	—	25.00	—

KM# 887 19.1000 g. Copper-Nickel 34.06 mm. **Subject:** Six-string national guitar **Obv:** Bust right

Obv. Legend: Elizabeth II DG Regina **Obv. Designer:** Susanna Blunt **Rev:** Hologram with 6 "strings" **Rev. Legend:** 50 cents Canada **Shape:** Triangle

Date	Mintage	MS-63	Proof
2009 Proof	30,000	—	50.00

KM# 936 9.3000 g. Nickel **Rev:** Vancouver Canucks goalie jersey

Date	Mintage	MS-63	Proof
2000	—	15.00	—

KM# 937 6.9000 g. Nickel Plated Steel 35 mm. **Rev:** Calgary Flames player - colorized

Date	Mintage	MS-63	Proof
2009	—	15.00	—

KM# 938 6.9000 g. Nickel Plated Steel 35 mm. **Rev:** Edmonton Oilers player

Date	Mintage	MS-63	Proof
2009	—	15.00	—

KM# 939 6.9000 g. Nickel Plated Steel 35 mm. **Rev:** Toronto Maple Leafs player

Date	Mintage	MS-63	Proof
2009	—	15.00	—

KM# 940 6.9000 g. Nickel Plated Steel 35 mm. **Rev:** Montreal Canadiens player

Date	Mintage	MS-63	Proof
2009	—	15.00	—

KM# 941 6.9000 g. Nickel Plated Steel 35 mm. **Rev:** Ottawa Senators player

Date	Mintage	MS-63	Proof
2009	—	15.00	—

KM# 1035 Brass Plated Steel **Subject:** Christmas toy train **Rev:** movement from far to close

Date	Mintage	MS-63	Proof
2009	—	17.50	—

KM# 961 6.9000 g. Nickel Plated Steel 35 mm. **Rev:** Bob sleigh

Date	Mintage	MS-63	Proof
2010	—	15.00	—

KM# 961a 6.9000 g. Nickel Plated Steel 35 mm. **Rev:** Bob sleigh - red enamel

Date	Mintage	MS-63	Proof
2010	—	15.00	—

KM# 962 6.9000 g. Nickel Plated Steel 35 mm.
Rev: Speed skating

Date	Mintage	MS-63	Proof
2010	—	15.00	—

KM# 962a 6.9000 g. Nickel Plated Steel 35 mm.
Rev: Speed skating - red enamel

Date	Mintage	MS-63	Proof
2010	—	15.00	—

KM# 963 6.9000 g. Nickel Plated Steel 35 mm.
Rev: Miga in bob sleigh

Date	Mintage	MS-63	Proof
2010	—	15.00	—

KM# 964 6.9000 g. Nickel Plated Steel 35 mm.
Rev: Miga in hockey

Date	Mintage	MS-63	Proof
2010	—	15.00	—

KM# 965 6.9000 g. Nickel Plated Steel 35 mm.
Rev: Quatchi in ice hockey

Date	Mintage	MS-63	Proof
2010	—	15.00	—

KM# 966 6.9000 g. Nickel Plated Steel 35 mm.
Rev: Sumi Para Sledge

Date	Mintage	MS-63	Proof
2010	—	15.00	—

KM# 967 6.9000 g. Nickel Plated Steel 35 mm.
Rev: Figure-skating mascot **Edge:** Reeded

Date	Mintage	MS-63	Proof
2010	—	15.00	—

KM# 968 6.9000 g. Nickel Plated Steel 35 mm.
Rev: Free-style mascot

Date	Mintage	MS-63	Proof
2010	—	15.00	—

KM# 969 6.9000 g. Nickel Plated Steel 35 mm.
Rev: Skeleton mascot

Date	Mintage	MS-63	Proof
2010	—	15.00	—

KM# 970 6.9000 g. Nickel Plated Steel 35 mm.
Rev: Parallel giant slalom mascot

Date	Mintage	MS-63	Proof
2010	—	15.00	—

KM# 971 6.9000 g. Nickel Plated Steel 35 mm.
Rev: Alpine skiing mascot

Date	Mintage	MS-63	Proof
2010	—	15.00	—

KM# 972 6.9000 g. Nickel Plated Steel 35 mm.
Rev: Para Olympic alpine skiing mascott

Date	Mintage	MS-63	Proof
2010	—	15.00	—

KM# 973 6.9000 g. Nickel Plated Steel 35 mm.
Rev: Snowboard mascot

Date	Mintage	MS-63	Proof
2010	—	15.00	—

KM# 974 6.9000 g. Nickel Plated Steel 35 mm.
Rev: Speed-skating mascott

Date	Mintage	MS-63	Proof
2010	—	15.00	—

KM# 986 12.6100 g. Brass Plated Steel **Rev:** Dasplerosaurus Torosus - 3-D lenticular movement

Date	Mintage	MS-63	Proof
2010 Specimen	—	—	40.00

KM# 1015 12.6100 g. Brass Plated Steel 35 mm. **Rev:** Sinosauropteryx

Date	Mintage	MS-63	Proof
2010	—	25.00	—

KM# 1016 12.6100 g. Brass Plated Steel 35 mm. **Rev:** Albertosaurus

Date	Mintage	MS-63	Proof
2010	—	25.00	—

KM# 1043   Nickel Plated Steel   **Rev:** Santa Claus transforms into Rudolf the red-nosed reindeer

Date	Mintage	MS-63	Proof
2010	—	17.50	—

DOLLAR

KM# 30   23.3276 g. 0.8000 Silver 0.6000 oz. ASW 36 mm.   **Subject:** Silver Jubilee **Obv:** Bust left **Obv. Designer:** Percy Metcalfe **Rev:** Voyager, date and denomination below **Rev. Designer:** Emanuel Hahn

Date	Mintage	F-12	VF-20	XF-40	AU-50	MS-60	MS-63	Proof
1935	428,707	20.00	25.00	37.50	42.00	49.00	85.00	4,500

KM# 31   23.3276 g. 0.8000 Silver 0.6000 oz. ASW 36 mm.   **Obv:** Crowned bust left **Obv. Designer:** E. B. MacKennal **Rev:** Voyageur, date and denomination below **Rev. Designer:** Emanuel Hahn

Date	Mintage	F-12	VF-20	XF-40	AU-50	MS-60	MS-63	Proof
1936	339,600	20.00	22.00	35.00	42.00	49.00	105	5,000

| Pointed 7 | Blunt 7 | Maple leaf |

KM# 37 23.3276 g. 0.8000 Silver 0.6000 oz. ASW 36 mm. **Obv:** Head left **Obv. Designer:** T. H. Paget **Rev:** Voyageur, date and denomination below **Rev. Designer:** Emanuel Hahn

Date	Mintage	F-12	VF-20	XF-40	AU-50	MS-60	MS-63	Proof
1937	207,406	20.00	21.00	22.50	27.50	30.00	120	—
1937 Mirror Proof	1,295	—	—	—	—	—	—	650
1937 Matte Proof	Inc. above	—	—	—	—	—	—	250
1938	90,304	30.00	42.00	80.00	95.00	120	210	6,000
1945	38,391	90.00	180	210	270	350	600	2,000
1946	93,055	20.00	30.00	42.00	55.00	115	350	1,800
1947 Pointed 7		70.00	95.00	150	180	350	1,700	3,500
1947 Blunt 7	65,595	55.00	70.00	95.00	125	150	300	4,500
1947 Maple leaf	21,135	150	180	210	240	300	600	1,800

KM# 38 23.3276 g. 0.8000 Silver 0.6000 oz. ASW 36 mm. **Subject:** Royal Visit **Obv:** Head left **Obv. Designer:** T. H. Paget **Rev:** Tower at center of building, date and denomination below **Rev. Designer:** Emanuel Hahn

Date	Mintage	F-12	VF-20	XF-40	AU-50	MS-60	MS-63	Proof
1939	1,363,816	—	—	BV	20.00	22.00	35.00	—
1939		—	—	—	—	—	—	475
Note: Matte specimen								
1939 Proof		—	—	—	—	—	—	750
Note: Mirror specimen								

KM# 46 23.3276 g. 0.8000 Silver 0.6000 oz. ASW 36 mm. **Obv:** Head left, modified left legend **Obv. Designer:** T. H. Paget **Rev:** Voyageur, date and denomination below **Rev. Designer:** Emanuel Hahn

Date	Mintage	F-12	VF-20	XF-40	AU-50	MS-60	MS-63	Proof
1948	18,780	750	900	1,500	1,650	1,950	3,000	4,500
1950	261,002	—	BV	20.00	22.00	30.00	75.00	1,200
Note: With 3 water lines								
1950 Matte Proof	—	—	—	—	—	—	—	—
Note: With 4 water lines, 1 known								
1950	Inc. above	20.00	22.00	31.50	42.00	60.00	135	2,250
Note: Amprior with 2-1/2 water lines								
1951	416,395	—	—	BV	20.00	25.00	34.50	975
Note: With 3 water lines								
1951	Inc. above	55.00	75.00	90.00	150	265	600	3,000
Note: Amprior with 1-1/2 water lines								
1952	406,148	—	—	BV	20.00	25.00	37.50	1,500
Note: With 3 water lines								
1952	Inc. above	BV	20.00	33.00	45.00	60.00	150	1,900
Note: Amprior type								
1952	Inc. above	—	BV	20.00	22.00	30.00	70.00	—
Note: Without water lines								

KM# 47 23.3276 g. 0.8000 Silver 0.6000 oz. ASW 36 mm.   **Subject:** Newfoundland **Obv:** Head left **Obv. Designer:** T. H. Paget **Rev:** "The Matthew", John Cabot's ship, date and denomination below **Rev. Designer:** Thomas Shingles

Date	Mintage	F-12	VF-20	XF-40	AU-50	MS-60	MS-63	Proof
1949	672,218	BV	20.00	25.00	27.50	34.50	42.00	—
1949 Specimen proof	—	—	—	—	—	—	—	1,350

KM# 54 23.3276 g. 0.8000 Silver 0.6000 oz. ASW 36 mm.   **Obv:** Laureate bust right **Obv. Designer:** Mary Gillick **Rev:** Voyageur, date and denomination below **Rev. Designer:** Emanuel Hahn **Note:** All genuine circulation strike 1955 Amprior dollars have a die break running along the top of TI in the word GRATIA on the obverse.

Date	Mintage	F-12	VF-20	XF-40	AU-50	MS-60	MS-63	Proof
1953	1,074,578	—	—	—	BV	20.00	37.50	600
Note: Without strap, wire rim								
1953	Inc. above	—	—	—	BV	20.00	37.50	—
Note: With strap, flat rim								
1954	246,606	—	BV	20.00	25.00	45.00	85.00	—
1955	268,105	—	BV	20.00	22.50	40.00	70.00	—
Note: With 3 water lines								
1955	Inc. above	70.00	100.00	135	150	285	600	—
Note: Amprior with 1-1/2 water lines* and die break								
1956	209,092	BV	20.00	22.00	25.00	45.00	115	—
1957	496,389	—	—	—	BV	20.00	25.00	—
Note: With 3 water lines								
1957	Inc. above	—	BV	20.00	22.00	24.00	45.00	—
Note: With 1 water line								
1959	1,443,502	—	—	—	—	BV	20.00	—
1960	1,420,486	—	—	—	—	BV	20.00	—
1961	1,262,231	—	—	—	—	BV	20.00	—

Date	Mintage	F-12	VF-20	XF-40	AU-50	MS-60	MS-63	Proof
1962	1,884,789	—	—	—	—	BV	20.00	—
1963	4,179,981	—	—	—	—	BV	20.00	—

KM# 55 23.3276 g. 0.8000 Silver 0.6000 oz. ASW 36 mm.   **Subject:** British Columbia **Obv:** Laureate bust right **Obv. Designer:** Mary Gillick **Rev:** Totem Pole, dates at left, denomination below **Rev. Designer:** Stephan Trenka

Date	Mintage	F-12	VF-20	XF-40	AU-50	MS-60	MS-63	Proof
ND(1958)	3,039,630	—	—	—	BV	20.00	22.50	—

KM# 58 23.3276 g. 0.8000 Silver 0.6000 oz. ASW 36 mm.   **Subject:** Charlottetown **Obv:** Laureate bust right **Rev:** Design at center, dates at outer edges, denomination below **Rev. Designer:** Dinko Voldanovic

Date	Mintage	F-12	VF-20	XF-40	AU-50	MS-60	MS-63	Proof
ND(1964)	7,296,832	—	—	—	—	BV	20.00	—
ND(1964) Specimen proof	Inc. above	—	—	—	—	—	—	250

Large beads   Medium beads   Small beads

KM# 64.1 23.3276 g. 0.8000 Silver 0.6000 oz. ASW 36 mm.   **Obv:** Young bust right **Obv. Designer:** Arnold Machin **Rev:** Voyageur, date and denomination below **Rev. Designer:** Emanual Hahn

Date	Mintage	F-12	VF-20	XF-40	AU-50	MS-60	MS-63	Proof
1965	10,768,569	—	—	—	—	BV	20.00	—
Note: Small beads, pointed 5								
1965	Inc. above	—	—	—	—	BV	20.00	—
Note: Small beads, blunt 5								
1965	Inc. above	—	—	—	—	BV	20.00	—
Note: Large beads, blunt 5								
1965	Inc. above	—	—	—	BV	20.00	23.00	—
Note: Large beads, pointed 5								
1965	Inc. above	—	—	BV	20.00	22.50	55.00	—
Note: Medium beads, pointed 5								
1966	9,912,178	—	—	—	—	BV	20.00	—
Note: Large beads								
1966	485	—	—	1,800	2,000	2,200	3,500	—
Note: Small beads								

KM# 70 23.3280 g. 0.8000 Silver 0.6000 oz. ASW 36 mm. **Subject:** Confederation Centennial **Obv:** Young bust right **Obv. Designer:** Arnold Machin **Rev:** Goose left, dates below, denomination above **Rev. Designer:** Alex Colville

Date	Mintage	MS-63	Proof
1967	6,767,496	20.00	22.00

KM# 76.1 15.6400 g. Nickel 32 mm. **Obv:** Young bust right **Obv. Designer:** Arnold Machin **Rev:** Voyageur, date and denomination below **Rev. Designer:** Emanuel Hahn

Date	Mintage	MS-63	P/L	Proof
1968 Small island	—	8.50	—	—
1968	1,408,143	1.50	2.00	—
1968 No Island	—	10.00	—	—
1968	—	—	25.00	—
Note: Doubled die; exhibits extra water lines				
1968	5,579,714	2.00	—	—
1969	4,809,313	2.00	—	—
1969	594,258	—	2.00	—
1972	2,676,041	2.25	—	—
1972	405,865	—	2.50	—

KM# 78 15.6000 g. Nickel 32 mm. **Subject:** Manitoba **Obv:** Young bust right **Rev:** Pasque flower divides dates and denomination **Rev. Designer:** Raymond Taylor

Date	Mintage	MS-63	P/L	Proof
1970	4,140,058	2.00	—	—
1970	645,869	—	2.50	—

KM# 79 15.7000 g. Nickel 32.1 mm. **Subject:** British Columbia **Obv:** Young bust right **Rev:** Shield divides dates, denomination below, flowers above **Rev. Designer:** Thomas Shingles

Date	Mintage	MS-63	P/L	Proof
1971	4,260,781	2.00	—	—
1971	468,729	—	2.25	—

KM# 80 23.3276 g. 0.5000 Silver 0.3750 oz. ASW 36 mm. **Subject:** British Columbia **Obv:** Young bust right **Rev:** Crowned arms with supporters divide dates, maple at top divides denomination, crowned lion atop crown on shield **Rev. Designer:** Patrick Brindley

Date	Mintage	MS-63	P/L	Proof
1971 Specimen	585,674	—	11.50	—

KM# 64.2a 23.3276 g. 0.5000 Silver 0.3750 oz. ASW 36 mm. **Obv:** Smaller young bust right **Obv. Designer:** Arnold Machin **Rev:** Voyageur **Rev. Designer:** Emanuel Hahn

Date	Mintage	MS-63	P/L	Proof
1972	341,598	—	—	11.50

KM# 82 Nickel 32 mm.   **Subject:** Prince Edward Island **Obv:** Young bust right **Rev:** Building, inscription below divides dates, denomination above **Rev. Designer:** Terry Manning

Date	Mintage	MS-63	P/L	Proof
1973	3,196,452	2.00	—	—
1973 (c)	466,881	—	2.50	—

KM# 83 23.3276 g. 0.5000 Silver 0.3750 oz. ASW 36 mm.   **Obv:** Young bust right **Rev:** Mountie left, dates below, denomination at right **Rev. Designer:** Paul Cedarberg

Date	Mintage	MS-63	P/L	Proof
1973 Specimen	1,031,271	—	11.50	—
1973 Specimen	—	—	25.00	—

Note: Dollar housed in special blue case with RCMP crest.

KM# 88 Nickel 32 mm.   **Subject:** Winnipeg Centennial **Obv:** Young bust right **Rev:** Zeros frame pictures, dates below, denomination at bottom **Rev. Designer:** Paul Pederson and Patrick Brindley

Date	Mintage	MS-63	P/L	Proof
1974	2,799,363	2.00	—	—
1974 (c)	363,786	—	2.50	—

KM# 88a 0.5000 Silver 36 mm.   **Subject:** Winnipeg Centennial **Obv:** Young bust right **Rev:** Zeros frame pictures, dates below, denomination at bottom **Rev. Designer:** Paul Pederson and Patrick Brindley

Date	Mintage	MS-63	P/L	Proof
1974 Specimen	728,947	—	11.50	—

KM# 76.2 15.6200 g. Nickel 32 mm.   **Obv:** Smaller young bust right **Obv. Designer:** Arnold Machin **Rev:** Voyageur **Rev. Designer:** Emanuel Hahn

Date	Mintage	MS-63	P/L	Proof
1975	3,256,000	1.50	—	—
1975	322,325	—	2.50	—
1976	2,498,204	1.50	—	—
1976	274,106	—	2.50	—

KM# 97 23.3276 g. 0.5000 Silver 0.3750 oz. ASW 36 mm.   **Subject:** Calgary **Obv:** Youmg bust right **Rev:** Figure on bucking horse, dates divided below, denomination above **Rev. Designer:** Donald D. Paterson

Date	Mintage	MS-63	P/L	Proof
1975 Specimen	930,956	—	11.50	—

KM# 76.3 Nickel 32 mm.   **Obv:** Young bust right **Obv. Designer:** Arnold Machin **Rev:** Voyageur **Rev. Designer:** Emanuel Hahn **Note:** Only known in prooflike sets with 1976 obverse slightly modified.

Date	Mintage	MS-63	P/L	Proof
1975	Inc. above	—	3.00	—

Note: mule with 1976 obv.

KM# 106 23.3276 g. 0.5000 Silver 0.3750 oz. ASW 36 mm.   **Subject:** Parliament Library **Obv:** Young bust right **Rev:** Library building, dates below, denomination above **Rev. Designer:** Walter Ott and Patrick Brindley

Date	Mintage	MS-63	P/L	Proof
1976 Specimen	578,708	—	11.50	—
1976 Proof	Inc. above	—	—	25.00

Note: Blue case VIP

KM# 117 Nickel 32 mm. **Obv:** Young bust right **Obv. Designer:** Arnold Machin **Rev:** Voyageur modified **Rev. Designer:** Emanuel Hahn

Date	Mintage	MS-63	P/L	Proof
1977	1,393,745	3.50	—	—
1977	—	—	4.00	—

KM# 118 23.3276 g. 0.5000 Silver 0.3750 oz. ASW 36 mm. **Subject:** Silver Jubilee **Obv:** Young bust right, dates below **Rev:** Throne, denomination below **Rev. Designer:** Raymond Lee

Date	Mintage	MS-63	P/L	Proof
1977 Specimen	744,848	—	11.50	—
1977 Specimen	Inc. above	—	45.00	—

Note: red case VIP

KM# 120.1 15.5000 g. Nickel 32.1 mm. **Obv:** Young bust right **Obv. Designer:** Arnold Machin **Rev:** Voyageur, date and denomination below **Rev. Designer:** Emanuel Hahn **Note:** Modified design.

Date	Mintage	MS-63	Proof
1978	2,948,488	1.50	—
1979	2,954,842	1.50	—
1980	3,291,221	1.50	—
1981	2,778,900	1.50	—
1981 Proof	—	—	5.25
1982	1,098,500	1.50	—
1982 Proof	180,908	—	5.25
1983	2,267,525	1.50	—
1983 Proof	166,779	—	5.25
1984	1,223,486	1.50	—
1984 Proof	161,602	—	6.00
1985	3,104,092	1.50	—
1985 Proof	153,950	—	7.00
1986	3,089,225	2.00	—
1986 Proof	176,224	—	7.50
1987	287,330	3.50	—
1987 Proof	175,686	—	7.50

KM# 121 23.3276 g. 0.5000 Silver 0.3750 oz. ASW 36 mm. **Subject:** XI Commonwealth Games **Obv:** Young bust right **Rev:** Commonwealth games, logo at center **Rev. Designer:** Raymond Taylor

Date	Mintage	MS-63	P/L	Proof
1978 Specimen	709,602	—	11.50	—

KM# 124 23.3276 g. 0.5000 Silver 0.3750 oz. ASW 36 mm. **Subject:** Griffon **Obv:** Young bust right **Rev:** Ship, dates below, denomination above **Rev. Designer:** Walter Schluep

Date	Mintage	MS-63	P/L	Proof
1979 Specimen	826,695	—	13.00	—

KM# 128 23.3276 g. 0.5000 Silver 0.3750 oz. ASW 36 mm. **Subject:** Arctic Territories **Obv:** Young bust right **Rev:** Bear right, date below, denomination above **Rev. Designer:** Donald D. Paterson

Date	Mintage	MS-63	P/L	Proof
1980 Specimen	539,617	—	22.00	—

KM# 130 23.3276 g. 0.5000 Silver 0.3750 oz. ASW 36 mm.   **Subject:** Transcontinental Railroad **Obv:** Young bust right **Rev:** Train engine and map, date below, denomination above **Rev. Designer:** Christopher Gorey

Date	Mintage	MS-63	P/L	Proof
1981	699,494	8.50	—	—
1981 Proof	—	—	—	14.00

KM# 133 23.3276 g. 0.5000 Silver 0.3750 oz. ASW 36 mm.   **Subject:** Regina **Obv:** Young bust right **Rev:** Cattle skull divides dates and denomination below **Rev. Designer:** Huntley Brown

Date	Mintage	MS-63	Proof
1982	144,930	11.50	—
1982 Proof	758,958	—	11.50

KM# 134 15.4200 g. Nickel 32 mm.   **Subject:** Constitution **Obv:** Young bust right **Rev:** Meeting of Government **Rev. Designer:** Ago Aarand

Date	Mintage	MS-63	P/L	Proof
1982	9,709,422	3.00	6.00	—

KM# 138 23.3276 g. 0.5000 Silver 0.3750 oz. ASW 36 mm.   **Subject:** Edmonton University Games **Obv:** Young bust right **Rev:** Athlete within game logo, date and denomination below **Rev. Designer:** Carola Tietz

Date	Mintage	MS-63	Proof
1983	159,450	11.50	—
1983 Proof	506,847	—	11.50

KM# 140 23.3276 g. 0.5000 Silver 0.3750 oz. ASW 36 mm. **Subject:** Toronto Sesquicentennial **Obv:** Young bust right **Rev. Designer:** D. J. Craig

Date	Mintage	MS-63	Proof
1984	133,610	11.50	—
1984 Proof	732,542	—	11.50

KM# 141 15.5000 g. Nickel 32 mm. **Subject:** Jacques Cartier **Obv:** Young bust right **Rev:** Cross with shield above figures **Rev. Designer:** Hector Greville

Date	Mintage	MS-63	Proof
1984	7,009,323	3.50	—
1984 Proof	87,760	—	6.00

KM# 143 23.3276 g. 0.5000 Silver 0.3750 oz. ASW 36 mm. **Subject:** National Parks **Obv:** Young bust right **Rev:** Moose right, dates above, denomination below **Rev. Designer:** Karel Rohlicek

Date	Mintage	MS-63	Proof
1985	163,314	11.50	—
1985 Proof	733,354	—	12.50

KM# 120.2 Nickel 32.13 mm. **Obv:** Young bust right **Rev:** Voyageur **Note:** Mule with New Zealand 50 cent, KM-37 obverse.

Date	Mintage	MS-63	Proof
1985	—	3,000	—

KM# 149 23.3276 g. 0.5000 Silver 0.3750 oz. ASW 36 mm. **Subject:** Vancouver **Obv:** Young bust right **Rev:** Train left, dates divided below, denomination above **Rev. Designer:** Elliot John Morrison

Date	Mintage	MS-63	Proof
1986	125,949	11.50	—
1986 Proof	680,004	—	11.50

DOLLAR

KM# 157 7.0000 g. Aureate-Bronze Plated Nickel 26.5 mm. **Obv:** Young bust right **Obv. Designer:** Arnold Machin **Rev:** Loon right, date and denomination below **Rev. Designer:** Robert R. Carmichael **Shape:** 11-sided

Date	Mintage	MS-63	Proof
1987	205,405,000	2.25	—
1987 Proof	178,120	—	8.00
1988	138,893,539	2.25	—
1988 Proof	175,259	—	6.75
1989	184,773,902	3.00	—
1989 Proof	170,928	—	6.75

KM# 154 23.3276 g. 0.5000 Silver 0.3750 oz. ASW 36 mm. **Subject:** John Davis **Obv:** Young bust right **Rev:** Ship "John Davis" with masts, rock in background, dates below, denomination at bottom **Rev. Designer:** Christopher Gorey

Date	Mintage	MS-63	Proof
1987	118,722	11.50	—
1987 Proof	602,374	—	12.00

KM# 161 23.3276 g. 0.5000 Silver 0.3750 oz. ASW 36 mm. **Subject:** Ironworks **Obv:** Young bust right **Rev:** Ironworkers, date and denomination below **Rev. Designer:** Robert R. Carmichael

Date	Mintage	MS-63	Proof
1988	106,872	11.50	—
1988 Proof	255,013	—	17.50

DOLLAR

KM# 168 23.3276 g. 0.5000 Silver 0.3750 oz. ASW 36 mm. **Subject:** MacKenzie River **Obv:** Young bust right **Rev:** People in canoe, date above, denomination below **Rev. Designer:** John Mardon

Date	Mintage	MS-63	Proof
1989	99,774	13.50	—
1989 Proof	244,062	—	17.50

KM# 186 7.0000 g. Aureate-Bronze Plated Nickel 26.5 mm. **Obv:** Crowned head right **Obv. Designer:** Dora dePedery-Hunt **Rev:** Loon right, date and denomination **Rev. Designer:** Robert R. Carmichael **Shape:** 11-sided

Date	Mintage	MS-63	Proof
1990	68,402,000	1.75	—
1990 Proof	140,649	—	7.00
1991	23,156,000	1.75	—
1991 Proof	131,888	—	13.00
1993	33,662,000	2.00	—
1993 Proof	143,065	—	6.00
1994	16,232,530	2.00	—
1994 Proof	104,485	—	7.00
1995	27,492,630	2.25	—
1995 Proof	101,560	—	7.00
1996	17,101,000	2.00	—
1996 Proof	112,835	—	7.50
1997	—	5.00	—
1997 Proof	113,647	—	8.00
1998	—	2.50	—
1998W Prooflike	—	—	—
1998 Proof	93,632	—	10.00
1999	—	2.00	—
1999 Proof	95,113	—	8.00
2000	—	2.00	—
2000W Prooflike	—	—	—
2000 Proof	90,921	—	8.00
2001	—	2.50	—
2001 Proof	74,194	—	8.00
2002	—	4.50	—
2002 Proof	65,315	—	7.50
2003	—	5.50	—

Note: Mintage of 5,101,000 includes both KM186 and KM495 examples.

| 2003 Proof | — | — | 12.00 |

KM# 170 23.3276 g. 0.5000 Silver 0.3750 oz. ASW 36 mm. **Subject:** Henry Kelsey **Obv:** Crowned head right **Rev:** Kelsey with natives, dates below, denomination above **Rev. Designer:** D. J. Craig

Date	Mintage	MS-63	Proof
1990	99,455	11.50	—
1990 Proof	254,959	—	20.00

KM# 179 23.3276 g. 0.5000 Silver 0.3750 oz. ASW 36 mm. **Subject:** S.S. Frontenac **Obv:** Crowned head right **Rev:** Ship,"Frontenac," date and denomination below, **Rev. Designer:** D. J. Craig

Date	Mintage	MS-63	Proof
1991	73,843	11.50	—
1991 Proof	195,424	—	25.00

KM# 210 25.1750 g. 0.9250 Silver 0.7487 oz. ASW 36 mm. **Subject:** Stagecoach service **Obv:** Crowned head right **Rev:** Stagecoach, date and denomination below **Rev. Designer:** Karsten Smith

Date	Mintage	MS-63	Proof
1992	78,160	22.50	—
1992 Proof	187,612	—	22.50

KM# 209 Aureate 26.5 mm. **Subject:** Loon right, dates and denomination **Obv:** Crowned head right **Rev.**
Designer: Robert R. Carmichael

Date	Mintage	MS-63	Proof
1992	4,242,085	2.00	—
1992 Proof	147,061	—	8.00

KM# 218 Aureate 26 mm. **Subject:** Parliament **Obv:** Crowned head right, dates below **Rev:** Backs of three seated figures in front of building, denomination below **Rev. Designer:** Rita Swanson

Date	Mintage	MS-63	Proof
1992	23,915,000	2.25	—
1992 Proof	24,227	—	9.00

KM# 235 25.1750 g. 0.9250 Silver 0.7487 oz. ASW 36 mm. **Subject:** Stanley Cup hockey **Obv:** Crowned head right **Rev:** Hockey players between cups, dates below, denomination above **Rev. Designer:** Stewart Sherwood

Date	Mintage	MS-63	Proof
1993	88,150	22.50	—
1993 Proof	294,314	—	22.50

KM# 248 7.0000 g. Aureate Bronze 26 mm. **Subject:** War Memorial **Obv:** Crowned head right, date below **Rev:** Memorial, denomination at right **Rev. Designer:** R. C. M. Staff

Date	Mintage	MS-63	Proof
1994	20,004,830	2.25	—
1994 Proof	54,524	—	7.50

DOLLAR

KM# 251 25.1750 g. 0.9250 Silver 0.7487 oz. ASW 36 mm.   **Subject:** Last RCMP sled-dog patrol **Obv:** Crowned head right **Rev:** Dogsled, denomination divides dates below **Rev. Designer:** Ian Sparks

Date	Mintage	MS-63	Proof
1994	61,561	22.50	—
1994 Proof	170,374	—	22.50

KM# 258 7.0000 g. Aureate 26 mm.   **Subject:** Peacekeeping Monument in Ottawa **Obv:** Crowned head right, date below **Rev:** Monument, denomination above right **Rev. Designer:** J. K. Harmon, R. G. Henriquez and C. H. Oberlander **Note:** Mintage included with KM#186.

Date	Mintage	MS-63	Proof
1995	18,502,750	2.25	—
1995 Proof	43,293	—	7.50

KM# 259 25.1750 g. 0.9250 Silver 0.7487 oz. ASW 36 mm.   **Subject:** Hudson Bay Co. **Obv:** Crowned head right **Rev:** Explorers and ship, date and denomination below **Rev. Designer:** Vincent McIndoe

Date	Mintage	MS-63	Proof
1995	61,819	22.50	—
1995 Proof	166,259	—	30.00

KM# 274 25.1750 g. 0.9250 Silver 0.7487 oz. ASW 36 mm. **Subject:** McIntosh Apple **Obv:** Crowned head right **Rev:** Apple, dates and denomination below **Rev. Designer:** Roger Hill

Date	Mintage	MS-63	Proof
1996	58,834	22.50	—
1996 Proof	133,779	—	25.00

KM# 282 25.1750 g. 0.9250 Silver 0.7487 oz. ASW 36 mm. **Subject:** 25th Anniversary Hockey Victory **Obv:** Crowned head right **Rev:** The winning goal by Paul Aenderson. Based on a painting by Andre l'Archeveque, dates at right, denomination at bottom **Rev. Designer:** Walter Burden

Date	Mintage	MS-63	Proof
1997	155,252	22.50	—
1997 Proof	184,965	—	30.00

KM# 291 97595.0000 g. Aureate Bronze 26 mm. **Subject:** Loon Dollar 10th Anniversary **Obv:** Crowned head right **Rev:** Loon in flight left, dates above, denomination below **Rev. Designer:** Jean-Luc Grondin

Date	Mintage	MS-63	P/L	Proof
1997	—	—	22.00	—

KM# 296 25.1750 g. 0.9250 Silver 0.7487 oz. ASW 36 mm.   **Subject:** Loon Dollar 10th Anniversary **Obv:** Crowned head right **Rev:** Loon in flight left, dates above, denomination below **Rev. Designer:** Jean-Luc Grondin

Date	Mintage	MS-63	Proof
1997 Proof	24,995	—	95.00

KM# 306 25.1750 g. 0.9250 Silver 0.7487 oz. ASW 36 mm.   **Subject:** 120th Anniversary Royal Canadian Mounted Police **Obv:** Crowned head right **Rev:** Mountie on horseback, dates at left, denomination above **Rev. Designer:** Adeline Halvorson **Note:** Individually cased prooflikes, proofs or specimens are from broken-up prooflike or specimen sets.

Date	Mintage	MS-63	P/L	Proof
1998	79,777	—	22.50	—
1998 Proof	120,172	—	—	35.00

KM# 355 25.1750 g. 0.9250 Silver 0.7487 oz. ASW 36 mm.   **Subject:** International Year of Old Persons **Obv:** Crowned head right **Rev:** Figures amid trees, date and denomination below **Rev. Designer:** S. Armstrong-Hodgson

Date	Mintage	MS-63	Proof
1999 Proof	24,976	—	40.00

KM# 356 25.1750 g. 0.9250 Silver 0.7487 oz. ASW 36 mm. **Subject:** Discovery of Queen Charlotte Isle **Obv:** Crowned head right **Rev:** Ship and three boats, dates at right, denomination below **Rev. Designer:** D. J. Craig

Date	Mintage	MS-63	P/L	Proof
1999	67,655	—	22.50	—
1999 Proof	126,435	—	—	35.00

KM# 401 25.1750 g. 0.9250 Silver 0.7487 oz. ASW 36 mm. **Subject:** Voyage of Discovery **Obv:** Crowned head right **Rev:** Human and space shuttle, date above, denomination below **Rev. Designer:** D. F. Warkentine

Date	Mintage	MS-63	P/L	Proof
2000	60,100	—	22.50	—
2000 Proof	114,130	—	—	30.00

KM# 414 25.1750 g. 0.9250 Silver 0.7487 oz. ASW 36 mm. **Subject:** National Ballet **Obv:** Crowned head right **Rev:** Ballet dancers **Rev. Designer:** Scott McKowen **Edge:** Reeded

Date	Mintage	MS-63	Proof
2001 Proof	225,000	—	35.00
2001	65,000	27.50	—

KM# 434 25.1750 g. 0.9250 Silver 0.7487 oz. ASW 36 mm.   **Obv:** Crowned head right **Rev:** Recycled 1911 pattern dollar design: denomination, country name and dates in crowned wreath **Edge:** Reeded

Date	Mintage	MS-63	Proof
2001 Proof	24,996	—	55.00

KM# 186a Gilt 26.5 mm.   **Subject:** Olympic Win

Date	Mintage	MS-63	Proof
2002 Proof	—	—	40.00

KM# 443 25.1750 g. 0.9250 Silver 0.7487 oz. ASW 36 mm.   **Subject:** Queen's Golden Jubilee **Obv:** Crowned head right, with anniversary date at left **Obv. Designer:** Dora dePédery-Hunt **Rev:** Queen in her coach and a view of the coach, denomination below **Edge:** Reeded

Date	Mintage	MS-63	Proof
2002	65,140	28.50	—
2002 Proof	29,688	—	40.00

KM# 443a 25.1800 g. 0.9250 Silver Gilt 0.7488 oz. ASW 36 mm.   **Subject:** Queen's Golden Jubilee **Obv:** Crowned head right with anniversary date **Rev:** Queen in her coach and a view of the coach **Edge:** Reeded **Note:** Special 24 karat gold plated issue of KM#443.

Date	Mintage	MS-63	Proof
2002 Proof	32,642	—	45.00

KM# 462 7.0000 g. Aureate-Bronze Plated Nickel   **Obv:** Commemorative dates 1952-2002 **Obv. Designer:** Dora dePédery-Hunt **Rev:** Family of Loons

Date	Mintage	MS-63	Proof
2002 Specimen	67,672	—	35.00

KM# 467 7.0000 g. Aureate-Bronze Plated Nickel   **Subject:** Elizabeth II Golden Jubilee **Obv:** Crowned head right, Jubilee commemorative dates 1952-2002 **Obv. Designer:** Dora dePédery-Hunt

Date	Mintage	MS-63	Proof
2002	2,302,000	2.50	—
2002 Proof	—	—	8.00

KM# 467a Gold   **Subject:** 50th Anniversary, Accession to the Throne **Obv:** Crowned head right **Note:** Sold on the internet.

Date	Mintage	MS-63	Proof
2002	1	—	55,500

KM# 503 25.1750 g. 0.9250 Silver 0.7487 oz. ASW 36 mm.   **Subject:** Queen Mother **Obv:** Crowned head right **Obv. Designer:** Dora de Pedery-Hunt **Rev:** Queen Mother facing

Date	Mintage	MS-63	Proof
2002 Proof	9,994	—	250

KM# 450 25.1750 g. 0.9999 Silver 0.8093 oz. ASW 36 mm.   **Subject:** Cobalt Mining Centennial **Obv:** Queens portrait right **Obv. Designer:** Dora dePédery-Hunt **Rev:** Mine tower and fox **Edge:** Reeded

Date	Mintage	MS-63	Proof
2003	51,130	30.00	—
2003 Proof	88,536	—	45.00

KM# 495 7.0000 g. Aureate-Bronze Plated Nickel 26.5 mm.   **Obv:** Bare head right **Obv. Designer:** Susanna Blunt **Rev:** Loon right **Rev. Designer:** Robert R. Carmichael **Shape:** 11-sided

Date	Mintage	MS-63	Proof
2003	5,102,000	5.50	—
Note: Mintage of 5,101,000 includes both KM 186 and 495 examples.			
2003W Prooflike	—	—	—
2003 Proof	62,507	—	7.50
2004	10,894,000	1.75	—
2004 Proof	—	—	12.00
2005	44,375,000	3.00	—
2005 Proof	—	—	7.50
2006	49,111,000	3.00	—
2006 Proof	—	—	7.50
2006(ml)	49,111,000	3.00	—
2006(ml) Proof	—	—	7.50
2007(ml)	38,045,000	3.00	—
2007(ml) Proof	—	—	7.50
2008(ml)	29,561,000	3.00	—
2008(ml) Proof	—	—	7.50
2009(ml)	39,601,000	3.00	—
2009(ml) Proof	—	—	7.50
2010(ml)	—	3.00	—
2010(ml) Proof	—	—	7.50
2011(ml)	—	3.00	—
2011(ml) Proof	—	—	7.50

KM# 473 25.1750 g. 0.9999 Silver 0.8093 oz. ASW   **Subject:** 50th Anniversary of the Coronation of Elizabeth II **Obv:** 1953 effigy of the Queen, Jubilee dates 1953-2003 **Obv. Designer:** Mary Gillick **Rev:** Voyageur, date and denomination below

Date	Mintage	MS-63	Proof
2003 Proof	29,586	—	45.00

KM# 473a Gold   **Subject:** 50th Anniversary of Coronation **Obv. Designer:** Mary Gilick **Rev:** Voyageur **Note:** Sold on the internet.

Date	Mintage	MS-63	Proof
2003	1	—	62,750

KM# 480 25.1750 g. 0.9999 Silver 0.8093 oz. ASW   **Subject:** Coronation of Queen Elizabeth II **Obv:** Head right **Rev:** Voyaguers **Rev. Designer:** Emanuel Hahn

Date	Mintage	MS-63	Proof
2003 Proof	21,400	—	50.00

DOLLAR

KM# 507 7.0000 g. Aureate-Bronze Plated Nickel 26.5 mm. **Obv:** Bare head right, date below **Obv. Designer:** Susanna Blunt **Rev:** Loon **Edge:** Plain **Shape:** 11-sided

Date	Mintage	MS-63	Proof
2004 Proof	12,550	—	75.00

KM# 512 25.1750 g. 0.9999 Silver 0.8093 oz. ASW 36 mm. **Subject:** First French Settlement in America **Obv:** Crowned head right **Rev:** Sailing ship **Edge:** Reeded

Date	Mintage	MS-63	Proof
2004	42,582	30.00	—
2004 Fleur-dis-lis	8,315	60.00	—
2004 Proof	106,974	—	50.00

KM# 513 7.0000 g. Aureate-Bronze Plated Nickel 26.5 mm. **Subject:** Olympics **Obv:** Bare head right **Rev:** Maple leaf, Olympic flame and rings above loon **Edge:** Plain **Shape:** 11-sided

Date	Mintage	MS-63	Proof
2004	6,526,000	8.00	—

KM# 513a 9.3100 g. 0.9250 Silver 0.2769 oz. ASW 26.5 mm. **Subject:** Olympics **Obv:** Bare head right **Rev:** Multicolor maple leaf, Olympic flame and rings above loon **Edge:** Plain **Shape:** 11-sided

Date	Mintage	MS-63	Proof
2004 Proof	19,994	—	50.00

KM# 549 25.1750 g. 0.9250 Silver 0.7487 oz. ASW 36.07 mm. **Subject:** 40th Anniversary of National Flag **Obv:** Head right **Obv. Designer:** Susanna Blunt **Rev. Designer:** William Woodruff

Date	Mintage	MS-63	Proof
2005	50,948	27.50	—
2005 Proof	95,431	—	40.00

KM# 549a 25.1750 g. 0.9250 Silver 0.7487 oz. ASW 36.07 mm. **Subject:** 40th Anniversary of National Flag **Obv:** Head right

Date	Mintage	MS-63	Proof
2005	62,483	75.00	—

KM# 549b 25.1800 g. 0.9250 Silver 0.7488 oz. ASW 36.07 mm. **Subject:** 40th Anniversary National Flag **Rev:** National flag, colorized

Date	Mintage	MS-63	Proof
2005 Proof	4,898	—	350

KM# 552 7.0000 g. Aureate-Bronze Plated Nickel **Subject:** Terry Fox **Obv:** Head right

Date	Mintage	MS-63	Proof
2005	1,290,900	3.50	—

KM# 553 7.0000 g. Aureate-Bronze Plated Nickel **Subject:** Tuffed Puffin **Obv:** Head right **Obv. Designer:** Susanna Blunt

Date	Mintage	MS-63	Proof
2005 Specimen	40,000	—	30.00

KM# 581 9.3100 g. 0.9250 Silver 0.2769 oz. ASW **Subject:** Lullabies Loonie **Obv:** Head right **Obv. Designer:** Susanna Blunt **Rev:** Loon and moon, teddy bear in stars

Date	Mintage	MS-63	Proof
2006	18,103	4.50	—

KM# 582 7.0000 g. Aureate-Bronze Plated Nickel 26.5 mm. **Subject:** Snowy owl **Obv:** Head right **Obv. Designer:** Susanna Blunt **Rev:** Snowy owl with year above

Date	Mintage	MS-63	Proof
2006 Specimen	40,000	—	30.00

KM# 583 25.1750 g. 0.9250 Silver 0.7487 oz. ASW 36 mm. **Obv:** Head right **Rev:** Victoria Cross

Date	Mintage	MS-63	Proof
2006	27,254	25.00	—
2006 Proof	59,599	—	45.00

KM# 583a 25.1750 g. 0.9250 Silver 0.7487 oz. ASW 36 mm. **Obv:** Head right **Rev:** Victoria Cross gilt

Date	Mintage	MS-63	Proof
2006 Proof	—	—	75.00

KM# 630 9.3100 g. 0.9250 Silver 0.2769 oz. ASW **Subject:** Olympic Games **Obv:** Crowned head right **Rev:** Loon in flight, colored olympic logo above

Date	Mintage	MS-63	Proof
2006	19,956	30.00	—

KM# 654 7.0000 g. 0.9250 Silver 0.2082 oz. ASW **Obv:** Head right **Rev:** Snowflake, colorized **Note:** Sold in a CD package.

Date	Mintage	MS-63	Proof
2006(ml)	34,014	35.00	—

KM# 655 7.0000 g. 0.9250 Silver 0.2082 oz. ASW **Subject:** Baby Rattle **Obv:** Head right **Rev:** Baby rattle

Date	Mintage	MS-63	Proof
2006	3,207	20.00	—

DOLLAR

KM# 656 28.1750 g. 0.9250 Silver 0.8379 oz. ASW **Subject:** Medal of Bravery **Obv:** Head right

Date	Mintage	MS-63	Proof
2006 Proof	8,343	—	50.00

KM# 656a 28.1750 g. 0.9250 Silver 0.8379 oz. ASW **Subject:** Medal of Bravery **Obv:** Head right **Rev:** Maple leaf within wreath. Colorized.

Date	Mintage	MS-63	Proof
2006 Proof	4,999	—	150

KM# 688 7.0000 g. Aureate Bronze 26.5 mm. **Obv:** Head right **Rev:** Trumpeter Swan

Date	Mintage	MS-63	Proof
2007(ml)	40,000	20.00	—

KM# 653 25.1750 g. 0.9250 Silver 0.7487 oz. ASW 36.07 mm. **Subject:** Thayendanegea **Obv:** Head right **Rev:** Bust 3/4 facing right

Date	Mintage	MS-63	Proof
2007	16,378	30.00	—
2007 Proof	—	—	40.00

KM# 655a 7.0000 g. 0.9250 Silver 0.2082 oz. ASW **Obv:** Bust right **Rev:** Baby Rattle, partially gilt

Date	Mintage	MS-63	Proof
2007	1,911	15.00	—

KM# 700 7.0000 g. 0.9250 Silver 0.2082 oz. ASW **Rev:** Alphabet Letter Blocks

Date	Mintage	MS-63	Proof
2007	3,229	—	25.00

KM# 719 25.1800 g. 0.9250 Silver 0.7488 oz. ASW 36.07 mm. **Subject:** Celebration of the Arts **Rev:** Book, TV set, musical instruments, film montage **Rev. Designer:** Friedrich Peter **Edge:** Reeded

Date	Mintage	MS-63	Proof
2007	6,466	—	55.00

KM# A727 7.0000 g. Aureate Bronze 26.5 mm. **Subject:** Vancouver Olympic Games **Rev:** Loon splashing in water, Olympics logo at right

Date	Mintage	MS-63	Proof
2007(ml)	30,000	3.00	—

KM# 767 25.1800 g. 0.9250 Silver 0.7488 oz. ASW 36.07 mm. **Rev:** Poppy at center of large maple leaf

Date	Mintage	MS-63	Proof
2008 Proof	—	—	50.00

KM# 781 25.1800 g. 0.9250 Silver 0.7488 oz. ASW 36.07 mm. **Subject:** Ottawa Mint Centennial 1908-2008 **Rev:** Maple leaf transforming into a common loon **Rev. Designer:** Jason Bowman

Date	Mintage	MS-63	Proof
2008 Proof	25,000	—	65.00

KM# 784 7.0000 g. Nickel-Bronze 26.5 mm. **Rev:** Common elder

Date	Mintage	MS-63	Proof
2008 Specimen	40,000	—	50.00

KM#785 25.1800 g. 0.9250 Silver 0.7488 oz. ASW 36.07 mm. **Subject:** Founding of Quebec 400th Anniversary **Rev:** Samuel de Champlain, ship and town view **Rev. Designer:** Susanne Duranceau

Date	Mintage	MS-63	Proof
2008 Proof	65,000	—	40.00

KM# 785a 25.1800 g. 0.9250 Silver 0.7488 oz. ASW 36.07 mm. **Subject:** Founding of Quebec 400th Anniversary **Rev:** Samuel de Champlain selectively gold plated, ship, town view **Rev. Designer:** Susanne Duranceau

Date	Mintage	MS-63	Proof
2008 Proof	—	—	75.00

KM# 787 7.0000 g. Nickel-Brass 26.5 mm. **Subject:** Lucky Loonie **Rev:** Loon splashing and Olympic logo at right **Rev. Designer:** Steve Hepurn

Date	Mintage	MS-63	Proof
2008	—	20.00	—

KM#787a 9.3100 g. 0.9250 Silver 0.2769 oz. ASW 26.5 mm. **Rev:** Loon splashing with Olympic logo and maple leaf in color above **Rev. Designer:** Steve Hepurn

Date	Mintage	MS-63	Proof
2008 Proof	30,000	—	25.00

KM# 791 6.5000 g. Nickel 26.5 mm. **Rev:** Edmonton Oilers

Date	Mintage	MS-63	Proof
2008	—	25.00	—

KM# 792 6.5000 g. Nickel 26.5 mm. **Rev:** Montreal Canadiens

Date	Mintage	MS-63	Proof
2008	—	25.00	—

KM# 793 6.5000 g. Nickel 26.5 mm. **Rev:** Ottawa Senators

Date	Mintage	MS-63	Proof
2008	—	25.00	—

KM# 794 6.5000 g. Nickel 26.5 mm. **Rev:** Toronto Maple Leafs

Date	Mintage	MS-63	Proof
2008	—	25.00	—

KM# 795 6.5000 g. Nickel 26.5 mm. **Rev:** Vancouver Canucks

Date	Mintage	MS-63	Proof
2008	—	25.00	—

DOLLAR

KM# 851 33.6500 g. Nickel 26.5 mm. **Rev:** Calgary Flames Jersey

Date	Mintage	MS-63	Proof
2009	—	25.00	—

KM# 852 33.6500 g. 0.9990 Nickel 1.0807 oz. 26.5 mm. **Rev:** Edmonton Oilers Jersey

Date	Mintage	MS-63	Proof
2009	—	25.00	—

KM# 853 33.6500 g. Nickel 26.5 mm. **Rev:** Montreal Canadians Jersey

Date	Mintage	MS-63	Proof
2009	—	25.00	—

KM# 854 33.6500 g. Nickel 26.5 mm. **Rev:** Ottawa Senators Jersey

Date	Mintage	MS-63	Proof
2009	—	25.00	—

KM# 855 33.6500 g. Nickel 26.5 mm. **Rev:** Toronto Maple Leafs Jersey

Date	Mintage	MS-63	Proof
2009	—	25.00	—

KM# 856 33.6500 g. Nickel 26.5 mm. **Rev:** Vancouver Canucks Jersey

Date	Mintage	MS-63	Proof
2009	—	25.00	—

KM# 864 7.0000 g. Aureate Bronze 26.5 mm. **Subject:** Montreal Canadiens, 100th Anniversary **Obv:** Bust right **Rev:** Montreal Canadiens logo and large 100 **Shape:** 11-sided

Date	Mintage	MS-63	Proof
2009	—	25.00	—

KM#865 25.1700 g. 0.9250 Silver 0.7485 oz. ASW 36.07 mm. **Subject:** Montreal Canadiens 100th Anniversary **Obv:** Bust right **Obv. Designer:** Susanna Blunt **Rev:** Montreal Canadiens logo partially gilt

Date	Mintage	MS-63	Proof
2009 Proof in black case	15,000	—	75.00
2009 Proof in acrillic stand	5,000	—	150

KM#889 25.1800 g. 0.9250 Silver 0.7488 oz. ASW 36.07 mm. **Subject:** 100th Anniversary of flight in Canada **Obv:** Bust right **Obv. Legend:** Elizabeth II DG Regina **Obv. Designer:** Susanna Blunt **Rev:** Silhouette with arms spread, 3 planes, plane cutout **Rev. Legend:** Canada Dollar 1909-2009 **Rev. Designer:** Jason Bouwman

Date	Mintage	MS-63	Proof
2009	50,000	35.00	—
2009 Proof	50,000	—	55.00

KM#889a 25.1800 g. 0.9250 Silver 0.7488 oz. ASW 36.07 mm. **Obv:** Bust right **Rev:** Silouette with arms spread, 3 planes, plane shadow partially gilt

Date	Mintage	MS-63	Proof
2009(ml) Proof	—	—	50.00

KM# 914 7.0000 g. Aureate-Bronze Plated Nickel 26.5 mm. **Obv:** Bust right **Obv. Designer:** Susanna Blunt **Rev:** Blue heron in flight

Date	Mintage	MS-63	Proof
2009 Specimen	40,000	50.00	—

KM# 883 7.0000 g. Aureate-Bronze Plated Nickel 26.5 mm. **Subject:** Lucky Loonie **Obv:** Bust right **Obv. Legend:** Elizabeth II DG Regina **Rev:** Canadian Olympic logo **Rev. Legend:** Canada Dollar

Date	Mintage	MS-63	Proof
2010	12,000	20.00	—

KM# 883a 9.3100 g. 0.9250 Silver 0.2769 oz. ASW 26.5 mm.   **Subject:** Lucky Loonie **Obv:** Bust right **Obv. Legend:** Elizabeth II DG Regina **Rev:** Canadian Olympic logo in color **Rev. Legend:** Vancouver 2010 Canada Dollar **Shape:** 11-sided

Date	Mintage	MS-63	Proof
2010 Proof	40,000	—	55.00

KM# 1046   Aureate Bronze 26.5 mm.   **Subject:** Roughriders **Rev:** S logo **Shape:** 11-sided

Date	Mintage	MS-63	Proof
2010(ml)	—	7.50	—

KM# 1027 25.1800 g. 0.9250 Silver 0.7488 oz. ASW 36.07 mm.   **Obv:** George V bust left **Rev:** Voyaguers, dual dates below

Date	Mintage	MS-63	Proof
2010 Proof	7,500	—	70.00

KM# 975 0.9250 Silver 36 mm.   **Rev:** Sun mask **Rev. Designer:** Xwa lack Tun

Date	Mintage	MS-63	Proof
2010 Proof	5,000	—	200

KM# 1050 25.1800 g. 0.9250 Silver 0.7488 oz. ASW 36.07 mm.   **Rev:** Red poppy in large field of poppies **Edge:** Reeded

Date	Mintage	MS-63	Proof
2010 Proof	—	—	55.00

KM# 1087a 25.1800 g. 0.9250 Silver 0.7488 oz. ASW 36.07 mm.   **Subject:** Parks Canada, 100th Anniversary **Rev:** Female head looking downward to hands holding nature scene, partially gilt **Rev. Designer:** Luc Normandin

Date	Mintage	MS-63	Proof
2010 Proof	45,000	—	75.00

KM# 1086 7.0000 g. Bronze Plated Nickel 26.5 mm.   **Rev:** Great Grey Owl **Rev. Designer:** Arnold Nagy

Date	Mintage	MS-63	Proof
2011	35,000	13.50	—

KM# 1087 25.1800 g. 0.9250 Silver 0.7488 oz. ASW 36.07 mm.   **Subject:** Parks Canada, 100th Anniversary **Rev:** Female head looking downward into hands holding nature scene **Rev. Designer:** Luc Normandin

Date	Mintage	MS-63	Proof
2011	25,000	50.00	—
2011 Proof	—	—	60.00

KM# 1017 Aureate Bronze   **Rev:** Male and female sailors saluting, HMCS Halifax and anchor above

Date	Mintage	MS-63	Proof
2010	—	5.00	—

DOLLAR (Louis)

KM# 652 1.5000 g. 0.9990 Gold 0.0482 oz. AGW 14.1 mm. **Subject:** Gold Louis **Obv:** Bust right **Obv. Designer:** Susanna Blunt **Rev:** Crowned double L monogram within wreath

Date	Mintage	MS-63	Proof
2006 Proof	5,648	—	100

KM# 756 1.5550 g. 0.9990 Gold 0.0499 oz. AGW 14.1 mm. **Obv:** Bust right **Obv. Designer:** Susanna Blunt **Rev:** Crown above two oval shields

Date	Mintage	MS-63	Proof
2007 Proof	3,457	—	100

KM# 834 1.5550 g. 0.9990 Gold 0.0499 oz. AGW 14.1 mm. **Obv:** Bust right **Obv. Designer:** Susanna Blunt **Rev:** Crowned double L monogram, three lis around

Date	Mintage	MS-63	Proof
2008 Proof	—	—	125

2 DOLLARS

KM# 270 7.3000 g. Bi-Metallic Aluminum-Bronze center in Nickel ring 28 mm. **Obv:** Crowned head right within circle, date below **Obv. Designer:** Dora dePedery-Hunt **Rev:** Polar bear right within circle, denomination below **Rev. Designer:** Brent Townsend **Edge:** Segmented reeding

Date	Mintage	MS-63	P/L	Proof
1996	375,483,000	3.25	5.00	—
1996 Proof	—	—	—	10.00
1997	16,942,000	3.25	—	—
1998	4,926,000	3.25	—	—
1998W	Inc. above	3.25	—	—
1999	25,130,000	3.25	—	—
2000	29,847,000	3.25	—	—
2000W	Inc. above	3.25	—	—
2001	27,008,000	5.00	—	—
2001 Proof	74,944	—	—	12.50
2002	11,910,000	5.00	—	—
2002 Proof	65,315	—	—	12.50
2003	7,123,697	5.00	—	—
2003 Proof	62,007	—	—	12.50

KM# 270b 25.0000 g. 0.9250 Bi-Metallic Gold plated silver center on Silver planchet 0.7435 oz. 28 mm. **Obv:** Crowned head right within circle, date below **Rev:** Polar bear right within circle, denomination below **Edge:** 4.5mm thick

Date	Mintage	MS-63	Proof
1996 Proof	10,000	—	55.00
1998 Proof	—	—	—

KM# 270c 8.8300 g. 0.9250 Silver gold plated center 0.2626 oz. ASW 28 mm. **Obv:** Crowned head right within circle, date below **Rev:** Polar bear right within circle, denomination below **Note:** 1.9mm thick.

Date	Mintage	MS-63	Proof
1996 Proof	10,000	—	12.00
1997 Proof	—	—	10.00
1998O Proof	—	—	12.00
1999 Proof	—	—	12.00

Date	Mintage	MS-63	Proof
2000 Proof	—	—	12.00
2001 Proof	—	—	12.00

KM# 270a 10.8414 g. Bi-Metallic .999 Gold 5.7456g center in .999 Silver 5.0958g ring 28 mm. **Obv:** Crowned head right within circle, date below **Rev:** Polar bear right within circle, denomination below

Date	Mintage	MS-63	Proof
1996 Proof	5,000	—	225

KM# 357 7.3000 g. Bi-Metallic Aluminumn-Bronze center in Nickel ring 28 mm. **Subject:** Nunavut **Obv:** Crowned head right **Rev:** Inuit person with drum, denomination below **Rev. Designer:** G. Arnaktavyok **Edge:** Segmented reeding

Date	Mintage	MS-63	Proof
1999	—	4.00	—

KM# 357a 8.5200 g. 0.9250 Silver gold plated center. 0.2534 oz. ASW 28 mm. **Subject:** Nunavut **Obv:** Crowned head right **Rev:** Drum dancer **Edge:** Interrupted reeding

Date	Mintage	MS-63	Proof
1999 Proof	39,873	—	15.00

KM# 357b Gold Yellow gold center in White Gold ring **Subject:** Nunavut **Obv:** Crowned head right **Rev:** Drum dancer

Date	Mintage	MS-63	Proof
1999 Proof	4,298	—	250

KM# 399 7.3000 g. Bi-Metallic Aluminum-Bronze center in Nickel ring 28 mm. **Subject:** Knowledge **Obv:** Crowned head right within circle, denomination below **Rev:** Polar bear and 2 cubs right within circle, date above **Rev. Designer:** Tony Bianco **Edge:** Segmented reeding

Date	Mintage	MS-63	P/L	Proof
2000 Specimen	1,500	—	5.00	—

KM# 399a 8.5200 g. 0.9250 Silver gold plated center. 0.2534 oz. ASW **Subject:** Knowledge **Obv:** Crowned head right within circle, denomination below **Rev:** Polar bear and 2 cubs within circle, date above

Date	Mintage	MS-63	Proof
2000 Proof	39,768	—	15.00

KM# 399b 6.3100 g. 0.9160 Gold Yellow gold center in White Gold ring 0.1858 oz. AGW **Subject:** Knowledge **Obv:** Crowned head right within circle, denomination below **Rev:** Polar bear and two cubs right within circle, date above

Date	Mintage	MS-63	Proof
2000 Proof	5,881	—	250

KM# 449 7.3000 g. Bi-Metallic Aluminum-Bronze center in Nickel ring 28 mm.   **Subject:** Elizabeth II Golden Jubilee **Obv:** Crowned head right, jubilee commemorative dates 1952-2002 **Edge:** Segmented reeding

Date	Mintage	MS-63	Proof
2002	27,020,000	4.00	

KM# 449a 8.8300 g. 0.9250 Silver gold plated center 0.2626 oz. ASW   **Subject:** Elizabeth II Golden Jubilee **Obv:** Crowned head right, jubilee commemorative dates 1952-2002

Date	Mintage	MS-63	Proof
2002 Proof	100,000	—	14.00

KM# 496 7.3000 g. Bi-Metallic Aluminum-Bronze center in Nickel ring 28 mm.   **Obv:** Head right **Obv. Designer:** Susanna Blunt **Rev:** Polar bear advancing right **Rev. Designer:** Brent Townsend **Edge:** Segmented reeding

Date	Mintage	MS-63	Proof
2003	11,244,000	5.00	—
2003W	71,142	25.00	—
2004	12,908,000	5.00	—
2004 Proof	—	—	12.50
2005	38,317,000	5.00	—
2005 Proof	—	—	12.50
2006(ml)	35,319,000	5.00	—
2006(ml) Proof	—	—	12.50
2007(ml)	38,957,000	5.00	—
2007(ml) Proof	—	—	12.50
2008(ml)	18,400,000	5.00	—
2008(ml) Proof	—	—	12.50
2009(ml)	38,430,000	5.00	—
2009(ml) Proof	—	—	12.50
2010(ml)	—	5.00	—
2010(ml) Proof	—	—	12.50
2011(ml)	—	5.00	—
2011(ml) Proof	—	—	12.50

KM# 270d 8.8300 g. 0.9250 Silver gold plated center 0.2626 oz. ASW   **Subject:** 100th Anniversary of the Cobalt Silver Strike **Obv:** Crowned head right, within circle, date below **Rev:** Polar bear right, within circle, denomination below

Date	Mintage	MS-63	Proof
2003 Proof	100,000	—	25.00

KM# 496a 10.8414 g. 0.9250 Bi-Metallic Gold plated Silver center in Silver ring 0.3224 oz. 28 mm.   **Obv:** Head right **Obv. Designer:** Susanna Blunt **Rev:** Polar Bear **Edge:** Segmented reeding

Date	Mintage	MS-63	Proof
2004 Proof	—	—	25.00

KM# 835 8.8000 g. 0.9250 Silver 0.2617 oz. ASW 27.95 mm.   **Rev:** Proud Polar Bear advancing right

Date	Mintage	MS-63	Proof
2004 Proof	12,607	—	40.00

KM# 837 7.3000 g. Bi-Metallic Aluminum-Bronze center in Nickel ring   **Obv:** Bust left, date at top **Rev:** Polar Bear advancing right

Date	Mintage	MS-63	Proof
2006(ml)	—	7.50	—
2007(ml)	38,957,000	7.50	—

KM# 631 7.3000 g. Bi-Metallic Aluminum-Bronze center in Nickel ring 28 mm.   **Subject:** 10th Anniversary of $2 coin **Obv:** Crowned head right **Edge:** Segmented reeding

Date	Mintage	MS-63	Proof
2006(ml)	5,005,000	25.00	—
2006(ml) Proof	—	—	40.00

KM# 631a Bi-Metallic 22 Kt Gold ring around 4.1 Kt. Gold core   **Subject:** 10th Anniversary of $2 coin **Obv:** Crowned head right **Rev:** Polar bear

Date	Mintage	MS-63	Proof
2006 Proof	2,068	—	400

KM# 836 7.3000 g. Bi-Metallic Aluminum-Bronze center in Nickel ring 28 mm.   **Subject:** $2 coin, 10th Anniversary **Rev:** "Churchill" Polar Bear, northern lights **Edge:** Segmented reeding

Date	Mintage	MS-63	Proof
2006(ml)	—	7.50	—

KM# 796 8.8300 g. 0.9250 Silver 0.2626 oz. ASW 28.07 mm.   **Rev:** Bear, gold plated center

Date	Mintage	MS-63	Proof
2008	—	25.00	—

KM# 1040 7.3000 g. Bi-Metallic Aluminumn-Bronze center in Nickel ring 27.95 mm. **Subject:** Quebec 400th Anniversary **Rev:** Lis and small sailing ship

Date	Mintage	MS-63	Proof
2008	—	7.50	—

KM# 1020 7.3000 g. Bi-Metallic Aluminum-Bronze center in Nickel ring 28 mm. **Rev:** Two lynx cubs **Rev. Designer:** Christie Paquet **Edge:** Segmented reeding

Date	Mintage	MS-63	Proof
2010 Specimen	15,000	—	40.00

KM# 1088 7.3000 g. Bi-Metallic Copper-Nickel center in Nickel ring 28.03 mm. **Rev:** Elk Calf **Rev. Designer:** Christine Paquet

Date	Mintage	MS-63	Proof
2011	—	7.50	—

3 DOLLARS

KM# 657 11.7200 g. 0.9250 Silver 0.3485 oz. ASW 27x27 mm. **Rev:** Beaver within wreath **Shape:** Square

Date	Mintage	MS-63	Proof
2006 Proof	19,963	—	225

KM# 1051 11.6000 g. 0.9250 Silver 0.3450 oz. ASW 27x27 mm. **Subject:** Wildlife conservation **Rev:** Stylized polar bear and northern lights **Shape:** square

Date	Mintage	MS-63	Proof
2010 Specimen	15,000	55.00	—

KM# 978 7.9600 g. Silver 27 mm. **Rev:** Return of the Tyee (giant salmon)

Date	Mintage	MS-63	Proof
2010 Proof	15,000	—	50.00

KM# 1011 11.6000 g. 0.9250 Silver 0.3450 oz. ASW 27x27 mm. **Rev:** Barn Owl **Rev. Designer:** Jason Bouwman **Shape:** Square

Date	Mintage	MS-63	Proof
2010 Proof	15,000	—	65.00

KM# 1089 11.6000 g. 0.9250 Silver 0.3450 oz. ASW 27x27 mm. **Rev:** Orca Whale **Rev. Designer:** Jason Bouwman **Shape:** Square

Date	Mintage	MS-63	Proof
2011 Proof	15,000	—	65.00

KM# 1090 7.9600 g. 0.9990 Silver 0.2557 oz. ASW 27 mm. **Rev:** Eskimo mother kneeling, child on back **Rev. Designer:** Andrew Oappik

Date	Mintage	MS-63	Proof
2011 Proof	10,000	—	65.00

4 DOLLARS

KM#728 15.8700 g. 0.9250 Silver 0.4719 oz. ASW
34 mm.   **Subject:** Dinosaur fossil **Obv:** Bust right
Rev: Parasaurolophus, selective enameling

Date	Mintage	MS-63	Proof
2007 Proof	13,010	—	200

KM#797 15.8700 g. 0.9990 Silver 0.5097 oz. ASW
34 mm.   **Subject:** Dinosaur fossil **Obv:** Bust right
Rev: Triceratops, enameled **Rev. Designer:** Kerri
Burnett

Date	Mintage	MS-63	Proof
2008 Proof	20,000	—	75.00

KM#890 15.8700 g. 0.9990 Silver 0.5097 oz. ASW
34 mm.   **Subject:** Tyrannosaurus Rex **Obv:** Bust

right **Obv. Legend:** Elizabeth II DG Regina **Obv.
Designer:** Susanna Blunt **Rev:** T-Rex skeleton in
selective aging **Rev. Legend:** Canada 4 Dollars
Rev. Designer: Kerri Burnette

Date	Mintage	MS-63	Proof
2009 Proof	20,000	—	55.00

KM# 942 15.8700 g. Silver 34 mm.   **Rev:** Kids
hanging stocking on fireplace, Christmas tree on
right

Date	Mintage	MS-63	Proof
2009 Proof	Est. 15,000	—	45.00

KM# 1014 15.8700 g. 0.9990 Silver 0.5097 oz.
ASW   **Rev:** Euoplocephalus **Rev. Designer:** Kerri
Burnett

Date	Mintage	MS-63	Proof
2010 Proof	13,000	—	55.00

KM# 1022 Silver   **Rev:** Dromaeosaurus

Date	Mintage	MS-63	Proof
2010 Proof	13,000	—	55.00

SOVEREIGN

KM# 14 7.9881 g. 0.9170 Gold 0.2355 oz. AGW **Rev:** St. George slaying dragon, mint mark below horse's rear hooves

Date	Mintage	F-12	VF-20	XF-40	AU-50	MS-60	MS-63
1908C	636	1,800	2,100	2,400	2,700	3,000	4,000
1909C	16,273	BV	350	400	450	500	1,800
1910C	28,012	—	BV	350	400	500	3,000

KM# 20 7.9881 g. 0.9170 Gold 0.2355 oz. AGW **Rev:** St. George slaying dragon, mint mark below horse's rear hooves

Date	Mintage	F-12	VF-20	XF-40	AU-50	MS-60	MS-63
1911C Specimen	—	—	—	—	—	—	—
1911C	256,946	—	—	—	BV	350	400
1913C	3,715	550	700	950	1,200	1,500	3,000
1914C	14,871	BV	350	400	450	600	950
1916C About 20 known	—	8,000	13,000	16,000	18,000	20,000	30,000
Note: Stacks' A.G. Carter Jr. Sale 12-89 Gem BU realized $82,500							
1917C	58,845	—	—	—	BV	350	700
1918C	106,514	—	—	—	BV	350	750
1919C	135,889	—	—	—	BV	350	700

5 DOLLARS

KM# 26 8.3592 g. 0.9000 Gold 0.2419 oz. AGW **Obv:** Crowned bust left **Obv. Designer:** E. B. MacKennal **Rev:** Arms within wreath, date and denomination below **Rev. Designer:** W. H. J. Blakemore

Date	Mintage	F-12	VF-20	XF-40	AU-50	MS-60	MS-63
1912	165,680	—	—	BV	350	400	550
1913	98,832	—	—	BV	350	400	700
1914	31,122	350	400	450	500	700	3,000

KM# 84 24.3000 g. 0.9250 Silver 0.7226 oz. ASW 38 mm. **Subject:** 1976 Montreal Olympics **Obv:** Young bust right, small maple below, date at right **Rev:** Sailboat "Kingston", date at left, denomination below **Rev. Designer:** Georges Huel **Note:** Series I.

Date	Mintage	MS-63	Proof
1973	—	22.50	—
1973 Proof	165,203	—	22.50

KM# 85 24.3000 g. 0.9250 Silver 0.7226 oz. ASW 38 mm. **Subject:** 1976 Montreal Olympics **Obv:** Young bust right, small maple leaf below, date at right **Rev:** North American map, denominaton below **Rev. Designer:** Georges Huel **Note:** Series I.

Date	Mintage	MS-63	Proof
1973	—	22.50	—
1973 Proof	165,203	—	22.50

KM# 90 24.3000 g. 0.9250 Silver 0.7226 oz. ASW 38 mm. **Subject:** 1976 Montreal Olympics **Obv:** Young bust right, small maple leaf below, date at right **Rev:** Athlete with torch, denomination below **Rev. Designer:** Anthony Mann **Note:** Series II.

Date	Mintage	MS-63	Proof
1974	—	22.50	—
1974 Proof	97,431	—	22.50

KM# 91 24.3000 g. 0.9250 Silver 0.7226 oz. ASW 38 mm. **Subject:** 1976 Montreal Olympics **Obv:** Young bust right, small maple leaf below, date at right **Rev:** Rower, denomination below **Rev. Designer:** Ken Danby **Note:** Series III.

Date	Mintage	MS-63	Proof
1974	—	22.50	—
1974 Proof	104,684	—	22.50

KM# 89 24.3000 g. 0.9250 Silver 0.7226 oz. ASW 38 mm. **Subject:** 1976 Montreal Olympics **Obv:** Young bust right, small maple leaf below, date at right **Rev:** Olympic rings, denomination below **Rev. Designer:** Anthony Mann **Note:** Series II.

Date	Mintage	MS-63	Proof
1974	—	22.50	—
1974 Proof	97,431	—	22.50

KM# 92 24.3000 g. 0.9250 Silver 0.7226 oz. ASW 38 mm. **Subject:** 1976 Montreal Olympics **Obv:**

Young bust right, small maple leaf below, date at right **Rev:** Canoeing, denomination below **Rev. Designer:** Ken Danby **Note:** Series III.

Date	Mintage	MS-63	Proof
1974	—	22.50	—
1974 Proof	104,684	—	22.50

KM# 98 24.3000 g. 0.9250 Silver 0.7226 oz. ASW 38 mm.   **Subject:** 1976 Montreal Olympics **Obv:** Young bust right, small maple leaf below, date at right **Rev:** Marathon, denomination below **Rev. Designer:** Leo Yerxa **Note:** Series IV.

Date	Mintage	MS-63	Proof
1975	—	22.50	—
1975 Proof	89,155	—	22.50

KM# 99 24.3000 g. 0.9250 Silver 0.7226 oz. ASW 38 mm.   **Subject:** Montreal 1976 - 21st Summer Olympic Games **Obv:** Young bust right, small maple leaf below, date at right **Rev:** Women's javelin event, denomination below **Rev. Designer:** Leo Yerxa **Note:** Series IV.

Date	Mintage	MS-63	Proof
1975	—	22.50	—
1975 Proof	89,155	—	22.50

KM# 100 24.3000 g. 0.9250 Silver 0.7226 oz. ASW 38 mm.   **Subject:** 1976 Montreal Olympics **Obv:** Young bust right, small maple leaf below, date at

right **Rev:** Swimmer, denomination below **Rev. Designer:** Lynda Cooper **Note:** Series V.

Date	Mintage	MS-63	Proof
1975	—	22.50	—
1975 Proof	89,155	—	22.50

KM# 101 24.3000 g. 0.9250 Silver 0.7226 oz. ASW 38 mm.   **Subject:** Montreal 1976 - 21st Summer Olympic Games **Obv:** Young bust right, small maple leaf below, date at right **Rev:** Platform Diver, denomination below **Rev. Designer:** Lynda Cooper **Note:** Series V.

Date	Mintage	MS-63	Proof
1975	—	22.50	—
1975 Proof	89,155	—	22.50

KM# 107 24.3000 g. 0.9250 Silver 0.7226 oz. ASW 38 mm.   **Subject:** 1976 Montreal Olympics **Obv:** Young bust right, small maple leaf below, date at right **Rev:** Fencing, denomination below **Rev. Designer:** Shigeo Fukada **Note:** Series VI.

Date	Mintage	MS-63	Proof
1976	—	22.50	—
1976 Proof	82,302	—	22.50

KM# 108 24.3000 g. 0.9250 Silver 0.7226 oz. ASW 38 mm.   **Subject:** 1976 Montreal Olympics **Obv:** Young bust right, small maple leaf below, date at right **Obv. Legend:** Boxing **Rev:** Boxers,

denomination below **Rev. Designer:** Shigeo
Fukada **Note:** Series VI.

Date	Mintage	MS-63	Proof
1976	—	22.50	—
1976 Proof	82,302	—	22.50

KM# 109 24.3000 g. 0.9250 Silver 0.7226 oz. ASW
38 mm.   **Subject:** 1976 Montreal Olympics **Obv:**
Young bust right, small maple leaf below, date at right
Rev: Olympic village, denomination below **Rev.
Designer:** Elliot John Morrison **Note:** Series VII.

Date	Mintage	MS-63	Proof
1976	—	22.50	—
1976 Proof	76,908	—	22.50

KM# 110 24.3000 g. 0.9250 Silver 0.7226 oz. ASW
38 mm.   **Subject:** 1976 Montreal Olympics **Obv:**
Young bust right, maple leaf below, date at right
Rev: Olympic flame, denomination below **Rev.
Designer:** Elliot John Morrison **Note:** Series VII.

Date	Mintage	MS-63	Proof
1976	—	22.50	—
1976 Proof	79,102	—	22.50

KM# 316 31.3900 g. 0.9999 Silver 1.0091 oz.
ASW   **Subject:** Dr. Norman Bethune **Obv:** Young
bust right **Rev:** Bethune and party, date at upper
right **Rev. Designer:** Harvey Chan

Date	Mintage	MS-63	Proof
1998 Proof	61,000	—	40.00

KM# 398 Copper-Nickel-Zinc   **Obv:** Young bust
right **Rev:** Viking ship under sail **Rev. Designer:**
Donald Curley **Note:** Sold in sets with Norway 20
kroner, KM#465.

Date	Mintage	MS-63	Proof
1999 Proof	28,450	—	18.50

KM# 435 16.8600 g. 0.9250 Silver 0.5014 oz. ASW
28.4 mm.   **Subject:** Guglielmo Marconi **Obv:**
Crowned head right **Rev:** Gold-plated cameo
portrait of Marconi **Rev. Designer:** Cosme Saffioti
Edge: Reeded **Note:** Only issued in two coin set
with British 2 pounds KM#1014a.

Date	Mintage	MS-63	Proof
2001 Proof	15,011	—	30.00

KM# 519 8.3600 g. 0.9000 Gold 0.2419 oz. AGW
21.6 mm.   **Obv:** Crowned head right **Rev:** National
arms **Edge:** Reeded

Date	Mintage	MS-63	Proof
2002 Proof	2,002	—	375

KM# 518 31.1200 g. 0.9999 Silver 1.0004 oz. ASW
38 mm.   **Subject:** F.I.F.A. World Cup Soccer ,
Germany 2006 **Obv:** Crowned head right,
denomination **Rev:** Goalie on knees **Edge:** Reeded

Date	Mintage	MS-63	Proof
2003 Proof	21,542	—	40.00

KM# 514 31.1200 g. 0.9999 Silver 1.0004 oz. ASW

38 mm. **Obv:** Crowned head right **Rev:** Moose
Edge: Reeded

Date	Mintage	MS-63	Proof
2004 Proof	12,822	—	175

KM# 527 31.1200 g. 0.9999 Silver 1.0004 oz.
ASW **Subject:** Golf, Championship of Canada,
Centennial **Obv:** Head right

Date	Mintage	MS-63	Proof
2004 Proof	18,750	—	30.00

KM# 554 31.1200 g. 0.9999 Silver 1.0004 oz.
ASW **Subject:** Alberta **Obv. Designer:** Head
right **Rev. Designer:** Michelle Grant

Date	Mintage	MS-63	Proof
2005 Proof	20,000	—	35.00

KM# 555 31.1200 g. 0.9999 Silver 1.0004 oz.
ASW **Subject:** Saskatchewan **Obv:** Head right
Obv. Designer: Susanna Blunt **Rev. Designer:**
Paulett Sapergia

Date	Mintage	MS-63	Proof
2005 Proof	20,000	—	35.00

KM# 556.1 31.1200 g. 0.9990 Silver 0.9995 oz.
ASW 38.02 mm. **Subject:** 60th Anniversay
Victory WWII - Veterans **Obv:** Bust right **Rev:** Large
V and heads of sailor, soldier and aviator on large
maple leaf **Edge:** Reeded

Date	Mintage	MS-63	Proof
2005	25,000	32.00	—

KM# 556.2 31.1200 g. 0.9999 Silver 1.0004 oz.
ASW 38.02 mm. **Subject:** 60th Anniversary
Victory WW II - Veterans **Obv:** Bust right **Rev:** Large
V and heads of sailor, soldier and aviator on maple
leaf with small maple leaf added at left and right
Edge: Reeded

Date	Mintage	MS-63	Proof
2005	10,000	125	—

KM# 557 31.1200 g. 0.9999 Silver 1.0004 oz. ASW
36 mm. **Subject:** Walrus and calf **Obv:** Head right
Obv. Designer: Susanna Blunt **Rev:** Two walruses
and calf **Rev. Designer:** Pierre Leduc

Date	Mintage	MS-63	Proof
2005 Proof	5,519	—	40.00

KM# 558 31.1200 g. 0.9999 Silver 1.0004 oz. ASW
36 mm. **Subject:** White tailed deer **Obv:** Head
right **Obv. Designer:** Susanna Blunt **Rev:** Two deer
standing **Rev. Designer:** Xerxes Irani

Date	Mintage	MS-63	Proof
2005 Proof	6,439	—	40.00

KM# 585 31.1200 g. 0.9999 Silver 1.0004 oz. ASW
36 mm. **Obv:** Head right **Obv. Designer:**
Susanna Blunt **Rev:** Peregrine Falcon feeding
young ones **Rev. Designer:** Dwayne Harty

Date	Mintage	MS-63	Proof
2006 Proof	6,145	—	45.00

KM# 586 31.1200 g. 0.9999 Silver 1.0004 oz. ASW
36 mm. **Subject:** Sable Island horses **Obv:** Head
right **Obv. Designer:** Susanna Blunt **Rev:** Horse
and foal standing **Rev. Designer:** Christie Paquet

Date	Mintage	MS-63	Proof
2006 Proof	7,589	—	45.00

KM# 658 31.1200 g. 0.9999 Silver 1.0004 oz. ASW
36.07 mm. **Subject:** Breast Cancer Awareness
Rev: Colorized pink ribbon

Date	Mintage	MS-63	Proof
2006 Proof	11,048	—	50.00

KM# 659 31.1200 g. 0.9999 Silver 1.0004 oz.
ASW **Subject:** C.A.F. Snowbirds Acrobatic Jet
Flying Team **Rev:** Image of fighter jets and piolt

Date	Mintage	MS-63	Proof
2006 Proof	7,896	—	50.00

KM# 1036 31.1200 g. 0.9990 Silver 0.9995 oz.
ASW **Subject:** 80th Anniversary **Rev:** Two deer
standing, one eating branch

Date	Mintage	MS-63	Proof
2009 Proof	—	—	70.00

KM# 1060 31.1050 g. 0.9999 Silver 0.9999 oz.
ASW 38 mm.   **Rev:** Maple leaf in color, yellow
ribbon honoring servicemen

Date	Mintage	MS-63	Proof
2009	—	70.00	—

KM# 995a 25.1700 g. 0.9250 Silver 0.7485 oz.
ASW 36.07 mm.   **Subject:** Navy Centennial **Rev:**
HMCS Sackville, gilt sea waves

Date	Mintage	MS-63	Proof
2010	—	—	110

KM#995 25.1700 g. 0.9250 Silver 0.7485 oz. ASW
36.07 mm.   **Rev:** HMCS Sackville **Rev. Designer:**
Yves Berube

Date	Mintage	MS-63	Proof
2010 Proof	Est. 50,000	—	50.00

KM#1077 31.3900 g. 0.9990 Silver 1.0082 oz. ASW
34 mm.   **Rev:** Maple leaf on 45 degree angle left

Date	Mintage	MS-63	Proof
2010 Proof	9,000	—	80.00

8 DOLLARS

KM# 515 28.8000 g. 0.9250 Silver 0.8565 oz. ASW 39 mm.   **Obv:** Head right **Obv. Designer:** Susanna Blunt
Rev: Grizzly bear walking left **Edge:** Reeded

Date	Mintage	MS-63	Proof
2004 Proof	12,942	—	85.00

KM# 597 32.1500 g. 0.9999 Silver 1.0335 oz. ASW   **Subject:** Canadian Pacific Railway, 120th Anniversary
Obv: Head right **Obv. Designer:** Susanna Blunt **Rev:** Railway bridge

Date	Mintage	MS-63	Proof
2005 Proof	9,892	—	65.00

KM# 598 32.1500 g. 0.9999 Silver 1.0335 oz. ASW   **Subject:** Canadian Pacific Railway, 120th Anniversary
Obv: Head right **Rev:** Railway memorial to the Chinese workers

Date	Mintage	MS-63	Proof
2005 Proof	9,892	—	65.00

KM# 730 25.1800 g. 0.9999 Silver 0.8094 oz. ASW 36.07 mm.   **Obv:** Queens's head at top in circle, three
Chinese characters **Rev:** Dragon and other creatures

Date	Mintage	MS-63	Proof
2007 Proof	19,954	—	55.00

KM# 943 25.1800 g. Silver 36.1 mm.
Rev: Hollgram maple of wisdom - crystal

Date	Mintage	MS-63	Proof
2009 Proof	11,624	—	90.00

KM# 1012 25.3000 g. 0.9250 Silver 0.7524 oz. ASW 36.07 mm. **Rev:** Horses around central maple leaf hologram **Rev. Designer:** Simon Ng

Date	Mintage	MS-63	Proof
2010 Proof	8,888	—	100

10 DOLLARS

KM# 27 16.7185 g. 0.9000 Gold 0.4837 oz. AGW 26.92 mm. **Obv:** Crowned bust left **Obv. Designer:** E. B. MacKennal **Rev:** Arms within wreath, date and denomination below **Rev. Designer:** W. H. J. Blakemore

Date	Mintage	F-12	VF-20	XF-40	AU-50	MS-60	MS-63
1912	74,759	—	BV	700	750	900	2,900
1913	149,232	—	BV	700	750	900	3,000
1914	140,068	BV	700	750	800	1,150	3,500

KM# 86.1 48.6000 g. 0.9250 Silver 1.4453 oz. ASW 45 mm.   **Subject:** 1976 Montreal Olympics **Obv:** Young bust right, maple leaf below, date at right **Rev:** World map, denomination below **Rev. Designer:** Georges Huel **Note:** Series I.

Date	Mintage	MS-63	Proof
1973	103,426	45.00	—
1973 Proof	165,203	—	45.00

KM# 87 48.6000 g. 0.9250 Silver 1.4453 oz. ASW 45 mm.   **Subject:** 1976 Montreal Olympics **Obv:** Young bust right, small maple leaf below, date at right **Rev:** Montreal skyline, denomination below **Rev. Designer:** Georges Huel **Note:** Series I.

Date	Mintage	MS-63	Proof
1973 Proof	165,203	—	45.00
1973	—	45.00	—

KM# 86.2 48.6000 g. 0.9250 Silver 1.4453 oz. ASW 45 mm.   **Subject:** 1976 Montreal Olympics **Obv:** Young bust right, small maple leaf below, date at right **Rev:** World map **Rev. Designer:** Georges Huel **Note:** Series I.

Date	Mintage	MS-63	Proof
1974	320	325	—

Note: Error: mule

KM# 93 48.6000 g. 0.9250 Silver 1.4453 oz. ASW 45 mm.   **Subject:** 1976 Montreal Olympics **Obv:** Young bust right, small maple leaf below, date at right **Rev:** Head of Zeus, denomination below **Rev. Designer:** Anthony Mann **Note:** Series II.

Date	Mintage	MS-63	Proof
1974	—	45.00	—
1974 Proof	104,684	—	45.00

KM# 94 48.6000 g. 0.9250 Silver 1.4453 oz. ASW 45 mm.   **Subject:** 1976 Montreal Olympics **Obv:** Young bust right, small maple leaf below, date at

right **Rev:** Temple of Zeus, denomination below
Rev. Designer: Anthony Mann **Note:** Series II.

Date	Mintage	MS-63	Proof
1974 Proof	104,684	—	45.00
1974	—	45.00	—

KM#102 48.6000 g. 0.9250 Silver 1.4453 oz. ASW
45 mm. **Subject:** 1976 Montreal Olympics **Obv:**
Young bust right, small maple leaf below, date at
right **Rev:** Men's hurdles, denomination below **Rev.
Designer:** Leo Yerxa **Note:** Series IV.

Date	Mintage	MS-63	Proof
1975 Proof	82,302	—	45.00
1975	—	45.00	—

KM# 95 48.6000 g. 0.9250 Silver 1.4453 oz. ASW
45 mm. **Subject:** 1976 Montreal Olympics **Obv:**
Young bust right, small maple leaf below, date at
right **Rev:** Cycling, denomination below **Rev.
Designer:** Ken Danby **Note:** Series III.

Date	Mintage	MS-63	Proof
1974 Proof	97,431	—	45.00
1974	—	45.00	—

KM# 96 48.6000 g. 0.9250 Silver 1.4453 oz. ASW
45 mm. **Subject:** 1976 Montreal Olympics **Obv:**
Young bust right, small maple leaf below, date at
right **Rev:** Lacrosse, denomination below **Rev.
Designer:** Ken Danby **Note:** Series III.

Date	Mintage	MS-63	Proof
1974	—	45.00	—
1974 Proof	97,431	—	45.00

KM#103 48.6000 g. 0.9250 Silver 1.4453 oz. ASW
45 mm. **Subject:** Montreal 1976 - 21st Summer
Olympic Games **Obv:** Young bust right, small maple
leaf below, date at right **Rev:** Women's shot put,
denomination below **Rev. Designer:** Leo Yerxa
Note: Series IV.

Date	Mintage	MS-63	Proof
1975 Proof	82,302	—	45.00
1975	—	45.00	—

10 DOLLARS

KM# 104 48.6000 g. 0.9250 Silver 1.4453 oz. ASW
45 mm.   **Subject:** 1976 Montreal Olympics **Obv:**
Young bust right, small maple leaf below, date at
right **Rev:** Sailing, denomination below **Rev.**
Designer: Lynda Cooper **Note:** Series V.

Date	Mintage	MS-63	Proof
1975 Proof	89,155	—	45.00
1975	—	45.00	—

KM# 105 48.6000 g. 0.9250 Silver 1.4453 oz. ASW
45 mm.   **Subject:** 1976 Montreal Olympics **Obv:**
Young bust right, small maple leaf below, date at
right **Rev:** Canoeing, denomination below **Rev.**
Designer: Lynda Cooper **Note:** Series V.

Date	Mintage	MS-63	Proof
1975	—	45.00	—
1975 Proof	89,155	—	45.00

KM# 111 48.6000 g. 0.9250 Silver 1.4453 oz. ASW
45 mm.   **Subject:** 1976 Montreal Olympics **Obv:**
Young bust right, small maple leaf below, date at

right **Rev:** Football, denomination below **Rev.**
Designer: Shigeo Fukada **Note:** Series VI.

Date	Mintage	MS-63	Proof
1976 Proof	76,908	—	45.00
1976	—	45.00	—

KM# 112 48.6000 g. 0.9250 Silver 1.4453 oz. ASW
45 mm.   **Subject:** 1976 Montreal Olympics **Obv:**
Young bust right, small maple leaf below, date at
right **Rev:** Field hockey **Rev. Designer:** Shigeo
Fukada **Note:** Series VI.

Date	Mintage	MS-63	Proof
1976	—	45.00	—
1976 Proof	76,908	—	45.00

KM# 113 48.6000 g. 0.9250 Silver 1.4453 oz. ASW
45 mm.   **Subject:** 1976 Montreal Olympics **Obv:**
Young bust right, small maple leaf below, date at right
Rev: Olympic Stadium, denomination below **Rev.**
Designer: Elliot John Morrison **Note:** Series VII.

Date	Mintage	MS-63	Proof
1976	—	45.00	—
1976 Proof	79,102	—	45.00

KM# 114 48.6000 g. 0.9250 Silver 1.4453 oz. ASW
45 mm. **Subject:** 1976 Montreal Olympics **Obv:**
Young bust right, small maple leaf below, date at right
Rev: Olympic Velodrome, denomination below **Rev.**
Designer: Elliot John Morrison **Note:** Series VII.

Date	Mintage	MS-63	Proof
1976	—	45.00	—
1976 Proof	79,102	—	45.00

KM# 520 16.7200 g. 0.9000 Gold 0.4838 oz. AGW
26.92 mm. **Obv:** Crowned head right **Rev:**
National arms **Edge:** Reeded

Date	Mintage	MS-63	Proof
2002 Proof	2,002	—	750

KM# 559 25.1750 g. 0.9999 Silver 0.8093 oz. ASW
36 mm. **Subject:** Pope John Paul II **Obv:** Head right

Date	Mintage	MS-63	Proof
2005 Proof	24,716	—	45.00

KM# 757 25.1750 g. 0.9999 Silver 0.8093 oz.
ASW **Subject:** Year of the Veteran **Rev:** Profile
left of young and old veteran

Date	Mintage	MS-63	Proof
2005 Proof	6,549	—	55.00

KM# 661 25.1750 g. 0.9999 Silver 0.8093 oz.
ASW **Subject:** National Historic Sites **Obv:** Head
right **Rev:** Fortress of Louisbourg

Date	Mintage	MS-63	Proof
2006 Proof	5,544	—	40.00

KM# 1010 0.9990 Silver **Subject:** 75th
Anniversary Canadian Bank Notes **Rev:** Female
seated

Date	Mintage	MS-63	Proof
2010 Proof	—	—	80.00

KM# 1096 27.7800 g. 0.9250 Silver 0.8261 oz.
ASW 40 mm. **Rev:** Blue whale diving

Date	Mintage	MS-63	Proof
2010 Proof	10,000	—	85.00

15 DOLLARS

KM# 215 33.6300 g. 0.9250 Silver 1.0000 oz. ASW
39 mm. **Subject:** 1992 Olympics **Obv:** Crowned
head right, date at left, denomination below **Rev:**
Coaching track **Rev. Designer:** Stewart Sherwood

Date	Mintage	MS-63	Proof
1992 Proof	275,000	—	32.50

KM# 216 33.6300 g. 0.9250 Silver 1.0000 oz.
ASW **Subject:** 1992 Olympics **Obv:** Crowned
head right, date at left, denomination below **Rev:**
High jump, rings, speed skating **Rev. Designer:**
David Craig

Date	Mintage	MS-63	Proof
1992 Proof	275,000	—	32.50

KM# 304 Bi-Metallic 40 mm.   **Subject:** Year of the Tiger **Obv:** Crowned head right **Rev:** Tiger within octagon at center, animal figures surround **Rev. Designer:** Harvey Chan

Date	Mintage	MS-63	Proof
1998 Proof	68,888	—	375

KM# 331 Bi-Metallic   **Subject:** Year of the Rabbitt **Obv:** Crowned head right **Rev:** Rabbit within octagon at center, animal figures surround **Rev. Designer:** Harvey Chan

Date	Mintage	MS-63	Proof
1999 Proof	77,791	—	100

KM# 387 Bi-Metallic   **Subject:** Year of the Dragon **Obv:** Crowned head right **Rev. Designer:** Harvey Chan

Date	Mintage	MS-63	Proof
2000 Proof	88,634	—	150

KM# 415 33.6300 g. 0.9250 Silver 1.0000 oz. ASW 40 mm.   **Subject:** Year of the Snake **Obv:** Crowned head right **Rev:** Snake within circle of lunar calendar signs **Rev. Designer:** Harvey Chan **Edge:** Reeded

Date	Mintage	MS-63	Proof
2001 Proof	60,754	—	85.00

KM# 463 33.6300 g. 0.9250 Silver 1.0000 oz. ASW   **Subject:** Year of the Horse **Obv:** Crowned head right **Obv. Designer:** Dora dePédery-Hunt **Rev:** Horse in center with Chinese Lunar calendar around **Rev. Designer:** Harvey Chain

Date	Mintage	MS-63	Proof
2002 Proof	59,395	—	85.00

KM# 481 33.6300 g. 0.9250 Silver 1.0000 oz. ASW 40 mm.   **Subject:** Year of the Sheep **Obv:** Crowned head right **Rev:** Sheep in center with Chinese Lunar calendar around **Rev. Designer:** Harvey Chain

Date	Mintage	MS-63	Proof
2003 Proof	53,714	—	85.00

KM# 610 33.6300 g. 0.9250 Silver 1.0000 oz. ASW   **Subject:** Year of the Monkey **Obv:** Crowned head right **Rev:** Monkey in center with Chinese Lunar calendar around

Date	Mintage	MS-63	Proof
2004 Proof	46,175	—	150

KM# 560 33.6300 g. 0.9250 Silver 1.0000 oz. ASW   **Subject:** Year of the Rooster **Obv:** Crowned head right **Rev:** Rooster in center with Chinese Lunar calendar around

Date	Mintage	MS-63	Proof
2005 Proof	44,690	—	125

KM# 587 33.6300 g. 0.9250 Silver 1.0000 oz. ASW   **Subject:** Year of the Dog **Obv:** Crowned head left **Rev:** Dog in center with Chinese Lunar calendar around

Date	Mintage	MS-63	Proof
2006 Proof	41,617	—	100

KM# 732 33.6300 g. 0.9250 Silver 1.0000 oz. ASW 40 mm.   **Subject:** Year of the Pig **Rev:** Pig at center of lunar characters

Date	Mintage	MS-63	Proof
2007 Proof	48,888	—	100

KM# 801 33.6300 g. 0.9250 Silver 1.0000 oz. ASW 40 mm.   **Subject:** Year of the Rat **Rev:** Rat, gold octagonal insert at center

Date	Mintage	MS-63	Proof
2008 Proof	48,888	—	90.00

KM# 807 31.5600 g. 0.9250 Silver 0.9385 oz. ASW 28.6x49.8 mm.   **Rev:** Jack of Hearts, multicolor playing card

Date	Mintage	MS-63	Proof
2008 Proof	25,000	—	90.00

KM#919 31.5600 g.0.9250 Silver 0.9385 oz. ASW 49.8 x 28.6 mm. **Obv:** Bust right **Obv. Designer:** Susanna Blunt **Rev:** Ten of spades, multicolor **Shape:** rectangle

Date	Mintage	MS-63	Proof
2009 Proof	25,000	—	90.00

KM#920 31.5600 g.0.9250 Silver 0.9385 oz. ASW 49.8 x 28.6 mm. **Obv:** Bust right **Obv. Designer:** Susanna Blunt **Rev:** King of hearts, multicolor **Shape:** Rectangle

Date	Mintage	MS-63	Proof
2009 Proof	25,000	—	90.00

KM# 1038 Silver 38 mm. **Subject:** Year of the tiger **Rev:** Tiger in forest **Shape:** scalloped

Date	Mintage	MS-63	Proof
2009 Proof	—	—	85.00

KM#866 33.6300 g. 0.9250 Silver 1.0000 oz. ASW 40 mm. **Subject:** Year of the Ox **Rev:** Ox, octagon gold insert

Date	Mintage	MS-63	Proof
2009 Proof	48,888	—	90.00

KM#922 30.0000 g. 0.9250 Silver 0.8921 oz. ASW 36.15 mm. **Obv:** Bust right **Obv. Designer:** Susanna Blunt **Rev:** Pages portrait of George VI

Date	Mintage	MS-63	P/L	Proof
2009(ml) Prooflike	10,000	100.00	100.00	—

KM#923 30.0000 g. 0.9250 Silver 0.8921 oz. ASW
36.15 mm.   **Obv:** Bust right **Obv. Designer:**
Susanna Blunt **Rev:** Gillick portrait of Queen
Elizabeth II

Date	Mintage	MS-63	Proof
2009(ml) Prooflike	10,000	100.00	

KM#980 34.0000 g. 0.9250 Silver 1.0111 oz. ASW
40 mm.   **Rev:** Tiger in gold insert

Date	Mintage	MS-63	Proof
2010 Proof	48,888	—	100

KM# 1032 0.9990 Silver   **Subject:** Year of the
tiger **Rev:** Tiger walking tiger

KM# 1055 31.1050 g. 0.9990 Silver 0.9990 oz.
ASW 38 mm.   **Rev:** Rabbit sitting, head turned left
Shape: scalloped

Date	Mintage	MS-63	Proof
2011 Proof	—	—	85.00

KM# 1091 25.1100 g. 0.9250 Silver 0.7467 oz.
ASW 36.15 mm.   **Rev:** Prince Charles bust **Rev.**
Designer: Laurie McGaw

Date	Mintage	MS-63	Proof
2011 Prooflike	10,000	100.00	

KM# 1092 25.1100 g. 0.9250 Silver 0.7467 oz.
ASW 36.15 mm.   **Rev:** Prince William **Rev.**
Designer: Laurie McGaw

Date	Mintage	MS-63	Proof
2011 Prooflike	10,000	100.00	—

KM# 1093 25.1800 g. 0.9250 Silver 0.7488 oz.
ASW 36.15 mm.   **Rev:** Prince Harry bust 1/4 right
Rev. Designer: Laurie McGaw

Date	Mintage	MS-63	Proof
2011 Prooflike	10,000	100.00	—

KM# 1094 31.3900 g. 0.9990 Silver 1.0082 oz.
ASW 38 mm.   **Rev:** Rabbit bounding left **Rev.**
Designer: Aries Cheung

Date	Mintage	MS-63	Proof
2011 Proof	9,999	—	100

20 DOLLARS

KM# 71 18.2733 g. 0.9000 Gold 0.5287 oz. AGW
27.05 mm.   **Subject:** Centennial **Obv:** Crowned
head right **Rev:** Crowned and supported arms
Edge: Reeded

Date	Mintage	MS-63	Proof
1967 Proof	337,688	—	775

KM# 145 33.6300 g. 0.9250 Silver 1.0000 oz. ASW
40 mm.   **Subject:** 1988 Calgary Olympics **Obv:**
Young bust right, maple leaf below, date at right
Rev: Downhill skier, denomination below **Rev.**
Designer: Ian Stewart **Edge:** Lettered

Date	Mintage	MS-63	Proof
1985 Proof	406,360	—	32.00
1985 Proof	Inc. above	—	200
Note: Plain edge			

Date	Mintage	MS-63	Proof
1986 Proof	Inc. above	—	200

Note: Plain edge

KM# 146 33.6300 g. 0.9250 Silver 1.0000 oz. ASW 40 mm. **Subject:** 1988 Calgary Olympics **Obv:** Young bust right, small maple leaf below, date at right **Rev:** Speed skater, denomination below **Rev. Designer:** Friedrich Peter **Edge:** Lettered

Date	Mintage	MS-63	Proof
1985 Proof	354,222	—	32.00
1985 Proof	Inc. above	—	200

Note: Plain edge

KM# 148 33.6300 g. 0.9250 Silver 1.0000 oz. ASW 40 mm. **Subject:** 1988 Calgary Olympics **Obv:** Young bust right, small maple leaf below, date at right **Rev:** Hockey, denomination below **Rev. Designer:** Ian Stewart **Edge:** Lettered

Date	Mintage	MS-63	Proof
1986 Proof	396,602	—	32.00
1986 Proof	Inc. above	—	200

Note: Plain edge

KM# 150 33.6300 g. 0.9250 Silver 1.0000 oz. ASW 40 mm. **Subject:** Calgary 1988 - 15th Winter Olympic Games **Obv:** Young bust right, small maple leaf below, date at right **Rev:** Cross-country skier, denomination below **Rev. Designer:** Ian Stewart **Edge:** Lettered

Date	Mintage	MS-63	Proof
1986 Proof	303,199	—	32.00

KM# 151 33.6300 g. 0.9250 Silver 1.0000 oz. ASW 40 mm. **Subject:** 1988 Calgary Olympics **Obv:** Young bust right, small maple leaf below, date at right **Rev:** Free-style skier, denomination below **Rev. Designer:** Walter Ott **Edge:** Lettered

Date	Mintage	MS-63	Proof
1986 Proof	294,322	—	32.00
1986 Proof	Inc. above	—	200

Note: Plain edge

KM# 147 33.6300 g. 0.9250 Silver 1.0000 oz. ASW 40 mm. **Subject:** 1988 Calgary Olympics **Obv:** Young bust right, small maple leaf below, date at right **Rev:** Biathlon, denomination below **Rev. Designer:** John Mardon **Edge:** Lettered

Date	Mintage	MS-63	Proof
1986 Proof	308,086	—	32.00

KM# 155 34.1070 g. 0.9250 Silver 1.0143 oz. ASW 40 mm. **Subject:** Calgary 1988 - 15th Winter Olympic Games **Obv:** Young bust right, small maple leaf below, date at right **Rev:** Figure skating pairs

20 DOLLARS

event, denomination below **Rev. Designer:**
Raymond Taylor **Edge:** Lettered

Date	Mintage	MS-63	Proof
1987 Proof	334,875	—	32.00

KM# 156 34.1070 g. 0.9250 Silver 1.0143 oz. ASW
40 mm.   **Subject:** 1988 Calgary Olympics **Obv:**
Young bust right, small maple leaf below, date at
right **Rev:** Curling, denomination below **Rev.**
Designer: Ian Stewart **Edge:** Lettered

Date	Mintage	MS-63	Proof
1987 Proof	286,457	—	32.00

KM# 172 31.1030 g. 0.9250 Silver 0.9249 oz. ASW
38 mm.   **Subject:** Aviation **Obv:** Crowned head
right, date below **Rev:** Lancaster, Fauquier in
cameo, denomination below **Rev. Designer:** Robert
R. Carmichael

Date	Mintage	MS-63	Proof
1990 Proof	43,596	—	125

KM# 159 34.1070 g. 0.9250 Silver 1.0143 oz. ASW
40 mm.   **Subject:** 1988 Calgary Olympics **Obv:**
Young bust right, small maple leaf below, date at
right **Rev:** Ski jumper, denomination below **Rev.**
Designer: Raymond Taylor **Edge:** Lettered

Date	Mintage	MS-63	Proof
1987 Proof	290,954	—	32.00

KM# 173 31.1030 g. 0.9250 Silver 0.9249 oz. ASW
38 mm.   **Subject:** Aviation **Obv:** Crowned head
right, date below **Rev:** Anson and Harvard, Air
Marshal Robert Leckie in cameo, denomination
below **Rev. Designer:** Geoff Bennett

Date	Mintage	MS-63	Proof
1990 Proof	41,844	—	45.00

KM# 160 34.1070 g. 0.9250 Silver 1.0143 oz. ASW
40 mm.   **Subject:** 1988 Calgary Olympics **Obv:**
Young bust right, maple leaf below, date at right
Rev: Bobsled, denomination below **Rev. Designer:**
John Mardon **Edge:** Lettered

Date	Mintage	MS-63	Proof
1987 Proof	274,326	—	32.00

KM# 196 31.1030 g. 0.9250 Silver 0.9249 oz. ASW
38 mm.   **Subject:** Aviation **Obv:** Crowned head
right, date below **Rev:** Silver Dart, John A. D.
McCurdy and F. W. "Casey" Baldwin in cameo,
denomination below **Rev. Designer:** George
Velinger

Date	Mintage	MS-63	Proof
1991 Proof	28,791	—	45.00

20 DOLLARS

KM#236 31.1030 g. 0.9250 Silver 0.9249 oz. ASW
38 mm. **Subject:** Aviation **Obv:** Crowned head
right, date below **Rev:** Fairchild 71C float plane,
James A. Richardson, Sr. in cameo, denomination
below **Rev. Designer:** Robert R. Carmichael

Date	Mintage	MS-63	Proof
1993 Proof	32,199	—	45.00

KM#197 31.1030 g. 0.9250 Silver 0.9249 oz. ASW
38 mm. **Subject:** Aviation **Obv:** Crowned head
right, date below **Rev:** de Haviland Beaver, Philip
C. Garratt in cameo, denomination below **Rev.
Designer:** Peter Massman

Date	Mintage	MS-63	Proof
1991 Proof	29,399	—	45.00

KM#224 31.1030 g. 0.9250 Silver 0.9249 oz. ASW
38 mm. **Subject:** Aviation **Obv:** Crowned head
right, date below **Rev:** Curtiss JN-4 Canick ("Jenny"),
Sir Frank W. Baillie in cameo, denomination below
Rev. Designer: George Velinger

Date	Mintage	MS-63	Proof
1992 Proof	33,105	—	45.00

KM#237 31.1030 g. 0.9250 Silver 0.9249 oz. ASW
38 mm. **Subject:** Aviation **Obv:** Crowned head
right, date below **Rev:** Lockheed 14, Zebulon Lewis
Leigh in cameo, denomination below **Rev.
Designer:** Robert R. Carmichael

Date	Mintage	MS-63	Proof
1993 Proof	32,550	—	45.00

KM#225 31.1030 g. 0.9250 Silver 0.9249 oz. ASW
38 mm. **Subject:** Aviation **Obv:** Crowned head
right, date below **Rev:** de Haviland Gypsy Moth,
Murton A. Seymour in cameo, denomination below
Rev. Designer: John Mardon

Date	Mintage	MS-63	Proof
1992 Proof	32,537	—	45.00

KM#246 31.1030 g. 0.9250 Silver 0.9249 oz. ASW
38 mm. **Subject:** Aviation **Obv:** Crowned head
right, date below **Rev:** Curtiss HS-2L seaplane,
Stewart Graham in cameo, denomination below
Rev. Designer: John Mardon

Date	Mintage	MS-63	Proof
1994 Proof	31,242	—	45.00

20 DOLLARS

KM#247 31.1030 g. 0.9250 Silver 0.9249 oz. ASW
38 mm.   Subject: Aviation Obv: Crowned head
right, date below Rev: Vickers Vedette, Wilfred T.
Reid in cameo, denomination below Rev. Designer:
Robert R. Carmichael

Date	Mintage	MS-63	Proof
1994 Proof	30,880	—	45.00

KM# 271 31.1030 g. 0.9250 Silver 0.9249 oz. ASW
38 mm.   Subject: Aviation Obv: Crowned head
right, date below Rev: C-FEA1 Fleet Cannuck,
denomination below Rev. Designer: Robert Bradford

Date	Mintage	MS-63	Proof
1995 Proof	17,438	—	45.00

KM# 272 31.1030 g. 0.9250 Silver 0.9249 oz. ASW
38 mm.   Subject: Aviation Obv: Crowned head
right, date below Rev: DHC-1 Chipmunk,
denomination below Rev. Designer: Robert Bradford

Date	Mintage	MS-63	Proof
1995 Proof	17,722	—	45.00

KM#276 31.1030 g. 0.9250 Silver 0.9249 oz. ASW
38 mm.   Subject: Aviation Obv: Crowned head
right, date below Rev: CF-100 Cannuck,
denomination below Rev. Designer: Jim Bruce

Date	Mintage	MS-63	Proof
1996 Proof	18,508	—	45.00

KM#277 31.1030 g. 0.9250 Silver 0.9249 oz. ASW
38 mm.   Subject: Aviation Obv: Crowned head
right, date below Obv. Legend: CF-105 Arrow,
denomination below Rev. Designer: Jim Bruce

Date	Mintage	MS-63	Proof
1996 Proof	27,163	—	100

KM#297 31.1030 g. 0.9250 Silver 0.9249 oz. ASW
38 mm.   Subject: Aviation Obv: Crowned head
right, date below Rev: Canadair F-86 Sabre,
denomination below Rev. Designer: Ross
Buckland

Date	Mintage	MS-63	Proof
1997 Proof	14,389	—	45.00

20 DOLLARS

KM#298 31.1030 g. 0.9250 Silver 0.9249 oz. ASW 38 mm. **Subject:** Aviation **Obv:** Crowned head right, date below **Rev:** Canadair CT-114 Tutor, denomination below **Rev. Designer:** Ross Buckland

Date	Mintage	MS-63	Proof
1997 Proof	15,669	—	45.00

KM#329 31.1030 g. 0.9250 Silver 0.9249 oz. ASW 38 mm. **Subject:** Aviation **Obv:** Crowned head, right, date below **Rev:** CP-107 Argus, denomination below

Date	Mintage	MS-63	Proof
1998 Proof	Est. 50,000	—	50.00

KM#330 31.1030 g. 0.9250 Silver 0.9249 oz. ASW 38 mm. **Subject:** Aviation **Obv:** Crowned head right, date below **Rev:** CP-215 Waterbomber, denomination below **Rev. Designer:** Peter Mossman

Date	Mintage	MS-63	Proof
1998 Proof	Est. 50,000	—	75.00

KM#339 31.1030 g. 0.9250 Silver 0.9249 oz. ASW 38 mm. **Subject:** Aviation **Obv:** Crowned head right, date below **Rev:** DHC-6 Twin Otter, denomination below **Rev. Designer:** Neil Aird

Date	Mintage	MS-63	Proof
1999 Proof	Est. 50,000	—	95.00

KM#340 31.1030 g. 0.9250 Silver 0.9249 oz. ASW 38 mm. **Subject:** Aviation **Obv:** Crowned head right, date below **Rev:** DHC-8 Dash 8, denomination below

Date	Mintage	MS-63	Proof
1999 Proof	50,000	—	100

KM# 395 0.9250 Silver 38 mm. **Subject:** First Canadian locomotive **Obv:** Crowned head right, date below **Rev:** Locomotive below multicolored cameo, denomination below

Date	Mintage	MS-63	Proof
2000 Proof	—	—	50.00

20 DOLLARS

KM# 396 0.9250 Silver 38 mm.   **Subject:** First Canadian self-propelled car **Obv:** Crowned head right, date below **Rev:** Car below multicolored cameo, denomination below

Date	Mintage	MS-63	Proof
2000 Proof	—	—	50.00

KM# 397 0.9250 Silver 38 mm.   **Subject:** Bluenose sailboat **Obv:** Crowned head right, date below **Rev:** Bluenose sailing left below multicolored cameo, denomination below

Date	Mintage	MS-63	Proof
2000 Proof	—	—	150

KM#411 31.1035 g. 0.9250 Silver 0.9250 oz. ASW 38 mm.   **Subject:** Transportation - Steam Locomotive **Obv:** Crowned head right **Obv. Designer:** Dora dePédery-Hunt **Rev:** First Canadian Steel Steam Locomotive and cameo hologram **Rev. Designer:** Don Curely **Edge:** Segmented reeding

Date	Mintage	MS-63	Proof
2001 Proof	15,000	—	45.00

KM#427 31.1030 g. 0.9250 Silver 0.9249 oz. ASW 38 mm.   **Series:** Transportation - The Marco Polo **Obv:** Crowned head right **Rev:** Sailship with hologram cameo **Rev. Designer:** J. Franklin Wright **Edge:** Segmented reeding

Date	Mintage	MS-63	Proof
2001 Proof	15,000	—	45.00

KM#428 31.1030 g. 0.9250 Silver 0.9249 oz. ASW 38 mm.   **Series:** Transportation - Russell Touring Car **Obv:** Crowned head right **Rev:** Russell touring car with hologram cameo **Rev. Designer:** John Mardon **Edge:** Segmented reeding

Date	Mintage	MS-63	Proof
2001 Proof	15,000	—	45.00

KM# 464 31.1030 g. 0.9250 Silver 0.9249 oz. ASW   **Obv:** Crowned head right **Obv. Designer:** Dora dePédery-Hunt **Rev:** Gray-Dort Model 25-SM with cameo hologram **Rev. Designer:** John Mardon

Date	Mintage	MS-63	Proof
2002 Proof	15,000	—	45.00

KM# 465 31.1030 g. 0.9250 Silver 0.9249 oz. ASW   **Obv:** Crowned head right **Obv. Designer:** Dora dePédery-Hunt **Rev:** Sailing ship William D. Lawrence **Rev. Designer:** Bonnie Ross

Date	Mintage	MS-63	Proof
2002 Proof	15,000	—	45.00

KM#482 31.3900 g. 0.9999 Silver 1.0091 oz. ASW 38 mm.   **Obv:** Crowned head right **Obv. Designer:** Dora dePédery-Hunt **Rev:** Niagara Falls hologram **Rev. Designer:** Gary Corcoran

Date	Mintage	MS-63	Proof
2003 Proof	29,967	—	75.00

KM# 483 31.1030 g. 0.9250 Silver 0.9249 oz. ASW   **Subject:** The HMCS Bras d'or (FHE-400) **Obv:** Crowned head right **Obv. Designer:** Dora dePédery-Hunt **Rev:** Ship in water **Rev. Designer:** Donald Curley, Stan Witten

Date	Mintage	MS-63	Proof
2003 Proof	15,000	—	45.00

20 DOLLARS

KM#523 31.3900 g. 0.9990 Silver 1.0082 oz. ASW 38 mm. **Obv:** Crowned head right **Obv. Designer:** Dora dePédery-Hunt **Rev:** Canadian Rockies, multicolor

Date	Mintage	MS-63	Proof
2003 Proof	29,967	—	50.00

KM# 484 31.1030 g. 0.9250 Silver 0.9249 oz. ASW **Subject:** Canadian National FA-1 diesel-electric locomotive **Obv:** Crowned head right **Obv. Designer:** Dora dePédery-Hunt **Rev. Designer:** John Mardon, William Woodruff

Date	Mintage	MS-63	Proof
2003 Proof	15,000	—	45.00

KM# 485 31.1030 g. 0.9250 Silver 0.9249 oz. ASW **Obv:** Crowned head right **Obv. Designer:** Dora dePédery-Hunt **Rev:** The Bricklin SV-1 **Rev. Designer:** Brian Hughes, José Oslo

Date	Mintage	MS-63	Proof
2003 Proof	15,000	—	45.00

KM#611 31.3900 g. 0.9999 Silver 1.0091 oz. ASW 38 mm. **Obv:** Head right **Obv. Designer:** Susanna Blunt **Rev:** Iceberg, hologram

Date	Mintage	MS-63	Proof
2004 Proof	24,879	—	45.00

KM#838 31.3900 g. 0.9999 Silver 1.0091 oz. ASW 38 mm. **Rev:** Hopewell Rocks, gilt

Date	Mintage	MS-63	Proof
2004 Proof	16,918	—	45.00

KM#561 31.3900 g. 0.9999 Silver 1.0091 oz. ASW 38 mm. **Subject:** Three-masted sailing ship, hologram **Obv:** Head right **Obv. Designer:** Susanna Blunt **Rev. Designer:** Bonnie Ross

Date	Mintage	MS-63	Proof
2005 Proof	18,276	—	55.00

KM# 562 31.3900 g. 0.9999 Silver 1.0091 oz. ASW 38 mm. **Subject:** Northwest Territories Diamonds **Obv:** Head right **Obv. Designer:** Susanna Blunt **Rev:** Multicolor diamond hologram on landscape **Rev. Designer:** José Oslo **Edge:** Reeded

Date	Mintage	MS-63	Proof
2005 Proof	35,000	—	45.00

KM# 563 31.3900 g. 0.9999 Silver 1.0091 oz. ASW **Subject:** Mingan Archcpelago **Obv:** Head right **Obv. Designer:** Susanna Blunt **Rev:** Cliffs with whale tail out of water **Rev. Designer:** Pierre Leduc

Date	Mintage	MS-63	Proof
2005 Proof	—	—	45.00

KM# 564 31.3900 g. 0.9999 Silver 1.0091 oz. ASW **Subject:** Rainforests of the Pacific Northwest **Obv:** Head right **Rev:** Open winged bird

Date	Mintage	MS-63	Proof
2005 Proof	—	—	45.00

KM#565 31.3900 g. 0.9999 Silver 1.0091 oz. ASW 38 mm. **Subject:** Toronto Island National Park **Obv:** Head right **Rev:** Toronto Island Lighthouse, Toronto skyline in background

Date	Mintage	MS-63	Proof
2005 Proof	—	—	45.00

KM# 588 31.3900 g. 0.9999 Silver 1.0091 oz. ASW **Subject:** Georgian Bay National Park **Obv:** Head right **Rev:** Canoe and small trees on island

Date	Mintage	MS-63	Proof
2006 Proof	—	—	60.00

KM#589 31.1000 g. 0.9999 Silver 0.9997 oz. ASW 38 mm. **Obv:** Head right **Rev:** Notre Dame Basilica, Montreal, as a hologram

Date	Mintage	MS-63	Proof
2006 Proof	15,000	—	50.00

KM#663 31.3900 g. 0.9999 Silver 1.0091 oz. ASW 38 mm. **Subject:** Nahanni National Park **Obv:** Head right **Rev:** Bear walking along sream, cliff in background

Date	Mintage	MS-63	Proof
2006 Proof	—	—	60.00

KM# 664 31.3900 g. 0.9999 Silver 1.0091 oz. ASW 38 mm. **Subject:** Jasper National Park **Obv:** Head right **Rev:** Cowboy on horseback in majestic scene

Date	Mintage	MS-63	Proof
2006 Proof	—	—	60.00

KM#665 31.1000 g. 0.9999 Silver 0.9997 oz. ASW 38 mm. **Obv:** Head right **Rev:** Holographic rendering of CN Tower

Date	Mintage	MS-63	Proof
2006 Proof	15,000	—	60.00

KM#666 31.1000 g. 0.9999 Silver 0.9997 oz. ASW **Subject:** Pengrowth (Calgary Saddledome) **Obv:** Head right **Rev:** Holographic view of Saddledome

Date	Mintage	MS-63	Proof
2006 Proof	15,000	—	55.00

20 DOLLARS

KM# 667 31.3900 g. 0.9999 Silver 1.0091 oz.
ASW   **Subject:** Tall Ship **Obv:** Head right **Rev:**
Ketch and holographic image

Date	Mintage	MS-63	Proof
2006 Proof	10,299	—	60.00

KM# 839 31.3900 g. 0.9999 Silver 1.0091 oz.
ASW   **Rev:** Northern lights in hologram

Date	Mintage	MS-63	Proof
2007	—	35.00	—

KM# 808 31.5000 g. 0.9250 Silver 0.9368 oz. ASW
38 mm.   **Subject:** Agriculture trade

Date	Mintage	MS-63	Proof
2008 Proof	10,000	—	70.00

KM# 809 31.1050 g. 0.9990 Silver 0.9990 oz. ASW
38 mm.   **Rev:** Royal Hudson Steam locomotive

Date	Mintage	MS-63	Proof
2008 Proof	10,000	—	70.00

KM# 734 31.1000 g. 0.9990 Silver 0.9988 oz. ASW
38 mm.   **Rev:** Holiday sleigh ride

Date	Mintage	MS-63	Proof
2007 Proof	6,041	—	70.00

KM# 735 31.1000 g. 0.9990 Silver 0.9988 oz. ASW
38 mm.   **Rev:** Snowflake, blue crystal

Date	Mintage	MS-63	Proof
2007 Proof	1,433	—	175

KM# 737 31.1000 g. 0.9990 Silver 0.9988 oz. ASW
38 mm.   **Subject:** International Polar Year

Date	Mintage	MS-63	Proof
2007 Proof	8,352	—	65.00

KM# 737a 31.1000 g. 0.9990 Silver 0.9988 oz.
ASW 38 mm.   **Subject:** International Polar Year
Rev: Blue plasma coating

Date	Mintage	MS-63	Proof
2007 Proof	3,005	—	250

KM# 738 31.3900 g. 0.9999 Silver 1.0091 oz. ASW
38 mm.   **Subject:** Tall ships **Rev:** Brigantine in
harbor, hologram

Date	Mintage	MS-63	Proof
2007 Proof	16,000	—	60.00

KM# 810 31.3900 g. 0.9990 Silver 1.0082 oz. ASW
38 mm.   **Rev:** Green leaf and crystal raindrop **Rev.**
Designer: Stanley Witten

Date	Mintage	MS-63	Proof
2008 Proof	15,000	—	110

KM# 811 31.1050 g. 0.9990 Silver 0.9990 oz.
ASW   **Rev:** Snowflake, amethyst crystal

Date	Mintage	MS-63	Proof
2008 Proof	15,000	—	90.00

KM#813 31.1050 g. 0.9990 Silver 0.9990 oz. ASW 38 mm.   **Rev:** Carolers around tree

Date	Mintage	MS-63	Proof
2008 Proof	10,000	—	70.00

KM#891 31.3900 g. 0.9990 Silver 1.0082 oz. ASW 38 mm.   **Subject:** Great Canadian Locomotives - Jubilee **Obv:** Bust right **Obv. Legend:** Elizabeth II DG Regina **Obv. Designer:** Susanna Blunt **Rev:** Jubilee locomotive side view **Rev. Legend:** Canada 20 Dollars **Edge Lettering:** Jubilee

Date	Mintage	MS-63	Proof
2009 Proof	10,000	—	70.00

KM#892 31.3900 g. 0.9990 Silver 1.0082 oz. ASW 38 mm.   **Subject:** Crystal raindrop **Obv:** Bust right **Obv. Legend:** Elizabeth II DG Regina **Obv. Designer:** Susanna Blunt **Rev:** Colored maple leaves with crystal raindrop **Rev. Legend:** Canada 20 Dollars **Rev. Designer:** Celia Godkin

Date	Mintage	MS-63	Proof
2009 Proof	10,000	—	95.00

KM#872 31.1050 g. 0.9990 Silver 0.9990 oz. ASW 38 mm.   **Rev:** Snowflake, sapphire crystal

Date	Mintage	MS-63	Proof
2008 Proof	15,000	—	85.00

KM#893 31.3900 g. 0.9990 Silver 1.0082 oz. ASW 38 mm.   **Subject:** Coal mining trade **Obv:** Bust right **Obv. Legend:** Elizabeth II DG Regina **Obv. Designer:** Susanna Blunt **Rev:** Miner pushing cart with coal **Rev. Legend:** Canada 20 Dollars **Rev. Designer:** John Marder

Date	Mintage	MS-63	Proof
2009 Proof	10,000	—	75.00

KM#870 27.7800 g. 0.9250 Silver 0.8261 oz. ASW 40 mm.   **Rev:** Calgary Flames goalie mask multicolor on goal net

Date	Mintage	MS-63	Proof
2009 Proof	10,000	—	70.00

KM#871 27.7800 g. 0.9250 Silver 0.8261 oz. ASW 40 mm.   **Rev:** Edmonton Oilers goalie mask, multicolor on goal net

Date	Mintage	MS-63	Proof
2009 Proof	10,000	—	70.00

20 DOLLARS

KM# 872A 27.7800 g. 0.9250 Silver 0.8261 oz.
ASW 40 mm.   **Rev:** Montreal Canadians goalie
mask multicolor

Date	Mintage	MS-63	Proof
2009 Proof	10,000	—	70.00

KM# 873 27.7800 g. 0.9250 Silver 0.8261 oz. ASW
40 mm.   **Rev:** Ottawa Senators goalie mask on
goal net

Date	Mintage	MS-63	Proof
2009 Proof	10,000	—	70.00

KM# 876 31.5000 g. 0.9250 Silver 0.9368 oz. ASW
40 mm.   **Rev:** Summer moon mask

Date	Mintage	MS-63	Proof
2009 Proof	10,000	—	75.00

KM# 874 27.7800 g. 0.9250 Silver 0.8261 oz. ASW
40 mm.   **Rev:** Toronto Maple Leafs goalie mask,
multicolor on goal net

Date	Mintage	MS-63	Proof
2009 Proof	10,000	—	70.00

KM# 944 31.1050 g. 0.9990 Silver 0.9990 oz. ASW
38 mm.   **Rev:** Snowflake - light blue crystal

Date	Mintage	MS-63	Proof
2009 Proof	15,000	—	95.00

KM# 875 27.7800 g. 0.9250 Silver 0.8261 oz. ASW
40 mm.   **Rev:** Vancouver Canucks goalie mask,
multicolor on goal net

Date	Mintage	MS-63	Proof
2009 Proof	10,000	—	70.00

KM# 945 31.1050 g. 0.9990 Silver 0.9990 oz. ASW
38 mm.   **Rev:** Snowflake - light red crystal

Date	Mintage	MS-63	Proof
2009 Proof	15,000	—	95.00

KM#946 31.3900 g. 0.9990 Silver 1.0082 oz. ASW
38 mm.   **Rev:** Maple leaf and rain drop - fall colors

Date	Mintage	MS-63	Proof
2009 Proof	10,000	—	75.00

KM# 1013 31.3900 g. 0.9990 Silver 1.0082 oz.
ASW 38 mm.   **Rev:** Maple leaf and crystal **Rev.**
Designer: Celia Godkin

Date	Mintage	MS-63	Proof
2010 Proof	10,000	—	95.00

KM#987 31.3900 g. 0.9999 Silver 1.0091 oz. ASW
31.39 mm.   **Rev:** Lotus Water Lilly in multicolor
and crystal **Rev. Designer:** Cladio D'Angelo

Date	Mintage	MS-63	Proof
2010 Proof	10,000	—	100

KM# 1018 31.3900 g. 0.9990 Silver 1.0082 oz.
ASW 38 mm.   **Rev:** Steam Locomotive Selkirk

Date	Mintage	MS-63	Proof
2010 Proof	10,000	—	80.00

KM# 1009 31.3900 g. 0.9990 Silver 1.0082 oz.
ASW   **Subject:** 75th Anniversary of Canadian
Bank Notes **Rev:** Female and farmer seated

Date	Mintage	MS-63	Proof
2010 Proof	—	—	70.00

KM# 1048 31.1050 g. 0.9999 Silver 0.9999 oz.
ASW 38 mm.   **Rev:** Snowflake, blue crystals

Date	Mintage	MS-63	Proof
2010 Proof	—	—	85.00

20 DOLLARS

KM# 1049 31.1050 g. 0.9999 Silver 0.9999 oz.
ASW 38 mm.   **Rev:** Snowflake, tanzanite crystals

Date	Mintage	MS-63	Proof
2010 Proof	—	—	85.00

KM# 1066 31.9900 g. 0.9990 Silver 1.0274 oz.
ASW 38 mm.   **Rev:** Pinecone with ruby crystals
Rev. Designer: Susan Taylor

Date	Mintage	MS-63	Proof
2010 Proof	5,000	—	120

KM# 1067 31.9900 g. 0.9990 Silver 1.0274 oz.
ASW 38 mm.   **Rev:** Pinecone with blue crystals
Rev. Designer: Susan Taylor

Date	Mintage	MS-63	Proof
2010 Proof	5,000	—	120

KM# 1075 27.7800 g. 0.9250 Silver 0.8261 oz.
ASW 40 mm.   **Subject:** Winter Scene **Rev:** Horse
pulling cut Christmas Tree **Rev. Designer:** Rene
Clark

Date	Mintage	MS-63	Proof
2011 Proof	8,000	—	70.00

25 DOLLARS

KM#743 27.7800 g. 0.9250 Silver 0.8261 oz. ASW
40 mm.   **Subject:** Vancouver Olympics **Rev:**
Athletics pride hologram

Date	Mintage	MS-63	Proof
2007 Proof	45,000	—	65.00

KM#744 27.7500 g. 0.9250 Silver 0.8252 oz. ASW
40 mm.   **Subject:** Vancouver Olympics **Rev:**
Biathleon hologram

Date	Mintage	MS-63	Proof
2007 Proof	54,000	—	65.00

KM#742 27.7800 g. 0.9250 Silver 0.8261 oz. ASW
40 mm.   **Subject:** Vancouver Olympics **Rev:**
Alpine skiing, hologram

Date	Mintage	MS-63	Proof
2007 Proof	45,000	—	65.00

KM#745 27.7800 g. 0.9250 Silver 0.8261 oz. ASW
40 mm.   **Subject:** Vancouver Olympics **Rev:**
Curling hologram

Date	Mintage	MS-63	Proof
2007 Proof	—	—	65.00

KM#816 27.7800 g. 0.9250 Silver 0.8261 oz. ASW 40 mm. **Subject:** Vancouver Olympics **Rev:** Freestyle skating, hologram

Date	Mintage	MS-63	Proof
2008 Proof	45,000	—	65.00

KM#746 27.7800 g. 0.9250 Silver 0.8261 oz. ASW 40 mm. **Subject:** Vancouver Olympics **Rev:** Hockey, hologram

Date	Mintage	MS-63	Proof
2007 Proof	45,000	—	65.00

KM#817 27.7800 g. 0.9250 Silver 0.8261 oz. ASW 40 mm. **Subject:** Vancouver Olympics **Rev:** Snowboarding, hologram

Date	Mintage	MS-63	Proof
2008 Proof	45,000	—	65.00

KM#814 27.7800 g. 0.9250 Silver 0.8261 oz. ASW 40 mm. **Subject:** Vancouver Olympics **Rev:** Bobsleigh, hologram

Date	Mintage	MS-63	Proof
2008 Proof	45,000	—	65.00

KM#815 27.7800 g. 0.9250 Silver 0.8261 oz. ASW 40 mm. **Subject:** Vancouver Olympics **Rev:** Figure skating, hologram

Date	Mintage	MS-63	Proof
2008 Proof	45,000	—	65.00

KM#818 27.7800 g. 0.9250 Silver 0.8261 oz. ASW 40 mm. **Subject:** Vancouver Olympics **Rev:** Home of the 2010 Olympics

Date	Mintage	MS-63	Proof
2008 Proof	45,000	—	65.00

25 DOLLARS

KM#906 27.7800 g. 0.9250 Silver 0.8261 oz. ASW
40 mm.   **Subject:** 2010 Vancouver Olympics
Obv: Bust right **Obv. Designer:** Susanna Blunt
Rev: Ski Jumper, hologram at left

Date	Mintage	MS-63	Proof
2009 Proof	45,000	—	65.00

KM#903 27.7800 g. 0.9250 Silver 0.8261 oz. ASW
40 mm.   **Subject:** 2010 Vancouver Olympics
Obv: Bust right **Obv. Designer:** Susanna Blunt
Rev: Cross Country Skiing and hologram at left

Date	Mintage	MS-63	Proof
2009 Proof	45,000	—	65.00

KM#907 27.7800 g. 0.9250 Silver 0.8261 oz. ASW
40 mm.   **Subject:** 2010 Vancouver Olympics
Obv: Bust right **Obv. Designer:** Susanna Blunt
Rev: Speed Skaters, hologram at left

Date	Mintage	MS-63	Proof
2009 Proof	45,000	—	65.00

KM#904 27.7800 g. 0.9250 Silver 0.8261 oz. ASW
40 mm.   **Subject:** 2010 Vancouver Olympics
Obv: Bust right **Obv. Designer:** Susanna Blunt
Rev: Olympians holding torch, hologram at left

Date	Mintage	MS-63	Proof
2009 Proof	45,000	—	65.00

30 DOLLARS

KM# 590 31.5000 g. 0.9250 Silver 0.9368 oz.
ASW   **Subject:** Pacific Northwest Wood Carvings
Obv: Head right **Rev:** Welcome figure totem pole

Date	Mintage	MS-63	Proof
2006 Proof	9,904	—	75.00

KM#905 27.7800 g. 0.9250 Silver 0.8261 oz. ASW
40 mm.   **Subject:** 2010 Vancouver Olympics
Obv: Bust right **Obv. Designer:** Susanna Blunt
Rev: Sled, hologram at left

Date	Mintage	MS-63	Proof
2009 Proof	45,000	—	65.00

KM# 668 31.5000 g. 0.9250 Silver 0.9368 oz.
ASW   **Subject:** Canadarm and Col. C. Hadfield
Obv: Head right **Rev:** Hologram of Canadarm

Date	Mintage	MS-63	Proof
2006 Proof	9,357	—	90.00

KM# 669 31.5000 g. 0.9250 Silver 0.9368 oz. ASW **Subject:** National War Memorial **Obv:** Head right **Rev:** Statue of three soldiers

Date	Mintage	MS-63	Proof
2006 Proof	8,876	—	85.00

KM# 670 31.5000 g. 0.9250 Silver 0.9368 oz. ASW **Subject:** Beaumont Hamel Newfoundland **Obv:** Head right **Rev:** Caribou statue on rock outcrop

Date	Mintage	MS-63	Proof
2006 Proof	15,325	—	95.00

KM# 671 31.5000 g. 0.9250 Silver 0.9368 oz. ASW **Subject:** Dog Sled Team **Obv:** Head right **Rev:** Colorized

Date	Mintage	MS-63	Proof
2006 Proof	7,384	—	85.00

KM#739 31.5000 g. 0.9250 Silver 0.9368 oz. ASW 40 mm. **Rev:** Niagra Falls panoramic hologram

Date	Mintage	MS-63	Proof
2007 Proof	5,181	—	85.00

KM#741 31.5000 g. 0.9250 Silver 0.9368 oz. ASW 40 mm. **Rev:** War Memorial, Vimy Ridge

Date	Mintage	MS-63	Proof
2007 Proof	5,190	—	85.00

KM#819 31.5000 g. 0.9250 Silver 0.9368 oz. ASW 40 mm. **Subject:** IMAX **Rev:** Youth reaching out to shark on large screen

Date	Mintage	MS-63	Proof
2008 Proof	15,000	—	75.00

KM#895 33.7500 g. 0.9250 Silver 1.0037 oz. ASW 40 mm. **Subject:** International year of astronomy

Obv: Bust right **Obv. Legend:** Elizabeth II 30 Dollars DG Regina **Obv. Designer:** Susanna Blunt **Rev:** Observatory with planets and colored sky **Rev. Legend:** Canada **Rev. Designer:** Colin Mayne

Date	Mintage	MS-63	Proof
2009 Proof	10,000	—	90.00

50 DOLLARS

KM# 566 12.0000 g. 0.5833 Gold 0.2250 oz. AGW 27 mm. **Subject:** WWII **Obv:** Head right **Rev:** Large V and three portraits

Date	Mintage	MS-63	Proof
2005 Specimen	4,000	—	375

KM# 672 31.1600 g. 0.9995 Palladium 1.0013 oz. **Subject:** Constellation in Spring sky position **Rev:** Large Bear at top

Date	Mintage	MS-63	Proof
2006 Proof	297	—	1,200

KM# 673 31.1600 g. 0.9995 Palladium 1.0013 oz. **Subject:** Constellation in Summer sky position **Rev:** Large Bear at left

Date	Mintage	MS-63	Proof
2006 Proof	296	—	1,200

KM# 674 31.1600 g. 0.9995 Palladium 1.0013 oz. **Subject:** Constellation in Autumn sky position **Rev:** Large Bear towards bottom

Date	Mintage	MS-63	Proof
2006 Proof	296	—	1,200

KM# 675 31.1600 g. 0.9995 Palladium
1.0013 oz.   **Subject:** Constellation in Winter sky
position **Rev:** Large Bear towards right

Date	Mintage	MS-63	Proof
2006 Proof	293	—	1,200

KM# 709 155.5000 g. 0.9999 Silver 4.9987 oz.
ASW   **Subject:** Queen's 60th Wedding
Anniversary **Rev:** Coat of Arms and Mascots of
Elizabeth and Philip

Date	Mintage	MS-63	Proof
2007 Proof	4,000	—	350

KM# 783 156.7700 g. 0.9990 Silver 5.0350 oz.
ASW 65 mm.   **Subject:** Ottawa Mint Centennial
1908-2008 **Rev:** Mint building facade **Note:** Photo
reduced.

Date	Mintage	MS-63	Proof
2008 Proof	4,000	—	400

KM# 896 156.7700 g. 0.9990 Silver 5.0350 oz.
ASW 65.25 mm.   **Subject:** 150 Anniversary of the
start of construction of the parliament buildings **Obv:**
Bust right **Obv. Legend:** Elizabeth II Canada DG
Regina **Obv. Designer:** Susanna Blunt **Rev:**
Incomplete west block, original architecture **Rev.
Legend:** 50 Dollars 1859-2009

Date	Mintage	MS-63	Proof
2009 Proof	2,000	—	450

KM# 1008 157.6000 g. 0.9990 Silver 5.0617 oz.
ASW 65.25 mm.   **Subject:** 75th Anniverary of
Canadian Bank Notes **Rev:** Female seated
speaking into microphone **Note:** Photo reduced.

Date	Mintage	MS-63	Proof
2010 Proof	2000	—	450

75 DOLLARS

KM# 567 31.4400 g. 0.4166 Gold 0.4211 oz. AGW
27 mm.   **Subject:** Pope John Paul II **Obv:** Head
right **Rev:** Pope giving blessing

Date	Mintage	MS-63	Proof
2005 Proof	1,870	—	650

KM# 747 12.0000 g. 0.5830 Gold 0.2249 oz. AGW
27 mm.   **Subject:** Vancouver Olympics **Rev:**
Athletics Pride, multicolor flag

Date	Mintage	MS-63	Proof
2007 Proof	8,000	—	350

50 DOLLARS

KM# 748 12.0000 g. 0.5830 Gold 0.2249 oz. AGW
27 mm. **Obv:** Bust right **Obv. Designer:** Susanna
Blunt **Rev:** Canada geese in flight left, multicolor

Date	Mintage	MS-63	Proof
2007 Proof	8,000	—	350

KM# 749 12.0000 g. 0.5830 Gold 0.2249 oz. AGW
27 mm. **Rev:** Mountie, multicolor

Date	Mintage	MS-63	Proof
2007 Proof	8,000	—	350

KM# 821 12.0000 g. 0.5830 Gold 0.2249 oz. AGW
27 mm. **Rev:** Four Host Nations mask emblems,
colored **Rev. Designer:** Jody Broomfield

Date	Mintage	MS-63	Proof
2008 Proof	8,000	—	350

KM# 908 12.0000 g. 0.5830 Gold 0.2249 oz. AGW
27 mm. **Subject:** 2010 Vancouver Olympics
Obv: Bust right **Obv. Designer:** Susana Blunt **Rev:**
Multicolor moose

Date	Mintage	MS-63	Proof
2009 Proof	8,000	—	400

KM# 909 12.0000 g. 0.5830 Gold 0.2249 oz. AGW
27 mm. **Subject:** 2010 Vancouver Olympics
Obv: Bust right **Obv. Designer:** Susanna Blunt
Rev: Multicolor athletics and torch

Date	Mintage	MS-63	Proof
2009 Proof	8,000	—	375

KM# 910 12.0000 g. 0.5830 Gold 0.2249 oz. AGW
27 mm. **Subject:** 2010 Vancouver Olympics
Obv: Bust right **Obv. Designer:** Susanna Blunt
Rev: Wolf, multicolor

Date	Mintage	MS-63	Proof
2009 Proof	8,000	—	400

KM# 947 12.0000 g. 0.5830 Gold 0.2249 oz. AGW
27 mm. **Subject:** Vancouver Olympics **Rev:** Tent
building at Olympic

Date	Mintage	MS-63	Proof
2009 Proof	8,000	—	375

KM# 1002 12.0000 g. 0.5830 Gold 0.2249 oz.
AGW 27 mm. **Rev:** Spring color maple leaves

Date	Mintage	MS-63	Proof
2010 Proof	1,000	—	600

75 DOLLARS

KM# 1003 12.0000 g. 0.5830 Gold 0.2249 oz.
AGW 27 mm.   **Rev:** Summer color maple leaves

Date	Mintage	MS-63	Proof
2010 Proof	1,000	—	600

KM# 1004 12.0000 g. 0.5830 Gold 0.2249 oz.
AGW 27 mm.   **Rev:** Fall color maple leaves

Date	Mintage	MS-63	Proof
2010 Proof	1,000	—	600

100 DOLLARS

KM# 115 13.3375 g. 0.5830 Gold 0.2500 oz. AGW
27 mm.   **Subject:** 1976 Montreal Olympics **Obv:**
Young bust right, maple leaf below, date at right,
beaded borders **Rev:** Past and present Olympic
figures, denomination at right **Rev. Designer:** Dora
dePedery-Hunt

Date	Mintage	MS-63	Proof
1976	650,000	350	—

KM# 116 16.9655 g. 0.9170 Gold 0.5002 oz. AGW
25 mm.   **Subject:** 1976 Montreal Olympics **Obv:**
Young bust right, maple leaf below, date at right,
plain borders **Rev:** Past and present Olympic
figures, denomination at right **Rev. Designer:** Dora
dePedery-Hunt

Date	Mintage	MS-63	Proof
1976 Proof	337,342	—	700

KM# 119 16.9655 g. 0.9170 Gold 0.5002 oz.
AGW   **Subject:** Queen's silver jubilee **Obv:** Young
bust right **Rev:** Bouquet of provincial flowers,
denomination below **Rev. Designer:** Raymond Lee

Date	Mintage	MS-63	Proof
ND(1977) Proof	180,396	—	700

KM# 122 16.9655 g. 0.9170 Gold 0.5002 oz.
AGW   **Subject:** Canadian unification **Obv:** Young
bust right, denomination at left, date upper right **Rev:**
Geese (representing the provinces) in flight
formation **Rev. Designer:** Roger Savage

Date	Mintage	MS-63	Proof
1978 Proof	200,000	—	700

KM# 126 16.9655 g. 0.9170 Gold 0.5002 oz.
AGW   **Subject:** International Year of the Child
Obv: Young bust right **Rev:** Children with hands
joined divide denomination and date **Rev.
Designer:** Carola Tietz

Date	Mintage	MS-63	Proof
1979 Proof	250,000	—	700

KM# 129 16.9655 g. 0.9170 Gold 0.5002 oz.
AGW   **Subject:** Arctic Territories **Obv:** Young bust
right, denomination at left, date above right **Rev:**
Kayaker **Rev. Designer:** Arnaldo Marchetti

Date	Mintage	MS-63	Proof
1980 Proof	300,000	—	700

KM# 131 16.9655 g. 0.9170 Gold 0.5002 oz.
AGW **Subject:** National anthem **Obv:** Young bust
right, denomination at left, date above right **Rev:**
Music score on map **Rev. Designer:** Roger Savage

Date	Mintage	MS-63	Proof
1981 Proof	102,000	—	700

KM# 137 16.9655 g. 0.9170 Gold 0.5002 oz.
AGW **Subject:** New Constitution **Obv:** Young
bust right, denomination at left **Rev:** Open book,
maple leaf on right page, date below **Rev. Designer:**
Friedrich Peter

Date	Mintage	MS-63	Proof
1982 Proof	121,708	—	700

KM# 139 16.9655 g. 0.9170 Gold 0.5002 oz.
AGW **Subject:** 400th Anniversary of St. John's,
Newfoundland **Obv:** Young bust right **Rev:** Anchor
divides building and ship, denomination below,
dates above **Rev. Designer:** John Jaciw

Date	Mintage	MS-63	Proof
ND(1983) Proof	83,128	—	700

KM# 142 16.9655 g. 0.9170 Gold 0.5002 oz.
AGW **Subject:** Jacques Cartier **Obv:** Young bust
right **Rev:** Cartier head on right facing left, ship on
left, date lower right, denomination above **Rev.
Designer:** Carola Tietz

Date	Mintage	MS-63	Proof
ND(1984) Proof	67,662	—	700

KM# 144 16.9655 g. 0.9170 Gold 0.5002 oz.
AGW **Subject:** National Parks **Obv:** Young bust
right **Rev:** Bighorn sheep, denomination divides
dates below **Rev. Designer:** Hector Greville

Date	Mintage	MS-63	Proof
ND(1985) Proof	61,332	—	700

KM# 152 16.9655 g. 0.9170 Gold 0.5002 oz.
AGW **Subject:** Peace **Obv:** Young bust right **Rev:**
Maple leaves and letters intertwined, date at right,
denomination below **Rev. Designer:** Dora
dePedery-Hunt

Date	Mintage	MS-63	Proof
1986 Proof	76,409	—	700

KM# 158 13.3375 g. 0.5830 Gold 0.2500 oz.
AGW **Subject:** 1988 Calgary Olympics **Obv:**
Young bust right, maple leaf below, date at right
Rev: Torch and logo, denomination below **Rev.
Designer:** Friedrich Peter **Edge Lettering:** In
English and French

Date	Mintage	MS-63	Proof
1987 Proof, letter edge	142,750	—	350
1987 Proof, plain edge	Inc. above	—	375

KM# 162 13.3375 g. 0.5830 Gold 0.2500 oz.
AGW **Subject:** Bowhead Whales, balaera
mysticetus **Rev:** Whales left, date below, within
circle, denomination below **Rev. Designer:** Robert
R. Carmichael

Date	Mintage	MS-63	Proof
1988 Proof	52,594	—	350

100 DOLLARS

KM# 169 13.3375 g. 0.5830 Gold 0.2500 oz.·
AGW   **Subject:** Sainte-Marie **Obv:** Young bust
right **Rev:** Huron Indian, Missionary and Mission
building, denomination below, dates above **Rev.**
Designer: D. J. Craig

Date	Mintage	MS-63	Proof
ND(1989) Proof	59,657	—	350

KM#171 13.3375 g. 0.5830 Gold 0.2500 oz. AGW
Subject: International Literacy Year **Obv:** Crowned
head right, date below **Rev:** Woman with children,
denomination below **Rev. Designer:** John Mardon

Date	Mintage	MS-63	Proof
1990 Proof	49,940	—	350

KM# 180 13.3375 g. 0.5830 Gold 0.2500 oz.
AGW   **Subject:** S.S. Empress of India **Obv:**
Crowned head right, date below **Rev:** Ship, "SS
Empress", denomination below **Rev. Designer:**
Karsten Smith

Date	Mintage	MS-63	Proof
1991 Proof	33,966	—	350

KM# 211 13.3375 g. 0.5830 Gold 0.2500 oz.
AGW   **Subject:** Montreal **Obv:** Crowned head
right, date below **Rev:** Half figure in foreground with
paper, buildings in back, denomination below **Rev.**
Designer: Stewart Sherwood

Date	Mintage	MS-63	Proof
1992 Proof	28,162	—	350

KM# 245 13.3375 g. 0.5830 Gold 0.2500 oz.
AGW   **Subject:** Antique Automobiles **Obv:**
Crowned head right, date below **Rev:** German Bene
Victoria; Simmonds Steam Carriage; French
Panhard-Levassor's Daimler; American Duryea;
Canadian Featherston Haugh in center,
denomination below **Rev. Designer:** John Mardon

Date	Mintage	MS-63	Proof
1993 Proof	25,971	—	350

KM# 249 13.3375 g. 0.5830 Gold 0.2500 oz.
AGW   **Subject:** World War II Home Front **Obv:**
Crowned head right, date below **Rev:** Kneeling
figure working on plane, denomination below **Rev.**
Designer: Paraskeva Clark

Date	Mintage	MS-63	Proof
1994 Proof	16,201	—	350

KM# 260 13.3375 g. 0.5830 Gold 0.2500 oz.
AGW   **Subject:** Louisbourg **Obv:** Crowned head
right, date below **Rev:** Ship and buildings, dates and
denomination above **Rev. Designer:** Lewis Parker

Date	Mintage	MS-63	Proof
1995 Proof	16,916	—	350

KM# 273 13.3375 g. 0.5830 Gold 0.2500 oz.
AGW   **Subject:** Klondike Gold Rush Centennial
Obv: Crowned head right, date below **Rev:** Scene of

Kate Carmack panning for gold, dates above, denomination lower left **Rev. Designer:** John Mantha

Date	Mintage	MS-63	Proof
ND(1996) Proof	17,973	—	350

KM# 287 13.3375 g. 0.5830 Gold 0.2500 oz. AGW **Subject:** Alexander Graham Bell **Obv:** Crowned head right, date below **Rev:** A. G. Bell head right, globe and telephone, denomination upper right **Rev. Designer:** Donald H. Carley

Date	Mintage	MS-63	Proof
1997 Proof	14,775	—	350

KM# 307 13.3375 g. 0.5830 Gold 0.2500 oz. AGW **Subject:** Discovery of Insulin **Obv:** Crowned head right, date below **Rev:** Nobel prize award figurine, dates at left, denomination at right **Rev. Designer:** Robert R. Carmichael

Date	Mintage	MS-63	Proof
1998 Proof	11,220	—	350

KM# 341 13.3375 g. 0.5830 Gold 0.2500 oz. AGW **Subject:** 50th Anniversary Newfoundland Unity With Canada **Obv:** Crowned head right, date below **Rev:** Two designs at front, mountains in back, denomination below **Rev. Designer:** Jackie Gale-Vaillancourt

Date	Mintage	MS-63	Proof
1999 Proof	10,242	—	350

KM# 402 13.3375 g. 0.5830 Gold 0.2500 oz. AGW

27 mm. **Subject:** McClure's Arctic expedition **Obv:** Crowned head right, date below **Rev:** Six men pulling supply sled to an icebound ship, denomination below **Rev. Designer:** John Mardon **Edge:** Reeded

Date	Mintage	MS-63	Proof
2000 Proof	9,767	—	350

KM# 416 13.3375 g. 0.5830 Gold 0.2500 oz. AGW 27 mm. **Subject:** Library of Parliament **Obv:** Crowned head right **Obv. Designer:** Dora dePedery-Hunt **Rev:** Statue in domed building **Rev. Designer:** Robert R. Carmichael **Edge:** Reeded

Date	Mintage	MS-63	Proof
2001 Proof	8,080	—	375

KM# 452 13.3375 g. 0.5830 Gold 0.2500 oz. AGW 27 mm. **Subject:** Discovery of Oil in Alberta **Obv:** Crowned head right **Rev:** Oil well with black oil spill on ground **Rev. Designer:** John Marden **Edge:** Reeded

Date	Mintage	MS-63	Proof
2002 Proof	9,994	—	425

KM# 486 13.3375 g. 0.5830 Gold 0.2500 oz. AGW **Subject:** 100th Anniversary of the Discovery of Marquis Wheat **Obv:** Head right

Date	Mintage	MS-63	Proof
2003 Proof	9,993	—	375

KM# 528 12.0000 g. 0.5830 Gold 0.2249 oz. AGW **Subject:** St. Lawrence Seaway, 50th Anniversary **Obv:** Head right

Date	Mintage	MS-63	Proof
2004 Proof	7,454	—	350

KM# 593 12.0000 g. 0.5833 Gold 0.2250 oz. AGW **Subject:** 130th Anniversary, Supreme Court **Obv:** Head right

Date	Mintage	MS-63	Proof
2005 Proof	5,092	—	420

KM# 591 12.0000 g. 0.5833 Gold 0.2250 oz.
AGW   **Subject:** 75th Anniversary, Hockey Classic
between Royal Military College and U.S. Military
Academy **Obv:** Head right

Date	Mintage	MS-63	Proof
2006 Proof	5,439	—	350

KM# 689 12.0000 g. 0.5833 Gold 0.2250 oz. AGW
27 mm.   **Subject:** 140th Anniversary Dominion
Obv: Head right

Date	Mintage	MS-63	Proof
2007 Proof	4,453	—	420

KM# 823 12.0000 g. 0.5830 Gold 0.2249 oz. AGW
27 mm.   **Rev:** Fraser River

Date	Mintage	MS-63	Proof
2008 Proof	5,000	—	375

KM# 898 12.0000 g. 0.5830 Gold 0.2249 oz. AGW
27 mm.   **Subject:** 10th Anniversary of Nunavut
Obv: Bust right **Obv. Legend:** Elizabeth II DG
Regina **Obv. Designer:** Susanna Blunt **Rev:** Inuit
dancer with 3 faces behind **Rev. Legend:** Canada
100 Dollars 1999-2009

Date	Mintage	MS-63	Proof
2009 Proof	5,000	—	500

KM# 997 12.0000 g. 0.5830 Gold 0.2249 oz. AGW
27 mm.   **Rev:** Henry Hudson, Map of Hudson's
Bay **Rev. Designer:** John Mantha

Date	Mintage	MS-63	Proof
2010 Proof	Est. 5,000	—	550

KM# 1073 12.0000 g. 0.5830 Gold 0.2249 oz.
AGW 27 mm.   **Subject:** Canadian Railroads,
175th Anniversary **Rev:** Early steam locomotive

Date	Mintage	MS-63	Proof
2011	3,000	—	640

150 DOLLARS

KM# 388 13.6100 g. 0.7500 Gold 0.3282 oz.
AGW   **Subject:** Year of the Dragon **Obv:** Crowned
head right **Rev. Designer:** Harvey Chan

Date	Mintage	MS-63	Proof
2000 Proof	8,851	—	650

KM# 417 13.6100 g. 0.7500 Gold 0.3282 oz. AGW
28 mm.   **Subject:** Year of the Snake **Obv:**
Crowned head right **Obv. Designer:** Dora
dePedery-Hunt **Rev:** Multicolor snake hologram
Edge: Reeded

Date	Mintage	MS-63	Proof
2001 Proof	6,571	—	475

KM# 604 13.6100 g. 0.7500 Gold 0.3282 oz.
AGW   **Obv:** Head right **Rev:** Stylized horse left

Date	Mintage	MS-63	Proof
2002 Proof	6,843	—	475

KM# 487 13.6100 g. 0.7500 Gold 0.3282 oz. AGW
28 mm.   **Subject:** Year of the Ram **Obv:** Crowned
head right **Rev:** Stylized ram left, hologram **Rev.
Designer:** Harvey Chan

Date	Mintage	MS-63	Proof
2003 Proof	3,927	—	475

KM# 614 13.6100 g. 0.7500 Gold 0.3282 oz.
AGW   **Obv:** Head right **Rev:** Year of the Monkey,
hologram

Date	Mintage	MS-63	Proof
2004 Proof	3,392	—	475

KM# 568 13.6100 g. 0.7500 Gold 0.3282 oz.
AGW   **Subject:** Year of the Rooster **Obv:** Head
right **Rev:** Rooster left, hologram

Date	Mintage	MS-63	Proof
2005 Proof	3,731	—	475

KM# 592 13.6100 g. 0.7500 Gold 0.3282 oz. AGW
28 mm.   **Subject:** Year of the Dog, hologram **Obv:**
Head right **Rev:** Stylized dog left

Date	Mintage	MS-63	Proof
2006 Proof	2,604	—	500

KM# 733 11.8400 g. 0.7500 Gold 0.2855 oz. AGW
28 mm.   **Subject:** Year of the Pig **Obv:** Head right
Rev: Pig in center with Chinese lunar calendar
around, hologram

Date	Mintage	MS-63	Proof
2007 Proof	4,888	—	525

KM# 802 11.8400 g. 0.7500 Gold 0.2855 oz. AGW 28 mm. Subject: Year of the Rat Rev: Rat, hologram

Date	Mintage	MS-63	Proof
2008 Proof	4,888	—	525

KM# 899 10.4000 g. 0.9990 Gold 0.3340 oz. AGW 22.5 mm. Subject: Blessings of wealth Obv: Bust right Obv. Legend: Elizabeth II, DG Regina, Fine Gold 99999 or PUR Obv. Designer: Susanna Blunt Rev: Three goldfish surround peony, clouds Rev. Legend: Canada 150 Dollars (Chinese symbols of good fortune) Rev. Designer: Harvey Chan Edge: Scalloped

Date	Mintage	MS-63	Proof
2009 Proof	50,000	—	750

KM# 867 11.8400 g. 0.7500 Gold 0.2855 oz. AGW 28 mm. Subject: Year of the Ox Rev: Ox, hologram

Date	Mintage	MS-63	Proof
2009 Proof	4,888	—	525

KM# 979 11.8400 g. 0.7500 Gold 0.2855 oz. AGW 28 mm. Subject: Year of the Tiger Rev: Tiger in hologram

Date	Mintage	MS-63	Proof
2010 Proof	48,888	—	550

KM# 1030 0.9999 Gold Subject: Blessing of Wealth Shape: Scalloped

Date	Mintage	MS-63	Proof
2010 Proof	—	—	650

KM# 1031 Gold Subject: Year of the Tiger Rev: Tiger walking

Date	Mintage	MS-63	Proof
2010 Proof	—	—	550

KM# 1053 13.6100 g. 0.7500 Gold 0.3282 oz. AGW 28 mm. Subject: Year of the rabbit Rev: Rabbit hologram

Date	Mintage	MS-63	P/L	Proof
2011 Proof	—	—	—	525

175 DOLLARS

KM# 217 16.9700 g. 0.9170 Gold 0.5003 oz. AGW Subject: 1992 Olympics Obv: Crowned head right, date at left, denomination below Rev: Passing the torch Rev. Designer: Stewart Sherwood Edge: Lettered

Date	Mintage	MS-63	Proof
1992 Proof	22,092	—	700

200 DOLLARS

KM# 178 17.1350 g. 0.9166 Gold 0.5049 oz. AGW
29 mm. **Subject:** Canadian flag silver jubilee
Obv: Crowned head right, date below **Rev:** People
with flag, denomination above **Rev. Designer:**
Stewart Sherwood

Date	Mintage	MS-63	Proof
1990 Proof	20,980	—	710

KM# 202 17.1350 g. 0.9166 Gold 0.5049 oz. AGW
29 mm. **Subject:** Hockey **Obv:** Crowned head
right **Rev:** Hockey players, denomination above
Rev. Designer: Stewart Sherwood

Date	Mintage	MS-63	Proof
1991 Proof	10,215	—	720

KM# 230 17.1350 g. 0.9166 Gold 0.5049 oz. AGW
29 mm. **Subject:** Niagara Falls **Obv:** Crowned
head right **Rev:** Niagara Falls, denomination above
Rev. Designer: John Mardon

Date	Mintage	MS-63	Proof
1992 Proof	9,465	—	720

KM# 244 17.1350 g. 0.9166 Gold 0.5049 oz. AGW
29 mm. **Subject:** Mounted police **Obv:** Crowned

head right, date below **Rev:** Mountie with children,
denomination above **Rev. Designer:** Stewart
Sherwood

Date	Mintage	MS-63	Proof
1993 Proof	10,807	—	720

KM# 250 17.1350 g. 0.9166 Gold 0.5049 oz. AGW
29 mm. **Subject:** Interpretation of 1908 novel by
Lucy Maud Montgomery, 1874-1942, Anne of Green
Gables **Obv:** Crowned head right **Rev:** Figure sitting
in window, denomination above **Rev. Designer:**
Phoebe Gilman

Date	Mintage	MS-63	Proof
1994 Proof	10,655	—	720

KM# 265 17.1350 g. 0.9166 Gold 0.5049 oz. AGW
29 mm. **Subject:** Maple-syrup production **Obv:**
Crowned head right, date below **Rev:** Maple syrup
making, denomination at right **Rev. Designer:** J. D.
Mantha

Date	Mintage	MS-63	Proof
1995 Proof	6,579	—	720

KM# 275 17.1350 g. 0.9166 Gold 0.5049 oz. AGW
29 mm. **Subject:** Transcontinental Canadian
Railway **Obv:** Crowned head right, date below **Rev:**
Train going through mountains, denomination below
Rev. Designer: Suzanne Duranceau

Date	Mintage	MS-63	Proof
1996 Proof	8,047	—	720

KM# 288 17.1350 g. 0.9166 Gold 0.5049 oz. AGW 29 mm. **Subject:** Haida mask **Obv:** Crowned head right, date below **Rev:** Haida mask **Rev. Designer:** Robert Davidson

Date	Mintage	MS-63	Proof
1997 Proof	11,610	—	720

KM# 418 17.1350 g. 0.9166 Gold 0.5049 oz. AGW 29 mm. **Subject:** Cornelius D. Krieghoff's "The Habitant farm" **Obv:** Queens head right **Edge:** Reeded

Date	Mintage	MS-63	Proof
2001 Proof	5,406	—	750

KM# 317 17.1350 g. 0.9166 Gold 0.5049 oz. AGW 29 mm. **Subject:** Legendary white buffalo **Obv:** Crowned head right, date below **Rev:** Buffalo **Rev. Designer:** Alex Janvler

Date	Mintage	MS-63	Proof
1998 Proof	7,149	—	720

KM# 466 17.1350 g. 0.9166 Gold 0.5049 oz. AGW 29 mm. **Subject:** Thomas Thompson "The Jack Pine" (1916-17) **Obv:** Crowned head right

Date	Mintage	MS-63	Proof
2002 Proof	5,264	—	750

KM# 358 17.1350 g. 0.9166 Gold 0.5049 oz. AGW 29 mm. **Subject:** Mikmaq butterfly **Obv:** Crowned head right **Rev:** Butterfly within design **Rev. Designer:** Alan Syliboy

Date	Mintage	MS-63	Proof
1999 Proof	6,510	—	720

KM# 488 17.1350 g. 0.9166 Gold 0.5049 oz. AGW **Subject:** Fitzgerald's "Houses" (1929) **Obv:** Crowned head right **Rev:** House with trees

Date	Mintage	MS-63	Proof
2003 Proof	4,118	—	750

KM# 516 16.0000 g. 0.9166 Gold 0.4715 oz. AGW 29 mm. **Subject:** "Fragments" **Obv:** Crowned head right **Rev:** Fragmented face **Edge:** Reeded

Date	Mintage	MS-63	Proof
2004 Proof	3,917	—	725

KM# 569 16.0000 g. 0.9166 Gold 0.4715 oz. AGW **Subject:** Fur traders **Obv:** Head right **Rev:** Men in canoe riding wave

Date	Mintage	MS-63	Proof
2005 Proof	3,669	—	725

KM# 594 16.0000 g. 0.9166 Gold 0.4715 oz. AGW **Subject:** Timber trade **Obv:** Head right **Rev:** Lumberjacks felling tree

Date	Mintage	MS-63	Proof
2006 Proof	3,185	—	725

KM# 403 17.1350 g. 0.9166 Gold 0.5049 oz. AGW 29 mm. **Subject:** Motherhood **Obv:** Crowned head right, date above, denomination at right **Rev:** Inuit mother with infant **Rev. Designer:** Germaine Arnaktauyak **Edge:** Reeded

Date	Mintage	MS-63	Proof
2000 Proof	6,284	—	720

KM# 691 16.0000 g. 0.9166 Gold 0.4715 oz. AGW 29 mm. **Subject:** Fishing Trade **Obv:** Head right **Rev:** Two fishermen hauling net

Date	Mintage	MS-63	Proof
2007 Proof	4,000	—	725

KM# 824 16.0000 g. 0.9170 Gold 0.4717 oz. AGW 29 mm. **Subject:** Commerce **Rev:** Horse drawn plow

Date	Mintage	MS-63	Proof
2008 Proof	4,000	—	725

KM# 894 16.0000 g. 0.9160 Gold 0.4712 oz. AGW 29 mm. **Subject:** Coal mining trade **Obv:** Bust right **Obv. Legend:** Elizabeth II DG Regina **Obv. Designer:** Susanna Blunt **Rev:** Miner pushing cart with black coal **Rev. Legend:** Canada 200 Dollars **Rev. Designer:** John Marder

Date	Mintage	MS-63	Proof
2009 Proof	4,000	—	800

KM# 1000 16.0000 g. 0.9160 Gold 0.4712 oz. AGW 29 mm. **Subject:** Petroleum and Oil Trade **Rev:** Oil railcar and well head

Date	Mintage	MS-63	Proof
2010 Proof	4,000	—	1,000

KM# 1074 16.0000 g. 0.9167 Gold 0.4715 oz. AGW 29 mm. **Rev:** SS Beaver - Seam Sail ship **Rev. Designer:** John Mardon

Date	Mintage	MS-63	Proof
2011 Proof	2,800	—	1,100

250 DOLLARS

KM# 677 45.0000 g. 0.5833 Gold 0.8439 oz. AGW **Subject:** Dog Sled Team

Date	Mintage	MS-63	Proof
2006 Proof	953	—	1,250

KM# 751 1000.0000 g. 0.9999 Silver 32.146 oz. ASW 101.6 mm. **Subject:** Vancouver Olympics, 2010 **Rev:** Early Canada motif **Note:** Illustration reduced.

Date	Mintage	MS-63	Proof
2007 Proof	2,500	—	1,250

KM# 833 1000.0000 g. 0.9990 Silver 32.117 oz. ASW 101.6 mm. **Subject:** Vancouver Olympics 2010 **Rev:** Towards confederation **Note:** Illustration reduced.

Date	Mintage	MS-63	Proof
2008 Proof	2,500	—	1,600

Date	Mintage	MS-63	Proof
2010 Antique Patina	1,500	1,650	—
2010 Proof	—	—	1,750

KM# 913 1000.0000 g. 0.9999 Silver 32.146 oz. ASW 101.5 mm. **Obv:** Bust right **Obv. Designer:** Susanna Blunt **Rev:** Mask with fish - Surviving the flood **Note:** Illustration reduced.

Date	Mintage	MS-63	Proof
2009 Proof	—	—	2,000

KM# 981a 1000.0000 g. 0.9990 Silver 32.117 oz. ASW 101.6 mm. **Rev:** Eagle head, blue enamel **Note:** Illustration reduced.

Date	Mintage	MS-63	Proof
2010 Proof	—	—	1,750

KM# 949 1000.0000 g. 0.9990 Silver 32.117 oz. ASW 101.6 mm. **Rev:** Modern Canada **Note:** Illustration reduced.

Date	Mintage	MS-63	Proof
2009 Proof	—	—	1,600

KM# 981 1000.0000 g. 0.9990 Silver 32.117 oz. ASW 101.6 mm. **Rev:** Eagle head **Note:** Illustration reduced.

KM# 1044 1000.0000 g. 0.9990 Silver 32.117 oz. ASW 101.6 mm. **Subject:** Baniff, 125th Anniversary of resort founding **Rev:** Features of Baniff **Note:** Illustration reduced.

Date	Mintage	MS-63	Proof
2010 Proof	—	—	1,650

300 DOLLARS

KM# 501 60.0000 g. 0.5833 Gold 1.1252 oz. AGW 50 mm.   **Obv:** Triple cameo portraits of Queen Elizabeth II by Gillick, Machin and de Pedery-Hunt, each in 14K gold, rose in center **Rev:** Dates "1952-2002" and denomination in legend, rose in center **Note:** Housed in anodized gold-colored aluminum box with cherrywood stained siding.

Date	Mintage	MS-63	Proof
ND(2002) Proof	999	—	1,750

KM# 517 60.0000 g. 0.5833 Gold 1.1252 oz. AGW 50 mm.   **Obv:** Four coinage portraits of Elizabeth II **Rev:** Canadian arms above value **Edge:** Plain

Date	Mintage	MS-63	Proof
2004 Proof	998	—	1,750

KM# 570.1 60.0000 g. 0.5833 Gold 1.1252 oz. AGW   **Subject:** Standard Time - 4 AM Pacific **Obv:** Head right **Rev:** Roman numeral clock with world inside

Date	Mintage	MS-63	Proof
2005 Proof	200	—	1,650

KM# 596 60.0000 g. 0.5833 Gold 1.1252 oz. AGW   **Subject:** Shinplaster **Obv:** Head right **Rev:** Britannia bust, spear over shoulder

Date	Mintage	MS-63	Proof
2005 Proof	994	—	1,700

KM# 600 60.0000 g. 0.5833 Gold 1.1252 oz. AGW   **Subject:** Welcome Figure Totem Pole **Obv:** Head right **Rev:** Men with totem pole

Date	Mintage	MS-63	Proof
2005 Proof	947	—	1,650

KM# 570.2 60.0000 g. 0.5830 Gold 1.1246 oz. AGW   **Subject:** Standard Time - Mountian 5 AM **Obv:** Head right **Rev:** Roman numeral clock with world inside.

Date	Mintage	MS-63	Proof
2005 Proof	200	—	1,650

KM# 570.3 60.0000 g. 0.5830 Gold 1.1246 oz. AGW   **Subject:** Standard Time - Central 6 PM **Obv:** Head right **Rev:** Roman numeral clock with world inside

Date	Mintage	MS-63	Proof
2005 Proof	200	—	1,650

KM# 570.4 60.0000 g. 0.5830 Gold 1.1246 oz. AGW   **Subject:** Standard Time - Eastern 7 AM **Obv:** Head right **Rev:** Roman numeral clock with world inside

Date	Mintage	MS-63	Proof
2005 Proof	200	—	1,650

KM# 570.5 60.0000 g. 0.5830 Gold 1.1246 oz. AGW   **Subject:** Standard Time - Atlantic 8 AM **Obv:** Head right **Rev:** Roman numeral clock with world inside

Date	Mintage	MS-63	Proof
2005 Proof	200	—	1,650

KM# 570.6 60.0000 g. 0.5830 Gold 1.1246 oz. AGW   **Subject:** Standard Time - Newfoundland 8:30 **Obv:** Head right **Rev:** Roman numeral clock with world inside

Date	Mintage	MS-63	Proof
2005 Proof	200	—	1,650

KM# 595 60.0000 g. 0.5833 Gold 1.1252 oz. AGW   **Subject:** Shinplaster **Obv:** Head right **Rev:** Seated Britannia with shield

Date	Mintage	MS-63	Proof
2006 Proof	940	—	1,700

KM# 678 45.0000 g. 0.5833 Gold 0.8439 oz. AGW **Subject:** Canadam and Col. C. Hadfield **Rev:** Hologram of Canadarm

Date	Mintage	MS-63	Proof
2006 Proof	581	—	1,250

KM# 679 60.0000 g. 0.5833 Gold 1.1252 oz. AGW **Subject:** Queen Elizabeth's 80th Birthday **Rev:** State Crown, colorized

Date	Mintage	MS-63	Proof
2006 Proof	996	—	1,250

KM# 680 60.0000 g. 0.5833 Gold 1.1252 oz. AGW **Subject:** Crystal Snowflake

Date	Mintage	MS-63	Proof
2006 Proof	998	—	1,850

KM# 692 60.0000 g. 0.5833 Gold 1.1252 oz. AGW **Subject:** Shinplaster **Rev:** 1923 25 cent bank note

Date	Mintage	MS-63	Proof
2007 Proof	778	—	1,700

KM# 740 45.0000 g. 0.5830 Gold 0.8434 oz. AGW 40 mm. **Rev:** Canadian Rockies panoramic hologram

Date	Mintage	MS-63	Proof
2007 Proof	511	—	1,250

KM# 752 60.0000 g. 0.5830 Gold 1.1246 oz. AGW 50 mm. **Subject:** Vancouver Olympics **Rev:** Olympic ideals, classic figures and torch

Date	Mintage	MS-63	Proof
2007 Proof	2,500	—	1,700

KM# 753 31.1050 g. 0.9999 Platinum 0.9999 oz. APW 50 mm. **Rev:** Wooly mammoth

Date	Mintage	MS-63	Proof
2007 Proof	400	—	3,200

KM# 825 45.0000 g. 0.5830 Gold 0.8434 oz. AGW 40 mm. **Rev:** Alberta Coat of Arms

Date	Mintage	MS-63	Proof
2008 Proof	—	—	1,250

KM# 826 45.0000 g. 0.5830 Gold 0.8434 oz. AGW 40 mm. **Rev:** Newfoundland and Labrador Coat of Arms

Date	Mintage	MS-63	Proof
2008 Proof	1,000	—	1,350

KM# 827 45.0000 g. 0.5830 Gold 0.8434 oz. AGW 40 mm. **Subject:** Canadian achievements **Rev:** IMAX

Date	Mintage	MS-63	Proof
2008 Proof	—	—	1,250

KM# 828 45.0000 g. 0.5830 Gold 0.8434 oz. AGW 40 mm. **Rev:** Four seasons moon mask

Date	Mintage	MS-63	Proof
2008 Proof	1,200	—	1,500

KM# 830 60.0000 g. 0.5830 Gold 1.1246 oz. AGW 50 mm. **Subject:** Vancouver Olympics **Rev:** Olympic competition, athletics and torch

Date	Mintage	MS-63	Proof
2008 Proof	—	—	1,700

KM# 831 31.1050 g. 0.9990 Platinum 0.9990 oz. APW **Rev:** Saber Tooth Scimitar cat

Date	Mintage	MS-63	Proof
2008 Proof	200	—	3,500

KM# 900 60.0000 g. 0.5830 Gold 1.1246 oz. AGW 50 mm. **Subject:** Yukon Coat of Arms **Obv:** Bust right **Obv. Legend:** Elizabeth II DG Regina **Obv. Designer:** Susanna Blunt **Rev:** Yukon Coat of Arms **Rev. Legend:** Canada 300 Dollars

Date	Mintage	MS-63	Proof
2009 Proof	1,000	—	1,850

KM# 911 60.0000 g. 0.5830 Gold 1.1246 oz. AGW 50 mm. **Subject:** 2010 Vancouver Olympics **Obv:** Bust right **Obv. Designer:** Susanna Blunt **Rev:** Athletics with torch - Olympic firendship

Date	Mintage	MS-63	Proof
2009 Proof	—	—	1,700

KM# 877 45.0000 g. 0.5830 Gold 0.8434 oz. AGW 40 mm. **Rev:** Summer moon mask, enameled

Date	Mintage	MS-63	Proof
2009 Proof	—	—	1,700

KM# 999 54.0000 g. 0.5830 Gold 1.0121 oz. AGW 40 mm. **Rev:** British Columbia Arms

Date	Mintage	MS-63	Proof
2010 Proof	500	—	1,750

KM# 1047 60.0000 g. 0.5830 Gold 1.1246 oz.
AGW 50 mm.   **Rev:** Snowflake, white crystals

Date	Mintage	MS-63	Proof
2010 Proof	—	—	1,850

KM# 1078 60.0000 g. 0.5830 Gold 1.1246 oz.
AGW 50 mm.   **Rev:** New Brunswick Coat of arms

Date	Mintage	MS-63	Proof
2010 Proof	500	—	2,450

KM# 1095 60.0000 g. 0.9167 Gold 1.7683 oz.
AGW 50 mm.   **Rev:** Manitoba Coat of arms

Date	Mintage	MS-63	Proof
2011 Proof	500	—	2,450

350 DOLLARS

KM# 308 38.0500 g. 0.9999 Gold 1.2232 oz.
AGW   **Subject:** Flowers of Canada's Coat of Arms
Obv: Crowned head right, date behind,
denomination at bottom **Rev:** Flowers **Rev.
Designer:** Pierre Leduc

Date	Mintage	MS-63	Proof
1998 Proof	664	—	1,750

KM# 370 38.0500 g. 0.9999 Gold 1.2232 oz.
AGW   **Rev:** Lady's slipper **Rev. Designer:** Henry
Purdy

Date	Mintage	MS-63	Proof
1999 Proof	1,990	—	1,750

KM# 404 38.0500 g. 0.9999 Gold 1.2232 oz. AGW
34 mm.   **Obv:** Crowned head right **Rev:** Three
Pacific Dogwood flowers **Rev. Designer:** Caren
Heine **Edge:** Reeded

Date	Mintage	MS-63	Proof
2000 Proof	1,506	—	1,750

KM# 433 38.0500 g. 0.9999 Gold 1.2232 oz. AGW
34 mm.   **Subject:** The Mayflower Flower **Obv:**
Crowned head right **Rev:** Two flowers **Rev.
Designer:** Bonnie Ross **Edge:** Reeded

Date	Mintage	MS-63	Proof
2001 Proof	1,988	—	1,850

KM# 502 38.0500 g. 0.9999 Gold 1.2232 oz. AGW
34 mm.   **Subject:** The Wild Rose **Obv:** Crowned
head right **Obv. Designer:** Dora de Pedery-Hunt
Rev: Wild rose plant **Rev. Designer:** Dr. Andreas
Kare Hellum

Date	Mintage	MS-63	Proof
2002 Proof	2,001	—	1,850

KM# 504 38.0500 g. 0.9999 Gold 1.2232 oz. AGW
34 mm.   **Subject:** The White Trillium **Obv:**
Crowned head right **Obv. Designer:** Dora de
Pedery-Hunt **Rev:** White Trillium

Date	Mintage	MS-63	Proof
2003 Proof	1,865	—	1,850

KM# 601 38.0500 g. 0.9999 Gold 1.2232 oz.
AGW   **Subject:** Western Red Lilly **Obv:** Head right
Rev: Western Red Lilies

Date	Mintage	MS-63	Proof
2005 Proof	1,634	—	1,850

350 DOLLARS

KM# 626 38.0500 g. 0.9999 Gold 1.2232 oz. AGW
34 mm.　**Subject:** Iris Vericolor **Obv:** Crowned
head right **Rev:** Iris

Date	Mintage	MS-63	Proof
2006 Proof	1,995	—	1,850

KM# 754 35.0000 g. 0.9999 Gold 1.1251 oz. AGW
34 mm.　**Rev:** Purple violet

Date	Mintage	MS-63	Proof
2007 Proof	1,171	—	1,850

KM# 832 35.0000 g. 0.9999 Gold 1.1251 oz. AGW
34 mm.　**Rev:** Purple saxifrage

Date	Mintage	MS-63	Proof
2008 Proof	1,400	—	1,850

KM# 901 35.0000 g. 0.9990 Gold 1.1241 oz. AGW
34 mm.　**Subject:** Pitcher plant **Obv:** Bust right
Obv. Legend: Elizabeth II Canada DG Regina Fine
Gold 350 Dollars or PUR 99999 **Obv. Designer:**
Susana Blunt **Rev:** Cluster of pitcher flowers **Rev.
Legend:** Julie Wilson

Date	Mintage	MS-63	Proof
2009 Proof	1,400	—	2,000

KM# 1019 35.0000 g. 0.9990 Gold 1.1241 oz.
AGW 34 mm.　**Rev:** Praire Crocus **Rev. Designer:**
Celia Godkin

Date	Mintage	MS-63	Proof
2010 Proof	1,400	—	2,600

500 DOLLARS

KM# 710 155.5000 g. 0.9999 Gold 4.9987 oz.
AGW 60 mm.　**Subject:** Queen's 60th Wedding
Rev: Coat of Arms and Mascots of Elizabeth and
Philip

Date	Mintage	MS-63	Proof
2007	198	8,500	—

KM# 782 155.7600 g. 0.9990 Gold 5.0026 oz.
AGW 60 mm.　**Subject:** Ottawa Mint Centennial
1908-2008 **Rev:** Mint building facade **Note:**
Illustration reduced.

Date	Mintage	MS-63	Proof
2008	250	8,500	—

KM# 897 156.0500 g. 0.9990 Gold 5.0119 oz.
AGW 60.15 mm.　**Subject:** 150th Anniversary of
the start of construction of the Parliament Buildings
Obv: Bust right **Rev:** Incomplete west block, original
architecture **Rev. Legend:** 500 Dollars 1859-2009

Date	Mintage	MS-63	Proof
2009 Proof	200	—	9,500

KM# 1007 156.5000 g. 0.9990 Gold 5.0263 oz.
AGW 60.15 mm.　**Subject:** 75th Anniversary of
Canadian Bank Notes **Rev:** Abundance seated
under tree **Note:** Illustration reduced.

Date	Mintage	MS-63	Proof
2010 Proof	300	—	10,000

2500 DOLLARS

KM#681 1000.0000 g. 0.9999 Gold 32.146 oz. AGW 101.6 mm.   **Subject:** Kilo **Rev:** Common Characters, Early Canada **Note:** Illustration reduced.

Date	Mintage	MS-63	Proof
2007	20	47,500	—

KM# 902 1000.0000 g. 0.9990 Silver 32.117 oz. ASW 101.6 mm.   **Series:** History and Culture Collection **Subject:** Modern Canada **Obv:** Bust right **Obv. Legend:** Vancouver 2010, 2500 Dollars, Elizabeth II **Obv. Designer:** Susanna Blunt **Rev:**

Canadian landscape with modern elements **Note:** Illustration reduced.

Date	Mintage	MS-63	Proof
2009 Proof	2,500	—	1,200

KM# 902a 1000.0000 g. 0.9990 Gold 32.117 oz. AGW 101.6 mm.   **Series:** History and Culture Collection **Subject:** Modern Canada **Obv:** Bust right **Obv. Legend:** Vancouver 2010, 2500 Dollars, Elizabeth II **Obv. Designer:** Susana Blunt **Rev:** Canadian landscape with modern elements

Date	Mintage	MS-63	Proof
2009 Proof	50	—	55,000

KM# 912 1000.0000 g. 0.9999 Gold 32.146 oz. AGW 101 mm.   **Obv:** Bust right **Obv. Designer:** Susanna Blunt **Rev:** Mask with fish - Surviving the flood **Note:** Illustration reduced.

Date	Mintage	MS-63	Proof
2009 Proof	—	—	50,000

KM# 984 1000.0000 g. 0.9990 Gold 32.117 oz. AGW 101 mm.   **Note:** Illustration reduced.

Date	Mintage	MS-63	Proof
2010 Proof	20	—	50,000

KM# 1045 1000.0000 g. 0.9999 Gold 32.146 oz. AGW 101 mm.   **Subject:** Baniff, 125th Anniversary **Rev:** Highlights of Baniff **Note:** Illustration reduced.

Date	Mintage	MS-63	Proof
2010	—	—	50,000

SILVER BULLION COINAGE

DOLLAR

KM# 617 1.5550 g. 0.9999 Silver 0.0500 oz. ASW 16 mm.   **Obv:** Crowned head right **Rev:** Holographic Maple leaf **Edge:** Reeded

Date	Mintage	MS-63	Proof
2003 Proof	—		4.50

KM# 621 1.5550 g. 0.9999 Silver 0.0500 oz. ASW 17 mm.   **Obv:** Crowned head right **Rev:** Maple leaf **Edge:** Reeded

Date	Mintage	MS-63	Proof
2004 Mint logo privy mark Proof	13,859	—	4.50

2 DOLLARS

KM# 618 3.1100 g. 0.9999 Silver 0.1000 oz. ASW 20.1 mm.   **Obv:** Crowned head right **Rev:** Holographic Maple leaf **Edge:** Reeded

Date	Mintage	MS-63	Proof
2003 Proof	—	—	7.50

KM# 622 3.1100 g. 0.9999 Silver 0.1000 oz. ASW 21 mm.   **Obv:** Crowned head right **Rev:** Maple leaf **Edge:** Reeded

Date	Mintage	MS-63	Proof
2004 Mint logo privy mark Proof	13,859	—	7.50

KM# 571 3.1050 g. 0.9999 Silver 0.0998 oz. ASW   **Obv:** Head right **Rev:** Lynx

Date	Mintage	MS-63	Proof
2005 Proof	—	—	7.50

3 DOLLARS

KM# 619 7.7760 g. 0.9999 Silver 0.2500 oz. ASW 26.9 mm.   **Obv:** Crowned head right **Rev:** Holographic Maple leaf **Edge:** Reeded

Date	Mintage	MS-63	Proof
2003 Proof	—	—	17.50

KM# 623 7.7760 g. 0.9999 Silver 0.2500 oz. ASW 27 mm.   **Obv:** Crowned head right **Rev:** Maple leaf **Edge:** Reeded

Date	Mintage	MS-63	Proof
2004 Mint logo privy mark Proof	13,859	—	16.00

KM# 572 7.7760 g. 0.9999 Silver 0.2500 oz. ASW   **Obv:** Head right **Rev:** Lynx

Date	Mintage	MS-63	Proof
2005 Proof	—	—	12.50

4 DOLLARS

KM#620 15.5500 g. 0.9999 Silver 0.4999 oz. ASW
33.9 mm. **Obv:** Crowned head right **Rev:**
Holographic Maple leaf **Edge:** Reeded

Date	Mintage	MS-63	Proof
2003 Proof	—	—	32.00

KM#624 15.5500 g. 0.9999 Silver 0.4999 oz. ASW
34 mm. **Obv:** Crowned head right **Rev:** Maple leaf
Edge: Reeded

Date	Mintage	MS-63	Proof
2004 Mint logo privy mark Proof	13,859	—	28.00

KM# 573 15.5500 g. 0.9999 Silver 0.4999 oz.
ASW **Obv:** Head right **Rev:** Lynx

Date	Mintage	MS-63	Proof
2005 Proof	—	—	25.00

5 DOLLARS

KM# 163 31.1000 g. 0.9999 Silver 0.9997 oz.
ASW **Obv:** Young bust right, denomination and
date below **Obv. Designer:** Arnold Machin **Rev:**
Maple leaf flanked by 9999

Date	Mintage	MS-63	Proof
1988	1,155,931	30.00	—
1989	3,332,200	30.00	—
1989 Proof	29,999	—	40.00

KM# 187 31.1000 g. 0.9999 Silver 0.9997 oz.
ASW **Obv:** Crowned head right, date and
denomination below **Obv. Designer:** Dora de
Pedery-Hunt **Rev:** Maple leaf flanked by 9999

Date	Mintage	MS-63	Proof
1990	1,708,800	30.00	—
1991	644,300	30.00	—
1992	343,800	30.00	—
1993	889,946	30.00	—
1994	1,133,900	30.00	—

Date	Mintage	MS-63	Proof
1995	326,244	30.00	—
1996	250,445	42.50	—
1997	100,970	32.00	—
1998	591,359	30.00	—
1998 90th Anniversary R.C.M. privy mark	13,025	30.00	—
1998 Tiger privy mark	25,000	32.00	—
1998 R.C.M.P. privy mark	25,000	42.50	—
1998 Titanic privy mark	26,000	85.00	—
1999	1,229,442	30.00	—
1999 Rabbit privy mark	25,000	32.50	—
1999 "Y2K" privy mark	9,999	37.50	—
2000 Expo Hanover privy mark	—	45.00	—
2000 Dragon privy mark	25,000	35.00	—
2000	403,652	30.00	—
2001	398,563	35.00	—
2001 Reverse proof, Snake privy mark	25,000	—	45.00
2002	576,196	35.00	—
2002 Reverse proof, Horse privy mark	25,000	—	45.00
2003	—	35.00	—
2003 Reverse proof, sheep privy mark	25,000	—	45.00

KM# 363 31.1000 g. 0.9999 Silver 0.9997 oz.
ASW **Obv:** Crowned head right, date and
denomination below **Rev:** Maple leaf flanked by 9999

Date	Mintage	MS-63	Proof
1999/2000 Fireworks privy mark	298,775	32.00	—

KM#437 31.1035 g. 0.9999 Silver 0.9999 oz. ASW
38 mm. **Obv:** Crowned head right, date and
denomination below **Rev:** Radiant maple leaf
hologram **Edge:** Reeded

Date	Mintage	MS-63	Proof
2001 Good fortune privy mark	29,906	75.00	—

KM#436 31.1035 g. 0.9999 Silver 0.9999 oz. ASW
38 mm. **Obv:** Crowned head right, date and
denomination below **Rev:** Three maple leaves in
autumn colors, 9999 flanks **Rev. Designer:** Debbie
Adams **Edge:** Reeded

Date	Mintage	MS-63	Proof
2001 Proof	49,709	—	40.00

KM#505 31.1035 g. 0.9999 Silver 0.9999 oz. ASW
38 mm.   **Obv:** Crowned head right, date and
denomination below **Rev:** Two maple leaves in
spring color (green) **Edge:** Reeded

Date	Mintage	MS-63	Proof
2002	29,509	37.50	—

KM# 603 31.1050 g. 0.9999 Silver 0.9999 oz.
ASW   **Obv:** Head right **Rev:** Loon splashing in the
water, hologram

Date	Mintage	MS-63	Proof
2002 Satin Proof	30,000	—	45.00

KM# 521 31.1035 g. 0.9999 Silver 0.9999 oz.
ASW   **Obv:** Head right **Rev:** Maple leaf, summer
colors **Rev. Designer:** Stan Witten

Date	Mintage	MS-63	Proof
2003	29,416	37.50	—

KM#508 31.1035 g. 0.9999 Silver 0.9999 oz. ASW
38 mm.   **Obv:** Crowned head right, date and
denomination below **Obv. Designer:** Dora de
Pedery-Hunt **Rev:** Holographic Maple leaf flanked
by 9999 **Edge:** Reeded

Date	Mintage	MS-63	Proof
2003 Proof	—	—	37.50

KM# 607 31.1200 g. 0.9999 Silver 1.0004 oz.
ASW   **Obv:** Head right **Rev:** Maple leaf, winter colors

Date	Mintage	MS-63	Proof
2004	—	37.50	—

KM#625 31.1035 g. 0.9999 Silver 0.9999 oz. ASW
38 mm.   **Obv:** Bust right **Obv. Designer:** Susanna
Blunt **Rev:** Maple leaf **Edge:** Reeded

Date	Mintage	MS-63	Proof
2004 Mint logo privy mark Specimen	13,859	—	37.50
2004 Monkey privy mark Specimen	25,000	—	37.50
2004 D-Day privy mark Specimen	11,698	—	37.50
2004 Desjardins privy mark	15,000	37.50	—
2004 Capricorn privy Mark Reverse proof	5,000	—	37.50
2004 Aquarius privy mark Reverse proof	5,000	—	37.50
2004 Pisces privy mark Reverse proof	5,000	—	37.50
2004 Aries privy mark Reverse proof	5,000	—	37.50
2004 Taurus privy mark Reverse proof	5,000	—	37.50
2004 Gemini privy mark Reverse proof	5,000	—	37.50
2004 Cancer privy mark Reverse proof	5,000	—	37.50
2004 Leo privy mark Reverse proof	5,000	—	37.50
2004 Virgo privy mark Reverse proof	5,000	—	37.50
2004 Libra privy mark Reverse proof	5,000	—	37.50
2004 Scorpio privy mark Reverse proof	5,000	—	37.50
2004 Sagittarius privy mark Reverse proof	5,000	—	37.50
2005	—	35.00	—
2005 Tulip privy mark Reverse proof	3,500	—	40.00
2005 Tank privy mark Reverse proof	7,000	—	60.00
2005 USS Missouri privy mark Reverse proof	7,000	—	60.00
2005 Rooster privy mark Reverse proof	15,000	—	50.00
2006	—	35.00	—
2006 Dog privy mark Reverse proof	—	—	50.00
2007	—	35.00	—
2007 F12 privy mark Reverse proof	—	—	130
2007 Pig privy mark Reverse proof	—	—	40.00
2008	—	35.00	—
2008 F12 privy mark Reverse proof	—	—	130
2008 Rat privy mark Reverse proof	—	—	40.00
2009	—	35.00	—
2009 Brandenberg Gate privy mark Reverse proof	—	—	50.00
2009 Tower Bridge privy mark Reverse proof	—	—	40.00
2009 Ox Privy mark Reverse proof	—	—	37.50
2010	—	35.00	—
2011	—	35.00	—

KM# 522 31.1050 g. 0.9999 Silver 0.9999 oz.
ASW   **Obv:** Head right **Rev:** Maple leaf, winter
color **Rev. Designer:** Stan Witten

Date	Mintage	MS-63	Proof
2004	26,763	35.00	—

KM# 574 31.1035 g. 0.9999 Silver 0.9999 oz.
ASW   **Obv:** Head right **Rev:** Lynx

Date	Mintage	MS-63	Proof
2005 Proof	—	—	37.50

KM# 924 31.1050 g. 0.9999 Silver 0.9999 oz.
ASW **Rev:** Maple Leaf, laser engraved **Rev.
Designer:** Joan Nguyen

Date	Mintage	MS-63	Proof
2005 Proof	25,000	—	60.00

KM# 550 31.1035 g. 0.9999 Silver 0.9999 oz.
ASW **Obv:** Head right **Rev:** Big Leaf Maple,
colorized **Rev. Designer:** Stan Witten

Date	Mintage	MS-63	Proof
2005	21,233	35.00	—

KM# 660 31.1035 g. 0.9990 Silver 0.9990 oz.
ASW **Obv:** Bust right **Obv. Designer:** Susanna
Blunt **Rev:** Silver maple, colorized **Rev. Designer:**
Stan Witten

Date	Mintage	MS-63	Proof
2006	14,157	37.50	—

KM#729 31.1050 g. 0.9990 Silver 0.9990 oz. ASW
38 mm. **Obv:** Bust right **Rev:** Maple leaf orange
multicolor

Date	Mintage	MS-63	Proof
2007 Proof	—	—	45.00

KM# 925 31.1050 g. 0.9990 Silver 0.9990 oz.
ASW **Obv:** Bust right **Obv. Designer:** Susanna
Blunt **Rev:** Sugar maple, colorized **Rev. Designer:**
Stan Witten

Date	Mintage	MS-63	Proof
2007	11,495	37.50	—

KM#928 31.3900 g. 0.9990 Silver 1.0082 oz. ASW
38 mm. **Rev:** Orange sugar maple leaf **Rev.
Designer:** Stan Witten

Date	Mintage	MS-63	Proof
2007 Specimen	20,000	—	100

KM#800 31.1050 g. 0.9990 Silver 0.9990 oz. ASW
38 mm. **Subject:** Vancouver Olympics **Obv:** Bust
right **Obv. Designer:** Susanna Blunt **Rev:** Maple
leaf, Olympic logo at left, turtle

Date	Mintage	MS-63	Proof
2008	—	37.50	—
2009	—	37.50	—
2010	—	37.50	—

KM#798 31.1050 g. 0.9990 Silver 0.9990 oz. ASW
38 mm. **Subject:** Maple Leaf 20th Anniversary
Rev: Maple Leaf, selective gold plating

Date	Mintage	MS-63	Proof
2008 Proof	10,000	—	110

KM#799 31.1050 g. 0.9990 Silver 0.9990 oz. ASW
38 mm. **Subject:** Breast Cancer Awareness **Rev:**
Multicolor, green maple leaf and pink ribbon

Date	Mintage	MS-63	Proof
2008	11,048	85.00	—

KM# 1056 31.1050 g. 0.9999 Silver 0.9999 oz.
ASW 38 mm. **Rev:** Maple leaf in brown color, card
diamond

Date	Mintage	MS-63	Proof
2008	—	60.00	—

KM# 1057 31.1050 g. 0.9999 Silver 0.9999 oz. ASW
38 mm. **Rev:** Maple Leaf in green color, card heart

Date	Mintage	MS-63	Proof
2008	—	60.00	—

KM# 1058 31.1050 g. 0.9999 Silver 0.9999 oz. ASW
38 mm. **Rev:** Maple leaf in green color, card club

Date	Mintage	MS-63	Proof
2008	—	60.00	—

KM# 1059 31.1050 g. 0.9999 Silver 0.9999 oz.
ASW 38 mm. **Rev:** Maple Leaf in red color, card
spade

Date	Mintage	MS-63	Proof
2008	—	60.00	—

KM#863 31.3900 g. 0.9990 Silver 1.0082 oz. ASW
38 mm. **Subject:** Vancouver Olympics **Rev:**
Thunderbird Totem **Rev. Designer:** Rick Harry

Date	Mintage	MS-63	Proof
2009	—	50.00	—

KM# 1061 31.1050 g. 0.9999 Silver 0.9999 oz.
ASW 38 mm.   **Rev:** Maple leaf in red color, support
our troups yellow ribbon

Date	Mintage	MS-63	Proof
2009	—	70.00	—

KM# 998 31.1200 g. 0.9990 Silver 0.9995 oz. ASW
38 mm.   **Rev:** Olympic Hockey

Date	Mintage	MS-63	Proof
2010 Proof	—	—	42.50

KM# 1052 31.1050 g. 0.9999 Silver 0.9999 oz.
ASW 38 mm.   **Rev:** Wolf standing with moonlight
in background

Date	Mintage	MS-63	P/L	Proof
2011	—	40.00	—	—

8 DOLLARS

KM# 731 0.9990 Silver   **Rev:** Maple leaf, long life
hologram

Date	Mintage	MS-63	Proof
2007	15,000	—	60.00

20 DOLLARS

KM# 1062 7.9600 g. Silver 27 mm.   **Rev:** Five
Maple leaves at left **Note:** Thick planchet

Date	Mintage	MS-63	Proof
2011	200,000	—	25.00

50 DOLLARS

KM# 326 311.0350 g. 0.9999 Silver 9.9986 oz.
ASW   **Subject:** 10th Anniversary Silver Maple
Leaf **Obv:** Crowned head right **Rev:** Maple leaf
flanked by 9999 **Edge:** 10th ANNIVERSARY 10e
ANNIVERSAIRE

Date	Mintage	MS-63	Proof
1998 Proof	25,000	—	300

250 DOLLARS

KM# 676 1000.0000 g. 0.9999 Silver 32.146 oz.
ASW   **Subject:** Kilo

Date	Mintage	MS-63	Proof
2006	—	1,200	—

GOLD BULLION COINAGE

50 CENTS

KM# 888 1.2700 g. 0.9990 Gold 0.0408 oz. AGW
13.92 mm.   **Subject:** Red maple **Obv:** Bust right
Obv. Legend: Elizabeth II 50 cents **Obv. Designer:**

Susanna Blunt **Rev:** Two maple leaves **Rev.
Legend:** Canada, Fine gold 1/25 oz or PUR 9999

Date	Mintage	MS-63	Proof
2009 Proof	150,000	—	65.00

KM# 1085 1.2700 g. 0.9990 Gold 0.0408 oz. AGW
13.92 mm.   **Rev:** Geese in flight left **Rev.
Designer:** Emily Damstra

Date	Mintage	MS-63	Proof
2011 Proof	10,000	—	110

SILVER BULLION

DOLLAR

KM# 238 1.5551 g. 0.9999 Gold 0.0500 oz.
AGW **Obv:** Crowned head right, denomination
and date below **Rev:** Maple leaf flanked by 9999

Date	Mintage	MS-63	Proof
1993	37,080	BV+37%	—
1994	78,860	BV+37%	—
1995	85,920	BV+37%	—
1996	56,520	BV+37%	—
1997	59,720	BV+37%	—
1998	44,260	BV+37%	—
1999 oval "20 YEARS ANS" privy mark	—	BV+46%	—
2000 oval "2000" privy mark	—	BV+46%	—

KM#365 1.5551 g. 0.9999 Gold 0.0500 oz. AGW
Obv: Crowned head right **Rev:** Maple leaf hologram

Date	Mintage	MS-63	Proof
1999	500	100.00	—

2 DOLLARS

KM# 256 2.0735 g. 0.9999 Gold 0.0667 oz.
AGW **Obv:** Crowned head right, denomination
and date below **Rev:** Maple leaf flanked by 9999

Date	Mintage	MS-63	Proof
1994	5,493	95.00	—

5 DOLLARS

KM# 135 3.1200 g. 0.9999 Gold 0.1003 oz.
AGW **Obv:** Young bust right, date and
denomination below **Obv. Designer:** Arnold Machin
Rev: Maple leaf flanked by 9999

Date	Mintage	MS-63	Proof
1982	246,000	BV+14%	—
1983	304,000	BV+14%	—
1984	262,000	BV+14%	—
1985	398,000	BV+14%	—
1986	529,516	BV+14%	—
1987	459,000	BV+14%	—
1988	506,500	BV+14%	—
1989	539,000	BV+14%	—
1989 Proof	16,992	—	185

KM# 188 3.1200 g. 0.9999 Gold 0.1003 oz.
AGW **Obv:** Elizabeth II effigy **Obv. Designer:**
Dora dePedery-Hunt **Rev:** Maple leaf

Date	Mintage	MS-63	Proof
1990	476,000	BV+14%	—
1991	322,000	BV+14%	—
1992	384,000	BV+14%	—
1993	248,630	BV+14%	—
1994	313,150	BV+14%	—
1995	294,890	BV+14%	—
1996	179,220	BV+14%	—
1997	188,540	BV+14%	—
1998	301,940	BV+14%	—
1999 oval "20 Years ANS" privy mark	—	BV+19%	—
2000 oval "2000" privy mark	—	BV+19%	—

KM# 366 3.1200 g. 0.9999 Gold 0.1003 oz.
AGW **Rev:** Maple leaf hologram

Date	Mintage	MS-63	Proof
1999	500	175	—

KM# 439 3.1310 g. 0.9999 Gold 0.1006 oz. AGW
16 mm. **Subject:** Holographic Maple Leaves
Obv: Crowned head right **Rev:** Three maple leaves
multicolor hologram **Edge:** Reeded

Date	Mintage	MS-63	Proof
2001	600	160	—

KM# 929 3.1300 g. 0.9990 Gold 0.1005 oz. AGW
16 mm. **Obv. Designer:** Susan Blunt **Rev:** Maple
leaf **Rev. Designer:** Walter Ott

Date	Mintage	MS-63	Proof
2007	—	—	170
2008	—	—	170
2009	—	—	170

10 DOLLARS

KM# 136 7.7850 g. 0.9999 Gold 0.2503 oz.
AGW **Obv:** Young bust right, date and
denomination below **Obv. Designer:** Arnold Machin
Rev: Maple leaf flanked by 9999

Date	Mintage	MS-63	Proof
1982	184,000	BV+10%	—
1983	308,800	BV+10%	—
1984	242,400	BV+10%	—
1985	620,000	BV+10%	—
1986	915,200	BV+10%	—
1987	376,000	BV+10%	—
1988	436,000	BV+10%	—
1989 Proof	6,998	—	400
1989	328,800	BV+10%	—

KM# 189 7.7850 g. 0.9999 Gold 0.2503 oz.
AGW **Obv:** Crowned head right, date and
denomination below **Obv. Designer:** Dora
dePedery-Hunt **Rev:** Maple leaf flanked by 9999

Date	Mintage	MS-63	Proof
1990	253,600	BV+10%	—
1991	166,400	BV+10%	—
1992	179,600	BV+10%	—
1993	158,452	BV+10%	—
1994	148,792	BV+10%	—
1995	127,596	BV+10%	—
1996	89,148	BV+10%	—
1997	98,104	BV+10%	—
1998	85,472	BV+10%	—
1999 oval "20 Years ANS" privy mark	—	BV+15%	—
2000 oval "2000" privy mark	—	BV+15%	—

KM# 367 7.7850 g. 0.9999 Gold 0.2503 oz.
AGW **Rev:** Maple leaf hologram

Date	Mintage	MS-63	Proof
1999	—	425	—

KM# 440 7.7970 g. 0.9999 Gold 0.2506 oz. AGW
20 mm. **Subject:** Holographic Maples Leaves
Obv: Crowned head right **Rev:** Three maple leaves
multicolor hologram **Edge:** Reeded

Date	Mintage	MS-63	Proof
2001	15,000	375	—

20 DOLLARS

KM# 153 15.5515 g. 0.9999 Gold 0.4999 oz. AGW 32 mm. **Obv:** Young bust right, date and denomination below **Obv. Designer:** Arnold Machin **Rev:** Maple leaf flanked by 9999

Date	Mintage	MS-63	Proof
1986	529,200	BV+7%	—
1987	332,800	BV+7%	—
1988	538,400	BV+7%	—
1989	259,200	BV+7%	—
1989 Proof	6,998	—	775

KM# 190 15.5515 g. 0.9999 Gold 0.4999 oz. AGW **Obv:** Crowned head right, date and denomination below **Obv. Designer:** Dora dePedery-Hunt **Rev:** Maple leaf flanked by 9999

Date	Mintage	MS-63	Proof
1990	174,400	BV+7%	—
1991	96,200	BV+7%	—
1992	108,000	BV+7%	—
1993	99,492	BV+7%	—
1994	104,766	BV+7%	—
1995	103,162	BV+7%	—
1996	66,246	BV+7%	—
1997	63,354	BV+7%	—
1998	65,366	BV+7%	—
1999 oval "20 Years ANS" privy mark	—	BV+12%	—
2000 oval "2000" privy mark	—	BV+12%	—

KM# 368 15.5515 g. 0.9999 Gold 0.4999 oz. AGW **Rev:** Maple leaf hologram

Date	Mintage	MS-63	Proof
1999	500	800	—

KM# 441 15.5840 g. 0.9999 Gold 0.5010 oz. AGW 25 mm. **Subject:** Holographic Maples Leaves **Obv:** Crowned head right **Rev:** Three maple leaves multicolor hologram **Edge:** Reeded

Date	Mintage	MS-63	Proof
2001	600	775	—

50 DOLLARS

KM# 125.1 31.1030 g. 0.9990 Gold 0.9989 oz. AGW **Obv:** Young bust right, denomination and date below **Rev:** Maple leaf flanked by .999

Date	Mintage	MS-63	Proof
1979	1,000,000	BV+4%	—
1980	1,251,500	BV+4%	—
1981	863,000	BV+4%	—
1982	883,000	BV+4%	—

KM# 125.2 31.1030 g. 0.9999 Gold 0.9998 oz. AGW **Obv:** Young bust right, date and denomination below **Rev:** Maple leaf flanked by .9999

Date	Mintage	MS-63	Proof
1983	843,000	BV+4%	—
1984	1,067,500	BV+4%	—
1985	1,908,000	BV+4%	—
1986	779,115	BV+4%	—
1987	978,000	BV+4%	—
1988	826,500	BV+4%	—
1989	856,000	BV+4%	—
1989 Proof	17,781	—	1,500

KM# 191 31.1030 g. 0.9999 Gold 0.9998 oz. AGW **Obv:** Crowned head right, date and denomination below **Obv. Designer:** Dora dePedery-Hunt **Rev:** Maple leaf flanked by .9999

Date	Mintage	MS-63	Proof
1990	815,000	BV+4%	—
1991	290,000	BV+4%	—
1992	368,900	BV+4%	—
1993	321,413	BV+4%	—
1994	180,357	BV+4%	—
1995	208,729	BV+4%	—
1996	143,682	BV+4%	—
1997	478,211	BV+4%	—
1998	593,704	BV+4%	—
1999 oval "20 Years ANS" privy mark	—	BV+7%	—
2000 oval "2000" privy mark	—	BV+7%	—
2000 oval fireworks privy mark	—	BV+7%	—

KM# 305 31.1030 g. 0.9999 Gold 0.9998 oz. AGW **Obv:** Crowned head denomination below, within circle, dates below **Rev:** Mountie at gallop right, within circle **Rev. Designer:** Ago Aarand **Shape:** 10-sided

Date	Mintage	MS-63	Proof
1997	12,913	1,500	—

KM# 369 31.1030 g. 0.9999 Gold 0.9998 oz.
AGW **Obv:** Crowned head right, date and
denomination below **Rev:** Maple leaf hologram
flanked by 9999, with fireworks privy mark

Date	Mintage	MS-63	Proof
2000	500	1,750	—

KM# 442 31.1500 g. 0.9999 Gold 1.0014 oz. AGW
30 mm. **Subject:** Holographic Maples Leaves
Obv: Crowned head right **Rev:** Three maple leaves
multicolor hologram **Edge:** Reeded

Date	Mintage	MS-63	Proof
2001	600	1,550	—

KM# 1042 31.1050 g. 0.9990 Gold 0.9990 oz.
AGW 30 mm. **Rev:** Vancouver logo and maple
leaf **Edge:** Reeded

Date	Mintage	MS-63	Proof
2008P	—	1,500	—

KM# 1037 31.1050 g. 0.9999 Gold 0.9999 oz.
AGW 30 mm. **Rev:** Native eagle **Edge:** Reeded

Date	Mintage	MS-63	Proof
2009	—	1,500	—

KM# 1029 31.1050 g. 0.9999 Gold 0.9999 oz.
AGW 31 mm. **Rev:** Hockey player

Date	Mintage	MS-63	Proof
2010	—	—	—

200 DOLLARS

KM# 750 31.1500 g. 1.0000 Gold 1.0014 oz. AGW
30 mm. **Rev:** Three maple leaves

Date	Mintage	MS-63	Proof
2007 Proof, T/E privy mark	500	—	1,550

KM# 786 31.1050 g. 1.0000 Gold 1.0000 oz. AGW
30 mm. **Obv:** Bust right on lathe-work
background **Rev:** Two maple leaves on lathe-work
background

Date	Mintage	MS-63	Proof
2008 Proof	—	—	1,550

1000000 DOLLARS

KM# 755 100000.0000 g. 0.9999 Gold 3214.6 oz.
AGW **Rev:** Maple leaf **Note:** Cast. Illustration
reduced

Date	Mintage	MS-63	Proof
2007	10	4,750,000	—

PLATINUM BULLION COINAGE

DOLLAR

KM# 239 1.5552 g. 0.9995 Platinum 0.0500 oz.
APW **Obv:** Crowned head right, date and
denomination below **Rev:** Maple leaf flanked by 9995

Date	Mintage	MS-63	Proof
1993	2,120	BV+35%	—
1994	4,260	BV+35%	—
1995	460	150	—
1996	1,640	BV+35%	—
1997	1,340	BV+35%	—
1998	2,000	BV+35%	—
1999	2,000	BV+35%	—

2 DOLLARS

KM# 257 2.0735 g. 0.9995 Platinum 0.0666 oz. APW **Obv:** Crowned head right, date and denomination below **Rev:** Maple leaf flanked by 9995

Date	Mintage	MS-63	Proof
1994	1,470	240	—

5 DOLLARS

KM# 164 3.1203 g. 0.9995 Platinum 0.1003 oz. APW **Obv:** Young bust right, date and denomination below **Obv. Designer:** Arnold Machin **Rev:** Maple leaf flanked by 9995

Date	Mintage	MS-63	Proof
1988	74,000	BV+18%	—
1989 Proof	11,999	—	250
1989	18,000	BV+18%	—

KM# 192 3.1203 g. 0.9995 Platinum 0.1003 oz. APW **Obv. Designer:** dePedery-Hunt **Rev:** Maple leaf

Date	Mintage	MS-63	Proof
1990	9,000	BV+18%	—
1991	13,000	BV+18%	—
1992	16,000	BV+18%	—
1993	14,020	BV+18%	—
1994	19,190	BV+18%	—
1995	8,940	BV+18%	—
1996	8,820	BV+18%	—
1997	7,050	BV+18%	—
1998	5,710	BV+18%	—
1999	2,000	BV+18%	—

10 DOLLARS

KM# 165 7.7857 g. 0.9995 Platinum 0.2502 oz. APW **Obv:** Young bust right, date and denomination below **Obv. Designer:** Machin **Rev:** Maple leaf flanked by 9995

Date	Mintage	MS-63	Proof
1988	93,600	BV+13%	—
1989 Proof	1,999	—	550
1989	3,200	BV+13%	—

KM# 193 7.7857 g. 0.9995 Platinum 0.2502 oz. APW **Obv. Designer:** dePedery-Hunt **Rev:** Maple leaf

Date	Mintage	MS-63	Proof
1990	1,600	BV+13%	—
1991	7,200	BV+13%	—

Date	Mintage	MS-63	Proof
1992	11,600	BV+13%	—
1993	8,048	BV+13%	—
1994	9,456	BV+13%	—
1995	6,524	BV+13%	—
1996	6,160	BV+13%	—
1997	4,552	BV+13%	—
1998	3,816	BV+13%	—
1999	2,000	BV+13%	—

20 DOLLARS

KM# 166 15.5519 g. 0.9995 Platinum 0.4997 oz. APW **Obv:** Young bust right, denomination and date below **Obv. Designer:** Machin **Rev:** Maple leaf flanked by 9995

Date	Mintage	MS-63	Proof
1988	23,600	BV+9%	—
1989	4,800	BV+9%	—
1989 Proof	1,999	—	1,000

KM# 194 15.5519 g. 0.9995 Platinum 0.4997 oz. APW **Obv. Designer:** dePedery-Hunt **Rev:** Maple leaf

Date	Mintage	MS-63	Proof
1990	2,600	BV+9%	—
1991	5,600	BV+9%	—
1992	12,800	BV+9%	—
1993	6,022	BV+9%	—
1994	6,710	BV+9%	—
1995	6,308	BV+9%	—
1996	5,490	BV+9%	—
1997	3,990	BV+9%	—
1998	5,486	BV+9%	—
1999	500	BV+15%	—

30 DOLLARS

KM# 174 3.1100 g. 0.9990 Platinum 0.0999 oz. APW **Obv:** Crowned head right **Rev:** Polar bear swimming, denomination below **Rev. Designer:** Robert Bateman

Date	Mintage	MS-63	Proof
1990 Proof	2,629	—	210

KM# 198 3.1100 g. 0.9990 Platinum 0.0999 oz. APW **Obv:** Crowned head right **Rev:** Snowy owl, denomination below **Rev. Designer:** Glen Loates

Date	Mintage	MS-63	Proof
1991 Proof	3,500	—	210

PLATINUM BULLION

KM# 226 3.1100 g. 0.9990 Platinum 0.0999 oz.
APW **Obv:** Crowned head right **Rev:** Cougar
head and shoulders, denomination below **Rev.
Designer:** George McLean

Date	Mintage	MS-63	Proof
1992 Proof	3,500	—	210

KM# 240 3.1100 g. 0.9990 Platinum 0.0999 oz.
APW **Obv:** Crowned head right **Rev:** Arctic fox,
denomination below **Rev. Designer:** Claude
D'Angelo

Date	Mintage	MS-63	Proof
1993 Proof	3,500	—	210

KM# 252 3.1100 g. 0.9990 Platinum 0.0999 oz.
APW **Obv:** Crowned head right, date below **Rev:**
Sea otter, denomination below **Rev. Designer:** Ron
S. Parker

Date	Mintage	MS-63	Proof
1994 Proof	1,500	—	210

KM# 266 3.1100 g. 0.9990 Platinum 0.0999 oz.
APW **Obv:** Crowned head right, date below **Rev:**
Canadian lynx, denomination below **Rev.
Designer:** Michael Dumas

Date	Mintage	MS-63	Proof
1995 Proof	620	—	210

KM# 278 3.1100 g. 0.9990 Platinum 0.0999 oz.
APW **Obv:** Crowned head right, date below **Rev:**
Falcon portrait, denomination below **Rev.
Designer:** Dwayne Harty

Date	Mintage	MS-63	Proof
1996 Proof	489	—	210

KM# 300 3.1100 g. 0.9995 Platinum 0.0999 oz.
APW **Obv:** Crowned head right, date below **Rev:**
Bison head, denomination below **Rev. Designer:**
Chris Bacon

Date	Mintage	MS-63	Proof
1997 Proof	5,000	—	210

KM# 322 3.1100 g. 0.9990 Platinum 0.0999 oz.
APW **Obv:** Crowned head right, date below **Rev:**
Grey wolf **Rev. Designer:** Kerr Burnett

Date	Mintage	MS-63	Proof
1998 Proof	2,000	—	210

KM# 359 3.1100 g. 0.9995 Platinum 0.0999 oz.
APW **Obv:** Crowned head right, date below **Rev:**
Musk ox **Rev. Designer:** Mark Hobson

Date	Mintage	MS-63	Proof
1999 Proof	1,500	—	210

KM# 405 3.1100 g. 0.9995 Platinum 0.0999 oz.
APW 16 mm. **Obv:** Crowned head right, date
below **Rev:** Pronghorn antelope head,
denomination below **Rev. Designer:** Mark Hobson
Edge: Reeded

Date	Mintage	MS-63	Proof
2000 Proof	600	—	210

KM# 429 3.1100 g. 0.9995 Platinum 0.0999 oz.
APW 16 mm. **Obv:** Crowned head right **Rev:**
Harlequin duck's head **Rev. Designer:** Cosme
Saffioti and Susan Taylor **Edge:** Reeded

Date	Mintage	MS-63	Proof
2001 Proof	448	—	200

KM# 1097 3.1100 g. 0.9995 Platinum 0.0999 oz.
APW 16 mm. **Rev:** Great Blue Heron

Date	Mintage	MS-63	Proof
2002 Proof	344	—	200

KM# 1101 3.1100 g. 0.9995 Platinum 0.0999 oz.
APW 16 mm. **Rev:** Atlantic Walrus

Date	Mintage	MS-63	Proof
2003	365	—	250

KM# 1105 3.1100 g. 0.9995 Platinum 0.0999 oz.
APW 16 mm. **Rev:** Grizzly Bear

Date	Mintage	MS-63	Proof
2004 Proof	380	—	250

50 DOLLARS

KM# 167 31.1030 g. 0.9995 Platinum 0.9994 oz.
APW   **Obv:** Young bust right, denomination and
date below **Obv. Designer:** Machin **Rev:** Maple leaf
flanked by 9995

Date	Mintage	MS-63	Proof
1988	37,500	BV+4%	—
1989 Proof	5,965	—	1,950
1989	10,000	BV+4%	—

KM# 195 31.1030 g. 0.9995 Platinum 0.9994 oz.
APW   **Obv. Designer:** dePedery-Hunt **Rev:**
Maple leaf

Date	Mintage	MS-63	Proof
1990	15,100	BV+4%	—
1991	31,900	BV+4%	—
1992	40,500	BV+4%	—
1993	17,666	BV+4%	—
1994	36,245	BV+4%	—
1995	25,829	BV+4%	—
1996	62,273	BV+4%	—
1997	25,480	BV+4%	—
1998	10,403	BV+4%	—
1999	1,300	BV+10%	—

75 DOLLARS

KM# 175 7.7760 g. 0.9990 Platinum 0.2497 oz.
APW   **Obv:** Crowned head right **Rev:** Polar bear
resting, denomination below **Rev. Designer:** Robert
Bateman

Date	Mintage	MS-63	Proof
1990 Proof	2,629	—	520

KM# 199 7.7760 g. 0.9990 Platinum 0.2497 oz.
APW   **Obv:** Crowned head right **Rev:** Snowy owls
perched on branch, denomination below **Rev.**
Designer: Glen Loates

Date	Mintage	MS-63	Proof
1991 Proof	3,500	—	520

KM# 227 7.7760 g. 0.9990 Platinum 0.2497 oz.
APW   **Obv:** Crowned head right **Rev:** Cougar
prowling, denomination below **Rev. Designer:**
George McLean

Date	Mintage	MS-63	Proof
1992 Proof	3,500	—	520

KM# 241 7.7760 g. 0.9990 Platinum 0.2497 oz.
APW   **Obv:** Crowned head right **Rev:** Two Arctic
foxes, denomination below **Rev. Designer:** Claude
D'Angelo

Date	Mintage	MS-63	Proof
1993 Proof	3,500	—	520

KM# 253 7.7760 g. 0.9990 Platinum 0.2497 oz.
APW   **Obv:** Crowned head right, date below **Rev:**
Sea otter eating urchin, denomination below **Rev.**
Designer: Ron S. Parker

Date	Mintage	MS-63	Proof
1994 Proof	1,500	—	520

KM# 267 7.7760 g. 0.9990 Platinum 0.2497 oz.
APW   **Obv:** Crowned head right, date below **Rev:**
Two lynx kittens, denomination below **Rev.**
Designer: Michael Dumas

Date	Mintage	MS-63	Proof
1995 Proof	1,500	—	520

KM# 279 7.7760 g. 0.9990 Platinum 0.2497 oz.
APW   **Obv:** Crowned head right, date below **Rev:**

Peregrine falcon, denomination below **Rev.**
Designer: Dwayne Harty

Date	Mintage	MS-63	Proof
1996 Proof	1,500	—	520

KM# 301 7.7760 g. 0.9990 Platinum 0.2497 oz.
APW **Obv:** Crowned head right, date below **Rev:**
Two bison calves, denomination below **Rev.**
Designer: Chris Bacon

Date	Mintage	MS-63	Proof
1997 Proof	1,500	—	520

KM# 323 7.7760 g. 0.9990 Platinum 0.2497 oz.
APW **Obv:** Crowned head right, date below **Rev:**
Gray wolf **Rev. Designer:** Kerr Burnett

Date	Mintage	MS-63	Proof
1998 Proof	1,000	—	520

KM# 360 7.7760 g. 0.9990 Platinum 0.2497 oz.
APW **Obv:** Crowned head right, date below **Rev:**
Musk ox **Rev. Designer:** Mark Hobson

Date	Mintage	MS-63	Proof
1999 Proof	500	—	520

KM# 406 7.7760 g. 0.9990 Platinum 0.2497 oz.
APW 20 mm. **Obv:** Crowned head right **Rev:**
Standing pronghorn antelope, denomination below
Rev. Designer: Mark Hobson **Edge:** Reeded

Date	Mintage	MS-63	Proof
2000 Proof	600	—	520

KM# 430 7.7760 g. 0.9995 Platinum 0.2499 oz.
APW 20 mm. **Obv:** Crowned head right **Rev:**
Harlequin duck in flight **Rev. Designer:** Cosme
Saffioti and Susan Taylor **Edge:** Reeded

Date	Mintage	MS-63	Proof
2001 Proof	448	—	500

KM# 1098 7.7700 g. 0.9995 Platinum 0.2497 oz.
APW 20 mm. **Rev:** Great Blue Heron

Date	Mintage	MS-63	Proof
2002 Proof	344	—	525

KM# 1102 7.7700 g. 0.9995 Platinum 0.2497 oz.
APW 20 mm. **Rev:** Atlantic Walrus

Date	Mintage	MS-63	Proof
2003 Proof	365	—	550

KM# 1106 7.7700 g. 0.9995 Platinum 0.2497 oz.
APW 20 mm. **Rev:** Grizzly Bear

Date	Mintage	MS-63	Proof
2004 Proof	380	—	550

150 DOLLARS

KM# 176 15.5520 g. 0.9990 Platinum 0.4995 oz.
APW **Obv:** Crowned head right **Rev:** Polar bear
walking, denomination below **Rev. Designer:**
Robert Bateman

Date	Mintage	MS-63	Proof
1990 Proof	2,629	—	1,000

KM# 200 15.5520 g. 0.9990 Platinum 0.4995 oz.
APW **Obv:** Crowned head right **Rev:** Snowy owl
flying, denomination below **Rev. Designer:** Glen
Loates

Date	Mintage	MS-63	Proof
1991 Proof	3,500	—	1,000

KM# 228 15.5520 g. 0.9990 Platinum 0.4995 oz.
APW **Obv:** Crowned head right **Rev:** Cougar
mother and cub, denomination below **Rev.**
Designer: George McLean

Date	Mintage	MS-63	Proof
1992 Proof	3,500	—	1,000

KM# 242 15.5520 g. 0.9990 Platinum 0.4995 oz.
APW **Obv:** Crowned head right **Rev:** Arctic fox
by lake, denomination below **Rev. Designer:**
Claude D'Angelo

Date	Mintage	MS-63	Proof
1993 Proof	3,500	—	1,000

KM# 254 15.5520 g. 0.9990 Platinum 0.4995 oz. APW **Obv:** Crowned head right, date below **Rev:** Sea otter mother carrying pup, denomination below **Rev. Designer:** Ron S. Parker

Date	Mintage	MS-63	Proof
1994 Proof	—	—	1,000

KM# 324 15.5520 g. 0.9990 Platinum 0.4995 oz. APW **Obv:** Crowned head right, date below **Rev:** Two gray wolf cubs, denomination below **Rev. Designer:** Kerr Burnett

Date	Mintage	MS-63	Proof
1998 Proof	2,000	—	1,000

KM# 268 15.5520 g. 0.9990 Platinum 0.4995 oz. APW **Obv:** Crowned head right, date below **Rev:** Prowling lynx, denomination below **Rev. Designer:** Michael Dumas

Date	Mintage	MS-63	Proof
1995 Proof	226	—	1,000

KM# 361 15.5520 g. 0.9990 Platinum 0.4995 oz. APW **Obv:** Crowned head right **Rev:** Musk ox, denomination below **Rev. Designer:** Mark Hobson

Date	Mintage	MS-63	Proof
1999 Proof	500	—	1,000

KM# 280 15.5520 g. 0.9990 Platinum 0.4995 oz. APW **Obv:** Crowned head right, date below **Rev:** Peregrine falcon on branch, denomination below **Rev. Designer:** Dwayne Harty

Date	Mintage	MS-63	Proof
1996 Proof	100	—	1,000

KM# 407 15.5500 g. 0.9990 Platinum 0.4994 oz. APW 25 mm. **Obv:** Crowned head right **Rev:** Two pronghorn antelope, denomination below **Rev. Designer:** Mark Hobson **Edge:** Reeded

Date	Mintage	MS-63	Proof
2000 Proof	600	—	1,000

KM# 302 15.5520 g. 0.9990 Platinum 0.4995 oz. APW **Obv:** Crowned head right, date below **Rev:** Bison bull, denomination below **Rev. Designer:** Chris Bacon

Date	Mintage	MS-63	Proof
1997 Proof	4,000	—	1,000

KM# 431 15.5500 g. 0.9995 Platinum 0.4997 oz. APW 25 mm. **Obv:** Crowned head right **Rev:** Two harlequin ducks **Rev. Designer:** Cosme Saffioti and Susan Taylor **Edge:** Reeded

Date	Mintage	MS-63	Proof
2001 Proof	448	—	1,000

KM# 1099 15.5500 g. 0.9995 Platinum 0.4997 oz. APW 25 mm. **Rev:** Great Blue Heron

Date	Mintage	MS-63	Proof
2002 Proof	344	—	1,000

KM# 1103 15.5500 g. 0.9995 Platinum 0.4997 oz.
APW 25 mm. **Rev:** Atlantic Walrus

Date	Mintage	MS-63	Proof
2003 Proof	365	—	1,000

KM# 1107 15.5500 g. 0.9995 Platinum 0.4997 oz.
APW 25 mm. **Rev:** Grizzly Bear

Date	Mintage	MS-63	Proof
2004 Proof	380	—	1,000

300 DOLLARS

KM# 177 31.1035 g. 0.9990 Platinum 0.9990 oz.
APW **Obv:** Crowned head right **Rev:** Polar bear
mother and cub, denomination below **Rev.**
Designer: Robert Bateman

Date	Mintage	MS-63	Proof
1990 Proof	2,629	—	1,950

KM# 201 31.1035 g. 0.9990 Platinum 0.9990 oz.
APW **Obv:** Crowned head right **Rev:** Snowy owl
with chicks, denomination below **Rev. Designer:**
Glen Loates

Date	Mintage	MS-63	Proof
1991 Proof	3,500	—	1,950

KM# 229 31.1035 g. 0.9990 Platinum 0.9990 oz.
APW **Obv:** Crowned head right **Rev:** Cougar
resting in tree, denomination below **Rev. Designer:**
George McLean

Date	Mintage	MS-63	Proof
1992 Proof	3,500	—	1,950

KM# 243 31.1035 g. 0.9990 Platinum 0.9990 oz.
APW **Obv:** Crowned head right **Rev:** Mother fox
and three kits, denomination below **Rev. Designer:**
Claude D'Angelo

Date	Mintage	MS-63	Proof
1993 Proof	3,500	—	1,950

KM# 255 31.1035 g. 0.9990 Platinum 0.9990 oz.
APW **Obv:** Crowned head right, date below **Rev:**
Two otters swimming, denomination below **Rev.**
Designer: Ron S. Parker

Date	Mintage	MS-63	Proof
1994 Proof	—	—	1,950

KM# 269 31.1035 g. 0.9990 Platinum 0.9990 oz.
APW **Obv:** Crowned head right, date below **Rev:**
Female lynx and three kittens, denomination below
Rev. Designer: Michael Dumas

Date	Mintage	MS-63	Proof
1995 Proof	1,500	—	1,950

KM# 281 31.1035 g. 0.9990 Platinum 0.9990 oz.
APW **Obv:** Crowned head right, date below **Rev:**
Peregrine falcon feeding nestlings, denomination
below **Rev. Designer:** Dwayne Harty

Date	Mintage	MS-63	Proof
1996 Proof	1,500	—	1,950

KM# 303 31.1035 g. 0.9990 Platinum 0.9990 oz.
APW   **Obv:** Crowned head right, date below **Rev:**
Bison family, denomination below **Rev. Designer:**
Chris Bacon

Date	Mintage	MS-63	Proof
1997 Proof	1,500	—	1,950

KM# 432 31.1035 g. 0.9995 Platinum 0.9995 oz.
APW 30 mm.   **Obv:** Crowned head right **Rev:** Two
standing harlequin ducks **Rev. Designer:** Cosme
Saffioti and Susan Taylor **Edge:** Reeded

Date	Mintage	MS-63	Proof
2001 Proof	448	—	1,900

KM# 1100 31.1050 g. 0.9995 Platinum 0.9995 oz.
APW 30 mm.   **Rev:** Great Blue Heron

Date	Mintage	MS-63	Proof
2002 Proof	344	—	1,950

KM# 1104 31.1050 g. 0.9995 Platinum 0.9995 oz.
APW 30 mm.   **Rev:** Atlantic Walrus

Date	Mintage	MS-63	Proof
2003 Proof	365	—	1,950

KM# 1108 31.1050 g. 0.9995 Platinum 0.9995 oz.
APW 30 mm.   **Rev:** Grizzly Bear

Date	Mintage	MS-63	Proof
2004 Proof	380	—	1,950

KM# 325 31.1035 g. 0.9990 Platinum 0.9990 oz.
APW   **Obv:** Crowned head right, date below **Rev:**
Gray wolf and two cubs, denomination below **Rev.**
Designer: Kerr Burnett

Date	Mintage	MS-63	Proof
1998 Proof	—	—	1,950

KM# 362 31.1035 g. 0.9990 Platinum 0.9990 oz.
APW   **Obv:** Crowned head right, date below **Rev:**
Musk ox **Rev. Designer:** Mark Hobson

Date	Mintage	MS-63	Proof
1999 Proof	500	—	1,950

KM# 951 31.1600 g. 0.9990 Platinum 1.0008 oz.
APW 30 mm.   **Rev:** Steppe Bison

Date	Mintage	MS-63	Proof
2009 Proof	200	—	3,500

KM# 408 31.1035 g. 0.9990 Platinum 0.9990 oz.
APW 30 mm.   **Obv:** Crowned head right, date
below **Rev:** Four pronghorn antelope, denomination
below **Rev. Designer:** Mark Hobson **Edge:** Reeded

Date	Mintage	MS-63	Proof
2000 Proof	600	—	1,950

SETS

Custom Proof-Like Sets (CPL)

KM#	Date	Mintage	Identification	Issue Price	Mkt. Value
CPL1	1971 (7)	33,517	KM59.1 (2 pcs.), 60.1, 62b, 75.1, 77.1 ,79	6.50	5.00
CPL2	1971 (6)	38,198	KM59.1 (2 pcs.), 60.1, 62b, 75.1, 77.1	6.50	5.00
CPL3	1973 (6)	35,676	KM59.1 (2 pcs.), 60.1, 75.1, 77.1, 81.1 obv. 120 beads, 82	6.50	6.50
CPL4	1973 (7)	Inc. above	KM59.1 (2 pcs.), 60.1, 75.1, 77.1, 81.1 obv. 132 beads, 82	6.50	200
CPL5	1974 (5)	44,296	KM59.1 (2 pcs.), 60.1, 62b-75.1, 88	8.00	5.00
CPL6	1975 (6)	36,851	KM59.1 (2 pcs.), 60.1, 62b-75.1, 76.2, 77.1	8.00	5.00
CPL7	1976 (6)	28,162	KM59.1 (2 pcs.), 60.1, 62b-75.1, 76.2, 77.1	8.00	5.50
CPL8	1977 (6)	44,198	KM59.1 (2 pcs.), 60.1, 62b-75.2, 77.1, 117	8.15	7.50
CPL9	1978 (6)	41,000	KM59.1 (2 pcs.), 60.1, 62b-75.3, 77.1, 120.1	—	5.00
CPL10	1979 (6)	31,174	KM59.2 (2 pcs.), 60.2, 74, 75.3, 77.2, 120.1	10.75	5.00
CPL11	1980 (7)	41,447	KM60.2, 74, 75.3, 77.2, 120.1, 127 (2 pcs.)	10.75	6.00

Mint Sets

KM#	Date	Mintage	Identification	Issue Price	Mkt. Value
MS1	1973 (4)	Inc. above	KM84, 85, 86.1, 87; Olympic Commemoratives, Series I	45.00	135
MS2	1974 (4)	Inc. above	KM89, 90, 93, 94; Olympic Commemoratives, Series II	48.00	135
MS3	1974 (4)	Inc. above	KM91-92, 95-96; Olympic Commemorative, Series III	48.00	135
MS4	1975 (4)	Inc. above	KM98, 99, 102, 103; Olympic Commemoratives, Series IV	48.00	135
MS5	1975 (4)	Inc. above	KM100, 101, 104, 105; Olympic Commemoratives, Series V	60.00	135
MS6	1976 (4)	Inc. above	KM107, 108, 111, 112; Olympic Commemoratives, Series VI	60.00	135
MS7	1976 (4)	Inc. above	KM109, 110, 113, 114; Olympic Commemoratives, Series VII	60.00	135
MS8	2001 (5)	600	KM438-442	1,996	2,950
MS10	2002 (7)	—	KM#444-449, 467, Oh! Canada! 135th Birthday Gift set.	17.00	16.00
MS11	2002 (7)	—	KM#444-449, 467, Tiny Treasures Uncirculated Gift Set	17.00	16.00
MS12	2003 (7)	135,000	KM#289, 182b, 183b, 184b, 290, 186, 270	12.00	16.00
MS13	2003 (7)	75,000	KM490-496	13.25	20.00
MS14	2003 (7)	—	KM289, 182-184, 290, 186, 270, Oh! Canada!	17.75	16.00
MS15	2003 (7)	—	KM289, 182-184, 290, 186, 270, Tiny Treasures Uncirculated Gift Set	17.75	16.00

Olympic Commemoratives (OCP)

KM#	Date	Mintage	Identification	Issue Price	Mkt. Value
OCP1	1973 (4)	Inc. above	KM84-87, Series I	78.50	135
OCP2	1974 (4)	Inc. above	KM89-90, 93-94, Series II	88.50	135
OCP3	1974 (4)	Inc. above	KM91-92, 95-96, Series III	88.50	135
OCP4	1975 (4)	Inc. above	KM98-99, 102-103, Series IV	88.50	135
OCP5	1975 (4)	Inc. above	KM100-101, 104-105, Series V	88.50	135
OCP6	1976 (4)	Inc. above	KM107-108, 111-112, Series VI	88.50	135
OCP7	1976 (4)	Inc. above	KM109-110, 113-114, Series VII	88.50	135

Proof Sets

KM#	Date	Mintage	Identification	Issue Price	Mkt. Value
XPS1	1952 (6)	—	X#MB41-MB46	—	—
XPS2	1979 (5)	100	X#Tn1a-Tn5a	—	40.00
XPS3	1980 (6)	1,500	X#MB51-MB56	—	110
PS1	1981 (7)	199,000	KM60.2, 74, 75.3, 77.2, 120.1, 127, 130	36.00	30.00
PS2	1982 (7)	180,908	KM60.2a, 74, 75.3, 77.2, 120.1, 132, 133	36.00	37.50
PS3	1983 (7)	166,779	KM60.2a, 74, 75.3, 77.2, 120.1, 132, 138	36.00	27.50
PS4	1984 (7)	161,602	KM60.2a, 74, 75.3, 77.2, 120.1, 132, 140	30.00	27.50
PS5	1985 (7)	157,037	KM60.2a, 74, 75.3, 77.2, 120.1, 132, 143	30.00	30.00
PS6	1986 (7)	175,745	KM60.2a, 74, 75.3, 77.2, 120.1, 132, 149	30.00	29.00
PS7	1987 (7)	179,004	KM60.2a, 74, 75.3, 77.2, 120.1, 132, 154	34.00	30.00
PS8	1988 (7)	175,259	KM60.2a, 74, 75.3, 77.2, 132, 157, 161	37.50	34.00
PS10	1989 (4)	6,823	KM125.2, 135-136, 153	1,190	2,900
PS11	1989 (4)	1,995	KM164-167	1,700	3,750
PS12	1989 (3)	2,550	KM125.2, 163, 167	1,530	3,500
PS13	1989 (3)	9,979	KM135, 163, 164	165	475
PS9	1989 (7)	170,928	KM60.2a, 74, 75.3, 77.2, 132, 157, 168	40.00	34.00
PS14	1990 (7)	158,068	KM170, 181, 182, 183, 184, 185, 186	41.00	42.50
PS15	1990 (4)	2,629	KM174-177	1,720	3,700
PS16	1991 (7)	14,629	KM179, 181, 182, 183, 184, 185, 186	—	80.00
PS17	1991 (4)	873	KM198-201	1,760	3,700
PS18	1992 (11)	84,397	KM203a, 212a-214a, 218, 220a-223a, 231a-234a	—	92.50
PS19	1992 (7)	147,061	KM204-210	42.75	65.00
PS20	1992 (4)	3,500	KM226-229	1,680	3,700
PS21	1993 (7)	143,065	KM181, 182, 183, 184, 185, 186, 235	42.75	40.00
PS22	1993 (4)	3,500	KM240-243	1,329	3,700
PS23	1994 (7)	47,303	KM181-186, 248	47.50	30.00
PS24	1994 (7)	99,121	KM181-186, 251	43.00	45.00
PS25	1994 (4)	1,500	KM252-255	915	3,700
PS26	1995 (7)	Inc. above	KM181-186, 259	37.45	52.00
PS27	1995 (7)	50,000	KM181-185, 258, 259	49.45	52.00
PS28	1995 (4)	Inc. above	KM261-264	42.00	95.00
PS29	1995 (4)	682	KM266-269	1,555	3,700

KM#	Date	Mintage	Identification	Issue Price	Mkt. Value
PS30	1995 (2)	Inc. above	KM261-262	22.00	48.00
PS31	1995 (2)	Inc. above	KM263-264	22.00	46.00
PS32	1996 (4)	423	KM278-281	1,555	3,700
PS33	1996 (7)	Inc. above	KM181, 182a, 183a, 184a, 185a, 186, 274	49.00	60.00
PS34	1996 (4)	Inc. above	KM283-286	44.45	80.00
PS35	1997 (7)	Inc. above	KM182a, 183a, 184a, 270c, 282, 289, 290	60.00	75.00
PS36	1997 (4)	Inc. above	KM292-295	44.45	68.00
PS37	1997 (4)	Inc. above	KM300-303	1,530	3,700
PS38	1998 (8)	Inc. above	KM182a, 183a, 184a, 186, 270b, 289, 290a, 306	59.45	80.00
PS39	1998 (5)	25,000	KM309-313	73.50	55.00
PS40	1998 (2)	61,000	KM316 w/China Y-727	72.50	40.00
PS41	1998 (4)	Inc. above	KM318-321	44.45	68.00
PS42	1998 (4)	1,000	KM322-325	1,552	3,700
PS43	1998 (5)	25,000	KM310-313, 332	73.50	68.00
PS44	1999 (7)	Inc. above	KM182a-184a, 186, 270c, 289, 290a,	59.45	55.00
PS45	1999 (4)	Inc. above	KM335-338	39.95	140
PS46	1999 (12)	Inc. above	KM342a-353a	99.45	115
PS47	1999 (4)	Inc. above	KM359-362	1,425	3,700
PS48	2000 (12)	—	KM373a-383a, 384.2a	101	110
PS49	2000 (4)	—	KM389-392	44.00	80.00
PS50	2000 (4)	600	KM405-408	1,416	3,700
PS51	2001 (4)	—	KM429, 430, 431, 432	—	3,600
PS54	2002 (2)	—	KM#519, 520	750	1,125
PS57	2004 (8)	—	KM#490, 491a-494a, 495, 496a, 512	—	115
PS58	2004 (5)	25,000	KM#621-625	—	100.00

Proof-Like Dollars

KM#	Date	Mintage	Identification	Issue Price	Mkt. Value
D1.1	1951 (1)	—	KM46, Canoe	—	200
D1.2	1951 (1)	—	KM46, Arnprior	—	1,000
D2.1	1952 (1)	—	KM46, water lines	—	1,100
D2.2	1952 (1)	—	KM46, without water lines	—	200
D3	1953 (1)	1,200	KM54, Canoe w/shoulder fold	—	350
D4	1954 (1)	5,300	KM54, Canoe	1.25	150
D5	1955 (1)	7,950	KM54, Canoe	1.25	125
D5a	1955 (1)	Inc. above	KM54, Arnprior	1.25	600
D6	1956 (1)	10,212	KM54, Canoe	1.25	115
D7	1957 (1)	16,241	KM54, Canoe	1.25	40.00
D8	1958 (1)	33,237	KM55, British Columbia	1.25	25.00
D9	1959 (1)	45,160	KM54, Canoe	1.25	20.00
D10	1960 (1)	82,728	KM54, Canoe	1.25	20.00
D11	1961 (1)	120,928	KM54, Canoe	1.25	20.00
D12	1962 (1)	248,901	KM54, Canoe	1.25	20.00
D13	1963 (1)	963,525	KM54, Canoe	1.25	20.00
D14	1964 (1)	2,862,441	KM58, Charlottetown	1.25	20.00
D15	1965 (1)	2,904,352	KM64.1, Canoe	—	20.00
D16	1966 (1)	672,514	KM64.1, Canoe	—	20.00
D17	1967 (1)	1,036,176	KM70, Confederation	—	20.00

Proof-Like Sets (PL)

KM#	Date	Mintage	Identification	Issue Price	Mkt. Value
PL1	1953 (6)	1,200	KM49 w/o shoulder fold, 50-54	2.20	1,250
PL3	1954 (6)	3,000	KM49-54	2.50	825
PL4	1954 (6)	Inc. above	KM49 w/o shoulder fold, 50-54	2.50	1,100
PL5	1955 (6)	6,300	KM49, 50a, 51-54	2.50	2,500
PL6	1955 (6)	Inc. above	KM49, 50a, 51-54, Arnprior	2.50	500
PL7	1956 (6)	6,500	KM49, 50a, 51-54	2.50	225
PL8	1957 (6)	11,862	KM49, 50a, 51-54	2.50	150
PL9	1958 (6)	18,259	KM49, 50a, 51-53, 55	2.50	100.00
PL10	1959 (6)	31,577	KM49, 50a, 51, 52, 54, 56	2.50	55.00
PL11	1960 (6)	64,097	KM49, 50a, 51, 52, 54, 56	3.00	40.00
PL12	1961 (6)	98,373	KM49, 50a, 51, 52, 54, 56	3.00	40.00
PL13	1962 (6)	200,950	KM49, 50a, 51, 52, 54, 56	3.00	37.50
PL14	1963 (6)	673,006	KM49, 51, 52, 54, 56, 57	3.00	37.50
PL15	1964 (6)	1,653,162	KM49, 51, 52, 56-58	3.00	35.00
PL16	1965 (4)	2,904,352	KM59.1-60.1, 61-63, 64.1	4.00	35.00
PL17	1966 (5)	672,514	KM59.1-60.1, 61-63, 64.1	4.00	35.00
PL18	1967 (6)	961,887	KM65-70 (pliofilm flat pack)	4.00	37.50
PL18A	1967 (6)	70,583	KM65-70 and Silver Medal (red box)	12.00	42.50
PL18B	1967 (7)	337,688	KM65-71 (black box)	40.00	800
PL19	1968 (6)	521,641	KM59.1-60.1, 62b, 72a, 75.1-76.1	4.00	2.25
PL20	1969 (4)	326,203	KM59.1-60.1, 62b, 75.1-77.1	4.00	3.00
PL21	1970 (4)	349,120	KM59.1-60.1, 62b, 75.1, 77.1, 78	4.00	3.50
PL22	1971 (4)	253,311	KM59.1-60.1, 62b, 75.1, 77.1, 79	4.00	3.00
PL23	1972 (3)	224,275	KM59.1-60.1, 62b-77.1	4.00	3.00
PL24	1973 (6)	243,695	KM59.1-60.1, 62b-75.1 obv. 120 beads, 77.1, 81.1, 82	4.00	4.00
PL25	1973 (3)	Inc. above	KM59.1-60.1, 62b-75.1 obv. 132 beads, 77.1, 81.2, 82	4.00	250
PL26	1974 (6)	213,589	KM59.1-60.1, 62b-75.1, 77.1, 88	5.00	3.00
PL27.1	1975 (4)	197,372	KM59.1, 60.1, 62b-75.1, 76.2, 77.1	5.00	3.50

KM#	Date	Mintage	Identification	Issue Price	Mkt. Value
PL27.2	1975 (6)	Inc. above	KM59.1, 60.1, 62b-75.1, 76.3, 77.1	5.00	5.00
PL28	1976 (4)	171,737	KM59.1, 60.1, 62b-75.1, 76.2, 77.1	5.15	3.00
PL29	1977 (4)	225,307	KM59.1-60.1, 62b, 75.2, 77.1, 117.1	5.15	3.00
PL30	1978 (6)	260,000	KM59.1-60.1, 62b, 75.3, 77.1, 120.1	5.25	4.25
PL31	1979 (6)	187,624	KM59.2-60.2, 74, 75.3, 77.2, 120.1	6.25	4.25
PL32	1980 (6)	410,842	KM60.2, 74, 75.3, 77.2, 120.1, 127	6.50	4.50
PL33	1981 (5)	186,250	KM60.2, 74, 75.3, 77.2, 120.1, 123	5.00	4.00
PL34	1982 (5)	203,287	KM60.2, 74, 75.3, 77.2, 120.1, 123	6.00	4.00
PL36	1983 (6)	190,838	KM60.2a, 74, 75.3, 77.2, 120.1, 132	5.00	5.00
PL36.1	1983 (6)	Inc. above	KM60.2a, 74, 75.3, 77.2, 120.1, 132; set in folder packaged by British Royal Mint Coin Club	—	10.00
PL37	1984 (6)	181,249	KM60.2a, 74, 75.3, 77.2, 120.1, 132	5.25	5.00
PL38	1985 (6)	173,924	KM60.2a, 74, 75.3, 77.2, 120.1, 132	5.25	24.00
PL39	1986 (6)	167,338	KM60.2a, 74, 75.3, 77.2, 120.1, 132	5.25	6.50
PL40	1987 (6)	212,136	KM60.2a, 74, 75.3, 77.2, 120.1, 132	5.25	7.00
PL41	1988 (6)	182,048	KM60.2a, 74, 75.3, 77.2, 132, 157	6.05	5.50
PL42	1989 (6)	173,622	KM60.2a, 74, 75.3, 77.2, 132, 157	6.60	8.00
PL43	1990 (6)	170,791	KM181-186	7.40	8.00
PL44	1991 (6)	147,814	KM181-186	7.40	25.00
PL45	1992 (6)	217,597	KM204-209	8.25	17.50
PL46	1993 (6)	171,680	KM181-186	8.25	5.00
PL47	1994 (6)	141,676	KM181-185, 258	8.50	5.50
PL48	1994 (6)	18,794	KM181-185, 258 (Oh Canada holder)	—	8.50
PL49	1995 (6)	143,892	KM181-186	6.95	5.50
PL50	1995 (6)	50,927	KM181-186 (Oh Canada holder)	14.65	8.50
PL51	1995 (6)	36,443	KM181-186 (Baby Gift holder)	—	9.00
PL52	1996 (4)	116,736	KM181-186	—	27.00
PL53	1996 (6)	29,747	KM181-186 (Baby Gift holder)	—	14.00
PL54	1996 (10)	Inc. above	KM181a-185a, 186	8.95	65.00
PL55	1996 (6)	Inc. above	KM181a-185a, 186 (Oh Canada holder)	14.65	12.00
PL56	1996 (6)	Inc. above	KM181a-185a, 186 (Baby Gift holder)	—	12.00
PL57	1997 (7)	Inc. above	KM182a-184a, 209, 270, 289-290	10.45	8.00
PL58	1997 (7)	Inc. above	KM182a-184a, 270, 289-291 (Oh Canada holder)	16.45	30.00
PL59	1997 (5)	Inc. above	KM182a-184a, 209, 270, 289-290 (Baby Gift holder)	18.50	25.00
PL60	1998 (7)	Inc. above	KM182-184, 186, 270, 289-290	10.45	25.00
PL61	1998 (7)	Inc. above	KM182-184, 186, 270, 289-290 (Oh Canada holder)	16.45	25.00
PL62	1998 (7)	Inc. above	KM182-184, 186, 270, 289-290 (Tiny Treasures holder)	16.45	25.00
PL63	1999 (12)	Inc. above	KM342-353	16.95	10.00
PL64	2000 (12)	—	KM373-384	16.95	10.00

Specimen Sets (SS)

KM#	Date	Mintage	Identification	Issue Price	Mkt. Value
SS1	1858 (4)	Inc. above	KM1-4, Reeded edge	—	12,000
SS2	1858 (4)	Inc. above	KM1-4, Plain edge	—	10,000
SS3	1858 (4)	Inc. above	KM1-4; Double Set	—	20,000
SS4	1858 (1)	Inc. above	KM1 (overdate), 2-4; Double Set	—	20,000
SS5	1870 (1)	100	KM2, 3, 5, 6 (reeded edges)	—	40,000
SS6	1870 (1)	Inc. above	KM2, 3, 5, 6; Double Set (plain edges)	—	80,000
SS7	1872 (4)	Inc. above	KM2, 3, 5, 6	—	12,500
SS8	1875 (2)	Inc. above	KM2 (Large date), 3, 5	—	100,000
SS9	1880 (2)	Inc. above	KM2, 3, 5 (Narrow 0)	—	55,000
SS10	1881 (5)	Inc. above	KM7, 2, 3, 5, 6	—	35,000
SS11	1892 (2)	Inc. above	KM3, 5	—	10,000
SS12	1902 (5)	100	KM8-12	—	65,000
SS13	1902 (3)	Inc. above	KM9 (Large H), 10, 11	—	40,000
SS14	1903 (3)	Inc. above	KM10, 12, 13	—	7,000
SS15	1908 (5)	1,000	KM8, 10-13	—	4,500
SS16	1911 (5)	1,000	KM15-19	—	6,000
SS17	1911/12 (7)	5	KM15-20, 26-27	—	55,000
SS18	1921 (5)	Inc. above	KM22a-25a, 28	—	157,000
SS19	1922 (2)	Inc. above	KM28, 29	—	2,500
SS20	1923 (2)	Inc. above	KM28, 29	—	5,000
SS21	1924 (2)	Inc. above	KM28, 29	—	4,000
SS22	1925 (2)	Inc. above	KM28, 29	—	7,000
SS23	1926 (2)	Inc. above	KM28, 29 (Near 6)	—	5,000
SS24	1927 (3)	Inc. above	KM24a, 28, 29	—	8,000
SS25	1928 (4)	Inc. above	KM23a, 24a, 28, 29	—	12,000
SS26	1929 (5)	Inc. above	KM23a,-25a, 28, 29	—	24,000
SS27	1930 (4)	Inc. above	KM23a, 24a. 28, 29	—	24,000
SS28	1931 (5)	Inc. above	KM23a-25a, 28, 29	—	45,000
SS29	1932 (5)	Inc. above	KM23a-25a, 28, 29	—	20,000
SS30	1934 (2)	Inc. above	KM23-25, 28, 29	—	40,000
SS31	1936 (5)	Inc. above	KM23a-25a, 28, 29	—	12,000
SS32	1936 (5)	Inc. above	KM23a(dot), 24a(dot), 25a, 28(dot), 29, 30	—	500,000
SS33	1937 (6)	1,025	KM32-37, Matte Finish	—	750
SS34	1937 (4)	Inc. above	KM32-35, Mirror Fields	—	1,350
SS35	1937 (6)	75	KM32-37, Mirror Fields	—	3,500
SS36	1938 (6)	Inc. above	KM32-37	—	30,000
SS-A36	1939 (5)	Inc. above	KM32-35, 38, Matte Finish	—	—

KM#	Date	Mintage	Identification	Issue Price	Mkt. Value
SS-B36	1939 (5)	Inc. above	KM32-35, 38, Mirror Fields	—	—
SS-C36	1942 (2)	Inc. above	KM32, 33	—	1,000
SS-D36	1943 (2)	Inc. above	KM32, 40	—	1,000
SS37	1944 (5)	3	KM32, 34-37, 40a	—	15,000
SS-A37	1944 (2)	Inc. above	KM32, 40a	—	1,000
SS38	1945 (6)	6	KM32, 34-37, 40a	—	4,650
SS-A38	1945 (2)	Inc. above	KM32, 40a	—	1,000
SS39	1946 (6)	15	KM32, 34-37, 39a	—	4,000
SS40	1947 (6)	Inc. above	KM32, 34-37(7 curved), 37(7 pointed),	—	8,750
SS41	1947 (6)	Inc. above	KM32, 34-36(7 curved), 37(blunt 7), 39a	—	6,200
SS42	1947 (6)	Inc. above	KM32, 34-36(7 curved right), 37, 39a	—	4,250
SS43	1948 (6)	30	KM41-46	—	7,500
SS44	1949 (4)	20	KM41-45, 47	—	6,500
SS44A	1949 (2)	Inc. above	KM47	—	1,550
SS45	1950 (4)	12	KM41-46	—	2,700
SS46	1950 (4)	Inc. above	KM41-45, 46 (Arnprior)	—	5,500
SS47	1951 (5)	12	KM41, 48, 42a, 43-46 (w/water lines)	—	2,800
SS48	1952 (5)	2,317	KM41, 42a, 43-46 (water lines)	—	3,500
SS48A	1952 (5)	Inc. above	KM41, 42a, 43-46 (w/o water lines)	—	3,000
SS49	1953 (6)	28	KM49 w/o straps, 50-54	—	2,400
SS50	1953 (6)	Inc. above	KM49 w/ straps, 50-54	—	875
SS51	1964 (5)	Inc. above	KM49, 51, 52, 56-58	—	1,800
SS52	1965 (4)	Inc. above	KM59.1-60.1, 61-63, 64.1	—	1,800
SS56	1971 (6)	66,860	KM59.1-60.1, 62b-75.1, 77.1, 79 (2 pcs.); Double Dollar Prestige Sets	12.00	14.50
SS57	1972 (5)	36,349	KM59.1,-60.1, 62b-75.1, 76.1 (2 pcs.)	12.00	18.00
SS58	1973 (6)	119,819	KM59.1-60.1, 75.1, 77.1, 81.1, 82, 83	12.00	16.00
SS59	1973 (6)	Inc. above	KM59.1-60.1, 75.1, 77.1, 81.2, 82, 83	—	1,600
SS60	1974 (5)	85,230	KM59.1-60.1, 62b-75.1, 77.1, 88, 88a	15.00	12.50
SS61	1975 (5)	97,263	KM59.1-60.1, 62b-75.1, 76.2, 77.1, 97	15.00	12.50
SS62	1976 (5)	87,744	KM59.1-60, 62b-75.1, 76.2, 77.1, 106	16.00	14.00
SS63	1977 (5)	142,577	KM59.1-60.1, 62b, 75.2, 77.1, 117.1, 118	16.50	14.50
SS64	1978 (6)	147,000	KM59.1-60.1, 62b, 75.3, 77.1, 120.1, 121	16.50	10.00
SS65	1979 (6)	155,698	KM59.2-60.2, 74, 75.3, 77.2, 120, 124	18.50	15.50
SS66	1980 (6)	162,875	KM60.2, 74-75.3, 77.2, 120, 127, 128	30.50	25.00
SS67	1981 (6)	71,300	KM60.2, 74, 75.3, 77.2, 120.1, 127; Regular Specimen Sets	10.00	5.50
SS68	1982 (10)	62,298	KM60.2a, 74, 75.3, 77.2, 120.1, 132	11.50	100.00
SS69	1983 (6)	60,329	KM60.2a, 74, 75.3, 77.2, 120.1, 132	12.75	9.00
SS70	1984 (2)	60,400	KM60.2a, 74, 75.3, 77.2, 120.1, 132	10.00	5.50
SS71	1985 (6)	61,553	KM60.2a, 74, 75.3, 77.2, 120.1, 132	10.00	23.50
SS72	1986 (6)	67,152	KM60.2a, 74, 75.3, 77.2, 120.1, 132	10.00	9.00
SS72A	1987 (6)	75,194	KM60.2a, 74, 75.3, 77.2, 120.1, 132	11.00	7.50
SS73	1988 (6)	70,205	KM60.2a, 74, 75.3, 77.2, 132, 157	12.30	7.50
SS74	1989 (6)	75,306	KM60.2a, 74, 75.3, 77.2, 132, 157	14.50	9.50
SS75	1990 (6)	76,611	KM181-186	15.50	8.50
SS76	1991 (6)	68,552	KM181-186	15.50	17.50
SS77	1992 (6)	78,328	KM204-209	16.25	17.50
SS78	1993 (6)	77,351	KM181-186; Regular Specimen Sets Resumed	16.25	13.00
SS79	1994 (6)	77,349	KM181-186	16.50	9.50
SS80	1995 (6)	Inc. above	KM181-186	13.95	9.50
SS82	1996 (4)	Inc. above	KM181a-185a, 186	18.95	35.00
SS83	1997 (7)	Inc. above	KM182a-184a, 270, 289-291	19.95	47.50
SS84	1998 (7)	Inc. above	KM182-184, 186, 270, 289, 290	19.95	18.00
SS85	1999 (7)	Inc. above	KM182-184, 186, 270, 289a, 290	19.95	20.00
SS91	2003 (3)	75,000	KM#(uncertain), 270, 289, 290	30.00	50.00

V.I.P. Specimen Sets (VS)

KM#	Date	Mintage	Identification	Issue Price	Mkt. Value
VS1	1969 (0)	4		—	2,000
VS2	1970 (0)	100	KM59.1-60.1, 74.1-75.1, 77.1, 78	—	525
VS3	1971 (0)	69	KM59.1-60.1, 74.1-75.1, 77.1, 79(2 pcs.)	—	525
VS4	1972 (0)	25	KM59.1-60.1, 74.1-75.1, 76.1, (2 pcs.), 77.1	—	650
VS5	1973 (0)	26	KM59.1-60.1, 75.1, 77.1, 81.1, 82, 83	—	650
VS6	1974 (0)	72	KM59.1-60.1, 74.1-75.1, 77.1, 88a	—	525
VS7	1975 (0)	94	KM59.1-60.1, 74.1-75.1, 76.2, 77.1, 97	—	525
VS8	1976 (0)	Inc. above	KM59.1-60.1, 74.1-75.1, 76.2, 77.1, 106	—	525

NEW BRUNSWICK
PROVINCE

STERLING COINAGE

HALFPENNY TOKEN

KM# 1 Copper   **Obv:** Crowned head left **Obv. Legend:** VICTORIA DEI GRATIA REGINA **Rev:** Three masted ship **Rev. Legend:** NEW BRUNSWICK

Date	Mintage	VG-8	F-12	VF-20	XF-40	MS-60	MS-63	Proof
1843	480,000	4.00	7.50	15.00	45.00	300	400	—
1843 Proof	—	—	—	—	—	—	—	750

KM# 3 Copper   **Obv:** Head left **Obv. Legend:** VICTORIA DEI GRATIA REGINA **Rev:** Three masted ship **Rev. Legend:** NEW BRUNSWICK

Date	Mintage	VG-8	F-12	VF-20	XF-40	MS-60	MS-63	Proof
1854	864,000	4.00	7.50	15.00	45.00	300	400	—

KM# 3a Bronze   **Obv:** Head left **Obv. Legend:** VICTORIA DEI GRATIA REGINA **Rev:** Three masted ship **Rev. Legend:** NEW BRUNSWICK

Date	Mintage	VG-8	F-12	VF-20	XF-40	MS-60	MS-63	Proof
1854 Proof	—	—	—	—	—	—	—	400

1 PENNY TOKEN

KM# 2 Copper   **Obv:** Crowned head left **Obv. Legend:** VICTORIA DEI GRATIA REGINA **Rev:** Three masted ship **Rev. Legend:** NEW BRUNSWICK

Date	Mintage	VG-8	F-12	VF-20	XF-40	MS-60	MS-63	Proof
1843	480,000	5.00	9.50	23.00	65.00	250	350	—
1843 Proof	—	—	—	—	—	—	—	800

KM# 4   Copper   **Obv:** Head left **Obv. Legend:** VICTORIA DEI GRATIA REGINA **Rev:** Three masted ship
Rev. Legend: NEW BRUNSWICK

Date	Mintage	VG-8	F-12	VF-20	XF-40	MS-60	MS-63	Proof
1854	432,000	3.75	7.50	22.00	65.00	300	400	—

DECIMAL COINAGE

HALF CENT

KM# 5   Bronze   **Obv:** Laureate bust left **Obv. Legend:** VICTORIA D:G: BRITT: REG: F:D: **Rev:** Crown and
date within beaded circle, wreath surrounds

Date	Mintage	VG-8	F-12	VF-20	XF-40	MS-60	MS-63	Proof
1861	222,800	125	175	225	350	650	1,500	—
1861 Proof	—	—	—	—	—	—	—	2,200

CENT

KM# 6   Bronze   **Obv:** Laureate bust left **Obv. Legend:** VICTORIA D:G: BRITT: REG: F:D: **Rev:** Crown and
date within beaded circle, wreath surrounds **Rev. Legend:** NEW BRUNSWICK

Date	Mintage	VG-8	F-12	VF-20	XF-40	MS-60	MS-63	Proof
1861	1,000,000	3.50	6.00	9.00	14.00	100.00	450	—
1861 Proof	—	—	—	—	—	—	—	450
1864 short 6	1,000,000	3.50	6.00	9.00	20.00	125	550	—
1864 long 6	Inc. above	4.00	6.50	13.00	24.00	175	650	—

5 CENTS

KM# 7   1.1620 g. 0.9250 Silver 0.0346 oz. ASW   **Obv:** Laureate head left **Obv. Legend:** VICTORIA D: G:
REG: / NEW BRUNSWICK **Rev:** Denomination and date within wreath, crown above

Date	Mintage	VG-8	F-12	VF-20	XF-40	MS-60	MS-63	Proof
1862	100,000	65.00	100.00	225	500	1,700	3,200	—
1862 Proof	—	—	—	—	—	—	—	3,500
1864 small 6	100,000	65.00	100.00	225	1,000	2,200	4,900	—
1864 large 6	Inc. above	75.00	125	300	600	2,500	5,000	—

10 CENTS

KM# 8 2.3240 g. 0.9250 Silver 0.0691 oz. ASW **Obv:** Laureate head left **Obv. Legend:** VICTORIA D: G: REG: / NEW BRUNSWICK **Rev:** Denomination and date within wreath, crown above

Date	Mintage	VG-8	F-12	VF-20	XF-40	MS-60	MS-63	Proof
1862	150,000	65.00	100.00	225	450	1,600	3,000	—
1862 recut 2	Inc. above	95.00	175	350	750	2,900	6,700	—
1862 Proof	—	—	—	—	—	—	—	2,850
1864	100,000	65.00	100.00	225	450	2,700	6,300	—

20 CENTS

KM# 9 4.6480 g. 0.9250 Silver 0.1382 oz. ASW **Obv:** Laureate head left **Obv. Legend:** VICTORIA D: G: REG: / NEW BRUNSWICK **Rev:** Denomination and date within wreath, crown above

Date	Mintage	VG-8	F-12	VF-20	XF-40	MS-60	MS-63	Proof
1862	150,000	29.00	50.00	100.00	225	1,050	4,400	—
1862 Proof	—	—	—	—	—	—	—	2,850
1864	150,000	29.00	50.00	100.00	225	1,600	4,600	—

NEWFOUNDLAND

PROVINCE

CIRCULATION COINAGE

LARGE CENT

KM# 1 Bronze **Obv:** Laureate bust left **Obv. Legend:** VICTORIA D:G: BRITT: REG:F:D: **Rev:** Crown and date within circle, florals surround **Rev. Legend:** NEWFOUNDLAND

Date	Mintage	VG-8	F-12	VF-20	XF-40	MS-60	MS-63	Proof
1865	240,000	3.50	5.50	12.00	30.00	175	900	—
1872H	200,000	2.50	4.00	7.00	17.00	70.00	250	—
1872H Proof	—	—	—	—	—	—	—	800
1873	200,025	4.00	6.50	20.00	40.00	300	1,600	—
1873 Proof	—	—	—	—	—	—	—	3,000

Date	Mintage	VG-8	F-12	VF-20	XF-40	MS-60	MS-63	Proof
1876H	200,000	3.50	7.00	15.00	60.00	300	1,600	—
1876H Proof, reported not confirmed	—	—	—	—	—	—	—	—
1880 round 0, even date	400,000	3.00	3.50	7.00	20.00	125	500	—
1880 round and low 0	Inc. above	4.50	12.00	20.00	50.00	400	2,600	—
1880 oval 0	Inc. above	200	300	500	950	2,000	6,000	—
1880 oval 0 Proof	—	—	—	—	—	—	—	2,500
1885	40,000	27.50	50.00	75.00	125	500	2,400	—
1885 Proof	—	—	—	—	—	—	—	2,500
1888	50,000	30.00	55.00	80.00	175	750	4,800	—
1890	200,000	3.00	6.00	15.00	45.00	300	1,200	—
1894	200,000	3.00	5.00	10.00	25.00	140	1,200	—
1894 Proof	—	—	—	—	—	—	—	1,500
1896	200,000	3.00	3.50	7.00	27.00	120	500	—
1896 Proof	—	—	—	—	—	—	—	1,500

KM# 9 Bronze **Obv:** Crowned bust right **Obv. Designer:** G.W. DeSaulles **Rev:** Crown and date within center circle, wreath surrounds, denomination above **Rev. Designer:** Horace Morehen

Date	Mintage	VG-8	F-12	VF-20	XF-40	MS-60	MS-63	Proof
1904H	100,000	11.00	20.00	30.00	85.00	450	1,050	—
1904H Proof	—	—	—	—	—	—	—	6,000
1907	200,000	3.00	6.00	12.00	45.00	325	975	—
1909	200,000	3.00	6.00	11.00	27.50	150	225	—
1909 Proof	—	—	—	—	—	—	—	600

KM# 16 Bronze **Obv:** Crowned bust left **Obv. Designer:** E.B. MacKennal **Rev:** Crown and date within center circle, wreath surrounds, denomination above **Rev. Designer:** Horace Morehen

Date	Mintage	VG-8	F-12	VF-20	XF-40	MS-60	MS-63	Proof
1913	400,000	2.00	3.00	6.00	14.00	60.00	190	—
1917C	702,350	2.00	3.00	6.00	12.00	115	500	—
1917C Proof	—	—	—	—	—	—	—	2,000
1919C	300,000	2.00	4.00	6.00	20.00	265	750	—
1919C Proof	—	—	—	—	—	—	—	2,500
1920C	302,184	2.00	4.00	10.00	36.00	450	2,500	—
1929	300,000	2.00	3.00	6.00	12.00	85.00	250	—
1929C Proof	—	—	—	—	—	—	—	2,500
1936	300,000	2.00	2.50	4.00	8.00	42.00	190	—

SMALL CENT

KM# 18 3.2000 g. Bronze 19 mm.   **Obv:** Crowned head left **Obv. Designer:** Percy Metcalfe **Rev:** Pitcher plant divides date, denomination below **Rev. Designer:** Walter J. Newman

Date	Mintage	VG-8	F-12	VF-20	XF-40	MS-60	MS-63	Proof
1938	500,000	0.80	1.25	2.50	4.00	25.00	65.00	—
1938 Proof	—	—	—	—	—	—	—	1,500
1940	300,000	2.00	3.00	5.00	16.00	120	400	—
1940 Re-engraved date	Inc. above	48.00	65.00	200	110	800	1,450	—
1940 Proof	—	—	—	—	—	—	—	1,500
1941C	827,662	0.60	0.70	1.00	3.00	32.00	190	—
1941C Re-engraved date	Inc. above	14.00	20.00	48.00	105	400	1,100	—
1942	1,996,889	0.60	0.70	1.00	3.00	48.00	200	—
1943C	1,239,732	0.60	0.70	1.00	3.00	22.50	110	—
1944C	1,328,776	1.50	3.00	16.00	48.00	400	875	—
1947C	313,772	1.50	2.75	8.00	19.00	130	325	—
1947C Proof	—	—	—	—	—	—	—	3,000

5 CENTS

KM# 2 1.1782 g. 0.9250 Silver 0.0350 oz. ASW   **Obv:** Laureate head left **Obv. Legend:** VICTORIA D: G: REG: / NEWFOUNDLAND **Rev:** Denomination and date within ornamental circle **Edge:** Reeded

Date	Mintage	VG-8	F-12	VF-20	XF-40	MS-60	MS-63	Proof
1865	80,000	35.00	50.00	150	300	1,200	3,000	—
1865 Proof	—	—	—	—	—	—	—	4,000
1870	40,000	65.00	125	225	500	1,900	3,000	—
1870 Proof	—	—	—	—	—	—	—	4,000
1872H	40,000	40.00	70.00	125	175	600	2,400	—
1873	44,260	125	200	450	1,100	4,600	—	—
1873H	Inc. above	950	1,400	2,000	3,700	12,500	22,000	—
1873 Proof	—	—	—	—	—	—	—	10,000
1876H	20,000	125	200	350	650	1,200	2,750	—
1880	40,000	45.00	65.00	150	300	1,600	2,400	—
1880 Proof	—	—	—	—	—	—	—	5,000
1881	40,000	45.00	65.00	150	300	1,900	2,500	—
1881 Proof	—	—	—	—	—	—	—	5,000
1882H	60,000	23.00	45.00	90.00	200	800	2,000	—
1882H Proof	—	—	—	—	—	—	—	2,000
1885	16,000	130	210	335	750	2,400	4,500	—
1885 Proof	—	—	—	—	—	—	—	7,500
1888	40,000	40.00	75.00	225	375	1,900	4,900	—
1888 Proof	—	—	—	—	—	—	—	7,500
1890	160,000	11.00	21.00	45.00	125	800	2,000	—
1890 Proof	—	—	—	—	—	—	—	5,000
1894	160,000	10.00	19.00	30.00	100.00	800	2,500	—
1894 Proof	—	—	—	—	—	—	—	5,000
1896	400,000	4.00	8.00	20.00	50.00	700	2,700	—
1896 Proof	—	—	—	—	—	—	—	5,000

KM# 7 1.1782 g. 0.9250 Silver 0.0350 oz. ASW **Obv:** Crowned bust right **Rev:** Denomination and date within circle

Date	Mintage	VG-8	F-12	VF-20	XF-40	MS-60	MS-63	Proof
1903	100,000	6.00	14.00	30.00	70.00	700	2,150	—
1903 Proof	—	—	—	—	—	—	—	3,000
1904H	100,000	5.00	8.00	22.50	55.00	255	450	—
1904H Proof	—	—	—	—	—	—	—	1,800
1908	400,000	5.00	10.00	18.00	48.00	425	1,200	—

KM# 13 1.1782 g. 0.9250 Silver 0.0350 oz. ASW **Obv:** Crowned bust left **Obv. Designer:** E.B. MacKennal **Rev:** Denomination and date within circle **Rev. Designer:** G.W. DeSaulles

Date	Mintage	VG-8	F-12	VF-20	XF-40	MS-60	MS-63	Proof
1912	300,000	1.75	2.50	6.00	25.00	150	325	—
1912 Proof	—	—	—	—	—	—	—	2,400
1917C	300,319	1.75	4.00	8.00	30.00	300	775	—
1917C Proof	—	—	—	—	—	—	—	2,400
1919C	100,844	6.00	11.00	30.00	120	1,150	3,350	—
1919C Proof	—	—	—	—	—	—	—	2,400
1929	300,000	1.75	3.00	4.00	14.00	200	425	—

KM# 19 1.1782 g. 0.9250 Silver 0.0350 oz. ASW **Obv:** Crowned head left **Obv. Designer:** Percy Metcalfe **Rev:** Denomination and date within circle **Rev. Designer:** G.W. DeSaulles

Date	Mintage	VG-8	F-12	VF-20	XF-40	MS-60	MS-63	Proof
1938	100,000	1.25	2.50	3.00	11.00	110	350	—
1938 Proof	—	—	—	—	—	—	—	1,600
1940C	200,000	1.25	2.50	3.00	11.00	135	475	—
1940C Proof	—	—	—	—	—	—	—	3,200
1941C	621,641	1.00	2.50	3.00	6.00	25.00	55.00	—
1942C	298,348	1.25	2.50	3.00	6.00	27.50	65.00	—
1943C	351,666	1.00	1.50	3.00	6.00	25.00	48.00	—

KM# 19a 1.1664 g. 0.8000 Silver 0.0300 oz. ASW 15.67 mm. **Obv:** Crowned head left **Obv. Designer:** Percy Metcalfe **Rev:** Denomination and date within circle **Rev. Designer:** G.W. DeSaulles **Edge:** Reeded

Date	Mintage	VG-8	F-12	VF-20	XF-40	MS-60	MS-63	Proof
1944C	286,504	2.00	2.75	5.00	11.00	80.00	190	—
1945C	203,828	1.00	1.50	3.00	6.00	22.50	50.00	—
1946C	2,041	325	475	550	650	1,900	3,050	—
1946C Prooflike	—	—	—	—	—	—	4,000	—
1947C	38,400	3.00	5.00	8.00	27.50	105	325	—
1947C Prooflike	—	—	—	—	—	—	600	—

10 CENTS

KM# 3 2.3564 g. 0.9250 Silver 0.0701 oz. ASW **Obv:** Laureate head left **Obv. Legend:** VICTORIA D: G: REG: / NEWFOUNDLAND **Rev:** Denomination and date within ornamental circle

Date	Mintage	VG-8	F-12	VF-20	XF-40	MS-60	MS-63	Proof
1865	80,000	27.00	45.00	75.00	250	1,100	2,250	—
1865 Proof, plain edge	—	—	—	—	—	—	—	5,500
1870	30,000	150	250	450	725	2,350	5,000	—
1870 Proof	—	—	—	—	—	—	—	10,000
1872H	40,000	22.00	35.00	80.00	200	800	1,700	—
1873 flat 3	23,614	55.00	70.00	250	650	4,000	5,000	—
1873 round 3	Inc. above	55.00	70.00	250	650	4,000	5,000	—
1873 Proof	—	—	—	—	—	—	—	12,000
1876H	10,000	55.00	70.00	225	350	1,400	2,500	—
1880/70	10,000	55.00	100.00	250	400	1,800	2,950	—
1880 Proof	—	—	—	—	—	—	—	7,500
1882H	20,000	30.00	55.00	150	475	2,200	6,700	—
1882H Proof	—	—	—	—	—	—	—	3,000
1885	8,000	70.00	130	300	800	2,200	4,250	—
1885 Proof	—	—	—	—	—	—	—	8,000
1888	30,000	35.00	70.00	200	700	4,000	5,000	—
1888 Proof	—	—	—	—	—	—	—	8,000
1890	100,000	9.00	19.00	35.00	150	1,100	3,200	—
1890 Proof	—	—	—	—	—	—	—	5,000
1894	100,000	8.50	12.00	25.00	125	1,200	3,000	—
1894 Proof	—	—	—	—	—	—	—	5,000
1896	230,000	5.00	10.00	25.00	90.00	1,200	3,200	—
1896 Proof	—	—	—	—	—	—	—	5,000

KM# 8 2.3564 g. 0.9250 Silver 0.0701 oz. ASW **Obv:** Crowned bust right **Rev:** Denomination and date within circle

Date	Mintage	VG-8	F-12	VF-20	XF-40	MS-60	MS-63	Proof
1903	100,000	12.00	37.50	105	300	1,800	6,600	—
1903 Proof	—	—	—	—	—	—	—	3,750
1904H	100,000	6.00	15.00	45.00	135	300	525	—
1904H Proof	—	—	—	—	—	—	—	2,250

KM# 14 2.3564 g. 0.9250 Silver 0.0701 oz. ASW   **Obv:** Crowned bust left **Obv. Designer:** E.B. MacKennal
Rev. Designer: G.W. DeSaulles

Date	Mintage	VG-8	F-12	VF-20	XF-40	MS-60	MS-63	Proof
1912	150,000	2.00	5.00	15.00	60.00	250	400	—
1917C	250,805	2.00	5.00	17.00	60.00	600	1,950	—
1919C	54,342	4.00	11.00	27.50	85.00	265	450	—

KM# 20 2.3564 g. 0.9250 Silver 0.0701 oz. ASW   **Obv:** Crowned head left **Obv. Designer:** Percy Metcalfe
Rev: Denomination and date within circle **Rev. Designer:** G.W. DeSaulles

Date	Mintage	VG-8	F-12	VF-20	XF-40	MS-60	MS-63	Proof
1938	100,000	2.25	4.00	6.00	18.00	130	475	—
1938 Proof	—	—	—	—	—	—	—	3,200
1940	100,000	2.25	3.00	6.00	16.00	130	475	—
1940 Proof	—	—	—	—	—	—	—	4,000
1941C	483,630	2.25	3.00	4.00	8.00	65.00	200	—
1942C	293,736	2.25	3.00	4.00	8.00	80.00	210	—
1943C	104,706	2.25	3.00	5.00	10.00	95.00	325	—
1944C	151,471	5.00	7.00	20.00	32.00	325	1,300	—

KM# 20a 2.3328 g. 0.8000 Silver 0.0600 oz. ASW   **Obv:** Crowned head left **Obv. Designer:** Percy Metcalfe
Rev. Designer: G.W. DeSaulles

Date	Mintage	VG-8	F-12	VF-20	XF-40	MS-60	MS-63	Proof
1945C	175,833	2.00	2.75	5.00	7.00	70.00	350	—
1946C	38,400	4.00	8.00	20.00	40.00	160	450	—
1946C Proof	—	—	—	—	—	—	—	1,200
1947C	61,988	3.00	6.00	9.00	22.50	105	450	—

20 CENTS

KM# 4 4.7127 g. 0.9250 Silver 0.1401 oz. ASW 23.19 mm.   **Obv:** Laureate head left **Rev:** Denomination and date within ornamental circle

Date	Mintage	VG-8	F-12	VF-20	XF-40	MS-60	MS-63	Proof
1865	100,000	16.00	30.00	60.00	225	950	2,600	—
1865 Proof, plain edge	—	—	—	—	—	—	—	6,500
1865 Proof, reeded edge	—	—	—	—	—	—	—	10,000
1870	50,000	21.00	45.00	100.00	250	1,250	2,600	—
1870 Proof, plain edge	—	—	—	—	—	—	—	6,500
1870 Proof, reeded edge	—	—	—	—	—	—	—	6,500
1872H	90,000	12.00	25.00	60.00	140	750	1,800	—
1873	45,797	21.00	65.00	175	550	5,400	8,000	—
1873 Proof	—	—	—	—	—	—	—	12,000
1876H	50,000	25.00	50.00	80.00	300	1,350	2,700	—
1880/70	30,000	27.00	55.00	100.00	350	2,000	3,000	—

NEWFOUNDLAND

Date	Mintage	VG-8	F-12	VF-20	XF-40	MS-60	MS-63	Proof
1880 Proof	—	—	—	—	—	—	—	8,000
1881	60,000	12.00	25.00	80.00	300	1,200	2,900	—
1881 Proof	—	—	—	—	—	—	—	8,000
1882H	100,000	9.00	19.00	50.00	140	1,000	3,400	—
1882H Proof	—	—	—	—	—	—	—	3,500
1885	40,000	14.00	30.00	80.00	300	2,900	4,500	—
1885 Proof	—	—	—	—	—	—	—	10,000
1888	75,000	12.00	25.00	70.00	225	1,400	4,200	—
1888 Proof	—	—	—	—	—	—	—	10,000
1890	100,000	9.00	15.00	45.00	225	1,400	3,500	—
1890 Proof	—	—	—	—	—	—	—	6,500
1894	100,000	12.00	24.00	50.00	175	1,200	—	—
1894 Proof	—	—	—	—	—	—	—	6,500
1896 small 96	125,000	6.00	12.00	35.00	150	1,400	3,600	—
1896 large 96	Inc. above	7.00	15.00	50.00	200	1,700	4,500	—
1896 large 96, Proof	—	—	—	—	—	—	—	6,500
1899 hook 99	125,000	27.00	50.00	125	350	1,800	4,900	—
1899 large 99	Inc. above	5.00	12.00	30.00	125	1,400	3,600	—
1900	125,000	5.00	8.00	25.00	80.00	1,100	3,400	—
1900 Proof	—	—	—	—	—	—	—	6,500

KM# 10 4.7127 g. 0.9250 Silver 0.1401 oz. ASW   **Obv:** Crowned bust right **Obv. Designer:** G.W. DeSaulles
Rev: Denomination and date within circle **Rev. Designer:** W.H.J. Blakemore

Date	Mintage	VG-8	F-12	VF-20	XF-40	MS-60	MS-63	Proof
1904H	75,000	13.00	39.00	70.00	350	3,250	7,800	—
1904H Proof	—	—	—	—	—	—	—	2,400

KM# 15 4.7127 g. 0.9250 Silver 0.1401 oz. ASW   **Obv:** Crowned bust left **Obv. Designer:** E.B. MacKennal
Rev: Denomination and date within circle **Rev. Designer:** W.H.J. Blakemore

Date	Mintage	VG-8	F-12	VF-20	XF-40	MS-60	MS-63	Proof
1912	350,000	4.50	7.50	20.00	65.00	325	850	—
1912 Proof	—	—	—	—	—	—	—	2,500

25 CENTS

KM# 17 5.8319 g. 0.9250 Silver 0.1734 oz. ASW   **Obv:** Crowned bust left **Obv. Designer:** E.B. MacKennal
Rev: Denomination and date within circle **Rev. Designer:** W.H.J. Blakemore

Date	Mintage	VG-8	F-12	VF-20	XF-40	MS-60	MS-63	Proof
1917C	464,779	5.50	7.50	10.00	18.00	200	375	—
1917C Proof	—	—	—	—	—	—	—	3,000
1919C	163,939	5.50	7.50	15.00	35.00	500	1,750	—
1919C Proof	—	—	—	—	—	—	—	3,000

50 CENTS

KM# 6 11.7818 g. 0.9250 Silver 0.3504 oz. ASW 29.85 mm.   **Obv:** Laureate head left **Obv. Legend:** VICTORIA DEI GRATIA REGINA NEWFOUNDLAND **Rev:** Denomination and date within ornamental circle

Date	Mintage	VG-8	F-12	VF-20	XF-40	MS-60	MS-63	Proof
1870	50,000	26.00	50.00	150	600	3,500	8,500	—
1870 Proof, plain edge	—	—	—	—	—	—	—	25,000
1870 Proof, reeded edge	—	—	—	—	—	—	—	25,000
1872H	48,000	18.00	35.00	90.00	400	1,600	3,600	—
1873	37,675	40.00	75.00	200	650	9,600	11,000	—
1873 Proof	—	—	—	—	—	—	—	40,000
1874	80,000	25.00	45.00	125	550	8,900	10,000	—
1874 Proof	—	—	—	—	—	—	—	40,000
1876H	28,000	35.00	85.00	150	450	2,250	5,250	—
1880	24,000	45.00	95.00	250	900	6,500	16,000	—
1880 Proof	—	—	—	—	—	—	—	40,000
1881	50,000	20.00	35.00	135	400	3,300	9,300	—
1881 Proof	—	—	—	—	—	—	—	40,000
1882H	100,000	12.00	30.00	95.00	350	1,600	5,400	—
1882H Proof	—	—	—	—	—	—	—	8,000
1885	40,000	30.00	60.00	175	650	2,800	7,100	—
1885 Proof	—	—	—	—	—	—	—	40,000
1888	20,000	50.00	90.00	250	925	11,000	13,000	—
1888 Proof	—	—	—	—	—	—	—	40,000
1894	40,000	12.00	28.00	75.00	300	3,700	9,700	—
1896	60,000	8.50	16.00	65.00	300	3,000	8,100	—
1896 Proof	—	—	—	—	—	—	—	25,000
1898	76,607	8.50	13.00	60.00	200	3,100	8,100	—
1899 wide 9's	150,000	8.50	13.00	60.00	200	2,800	7,200	—
1899 narrow 9's	Inc. above	8.50	13.00	45.00	150	2,600	7,700	—
1900	150,000	8.50	13.00	45.00	175	2,600	7,200	—

KM# 11 11.7800 g. 0.9250 Silver 0.3503 oz. ASW 30 mm.   **Obv:** Crowned bust right **Obv. Designer:** G.W. DeSaulles **Rev. Designer:** W.H.J. Blakemore

Date	Mintage	VG-8	F-12	VF-20	XF-40	MS-60	MS-63	Proof
1904H	140,000	10.00	12.00	20.00	55.00	300	925	—
1904H Proof	—	—	—	—	—	—	—	5,500
1907	100,000	10.00	12.00	25.00	65.00	375	1,100	—
1908	160,000	10.00	12.00	20.00	50.00	250	775	—
1909	200,000	10.00	15.00	22.00	60.00	325	875	—

KM# 12 11.7800 g. 0.9250 Silver 0.3503 oz. ASW 30 mm.   **Obv:** Crowned bust left **Obv. Designer:** E.B. MacKennal **Rev:** Denomination and date within circle **Rev. Designer:** W.H.J. Blakemore

Date	Mintage	VG-8	F-12	VF-20	XF-40	MS-60	MS-63	Proof
1911	200,000	10.00	12.00	15.00	45.50	260	725	—
1917C	375,560	10.00	12.00	15.00	36.50	190	450	—
1917C Proof	—	—	—	—	—	—	—	3,250
1918C	294,824	10.00	12.00	15.00	36.50	190	450	—
1919C	306,267	10.00	12.00	15.00	39.00	425	1,500	—
1919C Proof	—	—	—	—	—	—	—	3,250

2 DOLLARS

KM# 5 3.3284 g. 0.9170 Gold 0.0981 oz. AGW   **Obv:** Laureate head left **Obv. Legend:** VICTORIA D: G: REG: / NEWFOUNDLAND **Rev:** Denomination and date within circle

Date	Mintage	F-12	VF-20	XF-40	AU-50	MS-60	MS-63
1865	10,000	150	225	300	375	1,100	8,500
1865 plain edge, Specimen-63, $15,000.	Est. 10	—	—	—	—	—	—
1870	10,000	150	225	300	450	1,500	7,500
1870 reeded edge, Specimen-63 $20,000.	Est. 5	—	—	—	—	—	—
1872	6,050	220	400	500	900	2,200	8,800
1872 Specimen-63 $12,500.	Est. 10	—	—	—	—	—	—
1880	2,500	800	1,000	1,200	2,300	4,650	14,250
1880/70	—	—	—	—	—	—	—
Note: Specimen. Bowers and Merena Norweb sale 11-96, specimen 64 realized $70,400.							
1881	10,000	150	200	250	325	1,600	2,500
1881 Specimen; Rare	—	—	—	—	—	—	—
1882H	25,000	150	200	250	300	700	2,200
1882H Specimen $4,250.	—	—	—	—	—	—	—
1885	10,000	150	200	250	300	850	2,750
1885 Specimen	—	—	—	—	—	—	—
Note: Bowers and Merena Norweb sale 11-96, specimen 66 realized $44,000							
1888	25,000	150	175	200	250	600	2,000
1888 Specimen; Rare	—	—	—	—	—	—	—

NOVA SCOTIA

PROVINCE

DECIMAL COINAGE

HALF CENT

KM# 7 Bronze **Obv:** Laureate bust left **Obv. Legend:** VICTORIA D:G: BRITT: REG:F:D: **Rev:** Crown and date within beaded circle, wreath of roses surrounds **Rev. Legend:** NOVA SCOTIA

Date	Mintage	VG-8	F-12	VF-20	XF-40	MS-60	MS-63	Proof
1861	400,000	5.00	7.00	8.00	13.00	60.00	300	—
1864	400,000	5.00	7.00	8.00	13.00	55.00	250	—
1864 Proof	—	—	—	—	—	—	—	300

CENT

KM# 8.2 Bronze **Obv:** Laureate bust left **Obv. Legend:** VICTORIA D:G: BRITT: REG:F:D: **Rev:** Crown and date within beaded circle, wreath of roses surrounds **Rev. Legend:** NOVA SCOTIA **Note:** Prev. KM#8. Small rosebud right of SCOTIA. The Royal Mint report records mintage of 1 million for 1862, which is considered incorrect.

Date	Mintage	VG-8	F-12	VF-20	XF-40	MS-60	MS-63	Proof
1861	800,000	3.00	4.50	5.00	11.00	125	400	—
1862	Est. 1,000,000	45.00	75.00	150	300	1,300	—	—
1864	800,000	3.00	4.50	5.00	16.00	150	450	—

STERLING COINAGE

HALFPENNY TOKEN

KM# 1a Copper **Obv:** Laureate head left, draped collar **Obv. Legend:** PROVINCE OF NOVA SCOTIA **Rev:** Thistle

Date	Mintage	VG-8	F-12	VF-20	XF-40	MS-60	MS-63	Proof
1382 1382 (error)	—	500	700	1,650	—	—	—	—
1832/1382	—	10.00	15.00	50.00	150	—	—	—
1832 (imitation)	—	3.00	9.00	27.00	75.00	125	200	—

KM# 1 Copper **Obv:** Laureate head left **Obv. Legend:** PROVINCE OF NOVA SCOTIA **Rev:** Thistle

Date	Mintage	VG-8	F-12	VF-20	XF-40	MS-60	MS-63	Proof
1823	400,000	3.00	6.00	13.00	60.00	275	—	—
1823 without hyphen	Inc. above	5.00	10.00	35.00	125	325	—	—
1824	118,636	6.00	12.00	27.00	65.00	450	—	—
1832	800,000	3.00	5.00	13.50	40.00	225	—	—

KM# 3 Copper   **Obv:** Head left **Obv. Legend:** PROVINCE OF NOVA SCOTIA **Rev:** Thistle

Date	Mintage	VG-8	F-12	VF-20	XF-40	MS-60	MS-63	Proof
1840 small 0	300,000	3.50	10.00	25.00	60.00	175	—	—
1840 large 0	Inc. above	4.00	10.00	40.00	125	225	—	—
1840 medium 0	Inc. above	3.50	9.00	25.00	60.00	175	—	—
1843	300,000	3.00	6.00	24.00	60.00	175	—	—

KM# 5 Copper

Date	Mintage	VG-8	F-12	VF-20	XF-40	MS-60	MS-63	Proof
1856 without LCW	720,000	3.00	4.00	7.50	23.00	175	—	—
1856 without LCW, Proof	—	—	—	—	—	—	—	600
1856 without LCW, inverted A for V in PROVINCE, Proof	—	—	—	—	—	—	—	600

KM# 5a Bronze

Date	Mintage	VG-8	F-12	VF-20	XF-40	MS-60	MS-63	Proof
1856 with LCW, Proof	—	—	—	—	—	—	—	600

1 PENNY TOKEN

KM# 2 Copper   **Obv:** Laureate head left **Obv. Legend:** PROVINCE OF NOVA SCOTIA **Rev:** Thistle

Date	Mintage	VG-8	F-12	VF-20	XF-40	MS-60	MS-63	Proof
1824	217,776	4.00	10.00	26.00	85.00	400	—	—
1832	200,000	4.00	8.00	15.00	55.00	350	—	—

KM# 2a Copper   **Obv:** Laureate head left **Obv. Legend:** PROVINCE OF NOVA SCOTIA **Rev:** Thistle

Date	Mintage	VG-8	F-12	VF-20	XF-40	MS-60	MS-63	Proof
1832 (imitation)	—	3.75	7.50	22.50	85.00	—	—	—

KM# 4 Copper 32 mm.   **Obv:** Head left **Obv. Legend:** PROVINCE OF NOVA SCOTIA **Rev:** Thistle

Date	Mintage	VG-8	F-12	VF-20	XF-40	MS-60	MS-63	Proof
1840	150,000	3.50	9.00	23.00	60.00	450	—	—
1843/0	150,000	45.00	75.00	250	—	—	—	—
1843	Inc. above	4.00	12.00	24.00	60.00	450	—	—

KM# 6 Copper **Obv:** Crowned head left **Obv. Legend:** VICTORIA D: G: BRITANNIA R: REG: F: D: **Rev:** Plant **Rev. Legend:** PROVINCE OF NOVA SCOTIA

Date	Mintage	VG-8	F-12	VF-20	XF-40	MS-60	MS-63	Proof
1856 without LCW	360,000	4.00	7.50	13.00	35.00	300	—	—
1856 with LCW	Inc. above	2.50	5.00	12.00	35.00	350	—	—

KM# 6a Bronze **Obv:** Crowned head left **Obv. Legend:** VICTORIA D: G: BRITANNIA R: REG: F: D: **Rev:** Plant **Rev. Legend:** PROVINCE OF NOVA SCOTIA

Date	Mintage	VG-8	F-12	VF-20	XF-40	MS-60	MS-63	Proof
1856 Proof	—	—	—	—	—	—	—	400

PRINCE EDWARD ISLAND

PROVINCE

CUT & COUNTERMARKED COINAGE

ca. 1813

SHILLING

KM# 1 Silver **Countermark:** Sunburst **Note:** Countermark on center plug of Spanish or Spanish Colonial 8 Reales.

Date	Mintage	VG-8	F-12	VF-20	XF-40	MS-60	MS-63	Proof
ND	1,000	2,000	3,000	5,000	—	—	—	—

5 SHILLING

KM# 3 Silver **Countermark:** Sunburst **Note:** Countermark on holed Lima 8 Reales, KM#106.2.

Date	Mintage	VG-8	F-12	VF-20	XF-40	MS-60	MS-63	Proof
ND1809-11	1,000	2,000	3,000	5,000	—	—	—	—

KM# 2.1 Silver **Countermark:** Sunburst **Note:** Countermark on holed Mexico City 8 Reales, KM#109.

Date	Mintage	VG-8	F-12	VF-20	XF-40	MS-60	MS-63	Proof
1791-1808	—	1,400	1,800	2,250	—	—	—	—

KM# 2.2   Silver   **Countermark:** Sunburst **Note:** Countermark on holed Mexico City 8 Reales, KM#110.

Date	Mintage	VG-8	F-12	VF-20	XF-40	MS-60	MS-63	Proof
ND1808-11	—	1,400	1,800	2,250	—	—	—	—

DECIMAL COINAGE

CENT

KM# 4   Bronze   **Obv:** Crowned head left within beaded circle **Obv. Legend:** VICTORIA QUEEN **Rev:** Trees within beaded circle **Rev. Legend:** PRINCE EDWARD ISLAND

Date	Mintage	VG-8	F-12	VF-20	XF-40	MS-60	MS-63	Proof
1871	2,000,000	2.50	4.00	6.50	20.00	100.00	185	—
1871 Proof	—	—	—	—	—	—	—	2,000

MEXICO

The United States of Mexico, located immediately south of the United States has an area of 759,529 sq. mi. (1,967,183 sq. km.) and an estimated population of 100 million. Capital: Mexico City. The economy is based on agriculture, manufacturing and mining. Oil, cotton, silver, coffee, and shrimp are exported.

Mexico was the site of highly advanced Indian civilizations 1,500 years before conquistador Hernando Cortes conquered the wealthy Aztec empire of Montezuma, 1519-21, and founded a Spanish colony, which lasted for nearly 300 years. During the Spanish period, Mexico, then called New Spain, stretched from Guatemala to the present states of Wyoming and California, its present northern boundary having been established by the secession of Texas during 1836 and the war of 1846-48 with the United States.

Independence from Spain was declared by Father Miguel Hidalgo on Sept. 16, 1810, (Mexican Independence Day) and was achieved by General Agustin de Iturbide in1821. Iturbide became emperor in 1822 but was deposed when a republic was established a year later. For more than fifty years following the birth of the republic, the political scene of Mexico was characterized by turmoil, which saw two emperors (including the unfortunate Maximilian), several dictators and an average of one new government every nine months passing swiftly from obscurity to oblivion. The land, social, economic and labor reforms promulgated by the Reform Constitution of Feb. 5, 1917 established the basis for sustained economic development and participative democracy that have made Mexico one of the most politically stable countries of modern Latin America.

SPANISH COLONIAL

COB COINAGE

KM# 24 1/2 REAL
1.6900 g., 0.9310 Silver 0.0506 oz. ASW **Ruler:** Philip V
Obv: Legend around crowned PHILIPVS monogram **Rev:**
Legend around cross, lions and castles **Mint:** Mexico City
Note: Mint mark M, Mo. For this series completeness of date is a stronger determining factor of price than grade. The values listed below reflect a range for examples with an average amount of date visible.

Date	Mintage	Good	VG	F	VF	XF
ND(1701-28)	—	—	25.00	40.00	65.00	—
Date off flan						
1701 L	—	—	125	200	300	—
1702 L	—	—	125	200	300	—
1703 L	—	—	125	200	300	—
1704 L	—	—	125	200	300	—
1705 L	—	—	125	200	300	—
1706 J	—	—	125	200	300	—
1707 J	—	—	125	200	300	—
1708 J	—	—	125	200	285	—
1709 J	—	—	125	200	285	—
1710 J	—	—	125	200	285	—
1711 J	—	—	125	200	285	—
1712 J	—	—	125	200	285	—
1713 J	—	—	125	200	285	—
1714 J	—	—	125	200	285	—
1715 J	—	—	125	200	285	—
1716 J	—	—	125	200	285	—
1717 J	—	—	125	200	285	—
1718/7	—	—	—	—	—	—
1718 J	—	—	125	200	285	—
1719 J	—	—	125	200	285	—
1720 J	—	—	125	200	285	—
1721 J	—	—	125	200	285	—
1722 J	—	—	125	200	285	—
1723 J	—	—	125	200	285	—
1724 J	—	—	125	200	285	—
1724 D	—	—	125	200	285	—
1725 D	—	—	125	200	285	—
1726 D	—	—	125	200	285	—
1727 D	—	—	125	200	285	—
1728 D	—	—	125	200	285	—

KM# 25 1/2 REAL
1.6900 g., 0.9310 Silver 0.0506 oz. ASW **Ruler:** Luis I **Obv:**
Legend around crowned LVDOVICVS monogram **Rev:**
Legend around cross, lions and castles **Note:** Mint mark M, Mo.

Date	Mintage	Good	VG	F	VF	XF
ND(1724-25)	—	—	125	200	250	—
Date off flan						
1724 D Rare	—	—	—	—	—	—
1725 D Rare	—	—	—	—	—	—

KM# 24a 1/2 REAL
1.6900 g., 0.9160 Silver 0.0498 oz. ASW **Ruler:** Philip V

Obv: Legend around crowned PHILIPVS monogram **Rev:**
Legend around cross, lions and castles **Mint:** Mexico City
Note: Mint mark M, Mo.

Date	Mintage	Good	VG	F	VF	XF
ND(1729-33)	—	—	25.00	40.00	65.00	—
Date off flan						
1729 R	—	—	90.00	120	150	—
1730 R	—	—	90.00	120	150	—
1730 F Rare	—	—	—	—	—	—
1731 F	—	—	90.00	120	150	—
1732/1 F	—	—	90.00	120	150	—
1732 F	—	—	90.00	120	150	—
1733/2 F	—	—	90.00	120	150	—
1733 F	—	—	90.00	120	150	—

KM# 30 REAL
3.3800 g., 0.9310 Silver 0.1012 oz. ASW **Ruler:** Philip V
Obv: Legend and date around crowned arms **Obv. Legend:**
PHILIPVS V DEI G **Rev:** Lions and castles in angles of cross
Mint: Mexico City **Note:** Mint mark M, Mo. For this series completeness of date is a stronger determining factor of price than grade. The values listed below reflect a range for examples with an average amount of date visible.

Date	Mintage	Good	VG	F	VF	XF
ND(1701-28)	—	—	35.00	55.00	75.00	—
Date off flan						
1701 L	—	—	165	275	400	—
1702 L	—	—	165	275	400	—
1703 L	—	—	165	275	400	—
1704 L	—	—	165	275	400	—
1705 L	—	—	165	275	400	—
1706 J	—	—	165	275	400	—
1707 J	—	—	165	275	400	—
1708 J	—	—	165	275	400	—
1709 J	—	—	165	275	400	—
1710 J	—	—	165	275	400	—
1711 J	—	—	165	275	400	—
1712 J	—	—	165	275	400	—
1713 J	—	—	165	275	400	—
1714 J	—	—	165	275	400	—
1715 J	—	—	150	275	400	—
1716 J	—	—	150	275	400	—
1717 J	—	—	150	275	400	—
1718 J	—	—	150	275	400	—
1719 J	—	—	150	275	400	—
1720/19 J Rare	—	—	—	—	—	—
1720 J	—	—	150	275	400	—
1721 J	—	—	150	275	400	—
1722 J	—	—	150	275	400	—
1723 J	—	—	150	275	400	—
1726 D	—	—	150	275	400	—

SPANISH COLONIAL

SPANISH COLONIAL - COB

Date	Mintage	Good	VG	F	VF	XF
1727 D	—	—	150	275	400	—
1728 D	—	—	150	275	400	—

KM# A31 REAL

3.3834 g., 0.9310 Silver 0.1013 oz. ASW **Ruler:** Luis I **Mint:** Mexico City **Note:** A significant portion of the legend must be visibile for proper attribution. Mint mark M, Mo.

Date	Mintage	Good	VG	F	VF	XF
1724 D Rare	—	—	—	—	—	—
1725 D Rare	—	—	—	—	—	—

KM# 30a REAL

3.3800 g., 0.9160 Silver 0.0995 oz. ASW **Ruler:** Philip V **Obv:** Legend and date around crowned arms **Obv. Legend:** PHILIPVS V DEI G **Rev:** Lions and castles in angles of cross **Mint:** Mexico City **Note:** Mint mark M, Mo.

Date	Mintage	Good	VG	F	VF	XF
ND(1729-32) Date off flan	—	—	30.00	50.00	70.00	—
1729 R	—	—	90.00	125	175	—
1730 R	—	—	90.00	125	175	—
1730 F	—	—	90.00	125	175	—
1730 G	—	—	90.00	125	175	—
1731 F	—	—	90.00	125	175	—
1732 F	—	—	90.00	125	175	—

KM# 35 2 REALES

6.7700 g., 0.9310 Silver 0.2026 oz. ASW **Ruler:** Philip V **Obv:** Legend and date around crowned arms **Obv. Legend:** PHILIPVS V DEI G **Rev:** Lions and castles in angles of cross **Mint:** Mexico City **Note:** Mint mark M, Mo. For this series completeness of date is a stronger determining factor of price than grade. The values listed below reflect a range for examples with an average amount of date visible.

Date	Mintage	Good	VG	F	VF	XF
ND(1701-28) Date off flan	—	—	45.00	65.00	90.00	—
1701 L	—	—	175	300	450	—
1702 L	—	—	175	300	450	—
1703 L	—	—	175	300	450	—
1704 L	—	—	175	300	450	—
1705 L	—	—	175	300	450	—
1706 J	—	—	175	300	450	—
1707 J	—	—	175	300	450	—
1708 J	—	—	175	300	450	—
1710 J	—	—	175	300	450	—
1711 J	—	—	175	300	450	—
1712 J	—	—	175	300	450	—
1713 J	—	—	175	300	450	—
1714 J	—	—	185	325	475	—
1715 J	—	—	185	325	475	—
1716 J	—	—	185	325	475	—
1717 J	—	—	185	325	475	—
1718 J	—	—	185	325	475	—
1719 J	—	—	185	325	475	—
1720 J	—	—	185	325	475	—
1721 J	—	—	185	325	475	—
1722 J	—	—	185	325	475	—
1723 J	—	—	185	325	475	—
1724 J	—	—	185	325	475	—
1725 D Rare	—	—	—	—	—	—
1726 D	—	—	185	325	475	—
1727 D	—	—	185	325	475	—
1728 D	—	—	185	325	475	—

KM# 35a 2 REALES

6.7700 g., 0.9160 Silver 0.1994 oz. ASW **Ruler:** Philip V **Obv:** Legend and date around crowned arms **Obv. Legend:** PHILIPVS V DEI G **Rev:** Lions and castles in angles of cross **Mint:** Mexico City **Note:** Mint mark M, Mo.

Date	Mintage	Good	VG	F	VF	XF
ND(1729-32) Date off flan	—	—	40.00	60.00	90.00	—
1729 R	—	—	125	175	225	—
1730 R	—	—	125	175	225	—
1730 G Rare	—	—	—	—	—	—

Date	Mintage	Good	VG	F	VF	XF
1730 G/R Rare	—	—	—	—	—	—
1731 F	—	—	125	175	225	—
1731/0 F Reported, not confirmed	—	—	—	—	—	—
1732 F	—	—	125	175	225	—
1733 F Rare	—	—	—	—	—	—

KM# 40 4 REALES

13.5400 g., 0.9310 Silver 0.4053 oz. ASW **Ruler:** Philip V **Obv:** Legend and date around crowned arms **Obv. Legend:** PHILIPVS V DEI G **Rev:** Lions and castles in angles of cross **Mint:** Mexico City **Note:** Mint mark M, Mo. For this series completeness of date is a stronger determining factor of price than grade. The values listed below reflect a range for examples with an average amount of date visible.

Date	Mintage	Good	VG	F	VF	XF
ND (1701-28) Date off flan	—	—	50.00	75.00	100	—
1701 L	—	—	225	475	800	—
1702 L	—	—	225	475	800	—
1703 L	—	—	225	475	800	—
1704 L	—	—	225	475	800	—
1705 L	—	—	225	475	800	—
1706 J	—	—	225	475	800	—
1707 J	—	—	225	475	800	—
1708 J	—	—	225	475	800	—
1709 J	—	—	225	475	800	—
1710 J	—	—	225	475	800	—
1711 J	—	—	200	425	700	—
1712 J	—	—	200	425	700	—
1713 J	—	—	200	425	700	—
1714 J	—	—	200	425	700	—
1715 J Rare	—	—	—	—	—	—
1716 J	—	—	250	600	1,000	—
1717 J	—	—	250	600	1,000	—
1718 J	—	—	250	600	1,000	—
1719 J	—	—	250	600	1,000	—
1720 J	—	—	250	600	1,000	—
1721 J	—	—	250	600	1,000	—
1722 J	—	—	250	600	1,000	—
1723 J	—	—	250	600	1,000	—
1726 D	—	—	250	600	1,000	—
1727 D	—	—	250	600	1,000	—
1728 D	—	—	250	600	1,000	—

KM# 42 4 REALES

13.5400 g., 0.9310 Silver 0.4053 oz. ASW **Ruler:** Luis I **Obv:** Legend around crowned arms **Obv. Legend:** LVDOVICVS I

DEI G **Rev:** Lions and castles in angles of cross, legend around **Mint:** Mexico City **Note:** A significant portion of the legend must be visible for proper attribution. Mint mark M, Mo.

Date	Mintage	Good	VG	F	VF	XF
1724 D Rare	—	—	—	—	—	—
1725 D Rare	—	—	—	—	—	—

KM# 40a 4 REALES
13.5400 g., 0.9160 Silver 0.3987 oz. ASW **Ruler:** Philip V **Obv:** Legend and date around crowned arms **Obv. Legend:** PHILIPVS V DEI G **Rev:** Lions and castles in angles of cross **Mint:** Mexico City **Note:** Mint mark M, Mo.

Date	Mintage	Good	VG	F	VF	XF
ND(1729-33)	—	—	50.00	75.00	100	—
Date off flan						
1729 R	—	—	150	250	350	—
1730 R	—	—	150	250	350	—
1730 F/G	—	—	150	250	375	—
1730 G	—	—	150	250	350	—
1731/0 F	—	—	150	250	375	—
1731 F	—	—	150	250	350	—
1732/1 F	—	—	150	250	350	—
1732 F	—	—	150	250	350	—
1733 F Rare	—	—	—	—	—	—
1733/2 F Rare	—	—	—	—	—	—

KM# 41 4 REALES
13.5400 g., 0.9160 Silver 0.3987 oz. ASW **Ruler:** Philip V **Obv:** Legend and date around crowned arms **Obv. Legend:** PHILIPVS V DEI G **Rev:** Lions and castles in angles of cross, legend around **Mint:** Mexico City **Note:** Klippe. Similar to KM#40a. Mint mark M, Mo.

Date	Mintage	Good	VG	F	VF	XF
1733 MF	—	—	450	600	750	—
1734 MF Rare	—	—	—	—	—	—
1734/3 MF	—	—	450	600	750	—

KM# 47 8 REALES
27.0700 g., 0.9310 Silver 0.8102 oz. ASW **Ruler:** Philip V **Obv:** Legend and date around crowned arms **Obv. Legend:** PHILIPVS V DEI G **Rev:** Lions and castles in angles of cross, legend around **Mint:** Mexico City **Note:** Mint mark M, Mo. For this series completeness of date is a stronger determining factor of price than grade. The values listed below reflect a range for examples with an average amount of date visible.

Date	Mintage	Good	VG	F	VF	XF
ND(1701-28)	—	—	70.00	90.00	120	—
Date off flan						
1701 L Rare	—	—	—	—	—	—
1702 L Rare	—	—	—	—	—	—
1703 L Rare	—	—	—	—	—	—
1704 L Rare	—	—	—	—	—	—
1705 L Rare	—	—	—	—	—	—
1706 J Rare	—	—	—	—	—	—
1707 J Rare	—	—	—	—	—	—
1708 J Rare	—	—	—	—	—	—
1709 J Rare	—	—	—	—	—	—
1710 J Rare	—	—	—	—	—	—
1711 J	—	—	200	1,100	2,000	—
1712 J	—	—	200	1,100	2,000	—
1713 J	—	—	200	1,100	2,000	—
1714 J	—	—	200	1,100	2,000	—
1715 J	—	—	200	1,200	2,250	—
1716 J	—	—	575	2,300	4,500	—
1717 J	—	—	575	2,300	4,500	—
1718/7 J	—	—	575	2,300	4,500	—
1718 J	—	—	525	2,000	4,000	—
1719 J	—	—	525	2,000	4,000	—
1720 J	—	—	525	2,000	4,000	—
1721 J	—	—	525	2,000	4,000	—
1722 J	—	—	525	2,000	4,000	—
1723 J	—	—	525	2,000	4,000	—
1724 D	—	—	525	2,000	4,000	—
1725 D	—	—	525	2,000	4,000	—
1726 D	—	—	525	2,000	4,000	—
1727 D	—	—	525	2,000	4,000	—
1728 D	—	—	600	2,400	5,000	—

KM# 46 8 REALES
27.0700 g., 0.9310 Silver 0.8102 oz. ASW **Ruler:** Charles II **Obv:** Legend and date around crowned arms **Obv. Legend:** CAROLVS II DEI G **Rev:** Legend around cross, lions and castles **Note:** Struck at Mexico City Mint, mint mark M, Mo.

Date	Mintage	Good	VG	F	VF	XF
1701 L Rare	—	—	—	—	—	—

KM# 49 8 REALES
27.0700 g., 0.9310 Silver 0.8102 oz. ASW **Ruler:** Luis I **Obv:** Legend and date around crowned arms **Obv. Legend:** LVDOVICVS I DEI G **Rev:** Lions and castles in angles of cross, legend around **Rev. Legend:** INDIARVM * REX HISPANIARV ... **Mint:** Mexico City **Note:** A significant portion of the legend must be visible for proper attribution. Mint mark M, Mo.

Date	Mintage	Good	VG	F	VF	XF
ND(1724-25)	—	—	—	—	—	—
Date off flan;						
Rare						
1724 D Rare	—	—	—	—	—	—
1725 D Rare	—	—	—	—	—	—

Date	Mintage	Good	VG	F	VF	XF
ND(1733-34) Date off flan	—	—	200	350	500	—
1733 F	—	—	550	750	1,150	—
1733 MF	—	—	450	600	750	—
1734/3 MF	—	—	500	750	1,000	—
1734 MF	—	—	500	750	1,000	—

KM# 50   ESCUDO
3.3800 g., 0.9170 Gold 0.0996 oz. AGW   **Ruler:** Charles II
Obv: Legend and date around crowned arms **Obv. Legend:**
CAROLVS II DEI G **Rev:** Lions and castles in angles of cross,
legend around **Mint:** Mexico City

Date	Mintage	VG	F	VF	XF	Unc
1701/0MXo L Rare	—	—	—	—	—	—

KM# 47a   8 REALES
27.0700 g., 0.9160 Silver 0.7972 oz. ASW   **Ruler:** Philip V
Obv: Legend and date around crowned arms **Obv. Legend:**
PHILIPVS V DEI G **Rev:** Lions and castles in angles of cross,
legend around **Mint:** Mexico City **Note:** Mint mark M, Mo.

Date	Mintage	Good	VG	F	VF	XF
ND(1729-33) Date off flan	—	—	70.00	100	125	—
1729 R	—	—	150	225	350	—
1730 G/R	—	—	150	225	350	—
1730 G	—	—	150	225	350	—
1730 R	—	—	150	225	350	—
1730 F Reported, not confirmed	—	—	—	—	—	—
1731/0 F	—	—	150	225	350	—
1731/0 F/G Rare	—	—	—	—	—	—
1731 F	—	—	135	210	325	—
1732/1 F	—	—	135	210	325	—
1732 F	—	—	135	210	350	—
1733/2 F	—	—	200	300	400	—
1733 F	—	—	200	300	400	—

KM# 51.1   ESCUDO
3.3800 g., 0.9170 Gold 0.0996 oz. AGW **Ruler:** Philip V **Obv:**
Legend and date around crowned arms **Obv. Legend:**
PHILIPVS V DEI G **Rev:** Lions and castles in angles of cross,
legend around **Mint:** Mexico City

Date	Mintage	VG	F	VF	XF	Unc
ND(1702-13) Date off flan	—	—	1,000	1,350	1,500	—
1702MXo L Rare	—	—	—	—	—	—
1703/2MXo L Rare	—	—	—	—	—	—
1704MXo L Rare	—	—	—	—	—	—
1707MXo J Rare	—	—	—	—	—	—
1708MXo J Rare	—	—	—	—	—	—
1709MXo J Rare	—	—	—	—	—	—
1710MXo J Rare	—	—	—	—	—	—
1711MXo J	—	—	1,500	2,500	3,500	—
1712MXo J	—	—	1,500	2,500	3,500	—
1713MXo J	—	—	1,500	2,500	3,500	—

KM# 51.2   ESCUDO
3.3800 g., 0.9170 Gold 0.0996 oz. AGW **Ruler:** Philip V **Obv:**
Legend and date around crowned arms **Obv. Legend:**
PHILIPVS V DEI G **Rev:** Lions and castles in angles of cross,
legend around **Mint:** Mexico City

Date	Mintage	VG	F	VF	XF	Unc
1712Mo J	—	—	2,000	3,000	4,000	—
1714Mo J	—	—	1,400	2,000	3,000	—
1714Mo J J's 1's (J7J4J) Rare	—	—	—	—	—	—
1715Mo J	—	—	2,000	3,000	4,000	—
1727Mo J Rare	—	—	—	—	—	—
1728Mo J Rare	—	—	—	—	—	—
1731 F Rare	—	—	—	—	—	—

Note: Die-struck counterfeits of 1731 F exist

KM# 48   8 REALES
0.9160 g., Silver   **Ruler:** Philip V **Obv:** Legend around
crowned arms **Rev:** Lions and castles in angles of cross,
legend around **Mint:** Mexico City **Note:** Klippe. Similar to
KM#47a. Mint mark M, Mo.

KM# 52 2 ESCUDOS
6.7700 g., 0.9170 Gold 0.1996 oz. AGW **Ruler:** Philip V **Obv:** Legend and date around crowned arms **Obv. Legend:** CAROLVS II DEI G **Rev:** Legend around cross **Mint:** Mexico City

Date	Mintage	VG	F	VF	XF	Unc
1701MXo L Rare	—	—	—	—	—	—

KM# 53.1 2 ESCUDOS
6.7700 g., 0.9170 Gold 0.1996 oz. AGW **Ruler:** Philip V **Obv:** Legend and date around crowned arms **Obv. Legend:** PHILIPVS V DEI G **Rev:** Legend around cross **Mint:** Mexico City

Date	Mintage	VG	F	VF	XF	Unc
ND(1704-13) Date off flan	—	—	1,250	1,500	2,000	—
1704MXo L Rare	—	—	—	—	—	—
1708MXo J Rare	—	—	—	—	—	—
1710MXo J Rare	—	—	—	—	—	—
1711MXo J	—	—	2,500	3,500	4,500	—
1712MXo J	—	—	2,500	3,500	4,500	—
1713MXo J	—	—	2,500	3,500	4,500	—

KM# 53.2 2 ESCUDOS
6.7700 g., 0.9170 Gold 0.1996 oz. AGW **Ruler:** Philip V **Obv:** Legend and date around crowned arms **Obv. Legend:** PHILIPVS V DEI G **Rev:** Legend around cross **Mint:** Mexico City **Note:** Struck counterfeits exist for 1731.

Date	Mintage	VG	F	VF	XF	Unc
ND(1714-31) Date off flan	—	—	1,500	1,750	2,500	—
1714Mo J	—	—	—	2,500	3,500	—
1715Mo J	—	—	—	3,000	4,000	—
1717Mo J Rare	—	—	—	—	—	—
1722Mo J Rare	—	—	—	—	—	—
1729Mo R Rare	—	—	—	—	—	—
1731Mo F Rare	—	—	—	—	—	—

KM# A54 2 ESCUDOS
6.7700 g., 0.9170 Gold 0.1996 oz. AGW **Ruler:** Luis I **Obv:** Legend and date around crowned arms **Obv. Legend:** LVDOVICVS I DEI G. **Rev:** Legend around cross **Mint:** Mexico City **Note:** A significant portion of the legend must be visible for proper attribution.

Date	Mintage	VG	F	VF	XF	Unc
NDMo D Rare	—	—	—	—	—	—

KM# 54 4 ESCUDOS
13.5400 g., 0.9170 Gold 0.3992 oz. AGW **Ruler:** Charles II **Obv:** Legend and date around crowned arms **Obv. Legend:** CAROLVS II DEI G **Rev:** Legend around cross **Mint:** Mexico City

Date	Mintage	VG	F	VF	XF	Unc
1701MXo L Rare	—	—	—	—	—	—

KM# 55.1 4 ESCUDOS
13.5400 g., 0.9170 Gold 0.3992 oz. AGW **Ruler:** Philip V **Obv:** Legend and date around crowned arms **Obv. Legend:** PHILIPVS V DEI G **Rev:** Legend around cross **Mint:** Mexico City

Date	Mintage	VG	F	VF	XF	Unc
ND(1705-13) Date off flan	—	—	2,500	3,000	4,000	—
1705MXo J Rare	—	—	—	—	—	—
1706MXo L Rare	—	—	—	—	—	—
1711MXo J	—	—	3,500	4,750	6,000	—
1712MXo J	—	—	3,500	4,750	6,000	—
1713MXo J	—	—	3,500	4,750	6,000	—

KM# 55.2 4 ESCUDOS
13.5400 g., 0.9170 Gold 0.3992 oz. AGW **Ruler:** Philip V **Obv:** Legend and date around crowned arms **Obv. Legend:** PHILIPVS V DEI G **Rev:** Legend around cross **Mint:** Mexico City

Date	Mintage	VG	F	VF	XF	Unc
ND(1714-20) Date off flan	—	—	2,500	3,500	4,500	—
1714Mo J	—	—	—	5,500	7,000	—
1715Mo J	—	—	—	5,500	7,000	—
1720Mo J Rare	—	—	—	—	—	—

SPANISH COLONIAL - COB

KM# 57.1   8 ESCUDOS
27.0700 g., 0.9170 Gold 0.7981 oz. AGW **Ruler:** Philip V **Obv:** Legend and date around crowned arms **Obv. Legend:** PHILIPVS V DEI G **Rev:** Legend around cross **Mint:** Mexico City

Date	Mintage	VG	F	VF	XF	Unc
ND(1701-13)	—	—	2,500	3,500	4,500	—
Date off flan						
1701MXo L Rare	—	—	—	—	—	—
1703MXo L Rare	—	—	—	—	—	—
1706MXo J Rare	—	—	—	—	—	—
1708MXo J Rare	—	—	—	—	—	—
1709MXo J Rare	—	—	—	—	—	—
1710MXo J Rare	—	—	—	—	—	—
1711MXo J	—	—	3,500	4,500	6,000	—
1712MXo J	—	—	3,500	4,500	6,000	—
1713MXo J	—	—	3,500	4,500	6,000	—

KM# 57.2   8 ESCUDOS
27.0700 g., 0.9170 Gold 0.7981 oz. AGW **Ruler:** Philip V **Obv:** Legend and date around crowned arms **Obv. Legend:** PHILIPVS V DEI G **Rev:** Legend around cross **Mint:** Mexico City

Date	Mintage	VG	F	VF	XF	Unc
ND(1714-32)Mo	—	—	2,750	3,750	5,000	—
Date off flan						
1714Mo J	—	—	4,000	5,500	7,500	—
1714Mo Date over GRAT on obverse	—	—	6,000	7,500	9,000	—
1715Mo J	—	—	5,000	6,500	8,000	—
1717/6Mo J Rare	—	—	—	—	—	—
1720/19Mo J Rare	—	—	—	—	—	—
1723Mo J Rare	—	—	—	—	—	—
1727/6Mo D Rare	—	—	—	—	—	—
1728/7Mo D Rare	—	—	—	—	—	—
1729Mo R Rare	—	—	—	—	—	—
1730Mo R Rare	—	—	—	—	—	—
1730Mo F Rare	—	—	—	—	—	—
1731Mo F Rare	—	—	—	—	—	—
1732Mo F Rare	—	—	—	—	—	—

KM# 57.3   8 ESCUDOS
27.0700 g., 0.9170 Gold 0.7981 oz. AGW **Ruler:** Philip V **Obv:** Date around crowned arms **Obv. Legend:** PHILIPVS V DEI G **Rev:** Legend and date around cross **Mint:** Mexico City

Date	Mintage	VG	F	VF	XF	Unc
1714Mo J Date on reverse	—	—	6,000	7,500	9,000	—

KM# 58   8 ESCUDOS
27.0700 g., 0.9170 Gold 0.7981 oz. AGW **Ruler:** Luis I **Obv:** Legend and date around crowned arms **Obv. Legend:** LVDOVICVS I DEI G **Rev:** Legend around cross **Mint:** Mexico City **Note:** A significant portion of the legend must be visible for proper attribution.

Date	Mintage	VG	F	VF	XF	Unc
ND(1724-25)Mo D Rare	—	—	—	—	—	—

ROYAL COINAGE

Struck on specially prepared round planchets using well centered dies in excellent condition to prove the quality of the minting to the Viceroy or even to the King.

KM# R24   1/2 REAL
1.6917 g., 0.9310 Silver 0.0506 oz. ASW **Ruler:** Philip V **Mint:** Mexico City **Note:** Normally found holed. Mint mark Mo.

Date	Mintage	Good	VG	F	VF	XF
1715Mo J	—	—	250	400	575	750
1719Mo J	—	—	250	400	575	750
1721Mo J	—	—	250	400	575	750
1722Mo J	—	—	250	400	575	750
1726Mo D	—	—	250	400	575	750
1727Mo D	—	—	250	400	575	750

KM# R25   1/2 REAL
1.6917 g., 0.9310 Silver 0.0506 oz. ASW **Ruler:** Luis I **Obv:** Legend around crowned LVDOVICVS monogram **Rev:** Lions and castles in angles of cross, legend around **Mint:** Mexico City **Note:** Mint mark Mo.

Date	Mintage	Good	VG	F	VF	XF
1724Mo D Rare	—	—	—	—	—	—

KM# R24a   1/2 REAL
1.6917 g., 0.9170 Silver 0.0499 oz. ASW **Ruler:** Philip V **Mint:** Mexico City **Note:** Normally found holed. Mint mark Mo.

Date	Mintage	Good	VG	F	VF	XF
1730Mo D	—	—	250	400	575	750

KM# R30   REAL
3.3834 g., 0.9310 Silver 0.1013 oz. ASW **Ruler:** Philip V **Obv. Legend:** PHILIPVS V DEI G **Mint:** Mexico City **Note:** Mint mark Mo.

Date	Mintage	Good	VG	F	VF	XF
1715Mo J Rare	—	—	—	—	—	—
1716Mo J Rare	—	—	—	—	—	—
1718Mo J Rare	—	—	—	—	—	—

KM# R35   2 REALES
6.7668 g., 0.9310 Silver 0.2025 oz. ASW **Ruler:** Philip V **Obv. Legend:** PHILIPVS V DEI G **Mint:** Mexico City **Note:** Mint mark Mo.

Date	Mintage	Good	VG	F	VF	XF
1715Mo J Rare	—	—	—	—	—	—

KM# R35a   2 REALES
6.7668 g., 0.9170 Silver 0.1995 oz. ASW **Ruler:** Philip V **Mint:** Mexico City **Note:** Mint mark Mo.

Date	Mintage	Good	VG	F	VF	XF
1730Mo R Rare	—	—	—	—	—	—

KM# R40   4 REALES
13.5337 g., 0.9310 Silver 0.4051 oz. ASW **Ruler:** Philip V **Obv. Legend:** PHILIPVS V DEI G **Mint:** Mexico City **Note:** Mint mark Mo.

Date	Mintage	Good	VG	F	VF	XF
1716Mo J Rare	—	—	—	—	—	—
1719Mo J Rare	—	—	—	—	—	—
1721Mo J Rare	—	—	—	—	—	—

Date	Mintage	Good	VG	F	VF	XF
1722Mo J Rare	—	—	—	—	—	—
1723Mo J Rare	—	—	—	—	—	—

KM# R47 8 REALES
27.0674 g., 0.9310 Silver 0.8102 oz. ASW **Ruler:** Philip V
Obv. Legend: PHILIPVS V DEI G **Mint:** Mexico City **Note:**
Struck at Mexico City Mint, mint mark Mo.

Date	Mintage	Good	VG	F	VF	XF
1702Mo L Rare	—	—	—	—	—	—
1703Mo L Rare	—	—	—	—	—	—
1705Mo J Rare	—	—	—	—	—	—
1706Mo J Rare	—	—	—	—	—	—
1709Mo J Rare	—	—	—	—	—	—
1711Mo J Rare	—	—	—	—	—	—
1714Mo J Rare	—	—	—	—	—	—
1715Mo J Rare	—	—	—	—	—	—
1716Mo J Rare	—	—	—	—	—	—
1717Mo J Rare	—	—	—	—	—	—
1719Mo J Rare	—	—	—	—	—	—
1721Mo J Rare	—	—	—	—	—	—
1722Mo J Rare	—	—	—	—	—	—
1723Mo J Rare	—	—	—	—	—	—
1724Mo D Rare	—	—	—	—	—	—
1725Mo D Rare	—	—	—	—	—	—
1726/5Mo D Rare	—	—	—	—	—	—
1726Mo D Rare	—	—	—	—	—	—
1727Mo D Rare	—	—	—	—	—	—

KM# R49 8 REALES
27.0674 g., 0.9310 Silver 0.8102 oz. ASW **Ruler:** Luis I
Note: Mint mark Mo.

Date	Mintage	Good	VG	F	VF	XF
1724 D Rare	—	—	—	—	—	—
1725 D Rare	—	—	—	—	—	—

KM# R47a 8 REALES
27.0674 g., 0.9170 Silver 0.7980 oz. ASW **Ruler:** Philip V
Mint: Mexico City **Note:** Mint mark Mo.

Date	Mintage	Good	VG	F	VF	XF
1729Mo R Rare	—	—	—	—	—	—
1730Mo R/D Rare	—	—	—	—	—	—
1730Mo G Rare	—	—	—	—	—	—

KM# R51.2 ESCUDO
3.3834 g., 0.9170 Gold 0.0997 oz. AGW **Ruler:** Philip V
Mint: Mexico City

Date	Mintage	Good	VG	F	VF	XF
1714Mo J Rare	—	—	—	—	—	—
1715Mo J Rare	—	—	—	—	—	—

KM# R53.1 2 ESCUDOS
6.7668 g., 0.9170 Gold 0.1995 oz. AGW **Ruler:** Philip V
Mint: Mexico City

Date	Mintage	Good	VG	F	VF	XF
1711MXo J Rare	—	—	—	—	—	—
1712MXo J Rare	—	—	—	—	—	—

KM# R55.1 4 ESCUDOS
13.5337 g., 0.9170 Gold 0.3990 oz. AGW **Ruler:** Philip V
Mint: Mexico City **Note:** Mint mark M, Mo.

Date	Mintage	Good	VG	F	VF	XF
1711 Rare	—	—	—	—	—	—

KM# R55.2 4 ESCUDOS
13.5337 g., 0.9170 Gold 0.3990 oz. AGW **Ruler:** Philip V
Mint: Mexico City **Note:** Mint mark M, Mo.

Date	Mintage	Good	VG	F	VF	XF
1714 Rare	—	—	—	—	—	—

KM# R57.1 8 ESCUDOS
27.0674 g., 0.9170 Gold 0.7980 oz. AGW **Ruler:** Philip V
Mint: Mexico City

Date	Mintage	Good	VG	F	VF	XF
1702MXo L Rare	—	—	—	—	—	—
1711MXo J Rare	—	—	—	—	—	—
1712MXo J Rare	—	—	—	—	—	—
1713MXo J Rare	—	—	—	—	—	—

KM# R57.3 8 ESCUDOS
27.0674 g., 0.9170 Gold 0.7980 oz. AGW **Ruler:** Philip V
Mint: Mexico City

Date	Mintage	Good	VG	F	VF	XF
1714Mo J Rare	—	—	—	—	—	—
1715Mo J Rare	—	—	—	—	—	—
1717Mo J Rare	—	—	—	—	—	—
1718Mo J Rare	—	—	—	—	—	—
1723Mo J Rare	—	—	—	—	—	—

MILLED COINAGE

KM# 59 1/8 PILON (1/16 Real)
Copper **Ruler:** Ferdinand VII **Obv:** Crowned monogram **Rev:**
Castles and lions in wreath **Mint:** Mexico City **Note:** Mint mark
Mo.

Date	Mintage	VG	F	VF	XF	Unc
1814	—	12.00	25.00	55.00	145	—
1815	—	12.00	25.00	55.00	145	—

KM# 63 1/4 TLACO (1/8 Real)
Copper **Ruler:** Ferdinand VII **Obv:** Crowned monogram
flanked by value and mint mark **Obv. Legend:** FERDIN. VII...
Rev: Arms without shield within wreath **Mint:** Mexico City
Note: Mint mark Mo.

Date	Mintage	VG	F	VF	XF	Unc
1814	—	14.00	30.00	60.00	180	—
1815	—	14.00	30.00	60.00	180	—
1816	—	14.00	30.00	60.00	180	—

KM# 62 1/4 REAL
0.8458 g., 0.8960 Silver 0.0244 oz. ASW **Ruler:** Charles IV
Obv: Crowned rampant lion, left **Rev:** Castle **Mint:** Mexico
City **Note:** Mint mark Mo.

Date	Mintage	VG	F	VF	XF	Unc
1796	—	35.00	65.00	125	200	—
1797	—	35.00	65.00	125	200	—
1798	—	35.00	65.00	125	200	—
1799/8	—	35.00	65.00	125	200	—
1799	—	35.00	65.00	125	200	—

Date	Mintage	VG	F	VF	XF	Unc
1800	—	35.00	65.00	125	200	—
1801/0	—	10.00	20.00	40.00	70.00	—
1801	—	10.00	20.00	40.00	70.00	—
1802	—	10.00	20.00	40.00	70.00	—
1803	—	10.00	20.00	40.00	70.00	—
1804	—	10.00	20.00	40.00	75.00	—
1805/4	—	12.50	25.00	55.00	85.00	—
1805	—	10.00	22.00	50.00	75.00	—
1806	—	10.00	22.00	50.00	80.00	—
1807/797	—	15.00	30.00	55.00	85.00	—
1807	—	12.50	25.00	50.00	80.00	—
1808	—	12.50	25.00	50.00	80.00	—
1809/8	—	12.50	25.00	50.00	80.00	—
1809	—	12.50	25.00	50.00	80.00	—
1810	—	12.50	25.00	50.00	75.00	—
1811	—	12.50	25.00	50.00	75.00	—
1812	—	12.50	25.00	50.00	75.00	—
1813	—	10.00	20.00	40.00	70.00	—
1815	—	12.50	22.00	50.00	75.00	—
1816	—	10.00	20.00	40.00	70.00	—

KM# 64 2/4 SENAL (1/4 Real)
Copper **Ruler:** Ferdinand VII **Obv:** Legend around crowned monogram flanked by mint mark and value **Obv. Legend:** FERDIN. VII... **Rev:** Arms without shield within wreath **Mint:** Mexico City **Note:** Mint mark Mo.

Date	Mintage	VG	F	VF	XF	Unc
1814	—	14.00	30.00	60.00	180	—
1815/4	—	18.00	36.00	70.00	200	—
1815	—	14.00	30.00	60.00	180	—
1816	—	14.00	30.00	60.00	180	—
1821	—	25.00	48.00	90.00	240	—

KM# 65 1/2 REAL
1.6917 g., 0.9170 Silver 0.0499 oz. ASW **Ruler:** Philip V **Obv:** Crowned shield flanked by M F, rosettes and small cross **Obv. Legend:** PHILIP • V • D • G • HISPAN • ET IND • REX **Rev:** Crowned globes flanked by crowned pillars with banner, date below **Mint:** Mexico City **Note:** Mint mark M, Mo, MX.

Date	Mintage	VG	F	VF	XF	Unc
1732 Rare	—	—	—	—	—	—
1732 F	—	500	800	1,200	2,000	—
1733 MF (MX)	—	400	600	1,000	1,500	—
1733 F	—	200	325	550	800	—
1733/2 MF	—	300	400	600	800	—
1733 MF	—	300	400	600	800	—
1734/3 MF	—	20.00	50.00	100	150	—
1734 MF	—	20.00	50.00	100	150	—
1735/4 MF	—	20.00	50.00	100	150	—
1735 MF	—	20.00	50.00	100	150	—
1736/5 MF	—	20.00	50.00	100	150	—
1736 MF	—	20.00	50.00	100	150	—
1737/6 MF	—	20.00	50.00	100	150	—
1737 MF	—	20.00	50.00	100	150	—
1738/7 MF	—	20.00	50.00	100	150	—
1738 MF	—	20.00	50.00	100	150	—
1739 MF	—	20.00	50.00	100	150	—
1740/30 MF	—	20.00	50.00	100	150	—
1740 MF	—	20.00	50.00	100	150	—
1741 MF	—	20.00	50.00	100	150	—

KM# 66 1/2 REAL
1.6900 g., 0.9170 Silver 0.0498 oz. ASW **Ruler:** Philip V **Obv:** Crowned shield flanked by stars **Obv. Legend:** PHS • V • D • G • HISP • ET IND • R **Rev:** Crowned globes flanked by crowned pillars with banner, date below **Mint:** Mexico City **Note:** Mint mark M, Mo.

Date	Mintage	VG	F	VF	XF	Unc
1742 M	—	15.00	40.00	75.00	125	—
1743 M	—	15.00	40.00	75.00	125	—
1744/3 M	—	15.00	40.00	75.00	125	—
1744 M	—	15.00	40.00	75.00	125	—
1745 M Rare	—	—	—	—	—	—

Note: Legend variation: PHS. V. D. G. HISP. EST IND. R

Date	Mintage	VG	F	VF	XF	Unc
1745 M	—	15.00	40.00	75.00	125	—
1746/5 M	—	15.00	40.00	75.00	125	—
1746 M	—	15.00	40.00	75.00	125	—
1747 M	—	15.00	40.00	75.00	125	—

KM# 67.1 1/2 REAL
1.6900 g., 0.9170 Silver 0.0498 oz. ASW **Ruler:** Ferdinand VI **Obv:** Royal crown **Obv. Legend:** FRD • VI • D • G • HIPS • ET IND • R **Mint:** Mexico City **Note:** Mint mark M, Mo.

Date	Mintage	VG	F	VF	XF	Unc
1747/6 M	—	15.00	40.00	75.00	125	—
1747 M	—	15.00	40.00	75.00	125	—
1748/7 M	—	15.00	40.00	75.00	125	—
1748 M	—	15.00	40.00	75.00	125	—
1749 M	—	15.00	40.00	75.00	125	—
1750 M	—	15.00	40.00	75.00	125	—
1751 M	—	15.00	40.00	75.00	125	—
1752 M	—	15.00	40.00	75.00	125	—
1753 M	—	15.00	40.00	75.00	125	—
1754 M	—	15.00	40.00	75.00	125	—
1755/6 M	—	15.00	40.00	75.00	125	—
1755 M	—	15.00	40.00	75.00	125	—
1756/5 M	—	15.00	40.00	75.00	125	—
1756 M	—	15.00	40.00	75.00	125	—
1757/6 M	—	15.00	40.00	75.00	125	—
1757 M	—	15.00	40.00	75.00	125	—

KM# 67.2 1/2 REAL
1.6917 g., 0.9170 Silver 0.0499 oz. ASW **Ruler:** Ferdinand VI **Obv:** Different crown **Mint:** Mexico City **Note:** Mint mark M, Mo.

Date	Mintage	VG	F	VF	XF	Unc
1757 M	—	15.00	40.00	75.00	125	—
1758/7 M	—	15.00	40.00	75.00	125	—
1758 M	—	15.00	40.00	75.00	125	—
1759 M	—	15.00	40.00	75.00	125	—
1760/59 M	—	15.00	40.00	75.00	125	—
1760 M	—	15.00	40.00	75.00	125	—

KM# 68 1/2 REAL
1.6900 g., 0.9170 Silver 0.0498 oz. ASW **Ruler:** Charles III **Obv:** Crowned shield flanked by stars **Obv. Legend:** CAR • III • D • G • HISP • ET IND • R **Rev:** Crowned globes flanked by crowned pillars with banner, date below **Mint:** Mexico City **Note:** Mint mark M, Mo.

Date	Mintage	VG	F	VF	XF	Unc
1760/59 M	—	15.00	40.00	75.00	125	—
1760 M	—	15.00	40.00	75.00	125	—
1761 M	—	15.00	40.00	75.00	125	—
1762 M	—	15.00	40.00	75.00	125	—
1763/2 M	—	15.00	40.00	75.00	125	—
1763 M	—	15.00	40.00	75.00	125	—
1764 M	—	15.00	40.00	75.00	125	—
1765/4 M	—	15.00	40.00	75.00	125	—
1765 M	—	15.00	40.00	75.00	125	—
1766 M	—	15.00	40.00	75.00	125	—
1767 M	—	15.00	40.00	75.00	125	—
1768/6 M	—	15.00	40.00	75.00	125	—
1768 M	—	15.00	40.00	75.00	125	—
1769 M	—	15.00	40.00	75.00	125	—
1770 M	—	15.00	40.00	75.00	125	—
1770 F	—	15.00	40.00	75.00	125	—
1771 F	—	15.00	40.00	75.00	125	—

KM# 69.2   1/2 REAL
1.6917 g., 0.9030 Silver 0.0491 oz. ASW **Ruler:** Charles III
Obv: Armored bust of Charles III, right **Obv. Legend:**
CAROLUS • III • DEI • GRATIA **Rev:** Crown above shield
flanked by pillars with banner, normal initials and mint mark
Mint: Mexico City **Note:** Mint mark Mo.

Date	Mintage	VG	F	VF	XF	Unc
1772Mo FF	—	15.00	40.00	70.00	110	—
1773Mo FM	—	12.00	35.00	60.00	100	—
1773Mo FM CAROLS (error)	—	75.00	150	250	400	—
1774Mo FM	—	10.00	25.00	50.00	90.00	—
1775Mo FM	—	10.00	25.00	50.00	90.00	—
1776Mo FM	—	20.00	40.00	70.00	110	—
1777/6Mo FM	—	10.00	25.00	50.00	90.00	—
1777Mo FM	—	10.00	25.00	50.00	90.00	—
1778Mo FF	—	10.00	25.00	50.00	90.00	—
1779Mo FF	—	10.00	25.00	50.00	90.00	—
1780/79Mo FF	—	10.00	25.00	50.00	90.00	—
1780Mo FF	—	10.00	25.00	50.00	90.00	—
1781Mo FF	—	10.00	25.00	50.00	90.00	—
1782/1Mo FF	—	10.00	25.00	50.00	90.00	—
1782Mo FF	—	10.00	25.00	50.00	90.00	—
1783Mo FF	—	10.00	25.00	50.00	90.00	—
1783Mo FM	—	10.00	25.00	50.00	90.00	—
1784Mo FF	—	10.00	25.00	50.00	90.00	—
1784Mo FM	—	10.00	25.00	50.00	90.00	—

KM# 69.1   1/2 REAL
1.6900 g., 0.9030 Silver 0.0491 oz. ASW **Ruler:** Charles III
Obv. Legend: CAROLUS • III • DEI • GRATIA **Rev:** Inverted
FM and mint mark **Mint:** Mexico City **Note:** Mint mark Mo.

Date	Mintage	VG	F	VF	XF	Unc
1772Mo FM	—	12.00	35.00	60.00	100	—
1773Mo FM	—	10.00	25.00	50.00	90.00	—

KM# 69.2a   1/2 REAL
1.6917 g., 0.8960 Silver 0.0487 oz. ASW **Ruler:** Charles III
Rev: Normal initials and mint mark **Note:** Mint mark M, Mo.

Date	Mintage	VG	F	VF	XF	Unc
1785/4 FM	—	10.00	25.00	50.00	90.00	—
1785 FM	—	10.00	25.00	50.00	90.00	—
1786 FM	—	10.00	25.00	50.00	90.00	—
1787 FM	—	10.00	25.00	50.00	90.00	—
1788 FM	—	10.00	25.00	50.00	90.00	—
1789 FM	—	12.00	35.00	60.00	100	—

KM# 70   1/2 REAL
1.6917 g., 0.8960 Silver 0.0487 oz. ASW **Ruler:** Charles IV
Obv: Armored bust of Charles IV, right **Obv. Legend:**
CAROLUS • IV •... **Rev:** Crown above shield flanked by pillars
with banner **Mint:** Mexico City **Note:** Mint mark Mo.

Date	Mintage	VG	F	VF	XF	Unc
1789 FM	—	12.00	35.00	60.00	100	—
1790 FM	—	12.00	35.00	60.00	100	—

KM# 71   1/2 REAL
1.6917 g., 0.8960 Silver 0.0487 oz. ASW **Ruler:** Charles IV
Obv: Armored bust of Charles IIII, right **Obv. Legend:**
CAROLUS • IIII •... **Rev:** Crown above shield flanked by pillars
with banner **Mint:** Mexico City **Note:** Mint mark M, Mo.

Date	Mintage	VG	F	VF	XF	Unc
1790 FM	—	12.00	35.00	60.00	100	—

KM# 72   1/2 REAL
1.6900 g., 0.9030 Silver 0.0491 oz. ASW **Ruler:** Charles IV
Obv: Armored bust of Charles IIII, right **Obv. Legend:**
CAROLUS • IIII • ... **Rev:** Crowned shield flanked by pillars
with banner **Rev. Legend:** IND • R • .... **Mint:** Mexico City
Note: Mint mark Mo.

Date	Mintage	VG	F	VF	XF	Unc
1792 FM	—	10.00	20.00	55.00	85.00	—
1793 FM	—	10.00	20.00	55.00	85.00	—
1794/3 FM	—	10.00	20.00	55.00	85.00	—
1794 FM	—	10.00	20.00	55.00	85.00	—
1795 FM	—	10.00	20.00	55.00	85.00	—
1796 FM	—	10.00	20.00	55.00	85.00	—
1797 FM	—	10.00	20.00	55.00	85.00	—
1798/7 FM	—	10.00	20.00	55.00	85.00	—
1798 FM	—	10.00	20.00	55.00	85.00	—
1799 FM	—	10.00	20.00	55.00	85.00	—
1800/799 FM	—	10.00	20.00	55.00	85.00	—
1800 FM	—	10.00	20.00	55.00	85.00	—
1801 FM	—	8.00	17.00	33.00	85.00	—
1801 FT	—	4.00	11.00	25.00	50.00	—
1802 FT	—	4.00	11.00	25.00	50.00	—
1803 FT	—	6.00	13.00	27.50	55.00	—
1804 TH	—	4.00	11.00	25.00	50.00	—
1805 TH	—	4.00	11.00	25.00	50.00	—
1806 TH	—	4.00	11.00	25.00	50.00	—
1807/6 TH	—	6.00	13.00	27.50	55.00	—
1807 TH	—	4.00	11.00	25.00	50.00	—
1808/7 TH	—	6.00	13.00	27.50	55.00	—
1808 TH	—	4.00	11.00	25.00	50.00	—

KM# 73   1/2 REAL
1.6900 g., 0.9030 Silver 0.0491 oz. ASW **Ruler:**
Ferdinand VII **Obv:** Armored laureate bust right **Obv.
Legend:** FERDIN.VII... **Rev:** Crowned shield flanked by
pillars **Rev. Legend:** IND.R.... **Mint:** Mexico City **Note:** Mint
mark Mo.

Date	Mintage	VG	F	VF	XF	Unc
1808 TH	—	4.00	9.00	22.50	40.00	—
1809 TH	—	4.00	9.00	22.50	40.00	—
1810 TH	—	6.00	11.00	25.00	50.00	—
1810 HJ	—	4.00	9.00	22.50	40.00	—
1811 HJ	—	4.00	9.00	22.50	40.00	—
1812/1 HJ	—	8.00	17.00	38.50	85.00	—
1812 HJ	—	4.00	9.00	22.50	40.00	—
1812 JJ	—	13.00	27.50	49.50	105	—
1813/2 JJ	—	13.00	27.50	49.50	105	—
1813 TH	—	4.00	9.00	22.50	40.00	—
1813 JJ	—	7.00	13.00	27.50	80.00	—
1813 HJ	—	8.00	17.00	38.50	95.00	—
1814/3 JJ	—	8.00	17.00	38.50	95.00	—
1814 JJ	—	6.00	11.00	25.00	50.00	—

KM# 74   1/2 REAL
1.6900 g., 0.9030 Silver 0.0491 oz. ASW **Ruler:**
Ferdinand VII **Obv:** Draped laureate bust right **Obv. Legend:**
FERDIN.VII.... **Rev:** Crowned shield flanked by pillars **Rev.
Legend:** IND.R.... **Mint:** Mexico City **Note:** Mint mark Mo.

Date	Mintage	VG	F	VF	XF	Unc
1815 JJ	—	4.00	9.00	22.50	45.00	—

Date	Mintage	VG	F	VF	XF	Unc
1816 JJ	—	4.00	9.00	22.50	45.00	—
1817/6 JJ	—	13.00	27.50	55.00	125	—
1817 JJ	—	4.00	9.00	30.75	50.00	—
1818/7 JJ	—	4.00	9.00	27.50	55.00	—
1818 JJ	—	4.00	9.00	27.50	55.00	—
1819/8 JJ	—	7.00	13.00	38.50	95.00	—
1819 JJ	—	4.00	9.00	22.50	45.00	—
1820 JJ	—	4.00	9.00	27.50	55.00	—
1821 JJ	—	4.00	9.00	22.50	45.00	—

KM# 75.1 REAL
3.3834 g., 0.9170 Silver 0.0997 oz. ASW **Ruler:** Philip V
Obv: Crowned shield flanked by MF I ** **Obv. Legend:** PHILIP
• V • D • G • HISPAN • ET IND • REX **Rev:** Crowned globes
flanked by crowned pillars with banner, date below **Mint:**
Mexico City **Note:** Mint mark M, Mo, (MX).

Date	Mintage	VG	F	VF	XF	Unc
1732 Rare	—	—	—	—	—	—
1732 F	—	—	—	—	—	—
1733 F (MX)	—	150	350	425	750	—
1733 MF (MX)	—	150	350	425	750	—
1733 F Rare	—	—	—	—	—	—
1733 MF	—	100	200	300	500	—
1734/3 MF	—	35.00	60.00	125	175	—
1734 MF	—	35.00	60.00	125	175	—
1735 MF	—	35.00	60.00	125	175	—
1736 MF	—	35.00	60.00	125	175	—
1737 MF	—	35.00	60.00	125	175	—
1738 MF	—	35.00	60.00	125	175	—
1739 MF	—	35.00	60.00	125	175	—
1740 MF	—	35.00	60.00	125	175	—
1741 MF	—	35.00	60.00	125	175	—

KM# 75.2 REAL
3.3834 g., 0.9170 Silver 0.0997 oz. ASW **Ruler:** Philip V
Obv. Legend: PHS • V • D • G • HISP • ET • IND • R **Note:**
Mint mark M, Mo.

Date	Mintage	VG	F	VF	XF	Unc
1742 M	—	35.00	60.00	110	165	—
1743 M	—	35.00	60.00	110	165	—
1744/3 M	—	35.00	60.00	110	165	—
1744 M	—	35.00	60.00	110	165	—
1745 M	—	35.00	60.00	110	165	—
1746/5 M	—	35.00	60.00	110	165	—
1746 M	—	35.00	60.00	110	165	—
1747 M	—	35.00	60.00	110	165	—

KM# 76.1 REAL
3.3800 g., 0.9170 Silver 0.0996 oz. ASW **Ruler:**
Ferdinand VI **Obv:** Crowned shield flanked by R I **Obv.
Legend:** FRD • VI • D • G • HISP • ET IND • R **Rev:** Crowned
globes flanked by crowned pillars with banner, date below
Mint: Mexico City **Note:** Mint mark M, Mo.

Date	Mintage	VG	F	VF	XF	Unc
1747 M	—	30.00	50.00	100	150	—
1748/7 M	—	30.00	50.00	100	150	—
1748 M	—	30.00	50.00	100	150	—
1749 M	—	30.00	50.00	100	150	—
1750/40 M	—	30.00	50.00	100	150	—
1750 M	—	30.00	50.00	100	150	—
1751 M	—	30.00	50.00	100	150	—
1752 M	—	30.00	50.00	100	150	—
1753 M	—	30.00	50.00	100	150	—
1754 M	—	30.00	50.00	100	150	—

Date	Mintage	VG	F	VF	XF	Unc
1755/4 M	—	30.00	50.00	100	150	—
1755 M	—	30.00	50.00	100	150	—
1756 M	—	30.00	50.00	100	150	—
1757 M	—	30.00	50.00	100	150	—
1758/5 M	—	30.00	50.00	100	150	—
1758 M	—	30.00	50.00	100	150	—

KM# 76.2 REAL
3.3834 g., 0.9170 Silver 0.0997 oz. ASW **Ruler:**
Ferdinand VI **Obv:** Royal and Imperial crowns **Note:** Mint
mark M, Mo.

Date	Mintage	VG	F	VF	XF	Unc
1757 M	—	30.00	50.00	100	150	—
1758/7 M	—	30.00	50.00	100	150	—
1758 M	—	30.00	50.00	100	150	—
1759 M	—	30.00	50.00	100	150	—
1760 M	—	30.00	50.00	100	150	—

KM# 77 REAL
3.3800 g., 0.9170 Silver 0.0996 oz. ASW **Ruler:** Charles III
Obv: Crowned shield flanked by R I **Obv. Legend:** CAR • III
• D • G • HISP • ET IND • R **Rev:** Crowned globes flanked by
crowned pillars with banner, date below **Mint:** Mexico City
Note: Mint mark M, Mo.

Date	Mintage	VG	F	VF	XF	Unc
1760 M	—	30.00	50.00	100	150	—
1761/0 M	—	30.00	50.00	100	150	—
1761 M	—	30.00	50.00	100	150	—
1762 M	—	30.00	50.00	100	150	—
1763/2 M	—	30.00	50.00	100	150	—
1763 M	—	30.00	50.00	100	150	—
1764 M	—	30.00	50.00	100	150	—
1765 M	—	30.00	50.00	100	150	—
1766 M	—	30.00	50.00	100	150	—
1767 M	—	30.00	50.00	100	150	—
1768 M	—	30.00	50.00	100	150	—
1769 M	—	30.00	50.00	100	150	—
1769/70 M	—	30.00	50.00	100	150	—
1770 M	—	30.00	50.00	100	150	—
1770 F	—	30.00	50.00	100	200	—
1771 F	—	30.00	50.00	100	200	—

KM# 78.1 REAL
3.3834 g., 0.9030 Silver 0.0982 oz. ASW **Ruler:** Charles III
Obv. Legend: CAROLUS • III • DEI • GRATIA **Rev:** Inverted
FM and mint mark **Note:** Mint mark M, Mo.

Date	Mintage	VG	F	VF	XF	Unc
1772 FM	—	25.00	40.00	80.00	125	—
1773 FM	—	25.00	40.00	80.00	125	—

KM# 78.2 REAL
3.3800 g., 0.9030 Silver 0.0981 oz. ASW **Ruler:** Charles III
Obv: Armored bust of Charles III, right **Obv. Legend:**
CAROLUS • III • DEI • GRATIA **Rev. Legend:** Crowned shield
flanked by pillars with banner, normal initials and mint mark
Mint: Mexico City **Note:** Mint mark M, Mo.

Date	Mintage	VG	F	VF	XF	Unc
1774 FM	—	20.00	35.00	65.00	100	—
1775/4 FM	—	20.00	35.00	65.00	100	—
1775 FM	—	20.00	35.00	65.00	100	—
1776 FM	—	20.00	35.00	65.00	100	—
1777 FM	—	20.00	35.00	65.00	100	—
1778 FF/M	—	20.00	35.00	65.00	100	—
1778 FF	—	20.00	35.00	65.00	100	—
1779 FF	—	20.00	35.00	65.00	100	—
1780 FF	—	20.00	35.00	65.00	100	—
1780 F F/M	—	20.00	35.00	65.00	100	—
1781 FF	—	20.00	35.00	65.00	100	—
1782 FF	—	20.00	35.00	65.00	100	—
1783 FF	—	20.00	35.00	65.00	100	—
1784 FF	—	20.00	35.00	65.00	100	—

KM# 78.2a REAL
3.3834 g., 0.8960 Silver 0.0975 oz. ASW **Ruler:** Charles III
Rev: Normal initials and mint mark **Note:** Mint mark M, Mo.

Date	Mintage	VG	F	VF	XF	Unc
1785 FF	—	20.00	35.00	65.00	100	—

Date	Mintage	VG	F	VF	XF	Unc
1785 FM	—	20.00	35.00	65.00	100	—
1786 FM	—	20.00	35.00	65.00	100	—
1787 FF	—	20.00	35.00	65.00	125	—
1787 FF	—	20.00	35.00	65.00	100	—
1788 FF	—	50.00	100	200	—	—
1788 FM	—	20.00	35.00	65.00	100	—
1789 FM	—	20.00	35.00	65.00	100	—

KM# 79 REAL
3.3800 g., 0.9030 Silver 0.0981 oz. ASW **Ruler:** Charles IV
Obv: Armored bust of Charles III, right **Obv. Legend:**
CAROLUS • IV • ... **Rev:** Crown above shield flanked by pillars
with banner **Mint:** Mexico City **Note:** Mint mark M, Mo.

Date	Mintage	VG	F	VF	XF	Unc
1789 FM	—	20.00	35.00	65.00	150	—
1790 FM	—	20.00	35.00	65.00	150	—

KM# 80 REAL
3.3800 g., 0.9030 Silver 0.0981 oz. ASW **Ruler:** Charles IV
Obv: Armored bust of Charles IIII, right **Obv. Legend:**
CAROLUS • IIII • ... **Rev:** Crowned shield flanked by pillars
with banner **Mint:** Mexico City **Note:** Mint mark M, Mo.

Date	Mintage	VG	F	VF	XF	Unc
1790 FM	—	20.00	35.00	70.00	165	—

KM# 81 REAL
3.3834 g., 0.8960 Silver 0.0975 oz. ASW **Ruler:** Charles IV
Obv: Armored bust of Charles IIII, right **Obv. Legend:**
CAROLUS • IIII • ... **Rev:** Crowned shield flanked by pillars
with banner **Rev. Legend:** IND • REX ... **Mint:** Mexico City
Note: Mint mark Mo.

Date	Mintage	VG	F	VF	XF	Unc
1792 FM	—	15.00	30.00	60.00	90.00	—
1793 FM	—	15.00	30.00	60.00	150	—
1794 FM	—	25.00	50.00	100	250	—
1795 FM	—	15.00	30.00	60.00	150	—
1796 FM	—	15.00	30.00	60.00	90.00	—
1797/6 FM	—	15.00	30.00	60.00	90.00	—
1797 FM	—	15.00	30.00	60.00	90.00	—
1798/7 FM	—	15.00	30.00	60.00	90.00	—
1798 FM	—	15.00	30.00	60.00	90.00	—
1799 FM	—	15.00	30.00	60.00	90.00	—
1800 FM	—	15.00	30.00	60.00	90.00	—
1801 FT/M	—	6.00	11.00	27.50	65.00	—
1801 FT	—	6.00	11.00	27.50	65.00	—
1801 FM	—	9.00	17.00	30.75	65.00	—
1802 FM	—	6.00	11.00	27.50	65.00	—
1802 FT	—	6.00	11.00	27.50	65.00	—
1802 FT/M	—	6.00	11.00	27.50	65.00	—
1802/1 FT	—	6.00	11.00	27.50	65.00	—
1803 FT	—	6.00	11.00	27.50	65.00	—
1804 TH	—	6.00	11.00	27.50	65.00	—
1805 TH	—	6.00	11.00	27.50	65.00	—
1806 TH	—	6.00	11.00	27.50	65.00	—
1807/6 TH	—	6.00	11.00	27.50	65.00	—

Date	Mintage	VG	F	VF	XF	Unc
1807 TH	—	6.00	11.00	27.50	65.00	—
1808/7 TH	—	6.00	11.00	27.50	65.00	—
1808 FM	—	6.00	11.00	27.50	65.00	—

KM# 82 REAL
3.3800 g., 0.9030 Silver 0.0981 oz. ASW **Ruler:**
Ferdinand VII **Obv:** Armored laureate bust right **Obv.
Legend:** FERDIN.VII... **Rev:** Crowned shield flanked by
pillars **Rev. Legend:** IND.REX.... **Mint:** Mexico City **Note:**
Mint mark Mo.

Date	Mintage	VG	F	VF	XF	Unc
1809 TH	—	9.00	17.00	30.75	95.00	—
1810/09 TH	—	9.00	17.00	30.75	95.00	—
1810 TH	—	9.00	17.00	30.75	95.00	—
1811 TH	—	27.50	38.50	65.00	250	—
1811 HJ	—	9.00	17.00	30.75	95.00	—
1812 HJ	—	4.00	10.00	30.75	85.00	—
1812 JJ	—	11.00	22.50	44.00	125	—
1813 HJ	—	11.00	22.50	44.00	125	—
1813 JJ	—	55.00	110	165	250	—
1814 HJ	—	17.00	33.00	165	155	—
1814 JJ	—	55.00	110	195	300	—

KM# 83 REAL
3.3800 g., 0.9030 Silver 0.0981 oz. ASW **Ruler:**
Ferdinand VII **Obv:** Draped laureate bust right **Obv. Legend:**
FERDIN.VII... **Rev:** Crowned shield flanked by pillars **Rev.
Legend:** IND.REX... **Mint:** Mexico City **Note:** Mint mark Mo.

Date	Mintage	VG	F	VF	XF	Unc
1814 JJ	—	27.50	55.00	110	350	—
1815 HJ	—	17.00	33.00	65.00	150	—
1815 JJ	—	11.00	22.50	44.00	125	—
1816 JJ	—	6.00	11.00	27.50	75.00	—
1817 JJ	—	6.00	11.00	27.50	75.00	—
1818 JJ	—	33.00	65.00	140	500	—
1819 JJ	—	6.00	11.00	27.50	75.00	—
1820 JJ	—	6.00	11.00	27.50	75.00	—
1821/0 JJ	—	9.00	17.00	33.00	115	—
1821 JJ	—	6.00	11.00	27.50	55.00	—

KM# 84 2 REALES
6.7668 g., 0.9170 Silver 0.1995 oz. ASW **Ruler:** Philip V
Obv: Crowned shield flanked by M F 2 **Obv. Legend:** PHILIP
• V • D • G • HISPAN • ET IND • REX **Rev:** Crowned globes
flanked by crowned pillars with banner, date below **Rev.
Legend:** VTRAQUE VNUM **Mint:** Mexico City **Note:** Mint
mark M, Mo, (MX).

Date	Mintage	VG	F	VF	XF	Unc
1732 Rare	—	—	—	—	—	—
1732 F	—	800	1,300	1,750	2,750	—
1733 F	—	600	800	1,350	2,250	—
1733 MF (MX)	—	350	600	1,000	1,650	—
1733 MF	—	600	900	1,500	2,500	—

Date	Mintage	VG	F	VF	XF	Unc
1734/3 MF	—	45.00	75.00	135	200	—
1734 MF	—	45.00	75.00	135	200	—
1735/3 MF	—	45.00	75.00	135	200	—
1735/4 MF	—	45.00	75.00	135	200	—
1735 MF	—	45.00	75.00	135	200	—
1736/3 MF	—	45.00	75.00	135	200	—
1736/4 MF	—	45.00	75.00	135	200	—
1736/5 MF	—	45.00	75.00	135	200	—
1736 MF	—	45.00	75.00	135	200	—
1737/3 MF	—	45.00	75.00	135	200	—
1737 MF	—	45.00	75.00	135	200	—
1738/7 MF	—	45.00	75.00	135	200	—
1738 MF	—	45.00	75.00	135	200	—
1739 MF	—	45.00	75.00	135	200	—
1740/30 MF	—	45.00	75.00	135	200	—
1740 MF	—	45.00	75.00	135	200	—
1741 MF	—	45.00	75.00	135	200	—

KM# 85   2 REALES
6.7700 g., 0.9170 Silver 0.1996 oz. ASW   **Ruler:** Philip V
Obv: Crowned shield flanked by R 2 **Obv. Legend:** PHS • V
• D • G • HISP • ET IND • R * **Rev:** Crowned globes flanked
by crowned pillars with banner, date below **Rev. Legend:**
VTRA QUE VNUM **Mint:** Mexico City **Note:** Mint mark M, Mo.

Date	Mintage	F	VF	XF	Unc	BU
1742 M	—	70.00	125	185	—	—
1743/2 M	—	70.00	125	185	—	—
1743 M	—	70.00	125	185	—	—
1744/3 M	—	70.00	125	185	—	—
1744 M	—	70.00	125	185	—	—
1745/4 M	—	70.00	125	185	—	—
1745 M	—	70.00	125	185	—	—
1745 M HIP Rare	—	—	—	—	—	—
1746/5 M	—	70.00	125	185	—	—
1746 M	—	70.00	125	185	—	—
1747 M	—	70.00	125	185	—	—
1750 M Rare	—	—	—	—	—	—

Note: Posthumous mule.

KM# 86.1   2 REALES
6.7668 g., 0.9170 Silver 0.1995 oz. ASW   **Ruler:**
Ferdinand VI **Obv:** Crowned shield flanked by R 2 **Obv.**
Legend: FRD • VI • D • G • HISP • ET IND • R **Rev:** Crowned
globes flanked by crowned pillars with banner, date below
Rev. Legend: VTRA QUE VNUM **Mint:** Mexico City **Note:**
Mint mark M, Mo.

Date	Mintage	VG	F	VF	XF	Unc
1747 M	—	35.00	60.00	110	175	—
1748/7 M	—	35.00	60.00	110	175	—
1748 M	—	35.00	60.00	110	175	—
1749 M	—	35.00	60.00	110	175	—
1750 M	—	35.00	60.00	110	175	—
1751/41 M	—	35.00	60.00	110	175	—
1751 M	—	35.00	60.00	110	175	—
1752 M	—	35.00	60.00	110	175	—

Date	Mintage	VG	F	VF	XF	Unc
1753/2 M	—	35.00	60.00	110	175	—
1753 M	—	35.00	60.00	110	175	—
1754 M	—	35.00	60.00	110	175	—
1755/4 M	—	35.00	60.00	110	175	—
1755 M	—	35.00	60.00	110	175	—
1756/55 M	—	35.00	60.00	110	175	—
1756 M	—	35.00	60.00	110	175	—
1757/6 M	—	35.00	60.00	110	175	—
1757 M	—	35.00	60.00	110	175	—

KM# 86.2   2 REALES
6.7668 g., 0.9170 Silver 0.1995 oz. ASW   **Ruler:**
Ferdinand VI **Obv:** Royal and Imperial crowns **Note:** Mint
mark M, Mo.

Date	Mintage	VG	F	VF	XF	Unc
1757 M	—	35.00	60.00	110	175	—
1758 M	—	35.00	60.00	110	175	—
1759/8 M	—	35.00	60.00	110	175	—
1759 M	—	35.00	60.00	110	175	—
1760 M	—	35.00	60.00	110	175	—

KM# 87   2 REALES
6.7700 g., 0.9170 Silver 0.1996 oz. ASW   **Ruler:** Charles III
Obv: Crowned shield flanked by R 2 **Obv. Legend:** CAR • III
• D • G • HISP • ET IND • R **Rev:** Crowned globes flanked by
crowned pillars with banner, date below **Rev. Legend:** VTRA
QUE VNUM **Mint:** Mexico City **Note:** Mint mark M, Mo.

Date	Mintage	VG	F	VF	XF	Unc
1760 M	—	35.00	60.00	110	175	—
1761 M	—	35.00	60.00	110	175	—
1762/1 M	—	35.00	60.00	110	175	—
1762 M	—	35.00	60.00	110	175	—
1763/2 M	—	35.00	60.00	110	175	—
1763 M	—	35.00	60.00	110	175	—
1764 M	—	35.00	60.00	110	175	—
1765 M	—	35.00	60.00	110	175	—
1766 M	—	35.00	60.00	110	175	—
1767 M	—	35.00	60.00	110	175	—
1768/6 M	—	35.00	60.00	110	175	—
1768 M	—	35.00	60.00	110	175	—
1769 M	—	35.00	60.00	110	175	—
1770 M	—	350	550	—	—	—
1770 F Rare	—	—	—	—	—	—
1771 F	—	35.00	60.00	110	175	—

KM# 88.1   2 REALES
6.7668 g., 0.9030 Silver 0.1964 oz. ASW   **Ruler:** Charles III
Obv: Armored bust of Charles III, right **Obv. Legend:**
CAROLUS • III • DEI • GRATIA **Rev:** Inverted FM and mint
mark **Note:** Mint mark M, Mo.

Date	Mintage	VG	F	VF	XF	Unc
1772 FM	—	30.00	50.00	100	150	—
1773 FM	—	30.00	50.00	100	150	—

KM# 88.2 2 REALES
6.7700 g., 0.9030 Silver 0.1965 oz. ASW **Ruler:** Charles III
Obv: Armored bust od Charles III, right **Obv. Legend:**
CAROLUS • III • DEI • GRATIA • **Rev:** Crowned shield flanked
by pillars with banner, normal initials and mint mark **Rev.**
Legend: • HISPAN • ET IND • REX • ... **Mint:** Mexico City
Note: Mint mark M, Mo.

Date	Mintage	VG	F	VF	XF	Unc
1773 FM	—	25.00	40.00	80.00	125	—
1774 FM	—	25.00	40.00	80.00	125	—
1775 FM	—	25.00	40.00	80.00	125	—
1776 FM	—	25.00	40.00	80.00	125	—
1777 FM	—	25.00	40.00	80.00	125	—
1778/7 FF	—	25.00	40.00	80.00	125	—
1778 F F/M	—	25.00	40.00	80.00	125	—
1778 FF	—	25.00	40.00	80.00	125	—
1779/8 FF	—	25.00	40.00	80.00	125	—
1779 FF	—	25.00	40.00	80.00	125	—
1780 FF	—	25.00	40.00	80.00	125	—
1781 FF	—	25.00	40.00	80.00	125	—
1782/1 FF	—	25.00	40.00	80.00	125	—
1782 FF	—	25.00	40.00	80.00	125	—
1783 FF	—	25.00	40.00	80.00	125	—
1784 FF	—	25.00	40.00	80.00	125	—
1784 FF DEI GRTIA (error)	—	100	150	250	600	—
1784 FM	—	70.00	120	225	575	—

KM# 88.2a 2 REALES
6.7668 g., 0.8960 Silver 0.1949 oz. ASW **Ruler:** Charles III
Obv: Armored bust of Charles III, right **Rev:** Crowned shield
flanked by pillars with banner **Mint:** Mexico City **Note:** Mint
mark Mo.

Date	Mintage	VG	F	VF	XF	Unc
1785Mo FM	—	25.00	40.00	80.00	125	—
1786Mo FF	—	200	350	550	950	—
1786Mo FM	—	25.00	40.00	80.00	125	—
1787Mo FM	—	25.00	40.00	80.00	125	—
1788/98Mo FM	—	25.00	40.00	80.00	125	—
1788Mo FM	—	25.00	40.00	80.00	125	—
1789Mo FM	—	25.00	40.00	50.00	150	—

KM# 89 2 REALES
6.7700 g., 0.9030 Silver 0.1965 oz. ASW **Ruler:** Charles IV
Obv: Armored bust of Charles IV, right **Obv. Legend:**
CAROLUS • IV • DEI • GRATIA • **Rev:** Crowned shield flanked
by pillars with banner **Rev. Legend:** • HISPAN • ET IND •
REX • ... **Mint:** Mexico City **Note:** Mint mark M, Mo.

Date	Mintage	VG	F	VF	XF	Unc
1789 FM	—	25.00	40.00	75.00	200	—
1790 FM	—	25.00	40.00	75.00	200	—

KM# 90 2 REALES
6.7700 g., 0.9030 Silver 0.1965 oz. ASW **Ruler:** Charles IV
Obv: Armored bust of Charles IIII, right **Obv. Legend:**
CAROLUS • IIII • DEI • GRATIA • **Rev:** Crowned shield flanked
by pillars with banner **Rev. Legend:** • HISPAN • ET IND REX
• ... **Mint:** Mexico City **Note:** Mint mark M, Mo.

Date	Mintage	VG	F	VF	XF	Unc
1790 FM	—	25.00	40.00	80.00	200	—

KM# 91 2 REALES
6.7668 g., 0.8960 Silver 0.1949 oz. ASW **Ruler:** Charles IV
Obv: Armored bust of Charles IIII, right **Obv. Legend:**
CAROLUS • IIII • DEI • GRATIA • **Rev:** Crowned shield flanked
by pillars with banner **Rev. Legend:** • HISPAN • ET IND REX
• ... **Mint:** Mexico City **Note:** Mint mark Mo.

Date	Mintage	VG	F	VF	XF	Unc
1792 FM	—	20.00	35.00	60.00	200	—
1793 FM	—	20.00	35.00	60.00	200	—
1794/3 FM	—	50.00	100	200	450	—
1794 FM	—	40.00	75.00	150	400	—
1795 FM	—	20.00	35.00	70.00	100	—
1796 FM	—	20.00	35.00	70.00	100	—
1797 FM	—	20.00	35.00	70.00	100	—
1798 FM	—	20.00	35.00	70.00	100	—
1799/8 FM	—	20.00	35.00	70.00	100	—
1799 FM	—	20.00	35.00	70.00	100	—
1800 FM	—	20.00	35.00	70.00	100	—
1801 FT/M	—	7.00	15.00	30.00	85.00	—
1801 FT	—	7.00	15.00	30.00	85.00	—
1801 FM	—	20.00	40.00	75.00	250	—
1802 FT	—	7.00	15.00	30.00	85.00	—
1803 FT	—	7.00	15.00	30.00	85.00	—
1804/3 TH	—	7.00	15.00	30.00	85.00	—
1804 TH	—	7.00	15.00	30.00	85.00	—
1805 TH	—	7.00	15.00	30.00	85.00	—
1806/5 TH	—	7.00	15.00	32.00	90.00	—
1806 TH	—	7.00	15.00	30.00	85.00	—
1807/5 TH	—	7.00	15.00	32.00	90.00	—
1807/6 TH	—	15.00	30.00	60.00	200	—
1807 TH	—	7.00	15.00	30.00	85.00	—
1808/7 TH	—	7.00	15.00	32.00	90.00	—
1808 TH	—	7.00	15.00	30.00	85.00	—

KM# 92 2 REALES
6.7700 g., 0.9030 Silver 0.1965 oz. ASW **Ruler:**
Ferdinand VII **Obv:** Armored laureate bust right **Obv.**
Legend: FERDIN.VII... **Rev:** Crowned shield flanked by

pillars **Rev. Legend:** IND.REX... **Mint:** Mexico City **Note:** Mint mark Mo.

Date	Mintage	VG	F	VF	XF	Unc
1809 TH	—	15.00	30.00	75.00	200	—
181/00 TH	—	15.00	30.00	75.00	200	—
181/00 HJ	—	15.00	30.00	75.00	200	—
181/00 HJ/TH	—	15.00	30.00	75.00	200	—
1810 TH	—	15.00	30.00	75.00	200	—
1810 HJ	—	15.00	30.00	75.00	200	—
1811 TH	—	150	250	350	750	—
1811/0 HJ/TH	—	40.00	80.00	150	300	—
1811 HJ	—	15.00	30.00	75.00	200	—
1811 HJ/TH	—	40.00	80.00	150	300	—

KM# 93   2 REALES
6.7700 g., 0.9030 Silver 0.1965 oz. ASW   **Ruler:**
Ferdinand VII **Obv:** Draped laureate bust right **Obv. Legend:**
FERDIN.VII... **Rev:** Crowned shield flanked by pillars **Rev.**
Legend: IND.REX... **Mint:** Mexico City **Note:** Mint mark Mo.

Date	Mintage	VG	F	VF	XF	Unc
1812 TH	—	60.00	125	250	550	—
1812 HJ	—	40.00	100	200	500	—
1812 JJ	—	10.00	20.00	60.00	200	—
1813 TH	—	15.00	30.00	100	400	—
1813 JJ	—	20.00	60.00	125	350	—
1813 HJ	—	40.00	100	200	500	—
1814/2 JJ	—	15.00	30.00	100	400	—
1814/3 JJ	—	15.00	30.00	100	400	—
1814 JJ	—	15.00	30.00	100	400	—
1815 JJ	—	6.00	12.00	28.00	85.00	—
1816 JJ	—	6.00	12.00	28.00	85.00	—
1817 JJ	—	6.00	12.00	28.00	85.00	—
1818 JJ	—	6.00	12.00	28.00	85.00	—
1819/8 JJ	—	5.50	12.00	30.00	85.00	—
1819 JJ	—	6.00	12.00	28.00	85.00	—
1820 JJ	—	175	—	—	—	—
1821/0 JJ	—	7.00	15.00	30.00	90.00	—
1821 JJ	—	6.00	12.00	28.00	85.00	—

KM# 94   4 REALES
13.5337 g., 0.9170 Silver 0.3990 oz. ASW   **Ruler:** Philip V
Obv: Crowned shield flanked by F 4 **Obv. Legend:** PHILLIP
• V • D • G • HISPAN • ET IND • REX **Rev:** Crowned globes
flanked by crowned pillars with banner, date below **Rev.**
Legend: VTRAQUE VNUM **Mint:** Mexico City **Note:** Mint
mark M, Mo, MX.

Date	Mintage	VG	F	VF	XF	Unc
1732 Rare; Specimen	—	—	—	—	—	—
1732 F	—	2,000	3,000	5,000	10,000	—
1733/2 F	—	1,500	2,000	4,000	6,500	—
1733 MF	—	1,100	1,650	2,250	4,250	—
1733 MF (MX)	—	1,500	2,200	3,250	5,500	—
1733 MX/XM	—	1,500	2,200	3,250	5,500	—
1734/3 MF	—	150	300	600	1,200	—
1734 MF	—	150	300	600	1,200	—
1735/4 MF	—	125	200	300	600	—

Date	Mintage	VG	F	VF	XF	Unc
1735 MF	—	125	200	300	600	—
1736 MF	—	125	200	300	600	—
1737 MF	—	125	200	300	600	—
1738/7 MF	—	125	200	300	600	—
1738 MF	—	125	200	300	600	—
1739 MF	—	125	200	300	600	—
1740/30 MF	—	125	200	325	625	—
1740 MF	—	125	200	300	600	—
1741 MF	—	125	200	300	600	—
1742/1 MF	—	125	200	300	600	—
1742/32 MF	—	125	200	300	600	—
1742 MF	—	110	185	300	600	—
1743 MF	—	110	185	300	600	—
1744/3 MF	—	125	200	325	625	—
1744 MF	—	110	185	300	600	—
1745 MF	—	110	185	300	600	—
1746 MF	—	110	185	300	600	—
1747 MF	—	150	275	400	650	—

KM# 95   4 REALES
13.5400 g., 0.9170 Silver 0.3992 oz. ASW   **Ruler:**
Ferdinand VI **Obv:** Crowned shield flanked by M F 4 **Obv.**
Legend: FERDND • VI • D • G • HISPAN • ET IND • REX
Rev: Crowned globes flanked by crowned pillars with banner,
date below **Rev. Legend:** ...QUE VNUM **Mint:** Mexico City
Note: Struck at Mexico City Mint, mint mark M, Mo.

Date	Mintage	VG	F	VF	XF	Unc
1747 MF	—	125	175	300	550	—
1748/7 MF	—	125	175	300	550	—
1748 MF	—	125	175	250	500	—
1749 MF	—	150	225	350	650	—
1750/40 MF	—	125	175	250	500	—
1751/41 MF	—	125	175	250	500	—
1751 MF	—	125	175	250	500	—
1752 MF	—	125	175	250	500	—
1753 MF	—	125	175	300	550	—
1754 MF	—	250	375	500	850	—
1755 MM	—	125	175	300	550	—
1756 MM	—	125	175	300	550	—
1757 MM	—	125	175	300	550	—
1758 MM	—	125	175	250	500	—
1759 MM	—	125	175	250	500	—
1760/59 MM	—	125	175	350	600	—
1760 MM	—	125	175	350	600	—

KM# 96   4 REALES
13.5400 g., 0.9170 Silver 0.3992 oz. ASW   **Ruler:** Charles III
Obv: Crowned shield flanked by F M 4 **Obv. Legend:**
CAROLVS • III • D • G • HISPAN • ET IND • REX **Rev:** Crowned
globes flanked by crowned pillars with banner, date below
Rev. Legend: ...AQUE VNUM **Mint:** Mexico City **Note:** Mint
mark M, Mo.

Date	Mintage	VG	F	VF	XF	Unc
1760 MM	—	125	175	250	900	—
1761 MM	—	125	175	250	900	—

Date	Mintage	VG	F	VF	XF	Unc
1761 MM Cross between H and I	—	125	175	250	900	—
1762 MM	—	125	175	250	500	—
1763/1 MM	—	125	175	300	600	—
1763 MM	—	125	175	300	600	—
1764 MM	—	400	600	1,000	2,000	—
1764 MF	—	350	500	1,000	2,000	—
1765 MF	—	350	500	1,000	2,000	—
1766 MF	—	250	350	550	1,250	—
1767 MF	—	125	175	300	600	—
1768 MF	—	125	175	250	500	—
1769 MF	—	125	175	250	500	—
1770 MF	—	125	175	250	500	—
1771 MF	—	125	200	325	700	—

KM# 97.1   4 REALES
13.5337 g., 0.9030 Silver 0.3929 oz. ASW **Ruler:** Charles III **Obv:** Armored bust of Charles III, right **Obv. Legend:** CAROLUS • III • DEI • GRATIA • **Rev:** Crowned shield flanked by pillars with banner, inverted FM and mint mark **Rev. Legend:** • HISPAN • ET IND REX • ... **Mint:** Mexico City **Note:** Mint mark M, Mo.

Date	Mintage	VG	F	VF	XF	Unc
1772 FM	—	100	125	250	500	—
1773 FM	—	100	175	300	650	—

KM# 97.2   4 REALES
13.5400 g., 0.9030 Silver 0.3931 oz. ASW **Ruler:** Charles III **Obv:** Armored bust of Charles III, right **Obv. Legend:** CAROLUS • III • DEI • GRATIA • **Rev:** Crowned shield flanked by pillars with banner, normal initials and mint mark **Rev. Legend:** • HISPAN • ET IND REX • ... **Mint:** Mexico City **Note:** Mint mark M, Mo.

Date	Mintage	VG	F	VF	XF	Unc
1774 FM	—	70.00	100	200	500	—
1775 FM	—	70.00	100	200	500	—
1776 FM	—	70.00	100	200	500	—
1777 FM	—	70.00	100	200	500	—
1778 FF	—	70.00	100	200	500	—
1779 FF	—	70.00	100	200	500	—
1780 FF	—	70.00	100	200	500	—
1781 FF	—	70.00	100	200	500	—
1782 FF	—	70.00	100	200	500	—
1783 FF	—	70.00	100	200	500	—
1784 FF	—	70.00	100	200	500	—
1784 FM	—	100	200	350	600	—

KM# 97.2a   4 REALES
13.5337 g., 0.8960 Silver 0.3898 oz. ASW **Ruler:** Charles III **Obv:** Armored bust of Charles III, right **Obv. Legend:** CAROLUS • III • DEI • GRATIA • **Rev:** Crowned shield flanked by pillars with banner, normal initials and mint mark **Rev. Legend:** • HISPAN • ET IND REX • ... **Note:** Mint mark M, Mo.

Date	Mintage	VG	F	VF	XF	Unc
1785 FM	—	100	200	350	600	—
1786 FM	—	70.00	100	200	500	—
1787 FM	—	70.00	100	200	500	—
1788 FM	—	70.00	100	200	500	—
1789 FM	—	70.00	100	200	500	—

KM# 98   4 REALES
13.5400 g., 0.9030 Silver 0.3931 oz. ASW **Ruler:** Charles IV **Obv:** Armored bust of Charles III, right **Obv. Legend:** CAROLUS • IV • DEI • GRATIA • **Rev:** Crowned shield flanked by pillars with banner **Rev. Legend:** • HISPAN • ET IND REX • ... **Mint:** Mexico City **Note:** Mintint mark M, Mo, using old bust punch.

Date	Mintage	VG	F	VF	XF	Unc
1789 FM	—	75.00	125	250	550	—
1790 FM	—	70.00	100	200	500	—

KM# 99   4 REALES
13.5400 g., 0.9030 Silver 0.3931 oz. ASW **Ruler:** Charles IV **Obv:** Armored bust of Charles III, right **Obv. Legend:** CAROLUS • IIII • DEI • GRATIA • **Rev:** Crowned shield flanked by pillars with banner **Rev. Legend:** • HISPAN • ET IND • REX • ... **Mint:** Mexico City **Note:** Mint mark M, Mo, using old bust punch.

Date	Mintage	VG	F	VF	XF	Unc
1790 FM	—	75.00	125	250	550	—

KM# 100   4 REALES
13.5337 g., 0.8960 Silver 0.3898 oz. ASW **Ruler:** Charles IV **Obv:** Armored bust of Charles IIII, right **Obv. Legend:** CAROLUS • IIII • DEI • GRATIA • **Rev:** Crowned shield flanked by pillars with banner **Rev. Legend:** • HISPAN • ET IND • REX • ... **Mint:** Mexico City **Note:** Mint mark Mo.

Date	Mintage	VG	F	VF	XF	Unc
1792 FM	—	60.00	85.00	150	400	—
1793 FM	—	75.00	125	200	500	—
1794/3 FM	—	60.00	85.00	150	400	—
1794 FM	—	60.00	85.00	150	400	—
1795 FM	—	60.00	85.00	150	400	—

Date	Mintage	VG	F	VF	XF	Unc
1796 FM	—	150	250	400	800	—
1797 FM	—	70.00	120	200	500	—
1798/7 FM	—	60.00	85.00	150	400	—
1798 FM	—	60.00	85.00	150	400	—
1799 FM	—	60.00	85.00	150	400	—
1800 FM	—	60.00	85.00	150	400	—
1801 FM	—	35.00	65.00	150	425	—
1801 FT	—	60.00	120	200	525	—
1802 FT	—	200	300	500	1,000	—
1803 FT	—	75.00	135	225	575	—
1803 FM	—	200	300	500	1,000	—
1804 TH	—	40.00	75.00	175	475	—
1805 TH	—	35.00	65.00	150	425	—
1806 TH	—	35.00	65.00	150	425	—
1807 TH	—	35.00	65.00	150	425	—
1808/7 TH	—	40.00	75.00	175	475	—
1808 TH	—	40.00	75.00	175	475	—

KM# 103   8 REALES
27.0674 g., 0.9170 Silver 0.7980 oz. ASW   **Ruler:** Philip V
Obv: Crowned shield flanked by M F 8 **Obv. Legend:** PHILIP
• V • D • G • HISPAN • ET IND • REX **Rev:** Crowned globes
flanked by crowned pillars with banner, date below **Rev.**
Legend: ...VNUM **Mint:** Mexico City **Note:** Mint mark M, Mo,
MX.

Date	Mintage	VG	F	VF	XF	Unc
1732 F	—	2,750	4,750	8,000	15,000	—
1733/2 F (MX)	—	3,000	5,250	9,000	—	—
1733 F	—	2,000	3,000	5,000	9,000	—
1733 MF Large crown; Rare	—	—	—	—	—	—
1733 F (MX) Rare	—	—	—	—	—	—

Note: Bonhams Patterson sale 7-96 VF 1733 F (MX) realized $11,710

Date	Mintage	VG	F	VF	XF	Unc
1733 MF (MX) Rare	—	—	—	—	—	—
1733 MF Small crown	—	700	1,500	2,250	3,500	—
1734/3 MF	—	125	175	275	575	—
1734 MF	—	125	175	250	450	—
1735 MF	—	125	175	250	450	—
1736/5 MF	—	125	175	275	575	—
1736 MF	—	125	175	250	450	—
1736 MF Small planchet	—	125	175	250	450	—
1737 MF	—	100	150	250	400	—
1738/6 MF	—	100	150	250	400	—
1738/7 MF	—	100	150	250	400	—
1738 MF	—	100	150	250	400	—
1739 MF	—	100	150	250	400	—
1739/6 MF 9 over inverted 6	—	100	150	250	400	—
1740/30 MF	—	100	150	275	500	—
1740/39 MF	—	100	150	275	500	—
1740 MF	—	100	150	250	400	—
1741/31 MF	—	100	150	250	400	—
1741 MF	—	100	150	250	400	—
1742/32 MF	—	100	150	250	500	—
1742/1 MF	—	100	150	250	400	—
1742 MF	—	100	150	250	400	—
1743/2 MF	—	100	150	250	400	—
1743 MF	—	100	150	250	400	—
1744/34 MF	—	100	150	250	400	—
1744/3 MF	—	100	150	250	400	—
1744 MF	—	100	150	250	400	—
1745/4 MF	—	100	150	250	425	—
1745 MF	—	100	150	250	400	—
1746/5 MF	—	100	150	275	575	—
1746 MF	—	100	150	250	400	—
1747 MF	—	100	150	250	400	—

KM# 101   4 REALES
13.5400 g., 0.9030 Silver 0.3931 oz. ASW   **Ruler:**
Ferdinand VII **Obv:** Armored laureate bust right **Obv.**
Legend: FERDIN.VII... **Rev:** Crowned shield flanked by
pillars **Rev. Legend:** IND.REX... **Mint:** Mexico City **Note:** Mint
mark Mo.

Date	Mintage	VG	F	VF	XF	Unc
1809 HJ	—	75.00	135	250	750	—
1810 HJ	—	75.00	135	250	750	—
1811 HJ	—	75.00	135	250	750	—
1812 HJ	—	400	650	900	1,850	—

KM# 102   4 REALES
13.5400 g., 0.9030 Silver 0.3931 oz. ASW   **Ruler:**
Ferdinand VII **Obv:** Draped laureate bust right **Obv. Legend:**
FERDIN.VII... **Rev:** Crowned shield flanked by pillars **Rev.**
Legend: IND.REX... **Mint:** Mexico City **Note:** Mint mark Mo.

Date	Mintage	VG	F	VF	XF	Unc
1816 JJ	—	150	200	325	700	—
1817 JJ	—	250	400	500	1,000	—
1818/7 JJ	—	250	400	500	1,000	—
1819 JJ	—	175	250	325	700	—
1820 JJ	—	175	250	325	700	—
1821 JJ	—	75.00	135	250	650	—

KM# 104.1 8 REALES
27.0674 g., 0.9170 Silver 0.7980 oz. ASW **Ruler:**
Ferdinand VI **Obv:** Crowned shield flaned by M F 8 **Obv.**
Legend: FERDND • VI • D • G • HISPAN • ET IND • REX
Rev: Crowned globes flanked by crowned pillars with banner,
date below **Rev. Legend:** ...VNUM M **Mint:** Mexico City **Note:**
Mint mark M, Mo.

Date	Mintage	VG	F	VF	XF	Unc
1747 MF	—	100	140	200	300	—
1748/7 MF	—	100	140	200	450	—
1748 MF	—	100	140	200	300	—
1749 MF	—	100	140	200	300	—
1749/8 MF	—	100	140	200	300	—
1750 MF	—	100	140	200	300	—
1751/0 MF	—	100	140	200	300	—
1751 MF	—	100	140	200	300	—
1752/1 MF	—	100	140	200	300	—
1752 MF	—	100	140	200	300	—
1753/2 MF	—	100	140	200	300	—
1753 MF	—	100	140	200	300	—
1754/3 MF	—	100	140	200	325	—
1754 MF	—	100	140	200	300	—
1754 MM/MF	—	300	700	1,500	3,500	—
1754 MM	—	300	700	1,500	3,500	—

KM# 104.2 8 REALES
27.0674 g., 0.9170 Silver 0.7980 oz. ASW **Ruler:**
Ferdinand VI **Obv:** Crowned shield flanked by M M 8 **Obv.**
Legend: FERDND • VI • D • G • HISPAN • ET IND • REX
Rev: Imperial crown on left pillar **Rev. Legend:** ...VNUM M
Mint: Mexico City **Note:** Mint mark M, Mo.

Date	Mintage	VG	F	VF	XF	Unc
1754 MM	—	100	140	200	375	—
1754 MM/MF	—	100	140	250	500	—
1754 MF	—	150	285	550	950	—
1755/4 MM	—	100	140	200	325	—
1755 MM	—	100	140	200	300	—
1756/5 MM	—	100	140	200	300	—
1756 MM	—	100	140	200	300	—
1757/6 MM	—	100	140	200	300	—
1757 MM	—	100	140	200	325	—
1758 MM	—	100	140	200	300	—
1759 MM	—	100	140	200	300	—
1760/59 MM	—	100	140	200	300	—
1760 MM	—	100	140	200	300	—

KM# 105 8 REALES
27.0674 g., 0.9170 Silver 0.7980 oz. ASW **Ruler:** Charles III
Obv: Crowned shield flanked by M M 8 **Obv. Legend:**
CAROLUS • III • D • G • HISPAN • ET IND • REX **Rev:** Crowned
globes flanked by crowned pillars with banner, date below
Rev. Legend: ...E VNUM M **Mint:** Mexico City **Note:** Mint
mark M, Mo.

Date	Mintage	VG	F	VF	XF	Unc
1760/59 MM	—	450	700	—	—	—
Note: CAROLUS. III/Ferdin. Vi						
1760 MM	—	100	140	200	325	—
Note: CAROLUS. III/FERDIN. VI. recut die						
1760 MM	—	100	140	200	300	—
1761/50 MM	—	100	140	200	325	—
Note: Tip of cross between I and S in legend						
1761/51 MM	—	100	140	200	325	—
Note: Tip of cross between I and S in legend						
1761/0 MM	—	100	140	200	325	—
Note: Tip of cross between H and I in legend						
1761 MM	—	100	140	200	275	—
Note: Cross under I in legend						
1761 MM	—	100	140	200	275	—
Note: Tip of cross between H and I in legend						
1761 MM	—	100	140	200	325	—
Note: Tip of cross between I and S in legend						
1762/1 MM	—	100	140	200	450	—
Note: Tip of cross between H and I in legend						
1762/1 MM	—	100	140	200	450	—
1762 MM	—	100	140	200	275	—
Note: Tip of cross between H and I in legend						
1762 MM	—	100	140	200	250	—
Note: Tip of cross between I and S in legend						
1762 MF	—	500	750	1,250	2,300	—
1763/2 MM	—	300	450	750	1,350	—
1763 MM	—	450	650	1,150	2,250	—
1763/1 MF	—	100	140	200	250	—
1763/2 MF	—	100	140	200	250	—
1763 MF	—	100	140	200	250	—
1764 MF	—	100	140	200	275	—
Note: CAR/CRA						
1764 MF	—	100	140	200	250	—

Date	Mintage	VG	F	VF	XF	Unc
1765 MF	—	100	140	200	250	—
1766/5 MF	—	100	150	200	575	—
1766 MF	—	100	140	200	250	—
1767/6 MF	—	100	140	200	250	—
1767 MF	—	100	140	200	250	—
1768/7 MF	—	100	165	250	600	—
1768 MF	—	100	140	200	250	—
1769 MF	—	100	140	200	250	—
1770/60 MF	—	100	185	300	650	—
1770 MF	—	100	140	200	250	—
1770/60 FM	—	100	185	300	650	—
1770/69 FM	—	100	185	300	650	—
1770 FM/F	—	100	40.00	200	250	—
1770 FM	—	100	140	200	250	—
1771/0 FM	—	100	140	200	250	—
1771 FM	—	100	140	200	250	—

KM# 106.1   8 REALES
27.0674 g., 0.9030 Silver 0.7858 oz. ASW **Ruler:** Charles III
Obv: Armored bust of Charles III, right **Obv. Legend:**
CAROLUS • III • DEI • GRATIA • **Rev:** Crowned shield flanked
by pillars with banner, Assayer initials and mint mark inverted
from remainder of legend **Rev. Legend:** • HISPAN • ET IND
• REX • ... **Mint:** Mexico City **Note:** Mint mark M, Mo. Mintmark
and assayer initials bottom facing rim.

Date	Mintage	VG	F	VF	XF	Unc
1772 FM	—	100	150	225	350	—
1772 MF	—	150	350	750	1,250	—
1773 FM	—	75.00	100	160	240	—

KM# 106.2   8 REALES
27.0674 g., 0.9030 Silver 0.7858 oz. ASW **Ruler:** Charles III
Obv: Armored bust of Charles III, right **Obv. Legend:**
CAROLUS • III • DEI • GRATIA • **Rev:** Crowned shield flanked
by pillars with banner, normal initials and mint mark **Rev.**
Legend: • HISPAN • ET IND • REX • ... **Note:** Mint mark M, Mo.

Date	Mintage	VG	F	VF	XF	Unc
1773 FM	—	75.00	100	150	225	—
1774 FM	—	75.00	100	150	225	—
1775 FM	—	75.00	100	150	225	—
1776 FM	—	100	150	225	350	—
1776 FF	—	75.00	100	150	225	—
1777/6 FM	—	75.00	100	150	225	—
1777 FM	—	75.00	100	150	225	—
1777 FF	—	75.00	100	150	225	—
1778 FM	—	—	—	—	—	—

Note: Superior Casterline sale 5-89 VF realized $17,600

Date	Mintage	VG	F	VF	XF	Unc
1778/7 FF	—	75.00	100	150	225	—
1778 FF	—	75.00	100	150	225	—
1779 FF	—	75.00	100	150	225	—
1780 FF	—	75.00	100	150	225	—
1781 FF	—	75.00	100	150	225	—
1782 FF	—	75.00	100	150	225	—
1783 FF	—	75.00	100	150	225	—
1783 FM	—	4,000	6,000	9,000	—	—
1784 FF	—	150	300	500	1,250	—
1784 FM	—	75.00	100	150	225	—

KM# 106.2a   8 REALES
27.0674 g., 0.8960 Silver 0.7797 oz. ASW **Ruler:** Charles III
Obv: Armored bust of Charles III, right **Obv. Legend:**
CAROLUS • III • DEI • GRATIA • **Rev:** Crowned shield flanked
by pillars with banner, normal initials and mint mark **Rev.**
Legend: • HISPAN • ET IND • REX • ... **Note:** Mint mark M, Mo.

Date	Mintage	VG	F	VF	XF	Unc
1785 FM	—	75.00	100	140	200	—
1786/5 FM	—	75.00	100	200	400	—
1786 FM	—	75.00	100	140	200	—

Date	Mintage	VG	F	VF	XF	Unc
1787/6 FM	—	100	250	450	1,200	—
1787 FM	—	75.00	100	140	200	—
1788 FM	—	75.00	100	140	200	—
1789 FM	—	75.00	100	150	225	—

KM# 107 8 REALES
27.0674 g., 0.9030 Silver 0.7858 oz. ASW **Ruler:** Charles IV
Obv: Armored bust of Charles III, right **Obv. Legend:**
CAROLUS • IV • DEI • GRATIA • **Rev:** Crowned shield flanked
by pillars with banner **Rev. Legend:** • HISPAN • ET IND •
REX • ... **Mint:** Mexico City **Note:** Mint mark M, Mo, using old
bust punch.

Date	Mintage	VG	F	VF	XF	Unc
1789 FM	—	75.00	100	160	250	—
1790 FM	—	75.00	100	150	225	—

KM# 109 8 REALES
27.0674 g., 0.8960 Silver 0.7797 oz. ASW **Ruler:** Charles IV
Obv: Armored bust of Charles IIII, right **Obv. Inscription:**
CAROLUS • IIII • DEI • GRATIA • **Rev:** Crowned shield flanked
by pillars with banner **Rev. Legend:** • HISPAN • ET IND •
REX • ... **Mint:** Mexico City **Note:** Mint mark Mo.

Date	Mintage	VG	F	VF	XF	Unc
1791 FM	—	60.00	90.00	135	175	—
1792 FM	—	60.00	90.00	135	175	—
1793 FM	—	60.00	90.00	135	175	—
1794 FM	—	60.00	90.00	135	175	—
1795/4 FM	—	60.00	90.00	135	175	—
1795 FM	—	60.00	90.00	135	175	—
1796 FM	—	60.00	90.00	135	175	—
1797 FM	—	60.00	90.00	135	175	—
1798 FM	—	60.00	90.00	135	175	—
1799 FM	—	60.00	90.00	135	175	—
1800/700 FM	—	60.00	90.00	135	175	—
1800 FM	—	60.00	90.00	135	175	—
1801/0 FT/FM	—	60.00	90.00	135	175	—
1801/791 FM	—	38.50	65.00	110	275	—
1801/0 FM	—	38.50	65.00	110	275	—
1801 FM	—	22.50	44.00	110	275	—
1801 FT/M	—	38.50	65.00	110	275	—
1801 FT	—	22.50	38.50	55.00	115	—
1802/1 FT	—	38.50	65.00	110	275	—
1802 FT	—	22.50	38.50	55.00	115	—
1802 FT/M	—	22.50	38.50	55.00	115	—
1803 FT	—	22.50	38.50	55.00	125	—
1803 FT/M	—	22.50	38.50	55.00	115	—
1803 TH	—	85.00	165	275	500	—
1804 TH	—	22.50	38.50	55.00	115	—
Note: CARLUS (error)						
1804/3 TH	—	38.50	65.00	110	275	—
1805/4 TH	—	44.00	90.00	140	300	—
1805 TH	—	22.50	38.50	55.00	115	—
Note: Narrow date						
1805 TH	—	22.50	38.50	55.00	115	—
Note: Wide date						
1806 TH	—	22.50	38.50	55.00	115	—
1807/6 TH	—	165	275	375	775	—
1807 TH	—	22.50	38.50	55.00	115	—
1808/7 TH	—	22.50	38.50	55.00	115	—
1808 TH	—	22.50	38.50	55.00	115	—

KM# 108 8 REALES
27.0674 g., 0.9030 Silver 0.7858 oz. ASW **Ruler:** Charles IV
Obv: Armored bust of Charles III, right **Obv. Legend:**
CAROLUS • IIII • DEI • GRATIA • **Rev:** Crowned shield flanked
by pillars with banner **Rev. Legend:** • HISPAN • ET IND •
REX • ... **Mint:** Mexico City **Note:** Mint mark M, Mo, using old
portrait punch.

Date	Mintage	VG	F	VF	XF	Unc
1790 FM	—	75.00	100	150	225	—

KM# 110   8 REALES
27.0674 g., 0.8960 Silver 0.7797 oz. ASW **Ruler:**
Ferdinand VII **Obv:** Armored laureate bust right **Obv.**
Legend: FERDIN • VII... **Rev:** Crowned shield flanked by
pillars **Rev. Legend:** IND • REX... **Mint:** Mexico City **Note:**
Mint mark Mo.

Date	Mintage	VG	F	VF	XF	Unc
1808 TH	—	27.50	44.00	85.00	165	—
1809/8 TH	—	27.50	44.00	85.00	165	—
1809 TH	—	22.50	38.50	60.00	140	—
1809 HJ	—	27.50	44.00	85.00	165	—
1809 HJ/TH	—	22.50	38.50	60.00	140	—
1810/09 HJ	—	27.50	44.00	85.00	165	—
1810 TH	—	85.00	165	325	675	—
1810 HJ/TH	—	27.50	44.00	85.00	165	—
1810 HJ	—	27.50	44.00	85.00	165	—
1811/0 HJ	—	22.50	38.50	60.00	140	—
1811 HJ	—	22.50	38.50	60.00	140	—
1811 HJ/TH	—	22.50	38.50	55.00	115	—

KM# 111   8 REALES
27.0700 g., 0.9030 Silver 0.7859 oz. ASW **Ruler:**
Ferdinand VII **Obv:** Draped laureate bust right **Obv. Legend:**
FERDIN • VII... **Rev:** Crowned shield flanked by pillars **Rev.**
Legend: IND • REX... **Mint:** Mexico City **Note:** Mint mark Mo.

Date	Mintage	VG	F	VF	XF	Unc
1811 HJ	—	22.50	44.00	65.00	145	—
1812 HJ	—	55.00	85.00	140	290	—
1812 JJ/HJ	—	22.50	38.50	55.00	115	—
1812 JJ	—	22.50	38.50	55.00	115	—
1813 HJ	—	55.00	85.00	140	290	—
1813 JJ	—	22.50	38.50	55.00	115	—
1814/3 HJ	—	1,300	2,750	5,500	—	—
1814/3 JJ	—	22.50	38.50	55.00	115	—
1814 JJ	—	22.50	38.50	55.00	115	—
1815/4 JJ	—	22.50	38.50	55.00	115	—
1815 JJ	—	22.50	38.50	55.00	115	—
1816/5 JJ	—	22.50	38.50	55.00	105	—
1816 JJ	—	22.50	38.50	55.00	105	—
1817 JJ	—	22.50	38.50	55.00	105	—
1818 JJ	—	22.50	38.50	55.00	105	—
1819 JJ	—	22.50	38.50	55.00	105	—
1820 JJ	—	22.50	38.50	55.00	105	—
1821 JJ	—	22.50	38.50	55.00	105	—

KM# 112   1/2 ESCUDO
1.6917 g., 0.8750 Gold 0.0476 oz. AGW **Ruler:**
Ferdinand VII **Obv:** Laureate head right **Obv. Legend:** FERD
• VII • D • G • HISP • ET IND **Rev:** Crowned oval shield **Mint:**
Mexico City **Note:** Mint mark Mo.

Date	Mintage	VG	F	VF	XF	Unc
1814 JJ	—	100	150	225	375	525
1815/4 JJ	—	150	200	250	400	875
1815 JJ	—	150	200	250	400	—
1816 JJ	—	100	150	225	375	—
1817 JJ	—	150	200	250	400	—
1818 JJ	—	150	200	250	400	—
1819 JJ	—	150	200	250	400	—
1820 JJ	—	200	300	400	550	—

KM# 113   ESCUDO
3.3834 g., 0.9170 Gold 0.0997 oz. AGW **Ruler:** Philip V **Obv:**
Armored bust right **Obv. Legend:** PHILIP • V • D • G • HISPAN
• ET IND • REX **Rev:** Crowned shield flanked by M F I **Mint:**
Mexico City

Date	Mintage	VG	F	VF	XF	Unc
1732 F	—	1,000	2,000	3,000	4,000	—
1733/2 F	—	1,000	2,000	3,000	4,000	—
1734/3 MF	—	200	300	400	850	—
1735/4 MF	—	200	300	400	850	—
1735 MF	—	200	300	400	850	—
1736/5 MF	—	200	300	400	850	—
1736 MF	—	200	300	400	850	—
1737 MF	—	200	300	600	1,200	—
1738/7 MF	—	200	300	600	1,200	—
1738 MF	—	200	300	600	1,200	—
1739 MF	—	200	300	600	1,200	—
1740/30 MF	—	200	300	600	1,200	—
1741 MF	—	200	300	600	1,200	—
1742 MF	—	200	300	600	1,200	—
1743/2 MF	—	200	300	450	800	—
1743 MF	—	200	300	400	700	—
1744/3 MF	—	200	300	400	700	—
1744 MF	—	200	300	400	700	—
1745 MF	—	200	300	400	700	—
1746/5 MF	—	200	300	400	700	—
1747 MF Rare	—	—	—	—	—	—

KM# 114 ESCUDO
3.3834 g., 0.9170 Gold 0.0997 oz. AGW **Ruler:** Ferdinand VI
Obv: Armored bust right **Obv. Legend:** FERD • VI • D • G •
HISPAN • ET IND • REX **Rev:** Crowned shield flanked by M
F I **Mint:** Mexico City **Note:** Mint mark M, Mo.

Date	Mintage	VG	F	VF	XF	Unc
1747 MF	—	1,650	3,000	5,000	7,500	—

KM# 115.1 ESCUDO
3.3834 g., 0.9170 Gold 0.0997 oz. AGW **Ruler:** Ferdinand VI
Obv: Short armored bust right **Obv. Legend:** FERD • VI • D
• G • HISPAN • ET IND • REX **Rev:** Crowned shield **Mint:**
Mexico City **Note:** Mint mark M, Mo.

Date	Mintage	VG	F	VF	XF	Unc
1748 MF	—	250	350	550	950	—
1749 MF	—	300	450	700	1,150	—
1750 MF	—	200	300	400	800	—
1751 MF	—	200	300	400	800	—

KM# 115.2 ESCUDO
3.3834 g., 0.9170 Gold 0.0997 oz. AGW **Ruler:** Ferdinand VI
Obv: Short armored bust right **Obv. Legend:** FERD • VI • D
• G • HISPAN • ET IND • REX **Rev:** Without 1 S flanking
crowned shield **Mint:** Mexico City

Date	Mintage	VG	F	VF	XF	Unc
1752 MF	—	200	300	375	750	—
1753/2 MF	—	200	300	400	800	—
1753 MF	—	200	300	400	800	—
1754 MF	—	200	300	400	800	—
1755 MM	—	200	300	400	800	—
1756 MM	—	200	300	400	800	—

KM# A116 ESCUDO
3.3834 g., 0.9170 Gold 0.0997 oz. AGW **Ruler:** Ferdinand VI
Obv: Armored bust right **Obv. Legend:** FERDIND • VI • D •
G • HISPAN • ETIND • REX • **Rev:** Crowned shield **Rev.
Legend:** M • NOMINA MAGNA SEQUOR • M **Mint:** Mexico
City

Date	Mintage	VG	F	VF	XF	Unc
1757 MM	—	200	300	400	800	—
1759 MM	—	200	300	400	800	—

KM# 116 ESCUDO
3.3834 g., 0.9170 Gold 0.0997 oz. AGW **Ruler:** Charles III
Obv: Armored bust right **Obv. Legend:** CAROLVS • III • D •
G • HISPAN • ET IND • REX **Rev:** Crowned shield **Rev.
Legend:** M • NOMINA MAGNA SEQUOR • M • **Mint:** Mexico
City **Note:** Mint mark M, Mo.

Date	Mintage	VG	F	VF	XF	Unc
1760 MM	—	400	800	1,500	2,500	—
1761/0 MM	—	400	800	1,500	2,500	—
1761 MM	—	400	800	1,500	2,500	—

KM# 117 ESCUDO
3.3834 g., 0.9170 Gold 0.0997 oz. AGW **Ruler:** Charles III
Obv: Large armored bust right **Obv. Legend:** CAR • III • D •
G • HISP • ET IND • R **Rev:** Crowned shield **Rev. Legend:**
IN • UTROQ • FELIX • **Mint:** Mexico City **Note:** Mint mark M,
Mo.

Date	Mintage	VG	F	VF	XF	Unc
1762 MM	—	250	375	600	1,000	—
1763 MM	—	275	425	700	1,100	—
1764 MM	—	250	375	600	1,000	—
1765 MF	—	250	375	600	1,000	—
1766 MF	—	250	375	600	1,000	—
1767 MF	—	250	375	600	1,000	—
1768 MF	—	250	375	600	1,000	—
1769 MF	—	250	375	600	1,000	—
1770 MF	—	250	375	600	1,000	—
1771 MF	—	250	375	600	1,000	—

KM# 118.1 ESCUDO
3.3834 g., 0.9010 Gold 0.0980 oz. AGW **Ruler:** Charles III
Obv: Large armored bust right **Obv. Legend:** CAROL • III •
D • G • HISPAN • ET IND • R **Rev:** Crowned shield flanked
by 1 S within order chain **Rev. Legend:** FELIX • A • D • ...
Mint: Mexico City **Note:** Mint mark M, Mo.

Date	Mintage	VG	F	VF	XF	Unc
1772 MF	—	175	250	350	475	—
1772 FM	—	175	250	275	475	—
1773 FM	—	175	250	275	475	—

KM# 118.2 ESCUDO
3.3834 g., 0.9010 Gold 0.0980 oz. AGW **Ruler:** Charles III
Obv: Large armored bust right **Obv. Legend:** CAROL • III •
D • G • HISPAN • ET IND • R **Rev:** crowned shield in order
chain, initials and mint mark inverted **Rev. Legend:** FELIX •
A • D • ... **Mint:** Mexico City **Note:** Mint mark M, Mo.

Date	Mintage	VG	F	VF	XF	Unc
1773 FM	—	175	250	350	475	—
1774 FM	—	175	250	350	475	—
1775 FM	—	175	250	350	475	—
1776 FM	—	225	300	400	575	—
1777 FM	—	175	250	350	475	—
1778 FF	—	175	250	350	475	—
1779 FF	—	175	250	350	475	—
1780 FF	—	175	250	350	475	—
1781 FF	—	175	250	350	475	—
1782 FF	—	175	250	350	475	—
1783/2 FF	—	175	250	350	475	—
1783 FF	—	175	250	350	475	—
1784/3 FF	—	175	250	350	475	—
1784/3 FM/F	—	175	250	350	475	—

KM# 118.2a ESCUDO
3.3800 g., 0.8750 Gold 0.0951 oz. AGW **Ruler:** Charles III **Obv:** Large armored bust right **Obv. Legend:** CAROL • III • D • G • HISPAN • ET IND • R • **Rev:** Crowned shield in order chain, initials and mint mark inverted **Rev. Legend:** FELIX • A • D • ... **Mint:** Mexico City **Note:** Mint mark M, Mo.

Date	Mintage	VG	F	VF	XF	Unc
1785 FM	—	175	250	350	475	—
1786 FM	—	175	250	350	475	—
1787 FM	—	175	250	350	475	—
1788 FM	—	175	250	350	475	—

KM# 118.1a ESCUDO
3.3834 g., 0.8750 Gold 0.0952 oz. AGW **Ruler:** Charles III **Obv:** Large armored bust right **Obv. Legend:** CAROL • III • D • G • HISPAN • ET IND • R **Rev:** Crowned shield in order chain, initial letters and mint mark upright **Rev. Legend:** FELIX • A • D • ... **Mint:** Mexico City **Note:** Mint mark M, Mo.

Date	Mintage	VG	F	VF	XF	Unc
1788 FM	—	175	250	350	475	—

KM# 119 ESCUDO
3.3834 g., 0.8750 Gold 0.0952 oz. AGW **Ruler:** Charles IV **Obv:** Armored bust of Charles III, right **Obv. Legend:** CAROL • IV • D • G • ... **Rev:** Crowned shield in order chain, initial letters and mint mark upright **Rev. Legend:** FELIX • A • D • ... **Mint:** Mexico City **Note:** Mint mark M, Mo, using old portrait punch.

Date	Mintage	VG	F	VF	XF	Unc
1789 FM	—	300	550	1,000	2,000	—
1790 FM	—	300	550	1,000	2,000	—

KM# 120 ESCUDO
3.3834 g., 0.8750 Gold 0.0952 oz. AGW **Ruler:** Charles IV **Obv:** Armored bust right **Obv. Legend:** CAROL • IIII • D • G • ... **Rev:** Crowned shield in order chain, initial letters and mint mark upright **Rev. Legend:** FELIX • A • D • ... **Mint:** Mexico City **Note:** Mint mark Mo.

Date	Mintage	VG	F	VF	XF	Unc
1792 MF	—	150	225	300	375	—
1793 FM	—	150	225	300	375	—
1794 FM	—	150	225	300	375	—
1795 FM	—	150	225	300	375	—
1796 FM	—	150	225	300	375	—
1797 FM	—	150	225	300	375	—
1798 FM	—	150	225	300	375	—
1799 FM	—	150	225	300	375	—
1800 FM	—	150	225	300	375	—
1801 FM	—	125	165	235	345	—
1801 FT	—	125	165	235	345	650
1802 FT	—	125	165	235	345	—
1803 FT	—	125	165	235	345	—
1804/3 TH	—	125	165	235	345	750
1804 TH	—	125	165	235	345	—
1805 TH	—	125	165	235	345	—
1806/5 TH	—	125	165	235	345	—
1806 TH	—	125	165	235	345	—
1807 TH	—	125	165	235	345	—
1808 TH	—	125	165	235	345	—

KM# 121 ESCUDO
3.3834 g., 0.8750 Gold 0.0952 oz. AGW **Ruler:** Ferdinand VII **Obv:** Armored bust right **Obv. Legend:** FERDIN.VII... **Rev:** Crowned shield divides designed wreath **Rev. Legend:** FELIX. A. D, initial letters and mint mark upright **Mint:** Mexico City **Note:** Mint mark Mo.

Date	Mintage	VG	F	VF	XF	Unc
1809 HJ/TH	—	125	165	235	400	—
1809 HJ	—	125	165	235	400	1,150
1811/0 HJ	—	125	165	235	400	—
1812 HJ	—	150	250	300	500	—

KM# 122 ESCUDO
3.3834 g., 0.8750 Gold 0.0952 oz. AGW **Ruler:** Ferdinand VII **Obv:** Laureate head right **Obv. Legend:** FERDIN • VII • D • G... **Rev:** Crowned shield divides designed wreath, initial letters and mint mark upright **Rev. Legend:** FELIX • A • D... **Mint:** Mexico City **Note:** Mint mark Mo.

Date	Mintage	VG	F	VF	XF	Unc
1814 HJ	—	150	250	300	500	—
1815 HJ	—	150	250	300	500	—
1815 JJ	—	150	250	300	500	—
1816 JJ	—	175	275	325	550	—
1817 JJ	—	150	250	300	500	—
1818 JJ	—	150	250	300	500	—
1819 JJ	—	150	250	300	500	—
1820 JJ	—	150	250	300	500	—

KM# 124 2 ESCUDOS
6.7660 g., 0.9170 Gold 0.1995 oz. AGW **Ruler:** Philip V **Obv:** Armored bust right **Obv. Legend:** PHILIP • V • D • G • HISPAN • ET IND • REX **Rev:** Crowned shield flanked by M F 2 **Rev. Legend:** INITIUM SAPIENTIAE TIMOR DOMINI **Mint:** Mexico City

Date	Mintage	VG	F	VF	XF	Unc
1732 F	—	1,000	1,500	2,000	3,000	—
1733 F	—	750	1,000	1,500	2,500	—
1734/3 MF	—	400	500	900	1,400	—
1735 MF	—	400	500	900	1,400	—
1736/5 MF	—	400	500	900	1,400	—
1736 MF	—	400	500	900	1,400	—
1737 MF	—	400	500	900	1,400	—
1738/7 MF	—	400	500	900	1,400	—
1739 MF	—	400	500	900	1,400	—
1740/30 MF	—	400	500	900	1,400	—
1741 MF	—	400	500	900	1,400	—
1742 MF	—	400	500	900	1,400	—
1743 MF	—	400	500	900	1,400	—
1744/2 MF	—	400	500	900	1,400	—
1744 MF	—	400	500	900	1,400	—
1745 MF	—	400	500	900	1,400	—
1746/5 MF	—	400	500	900	1,400	—
1747 MF	—	400	500	900	1,400	—

KM# 125 2 ESCUDOS
6.7660 g., 0.9170 Gold 0.1995 oz. AGW **Ruler:** Ferdinand VI
Obv: Large armored bust right **Obv. Legend:** FERD • VI • D
• G • ... **Rev:** Crowned shield flanked by M F 2 **Rev. Legend:**
INITIUM... **Mint:** Mexico City

Date	Mintage	VG	F	VF	XF	Unc
1747 MF	—	3,000	5,500	9,000	15,000	—

KM# 126.1 2 ESCUDOS
6.7660 g., 0.9170 Gold 0.1995 oz. AGW **Ruler:** Ferdinand VI
Obv: Head right **Obv. Legend:** FERD • VI • D • G • ... **Rev:**
Crowned shield **Rev. Legend:** NOMINA MAGNA SEQUOR
Mint: Mexico City **Note:** Mint mark M, Mo.

Date	Mintage	VG	F	VF	XF	Unc
1748 MF	—	450	750	1,500	3,000	—
1749/8 MF	—	450	750	1,500	3,000	—
1750 MF	—	400	700	1,400	2,850	—
1751 MF	—	400	700	1,400	2,850	—

KM# 126.2 2 ESCUDOS
6.7660 g., 0.9170 Gold 0.1995 oz. AGW **Ruler:** Ferdinand VI
Obv: Head right **Obv. Legend:** FERD • VI • D • G • ... **Rev:**
Without 2 S by crowned shield **Rev. Legend:** NOMINA
MAGNA SEQUOR **Mint:** Mexico City **Note:** Mint mark M, Mo.

Date	Mintage	VG	F	VF	XF	Unc
1752 MF	—	400	700	1,400	2,850	—
1753 MF	—	400	700	1,400	2,850	—
1754 MF	—	600	850	1,750	3,500	—
1755 MM	—	400	700	1,400	2,850	—
1756 MM	—	600	850	1,750	3,500	—

KM# 127 2 ESCUDOS
6.7660 g., 0.9170 Gold 0.1995 oz. AGW **Ruler:** Ferdinand VI
Obv: Armored bust right **Obv. Legend:** FERDIND • VI • D •
G • ... **Rev:** Without 2 S by crowned shield **Rev. Legend:**
NOMINA MAGNA SEQUOR **Mint:** Mexico City **Note:** Mint
mark M, Mo.

Date	Mintage	VG	F	VF	XF	Unc
1757 MM	—	450	750	1,500	3,000	—
1759 MM	—	450	750	1,500	3,000	—

KM# 128 2 ESCUDOS
6.7660 g., 0.9170 Gold 0.1995 oz. AGW **Ruler:** Charles III
Obv: Armored bust right **Obv. Legend:** CAROLVS • III • D •
G • ... **Rev:** Without 2 S by crowned shield **Rev. Legend:**
NOMINA MAGNA SEQUOR **Mint:** Mexico City **Note:** Mint
mark M, Mo.

Date	Mintage	VG	F	VF	XF	Unc
1760 MM	—	550	1,000	2,000	4,000	—
1761 MM	—	550	1,000	2,000	4,000	—

KM# 129 2 ESCUDOS
6.7668 g., 0.9170 Gold 0.1995 oz. AGW **Ruler:** Charles III
Obv: Large armored bust right **Obv. Legend:** CAROLUS • III
• D • G • ... **Rev:** Without 2 S by crowned shield **Rev. Legend:**
IN • UTROQ • FELIX • AUSPICE • DEO **Mint:** Mexico City
Note: Mint mark M, Mo.

Date	Mintage	VG	F	VF	XF	Unc
1762 MF	—	500	900	1,850	3,750	—
1763 MF	—	500	900	1,850	3,750	—
1764/3 MF	—	500	900	1,850	3,750	—
1765 MF	—	500	900	1,850	3,750	—
1766 MF	—	500	900	1,850	3,750	—
1767 MF	—	500	900	1,850	3,750	—
1768 MF	—	500	900	1,850	3,750	—
1769 MF	—	500	900	1,850	3,750	—
1770 MF	—	500	900	1,850	3,750	—
1771 MF	—	500	900	1,850	3,750	—

KM# 130.1 2 ESCUDOS
6.7668 g., 0.9010 Gold 0.1960 oz. AGW **Ruler:** Charles III
Obv: Older, armored bust right **Obv. Legend:** CAROLUS •
III • D • G • ... **Rev:** Crowned shield in order chain, initials and
mint mark upright **Rev. Legend:** IN • UTROQ • FELIX •
AUSPICE • DEO **Mint:** Mexico City **Note:** Mint mark M, Mo.

Date	Mintage	VG	F	VF	XF	Unc
1772 FM	—	300	400	550	1,000	—
1773 FM	—	300	400	550	1,000	—

KM# 130.2 2 ESCUDOS
6.7668 g., 0.9010 Gold 0.1960 oz. AGW **Ruler:** Charles III
Obv: Older, armored bust right **Obv. Legend:** CAROLUS •
III • D • G • ... **Rev:** Crowned shield in order chain, initials and
mint mark inverted **Rev. Legend:** IN • UTROQ • FELIX •
AUSPICE • DEO **Mint:** Mexico City **Note:** Mint mark M, Mo.

Date	Mintage	VG	F	VF	XF	Unc
1773 FM	—	300	400	550	1,000	—
1774 FM	—	300	400	550	1,000	—
1775 FM	—	300	400	550	1,000	—
1776 FM	—	350	500	675	1,000	—
1777 FM	—	300	400	500	900	—
1778 FF	—	300	400	500	900	—
1779 FF	—	300	400	500	900	—
1780 FF	—	300	400	500	900	—
1781 FM/M	—	300	400	500	900	—
1781 FF	—	300	400	500	900	—
1782 FF	—	300	400	500	900	—
1783 FF	—	300	400	500	900	—
1784 FF	—	300	400	500	900	—
1784 FM/F	—	300	400	500	900	—

SPANISH COLONIAL - MILLED

KM# 130.2a 2 ESCUDOS
6.7668 g., 0.8750 Gold 0.1904 oz. AGW **Ruler:** Charles III
Obv: Older, armored bust right **Obv. Legend:** CAROLUS •
III • D • G • ... **Rev:** Crowned shield in order chain, initials and
mint mark inverted **Rev. Legend:** IN • UTROQ • FELIX •
AUSPICE • DEO **Mint:** Mexico City **Note:** Mint mark M, Mo.

Date	Mintage	VG	F	VF	XF	Unc
1785 FM	—	300	400	500	900	—
1786 FM	—	300	400	500	900	—
1787 FM	—	300	400	500	900	—
1788 FM	—	300	400	500	900	—

KM# 130.1a 2 ESCUDOS
6.7668 g., 0.8750 Gold 0.1904 oz. AGW **Ruler:** Charles III
Obv: Older, armored bust right **Obv. Legend:** CAROLUS •
III • D • G • ... **Rev:** Crowned shield in order chain, initials and
mint mark upright **Rev. Legend:** IN • UTROQ • FELIX •
AUSPICE • DEO **Mint:** Mexico City **Note:** Mint mark M, Mo.

Date	Mintage	VG	F	VF	XF	Unc
1788 FM	—	300	400	500	900	—

KM# 131 2 ESCUDOS
6.7668 g., 0.8750 Gold 0.1904 oz. AGW **Ruler:** Charles IV
Obv: Armored bust of Charles III, right **Obv. Legend:** CAROL
• IV • D • G • ... **Rev:** Crowned shield in order chain, initials
and mint mark upright **Rev. Legend:** IN • UTROQ • FELIX •
AUSPICE • DEO **Mint:** Mexico City **Note:** Mint mark M, Mo,
using old portrait punch.

Date	Mintage	VG	F	VF	XF	Unc
1789 FM	—	650	1,200	2,000	3,500	—
1790 FM	—	650	1,200	2,000	3,500	—

KM# 132 2 ESCUDOS
6.7668 g., 0.8750 Gold 0.1904 oz. AGW **Ruler:** Charles IV
Obv: Armored bust of Charles IIII, right **Obv. Legend:** CAROL
• IIII • D • G • ... **Rev:** Crowned shield flanked by 2 S in order
chain **Rev. Legend:** IN • UTROQ • FELIX • AUSPICE • DEO;
initials and mint mark upright **Mint:** Mexico City **Note:** Mint
mark Mo.

Date	Mintage	VG	F	VF	XF	Unc
1791 FM Mo over inverted Mo	—	300	400	600	950	—
1792 FM	—	250	350	450	575	—
1793 FM	—	250	350	450	575	—
1794 FM	—	250	350	450	575	—
1795 FM	—	250	350	450	575	—
1796 FM	—	250	350	450	575	—
1797 FM	—	250	350	450	575	—
1798 FM	—	250	350	450	575	—
1799 FM	—	250	350	450	575	—
1800 FM	—	250	350	450	575	—
1801 FT	—	185	225	350	575	—
1802 FT	—	185	225	350	575	—
1803 FT	—	185	225	350	575	—
1804 TH	—	185	225	350	575	—
1805 TH	—	185	225	350	575	—
1806/5 TH	—	185	225	350	575	—
1807 TH	—	185	225	350	575	—
1808 TH	—	185	225	350	575	1,500

KM# 134 2 ESCUDOS
6.7668 g., 0.8750 Gold 0.1904 oz. AGW **Ruler:**
Ferdinand VII **Obv:** Laureate head right **Obv. Legend:**
FERDIN • VII • D • G... **Rev:** Crowned shield divides designed
wreath, initials and mint mark upright **Rev. Legend:** IN •
UTROQ • FELIX • AUSPICE • DEO **Mint:** Mexico City **Note:**
Mint mark Mo.

Date	Mintage	VG	F	VF	XF	Unc
1814Mo HJ	—	250	425	700	1,150	—
1815 JJ	—	250	425	700	1,150	—
1816 JJ	—	250	425	700	1,150	—
1817 JJ	—	250	425	700	1,150	—
1818 JJ	—	250	425	700	1,150	3,750
1819 JJ	—	250	425	700	1,150	—
1820 JJ	—	250	425	700	1,150	—
1821 JJ	—	250	425	700	1,150	—

KM# 135 4 ESCUDOS
13.5337 g., 0.9170 Gold 0.3990 oz. AGW **Ruler:** Philip V
Obv: Armored bust right **Obv. Legend:** PHILIP • V • D • G •
HISPAN • ET IND • REX **Rev:** Crowned shield flanked by F
4 **Rev. Legend:** INITIUM SAPIENTIAE TIMOR DOMINI **Mint:**
Mexico City

Date	Mintage	VG	F	VF	XF	Unc
1732 Rare	—	—	—	—	—	—
1732 F Rare	—	—	—	—	—	—
1733 F Rare	—	—	—	—	—	—
1734/3 F	—	1,200	1,800	3,350	5,400	—
1734 MF	—	1,000	1,600	3,000	5,100	—
1735 MF	—	1,000	1,600	3,000	5,400	—
1736 MF	—	1,000	1,600	3,000	5,400	—
1737 MF	—	900	1,500	2,900	4,800	—
1738/7 MF	—	900	1,500	2,900	4,800	—
1738 MF	—	900	1,500	2,900	4,800	—
1739 MF	—	900	1,500	2,900	4,800	—
1740/30 MF	—	900	1,500	2,900	4,800	—
1740 MF	—	900	1,500	2,900	4,800	—
1741 MF	—	900	1,500	2,900	4,800	—
1742/32 MF	—	900	1,500	2,900	4,800	—
1743 MF	—	900	1,500	2,900	4,800	—
1744 MD	—	900	1,500	2,900	4,800	—
1745 MF	—	900	1,500	2,900	4,800	—
1746 MF	—	900	1,500	2,900	4,800	—
1747 MF	—	900	1,500	2,900	4,800	—
1746/5 MF	—	900	1,500	2,900	4,800	—

KM# 136 4 ESCUDOS
13.5337 g., 0.9170 Gold 0.3990 oz. AGW **Ruler:**
Ferdinand VI **Obv:** Large, armored bust right **Obv. Legend:**
FERDND • VI • D • G • ... **Rev:** Crowned shield flanked by F
4 **Rev. Legend:** INITIUM SAPIENTIAE TIMOR DOMINI **Mint:**
Mexico City **Note:** Mint mark M, Mo.

Date	Mintage	VG	F	VF	XF	Unc
1747 MF	—	7,500	13,500	20,000	30,000	—

KM# 137 4 ESCUDOS
13.5337 g., 0.9170 Gold 0.3990 oz. AGW **Ruler:**
Ferdinand VI **Obv:** Armored bust right **Obv. Legend:**
FERDND • VI • D • G • ... **Rev:** Crowned shield flanked by 4
S **Rev. Legend:** NOMINA MAGNA SEQUOR **Mint:** Mexico
City **Note:** Mint mark M, Mo.

Date	Mintage	VG	F	VF	XF	Unc
1748 MF	—	1,500	3,000	5,000	8,000	—
1749 MF	—	1,500	3,000	5,000	8,000	—
1750/48 MF	—	1,500	3,000	5,000	8,000	—
1750 MF	—	1,500	3,000	5,000	8,000	—
1751 MF	—	1,500	3,000	5,000	8,000	—

KM# 138 4 ESCUDOS
13.5337 g., 0.9170 Gold 0.3990 oz. AGW **Ruler:**
Ferdinand VI **Obv:** Small, armored bust right **Obv. Legend:**
FERDND • VI • D • G • ... **Rev:** Crowned shield, without value
Rev. Legend: NOMINA MAGNA... **Mint:** Mexico City **Note:**
Mint mark M, Mo.

Date	Mintage	VG	F	VF	XF	Unc
1752 MF	—	1,000	2,000	3,500	6,000	—
1753 MF	—	1,000	2,000	3,500	6,000	—
1754 MF	—	1,000	2,000	3,500	6,000	—
1755 MM	—	1,000	2,000	3,500	6,000	—
1756 MM	—	1,000	2,000	3,500	6,000	—

KM# 139 4 ESCUDOS
13.5337 g., 0.9170 Gold 0.3990 oz. AGW **Ruler:**
Ferdinand VI **Obv:** Armored bust right **Obv. Legend:**
FERDND • VI • D • G • ... **Rev:** Crowned shield, without value
Rev. Legend: NOMINA MAGNA... **Mint:** Mexico City **Note:**
Mint mark M, Mo.

Date	Mintage	VG	F	VF	XF	Unc
1757 MM	—	1,250	2,500	4,000	6,500	—
1759 MM	—	1,250	2,500	4,000	6,500	—

KM# 140 4 ESCUDOS
13.5337 g., 0.9170 Gold 0.3990 oz. AGW **Ruler:** Charles III
Obv: Armored bust right **Obv. Legend:** CAROLVS • III • D •
G • ... **Rev:** Crowned shield, without value **Rev. Legend:**
NOMINA MAGNA SEQUOR **Mint:** Mexico City **Note:** Mint
mark M, Mo.

Date	Mintage	VG	F	VF	XF	Unc
1760 MM	—	3,500	6,500	10,000	20,000	—
1761 MM	—	3,500	6,500	10,000	20,000	—

KM# 141 4 ESCUDOS
13.5337 g., 0.9170 Gold 0.3990 oz. AGW **Ruler:** Charles III
Obv: Large, armored bust right **Obv. Legend:** CAROLUS •
III • D • G • ... **Rev:** Crowned shield in order chain, without
value **Rev. Legend:** IN • UTROQ • FELIX • AUSPICE • DEO
Mint: Mexico City **Note:** Mint mark M, Mo.

Date	Mintage	VG	F	VF	XF	Unc
1762 MF	—	2,500	4,500	7,500	15,000	—
1763 MF	—	2,500	4,500	7,500	15,000	—
1764 MF	—	2,500	4,500	7,500	15,000	—
1765 MF	—	2,500	4,500	7,500	15,000	—
1766/5 MF	—	2,500	4,500	7,500	15,000	—
1767 MF	—	2,500	4,500	7,500	15,000	—
1768 MF	—	2,500	4,500	7,500	15,000	—
1769 MF	—	2,500	4,500	7,500	15,000	—
1770 MF	—	2,500	4,500	7,500	15,000	—
1771 MF	—	2,500	4,500	7,500	15,000	—

KM# 142.1   4 ESCUDOS
13.5337 g., 0.9010 Gold 0.3920 oz. AGW **Ruler:** Charles III
Obv: Large, armored bust right **Obv. Legend:** CAROL • III •
D • G • ... **Rev:** Crowned shield in order chain, initials and mint
mark upright **Rev. Legend:** IN • UTROQ • FELIX • AUSPICE
• DEO **Mint:** Mexico City **Note:** Mint mark M, Mo.

Date	Mintage	VG	F	VF	XF	Unc
1772 FM	—	600	975	1,500	3,000	—
1773 FM	—	600	975	1,500	3,000	—

KM# 142.2   4 ESCUDOS
13.5337 g., 0.9010 Gold 0.3920 oz. AGW **Ruler:** Charles III
Obv: Large, armored bust right **Obv. Legend:** CAROL • III •
D • G • ... **Rev:** Crowned shield flanked by 4 S in order chain,
initials and mint mark inverted **Rev. Legend:** IN • UTROQ •
FELIX • AUSPICE • DEO **Mint:** Mexico City **Note:** Mint mark
M, Mo.

Date	Mintage	VG	F	VF	XF	Unc
1773 FM	—	525	725	1,100	2,200	—
1774 FM	—	525	725	1,100	2,200	—
1775 FM	—	525	725	1,100	2,200	—
1776 FM	—	525	725	1,100	2,200	—
1777 FM	—	525	725	1,100	2,200	—
1778 FF	—	525	725	1,100	2,200	—
1779 FF	—	525	725	1,100	2,200	—
1780 FF	—	525	725	1,100	2,200	—
1781 FF	—	525	725	1,100	2,200	—
1782 FF	—	525	725	1,100	2,200	—
1783 FF	—	525	725	1,100	2,200	—
1784 FF	—	525	725	1,100	2,200	—
1784/3 FM/F	—	525	725	1,100	2,200	—

KM# 142.2a   4 ESCUDOS
13.5337 g., 0.8750 Gold 0.3807 oz. AGW **Ruler:** Charles III
Obv: Large, armored bust right **Obv. Legend:** CAROL • III •
D • G • ... **Rev:** Crowned shield in order chain, initials and mint
mark inverted **Rev. Legend:** IN • UTROQ • FELIX • AUSPICE
• DEO **Mint:** Mexico City **Note:** Mint mark M, Mo.

Date	Mintage	VG	F	VF	XF	Unc
1785 FM	—	525	725	1,100	2,200	—
1786 FM/F	—	525	725	1,100	2,200	—
1786 FM	—	525	725	1,100	2,200	—
1787 FM	—	525	725	1,100	2,200	—
1788 FM	—	525	725	1,100	2,200	—

KM# 142.1a   4 ESCUDOS
13.5337 g., 0.8750 Gold 0.3807 oz. AGW **Ruler:** Charles III
Obv: Large, armored bust right **Obv. Legend:** CAROL • III •
D • G • ... **Rev:** Crowned shield in order chain, initials and mint
mark upright **Rev. Legend:** IN • UTROQ • FELIX • AUSPICE
• DEO **Mint:** Mexico City **Note:** Mint mark M, Mo.

Date	Mintage	VG	F	VF	XF	Unc
1788 FM	—	600	975	1,500	3,000	—

KM# 143.1   4 ESCUDOS
13.5337 g., 0.8750 Gold 0.3807 oz. AGW **Ruler:** Charles IV
Obv: Armored bust of Charles III, right **Obv. Legend:** CAROL
• IV • D • G • ... **Rev:** Crowned shield in order chain, initials
and mint mark upright **Rev. Legend:** IN • UTROQ • FELIX •
AUSPICE • DEO **Mint:** Mexico City **Note:** Mint mark M, Mo,
using old portrait punch.

Date	Mintage	VG	F	VF	XF	Unc
1789 FM	—	550	750	1,100	2,150	—
1790 FM	—	550	750	1,100	2,150	—

KM# 143.2   4 ESCUDOS
13.5337 g., 0.8750 Gold 0.3807 oz. AGW **Ruler:** Charles IV
Obv: Armored bust of Charles III, right **Obv. Legend:** CAROL
• IIII • D • G • ... **Rev:** Crowned shield in order chain, initials
and mint mark upright **Rev. Legend:** IN • UTROQ • FELIX •
AUSPICE • DEO **Mint:** Mexico City **Note:** Mint mark M, Mo,
using old portrait punch.

Date	Mintage	VG	F	VF	XF	Unc
1790 FM	—	600	1,000	1,800	3,000	—

KM# 144   4 ESCUDOS
13.5337 g., 0.8750 Gold 0.3807 oz. AGW **Ruler:** Charles IV
Obv: Armored bust of Charles IIII, right **Obv. Legend:** CAROL
• IIII • D • G • ... **Rev:** Crowned shield in order
chain **Rev. Legend:** IN • UTROQ • FELIX • AUSPICE • DEO;
initials and mint mark upright **Mint:** Mexico City **Note:** Mint
mark Mo.

Date	Mintage	VG	F	VF	XF	Unc
1792 FM	—	500	600	750	1,500	—
1793 FM	—	500	600	750	1,500	—
1794/3 FM	—	500	600	750	1,500	—
1795 FM	—	500	600	750	1,500	—
1796 FM	—	500	600	750	1,500	—
1797 FM	—	500	600	750	1,500	—
1798/7 FM	—	500	600	750	1,500	—
1798 FM	—	500	600	750	1,500	—
1799 FM	—	500	600	750	1,500	—
1800 FM	—	500	600	750	1,500	—
1801 FM	—	375	500	750	1,500	—
1801 FT	—	375	500	750	1,500	—
1802 FT	—	375	600	850	1,650	—
1803 FT	—	375	500	750	1,500	—
1804/3 TH	—	375	500	750	1,500	—
1804 TH	—	375	500	750	1,500	—
1805 TH	—	375	500	750	1,500	—
1806/5 TH	—	375	500	750	1,500	—
1807 TH	—	375	600	850	1,650	—
1808/0 TH	—	375	500	750	1,500	—
1808 TH	—	375	500	750	1,500	—

KM# 145   4 ESCUDOS
13.5337 g., 0.8750 Gold 0.3807 oz. AGW **Ruler:**
Ferdinand VII **Obv:** Armored bust right **Obv. Legend:**
FERDIN • VII D • G... **Rev:** Crowned shield divides designed
wreath, initials and mint mark upright **Rev. Legend:** IN •
UTROQ • FELIX • AUSPICE • DEO **Mint:** Mexico City **Note:**
Mint mark Mo.

Date	Mintage	VG	F	VF	XF	Unc
1810 HJ	—	375	550	1,000	2,300	—
1811 HJ	—	375	550	1,000	2,300	—
1812 HJ	—	375	550	1,000	2,300	—

KM# 146   4 ESCUDOS
13.5337 g., 0.8750 Gold 0.3807 oz. AGW **Ruler:**

Ferdinand VII **Obv:** Laureate head right **Obv. Legend:** FERDIN. VII D. G... **Rev:** Crowned shield divides designed wreath **Rev. Legend:** IN. UTROQ. FELIX. AUSPICE. DEO; initials and mint mark upright **Mint:** Mexico City **Note:** Mint mark Mo.

Date	Mintage	VG	F	VF	XF	Unc
1814 HJ	—	400	700	1,150	2,500	—
1815 HJ	—	400	700	1,150	2,500	—
1815 JJ	—	400	700	1,150	2,500	—
1816 JJ	—	400	700	1,150	2,500	—
1817 JJ	—	400	700	1,150	2,500	—
1818 JJ	—	400	700	1,150	2,500	—
1819 JJ	—	400	700	1,150	2,500	—
1820 JJ	—	400	700	1,150	2,500	—

KM# 148   8 ESCUDOS
27.0674 g., 0.9170 Gold 0.7980 oz. AGW **Ruler:** Philip V **Obv:** Large, armored bust right **Obv. Legend:** PHILIP • V • D • G • HISPAN • ET IND • REX **Rev:** Crowned shield flanked by M F 8 in order chain **Rev. Legend:** INITIUM SAPIENTIAE TIMOR DOMINI **Mint:** Mexico City **Note:** Mint mark M, Mo.

Date	Mintage	VG	F	VF	XF	Unc
1732 Rare	—	—	—	—	—	—
1732 F Rare	—	—	—	—	—	—
1733 F Rare	—	—	—	—	—	—

Note: Heritage World Coin Auctions #3004, 1-09, MS64 realized $54,625

Date	Mintage	VG	F	VF	XF	Unc
1734 MF	—	1,500	2,000	3,300	5,800	—
1734 MF/F	—	1,500	2,000	3,300	5,800	—
1735 MF	—	1,500	1,800	3,000	5,400	—
1736 MF	—	1,500	1,800	3,000	5,400	—
1737 MF	—	1,500	1,800	3,000	5,400	—
1738/7 MF	—	1,500	1,800	3,000	5,400	—
1738 MF	—	1,500	1,800	3,000	5,400	—
1739 MF	—	1,500	1,800	3,000	5,400	—
1740 MF	—	1,500	1,800	3,000	5,400	—
1740/30 MF	—	1,500	1,800	3,000	5,400	—
1741 MF	—	1,500	1,800	3,000	5,400	—
1742 MF	—	1,500	1,800	3,000	5,400	—
1743 MF	—	1,500	1,800	3,000	5,400	—
1744 MF	—	1,500	1,800	3,000	5,400	—
1744/3 MF	—	1,500	1,800	3,000	5,400	—
1745 MF	—	1,500	1,800	3,000	5,400	—
1745/4 MF	—	1,500	1,800	3,000	5,400	—
1746 MF	—	1,500	1,800	3,000	5,400	—
1746/5 MF	—	1,500	1,800	3,000	5,400	—
1747 MF	—	1,500	2,100	3,400	6,000	—

KM# 149   8 ESCUDOS
27.0674 g., 0.9170 Gold 0.7980 oz. AGW **Ruler:** Ferdinand VI **Obv:** Large, armored bust right **Obv. Legend:** FERDND • VI • D • G • ... **Rev:** Crowned shield flanked by M F 8 in order chain **Rev. Legend:** INITIUM SAPIENTIAE TIMOR DOMINI **Mint:** Mexico City **Note:** Mint mark M, Mo.

Date	Mintage	VG	F	VF	XF	Unc
1747 MF	—	9,000	15,000	22,000	35,000	—

KM# 150   8 ESCUDOS
27.0674 g., 0.9170 Gold 0.7980 oz. AGW **Ruler:** Ferdinand VI **Obv:** Small, armored bust right **Obv. Legend:** FERDND • VI • D • G • ... **Rev:** Crowned shield flanked by 8 S in order chain **Rev. Legend:** NOMINA MAGNA SEQUOR **Mint:** Mexico City **Note:** Mint mark M, Mo.

Date	Mintage	VG	F	VF	XF	Unc
1748 MF	—	1,500	2,400	4,200	7,200	—
1749/8 MF	—	1,500	2,400	4,200	7,200	—
1749 MF	—	1,500	2,400	4,200	7,200	—
1750 MF	—	1,500	2,400	4,200	7,200	—
1751/0 MF	—	1,800	2,400	4,200	7,200	—
1751 MF	—	1,500	2,400	4,200	7,200	—

KM# 151   8 ESCUDOS
27.0674 g., 0.9170 Gold 0.7980 oz. AGW **Ruler:**

Ferdinand VI **Obv:** Armored bust right **Obv. Legend:**
FERDND • VI • D • G • ... **Rev:** Crowned shield in order chain
Rev. Legend: NOMINA MAGNA SEQUOR **Mint:** Mexico City
Note: Mint mark M, Mo.

Date	Mintage	VG	F	VF	XF	Unc
1752 MF	—	1,500	2,400	4,200	7,200	—
1753 MF	—	1,500	2,400	4,200	7,200	—
1754 MF	—	1,500	2,400	4,200	7,200	—
1755 MM	—	1,500	2,400	4,200	7,200	—
1756 MM	—	1,500	2,400	4,200	7,200	—

KM# 152   8 ESCUDOS
27.0674 g., 0.9170 Gold 0.7980 oz. AGW   **Ruler:**
Ferdinand VI **Obv:** Armored bust right **Obv. Legend:**
FERDND • VI • D • G • ... **Rev:** Crowned shield in order chain
Rev. Legend: NOMINA MAGNA SEQUOR **Mint:** Mexico City
Note: Mint mark M, Mo.

Date	Mintage	VG	F	VF	XF	Unc
1757 MM	—	1,500	2,400	4,200	7,200	—
1758 MM	—	1,500	2,400	4,200	7,200	—
1759 MM	—	1,500	2,400	4,200	7,200	—

KM# 154   8 ESCUDOS
27.0674 g., 0.9170 Gold 0.7980 oz. AGW   **Ruler:** Charles III
Obv: Armored bust right **Obv. Legend:** CAROLVS • III • D •
G • ... **Rev:** Crowned shield in order chain **Rev. Legend:**
NOMINA MAGNA SEQUOR **Mint:** Mexico City **Note:** Mint
mark M, Mo.

Date	Mintage	VG	F	VF	XF	Unc
1761 MM	—	2,100	3,600	6,300	11,500	—

KM# 153   8 ESCUDOS
27.0674 g., 0.9170 Gold 0.7980 oz. AGW   **Ruler:** Charles III
Obv: Armored bust right **Obv. Legend:** CAROLVS • III • D •
G • ... **Rev:** Crowned shield in order chain **Rev. Legend:**
NOMINA MAGNA SEQUOR **Mint:** Mexico City **Note:** Mint
mark M, Mo.

Date	Mintage	VG	F	VF	XF	Unc
1760 MM	—	2,100	3,600	6,000	11,000	—
1761/0 MM	—	2,400	4,200	6,600	12,000	—
1761 MM	—	2,400	4,200	6,600	12,000	—

KM# 155   8 ESCUDOS
27.0674 g., 0.9170 Gold 0.7980 oz. AGW   **Ruler:** Charles III
Obv: Large, armored bust right **Obv. Legend:** CAROLUS •
III • D • G • ... **Rev:** Crowned shield in order chain **Rev. Legend:**
IN • UTROQ • FELIX • AUSPICE • DEO • **Mint:** Mexico City
Note: Mint mark M, Mo.

Date	Mintage	VG	F	VF	XF	Unc
1762 MM	—	2,000	3,450	5,600	10,500	—
1763 MM	—	2,000	3,450	5,600	10,500	—
1764 MF	—	2,200	3,750	6,300	11,500	—
1764/2 MF	—	2,200	3,750	6,300	11,500	—
1764 MM	—	2,200	3,750	6,300	11,500	—
1765/4 MF	—	2,200	3,750	6,300	11,500	—
1765/4 MM	—	2,200	3,750	6,300	11,500	—
1765 MF	—	2,200	3,750	6,300	11,500	—
1765 MM	—	1,900	3,150	5,000	9,400	—
1766 MF	—	1,900	3,150	5,000	9,400	—
1767/6 MF	—	1,900	3,150	5,000	9,400	—
1767 MF	—	1,900	3,150	5,000	9,400	—
1768/7 MF	—	1,900	3,150	5,000	9,400	—
1768 MF	—	1,900	3,150	5,000	9,400	—
1769 MF	—	1,900	3,150	5,000	9,400	—
1770 MF	—	1,900	3,150	5,000	9,400	—
1771 MF	—	2,200	3,750	6,300	11,500	—

Date	Mintage	VG	F	VF	XF	Unc
1784 FM/F	—	1,100	1,350	1,500	2,400	—
1784 FM	—	1,100	1,350	1,500	2,400	—
1785 FM	—	1,100	1,350	1,500	2,400	—

KM# 156.1   8 ESCUDOS
27.0674 g., 0.9010 Gold 0.7841 oz. AGW **Ruler:** Charles III
Obv: Large, armored bust right **Obv. Legend:** CAROL • III •
D • G • ... **Rev:** Crowned shield flanked by 8 S in order chain,
initials and mint mark upright **Rev. Legend:** ... AUSPICE •
DEO • **Mint:** Mexico City **Note:** Mint mark M, Mo.

Date	Mintage	VG	F	VF	XF	Unc
1772 FM	—	1,100	1,500	2,000	2,750	—
1773 FM	—	1,100	1,500	2,000	2,750	—

KM# 156.2a   8 ESCUDOS
27.0674 g., 0.7614 oz. AGW **Ruler:** Charles III
Obv: Large, armored bust right **Obv. Legend:** CAROL • III •
D • G • ... **Rev:** Crowned shield flanked by 8 S in order chain,
initials and mint mark inverted **Rev. Legend:** ... AUSPICE •
DEO • **Mint:** Mexico City **Note:** Mint mark M, Mo.

Date	Mintage	VG	F	VF	XF	Unc
1786 FM	—	1,100	1,350	1,800	2,400	—
1787 FM	—	1,100	1,350	1,800	2,400	—
1788 FM	—	1,100	1,350	1,800	2,400	—

KM# 156.2   8 ESCUDOS
27.0674 g., 0.9010 Gold 0.7841 oz. AGW **Ruler:** Charles III
Obv: Large, armored bust right **Obv. Legend:** CAROL • III •
D • G • ... **Rev:** Crowned shield flanked by 8 S in order chain,
initials and mint mark inverted **Rev. Legend:** ... AUSPICE •
DEO • **Mint:** Mexico City **Note:** Mint mark M, Mo.

Date	Mintage	VG	F	VF	XF	Unc
1773 FM	—	1,100	1,350	1,800	2,400	—
1774 FM	—	1,100	1,350	1,800	2,400	—
1775 FM	—	1,100	1,350	1,800	2,400	—
1776 FM	—	1,500	1,850	2,250	3,000	—
1777/6 FM	—	1,100	1,350	1,500	2,400	—
1777 FM	—	1,100	1,350	1,500	2,400	—
1778 FF	—	1,100	1,350	1,500	2,400	—
1779 FF	—	1,100	1,350	1,500	2,400	—
1780 FF	—	1,100	1,350	1,500	2,400	—
1781 FF	—	1,100	1,350	1,500	2,400	—
1782 FF	—	1,100	1,350	1,500	2,400	—
1783 FF	—	1,100	1,350	1,500	2,400	—
1784 FF	—	1,100	1,350	1,500	2,400	—

KM# 156.1a   8 ESCUDOS
27.0674 g., 0.8750 Gold 0.7614 oz. AGW **Ruler:** Charles III
Obv: Large, armored bust right **Obv. Legend:** CAROL • III •
D • G • ... **Rev:** Crowned shield flanked by 8 S in order chain,
initials and mint mark upright **Rev. Legend:** ... AUSPICE •
DEO • **Mint:** Mexico City **Note:** Mint mark M, Mo.

Date	Mintage	VG	F	VF	XF	Unc
1788 FM	—	1,100	1,300	1,500	2,400	—

KM# 157   8 ESCUDOS
27.0674 g., 0.8750 Gold 0.7614 oz. AGW **Ruler:** Charles IV
Obv: Armored bust of Charles III, right **Obv. Legend:** CAROL
• IV • D • G • ... **Rev:** Crowned shield flanked by 8 S in order
chain **Rev. Legend:** IN • UTROQ • ... **Mint:** Mexico City **Note:**
Mint mark M, Mo, using old portrait punch.

Date	Mintage	VG	F	VF	XF	Unc
1789 FM	—	1,100	1,500	2,000	2,750	—
1790 FM	—	1,100	1,500	2,000	2,750	—

KM# 158   8 ESCUDOS
27.0674 g., 0.8750 Gold 0.7614 oz. AGW **Ruler:** Charles IV
Obv: Armored bust of Charles III, right **Obv. Legend:** CAROL
• IIII • D • G • ... **Rev:** Crowned shield flanked by 8 S in order
chain **Rev. Legend:** IN • UTROQ • ... **Mint:** Mexico City **Note:**
Mint mark M, Mo, using old portrait punch.

Date	Mintage	VG	F	VF	XF	Unc
1790 FM	—	1,100	1,500	2,000	2,750	—

KM# 159   8 ESCUDOS
27.0674 g., 0.8750 Gold 0.7614 oz. AGW **Ruler:** Charles IV
Obv: Armored bust right **Obv. Legend:** CAROL • IIII • D • G
• ... **Rev:** Crowned shield flanked by 8 S in order chain **Rev.
Legend:** IN • UTROQ • ... **Mint:** Mexico City **Note:** Mint mark
Mo.

Date	Mintage	VG	F	VF	XF	Unc
1791 FM	—	1,000	1,250	1,500	2,000	—
1792 FM	—	1,000	1,250	1,500	2,000	—
1793 FM	—	1,000	1,250	1,500	2,000	—
1794 FM	—	1,000	1,250	1,500	2,000	—
1795 FM	—	1,000	1,250	1,500	2,000	—
1796/5 FM	—	1,000	1,250	1,500	2,000	—
1796 FM	—	1,000	1,250	1,500	2,000	—
1797 FM	—	1,000	1,250	1,500	2,000	—
1797 FM EPLIX	—	1,000	1,250	1,500	2,000	—
1798 FM	—	1,000	1,250	1,500	2,000	—
1799 FM	—	1,000	1,250	1,500	2,000	—
1800 FM	—	1,000	1,250	1,500	2,000	—
1801/0 FT	—	750	750	925	1,750	—
1801 FM	—	750	750	850	1,500	—
1801 FT	—	750	750	850	1,500	—
1802 FT	—	750	750	850	1,500	—
1803 FT	—	750	775	875	1,500	—
1804/3 TH	—	750	775	900	1,750	—
1804 TH	—	750	750	850	1,500	5,300
1805 TH	—	750	750	850	1,500	—
1806 TH	—	750	750	850	1,500	5,300
1807 TH Mo over inverted Mo	—	750	775	900	1,750	
1807/6 TH	—	750	775	900	1,750	—
1808/7 TH	—	750	750	850	1,900	—
1807 TH	—	750	775	1,050	1,500	—
1808 TH	—	750	775	1,050	1,900	—

KM# 160   8 ESCUDOS
27.0674 g., 0.8750 Gold 0.7614 oz. AGW   **Ruler:**
Ferdinand VII **Obv:** Armored bust right **Obv. Legend:**
FERDIN • VII • D • G... **Rev:** Crowned shield divides designed
wreath **Rev. Legend:** IN UTROQ • FELIX **Mint:** Mexico City
Note: Mint mark Mo.

Date	Mintage	VG	F	VF	XF	Unc
1808 TH	—	750	775	1,050	2,150	—
1809 HJ	—	750	775	1,050	2,300	—
1810 HJ	—	750	775	1,000	2,050	—
1811 HJ H/T	—	750	775	1,100	2,300	—
1811/0 HJ	—	750	775	1,100	2,300	—
1811 HJ	—	750	775	1,100	2,300	—
1811 JJ	—	750	775	1,000	2,050	—
1812 JJ	—	750	775	1,000	2,050	—

KM# 161   8 ESCUDOS
27.0674 g., 0.8750 Gold 0.7614 oz. AGW **Ruler:**
Ferdinand VII **Obv:** Laureate head right **Obv. Legend:**
FERDIN • VII • D • G... **Rev:** Crowned shield divides designed
wreath **Rev. Legend:** IN UTROQ • FELIX **Mint:** Mexico City
Note: Mint mark Mo.

Date	Mintage	VG	F	VF	XF	Unc
1814 JJ	—	750	775	1,000	1,700	—
1815/4 JJ	—	750	775	1,050	1,950	—
1815/4 HJ	—	750	775	1,050	1,950	—
1815 JJ	—	750	775	1,000	1,700	—
1815 HJ	—	750	775	1,000	1,700	—
1816 JJ	—	750	775	1,000	1,700	—
1817 JJ	—	750	775	1,000	1,950	—
1818/7 JJ	—	750	775	1,000	1,850	—
1818 JJ	—	750	775	1,000	1,850	—
1819 JJ	—	750	775	1,000	1,850	—
1820 JJ	—	750	775	1,000	1,850	—
1821 JJ	—	750	775	1,050	2,200	—

PROCLAMATION
MEDALLIC COINAGE

The Q used in the following listings refer to Stan-
dard Catalog of Mexican Coins, Paper Money,
Stocks, Bonds, and Medals by Krause Publications,
Inc., ©1981.

KM# Q22   1/2 REAL
1.6000 g., Silver **Issuer:** Mexico City **Obv:** Crowned shield
flanked by crowned pillars with banner **Obv. Legend:** A
CARLOS IV REY DE ESPANA Y DE LAS YNDIAS **Rev:**
Legend, date within wreath **Rev. Legend:** PROCLAMADO
EN MEXICO ANO DE 1789

Date	Mintage	F	VF	XF	Unc	BU
1789	—	40.00	70.00	120	—	—

KM# Q22a   1/2 REAL
Bronze **Issuer:** Mexico City **Obv:** Crowned shield flanked
by crowned pillars with banner **Obv. Legend:** A CARLOS IV
REY DE ESPANA Y DE LAS YNDIAS **Rev:** Legend, date
within wreath **Rev. Legend:** PROCLAMADO EN MEXICO
ANO DE 1789

Date	Mintage	F	VF	XF	Unc	BU
1789	—	45.00	90.00	150	—	—

KM# Q23   1/2 REAL
Silver **Issuer:** Mexico City **Obv:** Crowned arms in double-
lined circle **Obv. Legend:** A CARLOS IV REY DE ESPANA
Y DE LAS YNDIAS **Rev. Legend:** PROCLAMADO EN
MEXICO ANO DE 1789

Date	Mintage	F	VF	XF	Unc	BU
1789	—	40.00	70.00	120	—	—

KM# Q23a   1/2 REAL
Bronze **Issuer:** Mexico City **Obv:** Crowned arms in double-
lined circle **Obv. Legend:** A CARLOS IV REY DE ESPANA
Y DE LAS YNDIAS **Rev. Legend:** PROCLAMADO EN
MEXICO ANO DE 1789

Date	Mintage	F	VF	XF	Unc	BU
1789	—	45.00	90.00	150	—	—

KM# Q24   REAL
Silver **Issuer:** Mexico City **Obv:** Crowned shield flanked by
crowned pillars with banner **Obv. Legend:** A CARLOS IV REY
DE ESPANA Y DE LAS YNDIAS **Rev:** Legend, date, value
within wreath **Rev. Legend:** PROCLAMADO EN MEXICO
ANO DE 1789

Date	Mintage	F	VF	XF	Unc	BU
1789	—	40.00	70.00	120	—	—

KM# Q24a   REAL
Bronze **Issuer:** Mexico City **Obv:** Crowned shield flanked
by crowned pillars with banner **Obv. Legend:** A CARLOS IV
REY DE ESPANA Y DE LAS YNDIAS **Rev:** Legend, date,
value within wreath **Rev. Legend:** PROCLAMADO EN
MEXICO ANO DE 1789

Date	Mintage	F	VF	XF	Unc	BU
1789	—	45.00	90.00	150	—	—

KM# Q-A24   REAL
Silver **Issuer:** Mexico City **Obv:** Crowned arms in double-
lined circle **Obv. Legend:** A CARLOS IV REY DE ESPANA
Y DE LAS YNDIAS **Rev. Legend:** PROCLAMADO EN
MEXICO ANO DE 1789

Date	Mintage	F	VF	XF	Unc	BU
1789	—	40.00	70.00	120	—	—

KM# Q-A24a   REAL
Copper **Issuer:** Mexico City **Obv:** Crowned arms in double-
lined circle **Obv. Legend:** A CARLOS IV REY DE ESPANA
Y DE LAS YNDIAS **Rev. Legend:** PROCLAMADO EN
MEXICO ANO DE 1789

Date	Mintage	F	VF	XF	Unc	BU
1789	—	45.00	90.00	150	—	—

KM# Q8   REAL
Silver **Issuer:** Chiapa **Obv:** Crowned shield flanked by pillars
Obv. Legend: FERNANDO. VII. REY DE ESPANA. Y DE
SUS IND. **Rev:** Legend within wreath **Rev. Legend:**
PROCLA/MADO ENCUID•R•DE/ CHIAPA•/•A1808•

Date	Mintage	F	VF	XF	Unc	BU
1808	—	25.00	40.00	65.00	115	—

KM# Q25   2 REALES
6.7000 g., Silver **Issuer:** Mexico City **Obv:** Crowned shield
flanked by crowned pillars with banner **Obv. Legend:** A
CARLOS IV REY DE ESPANA Y DE LAS YNDIAS **Rev:**
Legend, date, value within wreath **Rev. Legend:**
PROCLAMADO EN MEXICO ANO DE 1789

Date	Mintage	F	VF	XF	Unc	BU
1789	—	70.00	125	225	—	—

KM# Q25a   2 REALES
6.7000 g., Bronze **Issuer:** Mexico City **Obv:** Crowned shield
flanked by crowned pillars with banner **Obv. Legend:** A
CARLOS IV REY DE ESPANA Y DE LAS YNDIAS **Rev:**
Legend, date, value within wreath **Rev. Legend:**
PROCLAMADO EN MEXICO ANO DE 1789

Date	Mintage	F	VF	XF	Unc	BU
1789	—	60.00	115	180	—	—

KM# Q64   2 REALES
Silver **Issuer:** Queretaro **Obv:** Crowned shield flanked by
pillars **Obv. Legend:** FERNANDO VII REY DE ESPANA **Rev:**
Legend, date within wreath

Date	Mintage	F	VF	XF	Unc	BU
1808	—	25.00	45.00	90.00	150	—

KM# Q10   2 REALES
Silver **Issuer:** Chiapa **Obv:** Crowned shield flanked by pillars
Obv. Legend: FERNANDO VII REY DE ESPANA Y DE SUS
INDIAS **Rev:** Legend, date within wreath

Date	Mintage	F	VF	XF	Unc	BU
1808	—	45.00	70.00	100	175	—

KM# Q27   4 REALES
13.6000 g., Silver **Issuer:** Mexico City **Obv:** Crowned shield
flanked by crowned pillars with banner **Obv. Legend:** A
CARLOS IV REY DE ESPANA Y DE LAS YNDIAS **Rev:**
Legend date, value within wreath **Rev. Legend:**
PROCLAMADO EN MEXICO ANO DE 1789

Date	Mintage	F	VF	XF	Unc	BU
1789	—	200	375	675	1,150	—

KM# Q27a   4 REALES
13.6000 g., Bronze **Issuer:** Mexico City **Obv:** Crowned shield
flanked by crowned pillars with banner **Obv. Legend:** A
CARLOS IV REY DE ESPANA Y DE LAS YNDIAS **Rev:**
Legend, date, value within wreath **Rev. Legend:**
PROCLAMADO EN MEXICO ANO DE 1789

Date	Mintage	F	VF	XF	Unc	BU
1789	—	140	250	450	—	—

KM# Q-A66   4 REALES
Silver **Issuer:** Queretaro **Obv:** Crowned shield flanked by

pillars **Obv. Legend:** FERNANDO VII REY DE ESPANA **Rev:**
Legend, date within wreath

Date	Mintage	F	VF	XF	Unc	BU
1808	—	100	160	295	475	—

KM# Q28   8 REALES
27.0000 g., Silver **Issuer:** Mexico City **Obv:** Crowned shield
flanked by crowned pillars with banner **Obv. Legend:** A
CARLOS IV REY DE ESPANA Y DE LAS YNDIAS **Rev:**
Legend, date, value within wreath **Rev. Legend:**
PROCLAMADO EN MEXICO ANO DE 1789

Date	Mintage	F	VF	XF	Unc	BU
1789	—	400	700	1,200	2,000	—

KM# Q28a   8 REALES
27.0000 g., Bronze **Issuer:** Mexico City **Obv:** Crowned shield
flanked by crowned pillars with banner **Obv. Legend:** A
CARLOS IV REY DE ESPANA Y DE LAS YNDIAS **Rev:**
Legend, date, value within wreath **Rev. Legend:**
PROCLAMADO EN MEXICO ANO DE 1789

Date	Mintage	F	VF	XF	Unc	BU
1789	—	140	250	450	—	—

KM# Q68   8 REALES
Silver **Issuer:** Queretaro **Obv:** Crowned shield flanked by
pillars **Obv. Legend:** FERNANDO VII REY DE ESPANA **Rev:**
Legend, date within wreath

Date	Mintage	F	VF	XF	Unc	BU
1808	—	220	425	575	950	—

WAR OF INDEPENDENCE

CHIHUAHUA

The Chihuahua Mint was established by a decree of October 8, 1810 as a temporary mint. Their first coins were cast 8 Reales using Mexico City coins as patterns and obliterating/changing the mint mark and moneyer initials. Two c/m were placed on the obverse - on the left, a T designating receipt by the Royal Treasurer, crowned pillars of Hercules on the right with pomegranate beneath, the comptrollers symbol.

In 1814, standard dies were made available, thus machine struck 8 Reales were produced until 1822. Only the one denomination was made at Chihuahua.

Mint mark: CA.

ROYALIST COINAGE

KM# 123   8 REALES
Cast Silver **Ruler:** Ferdinand VII **Countermark:** T at left, pillars at right, pomegranate below **Obv:** Armored bust right **Obv. Legend:** FERDIN• VII • DEI • GRATIA **Rev:** Crowned shield flanked by pillars **Mint:** Chihuahua

Date	Mintage	Good	VG	F	VF	XF
1810CA RP Rare	—	—	—	—	—	—
1811CA RP	—	45.00	70.00	120	200	—
1812CA RP	—	40.00	65.00	90.00	175	—
1813CA RP	—	35.00	50.00	70.00	120	—

KM# 111.1   8 REALES
27.0700 g., 0.9030 Silver 0.7859 oz. ASW **Ruler:** Ferdinand VII **Obv:** Draped bust right **Obv. Legend:** FERDIN • VII • DEI • GRATIA **Rev:** Crowned shield flanked by pillars

Date	Mintage	VG	F	VF	XF	Unc
1815 RP	—	220	300	525	750	—
1816 RP	—	90.00	140	225	425	—
1817 RP	—	110	165	280	425	—
1818 RP	—	110	165	280	425	—
1819/8 RP	—	140	195	375	525	—
1819 RP	—	140	195	375	525	—
1820 RP	—	220	300	525	750	—
1821 RP	—	220	300	525	750	—
1822 RP	—	450	650	1,200	1,650	—

Note: KM#111.1 is normally found struck over earlier cast 8 Reales, KM#123 and Monclova (MVA) 1812 cast countermark 8 Reales, KM#202 and Zacatecas 8 Reales, KM#190

DURANGO

The Durango mint was authorized as a temporary mint on the same day as the Chihuahua Mint, October 8, 1810. The mint opened in 1811 and made coins of 6 denominations between 1811 and 1822.

Mint mark: D.

ROYALIST COINAGE

KM# 60   1/8 REAL
Copper **Ruler:** Ferdinand VII **Obv:** Crowned monogram **Rev:** EN DURANGO, value, date **Mint:** Durango

Date	Mintage	VG	F	VF	XF	Unc
1812D	—	40.00	75.00	125	250	—
1813D	—	65.00	135	185	375	—
1814D Rare	—	—	—	—	—	—

KM# 61   1/8 REAL
Copper **Ruler:** Ferdinand VII **Obv:** Crowned monogram **Rev:** Value within spray, date below **Rev. Legend:** ENDURANGO. **Mint:** Durango

Date	Mintage	VG	F	VF	XF	Unc
1814D	—	18.00	32.50	55.00	95.00	—
1815D	—	18.00	35.00	60.00	100	—
1816D	—	18.00	35.00	60.00	100	—
1817D	—	15.00	30.00	50.00	95.00	—
1818D	—	15.00	30.00	50.00	95.00	—
1818D	—	45.00	80.00	125	225	—

Note: OCTAVO DD REAL, error

KM# 74.1   1/2 REAL
1.6900 g., 0.9030 Silver 0.0491 oz. ASW **Ruler:** Ferdinand VII **Obv:** Draped laureate bust right **Rev:** Crowned shield flanked by pillars **Mint:** Durango

Date	Mintage	VG	F	VF	XF	Unc
1813D RM	—	250	450	750	1,850	—
1814D MZ	—	250	450	750	1,850	—
1816D MZ	—	250	450	750	1,850	—

KM# 83.1   REAL
3.3800 g., 0.9030 Silver 0.0981 oz. ASW **Ruler:** Ferdinand VII **Obv:** Draped laureate bust right **Obv. Legend:** FERDIN • VII... **Rev:** Crowned shield flanked by pillars **Rev. Legend:** IND • REX... **Mint:** Durango

Date	Mintage	VG	F	VF	XF	Unc
1813D RM	—	250	450	650	1,650	—
1814D MZ	—	250	450	650	1,650	—
1815D MZ	—	250	450	650	1,650	—

KM# 92.2   2 REALES
6.7700 g., 0.9030 Silver 0.1965 oz. ASW **Ruler:** Ferdinand VII **Obv:** Armored bust right **Rev:** Crowned shield flanked by pillars **Rev. Legend:** MON PROV DE DURANGO... **Mint:** Durango

Date	Mintage	VG	F	VF	XF	Unc
1811D RM	—	575	675	1,300	2,650	—

KM# 92.3   2 REALES
6.7700 g., 0.9030 Silver 0.1965 oz. ASW **Ruler:** Ferdinand VII **Obv:** Armored bust right **Rev:** Crowned shield flanked by pillars **Rev. Legend:** HISPAN ET IND REX...

Date	Mintage	VG	F	VF	XF	Unc
1812 RM	—	375	600	1,150	2,500	—

KM# 93.1   2 REALES
6.7700 g., 0.9030 Silver 0.1965 oz. ASW **Ruler:** Ferdinand VII **Obv:** Draped laureate bust right **Obv. Legend:** FERDIN • VII... **Rev:** Crowned shield flanked by pillars **Rev. Legend:** IND • REX... **Mint:** Durango

Date	Mintage	VG	F	VF	XF	Unc
1812D RM	—	350	550	1,050	2,300	—
1813D RM	—	425	850	1,400	3,850	—

WAR OF INDEPENDENCE

Date	Mintage	VG	F	VF	XF	Unc
1813D MZ	—	425	850	1,400	3,850	—
1814D MZ	—	425	850	1,400	3,850	—
1815D MZ	—	425	850	1,400	3,850	—
1816D MZ	—	425	850	1,400	3,850	—
1817D MZ	—	425	850	1,400	3,850	—

KM# 102.1   4 REALES
13.5400 g., 0.9030 Silver 0.3931 oz. ASW   **Ruler:**
Ferdinand VII **Obv:** Draped laureate bust right **Obv. Legend:**
FERDIN • VII... **Rev:** Crowned shield flanked by pillars **Rev.**
Legend: IND • REX... **Mint:** Durango

Date	Mintage	VG	F	VF	XF	Unc
1814D MZ	—	775	1,400	2,300	6,300	—
1816D MZ	—	625	1,250	1,950	5,600	—
1817D MZ	—	625	1,250	1,950	5,600	—

KM# 111.2   8 REALES
27.0700 g., 0.9030 Silver 0.7859 oz. ASW   **Ruler:**
Ferdinand VII **Obv:** Draped laureate bust right **Obv. Legend:**
FERDIN • VII... **Rev:** Crowned shield flanked by pillars **Rev.**
Legend: IND • REX... **Mint:** Durango

Date	Mintage	VG	F	VF	XF	Unc
1812D RM	—	125	175	275	825	—
1813D RM	—	150	200	325	875	—
1813D MZ	—	125	175	275	775	—
1814/2D MZ	—	150	200	300	775	—
1814D MZ	—	150	200	300	775	—
1815D MZ	—	75.00	125	225	625	—
1816D MZ	—	50.00	75.00	125	350	—
1817D MZ	—	30.00	50.00	90.00	275	—
1818D MZ	—	50.00	75.00	125	375	—
1818D RM	—	50.00	75.00	125	350	—
1818D CG/RM	—	100	125	150	375	—
1818D CG	—	50.00	75.00	125	350	—
1819D CG/RM	—	50.00	100	150	325	—
1819D CG	—	30.00	60.00	100	275	—
1820D CG	—	30.00	60.00	100	275	—
1821D CG	—	30.00	40.00	80.00	225	—
1822D CG	—	30.00	50.00	90.00	265	—

Note: Occasionally these are found struck over cast Chihuahua 8 reales and are very rare in general, specimens dated prior to 1816 are rather crudely struck

GUADALAJARA

The Guadalajara Mint made its first coins in 1812 and the mint operated until April 30, 1815. It was to reopen in 1818 and continue operations until 1822. It was the only Royalist mint to strike gold coins, both 4 and 8 Escudos. In addition to these it struck the standard 5 denominations in silver.
Mint mark: GA.

ROYALIST COINAGE

KM# 74.2   1/2 REAL
1.6900 g., 0.9030 Silver 0.0491 oz. ASW   **Ruler:**
Ferdinand VII **Obv:** Draped laureate bust right **Obv. Legend:**
FERDIN • VII... **Rev:** Crowned shield flanked by pillars **Rev.**
Legend: IND... **Mint:** Guadalajara

Date	Mintage	VG	F	VF	XF	Unc
1812GA MR Rare	—	—	—	—	—	—

KM# 110.1   8 REALES
27.0700 g., 0.9030 Silver 0.7859 oz. ASW   **Ruler:**
Ferdinand VII **Obv:** Armored bust right **Obv. Legend:** FERD
• VII... **Rev:** Crowned shield flanked by pillars **Rev. Legend:**
DURANGO • 8R R • M... **Mint:** Durango

Date	Mintage	VG	F	VF	XF	Unc
1811D RM	—	2,500	5,000	8,000	—	—
1812D RM	—	350	650	1,000	3,500	—
1814D MZ	—	350	650	1,000	3,500	—

Date	Mintage	VG	F	VF	XF	Unc
1814GA MR	—	48.00	120	240	350	—
1815GA MR	—	240	425	600	1,200	—

KM# 83.2 REAL
3.3800 g., 0.9030 Silver 0.0981 oz. ASW **Ruler:**
Ferdinand VII **Obv:** Draped laureate bust right **Obv. Legend:**
FERDIN • VII... **Rev:** Crowned shield flanked by pillars **Rev.**
Legend: IND • REX... **Mint:** Guadalajara

Date	Mintage	VG	F	VF	XF	Unc
1813GA MR	—	350	600	950	—	—
1814GA MR	—	180	240	425	775	—
1815GA MR	—	350	600	950	—	—

KM# 93.2 2 REALES
6.7700 g., 0.9030 Silver 0.1965 oz. ASW **Ruler:**
Ferdinand VII **Obv:** Draped laureate bust right **Obv. Legend:**
FERDIN • VII... **Rev:** Crowned shield flanked by pillars **Rev.**
Legend: IND • REX.... **Mint:** Guadalajara

Date	Mintage	VG	F	VF	XF	Unc
1812GA MR	—	300	500	800	2,500	—
1814/2GA MR	—	75.00	125	250	650	—
1814GA MR	—	75.00	125	250	650	—
1815/4GA MR	—	425	725	1,100	3,600	—
1815GA MR	—	400	700	1,000	3,500	—
1821GA FS	—	200	250	350	950	—

KM# 102.2 4 REALES
13.5400 g., 0.9030 Silver 0.3931 oz. ASW **Ruler:**
Ferdinand VII **Obv:** Draped laureate bust right **Obv. Legend:**
FERDIN • VII... **Rev:** Crowned shield flanked by pillars **Rev.**
Legend: IND • REX... **Mint:** Guadalajara

Date	Mintage	VG	F	VF	XF	Unc
1814GA MR	—	50.00	80.00	190	325	—
1815GA MR	—	100	190	375	625	—

KM# 102.3 4 REALES
13.5400 g., 0.9030 Silver 0.3931 oz. ASW **Ruler:**
Ferdinand VII **Obv:** Draped laureate bust right **Obv. Legend:**
FERDIN • VII... **Rev:** Crowned shield flanked by pillars **Rev.**
Legend: IND • REX... **Mint:** Guadalajara

Date	Mintage	VG	F	VF	XF	Unc
1814GA MR	—	65.00	125	250	500	—

KM# 102.4 4 REALES
13.5400 g., 0.9030 Silver 0.3931 oz. ASW **Ruler:**
Ferdinand VII **Obv:** Draped laureate bust right **Obv. Legend:**
FERDIN • VII... **Rev:** Crowned shield flanked by pillars **Rev.**
Legend: IND • REX... **Mint:** Guadalajara

Date	Mintage	VG	F	VF	XF	Unc
1814GA MR	—	75.00	150	325	575	—

KM# 111.3 8 REALES
27.0700 g., 0.9030 Silver 0.7859 oz. ASW **Ruler:**
Ferdinand VII **Obv:** Draped laureate bust right **Obv. Legend:**
FERDIN • VII... **Rev:** Crowned shield flanked by pillars **Rev.**
Legend: IND • REX... **Mint:** Guadalajara

Date	Mintage	VG	F	VF	XF	Unc
1812GA MR	—	2,500	4,400	6,300	8,800	—
1813/2GA MR	—	90.00	150	225	600	—

Date	Mintage	VG	F	VF	XF	Unc
1813GA MR	—	90.00	150	225	600	—
1814GA MR	—	30.00	55.00	90.00	270	—

Note: Several bust varieties exist for the 1814 issue

Date	Mintage	VG	F	VF	XF	Unc
1815GA MR	—	190	250	450	950	—
1818GA FS	—	45.00	75.00	115	300	—
1821/18GA FS	—	45.00	75.00	115	300	—
1821GA FS	—	37.50	55.00	90.00	250	—
1821/2GA FS	—	45.00	75.00	115	300	—
1822GA FS	—	37.50	65.00	95.00	250	—

Note: Die varieties exist. Early dates are also encountered struck over other types

Date	Mintage	VG	F	VF	XF	Unc
1822/1GA FS	—	45.00	75.00	115	300	—

KM# 147   4 ESCUDOS
13.5400 g., 0.8750 Gold 0.3809 oz. AGW   **Ruler:** Ferdinand VII **Obv:** Uniformed bust right **Rev:** Crowned shield divides designed wreath **Mint:** Guadalajara

Date	Mintage	VG	F	VF	XF	Unc
1812GA MR Rare	—	—	—	—	—	—

KM# 162   8 ESCUDOS
27.0700 g., 0.8750 Gold 0.7615 oz. AGW   **Ruler:** Ferdinand VII **Obv:** Large uniformed bust right **Obv. Legend:** FERDIN • VII • D • G... **Rev:** Crowned shield divides designed wreath **Rev. Legend:** UTROQ • FELIX... **Mint:** Guadalajara

Date	Mintage	VG	F	VF	XF	Unc
1812GA MR Rare	—	—	—	—	—	—
1813GA MR	—	6,000	9,000	15,000	25,000	—

Note: Heritage Long Beach sale 5-08, Choice AU realized $37,500. American Numismatic Rarities Eliasberg sale 4-05, VF-30 realized $23,000.

KM# 163   8 ESCUDOS
27.0700 g., 0.8750 Gold 0.7615 oz. AGW   **Ruler:** Ferdinand VII **Obv:** Small uniformed bust right **Obv. Legend:**

FERDIN • VII... **Rev:** Crowned shield divides designed wreath **Rev. Legend:** UTROQ • FELIX... **Mint:** Guadalajara

Date	Mintage	VG	F	VF	XF	Unc
1813GA MR	—	10,000	16,000	30,000	45,000	—

Note: Spink America Gerber sale 6-96 VF or better realized $46,200

KM# 161.1   8 ESCUDOS
27.0700 g., 0.8750 Gold 0.7615 oz. AGW   **Ruler:** Ferdinand VII **Obv:** Laureate head right **Obv. Legend:** FERDIN • VII • D • G... **Rev:** Crowned shield divides designed wreath **Rev. Legend:** UTROQ • FELIX... **Mint:** Guadalajara

Date	Mintage	VG	F	VF	XF	Unc
1821GA FS	—	2,000	4,000	10,000	17,000	—

Note: American Numismatic Rarities Eliasberg sale 4-05, AU-55 realized $20,700.

KM# 164   8 ESCUDOS
27.0700 g., 0.8750 Gold 0.7615 oz. AGW   **Ruler:** Ferdinand VII **Obv:** Draped laureate bust right **Rev:** Crowned shield flanked by pillars **Mint:** Guadalajara

Date	Mintage	VG	F	VF	XF	Unc
1821GA FS	—	5,500	8,000	14,500	23,500	—

GUANAJUATO

The Guanajuato Mint was authorized December 24, 1812 and started production shortly thereafter; closing for unknown reasons on May 15, 1813. The mint was reopened in April, 1821 by the insurgents, who struck coins of the old royal Spanish design to pay their army, even after independence, well into 1822.

Only the 2 and 8 Reales coins were made.

Mint mark: Go.

ROYALIST COINAGE

KM# 93.3   2 REALES
6.7700 g., 0.9030 Silver 0.1965 oz. ASW   **Ruler:** Ferdinand VII **Obv:** Draped laureate bust right **Obv. Legend:** FERDIN • VII... **Rev:** Crowned shield flanked bu pillars **Rev. Legend:** IND • REX... **Mint:** Guanajuato

Date	Mintage	VG	F	VF	XF	Unc
1821Go JM	—	42.00	80.00	120	220	—
1822Go JM	—	36.00	60.00	90.00	175	—

KM# 111.4   8 REALES
27.0700 g., 0.9030 Silver 0.7859 oz. ASW **Ruler:**
Ferdinand VII **Obv:** Draped laureate bust right **Obv. Legend:**
FERDIN • VII... **Rev:** Crowned shield flanked by pillars **Rev.
Legend:** IND • REX... **Mint:** Guanajuato

Date	Mintage	VG	F	VF	XF	Unc
1812Go JJ	—	3,500	6,000	—	—	—
1813Go JJ	—	150	210	325	725	—
1821Go JM	—	30.00	60.00	90.00	240	—
1822Go JM	—	25.00	42.00	70.00	220	—

NUEVA GALICIA

(Later became Jalisco State)

In early colonial times, Nueva Galicia was an extensive
province which substantially combined later provinces of
Zacatecas and Jalisco. These are states of Mexico today
although the name was revived during the War of Independence. The only issue was 2 Reales of rather enigmatic origin.
No decrees or other authorization to strike this coin has yet
been located or reported.

INSURGENT COINAGE

KM# 218   2 REALES
0.9030 Silver **Obv:** N. G. in center, date **Obv. Legend:**
PROVVICIONAL... **Rev:** 2R in center **Rev. Legend:** ... A.
JUNIANA...

Date	Mintage	Good	VG	F	VF	XF
1813	—	1,000	2,500	4,500	—	—
Note: Excellent struck counterfeits exist

NUEVA VISCAYA

(Later became Durango State)

This 8 Reales, intended for the province of Nueva Vis-
caya, was minted in the newly-opened Durango Mint during
February and March of 1811, before the regular coinage of
Durango was started.

ROYALIST COINAGE

KM# 181   8 REALES
27.0700 g., 0.9030 Silver 0.7859 oz. ASW **Ruler:**
Ferdinand VII **Obv:** Crowned shield within sprays **Obv.
Legend:** MON • PROV • DE NUEV • VIZCAYA **Rev:** Crowned
shield flanked by pillars

Date	Mintage	Good	VG	F	VF	XF
1811 RM	—	1,000	2,250	2,850	5,500	—
Note: Several varieties exist.

OAXACA

The city of Oaxaca was in the midst of a coin shortage
when it became apparent the city would be taken by the Insurgents. Royalist forces under Lt. Gen. Saravia had coins made.
They were cast in a blacksmith shop. 1/2, 1, and 8 Reales
were made only briefly in 1812 before the Royalists surren-
dered the city.

ROYALIST COINAGE

KM# 166   1/2 REAL
0.9030 Silver **Ruler:** Ferdinand VII **Obv:** Cross separating
castle, lion, Fo, 7o **Rev:** Legend around shield **Rev. Legend:**
PROV • D • OAXACA

Date	Mintage	Good	VG	F	VF	XF
1812	—	1,000	1,500	2,500	3,500	—

KM# 167   REAL
0.9030 Silver **Ruler:** Ferdinand VII **Obv:** Cross separating castle, lion, Fo, 7o **Rev:** Legend around shield **Rev. Legend:** PROV • D • OAXACA

Date	Mintage	Good	VG	F	VF	XF
1812	—	350	650	1,200	2,500	—

KM# 168   8 REALES
0.9030 Silver **Obv:** Cross separating castle, lion, Fo, 7o **Obv. Legend:** OAXACA 1812... **Rev:** Shield, authorization mark above **Note:** These issues usually display a second mark 'O' between the crowned pillars on the obverse. Varieties of large and small lion in shield also exist.

Date	Mintage	Good	VG	F	VF	XF
1812 "A"	—	1,300	1,900	3,300	5,500	—
1812 "B"	—	1,300	1,900	3,300	5,500	—
1812 "C"	—	1,300	1,900	3,300	5,500	—
1812 "D"	—	1,300	1,900	3,300	5,500	—
1812 "K"	—	1,300	1,900	3,300	5,500	—
1812 "L"	—	1,300	1,900	3,300	5,500	—
1812 "Mo"	—	1,300	1,900	3,300	5,500	—
1812 "N"	—	1,300	1,900	3,300	5,500	—
1812 "O"	—	1,300	1,900	3,300	5,500	—
1812 "R"	—	1,300	1,900	3,300	5,500	—
1812 "V"	—	1,300	1,900	3,300	5,500	—
1812 "Z"	—	1,300	1,900	3,300	5,500	—

INSURGENT COINAGE

Oaxaca was the hub of Insurgent activity in the south where coinage started in July 1811 and continued until October 1814. The Oaxaca issues represent episodic strikings, usually under dire circumstances by various individuals. Coins were commonly made of copper due to urgency and were intended to be redeemed at face value in gold or silver once silver was available to the Insurgents. Some were later made in silver, but most appear to be of more recent origin, to satisfy collectors.

KM# 219   1/2 REAL
Struck Copper **Issuer:** SUD, Under General Morelos **Obv:** Bow, arrow, SUD **Rev:** Morelos monogram Mo, date

Date	Mintage	Good	VG	F	VF	XF
1811	—	6.75	11.50	20.00	35.00	—
1812	—	6.75	11.50	20.00	35.00	—
1813	—	5.50	9.00	17.50	30.00	—
1814	—	9.00	16.50	25.00	40.00	—

Note: Uniface strikes exist of #219

KM# 220.1   1/2 REAL
Struck Silver **Issuer:** SUD, Under General Morelos **Obv:** Bow, arrow, SUD **Rev:** Morelos monogram Mo, date

Date	Mintage	Good	VG	F	VF	XF
1811	—	—	—	—	—	—
1812	—	—	—	—	—	—
1813	—	—	—	—	—	—

KM# 220.2   1/2 REAL
Struck Silver **Issuer:** SUD, Under General Morelos **Obv:** Bow, arrow, SUD **Rev:** Morelos monogram Mo, date

Date	Mintage	Good	VG	F	VF	XF
1811	—	—	—	—	—	—
1812	—	—	—	—	—	—
1813	—	27.50	55.00	110	165	—

Note: Use caution as silver specimens appear questionable and may be considered spurious

KM# 221   1/2 REAL
Struck Silver **Issuer:** SUD, Under General Morelos **Obv:** Bow, arrow **Obv. Legend:** PROVICIONAL DE OAXACA **Rev:** Lion **Rev. Legend:** AMERICA MORELOS

Date	Mintage	Good	VG	F	VF	XF
1812	—	38.50	65.00	110	165	—
1813	—	38.50	65.00	110	165	—

KM# 221a   1/2 REAL
Struck Copper **Issuer:** SUD, Under General Morelos **Obv:** Bow, arrow **Obv. Legend:** PROVICIONAL DE OAXACA **Rev:** Lion **Rev. Legend:** AMERICA MORELOS

Date	Mintage	Good	VG	F	VF	XF
1812	—	30.25	46.75	75.00	110	
1813	—	22.50	38.50	65.00	95.00	—

KM# A222   1/2 REAL
Struck Copper **Issuer:** SUD, Under General Morelos **Obv:** Similar to KM#220 **Rev:** Similar to KM#221 but with 1/2 at left of lion **Rev. Legend:** AMERICA MORELOS

Date	Mintage	Good	VG	F	VF	XF
1813	—	30.25	46.75	75.00	110	

KM# 243   1/2 REAL
Struck Copper **Issuer:** Tierra Caliente (Hot Country), Under General Morelos **Obv:** Bow, T.C., SUD **Rev:** Morelos monogram, value, date

Date	Mintage	Good	VG	F	VF	XF
1813	—	41.25	75.00	140	220	—

KM# 222 REAL
Struck Copper **Issuer:** SUD, Under General Morelos **Obv:**
Bow, arrow, SUD **Rev:** Morelos monogram, 1 R., date

Date	Mintage	Good	VG	F	VF	XF
1811	—	5.00	10.00	20.00	41.75	—
1812	—	4.00	8.00	15.00	33.00	—
1813	—	4.00	8.00	15.00	33.00	—

KM# 222a REAL
Struck Silver **Issuer:** SUD, Under General Morelos **Obv:**
Bow, arrow, SUD **Rev:** Morelos monogram, 1 R., date

Date	Mintage	Good	VG	F	VF	XF
1812	—	—	—	—	—	—
1813	—	—	—	—	—	—

KM# 223 REAL
Cast Silver **Issuer:** SUD, Under General Morelos **Obv:** Bow,
arrow, SUD with floral ornaments **Rev:** Morelos monogram,
1 R., date

Date	Mintage	Good	VG	F	VF	XF
1812	—	—	—	—	—	—
1813	—	30.25	65.00	125	175	—

Note: Use caution as many silver specimens appear questionable and may be considered spurious

KM# 224 REAL
Struck Copper **Issuer:** SUD, Under General Morelos **Obv:**
Bow, arrow/SUD **Rev:** Lion **Rev. Legend:** AMERICA
MORELOS

Date	Mintage	Good	VG	F	VF	XF
1813	—	30.25	46.75	85.00	120	—

KM# 225 REAL
Silver **Issuer:** SUD, Under General Morelos **Obv:** Bow,
arrow/SUD **Rev:** Lion **Rev. Legend:** AMERICA MORELOS

Date	Mintage	Good	VG	F	VF	XF
1813 Rare	—	—	—	—	—	—

KM# 244 REAL
Struck Copper **Issuer:** Tierra Caliente (Hot Country), Under
General Morelos **Obv:** Bow, T.C., SUD **Rev:** Morelos
monogram, value, date

Date	Mintage	Good	VG	F	VF	XF
1813	—	15.00	27.50	55.00	90.00	—

KM# 226.1 2 REALES
Struck Copper **Issuer:** SUD, Under General Morelos **Obv:**
Bow, arrow/SUD **Rev:** Morelos monogram, .2.R., date

Date	Mintage	Good	VG	F	VF	XF
1811	—	14.00	27.50	60.00	110	—
1811 inverted 2	—	17.00	33.00	65.00	130	—
1812	—	2.75	4.00	7.00	13.00	—
1813	—	3.00	6.00	9.00	17.00	—
1814	—	15.00	30.75	70.00	130	—

KM# 226.1a 2 REALES
Struck Silver **Issuer:** SUD, Under General Morelos **Obv:**
Bow, arrow/SUD **Rev:** Morelos monogram, .2.R., date

Date	Mintage	Good	VG	F	VF	XF
1812	—	195	325	550	825	—

KM# 229 2 REALES
Cast Silver **Issuer:** SUD, Under General Morelos **Obv:** Bow,
arrow, SUD **Rev:** Morelos monogram, value, date in center
with ornamentation around

Date	Mintage	Good	VG	F	VF	XF
1812	—	65.00	110	165	250	—
1812 Filled in D in SUD	—	65.00	110	165	250	—

Note: Use caution as many silver specimens appear questionable and may be considered spurious

KM# 245 2 REALES
Struck Copper **Issuer:** Tierra Caliente (Hot Country), Under
General Morelos **Obv:** Bow, T.C., SUD **Rev:** Morelos
monogram, value, date

Date	Mintage	Good	VG	F	VF	XF
1813	—	10.00	25.00	38.50	55.00	—

KM# 227 2 REALES
Struck Silver **Issuer:** SUD, Under General Morelos **Obv:**
Bow, arrow **Obv. Legend:** SUD-OXA **Rev:** Morelos
monogram, value, date

Date	Mintage	Good	VG	F	VF	XF
1813	—	65.00	110	220	325	—
1814	—	65.00	110	220	325	—

KM# 228 2 REALES
Struck Silver **Issuer:** SUD, Under General Morelos **Obv:**
Bow, arrow **Obv. Legend:** SUD. OAXACA **Rev:** Morelos
monogram, value, date

Date	Mintage	Good	VG	F	VF	XF
1814	—	65.00	110	220	350	—

KM# 226.2 2 REALES
Struck Silver **Issuer:** SUD, Under General Morelos **Obv:**
Three large stars added **Rev:** Morelos monogram, .2.R., date

Date	Mintage	Good	VG	F	VF	XF
1814	—	11.00	22.50	44.00	65.00	—

KM# 246 2 REALES
Struck Copper **Issuer:** Tierra Caliente (Hot Country), Under
General Morelos **Obv:** Bow, T.C., SUD **Rev:** Morelos
monogram, value, date

Date	Mintage	Good	VG	F	VF	XF
1814	—	27.50	60.00	120	210	—

KM# 234 8 REALES
Copper **Issuer:** SUD, Under General Morelos **Obv:** Bow,
arrow, SUD in floral ornamentation **Rev:** Morelos monogram,
.8.R., date surrounded by ornate flowery fields

Date	Mintage	Good	VG	F	VF	XF
1811	—	90.00	150	180	270	—
1812	—	8.00	12.00	20.00	40.00	—
1813	—	8.00	12.00	20.00	40.00	—
1814	—	15.00	22.50	37.50	75.00	—

KM# 235 8 REALES
Cast Silver **Issuer:** SUD, Under General Morelos **Obv:** Bow,
arrow, SUD in floral ornamentation **Rev:** Morelos monogram,
value, date surrounded by ornate flowery fields

Date	Mintage	Good	VG	F	VF	XF
1811	—	—	—	—	—	—
1812	—	90.00	150	240	425	—
1813	—	70.00	120	210	350	—
1814	—	—	—	—	—	—

Note: Most silver specimens available in today's market are
considered spurious

KM# 234a 8 REALES
Struck Silver **Issuer:** SUD, under General Morelos **Obv:**

Bow, arrow, SUD in floral ornamentation **Rev:** Morelos
monogram, .8.R., date surrounded by ornate flowery fields

Date	Mintage	Good	VG	F	VF	XF
1811	—	—	—	2,500	4,000	—
1812	—	—	—	1,200	2,000	—

KM# 233.5a 8 REALES
Silver **Issuer:** SUD, Under General Morelos **Obv:** 8 dots below
bow, SUD, plain fields **Rev:** Morelos monogram, 8.R., date

Date	Mintage	Good	VG	F	VF	XF
1812	—	—	—	1,200	2,000	—

KM# 236 8 REALES
0.9030 Struck Silver **Issuer:** SUD, Under General Morelos
Obv: M monogram **Obv. Legend:** PROV • D • OAXACA **Rev:**
Lion shield with or without bow above

Date	Mintage	Good	VG	F	VF	XF
1812 Rare	—	—	—	—	—	—

KM# 233.1 8 REALES
Copper **Issuer:** SUD, Under General Morelos **Obv:** Bow,
arrow, SUD **Rev:** Morelos monogram, 8.R., date, plain fields

Date	Mintage	Good	VG	F	VF	XF
1812	—	22.50	45.00	90.00	135	—

KM# 233.1a 8 REALES
Struck Silver **Issuer:** SUD, Under General Morelos **Obv:** Bow,
arrow, SUD **Rev:** Morelos monogram, 8.R., date, plain fields

Date	Mintage	Good	VG	F	VF	XF
1812	—	120	180	300	550	—

KM# 233.2 8 REALES
Copper **Issuer:** SUD, Under General Morelos **Obv:** Bow,
arrow, SUD **Rev:** Morelos monogram, 8 R, date, plain fields

Date	Mintage	Good	VG	F	VF	XF
1812	—	12.00	16.00	25.00	30.00	—
1813	—	12.00	16.00	25.00	30.00	—
1814	—	20.00	25.00	30.00	40.00	—

Note: Similar to KM#233.4 but lines below bow slant left

KM# 242 8 REALES
Copper **Issuer:** Huautla, Under General Morelos **Obv:** Legend around bow, arrow/SUD **Obv. Legend:** MONEDA PROVI • CIONAL PS • ES • **Rev. Legend:** FABRICADO EN HUAUTLA

Date	Mintage	Good	VG	F	VF	XF
1812	—	1,000	1,500	2,000	—	—

KM# 248 8 REALES
Struck Copper **Issuer:** Tierra Caliente (Hot Country), Under General Morelos **Obv:** Bow, T.C., SUD **Rev:** Morelos monogram, value, date

Date	Mintage	Good	VG	F	VF	XF
1813	—	14.00	30.00	60.00	115	—

KM# 249 8 REALES
Cast Silver **Issuer:** Tierra Caliente (Hot Country), Under General Morelos **Obv:** Bow, T.C., SUD **Rev:** Morelos monogram, value, date

Date	Mintage	Good	VG	F	VF	XF
1813	—	—	—	—	—	—

Note: Use caution as many silver specimens appear questionable and may be considered spurious

KM# 233.2a 8 REALES
Silver **Issuer:** SUD, Under General Morelos **Obv:** bow, arrow, SUD **Rev:** Morelos monogram, 8R, date, plain fields

Date	Mintage	Good	VG	F	VF	XF
1813	—	—	—	1,200	2,000	—

KM# 233.3 8 REALES
Struck Copper **Issuer:** SUD, Under General Morelos **Obv:** Bow, arrow, SUD, with left slant lines below bow **Rev:** Morelos monogram, 8.R., date, plain fields

Date	Mintage	Good	VG	F	VF	XF
1813	—	15.00	27.50	45.00	75.00	—

KM# 233.4 8 REALES
Struck Copper **Issuer:** SUD, Under General Morelos **Obv:** Bow, arrow, SUD, with right slant lines below bow **Rev:** Morelos monogram, 8.R., date, plain fields

Date	Mintage	Good	VG	F	VF	XF
1813	—	15.00	27.50	45.00	75.00	—

KM# 237 8 REALES
0.9250 Silver **Issuer:** SUD, Under General Morelos **Obv:** M monogram, without legend **Rev:** Lion shield with or without bow above

Date	Mintage	Good	VG	F	VF	XF
1813 Rare	—	—	—	—	—	—

KM# 238 8 REALES
0.9030 Struck Silver **Issuer:** SUD, Under General Morelos **Obv:** Bow/M/SUD **Rev:** PROV. DE. ... arms

Date	Mintage	Good	VG	F	VF	XF
1813 Rare	—	—	—	—	—	—

KM# 239 8 REALES
Cast Silver **Issuer:** SUD, Under General Morelos **Obv:** Bow, arrow **Obv. Legend:** SUD-OXA **Rev:** Morelos monogram

Date	Mintage	Good	VG	F	VF	XF
1814 Rare	—	—	—	—	—	—

KM# 240 8 REALES
Copper **Issuer:** SUD, Under General Morelos **Obv:** Bow, arrow **Obv. Legend:** SUD-OXA **Rev:** Morelos monogram, 8.R., date

Date	Mintage	Good	VG	F	VF	XF
1814	—	42.00	85.00	180	300	—

KM# 241 8 REALES
Copper **Issuer:** SUD, Under General Morelos **Obv:** Bow, arrow **Obv. Legend:** SUD-OAXACA **Rev:** Morelos monogram, 8.R., date

Date	Mintage	Good	VG	F	VF	XF
1814	—	100	200	350	550	—

PUEBLA

INSURGENT COINAGE

KM# 250 1/2 REAL
Copper **Issuer:** Zacatlan, struck by General Osorno **Obv:** Osorno monogram, ZACATLAN, date **Rev:** Crossed arrows, wreath, value

Date	Mintage	Good	VG	F	VF	XF
1813 Rare	—	—	—	—	—	—

KM# 251 REAL
Copper **Issuer:** Zacatlan, struck by General Osorno **Obv:** Osorno monogram, ZACATLAN, date **Rev:** Crossed arrows, wreath, value

Date	Mintage	Good	VG	F	VF	XF
1813	—	125	190	280	575	—

KM# 252 2 REALES
Copper **Issuer:** Zacatlan, struck by General Osorno **Obv:** Osorno monogram, ZACATLAN, date **Rev:** Crossed arrows, wreath, value

Date	Mintage	Good	VG	F	VF	XF
1813	—	155	220	350	625	—

REAL DEL CATORCE

(City in San Luis Potosi)

Real del Catorce is an important mining center in the Province of San Luis Potosi. In 1811 an 8 Reales coin was issued under very primitive conditions while the city was still in Royalist hands. Few survive.

ROYALIST COINAGE

KM# 169 8 REALES
0.9030 Silver **Ruler:** Ferdinand VII **Obv. Legend:** EL R • D • CATORC • POR FERNA • VII **Rev. Legend:** MONEDA • PROVISIONAL • VALE • 8R

Date	Mintage	VG	F	VF	XF	Unc
1811	—	7,000	15,000	35,000	65,000	—

Note: Spink America Gerber Sale 6-96 VF or XF realized $63,800

SAN FERNANDO DE BEXAR

TOKEN COINAGE

KM# Tn1   1/2 REAL (Jola)
Copper **Ruler:** Ferdinand VII **Note:** Prev. KM#170.

Date	Mintage	Good	VG	F	VF	XF
1818	8,000	—	—	—	25,000	30,000

KM# Tn2   1/2 REAL (Jola)
Copper **Ruler:** Ferdinand VII **Note:** Prev. KM#171.

Date	Mintage	Good	VG	F	VF	XF
1818	Inc. above	—	—	—	22,500	27,500

SAN LUIS POTOSI

Sierra de Pinos

ROYALIST COINAGE

KM# A172   1/4 REAL
Copper **Ruler:** Ferdinand VII **Issuer:** Sierra de Pinos, Villa

Date	Mintage	Good	VG	F	VF	XF
1814	—	100	150	250	400	—

KM# A172a   1/4 REAL
Silver **Ruler:** Ferdinand VII

Date	Mintage	Good	VG	F	VF	XF
1814 Rare	—	—	—	—	—	—

SOMBRERETE

(Under Royalist Vargas)

The Sombrerete Mint opened on October 8, 1810 in an area that boasted some of the richest mines in Mexico. The mint operated only until July 16, 1811, only to reopen in 1812 and finally close for good at the end of the year. Mines Administrator Fernando Vargas, was also in charge of the coining, all coins bear his name.

ROYALIST COINAGE

KM# 172   1/2 REAL
0.9030 Silver **Ruler:** Ferdinand VII **Obv:** Legend around

crowned globes **Obv. Legend:** FERDIN • VII • SOMBRERETE... **Rev:** Legend above lys in oval, sprays, date below **Rev. Legend:** VARGAS

Date	Mintage	Good	VG	F	VF	XF
1811	—	45.00	70.00	150	275	—
1812	—	50.00	90.00	175	300	—

KM# 173   REAL
0.9030 Silver **Ruler:** Ferdinand VII **Obv:** Legend around crowned globes **Obv. Legend:** FERDIN • VII • SOMBRERETE... **Rev:** Legend above lys in oval with denomination flanking, sprays, date below **Rev. Legend:** VARGAS

Date	Mintage	Good	VG	F	VF	XF
1811	—	45.00	70.00	150	275	—

Note: For 1811, denomination reads as '1R' or 'R1'

Date	Mintage	Good	VG	F	VF	XF
1812	—	50.00	90.00	175	300	—

KM# 174   2 REALES
0.9030 Silver **Ruler:** Ferdinand VII **Countermark:** VARGAS **Obv:** Royal arms **Obv. Legend:** R • CAXA • DE • SOMBRERETE **Rev:** 1811, S between crowned pillars

Date	Mintage	Good	VG	F	VF	XF
1811 SE	—	100	250	450	750	—

KM# 175   4 REALES
0.9030 Silver **Ruler:** Ferdinand VII **Obv:** Crowned Royal arms **Obv. Legend:** R • CAXA • DE • SOMBRERETE **Rev:** Large legend **Rev. Legend:** VARGAS / 1812 **Note:** Prev. KM#172.

Date	Mintage	Good	VG	F	VF	XF
1812	—	50.00	100	200	500	—

KM# 176   8 REALES
0.9030 Silver **Ruler:** Ferdinand VII **Countermark:** VARGAS, date, S **Obv:** Royal arms **Obv. Legend:** R • CAXA • DE • SOMBRERETE **Rev:** Several countermarks between crowned pillars

Date	Mintage	Good	VG	F	VF	XF
1810	—	1,000	1,750	2,750	4,500	8,750
1811	—	225	325	450	600	—

KM# 177   8 REALES
0.9030 Silver   **Ruler:** Ferdinand VII **Obv:** Crowned Royal arms **Obv. Legend:** R • CAXA • DE SOMBRETE **Rev. Legend:** VARGAS / date /3, S between crowned pillars

Date	Mintage	Good	VG	F	VF	XF
1811	—	140	200	400	800	—
1812	—	125	185	375	775	—

VALLADOLID MICHOACAN

ROYALIST COINAGE

KM# 178   8 REALES
0.9030 Silver   **Ruler:** Ferdinand VII **Obv:** Royal arms in wreath, value at sides **Rev. Legend:** PROVISIONAL / DE VALLADOLID / 1813

Date	Mintage	Good	VG	F	VF	XF
1813 Rare	—	—	—	—	—	—

KM# 179   8 REALES
0.9030 Silver   **Ruler:** Ferdinand VII **Obv:** Draped laureate bust right **Obv. Legend:** FERDIN • VII •... **Rev:** Crowned shield flanked by pillars, P. D. V. in legend **Rev. Legend:** REX • P • D • V...

Date	Mintage	Good	VG	F	VF	XF
1813 Rare	—	—	—	—	—	—

Note: Spink America Gerber sale 6-96 good realized $23,100

VERACRUZ

In Zongolica, in the province of Veracruz, 2 priests and a lawyer decided to raise an army to fight for independence. Due to isolation from other Insurgent forces, they decided to make their own coins. Records show that they intended to mint coins of 1/2, 1, 2, 4, and 8 Reales, but specimens are extant of only the three higher denominations.

INSURGENT COINAGE

KM# 253   2 REALES
0.9030 Silver   **Issuer:** Zongolica **Obv:** Bow and arrow **Obv. Legend:** VIVA FERNANDO VII Y AMERICA **Rev:** Value, crossed palm branch, sword, date **Rev. Legend:** ZONGOLICA

Date	Mintage	Good	VG	F	VF	XF
1812	—	100	200	350	650	—

KM# 255   8 REALES
0.9030 Silver   **Issuer:** Zongolica **Obv:** Bow and arrow **Obv. Legend:** VIVA FERNANDO VII Y AMERICA **Rev:** Value, crossed palm branch, sword, date **Rev. Legend:** ZONGOLICA **Note:** Similar to 2 Reales, KM#253.

Date	Mintage	Good	VG	F	VF	XF
1812 Rare	—	—	—	—	—	—

Note: Spink America Gerber sale 6-96 VF to XF realized $57,200

INSURGENT COUNTERMARKED COINAGE
CONGRESS OF CHILPANZINGO

Type A: Hand holding bow and arrow between quiver with arrows, sword and bow.

Type B: Crowned eagle on bridge.

KM# 256.1 1/2 REAL
Silver **Issuer:** Congress of Chilpanzingo **Countermark:** Type A hand holding bow and arrow between quiver with arrows, sword and bow **Note:** Countermark on cast Mexico City KM#72.

CM Date	Host Date	Good	VG	F	VF	XF
ND	1812	42.50	70.00	90.00	140	—

KM# 256.2 1/2 REAL
Silver **Issuer:** Congress of Chilpanzingo **Countermark:** Type A hand holding bow and arrow between quiver with arrows, sword and bow **Note:** Countermark on Zacatecas KM#181.

CM Date	Host Date	Good	VG	F	VF	XF
ND	1811	50.00	75.00	100	150	—

KM# A257 REAL
Cast Silver **Issuer:** Congress of Chilpanzingo **Countermark:** Type A hand holding bow and arrow between quiver with arrows, sword and bow **Note:** Countermark on cast Mexico City KM#81.

CM Date	Host Date	Good	VG	F	VF	XF
ND	1803	18.50	30.00	50.00	85.00	—

KM# 257.1 2 REALES
Silver **Issuer:** Congress of Chilpanzingo **Countermark:** Type B crowned eagle on bridge **Note:** Countermark on 1/4 cut of 8 Reales.

CM Date	Host Date	Good	VG	F	VF	XF
	ND Unique	—	—	—	—	—

KM# 257.2 2 REALES
Silver **Issuer:** Congress of Chilpanzingo **Countermark:** Type B crowned eagle on bridge **Note:** Countermark on Zacatecas KM#186.

CM Date	Host Date	Good	VG	F	VF	XF
ND	1811 Unique					

KM# 258.1 8 REALES
Silver **Issuer:** Congress of Chilpanzingo **Countermark:** Type A hand holding bow and arrow between quiver with arrows, sword and bow **Note:** Countermark on cast Mexico City KM#109.

CM Date	Host Date	Good	VG	F	VF	XF
ND	1805	45.00	65.00	85.00	150	—

Note: A countermark appears on coins dated 1805 TH

KM# 258.2 8 REALES
Silver **Issuer:** Congress of Chilpanzingo **Countermark:** Type A hand holding bow and arrow between quiver with arrows, sword and bow **Note:** Countermark on cast Mexico City KM#110.

CM Date	Host Date	Good	VG	F	VF	XF
ND	1810 HJ	50.00	75.00	100	175	—

KM# 258.3 8 REALES
Silver **Issuer:** Congress of Chilpanzingo **Countermark:** Type A hand holding bow and arrow between quiver with arrows, sword and bow **Note:** Countermark on cast Mexico City KM#111.

CM Date	Host Date	Good	VG	F	VF	XF
ND	1811 HJ	45.00	65.00	85.00	150	—
ND	1812 HJ	100	125	175	275	—

KM# 259.1 8 REALES
Silver **Issuer:** Congress of Chilpanzingo **Countermark:** Type B crowned eagle on bridge **Note:** Countermark on Chihuahua KM#111.1.

CM Date	Host Date	Good	VG	F	VF	XF
ND	1816 RP	200	250	300	400	—

KM# 259.2 8 REALES
Silver **Issuer:** Congress of Chilpanzingo **Countermark:** Type B crowned eagle on bridge **Note:** Countermark on cast Mexico City KM#111.

CM Date	Host Date	Good	VG	F	VF	XF
ND	1811 HJ	130	150	175	250	—

KM# 259.3 8 REALES
Silver **Issuer:** Congress of Chilpanzingo **Countermark:** Type B crowned eagle on bridge **Note:** Countermark on Valladolid KM#178.

CM Date	Host Date	Good	VG	F	VF	XF
ND	1813	1,000	2,000	3,000	5,000	—

KM# 259.4 8 REALES
Silver **Issuer:** Congress of Chilpanzingo **Countermark:** Type B crowned eagle on bridge **Note:** Countermark on Zacatecas KM#190.

CM Date	Host Date	Good	VG	F	VF	XF
ND	1810	400	500	600	775	—

DON JOSE MARIA DE LINARES

KM# 263.1 8 REALES
Silver **Issuer:** Don Jose Maria De Linares **Countermark:** LINA/RES* **Note:** Countermark on Mexico City KM#110.

CM Date	Host Date	Good	VG	F	VF	XF
ND	1808 TH	250	300	375	550	—

KM# 263.2 8 REALES
Silver **Issuer:** Don Jose Maria De Linares **Countermark:** LINA/RES * **Note:** Countermark on Zacatecas KM#190.

CM Date	Host Date	Good	VG	F	VF	XF
ND	1811	300	375	450	650	—

KM# 263.3 8 REALES
Silver **Issuer:** Don Jose Maria De Linares **Countermark:** LINA/RES* **Note:** Countermark on Zacatecas KM#191.

CM Date	Host Date	Good	VG	F	VF	XF
ND	1812	250	300	375	550	—

GENERAL VICENTE GUERRERO

The countermark of an eagle facing left within a pearled oval has been attributed by some authors as that of General Vicente Guerrero, a leader of the insurgents in the south, 1816-1821.

KM# 276 1/2 REAL
Silver **Issuer:** General Vicente Guerrero **Countermark:** Eagle **Note:** Countermark on Mexico City KM#72.

CM Date	Host Date	Good	VG	F	VF	XF
ND	ND	40.00	60.00	80.00	175	—

KM# 277 REAL
Silver **Issuer:** General Vicente Guerrero **Countermark:** Eagle **Note:** Countermark on Mexico City KM#78.

CM Date	Host Date	Good	VG	F	VF	XF
ND	1772 FM	35.00	50.00	75.00	165	—

KM# 278.1 2 REALES
Silver **Issuer:** General Vicente Guerrero **Countermark:** Eagle **Note:** Countermark on Mexico City KM#88.

CM Date	Host Date	Good	VG	F	VF	XF
ND	1784 FM	40.00	60.00	100	225	—
ND	1798	40.00	60.00	100	225	—

KM# 278.2 2 REALES
Silver **Issuer:** General Vicente Guerrero **Countermark:** Eagle **Note:** Countermark on Mexico City KM#91.

CM Date	Host Date	Good	VG	F	VF	XF
ND	1807 PJ	30.00	50.00	80.00	200	—

KM# 279 8 REALES
Silver **Issuer:** General Vicente Guerrero **Countermark:** Eagle **Note:** Countermark on Zacatecas KM#191.

CM Date	Host Date	Good	VG	F	VF	XF
ND	1811	100	150	200	350	—

ENSAIE

KM# 260.3 8 REALES
Silver **Issuer:** Ensaie **Countermark:** Eagle over ENSAIE,
crude sling below **Note:** Countermark on Zacatecas KM#190.

CM Date	Host Date	Good	VG	F	VF	XF
ND	1810	—	—	—	—	—
ND	1811	100	150	200	325	—

KM# 260.4 8 REALES
Silver **Issuer:** Ensaie **Countermark:** Eagle over ENSAIE,
crude sling below **Note:** Countermark on Zacatecas KM#191.

CM Date	Host Date	Good	VG	F	VF	XF
ND	1810	500	700	900	1,250	—
ND	1811	250	300	375	550	—
ND	1812	200	250	285	450	—

KM# 260.1 8 REALES
Silver **Issuer:** Ensaie **Countermark:** Eagle over ENSAIE,
crude sling below **Note:** Countermark on Mexico City
KM#110.

CM Date	Host Date	Good	VG	F	VF	XF
ND	1811 HJ	150	200	275	375	—

KM# 260.2 8 REALES
Silver **Issuer:** Ensaie **Countermark:** Eagle over ENSAIE,
crude sling below **Note:** Countermark on Zacatecas KM#189.

CM Date	Host Date	Good	VG	F	VF	XF
ND	1811	200	400	600	850	—

JOSE MARIA LICEAGA

J.M.L. with banner on cross, crossed olive
branches.

(J.M.L./V., D.s, S.M., S.Y.S.L., Ve, A.P., s.r.a.,
Sea, P.G., S., S.M., El)

KM# A260 1/2 REAL
Silver **Issuer:** Jose Maria Liceaga **Countermark:** JML/SM
with banner on cross, crossed olive branches **Note:**
Countermark on cast Mexico City 1/2 Real.

CM Date	Host Date	Good	VG	F	VF	XF
ND	ND	100	150	200	300	—

KM# 261.6 2 REALES
Silver **Issuer:** Jose Maria Liceaga **Countermark:** J.M.L./V.
with banner on cross, crossed olive branches **Note:**
Countermark on Zacatecas KM#187.

CM Date	Host Date	Good	VG	F	VF	XF
ND	1811	200	225	250	325	—

KM# 261.7 2 REALES
Silver **Issuer:** Jose Maria Liceaga **Countermark:** J.M.L./DS
with banner on cross, crossed olive branches **Note:**
Countermark on Zacatecas KM#187.

CM Date	Host Date	Good	VG	F	VF	XF
ND	1811	200	235	275	350	—

KM# 261.8 2 REALES
Silver **Issuer:** Jose Maria Liceaga **Countermark:** J.M.L./
S.M. with banner on cross, crossed olive branches **Note:**
Countermark on Zacatecas KM#187.

CM Date	Host Date	Good	VG	F	VF	XF
ND	1811	200	235	275	350	—

KM# 261.9 2 REALES
Silver **Issuer:** Jose Maria Liceaga **Countermark:** J.M.L./
S.Y. with banner on cross, crossed olive branches **Note:**
Countermark on Zacatecas KM#187.

CM Date	Host Date	Good	VG	F	VF	XF
ND	1811	200	235	275	350	—

KM# 261.1 2 REALES
Silver **Issuer:** Jose Maria Liceaga **Countermark:** J.M.L./Ve
with banner on cross, crossed olive branches **Note:**
Countermark on 1/4 cut of 8 Reales.

CM Date	Host Date	Good	VG	F	VF	XF
ND	ND	175	225	325	—	—

KM# 261.2 2 REALES
Silver **Issuer:** Jose Maria Liceaga **Countermark:** J.M.L./V
with banner on cross, crossed olive branchs **Note:**
Countermark on Zacatecas KM#186.

CM Date	Host Date	Good	VG	F	VF	XF
ND	1811	200	225	250	325	—

KM# 261.3 2 REALES
Silver **Issuer:** Jose Maria Liceaga **Countermark:** J.M.L./DS
with banner on cross, crossed olive branches **Note:**
Countermark on Zacatecas KM#186.

CM Date	Host Date	Good	VG	F	VF	XF
ND	1811	200	235	275	350	—

KM# 261.4 2 REALES
Silver **Issuer:** Jose Maria Liceaga **Countermark:** J.M.L./
S.M. with banner on cross, crossed olivo branches **Note:**
Countermark on Zacatecas KM#186.

CM Date	Host Date	Good	VG	F	VF	XF
ND	1811	200	235	275	350	—

KM# 261.5 2 REALES
Silver **Issuer:** Jose Maria Liceaga **Countermark:** J.M.L./
S.Y. with banner on cross, crossed olive branches **Note:**
Countermark on Zacatecas KM#186.

CM Date	Host Date	Good	VG	F	VF	XF
ND	1811	200	235	275	350	—

KM# 262.1 8 REALES
Silver **Issuer:** Jose Maria Liceaga **Countermark:** J.M.L./
D.S. with banner on cross, crossed olive branches **Note:**
Countermark on Zacatecas KM#190.

CM Date	Host Date	Good	VG	F	VF	XF
ND	1811	250	325	425	625	—

KM# 262.4 8 REALES
Silver **Issuer:** Jose Maria Liceaga **Countermark:** J.M.L./
S.F. with banner on cross, crossed olive branches **Note:**
Countermark on Zacatecas KM#190.

CM Date	Host Date	Good	VG	F	VF	XF
ND	1811	200	275	375	575	—

KM# 262.2 8 REALES
Silver **Issuer:** Jose Maria Liceaga **Countermark:** J.M.L./E
with banner on cross, crossed olive branches **Note:**
Countermark on Zacatecas KM#190.

CM Date	Host Date	Good	VG	F	VF	XF
ND	1811	225	300	400	600	—

KM# 262.3 8 REALES
Silver **Issuer:** Jose Maria Liceaga **Countermark:** J.M.L./
P.G. with banner on cross, crossed olive branches **Note:**
Countermark on Durango KM#111.2.

CM Date	Host Date	Good	VG	F	VF	XF
ND	1813 RM	200	275	375	575	—

KM# 262.5 8 REALES
Silver **Issuer:** Jose Maria Liceaga **Countermark:** J.M.L./
S.M. with banner on cross, crossed olive branches **Note:**
Countermark on Zacatecas KM#190.

CM Date	Host Date	Good	VG	F	VF	XF
ND	1811	200	275	375	550	—

KM# 262.10 8 REALES
Silver **Issuer:** Jose Maria Liceaga, J.M.L. with banner on
cross, crossed olive branches. (J.M.L./V. D.s., S.M.,
S.Y.S.L.,Ve, A.P., s.r.a., Sea, P.G., S., S.M., E.)
Countermark: J.M.L./S.M. **Note:** Countermark on Zacatecas
KM#190.

CM Date	Host Date	Good	VG	F	VF	XF
ND	1811	—	—	—	—	—

KM# 262.6 8 REALES
Silver **Issuer:** Jose Maria Liceaga **Countermark:** J.M.L./
V.E. with banner on cross, cross olive branches **Note:**
Countermark on Zacatecas KM#190.

CM Date	Host Date	Good	VG	F	VF	XF
ND	1811	200	275	375	550	—

KM# 262.12 8 REALES
Silver **Issuer:** Jose Maria Liceaga, Banner on cross, crossed olive branches **Countermark:** J.M.L. / P.G. **Note:** Countermark on Guanajuato 8 Reales, KM#111.4.

CM Date	Host Date	Good	VG	F	VF	XF
ND	ND1813	150	250	450	—	—

KM# 262.7 8 REALES
Silver **Issuer:** Jose Maria Liceaga, J.M.L with banner on cross, crossed olive branches. (J.M.L./V., D.s, S.M., S.Y.S.L., Ve, A.P., s.r.a., Sea, P.G., S., S.M., E.) **Countermark:** J.M.L./D.S. **Note:** Countermark on Zacatecas KM#190.

CM Date	Host Date	Good	VG	F	VF	XF
ND	1811	—	—	—	—	—

KM# 262.9 8 REALES
Silver **Issuer:** Jose Maria Liceaga, J.M.L. with banner on cross, crossed olive branches. (J.M.L./V. D.s., S.M., S.Y.S.L.,Ve, A.P., s.r.a., Sea, P.G., S., S.M., E.) **Countermark:** J.M.L./S.F. **Note:** Countermark on Zacatecas KM#190.

CM Date	Host Date	Good	VG	F	VF	XF
ND	1811	—	—	—	—	—

KM# 262.11 8 REALES
Silver **Issuer:** Jose Maria Liceaga, J.M.L. with banner on cross, crossed olive branches. (J.M.L./V. D.s., S.M., S.Y.S.L.,Ve, A.P., s.r.a., Sea, P.G., S., S.M., E.) **Countermark:** J.M.L./V.E. **Note:** Countermark on Zacatecas KM#190.

CM Date	Host Date	Good	VG	F	VF	XF
ND	1811	—	—	—	—	—

KM# 262.8 8 REALES
Silver **Issuer:** Jose Maria Liceaga, J.M.L. with banner on cross, crossed olive branches. (J.M.L./V. D.s., S.M., S.Y.S.L.,Ve, A.P., s.r.a., Sea, P.G., S., S.M., E.) **Countermark:** J.M.L./E **Note:** Countermark on Zacatecas KM#190.

CM Date	Host Date	Good	VG	F	VF	XF
ND	1811	—	—	—	—	—

L.V.S. - LABOR VINCIT SEMPER

Some authorities believe L.V.S. is for La Villa de Sombrerete.

KM# 264.1 8 REALES
Cast Silver **Issuer:** Labor Vincit Semper, Some authorities believe L.V.S. is for "La Villa de Sombrerete" **Countermark:** L.V.S. **Note:** Countermark on Chihuahua KM#123.

CM Date	Host Date	Good	VG	F	VF	XF
ND	1811 RP	275	350	450	600	—
ND	1812 RP	200	250	300	400	—

KM# 264.2 8 REALES
Silver **Issuer:** Labor Vincit Semper, Some authorities believe L.V.S. is for "La Villa de Sombrerete" **Countermark:** L.V.S. **Note:** Countermark on Chihuahua KM#111.1 overstruck on KM#123.

CM Date	Host Date	Good	VG	F	VF	XF
ND	1816 RP	250	300	325	425	—
ND	1817 RP	250	300	325	425	—
ND	1818 RP	250	300	325	425	—
ND	1819 RP	400	450	500	700	—
ND	1820 RP	450	500	550	350	—

KM# 264.3 8 REALES
Silver **Issuer:** Labor Vincit Semper, Some authorities believe L.V.S. is for "La Villa de Sombrerete" **Countermark:** L.V.S. **Note:** Countermark on Guadalajara KM#111.3.

CM Date	Host Date	Good	VG	F	VF	XF
ND	1817	185	220	250	350	—

KM# 264.4 8 REALES
Silver **Issuer:** Labor Vincit Semper, Some authorities believe L.V.S. is for "La Villa de Sombrerete" **Countermark:** L.V.S. **Note:** Countermark on Nueva Vizcaya KM#165.

CM Date	Host Date	Good	VG	F	VF	XF
ND	1811 RM	1,150	3,150	5,250	8,250	—

KM# 264.5 8 REALES
Silver **Issuer:** Labor Vincit Semper, Some authorities believe L.V.S. is for "La Villa de Sombrerete" **Countermark:** L.V.S. **Note:** Countermark on Sombrerete KM#177.

CM Date	Host Date	Good	VG	F	VF	XF
ND	1811	300	350	450	650	—
ND	1812	300	350	450	650	—

KM# 264.6 8 REALES
Silver **Issuer:** Labor Vincit Semper, Some authorities believe L.V.S. is for "La Villa de Sombrerete" **Countermark:** L.V.S. **Note:** Countermark on Zacatecas KM#190.

CM Date	Host Date	Good	VG	F	VF	XF
ND	1811	350	400	450	650	—

KM# 264.7 8 REALES
Silver **Issuer:** Labor Vincit Semper, Some authorities believe L.V.S. is for "La Villa de Sombrerete" **Countermark:** L.V.S. **Note:** Countermark on Zacatecas KM#192.

CM Date	Host Date	Good	VG	F	VF	XF
ND	1813	350	400	450	650	—

MORELOS
Morelos monogram

Type A: Stars above and below monogram in circle.

Type B: Dots above and below monogram in oval.

Type C: Monogram in rectangle.

Note: Many specimens of Type C available in to-days market are considered spurious.

KM# A265   2 REALES
Copper **Issuer:** Morelos **Countermark:** Type A stars above and below monogram in circle **Note:** Countermark on Oaxaca Sud, KM#226.1.

CM Date	Host Date	Good	VG	F	VF	XF
ND	1812	—	—	—	—	—

KM# A267   8 REALES
Silver   **Note:** Countermark Type C on Zacatecas KM#190.

CM Date	Host Date	Good	VG	F	VF	XF
ND	1811	300	350	450	750	—

KM# 265.1   8 REALES
Silver   **Issuer:** Morelos **Countermark:** Type A star above and below monogram in circle **Note:** Countermark on Mexico City KM#109.

CM Date	Host Date	Good	VG	F	VF	XF
ND	1797 FM	45.00	50.00	60.00	95.00	—
ND	1798 FM	45.00	50.00	60.00	95.00	—
ND	1800 FM	45.00	50.00	60.00	95.00	—
ND	1807 TH	45.00	50.00	60.00	95.00	—

KM# 265.2   8 REALES
Silver   **Issuer:** Morelos **Countermark:** Type A stars above and below monogram in circle **Note:** Countermark on Mexico City KM#110.

CM Date	Host Date	Good	VG	F	VF	XF
ND	1809 TH	55.00	75.00	120	200	—
ND	1811 HJ	55.00	75.00	120	200	—

KM# 265.3   8 REALES
Silver   **Issuer:** Morelos **Countermark:** Type A stars above and below monogram in circle **Note:** Countermark on Mexico City KM#111.

CM Date	Host Date	Good	VG	F	VF	XF
ND	1812 JJ	50.00	60.00	75.00	125	—

KM# 265.5   8 REALES
Cast Silver   **Issuer:** Morelos **Countermark:** Type A stars above and below monogram in circle **Note:** Countermark on Supreme National Congress KM#206.

CM Date	Host Date	Good	VG	F	VF	XF
ND	1811	200	250	375	600	—

KM# 266.1   8 REALES
Silver   **Issuer:** Morelos **Countermark:** Type B dots above and below monogram in oval **Note:** Countermark on Guatamala 8 Reales, C#67.

CM Date	Host Date	Good	VG	F	VF	XF
ND	1810 M Rare	—	—	—	—	—

KM# 266.2   8 REALES
Silver   **Issuer:** Morelos **Countermark:** Type B dots above and below monogram in oval **Note:** Countermark on Mexico City KM#110.

CM Date	Host Date	Good	VG	F	VF	XF
ND	1809 TH	45.00	55.00	65.00	100	—

WAR OF INDEPENDENCE

KM# 267.1   8 REALES
Silver **Issuer:** Morelos **Countermark:** Type C monogram in rectangle **Note:** Countermark on Zacatecas KM#189. Many specimens of Type C available in today's market are considered spurious.

CM Date	Host Date	Good	VG	F	VF	XF
ND	1811	300	350	450	750	—

KM# 265.4   8 REALES
Copper **Issuer:** Morelos **Countermark:** Type A stars above and below monogram in circle **Note:** Countermark on Oaxaca Sud KM#233.2.

CM Date	Host Date	Good	VG	F	VF	XF
ND	1812	19.00	27.50	37.50	60.00	—
ND	1813	19.00	27.50	37.50	60.00	—
ND	1814	19.00	27.50	37.50	60.00	—

KM# 265.6   8 REALES
Silver **Issuer:** Morelos **Countermark:** Type A stars above and below monogram in circle **Note:** Countermark on Zacatecas KM#190.

CM Date	Host Date	Good	VG	F	VF	XF
ND	1811	375	625	900	—	—

KM# 265.7   8 REALES
Silver **Issuer:** Morelos **Countermark:** Type A stars above and below monogram in circle **Note:** Countermark on Zacatecas KM#191.

CM Date	Host Date	Good	VG	F	VF	XF
ND	1811	200	250	375	600	—

KM# 267.2   8 REALES
Silver **Issuer:** Morelos **Countermark:** Type C: monogram in rectangle **Note:** Countermark Type C on Zacatecas KM#190. Many specimens of Type C available in today's market are considered spurious.

CM Date	Host Date	Good	VG	F	VF	XF
ND	1811	300	350	450	750	—

NORTE

Issued by the Supreme National Congress and the Army of the North.

Countermark: Eagle on cactus; star to left; NORTE below.

KM# 268   1/2 REAL
Silver **Issuer:** Supreme National Congress and the Army of the North **Countermark:** Eagle on cactus; star to left; NORTE below **Note:** Countermark on Zacatecas KM#180.

CM Date	Host Date	Good	VG	F	VF	XF
ND	1811	250	300	375	500	—

KM# 269   2 REALES
Silver **Issuer:** Supreme National Congress and the Army of the North **Countermark:** Eagle on cactus; star to left; NORTE below **Note:** Countermark on Zacatecas KM#187.

CM Date	Host Date	Good	VG	F	VF	XF
ND	1811	225	275	325	450	—

KM# A269   2 REALES
Silver **Issuer:** Supreme National Congress and the Army of the North **Countermark:** Eagle on cactus; star to left; NORTE below **Note:** Countermark on Zacatecas KM#188.

CM Date	Host Date	Good	VG	F	VF	XF
ND	1812	—	—	—	—	—

KM# B269   4 REALES
Silver **Issuer:** Supreme National Congress and the Army of the North **Countermark:** Eagle on cactus; star to left; NORTE below **Note:** Countermark on Sombrerete KM#175.

CM Date	Host Date	Good	VG	F	VF	XF
ND	1812	100	150	200	300	—

KM# 270.4   8 REALES
Silver **Issuer:** Supreme National Congress and the Army of the North **Countermark:** Eagle on cactus; star to left; NORTE below **Note:** Countermark on Zacatecas KM#191.

WAR OF INDEPENDENCE

CM Date	Host Date	Good	VG	F	VF	XF
ND	1811	200	300	400	550	—
ND	1811	200	300	400	550	—
ND	1812	200	300	400	550	—

KM# 270.1 8 REALES
Silver **Issuer:** Supreme National Congress and the Army of the North **Countermark:** Eagle on cactus; star to left; NORTE below **Note:** Countermark on Chihuahua KM#111.1.

CM Date	Host Date	Good	VG	F	VF	XF
ND	1813 RP	250	350	450	550	—

KM# 270.2 8 REALES
Silver **Issuer:** Supreme National Congress and the Army of the North **Countermark:** Eagle on cactus; star to left; NORTE below **Note:** Countermark on Guanajuato KM#111.4.

CM Date	Host Date	Good	VG	F	VF	XF
ND	1813 JM	400	550	700	850	—

KM# 270.3 8 REALES
Silver **Issuer:** Supreme National Congress and the Army of the North **Countermark:** Eagle on cactus; star to left; NORTE below **Note:** Countermark on Zacatecas KM#190.

CM Date	Host Date	Good	VG	F	VF	XF
ND	1811	300	400	500	675	—

OSORNO

Countermark: Osorno monogram. (Jose Francisco Osorno)

KM# 271.1 1/2 REAL
Silver **Issuer:** Jose Francisco Osorno **Countermark:** Osorno monogram **Note:** Countermark on Mexico City KM#72.

CM Date	Host Date	Good	VG	F	VF	XF
ND	1798 FM	65.00	100	150	225	—
ND	1802 FT	65.00	100	150	225	—
ND	1806	65.00	100	150	225	—

KM# 271.2 1/2 REAL
Silver **Issuer:** Jose Francisco Osorno **Countermark:** Osorno monogram **Note:** Countermark on Mexico City KM#73.

CM Date	Host Date	Good	VG	F	VF	XF
ND	1809 TH	65.00	100	150	225	—

KM# 272.1 REAL
Silver **Issuer:** Jose Francisco Osorno **Countermark:** Osorno monogram **Note:** Countermark on Mexico City KM#81.

CM Date	Host Date	Good	VG	F	VF	XF
ND	1803 FT	65.00	100	150	250	—

KM# 272.2 REAL
Silver **Issuer:** Jose Francisco Osorno **Countermark:** Osorno monogram **Note:** Countermark on Potosi KM#70.

CM Date	Host Date	Good	VG	F	VF	XF
ND	ND	75.00	115	175	275	—

KM# 272.3 REAL
Silver **Issuer:** Jose Francisco Osorno **Countermark:** Osorno monogram **Note:** Countermark on Guatemala KM#54.

CM Date	Host Date	Good	VG	F	VF	XF
ND	1804	75.00	115	175	275	—

KM# A272.1 2 REALES
Silver **Issuer:** Jose Francisco Osorno **Countermark:** Osorno monogram **Note:** Countermark on Mexico City KM#88.2.

CM Date	Host Date	Good	VG	F	VF	XF
ND	1788 FM	75.00	125	175	275	—

KM# A272.2 2 REALES
Silver **Issuer:** Jose Francisco Osorno **Countermark:** Osorno monogram **Note:** Countermark on Mexico City KM#91.

CM Date	Host Date	Good	VG	F	VF	XF
ND	1808 TH	75.00	125	175	275	—

KM# A272.3 2 REALES
Silver **Issuer:** Jose Francisco Osorno **Countermark:** Osorno monogram **Note:** Countermark on Mexico City KM#92.

CM Date	Host Date	Good	VG	F	VF	XF
ND	1809 TH	75.00	125	175	275	—

KM# A272.4 2 REALES
Silver **Issuer:** Jose Francisco Osorno **Countermark:** Osorno monogram **Note:** Countermark on Zacatlian KM#252.

CM Date	Host Date	Good	VG	F	VF	XF
ND	1813	150	200	350	500	—

KM# 273.1 4 REALES
Silver **Issuer:** Jose Francisco Osorno **Countermark:** Osorno monogram **Note:** Countermark on Mexico City KM#97.2.

CM Date	Host Date	Good	VG	F	VF	XF
ND	1782 FF	85.00	150	200	300	—

KM# 273.2 4 REALES
Silver **Issuer:** Jose Francisco Osorno **Countermark:** Osorno monogram **Note:** Countermark on Mexico City KM#100.

CM Date	Host Date	Good	VG	F	VF	XF
ND	1799 FM	85.00	150	200	300	—

KM# 274.1 8 REALES
Silver **Issuer:** Jose Francisco Osorno **Countermark:** Osorno monogram **Note:** Countermark on Lima 8 Reales, C#101.

CM Date	Host Date	Good	VG	F	VF	XF
ND	1811 JP	200	225	250	350	—

KM# 274.2 8 REALES
Silver **Issuer:** Jose Francisco Osorno **Countermark:** Osorno monogram **Note:** Countermark on Mexico City KM#110.

CM Date	Host Date	Good	VG	F	VF	XF
ND	1809 TH	125	150	225	375	—
ND	1810 HJ	125	150	225	375	—
ND	1811 HJ	125	150	225	375	—

VILLA / GRAN

(Julian Villagran)

KM# 298 2 REALES
Cast Silver , Julian Villagran **Countermark:** VILLA/GRAN **Note:** Countermark on cast Mexico City KM#91.

CM Date	Host Date	Good	VG	F	VF	XF
ND	1799 FM	150	200	250	350	—
ND	1802 FT	150	200	250	350	—

KM# 275 8 REALES
Cast Silver **Issuer:** Julian Villagran **Countermark:** VILLA/GRAN **Note:** Countermark on cast Mexico City KM#109.

CM Date	Host Date	Good	VG	F	VF	XF
ND	1796 FM	200	250	350	500	—
ND	1806 TH	200	250	350	500	—

ZMY

KM# 286 8 REALES
Silver **Issuer:** Unknown, presumed insurgent **Countermark:** ZMY **Note:** Countermark on Zacatecas KM#191.

CM Date	Host Date	Good	VG	F	VF	XF
ND	1812	100	150	200	350	—

COUNTERMARKED COINAGE

KM# 270.6 8 REALES
Silver **Issuer:** Issued by the Supreme National Congress and the Army of the North **Countermark:** Eagle on cactus; star to left; NORTE below. **Note:** Countermark on Sombrerete KM# 177.

CM Date	Host Date	Good	VG	F	VF	XF
ND	1812	1,000	1,450	1,875	—	—

KM# 263.4 8 REALES
Silver **Issuer:** Don Jose Maria De Linares **Countermark:** LINA/RES * **Note:** Countermark on Zacatecas KM#190.

CM Date	Host Date	Good	VG	F	VF	XF
ND	1811	—	—	—	—	—

KM# 263.5 8 REALES
Silver **Issuer:** Don Jose Maria De Linares **Countermark:** LINA/RES* **Note:** Countermark on Zacatecas KM#192.

CM Date	Host Date	Good	VG	F	VF	XF
ND	1812	—	—	—	—	—

KM# 270.5 8 REALES
Silver **Issuer:** Norte, Issued by the Supreme National Congress and the Army of the North **Countermark:** Eagle on cactus; star to left; NORTE below **Note:** Countermark on Zacatecas KM#190.

CM Date	Host Date	Good	VG	F	VF	XF
ND	1811	—	—	—	—	—

KM# 265.8 8 REALES
Silver **Issuer:** Morelos, Type A: Stars above and below monogram in circle. Type B: Dots above and below monogram in oval. Type C: Monogram in rectangle. Many specimens of Type C available in today's market are considered spurious. **Countermark:** Type A **Note:** Countermark on Zacatecas KM#190.

CM Date	Host Date	Good	VG	F	VF	XF
ND	1811	—	—	—	—	—

KM# 264.8 8 REALES
Cast Silver **Issuer:** Labor Vincit Semper, L.V.S.; Some authorities believe L.V.S. is for "La Villa de Sombrerete" **Countermark:** L.V.S. **Note:** Countermark on Zacatecas KM#190.

CM Date	Host Date	Good	VG	F	VF	XF
ND	1811	—	—	—	—	—

MULTIPLE COUNTERMARKS

Many combinations of Royalist and Insurgent countermarks are usually found on the cast copies produced by Chihuahua and Mexico City and on the other crude provisional issues of this period. Struck Mexico City coins were used to make molds for casting necessity issues and countermarked afterwards to show issuing authority. Some were marked again by either both or separate opposing friendly forces to authorize circulation in their areas of occupation. Some countermarks are only obtainable with companion markings.

KM# 289 2 REALES
Silver **Issuer:** C.M.S. and S.C.M. **Countermark:** C.M.S. (Comandancia Militar Suriana) and eagle with S.C.M. (Soberano Congreso Mexicano) **Note:** Countermark on Mexico City KM#91.

CM Date	Host Date	Good	VG	F	VF	XF
ND	ND	—	—	—	—	—

KM# 295 2 REALES
Silver **Issuer:** Militar del Sur and Soberano Congreso Mexicano **Countermark:** M.d.S. and eagle with S.C.M **Note:** Countermark on Mexico City KM#91.

CM Date	Host Date	Good	VG	F	VF	XF
ND	ND	150	250	450	—	—

KM# 296 2 REALES
Silver **Issuer:** Jose Francisco Osorno and Julian Villagran **Countermark:** Osorno monogram and VILLA/GRAN **Note:** Countermark on cast Mexico City KM#110.

CM Date	Host Date	Good	VG	F	VF	XF
ND	1809 TH	—	—	—	—	—

KM# A286 2 REALES
Silver **Issuer:** Jose Maria Liceaga and VTIL **Countermark:** J.M.L./D.S. AND VTIL **Note:** Countermark on Zacatecas KM#186.

CM Date	Host Date	Good	VG	F	VF	XF
ND	1811	75.00	125	175	275	—

KM# B286 2 REALES
Silver **Issuer:** Jose Maria Liceaga and VTIL **Countermark:**
J.M.L./V.E. and VTIL **Note:** Countermark on Zacatecas
KM#186.

CM Date	Host Date	Good	VG	F	VF	XF
ND	1810	75.00	125	175	275	—
ND	1811	75.00	125	175	275	—

KM# 285.2 8 REALES
Silver **Issuer:** Chilpanzingo and Morelos **Countermark:**
Chilpanzingo Type A and Morelos monogram Type A **Note:**
Countermark on cast Mexico City KM#110.

CM Date	Host Date	Good	VG	F	VF	XF
ND	1810 HJ	35.00	45.00	60.00	150	—
ND	1811 HJ	35.00	45.00	60.00	150	—

KM# C286 8 REALES
Silver **Issuer:** Chilpanzingo and Morelos and LVS
Countermark: Chilpanzingo Type A, Morelos Type A and
LVS monogram on cast Mexico City KM#110

CM Date	Host Date	Good	VG	F	VF	XF
ND	1809 HJ	50.00	75.00	125	325	—

KM# A298 8 REALES
Silver **Issuer:** S.J.N.G. and VTIL **Countermark:** S.J.N.G
and VTIL on Zacatecas KM#191

CM Date	Host Date	Good	VG	F	VF	XF
ND	ND	35.00	50.00	75.00	200	—

KM# A297 8 REALES
Silver **Issuer:** Chilpanzingo and ENSAIE **Countermark:**
Chilpanzingo Type B and ENSAIE **Note:** Countermark on
Zacatecas KM#189.

CM Date	Host Date	Good	VG	F	VF	XF
ND	ND	175	250	350	—	—

KM# 297 8 REALES
Silver **Issuer:** Chilpanzingo and LVA **Countermark:**
Chilpanzingo Type A and LVA **Note:** Countermark on Mexico
City KM#109.

CM Date	Host Date	Good	VG	F	VF	XF
ND	1805 TH	45.00	75.00	145	300	—

KM# 281 8 REALES
Silver **Issuer:** Chilpanzingo and LVS **Countermark:**
Chilpanzingo Type A and script LVS **Note:** Countermark on
cast Mexico City KM#110.

CM Date	Host Date	Good	VG	F	VF	XF
ND	1809 HJ	45.00	65.00	135	300	—

KM# 288.2 8 REALES
Silver **Issuer:** Chilpanzingo and Suprema Junta Nacional
Gubernativa **Countermark:** Chilpanzingo Type B **Note:**
Countermark on Zacatecas KM#190. Prev. KM#288.

CM Date	Host Date	Good	VG	F	VF	XF
ND	1811	—	—	—	—	—

KM# 290.2 8 REALES
Silver **Issuer:** ENSAIE and VTIL **Countermark:** ENSAIE
and VTIL **Note:** Countermark on Zacatecas KM#190. Prev.
KM#290.

CM Date	Host Date	Good	VG	F	VF	XF
ND	1811	100	175	275	375	—

KM# 291 8 REALES
Silver **Issuer:** Jose Maria Liceaga and VTIL **Countermark:**
J.M.L./D.S. and VTIL **Note:** Countermark on Mexico City
KM#110.

CM Date	Host Date	Good	VG	F	VF	XF
ND	1810 HJ	85.00	150	250	450	—

KM# 282 8 REALES
Silver **Issuer:** La Comandancia Militar and Morelos
Countermark: L.C.M and Morelos monogram Type A **Note:**
Countermark on cast Mexico City KM#109.

CM Date	Host Date	Good	VG	F	VF	XF
ND	1792 FM	—	—	—	—	—

KM# 283 8 REALES
Silver **Issuer:** Morelos and Morelos **Countermark:** Morelos
Type A and C **Note:** Countermark on cast Mexico City
KM#109.

CM Date	Host Date	Good	VG	F	VF	XF
ND	1806 TH	—	—	—	—	—

KM# 284 8 REALES
Silver **Issuer:** Chilpanzingo and Morelos **Countermark:**
Chilpanzingo Type A and Morelos monogram Type A **Note:**
Countermark on cast Mexico City KM#109.

CM Date	Host Date	Good	VG	F	VF	XF
ND	1806 TH	35.00	50.00	100	225	—
ND	1807 TH	35.00	50.00	100	225	—

KM# 285.1 8 REALES
Silver **Issuer:** Chilpanzingo and Morelos **Countermark:**
Chilpanzingo Type A and Morelos monogram Type A **Note:**
Countermark on struck Mexico City KM#110.

CM Date	Host Date	Good	VG	F	VF	XF
ND	1809 TH	45.00	65.00	135	300	—

KM# 285.3 8 REALES
Silver **Issuer:** Chilpanzingo and Morelos **Countermark:**
Chilpanzingo Type A and Morelos monogram Type A **Note:**
Countermark on cast Mexico City KM#111.

CM Date	Host Date	Good	VG	F	VF	XF
ND	1811 HJ	75.00	120	175	350	—

KM# A290 8 REALES
Silver **Issuer:** ENSAIE and Jose Maria Liceaga
Countermark: ENSAIE and J.M.L. **Note:** Countermark on
Zacatecas KM#190.

CM Date	Host Date	Good	VG	F	VF	XF
ND	1811	100	175	275	475	—

KM# 294 8 REALES
Silver **Issuer:** L.V.A. and Morelos **Countermark:** Script LVA
and Morelos monogram Type A **Note:** Countermark on cast
Mexico City KM#110.

CM Date	Host Date	Good	VG	F	VF	XF
ND	ND HJ	45.00	75.00	135	300	—

KM# 288.1 8 REALES
Silver **Issuer:** Chilpanzingo and Suprema Junta Nacional
Gubernativa **Countermark:** Chilpanzingo Type B and
S.J.N.G **Note:** Countermark on Zacatecas KM#189.

CM Date	Host Date	Good	VG	F	VF	XF
ND	1811	—	—	—	—	—

KM# 290.1 8 REALES
Silver **Issuer:** ENSAIE and VTIL **Countermark:** ENSAIE
and VTIL **Note:** Countermark on Zacatecas KM#189.

CM Date	Host Date	Good	VG	F	VF	XF
ND	1811	100	175	275	475	—

KM# 280.1 8 REALES
Silver **Issuer:** Chilpanzingo and Crown and flag
Countermark: Chilpanzingo Type B and Crown and flag
Note: Countermark on Zacatecas KM#189.

CM Date	Host Date	Good	VG	F	VF	XF
ND	1811	—	—	—	—	—

KM# 280.2 8 REALES
Silver **Issuer:** Chilpanzingo and crown and flag
Countermark: Chilpanzingo Type B and crown and flag **Note:**
Countermark on Zacatecas KM#190.

CM Date	Host Date	Good	VG	F	VF	XF
ND	1811	—	—	—	—	—

KM# 287   8 REALES
Silver **Issuer:** Chilpanzingo - Provisional De Valladolid
Countermark: Chilpanzingo Type B and P.D.V **Note:**
Countermark on Valladolid KM#178.

CM Date	Host Date	Good	VG	F	VF	XF
ND	1813	—	—	—	—	—

ZACATECAS

The city of Zacatecas, in a rich mining region has provided silver for the world since mid-1500. On November 14,
1810 a mint began production for the Royalist cause. Zacatecas was the most prolific during the War of Independence.
Four of the 5 standard silver denominations were made here,
4 Reales were not. The first, a local type showing mountains
of silver on the coins were made only in 1810 and 1811. Some
1811 coins were made by the Insurgents who took the city on
April 15, 1811, later retaken by the Royalists on May 21, 1811.
Zacatecas struck the standard Ferdinand VII bust type until
1922.
Mint marks: Z, ZS, Zs.

ROYALIST COINAGE

KM# 180   1/2 REAL
0.9030 Silver **Ruler:** Ferdinand VII **Obv:** Crowned shield
flanked by pillars **Obv. Legend:** FERDIN • VII... **Rev:**
Mountain within beaded circle **Mint:** Zacatecas **Note:** Mint
marks: Z, ZS, Zs.

Date	Mintage	Good	VG	F	VF	XF
1810	—	75.00	125	200	400	—
1811	—	30.00	50.00	90.00	200	—

Note: Date aligned with legend

KM# 181   1/2 REAL
0.9030 Silver **Ruler:** Ferdinand VII **Obv:** Crowned shield
flanked by pillars **Rev:** Mountain within beaded circle **Rev.
Legend:** MONEDA PROVISIONAL DE ZACATECAS **Mint:**
Zacatecas **Note:** Mint marks: Z, ZS, Zs.

Date	Mintage	Good	VG	F	VF	XF
1811	—	30.00	50.00	90.00	200	—

KM# 182   1/2 REAL
0.9030 Silver **Ruler:** Ferdinand VII **Obv:** Provincial bust right
Obv. Legend: FERDIN • VII **Rev:** Crowned shield flanked by
pillars **Rev. Legend:** MONEDA PROVISIONAL DE
ZACATECAS **Mint:** Zacatecas **Note:** Mint marks: Z, ZS, Zs.

Date	Mintage	Good	VG	F	VF	XF
1811	—	30.00	40.00	65.00	140	—
1812	—	25.00	35.00	60.00	125	—

KM# 73.1   1/2 REAL
1.6900 g., 0.9030 Silver 0.0491 oz. ASW **Ruler:**
Ferdinand VII **Obv:** Armored laureate bust right **Obv.
Legend:** FERDIN • VII... **Rev:** Crowned shield flanked by
pillars **Rev. Legend:** IND... **Mint:** Zacatecas **Note:** Mint
marks: Z, ZS, Zs.

Date	Mintage	Good	VG	F	VF	XF
1813 AG	—	20.00	40.00	60.00	110	—
1813 FP	—	25.00	45.00	85.00	185	—
1814 AG	—	15.00	30.00	60.00	110	—
1815 AG	—	12.50	25.00	40.00	70.00	—
1816 AG	—	10.00	15.00	25.00	55.00	—
1817 AG	—	10.00	15.00	25.00	55.00	—
1818 AG	—	10.00	15.00	25.00	55.00	—
1819 AG	—	10.00	15.00	25.00	55.00	—

KM# 74.3   1/2 REAL
1.6900 g., 0.9030 Silver 0.0491 oz. ASW **Ruler:**
Ferdinand VII **Obv:** Draped laureate bust right **Obv. Legend:**
FERDIN • VII... **Rev:** Crowned shield flanked by pillars **Rev.
Legend:** IND... **Mint:** Zacatecas **Note:** Mint marks: Z, ZS, Zs.

Date	Mintage	VG	F	VF	XF	Unc
1819 AG	—	8.00	12.00	25.00	50.00	—
1820 AG	—	8.00	12.00	25.00	50.00	—
1820 RG	—	5.00	10.00	20.00	45.00	—
1821 AG	—	150	250	450	850	—
1821 RG	—	5.00	10.00	20.00	45.00	—

KM# 183   REAL
0.9030 Silver **Ruler:** Ferdinand VII **Obv:** Crowned shield
flanked by pillars **Rev:** Mountain within beaded circle **Mint:**
Zacatecas **Note:** Mint marks: Z, ZS, Zs.

Date	Mintage	Good	VG	F	VF	XF
1810	—	100	150	300	500	—
1811	—	20.00	40.00	75.00	150	—

Note: Date aligned with legend

KM# 184   REAL
0.9030 Silver **Ruler:** Ferdinand VII **Obv:** Crowned shield
flanked by pillars **Rev:** Mountain within beaded circle **Rev.
Legend:** MONEDA PROVISIONAL DE ZACATECAS **Mint:**
Zacatecas **Note:** Mint marks: Z, ZS, Zs.

Date	Mintage	Good	VG	F	VF	XF
1811	—	15.00	30.00	60.00	135	—

KM# 185   REAL
0.9030 Silver **Ruler:** Ferdinand VII **Obv:** Provincial bust right
Obv. Legend: FERDIN • VII... **Rev:** Crowned shield flanked
by pillars **Rev. Legend:** MONEDA PROVISIONAL DE
ZACATECAS **Mint:** Zacatecas **Note:** Mint marks: Z, ZS, Zs.

Date	Mintage	Good	VG	F	VF	XF
1811	—	50.00	85.00	130	220	—
1812	—	40.00	70.00	110	195	—

KM# 82.1   REAL
3.3800 g., 0.9030 Silver 0.0981 oz. ASW **Ruler:**
Ferdinand VII **Obv:** Armored laureate bust right **Obv.
Legend:** FERDIN • VII... **Rev:** Crowned shield flanked by
pillars **Rev. Legend:** IND • REX... **Mint:** Zacatecas **Note:** Mint
marks: Z, ZS, Zs.

Date	Mintage	Good	VG	F	VF	XF
1813 FP	—	50.00	100	150	250	—
1814 AG	—	20.00	35.00	50.00	85.00	—
1814 FP	—	20.00	35.00	50.00	85.00	—
1815 AG	—	20.00	35.00	50.00	85.00	—
1816 AG	—	12.00	20.00	30.00	65.00	—
1817 AG	—	8.00	12.50	20.00	45.00	—
1818 AG	—	8.00	12.50	20.00	45.00	—
1819 AG	—	6.00	11.00	18.00	35.00	—

KM# 83.3   REAL
3.3800 g., 0.9030 Silver 0.0981 oz. ASW **Ruler:**
Ferdinand VII **Obv:** Draped laureate bust right **Obv. Legend:**
FERDIN • VII... **Rev:** Crowned shield flanked by pillars **Rev.
Legend:** REX • Z... **Mint:** Zacatecas **Note:** Mint marks: Z, ZS,
Zs.

Date	Mintage	VG	F	VF	XF	Unc
1820 AG	—	6.00	12.00	20.00	60.00	—
1820 RG	—	6.00	12.00	20.00	60.00	—
1821 AG	—	18.00	30.00	45.00	90.00	—
1821 AZ	—	12.00	20.00	40.00	85.00	—
1821 RG	—	7.00	12.50	25.00	65.00	—
1822 AZ	—	7.00	12.50	25.00	65.00	—
1822 RG	—	18.00	30.00	45.00	90.00	—

KM# 186   2 REALES
0.9030 Silver **Ruler:** Ferdinand VII **Obv:** Crowned shield
flanked by pillars **Obv. Legend:** FERDIN • VII... **Rev:**
Mountain within beaded circle **Rev. Legend:** MONEDA •
PROVISION... **Mint:** Zacatecas **Note:** Mint marks: Z, ZS, Zs.

Date	Mintage	Good	VG	F	VF	XF
1810 Rare	—	—	—	—	—	—
1811	—	30.00	48.00	85.00	145	—

Note: Date aligned with legend

KM# 187   2 REALES
0.9030 Silver **Ruler:** Ferdinand VII **Obv:** Crowned shield
flanked by pillars **Rev:** Mountain above L. V. O within beaded
circle **Rev. Legend:** MONEDA PROVISIONAL DE
ZACATECAS **Mint:** Zacatecas **Note:** Mint marks: Z, ZS, Zs.

Date	Mintage	Good	VG	F	VF	XF
1811	—	18.00	36.00	70.00	120	—

KM# 188   2 REALES
0.9030 Silver **Ruler:** Ferdinand VII **Obv:** Armored bust right
Obv. Legend: FERDIN • VII... **Rev:** Crowned shield flanked
by pillars **Rev. Legend:** MONEDA PROVISIONAL DE
ZACATECAS **Mint:** Zacatecas **Note:** Mint marks: Z, ZS, Zs.

Date	Mintage	Good	VG	F	VF	XF
1811	—	38.50	70.00	150	250	—
1812	—	33.00	65.00	140	220	—

KM# 92.1   2 REALES
6.7700 g., 0.9030 Silver 0.1965 oz. ASW **Ruler:**
Ferdinand VII **Obv:** Large armored bust right **Obv. Legend:**
FERDIN • VII **Rev:** Crowned shield flanked by pillars **Rev.
Inscription:** MONEDA • PROVISION... **Mint:** Zacatecas
Note: Mint marks: Z, ZS, Zs.

Date	Mintage	Good	VG	F	VF	XF
1813 FP	—	35.00	50.00	75.00	125	—
1814 FP	—	35.00	50.00	75.00	125	—
1814 AG	—	35.00	50.00	75.00	125	—
1815 AG	—	7.50	15.00	30.00	55.00	—
1816 AG	—	7.50	15.00	30.00	55.00	—
1817 AG	—	7.50	15.00	30.00	55.00	—
1818 AG	—	7.50	15.00	30.00	55.00	—

KM# 93.4   2 REALES
6.7700 g., 0.9030 Silver 0.1965 oz. ASW **Ruler:**
Ferdinand VII **Obv:** Draped laureate bust right **Obv. Legend:**

FERDIN • VII **Rev:** Crowned shield flanked by pillars **Rev.**
Legend: IND • REX... **Mint:** Zacatecas **Note:** Mint marks: Z,
ZS, Zs.

Date	Mintage	VG	F	VF	XF	Unc
1818 AG	—	7.50	15.00	30.00	55.00	—
1819 AG	—	10.00	20.00	40.00	85.00	—
1819 AG	—	10.00	20.00	40.00	85.00	—
Note: Reversed 'S' in HISPAN						
1820 AG	—	10.00	20.00	40.00	85.00	—
1820 RG	—	10.00	20.00	40.00	85.00	—
1821 AG	—	10.00	20.00	40.00	85.00	—
1821 AZ/RG	—	10.00	20.00	40.00	85.00	—
1821 AZ	—	10.00	20.00	40.00	85.00	—
1821 RG	—	10.00	20.00	40.00	85.00	—
1822 AG	—	10.00	20.00	40.00	85.00	—
1822 RG	—	10.00	20.00	40.00	85.00	—

KM# A92   2 REALES
6.7700 g., 0.9030 Silver 0.1965 oz. ASW   **Ruler:**
Ferdinand VII **Obv:** Small armored bust right **Obv. Legend:**
FERDIN • VII **Rev:** Crowned shield flanked by pillars **Rev.**
Legend: IND • REX... **Mint:** Zacatecas **Note:** Mint marks: Z,
ZS, Zs.

Date	Mintage	Good	VG	F	VF	XF
1819 AG	—	45.00	100	200	400	—

KM# 189   8 REALES
0.9030 Silver   **Ruler:** Ferdinand VII **Obv:** Crowned shield
flanked by pillars **Rev:** Mountain above L.V.O. within beaded
circle **Rev. Legend:** MONEDA.PROVISION... **Mint:**
Zacatecas **Note:** Mint Zacatecas.

Date	Mintage	Good	VG	F	VF	XF
1810	—	300	500	750	1,250	—
1811	—	100	150	225	350	—

Note: Date aligned with legend. Also exists with incomplete
date

KM# 190   8 REALES
0.9030 Silver   **Ruler:** Ferdinand VII **Obv:** Crowned shield
flanked by pillars **Obv. Legend:** FERDIN • VII • DEI... **Rev:**
Mountain above L. V. O within beaded circle **Rev. Legend:**
MONEDA PROVISIONAL DE ZACATECAS **Mint:** Zacatecas

Date	Mintage	Good	VG	F	VF	XF
1811	—	65.00	100	135	350	650
Note: Date aligned with legend						
1811 Error	—	—	—	—	3,000	5,000
FERDIN • VI						

KM# 191   8 REALES
0.9030 Silver   **Ruler:** Ferdinand VII **Obv:** Armored bust right
Obv. Legend: FERDIN • VII • 8 •R • DEI... **Rev:** Crowned
shield flanked by pillars **Rev. Legend:** MONEDA
PROVISIONAL DE ZACATECAS **Mint:** Zacatecas

Date	Mintage	Good	VG	F	VF	XF
1811	—	45.00	75.00	145	275	—
1812	—	50.00	85.00	160	300	—

KM# 192   8 REALES
0.9030 Silver   **Ruler:** Ferdinand VII **Obv:** Draped laureate
bust right **Obv. Legend:** FERDIN • VII • DEI... **Rev:** Crowned
shield flanked by pillars **Rev. Legend:** MONEDA
PROVISIONAL DE ZACATECAS **Mint:** Zacatecas

Date	Mintage	Good	VG	F	VF	XF
1812	—	75.00	150	275	450	—

KM# 111.5   8 REALES
27.0700 g., 0.9030 Silver 0.7859 oz. ASW **Ruler:**
Ferdinand VII **Obv:** Draped laureate bust right **Obv. Legend:**
FERDIN • VII • DEI • GRATIA **Rev:** Crowned shield flanked
by pillars **Rev. Legend:** HISPAN • ET IND • REX **Mint:**
Zacatecas **Note:** Mint mark: Zs. Several bust types exist for
the 1821 issues.

Date	Mintage	VG	F	VF	XF	Unc
1813 FP	—	75.00	125	175	275	—
1814 FP	—	150	250	350	450	—
1814 AG	—	100	150	200	300	—
1814 AG	—	125	175	225	325	—
Note: D over horizontal D in IND						
1814 AG/FP	—	100	150	200	300	—
1815 AG	—	50.00	100	150	250	—
1816 AG	—	35.00	50.00	65.00	125	—
1817 AG	—	35.00	50.00	65.00	125	—
1818 AG	—	30.00	40.00	50.00	100	—
1819 AG	—	30.00	40.00	50.00	100	—
1819 AG	—	100	200	300	400	—
'GRATIA' error						
1820 AG 18/11	—	100	200	300	400	—
error						
1820 AG	—	30.00	40.00	50.00	100	500
1820 RG	—	30.00	40.00	50.00	100	—
1821/81 RG	—	75.00	150	225	300	—
1821 RG	—	15.00	25.00	35.00	65.00	—
1821 AZ/RG	—	50.00	100	150	200	—
1821 AZ	—	50.00	100	150	200	—
1822 RG	—	40.00	60.00	100	175	650

KM# 111.6   8 REALES
27.0700 g., 0.9030 Silver 0.7859 oz. ASW **Ruler:**
Ferdinand VII **Obv:** Draped laureate bust right **Obv. Legend:**
FERDIN • VII • DEI • GRATIA **Rev:** Crowned shield flanked
by pillars **Rev. Legend:** HISAV • ET IND • REX **Mint:**
Zacatecas

Date	Mintage	VG	F	VF	XF	Unc
1821Zs	—	160	320	550	750	—

ROYALIST COUNTERMARKED COINAGE
LCM - LA COMANDANCIA MILITAR

Crown and Flag

This countermark exists in 15 various sizes.

KM# 193.1   2 REALES
0.9030 Silver **Issuer:** La Comandancia Militar **Countermark:**
LCM **Note:** Countermark on Mexico KM#92.

CM Date	Host Date	Good	VG	F	VF	XF
ND	1809 TH	85.00	165	250	450	—

KM# 193.2   2 REALES
0.9030 Silver **Issuer:** La Comandancia Militar, (The LCM
countermark exists in 15 various sizes) **Countermark:** LCM
Note: Countermark on Mexico KM#186.

CM Date	Host Date	Good	VG	F	VF	XF
ND	1811	85.00	165	250	450	—

KM# 194.1   8 REALES
Cast Silver **Issuer:** La Comandancia Militar, (The LCM
countermark exists in 15 various sizes) **Countermark:** LCM
Note: Countermark on Chihuahua KM#123.

CM Date	Host Date	Good	VG	F	VF	XF
ND	1811 RP	100	200	300	500	—
ND	1812 RP	100	200	300	500	—

KM# 194.6 8 REALES
0.9030 Silver **Issuer:** La Comandancia Militar, The LCM countermark exists in 15 different sizes **Countermark:** LCM
Note: Countermark on Nueva Viscaya KM#165.

CM Date	Host Date	Good	VG	F	VF	XF
ND	1811 RM Rare	—	—	—	—	—

KM# 194.7 8 REALES
0.9030 Silver **Issuer:** La Comandancia Militar, The LCM countermark exists in 15 different sizes **Countermark:** LCM
Note: Countermark on Mexico KM#111.

CM Date	Host Date	Good	VG	F	VF	XF
ND	1811 HJ	125	225	350	650	—
ND	1812 JJ	110	135	200	350	—
ND	1817 JJ	50.00	65.00	85.00	175	—
ND	1818 JJ	50.00	65.00	85.00	175	—
ND	1820 JJ	—	—	—	—	—

KM# 194.2 8 REALES
0.9030 Silver **Issuer:** La Comandancia Militar, The LCM countermark exists in 15 different sizes **Countermark:** LCM
Note: Countermark on Chihuahua KM#111.1 struck over KM#123.

CM Date	Host Date	Good	VG	F	VF	XF
ND	1815 RP	200	275	400	600	—
ND	1817 RP	125	175	225	350	—
ND	1820 RP	125	175	225	350	—
ND	1821 RP	125	175	225	350	—

KM# 194.3 8 REALES
0.9030 Silver **Issuer:** La Comandancia Militar, The LCM countermark exists in 15 different sizes **Countermark:** LCM
Note: Countermark on Durango KM#111.2.

CM Date	Host Date	Good	VG	F	VF	XF
ND	1812 RM	70.00	125	200	300	—
ND	1821 CG	70.00	125	200	300	—

KM# 194.4 8 REALES
0.9030 Silver **Issuer:** La Comandancia Militar, The LCM countermark exists in 15 different sizes **Countermark:** LCM
Note: Countermark on Guadalajara KM#111.3.

CM Date	Host Date	Good	VG	F	VF	XF
ND	1813 MR	150	225	300	500	—

KM# 194.5 8 REALES
0.9030 Silver **Issuer:** La Comandancia Militar, The LCM countermark exists in 15 different sizes **Countermark:** LCM
Note: Countermark on Guanajuato KM#111.4.

CM Date	Host Date	Good	VG	F	VF	XF
ND	1813 JJ	225	350	475	700	—

KM# 194.8 8 REALES
0.9030 Silver **Issuer:** La Comandancia Militar, The LCM countermark exists in 15 different sizes **Countermark:** LCM
Note: Countermark on Sombrerete KM#176.

CM Date	Host Date	Good	VG	F	VF	XF
ND	1811 Rare	—	—	—	—	—
ND	1812 Rare	—	—	—	—	—

KM# 194.9 8 REALES
0.9030 Silver **Issuer:** La Comandancia Militar, The LCM countermark exists in 15 different sizes **Countermark:** LCM
Note: Countermark on Zacatecas KM#190.

CM Date	Host Date	Good	VG	F	VF	XF
ND	1811	225	350	500	—	—

KM# 194.10   8 REALES
0.9030 Silver   **Issuer:** La Comandancia Militar, The LCM
countermark exists in 15 different sizes **Countermark:** LCM
Note: Countermark on Zacatecas KM#111.5.

CM Date	Host Date	Good	VG	F	VF	XF
ND	1813 FP	—	—	—	—	—
ND	1814 AG	—	—	—	—	—
ND	1822 RG	—	—	—	—	—

LCV - LAS CAJAS DE VERACRUZ

The Royal Treasury of the City of Veracruz

KM# 195   7 REALES
Silver   **Issuer:** Las Cajas de Veracruz, The Royal Treasury
of the City of Veracruz **Countermark:** LCV **Note:**
Countermark and 7 on underweight 8 Reales.

CM Date	Host Date	Good	VG	F	VF	XF
ND	ND Rare	—	—	—	—	—

Note: Most examples are counterfeit

KM# 196   7-1/4 REALES
Silver   **Issuer:** Las Cajas de Veracruz, The Royal Treasury
of the City of Veracruz **Countermark:** LCV **Note:**
Countermark and 7-1/4 on underweight 8 Reales.

CM Date	Host Date	Good	VG	F	VF	XF
ND	ND Rare	—	—	—	—	—

Note: Most examples are counterfeit

KM# 197   7-1/2 REALES
Silver   **Issuer:** Las Cajas de Veracruz, The Royal Treasury
of the City of Veracruz **Countermark:** LCV **Note:**
Countermark and 7-1/2 on underweight 8 Reales.

CM Date	Host Date	Good	VG	F	VF	XF
ND	ND Rare	—	—	—	—	—

Note: Most examples are counterfeit

KM# 198   7-3/4 REALES
Silver   **Issuer:** Las Cajas de Veracruz, The Royal Treasury
of the City of Veracruz **Countermark:** LCV **Note:**
Countermark and 7-3/4 on underweight 8 Reales.

CM Date	Host Date	Good	VG	F	VF	XF
ND	ND	300	375	450	700	—

Note: Many examples are counterfeit

KM# A198   8 REALES
Cast Silver   **Issuer:** Las Cajas de Veracruz, The Royal
Treasury of the City of Veracruz **Countermark:** LCV **Note:**
Countermark on Chihuahua KM#123.

CM Date	Host Date	Good	VG	F	VF	XF
ND	1811 RP	150	250	400	600	—

KM# 199   8 REALES
Silver   **Issuer:** Las Cajas de Veracruz, The Royal Treasury
of the City of Veracruz **Countermark:** LCV **Note:**
Countermark on Zacatecas KM#191.

CM Date	Host Date	Good	VG	F	VF	XF
ND	1811	175	225	275	375	—
ND	1812	175	225	275	375	—

MS (MONOGRAM) - MANUEL SALCEDO

KM# 200   8 REALES
Silver   **Issuer:** Manuel Salcedo **Countermark:** MS
monogram **Note:** Countermark on Mexico KM#110.

CM Date	Host Date	Good	VG	F	VF	XF
ND	1809 TH	150	250	400	600	—
ND	1810 HJ	150	250	400	600	—
ND	1811 HJ	150	250	400	600	—

MVA - MONCLOVA

KM# 202.3 8 REALES
Silver **Issuer:** Monclova, MVA **Countermark:** MVA/1812
Note: Countermark on cast Mexico KM#110.

CM Date	Host Date	Good	VG	F	VF	XF
1812	1809 HJ	100	150	250	375	—
1812	1809 TH	100	150	250	375	—
1812	1810 HJ	100	150	250	375	—

KM# 201 8 REALES
Silver **Issuer:** Monclova, MVA **Countermark:** MVA/1811
Note: Countermark on Chihuahua KM#111.1; struck over cast Mexico KM#110.

CM Date	Host Date	Good	VG	F	VF	XF
ND	1809	250	450	700	1,000	—
ND	1816 RP	250	450	700	1,000	—
ND	1821 RP	250	450	700	1,000	—

KM# 202.5 8 REALES
Silver **Issuer:** Monclova, MVA **Countermark:** MVA/1812
Note: Countermark on Zacatecas KM#189.

CM Date	Host Date	Good	VG	F	VF	XF
1812	1813	300	350	450	700	—

KM# 202.1 8 REALES
Silver **Issuer:** Monclova, MVA **Countermark:** MVA/1812
Note: Countermark on Chihuahua KM#111.1; struck over cast Mexico KM#109.

CM Date	Host Date	Good	VG	F	VF	XF
1812	1810	125	175	250	375	—

KM# 202.2 8 REALES
Silver **Issuer:** Monclova, MVA **Countermark:** MVA/1812
Note: Countermark on cast Mexico KM#109.

CM Date	Host Date	Good	VG	F	VF	XF
1812	1798 FM	100	150	250	375	—
1812	1802 FT	100	150	250	375	—

INSURGENT COINAGE

AMERICAN CONGRESS

KM# 216 REAL
0.9030 Silver **Issuer:** American Congress **Obv:** Eagle on cactus **Obv. Legend:** CONGRESO AMERICANO **Rev:** F. 7 on spread mantle **Rev. Legend:** DEPOSIT D.L. AUCTORI J **Mint:** Mexico City

Date	Mintage	Good	VG	F	VF	XF
ND(1813)	—	35.00	75.00	125	225	—

KM# 217 REAL
0.9030 Silver **Issuer:** American Congress **Obv:** Eagle on cactus **Obv. Legend:** CONGR. AMER. **Rev:** F. 7 on spread mantle **Rev. Legend:** DEPOS. D. L. AUT. D. **Mint:** Mexico City

Date	Mintage	Good	VG	F	VF	XF
ND(1813)	—	35.00	75.00	125	225	—

NATIONAL CONGRESS

KM# 209 1/2 REAL
Struck Copper **Issuer:** National Congress **Obv:** Eagle on bridge **Obv. Legend:** VICE FERD. VII DEI GRATIA ET **Rev:** Value, bow quiver, etc **Rev. Legend:** S. P. CONG. NAT. IND.

Date	Mintage	Good	VG	F	VF	XF
1811	—	45.00	85.00	150	250	—
1812	—	27.50	60.00	100	175	—
1813	—	27.50	60.00	100	175	—
1814	—	45.00	85.00	150	250	—

WAR OF INDEPENDENCE

KM# 210   1/2 REAL
0.9030 Silver   **Issuer:** National Congress **Obv:** Eagle on
bridge **Obv. Legend:** VICE FERD. VII DEI GRATIA ET **Rev:**
Value, bow quiver, etc **Rev. Legend:** S. P. CONG. NAT. IND.

Date	Mintage	Good	VG	F	VF	XF
1812	—	27.50	60.00	100	175	—
1813	—	45.00	90.00	175	275	—

Note: 1812 exists with the date reading inwards and out-
wards

KM# 211   REAL
0.9030 Silver   **Issuer:** National Congress **Obv:** Eagle on
bridge **Obv. Legend:** VICE FERD. VII DEI GRATIA ET **Rev:**
Value, bow quiver, etc **Rev. Legend:** S. P. CONG. NAT. IND.

Date	Mintage	Good	VG	F	VF	XF
1812	—	22.50	45.00	80.00	150	—
1813	—	22.50	45.00	80.00	150	—

Note: 1812 exists with the date reading either inward or
outward

KM# 212   2 REALES
Struck Copper   **Issuer:** National Congress **Obv:** Eagle on
bridge **Obv. Legend:** VICE FERD. VII DEI GRATIA ET **Rev:**
Value, bow quiver, etc **Rev. Legend:** S. P. CONG. NAT. IND.

Date	Mintage	Good	VG	F	VF	XF
1812	—	100	150	225	350	—
1813	—	23.50	50.00	75.00	150	—
1814	—	32.50	75.00	110	185	—

KM# A213   2 REALES
Struck Silver   **Issuer:** National Congress **Obv:** Eagle on bridge
Obv. Legend: VICE FERD. VII DEI GRATIA ET **Rev:** Value,
bow, quiver, etc **Rev. Legend:** S. P. CONG. NAT. IND.

Date	Mintage	Good	VG	F	VF	XF
1813	—	950	1,750	3,000	5,000	—

KM# 213   2 REALES
0.9030 Silver   **Issuer:** National Congress **Obv:** Eagle on
bridge in shield, denomination at sides **Obv. Legend:** VICE
FERD. VII DEI GRATIA ET **Rev:** Canon, quiver, arm, etc

Date	Mintage	Good	VG	F	VF	XF
1813	—	75.00	160	275	400	—

Note: These dies were believed to be intended for the striking of 2 Escudos

KM# 214   4 REALES
0.9030 Silver   **Issuer:** National Congress **Obv:** Eagle on
bridge **Obv. Legend:** VICE FERD. VII DEI GRATIA ET **Rev:**
Value, bow, quiver, etc **Rev. Legend:** S. P. CONG. NAT.
IND. **Mint:** Mexico City

Date	Mintage	Good	VG	F	VF	XF
1813	—	600	1,200	2,450	4,750	—

KM# 215.1   8 REALES
0.9030 Silver   **Issuer:** National Congress **Obv:** Small
crowned eagle **Obv. Legend:** VICE FERD. VII DEI GRATIA
ET **Rev:** Value, bow, quiver, etc **Rev. Legend:** S. P. CONG.
NAT. IND. **Mint:** Mexico City

Date	Mintage	Good	VG	F	VF	XF
1812Mo	—	600	1,150	2,350	4,500	—

KM# 215.2   8 REALES
0.9030 Silver   **Issuer:** National Congress **Obv:** Large
crowned eagle **Obv. Legend:** VICE FERD. VII DEI GRATIA
ET **Rev:** Value, bow, quiver, etc **Rev. Legend:** S. P. CONG.
NAT. IND. **Mint:** Mexico City

Date	Mintage	Good	VG	F	VF	XF
1813Mo	—	600	1,150	2,350	4,500	—

SUPREME NATIONAL CONGRESS OF AMERICA

PDV - Provisional de Valladolid

VTIL - Util = useful

(Refer to Multiple countermarks)

KM# 203 1/2 REAL
Struck Copper **Issuer:** Supreme National Congress of America **Obv:** Eagle on bridge **Obv. Legend:** FERDIN. VII DEI GRATIA **Rev:** Value, bow, quiver, etc **Rev. Legend:** S. P. CONG. NAT. IND. GUV.T.

Date	Mintage	Good	VG	F	VF	XF
1811	—	27.50	45.00	65.00	120	—
1812	—	27.50	45.00	65.00	120	—
1813	—	27.50	45.00	65.00	120	—
1814	—	27.50	45.00	65.00	120	—

KM# 204 REAL
Struck Copper **Issuer:** Supreme National Congress of America **Obv:** Eagle on bridge **Obv. Legend:** FERDIN. VII DEI GRATIA **Rev:** Value, bow, quiver, etc **Rev. Legend:** S. P. CONG. NAT. IND. GUV.T.

Date	Mintage	Good	VG	F	VF	XF
1811	—	45.00	75.00	125	200	—

KM# 205 2 REALES
Struck Copper **Issuer:** Supreme National Congress of America **Obv:** Eagle on bridge **Obv. Legend:** FERDIN. VII DEI GRATIA **Rev:** Value, bow, quiver, etc

Date	Mintage	Good	VG	F	VF	XF
1812	—	225	325	475	750	—

KM# 206 8 REALES
Cast Silver **Issuer:** Supreme National Congress of America **Obv:** Eagle on bridge **Obv. Legend:** FERDIN. VII DEI GRATIA **Rev:** Value, bow, quiver, etc

Date	Mintage	Good	VG	F	VF	XF
1811	—	150	250	350	550	—
1812	—	150	250	375	550	—

KM# 207 8 REALES
Struck Silver **Issuer:** Supreme National Congress of America **Obv:** Eagle on bridge **Obv. Legend:** FERDIN. VII DEI GRATIA **Rev:** Value, bow, quiver, etc

Date	Mintage	Good	VG	F	VF	XF
1811	—	—	—	—	—	—

Note: Ira & Larry Goldberg Millennia Sale 5-08, QU-55 realized $55,000.

1812	—	500	1,000	1,500	2,500	—

KM# 208 8 REALES
Struck Copper **Issuer:** Supreme National Congress of America **Obv:** Eagle on bridge **Obv. Legend:** FERDIN. VII... **Rev:** Bow, sword and quiver **Rev. Legend:** PROVICIONAL POR LA SUPREMA JUNTA DE AMERICA

Date	Mintage	Good	VG	F	VF	XF
1811	—	100	150	225	475	—
1812	—	100	150	225	475	—

EMPIRE OF ITURBIDE

RULER
Augustin I Iturbide, 1822-1823
MINT MARK
Mo - Mexico City
ASSAYERS' INITIALS
JA - Jose Garcia Ansaldo, 1812-1833
JM - Joaquin Davila Madrid, 1809-1833

MILLED COINAGE

KM# 299 1/8 REAL
Copper **Ruler:** Augustin I Iturbide **Obv:** Crowned shield within sprays **Rev:** Inscription, date **Rev. Inscription:** DE LA PROVINCIA DE NUEVA VISCAYA **Mint:** Durango

Date	Mintage	Good	VG	F	VF	XF
1821D	—	22.50	50.00	85.00	150	—
1822D	—	7.50	13.50	28.50	60.00	—
1823D	—	9.00	13.50	26.50	55.00	—

KM# 300 1/4 REAL
Copper **Ruler:** Augustin I Iturbide **Obv:** Crowned shield within sprays **Rev:** Inscription, date **Rev. Inscription:** DE LA PROVINCIA DE NUEVA VISCAYA **Mint:** Durango

Date	Mintage	Good	VG	F	VF	XF
1822D	—	160	275	400	550	—

KM# 301 1/2 REAL
0.9030 Silver **Ruler:** Augustin I Iturbide **Obv:** Head right
Obv. Legend: AUGUSTINUS DEI... **Rev:** Crowned eagle
Rev. Legend: I.M.E.X.I... **Mint:** Mexico City

Date	Mintage	F	VF	XF	Unc	BU
1822Mo JM	—	22.50	55.00	110	375	700
1823Mo JM	—	17.00	42.00	85.00	325	—

KM# 302 REAL
0.9030 Silver **Ruler:** Augustin I Iturbide **Obv:** Head right
Obv. Legend: AUGUSTINUS DEI... **Rev:** Crowned eagle
Rev. Legend: MEX.I.IMPERATOR... **Mint:** Mexico City

Date	Mintage	VG	F	VF	XF	Unc
1822Mo JM	—	100	175	350	550	1,150

KM# 303 2 REALES
6.7667 g., 0.9030 Silver 0.1964 oz. ASW **Ruler:**
Augustin I Iturbide **Obv:** Head right **Obv. Legend:**
AUGUSTINUS DEI... **Rev:** Crowned eagle **Rev. Legend:**
MEX • I • IMPERATOR... **Mint:** Mexico City

Date	Mintage	F	VF	XF	Unc	BU
1822Mo JM	—	60.00	120	350	1,000	—
1823Mo JM	—	40.00	80.00	250	850	—

KM# 304 8 REALES
27.0674 g., 0.9030 Silver 0.7858 oz. ASW **Ruler:**
Augustin I Iturbide **Obv:** Head right **Obv. Legend:**

AUGUST.... **Rev:** Crowned eagle **Rev. Legend:** ...MEX • I •
IMPERATOR... **Mint:** Mexico City

Date	Mintage	F	VF	XF	Unc	BU
1822Mo JM	—	75.00	150	300	1,100	—
1822Mo JM	—	—	—	—	—	—
Proof, 3 known						

Note: Ponterio & Associates Sale #86, 04-97, choice AU
Proof realized $12,650

KM# 305 8 REALES
0.9030 Silver **Ruler:** Augustin I Iturbide **Obv:** Bust similar to
8 Escudos, KM#131 **Rev:** Crowned eagle **Mint:** Mexico City

Date	Mintage	F	VF	XF	Unc	BU
1822Mo JM Rare	—	—	—	—	—	—

KM# 306.1 8 REALES
0.9030 Silver **Ruler:** Augustin I Iturbide **Obv:** Head right
Obv. Legend: AUGUST... **Rev:** Crowned eagle, 8 R.J.M. at
upper left of eagle **Rev. Legend:** MEX • I • IMPERATOR...
Mint: Mexico City **Note:** Type I.

Date	Mintage	F	VF	XF	Unc	BU
1822Mo JM	—	100	200	450	1,500	—

KM# 306.2 8 REALES
0.9030 Silver **Ruler:** Augustin I Iturbide **Obv:** Head right
Rev: Cross on crown **Mint:** Mexico City **Note:** Type I.

Date	Mintage	F	VF	XF	Unc	BU
1822Mo JM	—	650	1,000	—	—	—

KM# 307 8 REALES
0.9030 Silver **Ruler:** Augustin I Iturbide **Obv:** Head right
Rev: Crowned eagle **Mint:** Mexico City **Note:** Type II.

Date	Mintage	F	VF	XF	Unc	BU
1822Mo JM	—	150	350	700	2,500	—

KM# 308 8 REALES
0.9030 Silver **Ruler:** Augustin I Iturbide **Obv:** Head right,
continuous legend with long smooth truncation **Obv. Legend:**
AUGUSTINUS DEI... **Rev:** Crowned eagle **Mint:** Mexico City
Note: Type III.

Date	Mintage	F	VF	XF	Unc	BU
1822Mo JM	—	175	500	950	2,500	—

Note: Variety with long, straight truncation is valued at $5,000 in uncirculated condition

KM# 309   8 REALES

0.9030 Silver   **Ruler:** Augustin I Iturbide **Obv:** Head right
Obv. Legend: AUGUSTINUS DEI... **Rev:** Crowned eagle
Rev. Legend: MEX • I • IMPERATOR... **Mint:** Mexico City
Note: Type IV.

Date	Mintage	F	VF	XF	Unc	BU
1822Mo JM	—	50.00	120	250	850	—

KM# 310   8 REALES

0.9030 Silver   **Ruler:** Augustin I Iturbide **Obv:** Head right,
continuous legend with short irregular truncation **Obv.
Legend:** AUGUSTINUS DEI... **Rev:** Crowned eagle, 8 R.J.M.
below eagle **Rev. Legend:** MEX • I • IMPERATOR... **Mint:**
Mexico City **Note:** Type V.

Date	Mintage	F	VF	XF	Unc	BU
1822Mo JM	—	50.00	120	250	1,000	—
1823Mo JM	—	50.00	120	250	1,000	—

KM# 311   8 REALES

0.9030 Silver   **Ruler:** Augustin I Iturbide **Obv:** Head
right,long truncation **Rev:** Crowned eagle **Mint:** Mexico City
Note: Type VI.

Date	Mintage	F	VF	XF	Unc	BU
1822Mo JM Rare	—	—	—	—	—	—

KM# 312   4 SCUDOS

13.5334 g., 0.8750 Gold 0.3807 oz. AGW **Ruler:**
Augustin I Iturbide **Obv:** Head right **Obv. Legend:**
AUGUSTINUS DEI... **Rev:** Crowned eagle within ornate shield
Rev. Legend: CONSTITUT.4.S.I.M... **Mint:** Mexico City

Date	Mintage	F	VF	XF	Unc	BU
1823Mo JM	—	1,200	2,500	5,000	10,000	—

KM# 313.1   8 SCUDOS

27.0674 g., 0.8750 Gold 0.7614 oz. AGW **Ruler:** Augustin I
Iturbide **Obv:** Head right **Obv. Legend:** AUGUSTINUS . DEI...
Rev: Crowned eagle **Rev. Legend:** CONSTITUT.8.S.I.M...
Mint: Mexico City

Date	Mintage	F	VF	XF	Unc	BU
1822Mo JM	—	1,500	3,500	6,500	12,000	15,000

Note: American Numismatic Rarities Eliasberg sale 4-05,
MS-62 realized $20,700. Superior Casterline sale 5-89
choice AU realized $11,000

KM# 313.2   8 SCUDOS

0.8750 Gold   **Ruler:** Augustin I Iturbide **Obv:** Head right,
error in legend **Obv. Legend:** AUGUSTINUS • DEI... **Rev:**
Crowned eagle **Rev. Legend:** CONSTITUT • 8 • S • I • M...
Mint: Mexico City

Date	Mintage	F	VF	XF	Unc	BU
1822Mo JM	—	1,250	3,650	6,750	12,500	16,000

KM# 314   8 SCUDOS
0.8750 Gold **Ruler:** Augustin I Iturbide **Obv:** Head right **Obv.**
Legend: AUGUSTINUS DEI... **Rev:** Crowned eagle within
ornate shield **Rev. Legend:** CONSTITUT•8•S•I•M... **Mint:**
Mexico City

Date	Mintage	F	VF	XF	Unc	BU
1823Mo JM	—	1,200	2,500	6,000	10,000	—

REPUBLIC
First

MINT MARKS
A, AS - Alamos
CE - Real de Catorce
CA,CH - Chihuahua
C, Cn, Gn(error) - Culiacan
D, Do - Durango
EoMo - Estado de Mexico
Ga - Guadalajara
GC - Guadalupe y Calvo
G, Go - Guanajuato
H, Ho - Hermosillo
M, Mo - Mexico City
O, OA - Oaxaca
SLP, PI, P, I/P - San Luis Potosi
Z, Zs – Zacatecas
ASSAYERS' INITIALS

ALAMOS MINT

PG	1862-68	Pascual Gaxiola
DL, L	1866-79	Domingo Larraguibel
AM	1872-74	Antonio Moreno
ML, L	1878-95	Manuel Larraguibel

REAL DE CATORCE MINT

| ML | 1863 | Mariano Cristobal Ramirez |

CHIHUAHUA MINT

MR	1831-34	Mariano Cristobal Ramirez
AM	1833-39	Jose Antonio Mucharraz
MJ	1832	Jose Mariano Jimenez
RG	1839-56	Rodrigo Garcia
JC	1856-65	Joaquin Campa
BA	1858	Bruno Arriada
FP	1866	Francisco Potts
JC	1866-1868	Jose Maria Gomez del Campo
MM, M	1868-95	Manuel Merino
AV	1873-80	Antonio Valero
EA	1877	Eduardo Avila
JM	1877	Jacobo Mucharraz
GR	1877	Guadalupe Rocha
MG	1880-82	Manuel Gameros

CULIACAN MINT

CE	1846-70	Clemente Espinosa de los Monteros
C	1870	???
PV	1860-61	Pablo Viruega
MP, P	1871-76	Manuel Onofre Parodi
GP	1876	Celso Gaxiola & Manuel Onofre Parodi
CG, G	1876-78	Celso Gaxiola
JD, D	1878-82	Juan Dominguez
AM, M	1882-1899	Antonio Moreno
F	1870	Fernando Ferrari
JQ, Q	1899-1903	Jesus S. Quiroz

DURANGO MINT

RL	1825-1832	???
RM	1830-48	Ramon Mascarenas
OMC	1840	Octavio Martinez de Castro
CM	1848-76	Clemente Moron
JMR	1849-52	Jose Maria Ramirez
CP, P	1853-64, 1867-73	Carlos Leon de la Pena
LT	1864-65	???
JMP, P	1877	Carlos Miguel de la Palma
PE, E	1878	Pedro Espejo
TB, B	1878-80	Trinidad Barrera
JP	1880-94	J. Miguel Palma
MC, C,	1882-90	Manuel M. Canseco or Melchor Calderon
JB	1885	Jocobo Blanco
ND, D	1892-95	Norberto Dominguez

ESTADO DE MEXICO MINT

| L | 1828-30 | Luis Valazquez de la Cadena |
| F | 1828-30 | Francisco Parodi |

GUADALAJARA MINT

FS	1818-35	Francisco Suarez
JM	1830-32	???
JG	1836-39, 1842-67	Juan de Dios Guzman
MC	1839-46	Manuel Cueras
JM	1867-69	Jesus P. Manzano
IC, C	1869-77	Ignacio Canizo y Soto
MC	1874-75	Manuel Contreras
JA, A	1877-81	Julio Arancivia
FS, S	1880-82	Fernando Sayago
TB, B	1883-84	Trinidad Barrera
AH, H	1884-85	Antonio Hernandez y Prado
JS, S	1885-95	Jose S. Schiafino

GUADALUPE Y CALVO MINT

| MP | 1844-52 | Manuel Onofre Parodi |

GUANAJUATO MINT

JJ	1825-26	Jose Mariano Jimenez
MJ, MR, JM, PG, PJ, PF		???
PM	1841-48, 1853-61	Patrick Murphy
YF	1862-68	Yldefonso Flores
YE	1862-63	Ynocencio Espinoza
FR	1870-78	Faustino Ramirez
SB, RR		???
RS	1891-1900	Rosendo Sandoval

HERMOSILLO MINT

PP	1835-36	Pedro Peimbert
FM	1871-76	Florencio Monteverde
MP	1866	Manuel Onofre Parodi
PR	1866-75	Pablo Rubio
R	1874-75	Pablo Rubio
GR	1877	Guadalupe Rocha
AF, F	1876-77	Alejandro Fourcade
JA, A	1877-83	Jesus Acosta
FM, M	1883-86	Fernando Mendez
FG, G	1886-95	Fausto Gaxiola

MEXICO CITY MINT

Because of the great number of assayers for this mint (Mexico City is a much larger mint than any of the others)there is much confusion as to which initial stands for which assayer at any one time. Therefore we feel that it would be of no value to list the assayers.

OAXACA MINT

AE	1859-91	Agustin Endner
E	1889-90	Agustin Endner
FR	1861-64	Francisco de la Rosa
EN	1890	Eduardo Navarro Luna
N	1890	Eduardo Navarro Luna

POTOSI MINT

JS	1827-42	Juan Sanabria
AM	1838, 1843-49	Jose Antonio Mucharraz
PS	1842-43, 1848-49, 1857-61, 1867-70	Pompaso Sanabria
S	1869-70	Pomposo Sanabria
MC	1849-59	Mariano Catano
RO	1859-65	Romualdo Obregon
MH, H	1870-85	Manuel Herrera Razo
O	1870-73	Juan R. Ochoa
CA, G	1867-70	Carlos Aguirre Gomez
BE, E	1879-81	Blas Escontria
LC, C	1885-86	Luis Cuevas
MR, R	1886-93	Mariano Reyes

ZACATECAS MINT

A	1825-29	Adalco
Z	1825-26	Mariano Zaldivar
V	1824-31	Jose Mariano Vela
O	1829-67	Manuel Ochoa
M	1831-67	Manuel Miner
VL	1860-66	Vicente Larranaga
JS	1867-68, 1876-86	J.S. de Santa Ana
YH	1868-74	Ygnacio Hierro
JA	1874-76	Juan H. Acuna
FZ	18861905	Francisco de P. Zarate

PROFILE EAGLE COINAGE

The first coins of the Republic were of the distinctive Profile Eagle style, sometimes called the "Hooked Neck Eagle." They were struck first in Mexico City in 1823 in denominations of eight reales and eight escudos. In 1824, they were produced at the Durango and Guanajuato mints in addition to Mexico City. Denominations included the one half, one, two and eight reales. No gold escudos of this design were struck in 1824. In 1825, only the eight reales were struck briefly at the Guanajuato mint.

NOTE: For a more extensive examination of Profile Eagle Coinage, please refer to Hookneck - El Aguila de Perfil by Clyde Hubbard and David O Harrow.

KM# 369   1/2 REAL
1.6900 g., 0.9030 Silver 0.0491 oz. ASW   **Obv:** Full breast Profile eagle **Rev:** Cap and rays **Mint:** Mexico City **Note:** Die varieties exist.

Date	Mintage	F	VF	XF	Unc	BU
1824Mo JM	—	45.00	75.00	150	750	—

KM# 371.1   REAL
3.3800 g., 0.9030 Silver 0.0981 oz. ASW   **Obv:** Thin Profile eagle **Rev:** Superscript S reversed **Mint:** Durango

Date	Mintage	F	VF	XF	Unc	BU
1824Do RL	—	5,500	9,500	13,000	—	—

KM# 371.2   REAL
3.3800 g., 0.9030 Silver 0.0981 oz. ASW   **Obv:** Thin Profile eagle **Rev:** Superscript S normal **Mint:** Durango

Date	Mintage	F	VF	XF	Unc	BU
1824Do RL 3 known	—	—	—	—	—	—

Mint mark: Do

KM# 373.1   2 REALES
6.7600 g., 0.9030 Silver 0.1962 oz. ASW   **Obv:** Profile eagle, snake in beak **Obv. Legend:** REPUBLICA • MEXICANA **Rev:** Radiant cap **Mint:** Durango **Note:** Die varieties exist.

Date	Mintage	F	VF	XF	Unc	BU
1824Do RL	—	50.00	125	850	2,200	—

KM# 373.2   2 REALES
6.7600 g., 0.9030 Silver 0.1962 oz. ASW   **Obv:** Profile eagle, snake in beak **Rev:** Radiant cap **Rev. Legend:** Type 1, dot before 2R in legend **Mint:** Durango

Date	Mintage	F	VF	XF	Unc	BU
1824D RL	—	100	200	1,000	3,000	—

KM# 373.3   2 REALES
6.7600 g., 0.9030 Silver 0.1962 oz. ASW **Obv:** Profile eagle,
snake in beak **Obv. Legend:** Thin profile **Rev:** Radiant cap
Rev. Legend: Type II, no dot before 2R in legend **Mint:**
Durango

Date	Mintage	F	VF	XF	Unc	BU
1824D RL	—	100	200	1,000	3,000	—

KM# 373.4   2 REALES
Obv: Profile eagle, snake in beak **Obv. Legend:**
REPUBLICA • MEXICANA **Rev:** Radiant cap **Mint:** Mexico
City **Note:** Varieties exist.

Date	Mintage	F	VF	XF	Unc	BU
1824Mo JM	—	30.00	70.00	450	2,000	—

Note: No coins are known with visible feather details on the
eagle's breast

KM# A376.2   8 REALES
27.0700 g., 0.9030 Silver 0.7859 oz. ASW **Obv:** Full breast
profile eagle, snake in beak **Obv. Legend:** REPUBLICA
MEXICANA **Rev:** Radiant cap **Edge:** Standard or Republic
Mint: Mexico City

Date	Mintage	F	VF	XF	Unc	BU
1823Mo JM	—	150	300	800	4,500	—
1824Mo JM	—	125	250	700	4,000	—

KM# A376.1   8 REALES
27.0700 g., 0.9030 Silver 0.7859 oz. ASW **Obv:** Full breast
profile eagle, snake in beak **Obv. Legend:** REPUBLICA
MEXICANA. **Rev:** Radiant cap **Mint:** Guanajuato

Date	Mintage	F	VF	XF	Unc	BU
1824Go JM	—	250	400	1,100	3,500	—
1825/4Go JJ	—	600	1,200	2,750	7,000	—
1825Go JJ	—	500	750	1,400	5,500	—

KM# A376.3   8 REALES
27.0700 g., 0.9030 Silver 0.7859 oz. ASW **Obv:** Full breast
profile eagle, snake in beak **Rev:** Radiant cap **Edge:** Colonial
or circle and rectangle **Mint:** Mexico City

Date	Mintage	F	VF	XF	Unc	BU
1823Mo JM	—	—	—	—	—	—
Rare						

The Round-Topped Three

KM# A376.4   8 REALES
27.0700 g., 0.9030 Silver 0.7859 oz. ASW **Obv:** Full breast
profile eagle, snake in beak **Rev:** Radiant cap, round topped
three **Edge:** Standard or Republic **Mint:** Mexico City

Date	Mintage	F	VF	XF	Unc	BU
1823Mo JM	—	2,000	4,000	6,000	8,000	—

Note: Many die varieties exist; Illustrations of one of the die
differences is the size of the snake loop at the eagle's beak;
This difference is not apparent except on the 1824 Mo 8
Reales

KM# A376.5   8 REALES
27.0700 g., 0.9030 Silver 0.7859 oz. ASW **Obv:** Full breast
profile eagle, snake in beak, REPULICA (error) **Rev:** Radiant
cap **Mint:** Mexico City

Date	Mintage	F	VF	XF	Unc	BU
1824Mo JM	—	6,000	9,000	11,000	—	—

Note: Legible Libertads on the cap are not as prevalent on
the Mexico City 8 Reales as on the Durango 8 Reales; They
are much more numerous than on the Guanajuato 8 Reales

Typical Submissive
Snake Obverse

Typical Folded
Snake Obverse

NOTE: Legible Libertads on the Cap are common on Durango eight reales.

Med. Libertad **Small Libertad** **Large Libertad**
Cap Reverse **Cap Reverse** **Cap Reverse**

NOTE: The three styles of obverses and the three styles of reverses were combined to make six distinct varieties of coins.

KM# 376.1   8 REALES
27.0700 g., 0.9030 Silver 0.7859 oz. ASW **Obv:** Thin profile eagle, defiant snake **Rev:** Radiant cap, medium Libertad **Mint:** Durango

Date	Mintage	F	VF	XF	Unc	BU
1824Do RL	—	500	1,200	4,500	7,000	—

Note: Five die varieties are known, all are rare. Ira & Larry Goldberg Millennia Sale 5-08, MS-64 realized $25,000.

KM# 376.2   8 REALES
27.0700 g., 0.9030 Silver 0.7859 oz. ASW **Obv:** Thin profile eagle, defiant snake **Obv. Legend:** REPUBLICA MEXICANA **Rev:** Radiant cap, small Libertad **Mint:** Durango

Date	Mintage	F	VF	XF	Unc	BU
1824Do RL	—	300	400	1,600	3,500	—

Note: Eleven die varieties are known, some are rare

KM# 376.3   8 REALES
27.0700 g., 0.9030 Silver 0.7859 oz. ASW **Obv:** Thin profile eagle, submissive snake **Obv. Legend:** REPUBLICA • MEXICANA **Rev:** Radiant cap, small Libertad **Mint:** Durango

Date	Mintage	F	VF	XF	Unc	BU
1824Do RL	—	200	350	1,250	2,750	—

Note: Seven die varieties are known, some are rare

KM# 376.4   8 REALES
27.0700 g., 0.9030 Silver 0.7859 oz. ASW **Obv:** Thin profile eagle, submissive snake **Rev:** Radiant cap, large Libertad **Mint:** Durango

Date	Mintage	F	VF	XF	Unc	BU
1824Do RL	—	200	350	1,250	2,750	—

Note: Twelve die varieties known, some are rare

KM# 376.5   8 REALES
27.0700 g., 0.9030 Silver 0.7859 oz. ASW **Obv:** Thin profile eagle, folded snake **Rev:** Radiant cap, small Libertad **Mint:** Durango

Date	Mintage	F	VF	XF	Unc	BU
1824Do RL	—	200	350	1,200	2,500	—

Note: Only one die variety is known

KM# 376.6   8 REALES
27.0700 g., 0.9030 Silver 0.7859 oz. ASW **Obv:** Thin profile eagle, folded snake **Rev:** Radiant cap, large Libertad **Mint:** Durango

Date	Mintage	F	VF	XF	Unc	BU
1824Do RL	—	200	400	1,500	3,000	—

Note: Eleven die varieties known, some are rare

Type I Obverse/Reverse

NOTE: The cap on the reverse of the curved tail Type I points to the "A" of LIBERTAD.

KM# 382.1   8 ESCUDOS
27.0700 g., 0.8750 Gold 0.7615 oz. AGW **Obv:** Profile eagle, snake's tail curved **Obv. Legend:** REPUBLICA MEXICANA **Rev:** Open book, hand holding stick with cap, cap points to "A" of LIBERTAD **Rev. Legend:** LIBERTAD EN... **Mint:** Mexico City

Date	Mintage	F	VF	XF	Unc	BU
1823Mo JM	—	7,000	10,000	20,000	35,000	—

Note: American Numismatic Rarities Eliasberg sale 4-05, MS-61 realized $55,200.

Type II Obverse/Reverse

NOTE: The cap on the reverse of the looped tail Type I points to the "T" of LIBERTAD.

KM# 382.2   8 ESCUDOS
27.0700 g., 0.8750 Gold 0.7615 oz. AGW **Obv:** Profile eagle, snake's tail looped **Obv. Legend:** REPUBLICA MEXICANA **Rev:** Open book, hand holding stick with cap, cap points to "T" of LIBERTAD **Rev. Legend:** LIBERTAD EN... **Mint:** Mexico City

Date	Mintage	F	VF	XF	Unc	BU
1823Mo JM	—	6,000	9,000	18,000	35,000	—

Note: The quality of the strikes of Type I coins is almost always superior to that of the Type II; Details of the eagle feathers, cactus and lettering on the open book are better on most Type I coins but the Type II coins are scarcer; Type I coins outnumber Type II coins by about two to one

---

STATE COINAGE

KM# 316   1/16 REAL (Medio Octavo)
4.7500 g., Copper, 21 mm. **Obv:** Bow, quiver and flag **Obv. Legend:** DEPARTAMENTO DE JALISCO **Rev:** Seated figure, left, cap on pole **Edge:** Oblique reeding **Mint:** Guadalajara

Date	Mintage	Good	VG	F	VF	XF
1860	—	3.00	8.00	17.50	55.00	—

KM# 317   1/16 REAL (Medio Octavo)
4.7500 g., Copper, 21 mm. **Obv. Legend:** ESTADO LIBRE DE JALISCO **Edge:** Oblique reeding **Mint:** Guadalajara

Date	Mintage	Good	VG	F	VF	XF
1861	—	2.50	6.00	13.50	32.50	—

KM# 320   1/8 REAL (Octavo Real)
Copper **Obv:** Facing eagle, snake in beak, value at lower left **Rev:** Radiant Libertad above date within wreath **Rev. Legend:** LIBERTAD **Edge:** Oblique reeding **Mint:** Durango **Note:** Size varies 17-18mm. Weight varies 2.5-4 g. These pieces were frequently struck over 1/8 Real, dated 1821-23 of Nueva Vizcaya. All known examples struck over these coins are believed to be contemporary counterfeits.

Date	Mintage	Good	VG	F	VF	XF
1824D	—	5.00	12.50	35.00	85.00	—
1828D	—	150	250	400	1,000	—

KM# 338   1/8 REAL (Octavo Real)
4.0000 g., Brass, 21 mm. **Obv:** Monument **Obv. Legend:** ESTo LIBe FEDo DE ZACATECAS **Rev:** Floating angel holding radiant cap **Edge:** Oblique reeding **Mint:** Zacatecas

Date	Mintage	Good	VG	F	VF	XF
1825	—	3.00	5.50	12.00	25.00	—
1827	—	3.00	5.50	12.00	25.00	—
1827	—	12.00	20.00	40.00	100	—

Note: Inverted A for V in OCTAVO

1827	—	15.00	25.00	50.00	120	—

Note: OCTAVA (error)

1827 Inverted 1	—	12.00	20.00	40.00	100	—
1829 Rare	—	—	—	—	—	—
1830	—	2.75	5.00	8.00	20.00	—
1831	—	4.50	6.75	13.50	27.50	—
1832	—	2.75	5.00	8.00	20.00	—
1833	—	2.75	5.00	8.00	20.00	—
1835	—	3.50	6.00	10.00	25.00	—
1846	—	3.50	6.00	10.00	25.00	—
1851	—	38.00	70.00	115	220	—
1852	—	3.50	6.00	10.00	25.00	—
1858	—	2.75	5.00	8.00	20.00	—
1859	—	2.75	5.00	8.00	20.00	—
1862	—	2.75	5.00	8.00	20.00	—
1863 Reversed 6 in date	—	2.75	5.00	8.00	20.00	—

EMPIRE OF ITURBIDE

KM# 321 1/8 REAL (Octavo Real)
3.3000 g., Copper **Obv:** Child holding bow, right, small tree **Rev:** Radiant cap **Rev. Legend:** OCTo. DE. R. DE DO **Edge:** Oblique reeding **Mint:** Durango **Note:** Size varies 18-19mm.

Date	Mintage	Good	VG	F	VF	XF
1828D	—	7.50	18.50	40.00	115	—

KM# 335 1/8 REAL (Octavo Real)
Copper **Obv. Legend:** ESTADO DE OCCIDENTE **Edge:** Oblique reeding **Mint:** Alamos **Note:** Size varies: 17-18mm, weight varies: 2-3 g. The C before date on reverse may be a mint mark standing for Concepcion de Alamos.

Date	Mintage	Good	VG	F	VF	XF
1828 Reverse S	—	35.00	65.00	120	—	—
1829	—	30.00	60.00	110	—	—

KM# 329 1/8 REAL (Octavo Real)
4.8000 g., Copper, 21 mm. **Obv:** Bow, quiver and flag **Obv. Legend:** ESTADO LIBRE DE JALISCO **Rev:** Seated figure, left, cap on pole **Edge:** Oblique reeding **Mint:** Guadalajara

Date	Mintage	Good	VG	F	VF	XF
1828	—	3.00	5.00	8.00	22.50	—
1831	—	62.50	100	185	275	—
1832/28	—	4.50	6.50	11.00	27.50	—
1832	—	4.50	6.00	10.00	25.00	—
1833	—	3.50	5.50	9.00	23.50	—
1834	—	37.50	80.00	150	235	—

KM# 326 1/8 REAL (Octavo Real)
3.5000 g., Copper, 21 mm. **Obv:** Seated figure **Obv. Legend:** ESTADO LIBRE DE GUANAJUATO **Rev:** Cap within center wreath of stylized rays, date below **Edge:** Ornamented with incuse dots **Mint:** Guanajuato

Date	Mintage	Good	VG	F	VF	XF
1829	—	3.00	5.00	10.00	26.50	—
1829	—	4.00	6.50	12.50	28.50	—

Note: Error with GUANJUATO

1830	—	8.00	13.50	28.50	65.00	—

KM# 336 1/8 REAL (Octavo Real)
Copper, 21 mm. **Obv:** Value above divides wreath, open book within **Obv. Legend:** ESTADO LIBRE DE SAN LUIS POTOSI **Rev:** Seated figure **Edge:** Oblique reeding **Mint:** San Luis Potosi **Note:** Weight varies (1829-31) 4.5-5.5 g; (1859) 4-4.5 g.

Date	Mintage	Good	VG	F	VF	XF
1829	—	6.00	11.00	26.50	62.50	—
1830	—	8.50	15.00	30.00	70.00	—
1831	—	6.00	9.50	18.50	47.50	—

Date	Mintage	Good	VG	F	VF	XF
1859	—	5.00	8.00	16.50	45.00	—
1865/1	—	—	—	—	—	—

Note: Reported, not confirmed

KM# 318 1/8 REAL (Octavo Real)
3.5400 g., Copper, 20 mm. **Obv. Legend:** ESTADO SOBERANO DE CHIHUAHUA **Edge:** Plain **Mint:** Chihuahua

Date	Mintage	Good	VG	F	VF	XF
1833	—	350	750	—	—	—
1834	—	350	750	—	—	—
1835/3	—	350	750	—	—	—

KM# 322 1/8 REAL (Octavo Real)
3.5000 g., Copper, 20 mm. **Obv:** Profile eagle, snake in beak **Obv. Legend:** ESTADO DE DURANGO **Rev:** Value and date within circle and wreath **Mint:** Durango

Date	Mintage	Good	VG	F	VF	XF
1833	—	350	—	—	—	—

KM# 339 1/8 REAL (Octavo Real)
4.0000 g., Copper, 21 mm. **Obv:** Monument **Obv. Legend:** DEPARTAMENTO DE ZACATECAS **Rev:** Floating angel holding radiant cap **Edge:** Oblique reeding **Mint:** Zacatecas

Date	Mintage	Good	VG	F	VF	XF
1836	—	5.00	8.50	17.50	40.00	—
1845	—	7.50	12.50	22.50	50.00	—
1846	—	8.50	10.00	20.00	45.00	—

KM# 323 1/8 REAL (Octavo Real)
3.5000 g., Copper **Obv:** Facing eagle, snake in beak **Obv. Legend:** REPUBLICA MEXICANA **Rev:** Value and date within circle and wreath **Mint:** Durango **Note:** Size varies: 19-23mm.

Date	Mintage	Good	VG	F	VF	XF
1842/33	—	12.50	22.50	42.50	115	—
1842	—	8.50	15.00	32.50	100	—

KM# 324 1/8 REAL (Octavo Real)
Copper, 19 mm. **Obv:** Facing eagle, snake in beak **Obv. Legend:** REPUBLICA MEXICANA **Rev:** Value within circle **Rev. Legend:** DEPARTAMENTO DE DURANGO **Edge:** Ornamented with arc and dot pattern **Mint:** Durango **Note:** Weight varies: 3.5-3.8 g.

Date	Mintage	Good	VG	F	VF	XF
1845	—	22.50	55.00	115	250	—
1846 Rare	—	—	—	—	—	—
1847	—	3.50	7.50	17.50	37.50	—

KM# 325   1/8 REAL (Octavo Real)
Copper, 19 mm.   **Obv:** Facing eagle, snake in beak **Obv.
Legend:** REPUBLICA MEXICANA **Rev:** Value within circle
Rev. Legend: ESTADO DE DURANGO **Edge:** Ornamented
with arc and dot pattern **Mint:** Durango **Note:** Weight varies:
3.5-3.8 g.

Date	Mintage	Good	VG	F	VF	XF
1851	—	3.50	8.00	12.50	33.50	—
1852/1	—	3.50	6.50	11.00	33.50	—
1852	—	3.00	5.00	8.00	30.00	—
1854	—	7.00	13.50	28.50	62.50	—

KM# 319   1/8 REAL (Octavo Real)
3.5400 g., Copper, 20 mm.   **Obv:** Standing figure facing
holding bow and arrow **Obv. Legend:** ESTADO DE
CHIHUAHUA **Rev:** Date and value within wreath **Edge:** Plain
Mint: Chihuahua

Date	Mintage	Good	VG	F	VF	XF
1855	—	5.00	8.50	25.00	75.00	—

KM# 327   1/8 REAL (Octavo Real)
7.2000 g., Brass, 29 mm.   **Obv:** Facing eagle, snake in beak
Obv. Legend: ESTADO LIBRE DE GUANAJUATO **Rev:**
Oval arms within sprays below radiant cap **Edge:** Plain **Mint:**
Guanajuato

Date	Mintage	Good	VG	F	VF	XF
1856	—	7.50	12.00	20.00	75.00	—

KM# 330   1/8 REAL (Octavo Real)
9.5000 g., Copper, 28 mm.   **Obv. Legend:** ESTADO LIBRE
DE JALISCO **Rev:** Seated figure, left, cap on pole **Edge:**
Oblique reeding **Mint:** Guadalajara

Date	Mintage	Good	VG	F	VF	XF
1856	—	3.00	6.00	9.00	18.50	—
1857	—	3.00	6.00	9.00	18.50	—
1858	—	3.00	6.00	9.00	18.50	—
1861	—	75.00	135	200	300	—
1862/1	—	4.00	7.00	10.00	22.50	—
1862	—	4.00	7.00	10.00	22.50	—

KM# 328   1/8 REAL (Octavo Real)
Brass, 25 mm.   **Obv:** Facing eagle, snake in beak **Obv.
Legend:** ESTADO LIBRE DE GUANAJUATO **Rev:** Oval
arms within sprays below radiant cap **Edge:** Plain **Mint:**
Guanajuato **Note:** Weight varies: 7.1-7.2 g.

Date	Mintage	Good	VG	F	VF	XF
1856	—	4.00	7.50	12.50	35.00	—
1857	—	3.50	6.00	10.00	30.00	—

KM# 328a   1/8 REAL (Octavo Real)
Copper, 25 mm.   **Obv:** Facing eagle, snake in beak **Obv.
Legend:** ESTADO LIBRE DE GUANAJUATO **Rev:** Oval
arms within sprays below radiant cap **Edge:** Plain **Mint:**
Guanajuato **Note:** Weight varies: 7.1-7.2 g.

Date	Mintage	Good	VG	F	VF	XF
1857	—	7.00	16.50	32.50	55.00	—

KM# 331   1/8 REAL (Octavo Real)
9.5000 g., Copper, 28 mm.   **Obv:** Bow, quiver and flag **Obv.
Legend:** DEPARTAMENTO DE JALISCO **Edge:** Oblique
reeding **Mint:** Guadalajara

Date	Mintage	Good	VG	F	VF	XF
1858	—	4.00	7.00	13.50	28.50	—
1859	—	3.00	5.75	8.00	20.00	—
1860/59	—	3.25	6.00	9.00	22.50	—
1860	—	3.25	6.00	9.00	22.50	—
1862	—	4.00	8.00	17.50	37.50	—

KM# 337   1/8 REAL (Octavo Real)
6.7000 g., Copper, 28 mm.   **Obv. Legend:** ESTO LIBE Y
SOBO DE SONORA **Edge:** Reeded **Mint:** Hermosillo

Date	Mintage	Good	VG	F	VF	XF
1859 Rare	—	—	—	—	—	—

KM# 366   1/4 REAL (Un Quarto/Una Quartilla)
8.0000 g., Brass **Obv:** Monument **Obv. Legend:** ESTO LIBE
FEDO DE ZACATECAS **Rev:** Floating angel with radiant cap
on tip of arrow **Edge:** Oblique reeding **Mint:** Zacatecas **Note:**
Size varies: 28-29mm.

Date	Mintage	Good	VG	F	VF	XF
1824 Rare	—	—	—	—	—	—
1825	—	2.50	5.00	10.00	20.00	—
1826	—	75.00	130	220	325	—
1827/17	—	2.50	5.00	9.00	20.00	—
1829	—	2.50	5.00	9.00	20.00	—
1830	—	2.50	5.00	8.50	20.00	—
1831	—	40.00	85.00	140	220	—
1832	—	2.50	5.00	9.00	20.00	—
1833	—	2.50	5.00	9.00	20.00	—
1834 Rare	—	—	—	—	—	—

Date	Mintage	Good	VG	F	VF	XF
1835	—	2.50	5.00	9.00	20.00	—
1846	—	2.50	5.00	8.50	20.00	—
1847	—	2.50	5.00	8.50	20.00	—
1852	—	2.50	5.00	8.50	20.00	—
1853	—	2.50	5.00	8.50	20.00	—
1855	—	4.50	10.00	25.00	65.00	—
1858	—	2.50	5.00	8.50	20.00	—
1859	—	2.50	5.00	8.50	20.00	—
1860	—	75.00	125	200	310	—
1862/57	—	2.50	5.00	8.50	20.00	—
1862/59/7	—	8.00	18.00	37.50	75.00	—
1862	—	2.50	5.00	8.00	20.00	—
1863/2	—	2.50	5.00	8.00	20.00	—
1863	—	2.50	5.00	8.00	20.00	—
1864	—	4.00	11.00	25.00	60.00	—

KM# 359   1/4 REAL (Un Quarto/Una Quartilla)
Copper **Obv:** Value above divides wreath, open book within **Obv. Legend:** ESTADO LIBRE DE SAN LUIS POTOSI **Rev:** Seated figure with cap on tip of arrow **Rev. Legend:** MEXICO LIBRE **Edge:** Oblique reeding **Mint:** San Luis Potosi **Note:** Size varies: 25-31mm, weight varies: (1828-32) 9-10 g.; (1859-60) 8-9 g.

Date	Mintage	Good	VG	F	VF	XF
1828	—	2.25	4.00	9.00	19.00	—
1829	—	3.00	5.00	9.00	20.00	—
1830	—	2.25	4.00	8.00	17.00	—
1832	—	4.00	6.00	10.00	22.50	—
1859 Large LIBRE	—	2.75	4.00	8.00	18.00	—
1859 Small LIBRE	—	2.75	4.00	8.00	18.00	—
1860	—	2.75	4.00	8.00	18.00	—

KM# 351   1/4 REAL (Un Quarto/Una Quartilla)
7.0000 g., Copper, 27 mm. **Obv:** Seated figure with head right **Obv. Legend:** ESTADO LIBRE DE GUANAJUATO **Rev:** Cap within radiant wreath **Edge:** Ornamented with incuse dots **Mint:** Guanajuato

Date	Mintage	Good	VG	F	VF	XF
1828	—	3.75	8.00	18.50	40.00	—
1828	—	4.00	9.00	20.00	42.50	—

Note: Error with GUANJUATO

1829	—	5.50	12.00	22.50	47.50	—

KM# 353   1/4 REAL (Un Quarto/Una Quartilla)
9.3500 g., Copper, 28 mm. **Obv:** Oblique reeding **Obv. Legend:** ESTADO LIBRE DE JALISCO **Rev:** Seated figure, left, cap on pole **Mint:** Guadalajara

Date	Mintage	Good	VG	F	VF	XF
1828	—	3.75	7.00	15.00	37.50	—
1829/8	—	3.00	6.00	13.00	33.00	—
1829	—	3.00	6.00	13.00	33.00	—
1830/20	—	3.00	5.00	10.00	28.50	—
1830/29	—	3.00	5.00	10.00	28.50	—
1830	—	3.00	5.00	10.00	28.50	—
1831 Rare	—	—	—	—	—	—
1832/20	—	3.00	5.00	10.00	28.50	—
1832/28	—	3.00	5.00	10.00	28.50	—
1832	—	2.50	5.00	9.00	27.50	—
1833/2	—	3.00	5.00	9.00	27.50	—
1834	—	2.50	5.00	9.00	27.50	—
1835/3	—	3.00	5.00	9.00	27.50	—
1835	—	2.50	5.00	9.00	27.50	—
1836 Rare	—	—	—	—	—	—

KM# 364   1/4 REAL (Un Quarto/Una Quartilla)
Copper **Obv:** Arrow divides quivers **Obv. Legend:** EST. D. SONORA UNA CUART **Rev:** Stylized radiant cap **Edge:** Oblique reeding **Mint:** Hermosillo **Note:** Size varies: 21-22mm. Weight varies: 2.3-5.5 g.

Date	Mintage	Good	VG	F	VF	XF
1831 L.S. Rare	—	—	—	—	—	—
1832 L.S.	—	2.75	5.50	15.00	50.00	—
1833/2 L.S.	—	2.00	4.00	12.50	37.50	—
1833 L.S.	—	2.00	4.00	12.50	37.50	—
1834 L.S.	—	2.00	4.00	12.50	37.50	—
1835/3 L.S.	—	2.50	5.50	15.00	40.00	—
1835 L.S.	—	2.00	4.00	12.50	37.50	—
1836 L.S.	—	2.00	4.00	12.50	37.50	—

KM# 340   1/4 REAL (Un Quarto/Una Quartilla)
Copper, 27 mm. **Obv:** Child facing, holding bow and arrow **Obv. Legend:** ESTADO SOBERANO DE CHIHUAHUA **Rev:** Value and date within palm wreath **Edge:** Herringbone pattern **Mint:** Chihuahua

Date	Mintage	Good	VG	F	VF	XF
1833	—	7.50	16.50	37.50	85.00	—
1834	—	6.50	13.50	28.00	55.00	—
1835	—	5.00	10.00	22.00	50.00	—
1835 Plain edge	—	5.00	8.00	12.00	50.00	—

KM# 354   1/4 REAL (Un Quarto/Una Quartilla)
9.3500 g., Copper, 28 mm. **Obv. Legend:** DEPARTAMENTO DE JALISCO **Edge:** Oblique reeding **Mint:** Guadalajara

Date	Mintage	Good	VG	F	VF	XF
1836	—	120	200	350	—	—

KM# 367   1/4 REAL (Un Quarto/Una Quartilla)
8.0000 g., Brass **Obv:** Monument **Obv. Legend:**
DEPARTAMENTO DE ZACATECAS **Rev:** Floating angel with
radiant cap on tip of arrow **Edge:** Oblique reeding **Mint:**
Zacatecas **Note:** Size varies: 28-29mm.

Date	Mintage	Good	VG	F	VF	XF
1836	—	4.00	8.50	13.50	25.00	—
1845 Rare	—	—	—	—	—	—
1846	—	3.50	6.75	9.00	20.00	—

KM# 345   1/4 REAL (Un Quarto/Una Quartilla)
7.0000 g., Copper, 27 mm. **Obv:** Facing eagle, snake in beak
Obv. Legend: REPUBLICA MEXICANA **Rev:** Value and date
within circle, DURANGO above in wreath **Mint:** Durango

Date	Mintage	Good	VG	F	VF	XF
1845 Rare	—	—	—	—	—	—

KM# 341   1/4 REAL (Un Quarto/Una Quartilla)
7.0800 g., Copper, 27 mm. **Obv:** Stylized figure facing,
holding bow and arrow **Obv. Legend:** ESTADO LIBRE DE
CHIHUAHUA **Rev:** Value and date within designed wreath
Edge: Plain **Mint:** Chihuahua

Date	Mintage	Good	VG	F	VF	XF
1846	—	3.50	6.00	12.00	37.50	—
Note: With fraction bar						
1846	—	5.00	8.50	15.00	45.00	—
Note: Without fraction bar						

KM# 363   1/4 REAL (Un Quarto/Una Quartilla)
27.0000 g., Copper, 27 mm. **Obv:** Head left within wreath
Obv. Legend: ESTADO LIBRE Y SOBERANO DE SINALOA
Rev: Value and date within wreath **Edge:** Reeded **Mint:**
Culiacan

Date	Mintage	Good	VG	F	VF	XF
1847	—	3.50	5.50	12.00	23.50	—
1848	—	3.50	5.50	11.00	22.00	—
1859	—	3.00	4.50	7.50	16.50	—
1861	—	1.75	3.00	4.00	10.00	—
1862	—	1.75	3.00	4.00	11.00	—
1863	—	2.50	4.00	5.00	11.00	—
1864/3	—	2.50	4.00	5.00	11.00	—
1864	—	1.75	3.00	4.75	10.00	—
1865	—	3.00	5.50	8.50	18.50	—
1866/5	7,401,000	2.50	3.50	5.00	11.00	—
1866	Inc. above	1.75	3.00	4.00	10.00	—

KM# 363a   1/4 REAL (Un Quarto/Una Quartilla)
7.0000 g., Brass, 27 mm. **Obv:** Head left within wreath **Obv.
Legend:** ESTADO LIBRE Y SOBERANO DE SINALOA **Rev:**
Value and date within wreath **Edge:** Reeded **Mint:** Culiacan

Date	Mintage	Good	VG	F	VF	XF
1847	—	5.00	10.00	18.50	40.00	—

KM# 342   1/4 REAL (Un Quarto/Una Quartilla)
7.0800 g., Copper, 27 mm. **Obv:** Stylized figure facing,
holding bow and arrow **Obv. Legend:** ESTADO DE
CHIHUAHUA **Rev:** Value and date within designed wreath
Edge: Plain **Mint:** Chihuahua

Date	Mintage	Good	VG	F	VF	XF
1855	—	2.50	5.75	13.50	40.00	—
1856	—	2.50	5.75	13.50	40.00	—

KM# 343   1/4 REAL (Un Quarto/Una Quartilla)
7.0800 g., Copper, 27 mm. **Obv:** Stylized figure facing,
holding bow and arrow **Obv. Legend:** DEPARTAMENTO DE
CHIHUAHUA **Rev:** Value and date within designed wreath
Edge: Plain **Mint:** Chihuahua

Date	Mintage	Good	VG	F	VF	XF
1855	—	3.00	5.75	14.00	37.50	—
1855 DE	—	4.50	8.50	17.50	40.00	—
(reversed D)						

KM# 352   1/4 REAL (Un Quarto/Una Quartilla)
14.0000 g., Copper, 32 mm. **Obv:** Facing eagle, snake in
beak **Obv. Legend:** EST. LIB. DE GUANAXUATO **Rev:** Oval
arms within sprays below radiant cap **Rev. Legend:** OMNIA
VINCIT LABOR **Edge:** Plain **Mint:** Guanajuato

Date	Mintage	Good	VG	F	VF	XF
1856	—	7.50	18.50	37.50	70.00	—
1857	—	6.50	13.50	27.50	50.00	—

KM# 352a   1/4 REAL (Un Quarto/Una Quartilla)
14.0000 g., Brass, 32 mm. **Obv:** Facing eagle, snake in beak **Obv. Legend:** EST. LIB. DE GUANAXUATO **Rev:** Oval arms within sprays below radiant cap **Rev. Legend:** OMNIA VINCIT LABOR **Edge:** Plain **Mint:** Guanajuato

Date	Mintage	Good	VG	F	VF	XF
1856	—	3.25	6.75	13.50	30.00	—
1857	—	3.25	6.75	13.50	30.00	—

KM# 346   1/4 REAL (Un Quarto/Una Quartilla)
7.5000 g., Copper, 27 mm. **Obv:** Facing eagle, snake in beak **Obv. Legend:** REPUBLICA MEXICANA **Rev:** Value **Rev. Legend:** DURANGO **Edge:** Ornamented with arc and dot pattern **Mint:** Durango

Date	Mintage	Good	VG	F	VF	XF
1858 Rare	—	—	—	—	—	—

KM# 347   1/4 REAL (Un Quarto/Una Quartilla)
7.5000 g., Copper, 27 mm. **Obv:** Facing eagle, snake in beak **Obv. Legend:** ESTADO DE DURANGO **Rev:** Radiant cap above value and date within stylized sprays **Rev. Legend:** CONSTITUCION **Edge:** Ornamented with arc and dot pattern **Mint:** Durango **Note:** Brass examples have been reported, but not confirmed.

Date	Mintage	Good	VG	F	VF	XF
1858	—	4.00	8.50	22.00	50.00	—

KM# 355   1/4 REAL (Un Quarto/Una Quartilla)
19.0000 g., Copper, 32 mm. **Obv:** Bow, quiver and flag **Obv. Legend:** ESTADO LIBRE DE JALISCO **Rev:** Seated figure, left, cap on pole **Edge:** Oblique reeding **Mint:** Guadalajara

Date	Mintage	Good	VG	F	VF	XF
1858	—	3.00	6.00	11.00	25.00	—
1861	—	4.00	8.00	17.00	33.00	—
1862	—	3.00	6.00	11.00	25.00	—

KM# 356   1/4 REAL (Un Quarto/Una Quartilla)
19.0000 g., Copper, 32 mm. **Obv:** Bow, quiver and flag **Obv. Legend:** DEPARTAMENTO DE JALISCO **Rev:** Seated figure, left, cap on pole **Edge:** Oblique reeding **Mint:** Guadalajara

Date	Mintage	Good	VG	F	VF	XF
1858	—	3.00	6.00	9.00	20.00	—
1859/8	—	3.00	6.00	9.00	20.00	—
1859	—	3.00	6.00	9.00	20.00	—
1860	—	3.00	6.00	9.00	20.00	—

KM# 365   1/4 REAL (Un Quarto/Una Quartilla)
14.3000 g., Copper, 32 mm. **Obv:** Facing eagle, snake in beak **Obv. Legend:** ESTO. LIBE. Y SOBO. DE SONORA **Rev:** Seated figure, left, cap on pole **Edge:** Reeded **Mint:** Hermosillo

Date	Mintage	Good	VG	F	VF	XF
1859	—	3.00	8.00	12.00	30.00	—
1861/59	—	4.00	10.00	17.00	37.50	—
1861	—	3.00	8.00	12.00	30.00	—
1862	—	3.00	8.00	12.00	30.00	—
1863/2	—	8.00	19.00	37.50	85.00	—

KM# 344   1/4 REAL (Un Quarto/Una Quartilla)
Copper, 28 mm. **Obv:** Seated figure, right **Obv. Legend:** E. CHIHA LIBERTAD **Rev:** Value and date within wreath **Edge:** Plain **Mint:** Chihuahua **Note:** Weight varies 11-11.5 g.

Date	Mintage	Good	VG	F	VF	XF
1860	—	2.00	4.00	11.00	25.00	—
1861	—	2.00	4.00	11.00	25.00	—
1865/1	—	2.50	5.50	13.50	30.00	—
1865	—	6.00	14.00	28.50	65.00	—
1866/5	—	5.00	9.50	25.00	60.00	—
1866	—	2.00	4.00	11.00	25.00	—
Note: Coin rotation						
1866	—	2.00	4.00	11.00	25.00	—
Note: Medal rotation						

KM# 348   1/4 REAL (Un Quarto/Una Quartilla)
Copper, 27 mm.   **Obv:** Facing eagle, snake in beak **Obv.**
Legend: DEPARTAMENTO DE DURANGO **Rev:** Value and
date within circular legend and wreath **Rev. Legend:**
LIBERTAD EN EL ORDEN **Edge:** Ornamented with arc and
dot pattern **Mint:** Durango **Note:** Weight varies: 7-7.5 g.

Date	Mintage	Good	VG	F	VF	XF
1860	—	2.50	7.00	17.00	42.25	—
1866	—	3.00	8.00	18.00	46.75	—

KM# 360   1/4 REAL (Un Quarto/Una Quartilla)
Copper   **Obv:** Value above divides wreath, open book within
Obv. Legend: ESTADO LIBRE DE SAN LUIS POTOSI **Rev:**
Seated figure with cap on tip of arrow **Rev. Legend:**
REPUBLICA MEXICANA **Edge:** Oblique reeding **Mint:** San
Luis Potosi **Note:** Size varies: 25-31mm.

Date	Mintage	Good	VG	F	VF	XF
1862	1,367	2.75	4.00	8.00	17.00	—
1862 LIBR	Inc. above	4.00	6.00	9.00	18.00	—

KM# 349   1/4 REAL (Un Quarto/Una Quartilla)
7.0000 g., Copper   **Obv:** Facing eagle, snake in beak **Obv.**
Legend: ESTADO DE DURANGO **Rev:** Value and date
above sprays **Rev. Legend:** INDEPENDENCIA Y LIBERTAD
Edge: Ornamented with arc and dot pattern **Mint:** Durango
Note: Size varies: 26-27mm.

Date	Mintage	Good	VG	F	VF	XF
1866	—	4.00	9.00	25.00	55.00	—

KM# 361   1/4 REAL (Un Quarto/Una Quartilla)
Copper   **Obv. Legend:** ESTADO LIBRE Y SOBERANO DE
S.L. POTOSI **Rev:** Radiant cap and value within wrath, date
below **Rev. Legend:** LIBERTAD Y REFORMA **Edge:** Reeded
or plain **Mint:** San Luis Potosi **Note:** Size varies: 27-28mm.
Weight varies: 9-10 g.

Date	Mintage	Good	VG	F	VF	XF
1867	3,177,000	2.75	4.00	7.00	17.00	—
1867 AFG	Inc. above	2.75	4.00	7.00	17.00	—

Note: "AFG" are the coin designer/engraver initials

KM# 362   1/4 REAL (Un Quarto/Una Quartilla)
Copper   **Obv. Legend:** ESTADO LIBRE Y SOBERANO DE
S.L. POTOSI **Rev. Legend:** LIBERTAD Y REFORMA **Edge:**
Plain **Mint:** San Luis Potosi

Date	Mintage	Good	VG	F	VF	XF
1867	Inc. above	2.75	4.00	7.00	17.00	—
1867 AFG	Inc. above	2.75	4.00	7.00	17.00	—

Note: "AFG" are the coin designer/engraver initials

KM# 350   1/4 REAL (Un Quarto/Una Quartilla)
7.5000 g., Copper, 27 mm.   **Obv:** Facing eagle, snake in beak
Obv. Legend: ESTADO DE DURANGO **Rev:** Date and circular
legend, value within **Rev. Legend:** SUFRAGIO LIBRE **Edge:**
Ornamented with arc and dot pattern **Mint:** Durango **Note:** Brass
examples have been reported, but not confirmed.

Date	Mintage	Good	VG	F	VF	XF
1872	—	2.25	4.00	9.00	20.00	—

FEDERAL COINAGE

KM# 315   1/16 REAL (Medio Octavo)
1.7500 g., Copper, 17 mm.   **Obv. Legend:** REPUBLICA
MEXICANA **Edge:** Ornamented with small incuse rectangles
Mint: Mexico City

Date	Mintage	VG	F	VF	XF	Unc
1831	—	10.00	20.00	50.00	100	—
1832/1	—	12.00	22.00	55.00	125	—
1832	—	10.00	20.00	50.00	100	—
1833	—	10.00	20.00	50.00	100	—

KM# 315a   1/16 REAL (Medio Octavo)
1.7500 g., Brass, 17 mm.   **Obv. Legend:** REPUBLICA
MEXICANA **Edge:** Ornamented with small incuse rectangles
Mint: Mexico City

Date	Mintage	VG	F	VF	XF	Unc
1832	—	13.50	22.50	60.00	165	—
1833	—	10.00	17.50	50.00	135	—
1835	—	400	800	1,250	2,500	—

KM# 333   1/8 REAL (Octavo Real)
3.5000 g., Copper, 21 mm.   **Obv:** Facing eagle, snake in beak
Obv. Legend: REPUBLICA MEXICANA **Rev:** Value and date
within wreath **Edge:** Ornamented with small incuse rectangles
Mint: Mexico City

Date	Mintage	VG	F	VF	XF
1829	—	7.50	12.00	25.00	55.00
1830	—	1.00	2.00	6.00	20.00
1831	—	1.50	3.50	7.00	25.00
1832	—	1.50	3.50	7.00	25.00
1833/2	—	1.50	3.50	7.00	25.00
1833	—	1.50	2.75	6.00	20.00
1834	—	1.50	2.75	6.00	20.00
1835	—	1.50	2.75	6.00	20.00
1835/4	—	1.75	3.50	7.00	25.00

KM# 332   1/8 REAL (Octavo Real)
7.0000 g., Copper, 27 mm.   **Obv. Legend:** REPUBLICA
MEXICANA **Edge:** Ornamented with small incuse rectangles
Mint: Mexico City

Date	Mintage	VG	F	VF	XF	Unc
1829	—	450	900	1,500	2,500	—

KM# 334   1/8 REAL (Octavo Real)

14.0000 g., Copper **Obv:** Seated figure, right **Obv. Legend:** LIBERTAD **Rev:** Value and date within wreath **Edge:** Lettered (1841-42); Plain (1850-61) **Edge Lettering:** REPUBLICA MEXICANA **Mint:** Mexico City **Note:** Size varies: 29-30mm.

Date	Mintage	Good	VG	F	VF	XF
1841	—	6.00	15.00	30.00	75.00	—
1842	—	2.50	5.00	10.00	30.00	—
1850	—	12.50	20.00	30.00	80.00	—
1861	—	5.00	12.00	25.00	70.00	—

KM# 357   1/4 REAL (Un Quarto/Una Quartilla)

14.0000 g., Copper, 33 mm. **Obv:** Facing eagle, snake in beak **Obv. Legend:** REPUBLICA MEXICANA **Rev:** Value and date within wreath **Edge:** Ornamented with small incuse rectangles **Mint:** Mexico City

Date	Mintage	VG	F	VF	XF	Unc
1829	—	10.00	30.00	75.00	250	—

KM# 358   1/4 REAL (Un Quarto/Una Quartilla)

7.0000 g., Copper, 27 mm. **Obv:** Facing eagle, snake in beak **Obv. Legend:** REPUBLICA MEXICANA **Rev:** Value and date within wreath **Edge:** Ornamented with small incuse rectangles **Mint:** Mexico City **Note:** Reduced size.

Date	Mintage	VG	F	VF	XF	Unc
1829	—	12.00	25.00	50.00	150	—
1830	—	1.50	2.75	5.00	10.00	—
1831	—	1.50	2.75	5.00	10.00	—
1832	—	5.50	10.00	20.00	35.00	—
1833	—	1.50	2.75	5.00	10.00	—
1834/3	—	1.75	3.00	6.00	12.00	—
1834	—	1.50	2.75	5.00	10.00	—
1835	—	1.50	2.75	5.00	10.00	—
1836/5	—	1.75	3.00	6.00	12.00	—
1836	—	1.50	2.75	5.00	10.00	—
1837	—	6.50	13.50	22.50	45.00	—

KM# 358a.1   1/4 REAL (Un Quarto/Una Quartilla)

7.0000 g., Brass, 27 mm. **Countermark:** JM **Obv. Legend:** REPUBLICA MEXICANA **Edge:** Ornamented with small incuse rectangles **Mint:** Mexico City **Note:** Reduced size.

Date	Mintage	VG	F	VF	XF	Unc
1831	—	8.00	13.50	27.50	50.00	—

KM# 358a.2   1/4 REAL (Un Quarto/Una Quartilla)

7.0000 g., Brass, 27 mm. **Obv. Legend:** REPUBLICA MEXICANA **Edge:** Ornamented with small incuse rectangles **Mint:** Mexico City **Note:** Without countermark.

Date	Mintage	VG	F	VF	XF	Unc
1831	—	—	—	—	—	—

KM# 368.2   1/4 REAL (Un Quarto/Una Quartilla)

0.8450 g., 0.9030 Silver 0.0245 oz. ASW **Mint:** Durango **Note:** Struck at Durango Mint, mint mark Do.

Date	Mintage	VG	F	VF	XF	Unc
1842Do LR	—	12.00	20.00	40.00	125	—
1843Do	—	20.00	40.00	90.00	200	—

KM# 368   1/4 REAL (Un Quarto/Una Quartilla)

0.8450 g., 0.9030 Silver 0.0245 oz. ASW **Obv:** Head left **Rev:** Value **Mint:** Chihuahua **Note:** Mint mark CA.

Date	Mintage	VG	F	VF	XF	Unc
1843CA RG	—	75.00	125	300	500	—

KM# 368.3   1/4 REAL (Un Quarto/Una Quartilla)

0.8450 g., 0.9030 Silver 0.0245 oz. ASW **Mint:** Guadalajara **Note:** Mint mark Ga.

Date	Mintage	VG	F	VF	XF	Unc
1842Ga JG	—	2.50	5.50	8.00	20.00	—
1843/2Ga JG	—	—	—	—	—	—
1843Ga JG	—	6.00	9.00	12.50	30.00	—
1843Ga MC	—	4.00	6.50	9.00	25.00	—
1844Ga MC	—	4.00	6.50	9.00	25.00	—
1844Ga LR	—	2.50	5.00	10.00	20.00	—
1845Ga LR	—	8.00	20.00	40.00	75.00	—
1846Ga LR	—	10.00	25.00	40.00	60.00	—
1847Ga LR	—	8.00	20.00	40.00	60.00	—
1848Ga LR Rare	—	—	—	—	—	—
1850Ga LR Rare	—	—	—	—	—	—
1851Ga LR	—	6.00	10.00	20.00	50.00	—
1852Ga LR	—	50.00	100	135	200	—
1854/3Ga LR	—	50.00	100	135	200	—
1854Ga LR	—	10.00	20.00	50.00	100	—
1855Ga LR	—	10.00	20.00	50.00	100	—
1857Ga LR	—	10.00	20.00	50.00	100	—
1862Ga LR	—	10.00	20.00	50.00	100	—

KM# 368.5   1/4 REAL (Un Quarto/Una Quartilla)

0.8450 g., 0.9030 Silver 0.0245 oz. ASW **Mint:** Guanajuato **Note:** Mint mark Go.

Date	Mintage	VG	F	VF	XF	Unc
1842Go PM	—	5.00	15.00	35.00	75.00	—
1842Go LR	—	2.00	4.00	8.00	15.00	—
1843/2Go LR	—	4.00	6.00	10.00	20.00	—
1843Go LR	—	2.00	4.00	8.00	15.00	—
1844/3Go LR	—	—	—	—	—	—
1844Go LR	—	10.00	25.00	60.00	125	—
1845Go LR	—	8.00	17.00	40.00	80.00	—
1846/5Go LR	—	—	—	—	—	—
1846Go LR	—	6.00	15.00	30.00	60.00	—
1847Go LR	—	2.00	4.00	8.00	15.00	—
1848/7Go LR	—	2.00	4.00	8.00	15.00	—
1848Go LR	—	2.00	4.00	8.00	15.00	—
1849/7Go LR	—	8.00	15.00	30.00	60.00	—
1849Go LR	—	2.00	4.00	8.00	15.00	—
1850Go LR	—	2.00	4.00	8.00	15.00	—
1851Go LR	—	2.00	4.00	8.00	15.00	—
1852Go LR	—	2.00	4.00	8.00	15.00	—
1853Go LR	—	2.00	4.00	8.00	15.00	—
1855Go LR	—	4.00	8.00	15.00	30.00	—
1856/4Go LR	—	20.00	40.00	60.00	100	—
1856Go LR	—	5.00	10.00	20.00	35.00	—
1862/1Go LR	—	3.00	5.00	10.00	20.00	—
1862Go LR	—	2.00	4.00	8.00	15.00	—
1863Go	—	2.00	4.00	8.00	15.00	—

KM# 368.6   1/4 REAL (Un Quarto/Una Quartilla)

0.8450 g., 0.9030 Silver 0.0245 oz. ASW **Mint:** Mexico City **Note:** Mint mark Mo.

Date	Mintage	VG	F	VF	XF	Unc
1842Mo LR	—	2.00	4.00	8.00	15.00	—
1843Mo LR	—	2.00	4.00	8.00	15.00	—
1844/3Mo LR	—	20.00	30.00	75.00	125	—
1844Mo LR	—	4.00	6.00	10.00	20.00	—
1845Mo LR	—	6.00	15.00	35.00	70.00	—
1846Mo LR	—	10.00	20.00	35.00	65.00	—

Date	Mintage	VG	F	VF	XF	Unc
1850Mo LR Rare	—	—	—	—	—	—
1858Mo LR	—	4.00	8.00	15.00	30.00	—
1859Mo LR	—	4.00	6.00	10.00	20.00	—
1860Mo LR	—	4.00	6.00	10.00	20.00	—
1861Mo LR	—	4.00	6.00	10.00	20.00	—
1862Mo LR	—	4.00	6.00	10.00	20.00	—
1863/53Mo LR	—	4.00	6.00	10.00	20.00	—
1863Mo LR	—	4.00	6.00	10.00	20.00	—

KM# 368.7   1/4 REAL (Un Quarto/Una Quartilla)
0.8450 g., 0.9030 Silver 0.0245 oz. ASW   **Mint:** San Luis
Potosi **Note:** Mint mark SLP, PI, P, I/P.

Date	Mintage	VG	F	VF	XF	Unc
1842S.L.Pi	—	2.00	5.00	10.00	20.00	—
1843/2S.L.Pi	—	4.00	6.00	10.00	20.00	—
1843S.L.Pi	—	2.00	4.00	8.00	20.00	—
1844S.L.Pi	—	2.00	4.00	8.00	20.00	—
1845/3S.L.Pi	—	4.00	6.00	10.00	25.00	—
1845/4S.L.Pi	—	4.00	6.00	10.00	25.00	—
1845S.L.Pi	—	2.00	4.00	8.00	20.00	—
1847/5S.L.Pi	—	4.00	9.00	20.00	40.00	—
1847S.L.Pi	—	3.00	6.00	12.00	25.00	—
1851/47S.L.Pi	—	10.00	20.00	35.00	60.00	—
1854S.L.Pi	—	125	200	275	400	—
1856S.L.Pi	—	10.00	20.00	35.00	60.00	—
1857S.L.Pi	—	30.00	60.00	100	175	—
1862/57S.L.Pi	—	10.00	20.00	40.00	85.00	—

KM# 368.1   1/4 REAL (Un Quarto/Una Quartilla)
0.8450 g., 0.9030 Silver 0.0245 oz. ASW   **Mint:** Culiacan
Note: Mint mark C.

Date	Mintage	VG	F	VF	XF	Unc
1855C LR	—	50.00	100	225	475	—

KM# 368.4   1/4 REAL (Un Quarto/Una Quartilla)
0.8450 g., 0.9030 Silver 0.0245 oz. ASW   **Mint:** Guadalupe
y Calvo **Note:** Mint mark GC.

Date	Mintage	VG	F	VF	XF	Unc
1844GC LR	—	50.00	75.00	200	450	—

KM# 368.8   1/4 REAL (Un Quarto/Una Quartilla)
0.8450 g., 0.9030 Silver 0.0245 oz. ASW   **Mint:** Zacatecas
Note: Mint mark Zs.

Date	Mintage	VG	F	VF	XF	Unc
1842/1Zs LR	—	4.00	8.00	15.00	30.00	—
1842Zs LR	—	4.00	8.00	15.00	30.00	—

KM# 370.5   1/2 REAL
1.6900 g., 0.9030 Silver 0.0491 oz. ASW   **Obv:** Facing eagle,
snake in beak **Mint:** Guadalajara

Date	Mintage	F	VF	XF	Unc	BU
1825Ga FS	—	25.00	40.00	75.00	200	—
1826Ga FS	—	10.00	15.00	35.00	80.00	—
1828/7Ga FS	—	12.50	20.00	40.00	90.00	—
1829Ga FS	—	7.50	15.00	30.00	70.00	—
1830/29Ga FS	—	40.00	60.00	100	200	—
1831Ga LP	—	350	—	—	—	—
1832Ga FS	—	10.00	20.00	35.00	80.00	—
1834/3Ga FS	—	65.00	100	175	250	—
1834Ga FS	—	10.00	20.00	35.00	80.00	—
1835/4/3Ga FS/LP	—	15.00	25.00	40.00	90.00	—
1837/6Ga JG	—	100	250	500	1,000	—
1838/7Ga JG	—	15.00	25.00	40.00	90.00	—
1839/8Ga JG/FS	—	35.00	75.00	150	250	—
1839Ga MC	—	10.00	20.00	35.00	80.00	—
1840/39Ga MC/JG	—	—	—	—	—	—
1840Ga MC	—	15.00	25.00	40.00	90.00	—
1841Ga MC	—	20.00	35.00	50.00	100	—
1842/1Ga JG	—	15.00	25.00	40.00	90.00	—
1842Ga JG	—	10.00	20.00	35.00	80.00	—
1843/2Ga JG	—	15.00	30.00	50.00	100	—
1843Ga JG	—	10.00	20.00	35.00	80.00	—
1843Ga MC/JG	—	10.00	20.00	35.00	80.00	—
1843Ga MC	—	10.00	20.00	35.00	80.00	—
1844Ga MC	—	10.00	20.00	35.00	80.00	—
1845Ga MC	—	10.00	20.00	35.00	80.00	—
1845Ga JG	—	10.00	20.00	35.00	80.00	—
1846Ga MC	—	10.00	20.00	35.00	80.00	—
1846Ga JG	—	10.00	20.00	35.00	80.00	—
1847Ga JG	—	10.00	20.00	35.00	80.00	—
1848/7Ga JG	—	10.00	20.00	35.00	80.00	—
1849Ga JG	—	10.00	20.00	35.00	80.00	—
1850/49Ga JG	—	—	—	—	—	—
1850Ga JG	—	10.00	20.00	35.00	80.00	—
1851/0Ga JG	—	10.00	20.00	35.00	80.00	—

Date	Mintage	F	VF	XF	Unc	BU
1852Ga JG	—	10.00	20.00	35.00	80.00	—
1853Ga JG	—	10.00	20.00	35.00	80.00	—
1854Ga JG	—	10.00	20.00	35.00	80.00	—
1855/4Ga JG	—	10.00	20.00	35.00	80.00	—
1855Ga JG	—	10.00	20.00	35.00	80.00	—
1856Ga JG	—	10.00	20.00	35.00	80.00	—
1857Ga JG	—	10.00	20.00	35.00	80.00	—
1858/7Ga JG	—	10.00	20.00	35.00	80.00	—
1858Ga JG	—	10.00	20.00	35.00	80.00	—
1859/7Ga JG	—	10.00	20.00	35.00	80.00	—
1860/59Ga JG	—	10.00	20.00	35.00	80.00	—
1861Ga JG	—	5.00	12.50	25.00	60.00	—
1862/1Ga JG	—	15.00	25.00	40.00	90.00	—

KM# 370.6   1/2 REAL
1.6900 g., 0.9030 Silver 0.0491 oz. ASW   **Obv:** Facing eagle,
snake in beak **Mint:** Guadalupe y Calvo

Date	Mintage	F	VF	XF	Unc	BU
1844GC MP	—	50.00	100	150	375	—
1845GC MP	—	25.00	50.00	100	220	—
1846GC MP	—	25.00	50.00	100	220	—
1847GC MP	—	25.00	50.00	100	325	—
1848GC MP	—	20.00	40.00	75.00	165	—
1849GC MP	—	25.00	50.00	100	220	—
1850GC MP	—	30.00	60.00	125	275	—
1851GC MP	—	25.00	50.00	100	220	—

KM# 370.8   1/2 REAL
1.6900 g., 0.9030 Silver 0.0491 oz. ASW   **Obv:** Facing eagle,
snake in beak **Mint:** Hermosillo

Date	Mintage	F	VF	XF	Unc	BU
1839Ho PP Unique	—	—	—	—	—	—
1862Ho FM	—	500	650	1,000	—	—
1867Ho PR/FM Inverted 6, and 7/1	—	100	175	250	550	—

KM# 370.9   1/2 REAL
1.6900 g., 0.9030 Silver 0.0491 oz. ASW   **Obv:** Facing eagle,
snake in beak **Mint:** Mexico City

Date	Mintage	F	VF	XF	Unc	BU
1825Mo JM Short top 5	—	10.00	20.00	40.00	80.00	—
1825Mo JM Long top 5	—	10.00	20.00	40.00	80.00	—
1826/5Mo JM	—	10.00	20.00	40.00	80.00	—
1826Mo JM	—	5.00	10.00	20.00	60.00	—
1827/6Mo JM	—	5.00	10.00	20.00	60.00	—
1827Mo JM	—	5.00	10.00	20.00	60.00	—
1828/7Mo JM	—	7.50	15.00	25.00	85.00	—
1828Mo JM	—	10.00	20.00	40.00	90.00	—
1829Mo JM	—	7.50	15.00	25.00	75.00	—
1830Mo JM	—	5.00	10.00	20.00	60.00	—
1831Mo JM	—	5.00	10.00	20.00	60.00	—
1832Mo JM	—	7.50	12.50	27.50	60.00	—
1833Mo MJ	—	7.50	12.50	27.50	60.00	—
1834Mo ML	—	5.00	10.00	20.00	60.00	—
1835Mo ML	—	5.00	10.00	20.00	60.00	—
1836/5Mo ML/MF	—	7.50	15.00	25.00	65.00	—
1836Mo ML	—	7.50	15.00	25.00	65.00	—
1838Mo ML	—	5.00	10.00	20.00	60.00	—
1839/8Mo ML	—	5.00	10.00	25.00	65.00	—
1839Mo ML	—	5.00	10.00	20.00	50.00	—
1840Mo ML	—	5.00	10.00	20.00	50.00	—
1841Mo ML	—	5.00	10.00	20.00	50.00	—
1842Mo ML	—	15.00	35.00	80.00	200	—
1842Mo MM	—	5.00	10.00	20.00	50.00	—
1843Mo MM	—	10.00	20.00	40.00	80.00	—
1844Mo MF	—	5.00	10.00	20.00	50.00	—
1845/4Mo MF	—	5.00	10.00	25.00	60.00	—
1845Mo MF	—	5.00	10.00	20.00	50.00	—
1846Mo MF	—	5.00	10.00	20.00	50.00	—
1847Mo RC	—	10.00	20.00	40.00	80.00	—
1847Mo RC R/M	—	10.00	20.00	40.00	80.00	—
1848/7Mo GC/RC	—	5.00	10.00	20.00	50.00	—
1849Mo GC	—	5.00	10.00	20.00	50.00	—
1850Mo GC	—	5.00	10.00	20.00	50.00	—
1851Mo GC	—	5.00	10.00	20.00	50.00	—
1852Mo GC	—	5.00	10.00	20.00	50.00	—
1853Mo GC	—	5.00	10.00	20.00	50.00	—
1854Mo GC	—	5.00	10.00	20.00	50.00	—
1855Mo GC	—	5.00	10.00	20.00	50.00	—
1855Mo GF/GC	—	7.50	12.50	25.00	65.00	—
1856/5Mo GF	—	7.50	12.50	25.00	65.00	—

Date	Mintage	F	VF	XF	Unc	BU
1857Mo GF	—	5.00	10.00	20.00	50.00	—
1858Mo FH	—	3.00	5.00	12.50	40.00	—
1858Mo FH F/G	—	5.00	10.00	20.00	50.00	—
1858/9Mo FH	—	5.00	10.00	20.00	50.00	—
1859Mo FH/GC	—	5.00	10.00	20.00	50.00	—
1859Mo FH	—	3.00	6.00	15.00	50.00	—
1860Mo FH/GC	—	5.00	10.00	20.00	50.00	—
1860Mo FH	—	3.00	6.00	15.00	50.00	—
1860Mo TH	—	25.00	50.00	100	200	—
1860/59Mo FH	—	7.50	12.50	25.00	65.00	—
1861Mo CH	—	3.00	6.00	15.00	45.00	—
1862/52Mo CH	—	5.00	10.00	20.00	50.00	—
1862Mo CH	—	3.00	6.00	15.00	45.00	—
1863/55Mo TH/GC	—	5.00	10.00	20.00	50.00	—
1863Mo CH/GC	—	5.00	10.00	20.00	50.00	—
1863Mo CH	—	3.00	6.00	15.00	45.00	—

KM# 370.10 1/2 REAL
1.6900 g., 0.9030 Silver 0.0491 oz. ASW **Obv:** Facing eagle, snake in beak **Mint:** San Luis Potosi

Date	Mintage	F	VF	XF	Unc	BU
1831Pi JS	—	7.50	12.50	25.00	65.00	—
1841/36Pi JS	—	20.00	40.00	75.00	125	—
1842/1Pi PS	—	20.00	40.00	75.00	125	—
1842/1Pi PS P/J	—	60.00	80.00	150	300	—
1842Pi PS/PJ	—	50.00	75.00	125	250	—
1842 PS	—	60.00	80.00	150	300	—
1842Pi JS	—	20.00	40.00	75.00	125	—
1843/2Pi PS	—	17.50	25.00	40.00	80.00	—
1843Pi PS	—	15.00	25.00	35.00	70.00	—
1843Pi AM	—	10.00	15.00	25.00	60.00	—
1844Pi AM	—	10.00	15.00	30.00	65.00	—
1845Pi AM	—	250	375	500	1,500	—
1846/5Pi AM	—	40.00	75.00	125	200	—
1847/6Pi AM	—	15.00	25.00	40.00	80.00	—
1848Pi AM	—	15.00	25.00	40.00	80.00	—
1849Pi MC/AM	—	15.00	25.00	40.00	80.00	—
1849Pi MC	—	12.50	20.00	35.00	70.00	—
1850/49Pi MC	—	—	—	—	—	—
1850Pi MC	—	10.00	15.00	25.00	60.00	—
1850P MC	—	—	—	—	—	—
1851Pi MC	—	10.00	15.00	25.00	60.00	—
1852Pi MC	—	10.00	20.00	30.00	65.00	—
1853Pi MC	—	7.50	12.50	20.00	60.00	—
1854Pi MC	—	7.50	12.50	20.00	60.00	—
1855Pi MC	—	15.00	20.00	35.00	70.00	—
1856Pi MC	—	15.00	25.00	50.00	100	—
1856PI (no I)	—	—	—	—	—	—
1857Pi MC	—	7.50	12.50	20.00	60.00	—
1857Pi PS	—	10.00	15.00	30.00	65.00	—
1858Pi MC	—	12.50	20.00	35.00	70.00	—
1858Pi PS	—	12.50	20.00	35.00	70.00	—
1859Pi MC Rare	—	—	—	—	—	—
1860/59Pi PS	—	125	200	600	—	—
1861Pi RO	—	10.00	15.00	30.00	60.00	—
1862/1Pi RO	—	15.00	25.00	50.00	125	—
1862Pi RO	—	15.00	25.00	50.00	125	—
1863/2Pi RO	—	15.00	25.00	45.00	100	—

KM# 370.2 1/2 REAL
1.6900 g., 0.9030 Silver 0.0491 oz. ASW **Obv:** Facing eagle, snake in beak **Obv. Legend:** REPUBLICA MEXICANA **Rev:** Radiant cap **Mint:** Culiacan **Note:** Mint mark C.

Date	Mintage	F	VF	XF	Unc	BU
1846 CE	—	30.00	50.00	75.00	150	—
1848/7 CE	—	15.00	25.00	45.00	90.00	—
1849/8 CE	—	15.00	25.00	45.00	90.00	—
1849 CE	—	—	—	—	—	—
1852 CE	—	12.50	20.00	40.00	80.00	—
1853/1 CE	—	12.50	20.00	40.00	80.00	—
1854 CE	—	20.00	35.00	50.00	100	—
1856 CE	—	12.50	20.00	40.00	80.00	—
1857/6 CE	—	20.00	35.00	50.00	100	—

Date	Mintage	F	VF	XF	Unc	BU
1857 CE	—	15.00	25.00	45.00	90.00	—
1858 CE Error 1 for 1/2	—	12.50	20.00	40.00	80.00	—
1860/59 PV	—	20.00	35.00	50.00	100	—
1860 PV	—	12.50	20.00	40.00	80.00	—
1861 PV	—	12.50	20.00	40.00	80.00	—
1863 CE Error 1 for 1/2	—	15.00	25.00	45.00	90.00	—
1867 CE	—	12.50	20.00	40.00	80.00	—
1869 6/5 CE Error 1 for 1/2	—	12.50	20.00	40.00	80.00	—

KM# 370.3 1/2 REAL
1.6900 g., 0.9030 Silver 0.0491 oz. ASW **Obv:** Facing eagle, snake in beak **Mint:** Durango **Note:** Mint mark D, Do.

Date	Mintage	F	VF	XF	Unc	BU
1832 RM	—	125	225	350	600	—
1832 RM/L	—	—	—	—	—	—
1833/2 RM/L	—	75.00	100	150	225	—
1833/1 RM/L	—	12.50	20.00	40.00	80.00	—
1833 RM	—	25.00	40.00	75.00	150	—
1834/1 RM	—	25.00	40.00	75.00	150	—
1834 RM	—	12.50	20.00	40.00	80.00	—
1837/1 RM	—	12.50	30.00	60.00	200	—
1837/4 RM	—	12.50	30.00	60.00	200	—
1837/6 RM	—	12.50	30.00	60.00	200	—
1841/33 RM	—	15.00	30.00	60.00	250	—
1842/32 RM	—	12.50	20.00	40.00	80.00	—
1842 RM	—	12.50	20.00	40.00	80.00	—
1842 8R RM Error	—	12.50	20.00	40.00	80.00	—
1842 1/2/8R RM	—	12.50	20.00	40.00	80.00	—
1843/33 RM	—	15.00	25.00	50.00	100	—
1843 RM	—	15.00	25.00	50.00	100	—
1845/31 RM	—	12.50	20.00	40.00	80.00	—
1845/34 RM	—	12.50	20.00	40.00	80.00	—
1845/35 RM	—	12.50	20.00	40.00	80.00	—
1845 RM	—	15.00	25.00	50.00	100	—
1846 RM	—	30.00	50.00	80.00	200	—
1848/5 RM	—	35.00	55.00	110	250	—
1848/36 RM	—	25.00	40.00	75.00	200	—
1849 JMR	—	25.00	40.00	75.00	200	—
1850 RM Rare	—	—	—	—	—	—
1850 JMR	—	25.00	40.00	75.00	200	—
1851 JMR	—	20.00	35.00	50.00	100	—
1852/1 JMR	—	65.00	125	250	600	—
1852 JMR	—	30.00	50.00	80.00	200	—
1853 CP	—	12.50	20.00	40.00	80.00	—
1854 CP	—	25.00	40.00	75.00	200	—
1855 CP	—	25.00	40.00	60.00	150	—
1856/5 CP	—	20.00	35.00	50.00	100	—
1857 CP	—	20.00	35.00	50.00	100	—
1858/7 CP	—	20.00	35.00	50.00	100	—
1859 CP	—	20.00	35.00	50.00	100	—
1860/59 CP	—	40.00	65.00	135	300	—
1861 CP	—	125	250	400	700	—
1862 CP	—	25.00	40.00	60.00	125	—
1864 LT	—	100	300	500	1,000	—
1869 CP	—	40.00	65.00	125	275	—

KM# 370.11 1/2 REAL
1.6900 g., 0.9030 Silver 0.0491 oz. ASW **Obv:** Facing eagle, snake in beak **Mint:** Zacatecas **Note:** Mint mark Z, Zs.

Date	Mintage	F	VF	XF	Unc	BU
1826 AZ	—	5.00	10.00	20.00	60.00	—
1826 AO	—	5.00	10.00	20.00	60.00	—
1827 AO	—	5.00	10.00	20.00	60.00	—
1828/7 AO	—	5.00	10.00	20.00	60.00	—
1829 AO	—	5.00	10.00	20.00	60.00	—
1830 OV	—	5.00	10.00	20.00	60.00	—
1831 OV	—	25.00	50.00	75.00	150	—
1831 OM	—	5.00	10.00	20.00	60.00	—
1832 OM	—	5.00	10.00	20.00	60.00	—
1833 OM	—	5.00	10.00	20.00	60.00	—

FIRST REPUBLIC - FEDERAL

Date	Mintage	F	VF	XF	Unc	BU
1834 OM	—	5.00	10.00	20.00	60.00	—
1835/4 OM	—	5.00	10.00	20.00	60.00	—
1835 OM	—	5.00	10.00	20.00	60.00	—
1836 OM	—	5.00	10.00	20.00	60.00	—
1837 OM	—	10.00	20.00	40.00	80.00	—
1838 OM	—	5.00	10.00	20.00	60.00	—
1839 OM	—	7.50	15.00	30.00	65.00	—
1840 OM	—	10.00	20.00	45.00	90.00	—
1841 OM	—	10.00	25.00	45.00	90.00	—
1842/1 OM	—	5.00	10.00	20.00	60.00	—
1842 OM	—	5.00	10.00	20.00	60.00	—
1843 OM	—	40.00	75.00	115	250	—
1844 OM	—	5.00	10.00	20.00	60.00	—
1845 OM	—	5.00	10.00	20.00	60.00	—
1846 OM	—	7.50	15.00	30.00	65.00	—
1847 OM	—	5.00	10.00	20.00	50.00	—
1848 OM	—	5.00	10.00	20.00	50.00	—
1849 OM	—	5.00	10.00	20.00	50.00	—
1850 OM	—	5.00	10.00	20.00	50.00	—
1851 OM	—	5.00	10.00	20.00	50.00	—
1852 OM	—	5.00	10.00	20.00	50.00	—
1853 OM	—	5.00	10.00	20.00	50.00	—
1854/3 OM	—	5.00	10.00	20.00	50.00	—
1854 OM	—	5.00	10.00	20.00	50.00	—
1855/3 OM	—	7.50	15.00	30.00	65.00	—
1855 OM	—	5.00	10.00	20.00	50.00	—
1856 OM	—	5.00	10.00	20.00	50.00	—
1857 MO	—	5.00	10.00	20.00	50.00	—
1858 MO	—	5.00	10.00	20.00	50.00	—
1859 MO	—	6.00	8.50	17.50	35.00	—
1859 VL	—	6.00	8.50	17.50	40.00	—
1860/50 VL Inverted A for V	—	5.00	10.00	20.00	50.00	—
1860/59 VL Inverted A for V	—	5.00	10.00	20.00	50.00	—
1860 MO	—	5.00	10.00	20.00	50.00	—
1860 VL	—	5.00	10.00	20.00	50.00	—
1861/0 VL Inverted A for V	—	7.50	15.00	30.00	65.00	—
1861 VL Inverted A for V	—	5.00	10.00	20.00	50.00	—
1862 VL Inverted A for V	—	5.00	10.00	20.00	50.00	—
1863 VL Inverted A for V	—	5.00	10.00	20.00	50.00	—
1863/1 VL Inverted A for V	—	7.50	15.00	30.00	65.00	—
1869 YH	—	5.00	10.00	20.00	50.00	—

KM# 370.7 1/2 REAL
1.6900 g., 0.9030 Silver 0.0491 oz. ASW **Obv:** Facing eagle, snake in beak **Mint:** Guanajuato **Note:** Varieties exist.

Date	Mintage	F	VF	XF	Unc	BU
1826Go MJ	—	125	250	400	1,000	—
1827/6Go MJ	—	7.50	15.00	30.00	75.00	—
1828/7Go MJ	—	7.50	15.00	30.00	75.00	—
1828Go MJ	—	—	—	—	—	—
Note: Denomination 2/1						
1828Go JG	—	—	—	—	—	—
1828Go MR	—	50.00	100	150	250	—
1829/8Go MJ	—	5.00	10.00	25.00	50.00	—
1829Go MJ	—	5.00	10.00	25.00	50.00	—
1829Go MJ	—	5.00	10.00	25.00	50.00	—
Note: Reversed N in MEXICANA						
1830Go MJ	—	5.00	10.00	25.00	50.00	—
1831/29Go MJ	—	15.00	30.00	60.00	150	—
1831Go MJ	—	10.00	20.00	40.00	80.00	—
1832/1Go MJ	—	7.50	15.00	30.00	75.00	—
1832Go MJ	—	7.50	15.00	30.00	75.00	—
1833Go MJ Round top 3	—	10.00	20.00	40.00	80.00	—
1833Go MJ Flat top 3	—	10.00	20.00	40.00	80.00	—
1834Go PJ	—	5.00	10.00	25.00	50.00	—
1835Go PJ	—	5.00	10.00	25.00	50.00	—
1836/5Go PJ	—	7.50	15.00	30.00	75.00	—
1836Go PJ	—	5.00	10.00	25.00	50.00	—
1837Go PJ	—	5.00	10.00	25.00	50.00	—
1838/7Go PJ	—	5.00	10.00	25.00	50.00	—
1839Go PJ	—	5.00	10.00	25.00	50.00	—
1839Go PJ	—	5.00	10.00	25.00	50.00	—

Date	Mintage	F	VF	XF	Unc	BU
Note: Error: REPUBLIGA						
1840/39Go PJ	—	7.50	10.00	25.00	75.00	—
1840Go PJ Straight J	—	5.00	10.00	25.00	50.00	—
1840Go PJ Curved J	—	5.00	10.00	25.00	50.00	—
1841/31Go PJ	—	5.00	10.00	25.00	50.00	—
1841Go PJ	—	5.00	10.00	25.00	50.00	—
1842/1Go PJ	—	5.00	10.00	25.00	50.00	—
1842/1Go PM	—	5.00	10.00	25.00	50.00	—
1842Go PM/J	—	5.00	10.00	25.00	50.00	—
1842Go PJ	—	5.00	10.00	25.00	50.00	—
1842Go PM	—	5.00	10.00	25.00	50.00	—
1843/33Go PM 1/2 over 8	—	5.00	10.00	25.00	50.00	—
1843Go PM	—	5.00	10.00	25.00	50.00	—
Note: Convex wings						
1843Go PM	—	5.00	10.00	25.00	50.00	—
Note: Concave wings						
1844/3Go PM	—	5.00	10.00	25.00	50.00	—
1844Go PM	—	10.00	20.00	40.00	90.00	—
1845/4Go PM	—	5.00	10.00	25.00	50.00	—
1845Go PM	—	5.00	10.00	25.00	50.00	—
1846/4Go PM	—	5.00	10.00	25.00	50.00	—
1846/5Go PM	—	5.00	10.00	25.00	50.00	—
1846Go PM	—	5.00	10.00	25.00	50.00	—
1847/6Go PM	—	7.50	15.00	30.00	60.00	—
1847Go PM	—	7.50	15.00	30.00	60.00	—
1848/35Go PM	—	5.00	10.00	25.00	50.00	—
1848Go PM	—	5.00	10.00	25.00	50.00	—
1848Go PF/M	—	5.00	10.00	25.00	50.00	—
1849/39Go PF	—	5.00	10.00	25.00	50.00	—
1849Go PF	—	5.00	10.00	25.00	50.00	—
1849Go PF	—	5.00	10.00	25.00	50.00	—
Note: Error: MEXCANA						
1850Go PF	—	5.00	10.00	25.00	50.00	—
1851Go PF	—	5.00	10.00	25.00	50.00	—
1852/1Go PF	—	5.00	10.00	25.00	50.00	—
1852Go PF	—	2.50	7.50	17.50	40.00	—
1853Go PF/R	—	5.00	10.00	25.00	50.00	—
1853Go PF	—	5.00	10.00	25.00	50.00	—
1854Go PF	—	5.00	10.00	25.00	50.00	—
1855Go PF	—	5.00	10.00	25.00	50.00	—
1856/4Go PF	—	5.00	10.00	25.00	50.00	—
1856/5Go PF	—	5.00	10.00	25.00	50.00	—
1856Go PF	—	5.00	10.00	25.00	50.00	—
1857/6Go PF	—	5.00	10.00	25.00	50.00	—
1857Go PF	—	5.00	10.00	25.00	50.00	—
1858/7Go PF	—	7.50	15.00	30.00	60.00	—
1858Go PF	—	5.00	10.00	25.00	50.00	—
1859Go PF	—	5.00	10.00	25.00	50.00	—
1860Go PF Small 1/2	—	5.00	10.00	25.00	50.00	—
1860Go PF Large 1/2	—	5.00	10.00	25.00	50.00	—
1860/59Go PF	—	5.00	10.00	25.00	50.00	—
1861Go PF Small 1/2	—	5.00	10.00	25.00	50.00	—
1861Go PF Large 1/2	—	5.00	10.00	25.00	50.00	—
1862/1Go YE	—	5.00	10.00	25.00	50.00	—
1862Go YE	—	2.50	7.50	17.50	40.00	—
1862Go YF	—	5.00	10.00	25.00	50.00	—
1867Go YF	—	2.50	7.50	17.50	40.00	—
1868Go YF	—	2.50	7.50	17.50	40.00	—

KM# 370.1 1/2 REAL
1.6900 g., 0.9030 Silver 0.0491 oz. ASW **Obv:** Facing eagle **Mint:** Chihuahua

Date	Mintage	F	VF	XF	Unc	BU
1844Ca RG	—	75.00	125	175	300	—
1845Ca RG	—	75.00	125	150	275	—

KM# 370 1/2 REAL
1.6900 g., 0.9030 Silver 0.0491 oz. ASW **Obv:** Hooked-neck eagle **Mint:** Alamos

Date	Mintage	F	VF	XF	Unc	BU
1862A PG Rare	—	—	—	—	—	—

KM# 370.4 1/2 REAL
1.6900 g., 0.9030 Silver 0.0491 oz. ASW **Obv:** Facing eagle, snake in beak **Mint:** Estado de Mexico

Date	Mintage	F	VF	XF	Unc	BU
1829EoMo LF	—	175	300	500	1,500	—

KM# 372 REAL
3.3800 g., 0.9030 Silver 0.0981 oz. ASW **Obv:** Facing eagle, snake in beak **Mint:** Chihuahua

Date	Mintage	F	VF	XF	Unc	BU
1844Ca RG	—	500	1,000	1,500	2,750	—
1845Ca RG	—	500	1,000	1,500	2,750	—
1855Ca RG	—	100	150	225	475	—

KM# 372.1 REAL
3.3800 g., 0.9030 Silver 0.0981 oz. ASW **Obv:** Facing eagle, snake in beak **Mint:** Culiacan

Date	Mintage	F	VF	XF	Unc	BU
1846C CE	—	12.50	25.00	40.00	110	—
1848C CE	—	12.50	25.00	40.00	110	—
1850C CE	—	12.50	25.00	40.00	110	—
1851/0C CE	—	12.50	25.00	40.00	110	—
1852/1C CE	—	7.50	15.00	30.00	100	—
1853/2C CE	—	7.50	15.00	30.00	100	—
1854C CE	—	7.50	15.00	30.00	100	—
1856C CE	—	40.00	65.00	100	225	—
1857/4C CE	—	10.00	20.00	35.00	100	—
1857/6C CE	—	10.00	20.00	35.00	100	—
1858C CE	—	5.00	7.50	15.00	100	—
1859C CE	—	—	—	—	—	—
1860/9C PV/N	—	6.00	10.00	17.50	120	—
1860C PV	—	5.00	7.50	15.00	100	—
1861C PV	—	5.00	7.50	15.00	100	—
1863C CE	—	—	1,650	2,250	—	—
Note: 3 known						
1869C CE	—	—	7.50	15.00	100	—

KM# 372.2 REAL
3.3800 g., 0.9030 Silver 0.0981 oz. ASW **Obv:** Facing eagle, snake in beak **Mint:** Durango

Date	Mintage	F	VF	XF	Unc	BU
1832/1Do RM	—	5.00	10.00	20.00	90.00	—
1832Do RM/RL	—	10.00	15.00	30.00	100	—
1832Do RM	—	5.00	10.00	20.00	100	—
1834/24Do RM/RL	—	15.00	25.00	50.00	150	—
1834/3Do RM/RL	—	15.00	25.00	50.00	150	—
1834Do RM	—	10.00	20.00	40.00	110	—
1836/4Do RM	—	5.00	7.50	15.00	100	—
1836Do RM	—	5.00	7.50	15.00	100	—
1837Do RM 3/2	—	12.50	20.00	40.00	110	—
1837Do RM	—	12.50	20.00	40.00	110	—
1841Do RM	—	7.50	15.00	30.00	100	—
1842/32Do RM	—	10.00	20.00	40.00	110	—
1842Do RM	—	7.50	15.00	30.00	100	—
1843/37Do RM	—	10.00	20.00	40.00	110	—
1843Do RM	—	5.00	7.50	15.00	100	—
1844/34Do RM	—	15.00	25.00	45.00	125	—
1845Do RM	—	5.00	7.50	15.00	100	—
1846Do RM	—	7.50	15.00	30.00	100	—
1847Do RM	—	10.00	15.00	35.00	100	—
1848/31Do RM	—	10.00	15.00	35.00	100	—
1848/33Do RM	—	10.00	15.00	35.00	100	—
1848/5Do RM	—	10.00	15.00	35.00	100	—
1848Do RM	—	7.50	12.50	20.00	100	—
1849/8Do CM	—	10.00	15.00	30.00	100	—
1850Do JMR	—	20.00	40.00	75.00	175	—
1851Do JMR	—	20.00	40.00	75.00	175	—
1852Do JMR	—	20.00	40.00	75.00	175	—
1853Do CP	—	12.50	20.00	35.00	100	—
1854/1Do CP	—	10.00	15.00	25.00	100	—
1854Do CP	—	7.50	12.50	20.00	100	—
1855Do CP	—	10.00	15.00	25.00	100	—
1856Do CP	—	12.50	20.00	35.00	100	—
1857Do CP	—	12.50	20.00	35.00	100	—
1858Do CP	—	12.50	20.00	35.00	100	—
1859Do CP	—	7.50	12.50	20.00	100	—
1860/59Do CP	—	10.00	15.00	25.00	100	—
1861Do CP	—	15.00	25.00	40.00	110	—
1862/1Do CP	—	225	300	450	1,250	—
1864Do LT	—	15.00	25.00	40.00	110	—

KM# 372.4 REAL
3.3800 g., 0.9030 Silver 0.0981 oz. ASW **Obv:** Facing eagle, snake in beak **Mint:** Guadalajara

Date	Mintage	F	VF	XF	Unc	BU
1826Ga FS	—	15.00	30.00	50.00	125	—
1828/7Ga FS	—	15.00	30.00	50.00	125	—
1829/8/7Ga FS	—	—	—	—	—	—
1829Ga FS	—	15.00	30.00	50.00	125	—
1830Ga FS	—	250	425	600	—	—

Date	Mintage	F	VF	XF	Unc	BU
1831Ga LP	—	15.00	30.00	50.00	125	—
1831Ga LP/FS	—	300	450	600	—	—
1832Ga FS	—	250	350	500	—	—
1833/2Ga G FS	—	100	150	275	550	—
1833Ga FS	—	75.00	125	225	500	—
1834/3Ga FS	—	75.00	125	225	500	—
1835Ga FS	—	—	—	—	—	—
1837/6Ga JG/FS	—	12.50	20.00	35.00	100	—
1838/7Ga JG/FS	—	100	200	400	—	—
1839Ga JG	—	250	350	500	—	—
1840Ga JG	—	12.50	20.00	35.00	100	—
1840Ga MC	—	7.50	12.50	25.00	70.00	—
1841Ga MC	—	50.00	75.00	125	250	—
1842/0Ga JG/MC	—	10.00	15.00	30.00	100	—
1842Ga JG	—	7.50	12.50	20.00	100	—
1843Ga JG	—	150	200	300	750	—
1843Ga MC	—	5.00	7.50	15.00	100	—
1844Ga MC	—	7.50	12.50	20.00	100	—
1845Ga MC	—	10.00	15.00	25.00	100	—
1845Ga JG	—	5.00	7.50	20.00	100	—
1846Ga JG	—	12.50	20.00	35.00	100	—
1847/6Ga JG	—	10.00	15.00	25.00	100	—
1847Ga JG	—	10.00	15.00	25.00	100	—
1848Ga JG	—	400	550	700	—	—
1849Ga JG	—	7.50	12.50	20.00	100	—
1850Ga JG	—	175	275	400	—	—
1851Ga JG	—	10.00	15.00	25.00	100	—
1852Ga JG	—	10.00	15.00	25.00	100	—
1853/2Ga JG	—	10.00	15.00	25.00	100	—
1854Ga JG	—	10.00	15.00	25.00	100	—
1855Ga JG	—	15.00	25.00	40.00	100	—
1856Ga JG	—	7.50	12.50	20.00	100	—
1857/6Ga JG	—	12.50	20.00	35.00	100	—
1858/7Ga JG	—	15.00	25.00	40.00	110	—
1859/8Ga JG	—	25.00	50.00	75.00	150	—
1860/59Ga JG	—	30.00	60.00	90.00	225	—
1861/0Ga JG	—	20.00	30.00	50.00	125	—
1861Ga JG	—	25.00	50.00	100	250	—
1862Ga JG	—	7.50	12.50	20.00	100	—

KM# 372.5 REAL
3.3800 g., 0.9030 Silver 0.0981 oz. ASW **Obv:** Facing eagle, snake in beak **Obv. Legend:** REPUBLICA MEXICANA **Rev:** Radiant cap **Mint:** Guadalupe y Calvo

Date	Mintage	F	VF	XF	Unc	BU
1844GC MP	—	40.00	60.00	100	300	—
1845GC MP	—	40.00	60.00	100	300	—
1846GC MP	—	40.00	60.00	100	300	—
1847GC MP	—	40.00	60.00	100	300	—
1848GC MP	—	40.00	60.00	100	300	—
1849/7GC MP	—	40.00	60.00	100	300	—
1849/8GC MP	—	40.00	60.00	100	300	—
1849GC MP	—	40.00	60.00	100	300	—
1850GC MP	—	40.00	60.00	100	300	—
1851GC MP	—	40.00	60.00	100	300	—

KM# 372.6 REAL
3.3800 g., 0.9030 Silver 0.0981 oz. ASW **Obv:** Facing eagle, snake in beak **Mint:** Guanajuato

Date	Mintage	F	VF	XF	Unc	BU
1826/5Go JJ	—	5.00	7.50	15.00	85.00	—
1826Go MJ	—	4.00	6.00	15.00	85.00	—
1827Go MJ	—	4.00	6.00	15.00	65.00	—
1827Go JM	—	10.00	15.00	25.00	75.00	—
1828/7Go MR	—	4.00	6.00	15.00	85.00	—
1828Go MJ	—	4.00	6.00	15.00	85.00	—
Note: Straight J, small 8						
1828Go MJ	—	4.00	6.00	15.00	85.00	—
Note: Full J, large 8						
1828/6G MR/JJ	—	4.00	6.00	15.00	85.00	—
1828G MR/JJ	—	4.00	6.00	15.00	85.00	—
1828Go MR	—	4.00	6.00	15.00	85.00	—

Date	Mintage	F	VF	XF	Unc	BU
1829/8Go MG Small eagle	—	4.00	6.00	15.00	85.00	—
1829Go MJ Small eagle	—	4.00	6.00	15.00	85.00	—
1829Go MJ Large eagle	—	4.00	6.00	15.00	85.00	—
1830Go MJ Small initials	—	4.00	6.00	15.00	85.00	—
1830Go MJ Medium initials	—	4.00	6.00	15.00	85.00	—
1830Go MJ Large initials	—	4.00	6.00	15.00	85.00	—
1830Go MJ	—	4.00	6.00	15.00	85.00	—
Note: Reversed N in MEXICANA						
1830GC MJ 3/2	—	4.00	6.00	15.00	85.00	—
1831/0Go MJ	—	4.00	6.00	15.00	85.00	—
Note: Reversed N in MEXICANA						
1831Go MJ	—	4.00	6.00	15.00	85.00	—
1832/1Go MJ	—	15.00	30.00	50.00	125	—
1832Go MJ	—	15.00	30.00	50.00	125	—
1833Go MJ Top of 3 round	—	4.00	6.00	15.00	85.00	—
1833Go MJ Top of 3 flat	—	4.00	6.00	15.00	85.00	—
1834Go PJ	—	4.00	6.00	15.00	85.00	—
1835Go PJ	—	7.50	12.50	20.00	85.00	—
1836Go PJ	—	4.00	6.00	15.00	85.00	—
1837Go PJ	—	15.00	30.00	50.00	125	—
1838/7Go PJ	—	10.00	20.00	35.00	85.00	—
1839Go PJ	—	4.00	6.00	15.00	85.00	—
1840/39Go PJ	—	4.00	6.00	15.00	85.00	—
1840Go PJ	—	4.00	6.00	15.00	85.00	—
1841/31Go PJ	—	10.00	20.00	35.00	85.00	—
1841Go PJ	—	4.00	6.00	15.00	85.00	—
1842Go PJ	—	4.00	6.00	15.00	85.00	—
1842Go PM	—	4.00	6.00	15.00	85.00	—
1843Go PM Convex wings	—	4.00	6.00	15.00	85.00	—
1843Go PM Concave wings	—	4.00	6.00	15.00	85.00	—
1844Go PM	—	4.00	6.00	15.00	85.00	—
1845/4Go PM	—	4.00	6.00	15.00	85.00	—
1845Go PM	—	4.00	6.00	15.00	85.00	—
1846/5Go PM	—	7.50	12.50	20.00	85.00	—
1846Go PM	—	4.00	6.00	15.00	85.00	—
1847/6Go PM	—	4.00	6.00	15.00	85.00	—
1847Go PM	—	4.00	6.00	15.00	85.00	—
1848Go PM	—	4.00	6.00	15.00	85.00	—
1849Go PF	—	10.00	20.00	35.00	85.00	—
1850Go PF	—	4.00	6.00	15.00	85.00	—
1851Go PF	—	10.00	20.00	35.00	100	—
1853/2Go PF	—	7.50	12.50	20.00	75.00	—
1853Go PF	—	4.00	6.00	15.00	75.00	—
1853Go PF/M 5/4	—	7.50	12.50	20.00	75.00	—
1854/3Go PF	—	4.00	6.00	15.00	75.00	—
1854Go PF Large eagle	—	4.00	6.00	15.00	75.00	—
1854Go PF Small eagle	—	4.00	6.00	15.00	75.00	—
1855/3Go PF	—	4.00	6.00	15.00	75.00	—
1855/4Go PF	—	4.00	6.00	15.00	75.00	—
1855Go PF	—	4.00	6.00	15.00	75.00	—
1856/5Go PF	—	4.00	6.00	15.00	75.00	—
1856Go PF	—	4.00	6.00	15.00	75.00	—
1857/6Go PF	—	4.00	6.00	15.00	75.00	—
1857Go PF	—	4.00	6.00	15.00	75.00	—
1858Go PF	—	4.00	6.00	15.00	75.00	—
1859Go PF	—	4.00	6.00	15.00	75.00	—
1860/50Go PF	—	4.00	6.00	15.00	75.00	—
1860Go PF	—	4.00	6.00	15.00	75.00	—
1861Go PF	—	4.00	6.00	15.00	75.00	—
1862Go YE	—	4.00	6.00	15.00	75.00	—
1862/1Go YF	—	7.50	12.50	20.00	75.00	—
1862Go YF	—	4.00	6.00	15.00	75.00	—
1867Go YF	—	4.00	6.00	15.00	75.00	—
1868/7Go YF	—	4.00	6.00	15.00	75.00	—

KM# 372.7 REAL
3.3800 g., 0.9030 Silver 0.0981 oz. ASW **Obv:** Facing eagle, snake in beak **Mint:** Hermosillo

Date	Mintage	F	VF	XF	Unc	BU
1867Ho PR	—	38.50	75.00	120	250	—
Note: Small 7/1						
1867Ho PR	—	38.50	75.00	120	250	—
Note: Large 7/ small 7						
1868Ho PR	—	38.50	75.00	120	250	—

KM# 372.8 REAL
3.3800 g., 0.9030 Silver 0.0981 oz. ASW **Obv:** Facing eagle, snake in beak **Mint:** Mexico City

Date	Mintage	F	VF	XF	Unc	BU
1825Mo JM	—	10.00	20.00	40.00	125	—
1826Mo JM	—	7.50	15.00	30.00	115	—
1827/6Mo JM	—	7.50	15.00	30.00	85.00	—
1827Mo JM	—	5.00	10.00	20.00	80.00	—
1828Mo JM	—	7.50	15.00	30.00	110	—
1830/29Mo JM	—	5.00	10.00	20.00	110	—
1830Mo JM	—	5.00	12.50	25.00	110	—
1831Mo JM	—	100	200	300	800	—
1832Mo JM	—	5.00	10.00	20.00	110	—
1833/2Mo MJ	—	5.00	10.00	20.00	110	—
1850Mo GC	—	5.00	10.00	20.00	110	—
1852Mo GC	—	275	425	575	—	—
1854Mo GC	—	10.00	20.00	40.00	110	—
1855Mo GF	—	5.00	10.00	20.00	90.00	—
1856Mo GF	—	100	200	400	1,000	—
1857Mo GF	—	5.00	10.00	20.00	90.00	—
1858Mo FH	—	5.00	10.00	20.00	90.00	—
1859Mo FH	—	5.00	10.00	20.00	90.00	—
1861Mo CH	—	5.00	10.00	20.00	90.00	—
1862Mo CH	—	5.00	10.00	20.00	90.00	—
1863/2Mo CH	—	7.50	12.50	25.00	90.00	—

KM# 372.9 REAL
3.3800 g., 0.9030 Silver 0.0981 oz. ASW **Obv:** Facing eagle, snake in beak **Mint:** San Luis Potosi

Date	Mintage	F	VF	XF	Unc	BU
1831Pi JS	—	5.00	10.00	20.00	125	—
1837Pi JS	—	600	750	1,000	—	—
1838/7Pi JS	—	250	300	375	—	—
1838Pi JS	—	20.00	35.00	60.00	125	—
1840/39Pi JS	—	7.50	15.00	30.00	125	—
1840Pi JS	—	7.50	15.00	30.00	125	—
1841Pi JS	—	7.50	15.00	30.00	125	—
1842Pi JS	—	15.00	30.00	55.00	150	—
1842Pi PS	—	5.00	10.00	20.00	125	—
1843Pi PS	—	12.50	20.00	35.00	125	—
1843Pi AM	—	40.00	60.00	80.00	150	—
1844Pi AM	—	40.00	60.00	80.00	150	—
1845Pi AM	—	7.50	15.00	30.00	125	—
1846/5Pi AM	—	7.50	15.00	30.00	125	—
1847/6Pi AM	—	7.50	15.00	30.00	125	—
1847Pi AM	—	7.50	15.00	30.00	125	—
1848/7Pi AM	—	7.50	15.00	30.00	125	—
1849Pi PS	—	7.50	15.00	30.00	125	—
1849/8Pi SP	—	60.00	100	150	—	—
1849Pi SP	—	15.00	25.00	40.00	125	—
1850Pi MC	—	5.00	10.00	20.00	125	—
1851/0Pi MC	—	7.50	15.00	30.00	125	—
1851Pi MC	—	7.50	15.00	30.00	125	—
1852/1/0Pi MC	—	10.00	20.00	35.00	125	—
1852Pi MC	—	7.50	15.00	30.00	125	—
1853/1Pi MC	—	12.50	20.00	35.00	125	—
1853Pi MC	—	10.00	20.00	35.00	125	—
1854/2Pi MO	—	30.00	60.00	100	—	—
1854/3Pi MC	—	20.00	40.00	60.00	150	—
1855Pi MC	—	15.00	25.00	45.00	125	—
1855/4Pi MC	—	20.00	40.00	60.00	150	—
1856Pi MC	—	15.00	25.00	45.00	125	—
1857Pi PS	—	20.00	35.00	55.00	135	—
1857Pi MC	—	20.00	40.00	60.00	150	—
1858Pi MC	—	12.50	20.00	35.00	125	—
1859Pi PS	—	10.00	15.00	30.00	125	—
1860/59Pi PS	—	10.00	15.00	30.00	125	—
1861Pi PS	—	7.50	12.50	20.00	125	—
1861Pi RO	—	12.50	20.00	35.00	125	—
1862/1Pi RO	—	12.50	20.00	35.00	90.00	—
1862Pi RO	—	7.50	12.50	20.00	125	—

KM# 372.10 REAL
3.3800 g., 0.9030 Silver 0.0981 oz. ASW **Obv:** Facing eagle, snake in beak **Mint:** Zacatecas

Date	Mintage	F	VF	XF	Unc	BU
1826Zs AZ	—	5.00	12.50	35.00	120	—
1826Zs AO	—	5.00	12.50	35.00	120	—

Date	Mintage	F	VF	XF	Unc	BU
1827Zs AO	—	5.00	12.50	35.00	120	—
1828/7Zs AO	—	5.00	12.50	35.00	120	—
1828Zs AO	—	5.00	12.50	35.00	120	—
1828Zs AO Inverted V for A	—	5.00	12.50	35.00	120	—
1829Zs AO	—	5.00	12.50	35.00	120	—
1830Zs ZsOV	—	5.00	12.50	35.00	120	—
1830Zs ZOV	—	5.00	12.50	35.00	120	—
1831Zs OV	—	5.00	12.50	35.00	120	—
1831Zs OM	—	5.00	12.50	30.00	120	—
1832Zs OM	—	5.00	12.50	30.00	120	—
1833/2Zs OM	—	5.00	12.50	30.00	120	—
1833/2Zs OM/V	—	5.00	12.50	30.00	120	—
1833Zs OM	—	5.00	12.50	30.00	120	—
1834/3Zs OM	—	5.00	12.50	30.00	120	—
1834Zs OM	—	5.00	12.50	30.00	120	—
1835/4Zs OM	—	20.00	35.00	60.00	150	—
1835Zs OM	—	4.00	8.00	20.00	65.00	—
1836/5Zs OM	—	4.00	8.00	20.00	85.00	—
1836Zs OM	—	4.00	8.00	20.00	85.00	—
1837Zs OM	—	4.00	8.00	20.00	85.00	—
1838Zs OM	—	4.00	8.00	20.00	85.00	—
1839Zs OM	—	4.00	8.00	20.00	85.00	—
1840Zs OM	—	4.00	8.00	20.00	85.00	—
1841Zs OM	—	20.00	40.00	60.00	150	—
1842/1Zs OM	—	4.00	8.00	20.00	85.00	—
1842Zs OM	—	4.00	8.00	20.00	85.00	—
1843Zs OM	—	4.00	8.00	20.00	85.00	—
1844Zs OM	—	4.00	8.00	20.00	85.00	—
1845/4Zs OM	—	5.00	12.50	30.00	100	—
1845Zs OM	—	4.00	8.00	20.00	85.00	—
1846Zs OM	—	4.00	8.00	20.00	85.00	—
Note: Old font and obverse						
1846Zs OM	—	4.00	8.00	20.00	85.00	—
Note: New font and obverse						
1847Zs OM	—	4.00	8.00	20.00	85.00	—
1848Zs OM	—	4.00	8.00	20.00	85.00	—
1849Zs OM	—	10.00	25.00	50.00	125	—
1850Zs OM	—	4.00	6.00	15.00	85.00	—
1851Zs OM	—	4.00	6.00	15.00	85.00	—
1852Zs OM	—	4.00	6.00	15.00	85.00	—
1853Zs OM	—	4.00	6.00	15.00	85.00	—
1854/2Zs OM	—	4.00	6.00	15.00	85.00	—
1854/3Zs OM	—	4.00	6.00	15.00	85.00	—
1854Zs OM	—	4.00	6.00	15.00	85.00	—
1855/4Zs OM	—	4.00	6.00	15.00	85.00	—
1855Zs OM	—	4.00	6.00	15.00	85.00	—
1855Zs MO	—	4.00	6.00	15.00	85.00	—
1856Zs MO	—	4.00	6.00	15.00	85.00	—
1856Zs MO/OM	—	4.00	6.00	15.00	85.00	—
1857Zs MO	—	4.00	6.00	15.00	85.00	—
1858Zs MO	—	4.00	6.00	15.00	85.00	—
1859Zs MO	—	4.00	6.00	15.00	75.00	—
1860 MO	—	250	—	—	—	—
1860Zs VL	—	4.00	6.00	15.00	75.00	—
1860Zs VL Inverted A for V	—	4.00	6.00	15.00	75.00	—
1861Zs VL	—	4.00	6.00	15.00	75.00	—
1861Zs VL Inverted A for V	—	4.00	6.00	15.00	75.00	—
1862Zs VL	—	5.00	12.50	30.00	100	—
1868Zs JS	—	25.00	45.00	90.00	175	—
1869Zs YH	—	4.00	8.00	20.00	75.00	—

KM# 372.3 REAL
3.3800 g., 0.9030 Silver 0.0981 oz. ASW **Obv:** Facing eagle, snake in beak **Mint:** Estado de Mexico

Date	Mintage	F	VF	XF	Unc	BU
1828EoMo LF	—	200	300	450	1,600	—

KM# 374.2 2 REALES
6.7600 g., 0.9030 Silver 0.1962 oz. ASW **Obv:** Facing eagle, snake in beak **Edge:** Reeded **Mint:** Chihuahua

Date	Mintage	F	VF	XF	Unc	BU
1832Ca MR	—	30.00	60.00	100	200	—
1833Ca MR	—	30.00	60.00	125	500	—
1834Ca MR	—	35.00	75.00	125	500	—
1834Ca AM	—	35.00	75.00	125	500	—
1835Ca AM	—	35.00	75.00	125	500	—
1836Ca AM	—	20.00	40.00	80.00	200	—
1844Ca AM Rare	—	—	—	—	—	—
1844Ca RG Unique	—	—	—	—	—	—
1845Ca RG	—	20.00	40.00	80.00	200	—
1855Ca RG	—	20.00	40.00	80.00	200	—

KM# 374.3 2 REALES
6.7600 g., 0.9030 Silver 0.1962 oz. ASW **Obv:** Facing eagle, snake in beak **Edge:** Reeded **Mint:** Culiacan

Date	Mintage	F	VF	XF	Unc	BU
1846/1146C CE	—	25.00	50.00	100	225	—
1847C CE	—	12.50	20.00	40.00	200	—
1848C CE	—	12.50	20.00	40.00	200	—
1850C CE	—	25.00	50.00	75.00	200	—
1851C CE	—	12.50	20.00	40.00	200	—
1852/1C CE	—	12.50	20.00	40.00	200	—
1853/2C CE	—	12.50	20.00	40.00	200	—
1854C CE	—	15.00	30.00	50.00	200	—
1856C CE	—	20.00	35.00	70.00	200	—
1857C CE	—	12.50	20.00	40.00	200	—
1860C PV	—	12.50	20.00	40.00	200	—
1861C PV	—	12.50	20.00	40.00	200	—
1869C CE	—	12.50	20.00	40.00	200	—

KM# 374.4 2 REALES
6.7600 g., 0.9030 Silver 0.1962 oz. ASW **Obv:** Facing eagle, snake in beak **Edge:** Reeded **Mint:** Durango

Date	Mintage	F	VF	XF	Unc	BU
1826Do RL	—	20.00	40.00	60.00	200	—
1832Do RM	—	20.00	40.00	60.00	200	—
Note: Style of pre-1832						
1832Do RM	—	20.00	40.00	60.00	200	—
Note: Style of post-1832						
1834/2Do RM	—	20.00	40.00	60.00	200	—
1834/3Do RM	—	20.00	40.00	60.00	200	—
1835/4Do RM/RL	—	200	300	500	—	—
1841/31Do RM	—	50.00	75.00	125	250	—
1841Do RM	—	50.00	75.00	125	250	—
1842/32Do RM	—	12.50	20.00	40.00	200	—
1843Do RM/RL	—	12.50	20.00	40.00	200	—
1844Do RM	—	35.00	50.00	80.00	200	—
1845/34Do RM/RL	—	12.50	20.00	40.00	200	—
1846/36Do RM	—	100	150	200	350	—
1848/36Do RM	—	12.50	20.00	40.00	200	—
1848/37Do RM	—	12.50	20.00	40.00	200	—
1848/7Do RM	—	12.50	20.00	40.00	200	—
1848Do RM	—	12.50	20.00	40.00	200	—
1849Do CM/RM	—	12.50	20.00	40.00	200	—
1849Do CM	—	12.50	20.00	40.00	200	—
1851Do JMR/RL	—	12.50	20.00	40.00	200	—
1852Do JMR	—	12.50	20.00	40.00	200	—
1854Do CP/CR	—	30.00	50.00	80.00	200	—
1855Do CP	—	250	350	500	—	—
1856Do CP	—	100	150	250	500	—
1858Do CP	—	12.50	20.00	40.00	200	—
1859/8Do CP	—	12.50	20.00	40.00	200	—
1861Do CP	—	12.50	20.00	40.00	200	—

KM# 374.6 2 REALES
6.7600 g., 0.9030 Silver 0.1962 oz. ASW **Obv:** Facing eagle, snake in beak **Edge:** Reeded **Mint:** Guadalajara

Date	Mintage	F	VF	XF	Unc	BU
1825Ga FS	—	20.00	40.00	80.00	200	—
1826Ga FS	—	20.00	40.00	80.00	200	—
1828/7Ga FS	—	100	150	225	400	—
1829Ga FS Rare	—	—	—	—	—	—
1832/0Ga FS/LP	—	100	150	225	350	—
1832Ga FS	—	12.50	20.00	40.00	200	—
1833/2Ga FS/LP	—	12.50	20.00	40.00	200	—
1834/27Ga FS Rare	—	—	—	—	—	—
1834Ga FS	—	12.50	20.00	40.00	200	—
1835Ga FS	—	2,100	—	—	—	—
1837Ga JG	—	12.50	20.00	40.00	200	—
1838Ga JG	—	12.50	20.00	40.00	200	—
1840/30Ga MC	—	12.50	20.00	40.00	200	—
1841Ga MC	—	30.00	50.00	200	500	—
1842/32Ga JG/MC	—	35.00	50.00	100	200	—
1842Ga JG	—	20.00	40.00	80.00	200	—
1843Ga JG	—	12.50	20.00	40.00	200	—
1843Ga MC/JG	—	12.50	20.00	40.00	200	—
1844Ga MC	—	12.50	20.00	40.00	200	—
1845/3Ga MC/JG	—	12.50	20.00	40.00	200	—
1845/4Ga MC/JG	—	12.50	20.00	40.00	200	—
1845Ga JG	—	12.50	20.00	40.00	200	—

Date	Mintage	F	VF	XF	Unc	BU
1846Ga JG	—	12.50	20.00	40.00	200	—
1847/6Ga JG	—	25.00	40.00	80.00	200	—
1848/7Ga JG	—	12.50	20.00	40.00	200	—
1849Ga JG	—	12.50	20.00	40.00	200	—
1850/40Ga JG	—	12.50	20.00	40.00	200	—
1851Ga JG	—	250	350	500	—	—
1852Ga JG	—	12.50	20.00	40.00	200	—
1853/1Ga JG	—	12.50	20.00	40.00	200	—
1854/3Ga JG	—	250	350	500	—	—
1855Ga JG	—	35.00	50.00	80.00	200	—
1856Ga JG	—	12.50	20.00	40.00	200	—
1857Ga JG	—	250	350	500	—	—
1859/8Ga JG	—	12.50	20.00	40.00	200	—
1859Ga JG	—	12.50	20.00	40.00	200	—
1862/1Ga JG	—	12.50	20.00	40.00	200	—

KM# 374.7 2 REALES
6.7600 g., 0.9030 Silver 0.1962 oz. ASW **Obv:** Facing eagle, snake in beak **Edge:** Reeded **Mint:** Guadalupe y Calvo

Date	Mintage	F	VF	XF	Unc	BU
1844GC MP	—	40.00	60.00	125	275	—
1845GC MP	—	40.00	60.00	125	275	—
1846GC MP	—	50.00	100	150	300	—
1847GC MP	—	35.00	50.00	100	250	—
1848GC MP	—	50.00	100	150	300	—
1849GC MP	—	50.00	100	150	300	—
1850GC MP	—	125	250	—	—	—
1851/0GC MP	—	50.00	100	150	300	—
1851GC MP	—	50.00	100	150	300	—

KM# 374.9 2 REALES
6.7600 g., 0.9030 Silver 0.1962 oz. ASW **Obv:** Facing eagle, snake in beak **Edge:** Reeded **Mint:** Hermosillo

Date	Mintage	F	VF	XF	Unc	BU
1861Ho FM	—	200	300	400	650	—
1862/52Ho FM/C. CE	—	250	350	550	—	—
1867/1Ho PR/FM	—	75.00	150	250	500	—

KM# 374.11 2 REALES
6.7600 g., 0.9030 Silver 0.1962 oz. ASW **Obv:** Facing eagle, snake in beak **Edge:** Reeded **Mint:** San Luis Potosi

Date	Mintage	F	VF	XF	Unc	BU
1829Pi JS	—	10.00	15.00	30.00	200	—
1830/20Pi JS	—	20.00	30.00	60.00	200	—
1837Pi JS	—	10.00	15.00	30.00	200	—
1841Pi JS	—	10.00	15.00	30.00	200	—
1842/1Pi JS	—	10.00	15.00	30.00	200	—
1842Pi JS	—	10.00	15.00	30.00	200	—
1842Pi PS	—	20.00	35.00	60.00	200	—
1843Pi PS	—	12.50	20.00	40.00	200	—
1843Pi AM	—	10.00	15.00	30.00	200	—
1844Pi AM	—	10.00	15.00	30.00	200	—
1845Pi AM	—	10.00	15.00	30.00	200	—
1846Pi AM	—	10.00	15.00	30.00	200	—
1849Pi MC	—	10.00	15.00	30.00	200	—
1850Pi MC	—	10.00	15.00	30.00	200	—
1856Pi MC	—	40.00	60.00	125	250	—
1857Pi MC	—	—	—	—	—	—
1858Pi MC	—	12.50	20.00	40.00	200	—
1859Pi MC	—	50.00	70.00	100	200	—
1861Pi PS	—	10.00	15.00	30.00	200	—
1862Pi RO	—	12.50	20.00	40.00	200	—
1863Pi RO	—	100	250	350	500	—
1868Pi PS	—	10.00	15.00	30.00	200	—
1869/8Pi PS	—	10.00	15.00	30.00	200	—
1869Pi PS	—	10.00	15.00	30.00	200	—

KM# 374.8 2 REALES
6.7600 g., 0.9030 Silver 0.1962 oz. ASW **Obv:** Facing eagle, snake in beak **Edge:** Reeded **Mint:** Guanajuato **Note:** Varieties exist.

Date	Mintage	F	VF	XF	Unc	BU
1825Go JJ	—	7.50	15.00	30.00	150	—
1826/5Go JJ	—	7.50	15.00	30.00	150	—
1826Go JJ	—	7.50	10.00	25.00	150	—
1826Go MJ	—	7.50	10.00	25.00	150	—
1827/6Go MJ	—	7.50	10.00	25.00	150	—
1827Go MJ	—	7.50	10.00	25.00	150	—
1828/7Go MR	—	7.50	15.00	30.00	150	—
1828Go MJ	—	7.50	10.00	20.00	150	—
1828Go JM	—	7.50	10.00	20.00	150	—
1829Go MJ	—	7.50	10.00	20.00	150	—
1831Go MJ	—	7.50	10.00	20.00	150	—
1832Go MJ	—	7.50	10.00	20.00	150	—

Date	Mintage	F	VF	XF	Unc	BU
1833Go MJ	—	7.50	10.00	20.00	150	—
1834Go PJ	—	7.50	10.00	20.00	150	—
1835/4Go PJ	—	7.50	15.00	30.00	150	—
1835Go PJ	—	7.50	10.00	20.00	150	—
1836Go PJ	—	7.50	10.00	20.00	150	—
1837/6Go PJ	—	7.50	10.00	20.00	150	—
1837Go PJ	—	7.50	10.00	20.00	150	—
1838/7Go PJ	—	7.50	10.00	20.00	150	—
1838Go PJ	—	7.50	10.00	20.00	150	—
1839/8Go PJ	—	7.50	15.00	30.00	150	—
1839Go PJ	—	7.50	10.00	20.00	150	—
1840Go PJ	—	7.50	10.00	20.00	150	—
1841Go PJ	—	7.50	10.00	20.00	150	—
1842Go PJ	—	7.50	10.00	20.00	150	—
1842Go PM/PJ	—	7.50	10.00	20.00	150	—
1842Go PM	—	7.50	10.00	20.00	150	—
1843/2Go PM	—	7.50	10.00	20.00	150	—

Note: Concave wings, thin rays, small letters

Date	Mintage	F	VF	XF	Unc	BU
1843Go PM	—	7.50	10.00	20.00	150	—

Note: Convex wings, thick rays, large letters

Date	Mintage	F	VF	XF	Unc	BU
1844Go PM	—	7.50	10.00	20.00	150	—
1845/4Go PM	—	7.50	10.00	20.00	150	—
1845Go PM	—	7.50	10.00	20.00	150	—
1846/5Go PM	—	10.00	15.00	35.00	150	—
1846Go PM	—	7.50	10.00	20.00	150	—
1847Go PM	—	7.50	10.00	20.00	150	—
1848/7Go PM	—	7.50	15.00	30.00	150	—
1848Go PM	—	7.50	15.00	30.00	150	—
1848Go PF	—	100	150	250	500	—
1849/8Go PF/PM	—	7.50	10.00	20.00	150	—
1849Go PF	—	7.50	10.00	20.00	150	—
1850/40Go PF	—	7.50	10.00	20.00	150	—
1850Go PF	—	7.50	10.00	20.00	150	—
1851Go PF	—	7.50	10.00	20.00	150	—
1852/1Go PF	—	7.50	10.00	20.00	150	—
1852Go PF	—	7.50	10.00	20.00	150	—
1853Go PF	—	7.50	10.00	20.00	150	—
1854/3Go PF	—	7.50	10.00	20.00	150	—
1854Go PF	—	7.50	10.00	20.00	150	—

Note: Old font and obverse

1854Go PF	—	7.50	10.00	20.00	150	—

Note: New font and obverse

1855Go PF	—	7.50	10.00	20.00	150	—
1855Go PF	—	7.50	10.00	20.00	150	—

Note: Star in G of mint mark

1856/5Go PF	—	10.00	15.00	35.00	150	—
1856Go PF	—	10.00	15.00	25.00	150	—
1857/6Go PF	—	7.50	10.00	20.00	150	—
1857Go PF	—	7.50	10.00	20.00	150	—
1858/7Go PF	—	7.50	10.00	20.00	150	—
1858Go PF	—	7.50	10.00	20.00	150	—
1859/7Go PF	—	7.50	10.00	20.00	150	—
1859Go PF	—	7.50	10.00	20.00	150	—
1860/7Go PF	—	7.50	10.00	20.00	150	—
1860/50Go PF	—	7.50	10.00	20.00	150	—
1860/59Go PF	—	7.50	10.00	20.00	150	—
1860Go PF	—	7.50	10.00	20.00	150	—
1861/51Go PF	—	7.50	10.00	20.00	150	—
1861/57Go PF	—	7.50	10.00	20.00	150	—
1861/0Go PF	—	7.50	10.00	20.00	150	—
1861Go PF	—	7.50	10.00	20.00	150	—
1862/1Go YE	—	7.50	10.00	20.00	125	—
1862Go YE	—	7.50	10.00	20.00	125	—
1862/57Go YE	—	7.50	10.00	20.00	125	—
1862Go YE/PF	—	7.50	10.00	20.00	125	—
1862/57Go YF/E	—	7.50	10.00	20.00	125	—
1862/57Go YF	—	7.50	10.00	20.00	125	—
1862Go YF	—	7.50	10.00	20.00	125	—
1863/52Go YF/PE	—	7.50	10.00	20.00	125	—
1863/52Go YF	—	7.50	10.00	20.00	125	—
1863Go YF	—	7.50	10.00	20.00	125	—
1867/57Go YF	—	7.50	10.00	20.00	125	—
1868/57Go YF	—	10.00	15.00	25.00	125	—

KM# 374.10 2 REALES
6.7600 g., 0.9030 Silver 0.1962 oz. ASW **Obv:** Facing eagle, snake in beak **Obv. Legend:** REPUBLICA MEXICANA. **Rev:** Radiant cap **Edge:** Reeded **Mint:** Mexico City **Note:** Varieties exist.

Date	Mintage	F	VF	XF	Unc	BU
1825Mo JM	—	10.00	15.00	30.00	175	—
1826Mo JM	—	10.00	15.00	30.00	175	—
1827Mo JM	—	10.00	15.00	30.00	175	—
1828Mo JM	—	10.00	15.00	30.00	175	—
1829/8Mo JM	—	10.00	15.00	30.00	175	—
1829Mo JM	—	10.00	15.00	30.00	175	—
1830Mo JM	—	40.00	60.00	125	250	—
1831Mo JM	—	10.00	15.00	30.00	175	—
1832Mo JM	—	100	200	400	—	—
1833/2Mo MJ/JM	—	10.00	15.00	30.00	175	—
1834Mo ML	—	50.00	100	200	400	—
1836Mo MF	—	10.00	15.00	30.00	175	—
1837Mo ML	—	10.00	15.00	30.00	175	—
1840/7Mo ML	—	150	225	350	—	—
1840Mo ML	—	150	225	350	—	—
1841Mo ML	—	15.00	40.00	100	250	—
1842 ML Rare	—	—	—	—	—	—
1847Mo RC Narrow date	—	10.00	15.00	30.00	175	—
1847Mo RC Wide date	—	10.00	15.00	30.00	175	—
1848Mo GC	—	10.00	15.00	30.00	175	—
1849Mo GC	—	10.00	15.00	30.00	175	—
1850Mo GC	—	10.00	15.00	30.00	175	—
1851Mo GC	—	40.00	60.00	125	250	—
1852Mo GC	—	10.00	15.00	30.00	175	—
1853Mo GC	—	10.00	15.00	30.00	175	—
1854/44Mo GC	—	10.00	15.00	30.00	175	—
1855Mo GC	—	10.00	15.00	30.00	175	—
1855Mo GF/GC	—	10.00	15.00	30.00	175	—
1855Mo GF	—	10.00	15.00	30.00	175	—
1856/5Mo GF/GC	—	10.00	15.00	30.00	175	—
1857Mo GF	—	10.00	15.00	30.00	175	—
1858Mo FH	—	7.50	12.50	25.00	150	—
1858Mo FH/GF	—	7.50	12.50	25.00	150	—
1859Mo FH	—	7.50	12.50	25.00	150	—
1860Mo FH	—	7.50	12.50	25.00	150	—
1860Mo TH	—	7.50	12.50	25.00	150	—
1861Mo CH	—	7.50	12.50	25.00	150	—
1862Mo CH	—	7.50	12.50	25.00	150	—
1863Mo CH	—	7.50	12.50	25.00	150	—
1863Mo TH	—	7.50	12.50	25.00	150	—
1867Mo CH	—	7.50	12.50	25.00	150	—
1868Mo CH	—	10.00	15.00	30.00	150	—
1868Mo PH	—	7.50	12.50	25.00	150	—

KM# 374.12 2 REALES
6.7600 g., 0.9030 Silver 0.1962 oz. ASW **Obv:** Facing eagle, snake in beak **Edge:** Reeded **Mint:** Zacatecas **Note:** Varieties exist.

Date	Mintage	F	VF	XF	Unc	BU
1825Zs AZ	—	10.00	15.00	30.00	150	—
1826Zs AV	—	7.50	10.00	25.00	150	—
Note: A is inverted V						
1826Zs AZ	—	7.50	10.00	25.00	150	—
Note: A is inverted V						
1826Zs AO	—	10.00	15.00	30.00	150	—
1827Zs AO	—	6.00	8.00	12.00	150	—
Note: A is inverted V						
1827Zs AO	—	6.00	8.00	12.00	150	—
1828/7Zs AO	—	15.00	30.00	60.00	175	—
1828Zs AO	—	7.50	10.00	25.00	100	—
1828Zs AO	—	7.50	10.00	25.00	150	—
Note: A is inverted V						
1829Zs AO	—	7.50	10.00	25.00	150	—

Date	Mintage	F	VF	XF	Unc	BU
1829Zs OV	—	7.50	10.00	25.00	150	—
1830Zs OV	—	7.50	10.00	25.00	150	—
1831Zs OV	—	7.50	10.00	25.00	150	—
1831Zs OM/OV	—	7.50	10.00	25.00	150	—
1831Zs OM	—	7.50	10.00	25.00	150	—
1832/1Zs OM	—	15.00	30.00	60.00	150	—
1832Zs OM	—	7.50	10.00	25.00	150	—
1833/27Zs OM	—	7.50	10.00	25.00	150	—
1833/2Zs OM	—	7.50	10.00	25.00	150	—
1833Zs OM	—	7.50	10.00	25.00	150	—
1834Zs OM	—	40.00	60.00	125	200	—
1835Zs OM	—	7.50	10.00	25.00	150	—
1836Zs OM	—	7.50	10.00	25.00	150	—
1837Zs OM	—	7.50	10.00	25.00	150	—
1838Zs OM	—	15.00	30.00	60.00	150	—
1839Zs OM	—	7.50	10.00	20.00	150	—
1840Zs OM	—	7.50	10.00	20.00	150	—
1841/0Zs OM	—	7.50	10.00	20.00	150	—
1841Zs OM	—	7.50	10.00	20.00	150	—
1842Zs OM Narrow date	—	7.50	10.00	20.00	150	—
1842Zs OM Wide date	—	7.50	10.00	20.00	150	—
1843Zs OM	—	7.50	10.00	20.00	150	—
1844Zs OM	—	7.50	10.00	20.00	150	—
1845Zs OM	—	7.50	10.00	20.00	150	—
Note: Small letters with leaves						
1845Zs OM	—	7.50	10.00	20.00	150	—
Note: Large letters with leaves						
1846Zs OM	—	7.50	10.00	20.00	150	—
1847Zs OM	—	7.50	10.00	20.00	150	—
1848Zs OM	—	7.50	10.00	20.00	150	—
1849Zs OM	—	7.50	10.00	20.00	150	—
1850Zs OM	—	7.50	10.00	20.00	150	—
1851Zs OM	—	7.50	10.00	20.00	150	—
1852Zs OM	—	7.50	10.00	20.00	150	—
1853Zs OM	—	7.50	10.00	20.00	150	—
1854/3Zs OM	—	7.50	10.00	20.00	150	—
1854Zs OM	—	7.50	10.00	20.00	150	—
1855/4Zs OM	—	7.50	10.00	20.00	150	—
1855Zs OM	—	7.50	10.00	20.00	150	—
1855Zs MO	—	7.50	10.00	20.00	150	—
1856/5Zs MO	—	7.50	10.00	20.00	150	—
1856Zs MO	—	7.50	10.00	20.00	150	—
1857Zs MO	—	7.50	10.00	20.00	150	—
1858Zs MO	—	7.50	10.00	20.00	150	—
1859Zs MO	—	7.50	10.00	20.00	150	—
1860/59Zs MO	—	7.50	10.00	20.00	150	—
1860Zs MO	—	7.50	10.00	20.00	100	—
1860Zs VL	—	7.50	10.00	20.00	150	—
1861Zs VL	—	7.50	10.00	20.00	150	—
1862Zs VL	—	7.50	10.00	20.00	100	—
1863Zs MO	—	12.50	20.00	40.00	150	—
1863Zs VL	—	7.50	10.00	20.00	150	—
1864Zs MO	—	7.50	10.00	20.00	150	—
1864Zs VL	—	7.50	10.00	20.00	150	—
1865Zs MO	—	7.50	10.00	20.00	150	—
1867Zs JS	—	7.50	10.00	20.00	150	—
1868Zs JS	—	10.00	15.00	35.00	150	—
1868Zs YH	—	7.50	10.00	20.00	150	—
1869Zs YH	—	7.50	10.00	20.00	150	—
1870Zs YH	—	7.50	10.00	20.00	150	—

KM# 374 2 REALES
6.7600 g., 0.9030 Silver 0.1962 oz. ASW **Obv:** Facing eagle, snake in beak **Edge:** Reeded **Mint:** Alamos

Date	Mintage	F	VF	XF	Unc	BU
1872A AM	15,000	60.00	125	250	600	—

KM# 374.1 2 REALES
6.7600 g., 0.9030 Silver 0.1962 oz. ASW **Obv:** Facing eagle, snake in beak **Edge:** Reeded **Mint:** Real de Catorce

Date	Mintage	F	VF	XF	Unc	BU
1863Ce ML	—	125	200	325	700	—

KM# 374.5 2 REALES
6.7600 g., 0.9030 Silver 0.1962 oz. ASW **Obv:** Facing eagle, snake in beak **Edge:** Reeded **Mint:** Estado de Mexico

Date	Mintage	F	VF	XF	Unc	BU
1828EoMo LF	—	325	525	900	2,500	—

KM# 375.1 4 REALES
13.5400 g., 0.9030 Silver 0.3931 oz. ASW **Obv:** Facing eagle, snake in beak **Mint:** Culiacan

Date	Mintage	F	VF	XF	Unc	BU
1846C CE	—	400	550	950	—	—
1850C CE	—	75.00	125	250	—	—
1852C CE	—	200	300	500	—	—
1857C CE Rare	—	—	—	—	—	—
1858C CE	—	100	200	350	—	—
1860C PV	—	25.00	50.00	125	—	—

KM# 375.2 4 REALES
13.5400 g., 0.9030 Silver 0.3931 oz. ASW **Obv:** Facing eagle, snake in beak **Mint:** Guadalajara

Date	Mintage	F	VF	XF	Unc	BU
1843Ga MC	—	20.00	40.00	80.00	—	—
1844/3Ga MC	—	30.00	60.00	125	—	—
1844Ga MC	—	20.00	40.00	80.00	—	—
1845Ga MC	—	20.00	40.00	80.00	—	—
1845Ga JG	—	20.00	40.00	80.00	—	—
1846Ga JG	—	20.00	40.00	80.00	—	—
1847Ga JG	—	40.00	80.00	150	—	—
1848/7Ga JG	—	40.00	80.00	150	—	—
1849Ga JG	—	40.00	80.00	150	—	—
1850Ga JG	—	65.00	125	250	—	—
1852Ga JG Rare	—	—	—	—	—	—
1854Ga JG Rare	—	—	—	—	—	—
1855Ga JG	—	100	200	400	—	—
1856Ga JG Rare	—	—	—	—	—	—
1857/6Ga JG	—	65.00	125	250	—	—
1858Ga JG	—	125	250	450	—	—
1859/8Ga JG	—	125	250	450	—	—
1860Ga JG	—	850	1,450	—	—	—
1863/2Ga JG	—	150	300	1,250	—	—
1863Ga JG	—	150	300	1,250	—	—

KM# 375.3 4 REALES
13.5400 g., 0.9030 Silver 0.3931 oz. ASW **Obv:** Facing eagle, snake in beak **Mint:** Guadalupe y Calvo

Date	Mintage	F	VF	XF	Unc	BU
1844GC MP	—	3,000	5,000	—	—	—
1845GC MP	—	6,500	8,000	—	—	—

Date	Mintage	F	VF	XF	Unc	BU
1846GC MP	—	1,700	2,800	—	—	—
1847GC MP	—	1,500	2,500	—	—	—
1849GC MP	—	3,000	4,000	—	—	—
1850GC MP	—	1,500	2,500	—	—	—

KM# 375.5 4 REALES
13.5400 g., 0.9030 Silver 0.3931 oz. ASW **Obv:** Facing eagle, snake in beak **Mint:** Hermosillo

Date	Mintage	F	VF	XF	Unc	BU
1861Ho FM	—	200	350	500	—	—
1867/1Ho PR/FM	—	150	275	400	—	—

KM# 375.6 4 REALES
13.5400 g., 0.9030 Silver 0.3931 oz. ASW **Obv:** Facing eagle, snake in beak **Mint:** Mexico City

Date	Mintage	F	VF	XF	Unc	BU
1827/6Mo JM	—	200	400	800	—	—
1850Mo GC Rare	—	—	—	—	—	—
1852Mo GC Rare	—	—	—	—	—	—
1854Mo GC Rare	—	—	—	—	—	—
1855Mo GF/GC	—	50.00	100	200	—	—
1855Mo GF	—	100	200	350	—	—
1856Mo GF/GC	—	50.00	125	400	—	—
1856Mo GF Rare	—	—	—	—	—	—
1859Mo FH	—	20.00	50.00	150	—	—
1861Mo CH	—	15.00	35.00	125	—	—
1862Mo CH	—	20.00	50.00	150	—	—
1863/2Mo CH	—	20.00	50.00	150	—	—
1863Mo CH	—	75.00	150	300	—	—
1867Mo CH	—	20.00	50.00	150	—	—
1868Mo CH/PH	—	30.00	75.00	150	—	—
1868Mo CH	—	20.00	50.00	150	—	—
1868Mo PH	—	30.00	75.00	200	—	—

KM# 375.8 4 REALES
13.5400 g., 0.9030 Silver 0.3931 oz. ASW **Obv:** Facing eagle, snake in beak **Mint:** San Luis Potosi

Date	Mintage	F	VF	XF	Unc	BU
1837Pi JS	—	200	350	—	—	—
1838Pi JS	—	150	250	400	—	—
1842Pi PS	—	50.00	100	200	—	—
1843/2Pi PS	—	50.00	100	200	—	—
1843/2Pi PS	—	50.00	100	200	—	—
Note: 3 cut from 8 punch						
1843Pi AM	—	30.00	75.00	150	—	—
1843Pi PS	—	50.00	100	200	—	—
1844Pi AM	—	30.00	75.00	150	—	—
1845/4Pi AM	—	20.00	50.00	100	—	—
1845Pi AM	—	20.00	50.00	100	—	—
1846Pi AM	—	20.00	50.00	100	—	—
1847Pi AM	—	75.00	150	250	—	—
1848Pi AM Rare	—	—	—	—	—	—
1849Pi MC/AM	—	20.00	50.00	100	—	—
1849Pi MC	—	20.00	50.00	100	—	—
1849Pi PS	—	20.00	50.00	100	—	—
1850Pi MC	—	20.00	50.00	100	—	—
1851Pi MC	—	20.00	50.00	100	—	—
1852Pi MC	—	20.00	50.00	100	—	—
1853Pi MC	—	20.00	50.00	100	—	—
1854Pi MC	—	100	200	400	—	—
1855Pi MC	—	175	300	750	—	—
1856Pi MC	—	250	400	700	—	—
1857Pi MC Rare	—	—	—	—	—	—
1857Pi PS Rare	—	—	—	—	—	—

Date	Mintage	F	VF	XF	Unc	BU
1858Pi MC	—	100	200	400	—	—
1859Pi MC	—	2,000	3,000	—	—	—
1860Pi PS	—	300	450	700	—	—
1861Pi PS	—	150	300	600	—	—
1861/0Pi PS	—	300	600	—	—	—
1861Pi RO/PS	—	30.00	75.00	150	—	—
1861Pi RO	—	50.00	100	200	—	—
1862Pi RO	—	30.00	75.00	150	—	—
1863Pi RO	—	30.00	75.00	150	—	—
1864Pi RO	—	2,500	3,500	—	—	—
1868Pi PS	—	30.00	75.00	150	—	—
1869/8Pi PS	—	30.00	75.00	150	—	—
1869Pi PS	—	30.00	75.00	150	—	—

KM# 375.9 4 REALES
13.5400 g., 0.9030 Silver 0.3931 oz. ASW **Obv:** Facing eagle, snake in beak **Mint:** Zacatecas

Date	Mintage	F	VF	XF	Unc	BU
1830Zs OM	—	20.00	50.00	100	—	—
1831Zs OM	—	15.00	30.00	75.00	—	—
1832/1Zs OM	—	20.00	50.00	100	—	—
1832Zs OM	—	20.00	50.00	100	—	—
1833/2Zs OM	—	20.00	50.00	100	—	—
1833/27Zs OM	—	15.00	30.00	75.00	—	—
1833Zs OM	—	15.00	30.00	75.00	—	—
1834/3Zs OM	—	20.00	50.00	100	—	—
1834Zs OM	—	15.00	30.00	75.00	—	—
1835Zs OM	—	15.00	30.00	75.00	—	—
1836Zs OM	—	15.00	30.00	75.00	—	—
1837/5Zs OM	—	20.00	50.00	100	—	—
1837/6Zs OM	—	20.00	50.00	100	—	—
1837Zs OM	—	20.00	50.00	100	—	—
1838/7Zs OM	—	15.00	30.00	75.00	—	—
1839Zs OM	—	250	375	500	—	—
1840Zs OM	—	500	1,300	—	—	—
1841Zs OM	—	15.00	30.00	75.00	—	—
1842Zs OM Small letters	—	15.00	40.00	85.00	—	—
1842Zs OM Large letters	—	15.00	30.00	75.00	—	—
1843Zs OM	—	15.00	30.00	75.00	—	—
1844Zs OM	—	20.00	50.00	100	—	—
1845Zs OM	—	20.00	50.00	100	—	—
1846/5Zs OM	—	25.00	60.00	125	—	—
1846Zs OM	—	20.00	50.00	100	—	—
1847Zs OM	—	15.00	30.00	75.00	—	—
1848/6Zs OM	—	50.00	75.00	125	—	—
1848Zs OM	—	20.00	50.00	100	—	—
1849Zs OM	—	20.00	50.00	100	—	—
1850Zs OM	—	20.00	50.00	100	—	—
1851Zs OM	—	15.00	30.00	75.00	—	—
1852Zs OM	—	15.00	30.00	75.00	—	—
1853Zs OM	—	20.00	50.00	100	—	—
1854/3Zs OM	—	30.00	75.00	150	—	—
1855/4Zs OM	—	20.00	50.00	100	—	—
1855Zs OM	—	15.00	30.00	75.00	—	—
1856Zs OM	—	15.00	30.00	75.00	—	—
1856Zs MO	—	20.00	50.00	100	—	—
1857/5Zs MO	—	20.00	50.00	100	—	—
1857Zs O/M	—	20.00	50.00	100	—	—
1857Zs MO	—	15.00	30.00	75.00	—	—
1858Zs MO	—	20.00	50.00	100	—	—
1859Zs MO	—	15.00	30.00	75.00	—	—
1860/59Zs MO	—	20.00	50.00	100	—	—
1860Zs MO	—	15.00	30.00	75.00	—	—
1860Zs VL	—	20.00	50.00	100	—	—
1861/0Zs VL	—	20.00	50.00	100	—	—
1861Zs VL	—	15.00	30.00	75.00	—	—
1861Zs VL 6/5	—	20.00	50.00	100	—	—
1862/1Zs VL	—	20.00	50.00	100	—	—
1862Zs VL	—	20.00	50.00	100	—	—
1863Zs VL	—	20.00	50.00	100	—	—
1863Zs MO	—	20.00	50.00	100	—	—
1864Zs VL	—	15.00	30.00	75.00	—	—
1868Zs JS	—	20.00	50.00	100	—	—
1868Zs YH	—	15.00	30.00	75.00	—	—
1869Zs YH	—	15.00	30.00	75.00	—	—
1870Zs YH	—	15.00	30.00	75.00	—	—

KM# 375.4 4 REALES
13.5400 g., 0.9030 Silver 0.3931 oz. ASW **Obv:** Facing eagle, snake in beak **Obv. Legend:** REPUBLICA MEXICANA **Rev:** Radiant cap **Mint:** Guanajuato **Note:** Varieties exist. Some 1862 dates appear to be 1869 because of weak dies.

Date	Mintage	F	VF	XF	Unc	BU
1835Go PJ	—	12.50	25.00	60.00	—	—
1836/5Go PJ	—	15.00	30.00	75.00	—	—
1836Go PJ	—	15.00	30.00	75.00	—	—
1837Go PJ	—	12.50	25.00	60.00	—	—
1838/7Go PJ	—	15.00	30.00	75.00	—	—
1838Go PJ	—	12.50	30.00	75.00	—	—
1839Go PJ	—	12.50	25.00	60.00	—	—
1840/30Go PJ	—	20.00	50.00	100	—	—
1840 PJ	—	20.00	50.00	100	—	—
1841/30 PJ	—	200	325	600	—	—
1841/31Go PJ	—	150	250	450	—	—
1842Go PJ Rare	—	—	—	—	—	—
1842Go PM	—	15.00	30.00	75.00	—	—
1843/2Go PM	—	12.50	25.00	60.00	—	—

Note: Eagle with convex wings, thick rays

Date	Mintage	F	VF	XF	Unc	BU
1843Go PM	—	12.50	25.00	60.00	—	—

Note: Eagle with concave wings, thin rays

Date	Mintage	F	VF	XF	Unc	BU
1844/3Go PM	—	15.00	30.00	75.00	—	—
1844Go PM	—	20.00	50.00	100	—	—
1845/4Go PM	—	20.00	50.00	100	—	—
1845Go PM	—	20.00	50.00	100	—	—
1846/5Go PM	—	15.00	30.00	75.00	—	—
1846Go PM	—	15.00	30.00	75.00	—	—
1847/6Go PM	—	15.00	30.00	75.00	—	—
1847Go PM	—	15.00	30.00	75.00	—	—
1848/7Go PM	—	20.00	50.00	100	—	—
1848Go PM	—	20.00	50.00	100	—	—
1849Go PF	—	20.00	50.00	100	—	—
1850Go PF	—	12.50	25.00	60.00	—	—
1851Go PF	—	12.50	25.00	60.00	—	—
1852Go PF	—	15.00	30.00	75.00	—	—
1852Go PF 5/4	—	20.00	50.00	100	—	—
1853Go PF	—	15.00	30.00	75.00	—	—
1854Go PF	—	15.00	30.00	75.00	—	—

Note: Large eagle

Date	Mintage	F	VF	XF	Unc	BU
1854Go PF	—	15.00	30.00	75.00	—	—

Note: Small eagle

Date	Mintage	F	VF	XF	Unc	BU
1855/4Go PF	—	15.00	30.00	75.00	—	—
1855Go PF	—	12.50	25.00	60.00	—	—
1856Go PF	—	12.50	25.00	60.00	—	—
1857Go PF	—	20.00	50.00	100	—	—
1858Go PF	—	20.00	50.00	100	—	—
1859Go PF	—	20.00	50.00	100	—	—
1860/59Go PF	—	15.00	30.00	75.00	—	—
1860Go PF	—	15.00	30.00	75.00	—	—
1861/51Go PF	—	15.00	30.00	75.00	—	—
1861Go PF	—	20.00	50.00	100	—	—
1862/1Go YE	—	15.00	30.00	75.00	—	—
1862/1Go YF	—	15.00	30.00	75.00	—	—
1862Go YE/PF	—	15.00	30.00	75.00	—	—
1862Go YE	—	15.00	30.00	75.00	—	—
1862Go YF	—	15.00	30.00	75.00	—	—
1863/53Go YF	—	15.00	30.00	75.00	—	—
1863Go YF/PF	—	15.00	30.00	75.00	—	—
186/53Go YF	—	15.00	30.00	75.00	—	—
1863Go YF	—	15.00	30.00	75.00	—	—
1867/57Go YF/PF	—	15.00	30.00	75.00	—	—
1868/58Go YF/PF	—	15.00	30.00	75.00	—	—
1870Go FR	—	15.00	30.00	75.00	—	—

FIRST REPUBLIC · FEDERAL

KM# 375   4 REALES
13.5400 g., 0.9030 Silver 0.3931 oz. ASW **Obv:** Facing eagle, snake in beak **Obv. Legend:** REPUBLICA MEXICANA. **Rev:** Radiant cap **Mint:** Real de Catorce

Date	Mintage	F	VF	XF	Unc	BU
1863Ce ML Large C	—	200	500	850	—	—
1863Ce ML Small C	—	225	650	1,500	—	—

KM# 375.7   4 REALES
13.5400 g., 0.9030 Silver 0.3931 oz. ASW **Obv:** Facing eagle, snake in beak **Obv. Legend:** REPUBLICA MEXICANA. **Rev:** Radiant cap **Mint:** Oaxaca

Date	Mintage	F	VF	XF	Unc	BU
1861O FR	—	225	450	750	—	—
Note: Ornamental edge						
1861O FR	—	300	550	850	—	—
Note: Herringbone edge						
1861O FR	—	200	400	700	—	—
Note: Obliquely reeded edge						

KM# 377.5   8 REALES
27.0700 g., 0.9030 Silver 0.7859 oz. ASW **Obv:** Facing eagle, snake in beak **Rev:** Radiant cap **Mint:** Estado de Mexico

Date	Mintage	F	VF	XF	Unc	BU
1828EoMo LF/LP	—	350	850	2,150	—	—
1828EoMo LF	—	350	850	2,150	6,000	—
1829EoMo LF	—	300	750	1,850	4,800	—
1830/20EoMo LF	—	1,250	2,750	4,250	—	—
1830EoMo LF	—	1,000	2,000	3,250	6,500	—

KM# 377.7   8 REALES
27.0700 g., 0.9030 Silver 0.7859 oz. ASW **Obv:** Facing eagle, snake in beak **Obv. Legend:** REPUBLICA MEXICANA. **Rev:** Radiant cap **Mint:** Guadalupe y Calvo

Date	Mintage	F	VF	XF	Unc	BU
1844GC MP	—	350	500	1,000	2,000	—
1844GC MP	—	400	600	1,200	2,250	—
Note: Error, reversed S in Ds, Gs						
1845GC MP	—	125	200	325	700	—
Note: Eagle's tail square						
1845GC MP	—	175	350	650	1,200	—
Note: Eagle's tail round						
1846GC MP	—	175	350	750	1,650	—
Note: Eagle's tail square						
1846GC MP	—	125	200	350	750	—
Note: Eagle's tail round						
1847GC MP	—	150	250	400	800	—
1848GC MP	—	175	300	500	900	—
1849GC MP	—	175	300	525	1,000	—
1850GC MP	—	175	300	575	1,100	—
1851GC MP	—	300	500	900	1,600	—
1852GC MP	—	350	600	1,250	2,500	—

KM# 377   8 REALES
27.0700 g., 0.9030 Silver 0.7859 oz. ASW **Obv:** Facing eagle, snake in beak **Obv. Legend:** REPUBLICA MEXICANA. **Rev:** Radiant cap **Mint:** Alamos **Note:** Mint mark A, As. Varieties exist.

Date	Mintage	F	VF	XF	Unc	BU
1864 PG	—	750	1,250	2,000	—	—
1865/4 PG Rare	—	—	—	—	—	—
1865 PG	—	500	750	1,000	—	—
1866/5 PG Rare	—	—	—	—	—	—
1866 PG	—	1,250	2,250	—	—	—
1866 DL Rare	—	—	—	—	—	—
1867 DL	—	1,150	2,150	—	—	—
1868 DL	—	50.00	90.00	150	300	—
1869/8 DL	—	50.00	90.00	150	—	—
1869 DL	—	50.00	80.00	120	300	—
1870 DL	—	30.00	50.00	120	300	—
1871 DL	—	20.00	35.00	75.00	200	—
1872 AM/DL	—	25.00	50.00	100	300	—
1872 AM	—	25.00	50.00	100	250	—
1873 AM	509,000	18.00	25.00	50.00	150	—
1874/3As DL	—	25.00	50.00	100	250	—
1874 DL	—	18.00	25.00	50.00	150	—
1875A DL 7/7	—	40.00	80.00	120	300	—
1875A DL	—	18.00	25.00	50.00	150	—
1875As DL	—	30.00	60.00	110	250	—
1876 DL	—	18.00	25.00	50.00	150	—
1877 DL	515,000	18.00	25.00	50.00	150	—
1878 DL	513,000	18.00	25.00	50.00	150	—
1879 DL	—	20.00	35.00	75.00	175	—
1879 ML	—	30.00	60.00	125	350	—
1880 ML	—	16.00	18.00	30.00	140	—
1881 ML	966,000	16.00	18.00	30.00	140	—
1882 ML	480,000	16.00	18.00	30.00	140	—
1883 ML	464,000	16.00	18.00	30.00	140	—
1884 ML	—	16.00	18.00	30.00	140	—
1885 ML	280,000	16.00	18.00	30.00	140	—
1886 ML	857,000	16.00	18.00	25.00	115	—
1886/0As/Cn ML/JD	Inc. above	17.00	20.00	35.00	160	—
1887 ML	650,000	16.00	18.00	25.00	115	—
1888/7 ML	508,000	30.00	60.00	100	400	—
1888 ML	Inc. above	16.00	18.00	25.00	115	—
1889 ML	427,000	16.00	18.00	25.00	115	—
1890 ML	450,000	16.00	18.00	25.00	115	—
1891 ML	533,000	16.00	18.00	25.00	115	—
1892/0 ML	—	20.00	30.00	60.00	160	—
1892 ML	465,000	16.00	18.00	25.00	115	—
1893 ML	734,000	14.00	16.00	22.00	95.00	—
1894 ML	725,000	14.00	16.00	22.00	95.00	—
1895 ML	477,000	14.00	16.00	22.00	95.00	—

KM# 377.3   8 REALES
27.0700 g., 0.9030 Silver 0.7859 oz. ASW   **Obv:** Facing eagle, snake in beak **Obv. Legend:** REPUBLICA MEXICANA **Rev:** Radiant cap **Mint:** Culiacan **Note:** Mint mark C, Cn. Varieties exist.

Date	Mintage	F	VF	XF	Unc	BU
1846 CE	—	150	300	800	1,500	—
1846 CE	—	175	385	900	1,650	—

Date	Mintage	F	VF	XF	Unc	BU
Note: Dot after G						
1846 CE	—	125	265	750	1,450	—
Note: No dot after G						
1847 CE	—	400	700	1,500	—	—
1848 CE	—	125	250	450	1,000	—
1849 CE C/G	—	75.00	125	200	400	—
1849 CE	—	75.00	125	200	400	—
1850 CE	—	75.00	125	200	400	—
1851 CE	—	125	250	450	1,000	—
1852/1 CE	—	100	150	250	500	—
1852 CE	—	100	200	300	600	—
1853/0 CE	—	200	350	700	1,300	—
1853/2/0	—	200	400	750	1,400	—
1853 CE	—	100	175	300	600	—
Note: Thick rays						
1853 CE	—	200	350	650	—	—
Note: Error: MEXIGANA						
1854 CE	—	750	1,250	—	—	—
1854 CE	—	175	350	750	1,200	—
Note: Large eagle and hat						
1855/6 CE	—	40.00	60.00	100	200	—
1855 CE	—	25.00	40.00	75.00	150	—
1856 CE	—	50.00	100	175	350	—
1857 CE	—	20.00	35.00	75.00	160	—
1858 CE	—	30.00	40.00	75.00	160	—
1859 CE	—	20.00	35.00	75.00	160	—
1860/9 PV/CV	—	50.00	70.00	100	200	—
1860/9 PV/E	—	50.00	70.00	100	200	—
1860 CE	—	25.00	40.00	75.00	160	—
1860/9 PV	—	40.00	60.00	90.00	175	—
1860 PV	—	40.00	60.00	90.00	175	—
1861/0 CE	—	50.00	80.00	120	250	—
1861 PV/CE	—	75.00	125	200	350	—
1861 CE	—	20.00	35.00	60.00	150	—
1862 CE	—	20.00	35.00	60.00	150	—
1863/2 CE	—	30.00	50.00	75.00	200	—
1863 CE	—	20.00	30.00	60.00	150	—
1864 CE	—	30.00	60.00	100	300	—
1865 CE	—	125	200	325	650	—
1866 CE	—	400	750	1,250	2,250	—
1867 CE	—	125	200	350	700	—
1868/7 CE	—	30.00	40.00	75.00	160	—
1868/8	—	50.00	100	150	300	—
1868 CE	—	30.00	40.00	75.00	160	—
1869 CE	—	30.00	40.00	75.00	175	—
1870 CE	—	50.00	100	150	350	—
1873 MP	—	50.00	100	150	300	—
1874/3 MP	—	30.00	40.00	75.00	160	—
1874C MP	—	20.00	30.00	45.00	125	—
1874CN MP	—	125	200	300	600	—
1875 MP	—	16.00	18.00	22.00	95.00	—
1876 GP	—	16.00	18.00	30.00	100	—
1876 CG	—	16.00	18.00	22.00	95.00	—
1877 CG	339,000	16.00	18.00	22.00	95.00	—
1877Gn CG Error	—	65.00	125	200	400	—
1877 JA	Inc. above	35.00	75.00	125	250	—
1878/7 CG	483,000	35.00	75.00	125	250	—
1878 CG	Inc. above	18.00	25.00	35.00	125	—
1878 JD/CG	—	25.00	35.00	50.00	150	—
1878 JD	Inc. above	18.00	22.00	30.00	125	—
1878 JD	Inc. above	20.00	30.00	40.00	150	—
Note: D over retrograde D						
1879 JD	—	16.00	18.00	30.00	135	—
1880/70 JD	—	18.00	22.00	30.00	100	—
1880 JD	—	16.00	18.00	22.00	120	—
1881/0 JD	1,032,000	18.00	20.00	30.00	100	—
1881C JD	Inc. above	16.00	18.00	22.00	95.00	—
1881Cn JD	Inc. above	40.00	60.00	90.00	150	—
1882 JD	397,000	16.00	18.00	22.00	95.00	—
1882 AM	Inc. above	16.00	18.00	22.00	95.00	—
1883 AM	333,000	16.00	18.00	22.00	125	—
1884 AM	—	16.00	18.00	22.00	95.00	—
1885/6 AM	227,000	20.00	30.00	45.00	125	—
1885C AM	Inc. above	35.00	70.00	150	350	—
1885Cn AM	Inc. above	16.00	18.00	22.00	95.00	—
1885Gn AM Error	Inc. above	25.00	50.00	100	275	—
1886 AM	571,000	16.00	18.00	22.00	95.00	—

Date	Mintage	F	VF	XF	Unc	BU
1887 AM	732,000	16.00	18.00	22.00	95.00	—
1888 AM	768,000	16.00	18.00	22.00	95.00	—
1889 AM	1,075,000	16.00	18.00	22.00	95.00	500
1890 AM	874,000	14.00	16.00	20.00	90.00	—
1891 AM	777,000	14.00	16.00	20.00	90.00	—
1892 AM	681,000	14.00	16.00	20.00	90.00	—
1893 AM	1,144,000	14.00	16.00	20.00	90.00	—
1894 AM	2,118,000	14.00	16.00	20.00	90.00	—
1895 AM	1,834,000	14.00	16.00	20.00	90.00	—
1896 AM	2,134,000	14.00	16.00	20.00	90.00	—
1897 AM	1,580,000	14.00	16.00	20.00	90.00	—

Date	Mintage	F	VF	XF	Unc	BU
1889 AE	150,000	20.00	30.00	60.00	175	—
1890 AE	181,000	20.00	30.00	60.00	175	—
1891 EN	160,000	18.00	25.00	40.00	135	—
1892 EN	120,000	18.00	25.00	40.00	135	—
1893 EN	66,000	45.00	75.00	115	300	—

KM# 377.11 8 REALES
27.0700 g., 0.9030 Silver 0.7859 oz. ASW **Obv:** Facing eagle, snake in beak **Rev:** Radiant cap **Mint:** Oaxaca **Note:** Mint mark O, Oa. Varieties exist.

Date	Mintage	F	VF	XF	Unc	BU
18580 AE	—	2,500	4,000	—	—	—
18580a AE Unique	—	—	—	—	—	—
1859 AE	—	500	900	1,750	—	—
Note: A in O of mint mark						
1860 AE	—	200	450	800	—	—
Note: A in O of mint mark						
18610 FR	—	125	250	550	1,350	—
18610a FR	—	150	350	700	—	—
18620 FR	—	40.00	80.00	200	375	—
18620a FR	—	65.00	125	250	450	—
18630 FR	—	30.00	60.00	100	250	—
18630 AE	—	30.00	60.00	100	250	—
18630a AE	—	100	150	250	450	—
Note: A in O of mint mark						
18630a AE	—	1,000	1,750	2,750	—	—
Note: A above O in mint mark						
1864 FR	—	25.00	50.00	75.00	200	—
1865 AE	—	1,850	3,000	—	—	—
1867 AE	—	40.00	80.00	150	400	—
1868 AE	—	40.00	80.00	150	400	—
1869 AE	—	30.00	60.00	100	250	—
1873 AE	—	200	300	550	1,350	—
1874 AE	142,000	18.00	30.00	50.00	200	—
1875/4 AE	131,000	25.00	50.00	75.00	200	—
1875 AE	Inc. above	18.00	30.00	40.00	135	—
1876 AE	140,000	20.00	35.00	55.00	200	—
1877 AE	139,000	20.00	30.00	50.00	200	—
1878 AE	125,000	20.00	30.00	50.00	200	—
1879 AE	153,000	20.00	30.00	50.00	200	—
1880 AE	143,000	18.00	30.00	45.00	150	—
1881 AE	134,000	20.00	35.00	60.00	150	—
1882 AE	100,000	20.00	35.00	60.00	150	—
1883 AE	122,000	18.00	30.00	45.00	150	—
1884 AE	142,000	18.00	30.00	50.00	150	—
1885 AE	158,000	18.00	25.00	40.00	135	—
1886 AE	120,000	18.00	30.00	45.00	150	—
1887/6 AE	115,000	25.00	50.00	80.00	200	—
1887 AE	Inc. above	18.00	25.00	40.00	135	—
1888 AE	145,000	18.00	25.00	40.00	135	—

KM# 377.4 8 REALES
27.0700 g., 0.9030 Silver 0.7859 oz. ASW **Obv:** Facing eagle, snake in beak **Mint:** Durango **Note:** Varieties exist.

Date	Mintage	F	VF	XF	Unc	BU
1825Do RL	—	30.00	65.00	150	375	—
1826Do RL	—	40.00	85.00	200	475	—
1827/6Do RL	—	35.00	60.00	85.00	200	—
1827/8Do RL	—	150	275	500	—	—
1827Do RL	—	30.00	50.00	90.00	200	—
1828/7Do RL	—	35.00	60.00	90.00	200	—
1828Do RL	—	25.00	50.00	80.00	175	—
1829Do RL	—	25.00	50.00	80.00	175	—
1830Do RM	—	25.00	50.00	90.00	200	—
Note: B on eagle's claw						
1831Do RM	—	20.00	30.00	60.00	150	—
Note: B on eagle's claw						
1832Do RM	—	35.00	60.00	120	300	—
Note: Mexican dies, B on eagle's claw						
1832/1Do RM/RL	—	25.00	35.00	75.00	165	—
Note: French dies, REPUB MEX spaced						
1833/2Do RM/RL	—	20.00	30.00	75.00	165	—
1833Do RM	—	18.00	30.00	60.00	150	—
1834/3/2Do RM/RL	—	20.00	35.00	75.00	165	—
1834Do RM	—	18.00	25.00	50.00	150	—
1835/4Do RM/RL	—	20.00	35.00	65.00	150	—
1835Do RM	—	20.00	35.00	65.00	150	—
Note: Mexican dies, REPUBMEX not spaced						
1836/1Do RM	—	20.00	35.00	65.00	150	—
1836/4Do RM	—	20.00	35.00	65.00	150	—
1836/5/4Do RM/RL	—	75.00	150	250	500	—
1836Do RM	—	20.00	30.00	55.00	150	—
1836Do RM	—	20.00	30.00	55.00	150	—
Note: M on snake						
1837/1Do RM	—	20.00	30.00	55.00	150	—
1837Do RM	—	20.00	30.00	55.00	150	—
1838/1Do RM	—	20.00	30.00	60.00	165	—
1838/7Do RM	—	20.00	30.00	60.00	165	—
1838Do RM	—	20.00	30.00	55.00	150	—
1839/1Do RM/RL	—	20.00	30.00	55.00	150	—
1839/1Do RM	—	20.00	30.00	55.00	150	—
1839Do RM	—	20.00	30.00	55.00	150	—
1840/38/31Do RM	—	20.00	30.00	55.00	150	—
1840/39Do RM	—	20.00	30.00	55.00	150	—
1840Do RM	—	20.00	30.00	55.00	150	—
1841/31Do RM	—	65.00	125	275	450	—
1841/39Do RM/L	—	25.00	50.00	85.00	200	—
1841/39Do RM	—	25.00	50.00	85.00	200	—
1842/31Do RM	—	125	250	400	750	—
Note: B below cactus						
1842/31Do RM	—	40.00	80.00	125	250	—
1842/32Do RM	—	40.00	80.00	125	250	—

Date	Mintage	F	VF	XF	Unc	BU
1842Do RM	—	20.00	30.00	55.00	150	—
Note: Eagle of 1832-41						
1842Do RM	—	20.00	30.00	55.00	150	—
Note: Pre-1832 eagle resumed						
1842Do RM	—	40.00	80.00	125	250	—
1843/33Do RM	—	50.00	90.00	150	250	—
1843Do RM	—	50.00	90.00	150	250	—
1844/34Do RM	—	100	200	300	500	—
1844/35Do RM	—	100	200	300	500	—
1844/43Do RM	—	60.00	120	220	425	—
1845/31Do RM	—	100	200	300	500	—
1845/34Do RM	—	35.00	75.00	125	250	—
1845/35Do RM	—	35.00	75.00	125	250	—
1845Do RM	—	20.00	30.00	55.00	150	—
1846/31Do RM	—	20.00	30.00	55.00	150	—
1846/36Do RM	—	20.00	30.00	55.00	150	—
1846Do RM	—	20.00	30.00	55.00	150	—
1847Do RM	—	25.00	50.00	80.00	185	—
1848/7Do RM	—	125	250	400	750	—
1848/7Do CM/RM	—	100	200	350	700	—
1848Do CM/RM	—	100	200	350	700	—
1848Do RM	—	100	200	300	600	—
1848Do CM	—	50.00	100	200	400	—
1849/39Do CM	—	100	200	350	700	—
1849Do CM	—	65.00	125	250	550	—
1849Do JMR/CM Oval 0	—	200	400	450	800	—
1849Do JMR Oval 0	—	200	325	450	800	—
1849Do JMR Round 0	—	200	400	600	1,000	—
1850Do JMR	—	100	150	250	500	—
1851/0Do JMR	—	65.00	125	225	475	—
1851Do JMR	—	100	150	250	500	—
1852Do CP/JMR	—	450	800	1,500	—	—
1852Do CP	—	750	1,200	2,250	—	—
1852Do JMR	—	175	250	375	650	—
1853Do CP/JMR	—	125	235	350	600	—
1853Do CP	—	200	350	600	1,200	—
1854Do CP	—	25.00	35.00	65.00	300	—
1855Do CP	—	50.00	100	175	350	—
Note: Eagle type of 1854						
1855Do CP	—	50.00	100	175	350	—
Note: Eagle type of 1856						
1856Do CP	—	50.00	100	175	350	—
1857Do CP	—	35.00	65.00	125	250	—
1858/7Do CP	—	25.00	35.00	70.00	165	—
1858Do CP	—	20.00	30.00	60.00	165	—
1859Do CP	—	20.00	30.00	60.00	165	—
1860/59Do CP	—	30.00	50.00	100	200	—
1860Do CP	—	20.00	30.00	60.00	165	—
1861/0Do CP	—	20.00	30.00	60.00	165	—
1861Do CP	—	20.00	30.00	50.00	125	—
1862/1Do CP	—	25.00	35.00	60.00	125	—
1862Do CP	—	20.00	30.00	60.00	175	—
1863/1Do CP	—	30.00	60.00	90.00	200	—
1863/2Do CP	—	25.00	50.00	75.00	175	—
1863/53Do CP	—	30.00	60.00	90.00	200	—
1863Do CP	—	25.00	50.00	75.00	175	—
1864Do CP	—	100	150	250	500	—
1864Do LT	—	25.00	40.00	80.00	175	—
1864Do LT/T	—	25.00	40.00	80.00	175	—
1864Do LT/CP	—	50.00	100	175	350	—
1865Do LT Rare	—	—	—	—	—	—
1866/4Do CM	—	2,750	5,500	—	—	—
1866Do CM	—	1,750	3,250	5,500	8,500	—
1867Do CM	—	3,500	—	—	—	—
1867/6Do CP	—	200	400	600	1,200	—
1867Do CP	—	175	300	500	1,000	—
1867Do CP/CM	—	125	250	400	900	—
1867Do CP/LT	—	200	400	650	1,250	—
1868Do CP	—	25.00	40.00	80.00	175	—
1869Do CP	—	20.00	30.00	50.00	135	—
1870/69Do CP	—	20.00	30.00	50.00	125	—
1870/9Do CP	—	20.00	30.00	50.00	125	—
1870Do CP	—	20.00	30.00	50.00	125	—
1873Do CP	—	125	225	325	600	—
1873Do CM	—	30.00	50.00	100	200	—
1874/3Do CM	—	14.00	18.00	25.00	125	—
1874Do CM	—	14.00	18.00	25.00	125	—

Date	Mintage	F	VF	XF	Unc	BU
1874Do JH	—	1,150	1,750	2,750	—	—
1875Do CM	—	14.00	18.00	25.00	125	—
1875Do JH	—	80.00	150	250	450	—
1876Do CM	—	14.00	18.00	25.00	125	—
1877Do CM	431,000	1,450	2,500	—	—	—
1877Do CP	Inc. above	14.00	18.00	25.00	125	—
1877Do JMP	Inc. above	750	1,250	2,000	—	—
1878Do PE	409,000	18.00	25.00	40.00	125	—
1878Do TB	Inc. above	14.00	18.00	25.00	125	—
1879Do TB	—	14.00	18.00	25.00	125	—
1880/70Do TB	—	60.00	100	175	350	—
1880/70Do TB/JP	—	150	250	375	650	—
1880/70Do JP	—	18.00	25.00	40.00	125	—
1880Do TB	—	150	250	375	650	—
1881Do JP	928,000	14.00	18.00	25.00	125	—
1882Do JP	414,000	14.00	18.00	25.00	125	—
1882Do MC/JP	Inc. above	30.00	60.00	100	200	—
1882Do MC	Inc. above	25.00	50.00	75.00	150	—
1883/73Do MC	452,000	18.00	25.00	40.00	125	—
1883Do MC	Inc. above	14.00	18.00	25.00	125	—
1884/3Do MC	—	18.00	25.00	40.00	125	—
1884Do MC	—	14.00	18.00	25.00	125	—
1885Do MC M/J	—	18.00	25.00	40.00	125	—
1885Do JB	Inc. above	25.00	35.00	50.00	135	—
1885Do MC	547,000	14.00	16.00	22.00	125	—
1886/5Do MC	—	18.00	25.00	40.00	100	—
1886/3Do MC	955,000	18.00	25.00	40.00	100	—
1886Do MC	Inc. above	14.00	16.00	22.00	90.00	—
1887Do MC	1,004,000	14.00	16.00	22.00	90.00	—
1888/7Do MC	—	65.00	125	250	450	—
1888Do MC	996,000	14.00	16.00	22.00	90.00	—
1889Do MC	874,000	14.00	16.00	22.00	90.00	—
1890Do MC	1,119,000	14.00	16.00	22.00	90.00	—
1890Do JP	Inc. above	14.00	16.00	22.00	90.00	—
1891Do JP	1,487,000	14.00	16.00	22.00	90.00	—
1892Do JP	1,597,000	14.00	16.00	22.00	90.00	—
1892Do ND	Inc. above	25.00	50.00	100	200	—
1893Do ND	1,617,000	14.00	16.00	22.00	90.00	—
1894Do ND	1,537,000	14.00	16.00	22.00	90.00	—
1895/3Do ND	761,000	18.00	25.00	40.00	100	—
1895Do ND	Inc. above	14.00	16.00	22.00	90.00	—
1895Do ND/P	—	18.00	25.00	40.00	100	—

KM# 377.6   8 REALES
27.0700 g., 0.9030 Silver 0.7859 oz. ASW **Obv:** Facing eagle, snake in beak **Obv. Legend:** REPUBLICA MEXICANA. **Rev:** Radiant cap **Mint:** Guadalajara **Note:** Varieties exist.

Date	Mintage	F	VF	XF	Unc	BU
1825Ga FS	—	150	275	475	1,000	—
1826/5Ga FS	—	125	250	450	1,000	—
1826Ga FS	—	125	250	450	1,000	—
1827/87Ga FS	—	125	250	450	1,000	—
1827Ga FS	—	125	250	450	1,000	—
1287Ga FS Error	—	8,500	9,500	—	—	—
1828Ga FS	—	200	375	550	1,200	—

Date	Mintage	F	VF	XF	Unc	BU
1829/8Ga FS	—	200	375	550	1,200	—
1829Ga FS	—	175	325	475	950	—
1830/29Ga FS	—	100	175	300	600	—
1830Ga FS	—	100	175	300	600	—
1830Ga LP/FS	—	800	1,450	—	—	—

Note: The 1830 LP/FS is currently only known with a Philippine countermark

Date	Mintage	F	VF	XF	Unc	BU
1831Ga LP	—	200	400	600	1,200	—
1831Ga FS/LP	—	300	500	750	1,500	—
1831Ga FS	—	125	275	400	—	—
1832/1Ga FS	—	50.00	100	175	300	—
1832/1Ga FS/LP	—	50.00	100	175	300	—
1832Ga FS/LP	—	75.00	150	285	550	—
1832Ga FS	—	25.00	50.00	100	225	—
1833/2/1Ga FS/LP	—	45.00	75.00	125	250	—
1833/2Ga FS	—	25.00	50.00	100	225	—
1834/2Ga FS	—	60.00	125	200	350	—
1834/3Ga FS	—	60.00	125	200	350	—
1834/0Ga FS	—	50.00	100	150	300	—
1834Ga FS	—	50.00	100	150	300	—
1835Ga FS	—	25.00	50.00	100	225	—
1836/5Ga FS	—	175	350	—	—	—
1836/1Ga JG/FS	—	40.00	80.00	125	250	—
1836Ga FS	—	275	450	750	—	—
1836Ga JG/FS	—	25.00	50.00	100	225	—
1836Ga JG	—	25.00	50.00	100	225	—
1837/6Ga JG/FS	—	50.00	100	175	300	—
1837/6Ga JG	—	45.00	90.00	160	285	—
1837Ga JG	—	40.00	80.00	125	250	—
1838/7Ga JG	—	100	175	300	550	—
1838Ga JG	—	100	150	275	500	—
1839Ga MC	—	100	200	350	600	—
1839Ga MC/JG	—	100	200	300	550	—
1839Ga JG	—	60.00	125	200	350	—
1840/30Ga MC	—	50.00	75.00	150	275	—
1840Ga MC	—	30.00	60.00	125	250	—
1841Ga MC	—	30.00	60.00	125	250	—
1842/1Ga JG/MG	—	100	150	250	450	—
1842/1Ga JG/MC	—	100	150	250	450	—
1842Ga JG	—	25.00	50.00	100	225	—
1842Ga JG/MG	—	25.00	50.00	100	225	—
1843/2Ga MC/JG	—	25.00	50.00	100	225	—
1843Ga MC/JG	—	25.00	50.00	100	225	—
1843Ga JG	—	400	600	900	1,800	—
1843Ga MC	—	50.00	100	150	300	—
1844Ga MC	—	50.00	100	150	300	—
1845Ga MC	—	75.00	150	300	700	—
1845Ga JG	—	500	850	1,250	1,850	—
1846Ga JG	—	40.00	80.00	150	300	—
1847Ga JG	—	100	150	225	400	—
1848/7Ga JG	—	55.00	85.00	125	250	—
1848Ga JG	—	50.00	75.00	100	225	—
1849Ga JG	—	90.00	125	175	325	—
1849/39Ga JG	—	250	500	—	—	—
1850Ga JG	—	50.00	100	150	300	—
1851Ga JG	—	125	200	350	650	—
1852Ga JG	—	100	150	250	450	—
1853/2Ga JG	—	125	175	250	475	—
1853Ga JG	—	90.00	125	175	300	—
1854/3Ga JG	—	65.00	90.00	125	250	—
1854Ga JG	—	50.00	75.00	110	225	—
1855/4Ga JG	—	50.00	100	150	275	—
1855Ga JG	—	25.00	50.00	100	225	—
1856/4Ga JG	—	60.00	125	175	300	—
1856/5Ga 56	—	60.00	125	175	300	—
1856Ga JG	—	50.00	100	150	275	—
1857Ga JG	—	50.00	100	225	450	—
1858Ga JG	—	100	150	300	500	—
1859/7Ga JG	—	25.00	50.00	110	225	—
1859/8Ga JG	—	25.00	50.00	100	200	—
1859Ga JG	—	20.00	40.00	80.00	175	—
1860Ga JG Without dot	—	350	750	1,200	2,250	—
1860Ga JG	—	2,000	3,250	4,500	—	—

Note: Dot in loop of snake's tail, base alloy

Date	Mintage	F	VF	XF	Unc	BU
1861Ga JG	—	2,200	5,750	—	—	—
1862Ga JG	—	850	1,350	2,750	4,500	—
1863/52Ga JG	—	—	—	—	—	—
1863/59Ga JG	—	45.00	50.00	85.00	145	—

Date	Mintage	F	VF	XF	Unc	BU
1863/2Ga JG	—	30.00	50.00	90.00	175	—
1863/4Ga JG	—	40.00	75.00	150	250	—
1863Ga JG	—	25.00	45.00	75.00	150	—
1863Ga FV Rare	—	—	—	—	—	—
1867Ga JM Rare	—	—	—	—	—	—
1868/7Ga JM	—	50.00	75.00	125	200	—
1868Ga JM	—	50.00	75.00	125	200	—
1869Ga JM	—	50.00	75.00	125	200	—
1869Ga IC	—	75.00	125	200	375	—
1870/60Ga IC	—	60.00	90.00	150	275	—
1870Ga IC	—	60.00	90.00	150	275	—
1873Ga IC	—	15.00	25.00	50.00	135	—
1874Ga IC	—	14.00	15.00	22.00	90.00	—
1874Ga MC	—	25.00	50.00	100	200	—
1875Ga IC	—	18.00	30.00	60.00	135	—
1875Ga MC	—	14.00	15.00	22.00	125	—
1876Ga IC	559,000	18.00	30.00	50.00	125	—
1876Ga MC	Inc. above	125	175	250	375	—
1877Ga IC	928,000	14.00	18.00	25.00	125	—
1877/6Ga JA	—	14.00	18.00	25.00	125	—
1877Ga JA	Inc. above	14.00	18.00	25.00	125	—
1878Ga JA	764,000	14.00	18.00	25.00	125	—
1879Ga JA	—	14.00	18.00	25.00	125	—
1880/70Ga FS	—	18.00	25.00	50.00	135	—
1880Ga JA	—	14.00	18.00	25.00	125	—
1880Ga FS	—	14.00	18.00	25.00	125	—
1881Ga FS	1,300,000	14.00	18.00	25.00	125	—
1882/1Ga FS	537,000	18.00	25.00	50.00	135	—
1882Ga FS	Inc. above	14.00	18.00	25.00	125	—
1882Ga TB/FS	Inc. above	50.00	100	175	300	—
1882Ga TB	Inc. above	50.00	100	175	300	—
1883Ga TB	561,000	18.00	25.00	40.00	135	—
1884Ga TB	—	14.00	16.00	22.00	125	—
1884Ga AH	—	14.00	16.00	22.00	125	—
1885Ga AH	443,000	14.00	16.00	22.00	125	—
1885Ga JS	Inc. above	30.00	60.00	100	200	—
1886Ga JS/H	—	14.00	16.00	22.00	125	—
1886Ga JS	1,038,999	14.00	16.00	22.00	125	—
1887Ga JS	878,000	14.00	16.00	22.00	125	—
1888Ga JS	1,159,000	14.00	16.00	22.00	125	—
1889Ga JS	1,583,000	14.00	16.00	22.00	125	—
1890Ga JS	1,658,000	14.00	16.00	22.00	110	—
1891Ga JS	1,507,000	14.00	16.00	22.00	110	—
1892/1Ga JS	1,627,000	18.00	25.00	50.00	125	—
1892Ga JS	Inc. above	14.00	16.00	22.00	110	—
1893Ga JS	1,952,000	14.00	16.00	22.00	110	—
1894Ga JS	2,045,999	14.00	16.00	22.00	110	—
1895/3Ga JS	—	16.00	20.00	35.00	115	—
1895Ga JS	1,146,000	14.00	16.00	22.00	110	—

KM# 377.8   8 REALES
27.0700 g., 0.9030 Silver 0.7859 oz. ASW **Obv:** Facing eagle, snake in beak **Obv. Legend:** REPUBLICA MEXICANA. **Rev:** Radiant cap **Mint:** Guanajuato **Note:** Varieties exist.

Date	Mintage	F	VF	XF	Unc	BU
1825Go JJ	—	40.00	70.00	150	300	—
1825G JJ	—	1,250	1,650	—	—	—
Note: Error mint mark G						
1826Go JJ	—	40.00	80.00	175	350	—
Note: Straight J's						
1826Go JJ	—	30.00	60.00	125	250	—
Note: Full J's						
1826Go MJ	—	250	450	850	—	—
1827Go MJ	—	40.00	75.00	125	250	—
1827Go MJ/JJ	—	—	—	—	—	—
1827Go MR	—	100	200	350	600	—
1828Go MJ	—	—	—	—	—	—
Note: Error mint mark Goo						
1828Go MJ	—	30.00	60.00	125	250	—
1828/7Go MR	—	150	300	600	1,200	—
1828Go MR	—	150	300	600	1,200	—
1829Go MJ	—	20.00	35.00	55.00	165	—
1830Go MJ	—	20.00	30.00	55.00	165	—
Note: Oblong beading and narrow J						
1830Go MJ	—	20.00	30.00	55.00	165	—
Note: Regular beading and wide J						
1831Go MJ	—	15.00	20.00	40.00	150	—
Note: Colon after date						
1831Go MJ	—	15.00	20.00	40.00	150	—
Note: 2 stars after date						
1832Go MJ	—	15.00	20.00	40.00	150	—
1832Go MJ	—	20.00	35.00	65.00	175	—
Note: 1 of date over inverted 1						
1833Go MJ/1	—	20.00	35.00	65.00	175	—
1833Go MJ	—	15.00	20.00	40.00	150	—
1833Go JM	—	400	750	1,250	2,500	—
1834Go PJ	—	15.00	20.00	40.00	150	—
1835Go PJ	—	15.00	20.00	40.00	150	—
Note: Star on cap						
1835Go PJ	—	15.00	20.00	40.00	150	—
Note: Dot on cap						
1836Go PJ	—	15.00	20.00	40.00	150	—
1837Go PJ	—	15.00	20.00	40.00	150	—
1838Go PJ	—	15.00	20.00	40.00	150	—
1839Go PJ/JJ	—	15.00	20.00	40.00	150	—
1839Go PJ	—	15.00	20.00	40.00	150	—
1840/30Go PJ	—	20.00	30.00	50.00	150	—
1840Go PJ	—	15.00	20.00	35.00	125	—
1841/31Go PJ	—	15.00	20.00	35.00	125	—
1841Go PJ	—	15.00	20.00	35.00	125	—
1842/1Go PM	—	20.00	30.00	50.00	125	—
1842/31Go PM/PJ	—	25.00	35.00	60.00	150	—
1842/1Go PJ	—	20.00	30.00	50.00	125	—
1842Go PJ	—	20.00	30.00	50.00	125	—
1842Go PM/PJ	—	15.00	20.00	35.00	125	—
1842Go PM	—	15.00	20.00	35.00	125	—
1843Go PM	—	15.00	20.00	35.00	125	—
Note: Dot after date						
1843Go PM	—	15.00	20.00	35.00	125	—
Note: Triangle of dots after date						
1844Go PM	—	15.00	20.00	35.00	125	—
1845Go PM	—	15.00	20.00	35.00	125	—
1846/5Go PM	—	20.00	30.00	50.00	150	—
Note: Eagle type of 1845						
1846Go PM	—	20.00	30.00	50.00	150	—
Note: Eagle type of 1845						
1846Go PM	—	18.00	25.00	40.00	135	—
Note: Eagle type of 1847						
1847Go PM Narrow date	—	15.00	20.00	35.00	125	—
1847Go PM Wide date	—	15.00	20.00	35.00	125	—
1848/7Go PM	—	15.00	35.00	65.00	150	—
1848Go PM	—	20.00	35.00	65.00	150	—
1849Go PF	—	15.00	20.00	35.00	125	—
1850Go PF	—	15.00	20.00	35.00	125	—
1851/0Go PF	—	20.00	30.00	50.00	150	—
1851Go PF	—	15.00	20.00	35.00	125	—
1852/1Go PF	—	20.00	30.00	50.00	150	—
1852Go PF	—	15.00	20.00	35.00	125	—
1853/2Go PF	—	20.00	30.00	50.00	150	—
1853Go PF	—	15.00	20.00	35.00	125	—
1854Go PF	—	15.00	20.00	35.00	125	—

Date	Mintage	F	VF	XF	Unc	BU
1855Go PF Large letters	—	15.00	20.00	35.00	125	—
1855Go PF Small letters	—	15.00	20.00	35.00	125	—
1856/5Go PF	—	20.00	30.00	50.00	150	—
1856Go PF	—	15.00	20.00	35.00	125	—
1857/5Go PF	—	20.00	30.00	50.00	150	—
1857/6Go PF	—	20.00	35.00	70.00	200	—
1857Go PF	—	15.00	18.00	22.00	90.00	—
1858/7Go PI Narrow date	—	15.00	20.00	35.00	125	—
1858Go PF Wide date	—	15.00	20.00	35.00	125	—
1859/7Go PF	—	15.00	20.00	35.00	125	—
1859/8Go PF	—	20.00	30.00	50.00	150	—
1859Go PF	—	15.00	20.00	35.00	125	—
1860/50Go PF	—	20.00	30.00	50.00	150	—
1860/59Go PF	—	15.00	18.00	25.00	95.00	—
1860Go PF	—	15.00	18.00	22.00	90.00	—
1861/51Go PF	—	15.00	20.00	30.00	100	—
Note: Narrow and wide dates exist						
1861/0Go PF	—	15.00	18.00	22.00	90.00	—
1861Go PF	—	15.00	18.00	22.00	90.00	—
186/52Go YE	—	18.00	20.00	30.00	100	—
1862Go YE/PF	—	15.00	18.00	22.00	90.00	—
186/52Go YF	—	18.00	20.00	30.00	100	—
1862Go YE	—	15.00	18.00	22.00	90.00	—
1862Go YF	—	15.00	18.00	22.00	90.00	—
1862Go YF/PF	—	15.00	18.00	22.00	90.00	—
1863/53Go YF	—	15.00	18.00	25.00	90.00	—
1863/54Go YF	—	18.00	20.00	30.00	100	—
1863Go YE Rare	—	—	—	—	—	—
1863Go YF	—	15.00	18.00	22.00	90.00	—
1867/57Go YF	—	18.00	20.00	30.00	100	—
1867Go YF	—	15.00	18.00	22.00	90.00	—
1868/58Go YF	—	18.00	20.00	30.00	100	—
1868/7Go YF	—	18.00	20.00	30.00	100	—
1868Go YF	—	15.00	18.00	22.00	90.00	—
1870/60Go FR	—	20.00	30.00	50.00	150	—
1870Go YF	—	1,800	3,000	5,000	7,500	—
1870Go FR/YF	—	20.00	35.00	70.00	200	—
1873Go FR	—	15.00	18.00	22.00	90.00	—
1874/3Go FR	—	18.00	20.00	30.00	95.00	—
1874Go FR	—	18.00	25.00	35.00	100	—
1875/3Go FR	—	18.00	20.00	30.00	95.00	—
1875/6Go FR	—	18.00	20.00	30.00	95.00	—
1875Go FR	—	15.00	18.00	22.00	90.00	—
Note: Small circle with dot on eagle						
1876/5Go FR	—	18.00	20.00	30.00	95.00	—
1876Go FR	—	15.00	18.00	22.00	90.00	—
1877Go FR Narrow date	—	15.00	18.00	22.00	90.00	—
1877Go FR Wide date	2,477,000	15.00	18.00	22.00	90.00	—
1878/7Go FR	2,273,000	18.00	20.00	30.00	90.00	—
1878/7Go SM, S/F	—	18.00	20.00	30.00	90.00	—
1878/7Go SM	—	18.00	20.00	30.00	90.00	—
1878Go FR	Inc. above	15.00	18.00	22.00	90.00	—
1878Go SM, S/F	—	18.00	20.00	25.00	90.00	—
1878Go SM	—	15.00	18.00	22.00	90.00	—
1879/7Go SM	—	18.00	20.00	30.00	90.00	—
1879/8Go SM	—	18.00	20.00	30.00	90.00	—
1879/8Go SM/FR	—	18.00	20.00	30.00	90.00	—
1879Go SM	—	15.00	18.00	22.00	90.00	—
1879Go SM/FR	—	18.00	20.00	30.00	90.00	—
1880/70Go SB	—	18.00	20.00	30.00	90.00	—
1880Go SB/SM	—	15.00	18.00	22.00	90.00	—
1880Go SB	—	15.00	18.00	22.00	90.00	—
1881/71Go SB	3,974,000	18.00	20.00	30.00	90.00	—
1881/0Go SB	Inc. above	18.00	20.00	30.00	90.00	—
1881Go SB	Inc. above	15.00	18.00	22.00	90.00	—
1882Go SB	2,015,000	15.00	18.00	22.00	90.00	—
1883Go SB	2,100,000	35.00	75.00	125	250	—
1883Go BR	Inc. above	15.00	18.00	22.00	90.00	—
1883Go BR/SR	—	15.00	18.00	22.00	90.00	—
1883Go BR/SB	Inc. above	15.00	18.00	22.00	90.00	—
1884/73Go BR	—	20.00	30.00	40.00	100	—
1884/74Go BR	—	20.00	30.00	40.00	100	—
1884/3Go BR	—	20.00	30.00	60.00	150	—

Date	Mintage	F	VF	XF	Unc	BU
1884Go BR	—	15.00	18.00	22.00	90.00	—
1884/74Go RR	—	50.00	100	175	350	—
1884Go RR	—	25.00	50.00	100	250	—
1885/75Go RR/BR	—	18.00	20.00	300	90.00	—
1885/75Go RR	2,363,000	18.00	20.00	30.00	90.00	—
1885Go RR	Inc. above	15.00	18.00	22.00	90.00	—
1886/75Go RR/BR	—	18.00	20.00	25.00	90.00	—
1886/75Go RR	4,127,000	18.00	20.00	25.00	90.00	—
1886/76Go RR/BR	—	15.00	18.00	22.00	90.00	—
1886/76Go RR	Inc. above	15.00	18.00	22.00	90.00	—
1886/5Go RR/BR	Inc. above	15.00	18.00	22.00	90.00	—
1886Go RR	Inc. above	15.00	18.00	22.00	90.00	—
1887Go RR	4,205,000	14.00	18.00	22.00	90.00	—
1888Go RR	3,985,000	14.00	18.00	22.00	90.00	—
1889Go RR	3,646,000	14.00	18.00	22.00	90.00	—
1890Go RR	3,615,000	14.00	18.00	22.00	90.00	—
1891Go RS/R	—	14.00	18.00	22.00	90.00	—
1891Go RS	3,197,000	14.00	18.00	22.00	90.00	—
1892/0Go/A RS	—	14.00	18.00	22.00	90.00	—
1892/0Go RS	—	14.00	18.00	22.00	90.00	—
1892Go RS	3,672,000	14.00	18.00	22.00	90.00	—
1892Go/A RS	—	14.00	18.00	22.00	90.00	—
1893Go RS	3,854,000	14.00	18.00	22.00	90.00	—
1894Go RS	4,127,000	14.00	18.00	22.00	90.00	—
1895/1Go RS	3,768,000	18.00	20.00	22.00	90.00	—
1895/3Go RS	Inc. above	18.00	20.00	25.00	90.00	—
1895Go RS	Inc. above	14.00	18.00	22.00	90.00	—
1896/1Go/As RS/ML	5,229,000	18.00	20.00	25.00	90.00	—
1896/1Go RS	Inc. above	15.00	18.00	22.00	90.00	—
1896Go/Ga RS	Inc. above	—	—	—	—	—
1896Go RS	Inc. above	14.00	15.00	20.00	90.00	—
1897Go RS	4,344,000	14.00	15.00	20.00	90.00	—

Date	Mintage	F	VF	XF	Unc	BU
1865Ho FM	—	250	500	950	1,850	—
1866Ho FM	—	1,150	2,150	3,500	5,500	—
1866Ho MP	—	950	1,750	3,000	4,650	—
1867Ho PR	—	100	175	275	500	—
1868Ho PR	—	20.00	35.00	65.00	175	—
1869Ho PR	—	40.00	60.00	125	250	—
1870Ho PR	—	100	175	275	550	—
1871/0Ho PR	—	50.00	75.00	125	250	—
1871Ho PR	—	30.00	50.00	90.00	200	—
1872/1Ho PR	—	35.00	60.00	90.00	200	—
1872Ho PR	—	30.00	50.00	75.00	175	—
1873Ho PR	351,000	30.00	50.00	85.00	150	—
1874Ho PR	—	18.00	22.00	40.00	125	—
1875Ho PR	—	18.00	22.00	40.00	125	—
1876Ho AF	—	18.00	22.00	40.00	125	—
1877Ho AF	410,000	20.00	30.00	50.00	150	—
1877Ho GR	Inc. above	100	150	225	400	—
1877Ho JA	Inc. above	25.00	50.00	85.00	175	—
1878Ho JA	451,000	18.00	22.00	40.00	120	—
1879Ho JA	—	18.00	22.00	40.00	120	—
1880Ho JA	—	18.00	22.00	40.00	120	—
1881Ho JA	586,000	18.00	22.00	40.00	120	—
1882Ho JA	240,000	25.00	40.00	65.00	125	—
Note: O above H						
1882Ho JA	Inc. above	25.00	40.00	65.00	125	—
Note: O after H						
1883/2Ho JA	204,000	200	350	500	1,000	—
1883/2Ho FM/JA	Inc. above	25.00	40.00	75.00	150	—
1883Ho FM/JA	—	27.00	45.00	85.00	165	—
1883Ho FM	—	20.00	30.00	60.00	125	—
1883Ho JA	Inc. above	275	450	800	1,500	—
1884/3Ho FM	—	20.00	25.00	50.00	125	—
1884Ho FM	—	18.00	22.00	40.00	120	—
1885Ho FM	132,000	18.00	22.00	40.00	120	—
1886Ho FM	225,000	20.00	30.00	45.00	125	—
1886Ho FG	Inc. above	20.00	30.00	45.00	125	—
1887/6Ho FG	—	20.00	35.00	65.00	150	—
1887Ho FG	150,000	20.00	35.00	65.00	150	—
1888Ho FG	364,000	15.00	20.00	30.00	110	—
1889Ho FG	490,000	15.00	20.00	30.00	110	—
1890Ho FG	565,000	15.00	20.00	30.00	110	—
1891Ho FG	738,000	15.00	20.00	30.00	110	—
1892Ho FG	643,000	15.00	20.00	30.00	110	—
1893Ho FG	518,000	15.00	20.00	30.00	110	—
1894Ho FG	504,000	15.00	20.00	30.00	110	—
1895Ho FG	320,000	15.00	20.00	30.00	110	—

KM# 377.9   8 REALES
27.0700 g., 0.9030 Silver 0.7859 oz. ASW **Obv:** Facing eagle, snake in beak **Rev:** Radiant cap **Mint:** Hermosillo **Note:** Varieties exist.

Date	Mintage	F	VF	XF	Unc	BU
1835Ho PP Rare	—	—	—	—	—	—
1836Ho PP Rare	—	—	—	—	—	—
1839Ho PR Unique	—	—	—	—	—	—
1861Ho FM	—	4,500	7,500	—	—	—
Note: Reeded edge						
1862Ho FM Rare	—	—	—	—	—	—
Note: Plain edge, snakes tail left, long ray over *8R						
1862Ho FM	—	1,550	2,700	—	—	—
Note: Plain edge, snake's tail left						
1862Ho FM	—	1,650	2,750	—	—	—
Note: Reeded edge, snakes tail right						
1863Ho FM	—	150	300	800	—	—
1864Ho FM	—	850	1,650	2,750	—	—
1864Ho PR/FM	—	1,200	2,200	—	—	—
1864Ho PR	—	650	1,250	2,150	3,350	—

KM# 377.12   8 REALES
27.0700 g., 0.9030 Silver 0.7859 oz. ASW **Obv:** Facing eagle, snake in beak **Obv. Legend:** REPUBLICA MEXICANA **Rev:** Radiant cap **Mint:** San Luis Potosi **Note:** Varieties exist.

Date	Mintage	F	VF	XF	Unc	BU
1827Pi JS	—	3,800	—	—	—	—
Note: Heritage World Coin Auction #3004, 1-09, MS63 realized $63,250						

Date	Mintage	F	VF	XF	Unc	BU
1827Pi SA	—	6,000	9,000	—	—	—
1828/7Pi JS	—	275	425	650	1,350	—
1828Pi JS	—	225	375	550	1,200	—
1829Pi JS	—	35.00	65.00	125	250	—
1830Pi JS	—	30.00	50.00	100	200	—

Note: Varities with low cap or centered cap

Date	Mintage	F	VF	XF	Unc	BU
1831/0Pi JS	—	35.00	75.00	200	350	—
1831Pi JS	—	25.00	35.00	75.00	200	—
1832/22Pi JS	—	25.00	35.00	65.00	165	—
18/032Pi JS	—	40.00	80.00	175	300	—
1832Pi JS	—	25.00	35.00	65.00	165	—
1833/2Pi JS	—	30.00	45.00	80.00	250	—
1833Pi JS Narrow date	—	20.00	30.00	50.00	150	—

Note: Planchet diameter 37.5 mm

Date	Mintage	F	VF	XF	Unc	BU
1833Pi JS Wide date	—	20.00	30.00	50.00	150	—

Note: Planchet diameter 38.5 mm

Date	Mintage	F	VF	XF	Unc	BU
1834/3Pi JS	—	35.00	65.00	125	300	—
1834Pi JS	—	18.00	25.00	50.00	150	—

Note: Varieties with low cap or centered cap

Date	Mintage	F	VF	XF	Unc	BU
1835/4Pi JS		60.00	125	250	500	—
1835Pi JS	—	20.00	30.00	65.00	175	—

Note: Denomination as 8R

Date	Mintage	F	VF	XF	Unc	BU
1835Pi JS	—	18.00	25.00	50.00	150	—

Note: Denomination as 8Rs

Date	Mintage	F	VF	XF	Unc	BU
1836Pi JS	—	20.00	30.00	55.00	150	—
1837Pi JS	—	30.00	50.00	85.00	200	—
1838Pi JS	—	20.00	30.00	55.00	150	—
1839Pi JS	—	20.00	40.00	70.00	150	—

Note: Varieties with small low cap or large high cap

Date	Mintage	F	VF	XF	Unc	BU
1840Pi JS	—	20.00	30.00	60.00	150	—
184/31Pi JS	—	25.00	40.00	85.00	200	—
1841Pi JS	—	25.00	40.00	85.00	200	—
1841iP JS Error	—	200	350	550	—	—
1842/1Pi JS	—	40.00	65.00	125	300	—
1842/1Pi JS/PS	—	35.00	55.00	90.00	200	—
1842Pi JS	—	30.00	50.00	80.00	175	—

Note: Eagle type of 1843

Date	Mintage	F	VF	XF	Unc	BU
1842Pi PS	—	30.00	50.00	80.00	175	—
1842Pi PS/JS	—	30.00	50.00	80.00	175	—

Note: Eagle type of 1841

Date	Mintage	F	VF	XF	Unc	BU
1843/2Pi PS Round-top 3	—	50.00	75.00	150	300	—
1843Pi PS Flat-top 3	—	60.00	100	200	475	—
1843Pi AM Round-top 3	—	20.00	30.00	55.00	150	—
1843Pi AM Flat-top 3	—	20.00	30.00	55.00	150	—
1844Pi AM	—	20.00	30.00	55.00	150	—
1845/4Pi AM	—	35.00	55.00	120	250	—
1845Pi AM	—	25.00	50.00	100	225	—
1846/5Pi AM	—	40.00	65.00	125	300	—
1846Pi AM	—	18.00	25.00	50.00	150	—
1847Pi AM	—	30.00	50.00	85.00	175	—
1848/7Pi AM	—	30.00	60.00	100	200	—
1848Pi AM	—	30.00	50.00	85.00	175	—
1849/8Pi PS/AM	—	950	1,750	—	—	—
1849Pi PS	—	950	1,750	—	—	—
1849Pi MC/PS	—	60.00	125	250	500	—
1849Pi AM	—	1,850	3,250	5,000	—	—
1849Pi MC	—	60.00	125	250	500	—
1850Pi MC	—	40.00	80.00	150	300	—
185/41Pi MC	—	75.00	150	275	550	—
1851Pi MC	—	75.00	150	275	550	—
1852Pi MC	—	75.00	125	200	400	—
1853Pi MC	—	150	275	400	850	—
1854Pi MC	—	100	150	250	500	—
1855Pi MC	—	100	150	250	500	—
1856Pi MC	—	65.00	100	200	400	—
1857Pi MC	—	400	700	1,250	—	—
1857Pi PS/MC	—	150	250	450	1,000	—
1857Pi PS	—	125	200	350	650	—
1858Pi MC/PS	—	250	400	650	1,200	—
1858Pi MC	—	250	400	650	1,200	—
1858Pi PS	—	650	1,150	1,750	—	—
1859/8Pi MC/PS	—	3,650	5,750	—	—	—
1859Pi MC/PS	—	900	1,750	—	—	—
1859Pi MC	—	2,000	3,500	5,000	—	—
1859Pi PS/MC	—	800	1,500	2,500	—	—
1860Pi FC Rare	—	—	—	—	—	—
1860Pi FE Rare	—	—	—	—	—	—
1860Pi MC	—	1,750	2,750	6,000	—	—
1860Pi PS/FE	—	500	1,000	—	—	—
1860Pi RO Rare	—	—	—	—	—	—

Note: Spink America Gerber sale 6-96 cleaned VF or better realized $33,000

Date	Mintage	F	VF	XF	Unc	BU
1860Pi PS	—	400	600	900	1,750	—
1861Pi PS	—	30.00	60.00	90.00	175	—
1861Pi RO	—	25.00	35.00	55.00	135	—
1862/1Pi RO	—	20.00	25.00	50.00	135	—
1862Pi RO	—	18.00	22.00	45.00	120	—

Note: Round O/M

Date	Mintage	F	VF	XF	Unc	BU
1862Pi RO	—	18.00	22.00	45.00	120	—

Note: Oval O in RO

Date	Mintage	F	VF	XF	Unc	BU
1862Pi RO	—	20.00	30.00	50.00	135	—

Note: Round O in RO, 6 is an inverted 9

Date	Mintage	F	VF	XF	Unc	BU
1863/2Pi RO	—	25.00	35.00	65.00	150	—
1863Pi RO/MO/FC	—	20.00	30.00	50.00	150	—
1863/5Pi RO	—	20.00	25.00	45.00	150	—
1863Pi RO	—	18.00	25.00	40.00	135	—
1863	—	25.00	35.00	55.00	135	—

Note: 6 over inverted 6

Date	Mintage	F	VF	XF	Unc	BU
1863Pi FC	—	2,750	4,750	—	—	—
1864Pi RO Rare	—	—	—	—	—	—
1867Pi CA	—	300	500	—	—	—
1867Pi LR	—	250	400	650	—	—
1867Pi PS/CA	—	850	—	—	—	—
1867Pi PS	—	30.00	60.00	125	275	—
1868/7Pi PS	—	30.00	60.00	125	250	—
1868Pi PS	—	20.00	30.00	50.00	135	—
1869/8Pi PS	—	20.00	25.00	45.00	135	—
1869Pi PS	—	18.00	22.00	45.00	135	—
1870/69Pi PS	—	750	1,450	3,500	—	—
1870Pi PS	—	650	1,250	2,500	—	—
1873Pi MH	—	18.00	25.00	45.00	150	—
1874/3Pi MH	—	25.00	50.00	120	250	—
1874Pi MH	—	14.00	16.00	22.00	120	—
1875Pi MH	—	14.00	16.00	22.00	110	—
1876/5Pi MH	—	18.00	25.00	45.00	150	—
1876Pi MH	—	14.00	16.00	22.00	110	—
1877/6Pi MH	—	165	325	550	—	—
1877Pi MH	1,018,000	14.00	16.00	22.00	120	—
1878Pi MH	1,046,000	18.00	30.00	100	225	—
1879/8Pi MH	—	18.00	22.00	30.00	125	—
1879Pi MH	—	14.00	12.00	22.00	110	—
1879Pi BE	—	25.00	50.00	75.00	150	—
1879Pi MR	—	30.00	50.00	100	200	—
1880Pi MR	—	250	375	750	—	—
1880/70Pi MH/R	—	14.00	16.00	22.00	110	—
1880Pi MH/R	—	14.00	16.00	22.00	110	—
1880Pi MH	—	14.00	16.00	22.00	110	—
1881/71Pi MH/R	—	14.00	16.00	22.00	110	—
1881Pi MH/R	—	14.00	16.00	22.00	110	—
1881Pi MH	2,100,000	14.00	16.00	22.00	110	—
1882/1Pi MH	1,602,000	18.00	22.00	30.00	125	—
1882Pi MH	Inc. above	14.00	16.00	22.00	110	—
1883/2Pi MH	—	18.00	22.00	30.00	125	—
1883Pi MH	1,545,000	14.00	16.00	22.00	110	—
1884/3Pi MH	—	18.00	22.00	30.00	125	—
1884Pi MH/MM	—	16.00	18.00	22.00	95.00	—
1884Pi MH	—	14.00	16.00	20.00	90.00	—
1885/4Pi MH	1,736,000	18.00	22.00	30.00	125	—
1885/8Pi MH	Inc. above	18.00	22.00	30.00	125	—
1885Pi MH	Inc. above	14.00	16.00	20.00	90.00	—
1885Pi LC	Inc. above	16.00	20.00	25.00	110	—
1886Pi LC	3,347,000	14.00	16.00	20.00	90.00	—
1886Pi MH	Inc. above	14.00	16.00	20.00	90.00	—
1887Pi MR	2,922,000	14.00	16.00	20.00	90.00	—
1888/7Pi MR	—	18.00	22.00	30.00	125	—
1888Pi MR	2,438,000	14.00	16.00	20.00	90.00	—
1889Pi MR	2,103,000	14.00	16.00	20.00	90.00	—
1890Pi MR	1,562,000	14.00	16.00	20.00	90.00	—
1891Pi MR	1,184,000	14.00	16.00	20.00	90.00	—
1892Pi MR	1,336,000	14.00	16.00	20.00	90.00	—
1893Pi MR	530,000	14.00	16.00	20.00	90.00	—

KM# 377.13   8 REALES
27.0700 g., 0.9030 Silver 0.7859 oz. ASW **Obv:** Facing
eagle, snake in beak **Obv. Legend:** REPUBLICA
MEXICANA. **Rev:** Radiant cap **Mint:** Zacatecas **Note:**
Varieties exist.

Date	Mintage	F	VF	XF	Unc	BU
1825Zs AZ	—	25.00	35.00	65.00	175	—
1826/5Zs AZ	—	25.00	45.00	85.00	200	—
1826Zs AZ	—	100	200	400	800	—
1826Zs AV	—	175	350	600	1,500	—
1826/5Zs AO/AZ	—	300	600	1,000	2,000	—
1826Zs AO	—	200	350	750	2,000	—
1827Zs AO/AZ	—	35.00	50.00	125	250	—
1827Zs AO	—	25.00	45.00	85.00	200	—
1828Zs AO	—	18.00	22.00	45.00	165	—

Note: Wide and narrow date varieties exist

Date	Mintage	F	VF	XF	Unc	BU
1829Zs AO	—	18.00	2.00	45.00	165	—
1829Zs OV	—	50.00	90.00	150	300	—
1830Zs OM	—	—	—	—	—	—
1830Zs OV	—	18.00	22.00	45.00	165	—
1831Zs OV	—	25.00	50.00	90.00	200	—
1831Zs OM	—	18.00	25.00	55.00	165	—
1832/1Zs OM	—	20.00	25.00	45.00	165	—
1832Zs OM	—	18.00	22.00	40.00	150	—
1833/2Zs OM	—	20.00	30.00	45.00	165	—
1833Zs OM/MM	—	18.00	25.00	40.00	150	—
1833Zs OM	—	18.00	22.00	35.00	150	—
1834Zs OM	—	18.00	22.00	35.00	150	—

Note: Known with large, medium and small "34" in date

Date	Mintage	F	VF	XF	Unc	BU
1835Zs OM	—	18.00	22.00	40.00	150	—
1836/4Zs OM	—	20.00	30.00	50.00	165	—
1836/5Zs OM	—	20.00	30.00	50.00	165	—
1836Zs OM	—	18.00	22.00	35.00	150	—
1837Zs OM	—	18.00	22.00	35.00	150	—
1838/7Zs OM	—	20.00	30.00	45.00	165	—
1838Zs OM	—	18.00	22.00	35.00	150	—
1839Zs OM	—	18.00	22.00	35.00	150	—
1840Zs OM	—	18.00	22.00	35.00	150	—
1841Zs OM	—	18.00	22.00	35.00	150	—
1842Zs OM	—	18.00	22.00	35.00	150	—

Note: Eagle type of 1841

Date	Mintage	F	VF	XF	Unc	BU
1842Zs OM	—	18.00	22.00	35.00	150	—

Note: Eagle type of 1843

Date	Mintage	F	VF	XF	Unc	BU
1843Zs OM	—	18.00	22.00	35.00	150	—
1844Zs OM	—	18.00	22.00	35.00	150	—
1845Zs OM	—	18.00	22.00	35.00	150	—
1846Zs OM	—	18.00	22.00	35.00	150	—
1847Zs OM	—	18.00	22.00	35.00	150	—
1848/7Zs OM	—	20.00	30.00	45.00	165	—
1848Zs OM	—	18.00	22.00	35.00	150	—
1849Zs OM	—	18.00	22.00	35.00	150	—
1850Zs OM	—	18.00	22.00	35.00	150	—
1851Zs OM	—	18.00	22.00	35.00	150	—
1852Zs OM	—	18.00	22.00	35.00	150	—
1853Zs OM	—	30.00	45.00	75.00	200	—

Date	Mintage	F	VF	XF	Unc	BU
1854/3Zs OM	—	20.00	30.00	60.00	175	—
1854Zs OM	—	18.00	25.00	45.00	165	—
1855Zs OM	—	20.00	30.00	60.00	175	—
1855Zs MO	—	30.00	60.00	90.00	200	—
1856/5Zs MO	—	20.00	30.00	45.00	165	—
1856Zs MO	—	18.00	22.00	35.00	150	—
1857/5Zs MO	—	20.00	30.00	45.00	165	—
1857Zs MO	—	18.00	22.00	35.00	150	—
1858/7Zs MO	—	18.00	22.00	35.00	150	—
1858Zs MO	—	18.00	22.00	35.00	150	—
1859/8Zs MO	—	18.00	22.00	35.00	150	—
1859Zs MO	—	18.00	22.00	35.00	150	—
1859Zs VL/MO	—	25.00	50.00	75.00	175	—
1859Zs VL	—	20.00	40.00	60.00	165	—
1860/50Zs MO	—	14.00	16.00	22.00	90.00	—
1860/59Zs MO	—	14.00	16.00	22.00	90.00	—
1860Zs MO	—	14.00	16.00	22.00	90.00	—
1860Zs VL/MO	—	14.00	16.00	22.00	90.00	—
1860Zs VL	—	14.00	16.00	22.00	90.00	—
1861Zs VL	—	14.00	16.00	22.00	90.00	—
1861/0Zs VL/MO	—	14.00	16.00	22.00	90.00	—
1861/0Zs VL	—	14.00	16.00	22.00	90.00	—
1862/1Zs VL	—	16.00	22.00	35.00	110	—
1862Zs VL	—	14.00	16.00	22.00	90.00	—
1863Zs VL	—	14.00	16.00	22.00	90.00	—
1863Zs MO	—	14.00	16.00	22.00	90.00	—
1864/3Zs VL	—	16.00	22.00	35.00	110	—
1864Zs VL	—	14.00	16.00	22.00	90.00	—
1864Zs MO	—	16.00	22.00	35.00	110	—
1865/4Zs MO	—	200	450	800	1,550	—
1865Zs MO	—	150	300	600	1,250	—
1866Zs VL	—	—	—	—	—	—

Note: Contemporary counterfeit

Date	Mintage	F	VF	XF	Unc	BU
1867Zs JS Rare	—	—	—	—	—	—
1868Zs JS	—	14.00	16.00	22.00	90.00	—
1868Zs YH	—	14.00	16.00	22.00	90.00	—
1869Zs YH	—	14.00	16.00	22.00	90.00	—
1870Zs YH Rare	—	—	—	—	—	—
1873Zs YH	—	14.00	16.00	22.00	90.00	—
1874Zs YH	—	14.00	16.00	22.00	90.00	—
1874Zs JA/YA	—	14.00	16.00	22.00	90.00	—
1874Zs JA	—	14.00	16.00	22.00	90.00	—
1875Zs JA	—	14.00	16.00	22.00	90.00	—
1876Zs JA	—	14.00	16.00	22.00	90.00	—
1876Zs JS	—	14.00	16.00	22.00	90.00	—
1877Zs JS	2,700,000	14.00	16.00	22.00	90.00	—
1878Zs JS	2,310,000	14.00	16.00	2.00	90.00	—
1879/8Zs JS	—	18.00	22.00	35.00	110	—
1879Zs JS	—	14.00	16.00	22.00	90.00	—
1880Zs JS	—	14.00	16.00	22.00	90.00	—
1881Zs JS	5,592,000	14.00	16.00	22.00	90.00	—
1882/1Zs JS	2,485,000	18.00	22.00	35.00	110	—
1882Zs JS Straight J	Inc. above	14.00	16.00	22.00	90.00	—
1882Zs JS Full J	Inc. above	14.00	16.00	22.00	90.00	—
1883/2Zs JS	2,563,000	18.00	22.00	35.00	110	—
1883Zs JS	Inc. above	14.00	16.00	22.00	90.00	—
1884Zs JS	—	14.00	16.00	22.00	90.00	—
1885Zs JS	2,252,000	14.00	16.00	22.00	90.00	—
1886/5Zs JS	5,303,000	18.00	22.00	35.00	110	—
1886/8Zs JS	Inc. above	18.00	22.00	35.00	110	—
1886Zs JS	Inc. above	14.00	16.00	22.00	90.00	—
1886Zs FZ	Inc. above	14.00	16.00	22.00	90.00	—
1887Zs FZ	4,733,000	14.00	16.00	22.00	90.00	—
1887Z FZ	Inc. above	20.00	30.00	50.00	110	—
1888/7Zs FZ	5,132,000	16.00	18.00	25.00	95.00	—
1888Zs FZ	Inc. above	14.00	16.00	22.00	90.00	—
1889Zs FZ	4,344,000	14.00	16.00	22.00	90.00	—
1890Zs FZ	3,887,000	14.00	16.00	22.00	90.00	—
1891Zs FZ	4,114,000	14.00	16.00	22.00	90.00	—
1892/1Zs FZ	4,238,000	16.00	18.00	25.00	95.00	—
1892Zs FZ Narrow date	Inc. above	14.00	16.00	22.00	90.00	—
1892Zs FZ Wide date	—	14.00	16.00	22.00	90.00	—
1893Zs FZ	3,872,000	14.00	16.00	22.00	90.00	—
1894Zs FZ	3,081,000	14.00	16.00	22.00	90.00	—
1895Zs FZ	4,718,000	14.00	16.00	22.00	90.00	—
1896Zs FZ	4,226,000	14.00	16.00	22.00	90.00	—
1897Zs FZ	4,877,000	14.00	16.00	22.00	90.00	—

KM# 377.10   8 REALES
27.0700 g., 0.9030 Silver 0.7859 oz. ASW **Obv:** Facing
eagle, snake in beak **Obv. Legend:** REPUBLICA
MEXICANA. **Rev:** Radiant cap **Mint:** Mexico City **Note:**
Varieties exist. 1874 CP is a die struck counterfeit.

Date	Mintage	F	VF	XF	Unc	BU
1824Mo JM Round tail	—	75.00	125	250	500	—
1824Mo JM Square tail	—	75.00	125	250	500	—
1825Mo JM	—	25.00	40.00	75.00	200	—
1826/5Mo JM	—	25.00	40.00	75.00	200	—
1826Mo JM	—	20.00	30.00	55.00	165	—
1827Mo JM	—	25.00	35.00	60.00	175	—
Note: Medal alignment						
1827Mo JM	—	25.00	35.00	60.00	175	—
Note: Coin alignment						
1828Mo JM	—	30.00	60.00	100	250	—
1829Mo JM	—	20.00	30.00	90.00	220	—
1830/20Mo JM	—	35.00	5.00	150	300	—
1830Mo JM	—	30.00	50.00	90.00	220	—
1831Mo JM	—	30.00	50.00	100	240	—
1832/1Mo JM	—	25.00	40.00	65.00	180	—
1832Mo JM	—	20.00	30.00	55.00	165	—
1833Mo MJ	—	25.00	40.00	80.00	200	—
1833Mo ML	—	450	650	950	2,000	—
1834/3Mo ML	—	25.00	35.00	60.00	175	—
1834Mo ML	—	20.00	30.00	55.00	165	—
1835Mo ML Narrow date	—	20.00	30.00	55.00	165	—
1835Mo ML Wide date	—	20.00	30.00	55.00	165	—
1836Mo ML	—	50.00	100	150	325	—
1836Mo ML/MF	—	50.00	100	150	325	—
1836Mo MF	—	30.00	50.00	90.00	220	—
1836Mo MF/ML	—	35.00	60.00	100	240	—
1837/6Mo ML	—	30.00	50.00	80.00	200	—
1837/6Mo MM	—	30.00	50.00	80.00	200	—
1837/6Mo MM/ML	—	30.00	50.00	80.00	200	—
1837/6Mo MM/MF	—	30.00	50.00	80.00	200	—
1837Mo ML	—	30.00	50.00	80.00	200	—
1837Mo MM	—	75.00	125	175	325	—
1838Mo MM	—	30.00	50.00	80.00	200	—
1838Mo ML	—	20.00	35.00	60.00	180	—
1838Mo ML/MM	—	20.00	35.00	60.00	180	—
1839Mo ML Narrow date	—	18.00	25.00	50.00	165	—
1839Mo ML Wide date	—	18.00	25.00	50.00	165	—
1840Mo ML	—	18.00	25.00	50.00	165	—
1841Mo ML	—	18.00	25.00	45.00	150	—
1842Mo ML	—	18.00	25.00	45.00	150	—
1842Mo MM	—	18.00	25.00	45.00	150	—
1843Mo MM	—	18.00	25.00	45.00	150	—
1844Mo MF/MM	—	—	—	—	—	—
1844Mo MF	—	18.00	25.00	45.00	150	—

Date	Mintage	F	VF	XF	Unc	BU
1845/4Mo MF	—	18.00	25.00	45.00	150	—
1845Mo MF	—	18.00	25.00	45.00	150	—
1846/5Mo MF	—	18.00	25.00	50.00	165	—
1846Mo MF	—	18.00	25.00	50.00	165	—
1847/6Mo MF	—	2,000	3,550	—	—	—
1847Mo MF	—	1,500	2,750	5,000	7,500	—
1847Mo RC	—	20.00	30.00	55.00	165	—
1847Mo RC/MF	—	18.00	25.00	45.00	150	—
1848Mo GC	—	18.00	25.00	45.00	150	—
1849/8Mo GC	—	20.00	35.00	60.00	180	—
1849Mo GC	—	18.00	25.00	45.00	150	—
1850/40Mo GC	—	25.00	50.00	100	240	—
1850/49Mo GC	—	25.00	50.00	100	240	—
1850Mo GC	—	20.00	40.00	75.00	200	—
1851Mo GC	—	20.00	40.00	60.00	175	—
1852Mo GC	—	20.00	40.00	75.00	200	—
1853Mo GC	—	18.00	25.00	50.00	160	—
1854Mo GC	—	16.00	18.00	30.00	125	—
1855Mo GC	—	20.00	35.00	65.00	180	—
1855Mo GF	—	16.00	18.00	30.00	125	—
1855Mo GF/GC	—	16.00	18.00	30.00	125	—
1856/4Mo GF	—	18.00	25.00	45.00	145	—
1856/5Mo GF	—	18.00	25.00	45.00	145	—
1856Mo GF	—	16.00	18.00	30.00	125	—
1857Mo GF	—	14.00	18.00	30.00	125	—
1858Mo FH Narrow date	—	14.00	18.00	30.00	125	—
1858/7Mo FH/GF	—	14.00	18.00	30.00	125	—
1858Mo FH Wide date	—	14.00	18.00	30.00	125	—
1859Mo FH	—	14.00	18.00	30.00	125	—
1859/8Mo FH	—	25.00	50.00	100	240	—
1860/59Mo FH	—	18.00	20.00	30.00	125	—
1860Mo FH	—	14.00	18.00	30.00	125	—
1860Mo TH	—	16.00	18.00	40.00	145	—
1861Mo TH	—	16.00	18.00	40.00	145	—
1861Mo CH	—	14.00	18.00	22.00	90.00	—
1862Mo CH	—	14.00	18.00	22.00	90.00	—
1863Mo CH	—	14.00	18.00	22.00	90.00	—
1863Mo CH/TH	—	14.00	18.00	22.00	90.00	—
1863Mo TH	—	14.00	18.00	22.00	90.00	—
1867Mo CH	—	14.00	18.00	22.00	90.00	—
1867Mo CH/TH	—	20.00	45.00	70.00	185	—
1868Mo CH	—	14.00	18.00	22.00	90.00	—
1868Mo PH	—	14.00	18.00	22.00	90.00	—
1868Mo CH/PH	—	14.00	18.00	22.00	90.00	—
1868Mo PH Narrow date	—	14.00	18.00	22.00	90.00	—
1868Mo PH Wide date	—	14.00	18.00	22.00	90.00	—
1869Mo CH	—	14.00	18.00	22.00	—	—
1873Mo MH	—	14.00	18.00	22.00	90.00	—
1873Mo MH/HH	—	16.00	18.00	25.00	95.00	—
1874/69Mo MH	—	20.00	45.00	70.00	185	—
1874Mo MH	—	16.00	18.00	25.00	95.00	—
1874Mo BH/MH	—	16.00	18.00	25.00	95.00	—
1874Mo BH	—	16.00	18.00	25.00	95.00	—
1875Mo BH	—	14.00	18.00	22.00	90.00	—
1876/4Mo BH	—	16.00	18.00	25.00	95.00	—
1876/5Mo BH	—	16.00	18.00	25.00	95.00	—
1876Mo BH	—	14.00	18.00	22.00	90.00	—
1877Mo MH	898,000	14.00	18.00	22.00	90.00	—
1877Mo MH/BH	Inc. above	16.00	18.00	25.00	95.00	—
1878Mo MH	2,154,000	14.00	18.00	22.00	90.00	—
1879/8Mo MH	—	14.00	18.00	22.00	95.00	—
1879Mo MH	—	14.00	18.00	22.00	90.00	—
1880/79Mo MH	—	18.00	20.00	30.00	100	—
1880Mo MH	—	14.00	18.00	22.00	90.00	—
1881Mo MH	5,712,000	14.00	18.00	22.00	90.00	—
1882/1Mo MH	2,746,000	16.00	18.00	22.00	90.00	—
1882Mo MH	Inc. above	14.00	18.00	22.00	90.00	—
1883/2Mo MH	2,726,000	16.00	18.00	25.00	95.00	—
1883Mo MH Narrow date	Inc. above	14.00	18.00	22.00	90.00	—
1883Mo MH Wide date	—	14.00	18.00	22.00	90.00	—
1884/3Mo MH	—	18.00	20.00	30.00	100	—
1884Mo MH	—	14.00	18.00	22.00	90.00	—
1885Mo MH	3,649,000	14.00	18.00	22.00	90.00	—
1886Mo MH	7,558,000	14.00	16.00	20.00	90.00	—

Date	Mintage	F	VF	XF	Unc	BU
1887Mo MH	7,681,000	14.00	16.00	20.00	90.00	—
1888Mo MH Narrow date	7,179,000	14.00	16.00	20.00	90.00	—
1888Mo MH Wide date	—	14.00	16.00	20.00	90.00	—
1889Mo MH	7,332,000	14.00	18.00	22.00	90.00	—
1890Mo MH Narrow date	7,412,000	14.00	16.00	20.00	90.00	—
1890Mo AM Wide date	—	14.00	16.00	20.00	90.00	—
1890Mo AM	Inc. above	14.00	16.00	20.00	90.00	—
1891Mo AM	8,076,000	14.00	16.00	20.00	90.00	—
1892Mo AM	9,392,000	14.00	16.00	20.00	90.00	—
1893Mo AM	10,773,000	14.00	16.00	20.00	90.00	—
1894Mo AM	12,394,000	14.00	16.00	20.00	90.00	—
1895Mo AM	10,474,000	14.00	16.00	20.00	90.00	—
1895Mo AB	Inc. above	14.00	16.00	20.00	90.00	—
1896Mo AB	9,327,000	14.00	16.00	20.00	90.00	—
1896Mo AM	Inc. above	14.00	16.00	20.00	90.00	—
1897Mo AM	8,621,000	14.00	16.00	20.00	90.00	—

KM# 377.1 8 REALES
27.0700 g., 0.9030 Silver 0.7859 oz. ASW **Obv:** Facing
eagle, snake in beak **Obv. Legend:** REPUBLICA
MEXICANA. **Rev:** Radiant cap **Mint:** Real de Catorce

Date	Mintage	F	VF	XF	Unc	BU
1863Ce ME	—	425	700	1,350	3,000	—
1863Ce /PI ML/MC	—	425	750	1,500	3,250	—

KM# 377.2 8 REALES
27.0700 g., 0.9030 Silver 0.7859 oz. ASW **Obv:** Facing
eagle, snake in beak **Obv. Legend:** REPUBLICA
MEXICANA. **Rev:** Radiant cap **Mint:** Chihuahua **Note:**
Varieties exist.

Date	Mintage	F	VF	XF	Unc	BU
1831Ca MR	—	1,000	1,750	2,250	3,250	—
1832Ca MR	—	125	200	300	600	—
1833Ca MR	—	250	550	1,000	—	—
1834Ca MR	—	300	600	1,150	—	—
1834Ca AM	—	350	500	700	—	—
1835Ca AM	—	150	250	475	900	—
1836Ca AM	—	100	200	300	600	—
1837Ca AM	—	550	1,150	—	—	—
1838Ca AM	—	100	200	300	600	—
1839Ca RG	—	750	1,250	2,500	—	—
1840Ca RG	—	300	500	800	1,500	—
Note: 1 dot after date						
1840Ca RG	—	300	500	800	1,500	—
Note: 3 dots after date						
1841Ca RG	—	50.00	100	150	300	—
1842Ca RG	—	25.00	40.00	75.00	150	—
1843Ca RG	—	40.00	80.00	125	250	—
1844/1Ca RG	—	35.00	70.00	100	200	—
1844Ca RG	—	25.00	40.00	75.00	160	—
1845Ca RG	—	25.00	40.00	75.00	160	—
1846Ca RG	—	30.00	60.00	100	250	—
1847Ca RG	—	40.00	80.00	125	250	—
1848Ca RG	—	35.00	70.00	125	250	—
1849Ca RG	—	30.00	60.00	100	200	—
1850/40Ca RG	—	40.00	80.00	125	250	—
1850Ca RG	—	30.00	60.00	100	200	—
1851/41Ca RG	—	100	200	300	500	—
1851Ca RG	—	150	250	400	750	—
1852/42Ca RG	—	150	250	400	750	—
1852Ca RG	—	150	250	400	750	—
1853/43Ca RG	—	150	250	400	750	—
1853Ca RG	—	150	250	350	700	—
1854/44Ca RG	—	100	200	300	500	—
1854Ca RG	—	50.00	100	150	300	—
1855/45Ca RG	—	100	200	350	650	—
1855Ca RG	—	50.00	100	150	300	—
1856/45Ca RG	—	275	450	750	1,250	—
1856/5Ca RG	—	400	700	1,500	3,500	—
1857Ca JC/RG	—	40.00	80.00	125	250	—
1857Ca JC	—	50.00	100	150	250	—
1858Ca JC	—	35.00	70.00	125	250	—
1858Ca BA	—	2,000	3,500	—	—	—
1859Ca JC	—	40.00	80.00	125	250	—
1860Ca JC	—	20.00	40.00	90.00	175	—
1861Ca JC	—	18.00	25.00	55.00	135	—
1862Ca JC	—	18.00	25.00	55.00	135	—
1863Ca JC	—	20.00	35.00	75.00	150	—
1864Ca JC	—	20.00	35.00	75.00	150	—
1865Ca JC	—	100	200	350	600	—
1865Ca FP	—	1,275	2,150	3,250	—	—
1866Ca JC	—	750	1,150	2,250	—	—
1866Ca FP	—	1,000	2,000	3,250	5,000	—
1866Ca JG	—	850	1,650	2,750	4,250	—
1867Ca JG	—	100	200	350	600	—
1868Ca JG	—	75.00	150	250	400	—
1868Ca MM	—	65.00	125	200	350	—
1869Ca MM	—	20.00	35.00	65.00	145	—
1870Ca MM	—	20.00	35.00	65.00	145	—
1871/0Ca MM	—	18.00	25.00	55.00	135	—
1871Ca MM	—	18.00	25.00	55.00	135	—
1871Ca MM	—	20.00	35.00	65.00	145	—
Note: Known with first M over inverted M and second M over inverted M						
1873/5Ca MM	—	20.00	35.00	65.00	145	—
1873Ca MM	—	20.00	35.00	65.00	145	—
1873Ca MM/T	—	18.00	25.00	55.00	135	—
1874Ca MM	—	16.00	18.00	30.00	110	—
1875Ca MM	—	16.00	18.00	30.00	110	—
1876Ca MM	—	16.00	18.00	30.00	110	—
1877Ca EA E/G	—	20.00	40.00	85.00	200	—
1877Ca EA	472,000	20.00	40.00	85.00	200	—
1877Ca GR	Inc. above	25.00	45.00	65.00	150	—
1877Ca JM	Inc. above	16.00	18.00	30.00	110	—
1877Ca AV	Inc. above	100	200	350	750	—
1878Ca AV	439,000	16.00	18.00	25.00	90.00	—
1879Ca AV	—	16.00	18.00	25.00	90.00	—
1880Ca AV	—	200	350	600	1,250	—
1880Ca PM	—	500	800	1,250	2,500	—
1880Ca MG	—	16.00	18.00	25.00	110	—

Date	Mintage	F	VF	XF	Unc	BU
Note: Normal initials						
1880Ca MG	—	16.00	18.00	25.00	110	—
Note: Tall initials						
1880Ca MM	—	16.00	18.00	25.00	110	—
1881Ca MG	1,085,000	14.00	16.00	22.00	90.00	—
1882Ca MG	779,000	14.00	16.00	22.00	90.00	—
1882Ca MM	Inc. above	14.00	16.00	22.00	90.00	—
1882Ca MM	Inc. above	20.00	45.00	100	175	—
Note: Second M over sideways M						
1883Ca MM	818,000	—	—	—	—	—
Note: Sideways M						
1883/2Ca MM/G	—	16.00	18.00	30.00	95.00	—
1883Ca MM	Inc. above	14.00	16.00	22.00	90.00	—
1884/3Ca MM	—	16.00	18.00	30.00	90.00	—
1884Ca MM	—	14.00	16.00	22.00	90.00	—
1885/4Ca MM	1,345,000	18.00	25.00	55.00	135	—
1885/6Ca MM	Inc. above	18.00	25.00	55.00	135	—
1885Ca MM	Inc. above	14.00	16.00	22.00	90.00	—
1886Ca MM	2,483,000	14.00	16.00	22.00	90.00	—
1887Ca MM	2,625,000	14.00	16.00	22.00	90.00	—
1888/7Ca MM	2,434,000	18.00	25.00	65.00	145	—
1888Ca MM	Inc. above	14.00	16.00	22.00	90.00	—
1889Ca MM	2,681,000	14.00	16.00	22.00	90.00	—
1890/89Ca MM	—	18.00	25.00	55.00	135	—
1890Ca MM	2,137,000	14.00	16.00	22.00	90.00	—
1891/0Ca MM	2,268,000	18.00	25.00	55.00	135	—
1891Ca MM	Inc. above	14.00	16.00	22.00	95.00	—
1892Ca MM	2,527,000	14.00	16.00	22.00	90.00	—
1893Ca MM	2,632,000	14.00	16.00	22.00	90.00	—
1894Ca MM	2,642,000	14.00	16.00	22.00	90.00	—
1895Ca MM	1,112,000	14.00	16.00	22.00	90.00	—

KM# 378.2 1/2 ESCUDO
1.6900 g., 0.8750 Gold 0.0475 oz. AGW **Obv:** Facing eagle, snake in beak **Obv. Legend:** REPUBLICA MEXICANA **Rev:** Hand holding cap on stick, open book **Rev. Legend:** LIBERTAD... **Mint:** Guadalajara

Date	Mintage	VG	F	VF	XF	Unc
1825Ga FS	—	55.00	70.00	120	210	—
1829Ga FS	—	55.00	70.00	120	210	—
1831Ga FS	—	55.00	70.00	120	210	—
1834Ga FS	—	55.00	70.00	120	210	—
1835Ga FS	—	55.00	70.00	120	210	—
1837Ga JG	—	55.00	70.00	120	210	—
1838Ga JG	—	55.00	70.00	120	210	—
1839Ga JG	—	—	—	—	—	—
1840Ga MC Unique	—	—	—	—	—	—
1842Ga JG	—	—	—	—	—	—
1847Ga JG	—	55.00	70.00	120	210	—
1850Ga JG	—	55.00	80.00	150	270	—
1852Ga JG	—	48.00	80.00	90.00	180	—
1859Ga JG	—	55.00	70.00	120	210	—
1861Ga JG	—	48.00	65.00	90.00	180	—

KM# 378.3 1/2 ESCUDO
1.6900 g., 0.8750 Gold 0.0475 oz. AGW **Obv:** Facing eagle, snake in beak **Obv. Legend:** REPUBLICA MEXICANA. **Rev:** Hand holding cap on stick, open book **Rev. Legend:** LIBERTAD... **Mint:** Guadalupe y Calvo

Date	Mintage	VG	F	VF	XF	Unc
1846GC MP	—	60.00	90.00	120	210	—
1847GC MP	—	60.00	90.00	120	210	550
1848/7GC MP	—	60.00	90.00	120	240	775

Date	Mintage	VG	F	VF	XF	Unc
1850GC MP	—	60.00	90.00	120	210	—
1851GC MP	—	60.00	90.00	120	210	—
Revised eagle						

KM# 378.4 1/2 ESCUDO
1.6900 g., 0.8750 Gold 0.0475 oz. AGW **Obv:** Facing eagle, snake in beak **Rev:** Hand holding cap on stick, open book **Mint:** Guanajuato

Date	Mintage	VG	F	VF	XF	Unc
1845Go PM	—	42.00	55.00	80.00	150	—
1849Go PF	—	42.00	60.00	110	210	750
1851/41Go PF	—	42.00	60.00	80.00	150	—
1851Go PF	—	42.00	55.00	80.00	150	—
1852Go PF/FF	—	—	—	—	—	—
1852Go PF	—	42.00	55.00	80.00	150	—
1853Go PF	—	42.00	55.00	80.00	150	—
1855Go PF	—	42.00	60.00	95.00	180	—
1857Go PF	—	42.00	55.00	80.00	150	—
1858/7Go PF	—	42.00	55.00	80.00	150	—
1859Go PF	—	42.00	55.00	80.00	150	—
1860Go PF	—	42.00	55.00	80.00	150	—
1861Go PF	—	42.00	55.00	80.00	150	—
1862/1Go YE	—	42.00	55.00	80.00	150	—
1863Go PF	—	42.00	60.00	95.00	180	—
1863Go YF	—	42.00	55.00	80.00	150	—

KM# 378.5 1/2 ESCUDO
1.6900 g., 0.8750 Gold 0.0475 oz. AGW **Obv:** Facing eagle, snake in beak **Obv. Legend:** REPUBLICA MEXICANA. **Rev:** Hand holding cap on stick, open book **Rev. Legend:** LIBERTAD... **Mint:** Mexico City

Date	Mintage	VG	F	VF	XF	Unc
1825/1Mo JM	—	60.00	90.00	150	240	—
1825/4Mo JM	—	60.00	90.00	150	240	—
1825Mo JM	—	42.00	60.00	95.00	180	425
1827/6Mo JM	—	42.00	60.00	95.00	180	—
1827Mo JM	—	42.00	60.00	95.00	180	425
1829Mo JM	—	42.00	60.00	95.00	180	—
1831/0Mo JM	—	42.00	60.00	95.00	180	—
1831Mo JM	—	42.00	55.00	80.00	150	—
1832Mo	—	42.00	55.00	80.00	150	—
1833Mo MJ	—	42.00	60.00	110	210	550
Note: Olive and oak branches reversed						
1834Mo ML	—	42.00	55.00	90.00	180	475
1835Mo ML	—	42.00	55.00	95.00	180	—
1838Mo ML	—	42.00	60.00	110	210	—
1839Mo ML	—	42.00	60.00	110	210	—
1840Mo ML	—	42.00	55.00	80.00	150	—
1841Mo ML	—	42.00	55.00	80.00	150	—
1842Mo ML	—	42.00	55.00	95.00	180	—
1842Mo MM	—	42.00	55.00	95.00	180	—
1843Mo MM	—	42.00	55.00	80.00	150	—
1844Mo MF	—	42.00	55.00	80.00	150	300
1845Mo MF	—	42.00	55.00	80.00	150	—
1846/5Mo MF	—	42.00	55.00	80.00	150	—
1846Mo MF	—	42.00	55.00	80.00	150	—
1848Mo GC	—	42.00	60.00	110	210	550
1850Mo GC	—	42.00	55.00	80.00	150	—
1851Mo GC	—	42.00	55.00	80.00	150	—
1852Mo GC	—	42.00	55.00	80.00	150	—
1853Mo GC	—	48.00	70.00	120	240	775
1854Mo GC	—	42.00	55.00	80.00	150	—
1855Mo GF	—	42.00	55.00	90.00	180	425
1856/4Mo GF	—	42.00	55.00	80.00	150	—
1857Mo GF	—	42.00	55.00	80.00	150	—
1858/7Mo FH/GF	—	42.00	60.00	90.00	180	—
1858Mo FH	—	42.00	55.00	80.00	150	—
1859Mo FH	—	42.00	55.00	80.00	150	—
1860/59Mo FH	—	42.00	55.00	80.00	150	300
1861Mo CH/FH	—	42.00	55.00	95.00	180	—
1862Mo CH	—	42.00	55.00	80.00	150	240
1863/57Mo CH/GF	—	42.00	55.00	80.00	150	300
1868/58Mo PH	—	42.00	55.00	95.00	180	—
1869/59Mo CH	—	42.00	55.00	95.00	180	—

KM# 378.6   1/2 ESCUDO
1.6900 g., 0.8750 Gold 0.0475 oz. AGW **Obv:** Facing eagle, snake in beak **Obv. Legend:** REPUBLICA MEXICANA. **Rev:** Hand holding cap on stick, open book **Rev. Legend:** LIBERTAD... **Mint:** Zacatecas

Date	Mintage	VG	F	VF	XF	Unc
1860Zs VL	—	48.00	60.00	90.00	180	—
1862/1Zs VL	—	48.00	60.00	90.00	180	—
1862Zs VL	—	42.00	55.00	80.00	150	—

KM# 378   1/2 ESCUDO
1.6900 g., 0.8750 Gold 0.0475 oz. AGW **Obv:** Facing eagle, snake in beak **Obv. Legend:** REPUBLICA MEXICANA **Rev:** Hand holding cap on stick, open book **Rev. Legend:** LIBERTAD... **Mint:** Culiacan

Date	Mintage	VG	F	VF	XF	Unc
1848C CE	—	48.00	60.00	90.00	180	350
1853C CE	—	48.00	60.00	90.00	180	—
1854C CE	—	48.00	60.00	90.00	180	—
Revised eagle						

Note: Dates 1854-1870 of this type display the revised eagle

Date	Mintage	VG	F	VF	XF	Unc
1856C CE	—	60.00	120	180	300	—
1857C CE	—	48.00	60.00	90.00	180	—
1859C CE	—	48.00	60.00	90.00	180	—
1860C CE	—	48.00	60.00	90.00	180	—
1862C CE	—	48.00	60.00	90.00	150	—
1863C CE	—	48.00	60.00	90.00	150	350
1866C CE	—	48.00	60.00	90.00	150	—
1867C CE	—	48.00	60.00	90.00	150	300
1870C CE	—	90.00	180	325	550	—

KM# 378.1   1/2 ESCUDO
1.6900 g., 0.8750 Gold 0.0475 oz. AGW **Obv:** Facing eagle, snake in beak **Rev:** Hand holding cap on stick, open book **Mint:** Durango

Date	Mintage	VG	F	VF	XF	Unc
1833Do RM/RL	—	48.00	60.00	90.00	180	—
1834/1Do RM	—	48.00	60.00	90.00	180	—
1834/3Do RM	—	48.00	60.00	90.00	180	—
1835/2Do RM	—	48.00	60.00	90.00	180	—
1835/3Do RM	—	48.00	60.00	90.00	180	—
1835/4Do RM	—	48.00	60.00	90.00	180	—
1836/5/4Do RM/L	—	55.00	70.00	120	210	550
1836/4Do RM	—	48.00	60.00	90.00	180	—
1837Do RM	—	48.00	60.00	90.00	180	—
1838Do RM	—	55.00	70.00	120	210	—
1843Do RM	—	55.00	70.00	120	210	—
1844/33Do RM	—	55.00	70.00	120	210	—
1844/33Do R./RL	—	80.00	150	325	550	—
1845Do CM	—	55.00	70.00	120	210	—
1846Do RM	—	55.00	70.00	120	210	—
1848Do RM	—	55.00	70.00	120	210	—
1850/33Do JMR	—	55.00	70.00	120	210	575
1851Do JMR	—	55.00	70.00	120	240	—
1852Do JMR	—	55.00	70.00	120	210	—
1853/33Do CP	—	90.00	180	350	600	—
1853Do CP	—	60.00	85.00	180	300	650
1854Do CP	—	48.00	60.00	90.00	180	—
1855Do CP	—	48.00	60.00	90.00	180	—
1859Do CP	—	48.00	60.00	90.00	180	—
1861Do CP	—	48.00	60.00	90.00	180	—
1862Do CP	—	48.00	60.00	90.00	180	—
1864Do LT	—	90.00	150	300	475	—

KM# 379   ESCUDO
3.3800 g., 0.8750 Gold 0.0951 oz. AGW **Obv:** Facing eagle, snake in beak **Rev:** Hand holding cap on stick, open book **Mint:** Culiacan

Date	Mintage	VG	F	VF	XF	Unc
1846C CE	—	100	120	240	425	—
1847C CE	—	80.00	90.00	150	210	—
1848C CE	—	80.00	90.00	150	210	850
1849/8C CE	—	85.00	120	180	270	—
1850C CE	—	80.00	90.00	150	210	—
1851C CE	—	85.00	120	180	270	—
1853/1C CE	—	85.00	120	180	270	—
1854C CE	—	80.00	90.00	150	210	—
1856/5/4C CE	—	85.00	120	180	270	—
1856C CE	—	80.00	90.00	150	210	—
1857/1C CE	—	85.00	120	180	270	—
1857C CE	—	80.00	90.00	150	210	—
1861C PV	—	80.00	90.00	150	210	—
1862C CE	—	80.00	90.00	150	210	—
1863C CE	—	80.00	90.00	150	210	—
1866C CE	—	80.00	90.00	150	210	—
1870C CE	—	80.00	90.00	150	210	—

KM# 379.1   ESCUDO
3.3800 g., 0.8750 Gold 0.0951 oz. AGW **Obv:** Facing eagle, snake in beak **Obv. Legend:** REPUBLICA MEXICANA. **Rev:** Hand holding cap on stick, open book **Rev. Legend:** LIBERTAD... **Mint:** Durango

Date	Mintage	VG	F	VF	XF	Unc
1832Do R.L.	—	—	—	—	—	—
1833/2Do RM/R.L.	—	100	150	240	350	—
1834Do RM	—	85.00	120	180	300	—
1835Do RM	—	—	—	—	—	—
1836Do RM/RL	—	85.00	120	180	300	—
1838Do RM	—	85.00	120	180	300	—
1846/38Do RM	—	100	150	240	350	—
1850Do JMR	—	100	150	210	325	—
1851/31Do JMR	—	100	150	240	350	—
1851Do JMR	—	100	150	210	325	—
1853Do CP	—	100	150	210	325	—
1854/34Do CP	—	100	150	210	325	—
1854/44Do CP/RP	—	100	150	210	325	—
1855Do CP	—	100	150	210	325	—
1859Do CP	—	100	150	210	325	—
1861Do CP	—	100	150	210	325	—
1864Do LT/CP Rare	—	—	—	—	—	—

KM# 379.2   ESCUDO
3.3800 g., 0.8750 Gold 0.0951 oz. AGW **Obv:** Facing eagle, snake in beak **Obv. Legend:** REPUBLICA MEXICANA. **Rev:** Hand holding cap on stick, open book **Mint:** Guadalajara

Date	Mintage	VG	F	VF	XF	Unc
1825Ga FS	—	85.00	110	150	240	—
1826Ga FS	—	85.00	110	150	240	—
1829Ga FS	—	—	—	—	—	—
1831Ga FS	—	85.00	110	150	240	—
1834Ga FS	—	85.00	110	150	240	—
1835Ga JG	—	85.00	110	150	240	—
1842Ga JG/MC	—	85.00	110	150	240	—

Date	Mintage	VG	F	VF	XF	Unc
1843Ga MC	—	85.00	110	150	240	—
1847Ga JG	—	85.00	110	150	240	—
1848/7Ga JG	—	85.00	110	150	240	—
1849Ga JG	—	85.00	110	150	240	—
1850/40Ga JG	—	90.00	150	270	400	—
1850Ga JG	—	85.00	110	150	240	—
1852/1Ga JG	—	85.00	110	150	240	1,100
1856Ga JG	—	85.00	110	150	240	—
1857Ga JG	—	85.00	110	150	240	—
1859/7Ga JG	—	85.00	110	150	240	—
1860/59Ga JG	—	90.00	120	210	325	—
1860Ga	—	85.00	110	150	240	—

KM# 379.3 ESCUDO
3.3800 g., 0.8750 Gold 0.0951 oz. AGW **Obv:** Facing eagle, snake in beak **Obv. Legend:** REPUBLICA MEXICANA. **Rev:** Hand holding cap on stick, open book **Mint:** Guadalupe y Calvo

Date	Mintage	VG	F	VF	XF	Unc
1844GC MP	—	100	120	210	300	—
1845GC MP	—	100	120	210	300	—
1846GC MP	—	100	120	210	300	—
1847GC MP	—	100	120	210	300	—
1848GC MP	—	100	120	210	300	—
1849GC MP	—	100	120	210	300	—
1850GC MP	—	130	180	300	600	2,400
1851GC MP	—	100	120	210	300	—
Revised eagle						

KM# 379.4 ESCUDO
3.3800 g., 0.8750 Gold 0.0951 oz. AGW **Obv:** Facing eagle, snake in beak **Rev:** Hand holding cap on stick, open book **Mint:** Guanajuato

Date	Mintage	VG	F	VF	XF	Unc
1845Go PM	—	85.00	95.00	150	240	—
1849Go PF	—	85.00	95.00	150	240	—
1851Go PF	—	85.00	95.00	150	240	—
1853Go PF	—	85.00	95.00	150	240	—
1860Go PF	—	100	150	240	350	—
1862Go YE	—	85.00	95.00	150	240	725

KM# 379.5 ESCUDO
3.3800 g., 0.8750 Gold 0.0951 oz. AGW **Obv:** Facing eagle, snake in beak **Obv. Legend:** REPUBLICA MEXICANA. **Rev:** Hand holding cap on stick, open book **Mint:** Mexico City

Date	Mintage	VG	F	VF	XF	Unc
1825Mo JM/FM	—	80.00	85.00	120	180	425
1825Mo JM	—	80.00	85.00	120	180	—
1827/6Mo JM	—	80.00	85.00	120	180	—
1827Mo JM	—	80.00	85.00	120	180	—
1830/29Mo JM	—	80.00	85.00	120	180	—
1831Mo JM	—	80.00	90.00	150	210	650
1832Mo JM	—	80.00	90.00	150	210	—
1833Mo MJ	—	80.00	85.00	120	180	—
1834Mo ML	—	80.00	90.00	150	210	—
1841Mo ML	—	80.00	90.00	150	210	—
1843Mo MM	—	80.00	90.00	150	210	1,050
1845Mo MF	—	80.00	85.00	120	180	—
1846/5Mo MF	—	80.00	85.00	120	180	—
1848Mo GC	—	80.00	90.00	150	210	—
1850Mo GC	—	80.00	90.00	150	210	—
1856/4Mo GF	—	80.00	85.00	120	180	—
1856/5Mo GF	—	80.00	85.00	120	180	—
1856Mo GF	—	80.00	85.00	120	180	—
1858Mo FH	—	80.00	90.00	150	210	—
1859Mo FH	—	80.00	90.00	150	210	900
1860Mo TH	—	80.00	90.00	150	210	—

Date	Mintage	VG	F	VF	XF	Unc
1861Mo CH	—	80.00	90.00	150	210	1,200
1862Mo CH	—	80.00	90.00	150	210	—
1863Mo TH	—	80.00	85.00	120	180	—
1869Mo CH	—	80.00	90.00	150	210	775

KM# 379.6 ESCUDO
3.3800 g., 0.8750 Gold 0.0951 oz. AGW **Obv:** Facing eagle, snake in beak **Rev:** Hand holding cap on stick, open book **Mint:** Zacatecas **Note:** Struck at Zacatecas Mint, mint mark Zs.

Date	Mintage	VG	F	VF	XF	Unc
1853Zs OM	—	130	150	240	350	—
1860/59Zs VL V is inverted A	—	100	120	240	425	—
1860Zs VL	—	100	120	180	240	—
1862Zs VL	—	100	120	180	240	—

KM# 380.3 2 ESCUDOS
6.7700 g., 0.8750 Gold 0.1904 oz. AGW **Obv:** Facing eagle, snake in beak **Obv. Legend:** REPUBLICA MEXICANA. **Rev:** Hand holding cap on stick, open book **Rev. Legend:** LIBERTAD... **Mint:** Guadalajara

Date	Mintage	VG	F	VF	XF	Unc
1835Ga FS	—	165	190	270	400	—
1836/5Ga JG	—	190	240	475	600	—
1839/5Ga JG	—	—	—	—	—	—
1839Ga JG	—	165	180	240	350	—
1840Ga MC	—	165	180	240	350	—
1841Ga MC	—	165	200	300	475	—
1847/6Ga JG	—	165	190	270	350	—
1848/7Ga JG	—	165	190	270	350	—
1850/40Ga JG	—	165	180	240	350	—
1851Ga JG	—	165	180	240	350	—
1852Ga JG	—	165	190	270	400	—
1853Ga JG	—	165	180	240	350	—
1854/2Ga JG	—	—	—	—	—	—
1858Ga JG	—	165	180	240	350	—
1859/8Ga JG	—	165	190	270	350	—
1859Ga JG	—	165	190	270	350	—
1860/50Ga JG	—	165	190	270	350	—
1860Ga JG	—	165	190	270	350	900
1861/59Ga JG	—	165	180	240	350	—
1861/0Ga JG	—	165	180	240	350	—
1863/2Ga JG	—	165	190	270	350	950
1863/1Ga JG	—	165	180	240	350	—
1870Ga IC	—	165	180	240	350	—

KM# 380.4 2 ESCUDOS
6.7700 g., 0.8750 Gold 0.1904 oz. AGW **Obv:** Facing eagle, snake in beak **Rev:** Hand holding cap on stick, open book **Mint:** Guadalupe y Calvo

Date	Mintage	VG	F	VF	XF	Unc
1844GC MP	—	300	550	1,200	2,400	—
1845GC MP	—	900	1,500	2,400	3,600	—
1846GC MP	—	900	1,500	2,400	3,600	—
1847GC MP	—	600	1,200	2,400	3,600	—

Date	Mintage	VG	F	VF	XF	Unc
1848GC MP	—	195	240	475	725	—
1849GC MP	—	900	1,500	—	—	—
1850GC MP	—	300	550	1,200	2,400	—

KM# 380.5 2 ESCUDOS
6.7700 g., 0.8750 Gold 0.1904 oz. AGW **Obv:** Facing eagle, snake in beak **Rev:** Hand holding cap on stick, open book
Mint: Guanajuato

Date	Mintage	VG	F	VF	XF	Unc
1845Go PM	—	165	190	300	475	—
1849Go PF	—	165	190	300	475	—
1853Go PF	—	195	350	775	1,200	—
1856Go PF	—	—	—	—	—	—
1859Go PF	—	195	350	775	1,200	—
1860/59Go PF	—	—	—	—	—	—
1860Go PF	—	165	190	300	475	—
1862Go YE	—	165	190	300	475	—

KM# 380 2 ESCUDOS
6.7700 g., 0.8750 Gold 0.1904 oz. AGW **Obv:** Facing eagle, snake in beak **Obv. Legend:** REPUBLICA MEXICANA. **Rev:** Hand holding cap on stick, open book **Mint:** Culiacan

Date	Mintage	VG	F	VF	XF	Unc
1846C CE	—	165	190	270	400	—
1847C CE	—	165	190	270	400	—
1848C CE	—	165	190	270	400	—
1852C CE	—	165	190	270	400	—
1854C CE	—	165	210	300	450	—
1856/4C CE	—	165	210	300	450	—
1857C CE	—	165	190	270	400	—

KM# 380.1 2 ESCUDOS
6.7700 g., 0.8750 Gold 0.1904 oz. AGW **Obv:** Facing eagle, snake in beak **Obv. Legend:** REPUBLICA MEXICANA. **Rev:** Hand holding cap on stick, open book **Rev. Legend:** LIBERTAD... **Mint:** Durango

Date	Mintage	VG	F	VF	XF	Unc
1833Do RM	—	400	550	850	1,450	—
1837/4Do RM	—	—	—	—	—	—
1837Do RM	—	—	—	—	—	—
1844Do RM	—	350	475	725	1,200	—

KM# 380.7 2 ESCUDOS
6.7700 g., 0.8750 Gold 0.1904 oz. AGW **Obv:** Facing eagle, snake in beak **Obv. Legend:** REPUBLICA MEXICANA **Rev:** Hand holding cap on stick, open book **Rev. Legend:** LIBERTAD... **Mint:** Mexico City

Date	Mintage	VG	F	VF	XF	Unc
1825Mo JM	—	165	180	240	350	—
1827/6Mo JM	—	165	180	240	350	—
1827Mo JM	—	165	180	240	350	—
1830/29Mo JM	—	165	180	240	350	—
1831Mo JM	—	165	180	240	350	—
1833Mo ML	—	165	180	240	350	—

Date	Mintage	VG	F	VF	XF	Unc
1841Mo ML	—	165	180	240	350	—
1844Mo MF	—	165	180	240	350	—
1845Mo MF	—	165	180	240	350	—
1846Mo MF	—	180	240	475	725	—
1848Mo GC	—	165	180	240	350	—
1850Mo GC	—	165	180	240	350	—
1856/5Mo GF	—	165	180	240	350	—
1856Mo GF	—	165	180	240	350	—
1858Mo FH	—	165	180	240	350	—
1859Mo FH	—	165	180	240	350	—
1861Mo TH	—	165	180	240	350	—
1861Mo CH	—	165	180	240	350	—
1862Mo CH	—	165	180	240	350	—
1863Mo TH	—	165	180	240	350	900
1868Mo PH	—	165	180	240	350	—
1869Mo CH	—	165	180	240	350	—

KM# 380.8 2 ESCUDOS
6.7700 g., 0.8750 Gold 0.1904 oz. AGW **Obv:** Facing eagle, snake in beak **Obv. Legend:** REPUBLICA MEXICANA. **Rev:** Hand holding cap on stick, open book **Rev. Legend:** LA LIBERTAD... **Mint:** Zacatecas

Date	Mintage	VG	F	VF	XF	Unc
1860Zs VL	—	180	350	725	1,450	—
1862Zs VL	—	325	600	950	1,450	—
1864Zs MO	—	180	350	725	1,450	—

KM# 380.2 2 ESCUDOS
6.7700 g., 0.8750 Gold 0.1904 oz. AGW **Obv:** Facing eagle, snake in beak **Obv. Legend:** REPUBLICA MEXICANA. **Rev:** Hand holding cap on stick, open book **Rev. Legend:** LIBERTAD... **Mint:** Estado de Mexico

Date	Mintage	VG	F	VF	XF	Unc
1828EoMo LF	—	850	1,200	2,100	3,600	—

KM# 380.6 2 ESCUDOS
6.7700 g., 0.8750 Gold 0.1904 oz. AGW **Obv:** Facing eagle, snake in beak **Rev:** Hand holding cap on stick, open book
Mint: Hermosillo

Date	Mintage	VG	F	VF	XF	Unc
1861Ho FM	—	600	1,200	1,800	2,650	—

KM# 381 4 ESCUDOS
13.5400 g., 0.8750 Gold 0.3809 oz. AGW **Obv:** Facing eagle, snake in beak **Obv. Legend:** REPUBLICA MEXICANA. **Rev:** Hand holding cap on stick, open book **Rev. Legend:** LA LIBERTAD... **Mint:** Culiacan

Date	Mintage	VG	F	VF	XF	Unc
1846C CE	—	1,450	2,050	—	—	—
1847C CE	—	475	775	1,000	1,800	—
1848C CE	—	725	1,100	1,500	2,400	—

KM# 381.1 4 ESCUDOS
13.5400 g., 0.8750 Gold 0.3809 oz. AGW **Obv:** Facing eagle, snake in beak **Obv. Legend:** REPUBLICA MEXICANA. **Rev:** Hand holding cap on stick, open book **Rev. Legend:** LA LIBERTAD.... **Mint:** Durango

Date	Mintage	VG	F	VF	XF	Unc
1832Do RM/LR Rare	—	—	—	—	—	—
1832Do RM	—	725	1,100	1,500	2,400	—
1833Do RM/RL Rare	—	—	—	—	—	—
1852Do JMR Rare	—	—	—	—	—	—

KM# 381.3 4 ESCUDOS
13.5400 g., 0.8750 Gold 0.3809 oz. AGW **Obv:** Facing eagle, snake in beak **Obv. Legend:** REPUBLICA MEXICANA **Rev:** Hand holding cap on stick, open book **Rev. Legend:** LA LIBERTAD... **Mint:** Guadalupe y Calvo

Date	Mintage	VG	F	VF	XF	Unc
1844GC MP	—	475	775	1,000	1,600	—
1845GC MP	—	425	600	850	1,200	—
1846GC MP	—	475	775	1,000	1,600	—
1848GC MP	—	475	775	1,000	1,600	—
1850GC MP	—	550	825	1,200	1,900	—

KM# 381.4 4 ESCUDOS
13.5400 g., 0.8750 Gold 0.3809 oz. AGW **Obv:** Facing eagle, snake in beak **Obv. Legend:** REPUBLICA MEXICANA. **Rev:** Hand holding cap on stick, open book **Rev. Legend:** LA LIBERTAD... **Mint:** Guanajuato

Date	Mintage	VG	F	VF	XF	Unc
1829/8Go MJ	—	350	425	550	1,000	—
1829Go JM	—	350	425	550	1,000	—
1829Go MJ	—	350	425	550	1,000	—
1831Go MJ	—	350	425	550	1,000	—
1832Go MJ	—	350	425	550	1,000	—
1833Go MJ	—	350	450	600	1,100	—
1834Go PJ	—	375	625	775	1,200	—
1835Go PJ	—	375	625	775	1,200	—
1836Go PJ	—	350	450	600	1,100	—
1837Go PJ	—	350	450	600	1,100	3,300
1838Go PJ	—	350	450	600	1,100	—
1839Go PJ	—	375	625	775	1,200	—

Date	Mintage	VG	F	VF	XF	Unc
1840Go PJ	—	350	450	650	1,200	—
1841Go PJ	—	375	625	775	1,200	—
1845Go PM	—	350	450	600	1,100	—
1847/5Go YE	—	375	625	775	1,200	—
1847Go PM	—	375	625	775	1,200	—
1849Go PF	—	375	625	775	1,200	—
1851Go PF	—	375	625	775	1,200	—
1852Go PF	—	350	450	600	1,100	—
1855Go PF	—	350	450	600	1,100	—
1857/5Go PF	—	350	450	600	1,100	—
1858/7Go PF	—	350	450	600	1,100	—
1858Go PF	—	350	450	600	1,100	—
1859/7Go PF	—	375	625	775	1,200	—
1860Go PF	—	375	675	900	1,450	—
1862Go YE	—	350	450	600	1,100	—
1863Go YF	—	350	450	600	1,100	—

KM# 381.6 4 ESCUDOS
13.5400 g., 0.8750 Gold 0.3809 oz. AGW **Obv:** Facing eagle, snake in beak **Obv. Legend:** REPUBLICA MEXICANA. **Rev:** Hand holding cap on stick, open book **Rev. Legend:** LA LIBERTAD... **Mint:** Mexico City

Date	Mintage	VG	F	VF	XF	Unc
1825Mo JM	—	350	450	625	1,150	—
1827/6Mo JM	—	350	450	600	1,100	—
1829Mo JM	—	350	500	775	1,200	—
1831Mo JM	—	350	500	775	1,200	—
1832Mo JM	—	375	675	900	1,450	—
1844Mo MF	—	350	500	775	1,200	—
1850Mo GC	—	350	500	775	1,200	—
1856Mo GF	—	350	450	600	1,100	—
1857/6Mo GF	—	350	450	600	1,100	—
1857Mo GF	—	350	450	600	1,100	—
1858Mo FH	—	350	500	775	1,200	—
1859/8Mo FH	—	350	500	775	1,200	—
1861Mo CH	—	550	1,100	1,450	2,100	—
1863Mo CH	—	350	500	775	1,200	2,400
1868Mo PH	—	350	450	600	1,100	—
1869Mo CH	—	350	450	600	1,100	1,800

KM# 381.8 4 ESCUDOS
13.5400 g., 0.8750 Gold 0.3809 oz. AGW **Obv:** Facing eagle, snake in beak **Obv. Legend:** REPUBLICA MEXICANA. **Rev:** Hand holding cap on stick, open book **Rev. Legend:** LA LIBERTAD... **Mint:** Zacatecas

Date	Mintage	VG	F	VF	XF	Unc
1860Zs VL Rare	—	—	—	—	—	—
1862Zs VL	—	900	1,500	2,700	4,500	—

Note: American Numismatic Rarities Eliasberg sale 4-05, MS-64 realized $18,400.

KM# 381.2 4 ESCUDOS
13.5400 g., 0.8750 Gold 0.3809 oz. AGW **Obv:** Facing eagle, snake in beak **Obv. Legend:** REPUBLICA MEXICANA. **Rev:** Hand holding cap on stick, open book **Rev. Legend:** LA LIBERTAD... **Mint:** Guadalajara

Date	Mintage	VG	F	VF	XF	Unc
1844Ga MC	—	600	900	1,200	1,900	—
1844Ga JG	—	475	775	1,000	1,600	—

KM# 381.5 4 ESCUDOS
13.5400 g., 0.8750 Gold 0.3809 oz. AGW **Obv:** Facing eagle, snake in beak **Rev:** Hand holding cap on stick, open book **Mint:** Hermosillo

Date	Mintage	VG	F	VF	XF	Unc
1861Ho FM	—	1,200	1,800	3,000	4,800	—

KM# 383.1 8 ESCUDOS
27.0700 g., 0.8750 Gold 0.7615 oz. AGW **Obv:** Facing eagle, snake in beak **Obv. Legend:** REPUBLICA MEXICANA **Rev:** Hand holding cap on stick, open book **Rev. Legend:** LA LIBERTAD.... **Mint:** Chihuahua

Date	Mintage	F	VF	XF	Unc	BU
1841Ca RG	—	800	1,100	1,550	2,300	—
1842Ca RG	—	725	875	1,250	1,950	—
1843Ca RG	—	725	875	1,250	1,950	—
1844Ca RG	—	725	875	1,250	1,950	—
1845Ca RG	—	725	875	1,250	1,950	—
1846Ca RG	—	950	1,800	1,900	2,600	—
1847Ca RG	—	1,450	3,650	—	—	—
1848Ca RG	—	725	875	1,250	1,950	—
1849Ca RG	—	725	875	1,250	1,950	—
1850/40Ca RG	—	725	875	1,250	1,950	—
1851/41Ca RG	—	725	875	1,250	1,950	—
1852/42Ca RG	—	725	875	1,250	1,950	—
1853/43Ca RG	—	725	875	1,250	1,950	—
1854/44Ca RG	—	725	875	1,250	1,950	—
1855/43Ca RG	—	725	875	1,250	1,950	—
1856/46Ca RG	—	750	950	1,550	2,300	—
1857Ca JC/RG	—	725	800	1,000	1,650	—
1858Ca JC	—	725	800	1,000	1,650	—
1858Ca BA/RG	—	725	800	1,000	1,650	—
1859Ca JC/RG	—	725	800	1,000	1,650	—
1860Ca JC/RG	—	725	875	1,250	1,950	—
1861Ca JC	—	725	800	1,000	1,650	—
1862Ca JC	—	725	800	1,000	1,650	—
1863Ca JC	—	875	1,450	2,200	2,950	—
1864Ca JC	—	800	1,100	1,550	2,300	—
1865Ca JC	—	1,100	2,200	3,150	4,550	—
1866Ca JC	—	725	725	1,250	1,950	—
1866Ca FP	—	950	1,800	2,500	3,250	—
1866Ca JG	—	725	875	1,250	1,950	—
1867Ca JG	—	725	800	1,000	1,650	—
1868Ca JG Concave wings	—	725	800	1,000	1,650	—
1869Ca MM Regular eagle	—	725	800	1,000	1,650	—
1870/60Ca MM	—	725	800	950	1,650	—
1871/61Ca MM	—	725	800	950	1,650	—

KM# 381.7 4 ESCUDOS
13.5400 g., 0.8750 Gold 0.3809 oz. AGW **Obv:** Facing eagle, snake in beak **Obv. Legend:** REPUBLICA MEXICANA. **Rev:** Hand holding cap on stick, open book **Rev. Legend:** LA LIBERTAD EN LA LEY... **Mint:** Oaxaca **Note:** Mint mark O, Oa.

Date	Mintage	VG	F	VF	XF	Unc
1861O FR	—	1,800	3,000	4,800	8,400	—

KM# 383 8 ESCUDOS
27.0700 g., 0.8750 Gold 0.7615 oz. AGW **Obv:** Facing eagle, snake in beak **Obv. Legend:** REPUBLICA MEXICANA **Rev:** Hand holding cap on stick, open book **Rev. Legend:** LA LIBERTAD... **Mint:** Alamos

Date	Mintage	F	VF	XF	Unc	BU
1864A PG	—	875	1,550	3,000	—	—
1866A DL	—	—	—	9,000	—	—
1868/7A DL	—	2,500	4,400	6,600	—	—
1869A DL	—	—	5,000	7,200	—	—
1870A DL	—	—	3,150	6,000	—	—
1872A AM Rare	—	—	—	—	—	—

KM# 383.2   8 ESCUDOS
27.0700 g., 0.8750 Gold 0.7615 oz. AGW **Obv:** Facing eagle, snake in beak **Obv. Legend:** REPUBLICA MEXICANA. **Rev:** Hand holding cap on stick, open book **Rev. Legend:** LA LIBERTAD... **Mint:** Culiacan

Date	Mintage	F	VF	XF	Unc	BU
1846C CE	—	725	875	1,250	2,300	—
1847C CE	—	725	800	1,000	1,650	—
1848C CE	—	725	875	1,250	2,300	—
1849C CE	—	725	800	950	1,650	—
1850C CE	—	725	800	950	1,650	—
1851C CE	—	725	800	1,000	1,650	—
1852C CE	—	725	800	1,000	1,650	—
1853/1C CE	—	725	800	950	1,550	—
1854C CE	—	725	800	950	1,550	—
1855/4C CE	—	725	725	1,250	2,300	—
1855C CE	—	725	800	1,000	1,650	—
1856C CE	—	725	800	950	1,550	—
1857C CE	—	725	800	950	1,550	—
1857C CE	—	—	—	—	—	—
Note: Without periods after C's						
1858C CE	—	725	800	950	1,550	—
1859C CE	—	725	800	950	1,550	—
1860/58C CE	—	725	800	1,000	1,650	—
1860C CE	—	725	800	1,000	1,650	—
1860C PV	—	725	800	950	1,550	—
1861C PV	—	725	800	1,000	1,650	—
1861C CE	—	725	800	1,000	1,650	—
1862C CE	—	725	800	1,000	1,650	—
1863C CE	—	725	800	1,000	1,650	—
1864C CE	—	725	800	950	1,550	—
1865C CE	—	725	800	950	1,550	—
1866/5C CE	—	725	800	950	1,550	—
1866C CE	—	725	800	950	1,550	—
1867C CB Error	—	725	800	950	1,550	—
1867C CE/CB	—	725	800	950	1,550	—
1868C CB Error	—	725	800	950	1,550	—
1869C CE	—	725	800	950	1,550	—
1870C CE	—	725	800	1,000	1,650	—

KM# 383.3   8 ESCUDOS
27.0700 g., 0.8750 Gold 0.7615 oz. AGW **Obv:** Facing eagle, snake in beak **Obv. Legend:** REPUBLICA MEXICANA **Rev:** Hand holding cap on stick, open book **Rev. Legend:** LA LIBERTAD.... **Mint:** Durango

Date	Mintage	F	VF	XF	Unc	BU
1832Do RM	—	725	2,550	2,500	3,900	—
1833Do RM/RL	—	725	800	1,000	1,650	—
1834Do RM	—	725	800	1,000	1,650	—
1835Do RM	—	725	800	1,000	1,650	—
1836Do RM/RL	—	725	800	1,000	1,650	—

Date	Mintage	F	VF	XF	Unc	BU
1836Do RM	—	725	800	1,000	1,650	—
Note: M on snake						
1837Do RM	—	725	800	1,000	1,650	—
1838/6Do RM	—	725	800	1,000	1,650	—
1838Do RM	—	725	800	1,000	1,650	—
1839Do RM	—	725	800	950	1,650	2,600
1840/30Do RM/RL	—	725	950	1,250	2,300	—
1841/0Do RM	—	725	800	950	1,650	—
1841/30Do RM	—	800	1,100	1,550	2,600	—
1841/31Do RM	—	725	800	1,000	1,650	—
1841/34Do RM	—	725	800	1,000	1,650	—
1841Do RM/RL	—	725	800	1,000	1,650	—
1842/32Do RM	—	725	800	1,000	1,650	—
1843/33Do RM	—	800	1,100	1,550	2,600	—
1843/1Do RM	—	725	800	1,000	1,650	—
1843Do RM	—	725	800	1,000	1,650	—
1844/34Do RM/RL	—	875	1,450	1,900	3,250	—
1844Do RM	—	800	1,150	1,550	2,600	—
1845/36Do RM	—	725	950	1,250	2,300	—
1845Do RM	—	725	950	1,250	2,300	—
1846Do RM	—	725	800	1,000	1,650	—
1847/37Do RM	—	725	800	1,000	1,650	—
1848/37Do RM	—	—	—	—	—	—
1848/38Do CM	—	725	800	1,000	1,650	—
1849/39Do CM	—	725	800	1,000	1,650	—
1849Do J.M.R. Rare	—	—	—	—	—	—
1850Do .JMR.	—	725	1,100	1,550	2,600	—
1851Do JMR	—	725	1,100	1,550	2,600	—
1852/1Do JMR	—	725	1,150	1,550	2,600	—
1852Do CP	—	725	1,150	1,550	2,600	—
1853Do CP	—	725	1,150	1,550	2,600	—
1854Do CP	—	725	950	1,250	2,300	—
1855/4Do CP	—	725	800	1,000	1,650	—
1855Do CP	—	725	800	1,000	1,650	—
1856Do CP	—	725	875	1,150	2,150	—
1857Do CP	—	725	800	1,000	1,650	—
Note: French style eagle, 1832-57						
1857Do CP	—	725	800	1,000	1,650	—
Note: Mexican style eagle						
1858Do CP	—	725	875	1,150	2,150	—
1859Do CP	—	725	800	1,000	1,650	—
1860/59Do CP	—	725	1,100	1,550	2,850	—
1861/0Do CP	—	725	950	1,250	2,300	—
1862/52Do CP	—	725	800	1,000	1,650	—
1862/1Do CP	—	725	800	1,000	1,650	—
1862Do CP	—	725	800	1,000	1,650	—
1863/53Do CP	—	725	800	1,000	1,650	—
1864Do LT	—	725	800	1,000	1,650	2,600
1865/4Do LT	—	875	1,450	2,050	3,600	—
1866/4Do CM	—	1,800	2,900	3,150	—	—
1866Do CM	—	725	950	1,250	2,300	—
1867/56Do CP	—	725	950	1,250	2,300	—
1867/4Do CP	—	725	800	1,000	1,650	—
1868/4Do CP/LT	—	—	—	—	—	—
1869Do CP	—	950	1,800	2,200	3,600	—
1870Do CP	—	725	950	1,250	2,300	—

KM# 383.4   8 ESCUDOS
27.0700 g., 0.8750 Gold 0.7615 oz. AGW **Obv:** Facing eagle,

snake in beak **Obv. Legend:** REPUBLICA MEXICANA **Rev:** Hand holding cap on stick, open book **Rev. Legend:** LA LIBERTAD... **Mint:** Estado de Mexico

Date	Mintage	F	VF	XF	Unc	BU
1828EoMo LF Rare	—	—	—	—	—	—
1829EoMo LF	—	4,400	6,900	10,500	—	—

KM# 383.5 8 ESCUDOS
27.0700 g., 0.8750 Gold 0.7615 oz. AGW **Obv:** Facing eagle, snake in beak **Obv. Legend:** REPUBLICA MEXICANA **Rev:** Hand holding cap on stick, open book **Rev. Legend:** LA LIBERTAD... **Mint:** Guadalajara

Date	Mintage	F	VF	XF	Unc	BU
1825Ga FS	—	875	1,450	1,550	2,300	—
1826Ga FS	—	875	1,450	1,550	2,300	—
1830Ga FS	—	875	1,450	1,550	2,300	—
1836Ga FS	—	1,100	2,200	2,500	3,900	—
1836Ga JG	—	1,450	3,650	4,400	—	—
1837Ga JG	—	1,450	3,650	4,400	—	—
1840Ga MC Rare	—	—	—	—	—	—
1841/31Ga MC	—	1,450	3,650	—	—	—
1841Ga MC	—	1,250	2,400	2,800	—	—
1842Ga JG Rare	—	4,350	6,300	—	—	—
1843Ga MC	—	—	3,650	8,100	—	—
1845Ga MC Rare	—	—	—	—	—	—
1847Ga JG	—	3,250	—	—	—	—
1849Ga JG	—	875	1,450	1,550	2,300	—
1850Ga JG	—	800	1,250	1,400	2,150	—
1851Ga JG	—	1,450	3,650	4,400	—	—
1852/1Ga JG	—	875	1,450	1,550	2,300	—
1855Ga JG	—	1,450	3,650	4,400	—	—
1856Ga JG	—	800	1,250	1,400	2,150	—
1857Ga JG	—	800	1,250	1,400	2,150	—
1861/0Ga JG	—	875	1,450	1,550	2,300	—
1861Ga JG	—	725	1,000	1,500	2,300	—
1863/1Ga JG	—	875	1,450	1,550	2,300	—
1866Ga JG	—	800	1,250	1,400	2,150	—

KM# 383.6 8 ESCUDOS
27.0700 g., 0.8750 Gold 0.7615 oz. AGW **Obv:** Facing eagle,

snake in beak **Obv. Legend:** REPUBLICA MEXICANA **Rev:** Hand holding cap on stick, open book **Rev. Legend:** LA LIBERTAD... **Mint:** Guadalupe y Calvo

Date	Mintage	F	VF	XF	Unc	BU
1844GC MP	—	800	1,100	1,550	2,600	—
1845GC MP	—	800	1,100	1,550	2,600	—
Note: Eagle's tail square						
1845GC MP	—	800	1,100	1,550	2,600	—
Note: Eagle's tail round						
1846GC MP	—	725	950	1,250	2,300	—
Note: Eagle's tail square						
1846GC MP	—	725	950	1,250	2,300	—
Note: Eagle's tail round						
1847GC MP	—	725	950	1,250	2,300	—
1848GC MP	—	800	1,100	1,550	2,600	—
1849GC MP	—	800	1,100	1,550	2,600	—
1850GC MP	—	725	950	1,250	2,300	—
1851GC MP	—	725	950	1,250	2,300	—
1852GC MP	—	800	1,100	1,550	2,600	—

KM# 383.7 8 ESCUDOS
27.0700 g., 0.8750 Gold 0.7615 oz. AGW **Obv:** Facing eagle, snake in beak **Obv. Legend:** REPUBLICA MEXICANA **Rev:** Hand holding cap on stick, open book **Rev. Legend:** LA LIBERTAD... **Mint:** Guanajuato

Date	Mintage	F	VF	XF	Unc	BU
1828Go MJ	—	1,100	2,550	2,800	3,900	—
1829Go MJ	—	950	2,200	2,500	3,600	—
1830Go MJ	—	725	800	950	1,300	—
1831Go MJ	—	950	2,200	2,500	3,600	—
1832Go MJ	—	800	1,450	1,900	3,250	—
1833Go MJ	—	725	800	875	1,300	—
1834Go PJ	—	725	800	875	1,300	—
1835Go PJ	—	725	800	875	1,300	—
1836Go PJ	—	725	950	1,150	1,650	—
1837Go PJ	—	725	950	1,150	1,650	—
1838/7Go PJ	—	725	800	875	1,300	—
1838Go PJ	—	725	800	1,000	1,550	—
1839/8Go PJ	—	725	800	875	1,300	—
1839Go PJ	—	725	800	1,000	1,550	—
Note: Regular eagle						
1840Go PJ	—	725	800	875	1,300	—
Note: Concave wings						
1841Go PJ	—	725	800	875	1,300	—
1842Go PJ	—	725	800	750	1,150	—
1842Go PM	—	725	800	875	1,300	—
1843Go PM	—	725	800	875	1,300	—
Note: Small eagle						
1844/3Go PM	—	725	950	1,150	1,650	—
1844Go PM	—	725	800	825	1,300	—
1845Go PM	—	725	800	875	1,300	—
1846/5Go PM	—	725	800	1,000	1,550	—
1846Go PM	—	725	800	875	1,300	—
1847Go PM	—	725	950	1,150	1,650	—
1848/7Go PM	—	725	800	875	1,300	—
1848Go PM	—	725	800	875	1,300	—

Date	Mintage	F	VF	XF	Unc	BU
1848Go PF	—	725	800	875	1,300	—
1849Go PF	—	725	800	750	1,250	—
1850Go PF	—	725	800	750	1,250	—
1851Go PF	—	725	800	875	1,300	—
1852Go PF	—	725	800	825	1,300	—
1853Go PF	—	725	800	825	1,300	—
1854Go PF	—	725	800	875	1,300	—
Note: Eagle of 1853						
1854Go PF	—	725	800	875	1,300	—
Note: Eagle of 1855						
1855/4Go PF	—	725	800	875	1,300	—
1855Go PF	—	725	800	875	1,300	—
1856Go PF	—	725	800	875	1,300	—
1857Go PF	—	725	800	875	1,300	—
1858Go PF	—	725	800	875	1,300	—
1859Go PF	—	725	800	750	1,150	—
1860/50Go PF	—	725	800	750	1,150	—
1860/59Go PF	—	725	800	875	1,450	—
1860Go PF	—	725	800	875	1,450	—
1861/0Go PF	—	725	800	750	1,100	—
1861Go PF	—	725	800	750	1,100	—
1862/1Go YE	—	725	800	875	1,300	—
1862Go YE	—	725	800	825	1,250	—
1862Go YF	—	—	—	—	—	—
1863/53Go YF	—	725	800	875	1,300	3,250
1863Go PF	—	725	800	875	1,300	—
1867/57Go YF/PF	—	725	800	875	1,300	—
1867Go YF	—	725	800	825	1,250	—
1868/58Go YF	—	725	800	875	1,300	2,300
1870Go FR	—	725	800	750	1,150	—

KM# 383.10 8 ESCUDOS
27.0700 g., 0.8750 Gold 0.7615 oz. AGW **Obv:** Facing eagle, snake in beak **Obv. Legend:** REPUBLICA MEXICANA. **Rev:** Hand holding cap on stick, open book **Rev. Legend:** LA LIBERTAD... **Mint:** Oaxaca

Date	Mintage	F	VF	XF	Unc	BU
1858Oa AE	—	2,900	4,350	5,000	7,800	—
1859O AE	—	1,450	3,650	4,700	7,200	—
1860O AE	—	1,450	3,650	4,700	7,200	—
1861O FR	—	875	1,250	1,550	3,600	—
1862O FR	—	875	1,250	1,550	3,600	—
1863O FR	—	875	1,250	1,550	3,600	—
1864O FR	—	875	1,250	1,550	3,600	—
1867O AE	—	875	1,250	1,550	3,600	—
1868O AE	—	875	1,250	1,550	3,600	—
1869O AE	—	875	1,250	1,550	3,600	—

KM# 383.8 8 ESCUDOS
27.0700 g., 0.8750 Gold 0.7615 oz. AGW **Obv:** Facing eagle, snake in beak **Obv. Legend:** REPUBLICA MEXICANA. **Rev:** Hand holding cap on stick, open book **Rev. Legend:** LA LIBERTAD... **Mint:** Hermosillo

Date	Mintage	F	VF	XF	Unc	BU
1863Ho FM	—	800	1,000	1,250	2,600	—
1864Ho FM	—	950	1,800	2,200	3,600	—
1864Ho PR/FM	—	800	1,000	1,250	2,600	—
1865Ho FM/PR	—	875	1,150	1,550	3,250	—
1867/57Ho PR	—	800	1,000	1,250	2,600	—
1868Ho PR	—	875	1,150	1,550	3,250	—
1868Ho PR/FM	—	875	1,150	1,550	3,250	—
1869Ho PR/FM	—	800	1,000	1,250	2,600	—
1869Ho PR	—	800	1,000	1,250	2,600	—
1870Ho PR	—	875	1,150	1,550	3,600	7,200
1871/0Ho PR	—	875	1,150	1,550	3,250	—
1871Ho PR	—	875	1,150	1,550	3,250	—
1872/1Ho PR	—	950	1,800	2,200	3,600	—
1873Ho PR	—	800	1,000	1,250	2,600	—

KM# 383.11 8 ESCUDOS
27.0700 g., 0.8750 Gold 0.7615 oz. AGW **Obv:** Facing eagle, snake in beak **Obv. Legend:** REPUBLICA MEXICANA **Rev:** Hand holding cap on stick, open book **Rev. Legend:** LA LIBERTAD... **Mint:** Zacatecas

Date	Mintage	F	VF	XF	Unc	BU
1858Zs MO	—	800	1,100	1,250	2,600	—
1859Zs MO	—	725	800	750	1,300	—
1860/59Zs VL/MO	—	2,900	4,350	5,000	—	—
1860/9Zs MO	—	800	1,100	1,250	2,600	—
1860Zs MO	—	725	800	875	1,450	—
1861/0Zs VL	—	725	800	875	1,450	—
1861Zs VL	—	725	800	875	1,450	3,900
1862Zs VL	—	725	800	875	1,500	—
1863Zs VL	—	725	800	950	1,550	—
1863Zs MO	—	725	800	875	1,450	—
1864Zs MO	—	1,100	1,450	1,900	4,550	—
1865Zs MO	—	1,100	1,450	2,000	4,900	—
1868Zs JS	—	725	875	1,000	1,650	—
1868Zs YH	—	725	875	1,000	1,650	—
1869Zs YH	—	725	875	1,000	1,650	—
1870Zs YH	—	725	875	1,000	1,650	—
1871Zs YH	—	725	875	1,000	1,650	—

KM# 383.9   8 ESCUDOS
27.0700 g., 0.8750 Gold 0.7615 oz. AGW **Obv:** Facing eagle, snake in beak **Obv. Legend:** REPUBLICA MEXICANA **Rev:** Hand holding cap on stick, open book **Rev. Legend:** LA LIBERTAD... **Mint:** Mexico City **Note:** Formerly reported 1825/3 JM is merely a reworked 5.

Date	Mintage	F	VF	XF	Unc	BU
1824Mo JM	—	875	1,450	1,550	2,600	—
Note: Large book reverse						
1825Mo JM	—	725	800	875	1,300	2,600
Note: Small book reverse						
1826/5Mo JM	—	1,100	2,550	2,800	3,900	—
1827/6Mo JM	—	725	800	875	1,300	—
1827Mo JM	—	725	800	875	1,300	—
1828Mo JM	—	725	800	875	1,300	—
1829Mo JM	—	725	800	875	1,300	—
1830Mo JM	—	725	800	875	1,300	—
1831Mo JM	—	725	800	875	1,300	—
1832/1Mo JM	—	725	800	875	1,300	—
1832Mo JM	—	725	800	875	1,300	—
1833Mo MJ	—	800	1,100	1,250	1,950	—
1833Mo ML	—	725	800	825	1,300	—
1834Mo ML	—	800	1,100	1,250	1,950	—
1835/4Mo ML	—	875	1,450	1,550	2,600	—
1836Mo ML	—	725	800	825	1,300	—
1836Mo MF	—	800	1,100	1,500	2,600	—
1837/6Mo ML	—	725	800	825	1,300	—
1838Mo ML	—	725	800	825	1,300	—
1839Mo ML	—	725	800	825	1,300	—
1840Mo ML	—	725	800	825	1,300	—
1841Mo ML	—	725	800	825	1,300	—
1842/1Mo ML	—	—	—	—	—	—
1842Mo ML	—	725	800	825	1,300	—
1842Mo MM	—	—	—	—	—	—
1843Mo MM	—	725	800	825	1,300	—
1844Mo MF	—	725	800	825	1,300	—
1845Mo MF	—	725	800	825	1,300	—
1846Mo MF	—	875	1,450	1,550	2,600	—
1847Mo MF	—	1,450	3,250	—	—	—
1847Mo RC	—	725	875	1,000	1,650	—
1848Mo GC	—	725	800	825	1,300	—
1849Mo GC	—	725	800	825	1,300	—
1850Mo GC	—	725	800	825	1,300	2,600
1851Mo GC	—	725	800	825	1,300	—
1852Mo GC	—	725	800	825	1,300	—
1853Mo GC	—	725	800	825	1,300	—
1854/44Mo GC	—	725	800	825	1,300	—
1854/3Mo GC	—	725	800	825	1,300	—
1855Mo GF	—	725	800	825	1,300	—
1856/5Mo GF	—	725	800	750	1,250	—
1856Mo GF	—	725	800	750	1,250	—
1857Mo GF	—	725	800	750	1,250	—
1858Mo FH	—	725	800	750	1,250	—
1859Mo FH	—	800	1,100	1,250	1,950	—
1860Mo FH	—	725	800	750	1,250	—
1860Mo TH	—	725	800	750	1,250	—
1861/51Mo CH	—	725	800	750	1,250	—
1862Mo CH	—	725	800	750	1,250	—
1863/53Mo CH	—	725	800	750	1,250	6,200
1863/53Mo TH	—	725	800	750	1,250	—
1867Mo CH	—	725	800	750	1,250	—
1868Mo CH	—	725	800	750	1,250	—
1868Mo PH	—	725	800	750	1,250	—
1869Mo CH	—	725	800	750	1,250	—

EMPIRE OF MAXIMILIAN

RULER
Maximilian, Emperor, 1864-1867
MINT MARKS
Refer To Republic Coinage
MONETARY SYSTEM
100 Centavos = 1 Peso (8 Reales)

MILLED COINAGE

KM# 384   CENTAVO
Copper **Ruler:** Maximilian **Obv:** Crowned facing eagle, snake in beak **Obv. Legend:** IMPERIO MEXICANO **Rev:** Value and date within wreath **Edge:** Coarsely reeded **Mint:** Mexico City

Date	Mintage	F	VF	XF	Unc	BU
1864M	—	50.00	100	250	1,250	1,850

KM# 385   5 CENTAVOS
1.3537 g., 0.9030 Silver 0.0393 oz. ASW **Ruler:** Maximilian **Mint:** Guanajuato

Date	Mintage	F	VF	XF	Unc	BU
1864G	90,000	17.50	35.00	85.00	320	—
1865G	—	20.00	30.00	65.00	300	—
1866G	—	75.00	150	300	2,000	—

KM# 385.1   5 CENTAVOS
1.3537 g., 0.9030 Silver 0.0393 oz. ASW **Ruler:** Maximilian **Mint:** Mexico City

Date	Mintage	F	VF	XF	Unc	BU
1864M	—	12.50	20.00	55.00	300	—
1866/4M	—	25.00	40.00	75.00	425	—
1866M	—	20.00	35.00	65.00	400	—

KM# 385.2   5 CENTAVOS
1.3537 g., 0.9030 Silver 0.0393 oz. ASW **Ruler:** Maximilian **Mint:** San Luis Potosi

Date	Mintage	F	VF	XF	Unc	BU
1864P	—	150	400	1,500	2,500	—

KM# 385.3   5 CENTAVOS
1.3537 g., 0.9030 Silver 0.0393 oz. ASW **Ruler:** Maximilian **Obv:** Crowned facing eagle, snake in beak **Obv. Legend:** IMPERIO MEXICANO **Rev:** Value and date within wreath **Mint:** Zacatecas

Date	Mintage	F	VF	XF	Unc	BU
1865Z	—	25.00	45.00	150	450	—

KM# 386   10 CENTAVOS
2.7073 g., 0.9030 Silver 0.0786 oz. ASW **Ruler:** Maximilian **Obv:** Crowned facing eagle, snake in beak **Obv. Legend:** IMPERIO MEXICANO **Rev:** Value and date within wreath **Mint:** Guanajuato

Date	Mintage	F	VF	XF	Unc	BU
1864G	45,000	20.00	45.00	90.00	325	—
1865G	—	30.00	60.00	110	375	—

KM# 386.1 10 CENTAVOS
2.7073 g., 0.9030 Silver 0.0786 oz. ASW **Ruler:** Maximilian
Obv: Crowned facing eagle, snake in beak **Obv. Legend:**
IMPERIO MEXICANO **Rev:** Value and date within wreath
Mint: Mexico City **Note:** Struck at Mexico City Mint, mint mark
M.

Date	Mintage	F	VF	XF	Unc	BU
1864M	—	15.00	25.00	55.00	285	—
1866/4M	—	25.00	35.00	70.00	320	—
1866/5M	—	25.00	40.00	85.00	375	—
1866M	—	25.00	35.00	75.00	375	—

KM# 386.2 10 CENTAVOS
2.7073 g., 0.9030 Silver 0.0786 oz. ASW **Ruler:** Maximilian
Mint: San Luis Potosi

Date	Mintage	F	VF	XF	Unc	BU
1864P	—	70.00	150	300	700	—

KM# 386.3 10 CENTAVOS
2.7073 g., 0.9030 Silver 0.0786 oz. ASW **Ruler:** Maximilian
Mint: Zacatecas

Date	Mintage	F	VF	XF	Unc	BU
1865Z	—	22.50	55.00	165	525	750

KM# 387 50 CENTAVOS
13.5365 g., 0.9030 Silver 0.3930 oz. ASW **Ruler:** Maximilian
Obv: Head right, with beard **Obv. Legend:** MAXIMILIANO
EMPERADOR **Rev:** Crowned oval shield **Rev. Legend:**
IMPERIO MEXICANO **Mint:** Mexico City **Designer:** S.
Navalon

Date	Mintage	F	VF	XF	Unc	BU
1866Mo	31,000	40.00	95.00	200	750	2,250

KM# 388 PESO
27.0700 g., 0.9030 Silver 0.7859 oz. ASW **Ruler:** Maximilian
Obv: Head right, with beard **Obv. Legend:** MAXIMILIANO
EMPERADOR **Rev:** Crowned arms with supporters **Rev.**
Legend: IMPERIO MEXICANO **Mint:** Guanajuato **Designer:**
S. Navalon

Date	Mintage	F	VF	XF	Unc	BU
1866Go	—	300	450	950	3,500	—

KM# 388.1 PESO
27.0700 g., 0.9030 Silver 0.7859 oz. ASW **Ruler:** Maximilian
Obv: Head right, with beard **Obv. Legend:** MAXIMILIANO
EMPERADOR **Rev:** Crowned arms with supporters **Rev.**
Legend: IMPERIO MEXICANO **Mint:** Mexico City **Designer:**
S. Navalon

Date	Mintage	F	VF	XF	Unc	BU
1866Mo	2,148,000	30.00	45.00	135	400	—
1867Mo	1,238,000	40.00	65.00	185	450	—

KM# 388.2 PESO
27.0700 g., 0.9030 Silver 0.7859 oz. ASW **Ruler:** Maximilian
Obv: Head right, with beard **Obv. Legend:** MAXIMILIANO
EMPERADOR **Rev:** Crowned arms with supporters **Rev.**
Legend: IMPERIO MEXICANO **Mint:** San Luis Potosi
Designer: S. Navalon

Date	Mintage	F	VF	XF	Unc	BU
1866Pi	—	45.00	90.00	275	775	—

KM# 389 20 PESOS
33.8400 g., 0.8750 Gold 0.9519 oz. AGW **Ruler:** Maximilian
Obv: Head right, with beard **Obv. Legend:** MAXIMILIANO
EMPERADOR **Rev:** Crowned arms with supporters **Rev.**
Legend: IMPERIO MEXICANO **Mint:** Mexico City **Designer:**
S. Navalon

Date	Mintage	F	VF	XF	Unc	BU
1866Mo	8,274	1,100	1,350	2,200	3,500	—

REPUBLIC
Second

DECIMAL COINAGE

100 CENTAVOS = 1 PESO

KM# 390 CENTAVO
Copper, 25 mm. **Obv:** Seated Liberty **Rev:** Thick wreath.
Mint: Mexico City

Date	Mintage	F	VF	XF	Unc	BU
1863Mo	—	10.00	30.00	70.00	500	—
Note: Flat-top 3, reeded edge						
1863Mo	—	13.50	32.50	75.00	500	—
Note: Round-top 3, plain edge						
1863Mo	—	13.50	32.50	75.00	500	—
Note: Round-top 3, reeded edge						

KM# 390.1 CENTAVO
Copper, 26.5 mm. **Obv:** Seated liberty **Obv. Legend:** LIBERTAD V REFORMA. **Rev:** Value and date within wreath **Mint:** San Luis Potosi

Date	Mintage	F	VF	XF	Unc	BU
1863SLP	1,024,999	15.00	32.50	75.00	425	—

KM# 391 CENTAVO
Copper **Obv:** Facing eagle, snake in beak **Rev:** Value and date within wreath **Edge:** Reeded. **Mint:** Alamos

Date	Mintage	F	VF	XF	Unc	BU
1875As Rare	—	—	—	—	—	—
1876As	50,000	100	200	300	650	—
1880As	—	25.00	50.00	200	500	—
1881As	—	30.00	60.00	125	350	—

KM# 391.1 CENTAVO
Copper **Obv:** Facing eagle, snake in beak **Obv. Legend:** REPUBLICA MEXICANA **Rev:** Value and date within wreath **Edge:** Plain **Mint:** Culiacan

Date	Mintage	F	VF	XF	Unc	BU
1874Cn	266,000	12.50	17.50	35.00	250	—
1875/4Cn	153,000	15.00	20.00	45.00	250	—
1875Cn	Inc. above	10.00	15.00	25.00	250	—
1876Cn	154,000	5.00	8.00	15.00	200	—
1877/6Cn	993,000	7.50	11.50	17.50	200	—
1877Cn	Inc. above	6.00	9.00	15.00	200	—
1880Cn	142,000	7.50	10.00	12.50	200	—
1881Cn	167,000	7.50	10.00	25.00	200	—
1897Cn	300,000	2.50	5.00	12.00	50.00	—

Note: Large N in mint mark

Date	Mintage	F	VF	XF	Unc	BU
1897Cn	Inc. above	2.50	5.00	9.00	45.00	—

Note: Small N in mint mark

KM# 391.2 CENTAVO
Copper **Obv:** Facing eagle, snake in beak **Rev:** Value and date within wreath **Mint:** Durango

Date	Mintage	F	VF	XF	Unc	BU
1879Do	110,000	10.00	35.00	60.00	200	—
1880Do	69,000	40.00	90.00	175	500	—
1891Do	—	8.00	25.00	50.00	200	—
1891Do/Mo	—	8.00	25.00	50.00	200	—

KM# 391.3 CENTAVO
Copper **Obv:** Facing eagle, snake in beak **Obv. Legend:** REPUBLICA MEXICANA **Rev:** Value and date within wreath **Mint:** Guadalajara

Date	Mintage	F	VF	XF	Unc	BU
1872Ga	263,000	15.00	30.00	60.00	225	—
1873Ga	333,000	6.00	9.00	25.00	200	—
1874Ga	76,000	15.00	25.00	50.00	200	—

Date	Mintage	F	VF	XF	Unc	BU
1875Ga	—	10.00	15.00	30.00	200	—
1876Ga	303,000	3.00	6.00	17.50	200	—
1877Ga	108,000	4.00	6.00	20.00	200	—
1878Ga	543,000	4.00	6.00	15.00	200	—
1881/71Ga	975,000	7.00	9.00	20.00	—	—
1881Ga	Inc. above	7.00	9.00	20.00	200	—
1889Ga/Mo	—	3.50	5.00	25.00	200	—
1890Ga	—	4.00	7.50	20.00	200	—

KM# 391.4 CENTAVO
Copper **Obv:** Facing eagle, snake in beak **Rev:** Value and date within wreath **Mint:** Guanajuato

Date	Mintage	F	VF	XF	Unc	BU
1874Go	—	20.00	40.00	80.00	250	—
1875Go	190,000	11.50	20.00	60.00	200	—
1876Go	—	125	200	350	750	—
1877Go Rare	—	—	—	—	—	—
1878Go	576,000	8.00	11.00	30.00	200	—
1880Go	890,000	6.00	10.00	25.00	200	—

KM# 391.5 CENTAVO
Copper **Obv:** Facing eagle, snake in beak **Obv. Inscription:** REPUBLICA MEXICANA **Rev:** Value and date within wreath **Mint:** Hermosillo

Date	Mintage	F	VF	XF	Unc	BU
1875Ho	3,500	450	—	—	—	—
1876Ho	8,508	50.00	100	225	500	—
1880Ho Short H, round O	102,000	7.50	15.00	50.00	200	—
1880Ho Tall H, oval O	Inc. above	7.50	15.00	50.00	200	—
1881Ho	459,000	5.00	10.00	50.00	200	—

KM# 391.7 CENTAVO
Copper **Obv:** Facing eagle, snake in beak **Obv. Legend:** REPUBLICA MEXICANA **Rev:** Value and date within wreath **Mint:** Oaxaca

Date	Mintage	F	VF	XF	Unc	BU
1872Oa	16,000	300	500	1,200	—	—
1873Oa	11,000	350	600	—	—	—
1874Oa	4,835	450	—	—	—	—
1875Oa	2,860	500	—	—	—	—

KM# 391.8 CENTAVO
Copper **Obv:** Facing eagle, snake in beak **Obv. Legend:** REPUBLICA MEXICANA **Rev:** Value and date within wreath **Mint:** San Luis Potosi

Date	Mintage	F	VF	XF	Unc	BU
1871Pi Rare	—	—	—	—	—	—
1877Pi	249,000	15.00	50.00	200	—	—

Date	Mintage	F	VF	XF	Unc	BU
1878Pi	751,000	12.50	25.00	50.00	200	—
1878	—	—	—	—	—	—

Note: Pp error mintmark - rare

Date	Mintage	F	VF	XF	Unc	BU
1891Pi/Mo	—	10.00	50.00	150	300	—
1891Pi	—	8.00	25.00	125	250	—

KM# 391.9 CENTAVO
Copper **Obv:** Facing eagle, snake in beak **Rev:** Value and
date within wreath **Mint:** Zacatecas **Note:** Struck at Zacatecas
Mint, mint mark Zs.

Date	Mintage	F	VF	XF	Unc	BU
1872Zs	55,000	22.50	30.00	100	300	—
1873Zs	1,460,000	4.00	8.00	25.00	150	—
1874/3Zs	685,000	5.50	11.00	30.00	250	—
1874Zs	Inc. above	4.00	8.00	25.00	200	—
1875/4Zs	200,000	8.50	17.00	45.00	250	—
1875Zs	Inc. above	7.00	14.00	35.00	200	—
1876Zs	—	5.00	10.00	25.00	200	—
1877Zs	—	50.00	125	300	750	—
1878Zs	—	4.50	9.00	25.00	200	—
1880Zs	100,000	5.00	10.00	30.00	200	—
1881Zs	1,200,000	4.25	8.00	25.00	150	—

KM# 391.6 CENTAVO
7.4000 g., Copper **Obv:** Facing eagle, snake in beak **Obv.
Legend:** REPUBLICA MEXICANA **Rev:** Value and date
within wreath **Mint:** Mexico City **Note:** Varieties exist.

Date	Mintage	F	VF	XF	Unc	BU
1869Mo	1,874,000	7.50	25.00	60.00	200	—
1870/69Mo	1,200,000	10.00	25.00	60.00	225	—
1870Mo	Inc. above	8.00	20.00	50.00	200	—
1871Mo	918,000	8.00	15.00	40.00	200	—
1872/1Mo	1,625,000	6.50	10.00	30.00	200	—
1872Mo	Inc. above	6.00	9.00	25.00	200	—
1873Mo	1,605,000	4.00	7.50	20.00	200	—
1874/3Mo	1,700,000	5.00	7.00	15.00	100	—
1874Mo	Inc. above	3.00	5.50	15.00	100	—
1874Mo	Inc. above	5.00	10.00	25.00	200	—
1875Mo	1,495,000	6.00	8.00	30.00	100	—
1876Mo	1,600,000	3.00	5.50	12.50	100	—
1877Mo	1,270,000	3.00	5.50	13.50	100	—
1878/5Mo	1,900,000	7.50	11.00	22.50	125	—
1878/6Mo	Inc. above	7.50	11.00	22.50	125	—
1878/7Mo	Inc. above	7.50	11.00	20.00	125	—
1878Mo	Inc. above	6.00	9.00	13.50	100	—
1879/8Mo	1,505,000	4.50	6.50	13.50	100	—
1879Mo	Inc. above	3.00	5.50	12.50	75.00	—
1880/70Mo	1,130,000	5.50	7.50	15.00	100	—
1880/72Mo	Inc. above	20.00	50.00	100	250	—
1880/79Mo	Inc. above	15.00	35.00	75.00	175	—
1880Mo	Inc. above	4.25	6.00	12.50	75.00	—
1881Mo	1,060,000	4.50	7.00	15.00	75.00	—
1886Mo	12,687,000	1.50	2.00	10.00	40.00	—
1887Mo	7,292,000	1.50	2.00	10.00	35.00	—
1888/78Mo	9,984,000	2.50	3.00	10.00	30.00	—
1888/7Mo	Inc. above	2.50	3.00	10.00	30.00	—
1888Mo	Inc. above	1.50	2.00	10.00	30.00	—
1889Mo	19,970,000	2.00	3.00	10.00	30.00	—
1890/89Mo	18,726,000	2.50	3.00	12.00	40.00	—
1890/990Mo	Inc. above	2.50	3.00	12.00	40.00	—
1890Mo	Inc. above	1.50	2.00	10.00	30.00	—
1891Mo	14,544,000	1.50	2.00	10.00	30.00	—
1892Mo	12,908,000	1.50	2.00	10.00	30.00	—
1893/2Mo	5,078,000	2.50	3.00	12.00	35.00	—
1893Mo	Inc. above	1.50	2.00	10.00	30.00	—
1894/3Mo	1,896,000	3.00	6.00	15.00	50.00	—
1894Mo	Inc. above	2.00	3.00	12.00	35.00	—
1895/3Mo	3,453,000	3.00	4.50	12.50	35.00	—
1895/85Mo	Inc. above	3.00	6.00	15.00	50.00	—
1895Mo	Inc. above	2.00	3.00	10.00	30.00	—

Date	Mintage	F	VF	XF	Unc	BU
1896Mo	3,075,000	2.00	3.00	10.00	30.00	—
1897Mo	4,150,000	1.50	2.00	10.00	30.00	—

KM# 392 CENTAVO
Copper-Nickel **Obv:** Crossed bow and quiver above date
Obv. Legend: REPUBLICA MEXICANA **Rev:** Value within
wreath **Mint:** Mexico City

Date	Mintage	F	VF	XF	Unc	BU
1882Mo	99,955,000	7.50	12.50	17.50	35.00	—
1883Mo	Inc. above	0.50	0.75	1.00	1.50	—

KM# 393 CENTAVO
Copper **Obv:** Facing eagle, snake in beak **Obv. Legend:**
REPUBLICA MEXICANA **Rev:** Value and date within wreath
Mint: Mexico City **Note:** Varieties exist.

Date	Mintage	F	VF	XF	Unc	BU
1898Mo	1,529,000	4.00	6.00	15.00	50.00	—

KM# 394.1 CENTAVO
2.6100 g., Copper **Obv:** Facing eagle, snake in beak **Obv.
Legend:** REPUBLICA MEXICANA **Rev:** Value below date
within wreath **Mint:** Mexico City **Note:** Reduced size. Varieties
exist.

Date	Mintage	F	VF	XF	Unc	BU
1899M	51,000	150	175	300	800	—
1900M Wide date	4,010,000	2.50	4.00	8.00	28.00	—
1900M Narrow date	Inc. above	2.50	4.00	8.00	28.00	—
1901M	1,494,000	3.00	8.00	17.50	50.00	—
1902/899M	2,090,000	30.00	60.00	125	225	—
1902M	Inc. above	2.25	4.00	10.00	40.00	—
1903M	8,400,000	1.50	3.00	7.00	20.00	—
1904/3M	10,250,000	1.50	10.00	20.00	55.00	—
1904M	Inc. above	1.50	3.00	8.00	25.00	—
1905M	3,643,000	2.25	4.00	10.00	40.00	—

KM# 394 CENTAVO
Copper **Obv:** National arms **Rev:** Value below date within
wreath **Mint:** Culiacan **Note:** Reduced size. Varieties exist.

Date	Mintage	F	VF	XF	Unc	BU
1901C	220,000	15.00	22.50	35.00	65.00	—
1902C	320,000	15.00	22.50	50.00	90.00	—
1903C	536,000	7.50	12.50	20.00	50.00	—
1904/3C	148,000	35.00	50.00	75.00	125	—
1905C	110,000	100	150	300	600	—

KM# 395 2 CENTAVOS
Copper-Nickel **Obv:** Crossed bow and quiver above date **Obv. Legend:** REPUBLICA MEXICANA **Rev:** Value within wreath **Mint:** Mexico City

Date	Mintage	F	VF	XF	Unc	BU
1882	50,023,000	2.00	3.00	7.50	15.00	—
1883/2	Inc. above	2.00	3.00	7.50	15.00	—
1883	Inc. above	0.50	0.75	1.00	2.50	—

KM# 396.1 5 CENTAVOS
1.3530 g., 0.9030 Silver 0.0393 oz. ASW **Obv:** Facing eagle, snake in beak **Rev:** Value within wreath **Mint:** San Luis Potosi

Date	Mintage	F	VF	XF	Unc	BU
1863SLP	—	37.50	135	350	1,200	—

KM# 397 5 CENTAVOS
1.3530 g., 0.9030 Silver 0.0393 oz. ASW **Obv:** Facing eagle, snake in beak **Obv. Legend:** REPUBLICA MEXICANA **Rev:** Radiant cap **Mint:** Mexico City **Note:** Varieties exist.

Date	Mintage	F	VF	XF	Unc	BU
1867Mo	—	20.00	45.00	110	400	—
1867/3Mo	—	22.50	50.00	125	425	—
1868/7Mo	—	22.50	50.00	150	500	—
1868Mo	—	18.50	42.50	100	400	—

KM# 397.1 5 CENTAVOS
1.3530 g., 0.9030 Silver 0.0393 oz. ASW **Obv:** Facing eagle, snake in beak **Rev:** Radiant cap **Mint:** San Luis Potosi

Date	Mintage	F	VF	XF	Unc	BU
1868P	Inc. above	20.00	45.00	100	400	—
1868/7P	34,000	25.00	50.00	125	450	—
1869P	14,000	150	300	600	—	—

KM# 396 5 CENTAVOS
1.3530 g., 0.9030 Silver 0.0393 oz. ASW **Obv:** Facing eagle, snake in beak **Obv. Legend:** REPUBLICA MEXICANA **Rev:** Value within wreath **Mint:** Chihuahua

Date	Mintage	F	VF	XF	Unc	BU
1868Ca	—	40.00	65.00	125	450	—
1869Ca	30,000	25.00	40.00	100	400	—
1870/69Ca	—	35.00	55.00	120	425	—
1870Ca	35,000	30.00	50.00	100	400	—

KM# 398.7 5 CENTAVOS
1.3530 g., 0.9030 Silver 0.0393 oz. ASW **Obv:** Facing eagle, snake in beak **Obv. Legend:** REPUBLICA MEXICANA **Rev:** Value within 1/2 wreath **Mint:** Mexico City **Note:** Mint mark Mo. Varieties exist.

Date	Mintage	F	VF	XF	Unc	BU
1869/8Mo C	40,000	8.00	15.00	40.00	120	—
1870Mo C	140,000	4.00	7.00	20.00	60.00	—
1871Mo C	103,000	9.00	20.00	40.00	100	—
1871Mo M	Inc. above	7.50	12.50	25.00	60.00	—
1872Mo M	266,000	5.00	8.00	20.00	55.00	—
1873Mo M	20,000	40.00	60.00	100	225	—
1874/69Mo M	—	7.50	15.00	30.00	75.00	—
1874Mo M	—	4.00	7.00	17.50	50.00	—
1874/3Mo B	—	5.00	8.00	22.50	55.00	—

Date	Mintage	F	VF	XF	Unc	BU
1874Mo B	—	5.00	8.00	22.50	55.00	—
1875Mo B	—	4.00	7.00	15.00	50.00	—
1875Mo B/M	—	6.00	9.00	17.50	60.00	—
1876/5Mo B	—	4.00	7.00	15.00	50.00	—
1876Mo B	—	4.00	7.00	12.50	50.00	—
1877/6Mo M	80,000	4.00	7.00	15.00	60.00	—
1877Mo M	Inc. above	4.00	7.00	12.50	60.00	—
1878/7Mo M	100,000	4.00	7.00	15.00	55.00	—
1878Mo M	Inc. above	2.50	5.00	12.50	45.00	—
1879/8Mo M	—	8.00	12.50	22.50	55.00	—
1879Mo M	—	4.50	7.00	15.00	50.00	—
1879Mo M 9/ inverted 9	—	10.00	15.00	25.00	75.00	—
1880/76Mo M/B	—	5.00	7.50	15.00	50.00	—
1880/76Mo M	—	5.00	7.50	15.00	50.00	—
1880Mo M	—	4.00	6.00	12.00	40.00	—
1881/0Mo M	180,000	4.00	6.00	10.00	35.00	—
1881Mo M	Inc. above	3.00	4.50	9.00	35.00	—
1886/0Mo M	398,000	2.00	2.75	7.50	25.00	—
1886/1Mo M	Inc. above	2.00	2.75	7.50	25.00	—
1886Mo M	Inc. above	1.75	2.25	6.00	20.00	—
1887Mo m	720,000	1.75	2.00	6.00	20.00	—
1887Mo M/m	Inc. above	1.75	2.00	6.00	20.00	—
1888/7Mo M	1,360,000	2.25	2.50	6.00	20.00	—
1888Mo M	Inc. above	1.75	2.00	5.00	20.00	—
1889/8Mo M	1,242,000	2.25	2.50	6.00	20.00	—
1889Mo M	Inc. above	1.75	2.00	5.00	20.00	—
1890/00Mo M	1,694,000	1.75	2.75	6.00	20.00	—
1890Mo M	Inc. above	1.50	2.00	5.00	20.00	—
1891Mo M	1,030,000	1.75	2.00	5.00	20.00	—
1892Mo M	1,400,000	1.75	2.00	5.00	20.00	—
1892Mo M 9/ inverted 9	Inc. above	2.00	2.75	7.50	20.00	—
1893Mo M	220,000	1.75	2.00	5.00	15.00	—
1894Mo M	320,000	1.75	2.00	5.00	15.00	—
1895Mo M	78,000	3.00	5.00	8.00	25.00	—
1896Mo B	80,000	1.75	2.00	5.00	20.00	—
1897Mo B	160,000	1.75	2.00	5.00	15.00	—

KM# 398.1 5 CENTAVOS
1.3530 g., 0.9030 Silver 0.0393 oz. ASW **Obv:** Facing eagle, snake in beak **Rev:** Value within 1/2 wreath **Mint:** Chihuahua **Note:** Mint mark: *Ca or Ch*.

Date	Mintage	F	VF	XF	Unc	BU
1871* M	14,000	20.00	40.00	100	250	—
1873* M Crude date	—	100	150	250	500	—
1874* M Crude date	—	25.00	50.00	75.00	150	—
1886* M	25,000	7.50	15.00	30.00	100	—
1887* M	37,000	7.50	15.00	30.00	100	—
1887* Ca/MoM	Inc. above	10.00	20.00	40.00	125	—
1888* M	145,000	1.50	3.00	6.00	25.00	—
1889* M	44,000	5.00	10.00	20.00	50.00	—
1890* M	102,000	1.50	3.00	6.00	25.00	—
1891* M	164,000	1.50	3.00	6.00	25.00	—
1892* M	85,000	1.50	3.00	6.00	25.00	—
1892* M/U	—	2.00	4.00	7.50	30.00	—
1892* M 9/inverted 9	Inc. above	2.00	4.00	7.50	30.00	—
1893* M	133,000	1.50	3.00	6.00	25.00	—
1894* M	108,000	1.50	3.00	6.00	25.00	—
1895* M	74,000	2.00	4.00	7.50	30.00	—

KM# 398 5 CENTAVOS
1.3530 g., 0.9030 Silver 0.0393 oz. ASW **Obv:** Facing eagle, snake in beak **Rev:** Value within 1/2 wreath **Mint:** Alamos

Date	Mintage	F	VF	XF	Unc	BU
1874As DL	—	10.00	20.00	40.00	150	—
1875As DL	—	10.00	20.00	40.00	150	—
1876As L	—	22.00	45.00	70.00	160	—
1878As L	—	250	350	650	—	—
Note: Mule, gold peso reverse						
1879As L	—	40.00	65.00	120	275	—
Note: Mule, gold peso obverse						
1880As L	12,000	55.00	85.00	165	325	—
Note: Mule, gold peso obverse						
1886As L	43,000	12.00	25.00	50.00	165	—
1886As L	Inc. above	55.00	85.00	165	300	—
Note: Mule, gold peso obverse						
1887As L	20,000	25.00	50.00	75.00	165	—
1888As L	32,000	12.00	25.00	50.00	125	—
1889As L	16,000	25.00	50.00	100	200	—
1890As L	30,000	25.00	50.00	85.00	175	—
1891As L	8,000	65.00	125	200	400	—

Date	Mintage	F	VF	XF	Unc	BU
1892As L	13,000	20.00	40.00	60.00	125	—
1893As L	24,000	10.00	20.00	45.00	90.00	—
1895As L	20,000	10.00	20.00	45.00	90.00	—

KM# 398.2 5 CENTAVOS
1.3530 g., 0.9030 Silver 0.0393 oz. ASW **Obv:** Facing eagle, snake in beak **Rev:** Value within 1/2 wreath **Mint:** Culiacan

Date	Mintage	F	VF	XF	Unc	BU
1871Cn P	—	125	200	350	—	—
1873Cn P	4,992	50.00	100	200	400	—
1874Cn P	—	25.00	50.00	100	200	—
1875Cn P Rare	—	—	—	—	—	—
1876Cn P	—	25.00	50.00	100	200	—
1886Cn M	10,000	25.00	50.00	100	200	—
1887Cn M	10,000	25.00	50.00	100	200	—
1888Cn M	119,000	1.50	3.00	6.00	30.00	—
1889Cn M	66,000	4.00	7.50	15.00	50.00	—
189/80Cn M	—	2.00	4.00	8.00	40.00	—
1890Cn M	180,000	1.50	3.00	6.00	25.00	—
1890/9Cn M	—	2.00	4.00	8.00	40.00	—
1890Cn D Error	Inc. above	125	175	250	—	—
1891Cn M	87,000	2.00	4.00	7.50	25.00	—
1894Cn M	24,000	4.00	7.50	15.00	40.00	—
1896Cn M	16,000	7.50	12.50	25.00	75.00	—
1897Cn M	223,000	1.50	2.50	5.00	20.00	—

KM# 398.3 5 CENTAVOS
1.3530 g., 0.9030 Silver 0.0393 oz. ASW **Obv:** Facing eagle, snake in beak **Rev:** Value within 1/2 wreath **Mint:** Durango

Date	Mintage	F	VF	XF	Unc	BU
1874Do M	—	100	150	225	500	—
1877Do P	4,795	75.00	125	225	450	—
1878/7Do E/P	4,300	200	300	450	—	—
1879Do B	—	125	200	350	—	—
1880Do B Rare	—	—	—	—	—	—
1881Do P	3,020	300	500	800	—	—
1887Do C	42,000	5.00	8.00	17.50	60.00	—
1888/9Do C	91,000	6.00	10.00	20.00	70.00	—
1888Do C	Inc. above	4.00	7.50	15.00	55.00	—
1889Do C	49,000	3.50	6.00	12.50	55.00	—
1890Do C	136,000	4.00	7.50	15.00	55.00	—
1890Do P	Inc. above	5.00	8.00	17.50	60.00	—
1891/0Do P	48,000	3.50	6.00	12.50	50.00	—
1891Do P	Inc. above	3.00	5.00	10.00	45.00	—
1894Do D	38,000	3.50	6.00	12.50	50.00	—

KM# 398.4 5 CENTAVOS
1.3530 g., 0.9030 Silver 0.0393 oz. ASW **Obv:** Facing eagle, snake in beak **Rev:** Value within 1/2 wreath **Mint:** Guadalajara

Date	Mintage	F	VF	XF	Unc	BU
1877Ga A	—	15.00	30.00	60.00	150	—
1881Ga S	156,000	4.00	7.50	15.00	60.00	—
1886Ga S	87,000	2.00	4.00	7.50	25.00	—
1888Ga S Large G	262,000	2.00	4.00	10.00	30.00	—
1888Ga S Small G	Inc. above	2.00	4.00	10.00	30.00	—
1889Ga S	178,000	1.50	3.00	7.50	25.00	—
1890Ga S	68,000	4.00	7.50	12.50	35.00	—
1891Ga S	50,000	4.00	6.50	10.00	35.00	—
1892Ga S	78,000	2.00	4.00	7.50	25.00	—
1893Ga S	44,000	4.00	7.50	15.00	45.00	—

KM# 398.5 5 CENTAVOS
1.3530 g., 0.9030 Silver 0.0393 oz. ASW **Obv:** Facing eagle, snake in beak **Obv. Legend:** REPUBLICA MEXICANA **Rev:** Value within 1/2 wreath **Mint:** Guanajuato

Date	Mintage	F	VF	XF	Unc	BU
1869Go S	80,000	15.00	30.00	75.00	175	—
1871Go S	100,000	5.00	10.00	25.00	75.00	—
1872Go S	30,000	30.00	60.00	125	250	—
1873Go S	40,000	30.00	60.00	125	250	—
1874Go S	—	7.00	12.00	25.00	75.00	—
1875Go S	—	8.00	15.00	30.00	75.00	—
1876Go S	—	8.00	15.00	30.00	75.00	—
1877Go S	—	7.00	12.00	20.00	75.00	—
1878/7Go S	20,000	8.00	15.00	25.00	75.00	—
1879Go S	—	8.00	15.00	25.00	75.00	—
1880Go S	55,000	15.00	30.00	60.00	200	—

Date	Mintage	F	VF	XF	Unc	BU
1881/0Go S	160,000	5.00	8.00	17.50	60.00	—
1881Go S	Inc. above	4.00	6.00	12.00	45.00	—
1886Go R	230,000	1.50	3.00	6.00	30.00	—
1887Go R/S	—	1.50	3.00	6.00	30.00	—
1887Go R	230,000	1.50	2.50	5.00	30.00	—
1888Go R	320,000	1.50	2.50	5.00	20.00	—
1889Go R/S	—	4.00	6.00	12.00	45.00	—
1889Go R	60,000	4.00	6.00	12.00	45.00	—
1890/5Go R/S	—	1.50	3.00	6.00	30.00	—
1890Go R	250,000	1.50	2.50	5.00	20.00	—
1891/0Go R	168,000	1.80	3.00	6.00	30.00	—
1891Go R	Inc. above	1.50	2.50	5.00	20.00	—
1892Go R	138,000	1.50	3.00	6.00	25.00	—
1893Go R	200,000	1.25	2.50	5.00	20.00	—
1894Go R	200,000	1.25	2.50	5.00	20.00	—
1896Go R	525,000	1.25	2.00	4.00	15.00	—
1896Go R/S	—	1.50	3.00	6.00	25.00	—
1897Go R	596,000	1.50	2.00	4.00	15.00	—
1898Go R	—	—	—	—	—	—

KM# 398.6 5 CENTAVOS
1.3530 g., 0.9030 Silver 0.0393 oz. ASW **Obv:** Facing eagle, snake in beak **Rev:** Value within 1/2 wreath **Mint:** Hermosillo

Date	Mintage	F	VF	XF	Unc	BU
1874/69Ho R	—	125	225	350	—	—
1874Ho R	—	100	200	325	—	—
1878/7Ho A Rare	22,000	—	—	—	—	—
1878Ho A	Inc. above	20.00	40.00	80.00	175	—
1878Ho A	Inc. above	40.00	80.00	150	300	—
Note: Mule, gold peso obverse						
1880Ho A	43,000	7.50	15.00	30.00	75.00	—
1886Ho G	44,000	5.00	10.00	20.00	75.00	—
1887Ho G	20,000	5.00	10.00	20.00	75.00	—
1888Ho G	12,000	7.50	15.00	30.00	85.00	—
1889Ho G	67,000	3.00	6.00	12.50	40.00	—
1890Ho G	50,000	3.00	6.00	12.50	40.00	—
1891Ho G	46,000	3.00	6.00	12.50	40.00	—
1893Ho G	84,000	2.50	5.00	10.00	30.00	—
1894Ho G	68,000	2.00	4.00	10.00	30.00	—

KM# 398.9 5 CENTAVOS
1.3530 g., 0.9030 Silver 0.0393 oz. ASW **Obv:** Facing eagle, snake in beak **Rev:** Value within 1/2 wreath **Mint:** San Luis Potosi **Note:** Varieties exist.

Date	Mintage	F	VF	XF	Unc	BU
1869Pi S	—	300	400	500	—	—
1870Pi G/MoC	20,000	150	250	400	—	—
1870Pi O Rare	Inc. above	200	300	450	—	—
1871Pi O Rare	5,400	—	—	—	—	—
1872Pi O	—	75.00	100	175	400	—
1873Pi Rare	5,000	—	—	—	—	—
1874Pi H	—	30.00	50.00	100	225	—
1875Pi H	—	7.50	12.50	30.00	75.00	—
1876Pi H	—	10.00	20.00	45.00	100	—
1877Pi H	—	7.50	12.50	20.00	60.00	—
1878/7Pi H Rare	—	—	—	—	—	—
1878Pi H	—	60.00	90.00	150	300	—
1879 H	—	200	400	—	—	—
1880Pi H Rare	6,200	—	—	—	—	—
1881Pi H Rare	4,500	—	—	—	—	—
1886Pi R	33,000	12.50	25.00	50.00	125	—
1887/0Pi R	169,000	4.00	7.50	15.00	45.00	—
1887Pi R	Inc. above	3.00	5.00	10.00	32.00	—
1888Pi R	210,000	2.00	4.00	9.00	30.00	—
1889/7Pi R	197,000	2.50	5.00	10.00	32.00	—
1889Pi R	Inc. above	2.00	4.00	9.00	30.00	—
1890Pi R	221,000	2.00	3.00	6.00	25.00	—
1891/89Pi R/B	176,000	2.00	4.00	8.00	25.00	—
1891/0Pi R/B	—	2.00	4.00	8.00	25.00	—
1891Pi R	Inc. above	2.00	3.00	6.00	20.00	—
1892/89Pi R	182,000	2.00	4.00	8.00	25.00	—
1892/0Pi R	Inc. above	2.00	4.00	8.00	25.00	—
1892Pi R	Inc. above	2.00	3.00	6.00	20.00	—
1893Pi R	41,000	5.00	10.00	20.00	60.00	—

KM# 398.10 5 CENTAVOS
1.3530 g., 0.9030 Silver 0.0393 oz. ASW **Obv:** Facing eagle, snake in beak **Rev:** Value within 1/2 wreath **Mint:** Zacatecas

Date	Mintage	F	VF	XF	Unc	BU
1870Zs H	40,000	12.50	25.00	50.00	125	—
1871Zs H	40,000	12.50	25.00	50.00	125	—

Date	Mintage	F	VF	XF	Unc	BU
1872Zs H	40,000	12.50	25.00	50.00	125	—
1873/2Zs H	20,000	35.00	65.00	125	275	—
1873Zs H	Inc. above	25.00	50.00	100	250	—
1874Zs H	—	7.50	12.50	25.00	75.00	—
1874Zs A	—	40.00	75.00	150	300	—
1875Zs A	—	7.50	12.50	25.00	75.00	—
1876Zs A	—	50.00	75.00	150	500	—
1876/5Zs S	—	15.00	30.00	60.00	150	—
1876Zs S	—	12.50	25.00	50.00	125	—
1877Zs S	—	3.00	6.00	12.00	40.00	—
1878Zs S	60,000	3.00	6.00	12.00	40.00	—
1879/8Zs S	—	3.00	6.00	15.00	50.00	—
1879Zs S	—	3.00	6.00	12.00	40.00	—
1880/79Zs S	130,000	6.00	10.00	20.00	60.00	—
1880Zs S	Inc. above	5.00	8.00	16.00	45.00	—
1881Zs S	210,000	2.50	5.00	10.00	35.00	—
1886/4Zs S	360,000	6.00	10.00	20.00	60.00	—
1886Zs S	Inc. above	2.00	3.00	6.00	20.00	—
1886Zs Z	Inc. above	5.00	10.00	25.00	65.00	—
1887Zs Z	400,000	2.00	3.00	6.00	25.00	—
1888/7Zs Z	500,000	2.00	3.00	6.00	25.00	—
1888Zs Z	Inc. above	2.00	3.00	6.00	25.00	—
1889Zs Z	520,000	2.00	3.00	6.00	25.00	—
1889Zs Z 9/ inverted 9	Inc. above	2.00	3.00	6.00	25.00	—
1889Zs Z/MoM	Inc. above	2.00	3.00	6.00	25.00	—
1890Zs Z	580,000	1.75	2.50	5.00	20.00	—
1890Zs Z/MoM	Inc. above	2.00	3.00	6.00	25.00	—
1890Zs ZsZ 9/8	—	2.00	3.00	6.00	25.00	—
1890Zs ZsZ 0/9 Z/M	—	2.00	3.00	6.00	25.00	—
1891Zs Z	420,000	1.75	2.50	5.00	20.00	—
1892Zs Z	346,000	1.75	2.50	5.00	20.00	—
1893Zs Z	258,000	1.75	2.50	5.00	20.00	—
1894Zs Z	228,000	1.75	2.50	5.00	20.00	—
1894Zs ZoZ Error	Inc. above	2.00	4.00	8.00	30.00	—
1895Zs Z	260,000	1.75	2.50	5.00	20.00	—
1895/4Zs ZsZ	—	2.00	3.00	6.00	25.00	—
1896Zs Z	200,000	1.75	2.50	5.00	20.00	—
1896Zs 6/ inverted 6	Inc. above	2.00	3.00	6.00	25.00	—
1897/6Zs Z	200,000	2.00	3.00	6.00	25.00	—
1897Zs Z	Inc. above	1.75	2.50	5.00	20.00	—

KM# 398.8 5 CENTAVOS
1.3530 g., 0.9030 Silver 0.0393 oz. ASW **Obv:** Facing eagle, snake in beak **Obv. Legend:** REPUBLICA MEXICANA **Rev:** Value within 1/2 wreath **Mint:** Oaxaca

Date	Mintage	F	VF	XF	Unc	BU
1890Oa E Rare	48,000	—	—	—	—	—
1890Oa N	Inc. above	65.00	125	200	350	—

KM# 399 5 CENTAVOS
Copper-Nickel **Obv:** Crossed bow and quiver above date **Obv. Legend:** REPUBLICA MEXICANA **Rev:** Value within wreath **Mint:** Mexico City

Date	Mintage	F	VF	XF	Unc	BU
1882	Inc. above	0.50	1.00	2.50	7.50	—
1883	Inc. above	25.00	50.00	80.00	250	—

KM# 400.2 5 CENTAVOS
1.3530 g., 0.9027 Silver 0.0393 oz. ASW **Obv:** Facing eagle, snake in beak **Rev:** Value within 1/2 wreath **Mint:** Mexico City

Date	Mintage	F	VF	XF	Unc	BU
1898Mo M	80,000	2.50	5.00	8.00	30.00	—
1899Mo M	168,000	2.00	3.00	5.00	18.00	—
1900/800Mo M	300,000	5.00	8.00	12.00	36.00	—
1900Mo M	Inc. above	2.00	3.00	5.00	18.00	—
1901Mo M	100,000	2.00	3.00	5.00	18.00	20.00
1902Mo M	144,000	1.50	2.50	5.00	14.00	18.00
1902/1Mo MoM	—	2.00	4.00	8.00	20.00	22.50
1903Mo M	500,000	1.50	2.50	5.00	14.00	18.00
1904/804Mo M	1,090,000	2.00	4.00	10.00	20.00	22.50
1904/94Mo M	Inc. above	2.00	5.00	11.00	20.00	22.50
1904Mo M	Inc. above	2.00	4.00	7.00	18.00	20.00
1905Mo M	344,000	2.00	4.00	8.00	20.00	22.50

KM# 400.3 5 CENTAVOS
1.3530 g., 0.9027 Silver 0.0393 oz. ASW **Obv:** Facing eagle, snake in beak **Rev:** Value within 1/2 wreath **Mint:** Zacatecas

Date	Mintage	F	VF	XF	Unc	BU
1898Zs Z	100,000	2.00	2.75	5.00	15.00	—
1899Zs Z	50,000	2.50	4.00	8.00	25.00	—
1900Zs Z	55,000	2.00	3.00	6.00	20.00	—
1901Zs Z	40,000	2.00	3.00	6.00	20.00	22.50
1902/1Zs Z	34,000	2.50	5.00	11.00	27.50	30.00
1902Zs Z	Inc. above	2.00	5.00	9.00	22.50	27.50
1903Zs Z	217,000	1.50	2.50	6.00	15.00	19.00
1904Zs Z	191,000	2.00	3.00	6.00	15.00	19.00
1904Zs M	Inc. above	2.00	3.00	7.00	20.00	22.50
1905Zs M	46,000	2.50	5.00	11.00	27.50	30.00
1905Zs M Repullica; Rare	Inc. above	—	—	—	—	—

KM# 400 5 CENTAVOS
1.3530 g., 0.9027 Silver 0.0393 oz. ASW, 14 mm. **Obv:** Facing eagle, snake in beak **Obv. Legend:** REPUBLICA MEXICANA **Rev:** Value within 1/2 wreath **Mint:** Culiacan **Note:** Varieties exist.

Date	Mintage	F	VF	XF	Unc	BU
1898Cn M	44,000	2.00	5.00	10.00	25.00	—
1899Cn M	111,000	7.00	10.00	25.00	60.00	—
1899Cn Q	Inc. above	2.00	3.00	5.00	18.00	—
1900/800Cn Q	239,000	4.00	6.00	15.00	36.00	—
1900Cn Q	Inc. above	2.00	4.00	7.00	20.00	—
Note: Round Q, single tail						
1900Cn Q	Inc. above	2.00	4.00	7.00	20.00	—
Note: Narrow C, oval Q						
1900Cn Q	Inc. above	2.00	4.00	7.00	20.00	—
Note: Wide C, oval Q						
1901Cn Q	148,000	2.00	3.00	5.00	18.00	22.50
1902Cn Q	262,000	2.00	4.00	7.00	20.00	25.00
Note: Narrow C, heavy serifs						
1902Cn Q	Inc. above	2.00	4.00	7.00	20.00	25.00
Note: Wide C, light serifs						
1903/1Cn Q	331,000	2.50	4.00	7.00	20.00	25.00
1903Cn Q	Inc. above	2.00	3.00	5.00	18.00	22.50
1903/1898Cn V	Inc. above	4.00	5.00	11.00	27.50	27.50
1903Cn V	Inc. above	2.00	3.00	5.00	18.00	22.50
1904Cn H	352,000	2.00	2.75	6.00	20.00	25.00
1904Cn H/C	—	2.00	3.00	6.00	20.00	25.00
1904Cn H 0/9	—	2.00	3.00	6.00	20.00	25.00

KM# 400.1 5 CENTAVOS
1.3530 g., 0.9027 Silver 0.0393 oz. ASW **Obv:** Facing eagle, snake in beak **Rev:** Value within 1/2 wreath **Mint:** Guanajuato **Note:** Varieties exist.

Date	Mintage	F	VF	XF	Unc	BU
1898Go R	180,000	7.50	15.00	30.00	75.00	—
Note: Mule, gold peso obverse						
1899Go R	260,000	1.75	2.50	4.50	15.00	—
1900Go R	200,000	1.75	2.50	4.50	15.00	—

KM# 402 10 CENTAVOS
2.7070 g., 0.9030 Silver 0.0786 oz. ASW **Obv:** Facing eagle, snake in beak **Rev:** Radiant cap **Mint:** Mexico City

Date	Mintage	F	VF	XF	Unc	BU
1867/3Mo	—	50.00	100	200	550	—
1867Mo	—	20.00	50.00	150	450	—
1868/7Mo	—	20.00	50.00	175	500	—
1868Mo	—	20.00	55.00	175	500	—

KM# 402.1 10 CENTAVOS
2.7070 g., 0.9030 Silver 0.0786 oz. ASW **Obv:** Facing eagle, snake in beak **Obv. Legend:** REPUBLICA MEXICANA **Rev:** Radiant cap **Mint:** San Luis Potosi

Date	Mintage	F	VF	XF	Unc	BU
1868/7P	38,000	45.00	90.00	175	650	—
1868P	Inc. above	20.00	40.00	100	550	—
1869/7P	4,900	55.00	125	250	800	—

KM# 401.1 10 CENTAVOS
2.7070 g., 0.9030 Silver 0.0786 oz. ASW **Obv:** Facing eagle, snake in beak **Rev:** Value within wreath **Mint:** Chihuahua
Note: Previous KM#401.

Date	Mintage	F	VF	XF	Unc	BU
1868/7Ca	—	30.00	60.00	150	550	—
1868Ca	—	30.00	60.00	150	550	—
1869Ca	15,000	25.00	50.00	125	600	—
1870Ca	17,000	22.50	45.00	100	550	—

KM# 401.2 10 CENTAVOS
2.7070 g., 0.9030 Silver 0.0786 oz. ASW **Obv:** Facing eagle, snake in beak **Obv. Legend:** REPUBLICA MEXICANA **Rev:** Value and date within wreath **Mint:** San Luis Potosi

Date	Mintage	F	VF	XF	Unc	BU
1863SLP	—	75.00	150	275	900	—

KM# 403 10 CENTAVOS
2.7070 g., 0.9030 Silver 0.0786 oz. ASW **Obv:** Facing eagle, snake in beak **Rev:** Value within 1/2 wreath **Mint:** Alamos
Note: Varieties exist.

Date	Mintage	F	VF	XF	Unc	BU
1874As DL	—	20.00	40.00	80.00	175	—
1875As L	—	5.00	10.00	25.00	90.00	—
1876As L	—	10.00	18.00	40.00	110	—
1878As L	—	5.00	10.00	30.00	100	—
1878/7As L	—	10.00	18.00	45.00	120	—
1879As L	—	10.00	18.00	40.00	110	—
1880As L	13,000	10.00	18.00	40.00	110	—
1882As L	22,000	10.00	18.00	40.00	110	—
1883As L	8,520	25.00	50.00	100	225	—
1884As L	—	7.50	12.50	35.00	100	—
1885As L	15,000	7.50	12.50	35.00	100	—
1886As L	45,000	7.50	12.50	35.00	100	—
1887As L	15,000	7.50	12.50	35.00	100	—
1888As L	38,000	7.50	12.50	35.00	100	—
1889As L	20,000	7.50	12.50	35.00	100	—
1890As L	40,000	7.50	12.50	35.00	100	—
1891As L	38,000	7.50	12.50	35.00	100	—
1892As L	57,000	5.00	10.00	25.00	90.00	—
1893As L	70,000	10.00	18.00	40.00	110	—

Note: An 1891 As L over 1889 HoG exists which was evidently produced at the Alamos Mint using dies sent from the Hermosillo Mint

KM# 403.4 10 CENTAVOS
2.7070 g., 0.9030 Silver 0.0786 oz. ASW **Obv:** Facing eagle, snake in beak **Rev:** Value within 1/2 wreath **Mint:** Guadalajara
Note: Varieties exist.

Date	Mintage	F	VF	XF	Unc	BU
1871Ga C	4,734	75.00	125	200	500	—
1873/1Ga C	25,000	10.00	15.00	35.00	150	—
1873Ga C	Inc. above	10.00	15.00	35.00	150	—
1874Ga C	—	10.00	15.00	35.00	150	—
1877Ga A	—	10.00	15.00	30.00	150	—
1881Ga S	115,000	5.00	10.00	25.00	150	—
1883Ga B	90,000	4.00	8.00	15.00	90.00	—
1884Ga H	—	3.00	5.00	10.00	90.00	—
1884Ga B	—	5.00	10.00	20.00	90.00	—
1884Ga B/S	—	6.00	12.50	25.00	90.00	—
1885Ga H	93,000	3.00	5.00	10.00	90.00	—

Date	Mintage	F	VF	XF	Unc	BU
1886Ga S	151,000	2.50	4.00	9.00	90.00	—
1887Ga S	162,000	1.50	3.00	6.00	90.00	—
1888Ga GaS/ HoG	Inc. above	1.50	3.00	6.00	90.00	—
1888Ga S	225,000	1.50	3.00	6.00	90.00	—
1889Ga S	310,000	1.50	3.00	6.00	40.00	—
1890Ga S	303,000	1.50	3.00	6.00	40.00	—
1891Ga S	199,000	5.00	10.00	20.00	45.00	—
1892Ga S	329,000	1.50	3.00	6.00	40.00	—
1893Ga S	225,000	1.50	3.00	6.00	40.00	—
1894Ga S	243,000	3.00	6.00	12.00	40.00	—
1895Ga S	80,000	1.50	3.00	6.00	40.00	—

KM# 403.5 10 CENTAVOS
2.7070 g., 0.9030 Silver 0.0786 oz. ASW **Obv:** Facing eagle, snake in beak **Rev:** Value within 1/2 wreath **Mint:** Guanajuato
Note: Varieties exist.

Date	Mintage	F	VF	XF	Unc	BU
1869Go S	7,000	20.00	40.00	80.00	200	—
1871/0Go S	60,000	15.00	25.00	50.00	125	—
1872Go S	60,000	15.00	25.00	50.00	125	—
1873Go S	50,000	15.00	25.00	50.00	125	—
1874Go S	—	15.00	25.00	50.00	125	—
1875Go S	—	250	350	500	800	—
1876Go S	—	10.00	20.00	40.00	100	—
1877Go S	—	80.00	120	200	400	—
1878/7Go S	10,000	10.00	20.00	45.00	110	—
1878Go S	Inc. above	7.50	12.00	20.00	75.00	—
1879Go S	—	7.50	12.00	20.00	75.00	—
1880Go S	—	100	200	300	450	—
1881/71Go S	100,000	3.00	5.00	10.00	75.00	—
1881/0Go S	Inc. above	3.50	5.00	10.00	75.00	—
1881Go S	Inc. above	3.00	5.00	10.00	75.00	—
1882/1Go S	40,000	3.00	6.00	12.00	75.00	—
1883Go B	—	3.00	5.00	10.00	75.00	—
1884Go B	—	1.50	3.00	6.00	75.00	—
1884Go S	—	6.00	12.50	25.00	90.00	—
1885Go R	100,000	1.50	3.00	6.00	75.00	—
1886Go R	95,000	3.00	5.00	10.00	75.00	—
1887Go R	330,000	2.50	5.00	10.00	75.00	—
1888Go R	270,000	1.50	3.00	6.00	75.00	—
1889Go R	205,000	2.00	4.00	8.00	75.00	—
1889Go GoR/HoG	Inc. above	3.00	5.00	10.00	75.00	—
1890Go R	270,000	1.50	3.00	6.00	35.00	—
1890Go GoR/Cn M	Inc. above	1.50	3.00	6.00	35.00	—
1891Go R	523,000	1.50	3.00	6.00	35.00	—
1891Go R/G	—	1.50	3.00	6.00	35.00	—
1891Go GoR/HoG	Inc. above	1.50	3.00	6.00	35.00	—
1892Go R	440,000	1.50	3.00	6.00	35.00	—
1893/1Go R	389,000	3.00	5.00	10.00	35.00	—
1893Go R	Inc. above	1.50	3.00	6.00	35.00	—
1894Go R	400,000	1.50	2.50	5.00	35.00	—
1895Go R	355,000	1.50	2.50	5.00	35.00	—
1896Go R	190,000	1.50	2.50	5.00	35.00	—
1897Go R	205,000	1.50	2.50	5.00	35.00	—

KM# 403.7 10 CENTAVOS
2.7070 g., 0.9020 Silver 0.0785 oz. ASW **Obv:** Facing eagle, snake in beak **Obv. Legend:** REPUBLICA MEXICANA **Rev:** Value within 1/2 wreath **Mint:** Mexico City **Note:** Varieties exist.

Date	Mintage	F	VF	XF	Unc	BU
1869/8Mo C	30,000	10.00	20.00	40.00	100	—
1869Mo C	Inc. above	8.00	17.50	35.00	90.00	—
1870Mo C	110,000	4.00	7.50	15.00	50.00	—
1871Mo C	84,000	50.00	75.00	125	250	—
1871Mo M	Inc. above	12.00	17.50	45.00	125	—
1872/69Mo M	198,000	10.00	20.00	35.00	100	—
1872Mo M	Inc. above	4.00	7.50	15.00	65.00	—
1873Mo M	40,000	10.00	15.00	30.00	75.00	—
1874Mo M	—	5.00	10.00	20.00	65.00	—
1874Mo M/C	—	5.00	10.00	20.00	65.00	—
1874/64Mo B	—	5.00	10.00	20.00	65.00	—
1874Mo B/M	—	20.00	40.00	60.00	125	—

Date	Mintage	F	VF	XF	Unc	BU
1874Mo B	—	5.00	10.00	15.00	65.00	—
1875Mo B	—	20.00	40.00	60.00	125	—
1876/5Mo B	—	4.00	6.00	10.00	65.00	—
1876/5Mo B/M	—	4.00	6.00	10.00	65.00	—
1877/6Mo M	—	4.00	6.00	10.00	65.00	—
1877/6Mo M/B	—	4.00	6.00	10.00	65.00	—
1877Mo M	—	4.00	6.00	10.00	65.00	—
1878/7Mo M	100,000	4.00	6.00	10.00	65.00	—
1878Mo M	Inc. above	4.00	6.00	10.00	65.00	—
1879/69Mo M	—	4.00	6.00	10.00	65.00	—
1879Mo M/C	—	4.00	6.00	10.00	65.00	—
1880/79Mo M	—	4.00	6.00	10.00	65.00	—
1881/0Mo M	510,000	4.00	6.00	10.00	35.00	—
1881Mo M	Inc. above	4.00	6.00	10.00	35.00	—
1882/1Mo M	550,000	4.00	6.00	10.00	35.00	—
1882Mo M	Inc. above	4.00	6.00	10.00	35.00	—
1883/2Mo M	250,000	4.00	6.00	10.00	35.00	—
1884Mo M	—	4.00	6.00	10.00	35.00	—
1885Mo M	470,000	4.00	6.00	10.00	35.00	—
1886Mo M	603,000	4.00	6.00	10.00	35.00	—
1887/6Mo M	—	4.00	6.00	10.00	35.00	—
1887Mo M	580,000	4.00	6.00	10.00	35.00	—
1888/7Mo MoM	710,000	4.00	6.00	10.00	35.00	—
1888Mo MoM	Inc. above	4.00	6.00	10.00	35.00	—
1888Mo MOM	Inc. above	4.00	6.00	10.00	35.00	—
1889/8Mo M	622,000	4.00	6.00	10.00	35.00	—
1889Mo M	Inc. above	4.00	6.00	10.00	35.00	—
1890/89Mo M	815,000	4.00	6.00	10.00	35.00	—
1890Mo M	Inc. above	4.00	6.00	10.00	35.00	—
1891Mo M	859,000	2.00	4.00	8.00	25.00	—
1892Mo M	1,030,000	2.00	4.00	8.00	25.00	—
1893Mo M	310,000	2.00	4.00	8.00	25.00	—
1893Mo M/C	Inc. above	2.00	4.00	8.00	25.00	—
1893Mo Mo/Ho M/G	—	2.00	4.00	8.00	25.00	—
1894/3Mo M	—	5.00	10.00	20.00	60.00	—
1894Mo M	350,000	5.00	10.00	20.00	60.00	—
1895Mo M	320,000	2.00	4.00	8.00	25.00	—
1896Mo B/G	340,000	2.00	4.00	8.00	25.00	—
1896Mo M	Inc. above	35.00	70.00	100	150	—
1897Mo M	170,000	2.00	4.00	6.00	20.00	—

KM# 403.9   10 CENTAVOS
2.7070 g., 0.9030 Silver 0.0786 oz. ASW **Obv:** Facing eagle, snake in beak **Rev:** Value within 1/2 wreath **Mint:** San Luis Potosi **Note:** Varieties exist.

Date	Mintage	F	VF	XF	Unc	BU
1869/8Pi S Rare	4,000	—	—	—	—	—
1870/69Pi O Rare	18,000	—	—	—	—	—
1870Pi G	Inc. above	125	200	325	600	—
1871Pi O	21,000	50.00	100	150	300	—
1872Pi O	16,000	150	225	350	650	—
1873Pi O Rare	4,750	—	—	—	—	—
1874Pi H	—	25.00	50.00	100	200	—
1875Pi H	—	75.00	125	200	400	—
1876Pi H	—	75.00	125	200	400	—
1877Pi H	—	75.00	125	200	400	—
1878Pi H	—	250	500	750	—	—
1879Pi H	—	—	—	—	—	—
1880Pi H	—	150	250	350	—	—
1881Pi H	7,600	250	350	500	—	—
1882Pi H Rare	4,000	—	—	—	—	—
1883Pi H	—	125	200	300	500	—
1884Pi H	—	25.00	50.00	100	200	—
1885Pi H	51,000	25.00	50.00	100	200	—
1885Pi C Rare	Inc. above	—	—	—	—	—
1886Pi C	52,000	15.00	30.00	60.00	150	—
1886Pi R	Inc. above	5.00	10.00	20.00	65.00	—
1887Pi R	118,000	3.00	6.00	12.00	50.00	—
1888Pi R	136,000	3.00	6.00	12.00	50.00	—
1889/8Pi R/G	—	7.50	12.50	20.00	60.00	—
1889/7Pi R	131,000	7.50	12.50	20.00	60.00	—
1890Pi R/G	—	2.50	5.00	10.00	40.00	—
1890Pi R	204,000	2.00	4.00	8.50	40.00	—
1891/89Pi R	163,000	3.00	6.00	12.00	40.00	—
1891Pi R	Inc. above	2.00	4.50	8.00	30.00	—
1892/0Pi R/G	—	2.50	5.00	10.00	40.00	—
1892/0Pi R	200,000	2.50	3.50	10.00	40.00	—
1892Pi R	Inc. above	2.00	2.50	5.00	40.00	—
1892Pi R/G	—	2.50	5.00	10.00	40.00	—

Date	Mintage	F	VF	XF	Unc	BU
1893Pi R/G	—	2.00	10.00	17.50	60.00	—
1893Pi R	48,000	7.50	10.00	17.50	60.00	—

KM# 403.2   10 CENTAVOS
2.7070 g., 0.9030 Silver 0.0786 oz. ASW **Obv:** Facing eagle, snake in beak **Rev:** Value within 1/2 wreath **Mint:** Culiacan

Date	Mintage	F	VF	XF	Unc	BU
1871Cn P Rare	—	—	—	—	—	—
1873Cn P	8,732	20.00	50.00	100	225	—
1881Cn D	9,440	75.00	175	325	500	—
1882Cn D	12,000	75.00	125	200	400	—
1885Cn M	18,000	25.00	50.00	100	200	—
Note: Mule, gold 2-1/2 peso obverse						
1886Cn M	13,000	50.00	100	150	300	—
Note: Mule, gold 2-1/2 peso obverse						
1887Cn M	11,000	20.00	40.00	75.00	175	—
1888Cn M	56,000	5.00	10.00	25.00	125	—
1889Cn M	42,000	5.00	10.00	20.00	75.00	—
1890Cn M	132,000	2.50	5.00	9.50	75.00	—
1891Cn M	84,000	5.00	10.00	20.00	75.00	—
1892/1Cn M	37,000	4.00	8.00	15.00	75.00	—
1892Cn M	Inc. above	3.00	6.00	12.00	75.00	—
1894Cn M	43,000	3.00	6.00	12.00	75.00	—
1895Cn M	23,000	3.00	6.00	12.00	60.00	—
1896Cn M	121,000	2.00	3.50	7.00	50.00	—

KM# 403.3   10 CENTAVOS
2.7070 g., 0.9030 Silver 0.0786 oz. ASW **Obv:** Facing eagle, snake in beak **Rev:** Value within 1/2 wreath **Mint:** Durango

Date	Mintage	F	VF	XF	Unc	BU
1878Do E	2,500	100	175	300	600	—
1879Do B Rare	—	—	—	—	—	—
1880/70Do B Rare	—	—	—	—	—	—
1880/79Do B Rare	—	—	—	—	—	—
1884Do C	—	30.00	60.00	100	225	—
1886Do C	13,000	75.00	150	300	500	—
1887Do C	81,000	4.00	8.00	15.00	100	—
1888Do C	31,000	6.00	12.00	30.00	100	—
1889Do C	55,000	4.00	8.00	15.00	100	—
1890Do C	50,000	4.00	8.00	15.00	100	—
1891Do P	139,000	2.00	4.00	8.00	80.00	—
1892Do P	212,000	2.00	4.00	8.00	80.00	—
1892Do D	Inc. above	2.00	4.00	8.00	80.00	—
1893Do D	258,000	2.00	4.00	8.00	80.00	—
1893Do D/C	Inc. above	2.50	5.00	10.00	80.00	—
1894Do D	184,000	1.50	3.00	6.00	80.00	—
1894Do D/C	Inc. above	2.00	4.00	8.00	80.00	—
1895Do D	142,000	1.50	3.00	6.00	80.00	—

KM# 403.6   10 CENTAVOS
2.7070 g., 0.9030 Silver 0.0786 oz. ASW **Obv:** Facing eagle, snake in beak **Rev:** Value within 1/2 wreath **Mint:** Hermosillo

Date	Mintage	F	VF	XF	Unc	BU
1874Ho R	—	30.00	60.00	100	200	—
1876Ho F	3,140	200	300	450	750	—
1878Ho A	—	5.00	10.00	15.00	85.00	—
1879Ho A	—	25.00	50.00	90.00	175	—
1880Ho A	—	3.50	7.00	13.50	85.00	—
1881Ho A	28,000	4.00	8.00	17.00	85.00	—
1882/1Ho A	25,000	5.00	10.00	20.00	85.00	—
1882/1Ho a	Inc. above	6.00	12.50	25.00	85.00	—
1882Ho A	Inc. above	4.00	8.00	17.00	85.00	—
1883Ho	7,000	65.00	100	200	400	—
1884/3Ho M	—	10.00	20.00	40.00	90.00	—
1884Ho A	—	35.00	75.00	150	300	—
1884/3Ho M	—	7.50	15.00	30.00	85.00	—
1884Ho M	—	7.50	15.00	30.00	85.00	—
1885Ho M	21,000	12.50	25.00	50.00	100	—
1886Ho M Rare	10,000	—	—	—	—	—
1886Ho G	Inc. above	7.50	12.50	25.00	85.00	—
1887Ho G	—	25.00	50.00	75.00	150	—
1888Ho G	25,000	6.00	12.50	25.00	85.00	—
1889Ho G	42,000	3.50	7.00	12.00	85.00	—
1890Ho G	48,000	3.50	7.00	12.00	85.00	—
1891/80Ho G	136,000	3.50	7.00	12.00	85.00	—
1891/0Ho G	Inc. above	3.50	7.00	12.00	85.00	—
1891Ho G	Inc. above	3.50	7.00	12.00	85.00	—
1892Ho G	67,000	3.50	7.00	12.00	85.00	—
1893Ho G	67,000	3.50	7.00	12.00	85.00	—

KM# 403.8 10 CENTAVOS
2.7070 g., 0.9030 Silver 0.0786 oz. ASW **Obv:** Facing eagle, snake in beak **Rev:** Value within 1/2 wreath **Mint:** Oaxaca

Date	Mintage	F	VF	XF	Unc	BU
1889Oa E	21,000	200	400	600	—	—
1890Oa E	31,000	100	150	250	500	—
1890Oa N Rare	Inc. above	—	—	—	—	—

KM# 403.10 10 CENTAVOS
2.7070 g., 0.9030 Silver 0.0786 oz. ASW **Obv:** Facing eagle, snake in beak **Obv. Legend:** REPUBLICA MEXICANA **Rev:** Value within 1/2 wreath **Mint:** Zacatecas **Note:** Varieties exist.

Date	Mintage	F	VF	XF	Unc	BU
1870Zs H	20,000	100	150	200	400	—
1871Zs H	Inc. above	—	—	—	—	—
1871/0Zs H	10,000	—	—	—	—	—
1872Zs H	10,000	150	200	275	500	—
1873Zs H	10,000	250	350	600	—	—
1874Zs A	—	200	300	500	—	—
1874/3Zs H	—	50.00	75.00	150	300	—
1875Zs A	—	5.00	10.00	25.00	100	—
1876Zs A	—	5.00	10.00	25.00	100	—
1876Zs S	—	100	200	300	500	—
1877Zs S Small S	—	7.50	12.50	25.00	100	—
1877Zs Regular S over small S	—	7.50	12.50	25.00	100	—
1877Zs S Regular S	—	7.50	12.50	25.00	100	—
1878Zs S	Inc. above	5.00	10.00	20.00	80.00	—
1878/7Zs S	30,000	5.00	10.00	20.00	80.00	—
1879Zs S	—	5.00	10.00	20.00	80.00	—
1880Zs S	—	5.00	10.00	20.00	80.00	—
1881Zs S	Inc. above	3.50	7.00	12.50	50.00	—
1881/0Zs S	120,000	3.50	7.00	12.50	50.00	—
1882Zs S	Inc. above	12.50	25.00	50.00	125	—
1882/1Zs S	64,000	12.50	25.00	50.00	125	—
1883Zs S	Inc. above	2.50	5.00	10.00	50.00	—
1883/73Zs S	102,000	2.50	5.00	10.00	50.00	—
1884Zs S	—	2.50	5.00	10.00	50.00	—
1884/3Zs S	—	2.50	5.00	10.00	50.00	—
1885Zs S	297,000	2.00	3.50	7.00	50.00	—
1885Zs Z	Inc. above	4.00	8.50	17.00	65.00	—
Note: Without assayers initials, error						
1885Zs S Small S in mint mark	Inc. above	3.00	5.00	10.00	50.00	—
1886Zs Z	Inc. above	12.50	25.00	50.00	125	—
1886Zs S	274,000	2.00	3.50	7.00	30.00	—
1887Zs ZsZ	233,000	2.00	3.50	7.00	30.00	—
1887Zs Z Z Error	Inc. above	4.00	10.00	25.00	100	—
1888Zs ZsZ	270,000	2.00	3.50	7.00	30.00	—
1888Zs Z Z Error	Inc. above	4.00	10.00	25.00	100	—
1889/7Zs Z/S	240,000	4.50	8.00	12.50	40.00	—
1889Zs ZS	Inc. above	2.00	5.00	10.00	30.00	—
1889Zs Z/G	—	2.00	5.00	10.00	30.00	—
1889Zs Z	Inc. above	2.00	3.50	7.00	30.00	—
1890Zs ZsZ	410,000	2.00	3.50	7.00	30.00	—
1890Zs Z Z Error	Inc. above	4.25	10.00	25.00	100	—
1891Zs Z	1,105,000	2.00	3.50	7.00	30.00	—
1891Zs ZsZ Double s	Inc. above	2.50	5.00	9.00	30.00	—
1892Zs Z	1,102,000	2.00	3.50	7.00	30.00	—
1892Zs Z/G	—	2.50	5.00	9.00	30.00	—
1893/2Zs Z	—	2.50	5.00	10.00	40.00	—
1893Zs Z	1,010,999	2.00	3.50	7.00	25.00	—
1894Zs Z	892,000	2.00	3.50	7.00	30.00	—
1895Zs Z	920,000	2.00	3.50	7.00	30.00	—
1895Zs Z 9/5	—	2.50	5.00	10.00	30.00	—
1896/5Z S/O Z/G	—	2.50	5.00	10.00	30.00	—
1896/5Zs Z/G	—	2.00	3.50	7.00	30.00	—
1896Zs Z/G	—	2.00	3.50	7.00	30.00	—
1896/5Zs ZsZ	700,000	2.00	3.50	7.00	30.00	—
1896Zs ZsZ	Inc. above	2.00	3.50	7.00	30.00	—
1896Zs Z Z Error	Inc. above	4.25	10.00	25.00	100	—
1897Zs Z	Inc. above	2.00	3.50	7.00	30.00	—
1897/6Zs ZsZ	900,000	2.50	6.00	10.00	30.00	—
1897/6Zs Z Z Error	Inc. above	4.25	10.00	25.00	100	—

KM# 403.1 10 CENTAVOS
2.7070 g., 0.9030 Silver 0.0786 oz. ASW **Obv:** Facing eagle, snake in beak **Rev:** Value within 1/2 wreath **Mint:** Chihuahua **Note:** Mint mark CH, Ca. Varieties exist.

Date	Mintage	F	VF	XF	Unc	BU
1871 M	8,150	15.00	30.00	60.00	150	—
1873 M Crude date	—	35.00	75.00	125	175	—
1874 M	—	10.00	17.50	35.00	100	—
1880 G/g	Inc. above	15.00	25.00	50.00	125	—
1880/70 G	7,620	20.00	40.00	80.00	175	—
1881 Rare	340	—	—	—	—	—
1883 M	9,000	10.00	20.00	40.00	125	—
1884/73	—	5.00	30.00	60.00	150	—
1884 M	—	10.00	20.00	40.00	125	—
1886 M	45,000	7.50	12.50	30.00	100	—
1887/3 M/G	96,000	5.00	10.00	20.00	75.00	—
1887 M/G	—	2.50	5.00	10.00	75.00	—
1887 M	Inc. above	2.50	5.00	10.00	75.00	—
1888 M/G	—	2.50	5.00	10.00	75.00	—
1888 M	299,000	2.00	4.00	7.00	75.00	—
1888 Ca/Mo	Inc. above	2.00	4.00	7.00	75.00	—
1889 M	Inc. above	2.50	5.00	10.00	75.00	—
Note: Small 89 (5 Centavo font)						
1889/8 M	115,000	2.50	5.00	10.00	75.00	—
1890 M	Inc. above	2.00	4.00	9.00	75.00	—
1890/80 M	140,000	2.50	5.00	10.00	75.00	—
1890/89 M	Inc. above	2.50	5.00	10.00	75.00	—
1891 M	163,000	2.00	4.00	9.00	75.00	—
1892 M	169,000	2.00	4.00	9.00	75.00	—
1892 M 9/inverted 9	Inc. above	2.50	5.00	10.00	75.00	—
1893 M	246,000	2.00	4.00	9.00	75.00	—
1894 M	163,000	2.00	4.00	9.00	75.00	—
1895 M	127,000	2.00	4.00	9.00	75.00	—

KM# 404 10 CENTAVOS
2.7070 g., 0.9030 Silver 0.0786 oz. ASW **Obv:** Facing eagle, snake in beak **Obv. Legend:** REPUBLICA MEXICANA **Rev:** Value within 1/2 wreath **Mint:** Culiacan **Note:** Varieties exist.

Date	Mintage	F	VF	XF	Unc	BU
1898Cn M	9,870	50.00	100	200	500	—
1899Cn Q Oval Q, double tail	Inc. above	5.00	7.50	25.00	100	—
1899Cn Q Round Q, single tail	80,000	5.00	7.50	25.00	100	—
1900Cn Q	160,000	2.25	3.00	7.00	27.50	—
1901Cn Q	235,000	2.25	3.00	7.00	25.00	27.50
1902Cn Q	186,000	2.25	3.00	7.00	27.50	30.00
1903Cn V	Inc. above	2.25	3.00	7.00	20.00	30.00
1903Cn Q	256,000	2.25	3.00	8.00	27.50	22.50
1904Cn H	307,000	2.25	3.00	7.00	20.00	22.50

KM# 404.1 10 CENTAVOS
2.7070 g., 0.9030 Silver 0.0786 oz. ASW **Obv:** Facing eagle, snake in beak **Rev:** Value within 1/2 wreath **Mint:** Guanajuato

Date	Mintage	F	VF	XF	Unc	BU
1898Go R	435,000	2.00	3.50	7.00	20.00	—
1899Go R	270,000	2.00	3.50	7.00	25.00	—
1900Go R	130,000	7.50	12.50	25.00	60.00	—

KM# 404.2 10 CENTAVOS
2.7070 g., 0.9030 Silver 0.0786 oz. ASW **Obv:** Facing eagle, snake in beak **Obv. Legend:** REPUBLICA MEXICANA **Rev:** Value within 1/2 wreath **Mint:** Mexico City

Date	Mintage	F	VF	XF	Unc	BU
1898Mo M	130,000	2.75	5.00	8.00	27.50	—
1899Mo M	190,000	2.75	5.00	8.00	27.50	—
1900Mo M	311,000	2.75	5.00	8.00	27.50	—
1901Mo M	80,000	3.00	5.00	9.00	30.50	33.75
1902Mo M	181,000	2.25	3.00	8.00	27.50	30.00
1903Mo M	581,000	2.25	3.00	8.00	27.50	30.00
1904Mo M	1,266,000	2.25	3.00	6.00	25.00	27.50
1904Mo MM (Error)	Inc. above	3.00	7.00	14.00	33.75	37.75
1905Mo M	266,000	2.75	5.00	10.00	27.50	30.00

KM# 404.3   10 CENTAVOS
2.7070 g., 0.9020 Silver 0.0785 oz. ASW **Obv:** Facing eagle, snake in beak **Rev:** Value within 1/2 wreath **Mint:** Zacatecas

Date	Mintage	F	VF	XF	Unc	BU
1898Zs Z	240,000	2.75	5.00	13.00	27.50	—
1899Zs Z	105,000	2.75	5.00	16.00	30.00	—
1900Zs Z	219,000	10.00	14.00	27.50	60.00	—
1901Zs Z	70,000	3.00	7.00	14.00	33.75	37.75
1902Zs Z	120,000	3.00	7.00	14.00	33.75	37.75
1903Zs Z	228,000	2.25	4.00	12.00	25.00	27.50
1904Zs Z	368,000	2.25	4.00	12.00	25.00	27.50
1904Zs M	Inc. above	2.25	4.00	12.00	30.00	33.75
1905Zs M	66,000	10.00	27.50	70.00	270	—

KM# 405   20 CENTAVOS
5.4150 g., 0.9030 Silver 0.1572 oz. ASW **Obv:** Facing eagle, snake in beak **Rev:** Value within 1/2 wreath **Mint:** Culiacan

Date	Mintage	F	VF	XF	Unc	BU
1898Cn M	114,000	5.00	12.50	35.00	140	—
1899Cn M	44,000	12.00	20.00	45.00	225	—
1899Cn Q	Inc. above	20.00	35.00	100	250	—
1900Cn Q	68,000	6.50	12.50	35.00	140	—
1901Cn Q	185,000	6.00	12.00	36.00	145	—
1902/802Cn Q	98,000	7.00	12.00	36.00	145	—
1902Cn Q	Inc. above	5.00	11.00	36.00	145	—
1903Cn Q	93,000	5.00	11.00	36.00	145	—
1904/3Cn H	258,000	—	—	—	—	—
1904Cn H	Inc. above	6.00	12.00	36.00	145	—

KM# 405.1   20 CENTAVOS
5.4150 g., 0.9027 Silver 0.1572 oz. ASW **Obv:** Facing eagle, snake in beak **Obv. Legend:** REPUBLICA MEXICANA **Rev:** Value within 1/2 wreath **Mint:** Guanajuato

Date	Mintage	F	VF	XF	Unc	BU
1898Go R	135,000	5.00	10.00	20.00	100	—
1899Go R	215,000	5.00	10.00	20.00	100	—
1900/800Go R	38,000	10.00	20.00	60.00	250	—

KM# 405.3   20 CENTAVOS
5.4150 g., 0.9027 Silver 0.1572 oz. ASW **Obv:** Facing eagle, snake in beak **Obv. Legend:** REPUBLICA MEXICANA **Rev:** Value within 1/2 wreath **Mint:** Zacatecas

Date	Mintage	F	VF	XF	Unc	BU
1898Zs Z	195,000	6.00	12.00	25.00	100	—
1899Zs Z	210,000	6.00	12.00	25.00	100	—
1900/800Zs Z	97,000	6.00	12.00	45.00	200	—
1901Zs Z	Inc. above	6.00	12.00	25.00	120	—
1901/0Zs Z	130,000	30.00	60.00	120	300	—
1902Zs Z	105,000	6.00	12.00	25.00	120	—
1903Zs Z	143,000	6.00	12.00	25.00	120	—
1904Zs Z	246,000	6.00	12.00	25.00	120	—
1904Zs M	Inc. above	6.00	12.00	60.00	350	—
1905Zs M	59,000	12.00	85.00	60.00	475	—

KM# 405.2   20 CENTAVOS
5.4150 g., 0.9030 Silver 0.1572 oz. ASW **Obv:** Facing eagle, snake in beak **Rev:** Value within 1/2 wreath **Mint:** Mexico City
Note: Varieties exist.

Date	Mintage	F	VF	XF	Unc	BU
1898Mo M	150,000	5.00	10.00	20.00	125	—
1899Mo M	425,000	5.00	10.00	20.00	125	—
1900/800Mo M	295,000	5.00	10.00	20.00	125	—
1901Mo M	110,000	5.00	10.00	25.00	110	—
1902Mo M	120,000	5.00	10.00	25.00	110	—
1903Mo M	213,000	5.00	10.00	25.00	110	—

Date	Mintage	F	VF	XF	Unc	BU
1904Mo M	276,000	5.00	10.00	25.00	110	—
1905Mo M	117,000	8.00	25.00	60.00	180	—

KM# 406.2   25 CENTAVOS
6.7680 g., 0.9030 Silver 0.1965 oz. ASW **Obv:** Facing eagle, snake in beak **Rev:** Radiant cap above scales **Mint:** Culiacan

Date	Mintage	F	VF	XF	Unc	BU
1871Cn P	—	250	500	750	—	—
1872Cn P	2,780	300	550	800	—	—
1873Cn P	20,000	100	150	250	500	—
1874Cn P	—	20.00	50.00	125	250	—
1875Cn P	—	250	500	750	—	—
1876Cn P Rare	—	—	—	—	—	—
1878Cn Cn/Go D/S	—	100	150	250	500	—
1878/7Cn D/S	—	100	150	250	500	—
1878Cn D	—	100	150	250	500	—
1879Cn D	—	15.00	35.00	70.00	175	—
1880Cn D	—	250	500	750	—	—
1881/0Cn D	18,000	15.00	30.00	60.00	175	—
1882Cn D	—	200	350	600	—	—
1882Cn M Rare	—	—	—	—	—	—
1883Cn M	15,000	50.00	100	150	300	—
1884Cn M	—	20.00	40.00	80.00	175	—
1885/4Cn M	19,000	20.00	40.00	80.00	175	—
1886Cn M	22,000	12.50	20.00	50.00	175	—
1887Cn M	32,000	12.50	20.00	50.00	175	—
1888Cn M Cn/Mo	—	—	—	—	—	—
1888Cn M	86,000	8.00	15.00	30.00	175	—
1889Cn M	50,000	10.00	25.00	50.00	175	—
1890Cn M 9/8	—	9.00	17.50	40.00	175	—
1890Cn M	91,000	9.00	17.50	40.00	175	—
1892/0Cn M	16,000	20.00	40.00	80.00	200	—
1892Cn M	Inc. above	20.00	40.00	80.00	200	—

KM# 406.3   25 CENTAVOS
6.7680 g., 0.9030 Silver 0.1965 oz. ASW **Obv:** Facing eagle, snake in beak **Rev:** Radiant cap above scales **Mint:** Durango

Date	Mintage	F	VF	XF	Unc	BU
1873Do P Rare	892	—	—	—	—	—
1877Do P	—	25.00	50.00	100	200	—
1878/7Do E	—	250	500	750	—	—
1878Do B Rare	—	—	—	—	—	—
1879Do B	—	50.00	75.00	125	250	—
1880Do B Rare	—	—	—	—	—	—
1882Do C	17,000	25.00	50.00	100	225	—
1884/3Do C	—	25.00	50.00	100	200	—
1885Do C	15,000	20.00	40.00	80.00	200	—
1885Do C/S	—	20.00	40.00	80.00	200	—
1886Do C	33,000	15.00	30.00	60.00	200	—
1887Do C	27,000	10.00	20.00	50.00	200	—
1888Do C	25,000	10.00	20.00	50.00	200	—
1889Do C	29,000	10.00	20.00	50.00	200	—
1890Do C	68,000	8.00	15.00	40.00	200	—

KM# 406.4   25 CENTAVOS
6.7680 g., 0.9030 Silver 0.1965 oz. ASW **Obv:** Facing eagle, snake in beak **Rev:** Radiant cap above scales **Mint:** Guadalajara

Date	Mintage	F	VF	XF	Unc	BU
1880Ga A	38,000	25.00	50.00	100	200	—
1881/0Ga S	39,000	25.00	50.00	100	200	—
1881Ga S	Inc. above	25.00	50.00	100	200	—
1882Ga S	18,000	25.00	50.00	100	200	—
1883/2Ga B/S	—	50.00	100	150	300	—
1884Ga B	—	20.00	40.00	80.00	150	—
1889Ga S	30,000	20.00	40.00	80.00	150	—

KM# 406   25 CENTAVOS
6.7680 g., 0.9030 Silver 0.1965 oz. ASW **Obv:** Facing eagle, snake in beak **Rev:** Radiant cap above scales **Mint:** Alamos
Note: Mint mark A, As.

Date	Mintage	F	VF	XF	Unc	BU
1874 L	—	20.00	40.00	90.00	200	—
1875 L	—	15.00	30.00	70.00	200	—
1876 L	—	30.00	50.00	100	200	—
1877 L	11,000	200	300	500	—	—
1877.	Inc. above	10.00	25.00	60.00	200	—
1878 L	25,000	10.00	25.00	60.00	200	—
1879 L	—	10.00	25.00	60.00	200	—
1880 L	—	10.00	25.00	60.00	200	—
1880. L	—	10.00	25.00	60.00	200	—
1881 L	8,800	500	700	—	—	—
1882 L	7,777	15.00	35.00	80.00	200	—
1883 L	28,000	10.00	25.00	60.00	200	—
1884 L	—	10.00	25.00	60.00	200	—
1885 L	—	20.00	40.00	90.00	200	—
1886 L	46,000	15.00	30.00	70.00	200	—
1887 L	12,000	12.50	27.50	65.00	200	—
1888 L	20,000	12.50	27.50	65.00	200	—
1889 L	14,000	12.50	27.50	65.00	200	—
1890 L	23,000	10.00	25.00	60.00	200	—

KM# 406.1 25 CENTAVOS

6.7680 g., 0.9030 Silver 0.1965 oz. ASW **Obv:** Facing eagle, snake in beak **Rev:** Radiant cap above scales **Mint:** Chihuahua **Note:** Mint mark CA, CH, Ca.

Date	Mintage	F	VF	XF	Unc	BU
1871 M	18,000	25.00	50.00	100	200	—
1872 M Very crude date	24,000	50.00	100	150	300	—
1883 M	12,000	10.00	25.00	50.00	175	—
1885/3 M	35,000	10.00	25.00	50.00	175	—
1885 M	Inc. above	10.00	25.00	50.00	175	—
1886 M	22,000	10.00	25.00	50.00	175	—
1887/6 M	26,000	10.00	15.00	30.00	175	—
1887 M	Inc. above	10.00	15.00	30.00	175	—
1888 M	14,000	10.00	25.00	50.00	175	—
1889 M	50,000	10.00	15.00	30.00	175	—

KM# 406.5 25 CENTAVOS

6.7680 g., 0.9030 Silver 0.1965 oz. ASW **Obv:** Facing eagle, snake in beak **Rev:** Radiant cap above scales **Mint:** Guanajuato **Note:** Varieties exist.

Date	Mintage	F	VF	XF	Unc	BU
1870Go S	128,000	10.00	20.00	50.00	125	—
1871Go S	172,000	10.00	20.00	50.00	125	—
1872/1Go S	178,000	10.00	20.00	50.00	125	—
1872Go S	Inc. above	10.00	20.00	50.00	125	—
1873Go S	120,000	10.00	20.00	50.00	125	—
1874Go S	—	15.00	30.00	60.00	150	—
1875/4Go S	—	15.00	30.00	60.00	150	—
1875Go S	—	10.00	20.00	50.00	125	—
1876Go S	—	20.00	40.00	80.00	175	—
1877Go S	124,000	10.00	20.00	50.00	125	—
1878Go S	146,000	10.00	20.00	50.00	125	—
1879Go S	—	10.00	20.00	50.00	125	—
1880Go S	—	20.00	40.00	80.00	175	—
1881Go S	408,000	9.00	17.50	45.00	125	—
1882Go S	204,000	9.00	17.50	45.00	125	—
1883Go B	168,000	9.00	17.50	45.00	125	—
1884/69Go B	—	9.00	17.50	45.00	125	—
1884/3Go B	—	9.00	17.50	45.00	125	—
1884/3Go B/R	—	9.00	17.50	45.00	125	—
1884Go B	—	9.00	17.50	45.00	125	—
1885/65Go R	300,000	9.00	17.50	45.00	125	—
1885/69Go R	Inc. above	9.00	17.50	45.00	125	—
1885Go R	Inc. above	9.00	17.50	45.00	125	—
1886/65Go R	—	9.00	17.50	45.00	125	—
1886/66Go R	322,000	9.00	17.50	45.00	125	—
1886/69Go R/S	Inc. above	9.00	17.50	45.00	125	—
1886/5/69Go R	Inc. above	9.00	15.00	45.00	125	—
1886Go R	Inc. above	9.00	15.00	45.00	125	—
1887Go R	254,000	9.00	15.00	45.00	125	—
1887Go/Cn R/D	Inc. above	9.00	15.00	45.00	125	—
1888Go R	312,000	8.00	15.00	45.00	125	—
1889/8Go R RS inverted B	—	—	—	—	—	—
1889/8Go R	304,000	8.00	15.00	45.00	125	—
1889/8Go/Cn R/D	Inc. above	8.00	15.00	45.00	125	—
1889Go R	Inc. above	8.00	15.00	45.00	125	—
1890Go R	236,000	8.00	15.00	45.00	125	—

KM# 406.6 25 CENTAVOS

6.7680 g., 0.9030 Silver 0.1965 oz. ASW **Obv:** Facing eagle, snake in beak **Rev:** Radiant cap above scales **Mint:** Hermosillo **Note:** Varieties exist.

Date	Mintage	F	VF	XF	Unc	BU
1874/64Ho R	Inc. above	10.00	20.00	40.00	125	—
1874/69Ho R	—	10.00	20.00	40.00	125	—
1874Ho R	23,000	10.00	20.00	40.00	125	—
1875Ho R Rare	—	—	—	—	—	—
1876/4Ho F/R	34,000	10.00	20.00	50.00	150	—
1876Ho F/R	Inc. above	10.00	25.00	60.00	150	—
1876Ho F	Inc. above	10.00	25.00	55.00	135	—
1877Ho F	—	10.00	20.00	50.00	125	—
1878Ho A	23,000	10.00	20.00	50.00	125	—
1879Ho A	—	10.00	20.00	50.00	125	—
1880Ho A	—	15.00	30.00	60.00	125	—
1881Ho A	19,000	10.00	30.00	60.00	125	—
1882Ho A	8,120	20.00	40.00	80.00	150	—
1883Ho M	2,000	100	200	300	600	—
1884Ho M	—	12.50	25.00	50.00	150	—
1885Ho M	—	10.00	20.00	50.00	125	—
1886Ho G	6,400	30.00	60.00	125	250	—
1887Ho G	12,000	10.00	20.00	40.00	125	—
1888Ho G	20,000	10.00	20.00	40.00	125	—
1889Ho G	28,000	10.00	20.00	40.00	125	—
1890/80Ho G	18,000	25.00	50.00	100	125	—
1890Ho G	Inc. above	25.00	50.00	100	125	—

KM# 406.7 25 CENTAVOS

6.7680 g., 0.9027 Silver 0.1964 oz. ASW **Obv:** Facing eagle, snake in beak **Obv. Legend:** REPUBLICA MEXICANA **Rev:** Radiant cap above scales **Mint:** Mexico City **Note:** Varieties exist.

Date	Mintage	F	VF	XF	Unc	BU
1869Mo C	76,000	10.00	25.00	50.00	125	—
1870/69Mo C	—	6.50	12.00	30.00	125	—
1870/9Mo C	136,000	6.50	12.00	30.00	125	—
1870Mo C	Inc. above	6.50	12.00	30.00	125	—
1871Mo M	138,000	6.50	12.00	30.00	125	—
1872Mo M	220,000	6.50	12.00	30.00	125	—
1873/1Mo M	48,000	10.00	25.00	50.00	125	—
1873Mo M	Inc. above	10.00	25.00	50.00	125	—
1874/69Mo B/M	—	10.00	25.00	50.00	125	—
1874/3Mo M	—	10.00	25.00	50.00	125	—
1874/3Mo B	—	10.00	25.00	50.00	125	—
1874/3Mo B/M	—	10.00	25.00	50.00	125	—
1874Mo M	—	6.50	12.00	30.00	125	—
1874Mo B/M	—	10.00	25.00	50.00	125	—
1875Mo B	—	6.50	12.00	30.00	125	—
1876/5Mo B	—	8.00	15.00	40.00	125	—
1876Mo B	—	6.50	12.00	30.00	125	—
1877Mo M	56,000	10.00	25.00	50.00	125	—
1878/1Mo M	120,000	10.00	25.00	50.00	125	—
1878/7Mo M	Inc. above	10.00	25.00	50.00	125	—
1878Mo M	Inc. above	6.50	12.00	30.00	125	—
1879Mo M	—	10.00	20.00	40.00	125	—
1880Mo M	—	8.00	15.00	35.00	125	—
1881/0Mo M	300,000	10.00	25.00	50.00	125	—
1881Mo M	Inc. above	10.00	25.00	50.00	125	—
1882Mo M	212,000	8.00	15.00	35.00	125	—
1883Mo M	108,000	8.00	15.00	35.00	125	—
1884/3Mo M	—	10.00	25.00	50.00	125	—
1884Mo M	—	10.00	20.00	40.00	125	—
1885Mo M	216,000	10.00	20.00	40.00	125	—
1886/5Mo M	436,000	8.00	15.00	35.00	125	—
1886Mo M	Inc. above	8.00	15.00	35.00	125	—
1887Mo M	376,000	8.00	15.00	35.00	125	—
1888Mo M	192,000	8.00	15.00	35.00	125	—
1889Mo M	132,000	8.00	15.00	35.00	125	—
1890Mo M	60,000	10.00	20.00	40.00	125	—

KM# 406.8 25 CENTAVOS
6.7680 g., 0.9030 Silver 0.1965 oz. ASW **Obv:** Facing eagle, snake in beak **Rev:** Radiant cap above scales **Mint:** San Luis Potosi **Note:** Varieties exist.

Date	Mintage	F	VF	XF	Unc	BU
1869Pi S	—	25.00	75.00	150	300	—
1870Pi G	50,000	10.00	30.00	75.00	150	—
1870Pi O	Inc. above	15.00	35.00	85.00	175	—
1871Pi O	30,000	10.00	30.00	75.00	150	—
1872Pi O	46,000	10.00	30.00	75.00	150	—
1873Pi O	13,000	15.00	40.00	90.00	175	—
1874Pi H	—	15.00	40.00	90.00	200	—
1875Pi H	—	10.00	20.00	60.00	150	—
1876/5Pi H	—	15.00	30.00	80.00	175	—
1876Pi H	—	10.00	25.00	65.00	150	—
1877Pi H	19,000	10.00	25.00	65.00	150	—
1878Pi H	—	15.00	30.00	60.00	150	—
1879/8Pi H	—	10.00	25.00	60.00	150	—
1879Pi H	—	10.00	25.00	60.00	150	—
1879Pi E	—	100	200	300	600	—
1880Pi H	—	20.00	40.00	100	200	—
1880Pi H/M	—	20.00	40.00	100	200	—
1881Pi H	50,000	20.00	40.00	80.00	175	—
1881Pi E Rare	Inc. above	—	—	—	—	—
1882Pi H	20,000	10.00	20.00	60.00	150	—
1883Pi H	17,000	10.00	25.00	65.00	150	—
1884Pi H	—	10.00	25.00	65.00	150	—
1885/4Pi H	—	10.00	25.00	60.00	150	—
1885Pi H	43,000	10.00	25.00	60.00	150	—
1886Pi C	78,000	10.00	25.00	65.00	150	—
1886Pi R	Inc. above	9.00	20.00	50.00	150	—
1886Pi R 6/ inverted 6	Inc. above	9.00	20.00	50.00	150	—
1887Pi/ZsR	92,000	9.00	20.00	50.00	150	—
1887Pi/ZsB	Inc. above	100	150	300	500	—
1887Pi R	—	9.00	20.00	50.00	150	—
1888Pi R	106,000	9.00	20.00	50.00	150	—
1888Pi/ZsR	Inc. above	10.00	20.00	50.00	150	—
1888Pi R/B	Inc. above	10.00	20.00	50.00	150	—
1889Pi R	115,000	10.00	15.00	40.00	150	—
1889Pi/ZsR	Inc. above	10.00	20.00	50.00	150	—
1889Pi R/B	Inc. above	10.00	20.00	50.00	150	—
1890Pi R	64,000	10.00	20.00	50.00	150	—
1890Pi/ZsR/B	Inc. above	8.00	15.00	40.00	150	—
1890Pi R/B	Inc. above	10.00	20.00	50.00	150	—

KM# 406.9 25 CENTAVOS
6.7680 g., 0.9030 Silver 0.1965 oz. ASW **Obv:** Facing eagle, snake in beak **Rev:** Radiant cap above scales **Mint:** Zacatecas **Note:** Varieties exist.

Date	Mintage	F	VF	XF	Unc	BU
1870Zs H	152,000	8.00	15.00	50.00	125	—
1871Zs H	250,000	8.00	15.00	50.00	125	—
1872Zs H	260,000	8.00	15.00	50.00	125	—
1872Zs/Cn H	—	—	—	—	—	—
1872Zs H	—	—	—	—	—	—
1873Zs H	132,000	8.00	15.00	50.00	125	—
1874Zs H	—	10.00	20.00	60.00	125	—
1874Zs A	—	10.00	20.00	60.00	125	—
1875Zs A	—	9.00	20.00	60.00	125	—
1876Zs A	—	8.00	15.00	50.00	125	—
1876Zs S	—	8.00	15.00	50.00	125	—
1877Zs S	350,000	8.00	15.00	50.00	125	—
1878Zs S	252,000	8.00	15.00	50.00	125	—
1878/1Zs S	—	9.00	20.00	60.00	125	—
1878/7Zs S	—	9.00	20.00	60.00	125	—
1879Zs S	—	8.00	15.00	50.00	125	—
1880Zs S	—	8.00	15.00	50.00	125	—
1881/0Zs S	570,000	8.00	15.00	50.00	125	—
1881Zs S	Inc. above	8.00	15.00	50.00	125	—
1882/1Zs S	300,000	10.00	17.50	55.00	125	—
1882Zs S	Inc. above	8.00	15.00	50.00	125	—
1883/2Zs S	193,000	10.00	17.50	55.00	125	—
1883Zs S	Inc. above	8.00	15.00	50.00	125	—
1884/3Zs S	—	10.00	17.50	55.00	125	—
1884Zs S	—	8.00	15.00	50.00	125	—
1885Zs S	309,000	8.00	15.00	50.00	125	—
1886/2Zs S	—	10.00	17.50	55.00	125	—
1886/5Zs S	613,000	8.00	15.00	50.00	125	—
1886Zs S	Inc. above	8.00	15.00	50.00	125	—
1886Zs Z	Inc. above	8.00	15.00	55.00	125	—
1887Zs Z	389,000	8.00	15.00	50.00	125	—
1888Zs Z	408,000	8.00	15.00	50.00	125	—
1889Zs Z	400,000	8.00	15.00	50.00	125	—
1890Zs Z	269,000	8.00	15.00	50.00	125	—

KM# 407.7 50 CENTAVOS
13.5360 g., 0.9030 Silver 0.3930 oz. ASW **Obv:** Facing eagle, snake in beak **Rev:** Radiant cap above scales **Mint:** San Luis Potosi

Date	Mintage	F	VF	XF	Unc	BU
1870Pi G	Inc. above	20.00	40.00	100	450	—
1870/780Pi G	50,000	25.00	45.00	110	500	—
1870Pi O	Inc. above	20.00	40.00	100	450	—
1871Pi O	—	15.00	30.00	80.00	400	—
1871Pi O/G	64,000	15.00	30.00	80.00	400	—
1872Pi O	52,000	15.00	30.00	80.00	400	—
1872Pi O/G	Inc. above	15.00	30.00	80.00	400	—
1873Pi O	32,000	20.00	40.00	100	450	—
1873Pi H	Inc. above	25.00	50.00	125	550	—
1874Pi H/O	—	15.00	30.00	80.00	400	—
1875/3Pi H	—	15.00	30.00	80.00	400	—
1875Pi H	—	15.00	30.00	80.00	400	—
1876Pi H	—	30.00	60.00	150	700	—
1877Pi H	34,000	20.00	40.00	100	450	—
1878Pi H	9,700	20.00	40.00	100	450	—
1879Pi H	—	15.00	35.00	90.00	450	—
1879/7Pi H	—	15.00	35.00	90.00	450	—
1880Pi H	—	20.00	40.00	100	450	—
1881Pi H	28,000	20.00	40.00	100	450	—
1882Pi H	22,000	15.00	30.00	80.00	400	—
1883Pi H	Inc. above	15.00	30.00	80.00	400	—
1883Pi H 8/8	29,000	50.00	100	200	750	—
1884Pi H	—	50.00	100	175	600	—
1885/3Pi H	—	20.00	40.00	100	450	—
1885/0Pi H	45,000	20.00	40.00	100	450	—
1885/4Pi H	Inc. above	20.00	40.00	100	450	—
1885Pi H	Inc. above	25.00	50.00	125	450	—
1885Pi C	Inc. above	15.00	30.00	80.00	400	—
1886/1Pi R	92,000	50.00	100	175	600	—
1886/1Pi C	—	25.00	40.00	100	450	—
1886Pi C	Inc. above	15.00	30.00	80.00	400	—
1886Pi R	Inc. above	15.00	30.00	80.00	400	—
1887Pi R	32,000	15.00	30.00	90.00	450	—

KM# 407 50 CENTAVOS
13.5360 g., 0.9030 Silver 0.3930 oz. ASW **Obv:** Facing eagle, snake in beak **Rev:** Radiant cap above scales **Mint:** Alamos **Note:** Mint mark A, As.

Date	Mintage	F	VF	XF	Unc	BU
1875 L	—	12.00	25.00	70.00	400	—
1876/5 L	—	25.00	50.00	120	450	—
1876 L	—	12.00	25.00	70.00	400	—
1876. L	—	12.00	25.00	70.00	400	—
1877 L	26,000	15.00	30.00	85.00	450	—
1878 L	—	12.00	25.00	70.00	400	—
1879 L	—	25.00	50.00	120	450	—
1880 L	57,000	12.00	25.00	70.00	400	—
1881 L	18,000	15.00	30.00	80.00	450	—
1884 L	6,286	65.00	120	250	650	—
1885As/HoL	21,000	15.00	35.00	90.00	450	—
1888 L	—	4,000	5,000	7,000	—	—

KM# 407.1 50 CENTAVOS
13.5360 g., 0.9030 Silver 0.3930 oz. ASW **Obv:** Facing eagle, snake in beak **Rev:** Radiant cap above scales **Mint:** Chihuahua **Note:** Mint mark Ca, CHa.

Date	Mintage	F	VF	XF	Unc	BU
1883 M	12,000	30.00	60.00	125	500	—
1884 M	—	25.00	50.00	125	500	—
1885 M	13,000	15.00	35.00	90.00	400	—
1886 M	18,000	20.00	40.00	100	450	—
1887 M	26,000	25.00	65.00	150	500	—

KM# 407.4 50 CENTAVOS
13.5360 g., 0.9030 Silver 0.3930 oz. ASW **Obv:** Facing eagle, snake in beak **Rev:** Radiant cap above scales **Mint:** Guanajuato **Note:** Struck at Guanajuato Mint, mitn mark Go. Varieties exist.

Date	Mintage	F	VF	XF	Unc	BU
1869Go S	—	15.00	35.00	75.00	550	—
1870Go S	166,000	12.00	25.00	50.00	450	—
1871Go S	148,000	12.00	25.00	50.00	450	—
1872/1Go S	144,000	15.00	30.00	60.00	500	—
1872Go S	Inc. above	12.00	25.00	50.00	450	—
1873Go S	50,000	12.00	25.00	50.00	450	—
1874Go S	—	12.00	25.00	50.00	450	—

Date	Mintage	F	VF	XF	Unc	BU
1875Go S	—	15.00	35.00	75.00	450	—
1876/5Go S	—	12.00	25.00	50.00	450	—
1877Go S	76,000	12.00	25.00	60.00	450	—
1878Go S	37,000	15.00	30.00	75.00	550	—
1879/8Go S	—	15.00	30.00	60.00	500	—
1879Go S	—	12.00	25.00	50.00	450	—
1880Go S	—	12.00	25.00	50.00	450	—
1881/79Go S	32,000	15.00	30.00	60.00	500	—
1881Go S	Inc. above	12.00	25.00	50.00	450	—
1882Go S	18,000	12.00	25.00	50.00	450	—
1883/2Go B/S	—	15.00	30.00	60.00	500	—
1883Go B	—	12.00	25.00	50.00	450	—
1883Go S Rare	—	—	—	—	—	—
1884Go B/S	—	15.00	30.00	60.00	500	—
1885/4Go R/B	—	15.00	30.00	60.00	500	—
1885Go R	53,000	12.00	25.00	50.00	450	—
1886/5Go R/B	59,000	15.00	30.00	60.00	500	—
1886/5Go R/S	Inc. above	20.00	40.00	75.00	500	—
1886Go R	Inc. above	20.00	40.00	75.00	450	—
1887Go R	18,000	20.00	40.00	75.00	550	—
1888Go R 1 known; Rare	—	—	—	—	—	—

KM# 407.8 50 CENTAVOS
13.5360 g., 0.9030 Silver 0.3930 oz. ASW **Obv:** Facing eagle, snake in beak **Rev:** Radiant cap above scales **Mint:** Zacatecas **Note:** Varieties exist.

Date	Mintage	F	VF	XF	Unc	BU
1870Zs H	86,000	12.00	25.00	60.00	450	—
1871Zs H	146,000	12.00	25.00	50.00	400	—
1872Zs H	132,000	12.00	25.00	50.00	400	—
1873Zs H	56,000	12.00	25.00	50.00	400	—
1874Zs H	—	12.00	25.00	50.00	400	—
1874Zs A Rare	—	—	—	—	—	—
1875Zs A	—	12.00	25.00	50.00	400	—
1876Zs A	—	12.00	25.00	50.00	400	—
1876Zs S	—	100	200	350	750	—
1876/5Zs A	—	15.00	30.00	60.00	450	—
1877Zs S	100,000	12.00	25.00	50.00	400	—
1878Zs S	Inc. above	15.00	30.00	60.00	400	—
1878/7Zs S	254,000	15.00	30.00	60.00	450	—
1879Zs S	—	12.00	25.00	50.00	400	—
1880Zs S	—	12.00	25.00	50.00	400	—
1881Zs S	201,000	12.00	25.00	50.00	400	—
1882Zs S	Inc. above	50.00	100	250	650	—
1882/1Zs S	2,000	50.00	100	250	650	—
1883Zs S	Inc. above	25.00	50.00	100	450	—
1883Zs/Za S	31,000	30.00	60.00	100	450	—
1884Zs S	—	12.00	25.00	50.00	400	—
1884/3Zs S	—	15.00	30.00	60.00	450	—
1885Zs S	Inc. above	25.00	50.00	125	450	—
1885/4Zs S	2,000	25.00	50.00	125	450	—
1886Zs Z	2,000	150	275	400	1,000	—
1887Zs Z	63,000	30.00	60.00	125	450	—

KM# 407.5 50 CENTAVOS
13.5360 g., 0.9030 Silver 0.3930 oz. ASW **Obv:** Facing eagle, snake in beak **Rev:** Radiant cap above scales **Mint:** Hermosillo **Note:** With and without dot after 50 of denomination, in medal and coin alignment.

Date	Mintage	F	VF	XF	Unc	BU
1874Ho R	—	20.00	40.00	100	600	—
1875/4Ho R	—	20.00	50.00	125	600	—
1875Ho R	—	20.00	50.00	125	600	—
1876/5Ho F/R	—	15.00	35.00	100	550	—
1876Ho F	—	15.00	35.00	100	550	—
1877Ho F	—	50.00	75.00	150	650	—
1880/70Ho A	—	15.00	35.00	100	550	—

Date	Mintage	F	VF	XF	Unc	BU
1880Ho A	—	15.00	35.00	100	550	—
1881Ho A	13,000	15.00	35.00	100	550	—
1882Ho A	—	75.00	150	250	750	—
1888Ho G	—	2,000	3,000	6,000	—	—
1894Ho G	59,000	15.00	30.00	100	450	—
1895Ho G	8,000	250	350	700	1,500	—

KM# 407.2 50 CENTAVOS
13.5360 g., 0.9030 Silver 0.3930 oz. ASW **Obv:** Facing eagle, snake in beak **Obv. Legend:** REPUBLICA MEXICANA **Rev:** Radiant cap above scales **Mint:** Culiacan

Date	Mintage	F	VF	XF	Unc	BU
1871Cn P	—	400	550	750	1,500	—
1873Cn P	—	400	550	750	1,500	—
1874Cn P	—	200	300	500	1,000	—
1875/4Cn P	—	20.00	40.00	75.00	450	—
1875Cn P	—	12.00	25.00	50.00	450	—
1876Cn P	—	15.00	30.00	60.00	450	—
1877/6Cn G	—	15.00	30.00	60.00	450	—
1877Cn G	—	12.00	25.00	50.00	450	—
1878Cn G	18,000	20.00	40.00	75.00	450	—
1878Cn/Mo D	Inc. above	30.00	60.00	100	450	—
1878Cn D	Inc. above	15.00	35.00	75.00	450	—
1879Cn D	—	12.00	25.00	50.00	450	—
1879Cn D/G	—	12.00	25.00	50.00	450	—
1880/8Cn D	—	15.00	30.00	60.00	450	—
1880Cn D	—	15.00	30.00	60.00	450	—
1881/0Cn D	188,000	15.00	30.00	60.00	450	—
1881Cn D	Inc. above	15.00	30.00	60.00	450	—
1881Cn G	Inc. above	125	175	275	550	—
1882Cn D	—	175	300	500	2,000	—
1882Gn G	—	100	250	300	1,000	—
1883 D	19,000	25.00	50.00	100	500	—
1885Cn M/M/G	—	30.00	60.00	100	500	—
1885/3Cn M/H	9,254	30.00	60.00	100	500	—
1886Cn M/G	7,030	50.00	100	300	1,500	—
1886Cn M	Inc. above	40.00	80.00	150	800	—
1887Cn M	76,000	20.00	40.00	100	450	—
1888Cn M	—	4,000	6,000	—	—	—
1892Cn M	8,200	40.00	80.00	150	650	—

KM# 407.3 50 CENTAVOS
13.5360 g., 0.9030 Silver 0.3930 oz. ASW **Obv:** Facing eagle, snake in beak **Obv. Legend:** REPUBLICA MEXICANA **Rev:** Radiant cap above scales **Mint:** Durango

Date	Mintage	F	VF	XF	Unc	BU
1871Do P Rare	591	—	—	—	—	—
1873Do P	4,010	150	250	500	1,250	—
1873Do M/P	Inc. above	150	250	500	1,250	—
1874Do M	—	20.00	40.00	175	750	—
1875Do M	—	20.00	40.00	80.00	350	—
1875Do H	—	150	250	450	1,000	—
1876/5Do M	—	35.00	70.00	150	500	—
1876Do M	—	35.00	70.00	150	500	—
1877Do P	2,000	30.00	45.00	150	1,250	—
1878Do B Rare	—	—	—	—	—	—

Date	Mintage	F	VF	XF	Unc	BU
1879Do B Rare	—	—	—	—	—	—
1880Do P	—	30.00	60.00	125	500	—
1881Do P	10,000	40.00	80.00	150	550	—
1882Do C	8,957	30.00	75.00	200	800	—
1884/2Do C	—	20.00	50.00	125	600	—
1884Do C	—	—	—	—	—	—
1885Do B	—	15.00	40.00	100	500	—
1885Do B/P	—	15.00	40.00	100	500	—
1886Do C	16,000	15.00	40.00	100	500	—
1887Do/Mo C	28,000	15.00	40.00	100	500	—
1887Do C	—	15.00	40.00	100	500	—

KM# 407.6 50 CENTAVOS
13.5360 g., 0.9027 Silver 0.3928 oz. ASW **Obv:** Facing
eagle, snake in beak **Obv. Legend:** REPUBLICA MEXICANA
Rev: Radiant cap above scales **Mint:** Mexico City

Date	Mintage	F	VF	XF	Unc	BU
1869Mo C	46,000	15.00	35.00	95.00	600	—
1870Mo C	52,000	15.00	30.00	90.00	550	—
1871Mo M/C	Inc. above	35.00	75.00	150	600	—
1871Mo C	14,000	40.00	75.00	150	650	—
1872Mo M	Inc. above	35.00	75.00	150	550	—
1872/1Mo M	60,000	35.00	75.00	150	550	—
1873Mo M	6,000	35.00	75.00	150	600	—
1874/3Mo M	—	200	400	600	1,250	—
1874/2Mo B	—	15.00	30.00	75.00	500	—
1874/2Mo B/M	—	15.00	30.00	75.00	500	—
1874/3Mo B/M	—	15.00	30.00	75.00	500	—
1874Mo B	—	15.00	30.00	75.00	500	—
1875Mo B	—	15.00	30.00	75.00	550	—
1876Mo B	—	12.00	25.00	75.00	500	—
1876/5Mo B	—	15.00	30.00	75.00	500	—
1877Mo M	—	15.00	30.00	90.00	500	—
1877/2Mo M	—	20.00	40.00	100	550	—
1878Mo M	Inc. above	15.00	35.00	100	550	—
1878/7Mo M	8,000	25.00	50.00	125	600	—
1879Mo M	—	25.00	50.00	125	550	—
1880Mo M	—	100	150	250	750	—
1881Mo M	16,000	25.00	50.00	125	600	—
1881/0Mo M	—	30.00	50.00	125	600	—
1882/1Mo M	2,000	30.00	60.00	150	750	—
1883/2Mo M	4,000	150	225	350	1,000	—
1884Mo M	—	150	225	350	1,000	—
1885Mo M	12,000	30.00	60.00	150	600	—
1886Mo M	Inc. above	12.00	25.00	75.00	450	—
1886/5Mo M	66,000	15.00	35.00	90.00	475	—
1887Mo M	Inc. above	15.00	35.00	75.00	475	—
1887/6Mo M	88,000	15.00	35.00	90.00	475	—
1888Mo M	—	3,000	4,000	6,000	—	—

KM# 408 PESO
27.0730 g., 0.9030 Silver 0.7860 oz. ASW **Obv:** Facing
eagle, snake in beak **Rev:** Radiant cap above scales **Mint:**
Chihuahua

Date	Mintage	F	VF	XF	Unc	BU
1872CH P/M	747,000	750	1,500	3,500	—	—
1872CH P	Inc. above	350	700	1,500	—	—
1872/1CH M	Inc. above	27.50	45.00	80.00	400	—
1872CH M	Inc. above	20.00	30.00	55.00	250	—
1873CH M	320,000	22.50	35.00	65.00	265	—
1873CH M/P	Inc. above	27.50	45.00	80.00	350	—

KM# 408.1 PESO
27.0730 g., 0.9030 Silver 0.7860 oz. ASW **Obv:** Facing
eagle, snake in beak **Rev:** Radiant cap above scales **Mint:**
Culiacan

Date	Mintage	F	VF	XF	Unc	BU
1870Cn E	—	40.00	80.00	150	500	—
1871Cn P	Inc. above	20.00	40.00	75.00	300	—
1871/11Cn P	478,000	25.00	45.00	100	450	—

Date	Mintage	F	VF	XF	Unc	BU
1872/1Cn P	—	20.00	40.00	75.00	300	—
1872Cn P	209,000	20.00	40.00	75.00	300	—
1873Cn P Narrow date	527,000	20.00	40.00	75.00	300	—
1873Cn P Wide date	Inc. above	20.00	40.00	75.00	300	—

KM# 408.2 PESO
27.0730 g., 0.9027 Silver 0.7857 oz. ASW **Obv:** Facing
eagle, snake in beak **Obv. Legend:** REPUBLICA MEXICANA
Rev: Radiant cap above scales **Mint:** Durango

Date	Mintage	F	VF	XF	Unc	BU
1870Do P	—	50.00	100	175	450	—
1871Do P	427,000	27.50	52.50	80.00	300	—
1872Do P	296,000	22.50	42.50	80.00	350	—
1872Do PT	Inc. above	100	175	250	850	—
1873Do P	203,000	27.50	47.50	90.00	350	—

KM# 408.3 PESO
27.0730 g., 0.9030 Silver 0.7860 oz. ASW **Obv:** Facing
eagle, snake in beak **Obv. Legend:** REPUBLICA MEXICANA
Rev: Radiant cap above scales **Mint:** Guadalajara

Date	Mintage	F	VF	XF	Unc	BU
1870Ga C	—	650	850	—	—	—
1871Ga C	829,000	27.50	70.00	140	600	—
1872Ga C	485,000	42.50	95.00	180	650	—
1873/2Ga C	277,000	42.50	95.00	180	700	—
1873Ga C	Inc. above	27.50	70.00	140	600	—

KM# 408.4   PESO
27.0730 g., 0.9027 Silver 0.7857 oz. ASW   **Obv:** Facing
eagle, snake in beak **Obv. Legend:** REPUBLICA MEXICANA
Rev: Radiant cap above scales **Mint:** Guanajuato

Date	Mintage	F	VF	XF	Unc	BU
1871/0Go S	3,946,000	32.50	55.00	95.00	350	—
1871/3Go S	Inc. above	22.50	40.00	75.00	275	—
1871Go S	Inc. above	15.00	25.00	45.00	220	—
1872Go S	4,067,000	15.00	25.00	45.00	250	—
1873/2Go S	1,560,000	18.00	30.00	55.00	250	—
1873Go S	Inc. above	15.00	25.00	50.00	250	—
1873Go/Mo/S/M	Inc. above	15.00	25.00	50.00	250	—

KM# 408.6   PESO
27.0730 g., 0.9030 Silver 0.7860 oz. ASW   **Obv:** Facing
eagle, snake in beak **Obv. Legend:** REPUBLICA MEXICANA
Rev: Radiant cap above scales **Mint:** Oaxaca

Date	Mintage	F	VF	XF	Unc	BU
1869Oa E	—	275	400	600	2,000	—
1870Oa E Small A	Inc. above	17.50	35.00	80.00	400	—
1870Oa E Large A	Inc. above	100	150	300	900	—
1871/69Oa E	140,000	32.50	55.00	130	550	—
1871Oa E Small A	Inc. above	18.00	35.00	65.00	300	—
1871Oa E Large A	Inc. above	18.00	35.00	80.00	400	—
1872Oa E Small A	180,000	18.00	35.00	80.00	400	—
1872Oa E Large A	Inc. above	55.00	100	200	450	—
1873Oa E	105,000	18.00	35.00	80.00	350	—

KM# 408.5   PESO
27.0730 g., 0.9030 Silver 0.7860 oz. ASW   **Obv:** Facing
eagle, snake in beak **Rev:** Radiant cap above scales **Mint:**
Mexico City

Date	Mintage	F	VF	XF	Unc	BU
1869Mo C	—	37.50	70.00	140	600	—
1870Mo C	Inc. above	15.00	25.00	45.00	250	—
1870Mo M	Inc. above	20.00	35.00	65.00	275	—
1870Mo M/C	Inc. above	20.00	35.00	65.00	275	—
1870/69Mo C	5,115,000	18.00	30.00	60.00	275	—
1871Mo M	Inc. above	15.00	25.00	45.00	250	—
1871/0Mo M	6,974,000	18.00	30.00	60.00	275	—
1872/1Mo M	—	18.00	30.00	55.00	275	—
1872/1Mo M/C	4,801,000	18.00	30.00	55.00	275	—
1872Mo M	Inc. above	15.00	25.00	45.00	250	—
1873Mo M	1,765,000	15.00	25.00	45.00	250	—

Note: The 1869 C with large LEY on the scroll is a pattern

KM# 409   PESO
27.0730 g., 0.9030 Silver 0.7860 oz. ASW, 39 mm.   **Obv:**
Facing eagle, snake in beak **Rev:** Radiant cap **Mint:** Culiacan

Date	Mintage	F	VF	XF	Unc	BU
1898Cn/MoAM	Inc. above	17.50	32.50	95.00	155	—
1898Cn AM	1,720,000	14.50	17.50	30.00	70.00	—
1899Cn AM	1,722,000	27.50	52.50	95.00	180	—
1899Cn JQ	Inc. above	14.50	17.50	55.00	130	—
1900Cn JQ	1,804,000	14.50	17.50	30.00	80.00	—
1901Cn JQ	1,473,000	25.00	27.50	40.00	120	—
1902Cn JQ	1,194,000	25.00	27.50	70.00	200	—
1903Cn JQ	1,514,000	25.00	27.50	48.00	135	—
1903Cn FV	Inc. above	40.00	80.00	160	350	—
1904Cn MH	1,554,000	25.00	27.50	40.00	120	—
1904Cn RP	Inc. above	80.00	160	240	550	—
1905Cn RP	598,000	40.00	80.00	160	400	—

KM# 410.2 PESO
1.6920 g., 0.8750 Gold 0.0476 oz. AGW **Obv:** Facing eagle, snake in beak **Obv. Legend:** REPUBLICA MEXICANA **Rev:** Value within 1/2 wreath **Mint:** Culiacan

Date	Mintage	F	VF	XF	Unc	BU
1873Cn P	1,221	75.00	100	150	250	—
1875Cn P	—	85.00	125	150	250	—
1878Cn G	248	100	175	225	500	—
1879Cn D	—	100	150	200	475	—
1881/0Cn D	338	100	150	200	475	—
1882Cn D	340	100	150	200	475	—
1883Cn D	—	100	150	200	475	—
1884Cn M	—	100	150	200	475	—
1886/4Cn M	277	100	150	225	500	—
1888/7Cn M	2,586	100	175	225	450	—
1888Cn M	Inc. above	65.00	100	150	265	—
1889Cn M Rare	—	—	—	—	—	—
1891/89Cn M	969	75.00	100	150	275	—
1892Cn M	780	75.00	100	150	275	—
1893Cn M	498	85.00	125	150	275	—
1894Cn M	493	80.00	125	150	275	—
1895Cn M	1,143	65.00	100	150	250	350
1896/5Cn M	1,028	65.00	100	150	250	350
1897Cn M	785	65.00	100	150	250	350
1898Cn M	3,521	65.00	100	150	225	325
1898Cn/MoM	Inc. above	65.00	100	150	250	350
1899Cn Q	2,000	65.00	100	150	225	325
1901Cn Q	Inc. above	70.00	100	150	225	325
1901/0Cn Q	2,350	70.00	100	150	225	325
1902Cn Q	2,480	70.00	100	150	225	325
1902Cn/MoQ/C	Inc. above	70.00	100	150	225	325
1904Cn H	3,614	70.00	100	150	225	325
1904Cn/Mo/ H	Inc. above	70.00	100	150	250	350
1905Cn P	1,000	—	—	—	—	—

Note: Reported, not confirmed

KM# 410.3 PESO
1.6920 g., 0.8750 Gold 0.0476 oz. AGW **Obv:** Facing eagle, snake in beak **Obv. Legend:** REPUBLICA MEXICANA **Rev:** Value within 1/2 wreath **Mint:** Guanajuato

Date	Mintage	F	VF	XF	Unc	BU
1870Go S	—	100	125	150	265	—
1871Go S	500	100	175	225	475	—
1888Go R	210	125	200	250	550	—
1890Go R	1,916	75.00	100	150	265	—
1892Go R	533	100	150	175	350	—
1894Go R	180	150	200	250	550	—
1895Go R	676	100	150	175	325	—
1896/5Go R	4,671	65.00	100	150	250	—
1897/6Go R	4,280	65.00	100	150	250	—
1897Go R	Inc. above	65.00	100	150	250	—
1898Go R	5,193	65.00	100	150	250	750

Note: Regular obverse

1898Go R	Inc. above	75.00	100	150	250	750

Note: Mule, 5 Centavos obverse, normal reverse

1899Go R	2,748	65.00	100	150	250	—
1900/800Go R	864	75.00	125	150	285	—

KM# 410.4 PESO
1.6920 g., 0.8750 Gold 0.0476 oz. AGW **Obv:** Facing eagle, snake in beak **Obv. Legend:** REPUBLICA MEXICANA **Rev:** Value within 1/2 wreath **Mint:** Hermosillo

Date	Mintage	F	VF	XF	Unc	BU
1875Ho R Rare	310	—	—	—	—	—
1876Ho F Rare	—	—	—	—	—	—
1888Ho G/MoM Rare	—	—	—	—	—	—

KM# 410.5 PESO
1.6920 g., 0.8750 Gold 0.0476 oz. AGW **Obv:** Facing eagle, snake in beak **Obv. Legend:** REPUBLICA MEXICANA **Rev:** Value within 1/2 wreath **Mint:** Mexico City

Date	Mintage	F	VF	XF	Unc	BU
1870Mo C	2,540	50.00	65.00	95.00	185	250
1871Mo M/C	1,000	60.00	100	150	250	250
1872Mo M/C	3,000	50.00	65.00	95.00	185	300
1873/1Mo M	2,900	50.00	65.00	100	200	250
1873Mo M	Inc. above	50.00	65.00	95.00	185	250
1874Mo M	—	50.00	65.00	95.00	185	250
1875Mo B/M	—	50.00	65.00	95.00	185	250
1876/5Mo B/M	—	50.00	65.00	95.00	185	250
1877Mo M	—	50.00	65.00	95.00	185	250
1878Mo M	2,000	50.00	65.00	95.00	185	250
1879Mo M	—	50.00	65.00	95.00	185	250
1880/70Mo M	—	50.00	65.00	95.00	185	250
1881/71Mo M	1,000	50.00	65.00	95.00	185	250
1882/72Mo M	—	50.00	65.00	95.00	185	250
1883/72Mo M	1,000	50.00	65.00	95.00	185	250
1884Mo M	—	50.00	65.00	95.00	185	250
1885/71Mo M	—	50.00	65.00	95.00	185	250
1885Mo M	—	50.00	65.00	95.00	185	250
1886Mo M	1,700	50.00	65.00	95.00	185	250
1887Mo M	2,200	50.00	65.00	95.00	185	250
1888Mo M	1,000	50.00	65.00	95.00	185	250
1889Mo M	500	100	150	200	285	—
1890Mo M	570	100	150	200	285	—
1891Mo M	746	100	150	200	285	—
1892/0Mo M	2,895	50.00	65.00	95.00	185	250
1893Mo M	5,917	50.00	65.00	95.00	185	250
1894/3MMo	—	50.00	65.00	95.00	185	250
1894Mo M	6,244	50.00	65.00	95.00	185	250
1895Mo M	8,994	50.00	65.00	95.00	185	250
1895Mo B	Inc. above	50.00	65.00	95.00	185	250
1896Mo B	7,166	50.00	65.00	95.00	185	250
1896Mo M	Inc. above	50.00	65.00	95.00	185	250
1897Mo M	5,131	50.00	65.00	95.00	185	250
1898/7Mo M	5,368	50.00	65.00	95.00	185	250
1899Mo M	9,515	50.00	65.00	95.00	185	250
1900/800Mo M	9,301	50.00	65.00	95.00	185	250
1900/880Mo M	Inc. above	50.00	65.00	95.00	185	250
1900/890Mo M	Inc. above	50.00	65.00	95.00	185	250
1900Mo M	Inc. above	50.00	65.00	95.00	185	250
1901Mo M Small date	Inc. above	70.00	85.00	115	205	270
1901/801Mo M Large date	8,293	70.00	85.00	115	205	270
1902Mo M Large date	11,000	70.00	85.00	115	205	270
1902Mo M Small date	Inc. above	70.00	85.00	115	205	270
1903Mo M Large date	10,000	70.00	85.00	115	205	270
1903Mo M Small date	Inc. above	80.00	105	145	220	325
1904Mo M	9,845	70.00	85.00	115	205	270
1905Mo M	3,429	70.00	85.00	115	205	270

KM# 410.6 PESO
1.6920 g., 0.8750 Gold 0.0476 oz. AGW **Obv:** Facing eagle, snake in beak **Obv. Legend:** REPUBLICA MEXICANA **Rev:** Value within 1/2 wreath **Mint:** Zacatecas

Date	Mintage	F	VF	XF	Unc	BU
1872Zs H	2,024	125	150	175	275	—

Date	Mintage	F	VF	XF	Unc	BU
1875/3Zs A	—	125	150	200	325	—
1878Zs S	—	125	150	175	275	—
1888Zs Z	280	175	225	325	700	—
1889Zs Z	492	150	175	225	450	—
1890Zs Z	738	150	175	225	450	—

KM# 409.3 PESO
27.0730 g., 0.9030 Silver 0.7860 oz. ASW, 39 mm. **Obv:** Facing eagle, snake in beak **Rev:** Radiant cap **Mint:** Zacatecas **Note:** Mint mark Zs. Varieties exist.

Date	Mintage	F	VF	XF	Unc	BU
1898Zs FZ	5,714,000	22.50	27.50	40.00	105	—
1899Zs FZ	5,618,000	22.50	27.50	40.00	110	—
1900Zs FZ	5,357,000	22.50	27.50	40.00	110	—
1901Zs FZ	Inc. above	25.00	27.50	32.00	90.00	—
1901Zs AZ	5,706,000	6,400	10,500	16,000	—	—
1902Zs FZ	7,134,000	25.00	27.50	32.00	90.00	—
1903/2Zs FZ	3,080,000	25.00	27.50	80.00	200	—
1903Zs FZ	Inc. above	25.00	27.50	32.00	105	—
1904Zs FZ	2,423,000	25.00	27.50	40.00	135	—
1904Zs FM	Inc. above	25.00	27.50	40.00	120	—
1905Zs FM	995,000	32.00	65.00	95.00	240	—

KM# 408.7 PESO
27.0730 g., 0.9030 Silver 0.7860 oz. ASW **Obv:** Facing eagle, snake in beak **Rev:** Radiant cap above scales **Mint:** San Luis Potosi **Note:** Varieties exist.

Date	Mintage	F	VF	XF	Unc	BU
1870Pi S	1,967,000	200	350	500	1,000	—
1870Pi S/A	Inc. above	200	350	550	1,200	—
1870Pi G	Inc. above	27.50	45.00	80.00	550	—
1870Pi H	Inc. above	—	—	—	—	—

Note: Contemporary counterfeits

Date	Mintage	F	VF	XF	Unc	BU
1870Pi O/G	Inc. above	27.50	45.00	80.00	550	—
1870Pi O	Inc. above	22.50	35.00	105	400	—
1871Pi O	—	18.00	35.00	65.00	500	—
1871Pi O/G	Inc. above	18.00	35.00	65.00	500	—
1871/69Pi O	2,103,000	80.00	105	205	500	—
1872Pi O	1,873,000	18.00	35.00	65.00	500	—
1873Pi H	Inc. above	18.00	35.00	65.00	500	—
1873Pi O	893,000	18.00	35.00	65.00	500	—

KM# 408.8 PESO
27.0730 g., 0.9030 Silver 0.7860 oz. ASW **Obv:** Facing eagle, snake in beak **Rev:** Radiant cap above scales **Mint:** Zacatecas **Note:** Varieties exist.

Date	Mintage	F	VF	XF	Unc	BU
1870Zs H	4,519,000	15.00	35.00	45.00	220	—
1871Zs H	4,459,000	15.00	25.00	45.00	220	—
1872Zs H	4,039,000	15.00	25.00	45.00	220	—
1873/1Zs H	Inc. above	15.00	25.00	45.00	220	—
1873Zs H	1,782,000	15.00	25.00	45.00	220	—

KM# 409.1 PESO
27.0730 g., 0.9030 Silver 0.7860 oz. ASW, 39 mm. **Obv:** Facing eagle, snake in beak **Rev:** Radiant cap **Mint:** Guanajuato **Note:** Varieties exist.

Date	Mintage	F	VF	XF	Unc	BU
1898Go/MoRS	Inc. above	22.50	30.00	60.00	125	—
1898Go RS	4,256,000	14.00	19.00	38.00	80.00	—
1899Go RS	3,207,000	14.00	19.00	33.00	80.00	—
1900Go RS	1,489,000	27.50	50.00	100	250	—

KM# 409.2 PESO
27.0730 g., 0.9027 Silver 0.7857 oz. ASW, 39 mm. **Obv:** Facing eagle, snake in beak **Obv. Legend:** REPUBLICA MEXICANA **Rev:** Radiant cap **Mint:** Mexico City **Note:** Varieties exist.

Date	Mintage	F	VF	XF	Unc	BU
1898Mo AM	10,250,000	15.00	17.50	19.50	45.00	—

Note: Restrike (1949) - reverse with 134 beads

Date	Mintage	F	VF	XF	Unc	BU
1898Mo AM	10,156,000	15.00	17.50	21.50	65.00	—

Note: Original strike - reverse with 139 beads

Date	Mintage	F	VF	XF	Unc	BU
1899Mo AM	7,930,000	15.00	17.50	23.00	75.00	—
1900Mo AM	8,226,000	15.00	17.50	23.00	75.00	—
1901Mo AM	14,505,000	25.00	27.50	36.75	120	—
1902/1Mo AM	16,224,000	240	475	800	1,500	—
1902Mo AM	Inc. above	25.00	27.50	32.00	110	—
1903Mo AM	22,396,000	25.00	27.50	32.00	110	—
1903Mo MA (Error)	Inc. above	1,500	2,500	3,500	7,500	—
1904Mo AM	14,935,000	25.00	27.50	32.00	110	—
1905Mo AM	3,557,000	27.50	40.00	90.00	200	—
1908Mo AM	7,575,000	25.00	27.50	32.00	95.00	—
1908Mo GV	Inc. above	25.00	27.50	30.00	65.00	—
1909Mo GV	2,924,000	25.00	27.50	30.00	65.00	—

KM# 410 PESO
1.6920 g., 0.8750 Gold 0.0476 oz. AGW **Obv:** Facing eagle, snake in beak **Obv. Legend:** REPUBLICA MEXICANA **Rev:** Value within 1/2 wreath **Mint:** Alamos

Date	Mintage	F	VF	XF	Unc	BU
1888AsL/MoM Rare	—	—	—	—	—	—
1888As L Rare	—	—	—	—	—	—

KM# 410.1 PESO
1.6920 g., 0.8750 Gold 0.0476 oz. AGW **Obv:** Facing eagle, snake in beak **Obv. Legend:** REPUBLICA MEXICANA **Rev:** Value within 1/2 wreath **Mint:** Chihuahua

Date	Mintage	F	VF	XF	Unc	BU
1888Ca/MoM Rare	104	—	—	—	—	—

KM# 411.3   2-1/2 PESOS
4.2300 g., 0.8750 Gold 0.1190 oz. AGW **Obv:** Facing eagle, snake in beak **Obv. Legend:** REPUBLICA MEXICANA **Rev:** Value within 1/2 wreath **Mint:** Guanajuato

Date	Mintage	F	VF	XF	Unc	BU
1871Go S	600	1,250	2,000	2,500	3,250	—
1888Go/MoR	110	1,750	2,250	2,750	3,500	—

KM# 411.4   2-1/2 PESOS
4.2300 g., 0.8750 Gold 0.1190 oz. AGW **Obv:** Facing eagle, snake in beak **Obv. Legend:** REPUBLICA MEXICANA **Rev:** Value within 1/2 wreath **Mint:** Hermosillo

Date	Mintage	F	VF	XF	Unc	BU
1874Ho R Rare	—	—	—	—	—	—
1888Ho G Rare	—	—	—	—	—	—

KM# 411.5   2-1/2 PESOS
4.2300 g., 0.8750 Gold 0.1190 oz. AGW **Obv:** Facing eagle, snake in beak **Rev:** Value within 1/2 wreath **Mint:** Mexico City

Date	Mintage	F	VF	XF	Unc	BU
1870Mo C	820	150	250	350	750	—
1872Mo M/C	800	150	250	350	750	—
1873/2Mo M	—	200	350	750	1,350	—
1874Mo M	—	200	350	750	1,350	—
1874Mo B/M	—	200	350	750	1,350	—
1875Mo B	—	200	350	750	1,350	—
1876Mo B	—	250	500	1,000	1,850	—
1877Mo M	—	200	350	750	1,350	—
1878Mo M	400	200	350	750	1,350	—
1879Mo M	—	200	350	750	1,350	—
1880/79Mo M	—	200	350	750	1,350	—
1881Mo M	400	200	350	750	1,350	—
1882Mo M	—	225	400	850	1,500	2,000
1883/73Mo M	400	200	350	750	1,350	—
1884Mo M	—	250	500	1,000	1,600	—
1885Mo M	—	400	850	1,750	3,000	—
1886Mo M	400	200	350	750	1,350	—
1887Mo M	400	200	350	750	1,350	—
1888Mo M	540	200	350	750	1,350	—
1889Mo M	240	150	300	525	950	—
1890Mo M	420	200	350	750	1,350	—
1891Mo M	188	200	350	750	1,350	—
1892Mo M	240	200	350	750	1,350	—

KM# 411.6   2-1/2 PESOS
4.2300 g., 0.8750 Gold 0.1190 oz. AGW **Obv:** Facing eagle, snake in beak **Obv. Legend:** REPUBLICA MEXICANA **Rev:** Value within 1/2 wreath **Mint:** Zacatecas

Date	Mintage	F	VF	XF	Unc	BU
1872Zs H	1,300	200	350	500	1,200	—
1873/3Zs H	—	175	325	475	900	—
1875/3Zs A	—	200	350	750	1,350	—

Date	Mintage	F	VF	XF	Unc	BU
1877Zs S	—	200	350	750	1,350	—
1878Zs S	300	200	350	750	1,350	—
1888Zs/MoS	80	300	500	1,000	1,800	—
1889Zs/Mo Z	184	250	450	950	1,600	—
1890Zs Z	326	200	350	750	1,350	—

KM# 411   2-1/2 PESOS
4.2300 g., 0.8750 Gold 0.1190 oz. AGW **Obv:** Facing eagle, snake in beak **Obv. Legend:** REPUBLICA MEXICANA **Rev:** Value within 1/2 wreath **Mint:** Alamos

Date	Mintage	F	VF	XF	Unc	BU
1888As/MoL Rare	—	—	—	—	—	—

KM# 411.1   2-1/2 PESOS
4.2300 g., 0.8750 Gold 0.1190 oz. AGW **Obv:** Facing eagle, snake in beak **Rev:** Value within 1/2 wreath **Mint:** Culiacan

Date	Mintage	F	VF	XF	Unc	BU
1893Cn M	141	1,500	2,000	2,500	3,500	—

KM# 411.2   2-1/2 PESOS
4.2300 g., 0.8750 Gold 0.1190 oz. AGW **Obv:** Facing eagle, snake in beak **Rev:** Value within 1/2 wreath **Mint:** Durango

Date	Mintage	F	VF	XF	Unc	BU
1888Do C Rare	—	—	—	—	—	—

KM# 412.2   5 PESOS
8.4600 g., 0.8750 Gold 0.2380 oz. AGW **Obv:** Facing eagle, snake in beak **Obv. Legend:** REPUBLICA MEXICANA **Rev:** Radiant cap above scales **Mint:** Culiacan

Date	Mintage	F	VF	XF	Unc	BU
1873Cn P	—	300	600	1,000	2,000	—
1874Cn P	—	—	—	—	—	—
1875Cn P	—	300	500	800	1,750	—
1876Cn P	—	300	500	800	1,750	—
1877Cn G	—	300	500	800	1,750	—
1882Cn Rare	174	—	—	—	—	—
1888Cn M	—	500	1,000	1,350	2,000	—
1890Cn M	435	250	500	750	1,600	—
1891Cn M	1,390	250	400	550	1,000	—
1894Cn M	484	250	500	750	1,600	—
1895Cn M	142	500	750	1,500	2,500	—
1900Cn Q	1,536	240	300	475	900	—
1903Cn Q	1,000	350	375	550	1,000	—

KM# 412.3   5 PESOS
8.4600 g., 0.8750 Gold 0.2380 oz. AGW **Obv:** Facing eagle, snake in beak **Obv. Legend:** REPUBLICA MEXICANA **Rev:** Radiant cap above scales **Mint:** Durango

Date	Mintage	F	VF	XF	Unc	BU
1873/2Do P	—	700	1,250	1,800	3,000	—
1877Do P	—	700	1,250	1,800	3,000	—
1878Do E	—	700	1,250	1,800	3,000	—
1879Do B	—	700	1,250	1,800	3,000	—
1879/7Do B	—	700	1,250	1,800	3,000	—

Date	Mintage	F	VF	XF	Unc	BU
1904Mo M	1,415	350	375	500	800	1,300
1905Mo M	563	350	450	600	1,550	2,050

KM# 412.4 5 PESOS
8.4600 g., 0.8750 Gold 0.2380 oz. AGW **Obv:** Facing eagle, snake in beak **Obv. Legend:** REPUBLICA MEXICANA **Rev:** Radiant cap above scales **Mint:** Guanajuato

Date	Mintage	F	VF	XF	Unc	BU
1871Go S	1,600	400	800	1,250	2,250	—
1887Go R	140	600	1,200	1,600	3,000	—
1888Go R Rare	65	—	—	—	—	—
1893Go R Rare	16	—	—	—	—	—

KM# 412 5 PESOS
8.4600 g., 0.8750 Gold 0.2380 oz. AGW **Obv:** Facing eagle, snake in beak **Obv. Legend:** REPUBLICA MEXICANA **Rev:** Radiant cap above scales **Mint:** Alamos

Date	Mintage	F	VF	XF	Unc	BU
1875As L	—	—	—	—	—	—
1878As L	383	900	1,700	3,000	4,500	—

KM# 412.6 5 PESOS
8.4600 g., 0.8750 Gold 0.2380 oz. AGW **Obv:** Facing eagle, snake in beak **Obv. Legend:** REPUBLICA MEXICANA **Rev:** Radiant cap above scales **Mint:** Mexico City

Date	Mintage	F	VF	XF	Unc	BU
1870Mo C	550	240	400	600	1,500	—
1871/69Mo M	1,600	240	300	400	650	—
1871Mo M	Inc. above	240	300	400	650	—
1872Mo M	1,600	240	300	400	650	—
1873/2Mo M	—	240	400	550	850	—
1874Mo M	—	240	400	550	850	—
1875/3Mo B/M	—	240	400	550	950	—
1875Mo B	—	240	400	550	950	—
1876/5Mo B/M	—	240	400	550	1,000	—
1877Mo M	—	250	450	750	1,650	—
1878/7Mo M	400	240	400	550	1,250	—
1878Mo M	Inc. above	240	400	550	1,250	—
1879/8Mo M	—	240	400	550	1,250	—
1880Mo M	—	240	400	550	1,250	—
1881Mo M	—	240	400	550	1,250	—
1882Mo M	200	250	450	750	1,650	—
1883Mo M	200	250	450	750	1,650	—
1884Mo M	—	250	450	750	1,650	—
1886Mo M	200	250	450	750	1,650	—
1887Mo M	200	250	450	750	1,650	—
1888Mo M	250	240	400	550	1,650	—
1889Mo M	190	250	450	750	1,650	—
1890Mo M	149	250	450	750	1,650	—
1891Mo M	156	250	450	750	1,650	—
1892Mo M	214	250	450	750	1,650	—
1893Mo M	1,058	240	400	500	800	—
1897Mo M	370	240	400	550	1,000	—
1898Mo M	376	240	400	550	1,000	—
1900Mo M	1,014	290	350	450	700	1,050
1901Mo M	1,071	350	375	500	800	1,300
1902Mo M	1,478	350	375	500	800	1,300
1903Mo M	1,162	350	375	500	800	1,300

KM# 412.7 5 PESOS
8.4600 g., 0.8750 Gold 0.2380 oz. AGW **Obv:** Facing eagle, snake in beak **Obv. Legend:** REPUBLICA MEXICANA **Rev:** Radiant cap above scales **Mint:** Zacatecas

Date	Mintage	F	VF	XF	Unc	BU
1874Zs A	—	250	500	750	1,500	—
1875Zs A	—	240	400	500	1,000	—
1877Zs S/A	—	240	400	550	1,000	—
1878/7Zs S/A	—	240	400	550	1,000	—
1883Zs S	—	175	300	450	750	—
1888Zs Z	70	1,000	1,500	2,000	3,000	—
1889Zs Z	373	240	300	500	850	—
1892Zs Z	1,229	240	300	450	750	1,250

KM# 412.1 5 PESOS
8.4600 g., 0.8750 Gold 0.2380 oz. AGW **Obv:** Facing eagle, snake in beak **Obv. Legend:** REPUBLICA MEXICANA **Rev:** Radiant cap above scales **Mint:** Chihuahua

Date	Mintage	F	VF	XF	Unc	BU
1888Ca M Rare	120	—	—	—	—	—

KM# 412.5 5 PESOS
8.4600 g., 0.8750 Gold 0.2380 oz. AGW **Obv:** Facing eagle, snake in beak **Obv. Legend:** REPUBLICA MEXICANA **Rev:** Radiant cap above scales **Mint:** Hermosillo

Date	Mintage	F	VF	XF	Unc	BU
1874Ho R	—	1,750	2,500	3,000	4,500	—
1877Ho A	Inc. above	650	1,100	1,750	2,750	—
1877Ho R	990	750	1,250	2,000	3,000	—
1888Ho G Rare	—	—	—	—	—	—

KM# 413.2 10 PESOS
16.9200 g., 0.8750 Gold 0.4760 oz. AGW **Obv:** Facing eagle, snake in beak **Obv. Legend:** REPUBLICA MEXICANA **Rev:** Radiant cap above scales **Mint:** Culiacan

Date	Mintage	F	VF	XF	Unc	BU
1881Cn D	—	460	600	1,000	1,750	—
1882Cn D	874	460	600	1,000	1,750	—
1882Cn E	Inc. above	460	600	1,000	1,750	—
1883Cn D	221	—	—	—	—	—
1883Cn M	Inc. above	460	600	1,000	1,750	—

SECOND REPUBLIC

Date	Mintage	F	VF	XF	Unc	BU
1884Cn D	—	460	600	1,000	1,750	—
1884Cn M	—	460	600	1,000	1,750	—
1885Cn M	1,235	460	600	1,000	1,750	—
1886Cn M	981	460	600	1,000	1,750	—
1887Cn M	2,289	460	600	1,000	1,750	—
1888Cn M	767	460	600	1,000	1,750	—
1889Cn M	859	460	600	1,000	1,750	—
1890Cn M	1,427	460	600	1,000	1,750	—
1891Cn M	670	460	600	1,000	1,750	—
1892Cn M	379	460	600	1,000	1,750	—
1893Cn M	1,806	460	600	1,000	1,750	—
1895Cn M	179	500	1,000	1,500	2,500	—
1903Cn Q	774	700	800	1,100	2,100	—

KM# 413.3 10 PESOS
16.9200 g., 0.8750 Gold 0.4760 oz. AGW **Obv:** Facing eagle, snake in beak **Obv. Legend:** REPUBLICA MEXICANA **Rev:** Radiant cap above scales **Mint:** Durango

Date	Mintage	F	VF	XF	Unc	BU
1872Do P	1,755	455	500	800	1,250	—
1873/2Do P	1,091	455	500	850	1,350	—
1873/2Do M/P	Inc. above	455	550	900	1,450	—
1874Do M	—	455	550	900	1,450	—
1875Do M	—	55.00	550	900	1,450	—
1876Do M	—	470	750	1,250	2,000	—
1877Do P	—	455	550	900	1,450	—
1878Do E	582	455	550	900	1,450	—
1879/8Do B	—	455	550	900	1,450	—
1879Do B	—	455	550	900	1,450	—
1880Do P	2,030	455	550	900	1,450	3,750
1881/79Do P	2,617	455	550	900	1,450	—
1882Do P Rare	1,528	—	—	—	—	—
1882Do C	Inc. above	455	550	900	1,450	—
1883Do C	793	470	750	1,250	2,000	—
1884Do C	108	470	750	1,250	2,000	—

KM# 413.4 10 PESOS
16.9200 g., 0.8750 Gold 0.4760 oz. AGW **Obv:** Facing eagle, snake in beak **Obv. Legend:** REPUBLICA MEXICANA **Rev:** Radiant cap above scales **Mint:** Guadalajara

Date	Mintage	F	VF	XF	Unc	BU
1870Ga C	490	500	800	1,000	1,750	—
1871Ga C	1,910	475	800	1,250	2,250	—
1872Ga C	780	500	1,000	2,000	2,500	—
1873Ga C	422	500	1,000	2,000	3,000	—
1874/3Ga C	477	500	1,000	2,000	3,000	—
1875Ga C	710	500	1,000	2,000	3,000	—
1878Ga A	183	600	1,200	2,500	3,500	—
1879Ga A	200	600	1,200	2,500	3,500	—
1880Ga S	404	500	1,000	2,000	3,000	—
1881Ga S	239	600	1,200	2,500	3,500	—
1891Ga S	196	600	1,200	2,500	3,500	—

KM# 413.5 10 PESOS
16.9200 g., 0.8750 Gold 0.4760 oz. AGW **Obv:** Facing eagle, snake in beak **Obv. Legend:** REPUBLICA MEXICANA **Rev:** Radiant cap above scales **Mint:** Guanajuato

Date	Mintage	F	VF	XF	Unc	BU
1872Go S	1,400	2,000	4,000	6,500	10,000	—
1887Go R Rare	80	—	—	—	—	—

Note: Stack's Rio Grande Sale 6-93, P/L AU realized, $12,650

1888Go R Rare	68	—	—	—	—	—

KM# 413.6 10 PESOS
16.9200 g., 0.8750 Gold 0.4760 oz. AGW **Obv:** Facing eagle, snake in beak **Obv. Legend:** REPUBLICA MEXICANA **Rev:** Radiant cap above scales **Mint:** Hermosillo

Date	Mintage	F	VF	XF	Unc	BU
1874Ho R Rare	—	—	—	—	—	—
1876Ho F Rare	357	—	—	—	—	—
1878Ho A	814	1,750	3,000	3,500	5,500	—
1879Ho A	—	1,000	2,000	2,500	4,000	—
1880Ho A	—	1,000	2,000	2,500	4,000	—
1881Ho A Rare	—	—	—	—	—	—

Note: American Numismatic Rarities Eliasberg sale 4-05, MS-62 realized $34,500.

KM# 413.7 10 PESOS
16.9200 g., 0.8750 Gold 0.4760 oz. AGW **Obv:** Facing eagle, snake in beak **Obv. Legend:** REPUBLICA MEXICANA **Rev:** Radiant cap above scales **Mint:** Mexico City

Date	Mintage	F	VF	XF	Unc	BU
1870Mo C	480	500	900	1,200	2,000	—
1872/1Mo M/C	2,100	460	550	900	1,350	—
1873Mo M	—	460	600	950	1,450	—
1874/3Mo M	—	460	600	950	1,450	—
1875Mo B/M	—	460	600	950	1,450	—
1876Mo B Rare	—	—	—	—	—	—
1878Mo M	300	460	600	950	1,450	—
1879Mo M	—	—	—	—	—	—
1881Mo M	100	500	1,000	1,600	2,500	—
1882Mo M	—	460	600	950	1,450	—
1883Mo M	100	600	1,000	1,600	2,500	—
1884Mo M	—	600	1,000	1,600	2,500	—
1885Mo M	—	460	600	950	1,450	—
1886Mo M	100	600	1,000	1,600	2,500	—
1887Mo M	100	600	1,000	1,625	2,750	—
1888Mo M	144	460	750	1,200	2,000	—

Date	Mintage	F	VF	XF	Unc	BU
1889Mo M	88	600	1,000	1,600	2,500	—
1890Mo M	137	600	1,000	1,600	2,500	—
1891Mo M	133	600	1,000	1,600	2,500	—
1892Mo M	45	600	1,000	1,600	2,500	—
1893Mo M	1,361	460	550	900	1,350	—
1897Mo M	239	460	600	950	1,450	—
1898/7Mo M	244	460	625	1,000	1,750	—
1900Mo M	733	460	600	950	1,450	—
1901Mo M	562	700	725	950	1,600	—
1902Mo M	719	700	725	950	1,600	2,600
1903Mo M	713	700	725	950	1,600	2,600
1904Mo M	694	700	725	950	1,600	—
1905Mo M	401	700	750	1,100	1,800	—

Date	Mintage	F	VF	XF	Unc	BU
1882/1Zs Z	—	460	600	1,000	1,750	2,500
1882Zs S	1,599	455	550	950	1,450	—
1883/2Zs S	256	400	600	1,000	1,750	—
1884/3Zs S	—	455	550	950	1,600	—
1884Zs S	—	455	550	950	1,600	—
1885Zs S	1,588	455	550	950	1,450	—
1886Zs S	5,364	455	550	950	1,450	—
1887Zs Z	2,330	455	550	950	1,450	—
1888Zs Z	4,810	455	550	950	1,450	—
1889Zs Z	6,154	455	500	750	1,250	—
1890Zs Z	1,321	455	550	950	1,450	—
1891Zs Z	1,930	455	550	950	1,450	3,250
1892Zs Z	1,882	455	550	950	1,450	—
1893Zs Z	2,899	455	550	950	1,450	—
1894Zs Z	2,501	455	550	950	1,450	—
1895Zs Z	1,217	455	550	950	1,450	—

KM# 413.8 10 PESOS
16.9200 g., 0.8750 Gold 0.4760 oz. AGW **Obv:** Facing eagle, snake in beak **Obv. Legend:** REPUBLICA MEXICANA **Rev:** Radiant cap above scales **Mint:** Oaxaca

Date	Mintage	F	VF	XF	Unc	BU
1870Oa E	4,614	460	600	900	1,600	—
1871Oa E	2,705	460	600	950	1,650	—
1872Oa E	5,897	460	600	850	1,500	—
1873Oa E	3,537	460	600	850	1,500	—
1874Oa E	2,205	460	600	1,200	1,850	—
1875Oa E	312	475	750	1,400	2,250	—
1876Oa E	766	475	750	1,400	2,250	—
1877Oa E	463	475	750	1,400	2,250	—
1878Oa E	229	475	750	1,400	2,250	—
1879Oa E	210	475	750	1,400	2,250	—
1880Oa E	238	475	750	1,400	2,250	—
1881Oa E	961	460	600	1,200	2,000	—
1882Oa E	170	600	1,000	1,500	2,500	—
1883Oa E	111	600	1,000	1,500	2,500	—
1884Oa E	325	475	750	1,400	2,250	—
1885Oa E	370	475	750	1,400	2,250	—
1886Oa E	400	475	750	1,400	2,250	—
1887Oa E	—	700	1,250	2,250	4,000	—
1888Oa E	—	—	—	—	—	—

KM# 413 10 PESOS
16.9200 g., 0.8750 Gold 0.4760 oz. AGW **Obv:** Facing eagle, snake in beak **Obv. Legend:** REPUBLICA MEXICANA **Rev:** Radiant cap above scales **Mint:** Alamos

Date	Mintage	F	VF	XF	Unc	BU
1874As DL Rare	—	—	—	—	—	—
1875As L	642	600	1,250	2,500	3,500	—
1878As L	977	500	1,000	2,000	3,000	—
1879As L	1,078	500	1,000	2,000	3,000	—
1880As L	2,629	500	1,000	2,000	3,000	—
1881As L	2,574	500	1,000	2,000	3,000	—
1882As L	3,403	500	1,000	2,000	3,000	—
1883As L	3,597	500	1,000	2,000	3,000	—
1884As L Rare	—	—	—	—	—	—
1885As L	4,562	500	1,000	2,000	3,000	—
1886As L	4,643	500	1,000	2,000	3,000	—
1887As L	3,667	500	1,000	2,000	3,000	—
1888As L	4,521	500	1,000	2,000	3,000	—
1889As L	5,615	500	1,000	2,000	3,000	—
1890As L	4,920	500	1,000	2,000	3,000	—
1891As L	568	500	1,000	2,000	3,000	—
1892As L	—	—	—	—	—	—
1893As L	817	500	1,000	2,000	3,000	—
1894/3As L	1,658					
1894As L	Inc. above	500	1,000	2,000	3,000	—
1895As L	1,237	500	1,000	2,000	3,000	—

KM# 413.9 10 PESOS
16.9200 g., 0.8750 Gold 0.4760 oz. AGW **Obv:** Facing eagle, snake in beak **Obv. Legend:** REPUBLICA MEXICANA **Rev:** Radiant cap above scales **Mint:** Zacatecas

Date	Mintage	F	VF	XF	Unc	BU
1871Zs H	2,000	455	500	800	1,250	—
1872Zs H	3,092	455	500	750	1,150	—
1873Zs H	936	460	600	950	1,450	—
1874Zs H	—	460	600	950	1,450	—
1875/3Zs A	—	460	600	1,000	1,750	—
1876/5Zs S	—	460	600	1,000	1,750	—
1877Zs S/H	506	460	600	1,000	1,750	—
1878Zs S	711	460	600	1,000	1,750	—
1879/8Zs Z	—	475	750	1,400	2,250	—
1879Zs S	—	475	750	1,400	2,250	—
1880Zs S	2,089	455	550	950	1,450	—
1881Zs S	736	460	600	1,000	1,750	—

KM# 413.1 10 PESOS
16.9200 g., 0.8750 Gold 0.4760 oz. AGW **Obv:** Facing eagle, snake in beak **Obv. Legend:** REPUBLICA MEXICANA **Rev:** Radiant cap above scales **Mint:** Chihuahua

Date	Mintage	F	VF	XF	Unc	BU
1888Ca M	175	—	—	7,500	—	—

KM# 414 20 PESOS
33.8400 g., 0.8750 Gold 0.9519 oz. AGW **Obv:** Facing eagle, snake in beak **Rev:** Radiant cap above scales **Mint:** Alamos

Date	Mintage	F	VF	XF	Unc	BU
1876As L Rare	276	—	—	—	—	—
1877As L Rare	166	—	—	—	—	—
1878As L	—	—	—	—	—	—
1888As L Rare	—	—	—	—	—	—

KM# 414.2 20 PESOS
33.8400 g., 0.8750 Gold 0.9519 oz. AGW **Obv:** Facing eagle, snake in beak **Obv. Legend:** REPUBLICA MEXICANA **Rev:** Radiant cap above scales **Mint:** Culiacan

Date	Mintage	F	VF	XF	Unc	BU
1870Cn E	3,749	BV	925	1,200	2,500	—
1871Cn P	3,046	BV	925	1,200	2,500	—
1872Cn P	972	BV	925	1,200	2,500	—
1873Cn P	1,317	BV	925	1,200	2,500	—
1874Cn P	—	BV	925	1,200	2,500	—
1875Cn P	—	925	1,600	2,250	3,150	—
1876Cn P	—	BV	925	1,200	2,500	—
1876Cn G	—	BV	925	1,200	2,500	—
1877Cn G	167	925	1,350	1,900	3,750	—
1878Cn Rare	842	—	—	—	—	—
1881/0Cn D	2,039	—	—	—	—	—
1881Cn D	Inc. above	BV	925	1,200	2,500	—
1882/1Cn D	736	BV	925	1,200	2,500	—
1883Cn M	1,836	BV	925	1,200	2,500	—
1884Cn M	—	BV	925	1,200	2,500	—
1885Cn M	544	BV	925	1,200	2,500	—
1886Cn M	882	BV	925	1,200	2,500	—
1887Cn M	837	BV	925	1,200	2,500	—
1888Cn M	473	BV	925	1,200	2,500	—
1889Cn M	1,376	BV	925	1,200	2,500	—
1890Cn M	—	1,100	2,350	4,400	11,000	—
1891Cn M	237	BV	1,200	1,500	2,800	—
1892Cn M	526	BV	925	1,200	2,500	—
1893Cn M	2,062	BV	925	1,200	2,500	—
1894Cn M	4,516	BV	925	1,200	2,500	—
1895Cn M	3,193	BV	925	1,200	2,500	—
1896Cn M	4,072	BV	925	1,200	2,500	—
1897/6Cn M	959	BV	925	1,200	2,500	—
1897Cn M	Inc. above	BV	925	1,200	2,500	—
1898Cn M	1,660	BV	925	1,200	2,500	—
1899Cn M	1,243	BV	925	1,200	2,500	—
1899Cn Q	Inc. above	BV	1,200	1,500	2,800	—
1900Cn Q	1,558	BV	925	1,200	2,500	—
1901Cn Q	Inc. above	BV	1,450	1,550	2,950	—
1901/0Cn Q	1,496	—	—	—	—	—
1902Cn Q	1,059	BV	1,450	1,550	2,950	—
1903Cn Q	1,121	BV	1,450	1,550	2,950	—
1904Cn H	4,646	BV	1,450	1,550	2,950	—
1905Cn P	1,738	BV	1,500	1,700	3,150	—

KM# 414.3 20 PESOS
33.8400 g., 0.8750 Gold 0.9519 oz. AGW **Obv:** Facing eagle, snake in beak **Obv. Legend:** REPUBLICA MEXICANA **Rev:** Radiant cap above scales **Mint:** Durango

Date	Mintage	F	VF	XF	Unc	BU
1870Do P	416	1,100	1,650	2,500	3,150	—
1871Do P	Inc. above	1,100	1,650	2,500	3,150	—
1871/0Do P	1,073	1,100	1,950	2,800	3,450	—
1872/1Do PT	—	1,650	3,300	5,600	8,800	—
1876Do M	—	1,100	1,650	2,500	3,150	—
1877Do P	94	1,650	2,500	3,450	4,050	—
1878Do Rare	258					

KM# 414.4 20 PESOS
33.8400 g., 0.8750 Gold 0.9519 oz. AGW **Obv:** Facing eagle, snake in beak **Obv. Legend:** REPUBLICA MEXICANA **Rev:** Radiant cap above scales **Mint:** Guanajuato

Date	Mintage	F	VF	XF	Unc	BU
1870Go S	3,250	BV	925	1,150	1,900	—
1871Go S	20,000	BV	925	1,150	1,900	2,750
1872Go S	18,000	BV	925	1,150	1,900	—
1873Go S	7,000	BV	925	1,150	1,900	—
1874Go S	—	BV	925	1,150	1,900	—
1875Go S	—	BV	925	1,150	1,900	—
1876Go S	—	BV	925	1,150	1,900	—
1876Go M/S	—	—	—	—	—	—
1877Go M/S Rare	15,000	—	—	—	—	—
1877Go R	Inc. above	BV	925	1,150	1,900	—
1877Go S Rare	Inc. above					
1878/7Go M/S	13,000	950	1,750	2,500	3,500	—
1878Go M	Inc. above	950	1,750	2,500	3,500	—
1878Go S	Inc. above	BV	925	1,150	1,900	—
1879Go S	8,202	BV	1,100	1,500	2,900	—
1880Go S	7,375	BV	925	1,150	1,900	—
1881Go S	4,909	BV	925	1,150	1,900	—
1882Go S	4,020	BV	925	1,150	1,900	—
1883/2Go B	3,705	BV	1,050	1,450	2,800	—
1883Go B	Inc. above	BV	925	1,150	1,900	—
1884Go B	1,798	BV	925	1,150	1,900	—
1885Go B	2,660	BV	925	1,150	1,900	—
1886Go R	1,090	950	1,100	1,550	3,150	—
1887Go R	1,009	950	1,100	1,550	3,150	—
1888Go R	1,011	950	1,100	1,550	3,150	—
1889Go R	956	950	1,100	1,550	3,150	—
1890Go R	879	950	1,100	1,550	3,150	—
1891Go R	818	950	1,100	1,550	3,150	—
1892Go R	730	950	1,100	1,550	3,150	—
1893Go R	3,343	BV	925	1,250	2,500	—
1894/3Go R	6,734	BV	925	1,150	1,900	—
1894Go R	Inc. above	BV	925	1,150	1,900	—
1895/3Go R	7,118	BV	925	1,150	1,900	—
1895Go R	Inc. above	BV	925	1,150	1,900	—
1896Go R	9,219	BV	925	1,150	1,900	7,200
1897/6Go R	6,781	BV	925	1,150	1,900	—
1897Go R	Inc. above	BV	925	1,150	1,900	—
1898Go R	7,710	BV	925	1,150	1,900	—
1899Go R	8,527	BV	925	1,150	1,900	—
1900Go R	4,512	950	1,100	1,550	2,950	—

Date	Mintage	F	VF	XF	Unc	BU
1891Mo M	Inc. above	BV	920	1,150	1,950	—
1892Mo M	11,000	BV	920	1,150	1,900	—
1893Mo M	15,000	BV	920	1,150	1,900	—
1894Mo M	14,000	BV	920	1,150	1,900	—
1895Mo M	13,000	BV	920	1,150	1,900	—
1896Mo B	14,000	BV	920	1,150	1,900	—
1897/6Mo M	12,000	BV	920	1,150	1,900	—
1897Mo M	Inc. above	BV	920	1,150	1,900	—
1898Mo M	20,000	BV	920	1,150	1,900	—
1899Mo M	23,000	BV	920	1,150	1,900	—
1900Mo M	21,000	BV	920	1,150	1,900	—
1901Mo M	29,000	BV	1,350	1,500	2,250	—
1902Mo M	38,000	BV	1,350	1,500	2,250	—
1903/2Mo M	31,000	BV	1,350	1,500	2,250	—
1903Mo M	Inc. above	BV	1,350	1,500	2,250	—
1904Mo M	52,000	BV	1,350	1,500	2,250	—
1905Mo M	9,757	BV	1,350	1,500	2,250	—

KM# 414.5   20 PESOS
33.8400 g., 0.8750 Gold 0.9519 oz. AGW **Obv:** Facing eagle, snake in beak **Obv. Legend:** REPUBLICA MEXICANA **Rev:** Radiant cap above scales **Mint:** Hermosillo

Date	Mintage	F	VF	XF	Unc	BU
1874Ho R Rare	—	—	—	—	—	—
1875Ho R Rare	—	—	—	—	—	—
1876Ho F Rare	—	—	—	—	—	—
1888Ho g Rare	—	—	—	—	—	—

KM# 414.6   20 PESOS
33.8400 g., 0.8750 Gold 0.9519 oz. AGW **Obv:** Facing eagle, snake in beak **Obv. Legend:** REPUBLICA MEXICANA **Rev:** Radiant cap above scales **Mint:** Mexico City

Date	Mintage	F	VF	XF	Unc	BU
1870Mo C	14,000	BV	920	1,150	1,900	—
1871Mo M	21,000	BV	920	1,150	1,900	—
1872/1Mo M	11,000	BV	920	1,150	2,050	—
1872Mo M	Inc. above	BV	920	1,150	1,900	—
1873Mo M	5,600	BV	920	1,150	1,900	—
1874/2Mo M	—	BV	920	1,150	1,900	—
1874/2Mo B	—	BV	920	1,250	2,050	—
1875Mo B	—	BV	920	1,150	2,000	—
1876Mo B	—	BV	920	1,150	2,000	—
1876Mo M	—	—	—	—	—	—

Note: Reported, not confirmed

Date	Mintage	F	VF	XF	Unc	BU
1877Mo M	2,000	BV	1,150	1,400	2,500	—
1878Mo M	7,000	BV	920	1,150	2,000	—
1879Mo M	—	BV	920	1,150	2,200	—
1880Mo M	—	BV	920	1,150	2,200	—
1881/0Mo M	11,000	BV	920	1,150	1,900	—
1881Mo M	Inc. above	BV	920	1,150	1,900	—
1882/1Mo M	5,800	BV	920	1,150	1,900	—
1882Mo M	Inc. above	BV	920	1,150	1,900	—
1883/1Mo M	4,000	BV	920	1,150	1,900	—
1883Mo M	Inc. above	BV	920	1,150	1,900	—
1884/3Mo M	—	BV	920	1,150	2,000	—
1884Mo M	—	BV	920	1,150	2,000	—
1885Mo M	6,000	BV	920	1,150	2,200	—
1886Mo M	10,000	BV	920	1,150	1,900	—
1887Mo M	12,000	BV	1,150	1,900	3,150	—
1888Mo M	7,300	BV	920	1,150	1,800	—
1889Mo M	6,477	BV	1,150	2,050	4,700	—
1890Mo M	7,852	BV	920	1,150	1,950	—
1891/0Mo M	8,725	BV	920	1,150	1,950	—

KM# 414.7   20 PESOS
33.8400 g., 0.8750 Gold 0.9519 oz. AGW **Obv:** Facing eagle, snake in beak **Obv. Legend:** REPUBLICA MEXICANA **Rev:** Radiant cap above scales **Mint:** Oaxaca

Date	Mintage	F	VF	XF	Unc	BU
1870Oa E	1,131	1,000	2,050	3,150	6,300	—
1871Oa E	1,591	1,000	2,050	3,150	6,300	—
1872Oa E	255	1,000	1,750	3,750	8,800	—
1888Oa E	170	2,000	3,500	6,300	—	—

KM# 414.8   20 PESOS
33.8400 g., 0.8750 Gold 0.9519 oz. AGW **Obv:** Facing eagle, snake in beak **Rev:** Radiant cap above scales **Mint:** Zacatecas

Date	Mintage	F	VF	XF	Unc	BU
1871Zs H	1,000	3,500	6,500	8,800	11,500	—
1875Zs A	—	4,000	6,000	9,400	12,000	—
1878Zs S	441	4,000	6,000	9,400	12,000	—
1888Zs Z Rare	50	—	—	—	—	—
1889Zs Z	640	3,500	5,500	8,800	11,500	—

KM# 414.1   20 PESOS
33.8400 g., 0.8750 Gold 0.9519 oz. AGW **Obv:** Facing eagle, snake in beak **Rev:** Radiant cap above scales **Mint:** Chihuahua **Note:** Mint mark CH, Ca.

Date	Mintage	F	VF	XF	Unc	BU
1872CH M	995	BV	950	1,250	3,150	—
1873CH M	950	BV	950	1,250	3,150	—
1874CH M	1,116	BV	925	1,200	3,150	—
1875CH M	750	BV	950	1,250	3,150	—
1876CH M	600	BV	1,100	1,550	3,450	—
1877CH Rare	55	—	—	—	—	—
1882CH M	1,758	BV	925	1,200	3,150	—
1883CH M	161	950	1,350	1,900	3,750	—
1884CH M	496	BV	950	1,250	3,150	—
1885CH M	122	950	1,350	1,900	3,750	—
1887Ca M	550	BV	950	1,250	3,150	—
1888Ca M	351	BV	950	1,250	3,150	—
1889Ca M	464	BV	950	1,250	3,150	—
1890Ca M	1,209	BV	925	1,200	3,150	—
1891Ca M	2,004	BV	900	1,150	2,800	—
1893Ca M	418	BV	950	1,200	3,150	—
1895Ca M	133	950	1,350	1,900	3,750	—

ESTADOS UNIDOS

DECIMAL COINAGE

100 CENTAVOS = 1 PESO

KM# 415   CENTAVO
3.0000 g., Bronze, 20 mm. **Obv:** National arms **Rev:** Value below date within wreath **Mint:** Mexico City **Note:** Mint mark Mo.

Date	Mintage	F	VF	XF	Unc	BU
1905 Narrow date	6,040,000	4.00	6.50	14.00	90.00	—
1905 Wide date	—	4.00	6.50	14.00	90.00	—
1906 Narrow date	Est. 67,505,000	0.50	0.75	1.25	14.00	25.00

Note: 50,000,000 pcs. were struck at the Birmingham Mint

Date	Mintage	F	VF	XF	Unc	BU
1906 Wide date	Inc. above	0.75	1.50	2.50	22.00	—
1910 Narrow date	8,700,000	2.00	3.00	6.50	85.00	100
1910 Wide date	—	2.00	3.00	6.50	85.00	100
1911 Narrow date	16,450,000	0.60	1.00	2.75	22.50	—
1911 Wide date	Inc. above	0.75	1.00	4.00	35.00	—
1912	12,650,000	1.00	1.35	3.25	35.00	—
1913	12,850,000	0.75	1.25	3.00	35.00	—
1914 Narrow date	17,350,000	0.75	1.00	3.00	15.00	20.00
1914 Wide date	Inc. above	0.75	1.00	3.00	15.00	20.00
1915	2,277,000	11.00	25.00	67.50	250	—
1916	500,000	45.00	80.00	170	1,200	—
1920	1,433,000	22.00	50.00	115	400	—
1921	3,470,000	5.50	15.50	47.00	275	—
1922	1,880,000	9.00	17.00	50.00	250	—
1923	4,800,000	0.75	1.25	1.75	13.50	—
1924/3	2,000,000	65.00	170	275	525	—
1924	Inc. above	4.50	11.00	22.00	250	300
1925	1,550,000	4.50	10.00	25.00	220	—
1926	5,000,000	1.00	2.00	4.00	20.00	28.00
1927/6	6,000,000	30.00	45.00	70.00	175	—
1927	Inc. above	0.75	1.25	4.50	32.00	45.00
1928	5,000,000	0.75	1.00	3.25	16.50	25.00
1929	4,500,000	0.75	1.00	1.75	17.00	25.00
1930	7,000,000	0.75	1.00	2.50	20.00	—
1933	10,000,000	0.25	0.35	1.75	16.50	22.00
1934	7,500,000	0.25	0.95	3.25	40.00	—
1935	12,400,000	0.15	0.25	0.40	11.50	15.00
1936	20,100,000	0.15	0.20	0.30	9.00	—
1937	20,000,000	0.15	0.25	0.35	4.00	6.00
1938	10,000,000	0.10	0.15	0.30	2.00	3.00
1939	30,000,000	0.10	0.20	0.30	1.00	2.50
1940	10,000,000	0.20	0.30	0.60	5.50	8.50
1941	15,800,000	0.15	0.25	0.35	2.00	3.00
1942	30,400,000	0.15	0.20	0.30	1.25	2.00
1943	4,310,000	0.30	0.50	0.75	9.00	12.50
1944	5,645,000	0.15	0.25	0.50	6.00	8.50
1945	26,375,000	0.10	0.15	0.25	1.00	1.75
1946	42,135,000	—	0.15	0.20	0.60	1.50
1947	13,445,000	—	0.10	0.15	0.80	1.50
1948	20,040,000	0.10	0.15	0.30	1.10	2.25
1949	6,235,000	0.10	0.15	0.30	1.25	3.00

Note: Varieties exist

KM# 416   CENTAVO
1.5000 g., Bronze, 16 mm. **Obv:** National arms **Rev:** Value below date within wreath **Mint:** Mexico City **Note:** Zapata issue. Struck at Mexico City Mint, mint mark Mo. Reduced size. Weight varies 1.39-1.5g.

Date	Mintage	F	VF	XF	Unc	BU
1915	179,000	18.00	30.00	60.00	85.00	—

KM# 417   CENTAVO
2.0000 g., Brass, 16 mm. **Obv:** National arms, eagle left **Rev:** Oat sprigs **Mint:** Mexico City **Note:** Mint mark Mo.

Date	Mintage	F	VF	XF	Unc	BU
1950	12,815,000	—	0.15	0.35	1.65	2.25
1951	25,740,000	—	0.15	0.35	0.65	1.25
1952	24,610,000	—	0.10	0.25	0.40	0.85
1953	21,160,000	—	0.10	0.25	0.40	0.85
1954	25,675,000	—	0.10	0.15	0.85	1.50
1955	9,820,000	—	0.15	0.25	0.85	1.75
1956	11,285,000	—	0.15	0.25	0.80	1.75
1957	9,805,000	—	0.15	0.25	0.85	1.50
1958	12,155,000	—	0.10	0.25	0.45	0.75
1959	11,875,000	—	0.10	0.25	0.75	1.50
1960	10,360,000	—	0.10	0.15	0.40	0.65
1961	6,385,000	—	0.10	0.15	0.45	0.85
1962	4,850,000	—	0.10	0.15	0.55	0.90
1963	7,775,000	—	0.10	0.15	0.25	0.45
1964	4,280,000	—	0.10	0.15	0.20	0.30
1965	2,255,000	—	0.10	0.15	0.25	0.40
1966	1,760,000	—	0.10	0.25	0.60	1.00
1967	1,290,000	—	0.10	0.15	0.40	0.75
1968	1,000,000	—	0.10	0.20	0.85	1.45
1969	1,000,000	—	0.10	0.15	0.65	0.85

KM# 418   CENTAVO
1.5000 g., Brass, 13 mm. **Obv:** National arms, eagle left **Rev:** Oat sprigs **Mint:** Mexico City **Note:** Reduced size.

Date	Mintage	F	VF	XF	Unc	BU
1970	1,000,000	—	0.20	0.40	1.45	2.25
1972	1,000,000	—	0.20	0.45	2.50	4.00
1972/2	—	—	0.50	1.25	3.50	5.00
1973	1,000,000	—	1.65	2.75	9.00	17.50

KM# 419   2 CENTAVOS
6.0000 g., Bronze, 25 mm. **Obv:** National arms **Rev:** Value below date within wreath **Mint:** Mexico City **Note:** Mint mark Mo.

Date	Mintage	F	VF	XF	Unc	BU
1905	50,000	150	300	500	1,200	1,350
1906 Inverted 6	9,998,000	30.00	55.00	120	375	—
1906 Wide date	Inc. above	5.00	11.00	28.00	95.00	110
1906 Narrow date	Inc. above	6.50	14.00	30.00	95.00	—

Note: 5,000,000 pieces were struck at the Birmingham Mint

Date	Mintage	F	VF	XF	Unc	BU
1920	1,325,000	6.50	17.50	75.00	350	—
1921	4,275,000	2.50	4.75	15.00	100	—
1922	—	225	550	1,750	5,500	—
1924	750,000	8.50	27.50	75.00	450	—
1925	3,650,000	2.50	3.50	7.50	35.00	40.00
1926	4,750,000	1.00	2.25	5.50	40.00	—
1927	7,250,000	0.60	1.00	4.50	22.00	35.00
1928	3,250,000	0.75	1.50	4.75	25.00	35.00
1929	250,000	85.00	225	550	1,200	—
1935	1,250,000	4.25	9.25	65.00	225	275
1939	5,000,000	0.60	0.90	2.25	20.00	30.00
1941	3,550,000	0.45	0.60	1.25	18.00	28.00

KM# 420 2 CENTAVOS
3.0000 g., Bronze, 20 mm. **Obv:** National arms **Rev:** Value below date within wreath **Mint:** Mexico City **Note:** Zapata issue. Mint mark Mo. Reduced size. Weight varies 3-3.03g.

Date	Mintage	F	VF	XF	Unc	BU
1915	487,000	7.50	9.00	17.50	75.00	—

KM# 421 5 CENTAVOS
5.0000 g., Nickel, 20 mm. **Obv:** National arms **Rev:** Value and date within beaded circle **Mint:** Mexico City **Note:** Mint mark Mo. Varieties exist.

Date	Mintage	F	VF	XF	Unc	BU
1905	1,420,000	7.00	10.00	28.00	325	375
1906/5	10,615,000	13.00	30.00	70.00	375	—
1906	Inc. above	0.75	1.35	3.25	55.00	75.00
1907	4,000,000	1.25	4.00	35.00	350	450
1909	2,052,000	3.25	10.00	50.00	360	—
1910	6,181,000	1.30	3.50	9.00	85.00	125
1911 Narrow date	4,487,000	1.00	3.00	71.00	95.00	135
1911 Wide date	Inc. above	2.50	5.00	9.00	110	170
1912 Small mint mark	420,000	90.00	100	230	725	—
1912 Large mint mark	Inc. above	70.00	95.00	200	575	—
1913	2,035,000	1.75	4.25	30.00	200	300

Note: Wide and narrow dates exist for 1913

Date	Mintage	F	VF	XF	Unc	BU
1914	2,000,000	1.00	2.00	5.00	75.00	110

Note: 5,000,000 pieces appear to have been struck at the Birmingham Mint in 1914 and all of 1909-1911. The Mexican Mint report does not mention receiving the 1914 dated coins

KM# 422 5 CENTAVOS
9.0000 g., Bronze, 28 mm. **Obv:** National arms **Rev:** Value below date within wreath **Mint:** Mexico City

Date	Mintage	F	VF	XF	Unc	BU
1914Mo	2,500,000	10.00	23.00	65.00	300	—
1915Mo	11,424,000	3.00	5.00	35.00	165	265
1916Mo	2,860,000	15.00	35.00	175	650	—
1917Mo	800,000	75.00	225	400	900	—
1918Mo	1,332,000	35.00	90.00	250	675	—

Date	Mintage	F	VF	XF	Unc	BU
1919Mo	400,000	115	225	360	950	—
1920Mo	5,920,000	3.00	8.00	45.00	265	350
1921Mo	2,080,000	10.00	24.00	75.00	275	—
1924Mo	780,000	40.00	95.00	275	700	—
1925Mo	4,040,000	5.50	11.00	47.50	225	—
1926Mo	3,160,000	5.50	11.00	48.00	325	—
1927Mo	3,600,000	4.00	7.00	35.00	250	350
1928Mo Large date	1,740,000	11.00	18.00	65.00	250	325
1928Mo Small date	Inc. above	30.00	45.00	100	385	—
1929Mo	2,400,000	5.50	12.00	50.00	200	—
1930Mo	2,600,000	5.00	8.00	27.50	225	—

Note: Large oval O in date

Date	Mintage	F	VF	XF	Unc	BU
1930Mo	Inc. above	65.00	125	250	565	—

Note: Small square O in date

Date	Mintage	F	VF	XF	Unc	BU
1931Mo	—	475	750	1,450	4,000	—
1933Mo	8,000,000	1.50	2.25	3.50	27.50	45.00
1934Mo	10,000,000	1.25	1.75	2.75	25.00	50.00
1935Mo	21,980,000	0.75	1.20	2.50	22.50	40.00

KM# 423 5 CENTAVOS
4.0000 g., Copper-Nickel, 20.5 mm. **Obv:** National arms, eagle left **Rev:** Value and date within circle **Mint:** Mexico City

Date	Mintage	F	VF	XF	Unc	BU
1936M	46,700,000	—	0.65	1.25	7.50	8.50
1937M	49,060,000	—	0.50	1.00	7.00	8.00
1938M	3,340,000	—	4.00	10.00	80.00	200
1940M	22,800,000	—	0.75	1.25	8.00	10.00
1942M	7,100,000	—	1.50	3.00	35.00	50.00

KM# 424 5 CENTAVOS
6.5000 g., Bronze, 25.5 mm. **Obv:** National arms, eagle left **Rev:** Head left **Mint:** Mexico City

Date	Mintage	F	VF	XF	Unc	BU
1942Mo	900,000	—	25.00	75.00	375	550
1943Mo	54,660,000	—	0.50	0.75	2.50	3.50
1944Mo	53,463,000	—	0.25	0.35	0.75	1.00
1945Mo	44,262,000	—	0.25	0.35	0.75	1.25
1946Mo	49,054,000	—	0.50	1.00	2.00	3.00
1951Mo	50,758,000	—	0.75	0.90	3.00	5.00
1952Mo	17,674,000	—	1.50	2.50	9.50	11.50
1953Mo	31,568,000	—	1.25	2.00	6.00	9.00
1954Mo	58,680,000	—	0.40	1.00	2.75	4.00
1955Mo	31,114,000	—	2.00	3.00	11.00	14.00

KM# 425 5 CENTAVOS
4.0000 g., Copper-Nickel, 20.5 mm. **Obv:** National arms, eagle left **Rev:** Bust right flanked by date and value **Mint:** Mexico City

Date	Mintage	F	VF	XF	Unc	BU
1950Mo	5,700,000	—	0.75	1.50	6.00	7.00

Note: 5,600,000 pieces struck at Connecticut melted

KM# 426 5 CENTAVOS
4.0000 g., Brass, 20.4 mm. **Obv:** National arms, eagle left **Rev:** Bust right **Mint:** Mexico City

Date	Mintage	F	VF	XF	Unc	BU
1954Mo Dot	—	—	10.00	50.00	300	375
1954Mo Without dot	—	—	15.00	35.00	275	325
1955Mo	12,136,000	—	0.75	1.50	9.00	12.50
1956Mo	60,216,000	—	0.20	0.30	0.75	1.25
1957Mo	55,288,000	—	0.15	0.20	0.90	1.50
1958Mo	104,624,000	—	0.15	0.20	0.60	1.00
1959Mo	106,000,000	—	0.15	0.25	0.75	1.25
1960Mo	99,144,000	—	0.10	0.15	0.50	0.75
1961Mo	61,136,000	—	0.10	0.15	0.50	0.75
1962Mo	47,232,000	—	0.10	0.15	0.25	0.35
1963Mo	156,680,000	—	—	0.15	0.25	0.40
1964Mo	71,168,000	—	—	0.15	0.20	0.40
1965Mo	155,720,000	—	—	0.15	0.25	0.35
1966Mo	124,944,000	—	—	0.15	0.40	0.65
1967Mo	118,816,000	—	—	0.15	0.25	0.40
1968Mo	189,588,000	—	—	0.15	0.50	0.75
1969Mo	210,492,000	—	—	0.15	0.55	0.80

KM# 426a 5 CENTAVOS
Copper-Nickel, 20.5 mm. **Obv:** National arms, eagle left **Rev:** Bust right **Mint:** Mexico City

Date	Mintage	F	VF	XF	Unc	BU
1960Mo	—	—	250	300	375	—
1962Mo	19	—	250	300	375	—
1965Mo	—	—	250	300	375	—

KM# 427 5 CENTAVOS
2.7500 g., Brass, 18 mm. **Obv:** National arms, eagle left **Rev:** Bust right **Note:** Due to some minor alloy variations this type is often encountered with a bronze-color toning. Reduced size.

Date	Mintage	F	VF	XF	Unc	BU
1970	163,368,000	—	0.10	0.15	0.35	0.45
1971	198,844,000	—	0.10	0.15	0.25	0.30
1972	225,000,000	—	0.10	0.15	0.25	0.30
1973 Flat top 3	595,070,000	—	0.10	0.15	0.25	0.40
1973 Round top 3	Inc. above	—	0.10	0.15	0.20	0.30
1974	401,584,000	—	0.10	0.15	0.30	0.40
1975	342,308,000	—	0.10	0.15	0.25	0.35
1976	367,524,000	—	0.10	0.15	0.40	0.60

KM# 428 10 CENTAVOS
2.5000 g., 0.8000 Silver 0.0643 oz. ASW, 18 mm. **Obv:** National arms **Rev:** Value and date within 3/4 wreath with Liberty cap above **Mint:** Mexico City **Note:** Mint mark Mo.

Date	Mintage	F	VF	XF	Unc	BU
1905	3,920,000	—	6.00	8.00	40.00	50.00
1906	8,410,000	—	5.50	7.50	27.00	40.00
1907/6	5,950,000	—	50.00	135	325	375
1907	Inc. above	—	5.50	6.25	35.00	50.00
1909	2,620,000	—	8.50	13.00	80.00	110
1910/00	3,450,000	—	10.00	40.00	75.00	85.00
1910	Inc. above	—	7.00	15.00	25.00	40.00

Date	Mintage	F	VF	XF	Unc	BU
1911 Narrow date	2,550,000	—	11.00	17.00	88.00	125
1911 Wide date	Inc. above	—	7.50	10.00	45.00	65.00
1912	1,350,000	—	10.00	18.00	130	175
1912 Low 2	Inc. above	—	10.00	18.00	115	155
1913/2	1,990,000	—	10.00	25.00	40.00	70.00
1913	Inc. above	—	7.00	10.00	33.00	45.00
1914	3,110,000	—	5.50	7.00	15.00	25.00

Note: Wide and narrow dates exist for 1914

KM# 429 10 CENTAVOS
1.8125 g., 0.8000 Silver 0.0466 oz. ASW, 15 mm. **Obv:** National arms **Rev:** Value and date within 3/4 wreath with Liberty cap above **Mint:** Mexico City **Note:** Mint mark Mo. Reduced size.

Date	Mintage	F	VF	XF	Unc	BU
1919	8,360,000	—	10.00	15.00	95.00	125

KM# 430 10 CENTAVOS
12.0000 g., Bronze, 30.5 mm. **Obv:** National arms **Rev:** Value below date within wreath **Mint:** Mexico City **Note:** Mint mark Mo.

Date	Mintage	F	VF	XF	Unc	BU
1919	1,232,000	—	25.00	85.00	475	550
1920	6,612,000	—	15.00	50.00	400	475
1921	2,255,000	—	35.00	95.00	650	800
1935	5,970,000	—	14.00	35.00	125	200

KM# 431 10 CENTAVOS
1.6600 g., 0.7200 Silver 0.0384 oz. ASW, 15 mm. **Obv:** National arms **Rev:** Value and date within wreath with Liberty cap above **Mint:** Mexico City **Note:** Mint mark Mo.

Date	Mintage	F	VF	XF	Unc	BU
1925/15	5,350,000	—	30.00	75.00	125	175
1925/3	Inc. above	—	20.00	40.00	125	175
1925	Inc. above	—	2.00	5.00	40.00	50.00
1926/16	2,650,000	—	30.00	75.00	125	175
1926	Inc. above	—	3.50	7.50	65.00	95.00
1927	2,810,000	—	2.25	3.00	17.50	25.00
1928	5,270,000	—	2.00	2.75	13.50	20.00
1930	2,000,000	—	3.75	5.00	18.75	28.00
1933	5,000,000	—	1.50	3.00	10.00	17.00
1934	8,000,000	—	1.75	2.50	8.00	16.00
1935	3,500,000	—	2.75	5.00	11.00	18.00

KM# 432 10 CENTAVOS
5.5000 g., Copper-Nickel, 23.5 mm. **Obv:** National arms, eagle left **Rev:** Value and date within circle **Mint:** Mexico City **Note:** Mint mark Mo.

Date	Mintage	F	VF	XF	Unc	BU
1936	33,030,000	—	0.75	2.50	10.00	12.00
1937	3,000,000	—	10.00	50.00	215	250
1938	3,650,000	1.25	2.00	7.00	70.00	85.00
1939	6,920,000	—	1.00	3.50	27.50	35.00
1940	12,300,000	—	0.40	1.25	5.00	7.00
1942	14,380,000	—	0.60	1.50	7.00	10.00
1945	9,558,000	—	0.40	0.70	3.50	5.00
1946	46,230,000	—	0.40	0.60	2.50	4.00

KM# 433 10 CENTAVOS
5.5000 g., Bronze, 23.5 mm. **Obv:** National arms, eagle left **Rev:** Bust left **Mint:** Mexico City **Note:** Mint mark Mo.

Date	Mintage	F	VF	XF	Unc	BU
1955	1,818,000	—	0.75	3.25	23.00	35.00
1956	5,255,000	—	0.75	3.25	23.00	32.00
1957	11,925,000	—	0.20	0.40	5.50	9.00
1959	26,140,000	—	0.30	0.45	0.75	1.25
1966	5,873,000	—	0.15	0.25	0.60	1.75
1967	32,318,000	—	0.10	0.15	0.30	0.40

Sharp stem

KM# 434.1 10 CENTAVOS
1.5000 g., Copper-Nickel **Obv:** National arms, eagle left **Rev:** Upright ear of corn **Edge:** Reeded **Mint:** Mexico City **Note:** Variety I- Sharp stem and wide date

Date	Mintage	F	VF	XF	Unc	BU
1974Mo	6,000,000	—	—	0.35	0.75	1.00
1975Mo	5,550,000	—	0.10	0.35	0.75	1.00
1976Mo	7,680,000	—	0.10	0.20	0.30	0.40
1977Mo	144,650,000	—	1.25	2.25	3.50	5.50
1978Mo	271,870,000	—	—	1.00	1.50	2.25
1979Mo	375,660,000	—	—	0.50	1.00	1.75
1980/79Mo	21,290,000	—	2.45	3.75	7.00	9.00
1980Mo	Inc. above	—	1.50	2.00	4.50	6.50

Blunt stem

KM# 434.2 10 CENTAVOS
1.5000 g., Copper-Nickel **Obv:** National arms, eagle left **Rev:** Upright ear of corn **Edge:** Reeded **Mint:** Mexico City **Note:** Variety II- Blunt stem and narrow date

Date	Mintage	F	VF	XF	Unc	BU
1974Mo	Inc. above	—	—	0.10	0.20	0.30
1977Mo	Inc. above	—	0.15	0.50	1.25	2.25
1978Mo	Inc. above	—	—	0.10	0.30	0.40
1979Mo	Inc. above	—	0.15	0.35	0.85	1.50
1980Mo	Inc. above	—	—	0.10	0.20	0.30

KM# 434.4 10 CENTAVOS
1.5000 g., Copper-Nickel **Obv:** National arms, eagle left **Rev:** Upright ear of corn **Edge:** Reeded **Mint:** Mexico City **Note:** Variety IV- Sharp stem and narrow date

Date	Mintage	F	VF	XF	Unc	BU
1974Mo	—	—	—	—	1.50	2.50
1979Mo	—	—	—	—	1.50	2.50

KM# 434.3 10 CENTAVOS
1.5000 g., Copper-Nickel **Obv:** National arms, eagle left **Rev:** Upright ear of corn **Edge:** Reeded **Mint:** Mexico City **Note:** Variety III- Blunt stem and wide date

Date	Mintage	F	VF	XF	Unc	BU
1980/79Mo	—	—	—	—	7.00	9.00

KM# 435 20 CENTAVOS
5.0000 g., 0.8000 Silver 0.1286 oz. ASW, 22 mm. **Obv:** National arms **Rev:** Value and date within wreath with Liberty cap above **Mint:** Mexico City **Note:** Mint mark Mo.

Date	Mintage	F	VF	XF	Unc	BU
1905	2,565,000	—	12.00	25.00	175	195
1906	6,860,000	—	9.00	16.50	60.00	85.00
1907 Straight 7	4,000,000	—	11.50	22.00	75.00	125
1907 Curved 7	5,435,000	—	7.50	15.00	70.00	120
1908	350,000	50.00	95.00	250	1,800	—
1910	1,135,000	—	11.00	16.00	90.00	110
1911	1,150,000	12.00	15.00	40.00	145	175
1912	625,000	20.00	40.00	70.00	350	400
1913	1,000,000	—	14.50	30.00	100	125
1914	1,500,000	—	10.00	22.50	65.00	80.00

KM# 436 20 CENTAVOS
3.6250 g., 0.8000 Silver 0.0932 oz. ASW, 19 mm. **Obv:** National arms **Rev:** Value and date within wreath with Liberty cap above **Mint:** Mexico City **Note:** Mint mark Mo. Reduced size.

Date	Mintage	F	VF	XF	Unc	BU
1919	4,155,000	—	30.00	65.00	200	275

KM# 437 20 CENTAVOS
15.0000 g., Bronze, 32.5 mm. **Obv:** National arms **Rev:** Value below date within wreath **Mint:** Mexico City **Note:** Mint mark Mo.

Date	Mintage	F	VF	XF	Unc	BU
1920	4,835,000	—	45.00	155	650	775
1935	20,000,000	—	6.00	10.00	95.00	145

Date	Mintage	F	VF	XF	Unc	BU
1960	39,756,000	—	0.15	0.25	0.75	1.00
1963	14,869,000	—	0.25	0.35	0.80	1.00
1964	28,654,000	—	0.25	0.40	0.90	1.25
1965	74,162,000	—	0.20	0.35	0.80	1.00
1966	43,745,000	—	0.15	0.25	0.75	1.00
1967	46,487,000	—	0.20	0.50	1.00	1.25
1968	15,477,000	—	0.30	0.55	1.35	1.65
1969	63,647,000	—	0.20	0.35	0.80	1.00
1970	76,287,000	—	0.15	0.20	0.90	1.30
1971	49,892,000	—	0.30	0.50	1.25	2.00

KM# 438   20 CENTAVOS
3.3333 g., 0.7200 Silver 0.0772 oz. ASW, 19 mm. **Obv:** National arms **Rev:** Value and date within wreath with Liberty cap above **Mint:** Mexico City **Note:** Mint mark Mo.

Date	Mintage	F	VF	XF	Unc	BU
1920	3,710,000	—	9.00	20.00	175	220
1921	6,160,000	—	7.00	14.00	100	150
1925	1,450,000	—	12.00	20.00	155	165
1926/5	1,465,000	—	20.00	70.00	350	375
1926	Inc. above	—	5.00	11.00	90.00	110
1927	1,405,000	—	5.00	12.00	95.00	115
1928	3,630,000	—	6.00	8.00	19.00	27.50
1930	1,000,000	—	8.00	12.00	30.00	42.00
1933	2,500,000	—	3.00	5.00	12.00	16.00
1934	2,500,000	—	3.00	6.00	13.00	20.00
1935	2,460,000	—	3.00	6.00	13.00	20.00
1937	10,000,000	—	2.75	3.00	6.00	9.00
1939	8,800,000	—	2.75	3.00	6.00	9.00
1940	3,000,000	—	2.75	3.00	5.00	9.00
1941	5,740,000	—	2.25	3.00	5.00	8.00
1942	12,460,000	—	2.25	3.00	5.00	8.00
1943	3,955,000	—	3.00	4.00	5.00	9.00

KM# 441   20 CENTAVOS
10.0000 g., Bronze, 28.5 mm. **Obv:** National arms, eagle left **Rev:** Liberty cap divides value above Pyramid of the Sun at Teotihuacán, volcanos Ixtaccihuatl and Popocatepet in background **Edge:** Plain **Mint:** Mexico City

Date	Mintage	F	VF	XF	Unc	BU
1971 Inc. KM#440	Inc. above	—	0.20	0.35	1.85	2.50
1973	78,398,000	—	0.25	0.35	0.95	1.65
1974	34,200,000	—	0.20	0.35	1.25	2.00

KM# 439   20 CENTAVOS
10.0000 g., Bronze, 28.5 mm. **Obv:** National arms, eagle left **Rev:** Liberty cap divides value above Pyramid of the Sun at Teotihuacán, volcanos Ixtaccihuatl and Popocatepet in background **Edge:** Plain **Mint:** Mexico City **Note:** Mint mark Mo.

Date	Mintage	F	VF	XF	Unc	BU
1943	46,350,000	—	1.25	3.00	20.00	28.00
1944	83,650,000	—	0.40	0.65	8.00	12.00
1945	26,801,000	—	1.25	3.50	9.50	15.00
1946	25,695,000	—	1.10	2.25	6.00	9.00
1951	11,385,000	—	3.00	8.75	100	120
1952	6,560,000	—	3.00	5.00	25.00	35.00
1953	26,948,000	—	0.35	0.80	9.00	15.00
1954	40,108,000	—	0.35	0.80	9.00	15.00
1955	16,950,000	—	2.75	7.00	60.00	75.00

KM# 442   20 CENTAVOS
3.0000 g., Copper-Nickel, 20 mm. **Obv:** National arms, eagle left **Rev:** Bust 3/4 facing flanked by value and date **Edge:** Reeded **Mint:** Mexico City

Date	Mintage	F	VF	XF	Unc	BU
1974	112,000,000	—	0.10	0.15	0.25	0.30
1975	611,000,000	—	0.10	0.15	0.30	0.35
1976	394,000,000	—	0.10	0.15	0.35	0.45
1977	394,350,000	—	0.10	0.15	0.40	0.45
1978	527,950,000	—	0.10	0.15	0.25	0.30
1979	524,615,000	—	0.10	0.15	0.25	0.30
1979	—	—	1.25	2.00	4.00	8.00

Note: Doubled die obv. small letters

1979	—	—	1.25	2.00	4.00	8.00

Note: Doubled die obv. large letters

1980	326,500,000	—	0.15	0.20	0.30	0.40
1981 Open 8	106,205,000	—	0.30	0.50	1.00	2.00
1981 Closed 8, high date	248,500,000	—	0.30	0.50	1.00	2.00
1981 Closed 8, low date	—	—	1.00	1.50	3.50	4.25
1981/1982	—	—	40.00	75.00	175	195

Note: The 1981/1982 overdate is often mistaken as 1982/1981

1982	286,855,000	—	0.40	0.60	0.90	1.10
1983 Round top 3	100,930,000	—	0.25	0.40	1.75	2.25
1983 Flat top 3	Inc. above	—	0.25	0.50	1.25	1.75
1983 Proof	998	Value: 45.00				

KM# 440   20 CENTAVOS
10.0000 g., Bronze, 28.5 mm. **Obv:** National arms, eagle left **Rev:** Liberty cap divides value above Pyramid of the Sun at Teotihuacán, volcanos Ixtaccihuatl and Popocatepet in background **Edge:** Plain **Mint:** Mexico City **Note:** Mint mark Mo.

Date	Mintage	F	VF	XF	Unc	BU
1955 Inc. KM#439	Inc. above	—	0.75	1.75	17.00	22.00
1956	22,431,000	—	0.30	0.35	3.00	5.00
1957	13,455,000	—	0.45	1.25	9.00	13.00
1959	6,017,000	—	4.50	9.00	75.00	100

KM# 491   20 CENTAVOS
3.0000 g., Bronze, 20 mm. **Subject:** Olmec Culture **Obv:** National arms, eagle left **Rev:** Mask 3/4 right with value below **Mint:** Mexico City

Date	Mintage	F	VF	XF	Unc	BU
1983	260,000,000	—	0.20	0.25	1.25	1.75
1983 Proof	53	Value: 185				
1984	180,320,000	—	0.20	0.35	1.85	2.25

KM# 443 25 CENTAVOS
3.3330 g., 0.3000 Silver 0.0321 oz. ASW, 21.5 mm. **Obv:** National arms, eagle left **Rev:** Scale below Liberty cap **Edge:** Reeded **Mint:** Mexico City **Note:** Mint mark Mo.

Date	Mintage	F	VF	XF	Unc	BU
1950	77,060,000	—	1.00	1.25	2.00	2.50
1951	41,172,000	—	1.00	1.25	2.00	2.50
1952	29,264,000	—	1.25	1.50	2.25	2.75
1953	38,144,000	—	1.25	1.25	2.00	2.50

KM# 444 25 CENTAVOS
5.5000 g., Copper-Nickel, 23 mm. **Obv:** National arms, eagle left **Rev:** Bust 3/4 facing **Mint:** Mexico City

Date	Mintage	F	VF	XF	Unc	BU
1964	20,686,000	—	—	0.15	0.20	0.30
1966 Closed beak	180,000	—	0.65	1.00	2.75	4.00
1966 Open beak	Inc. above	—	1.75	3.50	12.00	15.00

KM# 445 50 CENTAVOS
12.5000 g., 0.8000 Silver 0.3215 oz. ASW, 30 mm. **Obv:** National arms **Rev:** Value and date within 3/4 wreath with Liberty cap above **Mint:** Mexico City **Note:** Mint mark Mo.

Date	Mintage	F	VF	XF	Unc	BU
1905	2,446,000	12.50	20.00	35.00	175	250
1906 Open 9	16,966,000	—	12.00	15.00	55.00	85.00
1906 Closed 9	Inc. above	—	10.00	14.00	48.00	70.00
1907 Straight 7	18,920,000	—	10.00	14.00	36.00	42.00
1907 Curved 7	14,841,000	—	11.00	14.00	36.00	45.50
1908	488,000	—	80.00	190	550	675
1912	3,736,000	—	22.50	20.00	55.00	85.00
1913/07	10,510,000	—	40.00	90.00	250	300
1913/2	Inc. above	—	20.00	27.50	75.00	100
1913	Inc. above	—	11.00	13.00	33.00	42.00
1914	7,710,000	—	14.00	20.00	42.00	65.00
1916 Narrow date	480,000	—	60.00	85.00	250	350
1916 Wide date	Inc. above	—	60.00	85.00	250	350
1917	37,112,000	—	12.00	14.00	27.50	33.00
1918	1,320,000	—	70.00	135	300	400

KM# 446 50 CENTAVOS
9.0625 g., 0.8000 Silver 0.2331 oz. ASW, 27 mm. **Obv:** National arms **Rev:** Value and date within 3/4 wreath with Liberty cap above **Mint:** Mexico City **Note:** Mint mark Mo. Reduced size.

Date	Mintage	F	VF	XF	Unc	BU
1918/7	2,760,000	—	525	700	1,450	—
1918	Inc. above	—	20.00	70.00	350	450
1919	29,670,000	—	12.00	25.00	150	180

KM# 447 50 CENTAVOS
8.3333 g., 0.7200 Silver 0.1929 oz. ASW, 27 mm. **Obv:** National arms **Rev:** Value and date within 3/4 wreath with Liberty cap above **Edge Lettering:** INDEPENDENCIA Y LIBERTAD **Mint:** Mexico City **Note:** Mint mark Mo.

Date	Mintage	F	VF	XF	Unc	BU
1919	10,200,000	—	12.00	22.00	100	130
1920	27,166,000	—	9.00	17.00	75.00	90.00
1921	21,864,000	—	9.00	17.00	95.00	120
1925	3,280,000	—	17.50	35.00	145	185
1937	20,000,000	—	7.00	9.00	13.00	18.00
1938	100,000	—	50.00	95.00	245	350
1939	10,440,000	—	7.00	9.00	16.00	25.00
1942	800,000	—	7.00	10.00	18.00	22.00
1943	41,512,000	—	6.00	9.00	12.00	15.00
1944	55,806,000	—	6.00	9.00	12.00	15.00
1945	56,766,000	—	6.00	9.00	12.00	15.00

KM# 448 50 CENTAVOS
7.9730 g., 0.4200 Silver 0.1077 oz. ASW, 27 mm. **Obv:** National arms **Rev:** Value and date within 3/4 wreath with Liberty cap above **Mint:** Mexico City **Note:** Mint mark Mo.

Date	Mintage	F	VF	XF	Unc	BU
1935	70,800,000	—	4.00	5.00	9.00	12.00

KM# 449 50 CENTAVOS
6.6600 g., 0.3000 Silver 0.0642 oz. ASW, 26 mm. **Obv:** National arms, eagle left **Rev:** Head with head covering right **Mint:** Mexico City **Note:** Mint mark Mo.

Date	Mintage	F	VF	XF	Unc	BU
1950	13,570,000	—	2.25	2.75	5.00	8.00
1951	3,650,000	—	3.00	4.00	6.00	9.00

KM# 450 50 CENTAVOS
14.0000 g., Bronze, 33 mm. **Obv:** National arms, eagle left **Rev:** Head with headdress left **Mint:** Mexico City **Note:** Mint mark Mo.

Date	Mintage	F	VF	XF	Unc	BU
1955	3,502,000	—	1.50	3.00	80.00	40.00
1956	34,643,000	—	0.75	1.50	7.00	6.00
1957	9,675,000	—	1.00	2.00	6.50	8.00
1959	4,540,000	—	0.50	0.75	2.00	3.50

KM# 451   50 CENTAVOS
6.5000 g., Copper-Nickel, 25 mm. **Obv:** National arms, eagle left **Rev:** Head with headdress left **Edge:** Reeded **Mint:** Mexico City

Date	Mintage	F	VF	XF	Unc	BU
1964	43,806,000	—	0.15	0.20	0.40	0.60
1965	14,326,000	—	0.20	0.25	0.45	0.65
1966	1,726,000	—	0.20	0.40	1.50	2.00
1967	55,144,000	—	0.20	0.30	0.75	1.25
1968	80,438,000	—	0.15	0.30	0.65	1.00
1969	87,640,000	—	0.20	0.35	0.80	1.25

KM# 452   50 CENTAVOS
6.5000 g., Copper-Nickel, 25 mm. **Obv:** National arms, eagle left **Rev:** Head with headdress left **Mint:** Mexico City **Note:** Coins dated 1975 and 1976 exist with and without dots in centers of three circles on plumage on reverse. Edge varieties exist.

Date	Mintage	F	VF	XF	Unc	BU
1970	76,236,000	—	0.15	0.20	0.80	1.35
1971	125,288,000	—	0.15	0.20	0.90	1.45
1972	16,000,000	—	1.25	2.00	3.50	5.50
1975 Dots	177,958,000	—	0.65	1.75	3.50	6.00
1975 No dots	Inc. above	—	0.15	0.20	0.75	1.25
1976 Dots	37,480,000	—	0.75	1.50	5.00	7.00
1976 No dots	Inc. above	—	0.15	0.20	0.50	0.90
1977	12,410,000	—	6.50	10.00	32.50	45.00
1978	85,400,000	—	0.15	0.25	0.50	1.20
1979 Round 2nd 9 in date	229,000,000	—	0.15	0.25	0.50	1.00
1979 Square 9's in date	Inc. above	—	0.20	0.40	1.60	2.25
1980 Narrow date, square 9	89,978,000	—	0.45	0.75	1.75	2.50
1980 Wide date, round 9	178,188,000	—	0.20	0.25	1.00	2.25
1981 Rectangular 9, narrow date	142,212,000	—	0.50	0.75	1.75	2.50
1981 Round 9, wide date	Inc. above	—	0.30	0.50	1.25	1.75
1982	45,474,000	—	0.20	0.40	1.95	1.75
1983	90,318,000	—	0.50	0.75	1.75	2.50
1983 Proof	998	Value: 45.00				

KM# 492   50 CENTAVOS
4.4000 g., Stainless Steel, 22 mm. **Subject:** Palenque

Culture **Obv:** National arms, eagle left **Rev:** Head with headdress 3/4 left **Mint:** Mexico City

Date	Mintage	F	VF	XF	Unc	BU
1983	99,540,000	—	—	0.30	1.50	2.50
1983 Proof	53	Value: 195				

KM# 453   PESO
27.0700 g., 0.9030 Silver 0.7859 oz. ASW, 39 mm. **Subject:** Caballito **Obv:** National arms **Rev:** Horse and rider facing left among sun rays **Mint:** Mexico City **Designer:** Charles Pillet **Note:** Mint mark Mo.

Date	Mintage	F	VF	XF	Unc	BU
1910	3,814,000	—	45.00	50.00	200	275
1911	1,227,000	—	45.00	75.00	200	300

Note: Long lower left ray on reverse

1911	Inc. above	—	145	250	750	950

Note: Short lower left ray on reverse

1912	322,000	—	100	210	365	500
1913/2	2,880,000	—	45.00	75.00	300	450
1913	Inc. above	—	45.00	70.00	200	300

Note: 1913 coins exist with even and unevenly spaced date

1914	120,000	—	700	1,200	4,000	—

KM# 454   PESO
18.1300 g., 0.8000 Silver 0.4663 oz. ASW, 34 mm. **Obv:** National arms **Rev:** Value and date within 3/4 wreath with Liberty cap above **Mint:** Mexico City **Note:** Mint mark Mo.

Date	Mintage	F	VF	XF	Unc	BU
1918/7	—	250	350	—	—	—
1918	3,050,000	—	45.00	150	1,350	2,500
1919	6,151,000	—	30.00	125	950	1,750

KM# 455   PESO
16.6600 g., 0.7200 Silver 0.3856 oz. ASW, 34 mm. **Obv:** National arms **Rev:** Value and date within 3/4 wreath with Liberty cap above **Edge Lettering:** INDEPENDENCIA Y LIBERTAD **Mint:** Mexico City **Note:** Mint mark Mo.

Date	Mintage	F	VF	XF	Unc	BU
1920/10	8,830,000	—	50.00	90.00	325	—
1920	Inc. above	—	14.00	35.00	195	350
1921	5,480,000	—	14.00	35.00	195	275
1922	33,620,000	—	BV	12.00	20.00	35.00
1923	35,280,000	—	BV	12.00	20.00	35.00
1924	33,060,000	—	BV	12.00	20.00	35.00
1925	9,160,000	—	12.00	14.00	60.00	85.00
1926	28,840,000	—	BV	12.00	25.00	40.00
1927	5,060,000	—	13.00	16.00	70.00	90.00
1932 Open 9	50,770,000	—	—	BV	12.00	16.00
1932 Closed 9	Inc. above	—	—	BV	12.00	16.00
1933/2	43,920,000	—	20.00	35.00	100	—
1933	Inc. above	—	—	14.00	12.00	16.00
1934	22,070,000	—	—	BV	14.00	22.00
1935	8,050,000	—	BV	12.00	15.50	24.00
1938	30,000,000	—	—	BV	12.00	14.00
1940	20,000,000	—	—	BV	12.00	14.00
1943	47,662,000	—	—	BV	12.00	14.00
1944	39,522,000	—	—	BV	12.00	14.00
1945	37,300,000	—	—	BV	12.00	14.00

KM# 456   PESO
14.0000 g., 0.5000 Silver 0.2250 oz. ASW, 32 mm. **Obv:** National arms, eagle left **Rev:** Head with headcovering right **Edge:** Reeded **Mint:** Mexico City **Note:** Mint mark Mo.

Date	Mintage	F	VF	XF	Unc	BU
1947	61,460,000	—	—	BV	7.00	10.00
1948	22,915,000	—	—	BV	8.00	10.00
1949	4,000,000	—	—	1,200	1,600	2,500

Note: Not released for circulation
1949 Proof   — Value: 4,000

KM# 457   PESO
13.3300 g., 0.3000 Silver 0.1286 oz. ASW, 32 mm. **Obv:** National arms, eagle left **Rev:** Armored bust 3/4 left **Mint:** Mexico City **Note:** Mint mark Mo.

Date	Mintage	F	VF	XF	Unc	BU
1950	3,287,000	—	4.00	6.00	10.00	15.00

KM# 458   PESO
16.0000 g., 0.1000 Silver 0.0514 oz. ASW, 34.5 mm. **Subject:** 100th Anniversary of Constitution **Obv:** National arms, eagle left within wreath **Obv. Designer:** Manuel L. Negrete **Rev:** Head left **Edge Lettering:** INDEPENDENCIA Y LIBERTAD **Mint:** Mexico City **Note:** Mint mark Mo.

Date	Mintage	F	VF	XF	Unc	BU
1957	500,000	—	4.00	6.00	12.50	16.50

KM# 459   PESO
16.0000 g., 0.1000 Silver 0.0514 oz. ASW, 34.5 mm. **Obv:** National arms, eagle left within wreath **Rev:** Armored bust right within wreath **Edge Lettering:** INDEPENDENCIA Y LIBERTAD **Mint:** Mexico City **Note:** Mint mark Mo.

Date	Mintage	F	VF	XF	Unc	BU
1957	28,273,000	—	BV	1.75	3.00	10.00
1958	41,899,000	—	—	BV	1.85	3.00
1959	27,369,000	—	BV	2.00	5.50	8.00
1960	26,259,000	—	BV	1.60	3.50	6.00
1961	52,601,000	—	—	BV	2.50	5.00
1962	61,094,000	—	—	BV	1.75	4.00
1963	26,394,000	—	—	BV	1.75	2.50
1964	15,615,000	—	—	BV	1.75	2.50
1965	5,004,000	—	—	BV	1.85	2.50
1966	30,998,000	—	—	BV	1.65	2.25
1967	9,308,000	—	—	BV	2.75	4.50

Tall date	Short date

KM# 460   PESO
9.0000 g., Copper-Nickel, 29 mm. **Obv:** National arms, eagle left **Rev:** Head left **Edge:** Reeded **Mint:** Mexico City

Date	Mintage	F	VF	XF	Unc	BU
1970 Narrow date	102,715,000	—	0.25	0.35	0.65	0.80
1970 Wide date	Inc. above	—	1.25	2.50	7.50	10.00
1971	426,222,000	—	0.20	0.25	0.55	0.75
1972	120,000,000	—	0.20	0.25	0.40	0.65
1974	63,700,000	—	0.20	0.25	0.65	0.90
1975 Tall narrow date	205,979,000	—	0.25	0.45	1.00	1.35
1975 Short wide date	Inc. above	—	0.30	0.40	0.75	1.00
1976	94,489,000	—	0.15	0.20	0.50	0.75
1977 Thick date close to rim	94,364,000	—	0.25	0.45	1.00	1.25
1977 Thin date, space between sideburns and collar	Inc. above	—	1.00	2.50	8.50	16.50
1978 Closed 8	208,300,000	—	0.20	0.30	1.00	1.50
1978 Open 8	55,140,000	—	1.00	2.50	14.00	20.00
1979 Thin date	117,884,000	—	0.20	0.30	1.15	1.50
1979 Thick date	Inc. above	—	0.20	0.30	1.25	1.75
1980 Closed 8	318,800,000	—	0.25	0.35	1.00	1.25
1980 Open 8	23,865,000	—	0.75	1.50	8.00	15.00
1981 Closed 8	413,349,000	—	0.20	0.30	0.75	0.90
1981 Open 8	58,616,000	—	0.50	1.25	6.50	9.00
1982 Closed 8	235,000,000	—	0.25	0.75	2.25	2.50
1982 Open 8	—	—	0.75	1.50	8.00	15.00
1983 Wide date	100,000,000	—	0.30	0.45	3.00	3.50
1983 Narrow date	Inc. above	—	0.30	0.45	3.00	4.50
1983 Proof	1,051,000	Value: 38.00				

KM# 496   PESO
5.7000 g., Stainless Steel, 24.5 mm. **Obv:** National arms, eagle left **Rev:** Armored bust right **Mint:** Mexico City

Date	Mintage	F	VF	XF	Unc	BU
1984	722,802,000	—	0.10	0.25	0.65	1.45
1985	985,000,000	—	0.10	0.25	0.50	1.25
1986	740,000,000	—	0.10	0.25	0.50	1.25
1987	250,000,000	—	0.10	0.25	0.50	1.25
1987 Proof; 2 known	—	Value: 1,000				

KM# 461   2 PESOS
1.6666 g., 0.9000 Gold 0.0482 oz. AGW, 13 mm. **Obv:** National arms **Rev:** Date above value within wreath **Mint:** Mexico City **Note:** Mint mark Mo.

Date	Mintage	F	VF	XF	Unc	BU
1919	1,670,000	—	BV	80.00	100	—
1920/10	—	BV	70.00	90.00	130	—
1920	4,282,000	—	BV	85.00	95.00	—
1944	10,000	BV	80.00	90.00	120	—
1945	Est. 140,000	—	—	—	BV+20%	—
1946	168,000	BV	80.00	90.00	150	—
1947	25,000	BV	80.00	90.00	130	—
1948 No specimens known	45,000	—	—	—	—	—

Note: During 1951-1972 a total of 4,590,493 pieces were restruck, most likely dated 1945. In 1996 matte restrikes were produced. An additional 260,000 pieces dated 1945 were struck during 2000-2009

KM# 462   2 PESOS
26.6667 g., 0.9000 Silver 0.7716 oz. ASW, 39 mm. **Subject:** Centennial of Independence **Obv:** National arms, eagle left within wreath **Rev:** Winged Victory **Mint:** Mexico City **Designer:** Emilio del Moral **Note:** Mint mark Mo.

Date	Mintage	F	VF	XF	Unc	BU
1921	1,278,000	—	45.00	75.00	450	700

KM# 463   2-1/2 PESOS
2.0833 g., 0.9000 Gold 0.0603 oz. AGW, 15.5 mm. **Obv:** National arms **Rev:** Miguel Hidalgo y Costilla **Mint:** Mexico City **Note:** Mint mark Mo.

Date	Mintage	F	VF	XF	Unc	BU
1918	1,704,000	—	BV	95.00	115	—
1919	984,000	—	BV	95.00	115	—
1920/10	607,000	—	BV	95.00	155	—
1920	Inc. above	—	BV	95.00	110	—
1944	20,000	—	BV	100	125	—
1945	Est. 180,000	—	—	—	BV+18%	—
1946	163,000	—	BV	100	125	—
1947	24,000	200	265	375	650	—
1948	63,000	—	BV	100	125	—

Note: During 1951-1972 a total of 5,025,087 pieces were restruck, most likely dated 1945. In 1996 matte restrikes were produced. An additional 517,000 pieces dated 1945 were struck during 2000-2009

KM# 464 5 PESOS
4.1666 g., 0.9000 Gold 0.1206 oz. AGW, 19 mm. **Obv:**
National arms **Rev:** Miguel Hidalgo y Costilla **Mint:** Mexico
City **Note:** Mint mark Mo.

Date	Mintage	F	VF	XF	Unc	BU
1905	18,000	175	200	275	600	—
1906	4,638,000	—	—	BV	180	—
1907/6	—	—	—	—	—	—
1907	1,088,000	—	—	BV	180	—
1910	100,000	—	—	BV	190	—
1918/7	609,000	—	—	BV	220	—
1918	Inc. above	—	—	BV	180	—
1919	506,000	—	—	BV	180	—
1920	2,385,000	—	—	BV	180	—
1955	Est. 48,000	—	—	—	BV+12%	—

Note: During 1955-1972 a total of 1,767,645 pieces were
restruck, most likely dated 1955. In 1996 matte restrikes
were produced. An additional 89,000 pieces dated 1955
were struck during 2000-2009

KM# 465 5 PESOS
30.0000 g., 0.9000 Silver 0.8680 oz. ASW, 40 mm. **Obv:**
National arms, eagle left **Rev:** Head with headdress left **Edge:**
Reeded **Mint:** Mexico City **Note:** Mint mark Mo.

Date	Mintage	F	VF	XF	Unc	BU
1947	5,110,000	—	—	BV	27.50	32.50
1948	26,740,000	—	—	BV	27.50	32.50

KM# 466 5 PESOS
27.7800 g., 0.7200 Silver 0.6430 oz. ASW, 40 mm. **Subject:**
Opening of Southern Railroad **Obv:** National arms, eagle left
Rev: Radiant sun flanked by palm trees above train **Edge
Lettering:** COMERCIO - AGRICULTURA - INDUSTRIA **Mint:**
Mexico City **Designer:** Manuel L. Negrete **Note:** Mint mark Mo.

Date	Mintage	F	VF	XF	Unc	BU
1950	200,000	—	27.50	45.00	65.00	75.00

Note: It is recorded that 100,000 pieces were melted to be
used for the 1968 Mexican Olympic 25 Pesos

KM# 467 5 PESOS
27.7800 g., 0.7200 Silver 0.6430 oz. ASW, 40 mm. **Obv:**
National arms, eagle left **Rev:** Head left within wreath **Edge
Lettering:** COMERCIO - AGRICULTURA - INDUSTRIA
Mint: Mexico City **Note:** Mint mark Mo.

Date	Mintage	F	VF	XF	Unc	BU
1951	4,958,000	—	—	BV	20.00	22.50
1952	9,595,000	—	—	BV	20.00	22.50
1953	20,376,000	—	—	BV	20.00	22.50
1954	30,000	—	30.00	60.00	70.00	85.00

KM# 468 5 PESOS
27.7800 g., 0.7200 Silver 0.6430 oz. ASW, 40 mm. **Subject:**
Bicentennial of Hidalgo's Birth **Obv:** National arms, eagle left
Rev: Half-length figure facing to right of building and dates
Edge Lettering: COMERCIO - AGRICULTURA -
INDUSTRIA **Mint:** Mexico City **Designer:** Manuel L. Negrete
Note: Mint mark Mo.

Date	Mintage	F	VF	XF	Unc	BU
1953	1,000,000	—	—	BV	20.00	25.00

KM# 469 5 PESOS
18.0500 g., 0.7200 Silver 0.4178 oz. ASW, 36 mm. **Obv:**
National arms, eagle left **Rev:** Head left **Mint:** Mexico City
Note: Mint mark Mo.

ESTADOS UNIDOS MEXICANOS

Date	Mintage	F	VF	XF	Unc	BU
1955	4,271,000	—	—	BV	13.50	15.00
1956	4,596,000	—	—	BV	13.50	15.00
1957	3,464,000	—	—	BV	13.50	15.00

Date	Mintage	F	VF	XF	Unc	BU
1973	19,405,000	—	1.25	2.00	4.50	5.50
1974	34,500,000	—	0.50	0.80	1.75	2.25
1976 Small date	26,121,000	—	0.75	1.45	3.25	4.00
1976 Large date	121,550,000	—	0.35	0.50	1.50	1.75
1977	102,000,000	—	0.35	0.50	1.50	1.75
1978	25,700,000	—	1.00	1.50	4.50	6.25

KM# 470   5 PESOS
18.0500 g., 0.7200 Silver 0.4178 oz. ASW, 36 mm. **Subject:** 100th Anniversary of Constitution **Obv:** National arms, eagle left **Rev:** Head left **Edge Lettering:** INDEPENDENCIA Y LIBERTAD **Mint:** Mexico City **Designer:** Manuel L. Negrete **Note:** Mint mark Mo.

Date	Mintage	F	VF	XF	Unc	BU
1957	200,000	—	BV	13.50	15.00	18.00

KM# 485   5 PESOS
10.2000 g., Copper-Nickel, 27 mm. **Subject:** Quetzalcoatl **Obv:** National arms, eagle left **Rev:** Native sculpture to lower right of value and dollar sign **Edge Lettering:** LIBERTAD Y INDEPENDENCIA **Mint:** Mexico City **Note:** Inverted and normal edge legend varieties exist for the 1980 and 1981 dates.

Date	Mintage	F	VF	XF	Unc	BU
1980	266,899,999	—	0.25	0.50	1.75	2.25
1981	30,500,000	—	0.45	0.65	2.75	3.25
1982	20,000,000	—	1.50	2.35	4.25	5.25
1982 Proof	1,051	Value: 50.00				
1983 Proof; 7 known	—	Value: 1,200				
1984	16,300,000	—	1.25	2.00	4.75	6.00
1985	76,900,000	—	2.00	3.25	4.25	5.00

KM# 471   5 PESOS
18.0500 g., 0.7200 Silver 0.4178 oz. ASW, 36 mm. **Subject:** Centennial of Carranza's Birth **Obv:** National arms, eagle left **Rev:** Head left **Edge:** Plain **Mint:** Mexico City **Designer:** Manuel L. Negrete **Note:** Mint mark Mo.

Date	Mintage	F	VF	XF	Unc	BU
1959	1,000,000	—	—	BV	13.50	15.00

KM# 502   5 PESOS
3.1000 g., Brass, 17 mm. **Obv:** National arms, eagle left **Rev:** Date and value **Edge:** Reeded **Mint:** Mexico City **Note:** Circulation coinage.

Date	Mintage	F	VF	XF	Unc	BU
1985	30,000,000	—	—	0.15	0.35	0.50
1987	81,900,000	—	8.00	9.50	12.50	16.50
1988	76,600,000	—	—	0.10	0.25	0.35
1988 Proof; 2 known	—	Value: 600				

Small date   Large date

KM# 472   5 PESOS
14.0000 g., Copper-Nickel, 33 mm. **Obv:** National arms, eagle left **Rev:** Armored bust right **Edge Lettering:** INDEPENDENCIA Y LIBERTAD **Mint:** Mexico City **Note:** Small date, large date varieties.

Date	Mintage	F	VF	XF	Unc	BU
1971	28,457,000	—	0.50	0.95	2.50	3.25
1972	75,000,000	—	0.60	1.25	2.00	2.50

KM# 473   10 PESOS
8.3333 g., 0.9000 Gold 0.2411 oz. AGW, 22.5 mm. **Obv:** National arms **Rev:** Miguel Hidalgo y Costilla **Mint:** Mexico City **Note:** Mint mark Mo.

Date	Mintage	F	VF	XF	Unc	BU
1905	39,000	—	BV	360	395	410
1906	2,949,000	—	BV	350	375	410
1907	1,589,000	—	BV	350	375	410
1908	890,000	—	BV	350	375	410
1910	451,000	—	BV	350	375	410
1916	26,000	—	BV	3,875	500	500
1917	1,967,000	—	BV	350	375	410
1919	266,000	—	BV	350	375	410
1920	12,000	—	BV	550	925	1,000
1959	Est. 50,000	—	—	—	BV+7%	—

Note: *During 1961-1972 a total of 954,983 pieces were restruck, most likely dated 1959. In 1996 matte restrikes were produced. An additional 59,500 pieces dated 1959 were struck during 2000-2009

KM# 474   10 PESOS
28.8880 g., 0.9000 Silver 0.8359 oz. ASW, 40 mm.   **Obv:** National arms **Rev:** Head left **Edge:** Reeded **Mint:** Mexico City **Note:** Mint mark Mo.

Date	Mintage	F	VF	XF	Unc	BU
1955	585,000	—	—	BV	27.50	30.00
1956	3,535,000	—	—	BV	26.50	28.50

KM# 475   10 PESOS
28.8800 g., 0.9000 Silver 0.8356 oz. ASW, 40 mm.   **Subject:** 100th Anniversary of Constitution **Obv:** National arms, eagle left **Rev:** Head left **Edge Lettering:** INDEPENDENCIA Y LIBERTAD **Mint:** Mexico City **Designer:** Manuel L. Negrete **Note:** Mint mark Mo.

Date	Mintage	F	VF	XF	Unc	BU
1957	100,000	—	26.50	38.50	55.00	60.00

KM# 476   10 PESOS
28.8880 g., 0.9000 Silver 0.8359 oz. ASW, 40 mm.   **Subject:** 150th Anniversary - War of Independence **Obv:** National arms, eagle left **Rev:** Conjoined busts facing flanked by dates **Edge:** Reeded **Mint:** Mexico City **Designer:** Manuel L. Negrete **Note:** Mint mark Mo.

Date	Mintage	F	VF	XF	Unc	BU
1960	1,000,000	—	—	BV	26.50	30.00

KM# 477.1   10 PESOS
10.0000 g., Copper-Nickel, 30.5 mm.   **Subject:** Miguel Hidalgo y Costilla **Obv:** National arms, eagle left **Rev:** Head left **Shape:** 7-sided **Mint:** Mexico City **Note:** Thin flan - 1.6mm

Date	Mintage	F	VF	XF	Unc	BU
1974	3,900,000	—	0.50	1.00	3.00	4.50
1974 Proof	—	Value: 650				
1975	1,000,000	—	2.25	3.25	7.50	8.50
1976	74,500,000	—	0.25	0.75	1.75	2.75
1977	79,620,000	—	0.50	1.00	2.00	3.00

KM# 477.2   10 PESOS
11.5000 g., Copper-Nickel, 30.5 mm.   **Subject:** Miguel Hidalgo y Costilla **Obv:** National arms, eagle left **Rev:** Head left **Shape:** 7-sided **Mint:** Mexico City **Note:** Thick flan - 2.3mm

Date	Mintage	F	VF	XF	Unc	BU
1978	124,850,000	—	0.50	0.75	2.50	2.75
1979	57,200,000	—	0.50	0.75	2.50	2.75
1980	55,200,000	—	0.50	0.75	2.50	3.75
1981	222,768,000	—	0.40	0.60	2.25	2.75
1982	151,770,000	—	0.50	0.80	2.50	3.50
1982 Proof	1,051	Value: 45.00				
1983 Proof; 3 known	—	Value: 1,800				
1985	58,000,000	—	1.25	1.75	5.75	8.00

KM# 512   10 PESOS
3.8400 g., Stainless Steel, 19 mm.   **Obv:** National arms, eagle left **Rev:** Head facing with diagonal value at left **Mint:** Mexico City **Note:** Date varieties exist.

Date	Mintage	F	VF	XF	Unc	BU
1985	257,000,000	—	—	0.15	0.50	0.75
1986	392,000,000	—	—	0.15	0.50	1.50
1987	305,000,000	—	—	0.15	0.35	0.50
1988	500,300,000	—	—	0.15	0.25	0.35
1989	—	—	0.20	0.25	0.75	1.50
1990	—	—	—	0.25	0.75	1.25
1990 Proof; 2 known	—	Value: 550				

KM# 478   20 PESOS
16.6666 g., 0.9000 Gold 0.4822 oz. AGW, 27.5 mm.   **Obv:**

National arms, eagle left **Rev:** Aztec Sunstone with denomination below **Edge:** Lettered **Edge Lettering:** INDEPEDENCIA Y LIBERTAD **Mint:** Mexico City **Note:** Mint mark Mo.

Date	Mintage	F	VF	XF	Unc	BU
1917	852,000	—	—	BV	700	—
1918	2,831,000	—	—	BV	700	—
1919	1,094,000	—	—	BV	700	—
1920/10	462,000	—	—	BV	700	—
1920	Inc. above	—	—	BV	725	—
1921/11	922,000	—	—	BV	700	—
1921/10	—	—	—	—	—	—
1921	Inc. above	—	—	BV	725	—
1959	Est. 13,000	—	—	—	BV+4%	—

Note: During 1960-1971 a total of 1,158,414 pieces were restruck, most likely dated 1959. In 1996 matte restrikes were produced. An additional 78,000 pieces dated 1959 were struck in 2000-2009

KM# 486   20 PESOS
15.2000 g., Copper-Nickel, 32 mm. **Obv:** National arms, eagle left **Rev:** Figure with headdress facing left within circle **Edge Lettering:** INDEPENDENCIA Y LIBERTAD **Mint:** Mexico City

Date	Mintage	F	VF	XF	Unc	BU
1980	84,900,000	—	0.50	0.85	2.25	3.25
1981	250,573,000	—	0.60	0.80	2.25	3.25
1982	236,892,000	—	1.00	1.75	2.50	3.75
1982 Proof	1,051	Value: 50.00				
1983 Proof; 3 known	—	Value: 575				
1984	55,000,000	—	1.00	1.50	2.50	4.75

KM# 508   20 PESOS
6.0000 g., Brass, 21 mm. **Obv:** National arms, eagle left **Rev:** Bust facing with diagonal value at left **Edge:** Reeded **Mint:** Mexico City

Date	Mintage	F	VF	XF	Unc	BU
1985 Wide date	25,000,000	—	0.10	0.20	1.00	1.50
1985 Narrow date	Inc. above	—	0.10	0.25	1.50	2.25
1986	10,000,000	—	1.00	1.75	5.00	6.00
1988	355,200,000	—	0.10	0.20	0.45	0.75
1989	—	—	0.15	0.30	1.50	2.00
1990	—	—	0.15	0.30	1.50	2.50
1990 Proof; 3 known	—	Value: 575				

Snake's tongue straight

KM# 479.1   25 PESOS
22.5000 g., 0.7200 Silver 0.5208 oz. ASW, 38 mm. **Obv:** National arms, eagle left **Rev:** Olympic rings below dancing native left, numeral design in background **Designer:** Lorenzo Rafael **Note:** Type I, Rings aligned.

Date	Mintage	F	VF	XF	Unc	BU
1968	27,182,000	—	—	BV	16.50	18.50

KM# 479.2   25 PESOS
22.5000 g., 0.7200 Silver 0.5208 oz. ASW, 38 mm. **Subject:** Summer Olympics - Mexico City **Obv:** National arms, eagle left **Rev:** Olympic rings below dancing native left, numeral design in background **Mint:** Mexico City **Note:** Type II, center ring low.

Date	Mintage	F	VF	XF	Unc	BU
1968	Inc. above	—	BV	16.50	18.50	20.00

Snake's tongue curved

KM# 479.3   25 PESOS
22.5000 g., 0.7200 Silver 0.5208 oz. ASW, 38 mm. **Subject:** Summer Olympics - Mexico City **Obv:** National arms, eagle left **Rev:** Olympic rings below dancing native left, numeral design in background **Mint:** Mexico City **Note:** Snake with long curved or normal tongue. Type III, center rings low.

Date	Mintage	F	VF	XF	Unc	BU
1968	Inc. above	—	BV	16.50	18.50	22.50

KM# 519 25 PESOS
8.4060 g., 0.9250 Silver 0.2500 oz. ASW **Subject:** 1986 World Cup Soccer Games **Obv:** National arms, eagle left **Rev:** Soccer ball within net, date and value to left **Mint:** Mexico City

Date	Mintage	F	VF	XF	Unc	BU
1986 Proof	—			Value: 15.00		

KM# 497a 25 PESOS
8.4060 g., 0.9250 Silver 0.2500 oz. ASW **Subject:** 1986 World Cup Soccer Games **Obv:** National arms, eagle left **Rev:** Value above soccerball with date below **Mint:** Mexico City **Note:** Without finess statement- reverse description

Date	Mintage	F	VF	XF	Unc	BU
1986 Proof	—			Value: 15.00		

KM# 480 25 PESOS
22.5000 g., 0.7200 Silver 0.5208 oz. ASW, 38 mm. **Obv:** National arms, eagle left **Rev:** Bust facing **Mint:** Mexico City

Date	Mintage	F	VF	XF	Unc	BU
1972	2,000,000	—	BV	16.50	18.50	20.00

KM# 497 25 PESOS
7.7760 g., 0.7200 Silver 0.1800 oz. ASW **Subject:** 1986 World Cup Soccer Games **Obv:** National arms, eagle left **Rev:** Value above soccer ball with date below **Mint:** Mexico City

Date	Mintage	F	VF	XF	Unc	BU
1985	354,000	—	—	—		10.00

KM# 503 25 PESOS
8.4060 g., 0.9250 Silver 0.2500 oz. ASW **Subject:** 1986 World Cup Soccer Games **Obv:** National arms, eagle left **Rev:** Pre-Columbian hieroglyphs, ojo de buey, and soccer ball **Mint:** Mexico City

Date	Mintage	F	VF	XF	Unc	BU
1985 Proof	277,000		Value: 15.00			

KM# 481 50 PESOS
41.6666 g., 0.9000 Gold 1.2056 oz. AGW, 37 mm. **Subject:** Centennial of Independence **Obv:** National arms **Rev:** Winged Victory **Edge:** Reeded **Mint:** Mexico City **Designer:** Emilio del Moral **Note:** During 1949-1972 a total of 3,975,654 pieces were restruck, most likely dated 1947 and an additional 302,000 pieces dated 1947 were struck during 2000-2009. In 1996 matte restrikes were produced. Mint mark Mo.

Date	Mintage	F	VF	XF	Unc	BU
1921	180,000	—	—	BV	1,850	3,200
1922	463,000	—	—	BV	1,700	1,900
1923	432,000	—	—	BV	1,700	1,900
1924	439,000	—	—	BV	1,700	1,900
1925	716,000	—	—	BV	1,700	1,900
1926	600,000	—	—	BV	1,700	1,900
1927	606,000	—	—	BV	1,700	1,900
1928	538,000	—	—	BV	1,700	1,900
1929	458,000	—	—	BV	1,700	1,900
1930	372,000	—	—	BV	1,700	1,900
1931	137,000	—	—	BV	1,700	1,900
1944	593,000	—	—	BV	1,700	1,900
1945	1,012,000	—	—	BV	1,700	1,900
1946	1,588,000	—	—	BV	1,700	1,900
1947	309,000	—	—	—	BV+3%	—
1947 Specimen	—	—	—	—	—	—

Note: Value, $6,500

KM# 514 25 PESOS
8.4060 g., 0.9250 Silver 0.2500 oz. ASW **Subject:** 1986 World Cup Soccer Games **Obv:** National arms, eagle left **Rev:** Value above soccer ball **Mint:** Mexico City

Date	Mintage	F	VF	XF	Unc	BU
1985 Proof	234,000		Value: 15.00			

Date	Mintage	F	VF	XF	Unc	BU
1984	94,216,000	—	0.65	1.25	2.70	3.25
1985	296,000,000	—	0.25	0.45	1.25	2.25
1986	50,000,000	—	6.00	10.00	12.00	14.00
1987	210,000,000	—	0.25	0.45	1.00	1.25
1988	80,200,000	—	6.25	9.00	13.50	16.00

KM# 495a 50 PESOS
7.1000 g., Stainless Steel, 23.5 mm. **Subject:** Benito Juarez **Obv:** National arms, eagle left **Rev:** Bust 1/4 left with diagonal value at left **Edge:** Plain **Mint:** Mexico City

Date	Mintage	F	VF	XF	Unc	BU
1988	353,300,000	—	—	0.20	1.25	1.75
1990	—	—	—	0.30	1.00	2.00
1992	—	—	—	0.25	1.00	2.75

KM# 504 50 PESOS
16.8310 g., 0.9250 Silver 0.5005 oz. ASW **Subject:** 1986 World Cup Soccer Games **Obv:** National arms, eagle left **Rev:** Stylized athlete as soccer forerunner **Mint:** Mexico City

Date	Mintage	F	VF	XF	Unc	BU
1985 Proof	347,000	Value: 25.00				

KM# 515 50 PESOS
16.8310 g., 0.9250 Silver 0.5005 oz. ASW **Subject:** 1986 World Cup Soccer Games **Obv:** National arms, eagle left **Rev:** Value to right of soccer player **Mint:** Mexico City

Date	Mintage	F	VF	XF	Unc	BU
1985 Proof	234,000	Value: 25.00				

KM# 498 50 PESOS
15.5520 g., 0.7200 Silver 0.3600 oz. ASW **Subject:** 1986 World Cup Soccer Games **Obv:** National arms, eagle left **Rev:** Pair of feet and soccer ball **Mint:** Mexico City

Date	Mintage	F	VF	XF	Unc	BU
1985	347,000	—	—	—	—	16.50

KM# 482 50 PESOS
41.6666 g., 0.9000 Gold 1.2056 oz. AGW, 39 mm. **Obv:** National arms **Rev:** Winged Victory

Date	Mintage	F	VF	XF	Unc	BU
1943	89,000	—	—	—	BV	1,800

KM# 481a 50 PESOS
Platinum APW **Subject:** Centennial of Independence **Obv:** National arms **Rev:** Winged Victory **Edge:** Reeded **Mint:** Mexico City

Date	Mintage	F	VF	XF	Unc	BU
1947Mo	Est. 5	—	—	—	—	13,500

KM# 490 50 PESOS
19.8400 g., Copper-Nickel, 35 mm. **Subject:** Coyolxauhqui **Obv:** National arms, eagle left **Rev:** Value to right of artistic designs **Edge:** Reeded **Mint:** Mexico City **Note:** Doubled die examples of 1982 and 1983 dates exist.

Date	Mintage	F	VF	XF	Unc	BU
1982	222,890,000	—	1.00	2.50	5.00	6.50
1983	45,000,000	—	1.50	3.00	6.00	7.00
1903 Proof	1,051	Value: 55.00				
1984	73,537,000	—	1.00	1.35	3.50	4.50
1984 Proof; 4 known	—	Value: 750				

KM# 495 50 PESOS
8.6000 g., Copper-Nickel, 23.5 mm. **Subject:** Benito Juarez **Obv:** National arms, eagle left **Rev:** Bust 1/4 left with diagonal value at left **Edge:** Reeded **Mint:** Mexico City

KM# 523 50 PESOS
16.8310 g., 0.9250 Silver 0.5005 oz. ASW **Subject:** 1986
World Cup Soccer Games **Obv:** National arms, eagle left **Rev:**
Value to left of soccer balls **Mint:** Mexico City

Date	Mintage	F	VF	XF	Unc	BU
1986 Proof	190,000	Value: 25.00				

KM# 498a 50 PESOS
16.8310 g., 0.9250 Silver 0.5005 oz. ASW **Subject:** 1986
World Cup Soccer Games **Obv:** National arms, eagle left **Rev:**
Without fineness statement **Mint:** Mexico City

Date	Mintage	F	VF	XF	Unc	BU
1986 Proof	10,000	Value: 25.00				

KM# 532 50 PESOS
15.5500 g., 0.9990 Silver 0.4994 oz. ASW **Subject:** 50th
Anniversary - Nationalization of Oil Industry **Obv:** National
arms, eagle left **Rev:** Monument **Mint:** Mexico City

Date	Mintage	F	VF	XF	Unc	BU
ND(1988)Mo	20,000	—	—	—	22.50	25.00

Low 7's

KM# 483.1 100 PESOS
27.7700 g., 0.7200 Silver 0.6428 oz. ASW, 39 mm. **Obv:**
National arms, eagle left **Rev:** Bust facing, sloping right
shoulder, round left shoulder with no clothing folds **Edge:**
Reeded **Mint:** Mexico City

Date	Mintage	F	VF	XF	Unc	BU
1977 Low 7's	5,225,000	—	—	BV	20.00	22.50
1977 High 7's	Inc. above	—	—	BV	20.00	22.50

High 7's

KM# 483.2 100 PESOS
27.7700 g., 0.7200 Silver 0.6428 oz. ASW, 39 mm. **Obv:**
National arms, eagle left **Rev:** Bust facing, higher right
shoulder, left shoulder with clothing folds. **Mint:** Mexico City
Note: Mintage inc. KM#483.1

Date	Mintage	F	VF	XF	Unc	BU
1977 Date in line	—	—	—	BV	20.00	22.50
1978	9,879,000	—	—	BV	20.00	22.50
1979	784,000	—	—	BV	20.00	22.50
1979 Proof	—	Value: 650				

KM# 493 100 PESOS
11.7000 g., Aluminum-Bronze, 26.5 mm. **Obv:** National
arms, eagle left **Rev:** Head 1/4 right with diagonal value at
right **Edge:** Segmented reeding **Mint:** Mexico City

Date	Mintage	F	VF	XF	Unc	BU
1984	227,809,000	—	0.45	0.60	2.50	4.00
1985	377,423,000	—	0.30	0.50	2.00	3.00
1986	43,000,000	—	1.00	2.50	4.75	7.50
1987	165,000,000	—	0.60	1.25	2.25	3.00
1988	433,100,000	—	0.30	0.50	2.00	2.75
1989	—	—	0.35	0.65	2.00	2.75
1990	—	—	0.15	0.40	1.50	2.50
1990 Proof; 1 known	—	Value: 650				
1991	—	—	0.15	0.25	1.00	2.50
1992	—	—	0.30	0.75	1.75	3.00

KM# 499   100 PESOS
31.1030 g., 0.7200 Silver 0.7200 oz. ASW **Subject:** 1986
World Cup Soccer Games **Obv:** National arms, eagle left **Rev:**
Value above artistic designs and soccer ball **Mint:** Mexico City

Date	Mintage	F	VF	XF	Unc	BU
1985	302,000	—	—	—	—	30.00

KM# 499a   100 PESOS
32.6250 g., 0.9250 Silver 0.9702 oz. ASW **Subject:** 1986
World Cup Soccer Games **Obv:** National arms, eagle left **Rev:**
Without fineness statement **Mint:** Mexico City

Date	Mintage	F	VF	XF	Unc	BU
1985 Proof	9,006	Value: 55.00				

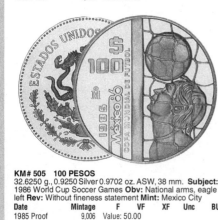

KM# 505   100 PESOS
32.6250 g., 0.9250 Silver 0.9702 oz. ASW, 38 mm. **Subject:**
1986 World Cup Soccer Games **Obv:** National arms, eagle
left **Rev:** Without fineness statement **Mint:** Mexico City

Date	Mintage	F	VF	XF	Unc	BU
1985 Proof	9,006	Value: 50.00				

KM# 521   100 PESOS
32.6250 g., 0.9250 Silver 0.9702 oz. ASW **Subject:** 1986
World Cup Soccer Games **Obv:** National arms, eagle left **Rev:**
Without fineness statement **Mint:** Mexico City

Date	Mintage	F	VF	XF	Unc	BU
1986 Proof	208,000	Value: 55.00				

KM# 524   100 PESOS
32.6250 g., 0.9250 Silver 0.9702 oz. ASW **Subject:** 1986
World Cup Soccer Games **Obv:** National arms, eagle left **Rev:**
Without fineness statement **Mint:** Mexico City

Date	Mintage	F	VF	XF	Unc	BU
1986 Proof	190,000	Value: 55.00				

KM# 537   100 PESOS
32.6250 g., 0.7200 Silver 0.7552 oz. ASW **Subject:** World
Wildlife Fund **Obv:** National arms, eagle left **Rev:** Monarch
butterflies **Mint:** Mexico City

Date	Mintage	F	VF	XF	Unc	BU
1987 Proof	28,500	Value: 65.00				

KM# 533   100 PESOS
31.1030 g., 0.9990 Silver 0.9989 oz. ASW   **Subject:** 50th Anniversary - Nationalization of Oil Industry **Obv:** National arms, eagle left **Rev:** Bust facing above sprigs and dates **Mint:** Mexico City

Date	Mintage	F	VF	XF	Unc	BU
1988Mo	20,000	—	—	—	40.00	55.00

KM# 539   100 PESOS
33.6250 g., 0.9250 Silver 0.9999 oz. ASW   **Subject:** Save the Children **Obv:** National arms, eagle left **Rev:** Child flying kite, two others sitting and playing **Mint:** Mexico City

Date	Mintage	F	VF	XF	Unc	BU
1991 Proof	11,000	Value: 50.00				

KM# 540   100 PESOS
27.0000 g., 0.9250 Silver 0.8029 oz. ASW   **Series:** Ibero - American Series **Obv:** National arms, eagle left within center of assorted arms **Rev:** Maps within circles flanked by pillars above sailboats **Mint:** Mexico City

Date	Mintage	F	VF	XF	Unc	BU
1991 Proof	50,000	Value: 85.00				
1992 Proof	75,000	Value: 80.00				

KM# 566   100 PESOS
31.1035 g., 0.9990 Silver 0.9990 oz. ASW   **Subject:** Save the Vaquita Porpoise **Obv:** National arms, eagle left **Rev:** Swimming vaquita porpoise **Mint:** Mexico City

Date	Mintage	F	VF	XF	Unc	BU
1992 Proof	28,007	Value: 60.00				

KM# 509   200 PESOS
Copper-Nickel, 29.5 mm.   **Subject:** 175th Anniversary of Independence **Obv:** National arms, eagle left **Rev:** Conjoined busts left **Mint:** Mexico City

Date	Mintage	F	VF	XF	Unc	BU
1985	75,000,000	—	—	2.00	3.50	5.50

KM# 510   200 PESOS
Copper-Nickel, 29.5 mm.   **Subject:** 75th Anniversary of 1910 Revolution **Obv:** National arms, eagle left **Rev:** Conjoined heads left below building **Mint:** Mexico City

Date	Mintage	F	VF	XF	Unc	BU
1985	98,590,000	—	—	2.00	4.00	6.00

KM# 525   200 PESOS
Copper-Nickel, 29.5 mm.   **Subject:** 1986 World Cup Soccer Games **Obv:** National arms, eagle left **Rev:** Soccer players **Edge:** Reeded **Mint:** Mexico City

Date	Mintage	F	VF	XF	Unc	BU
1986	50,000,000	—	—	2.50	4.00	6.00

KM# 526   200 PESOS
62.2060 g., 0.9990 Silver 1.9979 oz. ASW   **Subject:** 1986 World Cup Soccer Games **Obv:** National arms, eagle left **Rev:** Value above 3 soccer balls **Mint:** Mexico City

Date	Mintage	F	VF	XF	Unc	BU
1986	50,000	—	—	—	70.00	80.00

KM# 500.1   250 PESOS
8.6400 g., 0.9000 Gold 0.2500 oz. AGW   **Subject:** 1986 World Cup Soccer Games **Obv:** National arms, eagle left **Rev:** Soccer ball within top 1/2 of design with value, date, and state below **Mint:** Mexico City

Date	Mintage	F	VF	XF	Unc	BU
1985	100,000	—	—	—	—	400
1986	—	—	—	—	—	400

KM# 500.2   250 PESOS
8.6400 g., 0.9000 Gold 0.2500 oz. AGW   **Subject:** 1986 World Cup Soccer Games **Obv:** National arms, eagle left **Rev:** Without fineness statement **Mint:** Mexico City

Date	Mintage	F	VF	XF	Unc	BU
1985 Proof	4,506	Value: 400				
1986 Proof	—	Value: 400				

KM# 506.1   250 PESOS
8.6400 g., 0.9000 Gold 0.2500 oz. AGW   **Subject:** 1986 World Cup Soccer Games **Obv:** National arms, eagle left **Rev:** Equestrian left within circle **Mint:** Mexico City

Date	Mintage	F	VF	XF	Unc	BU
1985	88,000	—	—	—	—	400

KM# 506.2   250 PESOS
8.6400 g., 0.9000 Gold 0.2500 oz. AGW   **Subject:** 1986 World Cup Soccer Games **Obv:** National arms, eagle left **Rev:** Without fineness statement **Mint:** Mexico City

Date	Mintage	F	VF	XF	Unc	BU
1985 Proof	Est. 80,000	Value: 375				

KM# 501.1   500 PESOS
17.2800 g., 0.9000 Gold 0.5000 oz. AGW   **Subject:** 1986 World Cup Soccer Games **Obv:** National arms, eagle left **Rev:** Soccer player to right within emblem **Mint:** Mexico City

Date	Mintage	F	VF	XF	Unc	BU
1985	102,000	—	—	—	—	725
1986	—	—	—	—	—	725

KM# 501.2   500 PESOS
17.2800 g., 0.9000 Gold 0.5000 oz. AGW   **Subject:** 1986 World Cup Soccer Games **Obv:** National arms, eagle left **Rev:** Without fineness statement **Mint:** Mexico City

Date	Mintage	F	VF	XF	Unc	BU
1985 Proof	5,506	Value: 725				
1986 Proof	—	Value: 725				

KM# 507.1   500 PESOS
17.2800 g., 0.9000 Gold 0.5000 oz. AGW   **Subject:** 1986 World Cup Soccer Games **Obv:** National arms, eagle left **Rev:** Soccer ball within emblem flanked by value and date **Mint:** Mexico City

Date	Mintage	F	VF	XF	Unc	BU
1985	—	—	—	—	—	750

KM# 507.2   500 PESOS
17.2800 g., 0.9000 Gold 0.5000 oz. AGW   **Subject:** 1986 World Cup Soccer Games **Obv:** National arms, eagle left **Rev:** Without fineness statement **Mint:** Mexico City

Date	Mintage	F	VF	XF	Unc	BU
1985 Proof	—	Value: 750				

KM# 511   500 PESOS
33.4500 g., 0.9250 Silver 0.9947 oz. ASW   **Subject:** 75th Anniversary of 1910 Revolution **Obv:** National arms, eagle left **Rev:** Conjoined heads left below building **Mint:** Mexico City

Date	Mintage	F	VF	XF	Unc	BU
1985 Proof	40,000	Value: 65.00				

KM# 529 500 PESOS
12.6000 g., Copper-Nickel, 28.5 mm. **Obv:** National arms,
eagle left **Rev:** Head 1/4 right **Edge:** Reeded **Mint:** Mexico City

Date	Mintage	F	VF	XF	Unc	BU
1986	20,000,000	—	—	1.00	3.25	4.00
1987	180,000,000	—	—	0.75	2.25	3.00
1988	230,000,000	—	—	0.50	2.25	3.00
1988 Proof; 2 known	—	Value: 650				
1989	—	—	—	0.75	2.25	3.50
1992	—	—	—	1.00	2.25	4.00

KM# 534 500 PESOS
17.2800 g., 0.9000 Gold 0.5000 oz. AGW **Subject:** 50th
Anniversary - Nationalization of Oil Industry **Obv:** National
arms, eagle left **Rev:** Monument **Mint:** Mexico City **Note:**
Similar to 5000 Pesos, KM#531.

Date	Mintage	F	VF	XF	Unc	BU
1988Mo	611	—	—	—	—	750

KM# 513 1000 PESOS
17.2800 g., 0.9000 Gold 0.5000 oz. AGW **Subject:** 175th
Anniversary of Independence **Obv:** National arms, eagle left
Rev: Conjoined heads left below value **Mint:** Mexico City

Date	Mintage	F	VF	XF	Unc	BU
1985 Proof	—	Value: 750				

KM# 527 1000 PESOS
31.1050 g., 0.9990 Gold 0.9990 oz. AGW **Subject:** 1986 World
Cup Soccer Games **Obv:** National arms, eagle left **Rev:** Value
above soccer ball and two hemispheres **Mint:** Mexico City

Date	Mintage	F	VF	XF	Unc	BU
1986Mo	1,279	—	—	—	—	1,475

KM# 536 1000 PESOS
15.0000 g., Aluminum-Bronze, 30.5 mm. **Subject:** Juana de
Asbaje **Obv:** National arms, eagle left **Rev:** Bust 1/4 left with
diagonal value at left **Edge:** Reeded **Mint:** Mexico City

Date	Mintage	F	VF	XF	Unc	BU
1988	229,300,000	—	0.85	2.00	4.25	5.75
1989	—	—	0.85	2.00	4.25	5.75
1990	—	—	0.85	2.00	4.00	5.50
1990 Proof; 2 known	—	Value: 550				
1991	—	—	1.00	2.00	3.00	7.00
1992	—	—	1.00	2.00	3.50	7.50

KM# 535 1000 PESOS
34.5590 g., 0.9000 Gold 0.9999 oz. AGW **Subject:** 50th
Anniversary - Nationalization of Oil Industry **Obv:** National
arms, eagle left **Rev:** Portrait of Cardenas **Mint:** Mexico City
Note: Similar to 5000 Pesos, KM#531.

Date	Mintage	F	VF	XF	Unc	BU
1988 Proof	657	Value: 1,475				

KM# 643 1000 PESOS
Aluminum-Bronze, 22 mm. **Obv:** National arms, eagle left
Rev: Stylized boat and "ATLAN" above denomination **Mint:**
Mexico City **Note:** Unissued type due to currency reform.

Date	Mintage	F	VF	XF	Unc	BU
1991Mo	—	—	—	—	15.00	—

KM# 528 2000 PESOS
62.2000 g., 0.9990 Gold 1.9977 oz. AGW **Subject:** 1986 World
Cup Soccer Games **Obv:** National arms, eagle left **Rev:** Value
above soccer ball and two hemispheres **Mint:** Mexico City

Date	Mintage	F	VF	XF	Unc	BU
1986Mo	964	—	—	—	—	3,000

KM# 531 5000 PESOS
Copper-Nickel, 33.5 mm. **Subject:** 50th Anniversary -
Nationalization of Oil Industry **Obv:** National arms, eagle left
Rev: Monument above dates with diagonal value at left **Mint:**
Mexico City

Date	Mintage	F	VF	XF	Unc	BU
ND(1988)	50,000,000	—	—	4.75	7.75	10.00

REFORM COINAGE

1 NEW PESO = 1000 OLD PESOS; 100 CENTAVOS = 1 NEW PESO; 100 CENTAVOS = 1 PESO

KM# 546 5 CENTAVOS
1.5800 g., Stainless Steel, 15.5 mm. **Obv:** National arms **Rev:** Large value **Edge:** Plain **Mint:** Mexico City

Date	Mintage	F	VF	XF	Unc	BU
1992Mo	136,800,000	—	—	0.15	0.20	0.50
1993Mo	234,000,000	—	—	0.15	0.20	0.50
1994Mo	125,000,000	—	—	0.15	0.20	0.50
1995Mo	195,000,000	—	—	0.15	0.20	0.50
1995Mo Proof	6,981	Value: 2.00				
1996Mo	104,831,000	—	—	0.15	0.20	0.50
1997Mo	153,675,000	—	—	0.15	0.20	0.50
1998Mo	64,417,000	—	—	0.15	0.20	0.50
1999Mo	9,949,000	—	—	0.15	0.20	0.50
2000Mo	10,871,000	—	—	0.15	0.20	0.50
2001Mo	34,811,000	—	—	0.15	0.20	0.50
2002Mo	14,901,000	—	—	0.15	0.20	0.50

KM# 547 10 CENTAVOS
2.0800 g., Stainless Steel, 17 mm. **Obv:** National arms, eagle left **Rev:** Large value **Mint:** Mexico City

Date	Mintage	F	VF	XF	Unc	BU
1992Mo	121,250,000	Value: 0.75				
1993Mo	755,000,000	—	—	0.20	0.25	6.00
1994Mo	557,000,000	—	—	0.20	0.25	0.60
1995Mo	560,000,000	—	—	0.20	0.25	0.60
1995Mo Proof	6,981	Value: 2.00				
1996Mo	594,216,000	—	—	0.20	0.25	0.60
1997Mo	581,622,000	—	—	0.20	0.25	0.60
1998Mo	602,667,000	—	—	0.20	0.25	0.60
1999Mo	488,346,000	—	—	0.20	0.25	0.60
2000Mo	577,546,000	—	—	0.20	0.30	0.75
2001Mo	618,061,000	—	—	0.20	0.25	0.30
2002Mo	463,968,000	—	—	0.20	0.25	0.30
2003Mo	378,938,000	—	—	0.20	0.25	0.30
2004Mo	393,705,000	—	—	0.20	0.25	0.30
2005Mo	488,594,000	—	—	0.20	0.25	0.30
2006Mo	473,261,000	—	—	0.20	0.25	0.30
2007Mo	473,261,000	—	—	0.20	0.25	0.30
2008Mo	433,951,000	—	—	0.20	0.25	0.30
2009Mo	90,968,000	—	—	0.20	0.25	0.30

KM# 548 20 CENTAVOS
3.0400 g., Aluminum-Bronze, 19.5 mm. **Obv:** National arms, eagle left **Rev:** Value and date within 3/4 wreath **Shape:** 12-sided **Mint:** Mexico City

Date	Mintage	F	VF	XF	Unc	BU
1992Mo	95,000,000	—	—	0.25	0.35	1.00
1993Mo	95,000,000	—	—	0.25	0.35	1.00
1994Mo	105,000,000	—	—	0.25	0.35	11.00
1995Mo	180,000,000	—	—	0.25	0.35	1.00
1995Mo Proof	6,981	Value: 3.00				
1996Mo	54,896,000	—	—	0.25	0.35	1.00
1997Mo	178,807,000	—	—	0.25	0.35	1.00
1998Mo	223,847,000	—	—	0.25	0.35	1.00
1999Mo	233,753,000	—	—	0.25	0.35	1.00
2000Mo	223,973,000	—	—	0.25	0.35	1.00
2001Mo	234,360,000	—	—	0.25	0.35	0.40
2002Mo	229,256,000	—	—	0.25	0.35	0.40
2003Mo	149,518,000	—	—	0.25	0.35	0.40
2004Mo	174,351,000	—	—	0.25	0.35	0.40
2005Mo	204,426,000	—	—	0.25	0.35	0.40
2006Mo	234,263,000	—	—	0.25	0.35	0.40
2007Mo	234,301,000	—	—	0.25	0.35	0.40
2008Mo	214,303,000	—	—	0.25	0.35	0.40
2009Mo	41,167,000	—	—	0.25	0.35	0.40

KM# 549 50 CENTAVOS
4.3900 g., Aluminum-Bronze, 22 mm. **Obv:** National arms, eagle left **Rev:** Value and date within 1/2 designed wreath **Shape:** 12-sided **Mint:** Mexico City

Date	Mintage	F	VF	XF	Unc	BU
1992Mo	120,150,000	—	—	0.45	0.85	1.75
1993Mo	330,000,000	—	—	0.45	0.75	1.50
1994Mo	100,000,000	—	—	0.45	0.75	1.50
1995Mo	60,000,000	—	—	0.45	0.75	1.50
1995Mo Proof	6,981	Value: 5.00				
1996Mo	69,956,000	—	—	0.45	0.75	1.50
1997Mo	129,029,000	—	—	0.45	0.75	1.50
1998Mo	223,605,000	—	—	0.45	0.75	1.50
1999Mo	89,516,000	—	—	0.45	0.75	1.50
2000Mo	135,112,000	—	—	0.45	0.75	1.50
2001Mo	199,006,000	—	—	0.45	0.75	1.00
2002Mo	94,552,000	—	—	0.45	0.75	1.00
2003Mo	124,522,000	—	—	0.45	0.75	1.00
2004Mo	154,434,000	—	—	0.45	0.75	1.00
2005Mo	179,296,000	—	—	0.45	0.75	1.00
2006Mo	234,142,000	—	—	0.45	0.75	1.00
2007Mo	253,634,000	—	—	0.45	0.75	1.00
2008Mo	249,279,000	—	—	0.45	0.75	1.00
2009Mo	90,602,000	—	—	0.45	0.75	1.00

KM# 550 NUEVO PESO
3.9500 g., Bi-Metallic Aluminum-Bronze center in Stainless Steel ring, 21 mm. **Obv:** National arms, eagle left **Rev:** Value **Mint:** Mexico City

Date	Mintage	F	VF	XF	Unc	BU
1992Mo	144,000,000	—	—	0.60	1.50	2.75
1993Mo	329,860,000	—	—	0.60	1.50	2.75
1994Mo	221,000,000	—	—	0.60	1.50	2.75
1995Mo Small date	125,000,000	—	—	0.60	1.50	2.75
1995Mo Large date	Inc. above	—	—	0.60	1.50	2.75
1995Mo Proof	6,981	Value: 6.00				

KM# 603 PESO
3.9500 g., Bi-Metallic Aluminum-Bronze center in Stainless Steel ring, 21 mm. **Obv:** National arms, eagle left within circle **Rev:** Value and date within circle **Mint:** Mexico City **Note:** Similar to KM#550 but without N.

Date	Mintage	F	VF	XF	Unc	BU
1996Mo	169,510,000	—	—	—	1.25	2.25
1997Mo	222,870,000	—	—	—	1.25	2.25
1998Mo	261,942,000	—	—	—	1.25	2.25
1999Mo	99,168,000	—	—	—	1.25	2.25
2000Mo	158,379,000	—	—	—	1.25	2.25
2001Mo	208,576,000	—	—	—	1.25	2.75
2002Mo	119,514,000	—	—	—	1.25	2.75
2003Mo	169,320,000	—	—	—	1.25	2.75
2004Mo	208,611,000	—	—	—	1.25	2.75
2005Mo	253,923,000	—	—	—	1.25	2.75
2006Mo	289,834,000	—	—	—	1.25	2.75
2007Mo	368,408,000	—	—	—	1.25	2.75
2008Mo	393,878,000	—	—	—	1.25	2.75
2009Mo	239,229,000	—	—	—	1.25	2.75

KM# 551 2 NUEVO PESOS
5.1900 g., Bi-Metallic Aluminum-Bronze center in Stainless Steel ring, 23 mm. **Obv:** National arms, eagle left within circle **Rev:** Value and date within circle with assorted emblems around border **Mint:** Mexico City

Date	Mintage	F	VF	XF	Unc	BU
1992Mo	60,000,000	—	—	1.00	2.50	4.00
1993Mo	77,000,000	—	—	1.00	2.50	4.00
1994Mo	44,000,000	—	—	1.00	2.50	4.00
1995Mo	20,000,000	—	—	1.00	2.50	4.00
1995Mo Proof	6,981	Value: 6.00				

KM# 604 2 PESOS
5.1900 g., Bi-Metallic Aluminum-Bronze center in Stainless Steel ring, 23 mm. **Obv:** National arms, eagle left within circle **Rev:** Value and date within center circle of assorted emblems **Mint:** Mexico City **Note:** Similar to KM#551, but denomination without N.

Date	Mintage	F	VF	XF	Unc	BU
1996Mo	24,902,000	—	—	—	2.50	4.00
1997Mo	34,560,000	—	—	—	2.50	4.00
1998Mo	104,138,000	—	—	—	2.50	4.00
1999Mo	34,713,000	—	—	—	2.50	4.00
2000Mo	69,322,000	—	—	—	2.50	4.00
2001Mo	74,563,000	—	—	—	2.35	4.00
2002Mo	74,547,000	—	—	—	2.35	4.00
2003Mo	39,814,000	—	—	—	2.35	4.00
2004Mo	89,496,000	—	—	—	2.35	4.00
2005Mo	94,532,000	—	—	—	2.35	4.00
2006Mo	144,123,000	—	—	—	2.35	4.00
2007Mo	129,422,000	—	—	—	2.35	4.00
2008Mo	134,235,000	—	—	—	2.35	4.00
2009Mo	6,465,000	—	—	—	2.35	4.00

KM# 552 5 NUEVO PESOS
7.0700 g., Bi-Metallic Aluminum-Bronze center in Stainless Steel ring, 25.5 mm. **Obv:** National arms, eagle left within circle **Rev:** Value and date within circle with bow below **Mint:** Mexico City

Date	Mintage	F	VF	XF	Unc	BU
1992Mo	70,000,000	—	—	2.00	6.00	8.50
1993Mo	168,240,000	—	—	2.00	6.00	8.50
1994Mo	58,000,000	—	—	2.00	6.00	8.50
1995Mo Proof	6,981	Value: 25.00				

KM# 588 5 NUEVO PESOS
27.0000 g., 0.9250 Silver 0.8029 oz. ASW **Subject:** Environmental Protection **Obv:** National arms, eagle left within center of past and present arms **Rev:** Pacific Ridley Sea Turtle

Date	Mintage	F	VF	XF	Unc	BU
1994Mo Proof	20,000	Value: 50.00				

KM# 627 5 PESOS
31.1035 g., 0.9990 Silver 0.9990 oz. ASW **Subject:** World Wildlife Fund **Obv:** National arms, eagle left **Rev:** Wolf with pup

Date	Mintage	F	VF	XF	Unc	BU
1997	—	—	—	—	—	—
1998 Proof	13,004	Value: 95.00				

KM# 629 5 PESOS
27.0000 g., 0.9250 Silver 0.8029 oz. ASW **Subject:** Jarabe Tapatio **Obv:** National arms, eagle left within center of assorted arms **Rev:** Mexican dancers

Date	Mintage	F	VF	XF	Unc	BU
1997Mo Proof	20,000	Value: 350				
1998Mo Proof	—	Value: 350				

KM# 605 5 PESOS
7.0700 g., Bi-Metallic Aluminum-Bronze center in Stainless Steel ring, 25.5 mm. **Obv:** National arms, eagle left within circle **Rev:** Value within circle **Mint:** Mexico City **Note:** Similar to KM#552 but denomination without N.

Date	Mintage	F	VF	XF	Unc	BU
1997Mo	39,468,000	—	—	3.00	6.00	8.50
1998Mo	103,729,000	—	—	3.00	6.00	8.50
1999Mo	59,427,000	—	—	3.00	6.00	8.50
2000Mo	20,869,000	—	—	3.00	6.00	8.50
2001Mo	79,169,000	—	—	3.00	5.00	7.50
2002Mo	34,754,000	—	—	3.00	5.00	7.50
2003Mo	54,676,000	—	—	3.00	5.00	7.50
2004Mo	89,518,000	—	—	3.00	5.00	7.50
2005Mo	94,482,000	—	—	3.00	5.00	7.50
2006Mo	89,447,000	—	—	3.00	5.00	7.50
2007Mo	123,382,000	—	—	3.00	5.00	7.50
2008Mo	9,939,000	—	—	3.00	5.00	7.50
2009Mo	9,898,000	—	—	3.00	5.00	7.50

KM# 630   5 PESOS
31.1800 g., 0.9990 Silver 1.0014 oz. ASW **Subject:**
Millennium Series **Obv:** National arms, eagle left within center
of past and present arms **Rev:** Butterfly flanked by sprigs
above hands **Rev. Designer:** Francisco Ortega Romero

Date	Mintage	F	VF	XF	Unc	BU
1999-2000Mo Proof	47,435	Value: 60.00				

KM# 631   5 PESOS
31.1800 g., 0.9990 Silver 1.0014 oz. ASW **Subject:**
Millennium Series **Obv:** National arms, eagle left within center
of past and present arms **Rev:** Stylized dove as hand of peace
Rev. Designer: Omar Jiminez Torres

Date	Mintage	F	VF	XF	Unc	BU
1999-2000Mo Proof	47,389	Value: 55.00				

KM# 632   5 PESOS
31.1800 g., 0.9990 Silver 1.0014 oz. ASW **Subject:**
Millennium Series **Obv:** National arms, eagle left within center
of past and present arms **Rev:** Aztec bird design and value

Date	Mintage	F	VF	XF	Unc	BU
1999-2000Mo Proof	48,080	Value: 55.00				

KM# 635   5 PESOS
19.6000 g., 0.9250 Silver 0.5829 oz. ASW **Subject:**
Millennium Series **Obv:** National arms, eagle left **Rev:** Naval
training ship Cuauhtemoc sailing into world globe

Date	Mintage	F	VF	XF	Unc	BU
1999Mo Proof	15,504	Value: 45.00				

KM# 640   5 PESOS
31.1030 g., 0.9990 Silver 0.9989 oz. ASW, 40 mm. **Subject:**
UNICEF **Obv:** National arms, eagle left **Rev:** Two children
flying kite **Edge:** Reeded **Mint:** Mexico City

Date	Mintage	F	VF	XF	Unc	BU
1999Mo Proof	4,010	Value: 60.00				

KM# 652   5 PESOS
31.1710 g., 0.9990 Silver 1.0011 oz. ASW, 40 mm. **Series:**
Endangered Wildlife **Subject:** Aguila Real **Obv:** National
arms, eagle left within center of past and present arms **Rev:**
Golden Eagle on branch, value and date

Date	Mintage	F	VF	XF	Unc	BU
2000Mo	30,000	—	—	—	45.00	55.00

KM# 655 5 PESOS
31.1710 g., 0.9990 Silver 1.0011 oz. ASW, 40 mm. **Series:** Endangered Wildlife **Subject:** Cocodrilo de Rio **Obv:** National arms, eagle left within center of past and present arms **Rev:** American Crocodile, value and date

Date	Mintage	F	VF	XF	Unc	BU
2000Mo	30,000	—	—	—	45.00	55.00

KM# 656 5 PESOS
31.1710 g., 0.9990 Silver 1.0011 oz. ASW, 40 mm. **Series:** Endangered Wildlife **Subject:** Nutria de Rio **Obv:** National arms, eagle left within center of past and present arms **Rev:** Neotropical River Otter, value and date

Date	Mintage	F	VF	XF	Unc	BU
2000Mo	30,000	—	—	—	45.00	55.00

KM# 657 5 PESOS
31.1710 g., 0.9990 Silver 1.0011 oz. ASW, 40 mm. **Series:** Endangered Wildlife - Berrendo **Obv:** National arms, eagle left within center of past and present arms **Rev:** Peninsular Pronghorn, giant cardon cactus in back, value and date

Date	Mintage	F	VF	XF	Unc	BU
2000Mo	30,000	—	—	—	45.00	55.00

KM# 670 5 PESOS
27.0000 g., 0.9250 Silver 0.8029 oz. ASW, 40 mm. **Series:** Ibero-America **Obv:** National arms, eagle left within center of past and present arms **Rev:** Cowboy trick riding two horses **Edge:** Reeded **Mint:** Mexico City

Date	Mintage	F	VF	XF	Unc	BU
2000Mo Proof	—	Value: 85.00				

KM# 658 5 PESOS
31.1710 g., 0.9990 Silver 1.0011 oz. ASW, 40 mm. **Series:** Endangered Wildlife **Obv:** National arms in center of past and present arms **Rev:** Jaguar, value and date

Date	Mintage	F	VF	XF	Unc	BU
2001Mo	30,000	—	—	—	40.00	50.00

KM# 659 5 PESOS
31.1710 g., 0.9990 Silver 1.0011 oz. ASW, 40 mm. **Series:** Endangered Wildlife **Obv:** National arms in center of past and present arms **Rev:** Prairie dog, value and date

Date	Mintage	F	VF	XF	Unc	BU
2001Mo	30,000	—	—	—	40.00	50.00

KM# 660 5 PESOS
31.1710 g., 0.9990 Silver 1.0011 oz. ASW, 40 mm. **Series:** Endangered Wildlife **Obv:** National arms in center of past and present arms **Rev:** Volcano rabbit, value and date

Date	Mintage	F	VF	XF	Unc	BU
2001Mo	30,000	—	—	—	40.00	50.00

KM# 653 5 PESOS
31.1710 g., 0.9990 Silver 1.0011 oz. ASW, 40 mm. **Series:** Endangered Wildlife **Subject:** Aguila Arpia **Obv:** National arms in center of past and present arms **Rev:** Crowned Harpy Eagle perched on branch, value and date

Date	Mintage	F	VF	XF	Unc	BU
2001Mo	30,000	—	—	—	40.00	50.00

KM# 654 5 PESOS
31.1710 g., 0.9990 Silver 1.0011 oz. ASW, 40 mm. **Series:** Endangered Wildlife **Subject:** Oso Negro **Obv:** National arms in center of past and present arms **Rev:** Black bear, value and date

Date	Mintage	F	VF	XF	Unc	BU
2001Mo	30,000	—	—	—	40.00	50.00

KM# 651 5 PESOS
31.1710 g., 0.9990 Silver 1.0011 oz. ASW, 40 mm. **Series:** Endangered Wildlife **Obv:** National arms in center of past and present arms **Rev:** Manatee, value and date **Edge:** Reeded **Mint:** Mexico City

Date	Mintage	F	VF	XF	Unc	BU
2001Mo	30,000	—	—	—	40.00	50.00

KM# 678 5 PESOS
27.0000 g., 0.9250 Silver 0.8029 oz. ASW, 40 mm. **Subject:** Ibero-America: Acapulco Galleon **Obv:** National arms in center of past and present arms **Rev:** Spanish galleon with Pacific Ocean background and trading scene in foreground **Edge:** Reeded **Mint:** Mexico City

Date	Mintage	F	VF	XF	Unc	BU
2003Mo Proof	5,000	Value: 90.00				

KM# 765 5 PESOS
31.1035 g., 0.9250 Silver 0.9250 oz. ASW, 40 mm. **Subject:** Palacio de Bellas Artes **Obv:** Mexican Eagle and Snake **Rev:** Palace of Fine Arts **Edge:** Reeded **Mint:** Mexico City

Date	Mintage	F	VF	XF	Unc	BU
2005Mo Proof	—	Value: 90.00				

KM# 769 5 PESOS
15.5518 g., 0.9990 Silver 0.4995 oz. ASW, 33 mm. **Subject:** Monetary Reform of 1905 **Obv:** Mexican Eagle and Snake **Rev:** Cap and rays coin design **Mint:** Mexico City

Date	Mintage	F	VF	XF	Unc	BU
2005Mo Proof	1,505	Value: 45.00				

KM# 770 5 PESOS
31.1035 g., 0.9990 Silver 0.9990 oz. ASW, 40 mm. **Subject:** World Cup Soccer **Obv:** Mexican Eagle and Snake **Rev:** Mayan Pelota player and soccer ball **Mint:** Mexico City

Date	Mintage	F	VF	XF	Unc	BU
2006Mo Proof	40,000	Value: 65.00				

KM# 805 5 PESOS
31.1050 g., 0.9250 Silver 0.9250 oz. ASW **Obv:** Eagle on cactus **Rev:** Mayan ball game

Date	Mintage	F	VF	XF	Unc	BU
2006Mo Proof	—	Value: 75.00				

KM# 894 5 PESOS
7.0700 g., Bi-Metallic Aluminum-bronze center in stainless steel ring, 25.5 mm. **Subject:** Independence, 200th Anniversary **Obv:** National Arms - Eagle left **Rev:** Ignacio Rayon bust left **Mint:** Mexico City

Date	Mintage	F	VF	XF	Unc	BU
2008Mo	9,934,397	—	—	0.75	1.50	—
2008Mo Prooflike	4,267	—	—	—	—	7.50

KM# 895   5 PESOS
7.0700 g., Bi-Metallic Aluminum-bronze center in stainless
steel ring, 25.5 mm. **Subject:** Revolution 100th Anniversary
Obv: National Arms - Eagle left **Rev:** Alvaro Obregon bust 3/
4 facing left **Mint:** Mexico City

Date	Mintage	F	VF	XF	Unc	BU
2008Mo	9,948,722	—	—	0.75	1.50	—
2008Mo Prooflike	4,727	—	—	—	—	7.50

KM# 899   5 PESOS
7.0700 g., Bi-Metallic Aluminum-bronze center in stainless
steel ring, 25.5 mm. **Subject:** Revolution 100th Anniversary
Obv: National Arms - Eagle left **Rev:** Francisco Villa on
horseback left **Mint:** Mexico City

Date	Mintage	F	VF	XF	Unc	BU
2008Mo	—	—	—	0.75	1.50	—
2008Mo Prooflike	4,866	—	—	—	—	7.50

KM# 896   5 PESOS
7.0700 g., Bi-Metallic Aluninum-bronze in stainless steel ring,
25.5 mm. **Subject:** Independence 200th Anniversary **Obv:**
National Arms - Eagle left **Rev:** Carlos Maria de Bustamante
bust left **Mint:** Mexico City

Date	Mintage	F	VF	XF	Unc	BU
2008Mo	9,941,302	—	—	0.75	1.50	—
2008Mo Prooflike	4,852	—	—	—	—	7.50

KM# 900   5 PESOS
7.0700 g., Bi-Metallic Aluminum-Bronze center in Stainless
Steel ring, 25.5 mm. **Subject:** Independence 200th
Anniversary **Obv:** National Arms - Eagle left **Rev:** Francisco
Verdad y Rames bust right **Mint:** Mexico City

Date	Mintage	F	VF	XF	Unc	BU
2008Mo	9,937,000	—	—	0.75	1.50	—
2008Mo Prooflike	3,279	—	—	—	—	7.50

KM# 897   5 PESOS
7.0700 g., Bi-Metallic Aluminum-bronze center in stainless
steel ring, 25.5 mm. **Subject:** Revolution 100th Anniversary
Obv: National Arms - Eagle left **Rev:** Jose Vasconcelos bust
left **Mint:** Mexico City

Date	Mintage	F	VF	XF	Unc	BU
2008Mo	9,939,839	—	—	0.75	1.50	—
2008Mo Prooflike	4,767	—	—	—	—	7.50

KM# 901   5 PESOS
7.0700 g., Bi-Metallic Aluminum-Bronze center in Stainless
Steel ring, 25.5 mm. **Subject:** Revolution 100th Anniversary
Obv: National Arms - Eagle left **Rev:** Heriberto Jara bust 3/4
left **Mint:** Mexico City

Date	Mintage	F	VF	XF	Unc	BU
2008Mo	9,936,333	—	—	0.75	1.50	—
2008Mo Prooflike	4,870	—	—	—	—	7.50

KM# 898   5 PESOS
7.0700 g., Bi-Metallic Aluminum-bronze center in stainless
steel ring, 25.5 mm. **Subject:** Independence 200th
Anniversary **Obv:** National Arms - Eagle left **Rev:** Francisco
Mina bust 3/4 facing left **Mint:** Mexico City

Date	Mintage	F	VF	XF	Unc	BU
2008Mo	9,914,938	—	—	0.75	1.50	—
2008Mo Prooflike	4,523	—	—	—	—	7.50

KM# 902   5 PESOS
7.0700 g., Bi-Metallic Aluminum-Bronze center in Stainless
Steel ring, 25.5 mm. **Subject:** Independence 200th
Anniversary **Obv:** National Arms - Eagle left **Rev:** Mariano
Matamoros bust 3/4 facing right **Mint:** Mexico City

Date	Mintage	F	VF	XF	Unc	BU
2008Mo	9,947,802	—	—	0.75	1.50	—
2008Mo Prooflike	4,820	—	—	—	—	7.50

KM# 903 5 PESOS
7.0700 g., Bi-Metallic Aluminum-Bronze center Stainless Steel ring, 25.5 mm. **Subject:** Revolution 100th Anniversary **Obv:** National Arms - Eagle left **Rev:** Ricardo Magon bust right **Mint:** Mexico City

Date	Mintage	F	VF	XF	Unc	BU
2008Mo	9,940,278	—	—	0.75	1.50	—
2008Mo Prooflike	4,690	—	—	—	—	7.50

KM# 907 5 PESOS
7.0700 g., Bi-Metallic Aluminum-Bronze center in Stainless Steel ring., 25.5 mm. **Subject:** Revolution, 100th Anniversary **Obv:** National arms, eagle left **Rev:** Filomeno Mata facing. **Mint:** Mexico City

Date	Mintage	F	VF	XF	Unc	BU
2009Mo	9,935,689	—	—	0.75	1.50	—
2009Mo Prooflike	4,920	—	—	—	—	7.50

KM# 904 5 PESOS
7.0700 g., Bi-Metallic Aluminum-Bronze center in Stainless Steel ring, 25.5 mm. **Subject:** Independence 200th Anniversary **Obv:** National Arms - Eagle left **Rev:** Miguel Arizpe bust right **Mint:** Mexico City

Date	Mintage	F	VF	XF	Unc	BU
2008Mo	9,927,433	—	—	0.75	1.50	—
2008Mo Prooflike	4,863	—	—	—	—	7.50

KM# 908 5 PESOS
7.0700 g., Bi-Metallic Aluminum-Bronze cetner in Stainless Steel ring., 25.5 mm. **Obv:** National arms, eagle left. **Rev:** Jose Maria Cos bust right **Mint:** Mexico City

Date	Mintage	F	VF	XF	Unc	BU
2009Mo	9,935,040	—	—	0.75	1.50	—
2009Mo Prooflike	4,950	—	—	—	—	7.50

KM# 905 5 PESOS
7.0700 g., Bi-Metallic Aluminum-Bronze center in Stainless Steel ring, 25.5 mm. **Subject:** Revolution 100th Anniversary **Obv:** National arms, eagle left **Rev:** Francisco Mugica bust 3/4 facing left **Mint:** Mexico City

Date	Mintage	F	VF	XF	Unc	BU
2008Mo	9,926,537	—	—	0.75	1.50	—
2008Mo Prooflike	4,588	—	—	—	—	7.50

KM# 909 5 PESOS
7.0700 g., Bi-Metallic Aluminum-Bronze center in Stainless Steel ring, 25.5 mm. **Subject:** Revolution 100th Anniversary **Obv:** National Amrs, Eagle left **Rev:** Carmen Serdan bust facing **Mint:** Mexico City

Date	Mintage	F	VF	XF	Unc	BU
2009Mo	7,160,841	—	—	0.75	1.50	—
2009Mo Prooflike	4,787	—	—	—	—	7.50

KM# 906 5 PESOS
7.0700 g., Bi-Metallic Aluminum-Bronze center in Stainless Steel ring, 25.5 mm. **Subject:** Independence 200th Anniversary **Obv:** National Arms, eagle left **Rev:** Hermenegildo Galeana bust 3/4 facing left **Mint:** Mexico City

Date	Mintage	F	VF	XF	Unc	BU
2008Mo	9,935,901	—	—	0.75	1.50	—
2008Mo Prooflike	4,966	—	—	—	—	7.50

KM# 910 5 PESOS
7.0700 g., Bi-Metallic Aluminum-Bronze center in Stainless Steel ring, 25.5 mm. **Subject:** Independence, 200th Anniversary **Obv:** National arms, eagle left **Rev:** Pedro Moreno bust 3/4 right **Mint:** Mexico City

Date	Mintage	F	VF	XF	Unc	BU
2009Mo	6,942,480	—	—	0.75	1.50	—
2009Mo Prooflike	4,940	—	—	—	—	7.50

KM# 911   5 PESOS
7.0700 g., Bi-Metallic Aluminum-Bronze center in Stainless Steel ring, 25.5 mm. **Subject:** Revolution 100th Anniversary **Obv:** National arms, eagle left **Rev:** Andres Enriquezs bust 3/4 right **Mint:** Mexico City

Date	Mintage	F	VF	XF	Unc	BU
2009Mo	6,942,763	—	—	0.75	1.50	—
2009Mo Prooflike	4,666	—	—	—	—	7.50

KM# 912   5 PESOS
7.0700 g., Bi-Metallic Aluminum-Bronze center in Stainless Steel ring, 25.5 mm. **Subject:** Independence, 200th Anniversary **Obv:** National arms, eagle left **Rev:** Agustin de Iturbide bust left **Mint:** Mexico City

Date	Mintage	F	VF	XF	Unc	BU
2009Mo	6,944,222	—	—	0.75	1.50	—
2009Mo Prooflike	4,838	—	—	—	—	7.50

KM# 913   5 PESOS
7.0700 g., Bi-Metallic Aluminumn-Bronze center in Stainless Steel ring, 25.5 mm. **Subject:** Revolution 100th Anniversary **Obv:** National Arms, eagle left **Rev:** Luis Cabrera bust 3/4 facing left **Mint:** Mexico City

Date	Mintage	F	VF	XF	Unc	BU
2009Mo	—	—	—	0.75	1.50	—
2009Mo Prooflike	4,656	—	—	—	—	7.50

KM# 914   5 PESOS
7.0700 g., Bi-Metallic Aluminum-Bronze center Stainless Steel ring, 25.5 mm. **Subject:** Independence, 200th Anniversary **Obv:** National Arms, Eagle left **Rev:** Nicolas Bravo bust 3/4 facing left **Mint:** Mexico City

Date	Mintage	F	VF	XF	Unc	BU
2009Mo	—	—	—	0.75	0.50	—
2009Mo Prooflike	4,780	—	—	—	—	7.50

KM# 915   5 PESOS
7.0700 g., Bi-Metallic Aluminum-bronze center in Stainless steel ring, 25.5 mm. **Subject:** Revolution 100th Anniversary **Obv:** National Arms, eagle left **Rev:** Eulalio Gutierrez bust 3/4 right **Mint:** Mexico City

Date	Mintage	F	VF	XF	Unc	BU
2009Mo	6,908,760	—	—	0.75	1.50	—
2009Mo Prooflike	4,862	—	—	—	—	7.50

KM# 916   5 PESOS
7.0700 g., Bi-Metallic Aluminum-Bronze center in Stainless Steel ring, 25.5 mm. **Subject:** Independence 200th Anniversary **Obv:** National Arms, eagle left **Rev:** Servando de Mier bust left **Mint:** Mexico City

Date	Mintage	F	VF	XF	Unc	BU
2009Mo	6,937,421	—	—	0.75	1.50	—
2009Mo Prooflike	4,675	—	—	—	—	7.50

KM# 917   5 PESOS
7.0700 g., Bi-Metallic Aluminum-Bronze center in Stainless Steel ring, 25.5 mm. **Subject:** Revolution 100th Anniversary **Obv:** National Arms, eagle left **Rev:** Otilio Montano bust left **Mint:** Mexico City

Date	Mintage	F	VF	XF	Unc	BU
2009Mo	6,890,052	—	—	0.75	1.50	—
2009Mo Prooflike	4,923	—	—	—	—	7.50

KM# 918   5 PESOS
7.0700 g., Bi-Metallic Aluminum-Bronze center in Stainless Steel ring, 25.5 mm. **Series:** Revolution 100th Anniversary **Obv:** National Arms, eagle left **Rev:** Belisario Dominquez bust 3/4 left **Mint:** Mexico City

Date	Mintage	F	VF	XF	Unc	BU
2009Mo	6,926,606	—	—	0.75	1.50	—
2009Mo Prooflike	4,773	—	—	—	—	7.50

KM# 919   5 PESOS
7.0700 g., Bi-Metallic Aluminum-Bronze center in Stainless Steel ring, 25.5 mm. **Subject:** Independence 200th Anniversary **Obv:** National Arms, eagle left **Rev:** Leona Vicario bust left **Mint:** Mexico City

Date	Mintage	F	VF	XF	Unc	BU
2009Mo	6,937,872	—	—	0.75	1.50	—
2009Mo Prooflike	4,730	—	—	—	—	7.50

KM# 553 10 NUEVO PESOS
11.1800 g., Bi-Metallic 0.925 Silver center, .1667 oz. ASW within Aluminum-Bronze ring, 28 mm. **Obv:** National arms **Obv. Legend:** Estados Unidos Mexicanos **Rev:** Assorted shields within circle **Edge:** Groved **Mint:** Mexico City

Date	Mintage	F	VF	XF	Unc	BU
1992Mo	20,000,000	—	—	6.00	10.00	14.00
1993Mo	47,981,000	—	—	6.00	10.00	14.00
1994Mo	15,000,000	—	—	6.00	10.00	14.00
1995Mo	15,000,000	—	—	6.00	10.00	14.00
1995Mo Proof	6,981	Value: 20.00				

KM# 616 10 PESOS
10.3300 g., Bi-Metallic Copper-Nickel-Zinc center in Aluminum-Bronze ring, 28 mm. **Obv:** National arms **Obv. Legend:** ESTADOS UNIDOS MEXICANOS **Rev:** Aztec design **Mint:** Mexico City

Date	Mintage	F	VF	XF	Unc	BU
1997Mo	44,837,000	—	—	5.00	8.00	12.00
1998Mo	203,735,000	—	—	5.00	8.00	12.00
1999Mo	29,842,000	—	—	5.00	8.00	12.00
2002Mo	44,721,000	—	—	5.00	8.00	12.00
2004Mo	74,739,000	—	—	5.00	8.00	12.00
2005Mo	64,635,000	—	—	5.00	8.00	12.00
2006Mo	84,575,000	—	—	5.00	8.00	12.00
2007Mo	89,678,000	—	—	5.00	8.00	12.00
2008Mo	24,896,000	—	—	5.00	8.00	12.00
2009Mo	—	—	—	5.00	8.00	12.00

KM# 633 10 PESOS
62.0300 g., 0.9990 Silver 1.9922 oz. ASW **Subject:** Millennium Series **Obv:** National arms, eagle left within center of past and present arms **Rev:** Ancient and modern buildings within circle

Date	Mintage	F	VF	XF	Unc	BU
1999-2000Mo Proof	47,641	Value: 75.00				

KM# 636 10 PESOS
10.3300 g., Bi-Metallic Copper-Nickel-Zinc center in Aluminum-Bronze ring, 28 mm. **Series:** Millennium **Obv:** National arms **Obv. Legend:** ESTADOS UNIDOS MEXICANOS **Rev:** Aztec carving **Edge Lettering:** ANO (year) repeated 3 times **Mint:** Mexico City

Date	Mintage	F	VF	XF	Unc	BU
2000Mo	24,839,000	—	—	5.00	8.00	12.00
2001Mo	44,768,000	—	—	5.00	7.50	10.00

KM# 679 10 PESOS
31.1040 g., 0.9990 Silver 0.9990 oz. ASW, 39.9 mm. **Series:** First **Subject:** 180th Anniversary of Federation **Obv:** National arms **Obv. Legend:** ESTADOS UNIDOS MEXICANOS **Rev:** State Arms **Rev. Legend:** ESTADO DE ZACATECAS **Edge:** Reeded **Mint:** Mexico City

Date	Mintage	F	VF	XF	Unc	BU
2003Mo Proof	10,000	Value: 70.00				

KM# 680 10 PESOS
31.1040 g., 0.9990 Silver 0.9990 oz. ASW, 39.9 mm. **Series:** First **Subject:** 180th Anniversary of Federation **Obv:** National arms **Obv. Legend:** ESTADO UNIDOS MEXICANOS **Rev:** State arms **Rev. Legend:** ESTADO DE YUCATÁN **Edge:** Reeded **Mint:** Mexico City

Date	Mintage	F	VF	XF	Unc	BU
2003Mo Proof	10,000	Value: 70.00				

ESTADOS UNIDOS MEXICANOS

KM# 681   10 PESOS
31.1040 g., 0.9990 Silver 0.9990 oz. ASW, 39.9 mm. **Series:**
First **Subject:** 180th Anniversary of Federation **Obv:** National
arms **Obv. Legend:** ESTADOS UNIDOS MEXICANOS **Rev:**
State arms **Rev. Legend:** ESTADO DE VERACRUZ-LLAVE
Edge: Reeded **Mint:** Mexico City

Date	Mintage	F	VF	XF	Unc	BU
2003Mo Proof	10,000	Value: 70.00				

KM# 684   10 PESOS
31.1040 g., 0.9990 Silver 0.9990 oz. ASW, 39.9 mm. **Series:**
First **Subject:** 180th Anniversary of Federation **Obv:** National
arms **Obv. Legend:** ESTADOS UNIDOS DE MEXICANOS
Rev: State arms **Rev. Legend:** ESTADO DE TABASCO
Edge: Reeded **Mint:** Mexico City

Date	Mintage	F	VF	XF	Unc	BU
2004Mo Proof	10,000	Value: 70.00				

KM# 682   10 PESOS
31.1040 g., 0.9990 Silver 0.9990 oz. ASW, 39.9 mm. **Series:**
First **Subject:** 180th Anniversary of Frederation **Obv:**
National arms **Obv. Legend:** ESTADOS UNIDOS
MEXICANOS **Rev:** State arms **Rev. Legend:** ESTADO DE
TLAXCALA **Edge:** Reeded **Mint:** Mexico City

Date	Mintage	F	VF	XF	Unc	BU
2003Mo Proof	10,000	Value: 70.00				

KM# 685   10 PESOS
31.1040 g., 0.9990 Silver 0.9990 oz. ASW, 39.9 mm. **Series:**
First **Subject:** 180th Anniversary of Federation **Obv:** National
arms **Obv. Legend:** ESTADOS UNIDOS MEXICANOS **Rev:**
State arms **Rev. Legend:** ESTADO DE SONORA **Edge:**
Reeded **Mint:** Mexico City **Note:** Mexican States: Sonora

Date	Mintage	F	VF	XF	Unc	BU
2004Mo Proof	10,000	Value: 70.00				

KM# 683   10 PESOS
31.1040 g., 0.9990 Silver 0.9990 oz. ASW, 39.9 mm. **Series:**
First **Subject:** 180th Anniversary of Federation **Obv:** National
arms **Obv. Legend:** ESTADOS UNIDOS MEXICANOS **Rev:**
State arms **Rev. Legend:** ESTADO DE TAMAULIPAS **Edge:**
Reeded **Mint:** Mexico City

Date	Mintage	F	VF	XF	Unc	BU
2004Mo Proof	10,000	Value: 70.00				

KM# 686   10 PESOS
31.1040 g., 0.9990 Silver 0.9990 oz. ASW, 39.9 mm. **Series:**
First **Subject:** 180th Anniversary of Federation **Obv:** National
arms **Obv. Legend:** ESTADOS UNIDOS MEXICANOS
Rev: State arms **Rev. Legend:** ESTADO DE SINALOA **Edge:**
Reeded **Mint:** Mexico City **Note:** Mexican States: Sinaloa

Date	Mintage	F	VF	XF	Unc	BU
2004Mo Proof	10,000	Value: 70.00				

KM# 687   10 PESOS
31.1040 g., 0.9990 Silver 0.9990 oz. ASW, 39.9 mm. **Series:**
First **Subject:** 180th Anniversary of Federation **Obv:** National
arms **Obv. Legend:** ESTADOS UNIDOS MEXICANOS **Rev:**
State arms **Rev. Legend:** ESTADO DE SAN LUIS POTOSÍ
Edge: Reeded **Mint:** Mexico City

Date	Mintage	F	VF	XF	Unc	BU
2004Mo Proof	10,000	Value: 70.00				

KM# 737   10 PESOS
31.1040 g., 0.9990 Silver 0.9990 oz. ASW, 39.9 mm. **Series:**
First **Subject:** 180th Anniversary of Federation **Obv:** National
arms **Obv. Legend:** ESTADOS UNIDOS MEXICANOS **Rev:**
State arms **Rev. Legend:** ESTADO DE PUEBLA **Edge:**
Reeded **Mint:** Mexico City

Date	Mintage	F	VF	XF	Unc	BU
2004Mo Proof	10,000	Value: 70.00				

KM# 735   10 PESOS
31.1040 g., 0.9990 Silver 0.9990 oz. ASW, 39.9 mm. **Series:**
First **Subject:** 180th Anniversary of Federation **Obv:** National
arms **Obv. Legend:** ESTADOS UNIDOS MEXICANOS **Rev:**
State arms **Rev. Legend:** ESTADO DE QUINTANA ROO

Date	Mintage	F	VF	XF	Unc	BU
2004 Proof	10,000	Value: 70.00				

KM# 739   10 PESOS
31.1040 g., 0.9990 Bi-Metallic 0.9990 oz., 39.9 mm. **Series:**
First **Subject:** 180th Anniversary of Federation **Obv:** National
arms **Obv. Legend:** ESTADOS UNIDOS MEXICANOS **Rev:**
State arms **Rev. Legend:** ESTADO DE OAXACA **Edge:**
Reeded **Mint:** Mexico City

Date	Mintage	F	VF	XF	Unc	BU
2004Mo Proof	10,000	Value: 70.00				

KM# 733   10 PESOS
31.1040 g., 0.9990 Silver 0.9990 oz. ASW, 39.9 mm. **Series:**
First **Subject:** 180th Anniversary of Federation **Obv:** National
arms **Obv. Legend:** ESTADOS UNIDOS MEXICANOS **Rev:**
State arms **Rev. Legend:** ESTADO DE QUERÉTARO
ARTEAGA **Edge:** Reeded

Date	Mintage	F	VF	XF	Unc	BU
2004 Proof	10,000	Value: 70.00				

KM# 741   10 PESOS
31.1040 g., 0.9990 Silver 0.9990 oz. ASW, 39.9 mm. **Series:**
First **Subject:** 180th Anniversary of Federation **Obv:** National
arms **Obv. Legend:** ESTADOS UNIDOS MEXICANOS **Rev:**
State arms **Rev. Legend:** ESTADO DE NUEVO LEÓN **Edge:**
Reeded **Mint:** Mexico City

Date	Mintage	F	VF	XF	Unc	BU
2004Mo Proof	10,000	Value: 70.00				

ESTADOS UNIDOS MEXICANOS

KM# 743   10 PESOS
31.1040 g., 0.9990 Silver 0.9990 oz. ASW, 39.9 mm. **Series:**
First **Subject:** 180th Anniversary of Federation **Obv:** National
arms **Obv. Legend:** ESTADOS UNIDOS MEXICANOS **Rev:**
State arms **Rev. Legend:** ESTADO DE NAYARIT **Edge:**
Reeded **Mint:** Mexico City

Date	Mintage	F	VF	XF	Unc	BU
2004Mo Proof	10,000	Value: 70.00				

KM# 745   10 PESOS
31.1040 g., 0.9990 Silver 0.9990 oz. ASW, 39.9 mm. **Series:**
First **Subject:** 180th Anniversary of Federation **Obv:** National
arms **Obv. Legend:** ESTADOS UNIDOS MEXICANOS **Rev:**
State arms **Rev. Legend:** ESTADO DE MORELOS **Edge:**
Reeded **Mint:** Mexico City

Date	Mintage	F	VF	XF	Unc	BU
2004Mo Proof	10,000	Value: 70.00				

KM# 796   10 PESOS
31.1040 g., 0.9990 Silver 0.9990 oz. ASW, 39.9 mm. **Series:**
First **Subject:** 180th Anniversary of Federation **Obv:** National
arms **Obv. Legend:** ESTADOS UNIDOS MEXICANOS **Rev:**
State arms **Rev. Legend:** ESTADO DE MICHOACÁN DE
OCAMPO **Edge:** Reeded **Mint:** Mexico City

Date	Mintage	F	VF	XF	Unc	BU
2004Mo Proof	10,000	Value: 70.00				

KM# 747   10 PESOS
31.1040 g., 0.9990 Silver 0.9990 oz. ASW, 39.9 mm. **Series:**
First **Subject:** 180th Anniversary of Federation **Obv:** National
arms **Obv. Legend:** ESTADOS UNIDOS MEXICANOS **Rev:**
State arms **Rev. Legend:** ESTADO DE MÉXICO **Edge:**
Reeded **Mint:** Mexico City

Date	Mintage	F	VF	XF	Unc	BU
2004Mo Proof	10,000	Value: 70.00				

KM# 749   10 PESOS
31.1040 g., 0.9990 Silver 0.9990 oz. ASW, 39.9 mm. **Series:**
First **Subject:** 180th Anniversary of Federation **Obv:** National
arms **Obv. Legend:** ESTADOS UNIDOS MEXICANOS **Rev:**
State arms **Rev. Legend:** ESTADO DE JALISCO **Edge:**
Reeded **Mint:** Mexico City

Date	Mintage	F	VF	XF	Unc	BU
2004Mo Proof	10,000	Value: 70.00				

KM# 766   10 PESOS
31.1035 g., 0.9990 Silver 0.9990 oz. ASW, 40 mm. **Subject:**
Cervantes Festival **Obv:** Mexican Eagle and Snake **Rev:** Don
Quixote **Edge:** Reeded **Mint:** Mexico City

Date	Mintage	F	VF	XF	Unc	BU
2005Mo Proof	1,205	Value: 75.00				

KM# 768   10 PESOS
31.1035 g., 0.9990 Silver 0.9990 oz. ASW, 40 mm. **Subject:**
470th Anniversary - Mexico City Mint **Obv:** Mexican Eagle
and Snake **Rev:** Antique coin press **Mint:** Mexico City

Date	Mintage	F	VF	XF	Unc	BU
2005Mo Proof	2,005	Value: 65.00				

KM# 711   10 PESOS
31.1040 g., 0.9990 Silver 0.9990 oz. ASW, 39.9 mm. **Series:**

First **Subject:** 180th Anniversary of Federation **Obv:** National arms **Obv. Legend:** ESTADOS UNIDOS MEXICANOS **Rev:** State arms **Rev. Legend:** ESTADO DE HIDALGO **Edge:** Reeded **Mint:** Mexico City

Date	Mintage	F	VF	XF	Unc	BU
2005Mo Proof	10,000	Value: 70.00				

KM# 710 10 PESOS
31.1040 g., 0.9990 Silver 0.9990 oz. ASW, 39.9 mm. **Series:** First **Subject:** 180th Anniversary of Federation **Obv:** National arms **Obv. Legend:** ESTADOS UNIDOS MEXICANOS **Rev:** State arms **Rev. Legend:** ESTADO DE GUERRERO **Edge:** Reeded **Mint:** Mexico City

Date	Mintage	F	VF	XF	Unc	BU
2005Mo Proof	10,000	Value: 70.00				

KM# 709 10 PESOS
31.1040 g., 0.9990 Silver 0.9990 oz. ASW, 39.9 mm. **Series:** First **Subject:** 180th Anniversary of Federation **Obv:** National arms **Obv. Legend:** ESTADOS UNIDOS MEXICANOS **Rev:** State arms **Rev. Legend:** ESTADO DE GUANAJUATO **Edge:** Reeded **Mint:** Mexico City

Date	Mintage	F	VF	XF	Unc	BU
2005Mo Proof	10,000	Value: 70.00				

KM# 708 10 PESOS
31.1040 g., 0.9990 Silver 0.9990 oz. ASW, 39.9 mm. **Series:** First **Subject:** 180th Anniversary of Federation **Obv:** National arms **Obv. Legend:** ESTADOS UNIDOS MEXICANOS **Rev:** State arms **Rev. Legend:** ESTADO DE DURANGO **Edge:** Reeded **Mint:** Mexico City

Date	Mintage	F	VF	XF	Unc	BU
2005Mo Proof	10,000	Value: 70.00				

KM# 707 10 PESOS
31.1040 g., 0.9990 Silver 0.9990 oz. ASW, 39.9 mm. **Series:** First **Subject:** 180th Anniversary of Federation **Obv:** National arms **Obv. Legend:** ESTADOS UNIDOS MEXICANOS **Rev:** Federal District arms **Rev. Legend:** DISTRITO FEDERAL **Edge:** Reeded **Mint:** Mexico City

Date	Mintage	F	VF	XF	Unc	BU
2005Mo Proof	10,000	Value: 70.00				

KM# 753 10 PESOS
31.1040 g., 0.9990 Silver 0.9990 oz. ASW, 39.9 mm. **Series:** First **Subject:** 180th Anniversary of Federation **Obv:** National arms **Obv. Legend:** ESTADOS UNIDOS MEXICANOS **Rev:** State arms **Rev. Legend:** ESTADO DE CHIHUAHUA **Edge:** Reeded **Mint:** Mexico City

Date	Mintage	F	VF	XF	Unc	BU
2005Mo Proof	10,000	Value: 70.00				

KM# 706 10 PESOS
31.1040 g., 0.9990 Silver 0.9990 oz. ASW, 39.9 mm. **Series:** First **Subject:** 180th Anniversary of Federation **Obv:** National arms **Obv. Legend:** ESTADOS UNIDOS MEXICANOS **Rev:** State arms **Rev. Legend:** ESTADO DE CHIAPAS **Edge:** Reeded **Mint:** Mexico City

Date	Mintage	F	VF	XF	Unc	BU
2005Mo Proof	10,000	Value: 70.00				

KM# 728   10 PESOS
31.1040 g., 0.9990 Silver 0.9990 oz. ASW, 39.9 mm. **Series:**
First **Subject:** 180th Anniversary of Federation **Obv:** National
arms **Obv. Legend:** ESTADOS UNIDOS MEXICANOS **Rev:**
State arms **Rev. Legend:** ESTADO DE COLIMA **Edge:**
Reeded **Mint:** Mexico City

Date	Mintage	F	VF	XF	Unc	BU
2005Mo Proof	10,000	Value: 70.00				

KM# 724   10 PESOS
31.1040 g., 0.9990 Silver 0.9990 oz. ASW, 39.9 mm. **Series:**
First **Subject:** 180th Anniversary of Federation **Obv:** National
arms **Obv. Legend:** ESTADOS UNIDOS MEXICANOS **Rev:**
State arms **Rev. Legend:** ESTADO DE BAJA CALIFORNIA
SUR **Edge:** Reeded **Mint:** Mexico City

Date	Mintage	F	VF	XF	Unc	BU
2005Mo Proof	10,000	Value: 70.00				

KM# 751   10 PESOS
31.1040 g., 0.9990 Silver 0.9990 oz. ASW, 39.9 mm. **Series:**
First **Subject:** 180th Anniversary of Federation **Obv:** National
arms **Obv. Legend:** ESTADOS UNIDOS MEXICANOS **Rev:**
State arms **Rev. Legend:** ESTADO DE COAHUILA DE
ZARAGOZA **Edge:** Reeded **Mint:** Mexico City

Date	Mintage	F	VF	XF	Unc	BU
2005Mo Proof	10,000	Value: 70.00				

KM# 722   10 PESOS
31.1040 g., 0.9990 Silver 0.9990 oz. ASW, 39.9 mm. **Series:**
First **Subject:** 180th Anniversary of Federation **Obv:** National
arms **Obv. Legend:** ESTADOS UNIDOS MEXICANOS **Rev:**
State arms **Rev. Legend:** ESTADO DE BAJA CALIFORNIA
Edge: Reeded **Mint:** Mexico City

Date	Mintage	F	VF	XF	Unc	BU
2005Mo Proof	10,000	Value: 70.00				

KM# 726   10 PESOS
31.1040 g., 0.9990 Silver 0.9990 oz. ASW, 39.9 mm. **Series:**
First **Subject:** 180th Anniversary of Federation **Obv:** National
arms **Obv. Legend:** ESTADOS UNIDOS MEXICANOS **Rev:**
State arms **Rev. Legend:** ESTADO DE CAMPECHE **Edge:**
Reeded **Mint:** Mexico City

Date	Mintage	F	VF	XF	Unc	BU
2005Mo Proof	10,000	Value: 70.00				

KM# 720   10 PESOS
31.1040 g., 0.9990 Silver 0.9990 oz. ASW, 39.9 mm. **Series:**
First **Subject:** 180th Anniversary of Federation **Obv:** National
arms **Obv. Legend:** ESTADOS UNIDOS MEXICANOS **Rev:**
State arms **Rev. Legend:** ESTADO DE AGUASCALIENTES
Edge: Reeded **Mint:** Mexico City

Date	Mintage	F	VF	XF	Unc	BU
2005Mo Proof	10,000	Value: 70.00				

KM# 718   10 PESOS
31.1040 g., 0.9990 Silver 0.9990 oz. ASW, 40 mm. **Series:**
Second **Obv:** National arms **Obv. Legend:** ESTADOS
UNIDOS MEXICANOS **Rev:** Facade of the San Marcos
garden above sculpture of national emblem at left, San
Antonio Temple at right **Rev. Legend:** AGUASCALIENTES
Edge: Reeded **Mint:** Mexico City

Date	Mintage	F	VF	XF	Unc	BU
2005Mo Proof	6,000	Value: 65.00				

KM# 757   10 PESOS
31.1040 g., 0.9990 Silver 0.9990 oz. ASW, 40 mm. **Series:**
Second **Obv:** National arms **Obv. Legend:** ESTADOS
UNIDOS MEXICANOS **Rev:** Rams head, mountain outline in
background **Rev. Legend:** BAJA CALIFORNIA - GOBIERNO
DEL ESTADO **Edge:** Reeded **Mint:** Mexico City

Date	Mintage	F	VF	XF	Unc	BU
2005Mo Proof	6,000	Value: 65.00				

KM# 755   10 PESOS
31.1040 g., 0.9990 Silver 0.9990 oz. ASW, 40 mm. **Obv:**
National arms **Rev:** Baja California del Norte arms

Date	Mintage	F	VF	XF	Unc	BU
2005Mo Proof	—	Value: 75.00				

KM# 763   10 PESOS
31.1040 g., 0.9990 Silver 0.9990 oz. ASW, 40 mm. **Obv:**
National arms **Rev:** Benito Juarez **Edge:** Reeded **Mint:**
Mexico City

Date	Mintage	F	VF	XF	Unc	BU
2006Mo Proof	—	Value: 75.00				

KM# 761   10 PESOS
31.1040 g., 0.9990 Silver 0.9990 oz. ASW, 40 mm. **Series:**

Second **Obv:** National arms **Obv. Legend:** ESTADOS
UNIDOS MEXICANOS **Rev:** Outlined map of peninsula at
center, cave painting of deer behind, cactus at right **Rev.
Legend:** ESTADO DE BAJA CALIFORNIA SUR **Edge:**
Reeded **Mint:** Mexico City

Date	Mintage	F	VF	XF	Unc	BU
2006Mo Proof	6,000	Value: 65.00				

KM# 759   10 PESOS
31.1040 g., 0.9990 Silver 0.9990 oz. ASW, 40 mm. **Series:**
Second **Obv:** National arms **Obv. Legend:** ESTADOS
UNIDOS MEXICANOS **Rev:** Jade mask - Calakmul,
Campeche **Rev. Legend:** ESTADO DE CAMPECHE **Edge:**
Reeded **Mint:** Mexico City

Date	Mintage	F	VF	XF	Unc	BU
2006Mo Proof	6,000	Value: 65.00				

KM# 780   10 PESOS
31.1040 g., 0.9990 Silver 0.9990 oz. ASW, 40 mm. **Series:**
Second **Obv:** National arms **Obv. Legend:** ESTADOS
UNIDOS MEXICANOS **Rev:** Outlined map with turtle, mine
cart above grapes at center, Friendship dam above Christ of
the Nodas at left, chimneys above crucibles and bell tower of
Santiago's cathedral at right **Rev. Inscription:** COAHUILA
DE ZARAGOZA **Edge:** Reeded **Mint:** Mexico City

Date	Mintage	F	VF	XF	Unc	BU
2006Mo Proof	6,000	Value: 65.00				

KM# 776   10 PESOS
31.1040 g., 0.9990 Silver 0.9990 oz. ASW, 40 mm. **Series:**
Second **Obv:** National arms **Obv. Legend:** ESTADOS
UNIDOS MEXICANOS **Rev:** State arms at lower center,
Nevado de Colima and Volcan de Fuego volcanos in

background **Rev. Legend:** *Colima* **Rev. Inscription:**
GENEROSO **Edge:** Reeded **Mint:** Mexico City

Date	Mintage	F	VF	XF	Unc	BU
2006Mo Proof	6,000	Value: 65.00				

KM# 772   10 PESOS
31.1040 g., 0.9990 Silver 0.9990 oz. ASW, 40 mm. **Series:**
Second **Obv:** National arms **Obv. Legend:** ESTADOS
UNIDOS MEXICANOS **Rev:** Head of Pakal, ancient Mayan
king, Palenque **Rev. Legend:** ESTADO DE CHIAPAS -
CABEZA MAYA DEL REY PAKAL, PALENQUE **Edge:**
Reeded **Mint:** Mexico City

Date	Mintage	F	VF	XF	Unc	BU
2006Mo Proof	6,000	Value: 65.00				

KM# 774   10 PESOS
31.1040 g., 0.9990 Silver 0.9990 oz. ASW, 40 mm. **Series:**
Second **Obv:** National arms **Obv. Legend:** ESTADOS
UNIDOS MEXICANOS **Rev:** Angel of Liberty **Rev. Legend:**
MEXICO - ANGEL DE LA LIBERTAD, CHIHUAHUA **Edge:**
Reeded **Mint:** Mexico City

Date	Mintage	F	VF	XF	Unc	BU
2006Mo Proof	6,000	Value: 65.00				

KM# 778   10 PESOS
31.1040 g., 0.9990 Silver 0.9990 oz. ASW, 40 mm. **Series:**
Second **Obv:** National arms **Obv. Legend:** ESTADOS
UNIDOS MEXICANOS **Rev:** National Palace **Rev. Legend:**
DISTRITO FEDERAL - ANTIGUO AYUNTAMIENTO **Edge:**
Reeded **Mint:** Mexico City

Date	Mintage	F	VF	XF	Unc	BU
2006Mo Proof	6,000	Value: 65.00				

KM# 786   10 PESOS
31.1040 g., 0.9990 Silver 0.9990 oz. ASW, 40 mm. **Series:**
Second **Obv:** National arms **Obv. Legend:** ESTADOS
UNIDOS MEXICANOS **Rev:** Tree **Rev. Legend:** PRIMERA
RESERVA NACIONAL FORESTAL - DURANGO **Edge:**
Reeded **Mint:** Mexico City

Date	Mintage	F	VF	XF	Unc	BU
2006Mo Proof	6,000	Value: 65.00				

KM# 788   10 PESOS
31.1040 g., 0.9990 Silver 0.9990 oz. ASW, 40 mm. **Series:**
Second **Obv:** National arms **Obv. Legend:** ESTADOS
UNIDOS MEXICANOS **Rev:** State arms at center, statue of
Miguel Hidalgo at left, monument to Pípila at lower right **Rev.**
Inscription: *Guanajuato* **Edge:** Reeded **Mint:** Mexico City

Date	Mintage	F	VF	XF	Unc	BU
2006Mo Proof	6,000	Value: 65.00				

KM# 790   10 PESOS
31.1040 g., 0.9990 Silver 0.9990 oz. ASW, 40 mm. **Series:**
Second **Obv:** National arms **Obv. Legend:** ESTADOS
UNIDOS MEXICANOS **Rev:** Stylized portrait of Vicente
Guerrero at left, church of Taxco at upper center, Acapulco's
la Quebrada with diver above Christmas Eve flower and mask
Rev. Legend: GUERRERO **Edge:** Reeded **Mint:** Mexico City

Date	Mintage	F	VF	XF	Unc	BU
2006Mo Proof	6,000	Value: 65.00				

KM# 792   10 PESOS
31.1040 g., 0.9990 Silver 0.9990 oz. ASW, 40 mm. **Series:**
Second **Obv:** National arms **Obv. Legend:** ESTADOS
UNIDOS MEXICANOS **Rev:** Monument of Pachuca Hidalgo
Rev. Inscription: *RELOJ/MONUMENTAL/DE/PACHUCA*

/ HIDALGO - La / Bella / Airosa **Edge:** Reeded **Mint:** Mexico
City

Date	Mintage	F	VF	XF	Unc	BU
2006Mo Proof	6,000	Value: 65.00				

KM# 794   10 PESOS
31.1040 g., 0.9990 Silver 0.9990 oz. ASW, 40 mm. **Series:**
Second **Obv:** National arms **Obv. Legend:** ESTADOS
UNIDOS MEXICANOS **Rev:** Hospicio Cabañas orphanage
Rev. Legend: ESTADO DE JALISCCO **Edge:** Reeded **Mint:**
Mexico City

Date	Mintage	F	VF	XF	Unc	BU
2006Mo Proof	6,000	Value: 65.00				

KM# 830   10 PESOS
31.1040 g., 0.9990 Silver 0.9990 oz. ASW, 40 mm. **Series:**
Second **Obv:** National arms **Obv. Legend:** ESTADOS
UNIDOS MEXICANOS **Rev:** Pyramid de la Loona (Moon)
Rev. Legend: ESTADO DE MÉXICO **Edge:** Reeded **Mint:**
Mexico City

Date	Mintage	F	VF	XF	Unc	BU
2006Mo Proof	6,000	Value: 65.00				

KM# 831   10 PESOS
31.1040 g., 0.9990 Silver 0.9990 oz. ASW, 40 mm. **Series:**
Second **Obv:** National arms **Obv. Legend:** ESTADOS
UNIDOS MEXICANOS **Rev:** Four Monarch butterflies **Rev.
Legend:** ESTADO DE MICHOACÁN **Edge:** Reeded **Mint:**
Mexico City

Date	Mintage	F	VF	XF	Unc	BU
2006Mo Proof	6,000	Value: 65.00				

KM# 832   10 PESOS
31.1040 g., 0.9990 Silver 0.9990 oz. ASW, 40 mm. **Series:**
Second **Obv:** National arms **Obv. Legend:** ESTADOS
UNIDOS MEXICANOS **Rev:** 1/2 length figure of Chinelo (local
dancer) at right, Palacio de Cortes in background **Rev.
Inscription:** ESTADO DE / MORELOS **Edge:** Reeded **Mint:**
Mexico City

Date	Mintage	F	VF	XF	Unc	BU
2006Mo Proof	6,000	Value: 65.00				

KM# 833   10 PESOS
31.1040 g., 0.9990 Silver 0.9990 oz. ASW, 40 mm. **Series:**
Second **Obv:** National arms **Obv. Legend:** ESTADOS
UNIDOS MEXICANOS **Rev:** Isle de Mexcaltitlán **Rev.
Legend:** ESTADO DE NAYARIT **Edge:** Reeded **Mint:**
Mexico City

Date	Mintage	F	VF	XF	Unc	BU
2007Mo Proof	6,000	Value: 65.00				

KM# 834   10 PESOS
31.1040 g., 0.9990 Silver 0.9990 oz. ASW, 40 mm. **Series:**
Second **Obv:** National arms **Obv. Legend:** ESTADOS
UNIDOS MEXICANOS **Rev:** Old foundry in Pargue Fundidora
(public park) at right, Cerro de la Silla (Saddle Hill) in
background **Rev. Legend:** ESTADO DE NUEVO LEÓN
Edge: Reeded **Mint:** Mexico City

Date	Mintage	F	VF	XF	Unc	BU
2007Mo Proof	6,000	Value: 65.00				

KM# 835   10 PESOS
31.1040 g., 0.9990 Silver 0.9990 oz. ASW, 40 mm. **Series:**
Second **Obv:** National arms **Obv. Legend:** ESTADOS
UNIDOS MEXICANOS **Rev:** Teatro Macedonio Alcala
(theater) **Rev. Legend:** OAXACA **Edge:** Reeded **Mint:**
Mexico City

Date	Mintage	F	VF	XF	Unc	BU
2007Mo Proof	6,000	Value: 65.00				

KM# 838   10 PESOS
31.1040 g., 0.9990 Silver 0.9990 oz. ASW, 40 mm. **Series:**
Second **Obv:** National arms **Obv. Legend:** ESTADOS
UNIDOS MEXICANOS **Rev:** Acqueduct of Querétaro at left,
church of Santa Rosa de Viterbo at right **Rev. Legend:**
ESTADO DE QUERÉTARO ARTEAGA **Edge:** Reeded **Mint:**
Mexico City

Date	Mintage	F	VF	XF	Unc	BU
2007Mo Proof	6,000	Value: 65.00				

KM# 836   10 PESOS
31.1040 g., 0.9990 Silver 0.9990 oz. ASW, 40 mm. **Series:**
Second **Obv:** National arms **Obv. Legend:** ESTADOS
UNIDOS MEXICANOS **Rev:** Talavera porcelain dish **Rev.
Legend:** ESTADO DE PUEBLA **Edge:** Reeded **Mint:** Mexico
City

Date	Mintage	F	VF	XF	Unc	BU
2007Mo Proof	6,000	Value: 65.00				

KM# 839   10 PESOS
31.1040 g., Silver, 40 mm. **Series:** Second **Obv:** National
arms **Obv. Legend:** ESTADOS UNIDOS MEXICANOS **Rev:**
Facade of Caja Real **Rev. Legend:** • SAN LUIS POTOSÍ •
Edge: Reeded **Mint:** Mexico City

Date	Mintage	F	VF	XF	Unc	BU
2007Mo Proof	6,000	Value: 65.00				

KM# 837   10 PESOS
31.1040 g., 0.9990 Silver 0.9990 oz. ASW, 40 mm. **Series:**
Second **Obv:** National arms **Obv. Legend:** ESTADOS
UNIDOS MEXICANOS **Rev:** Mask at left, rays above state
arms at center, Mayan ruins at right **Rev. Legend:** QUINTANA
ROO **Edge:** Reeded **Mint:** Mexico City

Date	Mintage	F	VF	XF	Unc	BU
2007Mo Proof	6,000	Value: 65.00				

KM# 840   10 PESOS
31.1040 g., 0.9990 Silver 0.9990 oz. ASW, 40 mm. **Series:**
Second **Obv:** National arms **Obv. Legend:** ESTADOS
UNIDOS MEXICANOS **Rev:** Shield on pile of cactus fruits
Rev. Legend: ESTADO DE SINALOA - LUGAR DE
PITAHAYAS **Edge:** Reeded **Mint:** Mexico City

Date	Mintage	F	VF	XF	Unc	BU
2007Mo Proof	6,000	Value: 65.00				

KM# 841 10 PESOS
31.1040 g., 0.9990 Silver 0.9990 oz. ASW, 40 mm. **Series:**
Second **Obv:** National arms **Obv. Legend:** ESTADOS
UNIDOS MEXICANOS **Rev:** Local in Dance of the Deer at
left, cactus at right, mountains in background **Rev. Legend:**
ESTADO DE SONORA **Edge:** Reeded **Mint:** Mexico City

Date	Mintage	F	VF	XF	Unc	BU
2007Mo Proof	6,000	Value: 65.00				

KM# 844 10 PESOS
31.1040 g., 0.9990 Silver 0.9990 oz. ASW, 40 mm. **Series:**
Second **Obv:** National arms **Obv. Legend:** ESTADOS
UNIDOS MEXICANOS **Rev:** Basilica de Ocotlán at left, state
arms above Capilla Abierta, Plaza de Toros Ranchero Aguilar
below, Exconvento de San Francisco at right **Rev. Legend:**
ESTADO DE TLAXCALA **Edge:** Reeded **Mint:** Mexico City

Date	Mintage	F	VF	XF	Unc	BU
2007Mo Proof	6,000	Value: 65.00				

KM# 842 10 PESOS
31.1040 g., 0.9990 Silver 0.9990 oz. ASW, 40 mm. **Series:**
Second **Obv:** National arms **Obv. Legend:** ESTADOS
UNIDOS MEXICANOS **Rev:** Fuente de los Pescadores
(fisherman fountain) at lower left, giant head from the Olmec-
pre-Hispanic culture at right, Planetario Tabasco in
background **Rev. Legend:** TABASCO **Edge:** Reeded **Mint:**
Mexico City

Date	Mintage	F	VF	XF	Unc	BU
2007Mo Proof	6,000	Value: 65.00				

KM# 845 10 PESOS
31.1040 g., 0.9990 Silver 0.9990 oz. ASW, 40 mm. **Series:**
Second **Obv:** National arms **Obv. Legend:** ESTADOS
UNIDOS MEXICANOS **Rev:** Pyramid of El Tajín **Rev.
Legend:** • VERACRUZ • - • DE IGNACIO DE LA LLAVE •
Edge: Reeded **Mint:** Mexico City

Date	Mintage	F	VF	XF	Unc	BU
2007Mo Proof	6,000	Value: 65.00				

KM# 843 10 PESOS
31.1040 g., 0.9990 Silver 0.9990 oz. ASW, 40 mm. **Series:**
Second **Obv:** National arms **Obv. Legend:** ESTADOS
UNIDOS MEXICANOS **Rev:** Ridge - Cerro Del Bernal,
Gonzáles **Rev. Legend:** TAMAULIPAS **Edge:** Reeded **Mint:**
Mexico City

Date	Mintage	F	VF	XF	Unc	BU
2007Mo Proof	6,000	Value: 65.00				

KM# 846 10 PESOS
31.1030 g., 0.9990 Silver 0.9989 oz. ASW, 40 mm. **Series:**
Second **Obv:** National arms **Obv. Legend:** ESTADOS
UNIDOS MEXICANOS **Rev:** Stylized pyramid of Chichén-Itzá
Rev. Legend: Castillo de Chichén Itzá **Rev. Inscription:**
YUCATÁN **Edge:** Reeded **Mint:** Mexico City

Date	Mintage	F	VF	XF	Unc	BU
2007Mo Proof	6,000	Value: 65.00				

KM# 847 10 PESOS
31.1040 g., 0.9990 Silver 0.9990 oz. ASW, 40 mm. **Series:**
Second **Obv:** National arms **Obv. Legend:** ESTADOS
UNIDOS MEXICANOS **Rev:** Cable car above Monumento al
Minero at left, Cathedral de Zacatecas at center right **Rev.**
Legend: Zacatecas **Edge:** Reeded **Mint:** Mexico City

Date	Mintage	F	VF	XF	Unc	BU
2007Mo Proof	6,000	Value: 65.00				

KM# 561 20 NUEVO PESOS
16.9200 g., Bi-Metallic 0.925 Silver 16.9g, (.2500 oz. ASW)
center within Aluminum-Bronze ring, 31.86 mm. **Obv:**
National arms **Obv. Legend:** ESTADOS UNIDOS
MEXICANOS **Rev:** Head of Hidalgo left within wreath **Edge:**
Reeded **Mint:** Mexico City

Date	Mintage	F	VF	XF	Unc	BU
1993Mo	25,000,000	—	—	8.00	12.00	15.00
1994Mo	5,000,000	—	—	8.00	12.00	15.00
1995Mo	5,000,000	—	—	8.00	12.00	15.00

KM# 641 20 PESOS
6.2210 g., 0.9990 Gold 0.1998 oz. AGW, 21.9 mm. **Subject:**
UNICEF **Obv:** National arms, eagle left **Rev:** Child playing
with lasso **Edge:** Reeded **Mint:** Mexico City

Date	Mintage	F	VF	XF	Unc	BU
1999Mo Proof	1,510	Value: 375				

KM# 637 20 PESOS
Bi-Metallic Copper-Nickel center within Brass ring, 32 mm.

Subject: Xiuhtecuhtli **Obv:** National arms, eagle left within
circle **Rev:** Aztec with torch within spiked circle

Date	Mintage	F	VF	XF	Unc	BU
2000Mo	14,850,000	—	—	—	15.00	18.50
2001Mo	2,478,000	—	—	—	16.00	18.00

KM# 638 20 PESOS
Bi-Metallic Copper-Nickel center within Brass ring, 32 mm.
Subject: Octavio Paz **Obv:** National arms, eagle left within
circle **Rev:** Head 1/4 right within circle

Date	Mintage	F	VF	XF	Unc	BU
2000Mo	14,943,000	—	—	—	15.00	18.50
2001Mo	2,515,000	—	—	—	16.00	18.50

KM# 704 20 PESOS
62.4000 g., 0.9990 Silver 2.0041 oz. ASW, 48.1 mm.
Subject: 400th Anniversary of Don Quijote de la Manchia
Obv: National arms **Rev:** Skeletal figure horseback with spear
galloping right **Edge:** Plain **Mint:** Mexico City

Date	Mintage	F	VF	XF	Unc	BU
ND(2005)Mo Proof	10,000	Value: 85.00				

KM# 767 20 PESOS
62.4000 g., 0.9990 Silver 2.0041 oz. ASW, 48 mm. **Subject:**
80th Anniversary - Bank of Mexico **Obv:** National arms **Rev:**
100 Peso banknote design of 1925 **Mint:** Mexico City

Date	Mintage	F	VF	XF	Unc	BU
2005Mo	—	—	—	—	—	70.00
2005Mo Proof	3,005	Value: 90.00				

KM# 571   50 NUEVO PESOS
34.1100 g., Bi-Metallic 0.925 Silver .5000 ASW center within Brass ring, 38.87 mm. **Subject:** Nino Heroes **Obv:** National arms **Obv. Legend:** ESTADOS UNIDOS MEXICANOS **Rev:** Six heads facing with date at upper right, all within circle and 1/2 wreath **Edge:** Reeded **Mint:** Mexico City

Date	Mintage	F	VF	XF	Unc	BU
1993Mo	2,000,000	—	—	—	25.00	32.50
1994Mo	1,500,000	—	—	—	25.00	32.50
1995Mo	1,500,000	—	—	—	25.00	32.50

KM# 688   100 PESOS
33.9400 g., Bi-Metallic .925 Silver 20.1753g center in Aluminum-Bronze ring, 39.04 mm. **Series:** First **Subject:** 180th Anniversary of Federation **Obv:** National arms **Obv. Legend:** ESTADOS UNIDOS MEXICANOS **Rev:** State arms **Rev. Legend:** ESTADO DE ZACATECAS **Edge:** Segmented reeding **Mint:** Mexico City

Date	Mintage	F	VF	XF	Unc	BU
2003Mo	244,900	—	—	—	40.00	50.00

KM# 696   100 PESOS
29.1690 g., Bi-Metallic .999 Gold 17.154g center in .999 Silver 12.015g ring, 34.5 mm. **Series:** First **Subject:** 180th Anniversary of Federation **Obv:** National arms **Obv. Legend:** ESTADOS UNIDOS MEXICANOS **Rev:** State arms **Rev. Legend:** ESTADO DE ZACATECAS **Edge:** Segmented reeding **Mint:** Mexico City

Date	Mintage	F	VF	XF	Unc	BU
2003Mo Proof	1,000	Value: 850				

KM# 689   100 PESOS
33.9400 g., Bi-Metallic .925 Silver 20.1753g center in Aluminum-Bronze ring, 39.04 mm. **Series:** First **Subject:** 180th Anniversary of Federation **Obv:** National arms **Obv. Legend:** ESTADOS UNIDOS MEXICANOS **Rev:** State arms **Rev. Legend:** ESTADO DE YUCATÁN **Edge:** Segmented reeding **Mint:** Mexico City

Date	Mintage	F	VF	XF	Unc	BU
2003Mo	235,763	—	—	—	40.00	50.00

KM# 697   100 PESOS
29.1690 g., Bi-Metallic .999 Gold 17.154g center in .999 Silver 12.015g ring, 34.5 mm. **Series:** First **Subject:** 180th Anniversary of Federation **Obv:** National arms **Obv. Legend:** ESTADOS UNIDOS MEXICANOS **Rev:** State arms **Rev. Legend:** ESTADO DE YUCATÁN **Edge:** Segmented reeding **Mint:** Mexico City

Date	Mintage	F	VF	XF	Unc	BU
2003Mo Proof	1,000	Value: 850				

KM# 690   100 PESOS
33.9400 g., Bi-Metallic .925 Silver 20.1753g center in Aluminum-Bronze ring, 39.04 mm. **Series:** First **Subject:** 180th Anniversary of Federation **Obv:** National arms **Obv. Legend:** ESTADOS UNIDOS MEXICANOS **Rev:** State arms **Rev. Legend:** ESTADO DE VERACRUZ-LLAVE **Edge:** Segmented reeding **Mint:** Mexico City

Date	Mintage	F	VF	XF	Unc	BU
2003Mo	248,810	—	—	—	40.00	50.00

KM# 698   100 PESOS
29.1690 g., Bi-Metallic .999 Gold 17.154g center in .999 Silver 12.015g ring, 34.5 mm. **Series:** First **Subject:** 180th Anniversary of Federation **Obv:** National arms **Obv. Legend:** ESTADOS UNIDOS MEXICANOS **Rev:** State arms **Rev. Legend:** ESTADO DE VERACRUZ-LLAVE **Edge:** Segmented reeding **Mint:** Mexico City

Date	Mintage	F	VF	XF	Unc	BU
2003Mo Proof	1,000	Value: 850				

KM# 691   100 PESOS
33.9400 g., Bi-Metallic .925 Silver 20.1753g center in Aluminum-Bronze ring, 39.9 mm. **Series:** First **Subject:** 180th Anniversary of Federation **Obv:** National arms **Obv. Legend:** ESTADOS UNIDOS MEXICANOS **Rev:** State arms **Rev. Legend:** ESTADO DE TLAXCALA **Edge:** Segmented reeding **Mint:** Mexico City

Date	Mintage	F	VF	XF	Unc	BU
2003Mo	248,976	—	—	—	35.00	40.00

KM# 699   100 PESOS
29.1690 g., Bi-Metallic .999 Gold 17.154g center in .999 Silver
12.015g ring, 34.5 mm. **Series:** First **Subject:** 180th
Anniversary of Federation **Obv:** National arms **Obv. Legend:**
ESTADOS UNIDOS MEXICANOS **Rev:** State arms **Rev.**
Legend: ESTADO DE TLAXCALA **Edge:** Segmented
reeding **Mint:** Mexico City

Date	Mintage	F	VF	XF	Unc	BU
2003Mo Proof	1,000	Value: 850				

KM# 692   100 PESOS
33.9400 g., Bi-Metallic .925 Silver 20.1753g center in
Aluminum-Bronze ring, 39.04 mm. **Series:** First **Subject:**
180th Anniversary of Federation **Obv:** National arms **Obv.**
Legend: ESTADOS UNIDOS MEXICANOS **Rev:** State arms
Rev. Legend: ESTADO DE TAMAULIPAS **Edge:**
Segmented reeding **Mint:** Mexico City

Date	Mintage	F	VF	XF	Unc	BU
2004Mo	249,398	—	—	—	35.00	40.00

KM# 700   100 PESOS
29.1690 g., Bi-Metallic .999 Gold 17.154g center in .999 Silver
12.015g ring, 34.5 mm. **Series:** First **Subject:** 180th
Anniversary of Federation **Obv:** National arms **Obv. Legend:**
ESTADOS UNIDOS MEXICANOS **Rev:** State arms **Rev.**
Legend: ESTADO DE TAMAULIPAS **Edge:** Segmented
reeding **Mint:** Mexico City

Date	Mintage	F	VF	XF	Unc	BU
2004Mo Proof	1,000	Value: 850				

KM# 694   100 PESOS
33.9400 g., Bi-Metallic .925 Silver 20.1753g center in
Aluminum-Bronze ring, 39.04 mm. **Series:** First **Subject:**
180th Anniversary of Federation **Obv:** National arms **Obv.**
Legend: ESTADOS UNIDOS MEXICANOS **Rev:** State arms
Rev. Legend: ESTADO DE SONORA **Edge:** Segmented
reeding **Mint:** Mexico City

Date	Mintage	F	VF	XF	Unc	BU
2004Mo	249,300	—	—	—	35.00	40.00

KM# 702   100 PESOS
29.1690 g., Bi-Metallic .999 Gold 17.154g center in .999 Silver
12.015g ring, 34.5 mm. **Series:** First **Subject:** 180th
Anniversary of Federation **Obv:** National arms **Obv. Legend:**
ESTADOS UNIDOS MEXICANOS **Rev:** State arms **Rev.**
Legend: ESTADO DE SONORA **Edge:** Segmented reeding
Mint: Mexico City

Date	Mintage	F	VF	XF	Unc	BU
2004Mo Proof	1,000	Value: 850				

KM# 693   100 PESOS
33.9400 g., Bi-Metallic .925 Silver 20.1753g center in
Aluminum-Bronze ring, 39.04 mm. **Series:** First **Subject:**
180th Anniversary of Federation **Obv:** National arms **Obv.**
Legend: ESTADOS UNIDOS MEXICANOS **Rev:** State arms
Rev. Legend: ESTADO DE TABASCO **Edge:** Segmented
reeding **Mint:** Mexico City

Date	Mintage	F	VF	XF	Unc	BU
2004Mo	249,318	—	—	—	35.00	40.00

KM# 701   100 PESOS
29.1690 g., Bi-Metallic .999 Gold 17.154g center in .999 Silver
12.015g ring, 34.5 mm. **Series:** First **Subject:** 180th
Anniversary of Federation **Obv:** National arms **Obv. Legend:**
ESTADOS UNIDOS MEXICANOS **Rev:** State arms **Rev.**
Legend: ESTADO DE TABASCO **Edge:** Segmented reeding
Mint: Mexico City

Date	Mintage	F	VF	XF	Unc	BU
2004Mo Proof	1,000	Value: 850				

KM# 695   100 PESOS
33.9400 g., Bi-Metallic .925 Silver 20.1753g center in
Aluminum-Bronze ring, 39.04 mm. **Series:** First **Subject:**
180th Anniversary of Federation **Obv:** National arms **Obv.**
Legend: ESTADOS UNIDOS MEXICANOS **Rev:** State arms
Rev. Legend: ESTADO DE SINALOA **Edge:** Segmented
reeding **Mint:** Mexico City

Date	Mintage	F	VF	XF	Unc	BU
2004Mo	244,722	—	—	—	35.00	40.00

KM# 703   100 PESOS
29.1690 g., Bi-Metallic .999 Gold 17.154g center in .999 Silver
12.015g ring, 34.5 mm. **Series:** First **Subject:** 180th
Anniversary of Federation **Obv:** National arms **Obv. Legend:**
ESTADOS UNIDOS MEXICANOS **Rev:** State arms **Rev.**
Legend: ESTADO DE SINALOA **Edge:** Segmented reeding
Mint: Mexico City

Date	Mintage	F	VF	XF	Unc	BU
2004Mo Proof	1,000	Value: 850				

KM# 803   100 PESOS
33.9400 g., Bi-Metallic .925 Silver 20.1753g center in
Aluminum-Bronze ring, 39.04 mm. **Series:** First **Subject:**
180th Anniversary of Federation **Obv:** National arms **Obv.**
Legend: ESTADOS UNIDOS MEXICANOS **Rev:** State arms
Rev. Legend: ESTADO DE SAN LUIS POTOSÍ **Edge:**
Segmented reeding **Mint:** Mexico City

Date	Mintage	F	VF	XF	Unc	BU
2004Mo	249,662	—	—	—	35.00	40.00

KM# 806   100 PESOS
29.1690 g., Bi-Metallic .999 Gold 17.154g center in .999 silver
12.015 ring, 34.5 mm. **Series:** First **Subject:** 180th
Anniversary of Federation **Obv:** National arms **Obv. Legend:**
ESTADOS UNIDOS MEXICANOS **Rev:** State arms **Rev.**
Legend: ESTADO DE SAN LUIS POTOSÍ **Edge:** Segmented
reeding **Mint:** Mexico City

Date	Mintage	F	VF	XF	Unc	BU
2004Mo Proof	1,000	Value: 850				

KM# 734   100 PESOS
33.9400 g., Bi-Metallic .925 Silver 20.1753g center in
Aluminum-Bronze ring, 39.04 mm. **Series:** First **Subject:**
180th Anniversary of Federation **Obv:** National arms **Obv.**
Legend: ESTADOS UNIDOS MEXICANOS **Rev:** State arms
Rev. Legend: ESTADO DE QUERÉTARO ARTEAGA **Edge:**
Segmented reeding **Mint:** Mexico City

Date	Mintage	F	VF	XF	Unc	BU
2004Mo	249,263	—	—	—	35.00	40.00

KM# 808   100 PESOS
29.1690 g., Bi-Metallic .999 Gold 17.154g center in .999 Silver
12.015g ring, 34.5 mm. **Series:** First **Subject:** 180th
Anniversary of Federation **Obv:** National arms **Obv. Legend:**
ESTADOS UNIDOS MEXICANOS **Rev:** State arms **Rev.**
Legend: ESTADO DE QUERÉTARO ARTEAGA **Edge:**
Segmented reeding **Mint:** Mexico City

Date	Mintage	F	VF	XF	Unc	BU
2004Mo Proof	1,000	Value: 850				

KM# 736   100 PESOS
33.9400 g., Bi-Metallic .925 Silver 20.1753g center in
Aluminum-Bronze ring, 39.04 mm. **Series:** First **Subject:**
180th Anniversary of Federation **Obv:** National arms **Obv.**
Legend: ESTADOS UNIDOS MEXICANOS **Rev:** State arms
Rev. Legend: ESTADO DE QUINTANA ROO **Edge:**
Segmented reeding **Mint:** Mexico City

Date	Mintage	F	VF	XF	Unc	BU
2004Mo	249,134	—	—	—	35.00	40.00

KM# 807   100 PESOS
29.1690 g., Bi-Metallic .999 Gold 17.154g center in .999 Silver
12.015g ring, 34.5 mm. **Series:** First **Subject:** 180th
Anniversary of Federation **Obv:** National arms **Obv. Legend:**
ESTADOS UNIDOS MEXICANOS **Rev:** State arms **Rev.**
Legend: ESTADO DE QUINTANA ROO **Edge:** Segmented
reeding **Mint:** Mexico City

Date	Mintage	F	VF	XF	Unc	BU
2004Mo Proof	1,000	Value: 850				

KM# 738   100 PESOS
33.9400 g., Bi-Metallic .925 Silver 20.1753g center in
Aluminum-Bronze ring, 39.04 mm. **Series:** First **Subject:**
180th Anniversary of Federation **Obv:** National arms **Obv.**
Legend: ESTADOS UNIDOS MEXICANOS **Rev:** State arms
Rev. Legend: ESTADO DE PUEBLA **Edge:** Segmented
reeding **Mint:** Mexico City

Date	Mintage	F	VF	XF	Unc	BU
2004Mo	248,850	—	—	—	35.00	40.00

KM# 809   100 PESOS
Bi-Metallic .999 Gold 17.154g center in .999 Silver 12.015g
ring, 34.5 mm. **Series:** First **Subject:** 180th Anniversary of
Federation **Obv:** National arms **Obv. Legend:** ESTADOS
UNIDOS MEXICANOS **Rev:** State arms **Rev. Legend:**
ESTADO DE PUEBLA **Edge:** Segmented reeding **Mint:**
Mexico City

Date	Mintage	F	VF	XF	Unc	BU
2004Mo Proof	1,000	Value: 850				

KM# 740   100 PESOS
33.9400 g., Bi-Metallic .925 Silver 20.1753g center in
Aluminum-Bronze ring, 39.04 mm.   **Series:** First **Subject:**
180th Anniversary of Federation **Obv:** National arms **Obv.**
Legend: ESTADOS UNIDOS MEXICANOS **Rev:** State arms
Rev. Legend: ESTADO DE OAXACA **Edge:** Segmented
reeding **Mint:** Mexico City

Date	Mintage	F	VF	XF	Unc	BU
2004Mo	249,589	—	—	—	35.00	40.00

KM# 810   100 PESOS
29.1690 g., Bi-Metallic .999 Gold 17.154g center in .999 Silver
12.015g ring, 34.5 mm.   **Series:** 180th
Anniversary of Federation **Obv:** National arms **Obv. Legend:**
ESTADOS UNIDOS MEXICANOS **Rev:** State arms **Rev.**
Legend: ESTADO DE OAXACA **Edge:** Segmented reeding
Mint: Mexico City

Date	Mintage	F	VF	XF	Unc	BU
2004Mo Proof	1,000	Value: 850				

KM# 744   100 PESOS
33.9400 g., Bi-Metallic .925 Silver 20.1753g center in
Aluminum-Bronze ring, 39.04 mm.   **Series:** First **Subject:**
180th Anniversary of Federation **Obv:** National arms **Obv.**
Legend: ESTADOS UNIDOS MEXICANOS **Rev:** State arms
Rev. Legend: ESTADO DE NAYARIT **Edge:** Segmented
reeding **Mint:** Mexico City

Date	Mintage	F	VF	XF	Unc	BU
2004Mo	248,305	—	—	—	35.00	40.00

KM# 812   100 PESOS
29.1690 g., Bi-Metallic .999 Gold 17.154g center in .999 Silver
12.015g ring, 34.5 mm.   **Series:** First **Subject:** 180th
Anniversary of Federation **Obv:** National arms **Obv. Legend:**
ESTADOS UNIDOS MEXICANOS **Rev:** State arms **Rev.**
Legend: ESTADO DE NAYARIT **Edge:** Segmented reeding
Mint: Mexico City

Date	Mintage	F	VF	XF	Unc	BU
2004Mo Proof	1,000	Value: 850				

KM# 742   100 PESOS
33.9400 g., Bi-Metallic .925 Silver 20.1753g center in
Aluminum-Bronze ring, 39.04 mm.   **Series:** First **Subject:**
180th Anniversary of Federation **Obv:** National arms **Obv.**
Legend: ESTADOS UNIDOS MEXICANOS **Rev:** State arms
Rev. Legend: ESTADO DE NUEVO LEÓN **Edge:**
Segmented reeding **Mint:** Mexico City

Date	Mintage	F	VF	XF	Unc	BU
2004Mo	249,199	—	—	—	35.00	40.00

KM# 811   100 PESOS
29.1690 g., Bi-Metallic .999 Gold 17.154g center in .999 Silver
12.015g ring, 34.5 mm.   **Series:** First **Subject:** 180th
Anniversary of Federation **Obv:** National arms **Obv. Legend:**
ESTADOS UNIDOS MEXICANOS **Rev:** State arms **Rev.**
Legend: ESTADO DE NUEVO LEÓN **Edge:** Segmented
reeding **Mint:** Mexico City

Date	Mintage	F	VF	XF	Unc	BU
2004Mo Proof	1,000	Value: 850				

KM# 746   100 PESOS
33.9400 g., Bi-Metallic .925 Silver 20.1753g center in
Aluminum-Bronze ring, 39.04 mm.   **Series:** First **Subject:**
180th Anniversary of Federation **Obv:** National arms **Obv.**
Legend: ESTADOS UNIDOS MEXICANOS **Rev:** State arms
Rev. Legend: ESTADO DE MORELOS **Edge:** Segmented
reeding **Mint:** Mexico City

Date	Mintage	F	VF	XF	Unc	BU
2004Mo	249,260	—	—	—	35.00	40.00

KM# 813   100 PESOS
29.1690 g., Bi-Metallic .999 Gold 17.154g center in .999 Silver
12.015g ring, 34.5 mm.   **Series:** First **Subject:** 180th
Anniversary of Federation **Obv:** National arms **Obv. Legend:**
ESTADOS UNIDOS MEXICANOS **Rev:** State arms **Rev.**
Legend: ESTADO DE MORELOS **Edge:** Segmented reeding
Mint: Mexico City

Date	Mintage	F	VF	XF	Unc	BU
2004Mo Proof	1,000	Value: 850				

KM# 804   100 PESOS
33.9400 g., Bi-Metallic o.925 Silver 20.1763g center in
Aluminum-Bronze ring, 39.04 mm. **Series:** First **Subject:**
180th Anniversary of Federation **Obv:** National arms **Obv.**
Legend: ESTADOS UNIDOS MEXICANOS **Rev:** State arms
Rev. Legend: ESTADO DE MICHOACÁN DE OCAMPO
Edge: Segmented reeding **Mint:** Mexico City

Date	Mintage	F	VF	XF	Unc	BU
2004Mo	249,492	—	—	—	35.00	40.00

KM# 814   100 PESOS
29.1690 g., Bi-Metallic .999 Gold 17.154g center in .999
12.015g ring, 34.5 mm. **Series:** First **Subject:** 180th
Anniversary of Federation **Obv:** National arms **Obv. Legend:**
ESTADOS UNIDOS MEXICANOS **Rev:** State arms **Rev.**
Legend: ESTADO DE MICHOACÁN DE OCAMPO **Edge:**
Segmented reeding **Mint:** Mexico City

Date	Mintage	F	VF	XF	Unc	BU
2004Mo Proof	1,000	Value: 850				

KM# 750   100 PESOS
33.9400 g., Bi-Metallic .925 Silver 20.1753g center in
Aluminum-Bronze ring, 39.04 mm. **Series:** First **Subject:**
180th Anniversary of Federation **Obv:** National arms **Obv.**
Legend: ESTADOS UNIDOS MEXICANOS **Rev:** State arms
Rev. Legend: ESTADO DE JALISCO **Edge:** Segmented
reeding **Mint:** Mexico City

Date	Mintage	F	VF	XF	Unc	BU
2004Mo	249,115	—	—	—	35.00	40.00

KM# 816   100 PESOS
29.1690 g., Bi-Metallic .999 Gold 17.154g center in .999 Silver
12.015g ring, 34.5 mm. **Series:** First **Subject:** 180th
Anniversary of Federation **Obv:** National arms **Obv. Legend:**
ESTADOS UNIDOS MEXICANOS **Rev:** State arms **Rev.**
Legend: ESTADO DE JALISCO **Edge:** Segmented reeding
Mint: Mexico City

Date	Mintage	F	VF	XF	Unc	BU
2004Mo Proof	1,000	Value: 850				

KM# 748   100 PESOS
33.9400 g., Bi-Metallic .925 Silver 20.1753g center in
Aluminum-Bronze ring, 39.04 mm. **Series:** First **Subject:**
180th Anniversary of Federation **Obv:** National arms **Obv.**
Legend: ESTADOS UNIDOS MEXICANOS **Rev:** State arms
Rev. Legend: ESTADO DE MÉXICO **Edge:** Segmented
reeding **Mint:** Mexico City

Date	Mintage	F	VF	XF	Unc	BU
2004Mo	249,800	—	—	—	35.00	40.00

KM# 815   100 PESOS
29.1690 g., Bi-Metallic .999 Gold 17.154 center in .999 Silver
12.015 ring, 34.5 mm. **Series:** First **Subject:** 180th
Anniversary of Federation **Obv:** National arms **Obv. Legend:**
ESTADOS UNIDOS MEXICANOS **Rev:** State arms **Rev.**
Legend: ESTADO DE MÉXICO **Edge:** Segmented reeding
Mint: Mexico City

Date	Mintage	F	VF	XF	Unc	BU
2004Mo Proof	1,000	Value: 850				

KM# 705   100 PESOS
33.7400 g., Bi-Metallic .925 Silver center in Aluminum-Bronze
ring, 39 mm. **Subject:** 400th Anniversary of Don Quijote de
la Manchia **Obv:** National arms **Obv. Legend:** ESTADOS
UNIDOS MEXICANOS **Rev:** Skeletal figure on horseback
with spear galloping right **Edge:** Segmented reeding **Mint:**
Mexico City

Date	Mintage	F	VF	XF	Unc	BU
2005Mo	726,833	—	—	—	25.00	32.00
2005Mo Proof	3,761	Value: 75.00				

KM# 730   100 PESOS
33.8250 g., Bi-Metallic .925 Silver 20.1753g center in
Aluminum-Bronze ring, 39.9 mm. **Subject:** Monetary Reform
Centennial **Obv:** National arms **Rev:** Radiant Liberty Cap

ESTADOS UNIDOS MEXICANOS

divides date above value within circle **Edge:** Segmented reeding **Mint:** Mexico City

Date	Mintage	F	VF	XF	Unc	BU
2005Mo	49,716	—	—	—	40.00	45.00
2005Mo Proof	—	Value: 75.00				

KM# 731   100 PESOS
33.8250 g., Bi-Metallic .925 Silver 20.1753g center in Aluminum-Bronze ring, 39.9 mm. **Subject:** Mexico City Mint's 470th Anniversary **Obv:** National arms **Rev:** Screw press, value and date within circle **Edge:** Segmented reeding **Mint:** Mexico City

Date	Mintage	F	VF	XF	Unc	BU
2005Mo	49,895	—	—	—	40.00	45.00
2005Mo Proof	—	Value: 95.00				

KM# 732   100 PESOS
33.8250 g., Bi-Metallic .925 Silver 20.1753g center in Aluminum-Bronze ring, 39.9 mm. **Subject:** Bank of Mexico's 80th Anniversary **Obv:** National arms **Rev:** Back design of the 1925 hundred peso note **Edge:** Segmented reeding **Mint:** Mexico City

Date	Mintage	F	VF	XF	Unc	BU
2005Mo	49,712	—	—	—	40.00	45.00
2005Mo Proof	—	Value: 95.00				

KM# 717   100 PESOS
33.9400 g., Bi-Metallic .925 Silver center in Brass ring, 39.04 mm. **Series:** First **Subject:** 180th Anniversary of Federation **Obv:** National arms **Obv. Legend:** ESTADOS UNIDOS MEXICANOS **Rev:** State arms **Rev. Legend:** ESTADO DE HIDALGO **Edge:** Segmented reeding **Mint:** Mexico City

Date	Mintage	F	VF	XF	Unc	BU
2005Mo	249,820	—	—	—	35.00	40.00

KM# 817   100 PESOS
29.1690 g., Bi-Metallic .999 Gold 17.154g center in .999 Silver 12.015g ring, 34.5 mm. **Series:** First **Subject:** 180th Anniversary of Federation **Obv:** National arms **Obv. Legend:** ESTADOS UNIDOS MEXICANOS **Rev:** State arms **Rev. Legend:** ESTADO DE HIDALGO **Edge:** Segmented reeding **Mint:** Mexico City

Date	Mintage	F	VF	XF	Unc	BU
2005Mo Proof	1,000	Value: 850				

KM# 716   100 PESOS
33.9400 g., Bi-Metallic .925 Silver center in Brass ring, 39.04 mm. **Series:** First **Subject:** 180th Anniversary of Federation **Obv:** National arms **Obv. Legend:** ESTADOS UNIDOS MEXICANOS **Rev:** State arms **Rev. Legend:** ESTADO DE GUERRERO **Edge:** Segmented reeding **Mint:** Mexico City

Date	Mintage	F	VF	XF	Unc	BU
2005Mo	248,850	—	—	—	35.00	40.00

KM# 818   100 PESOS
29.1690 g., Bi-Metallic .999 Gold 17.154g center in .999 Silver 12.015 ring, 34.5 mm. **Series:** First **Subject:** 180th Anniversary of Federation **Obv:** National arms **Obv. Legend:** ESTADOS UNIDOS MEXICANOS **Rev:** State arms **Rev. Legend:** ESTADO DE GUERRERO **Edge:** Segmented reeding **Mint:** Mexico City

Date	Mintage	F	VF	XF	Unc	BU
2005Mo Proof	1,000	Value: 850				

KM# 715   100 PESOS
33.9400 g., Bi-Metallic .925 Silver center in Brass ring, 39.04 mm. **Series:** First **Subject:** 180th Anniversary of Federation **Obv:** National arms **Obv. Legend:** ESTADOS UNIDOS MEXICANOS **Rev:** State arms **Rev. Legend:** ESTADO DE GUANAJUATO **Edge:** Segmented reeding **Mint:** Mexico City

Date	Mintage	F	VF	XF	Unc	BU
2005Mo	249,489	—	—	—	35.00	40.00

KM# 819   100 PESOS
29.1690 g., Bi-Metallic .999 Gold 17.154g center in .999 Silver 12.015g ring, 34.5 mm. **Series:** First **Subject:** 180th Anniversary of Federation **Obv:** National arms **Obv. Legend:** ESTADOS UNIDOS MEXICANOS **Rev:** State arms **Rev. Legend:** ESTADO DE GUANAJUATO **Edge:** Segmented reeding **Mint:** Mexico City

Date	Mintage	F	VF	XF	Unc	BU
2005Mo Proof	1,000	Value: 850				

KM# 714   100 PESOS
33.9400 g., Bi-Metallic .925 Silver center in Brass ring, 39.04 mm. **Series:** First **Subject:** 180th Anniversary of Federation **Obv:** National arms **Obv. Legend:** ESTADOS UNIDOS MEXICANOS **Rev:** State arms **Rev. Legend:** ESTADO DE DURANGO **Edge:** Segmented reeding **Mint:** Mexico City

Date	Mintage	F	VF	XF	Unc	BU
2005Mo	249,774	—	—	—	35.00	40.00

KM# 820   100 PESOS
29.1690 g., Bi-Metallic .999 Gold 17.154g center in .999 silver 12.015g ring, 34.5 mm. **Series:** First **Subject:** 180th Anniversary of Federation **Obv:** National arms **Obv. Legend:** ESTADOS UNIDOS MEXICANOS **Rev:** State arms **Rev. Legend:** ESTADO DE DURANGO **Edge:** Segmented reeding **Mint:** Mexico City

Date	Mintage	F	VF	XF	Unc	BU
2005Mo Proof	1,000	Value: 850				

KM# 754   100 PESOS
33.9400 g., Bi-Metallic .925 Silver 20.1753g center in Aluminum-Bronze ring, 39.04 mm. **Series:** First **Subject:** 180th Anniversary of Federation **Obv:** National arms **Obv. Legend:** ESTADOS UNIDOS MEXICANOS **Rev:** State arms **Rev. Legend:** ESTADO DE CHIHUAHUA **Edge:** Segmented reeding **Mint:** Mexico City

Date	Mintage	F	VF	XF	Unc	BU
2005Mo	249,102	—	—	—	35.00	40.00

KM# 822   100 PESOS
29.1690 g., Bi-Metallic .999 Gold 17.154g center in .999 Silver 12.015g ring, 34.5 mm. **Series:** First **Subject:** 180th Anniversary of Federation **Obv:** National arms **Obv. Legend:** ESTADOS UNIDOS MEXICANOS **Rev:** State arms **Rev. Legend:** ESTADO DE CHIHUAHUA **Edge:** Segmented reeding **Mint:** Mexico City

Date	Mintage	F	VF	XF	Unc	BU
2005Mo Proof	1,000	Value: 850				

KM# 713   100 PESOS
33.9400 g., Bi-Metallic .925 Silver 20.1753g center in Brass ring, 39.04 mm. **Series:** First **Subject:** 180th Anniversary of Federation **Obv:** National arms **Obv. Legend:** ESTADOS UNIDOS MEXICANOS **Rev:** Federal District arms **Rev. Legend:** DISTRITO FEDERAL **Edge:** Segmented reeding **Mint:** Mexico City

Date	Mintage	F	VF	XF	Unc	BU
2005Mo	249,461	—	—	—	35.00	40.00

KM# 821   100 PESOS
29.1690 g., Bi-Metallic .999 Gold 17.154g center in .999 Silver 12.015g ring, 34.5 mm. **Series:** First **Subject:** 180th Anniversary of Federation **Obv:** National arms **Obv. Legend:** ESTADOS UNIDOS MEXICANOS **Rev:** Federal District arms **Rev. Legend:** DISTRITO FEDERAL **Edge:** Segmented reeding **Mint:** Mexico City

Date	Mintage	F	VF	XF	Unc	BU
2005Mo Proof	1,000	Value: 850				

KM# 712   100 PESOS
33.9400 g., Bi-Metallic .925 Silver 20.1753g center in Brass ring, 39.04 mm. **Series:** First **Subject:** 180th Anniversary of Federation **Obv:** National arms **Obv. Legend:** ESTADOS UNIDOS MEXICANOS **Rev:** State arms **Rev. Legend:** ESTADO DE CHIAPAS **Edge:** Segmented reeding **Mint:** Mexico City

Date	Mintage	F	VF	XF	Unc	BU
2005Mo	249,417	—	—	—	35.00	40.00

KM# 823   100 PESOS
29.1690 g., Bi-Metallic .999 Gold 17.154g center in .999 Silver 12.015g ring, 34.5 mm. **Series:** First **Subject:** 180th Anniversary of Federation **Obv:** National arms **Obv. Legend:** ESTADOS UNIDOS MEXICANOS **Rev:** State arms **Rev. Legend:** ESTADO DE CHIAPAS **Edge:** Segmented reeding **Mint:** Mexico City

Date	Mintage	F	VF	XF	Unc	BU
2005Mo Proof	1,000	Value: 850				

ESTADOS UNIDOS MEXICANOS

KM# 729   100 PESOS
33.8250 g., Bi-Metallic .925 Silver 20.1753g center in
Aluminum-Bronze ring, 39.04 mm. **Series:** First **Subject:**
180th Anniversary of Federation **Obv:** National arms **Obv.**
Legend: ESTADOS UNIDOS MEXICANOS **Rev:** State arms
Rev. Legend: ESTADO DE COLIMA **Edge:** Segmented
reeding **Mint:** Mexico City

Date	Mintage	F	VF	XF	Unc	BU
2005Mo	248,850	—	—	—	35.00	40.00

KM# 824   100 PESOS
29.1690 g., Bi-Metallic .999 Gold 17.154g center in .999 Silver
12.015g ring, 34.5 mm. **Series:** First **Subject:** 180th
Anniversary of Federation **Obv:** National arms **Obv. Legend:**
ESTADOS UNIDOS MEXICANOS **Rev:** State arms **Rev.**
Legend: ESTADO DE COLIMA **Edge:** Segmented reeding
Mint: Mexico City

Date	Mintage	F	VF	XF	Unc	BU
2005Mo Proof	1,000	Value: 850				

KM# 727   100 PESOS
33.9400 g., Bi-Metallic .925 Silver 20.1753g center in
Aluminum-Bronze ring, 39.04 mm. **Series:** First **Subject:**
180th Anniversary of Federation **Obv:** National arms **Obv.**
Legend: ESTADOS UNIDOS MEXICANOS **Rev:** State arms
Rev. Legend: ESTADO DE CAMPECHE **Edge:** Segmented
reeding **Mint:** Mexico City

Date	Mintage	F	VF	XF	Unc	BU
2005Mo	249,040	—	—	—	35.00	40.00

KM# 826   100 PESOS
29.1690 g., Bi-Metallic .999 Gold 17.154g center in .999 Silver
12.015g ring, 34.5 mm. **Series:** First **Subject:** 180th
Anniversary of Federation **Obv:** National arms **Obv. Legend:**
ESTADOS UNIDOS MEXICANOS **Rev:** State arms **Rev.**
Legend: ESTADO DE CAMPECHE **Edge:** Segmented
reeding **Mint:** Mexico City

Date	Mintage	F	VF	XF	Unc	BU
2005Mo Proof	1,000	Value: 850				

KM# 752   100 PESOS
33.9400 g., Bi-Metallic .925 Silver 20.1753g center in
Aluminum-Bronze ring, 39.04 mm. **Series:** First **Subject:**
180th Anniversary of Federation **Obv:** National arms **Obv.**
Legend: ESTADOS UNIDOS MEXICANOS **Rev:** State arms
Rev. Legend: ESTADO DE COAHUILA DE ZARAGOZA
Edge: Segmented reeding **Mint:** Mexico City

Date	Mintage	F	VF	XF	Unc	BU
2005Mo	247,991	—	—	—	35.00	40.00

KM# 825   100 PESOS
29.1690 g., Bi-Metallic .999 Gold 17.154g center in .999 Silver
12.015g ring, 34.5 mm. **Series:** First **Subject:** 180th
Anniversary of Federation **Obv:** National arms **Obv. Legend:**
ESTADOS UNIDOS MEXICANOS **Rev:** State arms **Rev.**
Legend: ESTADO DE COAHUILA DE ZARAGOZA **Edge:**
Segmented reeding **Mint:** Mexico City

Date	Mintage	F	VF	XF	Unc	BU
2005Mo Proof	1,000	Value: 850				

KM# 725   100 PESOS
33.9400 g., Bi-Metallic .925 Silver 20.1753g center in
Aluminum-Bronze ring, 39.04 mm. **Series:** First **Subject:**
180th Anniversary of Federation **Obv:** National arms **Obv.**
Legend: ESTADOS UNIDOS MEXICANOS **Rev:** State arms
Rev. Legend: ESTADO DE BAJA CALIFORNIA SUR **Edge:**
Segmented reeding **Mint:** Mexico City

Date	Mintage	F	VF	XF	Unc	BU
2005Mo	249,585	—	—	—	35.00	40.00

KM# 827   100 PESOS
29.1690 g., Bi-Metallic .999 Gold 17.154g center in .999 Silver
12.015g ring, 34.5 mm. **Series:** First **Subject:** 180th
Anniversary of Federation **Obv:** National arms **Obv. Legend:**
ESTADOS UNIDOS MEXICANOS **Rev:** State arms **Rev.**
Legend: ESTADO DE BAJA CALIFORNIA SUR **Edge:**
Segmented reeding **Mint:** Mexico City

Date	Mintage	F	VF	XF	Unc	BU
2005Mo Proof	—	Value: 850				

KM# 723 100 PESOS
33.9400 g., Bi-Metallic .925 Silver 20.1753g center in
Aluminum-Bronze ring, 39.04 mm. **Series:** First **Subject:**
180th Anniversary of Federation **Obv:** National arms **Obv.**
Legend: ESTADOS UNIDOS MEXICANOS **Rev:** State arms
Rev. Legend: ESTADO DE BAJA CALIFORNIA **Edge:**
Segmented reeding **Mint:** Mexico City

Date	Mintage	F	VF	XF	Unc	BU
2005Mo	249,263	—	—	—	35.00	40.00

KM# 828 100 PESOS
29.1690 g., Bi-Metallic .999 Gold 17.154g center in .999 Silver
12.015g ring, 34.5 mm. **Series:** First **Subject:** 180th
Anniversary of Federation **Obv:** National arms **Obv. Legend:**
ESTADOS UNIDOS MEXICANOS **Rev:** State arms **Rev.**
Legend: ESTADO DE BAJA CALIFORNIA **Edge:**
Segmented reeding **Mint:** Mexico City

Date	Mintage	F	VF	XF	Unc	BU
2005Mo Proof	1,000	Value: 850				

KM# 719 100 PESOS
33.8250 g., Bi-Metallic .925 Silver 20.1753g center in
Aluminum-Bronze ring, 39.04 mm. **Series:** Second **Obv:**
National arms **Obv. Legend:** ESTADOS UNIDOS
MEXICANOS **Rev:** Facade of the San Marcos garden above
sculpture of national emblem at left, San Antonio Temple at
right **Rev. Legend:** AGUASCALIENTES **Edge:** Segmented
reeding **Mint:** Mexico City

Date	Mintage	F	VF	XF	Unc	BU
2005Mo	149,705	—	—	—	25.00	30.00

KM# 862 100 PESOS
29.1690 g., Bi-Metallic .999 Gold 17.154g center in .999 Silver
12.015g ring, 34.5 mm. **Series:** Second **Obv:** National arms
Obv. Legend: ESTADOS UNIDOS MEXICANOS **Rev:**
Facade of the San Marcos garden above sculpture of national
emblem at left, San Antonio temple at right **Rev. Legend:**
AGUASCALIENTES **Edge:** Segmented reeding **Mint:**
Mexico City

Date	Mintage	F	VF	XF	Unc	BU
2005Mo Proof	600	Value: 875				

KM# 721 100 PESOS
33.9400 g., Bi-Metallic .925 Silver 20.1753g center in
Aluminum-Bronze ring, 39.04 mm. **Series:** First **Subject:**
180th Anniversary of Federation **Obv:** National arms **Obv.**
Legend: ESTADOS UNIDOS MEXICANOS **Rev:** Estados de
Aguascalientes state arms **Rev. Legend:** ESTADO DE
AGUASCALIENTES **Edge:** Segmented reeding **Mint:**
Mexico City

Date	Mintage	F	VF	XF	Unc	BU
2005Mo	248,410	—	—	—	35.00	40.00

KM# 829 100 PESOS
29.1690 g., Bi-Metallic .999 Gold 17.154g center in .999 Silver
12.015g ring, 34.5 mm. **Series:** First **Subject:** 180th
Anniversary of Federation **Obv:** National arms **Obv. Legend:**
ESTADOS UNIDOS MEXICANOS **Rev:** State arms **Rev.**
Legend: ESTADO DE AGUASCALIENTES **Edge:**
Segmented reeding **Mint:** Mexico City

Date	Mintage	F	VF	XF	Unc	BU
2005Mo Proof	1,000	Value: 850				

KM# 758 100 PESOS
33.9400 g., Bi-Metallic .925 Silver 20.1753g center in
Aluminum-Bronze ring, 39.04 mm. **Series:** Second **Obv:**
National arms **Obv. Legend:** ESTADOS UNIDOS
MEXICANOS **Rev:** Ram's head and value within circle **Rev.**
Legend: BAJA CALIFORNIA - GOBIERNO DEL ESTADO
Edge: Segmented reeding **Mint:** Mexico City

Date	Mintage	F	VF	XF	Unc	BU
2005Mo	—	—	—	—	25.00	30.00

KM# 863 100 PESOS
29.1690 g., Bi-Metallic .999 Gold 17.154g center in .999 Silver
12.015g ring, 34.5 mm. **Series:** Second **Obv:** National arms
Obv. Legend: ESTTADOS UNIDOS MEXICANOS **Rev:**
Ram's head, mountain outline in background **Rev. Legend:**
BAJA CALIFORNIA - GOBIERNO DEL ESTADO **Edge:**
Segmented reeding **Mint:** Mexico City

Date	Mintage	F	VF	XF	Unc	BU
2005Mo Proof	600	Value: 875				

ESTADOS UNIDOS MEXICANOS

KM# 762   100 PESOS
33.9400 g., Bi-Metallic .925 Silver 20.175g center in Aluminum-Bronze ring, 39.04 mm. **Series:** Second **Obv:** National arms **Obv. Legend:** ESTADOS UNIDOS MEXICANOS **Rev:** Outlined map of peninsula at center, cave painting of deer behind, cactus at right **Rev. Legend:** ESTADO DE BAJA CALIFORNIA SUR **Edge:** Segmented reeding **Mint:** Mexico City

Date	Mintage	F	VF	XF	Unc	BU
2005Mo	149,152	—	—	—	25.00	30.00

KM# 764   100 PESOS
33.7000 g., Bi-Metallic .925 Silver 20.1753g center in Aluminum-Bronze ring **Subject:** 200th Anniversary Birth of Benito Juarez Garcia **Obv:** National arms **Rev:** Bust 1/4 left within circle **Mint:** Mexico City

Date	Mintage	F	VF	XF	Unc	BU
2006Mo	49,913	—	—	—	40.00	45.00

KM# 864   100 PESOS
29.1690 g., Bi-Metallic .999 Gold 17.154g center in .999 Silver 12.015g ring, 34.5 mm. **Series:** Second **Obv:** National arms **Obv. Legend:** ESTADOS UNIDOS MEXICANOS **Rev:** Outlined map of peninsula at center, cave painting of deer behind, cactus at right **Rev. Legend:** ESTADO DE BAJA CALIFORNIA SUR **Edge:** Segmented reeding **Mint:** Mexico City

Date	Mintage	F	VF	XF	Unc	BU
2006Mo Proof	600	Value: 875				

KM# 760   100 PESOS
33.9400 g., Bi-Metallic .925 Silver 20.1753g center in Aluminum-Bronze ring, 39.04 mm. **Series:** Second **Subject:** Estado de Campeche **Obv:** National arms **Obv. Legend:**

ESTADOS UNIDOS MEXICANOS **Rev:** Jade mask - Calakmul, Campeche **Rev. Legend:** ESTADO DE CAMPECHE **Edge:** Segmented reeding **Mint:** Mexico City

Date	Mintage	F	VF	XF	Unc	BU
2006Mo	—	—	—	—	25.00	30.00

KM# 865   100 PESOS
29.1690 g., Bi-Metallic .999 Gold 17.154g center in .999 Silver 12.015g ring, 34.5 mm. **Series:** Second **Obv:** National arms **Obv. Legend:** ESTADOS UNIDOS MEXICANOS **Rev:** Jade mask - Calakmul, Campeche **Rev. Legend:** ESTADO DE CAMPECHE **Edge:** Segmented reeding **Mint:** Mexico City

Date	Mintage	F	VF	XF	Unc	BU
2006Mo Proof	600	Value: 875				

KM# 781   100 PESOS
33.7000 g., Bi-Metallic .925 Silver 20.1753g center in Aluminum-Bronze ring, 39.04 mm. **Series:** Second **Obv:** National arms **Obv. Legend:** ESTADOS UNIDOS MEXICANOS **Rev:** Outlined map with turtle, mine cart above grapes at center, Friendship Dam above Christ of the Nodas at left, chimneys above crucibles and bell tower of Santiago's cathedral at right **Rev. Legend:** COAHUILA DE ZARAGOZA **Edge:** Segmented reeding **Mint:** Mexico City

Date	Mintage	F	VF	XF	Unc	BU
2006Mo	—	—	—	—	25.00	30.00

KM# 866   100 PESOS
29.1690 g., Bi-Metallic .999 Gold 17.154g center in .999 Silver 12.015g ring, 34.5 mm. **Series:** Second **Obv:** National arms **Obv. Legend:** ESTADOS UNIDOS MEXICANOS **Rev:** Outlined map with turtle, mine cart above grapes at center, Friendship dam above Christ of the Nodas at left, chimneys above crucibles and bell tower of Santiago's cathedral at right **Rev. Inscription:** COAHUILA DE ZARAGOZA **Edge:** Segmented reeding **Mint:** Mexico City

Date	Mintage	F	VF	XF	Unc	BU
2006Mo Proof	600	Value: 875				

KM# 777   100 PESOS
33.9400 g., Bi-Metallic .925 Silver 20.1753g center in Aluminum-Bronze ring, 39.04 mm. **Series:** Second **Obv:** National arms **Obv. Legend:** ESTADOS UNIDOS MEXICANOS **Rev:** State arms at lower center, Nevado de Colima and Volcan de Fuego volcanos in background **Rev. Legend:** *Colima* **Rev. Inscription:** GENEROSO **Edge:** Segmented reeding **Mint:** Mexico City

Date	Mintage	F	VF	XF	Unc	BU
2006Mo	149,041	—	—	—	25.00	30.00

KM# 867 100 PESOS
29.1690 g., Bi-Metallic .999 Gold 17.154g center in .999 Silver 12.015 ring, 34.5 mm. **Series:** Second **Obv:** National arms **Obv. Legend:** ESTADOS UNIDOS MEXICANOS **Rev:** State arms at lower center, Nevado de Colima and Volcan de Fuego volcanos in background **Rev. Legend:** Colima **Rev.** **Inscription:** GENEROSO **Edge:** Segmented reeding **Mint:** Mexico City

Date	Mintage	F	VF	XF	Unc	BU
2006Mo Proof	600				Value: 875	

KM# 869 100 PESOS
29.1690 g., Bi-Metallic .999 Gold 17.154g center in .999 Silver 12.015g ring, 34.5 mm. **Series:** Second **Obv:** National arms **Obv. Legend:** ESTADOS UNIDOS MEXICANOS **Rev:** Angel of Liberty **Rev. Legend:** MÉXICO - ANGEL DE LA LIBERTAD, CHIHUAHUA **Edge:** Segmented reeding **Mint:** Mexico City

Date	Mintage	F	VF	XF	Unc	BU
2006Mo Proof	600				Value: 875	

KM# 773 100 PESOS
33.9400 g., Bi-Metallic .925 Silver 20.1753g center in Aluminum-Bronze ring, 39.04 mm. **Series:** Second **Obv:** National arms **Obv. Legend:** ESTADOS UNIDOS MEXICANOS **Rev:** Head of Pakal, ancient Mayan king, Palenque **Rev. Legend:** ESTADO DE CHIAPAS - CABEZA MAYA DEL REY PAKAL, PALENQUE **Edge:** Segmented reeding **Mint:** Mexico City

Date	Mintage	F	VF	XF	Unc	BU
2006Mo	149,491	—	—	—	25.00	30.00

KM# 868 100 PESOS
29.1690 g., Bi-Metallic .999 Gold 17.154g center in .999 Silver 12.015g ring, 34.5 mm. **Series:** Second **Obv:** National arms **Obv. Legend:** ESTADOS UNIDOS MEXICANOS **Rev:** Head of Pakal, ancient Mayan king, Palenque **Rev. Legend:** ESTADO DE CHIAPAS - CABEZA MAYA DEL REY PAKAL, PALENQUE **Edge:** Segmented reeding **Mint:** Mexico City

Date	Mintage	F	VF	XF	Unc	BU
2006Mo Proof	600				Value: 875	

KM# 779 100 PESOS
33.9400 g., Bi-Metallic .925 Silver 20.1753g center in Aluminum-Bronze ring, 39.04 mm. **Series:** Second **Obv:** National arms **Obv. Legend:** ESTADOS UNIDOS MEXICANOS **Rev:** National Palace **Rev. Legend:** DISTRITO FEDERAL - ANTIGUO AYUNTAMIENTO **Edge:** Segmented reeding **Mint:** Mexico City

Date	Mintage	F	VF	XF	Unc	BU
2006Mo	149,525	—	—	—	25.00	30.00

KM# 870 100 PESOS
29.1690 g., Bi-Metallic .999 Gold 17.154g center in .999 Silver 12.015g ring, 34.5 mm. **Series:** Second **Obv:** National arms **Obv. Legend:** ESTADOS UNIDOS MEXICANOS **Rev:** National palace **Rev. Legend:** DISTRITO FEDERAL - ANTIGUO AYUNTAMIENTO **Edge:** Segmented reeding **Mint:** Mexico City

Date	Mintage	F	VF	XF	Unc	BU
2006Mo Proof	600				Value: 875	

KM# 775 100 PESOS
33.9400 g., Bi-Metallic .925 Silver 20.1753g center in Aluminum-Bronze ring, 39.04 mm. **Series:** Second **Obv:** National arms **Obv. Legend:** ESTADOS UNIDOS MEXICANOS **Rev:** Angel of Liberty **Rev. Legend:** MÉXICO - ANGEL DE LA LIBERTAD, CHIHUAHUA **Edge:** Segmented reeding **Mint:** Mexico City

Date	Mintage	F	VF	XF	Unc	BU
2006Mo	149,557	—	—	—	25.00	30.00

KM# 787 100 PESOS
33.9400 g., Bi-Metallic .925 Silver 20.1753g center in Brass ring, 39.04 mm. **Series:** Second **Obv:** National arms **Obv. Legend:** ESTADOS UNIDOS MEXICANOS **Rev:** Tree **Rev. Legend:** PRIMERA RESERVA NACIONAL FORESTAL - DURANGO **Edge:** Segmented reeding **Mint:** Mexico City

Date	Mintage	F	VF	XF	Unc	BU
2006Mo	149,034	—	—	—	25.00	30.00

KM# 871 100 PESOS
29.1690 g., Bi-Metallic .999 Gold 17.154g center in .999 Silver 12.015g ring, 34.5 mm. **Series:** Second **Obv:** National arms **Obv. Legend:** ESYADOS UNIDOS MEXICANOS **Rev:** Tree **Rev. Legend:** PRIMERA RESERVA NACIONAL RORESTAL - DURANGO **Edge:** Segmented reeding **Mint:** Mexico City

Date	Mintage	F	VF	XF	Unc	BU
2006Mo Proof	600				Value: 875	

KM# 789   100 PESOS
33.9400 g., Bi-Metallic .925 Silver 20.1753g center in Brass ring, 39.04 mm. **Series:** Second **Obv:** National arms **Obv. Legend:** ESTADOS UNIDOS MEXICANOS **Rev:** State arms at center, statue of Miguel Hidalgo at left, monument to Pipla at lower right **Rev. Inscription:** *Guanajuato* **Edge:** Segmented reeding **Mint:** Mexico City

Date	Mintage	F	VF	XF	Unc	BU
2006Mo	149,921	—	—	—	25.00	30.00

KM# 872   100 PESOS
29.1690 g., Bi-Metallic .999 Gold 17.154g center in .999 Silver 12.015g ring, 34.50 mm. **Series:** Second **Obv:** National arms **Obv. Legend:** ESTADOS UNIDOS MEXICANOS **Rev:** State arms at lower center, statue of Miguel Hidalgo at left, monument to Pipila at lower right **Rev. Inscription:** *Guanajauto* **Edge:** Segmented reeding **Mint:** Mexico City

Date	Mintage	F	VF	XF	Unc	BU
2006Mo Proof	600	Value: 875				

KM# 793   100 PESOS
33.9400 g., Bi-Metallic .925 Silver 20.1753g center in Aluminum-Bronze ring, 39.04 mm. **Series:** Second **Obv:** National arms **Obv. Legend:** ESTADOS UNIDOS MEXICANOS **Rev:** Monument of Pachuca Hidalgo **Rev. Inscription:** *RELOJ / MONUMENTAL / DE / PACHUCA / HIDALGO - La / Bella / Airosa* **Edge:** Segmented reeding **Mint:** Mexico City

Date	Mintage	F	VF	XF	Unc	BU
2006Mo	149,273	—	—	—	25.00	30.00

KM# 874   100 PESOS
29.1690 g., Bi-Metallic .999 Gold 17.154g center in .999 Silver 12.015g ring, 34.5 mm. **Series:** Second **Obv:** National arms **Obv. Legend:** ESTADOS UNIDOS MEXICANOS **Rev:** Monument of Pachuca Hidalgo **Rev. Inscription:** *RELOJ / MONUMENTAL / DE / PACHUCA / HIDALGO* **Edge:** Segmented reeding **Mint:** Mexico City

Date	Mintage	F	VF	XF	Unc	BU
2006Mo Proof	600	Value: 875				

KM# 791   100 PESOS
33.9400 g., Bi-Metallic .925 Silver 20.1753g center in Brass ring, 39.04 mm. **Series:** Second **Obv:** National arms **Obv. Legend:** ESTADOS UNIDOS MEXICANOS **Rev:** Stylized portrait of Vicente Guerrero at left, church of Taxco at upper center, Acapulco's la Quebrada with diver above Christmas Eve flower and mask **Rev. Legend:** GUERRERO **Edge:** Segmented reeding **Mint:** Mexico City

Date	Mintage	F	VF	XF	Unc	BU
2006Mo	149,675	—	—	—	25.00	30.00

KM# 873   100 PESOS
29.1690 g., Bi-Metallic .999 Gold 17.154g center in .999 Silver 12.015g ring, 34.5 mm. **Series:** Second **Obv:** National arms **Obv. Legend:** ESTADOS UNIDOS MEXICANOS **Rev:** Stylized portrait of Vicente Guerrero at left, church of Taxco at upper center, Acapulco's la Quebrada with diver over Christmas Eve flower and mask **Rev. Legend:** GUERRERO **Edge:** Segmented reeding **Mint:** Mexico City

Date	Mintage	F	VF	XF	Unc	BU
2006Mo Proof	600	Value: 875				

KM# 795   100 PESOS
33.9400 g., Bi-Metallic .925 Silver 20.1753g center in Brass ring, 39.04 mm. **Series:** Second **Obv:** National arms **Obv. Legend:** ESTADOS UNIDOS MEXICANOS **Rev:** Hospicio Cabañas orphanage **Rev. Legend:** ESTADO DE JALISCO **Edge:** Segmented reeding **Mint:** Mexico City

Date	Mintage	F	VF	XF	Unc	BU
2006Mo	149,750	—	—	—	25.00	30.00

KM# 875   100 PESOS
29.1690 g., Bi-Metallic .999 Gold 17.154g center in .999 Silver 12.015g ring, 34.5 mm. **Series:** Second **Obv:** National arms **Obv. Legend:** ESTADOS UNIDOS MEXICANOS **Rev:** Hospicio Cabañas orphanage **Rev. Legend:** ESTADO DE JALISCO **Edge:** Segmented reeding **Mint:** Mexico City

Date	Mintage	F	VF	XF	Unc	BU
2006Mo Proof	600	Value: 875				

KM# 802   100 PESOS
33.9400 g., Bi-Metallic .925 Silver 20.1753g center in Aluminum-Bronze ring, 33.7, 39.04 mm. **Series:** Second **Obv:** National arms **Obv. Legend:** ESTADOS UNIDOS MEXICANOS **Rev:** Pyramid de la Loona (moon) **Rev. Legend:** ESTADO DE MÉXICO **Edge:** Segmented reeding **Mint:** Mexico City

Date	Mintage	F	VF	XF	Unc	BU
2006Mo	149,377	—	—	—	25.00	30.00

KM# 876 100 PESOS
29.1690 g., Bi-Metallic .999 Gold 17.154g center in .999 Silver
12.015g ring, 34.5 mm. **Series:** Second **Obv:** National arms
Obv. Legend: ESTADOS UNIDOS MEXICANOS **Rev:**
Pyramid de la Looona (moon) **Rev. Legend:** ESTADO DE
MÉXICO **Edge:** Segmented reeding **Mint:** Mexico City

Date	Mintage	F	VF	XF	Unc	BU
2006Mo Proof	600	Value: 875				

KM# 785 100 PESOS
33.9400 g., Bi-Metallic .925 Silver 20.1753g center in
Aluminum-Bronze ring, 33.7, 39.04 mm. **Series:** Second
Obv: National arms **Obv. Legend:** ESTADOS UNIDOS
MEXICANOS **Rev:** Four Monarch butterflies **Rev. Legend:**
ESTADO DE MICHOACÁN **Edge:** Segmented reeding **Mint:**
Mexico City

Date	Mintage	F	VF	XF	Unc	BU
2006Mo	149,730	—	—	—	25.00	30.00

KM# 877 100 PESOS
29.1690 g., Bi-Metallic .999 Gold 17.154g center in .999 Silver
12.015g ring, 34.5 mm. **Series:** Second **Obv:** National arms
Obv. Legend: ESTADOS UNIDOS MEXICANOS **Rev:** Four
Monarch butterflies **Rev. Legend:** ESTADO DE
MICHOACÁN **Edge:** Segmented reeding **Mint:** Mexico City

Date	Mintage	F	VF	XF	Unc	BU
2006Mo Proof	600	Value: 875				

KM# 800 100 PESOS
33.9400 g., Bi-Metallic .925 Silver 20.1753g center in
Aluminum-Bronze ring, 33.7, 39.04 mm. **Series:** Second
Obv: National arms **Obv. Legend:** ESTADOS UNIDOS
MEXICANOS **Rev:** 1/2 length figure of Chinelo (local dancer)
at right, Palacio de Cortes in background **Rev. Inscription:**
ESTADO DE / MORELOS **Edge:** Segmented reeding **Mint:**
Mexico City

Date	Mintage	F	VF	XF	Unc	BU
2006Mo	149,648	—	—	—	25.00	30.00

KM# 878 100 PESOS
29.1690 g., Bi-Metallic .999 Gold 17.154g center in .999 Silver
12.015g ring, 34.5 mm. **Series:** Second **Obv:** National arms
Obv. Legend: ESTADOS UNIDOS MEXICANOS **Rev:** 1/2
length figure of Chinelo (local dancer) at right, Palacio de
Cortes in background **Rev. Inscription:** ESTADO DE /
MORELOS **Edge:** Segmented reeding **Mint:** Mexico City

Date	Mintage	F	VF	XF	Unc	BU
2006Mo Proof	600	Value: 875				

KM# 798 100 PESOS
33.9400 g., 33.8250 Bi-Metallic 0.925 Silver 20.1753g center
in Aluminum-Bronze ring 36.908 oz., 39.04 mm. **Series:**
Second **Obv:** National arms **Obv. Legend:** ESTADOS
UNIDOS MEXICANOS **Rev:** Isle de Mexcaltitlán **Rev.
Legend:** ESTADO DE NAYARIT **Edge:** Segmented reeding
Mint: Mexico City

Date	Mintage	F	VF	XF	Unc	BU
2007Mo	149,560	—	—	—	25.00	30.00

KM# 879 100 PESOS
29.1690 g., Bi-Metallic .999 Gold 17.154g center in .999
12.015g ring, 34.5 mm. **Series:** Second **Obv:** National arms
Obv. Legend: ESTADOS UNIDOS MEXICANOS **Rev:** Isle
de Mexcaltitlán **Rev. Legend:** ESTADO DE NAYARIT **Edge:**
Segmented reeding **Mint:** Mexico City

Date	Mintage	F	VF	XF	Unc	BU
2007Mo Proof	600	Value: 875				

KM# 848 100 PESOS
33.9400 g., Bi-Metallic .925 Silver 20.1753 center in
Aluminum-Bronze ring, 39.04 mm. **Series:** Second **Obv:**
National arms **Obv. Legend:** ESTADOS UNIDOS
MEXICANOE **Rev:** Old foundry in Parque Fundidora (public
park) at right, Cerro de la Silla (Saddle Hill) in background
Rev. Legend: ESTADO DE NUEVO LEÓN **Edge:**
Segmented reeding **Mint:** Mexico City

Date	Mintage	F	VF	XF	Unc	BU
2007Mo	149,425	—	—	—	25.00	30.00

KM# 880 100 PESOS
29.1690 g., Bi-Metallic .999 Gold 17.154g center in .999 Silver
12.015g ring, 34.5 mm. **Series:** Second **Obv:** National arms
Obv. Legend: ESTADOS UNIDOS MEXICANOS **Rev:** Old
foundry in Parque Fundidora (public park) at right, Cerro de
la Silla (Saddle hill) in background **Rev. Legend:** ESTADO
DE NUEVO LEÓN **Edge:** Segmented reeding **Mint:** Mexico
City

Date	Mintage	F	VF	XF	Unc	BU
2007Mo Proof	600	Value: 875				

KM# 849   100 PESOS
33.9400 g., Bi-Metallic .925 Silver 20.1753g center in
Aluminum-Bronze ring, 39.04 mm.   **Series:** Second **Obv:**
National arms **Obv. Legend:** ESTADOS UNIDOS
MEXICANOS **Rev:** Teatro Macedonio Alcala (theater) **Rev.
Legend:** OAXACA **Edge:** Segmented reeding **Mint:** Mexico
City

Date	Mintage	F	VF	XF	Unc	BU
2007Mo	149,892	—	—	—	25.00	30.00

KM# 881   100 PESOS
29.1690 g., Bi-Metallic .999 Gold 17.154g center in .999 Silver
12.015g ring, 34.50 mm.   **Series:** Second **Obv:** National arms
Obv. Legend: ESTADOS UNIDOS MEXICANOS **Rev:**
Teatro Macedonio Alcala (theater) **Rev. Legend:** OAXACA
Edge: Segmented reeding **Mint:** Mexico City

Date	Mintage	F	VF	XF	Unc	BU
2007Mo Proof	600	Value: 875				

KM# 851   100 PESOS
33.9400 g., Bi-Metallic .925 Silver 20.1753g center in
Aluminum-Bronze ring, 39.04 mm.   **Series:** Second **Obv:**
National arms **Obv. Legend:** ESTADOS UNIDOS
MEXICANOS **Rev:** Mask at left, rays above state arms at
center, Mayan ruins at right **Rev. Legend:** QUINTANA ROO
Edge: Segmented reeding **Mint:** Mexico City

Date	Mintage	F	VF	XF	Unc	BU
2007Mo	149,582	—	—	—	25.00	30.00

KM# 883   100 PESOS
29.1690 g., Bi-Metallic .999 Gold 17.154g center in .999 Silver
12.015g ring, 34.5 mm.   **Series:** Second **Obv:** National arms
Obv. Legend: ESTADOS UNIDOS MEXICANOS **Rev:** Mask
at left, rays above state arms at center, Mayan ruins at right
Rev. Legend: QUINTANA ROO **Edge:** Segmented reeding
Mint: Mexico City

Date	Mintage	F	VF	XF	Unc	BU
2007Mo Proof	600	Value: 875				

KM# 850   100 PESOS
33.9400 g., Bi-Metallic .925 Silver 20.1753g center in
Aluminum-Bronze ring, 39.04 mm.   **Series:** Second **Obv:**
National arms **Obv. Legend:** ESTADOS UNIDOS
MEXICANOS **Rev:** Talavera porcelain dish **Rev. Legend:**
ESTADO DE PUEBLA **Edge:** Segmented reeding **Mint:**
Mexico City

Date	Mintage	F	VF	XF	Unc	BU
2007Mo	149,474	—	—	—	25.00	30.00

KM# 882   100 PESOS
29.1690 g., Bi-Metallic .999 Gold 17.154g center in .999 Silver
12.015g ring, 34.5 mm.   **Series:** Second **Obv:** National arms
Obv. Legend: ESTADOS UNIDOS MEXICANOS **Rev:**
Talavera porcelain dish **Rev. Legend:** ESTADO DE PUEBLA
Edge: Segmented reeding **Mint:** Mexico City

Date	Mintage	F	VF	XF	Unc	BU
2007Mo Proof	600	Value: 875				

KM# 852   100 PESOS
33.9400 g., Bi-Metallic .925 Silver 20.1753 center in
Aluminum-Bronze ring, 39.04 mm.   **Series:** Second **Obv:**
National arms **Obv. Legend:** ESTADOS UNIDOS
MEXICANOS **Rev:** Aqueduct of Querétaro at left, church of
Santa Rosa de Viterbo at right **Rev. Legend:** ESTADO DE
QUERÉTARO ARTEAGA **Edge:** Segmented reeding **Mint:**
Mexico City

Date	Mintage	F	VF	XF	Unc	BU
2007Mo	149,127	—	—	—	25.00	30.00

KM# 884   100 PESOS
29.1690 g., Bi-Metallic .999 Gold 17.154g center in .999 Silver
12.015g ring, 34.5 mm.   **Series:** Second **Obv:** National arms
Obv. Legend: ESTADOS UNIDOS MEXICANOS **Rev:**
Aqueduct of Querétaro at left, church of Santa Rosa de Viterbo
at right **Rev. Legend:** ESTADO DE QUERÉTARO ARTEAGA
Edge: Segmented reeding **Mint:** Mexico City

Date	Mintage	F	VF	XF	Unc	BU
2007Mo Proof	600	Value: 875				

KM# 853 100 PESOS
33.9400 g., Bi-Metallic .925 Silver 20.1753g center in
Aluminum-Bronze ring, 39.04 mm. **Series:** Second **Obv:**
National arms **Obv. Legend:** ESTADOS UNIDOS
MEXICANOS **Rev:** Facade of Caja Real **Rev. Legend:** • SAN
LUIS POTOSÍ • **Edge:** Segmented reeding **Mint:** Mexico City

Date	Mintage	F	VF	XF	Unc	BU
2007Mo	148,750	—	—	—	25.00	30.00

KM# 885 100 PESOS
29.1690 g., Bi-Metallic .999 Gold 17.154g center in .999 Silver
12.015 ring, 34.5 mm. **Series:** Second **Obv:** National arms
Obv. Legend: ESTADOS UNIDOS MEXICANOS **Rev:**
Facade of Caja Real **Rev. Legend:** • SAN LUIS POTOSÍ •
Edge: Segmented reeding **Mint:** Mexico City

Date	Mintage	F	VF	XF	Unc	BU
2007Mo Proof	600	Value: 875				

KM# 855 100 PESOS
33.9400 g., Bi-Metallic .925 Silver 20.1753g center in
Aluminum-Bronze ring, 39.04 mm. **Series:** Second **Obv:**
National arms **Obv. Legend:** ESTADOS UNIDOS
MEXICANOS **Rev:** Local in Dance of the Deer at left, cactus
at right, mountains in background **Rev. Legend:** ESTADO
DE SONORA **Edge:** Segmented reeding **Mint:** Mexico City

Date	Mintage	F	VF	XF	Unc	BU
2007Mo	149,891	—	—	—	25.00	30.00

KM# 887 100 PESOS
29.1690 g., Bi-Metallic .999 Gold 17.154g center in .999 Silver
12.015g ring, 34.5 mm. **Series:** Second **Obv:** National arms
Obv. Legend: ESTADOS UNIDOS MEXICANOS **Rev:** Local
in Dance of the Deer at left, cactus at right, mountains in
background **Rev. Legend:** ESTADO DE SONORA **Edge:**
Segmented reeding **Mint:** Mexico City

Date	Mintage	F	VF	XF	Unc	BU
2007Mo Proof	600	Value: 875				

KM# 854 100 PESOS
33.9400 g., Bi-Metallic .925 Silver 20.1753g center in
Aluminum-Bronze ring, 39.04 mm. **Series:** Second **Obv:**
National arms **Obv. Legend:** ESTADOS UNIDOS
MEXICANOS **Rev:** Shield on pile of cactus fruits **Rev.
Legend:** ESTADO DE SINALOA - LUGAR DE PITAHAYAS
Edge: Segmented reeding **Mint:** Mexico City

Date	Mintage	F	VF	XF	Unc	BU
2007Mo	149,032	—	—	—	25.00	30.00

KM# 886 100 PESOS
29.1690 g., Bi-Metallic .999 Gold 17.154 center in .999 Silver
12.015g ring, 34.5 mm. **Series:** Second **Obv:** National arms
Obv. Legend: ESTADOS UNIDOS MEXICANOS **Rev:**
Shield on pile of cactus fruits **Rev. Legend:** ESTADO DE
SINALOA - LUGAR DE PITAHAYES **Edge:** Segmented
reeding **Mint:** Mexico City

Date	Mintage	F	VF	XF	Unc	BU
2007Mo Proof	600	Value: 875				

KM# 856 100 PESOS
33.9400 g., Bi-Metallic .925 Silver 20.1753 center in
Aluminum-Bronze ring, 39.04 mm. **Series:** Second **Obv:**
National arms **Obv. Legend:** ESTADOS UNIDOS
MEXICANOS **Rev:** Fuente de los Pescadores (fisherman
fountain) at lower left, giant head from the Olmec-pre-Hispanic
culture at right, Planetario Tabasco in background **Rev.
Legend:** TABASCO **Edge:** Segmented reeding **Mint:** Mexico
City

Date	Mintage	F	VF	XF	Unc	BU
2007Mo	149,715	—	—	—	25.00	30.00

KM# 888 100 PESOS
29.1690 g., Bi-Metallic .999 Gold 17.154g center in .999 Silver
12.015g ring, 34.5 mm. **Series:** Second **Obv:** National arms
Obv. Legend: ESTADOS UNIDOS MEXICANOS **Rev:**
Fuente de los Pescadores (fisherman fountain) at lower left,
giant head from the Olmec-pre-Hispanic culture at right,
Planetario Tabasco in background **Rev. Legend:** TABASCO
Edge: Segmented reeding **Mint:** Mexico City

Date	Mintage	F	VF	XF	Unc	BU
2007Mo Proof	600	Value: 875				

KM# 857   100 PESOS
33.9400 g., Bi-Metallic .925 Silver 20.1753g center in
Aluminum-Bronze ring, 39.04 mm.   **Series:** Second **Obv:**
National arms **Obv. Legend:** ESTADOS UNIDOS
MEXICANOS **Rev:** Ridge - Cerro Del Bernal, Gonzáles **Rev.
Legend:** TAMAULIPAS **Edge:** Segmented reeding **Mint:**
Mexico City

Date	Mintage	F	VF	XF	Unc	BU
2007Mo	149,776	—	—	—	25.00	30.00

KM# 889   100 PESOS
29.1690 g., Bi-Metallic .999 Gold 17.154g center in .999 Silver
12.015g ring, 34.5 mm.   **Series:** Second **Obv:** National arms
Obv. Legend: ESTADOS DE MEXICANOS **Rev:** Ridge -
Cerro Del Bernal, Gonzáles **Rev. Legend:** TAMAULIPAS
Edge: Segmented reeding **Mint:** Mexico City

Date	Mintage	F	VF	XF	Unc	BU
2007Mo Proof	600	Value: 875				

KM# 859   100 PESOS
33.9400 g., Bi-Metallic .912 Silver 20.1753g center in
Aluminum-Bronze ring, 39.04 mm.   **Series:** Second **Obv:**
National arms **Obv. Legend:** ESTADOS UNIDOS
MEXICANOS **Rev:** Pyramid of El Tajín **Rev. Legend:** •
VERACRUZ • - • DE IGNACIO DE LA LLAVE • **Edge:**
Segmented reeding **Mint:** Mexico City

Date	Mintage	F	VF	XF	Unc	BU
2007Mo	149,703	—	—	—	25.00	30.00

KM# 891   100 PESOS
29.1690 g., Bi-Metallic .999 Gold 17.154g center in .999 Silver
12.015g ring, 34.5 mm.   **Series:** Second **Obv:** National arms
Obv. Legend: ESTADOS UNIDOS MEXICANOS **Rev:**
Pyramid of El Tajin **Rev. Legend:** • VERACRUZ • - • DE
IGNACIO DE LA LLAVE • **Edge:** Segmented reeding **Mint:**
Mexico City

Date	Mintage	F	VF	XF	Unc	BU
2007Mo Proof	600	Value: 875				

KM# 858   100 PESOS
33.9400 g., Bi-Metallic .925 Silver 20.1753g center in
Aluminum-Bronze ring, 39.04 mm.   **Series:** Second **Obv:**
National arms **Obv. Legend:** ESTADOS UNIDOS
MEXICANOS **Rev:** Basilica de Ocotlán at left, state arms
above Capilla Abierta, Plaza de Toros Ranchero Aguilar
below, Exconvento de San Francisco at right **Rev. Legend:**
ESTADO DE TLAXCALA **Edge:** Segmented reeding **Mint:**
Mexico City

Date	Mintage	F	VF	XF	Unc	BU
2007Mo	149,465	—	—	—	25.00	30.00

KM# 890   100 PESOS
29.1690 g., Bi-Metallic .999 Gold 17.154g center in .999 Silver
12.015g ring, 34.5 mm.   **Series:** Second **Obv:** National arms
Obv. Legend: ESTADOS UNIDOS MEXICANOS **Rev:**
Basilica de Ocotlán at left, state arms above Capilla Abierta,
Plaza de Toros Ranchero Aguilar below, Exconvento de San
Francisco at right **Rev. Legend:** ESTADO DE TLAXCALA
Edge: Segmented reeding **Mint:** Mexico City

Date	Mintage	F	VF	XF	Unc	BU
2007Mo Proof	600	Value: 875				

KM# 860   100 PESOS
33.9400 g., Bi-Metallic .925 Silver 20.1753 center in
Aluminum-Bronze ring, 39.04 mm.   **Series:** Second **Obv:**
National arms **Obv. Legend:** ESTADOS UNIDOS
MEXICANOS **Rev:** Stylized pyramid of Chichén Itzá **Rev.
Legend:** Castillo de Chichén Itzá **Edge:** Segmented reeding
Mint: Mexico City

Date	Mintage	F	VF	XF	Unc	BU
2007Mo	149,579	—	—	—	25.00	30.00

KM# 892   100 PESOS
29.1690 g., Bi-Metallic .999 Gold 17.154g center in .999 Silver
12.015g ring, 34.5 mm.   **Series:** Second **Obv:** National arms
Obv. Legend: ESTADOS UNIDOS MEXICANOS **Rev:**
Stylized pyramid of Chichén-Itzá **Rev. Inscription:**
YUCATÁN **Edge:** Segmented reeding **Mint:** Mexico City

Date	Mintage	F	VF	XF	Unc	BU
2007Mo Proof	600	Value: 875				

KM# 861 100 PESOS
33.9400 g., Bi-Metallic .925 Silver 20.1753g center in
Aluminum-Bronze ring, 39.04 mm. **Series:** Second **Obv:**
National arms **Obv. Legend:** ESTADOS UNIDOS
MEXICANOS **Rev:** Cable car above Monumento al Minero at
left, Cathedral de Zacatecas at center right **Rev. Legend:**
ZACATECAS **Edge:** Segmented reeding **Mint:** Mexico City

Date	Mintage	F	VF	XF	Unc	BU
2007Mo	148,833	—	—	—	25.00	30.00

KM# 893 100 PESOS
29.1690 g., Bi-Metallic .999 Gold 17.154g center in .999 Silver
12.015g ring, 34.5 mm. **Series:** Second **Obv:** National arms
Obv. Legend: ESTADOS UNIDOS MEXICANOS **Rev:** Cable
car above Monumento al Minero at left, Cathedral de
Zacatecas at center right **Rev. Legend:** Zacatecas **Edge:**
Segmented reeding **Mint:** Mexico City

Date	Mintage	F	VF	XF	Unc	BU
2007Mo Proof	600	Value: 875				

KM# 771 50000 PESOS
7.7700 g., 0.9990 Gold 0.2496 oz. AGW, 23 mm. **Subject:**
World Cup Soccer **Obv:** Mexican Eagle and Snake **Rev:**
Kneeling Mayan Pelota player and soccer ball **Mint:** Mexico
City

Date	Mintage	F	VF	XF	Unc	BU
2006Mo Proof	9,505	Value: 600				

SILVER BULLION COINAGE
LIBERTAD SERIES

KM# 542 1/20 ONZA (1/20 Troy Ounce of Silver)
1.5551 g., 0.9990 Silver 0.0499 oz. ASW **Obv:** National
arms, eagle left **Rev:** Winged Victory **Mint:** Mexico City

Date	Mintage	F	VF	XF	Unc	BU
1991Mo	50,017	—	—	—	—	5.50
1992Mo	295,783	—	—	—	—	4.50
1992Mo Proof	5,000	Value: 10.00				
1993Mo	100,000	—	—	—	—	4.50
1993Mo Proof	5,002	Value: 10.00				
1994Mo	90,100	—	—	—	—	4.50
1994Mo Proof	5,002	Value: 10.00				
1995Mo	50,000	—	—	—	—	5.50
1995Mo Proof	2,000	Value: 12.00				

KM# 609 1/20 ONZA (1/20 Troy Ounce of Silver)
1.5551 g., 0.9990 Silver 0.0499 oz. ASW **Obv:** National
arms, eagle left **Rev:** Winged Victory **Mint:** Mexico City

Date	Mintage	F	VF	XF	Unc	BU
1996Mo	50,000	—	—	—	—	20.00
1996Mo Proof	1,000	Value: 30.00				
1997Mo	20,000	—	—	—	—	20.00
1997Mo Proof	800	Value: 30.00				
1998Mo	6,400	—	—	—	—	30.00

Date	Mintage	F	VF	XF	Unc	BU
1998Mo Proof	300	Value: 37.00				
1999Mo	8,001	—	—	—	—	25.00
1999Mo Proof	600	Value: 33.00				
2000Mo	57,500	—	—	—	—	25.00
2000Mo Proof	900	Value: 33.00				
2001Mo	25,000	—	—	—	—	25.00
2001Mo Proof	45,000	Value: 30.00				
2002Mo	2,800	—	—	—	—	16.00
2002Mo Proof	50,000	Value: 25.00				
2003Mo	4,400	—	—	—	—	16.00
2003Mo Proof	30,000	Value: 25.00				
2004Mo	2,700	—	—	—	—	16.00
2004Mo Proof	15,000	Value: 25.00				
2005Mo	2,600	—	—	—	—	16.00
2005Mo Proof	1,500	Value: 25.00				
2006Mo	20,000	—	—	—	—	16.00
2006Mo Proof	3,500	Value: 25.00				
2007Mo	4,000	—	—	—	—	16.00
2007Mo Proof	7,000	Value: 25.00				
2008Mo	3,300	—	—	—	—	16.00
2008Mo Proof	10,000	Value: 25.00				
2009Mo	5,000	—	—	—	—	16.00
2009Mo Proof	—	Value: 25.00				

KM# 543 1/10 ONZA (1/10 Troy Ounce of Silver)
3.1103 g., 0.9990 Silver 0.0999 oz. ASW **Obv:** National
arms, eagle left **Rev:** Winged Victory **Mint:** Mexico City

Date	Mintage	F	VF	XF	Unc	BU
1991Mo	50,017	—	—	—	—	7.50
1992Mo	299,983	—	—	—	—	6.50
1992Mo Proof	5,000	Value: 12.00				
1993Mo	100,000	—	—	—	—	6.50
1993Mo Proof	5,002	Value: 12.00				
1994Mo	90,100	—	—	—	—	6.50
1994Mo Proof	5,002	Value: 12.00				
1995Mo	50,000	—	—	—	—	7.50
1995Mo Proof	2,000	Value: 13.50				

KM# 610 1/10 ONZA (1/10 Troy Ounce of Silver)
3.1103 g., 0.9990 Silver 0.0999 oz. ASW **Obv:** National
arms, eagle left **Rev:** Winged Victory **Mint:** Mexico City

Date	Mintage	F	VF	XF	Unc	BU
1996Mo	50,000	—	—	—	—	25.00
1996Mo Proof	1,000	Value: 35.00				
1997Mo	20,000	—	—	—	—	25.00
1997Mo Proof	800	Value: 35.00				
1998Mo	6,400	—	—	—	—	33.00
1998Mo Proof	300	Value: 45.00				
1999Mo	8,000	—	—	—	—	27.50
1999Mo Proof	600	Value: 40.00				
2000Mo	27,500	—	—	—	—	27.50
2000Mo Proof	1,000	Value: 40.00				
2001Mo	25,000	—	—	—	—	27.50
2001Mo Proof	1,500	Value: 36.00				
2002Mo	35,000	—	—	—	—	20.00
2002Mo Proof	2,800	Value: 30.00				
2003Mo	20,000	—	—	—	—	20.00
2003Mo Proof	4,900	Value: 30.00				
2004Mo	15,000	—	—	—	—	20.00
2004Mo Proof	2,500	Value: 30.00				
2005Mo	9,277	—	—	—	—	20.00
2005Mo Proof	3,000	Value: 27.50				
2006Mo	15,000	—	—	—	—	20.00

Date	Mintage	F	VF	XF	Unc	BU
2006Mo Proof	3,000	Value: 27.50				
2007Mo	3,500	—	—	—	—	20.00
2007Mo Proof	4,000	Value: 27.50				
2008Mo	10,000	—	—	—	—	20.00
2008Mo Proof	5,000	Value: 27.50				
2009Mo	10,000	—	—	—	—	20.00
2009Mo Proof	5,000	Value: 27.50				

KM# 544   1/4 ONZA (1/4 Troy Ounce of Silver)
7.7758 g., 0.9990 Silver 0.2497 oz. ASW **Obv:** National arms, eagle left **Rev:** Winged Victory **Mint:** Mexico City

Date	Mintage	F	VF	XF	Unc	BU
1991Mo	50,017	—	—	—	—	10.00
1992Mo	104,000	—	—	—	—	8.50
1992Mo Proof	5,000	Value: 15.00				
1993Mo	90,500	—	—	—	—	8.50
1993Mo Proof	5,002	Value: 15.00				
1994Mo	90,100	—	—	—	—	8.50
1994Mo Proof	5,002	Value: 15.00				
1995Mo	50,000	—	—	—	—	10.00
1995Mo Proof	2,000	Value: 16.50				

KM# 611   1/4 ONZA (1/4 Troy Ounce of Silver)
7.7758 g., 0.9990 Silver 0.2497 oz. ASW **Obv:** National arms, eagle left **Rev:** Winged Victory **Mint:** Mexico City

Date	Mintage	F	VF	XF	Unc	BU
1996Mo	50,000	—	—	—	—	32.00
1996Mo Proof	1,000	Value: 40.00				
1997Mo	20,000	—	—	—	—	32.00
1997Mo Proof	800	Value: 40.00				
1998Mo	6,400	—	—	—	—	40.00
1998Mo Proof	300	Value: 65.00				
1999Mo	7,000	—	—	—	—	36.00
1999Mo Proof	600	Value: 50.00				
2000Mo	21,000	—	—	—	—	36.00
2000Mo Proof	700	Value: 50.00				
2001Mo	25,000	—	—	—	—	36.00
2001Mo Proof	1,000	Value: 44.00				
2002Mo	35,000	—	—	—	—	27.50
2002Mo Proof	2,800	Value: 40.00				
2003Mo	22,000	—	—	—	—	27.50
2003Mo Proof	3,900	Value: 40.00				
2004Mo	15,000	—	—	—	—	27.50
2004Mo Proof	2,500	Value: 40.00				
2005Mo	15,000	—	—	—	—	27.50
2005Mo Proof	2,400	Value: 37.00				
2006Mo	15,000	—	—	—	—	25.00
2006Mo Proof	2,900	Value: 37.00				
2007Mo	3,500	—	—	—	—	25.00
2007Mo Proof	3,000	Value: 37.00				
2008Mo	9,000	—	—	—	—	25.00
2008Mo Proof	2,800	Value: 37.00				
2009Mo	10,000	—	—	—	—	25.00
2009Mo Proof	3,000	Value: 37.00				

KM# 545   1/2 ONZA (1/2 Troy Ounce of Silver)
15.5517 g., 0.9990 Silver 0.4995 oz. ASW **Obv:** National arms, eagle left **Rev:** Winged Victory **Mint:** Mexico City

Date	Mintage	F	VF	XF	Unc	BU
1991Mo	50,618	—	—	—	—	14.00
1992Mo	119,000	—	—	—	—	12.00
1992Mo Proof	5,000	Value: 17.50				
1993Mo	90,500	—	—	—	—	12.00
1993Mo Proof	5,002	Value: 17.50				
1994Mo	90,100	—	—	—	—	12.00
1994Mo Proof	5,002	Value: 17.50				
1995Mo	50,000	—	—	—	—	12.00
1995Mo Proof	2,000	Value: 18.50				

KM# 612   1/2 ONZA (1/2 Troy Ounce of Silver)
15.5517 g., 0.9990 Silver 0.4995 oz. ASW **Obv:** National arms, eagle left **Rev:** Winged Victory **Mint:** Mexico City

Date	Mintage	F	VF	XF	Unc	BU
1996Mo	50,000	—	—	—	—	40.00
1996Mo Proof	1,000	Value: 60.00				
1997Mo	20,000	—	—	—	—	40.00
1997Mo Proof	800	Value: 60.00				
1998Mo	6,400	—	—	—	—	60.00
1998Mo Proof	2,500	Value: 90.00				
1999Mo	2,000	—	—	—	—	44.00
1999Mo Proof	600	Value: 70.00				
2000Mo	20,000	—	—	—	—	44.00
2000Mo Proof	700	Value: 70.00				
2001Mo	20,000	—	—	—	—	44.00
2001Mo Proof	1,000	Value: 60.00				
2002Mo	35,000	—	—	—	—	36.00
2002Mo Proof	2,800	Value: 50.00				
2003Mo	28,000	—	—	—	—	36.00
2003Mo Proof	3,400	Value: 50.00				
2004Mo	20,000	—	—	—	—	36.00
2004Mo Proof	2,500	Value: 50.00				
2005Mo	10,000	—	—	—	—	36.00
2005Mo Proof	2,800	Value: 44.00				
2006Mo	15,000	—	—	—	—	36.00
2006Mo Proof	2,900	Value: 44.00				
2007Mo	3,500	—	—	—	—	36.00
2007Mo Proof	1,500	Value: 44.00				
2008Mo	9,000	—	—	—	—	36.00
2008Mo Proof	2,500	Value: 44.00				
2009Mo	10,000	—	—	—	—	36.00
2009Mo Proof	3,000	Value: 44.00				

KM# 494.1   ONZA (Troy Ounce of Silver)
31.1000 g., 0.9990 Silver 0.9988 oz. ASW **Subject:** Libertad **Obv:** National arms, eagle left **Rev:** Winged Victory **Edge:** Plain **Mint:** Mexico City

Date	Mintage	F	VF	XF	Unc	BU
1982Mo	1,049,680	—	—	—	BV	32.00
1983Mo	1,001,768	—	—	—	BV	40.00
1983Mo Proof	998	Value: 600				
1984Mo	1,014,000	—	—	—	BV	32.00
1985Mo	2,017,000	—	—	—	BV	32.00
1986Mo	1,699,426	—	—	—	BV	32.00
1986Mo Proof	30,006	Value: 40.00				
1987Mo	500,000	—	—	—	BV	50.00
1987Mo Doubled die	Inc. above	—	—	—	—	70.00
1987Mo Proof	12,000	Value: 55.00				
1988Mo	1,500,500	—	—	—	BV	55.00
1989Mo	1,396,500	—	—	—	BV	42.00
1989Mo Proof	10,000	Value: 85.00				

KM# 494.2   ONZA (Troy Ounce of Silver)
31.1000 g., 0.9990 Silver 0.9988 oz. ASW **Obv:** National arms, eagle left **Rev:** Winged Victory **Edge:** Reeded **Mint:** Mexico City

Date	Mintage	F	VF	XF	Unc	BU
1988Mo	10,000	Value: 95.00				
1990Mo	1,200,000	—	—	—	BV	32.00
1990Mo Proof	10,000	Value: 80.00				
1991Mo	1,650,518	—	—	—	BV	45.00

KM# 494.5   ONZA (Troy Ounce of Silver)
31.1000 g., 0.9990 Silver 0.9988 oz. ASW **Subject:** Libertad **Obv:** National arms, eagle left, KM#494.3 **Rev:** Winged Victory, KM#494.2 **Edge:** Reeded **Mint:** Mexico City **Note:** Mule

Date	Mintage	F	VF	XF	Unc	BU
1991Mo Proof	10,000	Value: 75.00				

KM# 494.3   ONZA (Troy Ounce of Silver)
31.1000 g., 0.9990 Silver 0.9988 oz. ASW **Subject:** Libertad **Obv:** National arms, eight dots below eagle's left talons **Rev:** Winged Victory with revised design and lettering **Edge:** Reeded **Mint:** Mexico City

Date	Mintage	F	VF	XF	Unc	BU
1991Mo	Inc. above	—	—	—	BV	47.00
1991Mo Proof	10,000	Value: 75.00				
1992Mo	2,458,000	—	—	—	BV	42.00
1992Mo Proof	10,000	Value: 75.00				

KM# 494.4   ONZA (Troy Ounce of Silver)
31.1000 g., 0.9990 Silver 0.9988 oz. ASW **Subject:** Libertad **Obv:** National arms, Seven dots below eagle's left talon, dull claws on right talon, thick lettering **Rev:** Winged Victory with revised design and lettering **Edge:** Reeded **Mint:** Mexico City

Date	Mintage	F	VF	XF	Unc	BU
1993Mo	1,000,000	—	—	—	BV	35.00
1993Mo Proof	5,002	Value: 80.00				
1994Mo	400,000	—	—	—	BV	40.00

Date	Mintage	F	VF	XF	Unc	BU
1994Mo Proof	5,002	Value: 75.00				
1995Mo	500,000	—	—	—	BV	40.00
1995Mo Proof	2,000	Value: 75.00				

KM# 613   ONZA (Troy Ounce of Silver)
33.6250 g., 0.9250 Silver 0.9999 oz. ASW **Obv:** National arms, eagle left **Rev:** Winged Victory **Mint:** Mexico City

Date	Mintage	F	VF	XF	Unc	BU
1996Mo	300,000	—	—	—	—	42.00
1996Mo Proof	2,000	Value: 80.00				
1997Mo	100,000	—	—	—	—	50.00
1997Mo Proof	1,500	Value: 60.00				
1998Mo	67,000	—	—	—	—	125
1998Mo Proof	500	Value: 195				
1999Mo	95,000	—	—	—	—	45.00
1999Mo Proof	600	Value: 85.00				

KM# 639   ONZA (Troy Ounce of Silver)
31.1000 g., 0.9990 Silver 0.9988 oz. ASW **Subject:** Libertad **Obv:** National arms, eagle left within center of past and present arms **Rev:** Winged Victory **Edge:** Reeded **Mint:** Mexico City

Date	Mintage	F	VF	XF	Unc	BU
2000Mo	340,000	—	—	—	—	80.00
2000Mo Proof	1,600	Value: 140				
2001Mo	725,000	—	—	—	—	60.00
2001Mo Proof	2,000	Value: 140				
2002Mo	854,000	—	—	—	—	55.00
2002Mo Proof	3,800	Value: 150				
2003Mo	805,000	—	—	—	—	55.00
2003Mo Proof	5,400	Value: 130				
2004Mo	450,000	—	—	—	—	75.00
2004Mo Proof	3,000	Value: 130				
2005Mo	698,281	—	—	—	—	90.00
2005Mo Proof	3,300	Value: 150				
2006Mo	300,000	—	—	—	—	55.00
2006Mo Proof	4,000	Value: 140				
2007Mo	200,000	—	—	—	—	95.00

Date	Mintage	F	VF	XF	Unc	BU
2007Mo Proof	5,800	Value: 150				
2008Mo	950,000	—	—	—	—	65.00
2008Mo Proof	11,000	Value: 150				
2009Mo	1,650,000	—	—	—	—	75.00
2009Mo Proof	10,000	Value: 150				

KM# 614 2 ONZAS (2 Troy Ounces of Silver)
62.2070 g., 0.9990 Silver 1.9979 oz. ASW, 48 mm. **Subject:**
Libertad **Obv:** National arms, eagle left within center of past
and present arms **Rev:** Winged Victory **Edge:** Reeded **Mint:**
Mexico City

Date	Mintage	F	VF	XF	Unc	BU
1996Mo	50,000	—	—	—	—	120
1996Mo Proof	1,200	Value: 180				
1997Mo	15,000	—	—	—	—	120
1997Mo Proof	1,300	Value: 150				
1998Mo	7,000	—	—	—	—	110
1998Mo Proof	400	Value: 450				
1999Mo	5,000	—	—	—	—	130
1999Mo Proof	280	Value: 7,100				
2000Mo	7,500	—	—	—	—	130
2000Mo Proof	500	Value: 190				
2001Mo	6,700	—	—	—	—	120
2001Mo Proof	500	Value: 160				
2002Mo	8,700	—	—	—	—	110
2002Mo Proof	1,000	Value: 190				
2003Mo	9,500	—	—	—	—	110
2003Mo Proof	800	Value: 190				
2004Mo	8,000	—	—	—	—	100
2004Mo Proof	1,000	Value: 160				
2005Mo	3,549	—	—	—	—	100
2005Mo Proof	600	Value: 150				
2006Mo	5,800	—	—	—	—	100
2006Mo Proof	1,100	Value: 150				
2007Mo	8,000	—	—	—	—	100
2007Mo Proof	500	Value: 170				
2008Mo	17,000	—	—	—	—	110
2008Mo Proof	1,000	Value: 170				
2009Mo	46,000	—	—	—	—	110
2009Mo Proof	6,200	Value: 170				

KM# 615 5 ONZAS (5 Troy Ounces of Silver)
155.5175 g., 0.9990 Silver 4.9948 oz. ASW, 65 mm.
Subject: Libertad **Obv:** National arms, eagle left within center
of past and present arms **Rev:** Winged Victory **Edge:** Reeded
Mint: Mexico City **Note:** Illustration reduced.

Date	Mintage	F	VF	XF	Unc	BU
1996Mo	20,000	—	—	—	—	265
1996Mo Proof	1,200	Value: 295				
1997Mo	10,000	—	—	—	—	265
1997Mo Proof	1,300	Value: 295				
1998Mo	3,500	—	—	—	—	325
1998Mo Proof	400	Value: 1,000				
1999Mo	2,800	—	—	—	—	255
1999Mo Proof	100	Value: 1,250				
2000Mo	4,000	—	—	—	—	255
2000Mo Proof	500	Value: 375				
2001Mo	4,000	—	—	—	—	180
2001Mo Proof	600	Value: 325				
2002Mo	5,200	—	—	—	—	180
2002Mo Proof	1,000	Value: 325				
2003Mo	6,000	—	—	—	—	165
2003Mo Proof	1,500	Value: 250				
2004Mo	3,923	—	—	—	—	165
2004Mo Proof	800	Value: 225				
2005Mo	2,401	—	—	—	—	205
2005Mo Proof	1,000	Value: 225				
2006Mo	3,000	—	—	—	—	165
2006Mo Proof	700	Value: 265				
2007Mo	3,000	—	—	—	—	165
2007Mo Proof	500	Value: 205				
2008Mo	9,000	—	—	—	—	205
2008Mo Proof	900	Value: 270				
2009Mo	21,000	—	—	—	—	225
2009Mo Proof	5,000	Value: 270				

KM# 677 KILO (32.15 Troy Ounces of Silver)
999.9775 g., 0.9990 Silver 32.116 oz. ASW, 110 mm.
Subject: Collector Bullion **Obv:** National arms in center of
past and present arms **Rev:** Winged Victory **Edge:** Reeded
Mint: Mexico City

Date	Mintage	F	VF	XF	Unc	BU
2001Mo Prooflike	—	—	—	—	—	2,200
2002Mo Prooflike	1,100	—	—	—	—	1,750
2003Mo Prooflike	2,234	—	—	—	—	1,650
2004Mo Prooflike	500	—	—	—	—	1,800
2005Mo Prooflike	874	—	—	—	—	1,750
2006Mo Prooflike	—	—	—	—	—	1,650
2007Mo Prooflike	—	—	—	—	—	1,650
2008Mo Prooflike	—	—	—	—	—	1,650
2009Mo Prooflike	—	—	—	—	—	1,650

GOLD BULLION COINAGE

KM# 530 1/20 ONZA (1/20 Ounce of Pure Gold)
1.7500 g., 0.9000 Gold 0.0506 oz. AGW **Obv:** Winged
Victory **Rev:** Calendar stone **Mint:** Mexico City

Date	Mintage	F	VF	XF	Unc	BU
1987Mo	—	—	—	—	—	275
1988Mo						

KM# 589 1/20 ONZA (1/20 Ounce of Pure Gold)
1.5551 g., 0.9990 Gold 0.0499 oz. AGW, 13 mm. **Obv:** Winged
Victory **Rev:** National arms, eagle left **Mint:** Mexico City

Date	Mintage	F	VF	XF	Unc	BU
1991Mo	10,000	—	—	—	—BV+30%	
1992Mo	65,225	—	—	—	—BV+30%	
1993Mo	10,000	—	—	—	—BV+30%	
1994Mo	10,000	—	—	—	—BV+30%	

KM# 642 1/20 ONZA (1/20 Ounce of Pure Gold)
1.5551 g., 0.9990 Gold 0.0499 oz. AGW **Obv:** National arms,
eagle left **Rev:** Native working **Mint:** Mexico City

Date	Mintage	F	VF	XF	Unc	BU
2000Mo Proof	—	Value: 95.00				

KM# 671 1/20 ONZA (1/20 Ounce of Pure Gold)
1.5551 g., 0.9990 Gold 0.0499 oz. AGW, 13 mm. **Obv:**
National arms, eagle left **Rev:** Winged Victory **Edge:** Reeded
Mint: Mexico City **Note:** Design similar to KM#609. Value
estimates do not include the high taxes and surcharges added
to the issue prices by the Mexican Government.

Date	Mintage	F	VF	XF	Unc	BU
2000Mo	5,300	—	—	—	—BV+30%	
2002Mo	5,000	—	—	—	—BV+30%	
2003Mo	800	—	—	—	—BV+32%	
2004Mo	7,000	—	—	—	—BV+30%	
2005Mo	3,200	—	—	—	—BV+30%	
2005Mo Proof	400	BV+35%				
2006Mo	3,200	—	—	—	—BV+30%	
2006Mo Proof	3,000	BV+35%				
2007Mo	1,200	—	—	—	—BV+30%	
2007Mo Proof	500	BV+35%				
2008Mo	800	—	—	—	—BV+30%	
2008Mo Proof	500	—	—	—	—BV+35%	
2009Mo	2,000	—	—	—	—BV+30%	
2009Mo Proof	600	—	—	—	—BV+35%	

KM# 628 1/15 ONZA (1/15 Ounce of Pure Gold)
0.9990 Gold **Obv:** Winged Victory above legend **Rev:**
National arms, eagle left within circle **Mint:** Mexico City

Date	Mintage	F	VF	XF	Unc	BU
1987Mo	—	—	—	—	—	275

KM# 541 1/10 ONZA (1/10 Ounce of Pure Gold)
3.1103 g., 0.9990 Gold 0.0999 oz. AGW, 16 mm. **Obv:** National
arms, eagle left **Rev:** Winged Victory **Mint:** Mexico City

Date	Mintage	F	VF	XF	Unc	BU
1991Mo	10,000	—	—	—	—BV+20%	

Date	Mintage	F	VF	XF	Unc	BU
1992Mo	50,777	—	—	—	—BV+20%	
1993Mo	10,000	—	—	—	—BV+20%	
1994Mo	10,000	—	—	—	—BV+20%	

KM# 672 1/10 ONZA (1/10 Ounce of Pure Gold)
3.1103 g., 0.9990 Gold 0.0999 oz. AGW, 16 mm. **Obv:**
National arms, eagle left **Rev:** Winged Victory **Edge:** Reeded
Mint: Mexico City **Note:** Design similar to KM#610. Value
estimates do not include the high taxes and surcharges added
to the issue prices by the Mexican Government.

Date	Mintage	F	VF	XF	Unc	BU
2000Mo	3,500	—	—	—	—BV+20%	
2002Mo	5,000	—	—	—	—BV+20%	
2003Mo	300	—	—	—	—BV+22%	
2004Mo	2,000	—	—	—	—BV+20%	
2005Mo	500	—	—	—	—BV+20%	
2005Mo Proof	400	BV+22%				
2006Mo	2,500	—	—	—	—BV+20%	
2006Mo Proof	520	BV+22%				
2007Mo	1,200	—	—	—	—BV+20%	
2007Mo Proof	500	BV+22%				
2008Mo	2,500	—	—	—	—BV+20%	
2008Mo Proof	500	BV+22%				
2009Mo	9,000	—	—	—	—BV+20%	
2009Mo Proof	600	BV+22%				

KM# 487 1/4 ONZA (1/4 Ounce of Pure Gold)
8.6396 g., 0.9000 Gold 0.2500 oz. **Obv:** National arms,
eagle left **Rev:** Winged Victory **Mint:** Mexico City **Note:**
Similar to KM#488.

Date	Mintage	F	VF	XF	Unc	BU
1981Mo	313,000	—	—	—	—BV+11%	
1982Mo					—BV+11%	

KM# 590 1/4 ONZA (1/4 Ounce of Pure Gold)
7.7758 g., 0.9990 Gold 0.2497 oz. AGW, 23 mm. **Obv:**
Winged Victory above legend **Rev:** National arms, eagle left
Mint: Mexico City

Date	Mintage	F	VF	XF	Unc	BU
1991Mo	10,000	—	—	—	—BV+11%	
1992Mo	28,106	—	—	—	—BV+11%	
1993Mo	2,500	—	—	—	—BV+11%	
1994Mo	2,500	—	—	—	—BV+11%	

KM# 673 1/4 ONZA (1/4 Ounce of Pure Gold)
7.7758 g., 0.9990 Gold 0.2497 oz. AGW, 23 mm. **Obv:**
National arms, eagle left **Rev:** Winged Victory **Edge:** Reeded
Mint: Mexico City **Note:** Design similar to KM#611. Value
estimates do not include the high taxes and surcharges added
to the issue prices by the Mexican Government.

Date	Mintage	F	VF	XF	Unc	BU
2000Mo	2,500	—	—	—	—BV+12%	
2002Mo	5,000	—	—	—	—BV+12%	
2003Mo	300	—	—	—	—BV+14%	
2004Mo	1,500	—	—	—	—BV+12%	
2004Mo Proof	1,000	BV+15%				
2005Mo	500	—	—	—	—BV+12%	
2005Mo Proof	2,600	BV+15%				
2006Mo	1,500	—	—	—	—BV+12%	
2006Mo Proof	2,120	BV+15%				
2007Mo	500	—	—	—	—BV+12%	
2007Mo Proof	1,500	BV+15%				
2008Mo	800	—	—	—	—BV+12%	
2008Mo Proof	800	BV+15%				
2009Mo	3,000	—	—	—	—BV+12%	
2009Mo Proof	1,700	BV+15%				

KM# 488 1/2 ONZA (1/2 Ounce of Pure Gold)
17.2792 g., 0.9000 Gold 0.5000 oz. AGW **Obv:** National
arms, eagle left **Rev:** Winged Victory **Mint:** Mexico City

Date	Mintage	F	VF	XF	Unc	BU
1981Mo	193,000	—	—	—	—BV+8%	

BULLION • LIBERTAD

Date	Mintage	F	VF	XF	Unc	BU
1982Mo	—	—	—	—	—	BV+8%
1989Mo Proof	704	Value: 775				

KM# 591   1/2 ONZA (1/2 Ounce of Pure Gold)
15.5517 g., 0.9990 Gold 0.4995 oz. AGW, 29 mm. **Obv:** Winged Victory above legend **Rev:** National arms, eagle left **Mint:** Mexico City

Date	Mintage	F	VF	XF	Unc	BU
1991Mo	10,000	—	—	—	—	BV+8%
1992Mo	25,220	—	—	—	—	BV+8%
1993Mo	2,500	—	—	—	—	BV+8%
1994Mo	2,500	—	—	—	—	BV+8%

KM# 674   1/2 ONZA (1/2 Ounce of Pure Gold)
15.5517 g., 0.9990 Gold 0.4995 oz. AGW, 29 mm. **Obv:** National arms, eagle left **Rev:** Winged Victory **Edge:** Reeded **Mint:** Mexico City **Note:** Design similar to KM#612. Value estimates do not include the high taxes and surcharges added to the issue prices by the Mexican Government.

Date	Mintage	F	VF	XF	Unc	BU
2000Mo	1,500	—	—	—	—	BV+8%
2002Mo	5,000	—	—	—	—	BV+8%
2003Mo	300	—	—	—	—	BV+10%
2004Mo	500	—	—	—	—	BV+8%
2005Mo	500	—	—	—	—	BV+8%
2005Mo Proof	400	BV+12%				
2006Mo	500	—	—	—	—	BV+8%
2006Mo Proof	520	BV+12%				
2007Mo	500	—	—	—	—	BV+8%
2007Mo Proof	500	BV+12%				
2008Mo	300	—	—	—	—	BV+8%
2008Mo Proof	500	BV+12%				
2009Mo	3,000	—	—	—	—	BV+8%
2009Mo Proof	600	BV+12%				

KM# 489   ONZA (Ounce of Pure Gold)
34.5585 g., 0.9000 Gold 0.9999 oz. AGW **Obv:** National arms, eagle left **Rev:** Winged Victory **Mint:** Mexico City **Note:** Similar to KM#488.

Date	Mintage	F	VF	XF	Unc	BU
1981Mo	596,000	—	—	—	—	BV+3%
1985Mo	—	—	—	—	—	BV+3%
1988Mo	—	—	—	—	—	BV+3%

KM# 592   ONZA (Ounce of Pure Gold)
31.1035 g., 0.9990 Gold 0.9990 oz. AGW, 34.5 mm. **Obv:** Winged Victory above legend **Rev:** National arms, eagle left **Mint:** Mexico City

Date	Mintage	F	VF	XF	Unc	BU
1991Mo	109,193	—	—	—	—	BV+3%
1992Mo	46,281	—	—	—	—	BV+3%
1993Mo	73,881	—	—	—	—	BV+3%
1994Mo	1,000	—	—	—	—	BV+3%

KM# 675   ONZA (Ounce of Pure Gold)
31.1035 g., 0.9990 Gold 0.9990 oz. AGW, 34.5 mm. **Obv:** National arms, eagle left **Rev:** Winged Victory **Edge:** Reeded **Mint:** Mexico City **Note:** Design similar to KM#639. Value estimates do not include the high taxes and surcharges added to the issue prices by the Mexican Government.

Date	Mintage	F	VF	XF	Unc	BU
2000Mo	2,370	—	—	—	—	BV+3%
2002Mo	15,000	—	—	—	—	BV+3%
2003Mo	500	—	—	—	—	BV+4%
2004Mo	3,000	—	—	—	—	BV+3%
2004Mo Proof	150	BV+5%				
2005Mo	3,000	—	—	—	—	BV+3%
2005Mo Proof	250	BV+5%				
2006Mo	4,000	—	—	—	—	BV+3%
2006Mo Proof	520	BV+5%				
2007Mo	2,500	—	—	—	—	BV+3%
2007Mo Proof	500	BV+5%				
2008Mo	800	—	—	—	—	BV+3%
2008Mo Proof	500	BV+5%				
2009Mo	6,200	—	—	—	—	BV+3%
2009Mo Proof	600	BV+5%				

PLATINUM BULLION COINAGE

KM# 538   1/4 ONZA (1/4 Ounce)
7.7775 g., 0.9990 Platinum 0.2498 oz. APW **Obv:** National arms, eagle left **Rev:** Winged Victory **Mint:** Mexico City

Date	Mintage	F	VF	XF	Unc	BU
1989Mo Proof	3,500	Value: 550				

BULLION COINAGE

PRE-COLUMBIAN • AZTECA SERIES

KM# 644   NUEVO PESO
7.7700 g., 0.9990 Silver 0.2496 oz. ASW, 26.8 mm. **Subject:** Eagle Warrior **Obv:** National arms, eagle left within D-shaped circle and dotted border **Rev:** Eagle warrior within D-shaped circle and dotted border **Edge:** Reeded **Mint:** Mexico City

Date	Mintage	F	VF	XF	Unc	BU
1993Mo	1,500	—	—	—	—	18.00
1993 Proof	900	Value: 30.00				

KM# 645   2 NUEVO PESOS
15.4200 g., 0.9990 Silver 0.4952 oz. ASW, 32.9 mm. **Subject:** Eagle Warrior **Obv:** National arms, eagle left **Rev:** Eagle warrior **Edge:** Reeded **Mint:** Mexico City

Date	Mintage	F	VF	XF	Unc	BU
1993Mo	1,500	—	—	—	—	20.00
1993 Proof	800	Value: 40.00				

KM# 646   5 NUEVO PESOS
31.0500 g., 0.9990 Silver 0.9972 oz. ASW, 40 mm. **Subject:** Eagle Warrior **Obv:** National arms, eagle left **Rev:** Eagle warrior **Edge:** Reeded **Mint:** Mexico City

Date	Mintage	F	VF	XF	Unc	BU
1993	2,000	—	—	—	—	35.00
1993 Proof	1,000	Value: 70.00				

KM# 647   5 NUEVO PESOS
31.0000 g., 0.9990 Silver 0.9956 oz. ASW, 40 mm. **Subject:** Xochipilli **Obv:** National arms, eagle left within D-shaped circle and flower blossom border **Rev:** Seated figure sculpture within D-shaped circle and flower blossom border **Edge:** Reeded **Mint:** Mexico City

Date	Mintage	F	VF	XF	Unc	BU
1993	2,000	—	—	—	—	35.00
1993 Proof	800	Value: 85.00				

KM# 649   5 NUEVO PESOS
31.0000 g., 0.9990 Silver 0.9956 oz. ASW, 40 mm. **Subject:** Huchucteotl **Obv:** National arms, eagle left within D-shaped circle and designed border **Rev:** Aztec sculpture within D-shaped circle and designed border **Edge:** Reeded

Date	Mintage	F	VF	XF	Unc	BU
1993	5,000	—	—	—	—	35.00
1993 Proof	800	Value: 85.00				

KM# 648   5 NUEVO PESOS
31.0000 g., 0.9990 Silver 0.9956 oz. ASW, 40 mm. **Subject:** Brasco Efigie **Obv:** National arms, eagle left within D-shaped circle and designed border **Rev:** Sculpture within D-shaped circle and designed border **Edge:** Reeded

Date	Mintage	F	VF	XF	Unc	BU
1993	2,000	—	—	—	—	50.00
1993 Proof	500	Value: 95.00				

KM# 650   10 NUEVO PESOS
155.3100 g., 0.9990 Silver 4.9881 oz. ASW, 65 mm.
Subject: Piedra de Tizoc **Obv:** National arms, eagle left **Rev:**
Warrior capturing woman **Edge:** Reeded **Mint:** Mexico City
Note: Illustration reduced, similar to 100 Pesos, KM# 557

Date	Mintage	F	VF	XF	Unc	BU
1992 Proof	—	Value: 300				
1993	1,000	—	—	—	—	150
1993 Proof	1,000	Value: 200				

KM# 554   25 PESOS
7.7758 g., 0.9990 Silver 0.2497 oz. ASW   **Obv:** National
arms, eagle left within D-shaped circle and designed border
Rev: Eagle warrior right within D-shaped circle and a designed
border **Mint:** Mexico City

Date	Mintage	F	VF	XF	Unc	BU
1992	50,000	—	—	—	18.00	—
1992 Proof	3,000	Value: 30.00				

KM# 555   50 PESOS
15.5517 g., 0.9990 Silver 0.4995 oz. ASW   **Obv:** National
arms, eagle left within D-shaped circle designed border **Rev:**
Eagle warrior right within D-shaped circle and designed
border **Mint:** Mexico City

Date	Mintage	F	VF	XF	Unc	BU
1992	50,000	—	—	—	25.00	—
1992 Proof	3,000	Value: 40.00				

KM# 556   100 PESOS
31.1035 g., 0.9990 Silver 0.9990 oz. ASW **Obv:** National
arms, eagle left **Rev:** Eagle warrior **Mint:** Mexico City

Date	Mintage	F	VF	XF	Unc	BU
1992	205,000	—	—	—	35.00	47.50
1992	4,000	Value: 75.00				

KM# 562   100 PESOS
31.1035 g., 0.9990 Silver 0.9990 oz. ASW   **Obv:** National
arms, eagle left within D-shaped circle and designed border
Rev: Seated figure sculpture within D-shaped circle and
designed border **Mint:** Mexico City

Date	Mintage	F	VF	XF	Unc	BU
1992 Proof	4,000	Value: 90.00				

KM# 563   100 PESOS
31.1035 g., 0.9990 Silver 0.9990 oz. ASW   **Obv:** National
arms, eagle left within D-shaped circle and designed border
Rev: Brasero Efigie - The God of Rain within D-shaped circle
and designed border **Mint:** Mexico City

Date	Mintage	F	VF	XF	Unc	BU
1992 Proof	4,000	Value: 75.00				

KM# 564   100 PESOS
31.1035 g., 0.9990 Silver 0.9990 oz. ASW   **Obv:** National
arms, eagle left within D-shaped circle and designed border
Rev: Huehueteotl - The God of Fire within D-shaped circle
and designed border **Mint:** Mexico City

Date	Mintage	F	VF	XF	Unc	BU
1992 Proof	4,000	Value: 70.00				

KM# 558   250 PESOS
7.7758 g., 0.9990 Gold 0.2497 oz. AGW **Subject:** Native Culture **Obv:** National arms, eagle left within D-shaped circle and designed border **Rev:** Sculpture of Jaguar head within D-shaped circle and designed border **Mint:** Mexico City

Date	Mintage	F	VF	XF	Unc	BU
1992	10,000	—	—	—	—	350
1992 Proof	2,000	Value: 375				

KM# 559   500 PESOS
15.5517 g., 0.9990 Gold 0.4995 oz. AGW **Subject:** Native Culture **Obv:** National arms, eagle left within D-shaped circle and designed border **Rev:** Sculpture of Jaguar head within D-shaped circle and designed border **Mint:** Mexico City

Date	Mintage	F	VF	XF	Unc	BU
1992	10,000	—	—	—	—	725
1992 Proof	2,000	Value: 750				

KM# 560   1000 PESOS
31.1035 g., 0.9990 Gold 0.9990 oz. AGW **Subject:** Native Culture **Obv:** National arms, eagle left within D-shaped circle and designed border **Rev:** Sculpture of Jaguar head within D-shaped circle and designed border **Mint:** Mexico City

Date	Mintage	F	VF	XF	Unc	BU
1992	17,850	—	—	—	—	1,450
1992 Proof	2,000	Value: 1,500				

KM# 557   10000 PESOS
155.5175 g., 0.9990 Silver 4.9948 oz. ASW, 64 mm. **Subject:** Pieora De Tizoc **Obv:** National arms, eagle left within D-shaped circle and designed border **Rev:** Native warriors within D-shaped circle and designed border **Mint:** Mexico City **Note:** Similar to 10 Nuevo Pesos, KM#650

Date	Mintage	F	VF	XF	Unc	BU
1992	51,900	—	—	—	—	150
1992 Proof	3,300	Value: 275				

CENTRAL VERACRUZ SERIES

KM# 567   NUEVO PESO
7.7601 g., 0.9990 Silver 0.2492 oz. ASW, 27 mm. **Subject:** Bajo relieve de el Tajin **Obv:** National arms, eagle left within D-shaped circle and designed border **Rev:** Design within D-shaped circle and designed border **Mint:** Mexico City

Date	Mintage	F	VF	XF	Unc	BU
1993Mo	100,005	—	—	—	—	20.00
1993Mo Proof	4,005	Value: 35.00				

KM# 568   2 NUEVO PESOS
15.5516 g., 0.9990 Silver 0.4995 oz. ASW, 33 mm. **Subject:** Bajo relieve de el Tajin **Obv:** National arms, eagle left within D-shaped circle and designed border **Rev:** Design within D-shaped circle and designed border **Mint:** Mexico City

Date	Mintage	F	VF	XF	Unc	BU
1993Mo	100,005	—	—	—	—	25.00
1993Mo Proof	3,005	Value: 35.00				

KM# 569   5 NUEVO PESOS
31.1035 g., 0.9990 Silver 0.9990 oz. ASW, 40 mm. **Subject:** Bajo relieve de el Tajin **Obv:** National arms, eagle left within D-shaped circle and designed border **Rev:** Design within D-shaped circle and designed border **Mint:** Mexico City

Date	Mintage	F	VF	XF	Unc	BU
1993Mo	100,005	—	—	—	—	35.00
1993Mo Proof	3,905	Value: 70.00				

KM# 582 5 NUEVO PESOS
31.1035 g., 0.9990 Silver 0.9990 oz. ASW, 40 mm. **Subject:** Palma Con Cocodrilo **Obv:** National arms, eagle left within D-shaped circle and designed border **Rev:** Aerial view of crocodile within D-shaped circle and designed border **Mint:** Mexico City

Date	Mintage	F	VF	XF	Unc	BU
1993Mo	4,605	—	—	—	—	35.00
1993Mo Proof	3,555	Value: 75.00				

KM# 583 5 NUEVO PESOS
31.1035 g., 0.9990 Silver 0.9990 oz. ASW, 40 mm. **Subject:** Anciano Con Brasero **Obv:** National arms, eagle left within D-shaped circle and designed border **Rev:** Kneeling figure sculpture within D-shaped circle and designed border **Mint:** Mexico City

Date	Mintage	F	VF	XF	Unc	BU
1993Mo	3,200	—	—	—	—	35.00
1993Mo Proof	3,660	Value: 75.00				

KM# 584 5 NUEVO PESOS
31.1035 g., 0.9990 Silver 0.9990 oz. ASW, 40 mm. **Subject:** Carita Sonriente **Obv:** National arms, eagle left **Rev:** Sculptured head **Mint:** Mexico City

Date	Mintage	F	VF	XF	Unc	BU
1993Mo	4,605	—	—	—	—	35.00
1993Mo Proof	4,205	Value: 75.00				

KM# 570 10 NUEVO PESOS
155.5175 g., 0.9990 Silver 4.9948 oz. ASW, 65 mm. **Subject:** Piramide Del El Tajin **Obv:** National arms, eagle left within flat shaped circle and designed border **Rev:** Pyramid within flat shaped circle and designed border **Note:** Illustration reduced.

Date	Mintage	F	VF	XF	Unc	BU
1993Mo	50,405	—	—	—	—	170
1993Mo Proof	3,948	Value: 185				

KM# 585 25 NUEVO PESOS
7.7758 g., 0.9990 Gold 0.2497 oz. AGW **Subject:** Hacha Ceremonial **Obv:** National arms, eagle left **Rev:** Mask left **Note:** Similar to 100 New Pesos, KM#587.

Date	Mintage	F	VF	XF	Unc	BU
1993Mo	15,508	—	—	—	—	375
1993Mo Proof	802	Value: 400				

KM# 586 50 NUEVO PESOS
15.5517 g., 0.9990 Gold 0.4995 oz. AGW **Subject:** Hacha Ceremonial **Obv:** National arms, eagle left **Rev:** Mask left **Note:** Similar to 100 New Pesos, KM#587.

Date	Mintage	F	VF	XF	Unc	BU
1993Mo	15,508	—	—	—	—	725
1993Mo Proof	802	Value: 775				

KM# 587 100 NUEVO PESOS
31.1035 g., 0.9990 Gold 0.9990 oz. AGW **Subject:** Hacha Ceremonial **Obv:** National arms, eagle left **Rev:** Mask left

Date	Mintage	F	VF	XF	Unc	BU
1993Mo	7,160	—	—	—	—	1,475
1993Mo Proof	500	Value: 1,550				

MAYAN SERIES

KM# 572 NUEVO PESO
7.7601 g., 0.9990 Silver 0.2492 oz. ASW **Subject:** Chaac Mool **Obv:** National arms, eagle left within six sided shield and designed border **Rev:** Reclining figure within six sided shield and designed border **Mint:** Mexico City

Date	Mintage	F	VF	XF	Unc	BU
1994 Matte	30,000	—	—	—	—	20.00
1994 Proof	2,500	Value: 35.00				

KM# 573 2 NUEVO PESOS
15.5516 g., 0.9990 Silver 0.4995 oz. ASW **Subject:** Chaac Mool **Obv:** National arms, eagle left within six sided shield and designed border **Rev:** Reclining figure within six sided shield and designed border **Mint:** Mexico City

Date	Mintage	F	VF	XF	Unc	BU
1994 Matte	30,000	—	—	—	—	25.00
1994 Proof	2,500	Value: 35.00				

KM# 574 5 NUEVO PESOS
31.1035 g., 0.9990 Silver 0.9990 oz. ASW **Subject:** Chaac Mool **Obv:** National arms, eagle left within six sided shield and designed border **Rev:** Reclining figure within six sided shield and designed border **Mint:** Mexico City

Date	Mintage	F	VF	XF	Unc	BU
1994 Matte	50,000	—	—	—	—	32.00
1994 Proof	3,000	Value: 70.00				

KM# 575 5 NUEVO PESOS
31.1035 g., 0.9990 Silver 0.9990 oz. ASW **Subject:** Chaac Mool **Obv:** National arms, eagle left within six sided shield and designed border **Rev:** Tomb of Palenque Memorial Stone within six sided shield and designed border **Mint:** Mexico City

Date	Mintage	F	VF	XF	Unc	BU
1994	4,500	—	—	—	—	32.00
1994 Proof	2,800	Value: 70.00				

KM# 577 5 NUEVO PESOS
31.1035 g., 0.9990 Silver 0.9990 oz. ASW **Subject:** Mascaron Del Dios Chaac **Rev:** Elaborately carved wall segment **Mint:** Mexico City

Date	Mintage	F	VF	XF	Unc	BU
1994	4,500	—	—	—	—	32.00
1994 Proof	2,500	Value: 70.00				

KM# 578 5 NUEVO PESOS
31.1035 g., 0.9990 Silver 0.9990 oz. ASW **Subject:** Dintel 26 **Obv:** National arms, eagle left within six sided shield and designed border **Rev:** Two seated figures wall carving within six sided shield and designed border

Date	Mintage	F	VF	XF	Unc	BU
1994	4,500	—	—	—	—	45.00
1994 Proof	2,600	Value: 75.00				

KM# 676 10 NUEVO PESOS
155.5175 g., 0.9990 Silver 4.9948 oz. ASW, 65 mm. **Subject:** Piramide Del Castillo **Obv:** National arms, eagle left above metal content statement **Rev:** Pyramid above two-line inscription **Rev. Inscription:** PIRAMIDE DEL CASTILLO / CHICHEN-ITZA **Edge:** Reeded **Mint:** Mexico City

Date	Mintage	F	VF	XF	Unc	BU
1993Mo Proof	—	Value: 650				

KM# 576 10 NUEVO PESOS
115.5170 g., 0.9990 Silver 3.7101 oz. ASW, 64 mm. **Subject:** Piramide del Castillo **Obv:** National arms, eagle left **Rev:** Pyramid **Note:** Illustration reduced.

Date	Mintage	F	VF	XF	Unc	BU
1994	20,000	—	—	—	—	125
1994 Proof	2,100	Value: 200				

KM# 579 25 NUEVO PESOS
7.7758 g., 0.9990 Gold 0.2497 oz. AGW **Subject:** Personaje de Jaina **Rev:** Seated figure

Date	Mintage	F	VF	XF	Unc	BU
1994Mo	2,000	—	—	—	—	375
1994Mo Proof	501	Value: 400				

KM# 580 50 NUEVO PESOS
15.5517 g., 0.9990 Gold 0.4995 oz. AGW **Subject:** Personaje de Jaina **Rev:** Seated figure

Date	Mintage	F	VF	XF	Unc	BU
1994Mo	1,000	—	—	—	—	725
1994Mo Proof	501	Value: 775				

KM# 581 100 NUEVO PESOS
31.1035 g., 0.9990 Gold 0.9990 oz. AGW **Subject:** Personaje de Jaina **Obv:** National arms, eagle left within six sided shield and designed border **Rev:** Seated figure within six sided shield and designed border

Date	Mintage	F	VF	XF	Unc	BU
1994Mo	1,000	—	—	—	—	1,475
1994Mo Proof	501	Value: 1,550				

OLMEC SERIES

KM# 593 PESO
7.7750 g., 0.9990 Silver 0.2497 oz. ASW **Subject:** Senor De Las Limas **Obv:** National arms, eagle left within square and designed border **Rev:** Sitting figure facing within square and designed border **Mint:** Mexico City **Note:** Similar to 5 Pesos, KM#595.

Date	Mintage	F	VF	XF	Unc	BU
1996Mo	6,400	—	—	—	—	20.00
1996Mo Proof	3,700	Value: 35.00				
1998 Matte	2,400	—	—	—	—	22.00

KM# 594 2 PESOS
15.5517 g., 0.9990 Silver 0.4995 oz. ASW **Subject:** Senor
De Las Limas **Obv:** National arms, eagle left within square
and designed border **Rev:** Sitting figure facing within square
and designed border **Mint:** Mexico City **Note:** Similar to 5
Pesos, KM#595.

Date	Mintage	F	VF	XF	Unc	BU
1996Mo	6,400	—	—	—	—	25.00
1996Mo Proof	2,200	Value: 35.00				
1998 Matte	2,400	—	—	—	—	28.00

KM# 596 5 PESOS
31.1035 g., 0.9990 Silver 0.9990 oz. ASW **Subject:** Hombre
Jaguar **Obv:** National arms, eagle left within square and
designed border **Rev:** Statue facing within square and
designed border

Date	Mintage	F	VF	XF	Unc	BU
1996Mo	5,300	—	—	—	—	90.00
1996Mo Proof	4,000	Value: 100				
1998 Matte	6,000	—	—	—	—	35.00
1998 Proof	4,800	Value: 75.00				

KM# 595 5 PESOS
31.1035 g., 0.9990 Silver 0.9990 oz. ASW **Subject:** Senor
De Las Limas **Obv:** National arms, eagle left within square
and designed border **Rev:** Seated figure facing within square
and designed border

Date	Mintage	F	VF	XF	Unc	BU
1996Mo	8,700	—	—	—	—	32.00
1996Mo Proof	3,800	Value: 70.00				
1998 Matte	3,400	—	—	—	—	35.00

KM# 597 5 PESOS
31.1035 g., 0.9990 Silver 0.9990 oz. ASW **Subject:** El
Luchador **Obv:** National arms, eagle left **Rev:** El Luchador

Date	Mintage	F	VF	XF	Unc	BU
1996Mo	6,600	—	—	—	—	32.00
1996Mo Proof	3,600	Value: 70.00				
1998 Matte	2,000	—	—	—	—	37.00

KM# 598 5 PESOS
31.1035 g., 0.9990 Silver 0.9990 oz. ASW **Subject:** Hacha
Ceremonial **Obv:** National arms, eagle left within square and
designed border **Rev:** Statue within square and designed
border

Date	Mintage	F	VF	XF	Unc	BU
1996Mo	7,000	—	—	—	—	32.00
1996Mo Proof	3,500	Value: 70.00				
1998 Matte	2,000	—	—	—	—	37.00

KM# 599 10 PESOS
155.5175 g., 0.9990 Silver 4.9948 oz. ASW, 64 mm.
Subject: Cabeza Olmeca **Obv:** National arms, eagle left **Rev:**
Native mask **Note:** Illustration reduced.

Date	Mintage	F	VF	XF	Unc	BU
1996Mo	5,060	—	—	—	—	125
1996Mo Proof	3,550	Value: 185				
1998 Matte	2,150	—	—	—	—	125

KM# 600 25 PESOS
7.7758 g., 0.9990 Gold 0.2497 oz. AGW **Subject:** Sacerdote
Obv: National arms, eagle left **Rev:** Sculpture **Note:** Similar
to 100 Pesos, KM#602.

Date	Mintage	F	VF	XF	Unc	BU
1996Mo	500	—	—	—	—	375
1996Mo Proof	750	Value: 400				

KM# 601 50 PESOS
15.5517 g., 0.9990 Gold 0.4995 oz. AGW **Subject:**
Sacerdote **Obv:** National arms, eagle left **Rev:** Sculpture
Note: Similar to 100 Pesos, KM#602.

Date	Mintage	F	VF	XF	Unc	BU
1996Mo	500	—	—	—	—	750
1996Mo Proof	500	Value: 775				

KM# 602   100 PESOS
31.1035 g., 0.9990 Gold 0.9990 oz. AGW **Subject:**
Sacerdote **Obv:** National arms, eagle left within square and
designed border **Rev:** Sculpture within square and designed
border

Date	Mintage	F	VF	XF	Unc	BU
1996Mo	500	—	—	—	—	1,500
1996Mo Proof	500	Value: 1,550				

TEOTIHUACAN SERIES

KM# 617   PESO
7.7759 g., 0.9990 Silver 0.2497 oz. ASW **Subject:** Disco De
La Muerte **Obv:** National arms, eagle left within oblong circle
and designed border **Rev:** Sculpture within oblong circle and
designed border **Mint:** Mexico City

Date	Mintage	F	VF	XF	Unc	BU
1997	3,000	—	—	—	—	20.00
1997 Proof	1,600	Value: 35.00				
1998 Matte	2,400	—	—	—	—	25.00
1998 Proof	500	Value: 45.00				

KM# 618   2 PESOS
15.5517 g., 0.9990 Silver 0.4995 oz. ASW **Subject:** Disco
De La Muerte **Obv:** National arms, eagle left within oblong
circle and designed border **Rev:** Sculpture within oblong circle
and designed border **Mint:** Mexico City

Date	Mintage	F	VF	XF	Unc	BU
1997	3,000	—	—	—	—	25.00
1997 Proof	1,600	Value: 35.00				
1998	2,400	—	—	—	—	30.00
1998 Proof	500	Value: 50.00				

KM# 621   5 PESOS
31.1035 g., 0.9990 Silver 0.9990 oz. ASW **Subject:**
Teotihuacan - Vasija **Obv:** National arms, eagle left within

oval and designed border **Rev:** Seated woman joined to
pottery vase within oval and designed border

Date	Mintage	F	VF	XF	Unc	BU
1997	4,500	—	—	—	—	32.00
1997 Proof	Est. 1,800	Value: 75.00				
1998 Matte	2,000	—	—	—	—	37.00
1998 Proof	500	Value: 150				

KM# 622   5 PESOS
31.1035 g., 0.9990 Silver 0.9990 oz. ASW **Subject:**
Teotihuacan - Jugador de Pelota **Obv:** National arms, eagle
left

Date	Mintage	F	VF	XF	Unc	BU
1997	4,500	—	—	—	—	32.00
1997 Proof	Est. 1,800	Value: 75.00				
1998 Matte	2,000	—	—	—	—	37.00
1998 Proof	500	Value: 150				

KM# 619   5 PESOS
31.1035 g., 0.9990 Silver 0.9990 oz. ASW **Subject:**
Teotihuacan - Disco de la Muerte **Obv:** National arms, eagle
left within oblong circle and designed border **Rev:** Sculpture
within oblong circle and designed border

Date	Mintage	F	VF	XF	Unc	BU
1997	3,500	—	—	—	—	32.00
1997 Proof	Est. 1,800	Value: 75.00				
1998	3,400	—	—	—	—	35.00
1998 Proof	500	Value: 150				

KM# 620   5 PESOS
31.1035 g., 0.9990 Silver 0.9990 oz. ASW **Subject:**
Teotihuacan - Mascara **Obv:** National arms, eagle left within
oblong circle and designed border **Rev:** Face sculpture within
oblong circle and designed border

Date	Mintage	F	VF	XF	Unc	BU
1997	4,500	—	—	—	—	32.00
1997 Proof	Est. 1,800	Value: 75.00				
1998	2,000	—	—	—	—	37.00
1998 Proof	500	Value: 150				

KM# 623   10 PESOS
155.5175 g., 0.9990 Silver 4.9948 oz. ASW, 64 mm.
Subject: Piramide Del Sol **Obv:** National arms, eagle left
within oblong circle and designed border **Rev:** Pyramid within
oblong circle and designed border **Note:** Illustration reduced.

Date	Mintage	F	VF	XF	Unc	BU
1997	1,500	—	—	—	—	160
1997 Proof	2,100	Value: 200				
1998 Matte	2,150	—	—	—	—	160

KM# 624   25 PESOS
7.7758 g., 0.9990 Gold 0.2497 oz. AGW **Subject:** Serpiente
Emplumada **Obv:** National arms, eagle left **Note:** Similar to
100 Pesos, KM#626.

Date	Mintage	F	VF	XF	Unc	BU
1997Mo	500	—	—	—	—	375
1997Mo Proof	206	Value: 425				

KM# 625   50 PESOS
15.5517 g., 0.9990 Gold 0.4995 oz. AGW **Subject:**
Serpiente Emplumada **Obv:** National arms, eagle left **Note:**
Similar to 100 Pesos, KM#626.

Date	Mintage	F	VF	XF	Unc	BU
1997Mo	500	—	—	—	—	750
1997Mo Proof	206	Value: 800				

KM# 626   100 PESOS
31.1035 g., 0.9990 Gold 0.9990 oz. AGW **Subject:**
Teotihuacan - Serpiente Emplumada **Obv:** National arms,
eagle left

Date	Mintage	F	VF	XF	Unc	BU
1997Mo	500	—	—	—	—	1,500
1997Mo Proof	206	Value: 1,600				

TOLTECA SERIES

KM# 661   PESO
7.7759 g., 0.9990 Silver 0.2497 oz. ASW, 27 mm. **Subject:**
Jaguar **Obv:** National arms, eagle left **Rev:** Jaguar carving
Edge: Reeded **Mint:** Mexico City

Date	Mintage	F	VF	XF	Unc	BU
1998Mo	6,400	—	—	—	—	20.00
1998Mo Proof	3,700	Value: 30.00				

KM# 662   2 PESOS
15.5517 g., 0.9990 Silver 0.4995 oz. ASW, 33 mm. **Subject:**
Jaguar **Obv:** National arms, eagle left **Rev:** Jaguar carving
Edge: Reeded **Mint:** Mexico City

Date	Mintage	F	VF	XF	Unc	BU
1998Mo	6,400	—	—	—	—	25.00
1998Mo Proof	2,200	Value: 35.00				

KM# 663   5 PESOS
31.1035 g., 0.9990 Silver 0.9990 oz. ASW, 40 mm. **Subject:**
Jaguar **Obv:** National arms, eagle left within shield and
designed border **Rev:** Jaguar carving within shield and
designed border **Edge:** Reeded **Mint:** Mexico City

Date	Mintage	F	VF	XF	Unc	BU
1998Mo	5,300	—	—	—	—	32.00
1998Mo Proof	4,000	Value: 75.00				

KM# 664   5 PESOS
31.1035 g., 0.9990 Silver 0.9990 oz. ASW, 40 mm. **Obv:**
National arms, eagle left **Rev:** Sacerdote sculpture **Edge:**
Reeded **Mint:** Mexico City

Date	Mintage	F	VF	XF	Unc	BU
1998Mo	7,000	—	—	—	—	32.00
1998Mo Proof	3,500	Value: 75.00				

KM# 666   5 PESOS
31.1035 g., 0.9990 Silver 0.9990 oz. ASW, 40 mm. **Subject:**

Serpiente con Craneo **Obv:** National arms, eagle left **Rev:**
Large sculpture **Edge:** Reeded **Mint:** Mexico City

Date	Mintage	F	VF	XF	Unc	BU
1998Mo	8,700	—	—	—	—	32.00
1998Mo Proof	3,800	Value: 75.00				

KM# 665   5 PESOS
31.1035 g., 0.9990 Silver 0.9990 oz. ASW, 40 mm. **Subject:**
Quetzalcoatl **Obv:** National arms, eagle left **Rev:** Quetzalcoatl
sculpture **Edge:** Reeded **Mint:** Mexico City

Date	Mintage	F	VF	XF	Unc	BU
1998Mo	6,600	—	—	—	—	32.00
1998Mo Proof	3,600	Value: 75.00				

KM# 634   10 PESOS
155.7300 g., 0.9990 Silver 5.0016 oz. ASW **Subject:**
Atlantes **Obv:** National arms, eagle left within shield and
designed border **Rev:** Three carved statues within shield and
designed border

Date	Mintage	F	VF	XF	Unc	BU
1998Mo	5,060	—	—	—	—	170
1998Mo Proof	3,550	Value: 200				

KM# 667   25 PESOS
7.7759 g., 0.9990 Gold 0.2497 oz. AGW, 23 mm. **Subject:**
Aguila **Obv:** National arms, eagle left **Rev:** Eagle sculpture
Edge: Reeded **Mint:** Mexico City

Date	Mintage	F	VF	XF	Unc	BU
1998Mo	303	—	—	—	—	400
1998Mo Proof	303	Value: 425				

KM# 668   50 PESOS
15.5517 g., 0.9990 Gold 0.4995 oz. AGW, 29 mm. **Subject:**
Aguila **Obv:** National arms, eagle left **Rev:** Eagle sculpture
Edge: Reeded **Mint:** Mexico City

Date	Mintage	F	VF	XF	Unc	BU
1998Mo	303	—	—	—	—	775
1998Mo Proof	303	Value: 825				

KM# 669   100 PESOS
31.1035 g., 0.9990 Gold 0.9990 oz. AGW, 34.5 mm.
Subject: Aguila **Obv:** National arms, eagle left within
designed shield **Rev:** Eagle sculpture within designed shield
Edge: Reeded **Mint:** Mexico City

Date	Mintage	F	VF	XF	Unc	BU
1998Mo	303	—	—	—	—	1,550
1998Mo Proof	303	Value: 1,600				

MEDALLIC SILVER
BULLION COINAGE

KM# M49a   ONZA
33.6250 g., 0.9250 Silver 0.9999 oz. ASW, 41 mm. **Obv:**
Mint mark above coin press

Date	Mintage	F	VF	XF	Unc	BU
1949	1,000,000	BV	32.00	35.00	40.00	50.00

KM# M49b.1   ONZA
33.6250 g., 0.9250 Silver 0.9999 oz. ASW, 41 mm. **Obv:**

Wide spacing between DE MONEDA **Rev:** Mint mark below balance scale **Mint:** Mexico City **Note:** Type I

Date	Mintage	F	VF	XF	Unc	BU
1978Mo	280,000	—	—	BV	32.00	40.00

KM# M49b.2 ONZA
33.6250 g., 0.9250 Silver 0.9999 oz. ASW, 41 mm. **Obv:** Close spacing between DE MONEDA **Rev:** Mint mark below balance scale **Mint:** Mexico City **Note:** Type II

Date	Mintage	F	VF	XF	Unc	BU
1978Mo	Inc. above	—	—	BV	35.00	45.00

KM# M49b.3 ONZA
33.6250 g., 0.9250 Silver 0.9999 oz. ASW, 41 mm. **Obv:** Close spacing between DE MONEDA **Rev:** Left scale pan points to U in UNA **Mint:** Mexico City **Note:** Type III

Date	Mintage	F	VF	XF	Unc	BU
1979Mo	4,508,000	—	—	BV	32.00	37.00

KM# M49b.4 ONZA
33.6250 g., 0.9250 Silver 0.9999 oz. ASW, 41 mm. **Obv:** Close spacing between DE MONEDA **Rev:** Left scale pan points between U and N of UNA **Mint:** Mexico City **Note:** Type IV

Date	Mintage	F	VF	XF	Unc	BU
1979Mo	Inc. above	—	—	BV	32.00	37.00

KM# M49b.5 ONZA
33.6250 g., 0.9250 Silver 0.9999 oz. ASW, 41 mm. **Obv:** Close spacing between DE MONEDA **Rev:** Left scale pan points between U and N of UNA **Mint:** Mexico City **Note:** Type V

Date	Mintage	F	VF	XF	Unc	BU
1980Mo	6,104,000	—	—	BV	32.00	37.00
1980/70Mo	Inc. above	—	—	BV	35.00	42.00

MEDALLIC GOLD COINAGE

KM# M91a 10 PESOS
8.3333 g., 0.9000 Gold 0.2411 oz. AGW **Subject:** 200th Anniversary - Birth of Hidalgo

Date	Mintage	F	VF	XF	Unc	BU
1953	—	—	—	—	BV	350

KM# M123a 10 PESOS
8.3333 g., 0.9000 Gold 0.2411 oz. AGW **Subject:** Centennial of Constitution

Date	Mintage	F	VF	XF	Unc	BU
1957	Est. 73,000	—	—	—	BV	350

Note: Mintage includes #M122a

KM# M92a 20 PESOS
16.6666 g., 0.9000 Gold 0.4822 oz. AGW **Subject:** 200th Anniversary - Birth of Hidalgo

Date	Mintage	F	VF	XF	Unc	BU
1953	—	—	—	—	BV	700

KM# M122a 50 PESOS
41.6666 g., 0.9000 Gold 1.2056 oz. AGW **Subject:** Centennial of Constitution

Date	Mintage	F	VF	XF	Unc	BU
1957	—	—	—	—	BV	1,750

Note: Mintage included in total for KM#M123a

MEXICO-REVOLUTIONARY

AGUASCALIENTES

Aguascalientes is a state in central Mexico. Its coin issues, struck by authority of Pancho Villa, represent his deepest penetration into the Mexican heartland. Lack of silver made it necessary to make all denominations in copper.

FRANCISCO PANCHO VILLA

REVOLUTIONARY COINAGE

KM# 601 CENTAVO
3.5500 g., Copper, 17 mm. **Obv:** Liberty cap **Rev:** Value within 3/4 wreath below date **Note:** Large date weight 3.55g.

Date	Mintage	VG	F	VF	XF	Unc
1915	—	250	350	450	—	—
Note: Large date, plain edge						
1915	—	30.00	60.00	100	200	—
Note: Large date, reeded edge						
1915	—	30.00	60.00	100	130	—
Note: Small date, plain edge						
1915	—	30.00	60.00	80.00	120	—
Note: Small date, reeded edge						

KM# 602.1 2 CENTAVOS
4.2800 g., Copper **Obv:** Liberty cap **Rev:** Value within 3/4 wreath below date

Date	Mintage	VG	F	VF	XF	Unc
1915	—	40.00	100	200	350	—
Note: Round front 2, plain edge						

KM# 602.2 2 CENTAVOS
3.3500 g., Copper, 19 mm. **Obv:** Liberty cap **Rev:** Value within 1/2 wreath below date

Date	Mintage	VG	F	VF	XF	Unc
1915	—	35.00	60.00	85.00	200	—
Note: Square front 2, reeded edge						
1915 Plain edge	—	50.00	90.00	200	325	—
Note: Square front 2						

KM# 603 5 CENTAVOS
Copper, 25 mm. **Obv:** National arms **Rev:** Liberty cap and value above sprigs

Date	Mintage	VG	F	VF	XF	Unc
1915 Plain edge; Rare	—	—	—	—	—	—
1915 Reeded edge	—	10.00	20.00	30.00	50.00	—

KM# 604.1 5 CENTAVOS
7.1300 g., Copper, 25 mm. **Obv:** National arms **Rev:** Vertically shaded 5 within sprigs

Date	Mintage	VG	F	VF	XF	Unc
1915	—	100	150	225	325	—
Note: Plain edge						
1915	—	20.00	40.00	50.00	100	—
Note: Reeded edge						

KM# 604.2 5 CENTAVOS
Copper, 25 mm. **Obv:** National arms **Rev:** Horizontally shaded 5 within sprigs

Date	Mintage	VG	F	VF	XF	Unc
1915	—	30.00	50.00	80.00	150	—
Note: Plain edge						
1915	—	25.00	40.00	65.00	125	—
Note: Reeded edge						

KM# 606 20 CENTAVOS
Copper, 29 mm. **Obv:** National arms **Rev:** Value below Liberty cap within sprigs

Date	Mintage	VG	F	VF	XF	Unc
1915 Reeded edge	—	10.00	20.00	50.00	80.00	—

KM# 605   20 CENTAVOS
Copper, 29 mm.   **Obv:** National arms **Rev:** Value below
Liberty cap within sprigs

Date	Mintage	VG	F	VF	XF	Unc
1915 Reeded edge	—	10.00	20.00	50.00	80.00	—

KM# 600   20 CENTAVOS
Copper   **Obv:** National arms **Rev:** Value below Liberty cap
within sprigs **Edge:** Reeded

Date	Mintage	VG	F	VF	XF	Unc
1915	—	15.00	20.00	35.00	65.00	—

Note: Varieties exist with both plain and milled edges and
many variations in the shading of the numerals

CHIHUAHUA

Chihuahua is a northern state of Mexico bordering the
U.S. It was the arena that introduced Pancho Villa to the world.
Villa, an outlaw, was given a title when asked by Madero to
participate in maintaining order during Madero's presidency.
After Madero's death in February 1913, Villa became a per-
suasive leader. Chihuahua was where he made his first coins -
the *Army of the North* pesos also came
from this state. This coin helped Villa recruit soldiers because
of his ability to pay in silver while others were paying in worth-
less paper money.

ARMY OF THE NORTH
Ejercito Del Norte

REVOLUTIONARY COINAGE

KM# 619   PESO
29.2700 g., Silver   **Obv:** National arms **Rev:** Liberty cap

Date	Mintage	VG	F	VF	XF	Unc
1915	—	25.00	40.00	75.00	200	500

KM# 619a   PESO
Copper   **Obv:** National arms **Rev:** Liberty cap

Date	Mintage	VG	F	VF	XF	Unc
1915	—	500	1,000	1,500	2,500	—

KM# 619b   PESO
Brass   **Obv:** National arms **Rev:** Liberty cap **Note:** Uniface
obverse

Date	Mintage	VG	F	VF	XF	Unc
1915 Rare	—	—	—	—	—	—

CONSTITUTIONALIST ARMY
Ejercito Constitucionalista

REVOLUTIONARY COINAGE

KM# 612   5 CENTAVOS
Copper   **Obv:** Liberty cap **Rev:** Value above date

Date	Mintage	VG	F	VF	XF	Unc
1914	—	25.00	45.00	80.00	125	—

KM# 613   5 CENTAVOS
6.6000 g., Copper, 25 mm.   **Obv:** Liberty cap **Rev:** Value
above date **Note:** Numerous varieties exist. Weight varies
6.3-6.93g.

Date	Mintage	VG	F	VF	XF	Unc
1914	—	1.00	2.50	4.00	10.00	—
1915	—	1.00	2.50	4.00	10.00	—

KM# 613a   5 CENTAVOS
Brass   **Obv:** Liberty cap **Rev:** Value above date **Note:**
Numerous varieties exist.

Date	Mintage	VG	F	VF	XF	Unc
1914	—	2.00	3.00	8.00	10.00	—
1915	—	2.00	3.00	8.00	10.00	—

KM# 613b   5 CENTAVOS
Cast Copper   **Obv:** Liberty cap **Rev:** Value above date

Date	Mintage	VG	F	VF	XF	Unc
1914	—	75.00	200	300	450	—

KM# 614a   5 CENTAVOS
Copper   **Obv:** National arms **Rev:** Value below date within
sprigs with solid V

Date	Mintage	VG	F	VF	XF	Unc
1915 Rare	—	—	—	—	—	—

KM# 614b   5 CENTAVOS
Copper   **Obv:** National arms **Rev:** Value above date **Note:**
Mule.

Date	Mintage	VG	F	VF	XF	Unc
1915	—	—	350	—	—	—

KM# 614c   5 CENTAVOS
Copper   **Obv:** National arms **Rev:** Liberty cap **Note:** Mule.

Date	Mintage	VG	F	VF	XF	Unc
1915 Rare	—	—	—	—	—	—

KM# 614   5 CENTAVOS
Copper   **Obv:** National arms **Rev:** Value below date within
sprigs with double-lined V

Date	Mintage	VG	F	VF	XF	Unc
1915 SS Unique	—	—	—	—	—	—

KM# 615 10 CENTAVOS
8.7900 g., Copper, 27.5 mm. **Obv:** Liberty cap **Rev:** Value above date

Date	Mintage	VG	F	VF	XF	Unc
1915	—	1.25	2.50	3.50	5.00	—

KM# 615a 10 CENTAVOS
8.8900 g., Brass, 27.5 mm. **Obv:** Liberty cap **Rev:** Value above date

Date	Mintage	VG	F	VF	XF	Unc
1915	—	5.00	10.00	30.00	50.00	—

Note: Many varieties exist

HIDALGO DEL PARRAL
Fuerzas Constitucionalistas

REVOLUTIONARY COINAGE

KM# 607 2 CENTAVOS
6.8500 g., Copper, 25 mm. **Obv:** Liberty cap within circle flanked by sprigs **Rev:** Value flanked by sprigs within circle

Date	Mintage	VG	F	VF	XF	Unc
1913	—	5.00	10.00	15.00	25.00	—

KM# 607a 2 CENTAVOS
Brass **Obv:** Liberty cap within circle flanked by sprigs **Rev:** Value flanked by sprigs within circle

Date	Mintage	VG	F	VF	XF	Unc
1913	—	95.00	150	200	350	—

KM# 608 50 CENTAVOS
12.6500 g., Silver **Obv:** Liberty cap **Rev:** Value flanked by sprigs below Liberty cap **Edge:** Reeded

Date	Mintage	VG	F	VF	XF	Unc
1913	—	18.00	40.00	60.00	85.00	—

KM# 609 50 CENTAVOS
12.1700 g., Silver, 30 mm. **Edge:** Plain

Date	Mintage	VG	F	VF	XF	Unc
1913	—	50.00	70.00	95.00	135	—

KM# 609a 50 CENTAVOS
Copper **Edge:** Plain

Date	Mintage	VG	F	VF	XF	Unc
1913 rare	—	200	400	525	850	—

KM# 610 PESO
30.0000 g., Silver **Obv:** Inscription **Rev:** 1 through PESO and small circle above sprigs **Note:** Weight varies 29.18-30.9g.

Date	Mintage	VG	F	VF	XF	Unc
1913	—	1,200	2,000	3,000	6,500	14,000

KM# 611 PESO
Silver, 38 mm. **Obv:** Inscription **Rev:** Value above sprigs **Note:** Well struck counterfeits of this coin exist with the dot at the end of the word Peso even with the bottom of the O. On legitimate pieces the dot is slightly higher. Weight varies 27.3-28.85g.

Date	Mintage	VG	F	VF	XF	Unc
1913	—	35.00	45.00	125	275	475

DURANGO

A state in north central Mexico. Another area of operation for Pancho Villa. The *Muera Huerta* peso originates in this state. The coins were made in Cuencame under the orders of Generals Cemceros and Contreras.

CUENCAME
Muera Huerta (Death to Huerta)

REVOLUTIONARY COINAGE

KM# 620   PESO
Silver, 38 mm.   **Obv:** National arms **Rev:** Liberty cap with written value flanked by stars

Date	Mintage	VG	F	VF	XF	Unc
1914	—	1,000	2,000	3,000	5,000	9,500

KM# 621   PESO
23.2000 g., Silver, 39 mm.   **Obv:** National arms with continuous border **Rev:** Liberty cap with continuous border

Date	Mintage	VG	F	VF	XF	Unc
1914	—	75.00	150	300	700	1,650

KM# 621a   PESO
Copper   **Obv:** National arms with continuous border **Rev:** Liberty cap with continuous border **Note:** Varieties exist.

Date	Mintage	VG	F	VF	XF	Unc
1914	—	400	600	1,000	2,000	—

KM# 621b   PESO
Brass   **Obv:** National arms **Rev:** Liberty cap

Date	Mintage	VG	F	VF	XF	Unc
1914	—	—	1,000	2,000	3,500	—

KM# 622   PESO
23.4000 g., Silver, 38.5 mm.   **Obv:** National arms with dot and dash border **Rev:** Liberty cap with continuous border
Note: The so-called 20 Pesos gold Muera Huerta pieces are modern fantasies. Refer to Unusual World Coins, 4th edition, ©2005, KP Books, Inc.

Date	Mintage	VG	F	VF	XF	Unc
1914	—	65.00	120	300	500	950

ESTADO DE DURANGO

REVOLUTIONARY COINAGE

KM# 625   CENTAVO
3.2900 g., Copper, 20 mm.   **Obv:** Large date in center **Rev:** Value within wreath

Date	Mintage	VG	F	VF	XF	Unc
1914	—	2.00	4.00	8.00	12.00	—

KM# 625a   CENTAVO
Brass   **Obv:** Large date in center **Rev:** Value within wreath

Date	Mintage	VG	F	VF	XF	Unc
1914	—	75.00	150	300	400	—

KM# 625b   CENTAVO
Lead   **Obv:** Large date in center **Rev:** Value within wreath

Date	Mintage	VG	F	VF	XF	Unc
1914	—	20.00	40.00	65.00	90.00	—

KM# 625c   CENTAVO
Copper   **Obv:** Large date in center **Rev:** Value within wreath

Date	Mintage	VG	F	VF	XF	Unc
1914	—	25.00	50.00	80.00	125	—

KM# 626a   CENTAVO
Brass   **Obv:** Date **Rev:** Value within wreath

Date	Mintage	VG	F	VF	XF	Unc
1914	—	75.00	100	200	350	—

KM# 626b   CENTAVO
Lead   **Obv:** Date **Rev:** Value within wreath

Date	Mintage	VG	F	VF	XF	Unc
1914	—	20.00	40.00	70.00	125	—

Note: Varieties in size exist

KM# 627   CENTAVO
Copper, 20 mm.   **Obv:** Stars below date **Rev:** Value with retrograde N

Date	Mintage	VG	F	VF	XF	Unc
1914	—	6.00	10.00	20.00	30.00	—

KM# 627a CENTAVO
Lead, 20 mm. **Obv:** Stars below date **Rev:** Value with retrograde N

Date	Mintage	VG	F	VF	XF	Unc
1914	—	20.00	40.00	60.00	100	—

KM# 628 CENTAVO
Aluminum **Obv:** National arms within sprigs **Rev:** Value

Date	Mintage	VG	F	VF	XF	Unc
1914	—	0.65	1.00	2.00	4.00	10.00

KM# 624 CENTAVO
Lead **Obv:** Date **Rev:** Value within wreath **Note:** Cast.

Date	Mintage	VG	F	VF	XF	Unc
1914	—	45.00	75.00	100	200	—

KM# 626 CENTAVO
2.8000 g., Copper, 20 mm. **Obv:** Date **Rev:** Value within wreath **Note:** Weight varies 2.46-2.78g.

Date	Mintage	VG	F	VF	XF	Unc
1914	—	15.00	20.00	35.00	45.00	—

KM# 634b 5 CENTAVOS
6.8900 g., Copper-Nickel, 25.53 mm. **Obv:** National arms above sprigs **Obv. Legend:** REPUBLICA MEXICANA **Rev:** Value **Rev. Legend:** ESTADO DE DURANGO **Edge:** Plain

Date	Mintage	F	VF	XF	Unc	BU
1914	—	25.00	50.00	85.00	135	175

KM# 629 5 CENTAVOS
6.2000 g., Copper, 24 mm. **Obv:** Date above sprigs **Obv. Legend:** ESTADO DE DURANGO **Rev:** Value within designed wreath

Date	Mintage	VG	F	VF	XF	Unc
1914	—	2.00	3.00	6.00	12.00	—

KM# 630 5 CENTAVOS
Copper **Obv:** Date above sprigs **Obv. Legend:** E. DE DURANGO **Rev:** Value within designed wreath

Date	Mintage	VG	F	VF	XF	Unc
1914	—	125	275	375	600	—

KM# 631 5 CENTAVOS
5.0500 g., Copper, 23.5 mm. **Obv:** Date above sprigs **Obv. Legend:** E. DE DURANGO **Rev:** Value within designed wreath

Date	Mintage	VG	F	VF	XF	Unc
1914	—	1.25	3.00	6.00	15.00	—

KM# 631a 5 CENTAVOS
Brass **Obv:** Date above sprigs **Obv. Legend:** E. DE DURANGO **Rev:** Value within designed wreath

Date	Mintage	VG	F	VF	XF	Unc
1914	—	30.00	40.00	50.00	85.00	—

KM# 631b 5 CENTAVOS
Lead **Obv:** Date above sprigs **Obv. Legend:** E. DE DURANGO **Rev:** Value within designed wreath

Date	Mintage	VG	F	VF	XF	Unc
1914	—	45.00	70.00	100	180	—

KM# 632 5 CENTAVOS
4.6100 g., Copper, 23.5 mm. **Obv:** Date above sprigs **Obv. Legend:** E. DE DURANGO **Rev:** Roman numeral value

Date	Mintage	VG	F	VF	XF	Unc
1914	—	4.00	8.00	15.00	35.00	—

KM# 632a 5 CENTAVOS
Lead **Obv:** Date above sprigs **Obv. Legend:** E. DE DURANGO **Rev:** Roman numeral value

Date	Mintage	VG	F	VF	XF	Unc
1914	—	50.00	75.00	100	150	—

KM# 634 5 CENTAVOS
Brass **Obv:** National arms above sprigs **Obv. Legend:** REPUBLICA MEXICANA **Rev:** Value **Rev. Legend:** ESTADO DE DURANGO

Date	Mintage	VG	F	VF	XF	Unc
1914	—	0.50	1.00	2.50	5.00	—

KM# 633 5 CENTAVOS
Lead **Obv:** Three stars below 1914 **Rev:** 5 CVS **Note:** Counterfeits are prevalent in the market

Date	Mintage	VG	F	VF	XF	Unc
1914	—	—	600	2,000	—	—

KM# 634a 5 CENTAVOS
Copper **Obv:** National arms above sprigs **Obv. Legend:** REPUBLICA MEXICANA **Rev:** Value **Rev. Legend:** ESTADO DE DURANGO **Note:** There are numerous varieties of these general types of the Durango 1 and 5 Centavo pieces.

Date	Mintage	VG	F	VF	XF	Unc
1914	—	75.00	125	175	250	—

GUERRERO

Guerrero is a state on the southwestern coast of Mexico. It was one of the areas of operation of Zapata and his forces in the south of Mexico. The Zapata forces operated seven different mints in this state. The date ranges were from 1914 to 1917 and denominations from 2 Centavos to 2 Pesos. Some were cast but most were struck and the rarest coin of the group is the Suriana 1915 2 Pesos.

EMILIANO ZAPATA
(General Salgado)

REVOLUTIONARY COINAGE

KM# 638   2 CENTAVOS
6.0000 g., Copper, 22 mm.   **Obv:** National arms **Obv. Legend:** REPUBLICA H MEXICANA **Rev:** Value within wreath **Note:** Weight varies 5.4-6.03g.

Date	Mintage	VG	F	VF	XF	Unc
1915	—	75.00	125	175	250	—

KM# 635   3 CENTAVOS
Copper, 25 mm.   **Obv:** National arms **Obv. Legend:** REPUBLICA MEXICANA **Rev:** Value within wreath **Note:** Weight varies 4.63-6.87g.

Date	Mintage	VG	F	VF	XF	Unc
1915	—	500	1,500	2,000	3,000	—

KM# 636   5 CENTAVOS
Copper, 26 mm.   **Obv:** National arms **Rev:** Value within wreath

Date	Mintage	VG	F	VF	XF	Unc
1915GRO	—	800	1,200	2,000	3,000	—

KM# 637.1   10 CENTAVOS
Copper, 27-28.5 mm.   **Obv:** National arms, snake head ends at L in REPUBLICA **Obv. Legend:** REPUBLICA MEXICANA **Rev:** Date and value within wreath

Date	Mintage	VG	F	VF	XF	Unc
1915GRO	—	600	1,000	1,500	2,000	—

KM# 637.2   10 CENTAVOS
Copper, 27-28.5 mm.   **Obv:** National arms, snake head ends at C in REPUBLICA **Obv. Legend:** REPUBLICA MEXICANA **Rev:** Value within wreath **Note:** Size varies.

Date	Mintage	VG	F	VF	XF	Unc
1915GRO	—	3.00	5.00	8.00	15.00	—

KM# 637.2a   10 CENTAVOS
8.2300 g., Brass, 26 mm.   **Obv:** National arms, snake head ends at C in REPUBLICA **Obv. Legend:** REPUBLICA MEXICANA **Rev:** Value within wreath

Date	Mintage	VG	F	VF	XF	Unc
1915GRO	—	8.00	15.00	25.00	50.00	—

KM# 637.2b   10 CENTAVOS
Lead   **Obv:** National arms, snake head ends at C in REPUBLICA **Obv. Legend:** REPUBLICA MEXICANA **Rev:** Value within wreath

Date	Mintage	VG	F	VF	XF	Unc
1915GRO	—	50.00	75.00	175	275	—

KM# 637.3   10 CENTAVOS
Copper   **Obv:** National arms, snake head ends before A in REPUBLICA **Obv. Legend:** REPUBLICA MEXICANA **Rev:** Date and value within wreath

Date	Mintage	VG	F	VF	XF	Unc
1915.GRO	—	3.00	5.00	8.00	15.00	—

KM# 637.3a   10 CENTAVOS
Brass   **Obv:** National arms, snake head ends before A in REPUBLICA **Obv. Legend:** REPUBLICA MEXICANA **Rev:** Value and date within wreath

Date	Mintage	VG	F	VF	XF	Unc
1915.GRO	—	12.00	20.00	50.00	100	—

KM# 639 25 CENTAVOS
7.5000 g., Silver, 25 mm. **Obv:** Liberty cap **Obv. Legend:** Mexicana REPUbLICA **Rev:** Value above date **Note:** Weight varies 7.41-7.5g.

Date	Mintage	VG	F	VF	XF	Unc
1915	—	125	300	500	900	—

KM# 640 50 CENTAVOS
14.8000 g., Silver, 34 mm. **Obv:** Liberty cap **Rev:** Date and value within beaded border **Note:** Weight varies 14.5-14.8g.

Date	Mintage	VG	F	VF	XF	Unc
1915	—	1,000	2,000	3,500	5,000	—

KM# 641a PESO (UN)
Copper **Obv:** National arms **Obv. Legend:** REPUBLICA MEXICANA - H UN PESO **Rev:** Liberty cap and rays within sprigs **Rev. Legend:** "REFORMA LIBERTAD JUSTICIA Y LEY"

Date	Mintage	Good	VG	F	VF	XF
1914GRO	—	32.00	80.00	200	500	1,500

KM# 641 PESO (UN)
Gold With Silver, 29-31 mm. **Obv:** National arms **Obv. Legend:** REPUBLICA MEXICANA - H UN PESO **Rev:** Liberty cap and rays within sprigs **Rev. Legend:** "REFORMA LIBERTAD JUSTICIA Y LEY" **Rev. Inscription:** Oro:0,300 **Note:** Many die varieties exist. Size varies. Weight varies 10.28-14.84g. Coin is 0.30g fine Gold.

Date	Mintage	VG	F	VF	XF	Unc
1914GRO	—	20.00	30.00	40.00	85.00	—

KM# 642 PESO (UN)
Gold With Silver, 30.5-31 mm. **Obv:** National arms **Obv.**

Legend: REPUBLICA MEXICANA - H UN PESO H **Rev:** Liberty cap and rays within sprigs **Rev. Legend:** "REFORMA.LIBERTAD.JUSTICIA Y LEY" **Rev. Inscription:** Oro:0,300 **Note:** Weight varies 12.93-14.66g. Coin is 0.300g fine Gold.

Date	Mintage	VG	F	VF	XF	Unc
1914GRO	—	50.00	75.00	100	180	—
1915GRO	—	600	1,000	1,500	1,850	—

KM# 643 2 PESOS (Dos)
Gold With Silver, 38.25-39.6 mm. **Obv:** National arms **Obv. Legend:** REPUBLICA MEXICANA **Rev:** Radiant sun face above high mountain peaks **Rev. Legend:** "REFORMA LIBERTAD, JUSTICIA Y LEY", **Rev. Inscription:** Oro:0,595 **Note:** Many varieties exist. Coin is 0.595g fine Gold.

Date	Mintage	VG	F	VF	XF	Unc
1914GRO	—	25.00	45.00	125	200	425

KM# 643a 2 PESOS (Dos)
Copper, 38-38.5 mm. **Obv:** National arms **Obv. Legend:** REPUBLICA MEXICANA **Rev:** Radiant sun face above high mountain peaks **Rev. Legend:** "REFORMA, LIBERTAD, JUSTICIA Y LEY" **Note:** Size varies.

Date	Mintage	Good	VG	F	VF	XF
1914GRO	—	—	—	1,200	1,400	2,000

KM# 644a 2 PESOS (Dos)
Copper **Obv:** National arms **Obv. Legend:** REPUBLICA MEXICANA **Rev:** Radiant sun face above high and low mountain peaks **Rev. Legend:** "REFORMA, LIBERTAD, JUSTICIA Y LEY"

Date	Mintage	VG	F	VF	XF	Unc
1915GRO	—	400	1,000	1,200	1,800	—

KM# 644 2 PESOS (Dos)
Gold With Silver, 39-40 mm. **Obv:** National arms **Obv. Legend:** REPUBLICA MEXICANA **Rev:** Radiant sun face above high and low mountain peaks **Rev. Legend:** "REFORMA, LIBERTAD, JUSTICIA Y LEY" **Rev. Inscription:** Oro:0,595 **Note:** Weight varies 21.71-26.54g. Coin is 0.595g fine Gold.

Date	Mintage	VG	F	VF	XF	Unc
1915GRO	—	65.00	85.00	160	250	550

ATLIXTAC

REVOLUTIONARY COINAGE

KM# 645 10 CENTAVOS
Copper, 27.5-28 mm. **Obv:** National arms **Obv. Legend:** REPUBLICA MEXICANA **Rev:** Value within sprigs **Note:** Size varies. Weight varies 4.76-9.74g.

Date	Mintage	VG	F	VF	XF	Unc
1915	—	3.00	5.00	8.00	15.00	—

KM# 646   10 CENTAVOS
Copper, 27.55-28 mm. **Obv:** National arms **Obv. Legend:**
REPUBLICA H MEXICANA **Rev:** Value within sprigs **Note:**
Size varies. Weight varies 6.13-7.94g.

Date	Mintage	VG	F	VF	XF	Unc
1915	—	3.00	5.00	8.00	15.00	—

CACAHUATEPEC

REVOLUTIONARY COINAGE

KM# 648   5 CENTAVOS
12.1900 g., Copper, 28 mm. **Obv:** National arms **Obv.**
Legend: ESTADOS UNIDOS MEXICANOS **Rev:** Value
within wreath

Date	Mintage	VG	F	VF	XF	Unc
1917	—	12.00	25.00	40.00	75.00	—

KM# 649   20 CENTAVOS
Silver, 21-23.8 mm. **Obv:** National arms **Obv. Legend:**
ESTADOS UNIDOS MEXICANOS **Rev:** Value within sprigs
below liberty cap and rays **Note:** Size varies. Weight varies
3.99-6.2g.

Date	Mintage	VG	F	VF	XF	Unc
1917	—	100	200	350	400	—

KM# 650   50 CENTAVOS
13.8000 g., Silver, 30-30.3 mm. **Obv:** National arms **Obv.**
Legend: ESTADOS UNIDOS MEXICANOS **Rev:** Value and

date within sprigs below Liberty cap **Note:** Size varies. Weight
varies 13.45-13.78g.

Date	Mintage	VG	F	VF	XF	Unc
1917	—	25.00	65.00	150	375	—

KM# 651   PESO (UN)
Silver, 38 mm. **Obv:** National arms **Rev:** Liberty cap **Note:**
Weight varies 26.81-32.05g.

Date	Mintage	VG	F	VF	XF	Unc
1917 L.V. Go	—	2,000	4,000	6,000	9,000	—

CACALOTEPEC

REVOLUTIONARY COINAGE

KM# 652   20 CENTAVOS
Silver, 22.5 mm. **Obv:** National arms **Obv. Legend:**
ESTADOS UNIDOS MEXICANOS **Rev:** Date and value
within sprigs below Liberty cap and rays **Note:** Weight varies
3.89-5.73g.

Date	Mintage	VG	F	VF	XF	Unc
1917	—	1,000	1,800	3,000	5,000	—

CAMPO MORADO

REVOLUTIONARY COINAGE

KM# 653   5 CENTAVOS
4.3700 g., Copper, 23.5-24 mm. **Obv:** National arms **Rev:**
Value within wreath **Note:** Size varies.

Date	Mintage	VG	F	VF	XF	Unc
1915 C.M.	—	9.00	15.00	22.50	35.00	—

KM# 654 10 CENTAVOS
Copper, 25.25-26 mm. **Obv:** National arms **Rev:** Value and date within wreath **Note:** Size varies. Weight varies. 4.48-8.77g.

Date	Mintage	VG	F	VF	XF	Unc
1915 C.M. GRO	—	6.00	10.00	20.00	30.00	—

KM# 655 20 CENTAVOS
Copper, 28 mm. **Obv:** National arms **Rev:** Date above star and value within wreath **Note:** Weight varies 4.48-9g.

Date	Mintage	VG	F	VF	XF	Unc
1915 C.M. GRO	—	15.00	25.00	35.00	50.00	—

KM# 657a 50 CENTAVOS
Billon **Obv:** National arms **Rev:** Date and value within wreath **Note:** Regular obverse.

Date	Mintage	VG	F	VF	XF	Unc
1915 C.M. GRO	—	200	300	500	1,000	—

KM# 657 50 CENTAVOS
Copper, 30-31 mm. **Obv:** National arms **Rev:** Date and value within wreath **Note:** Regular obverse. Size varies. Weight varies 6.49-13.19g.

Date	Mintage	VG	F	VF	XF	Unc
1915 C.M. GRO	—	6.00	10.00	15.00	25.00	—

KM# 656 50 CENTAVOS
Copper, 29-31 mm. **Obv:** National arms **Rev:** Date and value within wreath **Note:** Size varies. Weight varies 9.81-16.77g.

Date	Mintage	VG	F	VF	XF	Unc
1915 C.M. GRO	—	12.00	20.00	30.00	60.00	—

KM# 658a PESO (UN)
Brass **Obv:** National arms **Rev:** Liberty cap

Date	Mintage	VG	F	VF	XF	Unc
1914 Co Mo Gro	—	—	—	—	—	—
Unique						

KM# 659 PESO (UN)
Gold With Silver, 30-31 mm. **Obv:** National arms **Rev:** Liberty cap within sprigs **Rev. Inscription:** Oro:0,300 **Note:** Weight varies 12.26-15.81g. Coin is 0.300g fine Gold.

Date	Mintage	VG	F	VF	XF	Unc
1914 CAMPO Mo	—	20.00	35.00	50.00	85.00	—

KM# 658 PESO (UN)
Gold With Silver, 32-32.5 mm. **Obv:** National arms **Rev:** Liberty cap **Rev. Inscription:** Oro:0,300 **Note:** Weight varies 12.42-16.5g. Coin is 0.300g fine Gold.

Date	Mintage	VG	F	VF	XF	Unc
1914 Co Mo Gro	—	500	600	1,000	1,200	—

KM# 660a 2 PESOS (Dos)
Copper **Obv:** National arms **Rev:** Sun over mountains

Date	Mintage	VG	F	VF	XF	Unc
1915 Co. Mo.	—	—	800	1,000	1,200	—

KM# 662a.1 2 PESOS (Dos)
Copper **Obv:** National arms **Rev:** Liberty cap

Date	Mintage	VG	F	VF	XF	Unc
1915 C. M. GRO	—	—	—	—	1,200	—

KM# 662a.2 2 PESOS (Dos)
Copper **Obv:** National arms **Rev:** Liberty cap

Date	Mintage	VG	F	VF	XF	Unc
1915 C. M. GRO	—	—	—	—	—	—
Unique						

KM# 661 2 PESOS (Dos)
29.4400 g., Gold With Silver, 39 mm. **Obv:** National arms **Rev:** Sun and mountains **Rev. Inscription:** Oro:0,595 **Note:** Coin is 0.595g fine Gold.

Date	Mintage	VG	F	VF	XF	Unc
1915 Co. Mo.	—	2,500	5,000	9,000	15,000	—

KM# 662   2 PESOS (Dos)
0.5950 g., 1.0000 Gold With Silver 0.0191 oz., 34.5-35 mm.
Obv: National arms **Rev:** Liberty cap **Note:** Size varies.
Weight varies 18.27-20.08g.

Date	Mintage	VG	F	VF	XF	Unc
1915 C. M. GRO	—	25.00	35.00	65.00	125	—

KM# 660   2 PESOS (Dos)
Gold With Silver, 38.9-39 mm. **Obv:** National arms **Rev:** Sun
over mountains **Rev. Inscription:** Oro:0,595 **Note:** Weight
varies 20.6-26.02g. Coin is 0.595g fine Gold.

Date	Mintage	VG	F	VF	XF	Unc
1915 Co. Mo.	—	18.00	22.00	40.00	85.00	425

CHILPANCINGO

REVOLUTIONARY COINAGE

KM# 663   10 CENTAVOS
2.5200 g., Cast Silver, 18 mm. **Obv:** National arms **Rev:** Sun
above value and sprigs

Date	Mintage	VG	F	VF	XF	Unc
1914	—	700	1,000	1,200	1,500	—

Note: Many counterfeits exist

KM# 664   20 CENTAVOS
4.9400 g., Cast Silver, 21.5 mm. **Obv:** National arms **Rev:**
Sun above value and sprigs

Date	Mintage	VG	F	VF	XF	Unc
1914	—	700	1,000	1,200	1,500	—

Note: Many counterfeits exist

SURIANA

REVOLUTIONARY COINAGE

KM# 665   2 PESOS (Dos)
22.9300 g., Gold With Silver, 39 mm. **Obv:** National arms
Rev: Sun over mountains **Rev. Inscription:** Oro:0,595 **Note:**
Coin is 0.595g fine Gold.

Date	Mintage	VG	F	VF	XF	Unc
1915 Rare	—	—	—	20,000	35,000	—

Note: Ira & Larry Goldberg - Millenia sale, 5-08 AU-55 replica. Ponterio & Associates sale, 4-09 VF realized $17,000.
Spink America Gerber sale part 2, 6-96 VF realized $16,500

TAXCO

REVOLUTIONARY COINAGE

KM# 667   2 CENTAVOS
Copper, 25.25-26 mm. **Obv:** National arms **Obv. Legend:**
EDO.DE.GRO **Rev:** Value within sprigs **Note:** Size varies.
Weight varies 6.81-8.55g.

Date	Mintage	VG	F	VF	XF	Unc
1915 O/T	—	25.00	40.00	60.00	90.00	—

KM# 668   5 CENTAVOS
Copper **Obv:** National arms **Obv. Legend:** REPUBLICA H

MEXICANA **Rev:** Value within sprigs **Note:** Weight varies 7.13-7.39g.

Date	Mintage	VG	F	VF	XF	Unc
1915	—	10.00	20.00	30.00	50.00	—

KM# 669   10 CENTAVOS
Copper, 27-28 mm.   **Obv:** National arms **Obv. Legend:** REPUBLICA H MEXICANA **Rev:** Date and value within sprigs **Note:** Size varies. Weight varies 7.51-8.67g.

Date	Mintage	VG	F	VF	XF	Unc
1915	—	9.00	20.00	35.00	50.00	—

KM# 670   50 CENTAVOS
5.4500 g., Copper, 27-28 mm.   **Obv:** National arms with legend in large letters **Rev:** Value within sprigs **Note:** Size varies.

Date	Mintage	VG	F	VF	XF	Unc
1915	—	15.00	25.00	50.00	65.00	—

KM# 671   50 CENTAVOS
Silver, 27.6-28 mm.   **Obv:** National arms **Rev:** Sun above value and sprigs **Note:** Size varies. Weight varies 8.95-10.85g.

Date	Mintage	VG	F	VF	XF	Unc
1915	—	25.00	40.00	60.00	100	—

KM# 672a   PESO (UN)
Brass   **Obv:** National arms **Rev:** Liberty cap within sprigs

Date	Mintage	VG	F	VF	XF	Unc
1915	—	200	300	450	600	—

KM# 672b   PESO (UN)
Lead   **Obv:** National arms **Rev:** Liberty cap within sprigs

Date	Mintage	VG	F	VF	XF	Unc
1915	—	50.00	100	200	350	—

KM# 672c   PESO (UN)
Copper   **Obv:** National arms **Rev:** Liberty cap within sprigs

Date	Mintage	VG	F	VF	XF	Unc
1915	—	200	300	400	650	—

KM# 673   PESO (UN)
11.6000 g., Gold With Silver, 30 mm.   **Obv:** National arms **Rev:** Liberty cap within sprigs **Rev. Inscription:** Oro:0,300 **Note:** Coin is 0.300g fine Gold.

Date	Mintage	VG	F	VF	XF	Unc
1915	—	250	400	500	800	—

KM# 674   PESO (UN)
Gold With Silver, 30 mm.   **Obv:** National arms **Rev:** Liberty cap within sprigs **Rev. Inscription:** Oro:0,300 **Note:** Weight varies 10.51-12.79g. Coin is 0.300g fine Gold.

Date	Mintage	VG	F	VF	XF	Unc
1915	—	100	200	300	550	—

KM# 672   PESO (UN)
Gold With Silver, 30-31 mm.   **Obv:** National arms **Rev:** Liberty cap within sprigs **Rev. Inscription:** Oro:0,300 **Note:** Weight varies 30-31g. Coin is 0.300g fine Gold.

Date	Mintage	VG	F	VF	XF	Unc
1915	—	18.00	22.00	35.00	60.00	—

JALISCO

Jalisco is a state on the west coast of Mexico. The few coins made for this state show that the *Army of the North* did not restrict their operations to the northern border states. The coins were made in Guadalajara under the watchful eye of General Dieguez, commander of this segment of Villa's forces.

GUADALAJARA

REVOLUTIONARY COINAGE

KM# 675   CENTAVO
Copper   **Obv:** Liberty cap **Rev:** Value

Date	Mintage	VG	F	VF	XF	Unc
1915	—	9.50	15.00	20.00	30.00	—

KM# 675a   CENTAVO
Brass   **Obv:** Liberty cap **Rev:** Value

Date	Mintage	VG	F	VF	XF	Unc
1915	—	—	—	300	450	—

KM# A676   CENTAVO
Copper   **Obv:** Liberty cap **Rev:** Retrograde value **Note:** Varieties exist.

Date	Mintage	VG	F	VF	XF	Unc
1915	—	100	300	600	1,000	—

KM# 676.1   2 CENTAVOS
Copper, 20 mm.   **Obv:** Liberty cap **Rev:** Value

Date	Mintage	VG	F	VF	XF	Unc
1915	—	10.00	18.00	20.00	35.00	—

Note: Varieties exist.

KM# 676.2   2 CENTAVOS
Copper **Obv:** Liberty cap **Rev:** Value

Date	Mintage	VG	F	VF	XF	Unc
1915	—	200	300	500	800	—

KM# 677   5 CENTAVOS
Copper, 24 mm.   **Obv:** Liberty cap **Rev:** Value

Date	Mintage	VG	F	VF	XF	Unc
1915	—	6.50	12.00	15.00	25.00	—

KM# 677a   5 CENTAVOS
Brass   **Obv:** Liberty cap **Rev:** Value

Date	Mintage	VG	F	VF	XF	Unc
1915 rare	—	—	—	—	—	—

KM# 678   10 CENTAVOS
Copper   **Obv:** Liberty cap above value and date **Rev:** Crowned shield

Date	Mintage	VG	F	VF	XF	Unc
1915	—	—	—	3,000	5,000	—

KM# A678   PESO
Copper   **Obv:** Liberty cap above value and date **Rev:** Crowned shield

Date	Mintage	VG	F	VF	XF	Unc
1915	—	—	—	—	17,000	—

MEXICO, ESTADO DE

Estado de Mexico is a state in central Mexico that surrounds the Federal District on three sides. The issues by the Zapata forces in this state have two distinctions – the Amecameca pieces are the crudest and the Toluca cardboard piece is the most unusual. General Tenorio authorized the crude incuse Amecameca pieces.

AMECAMECA

REVOLUTIONARY COINAGE

KM# 679   5 CENTAVOS
12.5500 g., Brass, 24.5 mm.   **Obv:** Legend **Obv. Legend:** EJERCITO CONVENCIONISTA **Rev:** Value above cent sign

Date	Mintage	VG	F	VF	XF	Unc
ND unique	—	—	—	—	—	—

KM# 680   5 CENTAVOS
12.7700 g., Brass, 24.6 mm.   **Obv:** National arms above RM **Rev:** Value above cent sign **Note:** Hand stamped.

Date	Mintage	VG	F	VF	XF	Unc
ND	—	300	400	600	800	—

KM# 681a   10 CENTAVOS
Copper   **Obv:** National arms above RM **Rev:** Value above cent sign **Note:** Hand stamped.

Date	Mintage	VG	F	VF	XF	Unc
ND	—	75.00	125	225	350	—

KM# 681   10 CENTAVOS
15.0000 g., Brass, 24.5-24.8 mm.   **Obv:** National arms above RM **Rev:** Value above cent sign **Note:** Hand stamped. Varieties exist. Size varies.

Date	Mintage	VG	F	VF	XF	Unc
ND	—	60.00	90.00	150	200	—

KM# 682 20 CENTAVOS
Brass, 24-25 mm. **Obv:** National arms above RM **Rev:** Value above cent sign **Note:** Hand stamped. Varieties exist. Size varies. Weight varies 11.34-12.86g.

Date	Mintage	VG	F	VF	XF	Unc
ND	—	15.00	22.50	35.00	60.00	—

KM# 682a 20 CENTAVOS
Copper **Obv:** National arms above RM **Rev:** Value above cent sign **Note:** Hand stamped.

Date	Mintage	VG	F	VF	XF	Unc
ND	—	25.00	50.00	175	250	—

KM# 687 50 CENTAVOS
Copper, 23.5-29 mm. **Obv:** National arms above sprigs **Rev:** Large numeral value **Note:** Contemporary counterfeit, hand engraved. Size varies. Weight varies 8.8-10.8g.

Date	Mintage	VG	F	VF	XF	Unc
ND	—	12.00	30.00	50.00	80.00	—

Note: "¢" clears top of 5

KM# 683 20 CENTAVOS
Copper, 19-20 mm. **Obv:** National arms above A. D. J. **Rev:** Value **Note:** Size varies. Weight varies 3.99-5.35g.

Date	Mintage	VG	F	VF	XF	Unc
ND	—	7.50	12.50	20.00	35.00	—

KM# 683a 20 CENTAVOS
Brass **Obv:** National arms above A. D. J. **Rev:** Value

Date	Mintage	VG	F	VF	XF	Unc
ND	—	—	—	300	500	—

KM# 686a 50 CENTAVOS
16.0400 g., Brass, 28.5 mm. **Obv:** National arms above sprigs **Rev:** Large numeral value **Note:** Hand stamped.

Date	Mintage	VG	F	VF	XF	Unc
ND	—	100	200	300	400	—

Note: Stem of "¢" above the 5

KM# 684 25 CENTAVOS
Brass **Obv:** Legend **Obv. Legend:** EJERCITO CONVENCIONISTA **Rev:** Value above cent sign

Date	Mintage	VG	F	VF	XF	Unc
ND unique	—	—	—	—	—	—

KM# 686 50 CENTAVOS
Copper, 28-28.5 mm. **Obv:** Eagle over sprays **Note:** Hand stamped. Size varies.

Date	Mintage	VG	F	VF	XF	Unc
ND	—	8.00	10.00	18.00	30.00	—

TENANCINGO, TOWN
(Distrito Federal Mexico)

REVOLUTIONARY COINAGE

KM# 685 25 CENTAVOS
Copper, 25 mm. **Obv:** National arms above sprigs **Rev:** Large numeral value **Note:** Hand stamped. Many modern counterfeits exist in all metals. Weight varies 6.32-6.99g.

Date	Mintage	VG	F	VF	XF	Unc
ND	—	15.00	20.00	30.00	40.00	—

KM# 685a 25 CENTAVOS
7.9200 g., Brass, 25 mm. **Obv:** National arms above sprigs **Rev:** Large numeral value **Note:** Hand stamped.

Date	Mintage	VG	F	VF	XF	Unc
ND	—	—	—	100	300	—

KM# 685b 25 CENTAVOS
Silver **Obv:** National arms above sprigs **Rev:** Large numeral value **Note:** Hand stamped.

Date	Mintage	VG	F	VF	XF	Unc
ND	—	—	—	250	400	—

KM# 688.1 2 CENTAVOS
Copper **Obv:** National arms **Rev:** Value within wreath without TM below value

Date	Mintage	VG	F	VF	XF	Unc
1915	—	—	—	800	2,000	—

KM# 688.2 2 CENTAVOS
Copper **Obv:** National arms **Rev:** Value within wreath with TM below value

Date	Mintage	VG	F	VF	XF	Unc
1915	—	—	400	800	2,000	—

KM# 689.1 5 CENTAVOS
Copper, 19 mm. **Obv:** National arms **Rev:** Numeral value over lined C within wreath **Note:** Weight varies 2.83-2.84g.

Date	Mintage	VG	F	VF	XF	Unc
1915	—	10.00	20.00	30.00	50.00	—

KM# 689.2 5 CENTAVOS
Copper, 19 mm. **Obv:** National arms **Rev:** Numeral value over lined C within wreath **Note:** Weight varies 2.83-2.84g.

Date	Mintage	VG	F	VF	XF	Unc
1915	—	100	300	500	900	—

KM# 690.1 10 CENTAVOS
Copper, 25.25 mm. **Obv:** National arms **Rev:** Value over lined C within wreath below date **Note:** Weight varies 4.27-5.64g.

Date	Mintage	VG	F	VF	XF	Unc
1916	—	10.00	20.00	40.00	60.00	—

KM# 690.2 10 CENTAVOS
Copper, 25.25 mm. **Obv:** National arms **Rev:** Value over lined C within wreath **Note:** Weight varies 4.27-5.64g.

Date	Mintage	VG	F	VF	XF	Unc
1916	—	100	200	400	600	—

KM# 691 20 CENTAVOS
Copper, 27.5-28 mm. **Obv:** National arms **Rev:** Value and date above sprigs **Note:** Size varies. Weight varies 8.51-11.39g.

Date	Mintage	VG	F	VF	XF	Unc
1915	—	25.00	40.00	55.00	85.00	—

TOLUCA, CITY
(Distrito Federal Mexico)

REVOLUTIONARY COINAGE

KM# 692.1 5 CENTAVOS
Cardboard grey in color, 27-28 mm. **Obv:** Crowned shield within sprigs **Rev:** Banner accross large numeral value **Note:** Size varies. Weight varies 1.04-1.16g.

Date	Mintage	VG	F	VF	XF	Unc
1915	—	15.00	30.00	50.00	85.00	—

KM# 692.2 5 CENTAVOS
Cardboard grey in color, 27-28 mm. **Obv:** Crowned shield within sprigs **Rev:** Banner accross large numeral value **Note:** Size varies. Weight varies 1.04-1.16g.

Date	Mintage	VG	F	VF	XF	Unc
1915	—	15.00	30.00	50.00	85.00	—

COUNTERMARKED COINAGE

KM# 693.1 20 CENTAVOS
Copper, 20 mm. **Countermark:** 20 within C **Obv:** National arms **Rev:** Numeral 20 within C and inner circle within sprigs **Note:** Countermark on 1 Centavo, KM#415. Varieties exist. Weight varies 2.65-2.95g.

CM Date	Host Date	Good	VG	F	VF	XF
ND(1915)	ND	—	20.00	40.00	55.00	95.00

KM# 693.2 20 CENTAVOS
Copper, 20 mm. **Countermark:** 20 within C **Obv:** National arms **Rev:** Numeral 20 within C and inner circle within 3/4 wreath **Note:** Countermark on 1 Centavo, KM#394.1. Weight varies 2.65-2.95g.

CM Date	Host Date	Good	VG	F	VF	XF
ND(1915)	1904	—	30.00	50.00	90.00	165

KM# 694 40 CENTAVOS
5.8600 g., Copper, 24.75-25 mm. **Countermark:** 40 within C **Obv:** National arms **Rev:** Numeral 40 within C and inner circle within wreath **Note:** Countermark on 2 Centavos, KM#419. Varieties exist. Size varies.

CM Date	Host Date	Good	VG	F	VF	XF
ND(1915)	ND	—	25.00	40.00	60.00	100

MORELOS

Morelos is a state in south central Mexico, adjoining the federal district on the south. It was the headquarters of Emiliano Zapata. His personal quarters were at Tlatizapan in Morelos. The Morelos coins from 2 Centavos to 1 Peso were all copper except one type of 1 Peso in silver. The two operating Zapatista mints in Morelos were Atlihuayan and Tlaltizapan.

EMILIANO ZAPATA
(Zapatista)

REVOLUTIONARY COINAGE

KM# 695 2 CENTAVOS
Copper, 23 mm. **Obv:** National arms **Obv. Legend:** E.L. DE MORELOS **Rev:** Value within wreath

Date	Mintage	VG	F	VF	XF	Unc
1915	—	1,000	1,400	1,800	2,750	—

KM# 696 5 CENTAVOS
9.0000 g., Copper, 25.9 mm. **Obv:** National arms **Rev:** Value within 3/4 wreath **Rev. Legend:** E. DE MOR. 1915

Date	Mintage	VG	F	VF	XF	Unc
1915	—	300	500	1,000	3,500	—

KM# 697 10 CENTAVOS
8.6900 g., Copper, 24 mm. **Obv:** National arms **Rev:** Value within lined C and wreath

Date	Mintage	VG	F	VF	XF	Unc
1915	—	12.00	20.00	30.00	40.00	—

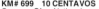

KM# 699 10 CENTAVOS
Copper **Obv:** National arms **Rev:** Date and value within wreath **Rev. Legend:** E. DE MOR

Date	Mintage	VG	F	VF	XF	Unc
1915	—	1,000	2,000	3,000	5,000	—

KM# 698 10 CENTAVOS
Copper, 24-24.5 mm. **Obv:** National arms **Rev:** Value within lined C and wreath with date effaced from die **Note:** Size varies. Weight varies 4.83-6.8g.

Date	Mintage	VG	F	VF	XF	Unc
ND	—	12.00	20.00	35.00	55.00	—

KM# 700   10 CENTAVOS
Copper, 28 mm. **Obv:** National arms **Rev:** Date and value within wreath **Rev. Legend:** MOR **Note:** Weight varies 5.56-8.36g.

Date	Mintage	VG	F	VF	XF	Unc
1916	—	5.00	20.00	30.00	50.00	—

KM# 701   20 CENTAVOS
Copper, 23.75-24.75 mm. **Obv:** National arms **Rev:** Value within lined C and 3/4 wreath **Note:** Size varies. Weight varies 3.88-4.15g.

Date	Mintage	VG	F	VF	XF	Unc
1915	—	9.00	15.00	25.00	35.00	—

KM# 702   50 CENTAVOS
Copper, 28.8 mm. **Obv:** National arms with MOR beneath eagle **Rev:** 50C monogram

Date	Mintage	VG	F	VF	XF	Unc
1915	—	300	500	900	1,450	—

KM# 703a   50 CENTAVOS
Brass **Obv:** National arms above sprigs **Rev:** 50C monogram

Date	Mintage	VG	F	VF	XF	Unc
1915	—	100	200	400	600	—

KM# 706   50 CENTAVOS
Copper, 28 mm. **Obv:** National arms **Rev:** Date above large numeral value **Rev. Legend:** REFORMA LIBERTAD JUSTICIA Y LEY

Date	Mintage	VG	F	VF	XF	Unc
1915	—	350	500	850	1,200	—

KM# 703   50 CENTAVOS
Copper, 28-29.5 mm. **Obv:** National arms **Rev:** Numeral value within lined C and 1/2 wreath **Note:** This coin exists with a silver and also a brass wash. Size varies. Weight varies 5.73-13.77g.

Date	Mintage	VG	F	VF	XF	Unc
1915	—	12.50	17.50	30.00	50.00	—

KM# 704   50 CENTAVOS
Copper, 29-30 mm. **Obv:** National arms with Morelos written below **Rev:** Value within wreath **Note:** Size varies. Weight varies 8.56-11.47g.

Date	Mintage	VG	F	VF	XF	Unc
1916	—	12.50	20.00	30.00	50.00	—

KM# 708   PESO (UN)
Silver **Obv:** National arms **Rev:** Liberty cap within wreath

Date	Mintage	VG	F	VF	XF	Unc
1916	—	450	750	1,150	1,850	—

KM# 708a   PESO (UN)
10.0000 g., Copper, 30 mm. **Obv:** National arms **Rev:** Liberty cap within wreath

Date	Mintage	VG	F	VF	XF	Unc
1916	—	500	1,000	1,200	2,300	—

OAXACA

Oaxaca is one of the southern states in Mexico. The coins issued in this state represent the most prolific series of the Revolution. Most of the coins bear the portrait of Benito Juarez, have corded or plain edges and were issued by a provisional government in the state. The exceptions are the rectangular 1 and 3 Centavos pieces that begin the series.

PROVISIONAL GOVERNMENT

REVOLUTIONARY COINAGE

KM# 709   CENTAVO (UN)
Copper, 19 mm. **Obv:** Legend within beaded rectangle **Rev:** Legend within beaded rectangle **Note:** Rectangular flan.

Date	Mintage	VG	F	VF	XF	Unc
1915	—	90.00	125	400	650	—

KM# 710   CENTAVO (UN)
Copper, 18 mm. **Obv:** Bust left with date flanked by stars

below **Rev:** Value within lined C and 1/2 wreath

Date	Mintage	VG	F	VF	XF	Unc
1915	—	12.00	17.50	25.00	40.00	—

KM# 710a CENTAVO (UN)
Brass **Obv:** Head left with date flanked by stars below **Rev:**
Value within lined C and 1/2 wreath

Date	Mintage	VG	F	VF	XF	Unc
1915	—	50.00	100	200	350	—

KM# 711 3 CENTAVOS (Tres)
Copper, 24 mm. **Obv:** Legend within rectangle with date below,
stars in corners **Rev:** Legend within rectangle with stars in
corners **Rev. Legend:** PROVISIO... **Note:** Rectangular flan.

Date	Mintage	VG	F	VF	XF	Unc
1915	—	100	200	400	600	—

KM# 712 3 CENTAVOS (Tres)
Copper **Obv:** Legend within rectangle with date below, stars
in corners **Rev:** Legend within rectangle with stars in corners
Rev. Legend: PROVISI... **Note:** Rectangular flan.

Date	Mintage	VG	F	VF	XF	Unc
1915	—	1,000	3,000	5,000	9,000	—

KM# 713.1 3 CENTAVOS (Tres)
2.2500 g., Copper, 20 mm. **Obv:** Bust left flanked by stars
below **Rev:** Value above sprigs **Note:** Without TM below value

Date	Mintage	VG	F	VF	XF	Unc
1915	—	3.00	5.00	12.00	25.00	—

KM# 713.2 3 CENTAVOS (Tres)
2.2500 g., Copper, 20 mm. **Obv:** Bust left flanked by stars
below **Rev:** Value above sprigs **Edge:** Plain **Note:** Without
TM below value

Date	Mintage	VG	F	VF	XF	Unc
1915	—	—	—	70.00	100	—

KM# 713.3 3 CENTAVOS (Tres)
2.2500 g., Copper, 20 mm. **Obv:** Bust left flanked by stars
below **Rev:** Value above sprigs **Note:** With TM below value

Date	Mintage	VG	F	VF	XF	Unc
1915	—	100	200	400	500	—

KM# 714 3 CENTAVOS (Tres)
Copper, 20 mm. **Obv:** Bust left **Rev:** Value above sprigs
Note: Small 3

Date	Mintage	VG	F	VF	XF	Unc
1915	—	6.00	10.00	15.00	30.00	—

KM# 715 5 CENTAVOS
Copper **Note:** JAN. 15 1915. incuse lettering

Date	Mintage	VG	F	VF	XF	Unc
1915 Rare	—	—	—	—	—	—

KM# 716 5 CENTAVOS
Copper **Obv:** Bust facing within circle **Rev:** Value above
sprigs

Date	Mintage	VG	F	VF	XF	Unc
1915	—	—	—	—	8,000	—

KM# 717 5 CENTAVOS
Copper, 22 mm. **Obv:** Low relief bust left with date flanked
by stars below **Rev:** Value above sprigs **Note:** Low relief with
long, pointed truncation

Date	Mintage	VG	F	VF	XF	Unc
1915	—	1.50	3.00	4.50	10.00	—

KM# 718 5 CENTAVOS
Copper, 22 mm. **Obv:** Raised bust left with date flanked by
stars below **Rev:** Value above sprigs **Note:** Heavy with short
unfinished lapels

Date	Mintage	VG	F	VF	XF	Unc
1915	—	1.50	2.50	4.00	10.00	—

KM# 719 5 CENTAVOS
Copper, 22 mm. **Obv:** Raised bust left with date flanked by
stars below **Rev:** Value above sprigs **Note:** Curved bottom

Date	Mintage	VG	F	VF	XF	Unc
1915	—	1.50	2.50	4.00	10.00	—

KM# 720 5 CENTAVOS
Copper, 22 mm. **Obv:** Bust left with date flanked by stars
below **Rev:** Value above sprigs **Note:** Short truncation with
closed lapels

Date	Mintage	VG	F	VF	XF	Unc
1915	—	1.50	3.00	4.50	10.00	—

KM# 721 5 CENTAVOS
Copper, 22 mm. **Obv:** Bust left with date flanked by stars below **Rev:** Value above sprigs **Note:** Short curved truncation

Date	Mintage	VG	F	VF	XF	Unc
1915	—	1.50	2.50	5.00	10.00	—

KM# 722 10 CENTAVOS
Copper **Obv:** Low relief bust left with date flanked by stars below **Rev:** Value above sprigs **Note:** Low relief with long pointed truncation

Date	Mintage	VG	F	VF	XF	Unc
1915	—	1.50	2.50	5.00	10.00	—

KM# 723 10 CENTAVOS
Copper **Obv:** Bust left with date flanked by stars below **Rev:** Value above sprigs **Note:** Obverse and reverse legend retrograde.

Date	Mintage	VG	F	VF	XF	Unc
1915 Rare	—	—	—	—	—	—

KM# 724 10 CENTAVOS
Copper, 26.5 mm. **Obv:** Raised bust left with date flanked by stars below **Rev:** Value above sprigs **Note:** Bold and unfinished truncation using 1 peso obverse die of km#740

Date	Mintage	VG	F	VF	XF	Unc
1915	—	3.00	5.00	7.00	10.00	—

KM# 725 10 CENTAVOS
Copper, 26.5 mm. **Obv:** Bust left with date flanked by stars below **Rev:** Value above sprigs **Note:** Heavy with short unfinished lapels centered high

Date	Mintage	VG	F	VF	XF	Unc
1915	—	1.50	2.50	4.00	10.00	—

KM# 726 10 CENTAVOS
Copper **Obv:** Raised bust left with date flanked by stars below **Rev:** Value above sprigs **Note:** Curved bottom

Date	Mintage	VG	F	VF	XF	Unc
1915	—	1.50	2.50	4.00	10.00	—

KM# 727.1 10 CENTAVOS
Copper **Obv:** Raised bust left with date flanked by stars below **Rev:** Value above sprigs **Note:** Short truncation with closed lapels

Date	Mintage	VG	F	VF	XF	Unc
1915	—	1.50	2.50	4.00	10.00	—

KM# 727.2 10 CENTAVOS
Copper **Obv:** Bust left with date flanked by stars below **Rev:** Value above sprigs **Note:** At present, only four pieces of this type are known. All are VF or better; T below bow with M below first leaf

Date	Mintage	VG	F	VF	XF	Unc
1915	—	—	—	400	550	—

KM# 727.3 10 CENTAVOS
Copper **Obv:** Raised bust left flanked by letters GV with date flanked by stars below **Rev:** Value above sprigs **Note:** This counterstamp appears on several different type host 10 cent coins.

Date	Mintage	VG	F	VF	XF	Unc
1915	—	100	200	300	450	—

Note: Letters GV correspond to General Garcia Vigil

KM# 730 20 CENTAVOS
Copper **Obv:** Bust left with date flanked by stars below **Rev:** Value above sprigs **Note:** 5th bust, heavy with short unfinished lapels using 20 Pesos obverse die

Date	Mintage	VG	F	VF	XF	Unc
1915	—	5.00	7.00	10.00	15.00	—

KM# 729.2 20 CENTAVOS
Copper **Counterstamp:** Liberty cap **Obv:** Bust left with date flanked by stars below **Rev:** Value above sprigs **Note:** Counterstamp: Liberty cap and rays with bold unfinished truncation using 1 peso obverse die

Date	Mintage	VG	F	VF	XF	Unc
1915	—	100	150	300	375	—

KM# 728 20 CENTAVOS
Silver, 19 mm. **Obv:** Low relief bust left with date flanked by stars below **Rev:** Value above sprigs **Note:** Low relief with long pointed truncation

Date	Mintage	VG	F	VF	XF	Unc
1915	—	800	2,000	3,000	4,000	—

KM# 728a 20 CENTAVOS
Copper, 19 mm. **Obv:** Bust left with date flanked by stars below **Rev:** Value above sprigs **Note:** Low relief with long pointed truncation

Date	Mintage	VG	F	VF	XF	Unc
1915 Rare	—	—	—	—	—	—

KM# 729.1 20 CENTAVOS
Copper **Obv:** Raised bust left with date flanked by stars below **Rev:** Value above sprigs **Note:** Unfinished truncation using 1 peso obverse die

Date	Mintage	VG	F	VF	XF	Unc
1915	—	1.50	3.00	4.50	10.00	—

KM# 731.1 20 CENTAVOS
Copper, 31 mm. **Obv:** Raised bust left with date flanked by stars below **Rev:** Value above sprigs **Note:** Curved bottom

Date	Mintage	VG	F	VF	XF	Unc
1915	—	1.50	2.50	5.00	10.00	—

KM# 731.2 20 CENTAVOS
Copper **Obv:** Raised bust left with date flanked by stars below **Rev:** Value above sprigs **Note:** Similar to KM#731.1 but with fourth bust.

Date	Mintage	VG	F	VF	XF	Unc
1915 Unique	—	—	—	—	—	—

KM# 732 20 CENTAVOS
Copper **Obv:** Raised bust left with date flanked by stars below **Rev:** Value above sprigs

Date	Mintage	VG	F	VF	XF	Unc
1915	—	1.50	2.50	4.00	10.00	—

KM# 733 20 CENTAVOS
Copper **Obv:** Bust left with date flanked by stars below **Rev:** Value above sprigs **Note:** 7th bust, short truncation with closed lapels

Date	Mintage	VG	F	VF	XF	Unc
1915	—	1.50	3.00	4.50	10.00	—

KM# 735 50 CENTAVOS
Silver, 22 mm. **Obv:** Raised bust left with date flanked by stars below **Rev:** Value above sprigs **Note:** Curved bottom

Date	Mintage	VG	F	VF	XF	Unc
1915	—	8.00	15.00	30.00	50.00	—

KM# 734 50 CENTAVOS
4.0700 g., Silver, 22 mm. **Obv:** Raised bust left with date flanked by stars below **Rev:** Value above sprigs **Note:** Heavy with short unfinished lapels

Date	Mintage	VG	F	VF	XF	Unc
1915	—	10.00	20.00	50.00	100	—

KM# 739 50 CENTAVOS
Billon, 28 mm. **Obv:** Raised bust left with date flanked by stars below **Rev:** Value above sprigs **Note:** Ninth bust, high nearly straight truncation

Date	Mintage	VG	F	VF	XF	Unc
1915	—	—	—	—	4,000	—

KM# 739a 50 CENTAVOS
Copper, 28 mm. **Obv:** Raised bust left with date flanked by stars below **Rev:** Value above sprigs **Note:** Ninth bust, high nearly straight truncation

Date	Mintage	VG	F	VF	XF	Unc
1915	—	—	—	—	—	—

KM# 736 50 CENTAVOS
Silver **Obv:** Bust left with date flanked by stars below **Rev:** Value above sprigs **Note:** Short truncation with closed lapels

Date	Mintage	VG	F	VF	XF	Unc
1915	—	8.00	15.00	30.00	50.00	—

KM# 737 50 CENTAVOS
4.5400 g., Silver, 22 mm. **Obv:** Bust left with date flanked by stars below **Rev:** Value above sprigs **Note:** Short truncation with pronounced curve

Date	Mintage	VG	F	VF	XF	Unc
1915	—	10.00	15.00	25.00	40.00	—

KM# 741 PESO (UN)
Silver **Obv:** Raised bust with date flanked by stars below **Rev:** Value above sprigs **Note:** Fifth bust, heavy with short unfinished lapels, centered high

Date	Mintage	VG	F	VF	XF	Unc
1915	—	8.00	10.00	25.00	35.00	—

KM# 740.1 PESO (UN)
Silver, 26 mm. **Obv:** Raised bust left with date flanked by stars below **Rev:** Written value above sprigs **Note:** Fourth bust with heavy unfinished truncation

Date	Mintage	VG	F	VF	XF	Unc
1915	—	7.00	12.00	25.00	40.00	—

KM# 740.2 PESO (UN)
Silver, 26 mm. **Obv:** Raised bust left with date flanked by stars below **Rev:** Written value above sprigs **Note:** Fourth bust with heavy unfinished truncation w/TM.

Date	Mintage	VG	F	VF	XF	Unc
1915	—	150	300	400	650	—

KM# 743 PESO (UN)
Silver **Obv:** Low relief bust left with date flanked by stars below **Rev:** Value above sprigs **Note:** Seventh bust, short truncation with closed lapels

Date	Mintage	VG	F	VF	XF	Unc
1915	—	10.00	20.00	30.00	50.00	—

KM# 743a PESO (UN)
Silver **Obv:** Low relief bust left with date flanked by stars below **Rev:** Value above sprigs **Note:** Seventh bust, short truncation with closed lapels

Date	Mintage	VG	F	VF	XF	Unc
1915	—	35.00	75.00	150	200	—

KM# 742 PESO (UN)
Silver **Obv:** Low relief bust left with date flanked by stars below **Rev:** Value above sprigs **Note:** Sixth bust; Curved bottom line

Date	Mintage	VG	F	VF	XF	Unc
1915	—	10.00	15.00	30.00	50.00	—

KM# 742a PESO (UN)
Copper **Obv:** Low relief bust left with date flanked by stars below **Rev:** Value above sprigs **Note:** Sixth bust; Curved bottom line

Date	Mintage	VG	F	VF	XF	Unc
1915	—	—	—	—	500	—

KM# 744 2 PESOS (Dos)
Silver, 30 mm. **Obv:** Raised bust left with date flanked by stars below **Rev:** Value above sprigs **Note:** Fourth bust, using 1 peso obverse die

Date	Mintage	VG	F	VF	XF	Unc
1915	—	18.00	28.00	45.00	75.00	—

KM# 744a 2 PESOS (Dos)
Copper **Obv:** Raised bust left with date flanked by stars below **Rev:** Value above sprigs **Note:** Fourth bust, using 1 peso obverse die

Date	Mintage	VG	F	VF	XF	Unc
1915 Rare	—	—	—	—	—	—

KM# 745 2 PESOS (Dos)
Gold With Silver, 22 mm. **Obv:** Low relief bust left with date flanked by stars below **Rev:** Value above sprigs **Note:** 0.9020 Silver, 0.0100 Gold. Fifth bust, curved bottom 2 over pesos

Date	Mintage	VG	F	VF	XF	Unc
1915	—	15.00	25.00	45.00	70.00	—

KM# 745a   2 PESOS (Dos)
Copper   **Obv:** Low relief bust left with date flanked by stars below **Rev:** Value above sprigs **Note:** Fifth bust, curved bottom 2 over pesos

Date	Mintage	VG	F	VF	XF	Unc
1915	—	75.00	100	150	250	—

KM# A746   2 PESOS (Dos)
Copper   **Obv:** Raised bust left with date flanked by stars below **Rev:** Balance scale below liberty cap **Note:** Seventh bust, short truncation with closed lapels

Date	Mintage	VG	F	VF	XF	Unc
1915 Unique	—	—	—	—	—	—

KM# 746   2 PESOS (Dos)
Silver   **Obv:** Raised bust left with date flanked by stars below **Rev:** Balance scale below liberty cap

Date	Mintage	VG	F	VF	XF	Unc
1915	—	22.00	28.00	50.00	75.00	—

KM# A747   2 PESOS (Dos)
Silver   **Obv:** Bust left with date flanked by stars below **Rev:** Balance scale below liberty cap **Note:** Obverse die is free hand engraved.

Date	Mintage	VG	F	VF	XF	Unc
1915	—	—	—	185	275	—

KM# 746a   2 PESOS (Dos)
Copper   **Obv:** Bust left with date flanked by stars below **Rev:** Balance scale below liberty cap

Date	Mintage	Good	VG	F	VF	XF
1915	—	—	150	200	600	1,000

KM# 747.1   2 PESOS (Dos)
13.4400 g., Silver, 33 mm.   **Obv:** Bust left with date flanked by stars below **Rev:** Balance scale below liberty cap

Date	Mintage	VG	F	VF	XF	Unc
1915	—	20.00	25.00	55.00	95.00	—

KM# 747.2   2 PESOS (Dos)
13.4400 g., Silver, 33 mm.   **Obv:** Bust left with date flanked by stars below **Rev:** Balance scale below liberty cap

Date	Mintage	VG	F	VF	XF	Unc
1915	—	22.00	28.00	60.00	100	—

KM# 747.3   2 PESOS (Dos)
13.4400 g., Silver, 33 mm.   **Obv:** Bust left with date flanked by stars below **Rev:** Balance scale below liberty cap

Date	Mintage	VG	F	VF	XF	Unc
1915	—	20.00	30.00	60.00	100	—

KM# 748   2 PESOS (Dos)
0.9020 Silver, 22 mm.   **Obv:** Bust left with date flanked by stars below **Rev:** Value above sprigs

Date	Mintage	VG	F	VF	XF	Unc
1915	—	20.00	30.00	60.00	100	—

KM# 749   2 PESOS (Dos)
Silver   **Obv:** Head left with date flanked by stars below **Rev:** Value above sprigs

Date	Mintage	VG	F	VF	XF	Unc
1915 Unique	—	—	—	—	3,000	—

KM# 751   5 PESOS
16.7700 g., Silver, 30 mm.   **Obv:** Low relief bust left with date flanked by stars below **Rev:** Value above sprigs **Note:** Seventh bust, short truncation with closed lapels

Date	Mintage	VG	F	VF	XF	Unc
1915	—	50.00	80.00	175	275	—

KM# 751a   5 PESOS
Copper   **Obv:** Low relief bust left with date flanked by stars below **Rev:** Value above sprigs **Note:** Seventh bust, short truncation with closed lapels

Date	Mintage	VG	F	VF	XF	Unc
1915	—	125	200	300	800	—

KM# 750   5 PESOS
0.1750 Gold, 19 mm.   **Obv:** Bust left **Rev:** Value above sprigs **Note:** Third bust, heavy, with short unfinished lapels

Date	Mintage	VG	F	VF	XF	Unc
1915	—	175	225	350	550	900

KM# 750a   5 PESOS
Copper   **Obv:** Bust left **Rev:** Value above sprigs **Note:** Third bust, heavy, with short unfinished lapels

Date	Mintage	VG	F	VF	XF	Unc
1915 Unique	—	—	—	—	—	—

KM# A752   10 PESOS
0.1500 Gold   **Obv:** Bust left with date flanked by stars below
Rev: Value above sprigs

Date	Mintage	VG	F	VF	XF	Unc
1915 Rare	—	—	—	—	—	—

KM# 752   10 PESOS
0.1750 Gold, 23 mm.   **Obv:** Bust left with date flanked by
stars below **Rev:** Value above sprigs

Date	Mintage	VG	F	VF	XF	Unc
1915	—	225	350	450	650	1,000

KM# 752a   10 PESOS
Copper   **Obv:** Bust left with date flanked by stars below **Rev:**
Value above sprigs

Date	Mintage	VG	F	VF	XF	Unc
1915	—	800	1,500	2,000	4,000	—

KM# 753   20 PESOS
0.1750 Gold   **Obv:** Bust left with date flanked by stars below
Rev: Value above sprigs

Date	Mintage	VG	F	VF	XF	Unc
1915	—	400	500	800	1,000	1,500

KM# 754   20 PESOS
0.1750 Gold, 27 mm.   **Obv:** Bust left with date flanked by
stars below **Rev:** Value above sprigs

Date	Mintage	VG	F	VF	XF	Unc
1915	—	250	450	650	950	1,700

KM# A753   20 PESOS
0.1500 Gold   **Obv:** Bust left with date flanked by stars below
Rev: Value above sprigs **Note:** Fourth bust

Date	Mintage	VG	F	VF	XF	Unc
1915 Unique	—	—	—	—	—	—

KM# 755   60 PESOS
50.0000 g., 0.8590 Gold 1.3808 oz. AGW   **Obv:** Head left
within 3/4 wreath **Rev:** Balance scale below liberty cap **Edge:**
Reeded

Date	Mintage	F	VF	XF	Unc	BU
1916 Rare	—	—	10,000	20,000	28,000	—

KM# 755a   60 PESOS
Silver   **Obv:** Head left within 3/4 wreath **Rev:** Balance scales
below liberty cap **Edge:** Reeded

Date	Mintage	F	VF	XF	Unc	BU
1916	—	—	—	—	1,800	—

KM# 755b   60 PESOS
Copper   **Obv:** Head left within 3/4 wreath **Rev:** Balance scales
below liberty cap **Edge:** Plain

Date	Mintage	F	VF	XF	Unc	BU
1916	—	—	—	1,000	1,800	—

PUEBLA

A state of central Mexico. Puebla was a state that occasionally saw Zapata forces active within its boundaries. Also active, and an issuer of coins, was the Madero brigade who issued coins with their name two years after Madero's death. The state issue of 2, 5, 10 and 20 Centavos saw limited circulation and recent hoards have been found of some values.

CHICONCUAUTLA
Madero Brigade

REVOLUTIONARY COINAGE

KM# 756 10 CENTAVOS
6.7300 g., Copper, 27 mm. **Obv:** Date below national arms **Rev:** Letters X and C entwined

Date	Mintage	VG	F	VF	XF	Unc
1915	—	7.50	12.50	17.50	25.00	—

KM# 758 20 CENTAVOS
Copper, 28 mm. **Obv:** Date below national arms **Rev:** Value

Date	Mintage	VG	F	VF	XF	Unc
1915	—	2.50	4.00	6.50	12.00	—

KM# 757 20 CENTAVOS
Copper, 28 mm. **Obv:** Date below national arms **Rev:** Value
Note: Varieties exist.

Date	Mintage	VG	F	VF	XF	Unc
1915	—	2.50	4.00	6.50	12.00	—

TETELA DEL ORO Y OCAMPO

REVOLUTIONARY COINAGE

KM# 759 2 CENTAVOS
Copper, 16 mm. **Obv:** National arms above date **Rev:** Value

Date	Mintage	VG	F	VF	XF	Unc
1915	—	12.50	20.00	28.00	45.00	—
1915 Restrikes	—	—	1.00	1.50	2.00	—

KM# 760 2 CENTAVOS
Copper, 20 mm. **Obv:** National arms within beaded circle
Rev: Value within beaded circle **Rev. Legend:** E. DE PU.

Date	Mintage	VG	F	VF	XF	Unc
1915	—	15.00	25.00	35.00	75.00	—

KM# 761 2 CENTAVOS
Copper, 20 mm. **Obv:** National arms within beaded circle
Rev: Value within beaded circle **Rev. Legend:** E. DE PUE.

Date	Mintage	VG	F	VF	XF	Unc
1915	—	9.00	20.00	25.00	50.00	—

KM# 762 5 CENTAVOS
Copper, 21 mm. **Obv:** National arms within beaded circle
Rev: Value within beaded circle

Date	Mintage	VG	F	VF	XF	Unc
1915	—	100	200	300	400	—

KM# 764 20 CENTAVOS
Copper, 24 mm. **Obv:** National arms **Rev:** Value above sprigs

Date	Mintage	VG	F	VF	XF	Unc
1915	—	50.00	100	150	225	—

SINALOA

A state along the west coast of Mexico. The cast pieces of this state have been attributed to two people - Generals Rafael Buelna and Juan Carrasco. The cap and rays 8 Reales is usually attributed to General Buelna and the rest of the series to Carrasco. Because of their crude nature it is questionable whether separate series or mints can be determined.

BUELNA / CARRASCO

CAST COINAGE
REVOLUTIONARY

KM# 766   50 CENTAVOS
Cast Silver, 29-31 mm. **Obv:** National arms **Rev:** Numeral value within wreath **Note:** Sand molded using regular 50 Centavos, KM#445. Size varies. Weight varies 12.81-14.8g.

Date	Mintage	Good	VG	F	VF	XF
ND(1905-1918)	—	200	300	—	—	—

COUNTERMARKED COINAGE
REVOLUTIONARY

These are all crude sand cast coins using regular coins to prepare the mold. Prices below give a range for how much of the original coin from which the mold was prepared is visible.

KM# 765   20 CENTAVOS
Cast Silver **Obv:** National arms within beaded circle **Rev:** Value within beaded circle **Note:** Sand molded using regular 20 Centavos.

CM Date	Host Date	Good	VG	F	VF	XF
ND(ca.1915)	ND(1898-1905)	200	300	—	—	—

KM# 767   50 CENTAVOS
Cast Silver **Countermark:** G.C. **Obv:** National arms with additional countermark **Rev:** Value and date within wreath with liberty cap above **Note:** Sand molded using regular 50 Centavos, KM#445.

CM Date	Host Date	Good	VG	F	VF	XF
ND	ND(1905-1918)	100	150	200	300	—

KM# 769   PESO
Cast Silver **Note:** Sand molded using regular Peso, KM#409.

CM Date	Host Date	Good	VG	F	VF	XF
	ND(1898-1909)	10.00	20.00	30.00	40.00	—

KM# 768.1   PESO
Cast Silver, 38.8-39 mm. **Note:** Sand molded using regular 8 Reales, KM#377. Size varies. Weight varies 26-33.67g.

CM Date	Host Date	Good	VG	F	VF	XF
ND(ca.1915)	ND(1824-97)	20.00	35.00	45.00	60.00	—

KM# 768.2   PESO
Cast Silver, 38.5-39 mm. **Countermark:** G.C. **Obv:** With additional countermark **Note:** Sand molded using regular 8 Reales, KM#377. Size varies. Weight varies 26-33.67g.

CM Date	Host Date	Good	VG	F	VF	XF
ND(ca.1915)	ND(1824-97)	25.00	45.00	100	150	—

KM# 770   PESO
Cast Silver, 38.5 mm. **Countermark:** G.C **Obv:** National arms with additional countermark **Rev:** Liberty cap with additional countermark **Note:** Sand molded using regular Peso, KM#409.

CM Date	Host Date	Good	VG	F	VF	XF
ND(ca.1915)	ND(1898-1909)	35.00	65.00	150	185	—